CASES AND MATERIALS ON
STATUTORY
INTERPRETATION

. . .

By
William N. Eskridge, Jr.
John A. Garver Professor of Jurisprudence
Yale University

Philip P. Frickey
The Late Alexander F. & May T. Morrison Professor of Law
University of California at Berkeley

Elizabeth Garrett
Frances R. and John J. Duggan Professor of Law,
Political Science and Public Policy
University of Southern California

AMERICAN CASEBOOK SERIES®

WEST®

A Thomson Reuters business

Mat #41195883

© 2012 Thomson Reuters
  610 Opperman Drive
  St. Paul, MN 55123
  1–800–313–9378
Printed in the United States of America

ISBN: 978–0–314–27818–0

In Memory of Phil Frickey, 1953–2010
Beloved colleague, friend, and co-author

PREFACE AND ACKNOWLEDGMENTS

This casebook is an adaptation, with a focus on statutory interpretation, of Eskridge, Frickey & Garrett's fourth edition of *Cases and Materials on Legislation: Statutes and the Creation of Public Policy*. The volume also updates the earlier materials and is current through the end of 2011.

In preparing this casebook, we have benefitted from the numerous comments from scholars and teachers of legislation and statutory interpretation. Although too numerous to identify everyone who contributed to this effort, we'd like to extend special thanks for ideas and insights to Victoria Nourse, Abbe Gluck, and James J. Brudney, as well as to Norman Dorsen, Guido Calabresi, Daniel Farber, John Ferejohn, David Grewal, Robert Katzmann, Jerry Mashaw, Richard Posner, Daniel Rodriguez, and Stephen Ross.

We are most grateful to Dean Robert Post of the Yale Law School for providing emotional and financial support, as well as a small army of research assistants who were essential to this project. Yale law students Diana Rusk (Class of 2009), Glenn Bridgman (Class of 2013), Amanda Elbogen (Class of 2013), Chris Lapinig (Class of 2013), and Brandon Trice (Class of 2012) were cheerful as well as brilliant and productive partners in this enterprise.

We dedicate this book to the memory of our cherished friend and co-author, Philip P. Frickey (1953–2010).

WILLIAM N. ESKRIDGE, JR.
New Haven, Connecticut

ELIZABETH GARRETT
Los Angeles, California

Summary of Contents

TABLE OF CONTENTS

TABLE OF CASES

The principal cases are in bold type. Cases cited or discussed in the text
are in roman type. References are to pages. Cases cited in principal
cases and within other quoted materials are not included.

CASES AND MATERIALS ON
STATUTORY INTERPRETATION

CHAPTER 1

AN INTRODUCTION TO STATUTES

■ ■ ■

We introduce the study of statutory interpretation through a case study, followed by descriptions of several theoretical frameworks for understanding that story. Section 1 of this chapter tells the story of the Civil Rights Act of 1964, Pub. L. No. 88–352, 78 Stat. 241 (codified as amended in scattered sections of 42 U.S.C.). We have chosen this law, in part, because it is a dramatic example of how statutes can and do make a significant difference in our society and our lives. The principles set forth in *Brown v. Board of Education*, 347 U.S. 483 (1954), would have been left largely unfulfilled were it not for the statute, which amplified and implemented the principles in ways which the Court was not able, or willing, to do. Also, the story of the law's enactment is itself a case study of the legislative process and of the unpredictable path followed by the official as well as private implementers of the statute. The path of the Civil Rights Act was atypical of the federal legislative process in 1964, and major legislation increasingly travels paths that diverge from the textbook descriptions of Congress.

The Civil Rights Act is also a useful starting point for a theoretical discussion of the legislative process in the United States. In Section 2, we offer three types of theories: pluralist theories, which focus on the role of interest groups in policymaking; proceduralist theories, which emphasize the many obstacles a bill must pass through before it becomes a law; and institutional theories, which approach statutes from the perspective of the various institutions charged with enacting, implementing, and overseeing them. Each theory has a descriptive feature (this is how the legislative process *does* work) and a normative dimension (this is how the legislative process *should* work).

In Section 3, we trace the dynamic interpretation of Title VII (the employment discrimination title) of the Civil Rights Act. We introduce you to theories of statutory interpretation through examination of an important case, *United Steelworkers v. Weber*, in which the Court interpreted the Act to allow voluntary affirmative action plans. We also consider the different interpretive methods used by the judges in light of the theories introduced in Section 2.

1

SECTION 1.   THE STORY OF THE CIVIL RIGHTS ACT OF 1964 AND THE PROCE-DURES OF STATUTE–CREATION[a]

Brown v. Board of Education declared a great principle—non-discrimination and racial equality—but the principle did little to change the day-to-day lives of most African Americans in the 1950s. *Brown* applied only to public institutions, leaving private hotels, restaurants, swimming pools, and employers free to continue racially discriminatory practices. Even public institutions (mainly schools) were only required to desegregate "with all deliberate speed." The pace of official desegregation was sloth-like. In 1961, seven years after *Brown*, it required a bevy of federal marshals to escort James Meredith through the doors of the University of Mississippi as its first African–American student.

On February 2, 1960, four black students from North Carolina A & T University sat down to order at a "whites only" lunch counter at a Woolworth's store in Greensboro, North Carolina. The store's manager refused to serve them. They remained seated, silently demanding equal treatment. Hundreds of similar "sit-ins" followed in other Southern locales.

In April 1963, the Reverend Dr. Martin Luther King, Jr. launched a nonviolent offensive to protest and boycott the segregated shops, churches, and restaurants of Birmingham, Alabama. When Dr. King defied an injunction and led a protest march, the Birmingham Police Commissioner, T. Eugene "Bull" Connor, had him and 54 others arrested and jailed. In May 1963, Connor and his cohorts brutally attacked hundreds of black schoolchildren marching and singing the anthem "We Shall Overcome." Front-page photos of Connor's hounds attacking African–American youths, of fire hose water pressing back the waves of black bodies, and of burly policemen sitting on a prostrate woman aroused the national conscience (Harvey 55).

---

a.   The authors gratefully acknowledge the critical assistance of John Rego, J.D., University of Virginia, 1986, in researching and writing this story. We relied on both primary and secondary sources for this account. The most informative source was Charles Whalen & Barbara Whalen, *The Longest Debate: A Legislative History of the 1964 Civil Rights Act* (1985) (cited in text as "Whalens," with page numbers). Not only does it provide valuable "inside" insights (Charles Whalen is a former Republican member of the House of Representatives), but its dramatic storytelling style inspired this short rendition. Quotations from *The Longest Debate* are reprinted with the permission of Charles Whalen, Barbara Whalen, and the publisher, Seven Locks Press, Inc., P.O. Box 27, Cabin John, Maryland 20818. Other useful sources were Carl Brauer, *John F. Kennedy and the Second Reconstruction* (1977) ("Brauer"); Hugh Davis Graham, *The Civil Rights Era: Origins and Development of National Policy, 1960–1972* (1990) ("Graham"); James Harvey, *Civil Rights During the Kennedy Administration* (1971) ("Harvey"); Hubert Humphrey, *Beyond Civil Rights: A New Day of Equality* (1968) ("Humphrey"); Neil MacNeil, *Dirksen: Portrait of a Public Man* (1970) ("MacNeil"); John Martin, *Civil Rights and the Crisis of Liberalism: The Democratic Party, 1945–76* (1979) ("Martin"); Merle Miller, *Lyndon: An Oral Biography* (1980) ("Miller"); Edward & Frederick Schapsmeier, *Dirksen of Illinois: Senatorial Statesman* (1985) ("Schapsmeier"); Bernard Schwartz, ed., *Statutory History of the United States: Civil Rights* (1970) ("Schwartz"); and Francis Vaas, *Title VII: Legislative History,* 7 B.C. Indus. & Com. L. Rev. 431 (1966) ("Vaas").

African–American leaders saw this as their historic moment. Dr. King wrote from his Birmingham jail cell:

> For years now I have heard the word "wait." It rings in the ear of every Negro with piercing familiarity. This "wait" has almost always meant "Never." * * * We have waited for more than 340 years for our constitutional and God-given rights. * * * [W]hen you take a cross-country drive and find it necessary to sleep night after night in the uncomfortable corners of your automobile because no motel will accept you; when you are humiliated day in and day out by nagging signs reading "white" and "colored"; when your first name becomes "nigger," your middle name becomes "boy" (however old you are) and your last name becomes "John," and your wife and mother are never given the respected title of "Mrs."; when you are harried by day and haunted by night by the fact that you are a Negro, living constantly at tiptoe stance, never quite knowing what to expect next, and plagued with inner fears and outer resentments; when you are forever fighting a degenerating sense of "no-bodiness"—then you will understand why we find it difficult to wait.

National media attention and outrage helped ensure the success of Dr. King's Birmingham campaign. On May 10, 1963, the city's businesses entered into a settlement in which the African–American community agreed to cease their boycott and the white-owned businesses agreed to hire blacks as clerks and salespeople, and to establish training programs in job categories previously closed to African Americans.

The Kennedy Administration was listening. Attorney General Robert Kennedy hailed the Birmingham settlement. On June 11, 1963, President John Kennedy addressed the country on national television and announced his intention to propose a comprehensive civil rights bill to the Congress:

> We are confronted primarily with a moral issue. It is as old as the Scriptures and it is as clear as the American Constitution. The heart of the question is whether all Americans are to be afforded equal rights and equal opportunities, whether we are going to treat our fellow Americans as we want to be treated. * * *

> One hundred years of delay have passed since President Lincoln freed the slaves, yet their heirs, their grandsons, are not fully free. They are not yet freed from the bonds of injustice. They are not yet freed from social and economic oppression. And this Nation, for all its hopes and all its boasts, will not be fully free until all its citizens are free.

> Now the time has come for this Nation to fulfill its promise.

Obstacles to Civil Rights Legislation

The President's proposed legislation concentrated on four areas of concern: discrimination in public accommodations, desegregation of public schools, fair employment, and discrimination by recipients of federal funds. Title II of the bill, the public accommodations provision, would guarantee equal access to all hotels, restaurants, places of amusement, and retail establishments. Title III covered school desegregation. It would give the federal government, particularly the Attorney General, greater authority to implement the *Brown* decision. Employment discrimination was treated, though some thought half-heartedly, in Title V of the President's bill, which expanded the powers of the Civil Rights Commission, and in Title VII, which would have established a Committee on Equal Employment to monitor the conduct of federal contractors. While not addressing private discrimination, the President reaffirmed his support for legislation addressing employment discrimination in the private sector. Finally, in Title VI, the President proposed that recipients of federal assistance be prohibited from discriminating on the basis of race.

The events of 1963 suggested the need for such legislation. But there was good reason to doubt that the President's bill would ever become law. The ambivalence of both political parties, the uncertain commitment of the President and Vice President, and significant unavoidable obstacles in the legislative process boded ill for the proposal.

1. *The Ambivalence of Both Political Parties.* On the issue of civil rights, the Democratic Party could be described as two parties. Throughout the century Southern Democrats normally controlled half or more of the party's votes in the Senate, and after the 1930s they systematically killed civil rights bills through parliamentary maneuvers (Martin 157). In 1948, the Democratic Party split when adoption of a civil rights plank at the national convention caused a walkout by segregationists. Efforts to heal those wounds led the Democrats to downplay civil rights in the 1952 and 1956 platforms. In contrast, the Republicans—the Party of Lincoln—showed renewed interest in civil rights. In 1957, President Eisenhower introduced a civil rights bill. The Republicans in the House of Representatives agreed to weaken the bill to enhance its chances for enactment. But a filibuster by Senate Democrats forced supporters to propose changes that made it an essentially toothless law. A similar presidential initiative in 1960 yielded a weak voting rights law, after Senate Democrats deleted school desegregation, employment, and housing discrimination provisions from the bill.

As the 1960 election approached, black leaders wondered which—if either—of the major parties was capable of delivering civil rights legislation. The Republicans had pushed for moderate civil rights laws in the 1950s but had been unable to deliver them. Democrats had both supported and torpedoed civil rights initiatives. The platforms of both parties called for civil rights legislation and prosecution of public segregation, but the support seemed increasingly rhetorical as the campaign wore on (Harvey 13). The Democrat (Kennedy) took stronger stands on the civil rights issue than did the Republican (Nixon), thereby winning the black vote. Indeed, his showing among African Americans and labor was the strongest since FDR (Martin 171) and was obviously crucial in that close election.

2. *The Uncertain Commitment of the President and Vice President.* Although President Kennedy opposed discrimination, he had no deep emotional concern for the issue. Kennedy saw his own family's Irish immigrant experience as proof that prejudice could be overcome without special assistance. Some have suggested that Kennedy was primarily concerned with foreign affairs and economic issues and thought of African Americans only in terms of votes (Harvey 19). As a senator in 1957, Kennedy had voted with the Democratic majority to weaken the Republicans' civil rights bill (Martin 167).

Thus it was hardly surprising that, after the 1960 election, President Kennedy disregarded his campaign rhetoric and decided not to seek legislation. He reasoned that such an effort would not only fail, but it would also delay enactment of important economic legislation (Harvey 19–20). Kennedy did use his powers as chief executive to appoint African Americans to important positions and to establish equal opportunity in federal employment. But he demonstrated no sense of urgency. It was not until November 1962, for example, that he issued the order prohibiting racial discrimination in federally financed housing, the same order he had, as a candidate in 1960, chastised Eisenhower for not issuing with a "stroke of his pen" (Martin 177). And it was not until he was faced with blatant defiance by Governors Ross Barnett (D–Miss.) and George Wallace (D–Ala.) that Kennedy, as Commander-in-Chief, used federal troops to enforce judicial desegregation orders.

Nor had the President's 1960 running mate displayed much enthusiasm for civil rights as a pressing item on the national agenda. In his 1948 campaign for the Senate, Lyndon Johnson had called President Truman's civil rights program (repeal of the poll tax; anti-lynching law; nondiscrimination in employment) "a farce and a sham—an effort to set up a police state in the guise of liberty" (Miller 118). Through his friendship with powerful Senator Richard Russell (D–Ga.), Johnson became the Democrats' Senate leader in 1953. More ambitious and opportunistic than ideological, Johnson adapted his agenda to the political needs of the time. Although few in 1963 considered LBJ a racist, he was not considered a civil rights activist, either.

3. *Obstacles in Congress.* Over 90% of bills introduced in Congress die in the legislative labyrinth. Though a senator for eight years and representative for six years before that, Kennedy was not a skilled legislative strategist. It was unlikely that he could move a civil rights bill through Congress.

Virtually all bills introduced in Congress are referred initially to a committee for consideration and cannot be voted on until the committee has reported them out.[b] Because a committee's chair controls the commit-

b. Current House Rule X, clause 1 and Senate Rule XXV, clause 1 identify the standing (permanent) committees in the two chambers and define the jurisdiction (area of exclusive authority) for each standing committee. House Rule XII, clause 2 and Senate Rule XVII, clause 3 govern referral to committees by the Speaker of the House and the Senate Majority Leader. (All citations to House and Senate Rules in this book are taken from *Standing Rules of the Senate*, in tee's staff and agenda, he or she has the power to effectively kill a bill by preventing the committee from considering it. Committee chairmanships have generally been awarded on the basis of seniority, and at the time of the deliberations on the Civil Rights Act, many powerful chairs were held by senior Members of Congress from the "one-party" states of the South and Southwest (Harvey 16–17).

In the Senate, civil rights legislation fell under the jurisdiction of the Judiciary Committee. The chairman, Senator James Eastland (D–Miss.), was notorious for killing civil rights bills. The situation was little better in the House, where the Rules Committee—the committee through which almost every bill passes on its way to the floor—was headed by Howard W. "Judge" Smith (D–Va.), also a foe of civil rights laws. In 1957, Smith stalled consideration of the civil rights bill simply by leaving Washington; he claimed that he needed to attend to his barn in Virginia that had recently burned down. Speaker of the House Sam Rayburn (D–Tex.) replied that he knew Smith was opposed to civil rights, but he never suspected that the Chairman would resort to arson (Martin 166).

Even if the civil rights bill were to survive the committee process, it faced a certain *filibuster* on the floor of the Senate. Senate rules allow unlimited debate of a question before voting, and civil rights opponents had successfully used this tactic in 1957 and 1960 to prevent consideration of civil rights bills, allowing a vote only after they had exacted tremendous concessions from the bills' supporters. The only ways to break a filibuster are by permitting it to continue until the filibusterers are physically exhausted or by invoking *cloture* (a two-thirds vote to end discussion).[c] The former had been tried and had failed in 1957, while the latter had been successfully invoked only five times in the history of the Senate and never to end debate on a civil rights bill (Whalens 126).

Passage in the House

The President's civil rights bill was introduced in both houses of Congress on June 19, 1963, but its supporters pushed for immediate consideration only in the House of Representatives. They believed that the obstacles would be less substantial in the House. If they could develop a strong record in support of the bill there, together with a large vote in favor of the bill, supporters hoped that political momentum would improve the bill's chances in the Senate.

Senate Manual, S. Doc. No. 107–1 (2002), and *Rules of the House of Representatives*, 111th Congress, http://www.rules.house.gov/ruleprec/111th.pdf (viewed Jan. 2, 2012)).

    c. Under current Senate Rule XXII, clause 2, cloture can be invoked in most cases by the vote of 60 of the 100 senators, but in 1963–64 the Rule provided for cloture of debate only by two-thirds of the senators voting on the question. Since important cloture votes could be expected to command all 100 senators, 67 votes were usually needed to close off debate. Even now, a two-thirds vote is required to end debate on any measure amending the Senate Rules, including the Rule governing cloture.

1. *Writing a Bill the Hard Way—The Judiciary Committee.* House Speaker John McCormack (D–Mass.) referred H.R. 7152[d] to the House Judiciary Committee, which had jurisdiction over civil rights bills. Chairman Emanuel Celler (D–N.Y.) referred the bill to Subcommittee No. 5. The Chairman referred the bill to this subcommittee, which normally handled antitrust matters, because it was dominated by civil rights advocates: its Chairman was Celler himself, the ranking Republican was William McCulloch (R–Ohio), and it had no senior Southern member (Harvey 60).

Chairman of the Judiciary Committee in 1949–53 and after 1955, Celler, a longtime representative from Brooklyn, had become one of Congress's leading civil rights advocates. Just after the 1960 election, Celler introduced a civil rights bill based on Kennedy's platform. (The bill died when the President failed to lend his support.) He was the House member chosen to sponsor President Kennedy's 1963 bill and was determined to see it become law. Bill McCulloch's district in rural Ohio was a universe away from Brooklyn. It was WASP and conservative, and it had an African–American population of only 2.7%. Although there was little interest in civil rights legislation at home, McCulloch's immense popularity allowed him latitude to pursue a personal legislative agenda. McCulloch was a man of firm principle, and a principle dear to him was antidiscrimination. McCulloch had worked hard to pass the Eisenhower civil rights bills in 1957 and 1960. In January 1963, he had introduced a civil rights bill of his own (Whalens 7–11). McCulloch's support, and the Republican votes he might bring with him, were essential to success in the House, where, because of the split in the Democratic ranks, the Republicans held the balance of power (Harvey 59).

Celler scheduled subcommittee hearings to start before the Fourth of July recess. The free ride that the bill was expected to get through the subcommittee hit a snag with the first witness, Attorney General Robert Kennedy. The Attorney General was unaware of McCulloch's earlier bill, as well as a bill introduced by John Lindsay (R–N.Y.), and his failure to acknowledge Republican civil rights efforts was interpreted as a Democratic attempt to take partisan advantage of the civil rights issue. The Republican members of the subcommittee threatened to scuttle H.R. 7152 if it became a partisan measure. To repair the nascent bipartisan coalition, the Administration dispatched Assistant Attorney General Burke Marshall to negotiate a deal with McCulloch during the recess (Whalens 5–11).

Marshall found that the Ohio Congressman agreed with the President, but McCulloch was unwilling to allow the Democrats to hog the civil rights issue (particularly since the Democrats heading the Administration had undermined his efforts in 1957 and 1960). A compromise was reached under which McCulloch pledged his support in exchange for two promises. First, the Administration agreed not to allow the Senate to water down the bill, as it had done in 1957 when Vice President Johnson was Majority

---

d. Bills introduced in the House and Senate are assigned identifying numbers—"H.R. ___" and "S. ___"—just as cases filed in U.S. courts are assigned a docket number.

Leader. This meant that McCulloch would be consulted on all changes to H.R. 7152 that the Administration wanted to accept after the bill passed the House. Second, President Kennedy agreed to keep the issue a bipartisan effort by giving the Republicans equal credit when the bill was passed (Whalens 10–14).

As the congressional hearings progressed, the Administration engaged in a campaign to build public support for H.R. 7152, meeting with over 1,600 members of interest groups in June and July. Receiving special attention were representatives of labor, the clergy, and civil rights groups (Brauer 273–74). The President was especially interested in a vigorous clerical lobby because it provided a means of influencing legislators from states where the impact of blacks and labor was minimal (Brauer 275). On the other hand, the Administration cautioned against lobbying *too* vigorously. At the meeting with members of the Leadership Conference on Civil Rights—an alliance of 74 organizations lobbying for civil rights legislation—the President argued against overly ambitious demands. But civil rights leaders wanted the strongest possible bill (Brauer 282), and a parade of such advocates appeared before Subcommittee No. 5.

By August 2, the subcommittee had held 22 days of hearings on H.R. 7152 and was ready to *mark up* the bill. A mark-up is a committee's drafting session, where members consider amendments and rewrite bills. President Kennedy had asked Celler to stall final consideration on the bill until his tax reform proposal was voted out of the House Ways and Means Committee, where it had been languishing since January. The highly controversial tax cut was a cornerstone in the President's economic program, and Kennedy feared that Southerners on Ways and Means might use the bill as a target for retaliation if the civil rights bill cleared Subcommittee No. 5 first. Therefore, Celler delayed substantive mark-up of H.R. 7152 until September (Whalens 22–23). Meanwhile, public pressure for legislation mounted.[e]

On September 10, the Ways and Means Committee approved the tax bill, and Celler prepared for the mark-up of H.R. 7152. Deputy Attorney General Nicholas Katzenbach had written Celler a letter setting forth the "tactics" that the Administration expected him to follow, pursuant to its deal with McCulloch. But Celler chose to pursue a more aggressive approach. He remembered that the Senate had watered down the moderate civil rights bills passed by the House in 1957 and 1960. Why not start with a very strong bill this time, so that a compromise version would still

---

e. While the Administration put the civil rights bill on the back burner, civil rights groups continued to lobby for it. On August 28, 1963, as Congress prepared to adjourn for the Labor Day recess, almost a quarter of a million people converged on Washington, D.C., in a peaceful demonstration for equal rights—the March on Washington for Jobs and Freedom (Martin 176–77). In his address to the crowd that afternoon, Dr. King argued that, one hundred years after the Emancipation Proclamation, African Americans were still not free. "One hundred years later, the life of the Negro is still sadly crippled by the manacles and the chains of discrimination. * * * One hundred years later, the Negro is still languishing in the corners of American society and finds himself an exile in his own land." Dr. King concluded: "I have a dream today that my four little children will one day live in a nation where they will not be judged by the color of their skin but by the content of their character. I have a dream today" (see Whalens 26).

be acceptable? Moreover, by publicly pushing a strong bill, Celler would be a hero to civil rights groups and would still be able to preserve his friendship with the conservatives by allowing them to score points with their constituents when the bill was inevitably weakened (Whalens 30–31).

Bill McCulloch watched in disbelief as Manny Celler and the liberal Democrats on the subcommittee proceeded to strengthen almost every title of the Administration bill, betraying the President's agreement with the Republican leadership in the process. Some of the changes were procedural. Byron Rogers (D–Colo.) offered a new Title III, which authorized the Attorney General to initiate or intervene in civil suits charging discrimination by state or local officials. Other changes were substantial and sweeping. Bob Kastenmeier (D–Wis.) offered an amendment to broaden Title II, the public accommodations provision, to include every private business—law firms, medical associations, and private schools—except rooming houses with five units or less (Whalens 34–35; Harvey 60). Finally, on September 25, the subcommittee replaced H.R. 7152's weak equal employment provisions with a new title, embodied in a 30–page amendment offered by Peter Rodino (D–N.J.). The new title would create an Equal Employment Opportunity Commission (EEOC) with authority to investigate employment discrimination on account of race, religion, or national origin and to issue enforceable cease-and-desist orders (Vaas 435; Whalens 35).

On October 2, Subcommittee No. 5 reported the new H.R. 7152 to the full Judiciary Committee. Civil rights leaders, who had received virtually every provision they had lobbied for, called the bill a triumph. But McCulloch labeled the bill "a pail of garbage" with no chance of passage on the floor of the House (Whalens 38). The Southerners on the Judiciary Committee who hoped to derail the bill apparently agreed; they joined the liberals and voted H.R. 7152 as amended out of subcommittee (Harvey 60).

House Minority Leader Charles Halleck (R–Ind.) met with Deputy Attorney General Katzenbach and Speaker McCormack on October 8 to tell them that the Republicans would allow the strengthened bill to go to the House floor, where it would probably die—unless the liberal Democrats themselves cooperated in weakening the bill. The Administration readily agreed to the Republicans' proposal and persuaded Celler to go along (Whalens 42–44). On October 15, the Attorney General testified before the Committee to recommend weakening changes (Brauer 304). On October 22, the amendments were to be offered, the first by Roland Libonati (D–Ill.). At the last moment Libonati backed out, leaving the Republicans feeling betrayed again. A Republican member moved to report the subcommittee bill to the full House. The motion would have easily passed had Celler not adjourned the Committee for the day. The situation was a mess.

Administration officials met with Halleck and McCulloch to work out a compromise bill that would satisfy the Republicans (Whalens 52–53).

The President agreed to Republican demands that the bill should be revised. The new bill reconciled a Republican redraft and the original Administration bill. The President and Republican leadership agreed that the compromise bill would be offered as a substitute for the subcommittee bill (Harvey 61). All that remained was to defeat the motion to report out the unacceptable subcommittee version of H.R. 7152. Halleck and McCulloch agreed to provide seven Republican votes if the Democrats would provide ten votes. The President twisted arms and Celler invoked loyalty to party and the chairman to meet their quota (Whalens 59–64).

Now uneasy with Chairman Celler's ability to run the Judiciary Committee, the Administration prepared a "six-point script" for him to follow on October 29, describing precisely the manner in which to proceed. For once, events went as planned (Whalens 64–66). (1) A roll call vote was taken on the pending motion to report the subcommittee bill. Democratic members were called first, according to tradition, allowing Halleck and McCulloch to see if the Democrats could deliver their share of the votes to defeat the motion before having to commit themselves. Celler delivered ten Democratic votes, and Halleck provided nine Republicans (more than he had promised) to defeat the motion. (2) Celler moved to strike all but the first sentence of the subcommittee bill and to insert the compromise bill as an amendment. (3) Celler and McCulloch quickly explained the substitute, and Celler brushed aside a *point of order* challenge. (4) Once the compromise was read in its entirety, Representative Rodino moved the *previous question*, cutting off any debate on the proposed amendment. The Committee voted 20–12 in favor of the previous question. (5) The Judiciary Committee passed the compromise substitute by a vote of 20–14. (6) The Committee reported H.R. 7152 to the House.

Although civil rights leaders criticized the Administration for favoring cutbacks in the subcommittee substitute, the Committee version was decidedly stronger than the Administration's original bill. For example, Title II (public accommodations) broadly prohibited discrimination in places of lodging, sports stadiums and arenas, theaters, restaurants, cafeterias, lunch counters, and gas stations. Title VII (equal employment) retained the main features of Rodino's substitute for the Administration's weak monitoring provisions, though the EEOC's adjudicatory powers were limited. The President praised the bill as "comprehensive and fair," and the Administration evenly distributed credit among Democrats and Republicans (Whalens 66).

2. *Surviving the Rules Committee.* On November 21, H.R. 7152 and the Judiciary Committee's report were conveyed to the Clerk of the House and then to the Rules Committee. Each bill reported out of committee passes through the Rules Committee, where a resolution (the *rule*) governing floor debate is prepared.[f] In addition to providing that high priority

---

f. Current House Rule XIII, clause 2 provides that all committee reports, including the views of the minority, shall be delivered to the Clerk for printing and reference to the proper *calendar* (described *infra*). Because House calendars contain many bills, and bills are to be considered in their order on the calendars, there is no assurance that the bill will be considered at all. The bills receive expedited consideration, the Committee determines the amount of time to be allowed for debate, how the time for debate will be allocated, and the scope of permissible amendments.

The Rules Committee stage often constitutes a substantive consideration of the bill, and it presents an opportunity to derail a bill before the House itself has a chance to consider it. Unfortunately, the chairman of the Rules Committee, 80–year–old Judge Howard Smith, had spent 33 years in the House killing or eviscerating progressive legislation in the areas of labor, public housing, education, medical care, and, of course, civil rights. His effectiveness had brought him a reputation as one of the most powerful members of the House (Whalens 84, 90).[g]

President Kennedy's assassination on November 22 meant that the task of getting H.R. 7152 through the Rules Committee fell to Lyndon Johnson. In an effort to seize the moral leadership of the nation, President Johnson addressed a joint session of Congress soon after Kennedy's death:

> [N]o memorial oration or eulogy could more eloquently honor President Kennedy's memory than the earliest possible passage of the civil rights bill for which he fought so long. We have talked long enough in this country about equal rights. We have talked for one hundred years or more. It is time now to write the next chapter and to write it in the books of law.

As a posthumous tribute to their martyred President, the American people were coming to support the civil rights bill in growing numbers and with increasing ardor. But none of this sentiment moved Judge Smith, who had a firm grip on the fate of H.R. 7152. Following the Southern strategy of delay, he declined even to hold hearings on the bill.

There were three procedural options capable of dislodging Smith's stranglehold on H.R. 7152, and each was tried by the bill's supporters (Whalens 84–85). First, under House Rule XV, a petition signed by a majority of the House's members (218) can remove any bill from committee, including the Rules Committee, after it has been in committee for 30 days. On December 9, Manny Celler began circulating such a *discharge petition*, but McCulloch and Halleck refused to deliver the needed Republican signatures, on the ground that such a course was antithetical to the committee process (Whalens 84). (Of 563 discharge petitions initiated between 1931 and 2002, only 47 were successful in forcing floor consideration. Nineteen of the discharged bills passed the House, but only two became law, with another two resulting in changes in the House's rules.

Rules Committee has the power to recommend a rule to expedite consideration of any bill—ahead of those previously placed on the calendars.

g. In an effort to curtail Smith's ability to bury the Administration's progressive legislative agenda, President Kennedy had worked prior to the 1961 session with then-Speaker of the House, Sam Rayburn, to enlarge the Rules Committee from ten to fifteen members (ten Democrats and five Republicans). The appointment of five new committee members allowed Rayburn and the Administration to create an 8–7 liberal majority on the Rules Committee and to increase the control of party leaders over it. While the enlargement improved prospects for the President's legislative agenda, highly controversial bills—like civil rights proposals—still faced unfavorable odds in Howard Smith's lair (Harvey 15–16).

Richard Beth, Congressional Research Service Report for Congress, *The Discharge Rule in the House: Use in Historical Context* (April 17, 2003).)

On December 11, the Republicans announced their intent to use a second device, *Calendar Wednesday*, to call up H.R. 7152. House Rule XXV allows the Speaker on each Wednesday to call the standing committees in alphabetical order to inquire whether the chairman wishes the House to consider any bill previously reported out of that committee. But with 11 committees coming alphabetically before the Judiciary Committee, including six chaired by Southerners, the bill's opponents could easily defeat the tactic by calling up other bills to exhaust the available time. To prevent an embarrassing display of intraparty divisions, the Democratic leadership simply adjourned the House before the Calendar Wednesday maneuver could be tried (Whalens 85).

The third mechanism was to be the key. House Rule XI permits any three members of a committee to request the chairman to call a meeting to consider a bill; if the meeting is not scheduled within three days, a majority of the committee may schedule one. Liberal Democrats numbered five on the Rules Committee, so three Republican votes were needed. The pivotal votes were controlled by 70–year–old Clarence Brown (R–Ohio), the ranking minority member on the Rules Committee (Whalens 85). The conservative Brown shared the commitment to civil rights of his friend and neighboring Congressman, Bill McCulloch.[h] Brown informed his friend Judge Smith of his plans to lead a mutiny, so to head off a confrontation, Smith announced that hearings would begin on January 9, 1964 (Whalens 86).

Between January 9 and January 30, the House Rules Committee heard testimony from 40 different members of Congress (Vaas 438). No one expected the hearings to have any effect on the outcome, but they provided the Southern Democrats a forum for airing their opposition to the bill. On January 30, 1964, the Rules Committee approved House Resolution 616, governing debate on H.R. 7152, by a vote of 11–4 (Whalens 99). The bill had not only survived the Rules Committee, it had survived without a single amendment (Vaas 438).

3. *Bipartisan House Victory.* The House of Representatives follows a rather formal six-step process in considering a bill called up from the floor. First, the House debates and votes on the bill's rule. If the rule is accepted, the body will resolve into the *Committee of the Whole House on the State of the Union*, which is simply the full House following simplified procedures for purposes of debate. Next, pursuant to the rule, members offer amendments, which are debated and then accepted or rejected by unrecorded votes. The members will then resume sitting formally as the House and, if requested by one-fifth of the members, take recorded votes on any accepted amendments. A minority party member will be recognized

---

h. Two major black universities (Wilberforce and Central State) were situated in Brown's district. The town of Xenia in his district was one of the major links in the Underground Railway, used by slaves to escape to Canada in the nineteenth century (Whalens 86).

to offer a motion to recommit the bill to committee. Finally, the House will vote on the bill, as amended by the Committee of the Whole (Whalens 101).

On January 3, 1964, Speaker John McCormack recognized a Rules Committee member to call up House Resolution 616 (the special rule) for immediate consideration. Under the rules of the House, debate on the resolution was limited to one hour, divided equally between each party. Clarence Brown spoke on behalf of the rule, and Rules Committee member William Colmer (D–Miss.) spoke against it. In a voice vote, the House ignored Colmer's plea not to succumb to the violent "blackmail" of civil rights activists, and approved the rule (Whalens 102–03). The House then resolved itself into the Committee of the Whole, and Speaker McCormack stepped down and handed the gavel to Eugene Keogh (D–N.Y.), who assumed his position as Chairman of the Committee of the Whole.

The rule approved for H.R. 7152 specified that general debate would be limited to ten hours, divided equally between the two parties (and further divided equally between North and South), after which amendments would be offered, title by title, in accordance with *the five minute rule*. Under this rule, all speakers—the amendment's sponsor, its proponents, and its opponents—were limited to five minutes of remarks each. Furthermore, in exchange for the bill's supporters' pledge not to limit debate on any amendment, the bill's opponents agreed not to bog down the proceedings with redundant quorum calls. This was to be a battle, but it would be a genteel one (Whalens 108).

Celler and McCulloch delivered the opening statements. Manny Celler chose to describe the bill in broad dramatic terms:

> The legislation before you seeks only to honor the constitutional guarantees of equality under the law for all. It bestows no preferences on any one group; what it does is to place into balance the scales of justice so that the living force of our Constitution shall apply to all people, not only to those who by accident of birth were born with white skins.

Bill McCulloch discussed H.R. 7152 more simply, explaining the need for federal legislation and its validity under the Constitution. He argued that "this bill is comprehensive in scope, yet moderate in application."

Not surprisingly, the Southern Congressmen cast the bill in a very different light. Edwin Willis (D–La.), for example, characterized the bill as "the most drastic and far-reaching proposal and grab for power ever to be reported out of a committee of Congress in the history of our Republic." Congressman Thomas Abernethy (D–Miss.) went even further:

> If this bill is enacted, I predict it will precipitate upheaval that will make the sit-ins, kneel-ins, lie-ins, stand-ins, mass picketing, chanting, the march on Washington, and all the other elements of the so-called Negro revolution, all of these—I predict—will look like kinder-

garten play in comparison with the counter-revolution that is bound to arise and continue to grow and grow and grow.

After ten hours of such general debate, H.R. 7152 prepared to meet its ultimate test in the House—the amendment process on the floor.

McCulloch and Celler had prepared carefully for this stage of the process. Each presided over a 20–foot–long table on their respective party's side of the chamber, on which they had assembled an impressive array of resources. There was a lengthy manual prepared by the Justice Department, containing a section-by-section defense of the bill and responding both to the opposing views expressed by the Southern Democratic minority in the Judiciary Committee's report and to expected amendments. The floor leaders had also assigned a member of the Judiciary Committee to each title with responsibility for becoming an expert on that particular area. Finally, there were eight Justice Department attorneys— one for each title of the bill—standing by for additional assistance (Whalens 103).

The major concern shared by Celler and McCulloch was their ability to keep sufficient members on the floor to defeat weakening amendments during the protracted debate. Because votes taken in the Committee of the Whole were unrecorded, constituents were not likely to find out how (or even if) their representatives had voted, and so marginally interested members often skipped those votes. Thus it was not unusual to find a determined minority passing substantial amendments to bills by simply waiting until enough of the bill's supporters left the floor. If such a situation arose, Celler and McCulloch planned to stall a final vote for ten minutes while they attempted to get their forces together. By objecting to the chair's call for a voice vote, they could force a standing vote. Then, with 20 members objecting to the standing vote, they could force a teller vote—a head count as the "yeas" and "nays" walked down the center aisle. During this delaying process, supporters could be rounded up.[i]

The amendment process began at noon on Monday, February 3, and continued, title-by-title and section-by-section, until 7:00 p.m. on February 10. Over the course of that week, 124 amendments were offered, debated, and voted on, but only 34 were accepted by the Committee of the Whole. Most were technical corrections, including 12 offered by Celler.

The most significant amendment expanded the scope of Title VII and was sponsored by none other than Judge Smith. He proposed the addition of the word "sex" to Title VII's list of impermissible bases for employment

---

i. Celler and McCulloch relied on a three-level organization. First, 17 members of the Democratic Study Group, each with responsibility for six to eight colleagues, would be responsible for directly contacting their respective Congressmen whenever a vote was about to occur. Second, a group of 25 volunteers under the direction of labor lobbyist Jane O'Grady, known as O'Grady's Raiders, would patrol the halls of the Congressional Office Buildings, making sure that representatives knew when a vote was coming up. Finally, in an effort to coerce some public accountability, hundreds of volunteers from the Leadership Conference on Civil Rights in the House gallery watched who voted and how. Because writing is forbidden in the galleries, members had to memorize the face of a particular member and then remember how he or she voted (Whalens 108–09).

decisions. In addition to his own personal commitment to equal opportunities for women, Smith hoped that by transforming the civil rights bill into a law guaranteeing women equal employment rights with men—thus drastically affecting virtually every employer, labor union, and governmental body in the country—the bill would become so controversial that it would fail, if not in the House, then certainly in the Senate (Vaas 441–42; Whalens 115–16).

A shocked, flustered (and perhaps chauvinist) Manny Celler immediately rose to oppose the amendment. While McCulloch sat on the sidelines, many Democratic liberals joined Celler in speaking against the amendment. Then five Congresswomen—Frances Bolton (R–Ohio), Martha Griffiths (D–Mich.), Katherine St. George (R–N.Y.), Catherine May (R–Wash.), and Edna Kelly (D–N.Y.)—rose in support "of this little crumb of equality. The addition of the little, terrifying word 's-e-x' will not hurt this legislation in any way," argued St. George. With a coalition of Southerners and women supporting it and the rest of the House hopelessly divided on the apparent choice between equal rights for blacks and equal rights for women, the Smith amendment passed, 168–133 (Vaas 442).

At the close of amendments on February 10, the Committee of the Whole dissolved, John McCormack reclaimed the Speaker's chair, and the members resumed sitting as the House. Chairman Keogh reported H.R. 7152, as amended, back to the House, and the Speaker prepared to complete the final three steps in the process. It was 7:00 p.m., and few were interested in prolonging the affair. Attempts to obtain recorded votes on certain substantive amendments failed to receive sufficient support, and the motion to recommit the bill to the Judiciary Committee failed on a voice vote. Finally it was time for the vote—up or down—on H.R. 7152. When the roll call was over, there were 152 Democratic votes and 138 Republican votes in favor, 96 Democratic votes and 34 Republican votes against. The civil rights bill passed overwhelmingly, 290–130 (Whalens 120–21). Now it was on to the Senate.

Passage in the Senate

The euphoria that accompanied passage in the House of Representatives was short-lived. H.R. 7152 next had to face the Senate, the body that had diluted civil rights bills in 1957 and 1960. Senator Eastland's Judiciary Committee had essentially ignored the Senate version of the Administration's bill (introduced in June 1963), holding only perfunctory hearings and calling only one witness: Attorney General Robert Kennedy.[j]

---

j. The Attorney General had opened his testimony by quoting from a couple of tourist guidebooks covering the South. According to the guides, there was only one hotel serving African Americans in the city of Montgomery, Alabama and none in Danville, Virginia. However, a dog, if traveling with a white person, would have his choice of five places in Montgomery and four in Danville (Brauer 279). Kennedy spent a large portion of his time sparring with Senator Sam Ervin (D–N.C.), later to be Chair of the Watergate Committee, who claimed to oppose the bill because it was both unnecessary and unconstitutional. When Ervin claimed to have no personal knowledge of racial discrimination in Mississippi, the Attorney General quickly offered to arrange for a guided tour of the state, but the Senator declined, saying he was too busy fighting to

At that time, consideration of a typical bill in the Senate followed an eight step process. First, the bill was read for the first time. If no objections were heard, the bill would immediately be read for the second time. After the second reading, the bill was generally referred to committee, unless a majority voted to place the bill directly on the Senate calendar. The fourth step was committee consideration where, as in the House, the bill could be amended or killed. If the bill survived committee action, it was placed on the Senate calendar. The sixth step was to call up the bill for consideration, and the seventh consisted of the actual debate of the bill under the Senate's unlimited debate rules. The final step was the third reading, followed by a vote on the bill, as amended by the committee and during floor debate (Whalens 131–32).

Majority Leader Mike Mansfield (D–Mont.) had a simple strategy. First, avoid referral of H.R. 7152 to Eastland's Judiciary Committee. Second, get the 67 votes needed to invoke cloture against the inevitable Southern filibuster.

1. *The Longest Debate Begins.* H.R. 7152 arrived in the Senate from the House on Monday, February 17, 1964. On Mike Mansfield's motion, the bill was read for the first time. However, Mansfield objected to a second reading of the bill because he wanted to delay a filibuster until the Senate had completed work on the tax bill. When the tax bill was completed on February 26, Mansfield called up the civil rights bill for its second reading. Mansfield then moved to have the bill placed directly on the Senate calendar, thereby bypassing the Judiciary Committee. Senator Richard Russell (D–Ga.), leader of the Southern bloc in the Senate, immediately objected and was joined by Minority Leader Everett Dirksen (R–Ill.) and others. Although Dirksen shared Mansfield's concern about referring a civil rights bill to Eastland's committee, he felt that a bill of this importance deserved the full legislative history that only committee consideration could provide. Mansfield persuaded 20 Republicans to join him and defeated Dirksen, 54–37, placing H.R. 7152 on the Senate calendar of pending bills (Whalens 132–35).

Mansfield delayed his next motion—to call up H.R. 7152 for debate— until after the Senate voted on a pending farm bill. This two-week hiatus provided an opportunity for the Senate leadership to organize for the coming battle. Although the chairman of the committee having jurisdiction over a bill is usually chosen to act as the primary floor leader during debate, Mansfield was not going to select Eastland. Instead he selected Hubert Horatio Humphrey (D–Minn.), the Democrats' Senate Whip. No one was more committed to civil rights legislation than Humphrey. In 1948, it was he who led the battle for a strong civil rights plank in the Democratic platform.[k] And the loquacious Humphrey had the energy and communication skills needed to organize the drive for 67 cloture votes.

"preserve constitutional principles and the individual freedoms of all citizens of the United States" (Brauer 280–81).

k. Hubert Humphrey's interest in the 1964 civil rights bill was not completely philosophical; he was a politically ambitious man who correctly saw the bill as an opportunity to establish

The Republican floor manager was Thomas Kuchel (R–Cal.), that party's Senate Whip. Kuchel was a popular choice for the position because he was a progressive Republican who was still accepted in the conservative camp (Whalens 137–38). Dirksen appointed seven other Republicans to assist Kuchel, selecting representatives from each region of the country to ensure that he was kept informed of the movements in all parts of the Party (MacNeil 232). Senators Joseph Clark (D–Pa.) and Clifford Case (R–N.J.) were the senators responsible for handling issues involving Title VII, the equal employment title (Vaas 445).

One of Mansfield's and Johnson's chief concerns was the ability of the liberal supporters of the bill to maintain their discipline throughout the ordeal of getting H.R. 7152 through the Senate. The liberals' disorganization had contributed to the success of the last two civil rights filibusters. Johnson challenged Humphrey to keep the troops together this time. "You have this great opportunity now, Hubert, but you liberals will never deliver. You don't know the rules of the Senate, and your liberal friends will be off making speeches when they ought to be present. You've got a great opportunity here, but I'm afraid it's going to fall between the boards" (Miller 368). Humphrey accepted the challenge. He organized a daily bipartisan newsletter, designed to inform members of the status of the debate, to refute arguments made on the floor by the bill's opponents, and to maintain a united front (Humphrey 86–87). The Democratic floor leader also set up a "quorum duty" system to ensure that there would always be sufficient senators on the floor to prevent the Southerners from adjourning the Senate. Finally, Humphrey scheduled regular strategy sessions with the bill's supporters (Humphrey 90).

By March 9, the Senate finished considering the farm bill, and Mike Mansfield moved to make H.R. 7152 the pending business of the Senate, a motion he knew would draw a filibuster by the Southern conservatives (Vaas 444).[1] For fourteen days the Senate debated this issue—not whether to pass H.R. 7152, but simply whether to consider the bill at all. Prior to moving for immediate consideration of the bill, Mansfield had met with the Southerners and had been assured that the filibuster on this preliminary issue would not last longer than four or five days. It became apparent, though, as debate dragged on, that the Southerners had merely been maneuvering to convince Mansfield not to call all-night sessions.[m]

himself a leader in the Democratic Party. Lyndon Johnson was conceded the Party's presidential nomination in 1964, but Humphrey believed that if he could lead the Democrats to a solid legislative accomplishment on civil rights, he would solidify his position as front-runner for the vice presidency.

1. Unlike the House, the Senate does not have a Rules Committee which recommends to the full house a rule allowing expedited consideration of important bills. Instead, the Majority Leader normally expedites consideration by negotiating a *unanimous consent agreement*, in which all interested senators agree to consider the bill on a stated date, sometimes with limitations on debate and amendments (like a House rule). But if even a single senator objects to this arrangement, it is nullified. Obviously, the Southern senators in 1964 were not going to agree readily to expedited consideration of the civil rights bill.

m. Mansfield was not inclined to hold all-night sessions in any event. Round-the-clock sessions had not worked in 1960 or in 1957, when Strom Thurmond (D–S.C.) had set the all-time

On March 23, Humphrey kept the Senate in session until 10:15 p.m.—not all night, but long enough to give the filibusterers a taste of what was to come. The next day, supporters announced that they would object to the holding of any committee hearings before the Senate had finished with the civil rights bill. The Southerners finally decided to allow a vote on Mansfield's motion. On March 26, 1964, the motion to take up H.R. 7152 passed 67–17, with only Southern Democrats opposing (Whalens 146–47).

On March 30, 1964, the Senate began debate on the merits of H.R. 7152. Hubert Humphrey delivered the opening statement. Knowing that with another filibuster around the corner there was no need to hurry (and never being the sort of speaker who strove for oratorical brevity), Humphrey treated the half-dozen Senators present to a 55–page, three and one-half hour speech. Tom Kuchel followed with an opening of a mere one and three-quarter hours (Whalens 150–51). Rather than let the Southerners monopolize debate, Humphrey decided to take the offensive early. His team held the floor for over 12 days, presenting a detailed, title-by-title defense of the bill. Senators were sent to appear on television and radio talk shows and were encouraged to send regular newsletters back to their constituents in an effort to maintain support for the bill in the press and public at large (Humphrey 89–90). Supporters of the civil rights bill emphasized the moral importance of the bill, attempting to elevate the issue above politics and appeal to a broad concept of justice (Humphrey 91–92).[n]

2. *Wooing the Wizard of Ooze.* The Southern filibusterers dominated debate after early April and seemed capable of talking the year away. Could Humphrey and Kuchel muster the 67 votes needed to invoke cloture? A block of about 20 Southern Democrats were certain to vote against cloture, and about 30 liberal Democrats, most representing the Northeast and Midwest, and 12 liberal Republicans were equally certain to vote for it. To reach the 67 votes needed for cloture, Humphrey and Kuchel needed to win the votes of 25 senators from two groups: 21 conservative Republicans and 17 moderate Democrats from Western and border states.

Invoking cloture would be tough. The crucial swing votes were expected to come from sparsely populated states in the West and Midwest

---

filibuster record of 24 hours and 18 minutes of uninterrupted talk. Mansfield thought the tactic was demeaning to the Senate. "This is not a circus or a sideshow. We are not operating in a pit with spectators coming into the galleries late at night to see senators of the republic come out in bedroom slippers without neckties, with their hair uncombed, and pajama tops sticking out of their necks." Also, Mansfield feared that some older senators would not survive the tactic (MacNeil 23).

n. As a consequence, Humphrey realized that among all the groups lobbying for passage, the religious lobby would be crucial. The support of this group was important for three reasons: (1) it reinforced the moral importance of the issue; (2) it provided a means of reaching senators not otherwise influenced by the labor and black lobbying efforts; and (3) it represented the form of lobbying least likely to alienate senators as unduly coercive. Therefore, Humphrey met with religious leaders and actively planned high-profile events to emphasize the interdenominational support for civil rights. Most successful of these efforts was a silent, 24–hour vigil maintained by Protestant, Catholic, and Jewish seminarians on the Capitol grounds throughout the Senate debate (Humphrey 93–94).

(Schapsmeier 156–57), which had traditionally relied upon the filibuster to protect themselves from more populous states. These senators would be hesitant to cast a vote that might later weaken their ability to filibuster to protect their own interests (Miller 370). Other senators considered the filibuster to be an essential element of the Senate's legislative process and hence might refuse to vote for cloture as a matter of principle (Miller 368). There was also the force of tradition working against cloture: since 1917, when the procedure was formally codified in the Senate's standing rules, cloture had been invoked successfully only once (Vaas 446). Finally, although some conservative Republicans were willing to support cloture, the bill needed them to vote as a virtual block—which seemed unlikely unless the Minority Leader himself became an enthusiastic supporter of the bill.

Although he led the minority party, with only 33 of the 100 senators, Everett Dirksen ruled the Senate along with Majority Leader Mike Mansfield (MacNeil 230–31). Over a 29–year career, Dirksen had risen to his position of power on the strength of an oratorical prowess that combined flowery language with a throatily mellifluous voice, and an uncanny ability to turn the most difficult political situations into personal triumphs. The former earned him the sobriquet "Wizard of Ooze"; the latter, "Old Doctor Snake Oil" (Whalens 151).

Publicly, Dirksen struck a Delphic pose in his attitude toward the civil rights bill. When President Kennedy's bill was introduced in June 1963, Dirksen expressed doubts about either a public accommodations provision or a fair employment practices section (Humphrey 85), and as late as August he told representatives of the NAACP that a public accommodations title was not acceptable (MacNeil 223). The momentum created by House passage and increasing public support for the bill led him to soften his position. In early November he assured Katzenbach that a civil rights bill would make it to a vote in the Senate (Brauer 308). The bill's strong support from McCulloch and Halleck in the House put further pressure on Dirksen to play a leadership role—a role that Humphrey urged upon him. One of Humphrey's key strategies for collecting the support of GOP conservatives was to cast Dirksen in the starring role of this battle (Humphrey 85–86).

By the time the filibuster began in earnest, Dirksen was in all probability going to support some kind of strong civil rights bill. But his support carried a price tag—namely Dirksen's own conservative stamp on the final product (MacNeil 232–33). The day after the Senate took up consideration of the bill, Dirksen met with the Senate Republican Policy Committee to discuss the amendments he wanted to propose, and the next day he met with the Republican caucus. A week later he unveiled a package of 40 weakening amendments to Title VII. The amendments pleased conservative Republicans but created great concern among the party's influential liberals, including Senators George Aiken (Vt.), John Sherman Cooper (Ky.), Jacob Javits (NY), Tom Kuchel (Cal.), Leverett Saltonstall (Mass.), Hugh Scott (Pa.), and Margaret Chase Smith (Me.).

The liberals' opposition forced Dirksen to trim the package to ten. On April 16, Dirksen publicly introduced his ten amendments, but did not seek a vote on the package (Whalens 159–64).

As April stretched on and Dirksen found himself unable to muster sufficient bipartisan support for his amendments, he decided to approach the President in an effort to bluff his way to a compromise. He met with Johnson on April 29 and offered to deliver 22 to 25 Republican votes for cloture if the Administration would go along with weakening the bill. By one account, Johnson and Humphrey refused to compromise, because they thought Dirksen had little choice but to support the civil rights bill (Whalens, 171–72). Another account, however, posits that Dirksen was in a much stronger bargaining position. When he met with Mansfield, Humphrey, and the Attorney General to hammer out a compromise on May 4, Dirksen achieved much of what he wanted to gain for the small businesses that were his primary concern. Thus, he procured the Administration's support for provisions in the jobs title limiting the authority of the EEOC, protecting employers against government-required quota programs, and expanding employer defenses.[o]

Dirksen spent the next week selling his deal to the Republican caucus. He presented his package—the most he thought he could get the Democrats to go along with—to the Republican senators (MacNeil 234–35). Just as his earlier amendments had been attacked by his party's liberals as going too far, Dirksen's latest proposal was attacked by some conservatives as not going nearly far enough. The Minority Leader's response was to go public, with a *fait accompli* challenging his Republicans to follow their Minority Leader. Following the caucus, Dirksen announced to stunned reporters that the time for action had arrived, that passage of the civil rights bill had become a moral imperative and that he was resolved to see it happen. Quoting Victor Hugo, Dirksen proclaimed, "No army is stronger than an idea whose time has come" (Whalens 185).

On May 26, Dirksen presented Amendment No. 656 to the Senate, an amendment in the nature of a substitute for H.R. 7152, known as the "Mansfield–Dirksen Amendment" (Vaas 445).[p] Although the Democrats and liberal Republicans were ultimately satisfied that the anti-discrimination goal of civil rights bill had not been significantly undermined (Whalens 188–89), the jobs title of the Mansfield–Dirksen substitute was in fact more business-friendly and less regulatory than the earlier version of the bill (Rodriguez & Weingast, 1487–96). Dirksen characteristically termed his bill "infinitely better than what came to us from the House" (Whalens 188), but Humphrey had little trouble concluding that he had kept his promise to Bill McCulloch not to support a weakened bill (Humphrey 85).

---

o. Indispensable for understanding Dirksen's success is the politically sophisticated account in Daniel A. Rodriguez & Barry R. Weingast, *The Positive Political Theory of Legislative History: New Perspectives on the 1964 Civil Rights Act and Its Interpretation*, 151 U. Pa. L. Rev. 1417 (2003).

p. An *amendment in the nature of a substitute* proposes a whole new bill to replace the bill under consideration. We will briefly discuss the various kinds of amendments in the "Note on How a Bill Becomes a Federal Law," *infra*.

With cloture now a tangible possibility, the bill's supporters—the President, the Senate Democratic leaders, and the Senate Republican leaders—spent the next two weeks stumping for votes. President Johnson used a combination of arm-twisting and inducements to lobby Senate Democrats. He spoke with Howard Cannon (D–Nev.), whom Majority Leader Johnson had appointed to critical Senate committees, and J. Howard Edmondson (D–Okla.), whom Johnson had supported during the state's Democratic primary. While Johnson only stressed the principles in the bill, his personal involvement indicated that he was calling in markers (Whalens 187–88). Both senators would vote for cloture. A devastating earthquake had struck Alaska on March 27, and Johnson had responded promptly, making Air Force Two available to Senators Bartlett and Gruening (both D–Alas.) and moving to free up $77.5 million in relief for the state. Although both senators had been considered questionable votes for cloture, the President's timely political favor pulled them into line (Whalens 200).

Mansfield and Humphrey concentrated on Democratic senators from the key Western states, attempting to disrupt a traditional understanding between Southern and Western senators involving the exchange of Southern votes on water projects for Western votes against civil rights (Whalens 201). Meanwhile, Everett Dirksen worked to pull in the 11 or more conservative Republicans he would need for cloture. In shifting H.R. 7152's focus toward federal intervention as a secondary, rather than primary, enforcement alternative, Dirksen argued to conservative colleagues from states with antidiscrimination laws that the federal legislation would have only a small incremental effect in their states. He complemented this approach by pointing to the Republican Party's heritage as the "Party of Lincoln." Conservatives were also influenced by the moral fervor of religious leaders who supported the bill. Finally, the effects of the filibuster itself were beginning to create pressure for cloture. The Senate had devoted 12 solid weeks to ducking the civil rights issue, and many senators were beginning to feel the embarrassment that came with public recognition of that fact (Whalens 202–03).

3. *Cloture and Victory in the Senate.* One by one the necessary commitments fell into place. On June 8, Mansfield and Dirksen moved for cloture: "We the undersigned Senators [27 Democrats, 11 Republicans], in accordance with the provisions of Rule XXII of the Standing Rules of the Senate, hereby move to bring to a close the debate on the bill * * *." After the required two-day wait, the time came to vote. Mansfield explained the importance of the cloture motion and then listened as a weary Richard Russell denounced the bill as contrary to both the spirit and the letter of the Constitution. After an uncharacteristically brief statement by Humphrey, Dirksen rose to make the final speech. He introduced Senate Amendment No. 1052, a second substitute for the entire bill to replace his earlier substitute amendment. Dirksen argued: "The time has come for equality of opportunity in sharing in government, in education, and in employment. It will not be stayed or denied."

The obligatory quorum call was a true formality on June 10: all 100 senators were present, including Clair Engle (D–Cal.), suffering from a brain tumor and unable to speak (Humphrey 91). The roll was called alphabetically by each senator's last name. Senator Engle cast his vote from his wheelchair by feebly lifting his left hand toward his eye. John Williams (R–Del.) cast the 67th vote for cloture. Hubert Humphrey raised his arms over his head in jubilation (Whalens 199). The final vote was 71–29, four votes more than required.

After over 534 hours of continuous debate, spanning 58 days, the longest filibuster in the history of the Senate had been broken—the first time ever that cloture had been achieved on a civil rights bill (Miller 368). The final breakdown was 44 Democrats and 27 Republicans in favor and 23 Democrats and 6 Republicans against. Johnson and Humphrey had succeeded in capturing the votes of 19 of the 21 Democrats from Western states, and Dirksen had convinced 16 of the 17 Republican senators from states with public accommodations and equal employment laws on the books (as well as eight of the ten senators from states with one or the other) to vote for cloture.

Even though cloture limited senators to sixty minutes of remarks—on both the bill and proposed amendments—the Southern opponents of H.R. 7152 continued to delay the bill's progress. They attempted to bog down the proceedings by calling up countless amendments, even though they knew their proposals had no chance of adoption. They slowed things down further by insisting on long roll-call votes (including a record 34 in one day) on virtually every question (Schwartz 1091).[q] But they succeeded only in delaying the inevitable for another eight days (Vaas 446). In all, 115 different amendments were defeated, 106 on roll-call votes (Miller 371), with only two amendments of substance being accepted (Schwartz 1091).

On June 19, 1964—one year after John Kennedy had sent his civil rights bill to Congress—the Senate finally voted on H.R. 7152, having accepted the second Mansfield–Dirksen substitute two days earlier by an overwhelming 76–18 margin. The bill was read for the third time and the Clerk called the roll (Vaas 446). At 7:40 p.m., to the applause of the observers in the gallery, the Clerk of the Senate announced the final vote: 73–27 in favor of H.R. 7152, as amended by the Mansfield–Dirksen substitute. The bill received the support of 46 Democrats and 27 Republicans, including four senators who had opposed cloture. Twenty-one Democrats and six Republicans voted nay (Whalens 215).

---

q. This phenomenon—the *post-cloture filibuster*—is made possible by the collegial Senate rules. During this period, absent a unanimous consent agreement, a Senator could propose any number of amendments, including those unrelated to the subject matter of the bill. (House Rule XVI, in contrast, limits amendments to those which are *germane* to the subject of the bill.) Moreover, any Senator could demand roll-call votes, not only on the amendments, but also on the normally routine motion to reconsider, and could seek repeated quorum calls. In 1979, the Senate amended Rule XXII, clause 2 to limit each Senator to calling up two amendments and to impose an overall 100 hour limit on post-cloture consideration.

Most important, the bill approved by the Senate was in substance virtually identical to the bill approved by the House in February (Miller 371). For example, of the 24 amendments to Title VII that were offered from the floor, only five were accepted. Even considering Dirksen's important changes, the title was not significantly weaker than the version delivered from the House in February.[r]

The Civil Rights Bill Becomes Law

A bill does not become a law unless both chambers of Congress agree to identical legislative language. Because the Senate had made a number of changes in H.R. 7152, it returned the bill to the House on June 27, 1964, together with a message asking for acquiescence in the Senate's changes. In a joint press release, Manny Celler and Bill McCulloch said that "none of the amendments do serious violence to the purpose of the bill. We are of a mind that a conference could fatally delay enactment of this measure" (Whalens 218). Celler and McCulloch knew that if the House refused to accept all of the Senate changes and a conference committee were called, the Senate conferees would be selected by Judiciary Chairman Eastland, guaranteeing further delay. Even if the conference committee did report out a bill, the Southerners would have another opportunity to filibuster in the Senate. On balance, the best strategy was simply to accept the Senate's changes (Whalens 218–19).

The revised H.R. 7152 returned to Judge Smith's Rules Committee. This time, with the national conventions of both parties approaching, supporters would tolerate no stalling by the Chairman. After a single day of hearings, the Rules Committee voted to report House Resolution 789, expressing the House's concurrence with the Senate's amendments to H.R. 7152. The Rules Committee also voted to limit debate to one hour prior to the final vote.

On July 2, the House took up consideration of House Resolution 789. Judge Smith spoke for 15 minutes, denouncing the Rules Committee's "exercise of raw, brutal power" in limiting debate to a single hour. But he conceded that "the bell has tolled. In a few minutes you will vote this monstrous instrument of oppression upon all of the American people." As he yielded the floor, Smith received applause from his Southern colleagues and a handshake from Manny Celler. Bill McCulloch, in his usual restrained manner, recommended approval of the Senate version of H.R. 7152 as a comprehensive, fair, and moderate statute. As he sat down, the

---

r. See Rodriguez & Weingast, *New Perspectives on the 1964 Civil Rights Act*, at 1487–96. A new provision specified that preferential hiring practices to correct racial imbalances in the workforce (*affirmative action*) would not be required. The authority of the EEOC to sue in court was eliminated and replaced with a provision authorizing the Commission, when conciliation efforts failed, to refer a case to the Attorney General for possible civil suit or to authorize private suit. However, the reduction in EEOC authority was agreed to only in exchange for the inclusion of provisions allowing the courts to appoint attorneys to represent private Title VII plaintiffs and providing for an award of attorney's fees to successful plaintiffs. The new version also allowed local authorities to retain jurisdiction over cases for a short time, to attempt conciliation, before the EEOC could step in (Vaas 447–56).

House rose in a rare standing ovation. Finally, Manny Celler claimed the floor to use the remaining six minutes of the allotted hour. When he finished, the House rose once again in a standing ovation, this time led by the redoubtable Judge Smith (Whalens 224–26).

The House vote on House Resolution 789 was 289–126. After the House accepted the Senate bill, Speaker McCormack signed the official copy of H.R. 7152 and handed it to the House Clerk for return to the Senate. When the bill arrived in the other chamber, business was suspended so that Carl Hayden, the Senate's President pro tempore, could place his signature alongside McCormack's. H.R. 7152, as amended, was now ready to be signed into law by the President. At 6:00 that evening, July 2, 1964, members of Congress and civil rights leaders arrived at the White House and, after brief remarks by President Johnson, witnessed the presidential signing of H.R. 7152 into law. H.R. 7152 had finally become "The Civil Rights Act of 1964."

Within days, Lyndon Johnson met with Nicholas Katzenbach, the new Attorney General, to discuss the President's plans for the next civil rights bill: "I want you to write me the goddamndest, toughest voting rights act that you can devise." As he had told Hubert Humphrey during the battle for the 1964 Act, "Yes, yes, Hubert, I want all of those other things— buses, restaurants, all of that—but the right to vote with no ifs, ands, or buts, that's the key. When the Negroes get that, they'll have every politician, north and south, east and west, kissing their ass, begging for their support" (Miller 371).[s] Johnson may have been overly optimistic (and typically crude), but he was astute enough to realize that the Civil Rights Act of 1964 was merely a start toward true equality and the end of discrimination.

NOTE ON HOW A BILL BECOMES A FEDERAL LAW

The Civil Rights Act illuminates the important features of the federal legislative process. The Constitution and its amendments set forth the basic structure: laws will be enacted by elected representatives, not by the people directly or by some authoritarian person or group. "All legislative powers herein granted shall be vested in a Congress of the United States, which shall consist of a Senate and House of Representatives." U.S. Const. art. I, § 1. House members are "chosen every second Year by the People of the several states," *id.* art. I, § 2, and each state has two Senators, "elected by the people thereof," *id.* amend. XVII. Laws must be approved by two legislative chambers (the *bicameralism* requirement) and the chief executive (the *presentment* requirement). If the President signs it, the "Bill" is "Law"; if he returns it without signature, it is not law unless two-thirds majorities of each chamber vote to override his *veto*. *Id.* art. I, § 7. If the President does not sign or return the bill within ten days and the Congress remains in session, the bill

---

s. Johnson was successful. In 1965, Congress adopted a strong Voting Rights Act, which was reenacted in 1970, 1975, 1982, and 2006 and remains a major component of federal civil rights law.

becomes law as though he had signed it. If Congress adjourns during the ten-day period, the bill does not become law, and the President has *pocket vetoed* the proposal.

Most of the procedures followed in Congress are the products of history and custom, rather than constitutional mandate.[a] It may be helpful to think about congressional rules as lying along a spectrum, with constitutional requirements such as bicameralism and presentment as the strongest and most durable. Each house also has a series of formal rules that bind it until they are changed by a vote of that house. As the Story of the Civil Rights Act demonstrates, there are many such rules affecting legislation, including committee consideration, scheduling procedures, and Senate rules allowing filibusters. All of these requirements are less durable than constitutional ones because, in most cases, they can be changed by a majority vote of the relevant house. Moreover, if the House or Senate violates the rules, there is often no effective enforcement mechanism to void the action. Courts have been reluctant to enforce congressional rules when they are ignored, holding instead that rulemaking and enforcement are committed by the Constitution to the discretion of each house. Finally, the least durable procedures are those that are matters of informal norms and practices, sometimes called the *folkways* of Congress. See Donald Matthews, *U.S. Senators and Their World* 151 (1960). One norm that played a role in the enactment of the Civil Rights Act was the seniority norm, which allocates power and position to members with long tenure and allows senior legislators and committee chairs to block bills they do not like even when a majority of the chamber or committee favors the legislation. The seniority norm is now weaker than it was at the time of our case study, perhaps because of higher turnover rates and an influx of junior members.

---

a. Among the best scholarly sources on legislative procedures are William J. Keefe & Morris S. Ogul, *The American Legislative Process: Congress and the States* (10th ed. 2001); Burdett A. Loomis & Wendy J. Schiller, *The Contemporary Congress* (5th ed. 2006); Walter J. Oleszek, *Congressional Procedures and the Policy Process* (8th ed. 2010); Steven S. Smith, Jason M. Roberts & Ryan J. Vander Wielen, *The American Congress* (4th ed. 2006).

Chart 1—1: How a Federal Bill Becomes a Law — Simplified Overview

HOUSE OF REPRESENTATIVES

Drafting of Bill or Resolution (e.g., by legislative staff, government agency, interest group, academic)

↓

Introduction of Bill by Member (revenue bills originate in House, see U.S. Const., art. I, § 7, cl. 1; customarily, appropriations bills do also)

↓

Referral to Standing Committee

↓

Committee Action
–can be referred to subcommittee
–hearings held on major bills
–committee resolution: take no action, defeat, accept or amend and report

↓

Major Calendars
–Union (appropriations and revenue)
–House (public)
–Discharge (extract bills from committee)

↓

Rules Committee (major bills) (closed rules possible but generally modified open or open rules)

↓

Floor Action (passage or defeat) ——

SENATE

Referred to standing committee

↓

Committee action (similar to House)

↓

Floor action (similar to House except that there is filibuster option in Senate; overriding filibuster requires 60 votes)

↓

CONFERENCE COMMITTEE (if House and Senate pass differing versions, a conference committee can be created with members from each house; each House must agree to the conference report)

↓

BILL SIGNED BY SPEAKER AND VICE PRESIDENT

↓

PRESENTMENT TO PRESIDENT (may sign, veto, or permit bill to become law without his/her signature; also possibility of "pocket veto" after adjournment)

The discussion that follows focuses on the traditional or "textbook" federal legislative process, which is presented in Chart 1–1. State legislatures usually follow similar procedures. In recent years, major federal legislation has often followed paths previously considered unorthodox. For example, Congress now enacts many major laws as part of complex omnibus legislation that is considered by several committees, may involve congressional party leaders and organizations in nontraditional ways, and provides challenges for congressional rules. Barbara Sinclair defines *omnibus legislation* as "[l]egislation that addresses numerous and not necessarily related subjects, issues, and programs, and therefore is usually highly complex and long." Sinclair, *Unorthodox Lawmaking: New Legislative Processes in the U.S. Congress* 71 (2d ed.

2000). In a few instances, party leaders appoint special task forces of sympathetic members to draft and negotiate important legislation, either bypassing committees entirely or reducing their role substantially. The Civil Rights Act is an early example of unorthodox lawmaking; as the case study reveals, party leaders were unusually influential in determining the path of enactment, and several strategies were used to bypass particular committees and undermine the power of senior lawmakers.

1. *Introduction of Bills.* More than 200,000 bills are introduced in the 50 state legislatures each biennium, and around 10,000 in each Congress. Only legislators can introduce bills, although in some states the governor is required to submit budget bills to the legislature. See, e.g., Ill. Const. art. VIII, § 2. The legislators themselves do not always come up with the ideas for major bills or draft them. The executive proposes or drafts much of the important legislation considered by the legislature.[b] Indeed, the President may be the country's chief law-initiator. For example, the Celler, Lindsay, and McCulloch civil rights bills went nowhere until President Kennedy publicized the issue; his Justice Department drafted the civil rights bill introduced in both the House and Senate in 1963. Private groups also present draft bills to members of the legislature or advise them about amendments to bills proposed by the executive. The NAACP, for example, probably helped draft liberalizing amendments to the Kennedy civil rights bill that were adopted by Subcommittee No. 5.

As the case study suggests, the President exerts substantial influence over the shape of the political agenda. John Kingdon defines *agenda* as "the list of subjects or problems to which governmental officials, and people outside of government closely associated with those officials, are paying some serious attention at any given time." Kingdon, *Agendas, Alternatives, and Public Policies* 3 (2d ed. 1995). Getting an issue on the agenda is a prerequisite to adopting a policy to address it. Kingdon identifies four aspects to policymaking: setting the agenda; specifying alternatives from which a policy choice is to be made; choosing among the alternatives; and implementing the decision. His work focuses on the first two processes and attempts to explain why some subjects and not others become salient to policymakers and the public, and why some alternatives receive serious consideration and others do not. With respect to the first, agenda setting, the President is the most influential political actor. "No other single actor in the political system has quite the capability of the president to set agendas in given policy areas for all who deal with those policies." *Id.* at 23. Interestingly, and consistent with the study of the Civil Rights Act, the President has substantially less control over which alternatives will then dominate the discussion concerning possible policies to deal with the salient issue. Thus, the President may be able to raise the issue of racial equality and force others to propose and adopt solutions; he has less ability to dominate the debate over the appropriate response.

State legislators are often even more dependent upon the offices of state attorneys general and private groups to draft legislation than members of Congress because they do not have the staff support of federal lawmakers.

---

b. See Paul C. Light, *The President's Agenda: Domestic Policy Choice from Kennedy to Clinton* (3d ed. 1999); Vasan Kesavan & J. Gregory Sidak, *The Legislator-in-Chief*, 44 Wm. & Mary L. Rev. 1, 48–55 (2002).

The staff situation in state legislatures has improved somewhat in the last 20 years, however. Since 1979, the size of state legislative staff has grown by about one-third. Many states provide personal staff to individual legislators, and most states have competent staff associated with legislative committees.

   2. *Committee Consideration.* Bills are routinely referred to standing committees by the presiding officer of the legislative chamber. House Rule XII, clause 2 requires the Speaker to refer a bill to the committee(s) having jurisdiction over its subject matter. Clause 2 was amended in 1975 to give the Speaker the power to send parts of the same bill to more than one committee, to send the whole bill to more than one committee, and/or to create an "ad hoc committee" to consider a bill. In 1995, the House modified the process for referring legislation to committee by abolishing joint referrals and mandating instead that the Speaker designate a committee of "primary" jurisdiction upon initial referral. Senate Rule XVII and the rules in many state legislatures do not require referral of bills to the appropriate committees, but the practice is to do so.

   Committee jurisdiction is akin to a property right over political issues, so lawmakers work hard to place important legislation within the jurisdiction of committees on which they serve. The parliamentarian, a relatively nonpartisan player, makes referral decisions using a "weight of the bill" test to assign a proposal to the committee or committees with the most compatible jurisdiction. In his study of changes in committee jurisdiction over time, David King argues that such change is incremental, resembling legal change in the courts.[c] Parliamentarians rely on congressional rules (a sort of *statutory jurisdiction*) and precedent (a sort of *common law jurisdiction*) to determine the appropriate referral. For example, congressional rules specify that tax legislation must be referred to the House Ways and Means and the Senate Finance Committees, but the rules provide only a partial list of all possible subject matter of federal legislation. When the rules are silent, the parliamentarian follows past practice to make the referral. This common law of jurisdiction is substantial; for example, Professor King estimates that more than two-thirds of the House Commerce Committee's activity focuses on issues assigned to it through common law means. An ambitious politician works to frame bills so they fall within jurisdictionally ambiguous areas and then to convince the parliamentarian to assign them to a committee on which she has influence. Once a precedent is established, the same committee will prevail on referrals of bills in related areas through the common law reasoning so familiar to lawyers.

   The emphasis on bill referrals underscores the importance of congressional committees. Perhaps the most important power of committees is the *power of negation*; the vast majority of bills referred to committees never emerge for consideration by the full body. In a typical Congress, only around 14% of the bills introduced survive committee consideration and actually make it to the floor of either chamber.[d] The key player is the chair of the committee. If the chair refuses to schedule hearings for a bill or refer the bill to subcommittee,

---

   c.   See David C. King, *Turf Wars: How Congressional Committees Claim Jurisdiction* (1997).

   d.   See Smith, Roberts & Vander Wielen, *supra*, at 99 (17% of bills referred to committees are reported to the House floor and 13% to the Senate floor).

or refers the bill to a hostile subcommittee, the bill will usually die—even if most of the committee members favor the bill. House Rule XI and Senate Rule XXVI permit a majority of the committee to compel the chair to place a bill on the agenda, as Representative Brown threatened to do in the House Rules Committee's consideration of the civil rights bill. This is a maneuver rarely threatened and almost never attempted.

In addition, a majority of the House can bypass a committee by filing a *discharge petition* calling for a measure to be brought to the floor. When half of the House members have signed the petition, the bill is taken away from the committee and brought to the full House. Before 1993, the names of members signing a discharge petition were kept confidential until 218 people had signed. Now, the list of signers is public from the first signature, making it easier for supporters to pressure members to sign and to check if those who promised to sign actually have. Although the discharge petition route is seldom successful, Barbara Sinclair concludes that committees have been bypassed more frequently in recent Congresses than, for example, during the time of our case study, when the path of the Civil Rights Act was truly anomalous. See Sinclair, *Unorthodox Lawmaking*, 93–94. In the Senate, circumventing committees is easier because bills languishing in committees can be added as nongermane amendments to most bills as they are considered on the floor.

The committee process is also crucial for bills that have a good chance of being enacted. The committee can iron out difficulties and build a consensus in favor of the bill. The chair is again the critical person when a bill is actively considered. The committee or subcommittee chair schedules hearings, determines who will testify at the hearings, and asks most of the questions. Recall Representative Celler's power to manipulate both the committee and subcommittee consideration of the civil rights bill (although he did not always act very skillfully). The power of the committee chair has waned in recent years, as more power has been claimed by party organizations[e] and as recent Congresses have adopted rules diminishing the influence of chairs. For example, in 1995 as part of Republicans' "Contract with America," the House voted to limit the terms of committee chairs to six years and abolished several subcommittees, thereby reducing the power of these positions and some of the more senior members of the body. (During Democratic Party control of the House, from 2007 to 2011, this term limit was not in force, but the Republican Party takeover of the House in 2011 reinstated this term limit.)

In short, committees are congressional players with great influence over the agenda and legislative outcomes. Unlike some other constitutions, the U.S. Constitution does not require that Congress establish committees; instead, this organizational pattern is entirely a matter of lawmaker preference. The description of committee activities suggests several reasons legislators might prefer to do work through committees, even though such an organiza-

---

e. Since the mid–1990s, more legislative work has been done in informal task forces or leadership committees, entirely controlled by the majority party and often followed by perfunctory or no formal hearings. Because these are not governed by open meeting rules, lobbyists and interest groups can have substantial influence. See Roger H. Davidson, *Building the Republican Regime: Leaders and Committees*, in *New Majority or Old Minority? The Impact of Republicans on Congress* 69, 79–80 (Nicol Rae & Colton Campbell eds., 1999).

tion transfers power from floor majorities to small groups of lawmakers and to committee chairs in particular.

First, committees allow members to specialize and accumulate expertise in a substantive area. Other members defer to the specialists, thereby avoiding the costly prospect of becoming experts in every matter raised for a vote. This *informational role* suggests that committees are part of an efficient congressional organization, particularly necessary in an increasingly complex world.[f] Members must monitor committees to ensure that they are faithful agents of the full body and that the information and recommendations they put forth are consistent with the wishes of the majority. As long as monitoring is less costly than developing expertise on all matters and allows members to detect divergence between committee activities and majority preferences, a committee structure is sensible.

Another theory of legislative organization, the *distributive theory*, describes committees as the engine of *rent-seeking*, or the distribution of unjustified benefits to interest groups. Members partly self-select their committee assignments, so they seek appointment to committees with jurisdiction over areas about which they and their constituents have particularly intense preferences. Accordingly, committees are typically composed of preference outliers.[g] In most cases, lawmakers specialize in areas that allow them to send benefits back to their constituents or to key special interests to improve their reelection chances. In other cases, they may seek committee assignments that allow them to capture personal benefits from interest groups (for example, the Senate Commerce Committee has wide jurisdiction over the telecommunications industry, full of wealthy interest groups willing to compensate its legislative friends) or that allow them to spend time on topics of interest to them or provide them national prominence (for example, the House International Relations and Senate Foreign Affairs Committees).[h]

The two explanations for committees are not necessarily exclusive.[i] Members may be willing to invest time and resources in developing expertise and producing helpful information for the full body because they have special interest in the issues that fall within the jurisdiction of a particular committee. A member from a largely urban state may be unwilling to specialize in agriculture topics because she and her constituents have no special interest in farm policy, other than an attenuated desire that farm interests not receive a disproportionate share of the government's limited resources. Members from farm states, on the other hand, who want to channel public benefits to their

---

f. See Keith Krehbiel, *Information and Legislative Organization* (1991); Arthur Lupia & Mathew D. McCubbins, *Who Controls? Information and the Structure of Legislative Decision Making*, 19 Legis. Studs. Q. 361 (1994).

g. See Glenn R. Parker, *Congress and the Rent–Seeking Society* 74–81 (1996); Barry R. Weingast & William J. Marshall, *The Industrial Organization of Congress; or, Why Legislatures, Like Firms, Are Not Organized as Markets*, 96 J. Pol. Econ. 132 (1988). See also E. Scott Adler, *Why Congressional Reforms Fail: Reelection and the House Committee System* (2002) (explaining the durability of committee structure and jurisdiction using the distributive theory).

h. See also Christopher J. Deering & Steven S. Smith, *Committees in Congress* 63–77 (3d ed. 1997) (discussing committees in terms of their primary benefits to lawmakers and providing tripartite classification: constituency, policy, and influence committees).

i. See Forrest Maltzman, *Competing Principals: Committees, Parties, and the Organization of Congress* (1997) (offering sophisticated theory of committee formation).

farmer-constituents and may have extensive knowledge of agriculture before coming to the legislature, will actively seek membership on the Agriculture Committee. The more likely it is that committees consist of preference outliers, however, the more diligence is required of the other members to monitor committee activity and ensure that extreme policies are not enacted.

A third theory posits that committees are primarily the *tools of the majority party*.[j] Majority-party committee members exclude members of the other party from decisionmaking and cooperate among themselves to further the majority party's collective goals. Again, consider the Agriculture Committee. Although most members of the majority party are likely to support only modest agriculture subsidies, there are some members whose reelection prospects are substantially affected by enactment of generous subsidies. Committees provide a mechanism for members of the majority party to defer to the wishes of the few with intense preferences and to ensure that those lawmakers in turn defer in the future on other issues vital to the reelection of their colleagues. This process allows the majority party to remain in power by enhancing the reelection prospects of its members; party dominance is a goal shared by all party members who want to continue to receive the benefits of majority control.

Once a committee marks up the bill to its satisfaction and votes to send it to the full legislative chamber, the committee staff drafts a report on the bill that will be circulated to the other legislators. This is mandatory in both chambers of Congress (House Rule XIII; Senate Rule XXVI) and is the prevailing practice in state legislatures as well. Committee reports in Congress set forth the procedural and substantive background of the reported bill, the exact language of the bill, and a section-by-section analysis of the bill. Such reports in state legislatures are often shorter, more general descriptions of reported bills; thus, they are often less helpful to interpreters than the more extensive federal legislative history (see Chapter 4).[k] Committee reports, or distillations of them prepared by party organizations, are frequently the only documents that most legislators and their staffs read before a vote is taken on the bill. Reports are not only the principal means of communicating committee decisions to the chamber, but they are also persuasive briefs setting forth the factual and policy reasons justifying the proposed legislation. Committee members dissenting from all or part of the report are entitled to set forth their views as well. Finally, provisions in several laws require committees to include certain information about bills in committee reports.

3. *Scheduling Legislative Consideration.* Bills reported by committee are placed on a calendar of the legislative chamber. The U.S. House's calendar arrangement is especially complex. It has three primary calendars. The most important calendar is the *Union Calendar*, or the "Calendar of the Committee of the Whole House on the State of the Union." Virtually all bills are placed on this calendar. Second is the *House Calendar*, which now contains few bills, mostly special rules from the Rules Committee, changes in House rules, ethics resolutions, and some constitutional amendments. Third, private bills, such as

---

j. See Gary W. Cox & Mathew D. McCubbins, *Legislative Leviathan: Party Government in the House* (2d ed. 2007).

k. See, e.g., Eric L. Lane, *How to Read a Statute in New York: A Response to Judge Kaye and Some More*, 28 Hofstra L. Rev. 85, 118–19 (1999) (describing committee reports in New York).

those for the relief of individual aliens seeking to remain in the country, are placed on the *Private Calendar*. In addition, there are two calendars to which bills on the three main ones may move. The *Consent Calendar* consists of bills involving spending of less than $1 million on the Union or House Calendar that a member anticipates will be passed by unanimous consent. Minor bills on the Consent Calendar are considered by the House twice a month. The *Discharge Calendar* lists motions to discharge bills that are pending in committee.[1] Additionally, bills may be called up and considered by the House under a process called *suspension of the rules*. Suspension of the rules allows the House, with the consent of the Speaker, to consider a bill in an expedited fashion with no amendments or motions, but it requires that the bill be passed by a two-thirds vote. The U.S. Senate has only two calendars, the *Calendar of General Orders* and the *Executive Calendar* for treaties and executive nominations.

Simply being on the appropriate calendar does not, of course, assure that the chamber will consider the bill. Salient or time-sensitive bills usually will be considered before other bills ahead of them on the calendar. In the House, major legislation moves to the floor from committees in two ways. Budget and appropriations bills are privileged matters and can be brought to the floor at virtually any time. For other major bills, and often for budget and appropriations bills when supporters want to structure deliberation in a particular way, the reporting committee will request a special order, or *rule*, from the Rules Committee to advance the bill for expedited floor consideration. The Rules Committee, which is essentially an arm of the majority party, then decides whether it will propose a rule for the bill (its refusal to grant a rule effectively kills the bill for that session); what kind of rule to grant (an *open rule* permitting amendments, a *closed rule* prohibiting all floor amendments, or a *modified closed rule* permitting specified floor amendments and structuring the order of their introduction); when a bill is to be considered; and how much time for debate. The full House votes on the proposed rule; such rules are almost always passed by party-line votes. Control of the legislative agenda, facilitated through the use of special rules, is a tactical advantage that accrues to the majority party; indeed, agenda control may well be the most significant power that the majority party wields.[m]

There is no Rules Committee in the Senate, and expedited consideration is usually accomplished by a *unanimous consent agreement* (Senate Rule V). Like a House rule, a unanimous consent agreement is a roadmap for the bill's consideration: when it may be brought up, what amendments may be proposed, and how much time may be spent on it. Unlike a House rule, a Senate unanimous consent agreement must be acceptable to all Senators; the objection of a single Senator kills it. Recall that the civil rights bill languished for weeks in a pre-consideration filibuster, during which Southern Senators objected to any expedition at all. Under current Senate rules, most bills are still susceptible to two filibuster threats: on the motion to proceed to consider

---

l. See Charles Tiefer, *Congressional Practice and Procedure: A Reference, Research, and Legislative Guide* 245–46 (1989).

m. Gary W. Cox & Mathew D. McCubbins, *Setting the Agenda: Responsible Party Government in the U.S. House of Representatives* (2005).

the bill and on final passage.[n] Most filibusters now are virtual ones, which may explain the recent increase in threatened and actual filibusters. Members threaten to engage in extended debate, placing a *hold* on the bill until floor leaders can work out a compromise. For years, holds were largely anonymous, but their widespread use has prompted cries for reforms, and now the names of members blocking consideration of legislation or nominations are sometimes revealed.

Most state legislatures use only a single calendar on which they list all pending bills ready for floor action. As in Congress, the order of listing is not a reliable indication of when the bill will actually be considered; priority items of consequence are mixed with unimportant bills. Oversimplifying a little, one can say that the actual order of consideration is determined in one of two ways, parallel to the two methods used in Congress. State legislatures with strong party caucus systems tend to have their agendas set by the majority leader and/or the majority party caucus. State legislatures in which parties are weak typically vest agenda control in calendar committees, rules committees, or informal but less partisan mechanisms. In some states, the two methods effectively merge. For instance, where the presiding officer of the legislative chamber is also the chair of the rules committee, there is little functional difference between the two methods.

4. *Floor Consideration: Debate, Amendment, Voting.* Once a bill has been placed on the agenda by the relevant committee and advanced for consideration by the full legislative chamber, the process is mostly automatic. Most legislators routinely vote "yes," and the bill is passed. In the Senate, for example, dozens of routine bills are adopted through unanimous consent agreements read quickly at the end of a day's session. Consistent with the informational theory of legislative organization, the chamber as a whole usually ratifies the decisions and compromises reached in the smaller, more expert groups (committees). Of course, much important legislation, such as the Civil Rights Act, is controversial and has to run the further gauntlet of floor consideration. Three important aspects of congressional decisionmaking occur during such floor consideration: debate, amendment, and vote.

In the U.S. House and most state chambers, debate is significantly limited by general or special rules. (Indeed, because many state legislatures still only meet for several months each year, there is simply not enough time for extended public debate on more than a few issues.) Even where debate is not formally limited, as in the U.S. Senate, it normally consists of "set" speeches read by members to virtually empty chambers (although many staffers and some lawmakers will watch the floor proceedings on closed circuit television) or of *colloquies*, rehearsed questions posed to the bill's sponsor in order to build a legislative record on some issue. Frequently, members of Congress simply submit statements for printing in the *Congressional Record*, and the statements are never uttered on the floor. The *Record* identifies such a statement by either a "bullet" (•) preceding it or by a different typeface.

---

n. Some forms of budget legislation cannot be filibustered because the Senate has adopted strict time limits on the consideration of these important legislative vehicles. See Sarah A. Binder & Steven S. Smith, *Politics or Principle? Filibustering in the United States Senate* 192–94 (1997) (contrasting budget rules from traditional rules allowing filibuster).

Few votes appear to be altered by floor debate; instead, debate is seen mainly in terms of its strategic value. Members may use it to demonstrate that they are competent in a certain field of policy; to gain publicity for their positions; and to attempt to pack the legislative history with remarks supporting an interpretation of the proposal that they favor. In the modern era of televised floor proceedings, members know that their constituents and lobbyists can easily monitor their activity and their positions. In addition, debate can be manipulated by organized minorities to delay passage of legislation that they oppose. For example, the filibuster used in the U.S. Senate enables a determined group of senators to kill a bill or force concessions from the majority by extended debate. Cloture (cutting off the debate) required a two-thirds vote of the Senators voting in 1964; under amended Senate Rule XXII, it now requires 60 votes except with respect to changes in the rules themselves.

More important than debate is amendment. Once they have been reported by committee, bills can be amended on "second reading," sometimes in the legislature sitting as a committee of the whole, or on "third reading" (just before the final up or down vote is taken on the bill). Amendment on third reading is rare and may require unanimous consent or some other special dispensation. Most legislative chambers do not follow the U.S. House practice of dissolving into a committee of the whole to consider amendments.

Major bills on controversial subjects will attract numerous proposed amendments. A first-degree amendment changing the text of the bill is a *perfecting amendment*, which can strike language, insert language, or do both. The reporting committee (through the chair or a sponsor) will sometimes propose perfecting amendments to correct minor problems with the bill or to attract more support for the bill. In the latter case, the amendment is often called a *saving amendment*. Perfecting amendments from the floor may include minor amendments addressed to a narrow problem with the bill; *riders*, or amendments seeking to add irrelevant matter to the bill (riders are prohibited by House Rule XVI and the rules of some state legislatures); and hostile amendments. Some floor amendments, called *killer amendments*, can be lethal to the bill's prospects. Killer amendments often appear friendly because they strengthen the bill, but they are designed to antagonize the bill's more moderate supporters. In the story of the Civil Rights Act, Judge Smith's amendment adding "sex" to the list of impermissible bases for employment decisions prompted the opposition of floor leaders worried that expanding the legislation would prove fatal. Amendments can be quite comprehensive; for example, *amendments in the nature of a substitute* seek to replace the entire bill, striking all after the enacting clause and inserting entirely new text. They can represent radically different approaches to the problem addressed by the bill, and adoption of such an amendment may spell the end of the bill either by ensuring its ultimate defeat or by impairing the operation of the bill, making passage useless. In other cases, the managers of the bill will propose an amendment in the nature of a substitute that reflects the results of negotiations on the proposal following committee action.

A different kind of amendment can be confused with amendments in the nature of a substitute because of its similar name. A *substitute amendment* is offered when another amendment is pending, and it changes part of the proposed amendment. This second-degree amendment can be minor—replacing only one word or phrase—or significant—proposing an entirely new text but in a way different from the pending amendment in the nature of a substitute. In the latter case, the amendment is both a substitute amendment and an amendment in the nature of a substitute. Both opponents and proponents of legislation use amendments strategically, seeking to fill up the complex *amendment tree* to foreclose other changes in the bill or to obtain a special rule in the House that favors a particular sequence of voting on amendments. In some cases, bill managers will accept floor amendments in order to move debate forward and ensure final passage, but they do not intend to support the amendment in the conference committee. Lawmakers often observe that amendments can be "lost" in the Capitol building when conferees walk across the Rotunda to the other chamber to begin negotiations on the final legislation.

The vote on an amendment or a bill may be taken in one of four ways: voice vote, division of the house, tellers, and roll calls (increasingly by use of electronic devices). The first three methods do not leave a record of how each member of the legislative chamber voted, but division (where the yeas and nays rise to be counted) and tellers (where the yeas pass down the aisle to be counted, then the nays) permit observers to record how each member voted. The U.S. House of Representatives uses all four methods, and the Senate uses all but tellers. One-fifth of a quorum may demand a roll-call vote in either chamber, except when the House committee of the whole is in session. Moreover, congressional rules can often require roll call votes on particular matters; for example, House Rule XX requires roll call votes on all tax rate increases and appropriations bills.

The number of votes needed to adopt an amendment or pass a bill is normally a majority of those voting in each house of Congress, assuming a quorum is present. Some state legislatures, in contrast, require the votes of a majority of the members elected; thus, members not wanting to commit themselves against a measure may help defeat it simply by staying away when the vote is taken. Two-thirds supermajorities are needed for Congress to propose a constitutional amendment, to override a presidential veto, to expel a member, or for the Senate to concur in a treaty. In states, supermajorities can be required to override gubernatorial vetoes, to pass emergency legislation or special appropriation bills, or to enact new tax legislation.

5. *The Reconciliation Process: Conference Committee.* In the prevailing system of bicameral legislatures, there must be a "meeting of the minds" of the two legislative chambers to enact statutes. If the version passed by the U.S. House differs in any respect from that passed by the U.S. Senate, there is no enactment—unless one chamber recedes from its differences and joins the version of the other (as was the case for the Civil Rights Act). Sometimes the House and Senate send bills back and forth several times, acceding to part of the other chamber's alterations each time, in an effort to reconcile the two versions.

After both chambers have voted themselves into a state of disagreement, the last chamber to disagree may request a conference. The Speaker of the House and the Presiding Officer of the Senate formally appoint the conferees, but in practice the chair and ranking minority member of each relevant committee will submit a list of proposed conferees, who are then appointed. Note that this involvement in the final conference committee allows congressional committees influence over legislation both before and after the main floor consideration. Knowing that they will have this ex post influence will affect the interaction of committee leaders and floor managers with rank-and-file members. In both state and the federal legislatures, all the members of the reporting committees in each chamber are often appointed. There can be any number of conferees from either chamber, and modern conference committees vary in size from more than 200 members to only a handful of party leaders. Any compromise adopted in conference must be approved by a majority of the conferees from each chamber.

The objectives of the conferees are, first, to preserve the provisions most important to their respective chambers and, second, to achieve an overall result acceptable to a majority in each chamber. In Congress and most state legislatures, conferees are only authorized to consider matters about which the bills passed by the two chambers are in disagreement. Thus, they may not strike or amend any part of the bill that is identical in both versions, nor may they insert new matter not germane to the differences, nor may they expand any provision beyond that found in either version. In practice, because congressional conference committees do much of their work in private, it is difficult for other members, interest groups, and the public to monitor conferees' behavior. Lengthy omnibus bills that have been the product of long negotiations often emerge from conference with provisions never considered by either house or by any substantive committee. If the bill is nevertheless enacted, the rule against new provisions in conference is considered waived. When the conferees have reached agreement, they set forth their recommendations in a conference report, which will be printed in both chambers and will include a statement explaining the effect of the amendments or propositions agreed upon by the conferees on the measure.

In recent years, the legislative path of major legislation has become a bit more like that of the Civil Rights Act in the 1960s in that the textbook version of the process is seldom followed. In fact, Barbara Sinclair concludes that "the legislative process for major legislation is now less likely to conform to the textbook model than to unorthodox lawmaking," a term she uses to emphasize the extent of the change in congressional procedures. Sinclair, *Unorthodox Lawmaking, supra*, at xiv. Sinclair defines major legislation according to contemporary views of what bills were significant, so she studies the 45 to 55 proposals identified as major by the *Congressional Quarterly Weekly Report* (with some additions). A significant number of bills are referred to at least two House committees; in contrast, some major proposals bypass committees altogether. For example, in 1995, one in ten major measures bypassed committee in the House, and one in four avoided committee consideration in the Senate.[o] Although these rates may be unusually high, stronger party leaders, increased partisanship, and committee gridlock are factors that have encouraged lawmakers to use unorthodox lawmaking techniques for significant legislation. Through an increased use of amendments in the nature of a

---

o. See Sinclair, *Unorthodox Lawmaking,* 15, 37.

substitute, committee leaders and floor managers often make substantial changes in bills after they leave committee but before floor consideration. Interestingly, unlike most legislation, major legislation, which is more often subject to unorthodox lawmaking, has considerably better chances of enactment. Since the 1990s, nearly 60% of major legislation has been enacted, perhaps because the more complicated procedures allow advocates to form supporting coalitions and find consensus.

Another modern phenomenon is the use of summits between congressional leaders and the executive branch to work on compromise legislation concerning controversial topics. Since the mid–1980s, budget summits have become biennial affairs. Summits can occur in other contexts as well, and they disrupt the traditional legislative dynamics. For example, summits may not include committee leaders but instead involve only the top political leaders in the House and Senate. Although party leaders, who may better represent median as opposed to outlying preferences, can often reach compromises more easily, and perhaps more legitimately, than committee chairs, they may lack the substantive expertise necessary to draft effective legislation. Summits also tend to take place in relative secrecy, allowing political actors to reach compromises without requiring that particular individuals take responsibility for advocating positions that their core constituencies view as "selling out." See generally John Gilmour, *Strategic Disagreement: Stalemate in American Politics* (1995).

In the normal course of events in which a bill goes to a conference committee rather than a summit, the chamber that did not request the conference acts first on the conference bill, because that chamber has the "papers" (the bill as originally introduced and the amendments to it). That chamber has three options—adopt the conference bill, reject it, or recommit it to conference (which is tantamount to killing the bill). If the first chamber adopts the conference bill, the conference committee is dissolved, and the other chamber is faced with a straight up-or-down vote on the bill. If the bill is agreed to by both chambers, a copy of the bill is enrolled for presentment to the President or the Governor for signature.

6. *Presentment for the Presidential or Gubernatorial Signature.* Under Article I, § 7 of the U.S. Constitution, once an enrolled bill is presented to the President, the Chief Executive has ten days (not including Sundays) to sign it or veto it. If the President vetoes the bill, it is returned to Congress, where the veto can be overridden by two-thirds of those voting in each chamber. If the veto is overridden, the bill then becomes law without the President's signature. In most cases, if no action is taken within the constitutional ten-day period, the bill also becomes law without the President's signature. The exception to this last rule is that if Congress adjourns before the end of the ten-day period and the President fails to sign the bill, it is killed by a *pocket veto.* Many major bills are passed in the waning days of each Congress, and so the President often has ample discretion to kill legislation without immediate congressional override.

The U.S. President must accept or reject the entire bill; if there are several provisions the President dislikes in the bill, the only formal option is to veto (or pocket veto) the entire bill. State Governors typically have more options, because they can veto individual provisions called *items* in bills presented to them. Congress attempted to delegate a similar power to the President in the Line Item Veto Act of 1996, Pub. L. No. 104–130, 110 Stat. 1200, codified at 2 U.S.C. §§ 691–92, but the Supreme Court struck down the federal act in *Clinton v. City of New York*, 524 U.S. 417 (1998).

T<small>ITLE</small> *VII* <small>OF THE</small> C<small>IVIL</small> R<small>IGHTS</small> A<small>CT:</small> A<small>N</small> I<small>NTRODUCTORY</small> P<small>ROBLEM</small>

The most complex, and most often litigated, portion of the Civil Rights Act has been Title VII, 78 Stat. 241, 253–66 (1964), codified as amended at 42 U.S.C. § 2000e *et seq.*, which prohibits job discrimination on the basis of race, sex, religion, or national origin. We shall now introduce you to the main provisions of the 1964 Act, before its amendments in 1972 and 1991. The prime directive of Title VII is found in § 703(a), 42 U.S.C. § 2000e–2(a):

It shall be an unlawful employment practice for an employer—

(1) to fail or refuse to hire or to discharge any individual, or otherwise to discriminate against any individual with respect to his compensation, terms, conditions, or privileges of employment, because of such individual's race, color, religion, sex, or national origin; or

(2) to limit, segregate, or classify his employees or applicants for employment in any way which would deprive or tend to deprive any individual of employment opportunities or otherwise adversely affect his status as an employee, because of such individual's race, color, religion, sex, or national origin.

Section 703(b)–(c), *id.* § 2000e–2(b)–(c), sets forth similar prohibitions of "unlawful employment practices" by employment agencies and labor organizations (unions). Section 703(d), *id.* § 2000e–2(d), applies the antidiscrimination principle specifically to apprenticeship or training programs.

The exact scope of this anti-discrimination rule (i.e., how broadly does the rule apply?) is provided by § 701's definitions of key terms. Thus "employer" is defined in § 701(b), *id.* § 2000e(b):

The term "employer" means a person engaged in an industry affecting commerce who has twenty-five or more employees for each working day in each of twenty or more calendar weeks in the current or preceding calendar year, and any agent of such a person, but such term does not include (1) the United States, a corporation wholly owned by the Government of the United States, an Indian tribe, or a State or political subdivision thereof, (2) a bona fide private membership club (other than a labor organization) which is exempt from taxation under section 501(c) of the Internal Revenue Code of 1954 * * *.

Section 701(h), *id.* § 2000e(h), defines "an industry affecting commerce" as "any activity, business, or industry in commerce or in which a labor dispute would hinder or obstruct commerce or the free flow of commerce and includes any activity or industry 'affecting commerce' within the meaning of the Labor–Management Reporting and Disclosure Act of 1959, and further includes any governmental industry, business, or activity." Section 701(g), *id.* § 2000e(g), defines "commerce" as "trade, traffic, commerce, transportation, transmission, or communication among the several States; or between a State and any place outside thereof; or within the District of Columbia, or a possession of the United States; or between points in the same State but through a point outside thereof." Section 701(i), *id.* § 2000e(i), defines "State" to include "a State of the United States, the District of Columbia, Puerto Rico, the Virgin Islands, American Samoa, Guam, Wake Island, the Canal Zone, and Outer Continental Shelf lands defined in the Outer Continental Shelf Lands Act." Definitions for "employment agency" and "labor organization" are set forth in § 701(c)–(e), *id.* § 2000e(c)–(e). There is no definition of "discriminate" or "discrimination" in Title VII.

There are various "exemptions" or "defenses" to the charge of unlawful employment practices under Title VII. Section 702, *id.* § 2000e–1, for example, exempts employment of aliens outside any State or employment of persons by religious groups from Title VII's application. But the main defenses are those which qualify the meaning of "unlawful employment practice" in § 703. Section 703(e), *id.* § 2000e–2(e), presents a defense for practices based on bona fide occupational qualifications:

> Notwithstanding any other provision of this subchapter, (1) it shall not be an unlawful employment practice for an employer to hire and employ employees, for an employment agency to classify, or refer for employment any individual, for a labor organization to classify its membership or to classify or refer for employment any individual, or for an employer, labor organization, or joint labor-management committee controlling apprenticeship or other training or retraining programs to admit or employ any individual in any such program, on the basis of his religion, sex, or national origin in those certain instances where religion, sex, or national origin is a bona fide occupational qualification reasonably necessary to the normal operation of that particular business or enterprise, and (2) it shall not be an unlawful employment practice for a school, college, university, or other educational institution or institution of learning to hire and employ employees of a particular religion if such school, college, university, or other educational institution or institution of learning is, in whole or in substantial part, owned, supported, controlled, or managed by a particular religion or by a particular religious corporation, association, or society, or if the curriculum of such school, college, university, or other educational institution or institution of learning is directed toward the propagation of a particular religion.

Section 703(f)–(g), *id.* § 2000e–2(f)–(g), relates to employment decisions based upon Communist Party membership and national security reasons. Section 703(h), *id.* § 2000e–2(h), protects employment decisions based upon bona fide seniority or merit systems:

> Notwithstanding any other provision of this subchapter, it shall not be an unlawful employment practice for an employer to apply different standards of compensation, or different terms, conditions, or privileges of employment pursuant to a bona fide seniority or merit system, or a system which measures earnings by quantity or quality of production or to employees who work in different locations, provided that such differences are not the result of an intention to discriminate because of race,

color, religion, sex, or national origin, nor shall it be an unlawful employment practice for an employer to give and to act upon the results of any professionally developed ability test provided that such test, its administration or action upon the results is not designed, intended, or used to discriminate because of race, color, religion, sex or national origin. It shall not be an unlawful employment practice under this subchapter for any employer to differentiate upon the basis of sex in determining the amount of the wages or compensation paid or to be paid to employees of such employer if such differentiation is authorized by the provisions of [section 206(d) of title 29].

Section 703(i), *id.* § 2000e–2(i), stipulates Title VII's inapplicability "to any business or enterprise on or near an Indian reservation with respect to any publicly announced employment practice of such business or enterprise under which a preferential treatment is given to any individual because he is an Indian living on or near a reservation." Section 703(j), *id.* § 2000e–2(j), deals with affirmative action under Title VII:

Nothing contained in this subchapter shall be interpreted to require any employer, employment agency, labor organization, or joint labor-management committee subject to this subchapter to grant preferential treatment to any individual or to any group because of the race, color, religion, sex, or national origin of such individual or group on account of an imbalance which may exist with respect to the total number or percentage of persons of any race, color, religion, sex, or national origin employed by any employer, referred or classified for employment by any employment agency or labor organization, admitted to membership or classified by any labor organization, or admitted to, or employed in, any apprenticeship or other training program, in comparison with the total number or percentage of persons of such race, color, religion, sex, or national origin in any community, State, section, or other area, or in the available work force in any community, State, section, or other area.

Section 713(b)(1), *id.* § 2000e–12(b)(1), provides a defense to a person charged with violating Title VII "if he pleads and proves that the act or omission complained of was in good faith, in conformity with, and in reliance on any written interpretation or opinion of the Commission."

A person "claiming to be aggrieved" may not file suit herself, but should file a "charge" with the EEOC asserting violation of the substantive norms of Title VII, pursuant to § 706(a), *id.* § 2000e–5(a). (Note that § 706(b), (d) sets forth time requirements within which the charge must be filed with the EEOC; the schedule depends in part on whether the state has a remedy for the violation.) Once the aggrieved person has filed a timely charge, the EEOC determines whether there is "reasonable cause to believe that the charge is true," and if so it will try to eliminate the unlawful practice informally through "conference, conciliation, and persuasion" (§ 706(a)). If the EEOC is unable to obtain voluntary compliance with Title VII, it notifies the aggrieved person and informs her that she may bring a lawsuit in federal court within thirty days (§ 706(e), *id.* § 2000e–5(e)). To remedy an unlawful employment practice, a court may enjoin the practice and order "such affirmative action as may be appropriate, which may include reinstatement or hiring of employees, with or without back pay" (§ 706(g), *id.* § 2000e–5(g)).[p]

Consider the following problem that arose soon after the statute's enactment. The Duke Power Company's electrical generating plant at Dan River Stream Station in Draper, North Carolina had ninety-five employees in 1966, including fourteen African Americans. Employees were divided into five departments: (1) Operations (responsible for the day-to-day operation of the plant's generating equipment); (2) Maintenance (fixing and maintaining equipment); (3) Laboratory and Testing (analysis of water and coal used in the plant's operation); (4) Coal Handling (unloading and handling coal); and (5) Labor (janitorial services). The Labor Department was the lowest paid, with its maximum wage of $1.565 per hour being lower than the lowest wage of $1.705 per hour paid in other departments, and much lower than the maximum wages in other departments, which ran from $3.18 to $3.65 per hour.

In 1955 Duke Power began requiring that every employee, except those in the Labor Department, had to have a high school diploma. The company also made the diploma a prerequisite for promotion of workers from the Labor Department into any of the others. Before 1955 the company's policy was to limit African–American workers to the Labor Department. Under that policy, every African–American employee in the Dan River plant continued to work in Labor, and none was promoted. In 1965, when Title VII went into effect, the company instituted a new policy under which employees could be promoted out of Labor by passing one of two high school equivalency tests—either the Wonderlic general intelligence test or the Bennett Mechanical AA general mechanical test. Duke promoted Jesse Martin, a black man, from Labor to Coal Handling in 1966. Two other African–American workers were promoted in 1968. All had high school degrees.

After exhausting their administrative remedies with the EEOC, 13 of the 14 African–American employees at Dan River sued Duke Power for job discrimination in violation of Title VII. Six of the plaintiffs had no high school diplomas and were hired in Labor before 1955—when Duke had no high school diploma requirement for promotion but when it refused to promote African Americans as a matter of company policy. Four plaintiffs had no high school diplomas but were hired after the company instituted the diploma

p. This is the typical enforcement scenario, but there are two variations in which the aggrieved person plays less of a role. One is that the Commission itself can initiate an unfair employment practice investigation, resulting in voluntary compliance *or* notification to the individuals of their rights to sue *or* referral to the Attorney General for suit (§§ 705(a), 706(a), (e)). Another enforcement mechanism is a "pattern or practice" lawsuit that can be brought by the Attorney General under § 707, 42 U.S.C. § 2000e–6.

Like the enforcement program, the remedial program is bifurcated. If conciliation by the EEOC fails and the aggrieved person successfully sues for an unlawful employment practice, the federal court may enjoin the practice and "order such affirmative action as may be appropriate, which may include reinstatement or hiring of employees, with or without back pay" (§ 706(g)). Also the court may allow the prevailing private plaintiff a "reasonable attorney's fee" as part of the costs awarded (§ 706(k)). The main relief in Attorney General pattern or practice suits has been injunctive relief (§ 707(a)). Some court decrees have been broad, ordering the merger of unions, the creation of revised seniority systems, and affirmative action plans where there has been continued discrimination.

requirement. The plaintiffs sought an injunction requiring Duke to discontinue its diploma and testing requirements for promotion.

You are the General Counsel for Duke Power. The company wants to retain its diploma and testing requirements, and you believe that company policy is no longer to exclude African Americans from higher positions simply because of their race. What do you advise the company? Do the diploma and testing requirements violate Title VII? There is no precedent on this issue in the court system in early 1966, when the lawsuits are brought. You understand that the EEOC is going to issue guidelines on the subject of testing later in 1966. Can you predict what the EEOC guidelines will say? Take a few minutes, and jot down your thoughts. Then read the following opinion.

GRIGGS v. DUKE POWER COMPANY
United States Court of Appeals for the Fourth Circuit, 1970
420 F.2d 1225

BOREMAN, CIRCUIT JUDGE.

[Writing for the panel majority, Judge Boreman ruled that the claims of three plaintiffs were moot, because the plaintiffs had been promoted. Further, his opinion held that Duke's application of the diploma and testing requirement to the six pre–1955 employees violated Title VII because these employees were treated differently from white employees of the same period. Prior to 1955 whites were sometimes hired or promoted into the other departments without high school diplomas. But Judge Boreman rejected the claims of the four employees hired after 1955 and held that Duke's diploma and testing requirements were not discriminatory within the meaning of Title VII.]

Pointing out that it uses an intra-company promotion system to train its own employees for supervisory positions inside the company rather than hire supervisory personnel from outside, Duke claims that it initiated the high school education requirement, at least partially, so that it would have some reasonable assurance that its employees could advance into supervisory positions; further, that its educational and testing requirements are valid because they have a legitimate business purpose, and because the tests are professionally developed ability tests, as sanctioned under § 703(h) of the Act, 42 U.S.C. § 2000e–2(h).

* * * [I]t seems reasonably clear that this requirement did have a genuine business purpose and that the company initiated the policy with no intention to discriminate against Negro employees who might be hired after the adoption of the educational requirement. This conclusion would appear to be not merely supported, but actually compelled by the following facts:

(1) Duke had long ago established the practice of training its own employees for supervisory positions rather than bringing in supervisory personnel from outside.

(2) Duke instituted its educational requirement in 1955, nine years prior to the passage of the Civil Rights Act of 1964 and well before the civil rights movement had gathered enough momentum to indicate the inevitability of the passage of such an act.

(3) Duke has, by plaintiffs' own admission, discontinued the use of discriminatory tactics in employment, promotions and transfers.

(4) The company's expert witness, Dr. Moffie, testified that he had observed the Dan River operation * * * and he concluded that a high school education would provide the training, ability and judgment to perform the tasks in the higher skilled classifications. This testimony is uncontroverted in the record.

(5) When the educational requirement was adopted it adversely affected the advancement and transfer of white employees who were Watchmen [a miscellaneous category] or were in the Coal Handling Department as well as Negro employees in the Labor Department.

(6) Duke has a policy of paying the major portion of the expenses incurred by an employee who secures a high school education or its equivalent. In fact, one of the plaintiffs recently obtained such equivalent, the company paying seventy-five percent of the cost.

[Having found the diploma requirement acceptable under Title VII, the Court then examined the testing requirement, which Judge Boreman found to be "professionally developed" and presumptively acceptable under § 703(h).]

The plaintiffs claim that tests must be *job-related* in order to be valid under § 703(h). The Equal Employment Opportunity Commission * * * supports plaintiffs' view. The EEOC has ruled that tests are unlawful " * * * in the absence of evidence that the tests are properly related to specific jobs and have been properly validated * * *." Decision of EEOC, December 2, 1966, reprinted in CCH Employment Practices Guide, ¶ 17,-304.53. * * *

[Judge Boreman conceded that courts should give "great weight" to agency interpretations of statutes they administer, citing *Udall v. Tallman*, 380 U.S. 1, 15 (1965). But such interpretations are not binding on courts.] We cannot agree with plaintiffs' contention that such an interpretation by [the] EEOC should be upheld where, as here, it is clearly contrary to compelling legislative history * * *.

The amendment which incorporated the testing provision of § 703(h) was proposed in modified form by Senator Tower, who was concerned about a then-recent finding by a hearing examiner for the Illinois Fair Employment Practices Commission in a case involving Motorola, Inc. The examiner had found that a pre-employment general intelligence test which Motorola had given to a Negro applicant for a job had denied the applicant an equal employment opportunity because Negroes were a culturally deprived or disadvantaged group. In proposing his original amendment, essentially the same as the version later unanimously accepted by the Senate, Senator Tower stated:

"It [the amendment which, in substance, became the ability testing provision of § 703(h)] is an effort to protect the system whereby employers give *general ability and intelligence tests to determine the trainability of prospective employees.* The amendment arises from my concern about what happened in the Motorola FEPC case * * *.

"If we should fail to adopt language of this kind, there could be an Equal Employment Opportunity Commission ruling which would in effect invalidate tests of various kinds of employees by both private business and Government to determine the professional competence or ability or trainability or suitability of a person to do a job." (Emphasis added.) 110 Congressional Record 13492, June 11, 1964.

The discussion which ensued among members of the Senate reveals that proponents and opponents of the Act agreed that general intelligence and ability tests, if fairly administered and acted upon, were not invalidated by the Civil Rights Act of 1964. See 110 Congressional Record 13503–13505, June 11, 1964.

The "Clark–Case" interpretive memorandum pertaining to Title VII fortifies the conclusion that Congress did not intend to invalidate an employer's use of bona fide general intelligence and ability tests. It was stated in said memorandum:

"There is no requirement in Title VII that employers abandon bona fide qualification tests *where, because of differences in background and education, members of some groups are able to perform better on these tests than members of other groups.* An employer may set his qualifications as high as he likes, he may test to determine which applicants have these qualifications, and he may hire, assign, and promote on the basis of test performance." (Emphasis added.) 110 Congressional Record 7213, April 8, 1964.

[When the Tower amendment was called up for a vote, Senator Humphrey urged its adoption, and it passed without dissent.]

SOBELOFF, CIRCUIT JUDGE [concurring in granting injunctive relief to the six pre–1955 employees and dissenting in refusing relief to the four post–1955 employees].

The pattern of racial discrimination in employment parallels that which we have witnessed in other areas. Overt bias, when prohibited, has oft-times been supplanted by more cunning devices designed to impart the appearance of neutrality, but to operate with the same invidious effect as before. Illustrative is the use of the Grandfather Clause in voter registration—a scheme that was condemned by the Supreme Court without dissent over a half century ago. *Guinn v. United States*, 238 U.S. 347 (1915). Another illustration is the resort to pupil transfer plans to nullify rezoning which would otherwise serve to desegregate school districts. Again, the illusory even-handedness did not shield the artifice from attack;

the Supreme Court unanimously repudiated the plan. *Goss v. Bd. of Education*, 373 U.S. 683 (1963). It is long-recognized constitutional doctrine that "sophisticated as well as simple-minded modes of discrimination" are prohibited. *Lane v. Wilson*, 307 U.S. 268, 275 (1938) (Frankfurter, J.). We should approach enforcement of the Civil Rights Act in much the same spirit. * * *

The statute is unambiguous. Overt racial discrimination in hiring and promotion is banned [by § 703(a)(1)]. So too, the statute [presumably § 703(a)(2)] interdicts practices that are fair in form but discriminatory in substance. Thus it has become well settled that "objective" or "neutral" standards that favor whites but do not serve business needs are indubitably unlawful employment practices. * * * For example, a requirement that all applicants for employment shall have attended a particular type of school would seem racially neutral. But what if it develops that the specified schools were open only to whites, and if, moreover, they taught nothing of particular significance to the employer's needs? No one can doubt that the requirement would be invalid. It is the position of the Equal Employment Opportunities Commission (EEOC) that educational or test requirements which are irrelevant to job qualifications and which put blacks at a disadvantage are similarly forbidden. * * *

Whites fare overwhelmingly better than blacks on all the criteria [imposed by Duke Power for promotion],[6] as evidenced by the relatively small promotion rate from the Labor Department since 1965. Therefore, the EEOC contends that use of the standards as condition for transfer, unless they have significant relation to performance on the job, is improper. The requirements, to withstand attack, must be shown to appraise accurately those characteristics (and only those) necessary for the job or jobs an employee will be expected to perform. In other words, the standards must be "job-related."

[Judge Sobeloff urged deference to the EEOC interpretation of § 703(h), as indeed other courts had done. He further maintained that the EEOC's interpretation was not only "not unreasonable, but it makes eminent common sense," especially compared with Duke Power's lenient approach, which only required tests to be "professionally developed" to assure protection under the statutory exemption.] But, what is professionally developed for one purpose is not necessarily so for another. * * * [A] test that is adequately designed to determine academic ability, such as a college entrance examination, may be grossly wide of the mark when used

---

6. * * * *High School Education.* In North Carolina, census statistics show, as of 1960, while 34% of white males had completed high school, only 12% of Negro males had done so. On a gross level, then, use of the high school diploma requirement would favor whites by a ratio of approximately 3 to 1.

Standardized Tests. * * * Since for generations blacks have been afforded inadequate educational opportunities and have been culturally segregated from white society, it is no more surprising that their performance on "intelligence" tests is significantly different than whites' than it is that fewer blacks have high school diplomas. In one instance, for example, it was found that 58% of whites could pass a battery of standardized tests, as compared with only 6% of the blacks. Included among those tests were the Wonderlic and Bennett tests.

in hiring a machine operator. * * * [M]y brethren's resolution of the issue contains a built-in invitation to evade the mandate of the statute. To continue his discriminatory practices an employer need only choose any test that favors whites and is irrelevant to actual job qualifications. * * *

[Judge Sobeloff then examined the legislative response to *Motorola*.] That case went to the extreme of suggesting that standardized tests on which whites performed better than Negroes could never be used. The decision was generally taken to mean that such tests could never be justified *even if the needs of the business required them.*

Understandably, there was an outcry in Congress that Title VII might produce a *Motorola* decision. [Judge Sobeloff quoted the same language from the Clark–Case memorandum quoted above by Judge Boreman.] Read against the context of the *Motorola* controversy, the import of the Clark–Case statement plainly appears: employers were not to be prohibited from using tests to determine *qualifications.* "Qualification" implies qualification *for* something. A reasonable interpretation of what the Senators meant, in light of the events, was that nothing in the Act prevents employers from requiring that applicants be fit for the job. * * *

[Judge Sobeloff quoted Senator Tower's amendment as targeted only to protect tests "designed to determine or predict whether such individual is suitable or trainable with respect to his employment in the particular business or enterprise involved." 110 Cong. Rec. 13492 (1964) (text of original Tower amendment). Senators Humphrey and Case opposed the amendment as redundant, and Senator Case feared it was too broad: "If this amendment were enacted, it * * * would give an absolute right to an employer to state as a fact that he had given a test to all applicants, whether it was a good test or not, so long as it was professionally designed." *Id.* at 13504. The original Tower amendment was then defeated. *Id.* at 13724. Tower revised his amendment to render it acceptable to Humphrey and Case, and as revised the amendment passed.]

[Judge Sobeloff concluded that the EEOC interpretation, that employment tests must be job-related, was consistent with the legislative history. The District Court had found the tests not to be job-related, and Duke Power did not produce evidence showing in any way that a high school education was necessary for jobs such as coal handling. He rejected Duke's argument that the tests were designed to identify future prospects rather than immediate promotion. Judge Sobeloff concluded his dissent with a separate, and broader, point.]

* * * [T]he Company's criteria unfairly apply only to outsiders seeking entrance to the inside departments. This policy disadvantages those who were not favored with the lax criteria used for whites before 1955. * * * [T]his when juxtaposed with the history of the Dan River plant, is itself sufficient to constitute a violation of Title VII. * * *

[While Duke's] practice does not constitute forthright racial discrimination, the policy disfavoring the outside employees has primary impact upon blacks. This effect is possible only because a history of overt bias caused the departments to become so imbalanced in the first place. The result is that in 1969, four years after the passage of Title VII, Dan River looks substantially like it did before 1965. The Labor Department is all black; the rest is virtually lily-white.

There no longer is room for doubt that a neutral superstructure built upon racial patterns that were discriminatorily erected in the past comes within the Title VII ban. * * *

A remedy for this kind of wrong is not without precedent. The "freezing" principle (more properly, the anti-freezing principle) developed by the Fifth Circuit in voting cases is analogous. In those cases a pattern or practice of discrimination excluded almost all eligible Negroes from the voting lists but enrolled the vast majority of whites. Faced with judicial attack, the authorities found that they could no longer avowedly employ discriminatory practices. They invented and put into effect instead new, unquestionably even-handed, but onerous voting requirements which had the effect of excluding new applicants of both races, but, as was to be expected, primarily affected Negroes, who in the main were the unlisted ones. [For this reason, the Fifth Circuit struck down the new rules, and the Supreme Court agreed. *Louisiana v. United States*, 380 U.S. 145 (1965).]

Title VII bars "freeze-outs" as well as pure discrimination, where the freeze is achieved by requirements that are arbitrary and have no real business justification. Thus Duke Power's discrimination against *all* those who did not benefit from the pre–1955 rule for whites operates as an illegal "freeze-out" of blacks from the inside departments.

NOTE ON GRIGGS AND BACKGROUND AGAINST WHICH STATUTES ARE READ

The NAACP Legal Defense & Education, Inc. Fund (the "Inc. Fund"), which represents the plaintiffs, appeals this decision's denial of relief for the post–1955 plaintiffs to the Supreme Court. Should defendant cross-appeal the Court's granting relief to the pre–1955 plaintiffs? Do you think the EEOC will join in plaintiffs' appeal? How will the Supreme Court rule on this issue?

As you ponder this last query, consider the issues that divide Judges Boreman and Sobeloff. Some are technical issues, such as how to read §§ 703(a), (h) and what to make of the legislative history of the Tower Amendment (§ 703(h)). Sympathetic to Judge Boreman's account, Professors Daniel B. Rodriguez and Barry R. Weingast focus on the pivotal legislators— conservative Republicans who were needed to break the Senate filibuster— and claim that those members had a narrower vision of equality of opportunity with minimal "meddling" from the EEOC. They cite the history of the Tower Amendment as evidence that the liberal sponsors of Title VII needed the support of conservative Republicans and, for that reason, made a costly concession by ultimately going along with the Tower Amendment. See Rodriguez & Weingast, *The Positive Political Theory of Legislative History: New Perspectives on the 1964 Civil Rights Act and Its Interpretation*, 151 U. Pa. L. Rev. 1417, 1501–10 (2003).

Sharply disputing this account is Victoria F. Nourse, *Misunderstanding Congress: Statutory Interpretation, the Supermajoritarian Difficulty, and the Separation of Powers*, 99 Geo. L.J. 1119 (2011). Professor Nourse observes that Senator Tower was *not* a Republican who was a possible vote for the civil rights bill (Tower was from Texas, a segregated state), and so his statements about the proposed legislation are precisely the sort of cheap talk that interpreters should not rely on. Moreover, Nourse points out that the Tower Amendment, ultimately accepted by the Senate, was a *post-cloture* amendment; in other words, it came *after* the pivotal legislators (namely, Senator Dirksen) had signed into the civil rights bill, with the changes reflected in the Mansfield–Dirksen substitute. By her account, the sponsors would *not* agree to make major changes to the civil rights bill after the consensus substitute had been introduced and cloture invoked. (Keep this debate in mind when you consider the utility of legislative history in judicial interpretation of statutes.)

There are also larger issues that separate the two opinions, including different visions of racial justice, different degrees of deference to the EEOC, and different visions of the role of courts in implementing Title VII? Indeed, reading the legislative record may reflect different visions. Professor Nourse's account focuses on the majority coalition of liberal Democrats and moderate Republicans, whose project was (as Judge Sobeloff emphasizes) racial integration of our country's segregated workforces. In contrast, Professors Rodriguez and Weingast's account focuses on legislators they consider pivotal, such as the conservative Republicans whose votes were needed to break the Senate filibuster.

SECTION 2.   DESCRIPTIVE AND NORMATIVE APPROACHES TO LEGISLATION

Griggs is just the starting point for the fascinating story of Title VII's evolution. Congress launched the statute in 1964; in the following decades, the statute has evolved in ways scarcely imaginable to its enactors. To understand the statute's evolution (explored in Section 3), it is useful to consider both theories of how the legislative process *actually* works in practice and of how it *should* work in the best of all worlds. Examine the two opinions in *Griggs* again. Note, for example, the significance that the different judges attributed to the Clark–Case memorandum, to the Senate rejection of the original Tower Amendment and then its adoption of the revised version of it, to Senator Case's objection to the original Tower Amendment, and to the EEOC's position. The interpretation of these events varies depending upon the interpreter's descriptive and normative assumptions about the congressional process in 1964.

In this section, we explore insights provided by three different approaches to lawmaking: *interest group* approaches, which focus on the influence and behavior of organized groups in the political process (Part A); *proceduralist* approaches such as the vetogates perspective, which focus on the procedures by which a bill becomes law (Part B); and *institutionalist* approaches, which focus on broad governmental structures (Part C). Each theory attempts to describe the congressional process, and each one also contains explicit or implicit assumptions about how that process should function. No single approach fully describes the rich and complex world of legislatures, lawmakers, interest groups, and constituents. Scholars often draw insights from several of the perspectives; each highlights important aspects of the legislative process for students, judges, legislators, and lawyers seeking to influence Congress and state legislatures or to understand the legislative product.

A. PLURALISM AND INTEREST GROUP APPROACHES TO LEGISLATION

1. Pluralism: The Importance of Groups in Legislation

Much thinking about the legislative process finds its genesis in *The Federalist Papers*, more specifically, in the political thought of James Madison. As he worked to construct institutions of governance, Madison started with the propensity of human society to contain "factions" of citizens "who are united and actuated by some common impulse or passion, or of interest, adverse to the rights of other citizens, or to the permanent and aggregate interests of the community." *Federalist* No. 10. Like the Anti–Federalists (who opposed adoption of the Constitution), Madison believed factions must be controlled. However, Madison rejected the Anti–Federalist view that government could educate people to avoid faction and petty self-interest. "The latent causes of faction are thus sown in the nature of man," and hence cannot be eliminated short of unacceptable limitations on liberty. Madison viewed institutions of government as ways to contain the effects of faction and to channel them in socially productive ways. We will talk about the proceduralist and institutional aspects of Madisonian thought below, but for the moment, let us focus on the notion of faction.

Madison's definition of faction, or interest group, was not neutral; he wrote that factions are driven by common interests that are "adverse" to the public good. Most modern American thinkers who have emphasized the role of organized interests have a more positive view of factions. These scholars write in the *pluralist* tradition, exemplified by Robert A. Dahl, *A Preface to Democratic Theory* (1956). For them, an interest group is "any group that, on the basis of one or more shared attitudes, makes certain claims upon other groups in the society for the establishment, maintenance, or enhancement of forms of behavior that are implied by the shared attitudes." David Truman, *The Governmental Process* 33 (1951). Peter Schuck articulates an even broader definition: "special interests * * * include any group that pursues contested political or policy goals, and that is widely regarded by the public as being one contending interest among others." Schuck, *Against (and For) Madison: An Essay in Praise of Factions*, 15 Yale L. & Pol'y Rev. 553, 558 (1997). Under some definitions, political parties would be interest groups; other theorists distinguish between the major political parties and other organized groups.

As we are using the term, pluralism entails a number of interrelated propositions and definitions. (1) *Citizens organize into groups for political action.* Citizens have different opinions and different economic interests, which leads to the formation of "interest groups." (2) *Interest group politics results in "pluralism"—the spreading of political power across many political actors.* "Actual authority tends to be dispersed and exercised not solely by governmental officials but also by private individuals and groups within the society. Moreover, the power structure tends to be segmented; authority over one question rests here and over another there. All this contrasts with the model of a clear and rigid hierarchical pattern of power." V.O. Key, *Politics, Parties, and Pressure Groups* 9 (1958). Strong interest groups, many of which are private or voluntary organizations, protect individuals against oppressive and tyrannical government. In a way, a decentralized pluralist system expands one of Madison's checks on self-serving factions, as the ambition of one group checks the ambition of others and of government actors. See *Federalist* No. 10. (3) *Politics can be conceptualized as the process by which conflicting interest-group desires are resolved.* Because the objectives of one interest group can often be obtained only at the expense of others, the groups will come into conflict. The state regulates that conflict, and indeed the political system might be seen as nothing more than the arena in which interest group conflict is played out.

This third assumption deserves special attention. The starkest models of pluralism assume that government officials simply enact into law whatever interest groups, on balance, want. Policymakers are little more than rubber stamps validating the deals struck by interest groups in private negotiation, or umpires enforcing the rules of the game but playing no role in its outcome. Optimistic pluralists are not concerned that the resulting policies will be ill-conceived or contrary to the public interest; instead, a political environment with many groups actively competing will tend to produce moderate and well-considered policies. In part, moderation results because of the connections among interest groups. All of us belong to many groups, and our overlapping memberships provide an effective restraint on the extremism of any one group. In addition, "[b]ecause constant negotiations among different centers of power are necessary in order to make decisions, citizens and leaders will perfect the precious art of dealing peacefully with their conflicts, and not merely to the benefit of one partisan but to the mutual benefit of all the parties to a conflict." Robert A. Dahl, *Pluralist Democracy in the United States: Conflict and Consent* 24 (1967).

Our pluralist system is a marketplace of ideas, where all perspectives are articulated forcefully and persuasively. The best ideas succeed, while the worst are discarded. Pluralists argue that groups have a degree of power proportionate to their numbers—the larger, more general interest will prevail over the smaller, special interest. In addition, they have a degree of power proportionate to the intensity with which they hold their views, a factor which can increase the influence of smaller groups. As

Nathaniel Persily explains the pluralist vision: " '[I]nterests' are not all equal: some are intensely felt, others only weakly so. 'Democracy' is more than a math problem. The *number* of people favoring a particular candidate or proposition is only one factor for which [a governance] system needs to account. The intensity of preferences also must weigh in the balance." Persily, *Toward a Functional Defense of Political Party Autonomy*, 76 N.Y.U. L. Rev. 750 (2001).[a] In short, bargaining among interest groups allows the system to reach a long-term equilibrium providing many interest groups one or a few policy objectives they care deeply about because they are willing to give up on issues about which they care much less.

A crucial assumption underlying such optimistic visions of pluralism is that all views and interests are represented. One might view the policies that emerge from interest group conflict and interaction with concern, however, if some interests are systematically unrepresented, or if some groups cannot accurately communicate to policymakers the intensity with which they support particular perspectives. Even early critics of interest-group liberalism noted pervasive disparities of access to the political process. One prominent skeptic, Elmer E. Schattschneider, in *The Semisovereign People: A Realist's View of Democracy in America* (1960), argued that interest groups are not broad-based or representative of all societal interests. "The flaw in the pluralist heaven is that the heavenly chorus sings with a strong upper-class accent. Probably about 90 percent of the people cannot get into the pressure system. * * * Pressure politics is a selective process ill designed to serve diffuse interests," such as the interests of consumers and other ordinary people. *Id.* at 34–35.

Professor Schattschneider based his observation in part on his study of the Smoot–Hawley Tariff, which he found to have been enacted as a result of deals struck by well-heeled special interest groups rather than any deliberative consideration of the public interest. See Elmer E. Schattschneider, *Politics, Pressures and the Tariff: A Study of Free Private Enterprise in Pressure Politics, as Shown in the 1929–1930 Revision of the Tariff* (1935). Professors Kay Lehman Schlozman and John T. Tierney have provided a stronger empirical basis for this observation, which seems at least intuitively plausible to any observer of politics. They found that "the pressure community [in Washington] is heavily weighted in favor of business organizations: 70 percent of all organizations having a Washington presence and 52 percent of those having their own offices represent business. The overrepresentation of business interests takes place at the expense of two other kinds of organizations: groups representing broad public interests and groups representing the less advantaged." Schlozman & Tierney, *Organized Interests and American Democracy* 68 (1986). These numbers may somewhat overstate the business community's influence

---

a. See also Robert A. Dahl, *Democracy and Its Critics* 150 (1989) (arguing that our system is one of "minorities rule" rather than of "majority rule"); Sidney Verba, Kay Lehman Schlozman & Henry E. Brady, *Voice and Equality: Civic Voluntarism in American Politics* 179–82 (1995) (explaining the importance of intensity of preference for pluralist democratic theory).

relative to citizen groups; although citizen groups may comprise less than the 7% of Washington representatives identified by Professors Schlozman and Tierney, they represent nearly 32% of all congressional testimony. Jeffrey Berry, *The New Liberalism: The Rising Power of Citizen Groups* 21–22 (1999).

In *The Logic of Collective Action* (1965), Mancur L. Olson Jr. elaborated on Schattschneider's thesis and provided a theory to explain why some groups form and work to influence politics and why some do not. Legislation is a *public good*; once the state has decided to provide clean waterways or safe highways, for example, all in society will benefit. Yet any individual effort to pass such laws will have only an infinitesimal effect on the probability of its enactment. Therefore, a rational person will not participate in the political process at all, preferring instead to *free-ride* on the efforts of others. As long as the free-rider cannot be excluded from enjoying the public goods that legislation and the efforts of groups lobbying in favor of new laws provide, she will have no incentive to join the group or to expend time and resources. If all citizens follow this rational course, then none will work to influence her representative to pass legislation providing diffuse benefits to the public at large.

Professor Olson's theory predicts, therefore, that groups will form most often when there are a few interested members. In that case, each member has a large enough stake in the sought-after law to justify its participation. Furthermore, in small groups, members can monitor the behavior of others, detect and punish shirking, and ensure collective action. In other cases, a group will form because one member will receive such a large fraction of the governmental benefit that it would work to obtain the legislation even if it had to internalize all the costs of political activity. Indeed, the interested party may expend significant resources forming an interest "group" as part of its political strategy. It may fare better in the political process if the policy it advocates appears to elicit broader support. For example, a great deal of modern grassroots activity is financed, and to some extent manufactured, by well-funded, relatively small groups that hope to lend populist credentials to their policy proposals.[b] Under both these scenarios of group formation, small groups have the advantage over larger ones, and they will work to obtain targeted benefits at the expense of the diffuse and unorganized public. As Olson concludes: "[T]here is a surprising tendency for the 'exploitation' of the great by the small." *The Logic of Collective Action, supra*, at 35 (emphasis omitted). Other groups form because they can successfully coerce members to participate. For example, some have argued labor unions' legislative and electoral clout results in part from their ability essentially to require workers to belong and to participate in their activities.

The work of Professors Olson and Schattschneider is necessary to understand interest group activity in politics and the threat that minority interests pose to the public good. Their work points out a flaw in

---

b. See Richard Davis, *The Web of Politics: The Internet's Impact on the American Political System* 81–83 (1999).

Madison's prediction of the threat of factions. In a democracy, Madison feared more the tyranny of majority factions that could adopt policies oppressing minorities. He dismissed concerns about minority factions in *Federalist* No. 10: "If a faction consists of less than a majority, relief is supplied by the republican principle, which enables a majority to defeat its sinister views by regular vote." As we will discuss in our survey of proceduralist and institutional theories of the legislative process, not only do minority factions possess organizational advantages over majority factions, they may also be adept in using aspects of the political process to dominate the discussion of policy alternatives, the selection of a particular course of action, and the implementation of the policy.

Although in some ways he completes and improves Madison's view of factions, Olson himself did not put forth an entirely satisfying theory. Large groups do form and influence political outcomes. Under the logic of collective action, such groups should remain latent, quietly footing the bill for the self-serving legislation that small groups manage to enact. Olson explained large groups in two ways. First, some form for nonpolitical reasons and then turn to political activity as a *byproduct*. For these groups, the initial costs of organizing, often the greatest hurdle facing those who seek to influence governmental policies, have already been met. Notably, these existing groups tend to comprise more privileged people— such as cartels, unions, farmer cooperatives, monopolies, and oligopolies— and therefore fit comfortably into Schattschneider's elite chorus. In the story of the Civil Rights Act, however, religious groups participated in political activity as a byproduct of their other activities. Their involvement demonstrates that not all such groups consist of the wealthy or advantaged classes.

Large groups can also form if they offer desirable *selective benefits* only to their members. For example, groups may offer life insurance, discounts on travel, dinners and events, and other goodies only to their members. The AARP offers members discounts on drugs; the NRA offers members discounts on bullets. To explain large political groups on the basis of this sort of selective benefit seems rather unpersuasive, however. Why pay dues that fund the Sierra Club's political activity just to get the calendar when one can buy a nature calendar for much less money? The kind of selective benefit that prompts people to join large groups must relate to the political activity itself. Accordingly, some public choice theorists argue that participation in group activity provides members with purposive or solidary benefits that justify any costs they incur.[c] *Purposive benefits* accrue to members who seek ideological or issue-oriented goals and find pursuit of those objectives more meaningful as part of an organized group.[d] *Solidary benefits* provide members social rewards, including the satisfaction of the desire to be politically motivated.

---

c. See Paul Johnson, *Interest Group Recruiting: Finding Members and Keeping Them*, in *Interest Group Politics* 35 (Allan J. Cigler & Burdett A. Loomis eds., 5th ed. 1998).

d. See Edward L. Rubin, *Getting Past Democracy*, 149 U. Pa. L. Rev. 711, 745–46 (2001) (describing social movement theorists and noting that "meaning, not self-interest, * * * motivated many citizens' participation.").

These sorts of benefits may explain the existence of groups representing the poor and powerless in society. People who do not vote or have economic resources to influence policymakers rely on others who receive purposive or solidary benefits from political activity on behalf of disempowered groups. In addition, such a group may be led by an activist who obtains nonpecuniary personal benefits, perhaps through publicity or by satisfying intense ideological preferences, and thus is willing to incur the costs of organizing and lobbying. Regardless of the existence of these altruistic groups, however, we might suspect that individuals who must rely on others to assert their interests face significant disadvantages in the political system and obtain fewer benefits than they would in an ideal world.

Olson's vision is also incomplete because legislators will sometimes pay attention to the concerns of the diffuse public even if no organized group works to place the concerns on the policy agenda. For example, Congress enacts environmental legislation with provisions that benefit the general public, and it would probably do so even if groups like the Sierra Club remained latent. And we all know that lawmakers work to avoid passing general tax rate increases even though taxpayers are largely unorganized and Congress could use the money to send targeted benefits to vocal and organized minority factions.

In *The Logic of Congressional Action* (1990), a book designed to expand on Olson's seminal work, R. Douglas Arnold explains why legislators respond to the general public, which he calls the *inattentive public*, and do not spend all their time legislating in favor of organized groups that comprise the *attentive public*. The simple explanation is the electoral connection between lawmakers and the public. Members of Congress want to be reelected, and they know that the inattentive public, many of whom will vote in the next election, can be roused into action on particular issues under certain conditions. To avoid reprisals at election time, legislators will consider the potential preferences of the inattentive public and the likelihood that voters will focus on these preferences at election time. Given their limited attention, however, the inattentive public may be satisfied with legislation that is largely symbolic, effecting no real change in policy.

Again, the mechanism that Arnold describes does not ensure that lawmakers will take into account all public preferences or the intensity with which citizens hold them. Instead, lawmakers will pay attention to issues affecting the diffuse public when they believe the issues are likely to influence votes in the next election. Arnold identifies several factors that affect the likelihood that a citizen will care about a given issue when she enters the voting booth. The *magnitude* of the cost or benefit affects the probability that a citizen will perceive it; and the *timing* of the cost or benefit is important because citizens can more easily trace the direct effects of a policy back to a legislative action than they can effects further down the causal chain. In addition, the *proximity* of a voter to others similarly affected will influence the probability that she will pay attention to the issue. Perhaps most importantly, the unorganized public is more likely to notice an issue when an *instigator* or *policy entrepreneur* brings the issue forcefully to its attention near election time. A policy entrepreneur is a person, sometimes but not necessarily a government official, who works to bring a particular issue to the forefront of the policy agenda and to mobilize public support for action.[e] Examples of policy entrepreneurs who can elevate an issue to the consciousness of the inattentive public are journalists or political opponents.

2. Public Choice Theory: A Transactional View of the Legislative Process

Based in part on the empirical work of scholars such as Schattschneider and on the theories of classical market economics, a group of pluralists called *public choice theorists* have developed a rich line of scholarship to explain the operation of the processes by which legislators are selected, take action and positions, and make collective decisions.[f] Public choice scholars apply economic models to political phenomena and decisionmaking. Politicians and voters are considered rational utility-maximizers operating in a competitive electoral market. One prominent aspect of public choice theory has been the creation of models treating the legislative process as a microeconomic system in which "actual political choices are determined by the efforts of individuals and groups to further their own interests." Gary Becker, *A Theory of Competition Among Pressure Groups for Political Influence*, 98 Q.J. Econ. 371, 371 (1983). "The basic assumption is that taxes, subsidies, regulations, and other political instruments are used to raise the welfare of more influential pressure groups." *Id.* at 373–74. Compared to the optimistic pluralists, who often adopt an avowedly normative position in their scholarship, public choice theorists claim to be less normative and more descriptive in their methods and objectives. They are not wholly descriptive, however; for example, they often criticize existing institutional arrangements and propose changes based on their assumptions about individual and group behavior.

True to their perspective as economists, public choice scholars model the legislative environment as a political market. Interest groups, and to a lesser extent the public, are the demanders of legislation. They send benefits to legislators, who can supply them with governmental largesse. Legislators can respond to demand by refusing to pass a bill, by avoiding a clear choice through delegation of broad decisionmaking authority to an agency in the executive branch, or by explicitly allocating tangible bene-

---

e. See, e.g., Frank Baumgartner & Bryan Jones, *Agendas and Instability in American Politics* 6 (1993) (discussing the importance of policy entrepreneurs); Gregory J. Wawro, *Legislative Entrepreneurship in the U.S. House of Representatives* (2000) (studying entrepreneurial behavior in Congress).

f. In addition to Professor Olson's book cited earlier, other prominent works of public choice theory include James M. Buchanan & Gordon Tullock, *The Calculus of Consent* (1962); Anthony Downs, *An Economic Theory of Democracy* (1957); William Riker, *Liberalism Against Populism* (1982).

fits. Based on Olson's *Logic of Collective Action* and James Q. Wilson's *Political Organizations* (1973), Michael T. Hayes posits a transactional theory of legislation in *Lobbyists and Legislators: A Theory of Political Markets* (1981). Inspired by the idea that political markets are analogous to economic markets, Hayes outlines the demand and supply patterns for several different categories of political issues.

a. *Demand Patterns in Political Markets.* On the demand side (what interest groups want out of the legislature), legislators are often faced with a myriad of interest groups on any given issue, and these groups may either agree (consensual pattern) or disagree (conflictual pattern) with each other. A consensual demand pattern is similar to a non-zero-sum situation, while a conflictual demand pattern is basically zero sum. If an issue is consensual, then everyone who is aware of and actively interested in the issue can come out a winner, while if it is conflictual, then the resolution of the conflict will necessarily result in immediately identifiable winners and losers. In a way, this dichotomy is unrealistic; in a world of limited resources, all policies are zero sum because someone, either now or later, has to pay for them. In the short run, however, government decisions can be relatively unconstrained by resource limitations if policy-makers can push the costs onto an inattentive group or a group that does not vote in the next election. For example, government benefits funded through deficit financing places the costs on future generations of taxpayers, some of whom have not yet been born. See Daniel Shaviro, *Do Deficits Matter?* (1997). Living voters may be harmed by higher interest rates as the government competes for credit or by inflation if the government just prints more money, but those costs can be hard for citizens to trace back to particular legislative decisions. In these essentially consensual circumstances, interest groups may cooperate, making deals among themselves to obtain benefits at the expense of the general public. This type of interest group behavior is often called *logrolling* as minority interests work together to enact a bill, providing goodies to the organized constituents of a majority of lawmakers. Examples of these kinds of bills include tax bills that enact tax benefits for hundreds of interest groups, military construction bills that send money to projects in hundreds of congressional districts, or tariff bills like the Smoot–Hawley Act that Schattschneider studied.

The extent to which an interest group is formally organized is one key to its effectiveness in demanding legislation. Organized groups provide useful information to political actors and tend to frame the issues more clearly and precisely for legislators. And, as we have learned, certain kinds of groups are more likely to succeed in surmounting the hurdles to effective organization than others, potentially skewing the market for legislation.

Increasingly, the demand side of the market is characterized by interest groups working in coalitions in which several groups with shared interests work together typically for a limited time.[g] Some coalitions are relatively permanent, however; for example, the American Chamber of Commerce or the National Association of Manufacturers are really coalitions of smaller groups. Coordination among groups can reveal to lawmakers that a policy's advocates span numerous congressional districts, and coalitions are often nonpartisan, giving them the advantage of bipartisan support. Of course, coalitions are not invincible. The larger and broader a coalition, the more susceptible it may be to tactics that divide members and dissipate its strength. Those forming coalitions thus face a difficult tension. On the one hand, larger coalitions have more clout because they command more resources and they can maintain relationships with more lawmakers. On the other hand, large coalitions often comprise groups whose interests are aligned but not identical. Thus, a large coalition may face collective action problems or may begin to splinter when compromises are developed through the legislative process.

Professor James Q. Wilson maintains that the degree and nature of interest group organization is determined by the perceived incidence of costs and benefits from a specified policy. Similarly, Theodore Lowi argues that the political relationship among demanders of the legislative product is "determined by the type of policy at stake, so that for every type of policy there is likely to be a distinctive type of political relationship." Lowi, *American Business, Public Policy, Case–Studies, and Political Theory*, 16 World Pol. 677, 688 (1964). Costs of a policy may be broadly *distributed*, such as a sales tax paid by all consumers, or may be *concentrated* on a small group, such as a license fee. Similarly, benefits may be widely distributed or shared by all, such as the benefits of national security, or they may be concentrated in the hands of a few, such as state subsidies to tobacco farmers. When Wilson's typology is combined with the insights of Olson's theory, a transactional theorist might surmise that because bills providing concentrated costs or benefits will affect smaller groups, they will *on average* stimulate more organizational activity than measures with distributed costs and benefits.[h] Table 1–1 sets forth this model.

Each of these quadrants produces a particular kind of political climate. Quadrant I is best described as *majoritarian politics*. Although there is little group activity on either side, some large groups of citizens will weigh in both in favor of distributed benefits (for example, environmental groups will favor clean air legislation) and against distributed costs (Citizens for a Sound Economy will oppose tax increases or the Concord Coalition will oppose deficit spending). Quadrant II fits the model of

---

g. See Kevin Hula, *Lobbying Together: Interest Group Coalitions in Legislative Politics* (2000).

h. Note the textual emphasis, *on average*; this is only a generalization, not an iron rule. Due to the free-rider problem, the formation of even small groups cannot be assumed. Extremely large groups sometimes organize. In addition, as our analysis of proceduralism will demonstrate, numerous advantages exist for groups in a defensive posture, which means that such groups are perhaps more likely to form. Also, an effective demand pattern is not limited to interest groups— the existence of an inattentive public can and does exert influence in certain situations. Finally, the work of interest groups can all be for naught due to the countervailing power of the latitude possessed by legislators.

entrepreneurial politics. Organized interests will form to derail the legislation; support is likely only if a policy entrepreneur is willing to push the proposal, rouse the inattentive public, and perhaps take the initiative in forming citizen groups offering purposive or solidary benefits to participants. *Client politics* describes the consensual interest group activity in Quadrant III, where logrolling dominates the essentially non-zero sum game that interest groups play. Finally, Quadrant IV is the area of conflictual *interest group politics* where the process produces identifiable and short-term winners and losers, and both sides are organized and active.

Table 1–1
Taxonomy of Demand for Legislation Based on Benefits/Costs

I *Distributed benefits/distributed costs*	**II** *Distributed benefits/concentrated costs*
A general benefit-general taxation case that usually involves public goods. Little group activity on either side of most cases.	A general benefit-specific taxation case in which the majority imposes its will on the minority up to the capacity of the minority to pay. Opposition will tend to be well organized.
III *Concentrated benefits/distributed costs*	**IV** *Concentrated benefits/concentrated costs*
Tends to have strong interest group support and weak, if any, organized opposition because of the free-rider problem. The benefit to an individual of having the policy changed is simply too immaterial.	Results in continuous organized conflict over payment of benefits and distribution of costs. A prime example is the NLRB and the conflicts between labor and management.

b. *Supply Patterns in Legislative Markets.* Public choice theorists tend to discount legislators' statements that they vote "for the public interest." Morris P. Fiorina, *Congress: Keystone of the Washington Establishment* (2d ed. 1989), and David R. Mayhew, *Congress: The Electoral Connection* (1974), posit that legislative behavior can best be explained by the assumption that the primary goal of legislators is to be reelected. Of course, regardless of the ultimate motivation for legislative behavior, the desire for reelection is a good focus of study because, as long as lawmakers do not face term limits, reelection is a prerequisite to achieving any other goals. To put it differently, legislators may ultimately want to enact particular policies that they believe benefit the country, or to receive benefits from interest groups, or to gain publicity because of their positions. But to achieve any of these goals, they must remain in office; thus, the electoral connection is a paramount concern.

A large majority of legislators respond to this electoral incentive effectively and are reelected time after time. Although the advantage of incumbency has declined slightly, it is still one of the strongest predictors of electoral success.[i] How can a politician ensure that she will remain undefeated if her elected position demands that she take public stands on controversial issues? Fiorina has suggested that *abstention* (the legislator does not take sides) or *casework* (the legislator dollops out individual, nonlegislative favors, such as intervention in agency decisionmaking, to the groups voted against) can ameliorate the harmful effects of conflicting constituent demands. Other transactional theorists argue that the most effective response is for the legislator to act so that each of the conflicting groups will believe it has won something. Thus, the legislator's best strategies for dealing with conflictual demand patterns are to persuade the conflicting groups to reach a compromise which the legislator will then support *or* to pass an ambiguous bill which delegates policy responsibility to an administrative agency which is even more prone to interest group manipulation. The capture theory has gained wide currency in administrative law: agencies charged with regulating an industry or making political value choices regarding a cluster of issues become tools of the interests they are supposed to be ruling.[j]

Again, Wilson's typology may be useful. If a policy imposes concentrated costs, legislators will want to avoid responsibility as much as possible, perhaps by delegating the cost-imposition to a regulatory agency, such as the Food and Drug Administration or the Environmental Protection Agency. The regulated interest may accept this outcome, hoping that its superior organization will allow it to capture the regulating agency and subvert the policy.[k] Even if the costs are distributed, such as in majoritarian politics, legislators may be wary of acting directly and decisively. Take, for example, the case of a clean air act funded through a general tax rate hike. The inattentive public is more likely to trace the immediate and somewhat costly increase in taxes back to lawmakers and vote against them than voters are apt to notice slight increases in air quality and to make the connection between cleaner air and a particular piece of legislation. In cases of concentrated benefits and distributed costs, however, legislators may risk the wrath of the electorate to gain the gratitude of the attentive and organized public, particularly if they believe that the cost-bearers will remain unaware of the costs or can be deceived by public-regarding half-truths about the statutory purposes. Thus, in the arena of client politics, legislators often reward friendly interest groups with self-regulation or distributive benefits.

Table 1–2 illustrates the transactional supply model. As you study the interest group dynamics in the various quadrants, ask yourself where the Civil Rights Act of 1964 fits. Businesses required to change their hiring and promotion practices may have believed they were subject to concen-

---

i. See Bruce E. Cain, *The American Electoral System,* in *Developments in American Politics* 37, 43–46 (Gillian Peele, Christopher Bailey & Bruce E. Cain eds., 1992).

j. See, e.g., Thomas A. Merrill, *Capture Theory and the Courts: 1967–1983,* 72 Chi.-Kent L. Rev. 1039, 1050–52 (1997).

k. See Peter H. Aranson, Ernest Gellhorn, & Glen O. Robinson, *A Theory of Legislative Delegation,* 69 Cornell L. Rev. 1 (1982).

trated costs. On the other hand, businesses in the South that wanted to expand their client base or expand their pool of potential workers may have preferred legislation that would allow them to integrate without violating ingrained racist norms in those regions.[1] What about the interest groups on the other side? As we have noted, the religious organizations favoring the bill were already organized; their political activity was a relatively cheap byproduct since the initial costs of organization had been defrayed and mechanisms of collecting financial support and harnessing human resources were well established. Policy entrepreneurs inside and outside of government abound, all with varying personal interests. And while blacks and other groups facing discrimination were relatively powerless in society, they had the potential to organize and affect electoral outcomes, particularly after President Johnson succeeded in meeting his subsequent objective of enacting strong voting rights laws.

Table 1–2
Taxonomy of Supply of Legislation Based on Benefits/Costs

I *Distributed benefits/distributed costs*	**II** *Distributed benefits/concentrated costs*
Because there is no strong pressure from organized interests, legislature will favor *no bill or symbolic action*. Sometimes delegation to agency regulation will occur.	Because the proposal will be opposed by organized interests, the best legislative solution is to draft an ambiguous bill and *delegate to agency regulation*, so all sides can claim victory. Regulatory capture can result.
III *Concentrated benefits/distributed costs*	**IV** *Concentrated benefits/concentrated costs*
Because the costs can be allocated to an uninformed public, legislature will follow a policy of *distribution* of subsidies and power to the organized beneficiaries. Often *self-regulation* is the chosen policy.	Because any policy choice will incur the wrath of opposing interest groups, legislators will favor *no bill* or delegation to *agency regulation*.

c. *The Implications of a Transactional Model of Legislation: Madison's Nightmare.* The transactional model developed in Tables 1–1 and 1–2 suggest considerable pessimism regarding the results of imperfect political markets. On the one hand, the public sector will tend to spend too much money on statutes that concentrate benefits on special interests while distributing their costs to the general, and often unsuspecting, public. There is an obvious tendency to logroll in a specific benefit-general taxation scheme such as ours, because legislators can please important groups with tax subsidies, while avoiding blame for the overspending that results.

---

1. But see Richard A. Epstein, *Forbidden Grounds: The Case Against Employment Discrimination Laws* 127–28 (1992) (contesting this prisoner's dilemma view and the conclusion that it justified regulation).

On the other hand, the public sector will tend to supply too few statutes that are likely to be public-regarding, namely, statutes that distribute benefits broadly (e.g., infrastructure programs, commercial codes, effective criminal laws). Legislators often have little interest in such statutes, because they do not as reliably generate votes in the next election. And even if the populace were appreciative of these statutes, it is possible that in many cases Congress will be unaware of the demand, because the free-rider problem precludes effective organization. This problem is particularly acute in Quadrant II because a statute that provides distributed benefits through enacting concentrated costs will face strong and organized opposition that is likely to prevail over the shallow support that a policy entrepreneur can create. Some of these laws, notably federal criminal laws when violence and crime are salient for voters, may produce political payoffs attractive enough to encourage lawmakers to spend some time on these proposals and to pass legislation that is often primarily symbolic.

This taxonomy may suggest reforms that are likely to improve the legislative process because it helps to identify the equivalents of market failures. For example, if legislation in the majoritarian and entrepreneurial arenas tends to be more consistent with the public good but is underproduced because of interest group dynamics, reforms might emphasize empowering people whose interests are not well represented by organized groups. Alternatively, it might suggest that we should identify proxy groups with related interests that can serve as champions for the unorganized. Criminals are, for the most part, not well-organized politically, but lawyers are well-organized and usually serve as virtual representatives for the interests of those accused of crimes.

If we notice that inefficient, private-regarding legislation is less likely when interest group behavior is conflictual and not cooperative, we might seek to structure the legislative process to force interest groups to compete for limited resources. Structuring legislative processes so that losers are more clearly identified will make such legislation more difficult to pass.[m] It is also worth considering how changing technology may affect the dynamics of the transactional model. For example, as the Internet makes communication and organization less costly, will larger groups form and influence the political process? Or will these technologies work primarily to the advantage of the already powerful and organized interests? See Bruce Bimber, *Information and American Democracy: Technology in the Evolution of Power* (2003) (discussing effect of Internet and new communication technology on political organizations, citizens and government).

3. Criticisms of the Pluralist or Public Choice Vision

You might consider the transactional model suggested by public choice theory a distressing vision of our polity. In fact, the descriptive

---

m. See Elizabeth Garrett, *Rethinking the Structures of Decisionmaking in the Federal Budget Process*, 35 Harv. J. Legis. 387 (1998).

vision of public choice theory and the normative vision of pluralism are controversial.

Public choice models of the legislative process have come under increasing attack in the last decade for their oversimplification of the political process and their failure to recognize its institutional richness.[n] Even some scholars writing in the public choice tradition have criticized the transactional model because it treats legislators as ciphers, merely implementing the deals that interest groups reach. Perhaps the most interesting public-choice-inspired critique of this view of legislators' role has been offered by Professor Fred S. McChesney. He notes that those who posit the economic theory of legislation and legal regulation largely ignore the ways in which politicians obtain benefits from their office other than by sending legislative goodies to interest groups. In *Money for Nothing: Politicians, Rent Extraction, and Political Extortion* 2–3 (1997), Professor McChesney argues that

> payments to politicians [campaign contributions, gifts, post-tenure employment] often are made, not for particular political favors, but to avoid particular political disfavor, that is, as part of a system of political extortion or 'rent extraction.' * * * Because the state, quite legally, can (and does) take money and other forms of wealth from its citizens, politicians can extort from private parties payments *not* to expropriate private wealth. * * * In that sense, rent extraction— receiving payments not to take or destroy private wealth—is "money for nothing" in the words of the song.

Rent extraction is theoretically possible in any field of legislation because lawmakers always have the capacity to repeal existing beneficial laws or to enact new taxes or fees burdening particular activities or industries. Practically, however, the threat to burden an interest group must be credible for successful rent extraction. In other words, the threatened group must believe that the chances are good that lawmakers will actually pass harmful legislation. One arena of particularly credible threats is the tax legislative arena because Congress frequently passes new tax laws decreasing some tax subsidies and increasing taxes on particular groups. This behavior produces enough uncertainty that current beneficiaries of tax subsidies are regularly worried that their provisions will be scaled back or modified and are willing to pay protection money to lawmakers.[o]

---

n. For commentary, see, e.g., Daniel A. Farber & Philip P. Frickey, *Law and Public Choice: A Critical Introduction* (1991); *The Rational Choice Controversy* (Jeffrey Friedman ed., 1996); Donald Green & Ian Shapiro, *Pathologies of Rational Choice Theory* (1994); Jerry L. Mashaw, *Greed, Chaos, and Governance: Using Public Choice To Improve Public Law* (1997); Maxwell L. Stearns, *Public Choice and Public Law: Readings and Commentary* (1997); Frank B. Cross, *The Judiciary and Public Choice*, 50 Hastings L.J. 355 (1999); Einer Elhauge, *Does Interest Group Theory Justify More Intensive Judicial Review?*, 101 Yale L.J. 31 (1991); Thomas A. Merrill, *Does Public Choice Justify Judicial Activism After All?*, 21 Harv. J.L. & Pub. Pol. 219 (1997); *Symposium: Getting Beyond Cynicism: New Theories of the Regulatory State*, 87 Cornell L. Rev. 267 (2002).

o. See, e.g., Richard L. Doernberg & Fred S. McChesney, *Doing Good or Doing Well?: Congress and the Tax Reform Act of 1986*, 62 N.Y.U. L. Rev. 891 (1987); Edward J. McCaffery &

Rent extraction helps to fill out the complex and varied reality of the legislative process, but it is not completely satisfying. First, it accepts the inaccurate view of legislators as one-dimensional seekers of financial rewards from special interest groups. As we will discuss below, although reelection and interest group considerations are important to lawmakers, most are also pursuing other objectives, such as affecting policy in ways consistent with their ideological commitments. Second, the theory of rent extraction combined with the transactional model of legislation allows public choice scholars to explain every possible congressional decision in terms of the market model; it thereby loses a great deal of its explanatory and predictive force. If legislation is enacted, then the beneficiaries must have outbid their rivals; if legislation is not enacted, then the rivals clearly won. If a particular tax subsidy is repealed in order to pay for a new tax benefit for another group, then the holders of the repealed provision must not have paid enough to avoid the burden, perhaps erroneously believing that Congress was bluffing. If the repeal is proposed but not enacted, then the holders of the targeted provision must have met the extortionate demand in order to continue enjoying the federal largesse.

Empirical studies also provide a basis for a critique of public choice, revealing that money and organization do not always translate into clout. See Jeffrey Berry, *The Interest Group Society* 226–33 (3d ed. 1997). Instead, an interest group's influence depends upon the context. First, interest groups are more successful at blocking legislation than enacting a new policy. See Schlozman and Tierney, *Organized Interests, supra,* at 314–15. Several factors make opposition an easier posture for interest groups. Groups defending the status quo need to prevail at only one stage in the convoluted legislative process. Proponents of new legislation must successfully navigate all of the procedural obstacles. In addition, cognitive psychology suggests that people work harder to preserve what they have than to gain a new benefit.[p] This finding is confirmed by leaders of interest groups who report it is easier to ward off an attack than to mount one. Second, interest groups succeed more frequently on issues that are not salient to the larger public and that are perceived as narrow, technical, nonpartisan issues. *Id.* at 314. Client politics is easier when it occurs outside the glare of publicity, and members are willing to trade support on minor issues in backroom deals. Finally, groups work to locate the decisionmaking in institutions that are sympathetic to their position or have procedures they can use to their advantage.[q]

Just as empirical studies have given us a different and more complex explanation than that provided by public choice theory for the demand side of legislation (interest group behavior), case studies of Congress by institutional political scientists have questioned the public choice explana-

---

Linda R. Cohen, *Shakedown at Gucci Gulch: The New Logic of Collective Action*, 84 N.C. L. Rev. 1159 (2006).

p.　See Cass R. Sunstein, *Behavioral Analysis of Law*, 64 U. Chi. L. Rev. 1175, 1179–81 (1997).

q.　See Neil K. Komesar, *Imperfect Alternatives: Choosing Institutions in Law, Economics, and Public Policy* (1994).

tion for the supply side (behavior of legislators). Richard Fenno's classic case study, *Congressmen in Committees* (1973), argues that legislators are interested in more than simply being reelected, contrary to the assumptions of public choice theory. While reelection is certainly a powerful motivating factor and a necessary intermediate goal, legislators also want to have "status" within government and to make some positive contribution to what they consider good public policy. Especially when an issue involves moral questions and is publicly visible, the legislator's vote depends on something more than her calculations about reelection.[r] Recall the behavior of the legislators in our story of the Civil Rights Act. Can it all be explained solely in terms of interest group influence, or were other factors at work?

Not only may public choice theory oversimplify legislator motivations, it may also misconceive the legislative process by viewing it statically and disregarding institutional changes that affect behavior. For example, centralized organizations like political parties have recently become stronger in the federal legislature, relative to committees and rank-and-file members, allowing lawmakers to coordinate their efforts more effectively and resist the urge to act in ways that benefit only narrow special interests or small constituencies. Lawmakers who serve in party leadership roles tend to come from relatively safe districts and therefore to be insulated from narrow constituent pressures. Thus, they can survive the electoral heat of authoring a compromise bill that offends the sensibilities of extremists or particular interest groups, and they may have more leeway in pursuing their vision of the public good without fearing electoral reprisals.[s] Counterbalancing this, however, is their desire to remain in the majority and an awareness that the reelection of some of their members may depend on legislation benefitting special interests.

Another institution that affects legislative behavior—the Presidency—was long slighted by traditional public choice theory. It is now receiving more attention.[t] The President may be the dominant influence in the national legislative process. As a unitary office backed by a more cohesive coalition than the multi-membered Congress, the Presidency is in a better position to develop coherent policies and, consequently, often initiates and propels controversial bills through the legislative labyrinth. As our nation's most visible public figure, the President is ideally situated to stimulate publicity about a public problem. As the chief of the executive branch, the President has access to an impressive brain trust (such as the Office of Management and Budget, the Treasury Department's Office of Tax Policy, and other prestigious executive branch entities), which can think creatively about a problem and draft proposed legislation. As the

---

r. See also Keith T. Poole & Howard Rosenthal, *Congress: A Political–Economic History of Roll Call Voting* (1997) (finding ideology was largest influence on roll call voting behavior).

s. See John Aldrich, *Why Parties? The Origin and Transformation of Political Parties in America* 205 (1995).

t. See, e.g., *The Presidency and the Political System* (Michael Nelson ed., 8th ed. 2006); Terry M. Moe & Scott A. Wilson, *Presidents and the Politics of Structure*, 57 Law & Contemp. Probs. 1 (Spring 1994).

head of one of the political parties, representative of a uniquely national constituency, and someone who controls a number of desirable benefits, the President can be the best possible lobbyist a bill can have. Something as controversial as the Civil Rights Act (or the tax reform legislation in 1986 or the radical reform of federal welfare programs in the 1990s) would have likely been impossible without the President's active involvement.[u]

An increasing focus of institutional political science theory has been the dynamic nature of the legislative process. John W. Kingdon, in *Agenda, Alternatives, and Public Policies* (2d ed. 1995), has developed a dynamic model of the legislative process which synthesizes prior political science scholarship and presents an alternative to the static public choice model. Kingdon de-emphasizes the role of interest groups and argues that public officials (the President, the Cabinet appointed by the President, Congress, as well as leaders of political parties) play the key roles in setting the nation's political agenda. The role of interest groups is usually to formulate and debate policy alternatives, a role they share with other less visible (but perhaps more public-regarding) participants, such as civil servants, academics and experts, the media, and legislative staff.

Professor Kingdon's model of the legislative process is drawn from the "garbage can model of organizational choice," described in Michael Cohen, James March & Johan Olsen, *A Garbage Can Model of Organizational Choice*, 17 Ad. L.Q. 1 (March 1972). Under this conceptualization, Congress operates through an "organized anarchy," in which there is no linear process for identifying a problem, defining alternative solutions, and reaching a decision. See also Charles Lindblom & Edward Woodhouse, *The Policy–Making Process* Chapters 1 & 2 (3d ed. 1993). Rather, salient problems, possible solutions, and choice opportunities will coexist as separate "streams" in the "garbage can" (the system). Sometimes problems are resolved; sometimes they go away; sometimes the system despairs of solving them. The outcome depends on the "coupling of the streams": a problem becomes salient at the same time a solution becomes well-regarded and participants favoring the solution can seize the legislative process for that end. To change policy, groups must have more than just political clout; they must draw attention to their proposal when the political environment is receptive to it. Activists need a focusing event, preferably after they have laid the groundwork necessary to increase the chances that the event will lead to movement in a direction they support. Sometimes streams connect and issues become prominent on the political agenda because of chance. Airline safety becomes a topic of national concern and attention after a tragic plane accident, for example. Political entrepreneurs, whether inside or out of government, need not leave matters completely to the vagaries of fate, however; they can manipulate the policy environment to increase receptivity to their objectives. When

u. But see Benjamin Ginsberg, Walter R. Mebane & Martin Shefter, *The President and the "Interests": Why the White House Cannot Govern*, in *The Presidency and the Political System* 361 (Michael Nelson ed., 6th ed. 2000); Michael A. Fitts, *The Paradox of Power in the Modern State: Why a Unitary, Centralized Presidency May Not Exhibit Effective or Legitimate Leadership*, 144 U. Pa. L. Rev. 827 (1996).

focusing events do not occur fortuitously, they can be created, much as Greenpeace has done in the environmental area when it confronts hunters and polluters on the high seas.

Public choice suffers from another static perspective: most scholars assume that preferences are independent of and prior to political activity. To use economic terminology, pluralism, particularly public choice, tends to view preferences as *exogenous* rather than *endogenous*. This assumption is clearly unrealistic; we all know that participating in decisionmaking, whether in the political realm or elsewhere, significantly affects the way we think and feel about a particular issue.[v] As the members of Congress deliberated about the Civil Rights Act of 1964 and discussed their views with their colleagues and constituents, their conclusions about integration and racism surely developed and changed. As we turn to theories of the legislative process that focus on the procedures shaping it, we will consider how the structures of deliberation affect our preferences about outcomes.

One can reject the public choice description of the legislative process in favor of one of the institutional political descriptions, yet still believe that some form of pluralism is and should be characteristic of our political system. But this normative vision has also become controversial. Typically, defenders of pluralism will now concede that interest group government sacrifices elements of fairness, rational social choice, and/or other values but will argue that pluralism is justified by its facilitation of stability, moderation, and broad satisfaction with the political system. This may not be a persuasive justification for those who consider social justice more important than stability.[w] Furthermore, by defining "politics" as the relatively narrow conflict among professional groups, pluralism implicitly denies the existence or feasibility of other forms of political struggle to change existing institutions and to organize around broader lines of cleavage (such as class). Because most of the political activity under pluralism is by and among elites, pluralist democracy may tend to reinforce already-existing social and economic inequalities.[x]

B. PROCEDURALIST APPROACHES TO LEGISLATION

Proceduralists also claim James Madison as their founding father, largely because his solution to the problem of faction lay in government design. Since the causes of faction cannot be eradicated except by destroying liberty or by somehow forcing all people to share identical opinions, interests, and passions, Madison reasoned the best strategy is to contain the effects of faction. Where the faction remains a minority, popular government is sufficient to contain it, because its views will not command

---

v.   See Amartya Sen, *Behavior and the Concept of Preference*, 40 Economica 241 (1973).

w.   See, e.g., Stuart Hampshire, *Justice in Conflict* (2000); Thomas Simon, *Democracy and Social Injustice: Law, Politics, and Philosophy* 151–71 (1995).

x.   See C. Wright Mills, *The Power Elite* (1959).

the necessary majority. But, noted Madison, sometimes a faction will temporarily command majority support because of inflamed passions, deception, and so forth. In that circumstance, a direct democracy would be little protection against oppression. In contrast, a representative government has the structural ability "to refine and enlarge the public views, by passing them through the medium of a chosen body of citizens, whose wisdom may best discern the true interest of their country * * *. The public voice, pronounced by the representatives of the people, will be more consonant to the public good than if pronounced by the people themselves, convened for the purpose." *Federalist* No. 10. Madison admitted the possibility of corruption of representatives but argued that republics of great size (such as the United States) would have a large enough number of representatives and a broad enough constituency for each as to minimize the possibility of corruption of a majority of the elected representatives.

In *Federalist* No. 51, Madison explained another protective strategy, the theory of *checks and balances* among the departments of government. If ill-motivated officials control one or more of the branches of the government, they are countered by those officials in the other branches—even when they, too, are not public-spirited. "Ambition," said Madison, "must be made to counteract ambition." Bicameralism is particularly important, not only because it provides a double review of proposed legislation and essentially requires supermajority support for any legislative proposal, but also because the two chambers perform complementary tasks. With its representatives being from smaller districts and subject to electoral scrutiny every two years, the House of Representatives would have an "immediate dependence on, and an intimate sympathy with, the people." *Federalist* No. 52. The Senate, whose members were originally elected by state legislatures for six-year terms, would have a stabilizing influence. Its members would have greater leisure to acquaint themselves with the issues and to discuss the issues deliberatively. *Federalist* No. 62.

1. Vetogates: Procedural Doors That Bills Must Pass Through

The most obvious feature of the legislative process described in the "Note on How a Bill Becomes a Federal Law," *supra*, is that any legislative proposal has to surmount a series of hurdles before it becomes a law. Most basically, Article I, § 7 of the Constitution requires endorsement of the proposal in identical form by both the House and Senate and then presentment to the President. Hence any of these bodies, and not just the President, can "veto" a proposal. The congressional process itself creates most of the "gates" that a bill must pass through and where it can be killed rather than moved along to the next stage of the process. Because of the nature of each of these obstacles, scholars have coined the term *vetogates*[y] to apply to the choke points in the process, some with the

---

y. See McNollgast [i.e., Mathew D. McCubbins, Roger Noll & Barry R. Weingast], *Legislative Intent: The Use of Positive Political Theory in Statutory Interpretation*, 57 Law & Contemp. Probs.

durability of constitutional requirements, others matters of congressional rule or norm. Opponents of a bill have many vetogates to exploit: (1) kill the bill in committee; (2) if committee approval cannot be avoided, stop the bill before full chamber consideration; (3) if full chamber consideration occurs, kill the bill there by filibustering it in the Senate, by amending it to death, or by outright defeating it on the chamber floor; (4) if one chamber has approved the bill, exploit the veto opportunities in the other chamber to prevent it from passing an identical measure; (5) if the other chamber produces a similar but not identical bill, amend or defeat it at the conference committee stage or in an interbranch summit; (6) if all else fails, persuade the President to veto it and then work against any congressional effort to override the veto.

Descriptively, the existence of vetogates means that determined minorities can often kill legislation or, in the alternative, maim legislation they cannot kill. Determined Southern opponents of civil rights legislation were able to stop or to dilute such bills until 1964 because they controlled pivotal vetogates (the House Rules Committee, the Senate Judiciary Committee). Rather than killing a measure, a minority controlling a vetogate may extract concessions from the enacting coalition by a threat to stall it or change it significantly. This was the approach taken by Senator Dirksen. Indeed, one way a small faction "exploits" majority factions, to use Mancur Olson's term, is the former's ability to influence those who control various vetogates. Interest groups spend time forming and maintaining connections with members of Congress and other participants in federal lawmaking. In this process, a group seeking to block legislation rather than to pass it has a tremendous advantage. Because legislation can be stopped at many points along the legislative path, groups need to secure the assistance of only one key player to succeed. The electoral strength of incumbents, combined with a strong seniority system that significantly influences committee assignments, gives organized groups great certainty about which legislator will occupy a strategic position in the system.

Normatively, the existence of vetogates may tell statutory interpreters (courts, administrative agencies, lawyers advising clients) to whom they should pay attention if they consult legislative history, as the Fourth Circuit judges thought they were doing in *Griggs*. Legislative statements are most important when they reflect assurances by the enacting coalition—especially promises to or by gatekeepers—to enable the bill to pass through a vetogate. Thus committee reports are conventionally referred to, both because they reflect the understanding of the key gatekeepers (the committee), but also because they are important representations by the floor managers of the bill (usually members of the committee) to attract votes on the floor. Thus, they reflect the expertise of the specialists in the area who act as the agents of the full body. Moreover, their statements are credible; if non-committee members discover that commit-

---

3 (1994). See also William N. Eskridge Jr., *Vetogates and American Public Law*, J.L. Econ. & Org. (2011).

tee reports contain inaccurate statements (perhaps because preference outliers dominate the drafting), then they will no longer trust the committee members' assurances and will be less likely to defer to them. To the extent that those who control vetogates are repeat players, they must maintain their reputations for honesty to assure their continuing influence.[z]

Note, however, that the *Griggs* judges gave weight to statements by Senator Tower for a different reason. Although he was not a supporter of the bill, his concerns were shared widely enough to assure the addition of the testing rule in § 703(h), his amendment. Representations made to him by Senator Humphrey were also considered because Humphrey was really speaking to all those Senators still on the fence and whose votes were needed to get the bill through its most difficult vetogate, the filibuster. It is not surprising, then, that all the judges in *Griggs* wanted their interpretation to be consistent with the assurances made to enable the bill to escape the filibuster.

2. Liberal Theory: Statutes Should Be Hard to Enact

The Framers believed that the Constitution's requirements of bicameral approval and presentment to the President (with the possibility of a veto) would assure that most social and economic problems would not generate legislation at all, because the two bodies would have different views about what should be done. *Federalist* No. 73. Hamilton saw proceduralism as "an additional security against the [enactment] of improper laws." However, he admitted that "the power of preventing bad laws includes that of preventing good ones; and may be used to the one purpose as well as to the other. * * * The injury that may possibly be done by defeating a few good laws will be amply compensated by the advantage of preventing a few bad ones." As Nelson Polsby observes, we should not be surprised that periods of stalemate are longer than periods of innovation because collective action is difficult "when formal power and autonomy are as dispersed as they are in the United States and it is necessary legislatively to mobilize the consent of majorities over and over—successively first in subcommittees, then in committees, then on the floors of the two legislative chambers, and finally behind the occupant of the White House." Polsby, *How Congress Evolves: Social Bases of Institutional Change* 147 (2004).

These consequences are consistent with some versions of *liberal theory*, which favors private autonomy and free economic markets and thus generally disfavors government regulation. To what extent do these assumptions remain robust today? Perhaps they are outdated: the post-New Deal regulatory state may assume that governmental regulation is the norm and indeed is perhaps even essential for the proper functioning

---

z. See Victoria F. Nourse, *Misunderstanding Congress: Statutory Interpretation, the Supermajoritarian Difficulty, and the Separation of Powers*, 99 Geo. L.J. 1119 (2011); Daniel B. Rodriguez & Barry R. Weingast, *The Positive Political Theory of Legislative History: New Perspectives on the 1964 Civil Rights Act and its Interpretation*, 151 U. Pa. L. Rev. 1417, 1442–51 (2003).

of the private market.[aa] Common law ordering is not the natural order of things; instead, it is just another kind of regulatory regime. Thus, to the extent that proceduralism protects one vision of regulation—a particular liberal vision—and reduces the ability of lawmakers to adopt different regulatory systems, it must be defended on that basis. It is not a neutral decision.

Moreover, the extreme liberal distaste for legislation may not be the political vision that the authors of *The Federalist Papers* subscribed to. They were not hostile to all legislative intrusions, and they did not believe that congressional enactments were inherently untrustworthy or harmful. Indeed, Madison and Hamilton expected that proceduralism would improve, not inevitably block, legislation designed to solve social or economic problems because the Article I, § 7 structure militates in favor of moderate rather than radical shifts from the status quo. See *Federalist* No. 63. But, some proposals are hastily conceived and unwise, incapable of being improved through delay, deliberation and compromise. Procedures serve to make their enactment difficult. Because we cannot require that enhanced procedures apply only to "unwise laws" and allow fewer procedures to stand in the way of "laws serving the public good," the protection we obtain from structural constraints is necessarily overinclusive. It will impede the passage of good laws as well as bad. This cost is one that we should not dismiss without some concern. For example, bicameralism and the Senate filibuster gutted civil rights bills in the 1950s, delaying such legislation for a decade. Hamilton argued that the loss of some good bills was a price worth paying. Is that right? What was the cost of delay in the civil rights context? Was that cost less than the cost of additional private-regarding laws that might have been passed in a world of more streamlined legislative procedures?

3. Civic Republican Theory: The Deliberative Value of Process

Rather than blocking enactment of most legislation, procedures can be seen as the way to shape public deliberation on legislative proposals so that they better serve the public good. This view of proceduralism is consistent with *civic republican theory*, and such theorists also lay claim to *The Federalist Papers* as inspiration. Although the republican tradition was espoused by the Anti–Federalists, who opposed adoption of the Constitution, many political philosophers and historians now believe that the Federalists did not utterly reject republican concerns.[bb] Under this view, Madison's *Federalist* No. 10 is, in fact, a redefinition of the republicans' concern about corruption of the common good (focusing on factions) and an argument that republican virtue might best be preserved through

---

aa. See Cass R. Sunstein, *After the Rights Revolution: Reconceiving the Regulatory State* 19–20 (1990); Bruce A. Ackerman, *Constitutional Law/Constitutional Politics*, 99 Yale L.J. 453 (1989).

bb. See David Epstein, *The Political Theory of the Federalist* (1984); Edmund Morgan, *Madison's Theory of Representation in the Tenth Federalist*, 36 J. Pol. 852 (1974). See also Larry Kramer, *Madison's Audience*, 112 Harv. L. Rev. 611 (1999).

a national political structure with checks and balances than through local government.

In *Federalist* No. 39, James Madison defined the sort of government created by the Constitution as a *republic*—a "government which derives all its powers directly or indirectly from the great body of the people, and is administered by persons holding their offices during pleasure, for a limited period, or during good behavior." Less democratic forms, such as monarchy or oligarchy, would be inconsistent with the "genius of the people of America," Madison argued, invoking memories of "taxation without representation" that inspired the American Revolution. More democratic forms, such as direct democracy, in which important matters would be decided by an immediate vote of the people, were unacceptable as well because such structures would not restrain the tyranny of majority factions. A republican form of government, shaped by a variety of counter-majoritarian or supermajoritarian procedures, would allow for deliberation among lawmakers, communication with constituents, and informed decisionmaking. For example, Madison justified the arguably duplicative role of the Senate as useful "to check the misguided career" of bills inspired by temporary passions or deception "and to suspend the blow mediated by the people against themselves, until reason, justice, and truth can regain their authority over the public mind." *Federalist* No. 63.

Many believe that the story of the Civil Rights Act of 1964 supports this optimism about the legislative process. Does a republican perspective also help resolve questions arising under the Act, such as in *Griggs*? Should the court decide open questions under the Act by interpreting it to promote the public interest in remedying racial injustice—or is that too one-sided a way to decide cases? Or is the more basic problem that this view of the legislative process is too optimistic?

Republican theorists, both past and current, emphasize the importance of deliberation to a normatively attractive legislative process. Deliberation shapes and changes public preferences on issues; it allows lawmakers to modify, amend, or discard proposals on the basis of new thinking and information; and it facilitates the development of civic virtue in citizens. Deliberation thus is an end in itself, and it serves the larger instrumental purpose of improving public policy. Madisonian deliberation remains a robust theory today as a justification for the procedurally complex legislative process. Professors Henry Hart and Albert Sacks, in their classic *legal process* materials, argued for the "vitally important relationship between procedure and substance. A procedure which is soundly adapted to the type of power to be exercised is conducive to well-informed and wise decisions. An unsound procedure invites ill-informed and unwise ones." Hart and Sacks reported a "general agreement" that "the best criterion of sound legislation is * * * whether it is the product of a sound process of enactment," namely, a process that is informed, deliberative, and efficient. Henry M. Hart, Jr. & Albert M. Sacks, *The Legal Process: Basic Problems in the Making and Application of Law* 154,

695 (William N. Eskridge Jr. & Philip P. Frickey pub. eds., 1994) (from the 1958 "tentative edition").

Notice that this formulation attempts to defend the process of deliberation on the ground that it will improve the substance of legislation. Such a claim requires a metric to measure outcomes—what counts as "sound legislation"—and the metric is inevitably tied up with a normative vision of the public good. Joseph M. Bessette defines the special reasoning process of policy deliberation as "necessarily involv[ing] reasoning about the substantive benefits of public policy, reasoning about some *public good*—some good external to the decisionmakers themselves." Bessette, *The Mild Voice of Reason: Deliberative Democracy and American National Government* 48 (1994).[cc]

Many scholars educated under the aegis of the legal process materials emphasize deliberation as an achievable ideal in our representative democracy. Theories of "neo-republicanism" integrate earlier theories of politics with this legal process heritage.[dd] Their essential point is that the legitimacy of government rests not just upon its democratic pedigree, but also upon the commitment of its officials to engage in a process of practical reasoning, deliberating for the common good. See Amy Gutmann & Dennis Thompson, *Democracy and Disagreement* (1996). The effect of proceduralism on deliberation and, in turn, the effect of deliberation on legislative outcomes are difficult to understand completely. Procedures cannot guarantee that deliberation will occur at all, or that any deliberation will be enlightened and positive. At the most, rules and structure provide an opportunity for deliberation and an environment conducive to public dialogue.

To be sure, the American public is unhappy with the congressional gridlock resulting from the vetogates described above. See John Hibbing and Elizabeth Theiss–Morse, *Congress as Public Enemy: Public Attitudes Toward American Political Institutions* 60–61 (1995). One positive response to this dissatisfaction would be to improve the conditions of deliberation and to educate the public to appreciate the benefits of public consideration of alternatives by representatives. Sociologists have also found that some amount of public participation and deliberation in deci-

---

cc. See also Larry Alexander, *Are Procedural Rights Derivative of Substantive Rights?*, 17 Law & Phil. 19, 36–42 (1998). But see Mathew D. McCubbins & Daniel B. Rodriguez, *When Does Deliberating Improve Decisionmaking?*, 15 J. Contemp. Legal Iss. 9 (2006) (providing results from experiments suggesting that deliberation does not improve social welfare and "in all but rare circumstances, may decrease it").

dd. For one of the leading republican statements, see Frank I. Michelman, *The Supreme Court, 1985 Term—Foreword: Traces of Self-Government*, 100 Harv. L. Rev. 4 (1986). Other important sources include Philip N. Pettit, *Republicanism: A Theory of Freedom and Government* (1997); Michael J. Sandel, *Liberalism and the Limits of Justice* (2d ed. 1998); Marci A. Hamilton, *Discussion and Decisions: A Proposal to Replace the Myth of Self-Rule With an Attorneyship Model of Representation*, 69 N.Y.U. L. Rev. 477 (1994); Mark B. Seidenfeld, *A Civic Republican Justification for the Bureaucratic State*, 105 Harv. L. Rev. 1511 (1992); Suzanna Sherry, *Responsible Republicanism: Educating for Citizenship*, 62 U. Chi. L. Rev. 131 (1995); *Symposium: The Republican Civic Tradition*, 97 Yale L.J. 1043 (1988). The historical discussion in these legal materials should be supplemented by reference to the historiographical literature, especially Daniel Rodgers, *Republicanism: The Career of a Concept*, 79 J. Am. Hist. 11 (1992).

sionmaking is necessary for citizens to view outcomes as legitimate and just. See, e.g., Tom Tyler, *Why People Obey the Law* (rev. ed. 2006). As philosopher Jeremy Waldron has observed, at least part of law's legitimacy and authority comes from the fact that multi-member assemblies pass statutes through collective decisionmaking after some discussion that allows for an airing of diverse viewpoints. The "dignity of legislation" is a result of the ability of a legislature to act in concert in what Waldron terms "circumstances of politics"; such collective action in the face of disagreement is a significant achievement that deserves our respect. See Waldron, *The Dignity of Legislation* 156–57 (1999). Importantly, the diversity of views represented in a deliberative body is related to the decisions that the group reaches. When people only hear "echoes of their own voices," the deliberating group may reach more extreme positions than its members' pre-deliberation tendencies suggested. See Cass R. Sunstein, *Deliberating Trouble? Why Groups Go to Extremes*, 110 Yale L.J. 71, 75–76 (2000). The conditions that shape deliberation, including the procedures governing it, play a role in whether group polarization develops, or more moderate compromise is reached.

C.　INSTITUTIONAL THEORIES OF LEGISLATION

1.　Introduction to the Institutional Perspective

A body of political theory variously called the *new institutionalism* or *positive political theory* grows out of the public choice tradition and has been influenced by game theory developed by economists.[ee] As with the other two groups, institutional theorists also claim the Madisonian tradition as their own. Like Madison, they emphasize the importance of institutional structures to constrain and shape behavior, and they characterize outcomes in terms of "balance" or "equilibrium." Modern institutional theory is characterized by certain crucial assumptions.

The first and most important is that political outcomes are dependent on the actions of several decisionmakers, who sometimes act simultaneously and sometimes consecutively. Moreover, each decisionmaker is aware of this interdependence. Thus, it is not enough to say that Senators Dirksen and Mansfield entered into a deal which enabled the civil rights bill to escape the Senate filibuster. They entered into the deal, knowing that the House and President had to accept their compromise. See Daniel A. Rodriguez & Barry R. Weingast, *The Positive Political Theory of Legislative History: New Perspectives on the 1964 Civil Rights Act and its Interpretation*, 151 U. Pa. L. Rev. 1417, 1474–87 (2003). The formulation the Senate leaders devised not only reflected their own preferences but also took into account the reactions it would spark in other players in the legislative game and any continuing influence the Senate might have on

---

ee. See generally Douglas G. Baird et al., *Game Theory and the Law* (1994); Peter Ordeshook, *A Political Theory Primer* (1992); Eric Posner, *Law and Social Norms* (2000); Kenneth A. Shepsle & Mark Bonchek, *Analyzing Politics: Rationality, Behavior, and Institutions* (1997); *Symposium on Positive Political Theory and Law*, 69 S. Cal. L. Rev. 1447 (1995).

subsequent developments. Relatedly, all the parties to the deal operate under assumptions about how the courts will interpret their bargain. They anticipate the judicial response as they draft and produce committee reports and floor debates. Depending on the issue, the federal actors may have to consider the response of state and local officials who may be required to implement some provisions of the legislation. Or, in some states, legislators are aware that the people can modify some laws through the referendum process, or they can enact their own through popular votes on initiatives. See Elisabeth R. Gerber, *The Populist Paradox* (1999). In other words, the representative institutions may have to take account of the reaction of constituents both at reelection time and through mechanisms of direct democracy.

This *anticipated response* feature of institutionalism is key. It requires us to think in a more complicated way about political actors. Dirksen chose the deal, not because the bill as modified reflected his own preferences, but because Dirksen believed that the other relevant actors (Senators, President, House Members) would otherwise make choices that had consequences he liked much less. Anticipating the responses of other players and calculating their consequences, Dirksen strategically "chose" the Dirksen–Mansfield substitute. This analysis implies another feature of institutionalism: political players are goal-oriented. Thus, when they anticipate the responses of other players, their preference for one scenario over others is determined by which scenario will ultimately achieve an outcome closest to their own preferred policies. Institutionalism does not assume that people's goals are economic or self-centered (though they often are). One goal that impelled Dirksen to support a compromise, for example, was his goal to position the Republican Party (of which he was a leader) advantageously on this issue.

One limitation of some of the institutional scholarship, however, is the simplifying view of preferences as stable and unchanging. Of course, preferences can be profoundly affected by deliberation and other aspects of the legislative process. Another unrealistic but simplifying assumption often used in the scholarship is that players have full information about the preferences of all the other players, even though we know that information is costly and therefore often incomplete and that players can make mistakes in their predictions of subsequent moves and reactions. For example, Manny Cellar decided to strengthen the committee version of the Civil Rights bill for strategic reasons, but he miscalculated and nearly scuttled the chances for success. Only the intervention of party leaders and the Administration assured that a palatable bill would emerge from committee. Using somewhat simplified models is justified, however, because it focuses attention on the interdependence of actions, the role of all players, including non-legislative ones, in the formation of policy, and the effect of anticipated responses. As we use this perspective, however, it is important to remember that it does not fully capture the complex and intricate world of the legislative process, and it should be used as a complement to the other theories to generate more accurate descriptions and predictions.

Finally, positive political theory emphasizes that institutions are the context in which political interdependence is shaped and people's goals are pursued. The structure of institutions makes a difference in the way people interact. Institutional theorists develop formal models which reveal regularities in such interaction. Just as the structures of institutions alter the ways in which players interact, players can also modify the contours of institutions in ways that allow them to reach their objectives with less difficulty. Institutions are seldom immutable; they can be reshaped, although the way that they have developed in the past may limit the possible range of alterations available to the players. See Sarah A. Binder, *Minority Rights, Majority Rule: Partisanship and the Development of Congress* 14 (1997).

Institutional models are often in the form of sequential anticipated response "games," in which each player's choice is determined not only by her own raw preferences about an issue, but also by her place in the decision process and her understanding of the preferences of players who follow her. Consider the following example of institutional game theory in the context of legislation.

2. The Article I, § 7 Game

The procedural requirements of Article I, § 7 (bicameralism and presentment) can be modeled as a sequential game, in which all players want to enact legislation reflecting their own preferences, but the players realize that their preferences may have to be compromised to guarantee the cooperation of other players as required by the constitutional structure. See William N. Eskridge Jr. & John Ferejohn, *The Article I, Section 7 Game*, 80 Geo. L.J. 523 (1992).

The game starts with the status quo, which prevails in the absence of legislation. Members of the House have preferences about policies that depart from the status quo, and committees help the chamber figure out the policy that will appeal to the preference of the *median legislator* (the one right in the middle of the 435 Representatives whose vote is needed to enact the legislation under majority-voting rules). See Duncan Black, *The Theory of Committees and Elections* (1958) (policy equilibrium rests with the preference of the median voter if preferences over policies are single-peaked). In writing legislation, the committee will be aware that the Senate has to agree, too; hence, it might adjust the legislation to anticipate and head off problems in the Senate (as the House Judiciary Committee did in 1963). The same process will occur in the Senate if it acts on the legislation first. Sometimes, both houses consider companion legislation at the same time, and the proponents of the bill will watch the deliberation in the other chamber closely to learn as much as they can about the preferences of the other key player. Both the House and the Senate will consider the preferences of the President, who must sign the bill. See Charles Cameron, *Veto Bargaining: Presidents and the Politics of*

Negative Power (2000). If the President is hostile to the legislation (not the case with the civil rights bill in 1963–64), the chambers usually will not go forward with a bill that does not have a chance of commanding the two-thirds majorities required to override a presidential veto. In a few cases, Congress will enact a bill that members know will be vetoed in order to gain partisan points in the next election.

Each participant in the game wants to impose its own policy preferences on federal statutory policy, but in most cases none will act in a way that subjects it to an immediate override. Each participant anticipates the moves that will be made by the next participants. The following notations describe the important points in this model:

SQ   =   Existing policy (status quo)

H and S   =   Preferences of the median legislator in the two chambers of the legislature

P   =   Preferences of the President

h and s   =   Pivotal voter in veto override in the two chambers of the bicameral legislature

x   =   Statutory policy resulting from model

Assume that the status quo is objectionable from the perspectives of both Congress and the President—but preferences for changing the status quo run in different directions, as they will often do under circumstances of divided government.

FIGURE 1
Legislative Compromise Involving Two Chambers and the President

				x	
H	**h**	**S**	**s**	**SQ**	**P**

In such a case, the House and the Senate will work out a compromise proposal, either through informal signals or a formal conference committee, because a majority of both chambers want to change the status quo and differ only as to how much to change it. Although the President does not have enough leverage to stop a statutory change contrary to his preferences, his veto power does give him leverage to moderate that change. The ultimate statutory policy (x) will fall closer to the status quo than it would in a parliamentary system. In a game of perfect information and strategic behavior, the ultimate policy ought to fall at that point where the veto median (the senator needed to override the potential presidential veto) would prefer the proposal to the status quo.

This example demonstrates the importance of the *pivotal voter* in determining legislative outcomes. Although the median voter's preference may exert a strong pull on the policy equilibrium, the existence of supermajoritarian procedures such as cloture rules and veto overrides allows pivotal voters to "dampen policy convergence to the median legislator's ideal point." Keith Krehbiel, *Pivotal Politics: A Theory of U.S. Lawmaking* 232 (1998). Krehbiel argues that the influence of the pivotal voter in Congress entrenches the status quo even further, leads to widespread gridlock, and explains why much major legislation is passed by relatively wide margins and with bipartisan support. In later chapters we will discuss other congressional procedures and institutional structures that allow different players or minority coalitions to block policies. All of these complicate the legislative game and move the point of policy equilibrium to different places along the spectrum of possibilities.

Notice that this Article I, § 7 model makes more precise the Framers' intuitions about the constitutional structure for lawmaking: Many problems will not generate statutory solutions (as when H < SQ < S), and the ones that do will generate statutes reflecting moderate rather than strong responses to the problem (such as the solution in Figure 1). The model also demonstrates some of the ways in which the President's preferences affect statutory policy, and the circumstances under which they will do so. Most important, the model suggests that even when the political system does "nothing" (no bill is proposed or acted on), the system might actually be "working" (no bill is proposed because everyone realizes it would be a waste of time).

3. Statutory Implementation as an Anticipated Response Game

A further consequence of institutional game theory is that statute-making must consider statute-implementing. The players in the legislative process (Senators, House Members, the President) not only act in response to the anticipated preferences of one another, but they also anticipate and consider the preferences of subsequent implementers and interpreters of the statute. See Jonathan R. Macey, *Separated Powers and Positive Political Theory: The Tug of War Over Administrative Agencies*, 60 Geo. L.J. 671 (1992). That is, when Senator Dirksen signed onto the Dirksen–Mansfield compromise, he was anticipating how that compromise would be implemented. Hence, he was acting in accord with theories he had about the administrative process (and the newly created EEOC) and the judicial process. For example, he thought that employers would be insulated from "overenforcement" of the statute by requiring complainants to exhaust lengthy administrative procedures before they could bring suit and by hamstringing the EEOC itself with limited powers.[ff] Additionally, Dirksen assumed that the judiciary would enforce the deals which he insisted be encoded in the statutory text. An example of such a deal was § 703(j), which prevents the government from "requiring" companies to adopt affirmative action plans.

---

ff. See Mathew D. McCubbins, Roger G. Noll & Barry R. Weingast, *Administrative Procedures as Instruments of Political Control*, 3 J.L. Econ. & Org. 243 (1987) (this is a typical legislative strategy); Kathleen Bawn, *Political Control Versus Expertise: Congressional Choices About Administrative Procedures*, 89 Am. Pol. Sci. Rev. 62 (1995).

Shift focus from the legislature to the agency and the courts. When the statute is enacted, the agency and the judiciary might be expected to follow the dictates of the enacting coalition, not only because these officials have internalized the norm of legislative supremacy, but also because their failure to do so would subject them to legislative override and perhaps some kind of discipline. In other words, agencies and courts, like Congress and the President, will consider the preferences and possible responses of other political actors before they choose a course of action. The EEOC, for example, would not have announced nonenforcement of a provision of the recently enacted statute, because the President would have quashed any such revolt, and Congress would have punished the agency (perhaps by abolishing it, severely reducing its funding, or calling the agency head to testify and answer the questions of angry lawmakers). The game is further complicated when there is divided government, where the executive branch and at least one house of the legislature are consistently controlled by different parties. See Morris Fiorina, *Divided Government* (2d ed. 1996); David Mayhew, *Divided We Govern: Party Control, Lawmaking and Investigations, 1946–1990* (2d ed. 2005). In the current era of relatively polarized parties, congressional and presidential preferences may be widely separated and make legislative action difficult.

In short, there is often no clear end to the legislative game. After Congress and the President enact a law, agencies, more or less under the control of the President, implement it. Judges oversee the implementation by requiring fidelity between execution and their interpretation of the statute's requirements. Congress can usually modify a law to take account of judicial interpretation or agency action, and it can bring influence to bear on at least the executive branch and sometimes indirectly on courts themselves. After such a congressional reaction, the agencies and courts have their turn in implementing and interpreting the new policy. Institutional theorists have also turned their attention to courts, applying their tools to understanding and predicting to judicial actors.[gg]

The Fourth Circuit's deliberation in *Griggs* can also be analyzed as an anticipated response game, albeit one where the players had incomplete information. In deciding whether to sustain plaintiffs' claims, the judges would surely have considered the preferences of the Supreme Court, which had the formal power to reverse the Fourth Circuit. In figuring those preferences, the Fourth Circuit had little information because there was no Supreme Court decision interpreting the Civil Rights Act. Hence, the circuit judges looked to analogous Supreme Court decisions in the voting and school desegregation arenas, and to the kind of evidence (legislative history, such as the Tower colloquies) that the Supreme Court often invoked in construing statutes.

---

gg. See, e.g., Cornell Clayton & Howard A. Gillman, *Supreme Court Decision–Making: New Institutionalist Approaches* (1999); Maxwell L. Stearns, *Constitutional Process: A Social Choice Analysis of Supreme Court Decision Making* (2000); Lee Epstein et al., *Dynamic Agenda–Setting on the United States Supreme Court: An Empirical Assessment*, 39 Harv. J. Legis. 395 (2002).

If the circuit judges were being particularly strategic, they would also have considered broader political currents that might, in turn, have influenced the Supreme Court's preferences. In 1969, Republican Richard Nixon had just been elected President, but his administration fully accepted the Civil Rights Act as a good statute and his Department of Justice Civil Rights Division was headed by a liberal, Stanley Pottinger. The EEOC remained a hotbed of liberal sentiment. Several of the prominent congressional opponents of civil rights laws had been defeated (Judge Smith) or had died or retired from Congress (Senators Harry Byrd [D–Va.] and Spessard Holland [D–Fla.]), and the new generation of southern Senators and Representatives were more moderate (e.g., Senators Charles Mathias [R–Md.], Howard Baker [R–Tenn.], Ernest Hollings [D–S.C.], Thomas Eagleton [D–Mo.], William Spong [D–Va.], all of whom came to the Senate by defeating segregationist Democrats in the elections of 1966 and 1968), perhaps reflecting the new voting clout of African Americans after enactment of the Voting Rights Act of 1965. We concede that "knowing" all this (and more) required a good deal of political sophistication, but Judge Sobeloff was himself a Washington insider, having served as President Eisenhower's Solicitor General in the early 1950s. Most federal judges have extensive political experience and sophistication.

Given this political context, the NAACP Inc. Fund appealed the Fourth Circuit loss to the Supreme Court. If the Court were to take the case (which became highly probable when the Nixon Administration joined the Inc. Fund in petitioning the Court for review), what do you predict the Supreme Court would do with *Griggs*? Is this what the Court *should* do? Jot down your thoughts in the margin.

SECTION 3.　TITLE VII AND AFFIRMATIVE ACTION: AN INTRODUCTION TO STATUTORY INTERPRETATION

This section will introduce you to important themes of statutory implementation and will suggest that issues of legal theory and political theory are inextricably intertwined. We shall revisit the *Griggs* problem from Section 1 and provide a more detailed political account of the problem's resolution in the early 1970s (Part A). The Supreme Court's resolution of *Griggs* raised new problems, of course. The most notable is whether Title VII permits employers to engage in "affirmative action" to rectify underrepresentation of minority employees. That issue has been a vexing one and impelled the Rehnquist Court to revisit both affirmative action and disparate impact decisions (Part B). Congress sought to restore the liberal regime developed by the Burger Court in a 1991 override statute—but the Roberts Court has construed the 1991 law in a narrow manner that destabilizes at least some affirmative action plans in the new millennium.

A. THE BURGER COURT'S LIBERAL CONSTRUCTION OF TITLE VII: *GRIGGS* AND *WEBER*

The *Griggs* problem analyzed in Section 1 is an example of a larger tension within Title VII: the statute that was enacted in 1964 focused on intentional discrimination (reread § 703) and set up a cumbersome administrative apparatus designed to minimize the role of the EEOC in the statute's development (see § 706). Both trade-offs were necessary to pass the statute. The former ensured broad middle class support and an expansive coalition because it suggested that this would not be a redistributive statute. The latter was the price exacted by Senator Dirksen to get the bill through the filibuster vetogate. Yet Title VII's focus on intentional discrimination changed shortly after the statute went into force. The engine of this change was the declawed EEOC, as the activists who had worked to enact the statute—civil rights leaders and litigators, bureaucrats, law professors—turned to the task of making the statute work to implement President Johnson's goal of "not just equality as a right and a theory but equality as a fact and equality as a result."[a]

From its first year in operation, key players at all levels of the EEOC believed that racial inequality in employment was the result of structural factors, not just intentional discrimination, and that affirmative results were more important than formal requirements.[b] Based upon her labor law experience, EEOC staff member Sonia Pressman argued that it would be impractical to expect evidence of discriminatory intent in most cases. Just as litigants challenging racial discrimination in jury selection could rely on underrepresentation of minorities, Pressman urged that plaintiffs be permitted to make out a claim of employment discrimination based upon underrepresentation of minorities. Memorandum from Sonia Pressman to EEOC General Counsel Charles Duncan, 31 May 1966, described and quoted in Graham, *Civil Rights Era* 244–47. The EEOC legal staff were candid about the tension between their views and the apparent compromises adopted in the 1964 statute, but they urged their approach as the most practical way to enforce the statute. By the end of the Johnson Administration, the EEOC Commissioners publicly interpreted the statute to bar employer practices "which prove to have a demonstrable racial effect." EEOC Commissioner Samuel Jackson, *EEOC vs. Discrimination, Inc.*, The Crisis, Jan. 1968, 16–17.

---

a. *Public Papers: Lyndon B. Johnson, 1965*, at 636 (1966) (June 1965 speech by President Johnson at Howard University). The story that follows is drawn from the records in the main cases and from recent archival research set forth in Hugh Davis Graham, *The Civil Rights Era: Origins and Development of National Policy, 1962–1971* (1990), reviewed and supplemented by Neal Devins, *The Civil Rights Hydra*, 89 Mich. L. Rev. 1723 (1991). See also Herman Belz, *Equality Transformed: A Quarter–Century of Affirmative Action* (1991).

b. See White House Conference on Equal Educational Opportunity (EEOC, 1965). Several key agency players published explanations and defenses of this ideology. See EEOC Executive Director Herman Edelsberg, *Title VII of the Civil Rights Act: The First Year*, 19 N.Y.U. Conf. on Labor 289–295 (1967), and EEOC staff member Alfred Blumrosen, *Black Employment and the Law* (1971).

The EEOC's rationale for an effects-based approach was that such an interpretation better served the statutory purpose. This position was shared by the Inc. Fund and other civil rights litigation groups. Directly encouraged by the EEOC, which filed helpful *amicus* briefs, civil rights litigation groups challenged employer testing and union seniority arrangements which had disproportionate and negative effects upon African Americans. These groups sometimes found a receptive audience in Eisenhower- and Johnson-appointed federal judges who were struggling with similar issues of racially discriminatory effects of arguably "neutral" state policies in the areas of education, voting, and jury selection. See, e.g., Judge Butzner's opinion in *Quarles v. Philip Morris, Inc.*, 279 F.Supp. 505 (E.D. Va. 1968), and Judge Wisdom's opinion in *Local 189, United Papermakers v. United States*, 416 F.2d 980 (5th Cir. 1969). Judge Sobeloff, dissenting in *Griggs*, relied on *Quarles* and *Local 189* to argue for a results-oriented rather than just intent-focused inquiry in Title VII.

The Inc. Fund appealed its loss in *Griggs*, with the support of the EEOC and the Nixon Administration's Solicitor General, Erwin Griswold. To the surprise of many pundits, the Supreme Court not only unanimously reversed in *Griggs v. Duke Power Co.*, 401 U.S. 424 (1971), but expanded upon Sobeloff's opinion. The Supreme Court held that a facially neutral employment practice that was not demonstrably discriminatory in purpose was nonetheless unlawful if it had the effect of excluding a group on the basis of race and without a strict showing of business necessity. Although the Court reaffirmed the colorblindness of Title VII, its rationale stressed that "Congress directed the thrust of the Act to the *consequences* of employment practices." This appeared to be a recognition that while § 703(a) speaks in terms of individuals, the underlying problems addressed by Title VII are institutionalized societal practices that systematically exclude minority groups from employment opportunities. The lower courts, especially those in the South, viewed *Griggs* as a mandate to use Title VII to reform group employment practices in entire companies, based upon the disparate impact idea.[c]

Some commentators have criticized the Supreme Court's decision as inconsistent with the original "deal" needed to get Title VII's protections through the vetogates, specifically, past the Senate filibuster. E.g., Daniel

---

c. Thus the Fifth Circuit sustained affirmative action remedies, finding that "[i]t is the collective interest, governmental as well as social, in effectively ending unconstitutional racial discrimination that justifies temporary, carefully circumscribed resort to racial criteria, whenever the chancellor determines that it represents the only rational, nonarbitrary means of eradicating past evils." *NAACP v. Allen*, 493 F.2d 614, 619 (5th Cir. 1974). "By reasonable affirmative action programs, courts can order employers to use ratios, percentages and quotas to ensure that members of minority groups traditionally discriminated against have reasonable opportunities to be hired." 2 Chester Antieau, *Federal Civil Rights Act: Civil Practice* § 528, at 237 (1980) (citing cases). Additional pressures for preferential hiring were generated by Executive Order 11,246, which required government contracts to include an affirmative action clause. 3 C.F.R. page 339 (1964–65). As elaborated in 1970, the Order required government contractors to establish "a set of specific and result-oriented procedures" to yield "equal employment opportunity." 35 Fed. Reg. 2586, 2587 (1970). For a discussion of the role of executive orders to expand civil rights, perhaps beyond what Congress would enact, see Kenneth Mayer, *With the Stroke of a Pen: Executive Orders and Presidential Power* Chapter 6 (2001).

B. Rodriguez & Barry R. Weingast, *The Positive Political Theory of Legislative History: New Perspectives on the 1964 Civil Rights Act and Its Interpretation*, 151 U. Pa. L. Rev. 1417, 1501–10 (2003). Assume that they are right. What, then, explains *Griggs*?

Judge Sobeloff's opinion in the lower court suggests one way of explaining an effects-based inquiry: it is needed to fulfill the statute's purpose. Congress in 1964 did not focus on the possibility that pre–1964 discrimination would have continuing effects, but once that became clear to the EEOC and the courts, they had a responsibility to apply the statute to new circumstances in a way that carried out the original purpose. One way to think of this approach is as a *translation* of the statute, moving it away from its apparent textual mandates on the ground that new approaches are required to fulfill the objectives of the enactors. In other words, an interpretation that departs from the terms of the deal, as reflected in the text of the statute, is actually more faithful to legislative intent than a more literal interpretation. This sort of dynamic statutory interpretation is controversial because it places a great deal of discretionary power in the unelected judiciary. On the other hand, at least in theory, it requires judges to be the faithful and careful agents of the legislative drafters, modifying or enhancing statutory provisions only when necessary to avoid undermining legislative purpose and intent.

Another way of explaining *Griggs* is that the liberal EEOC and Supreme Court were moving statutory policy in a leftward direction away from original legislative intent. This can be expressed in the game-theoretic terms familiar to us from our study of institutional theories of the legislative process. See Lee Epstein & Jack Knight, *The Choices Justices Make* (1999) (applying positive political theory to judicial behavior). Remember that positive political theory underscores the importance of all the players in the policymaking game, including the executive branch agencies that will implement the statute and the judges who will interpret it. If their preferences diverge from the legislature's, they will try to move policy closer to their ideal point, realizing that the Congress will monitor them and try to avert any substantial change in the outcome. Consider the following diagram, similar to the earlier ones but with positions added to represent the EEOC (the agency, "A") and the Supreme Court (the judiciary, "J"):

FIGURE 2
Movement of Title VII Policy Away from the Original Deal

	x*		x		
	H	S	s		SQ
	P				
	A				
	J				

The dynamics illustrated by Figure 2 start with the fact that the "filibuster median" (Senator Dirksen) needed to secure legislation was much more conservative than the median voter of the enforcing institutions, namely, the EEOC (filled with civil rights advocates) and the Supreme Court (egged on by the liberal Solicitor General). Hence, the new policy (x*) represented a shift to the left from the original deal, at least as hypothesized by this diagram.

Notice that the new interpretation (x*) represents a stable solution, unless Congress can override it. And to override the interpretation, a proposal must surmount all the vetogates that the original enactment did. It appears that the House, at least, was okay with *Griggs*, and even clearer that the House and Senate labor committees were delighted with *Griggs*. See H.R. Rep. No. 238, 92d Cong., 1st Sess. 21–22 (1971), reprinted in 1972 U.S.C.C.A.N. 2137, 2156–57; Sen. Rep. No. 415, 92d Cong., 1st Sess. 14 (1971). Because those committees exercised gatekeeping power over issues on the legislative agenda, they had substantial ability to head off overrides of agency policies or judicial decisions, especially when they were supported by the majority party leadership, which was similarly liberal on civil rights issues and exerted great control over the congressional agenda and floor politics.

Under the foregoing analysis, the EEOC and the Supreme Court can sometimes set policy at the point reflecting the preferences of the median member of the House Committee on Education and Labor, rather than the median member of the House. This institutional dynamic alone gives the agency and the courts substantial discretion to move statutory policy away from the original statutory deal (x). Note that under the foregoing analysis the EEOC and the Court are more strongly influenced by the preferences of members of the *current* Congress than they are by the preferences of the *enacting* Congress. Thus, our study reveals that the notion of legislative intent has a temporal element. Although many think of courts and executive branch officials as the agents of the enacting Congress, current Congresses can exert substantial influence over policies because they control the budget and have close connections with agency personnel with day-to-day oversight of federal programs.

Under a game-theoretic analysis, *Griggs* itself might be subject to reinterpretation. After Justices Lewis Powell and William Rehnquist took their seats in 1972, the Burger Court became much more ambivalent about broadly defined antidiscrimination duties. In constitutional cases, where the Court is better protected against political overrides, the Burger Court rejected the *Griggs* approach and held that race-based or gender-based effects do not amount to unlawful discrimination. See *Washington v. Davis*, 426 U.S. 229 (1976); *Personnel Administrator of Massachusetts v. Feeney*, 442 U.S. 256 (1979); see also Jeffrey Segal & Albert Cover, *Ideological Values and the Votes of U.S. Supreme Court Justices*, 83 Am. Pol. Sci. Rev. 557, 560 (1989) (Table 1). The Burger Court narrowed *Griggs* itself only by tightening up proof burdens on plaintiffs but did not directly attack the decision.

The survival of *Griggs* through the 1970s is remarkable. Not only was the decision vulnerable to the charge that it was a significant leap from the expectations of the enacting Congress (x* is a long way down the line from x), but also a majority on the Court in the 1970s was not enthusiastic about outlawing discriminatory effects. *Griggs* remained safe from being overruled in a period in which the Court was moving to the right, because Congress moved further to the left on civil rights issues in the 1970s. Thus the new policy (x*) was one that was acceptable to most Members of Congress by the late 1970s. Any open retreat from *Griggs* would have generated immediate controversy because the civil rights community, the EEOC, and the gatekeeping (labor) committees would have mobilized for an override. In fact, this is precisely what happened when the Court retreated from *Griggs* by refusing to treat pregnancy discrimination as sex discrimination under Title VII: the Court suffered a firestorm of protest and was promptly overridden. See Pregnancy Discrimination Act of 1978, Pub. L. No. 95–555, 92 Stat. 2076 (1978), overriding *General Electric Co. v. Gilbert*, 429 U.S. 125 (1976); William N. Eskridge Jr., *Reneging on History? Playing the Court/Congress/President Civil Rights Game*, 79 Calif. L. Rev. 613 (1991).

If you were counsel to a big company or a labor union in the 1970s, you would probably be very concerned about the representation of people of color in your company's workforce. Under *Griggs*, your company or union might be subject to a disparate impact lawsuit if bad numbers were not justified. And if your company did business with the federal government, the Johnson and Nixon Administrations had implemented a policy under which such companies had to improve their numbers or lose their lucrative contracts. In short, companies faced the loss of government contracts and judicially imposed back-pay awards and quota systems if their hiring efforts did not produce concrete results.

At the same time, consistent with *Griggs*, the Supreme Court encouraged companies to adopt their own plans. For example, in *Albemarle Paper Co. v. Moody*, 422 U.S. 405, 417–18 (1975), the Court approved broad EEOC guidelines out of an announced desire to provide the "spur or catalyst which causes employers and unions to self-examine and to self-evaluate their employment practices and to endeavor to eliminate, so far as possible, the last vestiges of an unfortunate and ignominious page in this country's history." See also *Franks v. Bowman Transp. Co.*, 424 U.S. 747, 778 (1976) (upholding retroactive award of seniority to African–American victims of discrimination and saying that "a collective bargaining agreement may go further, enhancing the seniority status of certain employees for purposes of furthering public policy interests beyond what is required by statute").

As a result of these developments, companies like Kaiser Aluminum and Chemical Corp. and labor unions like the United Steelworkers of America had incentives to adopt their own preferential hiring programs, with the hope that they could avoid having one thrust upon them by a court. In *McDonald v. Santa Fe Trail Transp. Co.*, 427 U.S. 273 (1976), however, the Court held that Title VII prohibits racial discrimination against whites as well as African Americans. The upshot of that case was that displaced white employees like Brian Weber had a colorable argument that voluntary affirmative action programs were unlawfully discriminatory against them as well—and that they had a cause of action under Title VII. That clash of different statutory purposes, different legally protected civil rights, and different Supreme Court signals generated the following case.

UNITED STEELWORKERS OF AMERICA v. WEBER

Supreme Court of the United States, 1979
443 U.S. 193, 99 S.Ct. 2721, 61 L.Ed.2d 480

MR. JUSTICE BRENNAN delivered the opinion of the Court. * * *

In 1974, petitioner United Steelworkers of America (USWA) and petitioner Kaiser Aluminum & Chemical Corp. (Kaiser) entered into a master collective-bargaining agreement covering terms and conditions of employment at 15 Kaiser plants. The agreement contained, *inter alia*, an affirmative action plan designed to eliminate conspicuous racial imbalances in Kaiser's then almost exclusively white craft-work forces. Black craft-hiring goals were set for each Kaiser plant equal to the percentage of blacks in the respective local labor forces. To enable plants to meet these goals, on-the-job training programs were established to teach unskilled production workers—black and white—the skills necessary to become craftworkers. The plan reserved for black employees 50% of the openings in these newly created in-plant training programs.

This case arose from the operation of the plan at Kaiser's plant in Gramercy, La. Until 1974, Kaiser hired as craftworkers for that plant only persons who had had prior craft experience. Because blacks had long been excluded from craft unions, few were able to present such credentials. As a consequence, prior to 1974 only 1.83% (5 out of 273) of the skilled craftworkers at the Gramercy plant were black, even though the work force in the Gramercy area was approximately 39% black.

Pursuant to the national agreement Kaiser altered its craft-hiring practice in the Gramercy plant. Rather than hiring already trained outsiders, Kaiser established a training program to train its production workers to fill craft openings. Selection of craft trainees was made on the basis of seniority, with the proviso that at least 50% of the new trainees were to be black until the percentage of black skilled craftworkers in the Gramercy plant approximated the percentage of blacks in the local labor force.

During 1974, the first year of the operation of the Kaiser–USWA affirmative action plan, 13 craft trainees were selected from Gramercy's production work force. Of these, seven were black and six white. The most senior black selected into the program had less seniority than several white production workers whose bids for admission were rejected. Thereafter one of those white production workers, respondent Brian Weber (hereafter respondent), instituted this class action in the United States District Court for the Eastern District of Louisiana.

The complaint alleged that the filling of craft trainee positions at the Gramercy plant pursuant to the affirmative action program had resulted in junior black employees' receiving training in preference to senior white employees, thus discriminating against respondent and other similarly situated white employees in violation of §§ 703(a)[2] and (d)[3] of Title VII. The District Court held that the plan violated Title VII, entered a judgment in favor of the plaintiff class, and granted a permanent injunction prohibiting Kaiser and the USWA "from denying plaintiffs, Brian F. Weber and all other members of the class, access to on-the-job training programs on the basis of race." A divided panel of the Court of Appeals for the Fifth Circuit affirmed, holding that all employment preferences based upon race, including those preferences incidental to bona fide affirmative action plans, violated Title VII's prohibition against racial discrimination in employment. * * * We reverse.

We emphasize at the outset the narrowness of our inquiry. * * * [S]ince the Kaiser–USWA plan was adopted voluntarily, we are not concerned with what Title VII requires or with what a court might order to remedy a past proved violation of the Act. The only question before us is the narrow statutory issue of whether Title VII *forbids* private employers and unions from voluntarily agreeing upon bona fide affirmative action plans that accord racial preferences in the manner and for the purpose provided in the Kaiser–USWA plan. * * *

Respondent argues that Congress intended in Title VII to prohibit all race-conscious affirmative action plans. Respondent's argument rests upon a literal interpretation of §§ 703(a) and (d) of the Act. Those sections make it unlawful to "discriminate * * * because of * * * race" in hiring and in the selection of apprentices for training programs. Since, the argument runs, *McDonald v. Santa Fe Trail Transp. Co.,* [427 U.S. 273, 281 n.8 (1976)], settled that Title VII forbids discrimination against whites as well as blacks, and since the Kaiser–USWA affirmative action plan operates to discriminate against white employees solely because they are white, it follows that the Kaiser–USWA plan violates Title VII.

Respondent's argument is not without force. But it overlooks the significance of the fact that the Kaiser–USWA plan is an affirmative

---

2. Section 703(a), 78 Stat. 255, as amended, 86 Stat. 109, 42 U.S.C. § 2000e–2(a), provides:

"(a) * * * It shall be an unlawful employment practice for an employer—

(1) to fail or refuse to hire or to discharge any individual, or otherwise to discriminate against any individual with respect to his compensation, terms, conditions, or privileges of employment, because of such individual's race, color, religion, sex, or national origin; or

(2) to limit, segregate, or classify his employees or applicants for employment in any way which would deprive or tend to deprive any individual of employment opportunities or otherwise adversely affect his status as an employee, because of such individual's race, color, religion, sex, or national origin."

3. Section 703(d), 78 Stat. 256, 42 U.S.C. § 2000e–2(d), provides:

"It shall be an unlawful employment practice for any employer, labor organization, or joint labor-management committee controlling apprenticeship or other training or retraining, including on-the-job training programs to discriminate against any individual because of his race, color, religion, sex, or national origin in admission to, or employment in, any program established to provide apprenticeship or other training."

action plan voluntarily adopted by private parties to eliminate traditional patterns of racial segregation. In this context respondent's reliance upon a literal construction of §§ 703(a) and (d) and upon *McDonald* is misplaced. It is a "familiar rule, that a thing may be within the letter of the statute and yet not within the statute, because not within its spirit, nor within the intention of its makers." *Holy Trinity Church v. United States*, 143 U.S. 457, 459 (1892). The prohibition against racial discrimination in §§ 703(a) and (d) of Title VII must therefore be read against the background of the legislative history of Title VII and the historical context from which the Act arose. Examination of those sources makes clear that an interpretation of the sections that forbade all race-conscious affirmative action would "bring about an end completely at variance with the purpose of the statute" and must be rejected. *United States v. Public Utilities Comm'n*, 345 U.S. 295, 315 (1953).

Congress's primary concern in enacting the prohibition against racial discrimination in Title VII of the Civil Rights Act of 1964 was with "the plight of the Negro in our economy." 110 Cong. Rec. 6548 (1964) (remarks of Sen. Humphrey). Before 1964, blacks were largely relegated to "unskilled and semiskilled jobs." *Ibid.* (remarks of Sen. Humphrey); *id.*, at 7204 (remarks of Sen. Clark); *id.*, at 7379–7380 (remarks of Sen. Kennedy). Because of automation the number of such jobs was rapidly decreasing. See *id.*, at 6548 (remarks of Sen. Humphrey); *id.*, at 7204 (remarks of Sen. Clark). As a consequence, "the relative position of the Negro worker [was] steadily worsening." * * *

Congress feared that the goals of the Civil Rights Act—the integration of blacks into the mainstream of American society—could not be achieved unless this trend were reversed. And Congress recognized that that would not be possible unless blacks were able to secure jobs "which have a future." *Id.*, at 7204 (remarks of Sen. Clark). See also *id.*, at 7379–7380 (remarks of Sen. Kennedy). As Senator Humphrey explained to the Senate:

> "What good does it do a Negro to be able to eat in a fine restaurant if he cannot afford to pay the bill? What good does it do him to be accepted in a hotel that is too expensive for his modest income? How can a Negro child be motivated to take full advantage of integrated educational facilities if he has no hope of getting a job where he can use that education?" *Id.*, at 6547. * * *

Accordingly, it was clear to Congress that "[t]he crux of the problem [was] to open employment opportunities for Negroes in occupations which have been traditionally closed to them," 110 Cong. Rec. 6548 (1964) (remarks of Sen. Humphrey), and it was to this problem that Title VII's prohibition against racial discrimination in employment was primarily addressed.

It plainly appears from the House Report accompanying the Civil Rights Act that Congress did not intend wholly to prohibit private and voluntary affirmative action efforts as one method of solving this problem. The Report provides:

"No bill can or should lay claim to eliminating all of the causes and consequences of racial and other types of discrimination against minorities. There is reason to believe, however, that national leadership provided by the enactment of Federal legislation dealing with the most troublesome problems *will create an atmosphere conducive to voluntary or local resolution of other forms of discrimination.*" H.R. Rep. No. 914, 88th Cong., 1st Sess., pt. 1, p. 18 (1963). (Emphasis supplied.) * * *

Given this legislative history, we cannot agree with respondent that Congress intended to prohibit the private sector from taking effective steps to accomplish the goal that Congress designed Title VII to achieve. * * * It would be ironic indeed if a law triggered by a Nation's concern over centuries of racial injustice and intended to improve the lot of those who had "been excluded from the American dream for so long," 110 Cong. Rec. 6552 (1964) (remarks of Sen. Humphrey), constituted the first legislative prohibition of all voluntary, private, race-conscious efforts to abolish traditional patterns of racial segregation and hierarchy.

Our conclusion is further reinforced by examination of the language and legislative history of § 703(j) of Title VII.[5] Opponents of Title VII raised two related arguments against the bill. First, they argued that the Act would be interpreted to *require* employers with racially imbalanced work forces to grant preferential treatment to racial minorities in order to integrate. Second, they argued that employers with racially imbalanced work forces would grant preferential treatment to racial minorities, even if not required to do so by the Act. See 110 Cong. Rec. 8618–8619 (1964) (remarks of Sen. Sparkman). Had Congress meant to prohibit all race-conscious affirmative action, as respondent urges, it easily could have answered both objections by providing that Title VII would not require or *permit* racially preferential integration efforts. But Congress did not choose such a course. Rather, Congress added § 703(j) which addresses only the first objection. The section provides that nothing contained in Title VII "shall be interpreted to *require* any employer * * * to grant preferential treatment * * * to any group because of the race * * * of such * * * group on account of" a *de facto* racial imbalance in the employer's work force. The section does *not* state that "nothing in Title

---

5. Section 703(j) of Title VII, 78 Stat. 257, 42 U.S.C. § 2000e–2(j), provides:

"Nothing contained in this title shall be interpreted to require any employer, employment agency, labor organization, or joint labor-management committee subject to this title to grant preferential treatment to any individual or to any group because of the race, color, religion, sex, or national origin of such individual or group on account of an imbalance which may exist with respect to the total number or percentage of persons of any race, color, religion, sex, or national origin employed by any employer, referred or classified for employment by any employment agency or labor organization, admitted to membership or classified by any labor organization, or admitted to, or employed in, any apprenticeship or other training program, in comparison with the total number or percentage of persons of such race, color, religion, sex, or national origin in any community, State, section, or other area, or in the available work force in any community, State, section, or other area."

Section 703(j) speaks to substantive liability under Title VII, but it does not preclude courts from considering racial imbalance as evidence of a Title VII violation. * * * Remedies for substantive violations are governed by § 706(g), 42 U.S.C. § 2000e–5(g).

VII shall be interpreted to *permit*" voluntary affirmative efforts to correct racial imbalances. The natural inference is that Congress chose not to forbid all voluntary race-conscious affirmative action.

The reasons for this choice are evident from the legislative record. Title VII could not have been enacted into law without substantial support from legislators in both Houses who traditionally resisted federal regulation of private business. Those legislators demanded as a price for their support that "management prerogatives, and union freedoms * * * be left undisturbed to the greatest extent possible." H.R. Rep. No. 914, 88th Cong., 1st Sess., pt. 2, p. 29 (1963). Section 703(j) was proposed by Senator Dirksen to allay any fears that the Act might be interpreted in such a way as to upset this compromise. The section was designed to prevent § 703 of Title VII from being interpreted in such a way as to lead to undue "Federal Government interference with private businesses because of some Federal employee's ideas about racial balance or racial imbalance." 110 Cong. Rec. 14314 (1964) (remarks of Sen. Miller). See also *id.*, at 9881 (remarks of Sen. Allott); *id.*, at 10520 (remarks of Sen. Carlson); *id.*, at 11471 (remarks of Sen. Javits); *id.*, at 12817 (remarks of Sen. Dirksen). Clearly, a prohibition against all voluntary, race-conscious, affirmative action efforts would disserve these ends. Such a prohibition would augment the powers of the Federal Government and diminish traditional management prerogatives while at the same time impeding attainment of the ultimate statutory goals. In view of this legislative history and in view of Congress's desire to avoid undue federal regulation of private businesses, use of the word "require" rather than the phrase "require or permit" in § 703(j) fortifies the conclusion that Congress did not intend to limit traditional business freedom to such a degree as to prohibit all voluntary, race-conscious affirmative action.[7]

---

7. Respondent argues that our construction of § 703 conflicts with various remarks in the legislative record. See, *e.g.*, 110 Cong. Rec. 7213 (1964) (Sens. Clark and Case); *id.*, at 7218 (Sens. Clark and Case); *id.*, at 6549 (Sen. Humphrey); *id.*, at 8921 (Sen. Williams). We do not agree. In Senator Humphrey's words, these comments were intended as assurances that Title VII would not allow establishment of systems "to *maintain* racial balance in employment." *Id.*, at 11848 (emphasis added). They were not addressed to temporary, voluntary, affirmative action measures undertaken to eliminate manifest racial imbalance in traditionally segregated job categories. Moreover, the comments referred to by respondent all preceded the adoption of § 703(j), 42 U.S.C. § 2000e–2(j). After § 703(j) was adopted, congressional comments were all to the effect that employers would not be *required* to institute preferential quotas to avoid Title VII liability, see, *e.g.*, 110 Cong. Rec. 12819 (1964) (remarks of Sen. Dirksen); *id.*, at 13079–13080 (remarks of Sen. Clark); *id.*, at 15876 (remarks of Rep. Lindsay). There was no suggestion after the adoption of § 703(j) that wholly voluntary, race-conscious, affirmative action efforts would in themselves constitute a violation of Title VII. On the contrary, as Representative MacGregor told the House shortly before the final vote on Title VII:

"Important as the scope and extent of this bill is, it is also vitally important that all Americans understand what this bill does not cover.

"Your mail and mine, your contacts and mine with our constituents, indicates a great degree of misunderstanding about this bill. People complain about * * * preferential treatment or quotas in employment. There is a mistaken belief that Congress is legislating in these areas in this bill. When we drafted this bill we excluded these issues largely because the problems raised by these controversial questions are more properly handled at a governmental level closer to the American people and by communities and individuals themselves." 110 Cong. Rec. 15893 (1964).

We therefore hold that Title VII's prohibition in §§ 703(a) and (d) against racial discrimination does not condemn all private, voluntary, race-conscious affirmative action plans. * * * [The Court held that the Kaiser plan was lawful under Title VII because both its purpose and effect were permissible: it was "designed to eliminate conspicuous racial imbalance in traditionally segregated job categories," and it "does not unnecessarily trammel the interests of white employees" because no white employees lost their jobs, half of those trained in the program will be white, and it was a temporary measure ending when "the percentage of black skilled craftworkers in the Gramercy plant approximates the percentage of blacks in the local labor force."]

MR. JUSTICE POWELL and MR. JUSTICE STEVENS took no part in the consideration or decision of these cases.

MR. JUSTICE BLACKMUN, concurring.

While I share some of the misgivings expressed in MR. JUSTICE REHNQUIST's dissent concerning the extent to which the legislative history of Title VII clearly supports the result the Court reaches today, I believe that additional considerations, practical and equitable, only partially perceived, if perceived at all, by the 88th Congress, support the conclusion reached by the Court today, and I therefore join its opinion as well as its judgment.

In his dissent from the decision of the United States Court of Appeals for the Fifth Circuit, Judge Wisdom pointed out that this litigation arises from a practical problem in the administration of Title VII. The broad prohibition against discrimination places the employer and the union on what he accurately described as a "high tightrope without a net beneath them." 563 F.2d 216, 230. If Title VII is read literally, on the one hand they face liability for past discrimination against blacks, and on the other they face liability to whites for any voluntary preferences adopted to mitigate the effects of prior discrimination against blacks.

In this litigation, Kaiser denies prior discrimination but concedes that its past hiring practices may be subject to question. Although the labor force in the Gramercy area was proximately 39% black, Kaiser's work force was less than 15% black, and its craftwork force was less than 2% black. Kaiser had made some effort to recruit black painters, carpenters, insulators, and other craftsmen, but it continued to insist that those hired have five years' prior industrial experience, a requirement that arguably was not sufficiently job related to justify under Title VII any discriminatory impact it may have had. * * * The parties dispute the extent to which black craftsmen were available in the local labor market. They agree, however, that after critical reviews from the Office of Federal Contract Compliance, Kaiser and the Steelworkers established the training program in question here and modeled it along the lines of a Title VII consent decree later entered for the steel industry. * * * Yet when they did this, respondent Weber sued, alleging that Title VII prohibited the program because it discriminated against him as a white person and it was not supported by a prior judicial finding of discrimination against blacks.

Respondent Weber's reading of Title VII, endorsed by the Court of Appeals, places voluntary compliance with Title VII in profound jeopardy. The only way for the employer and the union to keep their footing on the "tightrope" it creates would be to eschew all forms of voluntary affirmative action. Even a whisper of emphasis on minority recruiting would be forbidden. Because Congress intended to encourage private efforts to come into compliance with Title VII, see *Alexander v. Gardner–Denver Co.*, 415 U.S. 36, 44 (1974), Judge Wisdom concluded that employers and unions who had committed "arguable violations" of Title VII should be free to make reasonable responses without fear of liability to whites. Preferential hiring along the lines of the Kaiser program is a reasonable response for the employer, whether or not a court, on these facts, could order the same step as a remedy. The company is able to avoid identifying victims of past discrimination, and so avoids claims for backpay that would inevitably follow a response limited to such victims. If past victims should be benefited by the program, however, the company mitigates its liability to those persons. Also, to the extent that Title VII liability is predicated on the "disparate effect" of an employer's past hiring practices, the program makes it less likely that such an effect could be demonstrated. And the Court has recently held that work-force statistics resulting from private affirmative action were probative of benign intent in a "disparate treatment" case. *Furnco Construction Corp. v. Waters*, 438 U.S. 567 (1978).

The "arguable violation" theory has a number of advantages. It responds to a practical problem in the administration of Title VII not anticipated by Congress. It draws predictability from the outline of present law and closely effectuates the purpose of the Act. Both Kaiser and the United States urge its adoption here. Because I agree that it is the soundest way to approach this case, my preference would be to resolve this litigation by applying it and holding that Kaiser's craft training program meets the requirement that voluntary affirmative action be a reasonable response to an "arguable violation" of Title VII. * * *

MR. JUSTICE REHNQUIST, with whom THE CHIEF JUSTICE joins, dissenting.

In a very real sense, the Court's opinion is ahead of its time: it could more appropriately have been handed down five years from now, in 1984, a year coinciding with the title of a book from which the Court's opinion borrows, perhaps subconsciously, at least one idea. Orwell describes in his book a governmental official of Oceania, one of the three great world powers, denouncing the current enemy, Eurasia, to an assembled crowd:

"It was almost impossible to listen to him without being first convinced and then maddened. * * * The speech had been proceeding for perhaps twenty minutes when a messenger hurried onto the platform and a scrap of paper was slipped into the speaker's hand. He unrolled and read it without pausing in his speech. Nothing altered in his voice or manner, or in the content of what he was saying, but suddenly the names were different. Without words said, a wave of understanding rippled through the crowd. Oceania was at war with Eastasia! * * * The banners and posters with which the square was decorated were all wrong! * * *

"[T]he speaker had switched from one line to the other actually in mid-sentence, not only without a pause, but without even breaking the syntax."—G. Orwell, Nineteen Eighty–Four 181–182 (1949).

Today's decision represents an equally dramatic and equally unremarked switch in this Court's interpretation of Title VII. * * *

[II] Were Congress to act today specifically to prohibit the type of racial discrimination suffered by Weber, it would be hard pressed to draft language better tailored to the task than that found in § 703(d) of Title VII:

"It shall be an unlawful employment practice for any employer, labor organization, or joint labor-management committee controlling apprenticeship or other training or retraining, including on-the-job training programs to discriminate against any individual because of his race, color, religion, sex, or national origin in admission to, or employment in, any program established to provide apprenticeship or other training." 78 Stat. 256, 42 U.S.C. § 2000e–2(d).

Equally suited to the task would be § 703(a)(2), which makes it unlawful for an employer to classify his employees "in any way which would deprive or tend to deprive any individual of employment opportunities or otherwise adversely affect his status as an employee, because of such individual's race, color, religion, sex, or national origin." 78 Stat. 255, 42 U.S.C. § 2000e–2(a)(2).

Entirely consistent with these two express prohibitions is the language of § 703(j) of Title VII, which provides that the Act is not to be interpreted "to require any employer * * * to grant preferential treatment to any individual or to any group because of the race * * * of such individual or group" to correct a racial imbalance in the employer's work force. 42 U.S.C. § 2000e–2(j). Seizing on the word "require," the Court infers that Congress must have intended to "permit" this type of racial discrimination. Not only is this reading of § 703(j) outlandish in the light of the flat prohibitions of §§ 703(a) and (d), but also, as explained in Part III, it is totally belied by the Act's legislative history.

Quite simply, Kaiser's racially discriminatory admission quota is flatly prohibited by the plain language of Title VII. This normally dispositive fact, however, gives the Court only momentary pause. An "interpretation" of the statute upholding Weber's claim would, according to the Court, " 'bring about an end completely at variance with the purpose of the statute.' " To support this conclusion, the Court calls upon the "spirit" of the Act, which it divines from passages in Title VII's legislative history indicating that enactment of the statute was prompted by Congress's desire " 'to open employment opportunities for Negroes in occupations which [had] been traditionally closed to them.' " But the legislative history invoked by the Court to avoid the plain language of §§ 703(a) and (d) simply misses the point. To be sure, the reality of employment discrimination against Negroes provided the primary impetus for passage of Title VII. But this fact by no means supports the proposition that Congress intended to leave employers free to discriminate against white persons. In most cases, "[l]egislative history . . . is more vague than the statute we are called upon to interpret." [*United States v. Public Utilities Comm'n*, 345 U.S. 295, 320 (1953) (Jackson, J., concurring).] Here, however, the legislative history of Title VII is as clear as the language of §§ 703(a) and (d), and it irrefutably demonstrates that Congress meant precisely what it said in §§ 703(a) and (d)—that *no* racial discrimination in employment is permissible under Title VII, not even preferential treatment of minorities to correct racial imbalance.

[III] In undertaking to review the legislative history of Title VII, I am mindful that the topic hardly makes for light reading, but I am also fearful that nothing short of a thorough examination of the congressional debates will fully expose the magnitude of the Court's misinterpretation of Congress's intent.

[A] Introduced on the floor of the House of Representatives on June 20, 1963, the bill—H.R. 7152—that ultimately became the Civil Rights Act of 1964 contained no compulsory provisions directed at private discrimination in employment. The bill was promptly referred to the Committee on the Judiciary, where it was amended to include Title VII. With two exceptions, the bill reported by the House Judiciary Committee contained §§ 703(a) and (d) as they were ultimately enacted. Amendments subsequently adopted on the House floor added § 703's prohibition against sex discrimination and § 703(d)'s coverage of "on-the-job training."

After noting that "[t]he purpose of [Title VII] is to eliminate * * * discrimination in employment based on race, color, religion, or national origin," the Judiciary Committee's Report simply paraphrased the provisions of Title VII without elaboration. H.R. Rep., pt. 1, p. 26. In a separate Minority Report, however, opponents of the measure on the Committee advanced a line of attack which was reiterated throughout the debates in both the House and Senate and which ultimately led to passage of § 703(j). Noting that the word "discrimination" was nowhere defined in H.R. 7152, the Minority Report charged that the absence from Title VII of any reference to "racial imbalance" was a "public relations" ruse and that "the administration intends to rely upon its own construction of 'discrimination' as including the lack of racial balance. . . ." H.R. Rep., pt. 1, pp. 67–68. To demonstrate how the bill would operate in practice, the Minority Report posited a number of hypothetical employment situations, concluding in each example that the employer "*may be forced to hire according to race*, to 'racially balance' those who work for him *in every job classification* or be in violation of Federal law." *Id.*, at 69 (emphasis in original).

When H.R. 7152 reached the House floor, the opening speech in support of its passage was delivered by Representative Celler, Chairman of the House Judiciary Committee and the Congressman responsible for introducing the legislation. A portion of that speech responded to criticism "seriously misrepresent[ing] what the bill would do and grossly distort[ing] its effects":

"[T]he charge has been made that the Equal Employment Opportunity Commission to be established by title VII of the bill would have the power to prevent a business from employing and promoting the people it wished, and that a 'Federal inspector' could then order the hiring and promotion only of employees of certain races or religious groups. This description of the bill is entirely wrong. * * *

"Even [a] court could not order that any preference be given to any particular race, religion or other group, but would be limited to ordering an end of discrimination. The statement that a Federal inspector could order the employment and promotion only of members of a specific racial or religious group is therefore patently erroneous. * * *

" * * * The Bill would do no more than prevent * * * employers from discriminating against *or in favor* of workers because of their race, religion, or national origin.

"It is likewise not true that the Equal Employment Opportunity Commission would have power to rectify existing 'racial or religious imbalance' in employment by requiring the hiring of certain people without regard to their qualifications simply because they are of a given race or religion. Only actual discrimination could be stopped." 110 Cong. Rec. 1518 (1964) (emphasis added).

Representative Celler's construction of Title VII was repeated by several other supporters during the House debate.

Thus, the battle lines were drawn early in the legislative struggle over Title VII, with opponents of the measure charging that agencies of the Federal Government such as the Equal Employment Opportunity Commission (EEOC), by interpreting the word "discrimination" to mean the existence of "racial imbalance," would "require" employers to grant preferential treatment to minorities, and supporters responding that the EEOC would be granted no such power and that, indeed, Title VII prohibits discrimination "in favor of workers because of their race." Supporters of H.R. 7152 in the House ultimately prevailed by a vote of 290 to 130, and the measure was sent to the Senate to begin what became the longest debate in that body's history.

[B] The Senate debate was broken into three phases: the debate on sending the bill to Committee, the general debate on the bill prior to invocation of cloture, and the debate following cloture. * * *

Formal debate on the merits of H.R. 7152 began on March 30, 1964. Supporters of the bill in the Senate had made elaborate preparations for this second round. Senator Humphrey, the majority whip, and Senator Kuchel, the minority whip, were selected as the bipartisan floor managers on the entire civil rights bill. Responsibility for explaining and defending each important title of the bill was placed on bipartisan "captains." Senators Clark and Case were selected as the bipartisan captains responsible for Title VII. Vaas, Title VII: Legislative History, 7 B.C. Ind. & Com. L. Rev. 431, 444–445 (1966) (hereinafter Title VII: Legislative History).

In the opening speech of the formal Senate debate on the bill, Senator Humphrey addressed the main concern of Title VII's opponents, advising that not only does Title VII not require use of racial quotas, *it does not permit* their use. "The truth," stated the floor leader of the bill, "is that this title forbids discriminating against anyone on account of race. This is the simple and complete truth about title VII." 110 Cong. Rec. 6549 (1964). Senator Humphrey continued:

> "Contrary to the allegations of some opponents of this title, there is nothing in it that will give any power to the Commission or to any court to require hiring, firing, or promotion of employees in order to meet a racial 'quota' or to achieve a certain racial balance.
>
> "That bugaboo has been brought up a dozen times; but it is nonexistent. In fact, *the very opposite is true. Title VII prohibits discrimination.* In effect, it says that race, religion and national origin are not to be used as the basis for hiring and firing. Title VII is designed to encourage hiring on the basis of ability and qualifications, not race or religion." *Ibid.* (emphasis added).

At the close of his speech, Senator Humphrey returned briefly to the subject of employment quotas: "It is claimed that the bill would require racial quotas for all hiring, when in fact it provides that race shall not be a basis for making personnel decisions." *Id.*, at 6553. * * *

A few days later the Senate's attention focused exclusively on Title VII, as Senators Clark and Case rose to discuss the title of H.R. 7152 on which they shared floor "captain" responsibilities. In an interpretative memorandum submitted jointly to the Senate, Senators Clark and Case took pains to refute the opposition's charge that Title VII would result in preferential treatment for minorities. * * * Of particular relevance to the instant litigation were their observations regarding seniority rights. As if directing their comments at Brian Weber, the Senators said:

> "Title VII would have no effect on established seniority rights. Its effect is prospective and not retrospective. Thus, for example, if a business has been discriminating in the past and as a result has an all-white working force, when the title comes into effect the employer's obligation would be simply to fill future vacancies on a nondiscriminatory basis. He would not be obliged—*or indeed permitted*—to fire whites in order to hire Negroes, *or to prefer Negroes for future vacancies, or, once Negroes are hired, to give them special seniority rights at the expense of the white workers hired earlier.*" *Id.*, at 7213 (emphasis added).

[In addition, Senator Kuchel made similar comments. Southern opponents to the bill were still not satisfied, though. Senator Robertson (D–Va.) argued that the bill would mandate quotas. Senator H. Williams (D–N.J.) responded:]

"Those opposed to H.R. 7152 should realize that to hire a Negro solely because he is a Negro is racial discrimination, just as much as a 'white only' employment policy. Both forms of discrimination are prohibited by title VII of this bill. The language of that title simply states that race is not a qualification for employment.... Some people charge that H.R. 7152 favors the Negro, at the expense of the white majority. But how can the language of equality favor one race or one religion over another? Equality can have only one meaning, and that meaning is self-evident to reasonable men. Those who say that equality means favoritism do violence to common sense." *Id.*, at 8921. * * *

While the debate in the Senate raged, a bipartisan coalition under the leadership of Senators Dirksen, Mansfield, Humphrey, and Kuchel was working with House leaders and representatives of the Johnson administration on a number of amendments to H.R. 7152 designed to enhance its prospects of passage. The so-called "Dirksen–Mansfield" amendment was introduced on May 26 by Senator Dirksen as a substitute for the entire House-passed bill. The substitute bill, which ultimately became law, left unchanged the basic prohibitory language of §§ 703(a) and (d), as well as the remedial provisions in § 706(g). It added, however, several provisions defining and clarifying the scope of Title VII's substantive prohibitions. One of those clarifying amendments, § 703(j), was specifically directed at the opposition's concerns regarding racial balancing and preferential treatment of minorities, providing in pertinent part: "Nothing contained in [Title VII] shall be interpreted to require any employer ... to grant preferential treatment to any individual or to any group because of the race ... of such individual or group on account of" a racial imbalance in the employer's work force. 42 U.S.C. § 2000e–2(j). * * *

Contrary to the Court's analysis, the language of § 703(j) is precisely tailored to the objection voiced time and again by Title VII's opponents. Not once during the 83 days of debate in the Senate did a speaker, proponent or opponent, suggest that the bill would allow employers *voluntarily* to prefer racial minorities over white persons. In light of Title VII's flat prohibition on discrimination "against any individual ... because of such individual's race," § 703(a), 42 U.S.C. § 2000e–2(a), such a contention would have been, in any event, too preposterous to warrant response. Indeed, speakers on both sides of the issue, as the legislative history makes clear, recognized that Title VII would tolerate no *voluntary* racial preference, whether in favor of blacks or whites. The complaint consistently voiced by the opponents was that Title VII, particularly the word "discrimination," would be *interpreted* by federal agencies such as the EEOC to *require* the correction of racial imbalance through the granting of preferential treatment to minorities. Verbal assurances that

Title VII would not require—indeed, would not permit—preferential treatment of blacks having failed, supporters of H.R. 7152 responded by proposing an amendment carefully worded to meet, and put to rest, the opposition's charge. Indeed, unlike §§ 703(a) and (d), which are by their terms directed at entities—*e.g.*, employers, labor unions—whose actions are restricted by Title VII's prohibitions, the language of § 703(j) is specifically directed at entities—federal agencies and courts—charged with the responsibility of interpreting Title VII's provisions.

In light of the background and purpose of § 703(j), the irony of invoking the section to justify the result in this case is obvious. The Court's frequent references to the "voluntary" nature of Kaiser's racially discriminatory admission quota bear no relationship to the facts of this case. Kaiser and the Steelworkers acted under pressure from an agency of the Federal Government, the Office of Federal Contract Compliance, which found that minorities were being "underutilized" at Kaiser's plants. That is, Kaiser's work force was racially imbalanced. Bowing to that pressure, Kaiser instituted an admissions quota preferring blacks over whites, thus confirming that the fears of Title VII's opponents were well founded. Today, § 703(j), adopted to allay those fears, is invoked by the Court to uphold imposition of a racial quota under the very circumstances that the section was intended to prevent. * * *

[Justice Rehnquist also pointed to Senator Ervin's June 9 amendment to delete Title VII. Responding for the sponsors, Senator Clark emphasized that the bill "establishes no quotas." Senator Cotton (R–N.H.) offered an amendment to limit Title VII to firms having more than 100 employees. He opined that Title VII would forbid quotas. Although his amendment was defeated, Justice Rehnquist observed that the sponsors did not dispute the Cotton view.

[When cloture was invoked June 10, 1964, debate was limited, but several post-cloture statements by the bill's supporters reinforced the earlier view that Title VII imposed no quotas. The substitute bill was passed June 19. In final form, the bill was passed by the House on July 2 and signed by the President the same day.]

[V] Our task in this case, like any other case involving the construction of a statute, is to give effect to the intent of Congress. To divine that intent, we traditionally look first to the words of the statute and, if they are unclear, then to the statute's legislative history. Finding the desired result hopelessly foreclosed by these conventional sources, the Court turns to a third source—the "spirit" of the Act. But close examination of what the Court proffers as the spirit of the Act reveals it as the spirit animating the present majority, not the 88th Congress. For if the spirit of the Act eludes the cold words of the statute itself, it rings out with unmistakable clarity in the words of the elected representatives who made the Act law. It is *equality*. Senator Dirksen, I think, captured that spirit in a speech delivered on the floor of the Senate just moments before the bill was passed:

" * * * [T]oday we come to grips finally with a bill that advances the enjoyment of living; but, more than that, it advances the equality of opportunity.

"I do not emphasize the word 'equality' standing by itself. It means equality of opportunity in the field of education. It means equality of opportunity in the field of employment. It means equality of opportunity in the field of participation in the affairs of government * * *.

"That is it.

"Equality of opportunity, if we are going to talk about conscience, is the mass conscience of mankind that speaks in every generation, and it will continue to speak long after we are dead and gone." 110 Cong. Rec. 14510 (1964).

There is perhaps no device more destructive to the notion of equality than the *numerus clausus*—the quota. Whether described as "benign discrimination" or "affirmative action," the racial quota is nonetheless a creator of castes, a two-edged sword that must demean one in order to prefer another. In passing Title VII, Congress outlawed *all* racial discrimination, recognizing that no discrimination based on race is benign, that no action disadvantaging a person because of his color is affirmative. With today's holding, the Court introduces into Title VII a tolerance for the very evil that the law was intended to eradicate, without offering even a clue as to what the limits on that tolerance may be. We are told simply that Kaiser's racially discriminatory admission quota "falls on the permissible side of the line." By going not merely *beyond*, but directly *against* Title VII's language and legislative history, the Court has sown the wind. Later courts will face the impossible task of reaping the whirlwind.

NOTES ON WEBER AND MODES OF INTERPRETATION

We believe the three opinions in this case present strikingly different normative visions of the Court's role in statutory interpretation. See William N. Eskridge Jr., *Dynamic Statutory Interpretation* 13–31, 35–44 (1994); Philip P. Frickey, *Wisdom on* Weber, 74 Tulane L. Rev. 1169 (2000). Each vision is beset with practical problems of evidence, however. See Philip P. Frickey & William N. Eskridge Jr., *The Story of* United Steelworkers of America v. Weber: *Statutory Text, Spirit, and Practical Reasoning*, in *Statutory Interpretation Stories* 92–124 (Eskridge, Frickey & Garrett eds., 2011).

1. *Divining the "Intent" of Congress: Did the Court Invalidate the Original Legislative "Deal"?* One way to look at the role of the interpreter of a statute is to say that she is seeking the original intent of the author (the enacting Congress). Justices Brennan and Rehnquist both purport to be performing this interpretive role, with four Justices agreeing with Justice Brennan and only the Chief Justice agreeing with Justice Rehnquist. But many of the commentators agree with Justice Rehnquist that the Court "changed" the meaning of the statute by judicial fiat, and "[t]hat change goes to the roots of the bargain struck by the 88th Congress, and the roots of our color-blind aspiration." Bernard Meltzer, *The* Weber *Case: The Judicial*

Abrogation of the Antidiscrimination Standard in Employment, 47 U. Chi. L. Rev. 423, 456 (1980).[d] Do you agree?

Is Justice Rehnquist right in charging that Congress would have been "hard pressed" to have chosen language more clearly protecting Brian Weber than that of § 703(d), which makes it an unlawful practice for an employer "to discriminate against any individual because of his race * * * in admission to, or employment in, any program established to provide apprenticeship or other training"? What about the following:

> It shall be an unlawful employment practice for the employer * * * not to include any individual in any program established to provide apprenticeship or other training as a result of prohibited criteria, namely race * * *.

Wouldn't that have been clearer? Can we expect Congress, drafting statutory language in an environment of imperfect information and substantial time pressure, to anticipate specific questions that will arise under the law, or is it more realistic to expect general statements of policy that will require agencies and courts to use discretion in executing and interpreting the law?

Does Justice Rehnquist overstate the clarity of § 703(d)? The language enacted by Congress is amenable to another plausible interpretation supporting Justice Brennan's decision. Justice Rehnquist's dissent assumed, as many dictionaries say, that an employer *discriminates* on the basis of race if it makes a race-based *differentiation*. In a dictionary sense, it is a correct use of the term to say "I discriminate against peaches," if I prefer pears to peaches. But that is not the way we usually use the word *discriminate*, which connotes an *invidious* differentiation. Consider the definition of *discriminate* found in a desk dictionary published in 1968, just four years after Congress enacted Title VII. In this dictionary, the "prejudice" meaning is the first definition given. If one consults a newer desk dictionary, the "clear distinction" meaning is the first definition given. Is there a single "plain meaning" of "discriminate"? Are there other text-based arguments that Justice Rehnquist should have emphasized? See Eskridge, *Dynamic Statutory Interpretation*, 42–43 (laying out arguments for his position based on the structure of § 703).

Perhaps it is not so clear that the "deal" described by Meltzer and Justice Rehnquist is inscribed in the language of the statute. For that reason, statutory interpreters often look to the legislative history to elucidate the "intent" of Congress. As a rule, the most authoritative legislative history is the House and Senate committee reports, but Justice Rehnquist does not rely on them. Instead, like Justice Brennan, he relies on the colloquies between the bill's sponsors and the bill's opponents. Does this tell us anything about the "intent" of the 73 Senators and 290 Representatives who voted for the bill? Indeed, how can we know how many legislators actually heard the colloquies? Suppose Senator Humphrey was simply lying to the Southern opponents when he reassured them that the bill would not require preferential treatment—should his "lie" be binding not only on him, but also on his 72 colleagues who also voted for the bill? (There is no evidence that Senator

---

d. See also Nelson Lund, *The Law of Affirmative Action In and After the Civil Rights Act of 1991: Congress Invites Judicial Reform*, 6 Geo. Mason L. Rev. 87, 90–101 (1997); Daniel B. Rodriguez & Barry R. Weingast, *The Positive Political Theory of Legislative History: New Perspectives on the 1964 Civil Rights Act and Its Interpretation*, 151 U. Pa. L. Rev. 1417 (2003).

Humphrey's statements "persuaded" any of the Southern senators to vote for the bill.) Did Senator Humphrey have an incentive to tell the truth to his colleagues, perhaps because as a leader in the Senate he was a repeat player who wanted to establish a reputation for truthfulness so he could make credible deals in future negotiations?

Suppose that the statements of the sponsors are binding on everyone. Does anyone say: "We never want preferences for whites or blacks. By that we mean either governmentally required preferences, or preferences voluntarily agreed to by an employer or union to redress past discrimination." Did Justice Rehnquist discover such a "smoking gun" in the Clark–Case memorandum's passage that he claimed spoke directly to Brian Weber's situation?

Finally, note that most of Justice Rehnquist's evidence comes from legislative discussions *before* the final deal was reached, namely, the Mansfield–Dirksen substitute. Participants in the congressional process point out that anything that happens *before* the final deal is irrelevant if inconsistent with the final deal. The Mansfield–Dirksen substitute added § 703(j), which provides some support to Justice Brennan's position, and none to Justice Rehnquist's. To be sure, the latter would vehemently object that Senator Dirksen (a conservative Republican like Rehnquist) would *never* have read § 703(j) that way—but Rehnquist cites nothing to support his view, and Brennan cites Representative MacGregor (also a conservative Republican), who defended the Mansfield–Dirksen substitute precisely along the give-business-discretion lines that Justice Brennan does.

2. *Pitfalls of a Purpose–Oriented Interpretation.* Supporting the "spirit" approach taken by Justice Brennan, Professor Burt Neuborne (ACLU counsel in *Weber*) argues:

> At best, the concept of legislative intent is discernible primarily by the judges who claim to have deciphered it. The truth of the matter is that a legislature, especially in the civil rights area, generally enacts a statute aimed at a broad philosophical concept—in this case, equality in employment. It does not and cannot foresee, much less resolve, the myriad questions which must arise whenever a broad philosophical proposition is applied to the protean complexity of everyday life * * *.

Burt Neuborne, *Observations on* Weber, 54 N.Y.U. L. Rev. 546, 553 (1979). Is this a more realistic way of looking at the Civil Rights Act than Meltzer's specific bargain idea?

Is Justice Brennan right about the "spirit" of the Act? There is much to be said for Justice Rehnquist's position that when you read the committee report and the debate, you come away with the impression that the Act was mainly intended to eradicate racial criteria in hiring. Supporting Justice Brennan, Ronald Dworkin argues that the judge should interpret the statute to advance the policy that furnishes "the best political justification for the statute," because the "intent" of Congress on this issue is indeterminate. *How to Read the Civil Rights Act*, in *A Matter of Principle* 316, 327 (1985). Upon what model of the legislative process might this suggestion rest? Even if it is a valid approach, there seem to be two purposes in the Act—jobs for African Americans and creation of a color-blind society. How does the judge choose one politically coherent purpose over the other?

If we decide to interpret Title VII in light of its equal results spirit, will encouraging unions and companies to set up their own affirmative action programs (effectively shifting the costs of past discrimination from them onto "innocent" white employees) really contribute to this spirit? Consider some questions raised about *Weber*:

> In the longer run, the Court is taking frightful risks. (1) Can the Court insist on such intrusive use of racial classification without teaching the country that policies based on racial classification are legitimate? (2) Will those who are asked to step aside for the benefit of blacks not harbor ill will against them? Will this not be a particular problem for the young, who, having grown up on this side of the civil rights revolution, disassociate themselves from the racism of the old America, and may be surprised to learn that they are asked to pay for it? (3) Will the effect of pervasive affirmative action for blacks—combined with an equal pay principle—be to ensure that blacks are systematically promoted to the level just above their competence and cause affirmative action to become an engine of group defamation? * * * (5) Will affirmative action create incentives for employers to locate jobs away from black labor [so that they can avoid high black quotas]?

Edmund Kitch, *The Return of Color Consciousness to the Constitution*: Weber, Dayton, *and* Columbus, 1979 Sup. Ct. Rev. 1, 12–13. Indeed, in 1979 African–American unemployment was no less a problem than it had been in 1964 (in part because some companies did avoid African–American communities).

Judge Wisdom's dissenting opinion in the court below recognized several purposes for the statute—integration, color-blindness, and flexible voluntary remedies—and concluded that the "arguable violation" approach best balanced these competing purposes. See Frickey & Eskridge, *Story of* Weber, 112–14. Yet only Justice Blackmun accepted that argument. Why did it not have more traction among the Court majority?

3. *Reading Statutes Dynamically.* Both Justices Brennan and Rehnquist purport to be interpreting the "will" of Congress on this issue as of 1964, when the statute was enacted. The implicit argument of each opinion is that on the day Title VII became law, this is the answer the interpreter (be it court or Congress) would have given to the *Weber* question. Does that make sense to you? For purposes of statutory interpretation, the *Weber* issue is so important because it represents a tension that did not really exist in the statute as enacted, as Justice Blackmun's concurring opinion suggests. In a functional sense, the Title VII of 1964 was not the same statute as the Title VII of 1979, not because the statute was formally amended (as it was in 1972), but because the ongoing process of interpretation and elaboration altered the statute in response to evolving circumstances—*Griggs* as well as other decisions changed not only the statute, but the society on which the statute operated. Justice Blackmun therefore urged that the interpretation of Title VII reflect the unanticipated tension created by the ongoing application and interpretation process and permit the affirmative action plan in *Weber*. Upon what model of legislation was Justice Blackmun operating?

Two of us have argued that the most persuasive approach to *Weber* is Justice Blackmun's pragmatic appeal to current problems of statutory fairness and workability, not just the historical choices allegedly made in 1964.[e] The argument is that statutes start with gaps and ambiguities (including the precise meaning of "discriminate," a term that is not self-defining), which the EEOC and the Court had to interpret in light of factual settings they faced, and their interpretations went "beyond" Congress's original expectations. The gaps and ambiguities proliferated as the world changed—often in response to the statute and its applications—and offered more radical variations, including repeated fact patterns like *Weber*, where past discrimination continued to have present effects. Moreover, Title VII changed, often "against" the original legislative expectations, because the EEOC and the Court had their own values and "spin" on the statute, because the Congress with power to discipline these interpreters was the current rather than the enacting Congress (and the latter had a different spin on the statute than the former), and because the legal and social context changed over time. This is offered as a description of what interpreters do with the statute. Do you find it normatively acceptable? In particular, is it appropriate for the judiciary to undertake this task of updating the statute and filling gaps with new policies, or should Congress have the sole responsibility for amending old statutes to account for new social and economic developments? Does the answer change when the new conditions have resulted in large part from prior judicial opinions interpreting the act in unexpected ways?

You should be aware that liberals have no monopoly on dynamic interpretation. The conservative Justices on the Burger Court had their own spin on affirmative action, and the cases after *Weber* were harder on affirmative action plans. See *Local 28 of Sheet Metal Workers v. EEOC*, 478 U.S. 421 (1986); *Local No. 93, Int'l Ass'n of Firefighters v. Cleveland*, 478 U.S. 501 (1986); *Local Union No. 1784 Firefighters v. Stotts*, 467 U.S. 561 (1984).

B. AFFIRMATIVE ACTION AND *STARE DECISIS* IN STATUTORY CASES

The Supreme Court drifted further to the right soon after *Johnson*, when Justice Rehnquist became Chief Justice and yielded his seat to Judge Antonin Scalia, one of the most aggressive conservatives in the Court's history and a devout foe of affirmative action. Would the new Court move Title VII policy in a more conservative direction? An argument *against* such a move is *stare decisis*: the Court is obliged to follow its own precedents, with a narrow exception: the precedent was wrongly decided *and* there is positive harm in continuing its error. Indeed, in statutory cases, the Court says it follows a super-strong form of *stare decisis*, where courts should leave correction of its own errors to Congress. Does this precept make sense to you? Should it save *Weber*? If you think it should save *Weber*, should it save precedents you think are very wrong? Consider the follow-up to *Weber*, as well as a classic case where *stare decisis* saved a precedent everyone thought was wrong.

---

e. See Eskridge, *Dynamic Statutory Interpretation*, 24–25; Philip P. Frickey, *From the Big Sleep to the Big Heat: The Revival of Theory in Statutory Interpretation*, 77 Minn. L. Rev. 241, 245–47, 259 (1992); Frickey & Eskridge, *Story of* Weber, *supra*.

JOHNSON v. TRANSPORTATION AGENCY, SANTA CLARA COUNTY

Supreme Court of the United States, 1987
480 U.S. 616, 107 S.Ct. 1442, 94 L.Ed.2d 615

JUSTICE BRENNAN delivered the opinion of the Court.

[The Transportation Agency of Santa Clara County, California promulgated an Affirmative Action Plan to remedy historic patterns of discrimination against women and minorities in some job categories. The Plan provided that, in making promotions to positions within a traditionally segregated job classification in which women had been significantly underrepresented, the Agency was authorized to consider as one factor the sex of a qualified applicant. The Agency found women significantly underrepresented in its work force generally, and virtually unrepresented in the 238 Skilled Craft Worker positions. Pursuant to the Plan, the Agency promoted Diane Joyce to the position of road dispatcher in the Agency's Roads Division. Dispatchers assign road crews, equipment, and materials, and maintain records pertaining to road maintenance jobs. One of the applicants passed over was Paul Johnson, who had a slightly higher score than Joyce based upon his paper credentials and an oral interview.]

[Johnson filed a complaint with the EEOC, and subsequently a federal lawsuit. The district court granted Johnson relief, based upon its finding that Johnson was more qualified for the position than Joyce, and that sex was the "determining factor" in Joyce's selection. The Ninth Circuit reversed.]

[*Weber*] upheld the employer's decision to select less senior black applicants over the white respondent, for we found that taking race into account was consistent with Title VII's objective of "break[ing] down old patterns of racial segregation and hierarchy." As we stated:

> "It would be ironic indeed if a law triggered by a Nation's concern over centuries of racial injustice and intended to improve the lot of those who had 'been excluded from the American dream for so long' constituted the first legislative prohibition of all voluntary, private, race-conscious efforts to abolish traditional patterns of racial segregation and hierarchy." *Id.* (quoting remarks of Sen. Humphrey).[7]

---

7. JUSTICE SCALIA's dissent maintains that *Weber*'s conclusion that Title VII does not prohibit voluntary affirmative action programs "rewrote the statute it purported to construe." *Weber*'s decisive rejection of the argument that the "plain language" of the statute prohibits affirmative action rested on (1) legislative history indicating Congress' clear intention that employers play a major role in eliminating the vestiges of discrimination, and (2) the language and legislative history of section 703(j) of the statute, which reflect a strong desire to preserve managerial prerogatives so that they might be utilized for this purpose. As JUSTICE BLACKMUN said in his concurrence in *Weber*, "[I]f the Court has misconceived the political will, it has the assurance that because the question is statutory Congress may set a different course if it so chooses." Congress has not amended the statute to reject our construction, nor have any such amendments even been proposed, and we therefore may assume that our interpretation was correct.

JUSTICE SCALIA's dissent faults the fact that we take note of the absence of Congressional efforts to amend the statute to nullify *Weber*. It suggests that Congressional inaction cannot be regarded

* * * As JUSTICE BLACKMUN'S concurrence made clear, *Weber* held that an employer seeking to justify the adoption of a plan need not point to its own prior discriminatory practices, nor even to evidence of an "arguable violation" on its part. Rather, it need point only to a "conspicuous ... imbalance in traditionally segregated job categories." * * *

In reviewing the employment decision at issue in this case, we must first examine whether that decision was made pursuant to a plan prompted by concerns similar to those of the employer in *Weber.* Next, we must determine whether the effect of the plan on males and nonminorities is comparable to the effect of the plan in that case.

The first issue is therefore whether consideration of the sex of applicants for skilled craft jobs was justified by the existence of a "manifest imbalance" that reflected underrepresentation of women in "traditionally segregated job categories." In determining whether an imbalance exists that would justify taking sex or race into account, a comparison of the percentage of minorities or women in the employer's work force with the percentage in the area labor market or general population is appropriate in analyzing jobs that require no special expertise, or training programs designed to provide expertise. Where a job requires special training, however, the comparison should be with those in the labor force who possess the relevant qualifications. The requirement that the "manifest imbalance" relate to a "traditionally segregated job category" provides assurance both that sex or race will be taken into account in a manner consistent with Title VII's purpose of eliminating the effects of employment discrimination, and that the interests of those employees not benefitting from the plan will not be unduly infringed.

A manifest imbalance need not be such that it would support a prima facie case against the employer, as suggested in JUSTICE O'CONNOR'S concurrence, since we do not regard as identical the constraints of Title VII and the Federal Constitution on voluntarily adopted affirmative action plans. Application of the "prima facie" standard in Title VII cases would

---

as acquiescence under all circumstances, but then draws away from that unexceptional point the conclusion that *any* reliance on Congressional failure to act is necessarily a "canard." The fact that inaction may not always provide crystalline revelation, however, should not obscure the fact that it may be probative to varying degrees. *Weber,* for instance, was a widely-publicized decision that addressed a prominent issue of public debate. Legislative inattention thus is not a plausible explanation for Congressional inaction. Furthermore, Congress not only passed no contrary legislation in the wake of *Weber,* but not one legislator even proposed a bill to do so. The barriers of the legislative process therefore also seem a poor explanation for failure to act. By contrast, when Congress has been displeased with our interpretation of Title VII, it has not hesitated to amend the statute to tell us so. For instance, when Congress passed the Pregnancy Discrimination Act of 1978, 42 U.S.C. section 2000e(k), "it unambiguously expressed its disapproval of both the holding and the reasoning of the Court in [*General Electric v. Gilbert,* 429 U.S. 125 (1976)]." *Newport News Shipbuilding & Dry Dock v. EEOC,* 462 U.S. 669, 678 (1983). Surely, it is appropriate to find some probative value in such radically different Congressional reactions to this Court's interpretations of the same statute.

As one scholar has put it, "When a court says to a legislature: 'You (or your predecessor) meant X,' it almost invites the legislature to answer: 'We did not.' " G. Calabresi, A Common Law for the Age of Statutes 31–32 (1982). Any belief in the notion of a dialogue between the judiciary and the legislature must acknowledge that on occasion an invitation declined is as significant as one accepted.

be inconsistent with *Weber*'s focus on statistical imbalance, and could inappropriately create a significant disincentive for employers to adopt an affirmative action plan. A corporation concerned with maximizing return on investment, for instance, is hardly likely to adopt a plan if in order to do so it must compile evidence that could be used to subject it to a colorable Title VII suit.

It is clear that the decision to hire Joyce was made pursuant to an Agency plan that directed that sex or race be taken into account for the purpose of remedying underrepresentation. The Agency Plan acknowledged the "limited opportunities that have existed in the past" for women to find employment in certain job classifications "where women have not been traditionally employed in significant numbers." As a result, observed the Plan, women were concentrated in traditionally female jobs in the Agency, and represented a lower percentage in other job classifications than would be expected if such traditional segregation had not occurred. Specifically, 9 of the 10 Para–Professionals and 110 of the 145 Office and Clerical Workers were women. By contrast, women were only 2 of the 28 Officials and Administrators, 5 of the 58 Professionals, 12 of the 124 Technicians, none of the Skilled Craft Workers, and 1—who was Joyce—of the 110 Road Maintenance Workers. The Plan sought to remedy these imbalances through "hiring, training and promotion of ... women throughout the Agency in all major job classifications where they are underrepresented." * * *

We next consider whether the Agency Plan unnecessarily trammeled the rights of male employees or created an absolute bar to their advancement. In contrast to the plan in *Weber*, which provided that 50% of the positions in the craft training program were exclusively for blacks, and to the consent decree upheld last term in *Firefighters v. Cleveland*, 478 U.S. 501 (1986), which required the promotion of specific numbers of minorities, the Plan sets aside no positions for women. The Plan expressly states that "[t]he 'goals' established for each Division should not be construed as 'quotas' that must be met." Rather, the Plan merely authorizes that consideration be given to affirmative action concerns when evaluating qualified applicants. As the Agency Director testified, the sex of Joyce was but one of numerous factors he took into account in arriving at his decision. The Plan thus resembles the "Harvard Plan" approvingly noted by JUSTICE POWELL in *University of California Regents v. Bakke*, 438 U.S. 265, 316–319 (1978), which considers race along with other criteria in determining admission to the college. As JUSTICE POWELL observed: "In such an admissions program, race or ethnic background may be deemed a 'plus' in a particular applicant's file, yet it does not insulate the individual from comparison with all other candidates for the available seats." Similarly, the Agency Plan requires women to compete with all other qualified applicants. No persons are automatically excluded from consideration; all are able to have their qualifications weighed against those of other applicants. * * *

We therefore hold that the Agency appropriately took into account as one factor the sex of Diane Joyce in determining that she should be promoted to the road dispatcher position. The decision to do so was made pursuant to an affirmative action plan that represents a moderate, flexible, case-by-case approach to effecting a gradual improvement in the representation of minorities and women in the Agency's work force. Such a plan is fully consistent with Title VII, for it embodies the contribution that voluntary employer action can make in eliminating the vestiges of discrimination in the workplace. * * *

JUSTICE STEVENS, concurring. * * *

Prior to 1978 the Court construed the Civil Rights Act of 1964 as an absolute blanket prohibition against discrimination which neither required nor permitted discriminatory preferences for any group, minority or majority. * * * As I explained in my separate opinion in *Bakke*, and as the Court forcefully stated in *McDonald v. Santa Fe Trail Transportation Co.*, Congress intended " 'to eliminate all practices which operate to disadvantage the employment opportunities of any group protected by Title VII including Caucasians.' " If the Court had adhered to that construction of the Act, petitioner would unquestionably prevail in this case. But it has not done so.

In the *Bakke* case in 1978 and again in *Weber*, a majority of the Court interpreted the antidiscriminatory strategy of the statute in a fundamentally different way. * * * [T]he only problem for me is whether to adhere to an authoritative construction of the Act that is at odds with my understanding of the actual intent of the authors of the legislation. I conclude without hesitation that I must answer that question in the affirmative[.]

Bakke and *Weber* have been decided and are now an important part of the fabric of our law. This consideration is sufficiently compelling for me to adhere to the basic construction of this legislation that the Court adopted in *Bakke* and in *Weber*. There is an undoubted public interest in "stability and orderly development of the law."

The logic of antidiscrimination legislation requires that judicial constructions of Title VII leave "breathing room" for employer initiatives to benefit members of minority groups. If Title VII had never been enacted, a private employer would be free to hire members of minority groups for any reason that might seem sensible from a business or a social point of view. The Court's opinion in *Weber* reflects the same approach; the opinion relied heavily on legislative history indicating that Congress intended that traditional management prerogatives be left undisturbed to the greatest extent possible. * * *

As construed in *Weber* * * * the statute does not absolutely prohibit preferential hiring in favor of minorities; it was merely intended to protect historically disadvantaged groups *against* discrimination and not to hamper managerial efforts to benefit members of disadvantaged groups that are consistent with that paramount purpose. The preference granted by respondent in this case does not violate the statute as so construed; the record amply supports the conclusion that the challenged employment decision served the legitimate purpose of creating diversity in a category of employment that had been almost an exclusive province of males in the past. Respondent's voluntary decision is surely not prohibited by Title VII as construed in *Weber*.

Whether a voluntary decision of the kind made by respondent would ever be prohibited by Title VII is a question we need not answer until it is squarely presented. Given the interpretation of the statute the Court adopted in *Weber*, I see no reason why the employer has any duty, prior to granting a preference to a qualified minority employee, to determine whether his past conduct might constitute an arguable violation of Title VII. Indeed, in some instances the employer may find it more helpful to focus on the future. Instead of retroactively scrutinizing his own or society's possible exclusions of minorities in the past to determine the outer limits of a valid affirmative-action program—or indeed, any particular affirmative-action decision—in many cases the employer will find it more appropriate to consider other legitimate reasons to give preferences to members of underrepresented groups. Statutes enacted for the benefit of minority groups should not block these forward-looking considerations. * * *

JUSTICE O'CONNOR, concurring in the judgment. * * *

In my view, the proper initial inquiry in evaluating the legality of an affirmative action plan by a public employer under Title VII is no different from that required by the Equal Protection Clause. In either case, consistent with the congressional intent to provide some measure of protection to the interests of the employer's nonminority employees, the employer must have had a firm basis for believing that remedial action was required. An employer would have such a firm basis if it can point to a statistical disparity sufficient to support a prima facie claim under Title VII by the employee beneficiaries of the affirmative action plan of a pattern or practice claim of discrimination.

In *Weber*, this Court balanced two conflicting concerns in construing § 703(d): Congress's intent to root out invidious discrimination against *any* person on the basis of race or gender, and its goal of eliminating the lasting effects of discrimination against minorities. Given these conflicting concerns, the Court concluded that it would be inconsistent with the background and purpose of Title VII to prohibit affirmative action in all cases. As I read *Weber*, however, the Court also determined that Congress had balanced these two competing concerns by permitting affirmative action only as a remedial device to eliminate actual or apparent discrimination or the lingering effects of this discrimination. * * *

[Justice O'Connor argued that the constitutional standard for public employer affirmative action plans is consistent with the *Weber* standard for private employer affirmative action plans. In both cases, the Court has required that the employer have a "firm basis" for concluding that action be necessary to remedy past discrimination. In neither case has the Court required an employer to prove or admit that it "actually discriminated against women or minorities." Hence, evidence sufficient for a prima facie case under Title VII would justify an employer's adoption of voluntary affirmative action.]

In applying these principles to this case, it is important to pay close attention to both the affirmative action plan, and the manner in which that plan was applied to the specific promotion decision at issue in this case. * * * At the time the plan was adopted, not one woman was employed in respondents' 238 skilled craft positions, and the plan recognized that women "are not strongly motivated to seek employment in job classifications where they have not been traditionally employed because of the limited opportunities that have existed in the past for them to work in such classifications." Additionally, the plan stated that respondents "recognize[d] that mere prohibition of discriminatory practices is not enough to remedy the effects of past practices and to permit attainment of an equitable representation of minorities, women and handicapped persons," and that "the selection and appointment processes are areas where hidden discrimination frequently occurs." Thus, the respondents had the expectation that the plan "should result in improved personnel practices that will benefit all Agency employees who may have been subjected to discriminatory personnel practices in the past." * * *

[Justice O'Connor rejected Justice Scalia's characterization of the decision as resting upon a single factor, sex. She credited the Director's testimony that he looked at the "whole picture," and chose Joyce for a variety of reasons, one of which was her sex.] While I agree * * * that an affirmative action program that automatically and blindly promotes those marginally qualified candidates falling within a preferred race or gender category, or that can be equated with a permanent plan of "proportionate representation by race and sex," would violate Title VII, I cannot agree that this was such a case. Rather, as the Court demonstrates, Joyce's sex was simply used as a "plus" factor.

In this case, I am also satisfied that the respondent had a firm basis for adopting an affirmative action program. Although the District Court found no discrimination against women in fact, at the time the affirmative action plan was adopted, there were *no* women in its skilled craft positions. Petitioner concedes that women constituted approximately 5% of the local labor pool of skilled craft workers in 1970. Thus, when compared to the percentage of women in the qualified work force, the statistical disparity would have been sufficient for a prima facie Title VII case brought by unsuccessful women job applicants. * * *

[JUSTICE WHITE's dissenting opinion is omitted. Justice White indicated that he would overrule *Weber* (an opinion he joined in 1979), because the Court's reinterpretation of it was "a perversion of Title VII."]

JUSTICE SCALIA, with whom THE CHIEF JUSTICE [REHNQUIST] joins and with whom JUSTICE WHITE joins in Parts I and II, dissenting.

With a clarity which, had it not proven so unavailing, one might well recommend as a model of statutory draftsmanship, Title VII of the Civil Rights Act of 1964 declares:

"It shall be an unlawful employment practice for an employer—

"(1) to fail or refuse to hire or to discharge any individual, or otherwise to discriminate against any individual with respect to his compensation, terms, conditions, or privileges of employment, because of such individual's race, color, religion, sex, or national origin; or

"(2) to limit, segregate, or classify his employees or applicants for employment in any way which would deprive or tend to deprive any individual of employment opportunities or otherwise adversely affect his status as an employee, because of such individual's race, color, religion, sex, or national origin."

The Court today completes the process of converting this from a guarantee that race or sex will *not* be the basis for employment determinations, to a guarantee that it often *will*. Ever so subtly, without even alluding to the last obstacles preserved by earlier opinions that we now push out of our path, we effectively replace the goal of a discrimination-free society with the quite incompatible goal of proportionate representation by race and by sex in the workplace. * * *

[In Part I of his dissent, Justice Scalia argued that the Court and Justice O'Connor wrongly ignored the District Court's finding of fact that "if the Affirmative Action Coordinator had not intervened, 'the decision as to whom to promote ... would have been made by [the Road Operations Division Director],' who had recommended that Johnson be appointed to the position"; and the further findings of fact that Johnson was "more qualified for the position" and that Joyce's gender was "the determining factor" in her selection. Justice Scalia maintained in Part II maintains that the Court's opinion basically sanctions affirmative action plans that remedy societal rather than employer discrimination, a holding flatly contrary to *Wygant* and in tension with the Court's holding in *Bakke*.]

[III] I have omitted from the foregoing discussion the most obvious respect in which today's decision o'erleaps, without analysis, a barrier that was thought still to be overcome. In *Weber*, this Court held that a private-sector affirmative action training program that overtly discriminated against white applicants did not violate Title VII. However, although the majority does not advert to the fact, until today the applicability of *Weber* to public employers remained an open question. In *Weber* itself, and in later decisions, this Court has repeatedly emphasized that *Weber* involved only a private employer. This distinction between public and private employers has several possible justifications. *Weber* rested in part on the assertion that the 88th Congress did not wish to intrude too deeply into private employment decisions. Whatever validity that assertion may have with respect to private employers (and I think it negligible), it has none with respect to public employers or to the 92d Congress that brought them within Title VII. Another reason for limiting *Weber* to private employers is that state agencies, unlike private actors, are subject to the Fourteenth Amendment. As noted earlier, it would be strange to construe Title VII to permit discrimination by public actors that the Constitution forbids.

In truth, however, the language of 42 U.S.C. § 2000e–2 draws no distinction between private and public employers, and the only good reason for creating such a distinction would be to limit the damage of *Weber.* It would be better, in my view, to acknowledge that case as fully applicable precedent, and to use the Fourteenth Amendment ramifications—which *Weber* did not address and which are implicated for the first time here—as the occasion for reconsidering and overruling it. It is well to keep in mind just how thoroughly *Weber* rewrote the statute it purported to construe. The language of that statute, as quoted at the outset of this dissent, is unambiguous[.] *Weber* disregarded the text of the statute, invoking instead its " 'spirit,' " and "practical and equitable [considerations] only partially perceived, if perceived at all, by the 88th Congress" (Blackmun, J., concurring). It concluded, on the basis of these intangible guides, that Title VII's prohibition of intentional discrimination on the basis of race and sex does not prohibit intentional discrimination on the basis of race and sex, so long as it is "designed to break down old patterns of racial [or sexual] segregation and hierarchy," "does not unnecessarily trammel the interests of the white [or male] employees," "does not require the discharge of white [or male] workers and their replacement with new black [or female] hirees," "does [not] create an absolute bar to the advancement of white [or male] employees," and "is a temporary measure ... not intended to maintain racial [or sexual] balance, but simply to eliminate a manifest racial [or sexual] imbalance." In effect, *Weber* held that the legality of intentional discrimination by private employers against certain disfavored groups or individuals is to be judged not by Title VII but by a judicially crafted code of conduct, the contours of which are determined by no discernible standard, aside from (as the dissent convincingly demonstrated) the divination of congressional "purposes" belied by the face of the statute and by its legislative history. We have been recasting that self-promulgated code of conduct ever since—and what it has led us to today adds to the reasons for abandoning it.

The majority's response to this criticism of *Weber* [see note 7 of the majority opinion] asserts that, since "Congress has not amended the statute to reject our construction, ... we ... may assume that our interpretation was correct." This assumption, which frequently haunts our opinions, should be put to rest. It is based, to begin with, on the patently false premise that the correctness of statutory construction is to be measured by what the current Congress desires, rather than by what the law as enacted meant. To make matters worse, it assays the current Congress's desires *with respect to the particular provision in isolation,* rather than (the way the provision was originally enacted) as part of a total legislative package containing many *quids pro quo.* Whereas the statute as originally proposed may have presented to the enacting Congress a question such as "Should hospitals be required to provide medical care for indigent patients, with federal subsidies to offset the cost?," the question theoretically asked of the later Congress, in order to establish the "correctness" of a judicial interpretation that the statute provides no subsidies, is simply "Should the medical care that hospitals are required to provide for indigent patients be federally subsidized?" Hardly the same question—and many of those legislators who accepted the subsidy provisions in order to gain the votes necessary for enactment of the care requirement would not vote for the subsidy in isolation, now that an unsubsidized care requirement is, thanks to the judicial opinion, safely on the books. But even accepting the flawed premise that the intent of the current Congress, with respect to the provision in isolation, is determinative, one must ignore rudimentary principles of political science to draw any conclusions regarding that intent from the *failure* to enact legislation. The "complicated check on legislation," The Federalist No. 62, p. 378 C. Rossiter ed. (1961), erected by our Constitution creates an inertia that makes it impossible to assert with any degree of assurance that congressional failure to act represents (1) approval of the status quo, as opposed to (2) inability to agree upon how to alter the status quo, (3) unawareness of the status quo, (4) indifference to the status quo, or even (5) political cowardice * * *. I think we should admit that vindication by congressional inaction is a canard.

JUSTICE STEVENS' concurring opinion emphasizes "the underlying public interest in 'stability and orderly development of the law' " that often requires adherence to an erroneous decision. As I have described above, however, today's decision is a demonstration not of stability and order but of the instability and unpredictable expansion which the substitution of judicial improvisation for statutory text has produced. For a number of reasons, *stare decisis* ought not to save *Weber*. First, this Court has applied the doctrine of stare decisis to civil rights statutes less rigorously than to other laws. See *Maine v. Thiboutot*, 448 U.S. 1, 33 (1980) (Powell, J., dissenting); *Monroe v. Pape*, [365 U.S. 167, 221–22 (1961)] (Frankfurter, J., dissenting in part). Second, * * * *Weber* was itself a dramatic departure from the Court's prior Title VII precedents, and can scarcely be said to be "so consistent with the warp and woof of civil rights law as to be beyond question." Third, *Weber* was decided a mere seven years ago, and has provided little guidance to persons seeking to conform their conduct to the law, beyond the proposition that Title VII does not mean what it says. Finally, "even under the most stringent test for the propriety of overruling a statutory decision . . . —'that it appear beyond doubt . . . that [the decision] misapprehended the meaning of the controlling provision,' " *Weber* should be overruled.

In addition to complying with the commands of the statute, abandoning *Weber* would have the desirable side effect of eliminating the requirement of willing suspension of disbelief that is currently a credential for reading our opinions in the affirmative action field—from *Weber* itself, which demanded belief that the corporate employer adopted the affirmative action program "voluntarily," rather than under practical compulsion from government contracting agencies, to *Bakke*, a Title VI case cited as authority by the majority here, which demanded belief that the University of California took race into account as merely one of the many diversities to which it felt it was educationally important to expose its medical students, to today's opinion, which—in the face of a plan obviously designed to force promoting officials to prefer candidates from the favored racial and sexual classes, warning them that their "personal commitment" will be determined by how successfully they "attain" certain numerical goals, and in the face of a particular promotion awarded to the less qualified applicant by an official who "did little or nothing" to inquire into sources "critical" to determining the final candidates' relative qualifications other than their sex—in the face of all this, demands belief that we are dealing here with no more than a program that "merely authorizes that consideration be given to affirmative action concerns when evaluating qualified applicants." Any line of decisions rooted so firmly in naivete must be wrong. * * *

Today's decision does more, however, than merely reaffirm *Weber*, and more than merely extend it to public actors. It is impossible not to be aware that the practical effect of our holding is to accomplish *de facto* what the law—in language even plainer than that ignored in *Weber*, see 42 U.S.C. § 2000e-2(j)—forbids anyone from accomplishing *de jure*: in many contexts it effectively *requires* employers, public as well as private, to engage in intentional discrimination on the basis of race or sex. This Court's prior interpretations of Title VII, especially *Griggs*, subject employers to a potential Title VII suit whenever there is a noticeable imbalance in the representation of minorities or women in the employer's work force. Even the employer who is confident of ultimately prevailing in such a suit must contemplate the expense and adverse publicity of a trial, because the extent of the imbalance, and the "job relatedness" of his selection criteria, are questions of fact to be explored through rebuttal and counterrebuttal of a "prima facie case" consisting of no more than the showing that the employer's selection process "selects those from the protected class at a 'significantly' lesser rate than their counterparts." B. Schlei & P. Grossman, Employment Discrimination Law 91 (2d ed. 1983). If, however, employers are free to discriminate through affirmative action, without fear of "reverse discrimination" suits by their nonminority or male victims, they are offered a threshold defense against Title VII liability premised on numerical disparities. Thus, after today's decision the *failure* to engage in reverse discrimination is economic folly, and arguably a breach of duty to shareholders or taxpayers, wherever the cost of anticipated Title VII litigation exceeds the cost of hiring less capable (though still minimally capable) workers. (This situation is more likely to obtain, of course, with respect to the least skilled jobs—perversely creating an incentive to discriminate against precisely those members of the nonfavored groups *least* likely to have profited from societal discrimination in the past.) It is predictable, moreover, that this incentive will be greatly magnified by economic pressures brought to bear by government contracting agencies upon employers who refuse to discriminate in the fashion we have now approved. A statute designed to establish a color-blind and gender-blind workplace has thus been converted into a powerful engine of racism and sexism, not merely *permitting* intentional race- and sex-based discrimination, but often making it, through operation of the legal system, practically compelled.

It is unlikely that today's result will be displeasing to politically elected officials, to whom it provides the means of quickly accommodating the demands of organized groups to achieve concrete, numerical improvement in the economic status of particular constituencies. Nor will it displease the world of corporate and governmental employers (many of whom have filed briefs as amici in the present case, all on the side of Santa Clara) for whom the cost of hiring less qualified workers is often substantially less—and infinitely more predictable—than the cost of litigating Title VII cases and of seeking to convince federal agencies by nonnumerical means that no discrimination exists. In fact, the only losers in the process are the Johnsons of the country, for whom Title VII has been not merely repealed but actually inverted. The irony is that these individuals—predominantly unknown, unaffluent, unorganized—suffer this injustice at the hands of a Court fond of thinking itself the champion of the politically impotent. I dissent.

NOTES ON *JOHNSON*

1. *What Happened to* Weber? The debate in *Weber* is hardly recognizable in *Johnson*, not only because there are two new players (O'Connor and Scalia), but also because the old players changed their positions. Most dramatic were Justice White's switch from part of the *Weber* majority to a vote for overruling the decision, Justice Stevens' switch from dissent from *Weber* (a case where he did not actually vote) to a more aggressive approval of affirmative action than Justice Brennan's opinion, and Justice Powell's unexplained decision to join the Brennan opinion (he, too, had not voted in *Weber*, but his opinion in *Regents of the University of California v. Bakke*, 438 U.S. 265 (1978), suggests a sympathy with the O'Connor position, and an internal memorandum written before his recusal in *Weber* states that he was on the fence in that case).

Almost as dramatic is Justice Brennan's new rationale for affirmative action. Recall that in *Weber* affirmative action was defended on the ground that it contributed to Title VII's main purpose, to get jobs for racial minorities (all of the evidence cited by Justice Brennan adverted to helping African Americans). In *Johnson*, affirmative action is extended to help women—but without any evidence from the legislative history that this was a primary purpose of the statute. Recall the humble origins of Title VII's prohibition of sex discrimination, namely, Judge Smith's killer amendment. Note, too, that the dissenting Justices (including Chief Justice Rehnquist) in *Johnson* pretty much ignore the legislative history of the 1964 statute, as well, although Justice Scalia's dissent incorporates Rehnquist's lengthy *Weber* dissent by reference.

2. *Stare Decisis in Statutory Cases.* Justices O'Connor and Stevens accepted *Weber* as a starting point even though they would not have joined the Court's opinion or judgment in the earlier case. This is the idea of *stare decisis*: for reasons of efficient decisionmaking, legitimacy, and reliance, courts are obliged to follow precedents even if incorrectly decided. Indeed, the Supreme Court says it gives statutory precedents a super-strong presumption of correctness, in large part because Congress—not the Court—ought to be the primary institution charged with correcting judicial errors. See William N. Eskridge Jr., *Overruling Statutory Precedents*, 76 Geo. L.J. 1361 (1988). The case that follows, *Flood v. Kuhn*, is arguably the leading authority for this proposition, but note that Justice Brennan dissented in that case and would have overruled the statutory precedent.

Justice Scalia vigorously argued that *Weber* should be overruled, not just because it was egregiously wrong (why?), but also because it was a harmful decision (how?). Justice Brennan responded in footnote 7: whatever the original validity of *Weber* as implementing the intent or purpose of the 1964 Congress, it should not be reconsidered because Congress in the 1980s approved of the decision. Justice Scalia considered this argument a "canard" (and study the perceptive political analysis he provides to support his charge), but the end of his opinion suggests that Justice Brennan may be right: the powerful political forces inside the Beltway—labor unions, civil rights groups, and the Chamber of Commerce—were all satisfied with *Weber*, because it allowed them to advance their own goals (such as avoiding *Griggs* lawsuits) rather costlessly, at least to them. The cost-payers were the diffuse group of blue-collar males like Paul Johnson and Brian Weber, unorganized and ill-represented on Capitol Hill. This point seems accurate, and it suggests that Congress in the 1980s was also happy with *Weber*. (Contrary to footnote 7, congressional hearings were held in 1981 on a constitutional amendment introduced to override *Weber* and other affirmative action cases; none of the political powerhouses showed up, demonstrating the absence of interest among the powerful lobbies to override *Weber*.)

Justice Scalia's main point is a normative one, of course. He considers it objectionable for the Court to pay any attention to what goes on, or doesn't go on, in Congress short of formal bicameral approval mandated by Article I, § 7. And he also seems to have sympathy for the downtrodden, politically power-less, blue-collar white men who pay the price for affirmative action. Is this an appropriate factor to consider in statutory interpretation? Should statutory ambiguities be resolved *against* the more politically potent interests?

3. *The Court/Congress/President Civil Rights Game.* Recall that the blue-collar men whom Justice Scalia claims are politically "impotent" elected President Reagan twice, based upon a platform hostile to affirmative action— and Reagan delivered on his platform by appointing Rehnquist Chief Justice, elevating Scalia to the Court, and trying to elevate Judge Robert Bork to the Court (after *Johnson*). Although Bork was defeated, Reagan ended up ap-pointing someone nearly as conservative, Judge Anthony Kennedy of the Ninth Circuit. Since Kennedy replaced Justice Powell—Brennan's critical fifth vote in *Johnson*—the Court in 1988 was poised to shift civil rights policy rightward: four Justices (Rehnquist, White, Scalia, Kennedy) were openly opposed to affirmative action, and one (O'Connor) was skeptical. The Court

had a great deal of room to maneuver, since a rightward shift in policy could be protected against congressional override by a presidential veto (by Reagan or his successor, George H.W. Bush).

FLOOD v. KUHN

Supreme Court of the United States, 1972
407 U.S. 258, 92 S.Ct. 2099, 32 L.Ed.2d 728.

MR. JUSTICE BLACKMUN delivered the opinion of the Court.

[I. *The Game*] It is a century and a quarter since the New York Nine defeated the Knickerbockers 23 to 1 on Hoboken's Elysian Fields June 19, 1846, with Alexander Jay Cartwright as the instigator and the umpire. The teams were amateur, but the contest marked a significant date in baseball's beginnings. That early game led ultimately to the development of professional baseball and its tightly organized structure.

The Cincinnati Red Stockings came into existence in 1869 upon an outpouring of local pride. With only one Cincinnatian on the payroll, this professional team traveled over 11,000 miles that summer, winning 56 games and tying one. Shortly thereafter, on St. Patrick's Day in 1871, the National Association of Professional Baseball Players was founded and the professional league was born.

The ensuing colorful days are well known. The ardent follower and the student of baseball know of General Abner Doubleday; the formation of the National League in 1876; Chicago's supremacy in the first year's competition under the leadership of Al Spalding and with Cap Anson at third base; the formation of the American Association and then of the Union Association in the 1880's; the introduction of Sunday baseball; interleague warfare with cut-rate admission prices and player raiding; the development of the reserve "clause"; the emergence in 1885 of the Brotherhood of Professional Ball Players, and in 1890 of the Players League; the appearance of the American League, or "junior circuit," in 1901, rising from the minor Western Association; the first World Series in 1903, disruption in 1904, and the Series' resumption in 1905; the short-lived Federal League on the majors' scene during World War I years; the troublesome and discouraging episode of the 1919 Series; the home run ball; the shifting of franchises; the expansion of the leagues; the installation in 1965 of the major league draft of potential new players; and the formation of the Major League Baseball Players Association in 1966.

Then there are the many names, celebrated for one reason or another, that have sparked the diamond and its environs and that have provided tinder for recaptured thrills, for reminiscence and comparisons, and for conversation and anticipation in-season and off-season: Ty Cobb, Babe Ruth, Tris Speaker, Walter Johnson, Henry Chadwick, Eddie Collins, Lou Gehrig, Grover Cleveland Alexander, Rogers Hornsby, Harry Hooper, Goose Goslin, Jackie Robinson, Honus Wagner, Joe McCarthy, John McGraw, Deacon Phillippe, Rube Marquard, Christy Mathewson, Tommy Leach, Big Ed Delahanty, Davy Jones, Germany Schaefer, King Kelly, Big

Dan Brouthers, Wahoo Sam Crawford, Wee Willie Keeler, Big Ed Walsh, Jimmy Austin, Fred Snodgrass, Satchel Paige, Hugh Jennings, Fred Merkle, Iron Man McGinnity, Three–Finger Brown, Harry and Stan Coveleski, Connie Mack, Al Bridwell, Red Ruffing, Amos Rusie, Cy Young, Smokey Joe Wood, Chief Meyers, Chief Bender, Bill Klem, Hans Lobert, Johnny Evers, Joe Tinker, Roy Campanella, Miller Huggins, Rube Bressler, Dazzy Vance, Edd Roush, Bill Wambsganss, Clark Griffith, Branch Rickey, Frank Chance, Cap Anson, Nap Lajoie, Sad Sam Jones, Bob O'Farrell, Lefty O'Doul, Bobby Veach, Willie Kamm, Heinie Groh, Lloyd and Paul Waner, Stuffy McInnis, Charles Comiskey, Roger Bresnahan, Bill Dickey, Zack Wheat, George Sisler, Charlie Gehringer, Eppa Rixey, Harry Heilmann, Fred Clarke, Dizzy Dean, Hank Greenberg, Pie Traynor, Rube Waddell, Bill Terry, Carl Hubbell, Old Hoss Radbourne, Moe Berg, Rabbit Maranville, Jimmie Foxx, Lefty Grove. The list seems endless.

And one recalls the appropriate reference to the "World Serious," attributed to Ring Lardner, Sr.; Ernest L. Thayer's "Casey at the Bat"; the ring of "Tinker to Evers to Chance"; and all the other happenings, habits, and superstitions about and around baseball that made it the "national pastime" or, depending upon the point of view, "the great American tragedy."

[Curt Flood, the petitioner, was a star center fielder with the St. Louis Cardinals. Under the "reserve clause" in his contract he was required to play for the Cardinals, the Cardinals could unilaterally assign his contract to another team, and the Cardinals could annually renew that contract so long as the minimum salary was provided.

[In October 1969, the Cards traded Flood to the Philadelphia Phillies. Flood refused to report to the Phillies and asked Bowie Kuhn, the Commissioner of Baseball, to be allowed to negotiate a contract with the team of his choice. Kuhn refused. Flood filed a lawsuit claiming, *inter alia*, that the reserve clause violated the antitrust laws because it prevented him from contracting with the team of his choice. Lower courts denied relief based on Supreme Court precedents holding baseball immune from the antitrust laws.]

[IVA. *The Legal Background*] *Federal Baseball Club v. National League*, 259 U.S. 200 (1922), was a suit for treble damages instituted by a member of the Federal League (Baltimore) against the National and American Leagues and others. The plaintiff obtained a verdict in the trial court, but the Court of Appeals reversed. The main brief filed by the plaintiff with this Court discloses that it was strenuously argued, among other things, that the business in which the defendants were engaged was interstate commerce; that the interstate relationship among the several clubs, located as they were in different States, was predominant; that organized baseball represented an investment of colossal wealth; that it was an engagement in moneymaking; that gate receipts were divided by agreement between the home club and the visiting club; and that the business of baseball was to be distinguished from the mere playing of the game as a sport for physical exercise and diversion.

Mr. Justice Holmes, in speaking succinctly for a unanimous Court, said:

> "The business is giving exhibitions of base ball, which are purely state affairs. * * * But the fact that in order to give the exhibitions the Leagues must induce free persons to cross state lines and must arrange and pay for their doing so is not enough to change the character of the business. * * * [T]he transport is a mere incident, not the essential thing. That to which it is incident, the exhibition, although made, for money would not be called trade or commerce in the commonly accepted use of those words. As it is put by the defendant, personal effort, not related to production, is not a subject of commerce. That which in its consummation is not commerce does not become commerce among the States because the transportation that we have mentioned takes place. To repeat the illustrations given by the Court below, a firm of lawyers sending out a member to argue a case, or the Chautauqua lecture bureau sending out lecturers, does not engage in such commerce because the lawyer or lecturer goes to another State.

> "If we are right the plaintiff's business is to be described in the same way and the restrictions by contract that prevented the plaintiff from getting players to break their bargains and the other conduct charged against the defendants were not an interference with commerce among the States." 259 U.S., at 208–209. * * *

In the years that followed, baseball continued to be subject to intermittent antitrust attack. The courts, however, rejected these challenges on the authority of *Federal Baseball*. In some cases stress was laid, although unsuccessfully, on new factors such as the development of radio and television with their substantial additional revenues to baseball. For the most part, however, the Holmes opinion was generally and necessarily accepted as controlling authority. And in the 1952 Report of the Subcommittee on Study of Monopoly Power of the House Committee on the Judiciary, H.R.Rep. No. 2002, 82d Cong., 2d Sess., 229, it was said, in conclusion:

> "On the other hand the overwhelming preponderance of the evidence established baseball's need for some sort of reserve clause. Baseball's history shows that chaotic conditions prevailed when there was no reserve clause. Experience points to no feasible substitute to protect the integrity of the game or to guarantee a comparatively even competitive struggle. The evidence adduced at the hearings would clearly not justify the enactment of legislation flatly condemning the reserve clause."

C.   The Court granted certiorari in [*Toolson, Kowalski,* and *Corbett*], and, by a short per curiam (Warren, C.J., and Black, Frankfurter, Douglas, Jackson, Clark, and Minton, JJ.), affirmed the judgments of the respective courts of appeals in those three cases. *Toolson v. New York Yankees, Inc.*, 346 U.S. 356 (1953). *Federal Baseball* was cited as holding "that the business of providing public baseball games for profit between clubs of professional baseball players was not within the scope of the federal antitrust laws," and:

> "Congress has had the ruling under consideration but has not seen fit to bring such business under these laws by legislation having prospective effect. The business has thus been left for thirty years to develop, on the understanding that it was not subject to existing antitrust legislation. The present cases ask us to overrule the prior decision and, with retrospective effect, hold the legislation applicable. We think that if there are evils in this field which now warrant application to it of the antitrust laws it should be by legislation. Without re-examination of the underlying issues, the judgments below are affirmed on the authority of *Federal Baseball Club of Baltimore v. National League of Professional Baseball Clubs, supra,* so far as that decision determines that Congress had no intention of including the business of baseball within the scope of the federal antitrust laws."

This quotation reveals four reasons for the Court's affirmance of *Toolson* and its companion cases: (a) Congressional awareness for three decades of the Court's ruling in *Federal Baseball*, coupled with congressional inaction. (b) The fact that baseball was left alone to develop for that period upon the understanding that the reserve system was not subject to existing federal antitrust laws. (c) A reluctance to overrule *Federal Baseball* with consequent retroactive effect. (d) A professed desire that any needed remedy be provided by legislation rather than by court decree. The emphasis in *Toolson* was on the determination, attributed even to *Federal Baseball*, that Congress had no intention to include baseball within the reach of the federal antitrust laws. * * *

[Justice Blackmun recounted three subsequent opinions. In *United States v. Shubert*, 348 U.S. 222 (1955), the Court reversed a dismissal of an antitrust suit against defendants engaged in theatrical attractions across the country, indicating that *Federal Baseball* and *Toolson* gave no general antitrust exemption for businesses built around local exhibitions. Similarly, the Court in *United States v. International Boxing Club*, 348 U.S. 236 (1955), reversed a district court for dismissing the antitrust complaint; the Court denied that *Federal Baseball* gave sports other than baseball an exemption from the antitrust laws. Finally, in *Radovich v. National Football League*, 352 U.S. 445 (1957), the Supreme Court reversed the lower courts for dismissing another antitrust complaint against a football league. Justice Clark's opinion for the Court noted that *Toolson* upheld baseball's immunity, "because it was concluded that more harm would be done in overruling *Federal Base Ball* than in upholding a ruling which at best was of dubious validity." The opinion said:]

> "All this, combined with the flood of litigation that would follow its repudiation, the harassment that would ensue, and the retroactive

effect of such a decision, led the Court to the practical result that it should sustain the unequivocal line of authority reaching over many years.

"[S]ince *Toolson* and *Federal Base Ball* are still cited as controlling authority in antitrust actions involving other fields of business, we now specifically limit the rule there established to the facts there involved, *i.e.*, the business of organized professional baseball. As long as the Congress continues to acquiesce we should adhere to—but not extend—the interpretation of the Act made in those cases. * * *

"If this ruling is unrealistic, inconsistent, or illogical, it is sufficient to answer, aside from the distinctions between the businesses,that were we considering the question of baseball for the first time upon a clean slate we would have no doubts. But *Federal Base Ball* held the business of baseball outside the scope of the Act. No other business claiming the coverage of those cases has such an adjudication. We therefore, conclude that the orderly way to eliminate error or discrimination, if any there be, is by legislation and not by court decision. Congressional processes are more accommodative, affording the whole industry hearings and an opportunity to assist in the formulation of new legislation. The resulting product is therefore more likely to protect the industry and the public alike. The whole scope of congressional action would be known long in advance and effective dates for the legislation could be set in the future without the injustices of retroactivity and surprise which might follow court action."

Mr. Justice Frankfurter dissented essentially for the reasons stated in his dissent in *International Boxing*. Mr. Justice Harlan, joined by Mr. Justice Brennan, also dissented because he, too, was "unable to distinguish football from baseball." Here again the dissenting Justices did not call for the overruling of the baseball decisions. They merely could not distinguish the two sports and, out of respect for *stare decisis*, voted to affirm.

G.　Finally, in *Haywood v. National Basketball Assn.*, 401 U.S. 1204 (1971), Mr. Justice Douglas, in his capacity as Circuit Justice, reinstated a District Court's injunction *pendente lite* in favor of a professional basketball player and said, "Basketball * * * does not enjoy exemption from the antitrust laws."

H.　This series of decisions understandably spawned extensive commentary, some of it mildly critical and much of it not; nearly all of it looked to Congress for any remedy that might be deemed essential.

I.　Legislative proposals have been numerous and persistent. Since *Toolson* more than 50 bills have been introduced in Congress relative to the applicability or nonapplicability of the antitrust laws to baseball. A few of these passed one house or the other. Those that did would have expanded, not restricted, the reserve system's exemption to other professional league sports. And the Act of Sept. 30, 1961, Pub.L. 87–331, 75 Stat.

732, and the merger addition thereto effected by the Act of Nov. 8, 1966, Pub.L. 89–800, § 6(b), 80 Stat. 1515, 15 U.S.C. §§ 1291–1295, were also expansive rather than restrictive as to antitrust exemption.

[V.] In view of all this, it seems appropriate now to say that:

1.   Professional baseball is a business and it is engaged in interstate commerce.

2.   With its reserve system enjoying exemption from the federal antitrust laws, baseball is, in a very distinct sense, an exception and an anomaly. *Federal Baseball* and *Toolson* have become an aberration confined to baseball.

3.   Even though others might regard this as "unrealistic, inconsistent, or illogical," see *Radovich*, the aberration is an established one, and one that has been recognized not only in *Federal Baseball* and *Toolson*, but in *Shubert, International Boxing*, and *Radovich*, as well, a total of five consecutive cases in this Court. It is an aberration that has been with us now for half a century, one heretofore deemed fully entitled to the benefit of *stare decisis*, and one that has survived the Court's expanding concept of interstate commerce. It rests on a recognition and an acceptance of baseball's unique characteristics and needs.

4.   Other professional sports operating interstate—football, boxing, basketball, and, presumably, hockey and golf—are not so exempt.

5.   The advent of radio and television, with their consequent increased coverage and additional revenues, has not occasioned an overruling of *Federal Baseball* and *Toolson*.

6.   The Court has emphasized that since 1922 baseball, with full and continuing congressional awareness, has been allowed to develop and to expand unhindered by federal legislative action. Remedial legislation has been introduced repeatedly in Congress but none has ever been enacted. The Court, accordingly, has concluded that Congress as yet has had no intention to subject baseball's reserve system to the reach of the antitrust statutes. This, obviously, has been deemed to be something other than mere congressional silence and passivity.

7.   The Court has expressed concern about the confusion and the retroactivity problems that inevitably would result with a judicial overturning of *Federal Baseball*. It has voiced a preference that if any change is to be made, it come by legislative action that, by its nature, is only prospective in operation.

8.   The Court noted in *Radovich* that the slate with respect to baseball is not clean. Indeed, it has not been clean for half a century.

This emphasis and this concern are still with us. We continue to be loath, 50 years after *Federal Baseball* and almost two decades after *Toolson*, to overturn those cases judicially when Congress, by its positive inaction, has allowed those decisions to stand for so long and, far beyond mere inference and implication, has clearly evinced a desire not to disapprove them legislatively.

Accordingly, we adhere once again to *Federal Baseball* and *Toolson* and to their application to professional baseball. We adhere also to *International Boxing* and *Radovich* and to their respective applications to professional boxing and professional football. If there is any inconsistency or illogic in all this, it is an inconsistency and illogic of long standing that is to be remedied by the Congress and not by this Court. If we were to act otherwise, we would be withdrawing from the conclusion as to congressional intent made in *Toolson* and from the concerns as to retrospectivity therein expressed. Under these circumstances, there is merit in consistency even though some might claim that beneath that consistency is a layer of inconsistency.

* * * [W]hat the Court said in *Federal Baseball* in 1922 and what it said in *Toolson* in 1953, we say again here in 1972: the remedy, if any is indicated, is for congressional, and not judicial, action.

MR. JUSTICE WHITE joins in the judgment of the Court, and in all but Part I of the Court's opinion.

MR. JUSTICE POWELL took no part in the consideration or decision of this case.

MR. CHIEF JUSTICE BURGER, concurring.

I concur in all but Part I of the Court's opinion but, like Mr. Justice Douglas, I have grave reservations as to the correctness of *Toolson*; as he notes in his dissent, he joined that holding but has "lived to regret it." The error, if such it be, is one on which the affairs of a great many people have rested for a long time. Courts are not the forum in which this tangled web ought to be unsnarled. I agree with Mr. Justice Douglas that congressional inaction is not a solid base, but the least undesirable course now is to let the matter rest with Congress; it is time the Congress acted to solve this problem.

MR. JUSTICE DOUGLAS, with whom MR. JUSTICE BRENNAN concurs, dissenting.

This Court's decision in *Federal Baseball Club*, made in 1922, is a derelict in the stream of the law that we, its creator, should remove. Only a romantic view of a rather dismal business account over the last 50 years would keep that derelict in midstream.

In 1922 the Court had a narrow, parochial view of commerce. With the demise of the old landmarks of that era, the whole concept of commerce has changed.

Under the modern [commerce clause] decisions, the power of Congress was recognized as broad enough to reach all phases of the vast operations of our national industrial system. An industry so dependent on radio and television as is baseball and gleaning vast interstate revenues (see H.R.Rep. No. 2002, 82d Cong., 2d Sess., 4, 5 (1952)) would be hard put today to say with the Court in the *Federal Baseball Club* case that baseball was only a local exhibition, not trade or commerce.

Baseball is today big business that is packaged with beer, with broadcasting, and with other industries. The beneficiaries of the *Federal Baseball Club* decision are not the Babe Ruths, Ty Cobbs, and Lou Gehrigs.

The owners, whose records many say reveal a proclivity for predatory practices, do not come to us with equities. The equities are with the victims of the reserve clause. I use the word "victims" in the Sherman Act sense, since a contract which forbids anyone to practice his calling is commonly called an unreasonable restraint of trade.

If congressional inaction is our guide, we should rely upon the fact that Congress has refused to enact bills broadly exempting professional sports from antitrust regulation. H.R.Rep. No. 2002, 82nd Cong., 2d Sess. (1952). The only statutory exemption granted by Congress to professional sports concerns broadcasting rights. 15 U.S.C. §§ 1291–1295. I would not ascribe a broader exemption through inaction than Congress has seen fit to grant explicitly.

There can be no doubt "that were we considering the question of baseball for the first time upon a clean slate" we would hold it to be subject to federal antitrust regulation. *Radovich.* The unbroken silence of Congress should not prevent us from correcting our own mistakes.

MR. JUSTICE MARSHALL, with whom MR. JUSTICE BRENNAN joins, dissenting.

This is a difficult case because we are torn between the principle of *stare decisis* and the knowledge that the decisions in *Federal Baseball Club* and *Toolson* are totally at odds with more recent and better reasoned cases. * * *

Has Congress acquiesced in our decisions in *Federal Baseball Club* and *Toolson?* I think not. Had the Court been consistent and treated all sports in the same way baseball was treated, Congress might have become concerned enough to take action. But, the Court was inconsistent, and baseball was isolated and distinguished from all other sports. In *Toolson* the Court refused to act because Congress had been silent. But the Court may have read too much into this legislative inaction.

Americans love baseball as they love all sports. Perhaps we become so enamored of athletics that we assume that they are foremost in the minds of legislators as well as fans. We must not forget, however, that there are only some 600 major league baseball players. Whatever muscle they might have been able to muster by combining forces with other athletes has been greatly impaired by the manner in which this Court has isolated them. It is this Court that has made them impotent, and this Court should correct its error.

We do not lightly overrule our prior constructions of federal statutes, but when our errors deny substantial federal rights, like the right to compete freely and effectively to the best of one's ability as guaranteed by the antitrust laws, we must admit our error and correct it. We have done so before and we should do so again here. See, *e.g.*, *Blonder–Tongue Laboratories, Inc. v. University of Illinois Foundation*, 402 U.S. 313 (1971); *Boys Markets, Inc. v. Retail Clerks Union*, 398 U.S. 235, 241 (1970).

To the extent that there is concern over any reliance interests that club owners may assert, they can be satisfied by making our decision prospective only. Baseball should be covered by the antitrust laws beginning with this case and henceforth, unless Congress decides otherwise.

NOTES ON *FLOOD v. KUHN* AND *STARE DECISIS* IN STATUTORY CASES

1. *Is There a Rationale for* Flood? *What of Its Aftermath?* It appears that every member of the Court thought that *Federal Baseball* was wrongly decided, yet a majority nevertheless applied the wrongheaded precedent. Why should the Court reaffirm this "inconsistency and illogic of long standing"? The Court notes "retrospectivity" problems that would inhere if it were to overturn *Toolson* and *Federal Baseball*, suggesting that the industry had been "relying" on these precedents in conducting its affairs. Yet the testimony of post-*Toolson* purchasers of baseball teams indicated that they had been advised of the distinct possibility of changes in the antitrust exemption. *Flood v. Kuhn*, Brief for Petitioner, at 24.

The Chief Justice suggested that "[c]ourts are not the forum in which this tangled web ought to be unsnarled." Let Congress make the change. Yet, given the past history of congressional involvement, recounted by the Court, was there any reason to believe that Congress would do anything? The reaction to *Flood* in Congress was, indeed, immediate. Two bills were introduced in the House of Representatives, H.R. 12401 and H.R. 14614, 92d Cong., 2d Sess. (1972), and a hearing was held by the appropriate subcommittee, but neither bill went anywhere. Is that because Congress "liked" the Court's decision? Or didn't "dislike" it enough to revoke it? Or was lobbied very hard by the baseball owners?[f]

Could *Flood v. Kuhn* be an example of *stare nostalgia*? Consider Justice Blackmun's "Ode to Baseball" in Part I of the opinion. Was that an appropriate matter to be included in a judicial opinion? Even if not, were Chief Justice Burger and Justice White right in making a point of not joining Part I? (We think this is the only time in history that all of an opinion commanded a Court majority except for its statement of facts!)

2. *The Aftermath of* Flood v. Kuhn. The Court never returned to the *Flood* issue (maybe on the ground that, after *Federal Baseball*, *Toolson*, and *Flood*, three strikes and you're out?). Thwarted on antitrust grounds, players used labor law to their advantage. They formed a union and agitated for

---

f. In the 1970s, Members of Congress were promoting the return of major league baseball to the nation's capital, leading one commentator to opine: "It thus appears that there is more bicameral interest in where baseball will be played than in the legalities of the sport." Philip Martin, *The Aftermath of* Flood v. Kuhn: *Professional Baseball's Exemption from Antitrust Regulation*, 3 West. St. U.L. Rev. 262, 280 (1976). For the argument that *Federal Baseball* was ripe for overruling, see Stephen Ross, *Reconsidering* Flood v. Kuhn, 12 U. Miami Ent. & Sports L. Rev. 169 (1995).

change. Five years after *Flood*, an arbitrator awarded free-agent status to two players; the collective bargaining between owners and the players' union that followed, with impasses sometimes resulting in strikes, led to labor agreements that provided players with significant freedom. In the mid–1990s, following particularly acrimonious labor conflict, management agreed with the union to approach Congress jointly and request legislation effectively overriding *Flood*.

Congress responded by enacting the Curt Flood Act of 1998, Pub. L. 105–297, 112 Stat. 2824. The statute subjects any business practices "directly relating to or affecting employment of major league baseball players * * * to the antitrust laws to the same extent such * * * practices * * * would be subject to the antitrust laws if engaged in by persons in any other professional sports business affecting interstate commerce." Drafted to avoid any application of the antitrust laws to such matters as franchise relocation and the treatment of minor-league players, it is not clear that the statute changed the law in general or, in particular, provides any rights to players that they had not already achieved through collective bargaining.

Nonetheless, the statute was at least a symbolic victory. When Flood decided that he would not accept his trade, he wrote the baseball commissioner: "After 12 years in the Major Leagues, I do not feel I am a piece of property to be bought and sold irrespective of my wishes. I believe that any system which produces that result violates my basic rights as a citizen." A year before Congress belatedly agreed, Flood died of cancer at age 59.

3. *When Is It Appropriate To Overrule a Statutory Precedent?* As *Flood* suggests, the Supreme Court will not routinely overrule a prior interpretation of a statute. State courts are even more emphatic that statutory precedents should rarely, or never (in some states), be overruled, since the legislature can change the statute. Thus, even though the extra-strong presumption of stare decisis for statutory precedents may lack historical support in practices before the twentieth century, it seems to be deeply rooted at the beginning of the twenty-first. Is it ever appropriate to overrule a statutory precedent? Consider some hypotheses:

(a) **Constitutionalized Recent Decisions.** Justice Scalia (in *Johnson*) says the Court should terminate bad civil rights precedents before they get entrenched. The Court does sometimes overrule civil rights precedents overtaken by normative constitutional thinking, e.g., *Monell v. Department of Social Servs.*, 436 U.S. 658 (1978) (overruling a 1961 precedent excluding municipalities from § 1983, which holds state governments accountable for violation of federal law), but not with unusual frequency. Overruling decisions quickly is a better idea, because it reduces reliance interests. In *Flood*, for example, the whole industry had developed in reliance of the antitrust exemption.

(b) **Common Law Statutes.** Justice Stevens once argued that statutes, like the Sherman Act (*Flood*) and section 1983 (*Monell*), that deployed open-textured common law terminology were, effectively, delegations to the judiciary to develop norms, common law style. Hence, ordinary *stare decisis* ought to apply. Although *Flood* is inconsistent with this idea, the Court has in fact overruled a lot more Sherman Act precedents than it has done for any other federal statute. See William N. Eskridge Jr. & John Ferejohn, *A Republic of Statutes: The New American Constitution* ch. 3 (2010).

(c) Subsequent Statutory Developments. If subsequent statutory developments support the precedent, that is a good reason not to overrule, as in *Flood*; if the subsequent developments cut against the precedent, that supports an overruling, as in *Monell*.

C. THE REHNQUIST COURT'S RETREAT FROM *GRIGGS* AND CONGRESS'S RESPONSE (THE CIVIL RIGHTS ACT OF 1991)

The 1988 Term of the Court included several employment discrimination cases that bitterly divided the Court. The most important case was *Wards Cove Packing Co. v. Atonio*, 490 U.S. 642 (1989), which evaluated a Title VII claim against the operation of two salmon canneries in Alaska. Unskilled positions at the canneries were staffed almost entirely by Pacific Americans (Filipinos and Native Alaskans) hired on the site of the canneries, while about half of the skilled office positions were filled by whites hired in the firm's Oregon and Washington offices, usually through word-of-mouth (and sometimes through nepotism). A cannery employee could not be promoted to an office position. The cannery jobs paid a lot less than the office jobs. Cannery employees ate and lived in separate areas from the office employees.

This arrangement may be viewed as a classic "plantation" set-up, and plaintiff cannery employees sued Wards Cove for discriminating against them in making its office hires. The Ninth Circuit (en banc) held that plaintiffs made out a prima facie case of disparate impact employment discrimination under *Griggs*. The Supreme Court reversed. The majority opinion was written by Justice White and was joined by Chief Justice Rehnquist and Justices O'Connor, Scalia, and Kennedy.

The Supreme Court majority held that the lower court's approach would impose excessive burdens on employers to get good numbers, and would encourage such employers to adopt quotas—which the Court found inconsistent with § 703(j). Thus, the Court held that a prima facie case of disparate impact discrimination is not made out unless the plaintiffs demonstrate that the bad numbers are out of line with the number of "qualified" minority applicants for the positions in question. "As long as there are no barriers or practices deterring qualified nonwhites from applying for noncannery positions, if the percentage of selected applicants who are nonwhite is not significantly less than the percentage of qualified applicants who are nonwhite, the employer's selection mechanism probably does not operate with a disparate impact upon minorities." The Court disapproved the Ninth Circuit's focus on the substantial disparity between the overwhelming minority composition of cannery workers and their trivial representation among office workers. To make out a prima facie case, the plaintiffs would have to show that the poor representation among office workers is disproportionate to the percentage of qualified minority applicants for those positions.

The Court remanded the case to the lower courts to reevaluate the disparate impact claim, but (in what may or may not be dicta) it also set forth some guidelines for the lower courts to follow: Plaintiffs' burden of proof in disparate impact cases includes the burden of identifying to the factfinder not only a statistical disparity (see the above discussion), but also the specific employment practice that caused the disparity. The *Wards Cove* plaintiffs argued that a congeries of practices contributed to the bad numbers—nepotism in hiring for office positions, the firm's refusal to advertise such positions locally, and the firm's failure to consider cannery employees for promotions. The Court admonished the plaintiffs "to demonstrate that the disparity they complain of is the result of one or more of the employment practices that they are attacking here, specifically showing that each challenged practice has a significantly disparate impact on employment opportunities for whites and nonwhites." In response to plaintiffs' argument that such a burden is unfair, the Court noted that "liberal civil discovery rules give plaintiffs access to employers' records in an effort to document their claims," and that most employers are required to keep impact-related employment records as a matter of federal law.

If plaintiffs were to succeed in establishing a prima facie disparate impact case, the Court further stated (again in what may be dicta) that the employer would have the burden of producing some evidence that the challenged practices were justified business practices. The Court carefully noted that the burden of persuasion would remain with the plaintiffs. Hence, plaintiffs would ultimately have to persuade the finder of fact (1) that there was a statistical disparity, (2) that the disparity can be linked to specific employment practices, and (3) that those practices do not have a substantial business justification.

Four Justices (Brennan, Marshall, Blackmun, and Stevens) dissented. The dissenting Justices argued that the Court's opinion, especially its dicta about plaintiffs' burden of persuasion on the business justification defense, represented a striking departure from existing law and a partial renunciation of *Griggs*. At about the same time it was deciding *Wards Cove* (June 5, 1989), the Supreme Court handed down five other decisions that gave a narrow construction to Title VII and related statutes.

These decisions created a number of practical difficulties for litigants challenging discriminatory employment practices. More generally, they signaled a determination by five Justices to close off the expansion of civil rights statutes and, more important, to discourage employers from adopting affirmative action programs. The Court earlier in the Term had struck down the Richmond municipal program for setting aside business for minority-owned enterprises in *City of Richmond v. J.A. Croson Co.*, 488 U.S. 469 (1989).

These decisions produced a collective shock to the nation's civil rights community, which immediately sought to override them legislatively. On February 27, 1990, Senator Edward Kennedy (D–Mass.) and 33 co-sponsors introduced S. 2104, the Civil Rights Act of 1990. A similar House bill, H.R. 4000, was introduced by Representative Augustus Hawkins (D–Cal.) at the same time. The bill's purpose was "to respond to the Supreme Court's recent decisions by restoring the civil rights protections that were dramatically limited by those decisions." The substantive sections of the bill then amended Title VII and § 1981 to override one or more of the offending Supreme Court cases. With complex transition rules, the bill would have overridden all six of the 1989 Supreme Court decisions, plus three earlier ones as well. The sponsors of the bill roundly condemned the Supreme Court's performance. "I believe the Supreme Court's recent rulings represent an effort to renege on history," said Senator Jeffords (R–Vt.). 136 Cong. Rec. S1022 (daily ed. Feb. 7, 1990).

The George H.W. Bush Administration agreed that some of the decisions should have been overridden—but not *Wards Cove*; the Administration defended that decision on the ground that the overrides as drafted encouraged employers to adopt racial quotas, in violation of § 703(j). See Letter from Attorney General Richard Thornburgh to Senator Kennedy, Apr. 3, 1990. The sponsors realized that they did not have enough votes to override a presidential veto, and the result was a series of negotiations to work out a compromise bill. Between June and October 1990, rotating groups representing liberal Democrats, moderate Republicans, and the Administration engaged in such negotiations—which continued after the Senate passed a revised bill on July 18 (by a vote of 65–34) and the House passed its own bill on August 3 (by a vote of 272–154), and after the submission of conference reports on September 26 and October 12.

The final conference bill made a number of changes in the controversial *Wards Cove* provision in a final effort to appease the White House and/or to obtain Republican support for the bill. Specifically, the bill included a more liberal definition of the business necessity defense in disparate impact cases, required that plaintiffs prove which employer practices caused the disparate impact alleged, confirmed that bad numbers alone do not violate Title VII, and reiterated that Title VII does not require quotas. See 136 Cong. Rec. S15,327 (daily ed. Oct. 16, 1990) (statement of Sen. Kennedy). Nonetheless, the President vetoed the bill, *id.* at S16,562–63 (daily ed. Oct. 24, 1990), and the Senate failed to override the veto by one vote (66–34). *Id.* at S16,589.

The *Wards Cove* issue was a minor theme of the 1990 off-year elections, which yielded a net gain to the Democrats of one Senator (albeit by defeating a Republican who had voted to override the veto) and about a dozen House Members. On January 3, 1991, the bill that had come so close in 1990 was reintroduced as the Civil Rights and Women's Equity in Employment Act of 1991, H.R. 1, 102d Cong., 1st Sess. (1991). Hearings were held before the Education & Labor and the Judiciary Committees in February and March 1991, the Committees turned back Republican amendments and reported a very liberal bill, and the House passed H.R. 1 on June 5, 1991. See 137 Cong. Rec. H3924–25 (daily ed. June 5, 1991). It was a bill certain to be vetoed.

Again, once the bill reached the Senate floor, ongoing negotiations among liberal Democrats, moderate Republicans, and the Administration intensified. Negotiations yielded a new bipartisan compromise bill, the Danforth–Kennedy substitute, S. 1745, which significantly rewrote the House bill, just as the Senate had done in 1990. On the *Wards Cove* issues, S. 1745 simplified the burdens of proof in disparate impact cases (by adding new § 703(k)(1)(A)), generally required that plaintiffs link specific employer practices to their claimed disparate impact (see new § 703(k)(1)(B)), and abandoned prior efforts to define "business necessity" and left the definition to pre-*Wards Cove* case law (see § 3(2) of the Act). Importantly, new § 703(k) represented a clear congressional ratification of *Griggs* in the text of the job discrimination law, but a ratification setting limits on disparate impact lawsuits.

Notwithstanding the freshly revised S. 1745, there was still some doubt whether there would be civil rights legislation in 1991, because the Administration remained publicly unpersuaded that it was not a "quota bill" and because it was not clear how many Republicans would support the bill (eleven GOP Senators voted to override the 1990 veto). According to some inside-the-beltway accounts, the key event was a meeting between President Bush and several GOP Senators in mid-October, in which the Senators told the President that they wanted to vote for a civil rights bill and would vote to override a veto. After the meeting, President Bush dramatically changed his mind and announced he would sign the legislation, after a few more changes.

The final language of the bill (with much focus on § 703(k)) was hammered out during the week of October 21. During the Senate's debate upon the compromise bill, between October 25 and 30, numerous amendments were accepted and rejected and—perhaps not surprisingly given the tools of interpretation used by the courts—a flurry of "interpretive statements" or "memoranda" were inserted into the Congressional Record to "explain" what the bill now "meant." Senator Danforth (R–Mo.), a key architect of the compromise, offered his own interpretive memorandum, as well as the following wisdom, in response to attempts to amend the bill to forbid courts from using legislative history to interpret provisions of the 1991 Act (137 Cong. Rec. S15325 (daily ed. Oct. 29, 1991)):

> It is very common for Members of the Senate to try to affect the way in which a court will interpret a statute by putting things into the Congressional Record. * * * [A] court would be well advised to take with a large grain of salt floor debate and statements placed into the Congressional Record which purport to create an interpretation for the legislation that is before us. * * * [A]ny judge who tries to make legislative history out of the free-for-all that takes place on the floor of the Senate is on very dangerous grounds.

The Senate passed S. 1745 on October 30, and the House passed it on November 7, 1991, in both cases by overwhelming margins (reflecting the new bipartisan consensus). The President signed the bill on November 21, 1991, as the "Civil Rights Act of 1991," Pub. L. No. 102–166, 105 Stat. 1071. See 1991 U.S. Code Cong. & Admin. News 768, for the President's signing statement.

PROBLEM 1–1

Justice Scalia's Position on Affirmative Action After the Civil Rights Act of 1991?

You are a law clerk to *Weber*-hating Justice Scalia. The Civil Rights Act of 1991 has been enacted, and a new race-based affirmative action case comes before the Supreme Court, where a city has rejected promotions of municipal firefighters awarded on the basis of professionally developed tests, allegedly because there were not enough Latino– and African–American candidates awarded promotions. Does Justice Scalia have any *legal* basis for overruling *Weber* in, say, 2009? Does he have any *legal* basis for finding that Caucasian–American firefighters should have a Title VII claim for relief?

Consider the text of the 1991 act. New § 703(m), added in 1991, says this:

(m) Except as otherwise provided in this title, an unlawful employment practice is established when the complaining party demonstrates that race, color, religion, sex, or national origin was a motivating factor for any employment practice, even though other factors also motivated the practice.

Section 116 of the Civil Rights Act of 1991 said this: "Nothing in the amendments made by this title shall be construed to affect court-ordered remedies, affirmative action, or conciliation agreements, that are in accordance with the law." Jot down your answer and consider the most recent case.

Ricci v. DeStefano, 557 U.S. 557 (2009). In 2003, 118 New Haven firefighters took examinations to qualify for promotion to the rank of lieutenant or captain. Promotion examinations were infrequent, so the stakes were high. The results would determine which firefighters would be considered for promotions during the next two years, and the order in which they would be considered. The city contracted with Industrial/Organizational Solutions, Inc. (IOS), a well-regarded job-testing firm for police and fire departments, to develop and administer the examinations. IOS representatives worked with officials and firefighters (including minority firefighters) within the department to develop written and oral tests that would be related to the job requirements and fair to all groups.

Seventy-seven candidates completed the lieutenant examination—43 persons of European ancestry, 19 African ancestry, and 15 Latino ancestry. Of those, 34 candidates passed—25 European Americans, 6 African Americans, and 3 Latino Americans. Eight lieutenant positions were vacant at the time of the examination; the top 10 candidates were eligible for an immediate promotion to lieutenant, and all were of European ancestry. Subsequent vacancies would have allowed at least three African–American candidates to be considered for promotion to lieutenant.

Forty-one candidates completed the captain examination—25 European Americans, 8 African Americans, and 8 Latino Americans. Of those, 22 candidates passed—16 European Americans, 3 African Americans, and 3 Latino Americans. Seven captain positions were vacant at the time of the examination; 9 candidates were eligible for an immediate promotion to captain—7 European Americans and 2 Latino Americans.

When the examination results showed that European–American candidates had outperformed minority candidates, Mayor John DeStefano and other local politicians opened a public debate that turned rancorous. Some firefighters argued the tests should be discarded because the results showed the tests to be discriminatory. They threatened a discrimination lawsuit if New Haven made promotions based on the tests. Other firefighters said the exams were neutral, and they threatened a discrimination lawsuit if the city, relying on the statistical racial disparity, ignored the test results and denied promotions to the candidates who had performed well. In the end the, city took the side of those who protested the test results. The mayor threw out the examinations.

Certain Caucasian and Latino firefighters, who likely would have been promoted based on their good test performance, sued New Haven, Mayor DeStefano, and other officials. They alleged that, by discarding the test results, the defendants discriminated against the plaintiffs based on their race, in violation of Title VII and the Equal Protection Clause. New Haven defended its actions, arguing that, if officials had certified the results, they could have faced liability under Title VII for adopting a practice that had a disparate impact on the minority firefighters.

The District Court granted summary judgment for the defendants, and the Court of Appeals (in a panel that included Judge, now Justice, Sonia Sotomayor) affirmed. Joined by Chief Justice Roberts and Justices Scalia, Thomas, and Alito, **Justice Kennedy**'s opinion for the Court ruled that "race-based action like [New Haven's] in this case is impermissible under Title VII unless the employer can demonstrate a strong basis in evidence that, had it not taken the action, it would have been liable under the disparate-impact statute. The respondents, we further determine, cannot meet that threshold standard. As a result, the City's action in discarding the tests was a violation of Title VII." Because New Haven's action violated Title VII, the Court did not reach the constitutional (equal protection) challenge.

Justice Kennedy's opinion rejected the firefighters' arguments that New Haven's disparate treatment of them (because of their white race) could not be justified by the threat of disparate impact lawsuits if the city had followed the test results. Reading the 1964 and 1991 Acts together, the Court held that an employer may adopt voluntary race-based remedies for apparent violations of the disparate impact provision of the 1991 Act, without violating the disparate treatment provision of the 1964 Act. The opinion also rejected the city's argument that a "good faith" belief that the tests violated the disparate impact provision would justify race-based remedies; such a lenient standard would, Justice Kennedy feared, open the door to a "de facto quota system," inconsistent with the premises of Title VII. Cf. § 703(j).

"In searching for a standard that strikes a more appropriate balance, we note that this Court has considered cases similar to this one, albeit in the context of the Equal Protection Clause of the Fourteenth Amendment. The Court has held that certain government actions to remedy past racial discrimination—actions that are themselves based on race—are constitutional only where there is a 'strong basis in evidence' that the remedial actions were necessary." *Richmond v. J.A. Croson Co.*, 488 U.S. 469, 500 (1989) (O'Connor, J., for a majority), quoting *Wygant v. Jackson Bd. of Educ.*, 476 U.S. 267, 277 (1986) (Powell, J., for a plurality).

"The standard leaves ample room for employers' voluntary compliance efforts, which are essential to the statutory scheme and to Congress's efforts to eradicate workplace discrimination. And the standard appropriately constrains employers' discretion in making race-based decisions: It limits that discretion to cases in which there is a strong basis in evidence of disparate-impact liability, but it is not so restrictive that it allows employers to act only when there is a provable, actual violation." At no point did Justice Kennedy cite *Weber*, and his opinion paid only glancing reference to *Johnson*.

Was there a "strong basis in evidence" for the city to conclude that it would face disparate impact liability if it followed the test results? The disparate racial impact of the tests made out a prima facie case for liability under the 1991 Act, but Justice Kennedy ruled that New Haven had no "strong basis" to believe that its business necessity defense would not prevail in potential lawsuits.

Writing also for Justices Stevens, Souter, and Breyer, **Justice Ginsburg** dissented. She started with a broader context, namely, the long history of exclusion for African- and Latino–American citizens from municipal police and firefighting jobs, including near-total exclusion for most of New Haven's history. In light of this history of exclusion, especially in the officer ranks, New Haven had a great deal of discretion to question the results of a test that statistically favored persons of European descent. At public meetings (before the test results had been released), several observers claimed that the test had several questions not relevant to firefighting duties or command; others pointed out that some firefighters had earlier access to study materials than others did; one participant pointed out that a neighboring city had a racially imbalanced force until it abandoned the use of standardized tests such as this one. Experts told the city that a more problem-oriented approach would have been practical and would probably have had a less racially discriminatory impact.

"Congress [has] declared unambiguously that selection criteria operating to the disadvantage of minority group members can be retained only if justified by business necessity. In keeping with Congress's design, employers who reject such criteria due to reasonable doubts about their reliability can hardly be held to have engaged in discrimination 'because of' race. A reasonable endeavor to comply with the law and to ensure that qualified candidates of all races have a fair opportunity to compete is simply not what Congress meant to interdict. I would therefore hold that an employer who jettisons a selection device when its disproportionate racial impact becomes apparent does not violate Title VII's disparate-treatment bar automatically or at all, subject to this key condition: The employer must have good cause to believe the device would not withstand examination for business necessity."

Justice Ginsburg maintained that her approach was more consistent with the EEOC's longstanding guidance on remedial race-based affirmative action permissible under Title VII and with the Court's precedents, specifically *Johnson*. She also argued that equal protection precedents were of "limited utility" because the Equal Protection Clause does **not** regulate state rules that only have a disparate race-based impact; there is no equal protection parallel to *Griggs*, and the 1991 Act's provision for disparate impact liability. Even under the Court's announced standard, Justice Ginsburg maintained that New Haven had a "strong basis in evidence" to question whether the IOS-developed test really met the business necessity requirement of the 1991 Act. So many questions were raised about the test, and the city had followed it simply because the union insisted on such a test.

Writing also for Justices Scalia and Thomas, **Justice Alito** wrote a concurring opinion that responded to Justice Ginsburg's factual points. Justice Alito's understanding was that New Haven's volte-face was politically motivated. "Taking into account all the evidence in the summary judgment record, a reasonable jury could find the following. Almost as soon as the City disclosed the racial makeup of the list of firefighters who scored the highest on the exam, the City administration was lobbied by an influential community leader to scrap the test results, and the City administration decided on that course of action before making any real assessment of the possibility of a disparate-impact violation. To achieve that end, the City administration concealed its internal decision but worked—as things turned out, successfully—to persuade the [review board] that acceptance of the test results would be illegal and would expose the City to disparate-impact liability. But in the event that the [review board] was not persuaded, the Mayor, wielding ultimate decisionmaking authority, was prepared to overrule the [board] immediately. Taking this view of the evidence, a reasonable jury could easily find that the City's real reason for scrapping the test results was not a concern about violating the disparate-impact provision of Title VII but a simple desire to please a politically important racial constituency."

Justice Ginsburg responded that she would be in favor of a remand to see precisely what various options a "reasonable" jury would have accepted. Moreover, Justice Alito's understanding of the decisionmaking ignored the fact that the reviewing board—an unelected, politically insulated group of experts—made the actual decision, and the mayor did not. Finally, are all "political considerations" tantamount to race discrimination itself? "The real issue, then, is not whether the mayor and his staff were politically motivated; it is whether their attempt to score political points was legitimate (*i.e.,* nondiscriminatory). Were they seeking to exclude white firefighters from promotion (unlikely, as a fair test would undoubtedly result in the addition of white firefighters to the officer ranks), or did they realize, at least belatedly, that their tests could be toppled in a disparate-impact suit? In the latter case, there is no disparate-treatment violation. Justice Alito, I recognize, would disagree. In his view, an employer's action to avoid Title VII disparate-impact liability qualifies as a presumptively improper race-based employment decision. I reject that construction of Title VII. As I see it, when employers endeavor to avoid exposure to disparate-impact liability, they do not thereby encounter liability for disparate treatment."

Notes on the New Haven Firefighters Case

1. *What Is the Law Now?* Current Title VII law is the interpretation rendered by the Court majority in *Ricci*—but what is a "strong basis in evidence" for the existence of a *Griggs* violation? For example, would the *Ricci* Court have followed Justice O'Connor in *Johnson*, where she found that the employer had a "firm basis" for remedying prior discrimination? Recall that Justice Scalia (now part of the Court majority) rejected Justice O'Connor's reading of the record, in part because the District Court had found, as a matter of fact, that there had been "no discrimination" against women in *Johnson*.

How can the "strong basis in evidence" standard be administered? Should the EEOC issue a guidance along these lines? If so, what should it say?

2. *Impact of the 1991 Amendments on the Affirmative Action Issue?* The *Ricci* Court rejected a hard no-race-factors-ever interpretation of Title VII in light of the 1991 Amendments. (In a concurring opinion we omitted, Justice Scalia suggested that this might be unconstitutional in a future case.) Interestingly, there was a provision that some lower court judges thought barred affirmative action, namely, new § 703(m), quoted above. Why did the Court not consider § 703(m) in its construction of Title VII? Indeed, why did über-textualist Justice Scalia not insist upon following § 703(m), to stick to his absolutist position in *Johnson*? (From his perspective, § 703(m) would have the virtues of codifying his *Johnson* position and avoiding the potential constitutional problems with § 703(a) as construed in *Ricci*.)

A reader of legislative history, Justice Kennedy might have been reluctant to rely on § 703(m), because it was added to the 1991 Amendments to override *Price Waterhouse v. Hopkins*, a 1989 mixed-motives case. There is no evidence that anyone in Congress thought that § 703(m) affected *Johnson* or *Weber*. But why should Justice Scalia care about this kind of evidence?

3. *Continuing the Court/Congress/President Civil Rights Game.* Notice how *Ricci* reflects the dynamic potential of the law-implementation process. Soon after the 1964 Act was adopted, the EEOC and the Court pushed Title VII to the left through liberal construction of the disparate impact claim for relief. Congress rejected proposals to trim back Title VII in the 1972 Amendments, and *Weber–Johnson* confirmed the evolution of Title VII toward a more strongly integrationist stance than Congress had probably assumed in 1964.

But the Rehnquist Court pushed the statute in a more conservative direction—and Congress pushed back with the 1991 Amendments. As *Ricci* dramatically illustrates, the 1989 Supreme Court decisions did not push Title VII back to 1964—nor did the 1991 Amendments push Title VII back to the heyday of liberal interpretation in the 1970s. Instead, Title VII's text represents a pretty detailed compromise between the Brennan (Ginsburg) vision for workplace diversity and the Rehnquist (Scalia–Alito) vision for employer color-blindness.

CHAPTER 2

THEORIES OF STATUTORY INTERPRETATION

■ ■ ■

Statutes, rather than the common law or constitutional law, have created the modern structure for American governance, most of our nation's fundamental public policies, and even many of its basic norms. Notwithstanding the "statutorification" of American law (Grant Gilmore's phrase), courts and agencies retain an important role, because they apply and interpret statutes in the "hard cases" not clearly answered by the statutory language. Such hard cases are inevitable, partly because of the inherent imprecision of language and partly because of the inability of statute drafters to anticipate all problems or circumstances within the statute's ambit. Justice Felix Frankfurter, in *Some Reflections on the Reading of Statutes*, 47 Colum. L. Rev. 527, 528 (1947), expressed this problem in his own distinctive style:

> [U]nlike mathematical symbols, the phrasing of a document, especially a complicated enactment, seldom attains more than approximate precision. If individual words are inexact symbols, with shifting variables, their configuration can hardly achieve invariant meaning or assured definiteness. Apart from the ambiguity inherent in its symbols, a statute suffers from dubieties. It is not an equation or a formula representing a clearly marked process, nor is it an expression of individual thought to which is imparted the definiteness a single authorship can give. A statute is an instrument of government partaking of its practical purposes but also of its infirmities and limitations, of its awkward and groping efforts. * * *

Thus, while Frankfurter, as a professor at Harvard Law School, had developed "his threefold imperative to law students: (1) Read the statute; (2) read the statute; (3) read the statute," Henry Friendly, *Mr. Justice Frankfurter and the Reading of Statutes*, in Friendly, *Benchmarks* 202 (1967), he appreciated the difficulty of understanding a statute simply by parsing its language. The following example illustrates Frankfurter's point. A municipal ordinance provides that "all drug shops * * * shall be closed * * * at 10 p.m. on each and every day of the week." Does this require all such shops to remain open until 10 p.m., at which time they must be closed (i.e., is "closed" used as a verb or an adjective)? If a shop is closed at 10 p.m., may it lawfully open ten minutes later? In *Rex v. Liggetts–Findlay Drug–Stores Ltd.*, [1919] 3 W.W.R. 1025, the Supreme Court of Alberta answered the latter of these questions in the negative. The judge delivering the judgment stated:

> I think no one but a lawyer—I mean a person trained in legal technicalities such as a Judge or a lawyer—would ever think of imputing such a meaning to the [ordinance]. Everyone knows what is meant by closing a shop at 10 o'clock p.m. The meaning conveyed by the words used is too obvious for doubt. The rule, of course, is that the grammatical sense must in general be adhered to but with this limitation that if it leads to an absurdity or to something meaningless an effort must be made to give some sensible reading unless the language is absolutely intractable. * * * I think we should take the words to mean what they would quite clearly mean to the ordinary person and that is that shops should be closed not only at the moment of 10 o'clock but for the rest of that day.

Under this decision, could a store lawfully open at one minute after midnight?

Most statutes do not clearly answer all the questions that might arise, and over time the number of ambiguities or unanswered questions tends to increase. This gives rise to a predicament in our constitutional system. On the one hand, it is generally assumed that "any conflict between the legislative will and the judicial will must be resolved in favor of the former." Reed Dickerson, *The Interpretation and Application of Statutes* 8 (1975). Thus, statutory interpretation is not "an opportunity for a judge to use words as 'empty vessels into which he can pour anything he will'— his caprices, fixed notions, even statesmanlike beliefs in a particular policy." Frankfurter, *Reading of Statutes, supra*, at 529. On the other hand, statutory interpretation cannot be appropriately undertaken by a mechanical application of rules or "unimaginative adherence to well-worn professional phrases." *Id.* The proper interplay among statutory language, legislative purposes, extrinsic material such as other statutes and legislative history, and the particular facts of the case at hand may not be discerned by any formula. As a consequence, statutory interpretation in the hard cases involves substantial judicial discretion and political judgment. See Richard A. Posner, *Legal Formalism, Legal Realism and the Interpretation of Statutes and the Constitution*, 37 Case W. Res. L. Rev. 179 (1987). It is very much an art and not a science.

Three different theoretical approaches have dominated the history of American judicial practice: *intentionalism*, in which the interpreter identifies and then follows the original intent of the statute's drafters; *purposivism*, in which the interpreter chooses the interpretation that best carries out the statute's purpose; and *textualism*, in which the interpreter follows the "plain meaning" of the statute's text. These different approaches rest upon different visions of the role of the interpreter and the nature of our constitutional system. Each is, of course, subject to critique.

We have organized this chapter around the following historical dynamic. For most of this country's history, both the theory and the practice of statutory interpretation have been "eclectic" rather than systematic—that is, more case-by-case and inductive than rule-oriented and deductive. After the turn of the twentieth century, judges and scholars began to formulate their thoughts more systematically. An initial impulse was to emphasize original legislative intent as the foundational enterprise in statutory cases. In turn, beginning in the 1930s an influential group of skeptics, the "legal realists," debunked original intent as an indeterminate and incoherent concept for statutory interpretation. During the New Deal, American public law turned toward purpose-based approaches as the foundation for statutory meaning. This purpose approach was reflected in the influential Hart and Sacks materials on "The Legal Process" and in opinions of both state and federal courts. Purposivism was in turn criticized for slighting traditional rule-of-law values (e.g., predictability of law, limiting judicial discretion) and for engaging courts in policy analysis for which they are ill-equipped. The "new textualism" that arose in the 1980s seeks to return statutory interpretation to textual analysis, although this approach has in turn been criticized as impractical and unrealistic.

Our goal in this theoretical and historical survey is to offer you different theories from which you can learn, even as you criticize each of them. We think you will find the history and the theory useful, both in developing your own analytical skills in interpreting statutes and in appreciating the doctrinal material presented in the remaining chapters.

SECTION 1.   FROM ECLECTICISM TO SYSTEMATIC THEORY, 1789–1938

The early history of statutory interpretation in the United States is a complicated one, with American courts employing a grab-bag variety of approaches. Following English rhetoric and practice,[a] American courts in the eighteenth and early nineteenth centuries generally proclaimed their fidelity to legislative "intent" but would consider as evidence of such intent the statute's text, canons of statutory construction, the common law, the circumstances of enactment, principles of equity, and so forth.[b] Indeed, the big debate at the time of the drafting of the Constitution was how much discretion a court's *equity* powers gave it to ameliorate or extend the letter of the statute.

---

a. See Samuel E. Thorne, *A Discourse upon the Exposicion & Understanding of Statutes* (1942) (reprinting leading early modern English treatise developing intent as lodestar of statutory interpretation). See also Peter M. Tiersma, *A Message in a Bottle: Text, Autonomy, and Statutory Interpretation*, 76 Tul. L. Rev. 431 (2001) (medieval English law treated statutes as mere "evidence of law").

b. See Hans W. Baade, *"Original Intent" in Historical Perspective: Some Critical Glosses*, 69 Tex. L. Rev. 1001, 1062–1107 (1991); Hans W. Baade, *The Casus Omissus: A Pre-History of Statutory Analogy*, 20 Syr. J. Int'l L. 45 (1994). See also William D. Popkin, *Statutes in Court: The History and Theory of Statutory Interpretation* (1999); William S. Blatt, *The History of Statutory Interpretation: A Study in Form and Substance*, 6 Cardozo L. Rev. 799 (1985).

Chief Justice John Marshall was the first great American statutory interpreter, vigorously exercising equitable powers of construction in pursuit of his nationalist understanding of the Constitution, but under cover of rigorous and sometimes brilliant textual analysis.[c] For example, his opinion in *Ex parte Bollman*, 8 U.S. (4 Cranch) 75 (1807), remains a leading construction of the federal habeas corpus law. Section 14 of the Judiciary Act of 1789 provided, in its first sentence, that the Supreme Court and other federal courts "shall have power to issue writs of *scire facias, habeas corpus*, and all other writs not specially provided for by statute, which may be necessary for the exercise of their respective jurisdictions * * *." The second sentence provided that Supreme Court Justices and district judges, in their chambers, "shall have power to grant writs of *habeas corpus* for the purpose of an inquiry into the cause of commitment." The government maintained that the Supreme Court had no jurisdiction to inquire into the legality of Bollman's confinement, as that power was only given to individual judges.

This was a good plain meaning argument, yet not one the Court was prepared to accept. Marshall suggested there was a grammatical objection to this argument but declined to rest the decision on linguistic niceties.[d] Instead, "the sound construction, which the court thinks it safer to adopt," was the one consistent with a central goal of the Constitution—to assure "that the privilege of the writ of *Habeas Corpus* should not be suspended unless when in cases of rebellion or invasion the public safety might require it." *Id.* at 95. "Acting under the immediate influence of this injunction, [Congress in 1789] must have felt, with peculiar force, the obligation of providing efficient means by which this great constitutional privilege should receive life and activity." *Id.* Given the centrality of this writ to the liberty assured by the Constitution as well as the common law, the Chief Justice reasoned "that [C]ongress could never intend to give a power of this kind, to one of the judges of this court which is refused to all of them when assembled. * * * This is not consistent with the genius of our legislation, nor with the course of our judicial proceedings." *Id.* at 96. To reconcile the first and second sentences of the confusing statute, Marshall concluded that "the first sentence vests this power in all courts of the United States; but as those courts are not always in session, the second sentence vests it in every justice or judge of the United States." *Id.* Marshall cemented his argument with precedent: the Court had implicitly

---

c. See G. Edward White, *The Marshall Court and Cultural Change, 1815–1835*, in 3 *Oliver Wendell Holmes Devise, History of the Supreme Court of the United States* (1988); William N. Eskridge Jr., *All About Words*, 101 Colum. L. Rev. (2001); John Choon Yoo, Note, *Marshall's Plan: The Early Supreme Court and Statutory Interpretation*, 101 Yale L.J. 1607 (1991).

d. Marshall noted the rule of the last antecedent: because the limiting language of the first sentence followed "and all other writs etc.," it only modified that item in the list, and not the habeas corpus item. 8 U.S. at 95. As the Chief surely recognized, this was a weak argument, in part because a comma set off the qualifying phrase from the items in the list, see Lawrence M. Solan, *The Language of Judges* 29–38 (1993) (showing that the last antecedent rule—weak to begin with—does not apply when the modifying phrase is set off from the list by a comma), and in part because the point of the first sentence seems to be the qualification, with no apparent reason for limiting it only to the third catch-all item in the list.

resolved the issue of its habeas jurisdiction by granting the writ in the 1795 case of *United States v. Hamilton*, 3 U.S. (3 Dall.) 17 (1795).

Note the eclectic mode of argumentation in *Bollman*: Marshall's opinion considered the statutory text, its purpose in light of the constitutional background, and prior precedent. Such eclecticism was characteristic of American practice throughout the nineteenth century.

Treatise-writers sought to systematize Anglo–American practice by developing elaborate lists of "canons" of statutory interpretation—most of them borrowed or derived from English treatises.[e] By the end of the century, statutory interpretation was pretty settled in practice, but was theoretically chaotic. Consider the sampler of general theoretical approaches, which we have excerpted from the Hart and Sacks "Legal Process" materials, and then consider a leading case that unsettled practice—*Holy Trinity Church.*

HENRY M. HART, JR. AND ALBERT M. SACKS, THE LEGAL PROCESS: BASIC PROBLEMS IN THE MAKING AND APPLICATION OF LAW

1111–15 (William N. Eskridge Jr. & Philip P. Frickey eds., 1994) (1958 tent. ed.)

A.　*The Mischief Rule*

HEYDON'S CASE

Exchequer, 1584
30 Co. 7a, 76 Eng. Rep. 637

* * * And it was resolved by them, that for the sure and true interpretation of all statutes in general (be they penal or beneficial, restrictive or enlarging of the common law,) four things are to be discerned and considered:—

1st. What was the common law before the making of the Act.

2nd. What was the mischief and defect for which the common law did not provide.

3rd. What remedy the Parliament hath resolved and appointed to cure the disease of the commonwealth.

And, 4th. The true reason of the remedy; and then the office of all the Judges is always to make such construction as shall suppress the mischief, and advance the remedy, and to suppress subtle inventions and evasions for continuance of the mischief, and *pro privato commodo*, and to add force and life to the cure and remedy, according to the true intent of the makers of the Act, *pro bono publico*.

---

e. See, e.g., Theodore Sedgwick, *A Treatise on the Rules Which Govern the Interpretation and Application of Statutory and Constitutional Law* (1857); J.G. Sutherland, *Statutes and Statutory Construction* (1st ed. 1891).

B. *The "Golden" Rule*

Lord Blackburn, in *River Wear Comm'rs v. Adamson*, 2 App. Cas. 743, 764 (House of Lords, 1877):

* * * But it is to be borne in mind that the office of the Judges is not to legislate, but to declare the expressed intention of the Legislature, even if that intention appears to the Court injudicious; and I believe that it is not disputed that what *Lord Wensleydale* used to call the golden rule is right, viz., that we are to take the whole statute together, and construe it all together, giving the words their ordinary signification, unless when so applied they produce an inconsistency, or an absurdity or inconvenience so great as to convince the Court that the intention could not have been to use them in their ordinary signification, and to justify the Court in putting on them some other signification, which, though less proper, is one which the Court thinks the words will bear.

C. *The Literal Rule*

Lord Atkinson, in *Vacher & Sons, Ltd. v. London Soc'y of Compositers*, [1913] App. Cas. 107, 121–22 (House of Lords):

If the language of a statute be plain, admitting of only one meaning, the Legislature must be taken to have meant and intended what it has plainly expressed, and whatever it has in clear terms enacted must be enforced though it should lead to absurd or mischievous results. If the language of this subsection be not controlled by some of the other provisions of the statute, it must, since its language is plain and unambiguous, be enforced, and your Lordships' House sitting judicially is not concerned with the question whether the policy it embodies is wise or unwise, or whether it leads to consequences just or unjust, beneficial or mischievous.

Lord Bramwell, in *Hill v. East and West India Dock Co.*, 9 App. Cas. 448, 464–65 (House of Lords, 1884):

I should like to have a good definition of what is such an absurdity that you are to disregard the plain words of an Act of Parliament. It is to be remembered that what seems absurd to one man does not seem absurd to another. * * * I think it is infinitely better, although an absurdity or an injustice or other objectionable result may be evolved as the consequence of your construction, to adhere to the words of an Act of Parliament and leave the legislature to set it right than to alter those words according to one's notion of an absurdity.

* * *

F. *A Second Breath of Fresh Air*

LIEBER, LEGAL AND POLITICAL HERMENEUTICS

(2d ed. St. Louis, 1880) pp. 17–20

IV. Let us take an instance of the simplest kind, to show in what degree we are continually obliged to resort to interpretation. By and by we shall find that the same rules which common sense teaches every one to use, in order to understand his neighbor in the most trivial intercourse, are necessary likewise, although not sufficient, for the interpretation of documents or texts of the highest importance, constitutions as well as treaties between the great nations.

Suppose a housekeeper says to a domestic: "fetch some soupmeat," accompanying the act with giving some money to the latter; he will be unable to execute the order without interpretation, however easy and, consequently, rapid the performance of the process may be. Common sense and good faith tell the domestic, that the housekeeper's meaning was this: 1. He should go immediately, or as soon as his other occupations are finished; or, if he be directed to do so in the evening, that he should go next day at the *usual* hour; 2. that the money handed him by the housekeeper is intended to pay for the meat thus ordered, and not as a present to him; 3. that he should buy such meat and of such part of the animal, as, to his knowledge, has commonly been used in the house he stays at, for making soups; 4. that he buy the best meat he can obtain, for a fair price; 5. that he go to that butcher who usually provides the family, with whom the domestic resides, with meat, or to some convenient stall, and not to any unnecessarily distant place; 6. that he return the rest of the money; 7. that he bring home the meat in good faith, neither adding anything disagreeable nor injurious; 8. that he fetch the meat for the use of the family and not for himself. Suppose, on the other hand, the housekeeper, afraid of being misunderstood, had mentioned these eight specifications, she would not have obtained her object, if it were to exclude all *possibility* of misunderstanding. For, the various specifications would have required new ones. Where would be the end? We are constrained then, always, to leave a considerable part of our meaning to be found out by interpretation, which, in many cases must necessarily cause greater or less obscurity with regard to the exact meaning, which our words were intended to convey.

Experience is a plant growing as slowly as confidence, which Chatham said increased so tardily. In fact, confidence grows slowly because it depends upon experience. The British spirit of civil liberty induced the English judges to adhere strictly to the law, to its exact expressions. This again induced the law-makers to be, in their phraseology, as explicit and minute as possible, which causes such a tautology and endless repetition in the statutes of that country that even so eminent a statesman as Sir Robert Peel declared, in parliament, that he "contemplates no task with so much distaste as the reading through an ordinary act of parliament."

Men have at length found out that little or nothing is gained by attempting to speak with absolute clearness and endless specifications, but that human speech is the clearer, the less we endeavor to supply by words and specifications that interpretation which common sense must give to human words. However minutely we may define, somewhere we [must] trust at last to common sense and good faith. * * *

RECTOR, HOLY TRINITY CHURCH v. UNITED STATES

Supreme Court of the United States, 1892
143 U.S. 457, 12 S.Ct. 511, 36 L.Ed. 226

MR. JUSTICE BREWER delivered the opinion of the Court.

Plaintiff in error is a corporation, duly organized and incorporated as a religious society under the laws of the State of New York. E. Walpole Warren was, prior to September, 1887, an alien residing in England. In that month the plaintiff in error made a contract with him, by which he was to remove to the city of New York and enter into its service as rector and pastor; and in pursuance of such contract, Warren did so remove and enter upon such service. It is claimed by the United States that this contract on the part of the plaintiff in error was forbidden by the act of February 26, 1885, 23 Stat. 332, c. 164, and an action was commenced to recover the penalty prescribed by that act. The Circuit Court held that the contract was within the prohibition of the statute, and rendered judgment accordingly, and the single question presented for our determination is whether it erred in that conclusion.

The first section describes the act forbidden, and is in these words:

"*Be it enacted by the Senate and House of Representatives of the United States of America in Congress assembled*, That from and after the passage of this act it shall be unlawful for any person, company, partnership, or corporation, in any manner whatsoever, to prepay the transportation, or in any way assist or encourage the importation or migration of any alien or aliens, any foreigner or foreigners, into the United States, its Territories, or the District of Columbia, under contract or agreement, parol or special, express or implied, made previous to the importation or migration of such alien or aliens, foreigner or foreigners, to perform labor or service of any kind in the United States, its Territories, or the District of Columbia."

It must be conceded that the act of the corporation is within the letter of this section, for the relation of rector to his church is one of service, and implies labor on the one side with compensation on the other. Not only are the general words labor and service both used, but also, as it were to guard against any narrow interpretation and emphasize a breadth of meaning, to them is added "of any kind;" and, further, as noticed by the Circuit Judge in his opinion, the fifth section, which makes specific exceptions, among them professional actors, artists, lecturers, singers and domestic servants, strengthens the idea that every other kind of labor and service was intended to be reached by the first section. While there is great force to this reasoning, we cannot think Congress intended to denounce with penalties a transaction like that in the present case. It is a familiar rule, that a thing may be within the letter of the statute and yet not within the statute, because not within its spirit, nor within the intention of its makers. This has been often asserted, and the reports are full of cases illustrating its application. This is not the substitution of the will of the judge for that of the legislator, for frequently words of general meaning are used in a statute, words broad enough to include an act in question, and yet a consideration of the whole legislation, or of the circumstances surrounding its enactment, or of the absurd results which follow from giving such broad meaning to the words, makes it unreasonable to believe that the legislator intended to include the particular act. As said in Plowden, 205: "From which cases, it appears that the sages of the law heretofore have construed statutes quite contrary to the letter in some appearance, and those statutes which comprehend all things in the letter they have expounded to extend to but some things, and those which generally prohibit all people from doing such an act they have interpreted to permit some people to do it, and those which include every person in the letter, they have adjudged to reach to some persons only, which expositions have always been founded upon the intent of the legislature, which they have collected sometimes by considering the cause and necessity of making the act, sometimes by comparing one part of the act with another, and sometimes by foreign circumstances." * * *

* * * [T]he title of this act is, "An act to prohibit the importation and migration of foreigners and aliens under contract or agreement to perform labor in the United States, its Territories and the District of Columbia." Obviously the thought expressed in this reaches only to the work of the manual laborer, as distinguished from that of the professional man. No one reading such a title would suppose that Congress had in its mind any purpose of staying the coming into this country of ministers of the gospel, or, indeed, of any class whose toil is that of the brain. The common understanding of the terms labor and laborers does not include preaching and preachers; and it is to be assumed that words and phrases are used in their ordinary meaning. So whatever of light is thrown upon the statute by the language of the title indicates an exclusion from its penal provisions of all contracts for the employment of ministers, rectors and pastors.

Again, another guide to the meaning of a statute is found in the evil which it is designed to remedy; and for this the court properly looks at contemporaneous events, the situation as it existed, and as it was pressed upon the attention of the legislative body. The situation which called for this statute was briefly but fully stated by Mr. Justice Brown when, as District Judge, he decided the case of *United States v. Craig*, 28 Fed. Rep. 795, 798: "The motives and history of the act are matters of common knowledge. It had become the practice for large capitalists in this country to contract with their agents abroad for the shipment of great numbers of an ignorant and servile class of foreign laborers, under contracts, by which the employer agreed, upon the one hand, to prepay their passage, while, upon the other hand, the laborers agreed to work after their arrival for a certain time at a low rate of wages. The effect of this was to break down the labor market, and to reduce other laborers engaged in like occupations to the level of the assisted immigrant. The evil finally became so flagrant that an appeal was made to Congress for relief by the passage of the act in question, the design of which was to raise the standard of foreign immigrants, and to discountenance the migration of those who had not sufficient means in their own hands, or those of their friends, to pay their passage."

It appears, also, from the petitions, and in the testimony presented before the committees of Congress, that it was this cheap unskilled labor which was making the trouble, and the influx of which Congress sought to prevent. It was never suggested that we had in this country a surplus of brain toilers, and, least of all, that the market for the services of Christian ministers was depressed by foreign competition. Those were matters to which the attention of Congress, or of the people, was not directed. So far, then, as the evil which was sought to be remedied interprets the statute, it also guides to an exclusion of this contract from the penalties of the act.

A singular circumstance, throwing light upon the intent of Congress, is found in this extract from the report of the Senate Committee on Education and Labor, recommending the passage of the bill: "The general facts and considerations which induce the committee to recommend the passage of this bill are set forth in the Report of the Committee of the House. The committee report the bill back without amendment, although there are certain features thereof which might well be changed or modified, in the hope that the bill may not fail of passage during the present session. Especially would the committee have otherwise recommended amendments, substituting for the expression 'labor and service,' whenever it occurs in the body of the bill, the words 'manual labor' or 'manual service,' as sufficiently broad to accomplish the purposes of the bill, and that such amendments would remove objections which a sharp and perhaps unfriendly criticism may urge to the proposed legislation. The committee, however, believing that the bill in its present form will be construed as including only those whose labor or service is manual in character, and being very desirous that the bill become a law before the adjournment, have reported the bill without change." Page 6059, Congressional Record, 48th Congress. And, referring back to the report of the Committee of the House, there appears this language: "It seeks to restrain and prohibit the immigration or importation of laborers who would have never seen our shores but for the inducements and allurements of men whose only object is to obtain labor at the lowest possible rate, regardless of the social and material well-being of our own citizens and regardless of the evil consequences which result to American laborers from such immigration. This class of immigrants care nothing about our institutions, and in many instances never even heard of them; they are men whose passage is paid by the importers; they come here under contract to labor for a certain number of years; they are ignorant of our social condition, and that they may remain so they are isolated and prevented from coming into contact with Americans. They are generally from the lowest social stratum, and live upon the coarsest food and in hovels of a character before unknown to American workmen. They, as a rule, do not become citizens, and are certainly not a desirable acquisition to the body politic. The inevitable tendency of their presence among us is to degrade American labor, and to reduce it to the level of the imported pauper labor." Page 5359, Congressional Record, 48th Congress.

We find, therefore, that the title of the act, the evil which was intended to be remedied, the circumstances surrounding the appeal to Congress, the reports of the committee of each house, all concur in affirming that the intent of Congress was simply to stay the influx of this cheap unskilled labor.

But beyond all these matters no purpose of action against religion can be imputed to any legislation, state or national, because this is a religious people. This is historically true. From the discovery of this continent to the present hour, there is a single voice making this affirmation. The commission to Christopher Columbus, prior to his sail westward, is from "Ferdinand and Isabella, by the grace of God, King and Queen of Castile," etc., and recites that "it is hoped that by God's assistance some of the continents and islands in the ocean will be discovered," etc. The first colonial grant, that made to Sir Walter Raleigh in 1584, was from "Elizabeth, by the grace of God, of England, Fraunce and Ireland, queene, defender of the faith," etc.; and the grant authorizing him to enact statutes for the government of the proposed colony provided that "they be not against the true Christian faith nowe professed in the Church of England." * * *

If we examine the constitutions of the various States we find in them a constant recognition of religious obligations. Every constitution of every one of the forty-four States contains language which either directly or by clear implication recognizes a profound reverence for religion and an assumption that its influence in all human affairs is essential to the well being of the community. This recognition may be in the preamble, such as is found in the constitution of Illinois, 1870; "We, the people of the State of Illinois, grateful to Almighty God for the civil, political and religious liberty which He hath so long permitted us to enjoy, and looking to Him for a blessing upon our endeavors to secure and transmit the same unimpaired to succeeding generations," etc. * * *

Even the Constitution of the United States, which is supposed to have little touch upon the private life of the individual, contains in the First Amendment a declaration common to the constitutions of all the States, as follows: "Congress shall make no law respecting an establishment of religion, or prohibiting the free exercise thereof," etc. And also provides in Article 1, section 7, (a provision common to many constitutions,) that the Executive shall have ten days (Sundays excepted) within which to determine whether he will approve or veto a bill. * * *

If we pass beyond these matters to a view of American life as expressed by its laws, its business, its customs and its society, we find everywhere a clear recognition of the same truth. Among other matters note the following: The form of oath universally prevailing, concluding with an appeal to the Almighty; the custom of opening sessions of all deliberative bodies and most conventions with prayer; the prefatory words of all wills, "In the name of God, amen;" the laws respecting the observance of the Sabbath, with the general cessation of all secular business, and the closing of courts, legislatures, and other similar public assemblies on that day; the churches and church organizations which abound in every city, town and hamlet; the multitude of charitable organizations existing everywhere under Christian auspices; the gigantic missionary associations, with general support, and aiming to establish Christian missions in every quarter of the globe. These, and many other matters which might be noticed, add a volume of unofficial declarations to the mass of organic utterances that this is a Christian nation. In the face of all these, shall it be believed that a Congress of the United States intended to make it a misdemeanor for a church of this country to contract for the services of a Christian minister residing in another nation?

NOTES ON HOLY TRINITY AND ECLECTICISM IN STATUTORY INTERPRETATION

1. *The Court's Eclectic Approach and the Text of the Statute.* Justice Brewer's opinion seems to follow all the theories introduced at the beginning of this section—except that it seems to violate the "literal rule" of *Vacher & Sons*. Brewer concedes that his interpretation is not "within the letter of the statute." Was his concession too quickly made?

The first definition of the term "labor" listed in the 1879 and 1886 editions of *Webster's Dictionary* was "[p]hysical toil or bodily exertion * * * hard muscular effort directed to some useful end, as agriculture, manufactures, and the like." The second definition was "[i]ntellectual exertion, mental effort." In the 1880s, judges interpreting the laws and treaties excluding Chinese "laborers" or persons brought over for "labor" held that the terms should be read in their primary popular senses, to mean "physical labor for another for wages," and therefore not to include actors, teachers, or merchants, for example. See, e.g., *In re Ho King*, 14 F. 724 (D. Or. 1883). *Webster's Dictionary's* (1879 and 1886) first, and only relevant, definition of "service" was this: "The act of serving; the occupation of a servant; the performance of labor for the benefit of another, or at another's command; the attendance of an inferior, or hired helper or slave, etc., on a superior employer, master, and the like." *Black's Law Dictionary* (1891) defined service as "being employed to serve another; duty or labor to be rendered by one person to another." Is it 100% clear that the letter of the law unambiguously supported the prosecution?[f]

---

f. See William N. Eskridge Jr., *Textualism, The Unknown Ideal?*, 96 Mich. L. Rev. 1509, 1517–19, 1533, 1539–40 (1998).

2. *The Structure of the Statute.* The prohibition is found in § 1 of the 1885 law. (Section 2 voids contracts made in violation of § 1, and § 3 provides for criminal penalties for such alien labor contracts.) Although ignored by the Court, § 4 is also relevant, holding criminally accountable the master of a ship "who shall knowingly bring within the United States * * * any alien *laborer, mechanic or artisan*" who had contracted to perform "labor or service in the United States." What light does § 4 shed on the meaning of "labor or service of any kind" in § 1? Should § 1 be read narrowly, to track the terms in § 4, or does the narrowness of § 4 confirm a broader reading for § 1? The marginal note (not part of the enacted law) describes § 4 as applying to the master of a vessel who knowingly brings "such emigrant laborer" to our shores. 23 Stat. 332 (1885).

Justice Brewer does mention § 5, a list of exemptions to the liabilities imposed by §§ 1–4. Section 5 exempts "professional actors, artists, lecturers, or singers" as well as "persons employed strictly as personal or domestic servants" from the "provisions of this act." Does the omission of ministers from § 5 confirm their inclusion in § 1? To § 4, which is also subject to the § 5 exclusions? Might a minister fall under one of the exemptions? Section 5 also provides that §§ 1–4 shall not be construed to bar "any individual from assisting any member of his family or any relative or personal friend" in migrating to the United States. If a member of the Church were a "personal friend" of Reverend Warren, would that defeat the prosecution?

3. *Legislative History as Evidence of Legislative "Intent."* To narrow what he views as the apparent plain meaning of the law, Brewer relies on the evil (or mischief) against which the Act was aimed and the inapplicability to a "brain toiler" of a statute seeking to exclude "laborers." Brewer further cites a "smoking gun" in the legislative history, specifically the Senate committee report saying that the bill was only intended to exclude people engaged in "manual labor" but that it was too late in the session to amend the statute to add that precise language. Note the two ways that Brewer deploys the idea of legislative intent: one looks to the general goal of the law and tailors the text to meet the goal ("general intent"), and the other asks what the legislators thought they were doing as to the particular issue ("specific intent"). Recall these two levels of intent at work in *Weber*, the affirmative action case in Chapter 1, § 3. Recall, too, that the *Weber* majority quoted and followed *Holy Trinity*.

The Supreme Court had essentially rewritten statutes in earlier cases, in order to avoid absurd consequences (the golden rule) or where required by common law or constitutional maxims, but both the Court and commentators followed a rule whereby legislative materials were inadmissible evidence to alter "plain" statutory meanings. Cf. *Marshall Field & Co. v. Clark*, 143 U.S. 649 (1892) (refusing to examine legislative record to evaluate argument that enrolled bill was not same as bill that passed Congress). *Holy Trinity Church* seems to be the first case where the Supreme Court rewrote the statute based upon evidence from the legislative record. A revised edition of the leading treatise cited it repeatedly and endorsed its proposition that courts could consider legislative records to figure out what the intent of the legislature was on a particular issue. See J.G. Sutherland, *Statutes and Statutory Construction* 879–83 (John Lewis ed., 2d ed. 1904). (The first edition of the Sutherland treatise, published in 1891, followed the English practice of excluding extrinsic legislative materials from consideration in statutory cases.) The federal courts in the twentieth century cited an increasing amount and variety of legislative history, a trend that abated only in the late 1980s.

4. *Legislative History the Court Missed.* Independent examination by modern scholars suggests that Brewer was right about the general intent of Congress and the problem it was addressing, see Carol Chomsky, *The Story of Holy Trinity Church v. United States: Spirit and History in Statutory Interpretation,* in *Statutory Interpretation Stories* 2, 15–23 (Eskridge, Frickey & Garrett eds. 2010), but missed important evidence bearing on legislators' specific intent. Contrary to Brewer's opinion, the alien contract labor bill was not enacted in 1884, as the Senate committee had hoped, and was brought up in the 1885 session of the 48th Congress, just before the Cleveland Administration took office. The Senate had a lengthy debate about the bill, which was amended in minor ways. Among the amendments were those expanding the exempted classes, but no amendment was proposed to make clear that "labor" referred only to "manual labor." When pressed by an opponent of the bill, who argued that § 5 discriminated against "other classes of professional men" by granting exemptions to singers and lecturers and actors, Senator Blair, the floor manager, engaged in this exchange with the opponent:

> Mr. MORGAN: * * * [If the alien] happens to be a lawyer, an artist, a painter, an engraver, a sculptor, a great author, or what not, and he comes under employment to write for a newspaper, or to write books, or to paint pictures * * * he comes under the general provisions of the bill. * * *

> Mr. BLAIR: *If that class of people are liable to become the subject-matter of such importation, then the bill applies to them. Perhaps the bill ought to be further amended.*

> Mr. MORGAN: * * * I shall propose when we get to it to put an amendment in there. I want to associate with the lecturers and singers and actors, painters, sculptors [etc.], or any person having special skill in any business, art, trade or profession. * * *

16 Cong. Rec. 1633 (1885) (emphasis added). The House floor manager, Representative Hopkins, responded to an inquiry regarding agricultural workers by saying that the bill "prohibits the importation under contract of all classes with the exceptions named in [§ 5]." 16 Cong. Rec. 2032 (1885). Does this more complete record undermine Brewer's conclusion? See Adrian Vermeule, *Judging Under Uncertainty* 86–117 (2006) (filling in this gap in Brewer's deployment of legislative history and concluding that the judiciary was and remains incompetent to evaluate legislative history).

There is more legislative history that both the Court and subsequent commentators also missed. What is the relationship between § 1, with seemingly broad application to "labor or service of any kind," and § 4, with narrower application only to "labor or service" by "any alien laborer, mechanic, or artisan"? Senator Blair repeatedly assured his colleagues that § 4 was aimed at "the man who knowingly brings an immigrant * * * who comes here under and by virtue of a contract such as is prohibited by [§ 1] of the bill." 16 Cong. Rec. 1630 (1885); accord *id.* at 779 (Senator Miller), 1626

(Blair), 1629 (Senator McPherson), 1785 (Blair). We are not aware of any on-the-record statement to the contrary. Should this evidence influence the Court's understanding of the relationship between §§ 1 and 4? See William N. Eskridge Jr., *No Frills Textualism*, 119 Harv. L. Rev. 2041, 2065–70 (2006).

5. *Subsequent Legislation.* After the federal circuit court in the Southern District of New York construed the statute to apply to Reverend Warren in the *Holy Trinity Church* litigation, Congress amended the alien contract labor law to exempt ministers and professionals generally. Reversing the lower court, the Supreme Court in *Holy Trinity* did not mention the 1891 statute, which by its terms did not apply to pending proceedings, Act of March 3, 1891, § 12, 26 Stat. 1084, 1086. Does this later statute vindicate, or undermine, the Court's holding? Cf. *United States v. Laws*, 163 U.S. 258, 265 (1896) (discussing the 1891 amendment).

6. *What About the "Christian Nation" Discussion?* We are not aware of any strong reaction in 1892, but current readers might be taken aback by *Holy Trinity*'s invocation of the "Christian nation" analysis to clinch the Court's argument. (Born of Christian missionaries in Asia Minor, Justice Brewer was something of an evangelical jurist.) Was this critical to the Court's opinion? Would Justice Brewer have exempted a doctor from the statute's exclusion, for example? Cf. *Laws* (determining whether the 1885 law covered chemists).

Review the competing English approaches to statutory interpretation presented by Hart and Sacks. Note that *Holy Trinity Church* draws from two of them—the golden rule, under which statutory text need not be followed if it produces an absurd result, and the mischief rule, promoting statutory purpose as the touchstone of statutory meaning. The doctrine of precedent in the United States, however, only counsels later courts to adhere to the holding of prior cases, not to the methodology used in those cases to reach the holding; consequently, *Holy Trinity Church* in no way conclusively resolved how federal courts would henceforth undertake the interpretation of statutes.[g] Indeed, although *Holy Trinity Church* gave barely a passing reference to the force of literalism in statutory interpretation, the other English approach identified by Hart and Sacks, some other Supreme Court cases around the turn of the twentieth century embraced literalism. These cases promoted the *plain meaning rule*—if the statutory text had a "plain meaning," that was the end of the interpretive enterprise (one did not go on to consult legislative

---

g. In other words, under *stare decisis*, the lower courts were bound to interpret the immigration statute at issue in *Holy Trinity Church* as authorizing the entry of "brain toilers" into the United States, but not strictly bound to follow the golden rule and mischief rule in determining the meaning of statutes. To take another example, consistent with *Weber* (Chapter 1, § 3), lower courts are required to interpret Title VII of the 1964 Civil Rights Act as not prohibiting certain kinds of affirmative action in employment—but not bound to use *Weber*'s strongly purposive, nonliteral, *Holy Trinity Church* approach to the interpretation of statutes in general. At most, under the idea of adhering to judicial tradition, *Weber* might most strongly influence the interpretive method taken to other sections of the Civil Rights Act, less so that taken to other civil rights statutes, and even less so that taken to different sorts of statutes. The judge who uses the *Weber* method outside the civil rights area is using the method because she finds it persuasive on its own terms, not because of any strong sense of obligation. For discussion of the difference between *stare decisis* as to holding and as to methodology used to reach the holding, see Sydney Foster, *Should Courts Give Stare Decisis Effect to Statutory Interpretation Methodology?*, 96 Geo. L.J. 1863 (2008); Philip P. Frickey, *Interpretive–Regime Change*, 38 Loy. L.A. L. Rev. 1971 (2005).

history, statutory purpose, or other potential sources of meaning). The most famous of these cases follows.

Caminetti v. United States, 242 U.S. 470 (1917). A federal statute criminalized the transportation of, or the inducement to travel of, "any woman or girl to go from one place to another in interstate or foreign commerce, or in any territory or the District of Columbia, for the purpose of prostitution or debauchery, or for any other immoral purpose * * *." The case concerned a man who brought a woman from Sacramento, California, to Reno, Nevada, to "become his mistress and concubine." The Court, per **Justice Day**, stated that "it is elementary that the meaning of a statute must, in the first instance, be sought in the language in which the act is framed, and if that is plain, and if the law is within the constitutional authority of the lawmaking body which passed it, the sole function of the courts is to enforce it according to its terms." The majority found the statutory meaning plain—the conduct in question was for an "immoral purpose"—and held that Caminetti violated the statute. It refused to consider the title to the Act ("the White Slave Traffic Act") or legislative history suggesting that the purpose of the statute was narrower than its plain meaning (to reach only "commercialized vice").

The majority did not cite *Holy Trinity Church*, but **Justice McKenna**, joined in dissent by two other Justices, relied on it for the proposition that "the words of the statute should be construed to execute [the statutory purpose], and they may be so construed even if their literal meaning be otherwise." The dissent also argued that the statutory text was not plain: "other immoral purpose" should not be read literally and in isolation, but in light of the limiting words preceding them. As illuminated by the legislative history and by the principle that statutes should be read with "common sense" to avoid absurd applications, the statute should not reach "the occasional immoralities of men and women," but rather the "systematized and mercenary immorality epitomized in the statute's graphic phrase 'white slave traffic.'"

Although the free-wheeling approach of *Holy Trinity Church* may seem worlds apart from the mechanical approach of *Caminetti*, one might worry that unarticulated judicial values played a heavy role in both cases. That is, the Court would stick with literalism (*Caminetti*), or trump literalism with the mischief approach and the golden rule (*Holy Trinity Church*), in order to reach the interpretation that better matched its sensibilities. In *Caminetti*, for example, Justice McKenna's dissent stated that "[t]here is much in the present case to tempt to a violation of the [mischief] rule. Any measure that protects the purity of women from assault or enticement to degradation finds an instant advocate in our best emotions; but the judicial function cannot yield to emotion * * *." Similarly, in *Holy Trinity Church* the Court's importation of "Christian nation" and other reasoning to rework the statute caused anxiety among progressive commentators, the same people who would later decry the Court's opinion in *Lochner v. New York*, 198 U.S. 45 (1905) (invalidating a state statute establishing the maximum hours per week certain employees could be required to work on the ground that the due process clause protects economic liberty against unjustified regulation). For progressives who favored aggressive legislation supplanting the common law, decisions like *Lochner* and *Holy Trinity Church* sent the same message of judicial reluctance to accept new statutes. Dean Roscoe Pound of Harvard, the founder of sociological jurisprudence, laid out the following theory of statutory interpretation, designed to cabin judicial willfulness. Recall his argument that statutes should be a source of principles affecting the common law (Chapter 6, § 1).

Roscoe Pound, *Spurious Interpretation*, 7 Colum. L. Rev. 379, 381 (1907). "The object of genuine interpretation is to discover the rule which the law-maker intended to establish; to discover the intention which the law-maker made the rule, or the sense which he attached to the words wherein the rule is expressed. Its object is to enable others to derive from the language used 'the same idea which the author intended to convey.' Employed for these purposes, interpretation is purely judicial in character; and so long as the ordinary means of interpretation, namely the literal meaning of the language used and the context, are resorted to, there can be no question. But when, as often happens, these primary indices to the meaning and intention of the law-maker fail to lead to a satisfactory result, and recourse must be had to the reason and spirit of the rule, or to the intrinsic merit of the several possible interpretations, the line between a genuine ascertaining of the meaning of the law, and the making over of the law under guise of interpretation, becomes more difficult. Strictly, both are means of genuine interpretation. * * * The former means of interpretation tries to find out directly what the law-maker meant by assuming his position, in the surroundings in which he acted, and endeavoring to gather from the mischiefs he had to meet and the remedy by which he sought to meet them, his intention with respect to the particular point in controversy. The latter, if the former fails to yield sufficient light, seeks to reach the intent of the law-maker indirectly. It assumes that the law-maker thought as we do on general questions of morals and policy and fair dealing. Hence it assumes that of several possible interpretations the one which appeals most to our sense of right and justice for the time being is most likely to give the meaning of those who framed the rule. If resorted to in the first instance, or without regard to the other means of interpretation, this could not be regarded as a means of genuine interpretation. But inherent difficulties of expression and want of care in drafting require continual resort to this means of interpretation for the legitimate purpose of ascertaining what the law-maker in fact meant.

"On the other hand, the object of spurious interpretation is to make, unmake, or remake, and not merely to discover. It puts a meaning into the text as a juggler puts coins, or what not, into a dummy's hair, to be pulled forth presently with an air of discovery. It is essentially a legislative, not a judicial process, made necessary in formative periods by the paucity of principles, feebleness of legislation, and rigidity of rules characteristic of archaic law. * * *

"Spurious interpretation is an anachronism in an age of legislation. It is a fiction. * * *

" * * * Rigid constitutions, difficult of amendment, * * * are presenting to modern common-law courts the same problem which the rigid formalism of archaic procedure, and the terse obscurity of ancient codes, put before the jurists of antiquity. Cases must be decided, and they must be decided in the long run so as to accord with the moral sense of the community. This is the good side of spurious interpretation. It is this situation that provokes the general popular demand for judicial amendment of constitutions, state and federal, under the guise of interpretation.

"Looking at the matter purely from the standpoint of expediency, * * * the bad features of spurious interpretation, as applied to the modern state, may be said to be three: (1) That it tends to bring law into disrepute, (2) that it subjects the courts to political pressure, (3) that it reintroduces the personal element into judicial administration. * * * "

NOTES ON INTERPRETATION AS DETERMINATION OF LEGISLATIVE *"INTENT"*

1. *"Genuine Interpretation" versus "Spurious Interpretation."* Dean Pound assumes that "genuine interpretation" means ascertaining the meaning a speaker intended to convey when uttering a statement. His approach may seem simple, but in fact it raises highly controversial questions at the core of statutory interpretation theory. On his understanding, textual meaning and authorial intent are not separable concepts: the text has no autonomous significance; it merely consists of signifiers encoding an intended message, however difficult it might be for the interpreter to decode that message. This understanding retains force for some students of interpretation today, both in law and other fields.[h]

Thus, one cannot speak about the "plain meaning" of statutory text in isolation and be engaged in "interpretation" at all. In this way, Pound denies that the "plain meaning" approach to statutory construction constitutes "interpretation"—unless the best textual meaning is simply used as good evidence of legislative intent, to be supplemented by any other evidence of legislative intent available. On this reading, his argument is a remarkable rejection of literalism in statutory interpretation. It also suggests that purposivism is "genuine interpretation," but only so long as the interpreter sticks as closely as possible to the probable purposes that animated the enacting legislature and avoids imposing her own views of appropriate public-policy purposes upon the statute.

What should we make of Pound's analysis? Is it merely a definitional fight, or is more at stake than that? For example, one might speculate that Pound wants interpreters who deviate from legislative intentions to call their approach something other than "interpretation"—that term sounds neutral and legitimate, and its usage may conceal the difficult normative questions that arise when, in a democracy such as ours, interpreters essentially revise

---

h. Joseph Raz, *Intention in Interpretation*, in *The Autonomy of Law: Essays on Legal Positivism* 249, 258 (Robert George ed. 1996); Lawrence M. Solan, *The Language of Statutes* (2010) (detailed examination of "intent" for corporate bodies, including legislatures). See also Paul Campos, *That Obscure Object of Desire: Hermeneutics and the Autonomous Text*, 77 Minn. L. Rev. 1065 (1993); Paul Campos, *Against Constitutional Theory*, 4 Yale J.L. & Human. 279 (1992); Caleb Nelson, *What Is Textualism?*, 91 Va. L. Rev. 347 (2005) (arguing that both textualists and legislative history readers are, at bottom, seeking evidence of "legislative intent"). Compare John F. Manning, *Textualism and Legislative Intent*, 91 Va. L. Rev. 419 (2005) (arguing that textualists are not fundamentally seeking to apply "intent," which they consider an unhelpful and misleading construct).

statutes contrary to original legislative expectations, even if the revised understanding of the statute promotes justice or other laudable goals. Pound is not saying that what he calls "spurious interpretation" is always illegitimate; his point is that it should be called what it actually is—"revising to promote justice" or whatever—and debated on its own merits.

2. *Ascertaining Legislative Intent: Actual/Specific Intent versus Imaginative Reconstruction.* Pound proposes that interpreters follow legislative "intent," but admits that this method is frequently difficult to implement. Based on his excerpt, one might divide his vision of interpretation into two categories. First, and foremost, if the interpreter has clear evidence of the *actual (specific) intent* of the enacting legislature about what the statute should mean in the context under consideration, the interpreter should, of course, follow it. Second, because strong evidence of actual intent will often be absent, the interpreter usually must engage in a second-best inquiry, what we might call the *imaginative reconstruction of legislative intent.* This approach requires the interpreter to put herself in the position of the enacting legislature and, like a historian, examine the available historical evidence against a background of assumptions about the legislature (that it would prefer justice to injustice, for example) that are commonplace to our legal system, but can be rebutted by evidence that this enacting legislature had a different view (for example, that it defined "justice" and "injustice" differently than the interpreter would).[i] These remain the two fundamental inquiries of intentionalist interpretation today. Note that for both, the statutory text is important because it frequently will be the best evidence of legislative intent.

3. *Federal Court Reception of the Pound Approach.* The Supreme Court grew increasingly interested in what legislators actually expected out of their statutes, e.g., *Johnson v. Southern Pacific Company,* 196 U.S. 1 (1904), though the Court did not always follow legislative history (recall *Caminetti*). Consider *Duplex Printing Press Co. v. Deering,* 254 U.S. 443 (1921), which interpreted the Clayton Act to justify an injunction against a secondary boycott by print workers against an "unfair" employer. Although the Clayton Act contained two broad provisions exempting most labor activity from antitrust regulation, the Court held that it was not the actual intent of Congress to insulate labor boycotts from regulation. The Court relied on a statement by the Clayton Act's House floor manager that neither he nor any member of the reporting committee intended the bill to exempt boycotts from the regulation courts had imposed on them under the older Sherman Act. Justice Brandeis's dissenting opinion railed against this narrowing interpretation, also based upon the actual, subjective expectations of the enacting Congress. (Brandeis was a close adviser of President Wilson, who had proposed the Clayton Act, and hence had an "inside view" of the Act.)

The classic early practitioner of imaginative reconstruction was Judge Learned Hand of the Second Circuit, one of the judges reversed in *Duplex Printing.* See, e.g., *Lehigh Valley Coal Co. v. Yensavage,* 218 F. 547, 553 (2d

---

i. Pound's statement of imaginative reconstruction is taken from the commentary to *Eyston v. Studd,* (1574) 2 Plowden 459, 467, 75 Eng. Rep. 688, 699 (K.B), paraphrasing Aristotle, *The Nicomachean Ethics* bk. V, ch. 10 (J.O. Urmson ed., W.D. Ross tr., rev. ed. 1984). For a modern exposition of this approach, see Richard A. Posner, *The Federal Courts: Crisis and Reform* 286–93 (1985).

Cir. 1914); Archibald Cox, *Judge Learned Hand and the Interpretation of Statutes*, 60 Harv. L. Rev. 370 (1947). Consider the following exemplar of Pound's theory.

Fishgold v. Sullivan Drydock and Repair Corp., 154 F.2d 785 (2d Cir. 1946), *aff'd*, 328 U.S. 275 (1946). Section 8(b)(B) of the Selective Training & Service Act of 1940, 49 Stat. 888, 890, as amended in 1944, provided that the private employer of a person who had left employment for U.S. military service and then sought to return to the same position after discharge from the service "shall restore such person to such position or to a position of like seniority, status, and pay unless the employer's circumstances have so changed as to make it impossible or unreasonable to do so." Section 8(c) provided:

> Any person who is restored to a position in accordance with the provisions of paragraph (A) or (B) of subsection (b) shall be considered as having been on furlough or leave of absence during his period of training and service in the land or naval forces, shall be so restored without loss of seniority * * * and shall not be discharged from such position without cause within one year after such restoration.

Fishgold returned from service in the army during World War II and then was laid off within a year, while non-veteran employees who had more seniority were not laid off. Fishgold challenged the decision to lay him off, relying on § 8(c). **Judge Hand**'s opinion concluded that the layoff was legal. He avoided the thrust of § 8(c)'s protection against "discharge" by noting that its dictionary definition was a permanent termination of employment, rather than the temporary termination denoted by "layoff." This reflects the traditional labor law distinction between being terminated or fired (the employment relationship is severed) and being laid off (the employee is not employed but might be recalled to employment). Seniority typically affords virtually absolute protection against discharge or termination but only limited protection against layoffs.

Judge Hand was also sensitive to the general policy preferences favoring veterans that were being considered and enacted after World War II, but dispatched the policy argument as follows:

> When we consider the situation at the time that the Act was passed— September, 1940—it is extremely improbable that Congress should have meant to grant any broader privilege than as we are measuring it. * * * The original act limited service to one year, and it was most improbable that within that time we should be called upon to fight upon our own soil; as indeed the event proved, for we were still at peace in September, 1941. Congress was calling young men to the colors to give them an adequate preparation for our defence, but with no forecast of the appalling experiences which they were later to undergo. Against that background it is not likely that a proposal would then have been accepted which gave industrial priority, regardless of their length of employment, to unmarried men— for the most part under thirty—over men in the thirties, forties or fifties, who had wives and children dependent upon them. Today, in the light of what has happened, the privilege then granted may appear an altogether inadequate equivalent for their services; but we have not to decide what

is now proper; we are to reconstruct, as best we may, what was the purpose of Congress when it used the words in which § 8(b) and § 8(c) were cast.

Judge Chase dissented, based upon a broader view of the statute's purpose.

Max Radin, Statutory Interpretation, 43 Harv. L. Rev. 863, 870–71 (1930). "It has frequently been declared that the most approved method is to discover the intent of the legislator. * * * On this transparent and absurd fiction it ought not to be necessary to dwell. It is clearly enough an illegitimate transference to law of concepts proper enough in literature and theology. * * *

"That the intention of the legislature is undiscoverable in any real sense is almost an immediate inference from a statement of the proposition. The chances that of several hundred men each will have exactly the same determinate situations in mind as possible reductions of a given [statutory issue], are infinitesimally small. * * * In an extreme case, it might be that we could learn all that was in the mind of the draftsman, or of a committee of half a dozen men who completely approved of every word. But when this draft is submitted to the legislature and at once accepted without a dissentient voice and without debate, what have we then learned of the intentions of the four or five hundred approvers? Even if the contents of the minds of the legislature were uniform, we have no means of knowing that content except by the external utterances or behavior of these hundreds of men, and in almost every case the only external act is the extremely ambiguous one of acquiescence, which may be motivated in literally hundreds of ways, and which by itself indicates little or nothing of the pictures which the statutory descriptions imply. * * *

"And if [legislative intent] were discoverable, it would be powerless to bind us. What gives the intention of the legislature obligating force? * * * [I]n law, the specific individuals who make up the legislature are men to whom a specialized function has been temporarily assigned. That function is not to impose their will even within limits on their fellow citizens, but to 'pass statutes,' which is a fairly precise operation. That is, they make statements in general terms of undesirable and desirable situations, from which flow certain results. * * * When the legislature has uttered the words of a statute, it is *functus officio*, not because of the Montesquieuean separation of powers, but because that is what legislating means. The legislature might also be a court and an executive, but it can never be all three things simultaneously.

"And once the words are out, recorded, engrossed, registered, proclaimed, inscribed in bronze, they in turn become instrumentalities which administrators and courts must use in performing their own specialized functions. The principal use is that of 'interpretation.' Interpretation is an act which requires an existing determinate event—the issue to be litigated—and obviously that determinate event cannot exist until after the statute has come into force. To say that the intent of the legislature decides the interpretation is to say that the legislature interprets in advance * * * a situation which does not exist."

NOTES ON EARLY CRITIQUES OF INTENTIONALIST APPROACHES

1. *The Narrow Role of Legislatures.* Radin's last point, that legislatures exist only to pass statutes and not to impose their will on the citizenry, echoed Oliver Wendell Holmes, who insisted that in a "government of laws, not men," legal standards must be external to the decisionmaker. Oliver Wendell Holmes, *The Common Law* 41, 44 (1881). "[W]e ask, not what this man meant, but what those words would mean in the mouth of a normal speaker of English, using them in the circumstances in which they were used. * * * [T]he normal speaker of English is merely a special variety, a literary form, so to speak, of our old friend the prudent man. He is external to the particular writer, and a reference to him as the criterion is simply another instance of the externality of law. * * * We do not inquire what the legislature meant; we ask only what the statute means." Oliver Wendell Holmes, *The Theory of Legal Interpretation*, 12 Harv. L. Rev. 417, 417–18, 419 (1899).

But "what the statute means" is not always clear. If the law is ambiguous, should interpreters consider the expectations of the legislators who wrote the statute?[j] If a judge were interpreting a contract, would the judge prefer an interpretation that reconstructs the intent or expectations of the parties to one that the parties did not want? Shouldn't a court pay at least as much attention to the intent of Congress, not only because Congress drafts and enacts statutes, but also because Congress-acting-with-the-President (as required by Article I, § 7) is the "supreme" lawmaking authority in our constitutional democracy?[k]

2. *The Incoherence or Indeterminacy of Collective Intent.* Radin responds that legislative intent is incoherent or undiscoverable. It is incoherent to the extent that a collective body cannot easily be charged with having an "intent." As political scientist Kenneth Shepsle subsequently put it, "Congress is a They, not an It."[l] Intent is undiscoverable because too little evidence of collective understanding finds its way into the public record, and even when reported is hard to interpret. Also, how can the different "intents" of the House, Senate, and President be aggregated?

These are logical quarrels, but there is another way of looking at this matter. If the President or the Board of Directors of a company negotiates a contract with Joan Doe, the President's or Board's representations might be taken to be those of the company itself. As linguist and legal scholar Lawrence Solan has argued, both common sense and the law routinely attribute "intent" to collective bodies based upon the purposive declarations made by subgroups or agents publicly deputized to deliberate for the whole group.[m]

---

j. See Frederick de Sloovère, *Textual Interpretation of Statutes*, 11 N.Y.U. L. Rev. 538 (1934); cf. *Boston Sand & Gravel Co. v. United States*, 278 U.S. 41, 48 (1928) (Holmes, J.) (consulting legislative history to figure out "what the statute means").

k. For elaboration, see Daniel A. Farber, *Statutory Interpretation and Legislative Supremacy*, 78 Geo. L.J. 281 (1989).

l. Kenneth A. Shepsle, *Congress Is a "They," Not an "It": Legislative Intent as Oxymoron*, 12 Int'l Rev. L. & Econ. 239 (1992). See also Frank Easterbrook, *Text, History, and Structure in Statutory Interpretation*, 17 Harv. J.L. & Pub. Pol'y 61 (1994).

m. Lawrence M. Solan, *Private Language, Public Laws: The Central Role of Legislative Intent in Statutory Interpretation*, 93 Geo. L.J. 427, 437–49 (2005). See also Margaret Gilbert, *Sociability*

Political scientists make the same point about committees and sponsors in Congress.[n] In the same manner, statements by sponsors and committees might reasonably be thought to represent congressional consensus unless denied by other Members. Arguably, this is an institutional convention that is reasonable, and that Congress can be expected to adjust to (through better monitoring) if it yields results that systematically fail to reflect legislative bargains or consensuses.[o]

3. *The Inevitability of Interpretive Discretion and Interstitial Lawmaking?* A further critique of imaginative reconstruction is that it is more "imaginative" than it is "reconstruction." Judges in the early twentieth century were considered hidebound and hostile to many legislative innovations. The enthusiasm Pound and Hand felt for imaginative reconstruction was, in part, motivated by the need to tie judges more closely to progressive developments in the legislature. This was only partially achieved at the Supreme Court level, for imaginative reconstruction could also be utilized by conservatives bending statutes their way, as in *Duplex Printing* and *Holy Trinity Church*, and then ignoring legislative expectations in cases like *Caminetti*.

An underlying theme of Radin's article is that the nature of the judicial process—application of generally phrased statutes to unforeseen fact situations by an independent and co-equal branch of government—assures discretion. Cf. Benjamin Cardozo, *The Nature of the Judicial Process* 166 (1921) (asserting that judicial decisionmaking "in its highest reaches is not discovery but creation"). This suggests the possibility that often statutory interpretation might be "spurious," to use Pound's provocative label, or at least not an easy exercise in imaginative reconstruction.

The debates over statutory interpretation took several important turns in the 1930s.[p] The unprecedented degree of statute-making during the New Deal vindicated Pound's earlier arguments that the twentieth century would be the age of legislatures rather than courts, but this statutory binge also vindicated Radin's points that there was unlikely to be a clear legislative intent (reconstructed or otherwise) on any but a handful of issues and that interpretive discretion was required. During the New Deal and right before U.S. entry into World War II, an academic consensus found a way to accept both points of view. This approach, whose outlines were clear in the period from 1938–41,[q]

---

and Responsibility: New Essays in Plural Subject Theory (2000) (developing this idea along the lines of linguistic theory).

n. Daniel B. Rodriguez & Barry R. Weingast, *The Positive Political Theory of Legislative History: New Perspectives on the 1964 Civil Rights Act and Its Interpretation*, 151 U. Pa. L. Rev. 1417 (2003).

o. See James M. Landis, *A Note on "Statutory Interpretation,"* 43 Harv. L. Rev. 886, 888–90 (1930) (responding to Radin's article); McNollgast, *Positive Canons: The Role of Legislative Bargains in Statutory Interpretation*, 80 Geo. L.J. 705 (1992).

p. See our "Historical and Critical Introduction," in Henry M. Hart Jr. & Albert M. Sacks, *The Legal Process: Basic Problems in the Making and Application of Law* (William N. Eskridge Jr. & Philip P. Frickey eds. 1994).

q. The leading precursors of the budding legal process theory were Lon L. Fuller, *The Law in Quest of Itself* (1940); Harry Willmer Jones, *Statutory Doubts and Legislative Intention*, 40 Colum. L. Rev. 957 (1940); Frederick de Sloovère, *Extrinsic Aids in the Interpretation of Statutes*, 88 U. Pa. L. Rev. 527 (1940); A.B. Feller, Walter Gellhorn & Henry M. Hart Jr., "Materials on blossomed into "legal process" theory after World War II, to which our next Section turns.

PROBLEM 2–1

Imaginative Reconstruction Applied

(A) How would Judge Hand and Dean Pound have voted if they were presented with the statutory issue in *Holy Trinity Church*?

(B) Recall the *Weber* case from Chapter 1. How would Judge Hand and Dean Pound have voted in *Weber*? What might Professor Radin have said in that case?

(C) Williams tells her servant to "fetch me some soupmeat" from "Store X" (recall Lieber's hypothetical). The servant goes to Store X and discovers that the store only has one pound of soupmeat left, and it looks old and wormy. The servant knows that Store Y also carries soupmeat and, upon inspection, sees that Store Y's soupmeat looks pretty good. How would the following "servants" interpret the boss' command: Judge Hand? Justice Holmes? What do you think the proper interpretation is? Is statutory interpretation similar to this example?

SECTION 2. LEGAL PROCESS THEORIES OF INTERPRETATION

A. THE LEGAL PROCESS CLASSICS, 1940s–50s

The consensus about public law issues reached by intellectuals between 1938 and 1941 was reflected, after World War II, in Supreme Court decisions, law review articles, and teaching materials dealing with statutory issues. This consensus gave rise to "legal process theory." The following materials are the two legal process classics regarding issues of statutory interpretation.

LON L. FULLER, THE CASE OF THE SPELUNCEAN EXPLORERS

62 Harv. L. Rev. 616, 619–21, 623–26, 628–40 (1949) (tent. ed. 1958)*

TRUEPENNY, C.J. [The members of the Speluncean Society were amateur cave explorers. In May 4299, several members, including Roger Whetmore, were trapped in a cave because of a rockslide. Rescue efforts were delayed for various reasons, such as fresh rockslides, and the explorers were not rescued until the 32d day of their ordeal. Communication with the explorers was established on day 20 of the ordeal, and the explorers learned that they would not likely be rescued for another ten days, that they would probably die if they did not have sustenance within

---

Legislation" (1st ed. 1941–42) (teaching materials at Columbia, Yale, Harvard); Lloyd K. Garrison & J. Willard Hurst, "Law in Society" (1940 & 1941) (teaching materials at Wisconsin).

* Copyright 1949 by the Harvard Law Review Association. Reprinted by permission.

that period, and that they would probably not die if they cannibalized one of their number; the last datum was reluctantly conveyed by a doctor in response to the explorers' specific inquiry. After assimilating the doctor's predictions, all of the explorers agreed that one of them must die, and they further agreed that the person to die would be chosen by lots (rolls of the dice). Whetmore agreed to both propositions and suggested the method of lots, but before the dice were rolled he declared his withdrawal from the plan. The other explorers proceeded with the agreement, and Whetmore was the one chosen by lots. On the 23d day of their ordeal, the explorers killed and dined on Whetmore. After the surviving explorers were saved, they were indicted for the murder of Whetmore.]

[At trial, the foreman of the jury (a lawyer) asked the judge whether the jury could return a special verdict and leave it to the judge to determine guilt or innocence. With the agreement of the prosecutor and counsel for defendants, the judge agreed. The jury found the facts as related above. The trial judge ruled the defendants guilty based upon these facts and (according to the nondiscretionary requirement of the sentencing law) sentenced them to death by hanging. Both jury and judge issued communications to the Chief Executive seeking commutation of defendants' sentence to six months' imprisonment.]

* * * The language of our statute is well known: "Whoever shall willfully take the life of another shall be punished by death." N. C. S. A. (N. S.) § 12–A. This statute permits of no exception applicable to this case, however our sympathies may incline us to make allowance for the tragic situation in which these men found themselves.

In a case like this the principle of executive clemency seems admirably suited to mitigate the rigors of the law, and I propose to my colleagues that we follow the example of the jury and the trial judge by joining in the communications they have addressed to the Chief Executive. * * * I think we may therefore assume that some form of clemency will be extended to these defendants. If this is done, then justice will be accomplished without impairing either the letter or spirit of our statutes and without offering any encouragement for the disregard of law.

FOSTER, J. * * * If this Court declares that under our law these men have committed a crime, then our law is itself convicted in the tribunal of common sense * * *.

* * * I take the view that the enacted or positive law of this Commonwealth, including all of its statutes and precedents, is inapplicable to this case, and that the case is governed instead by what ancient writers in Europe and America called "the law of nature." [Judge Foster argued that once the reason for law disappears, so too does the law itself. As a matter of political morality, the defendants' conduct was justified by the agreement they entered into that ensured the survival of five at the expense of one.]

This concludes the exposition of the first ground of my decision. My second ground proceeds by rejecting hypothetically all the premises on which I have so far proceeded. I concede for purposes of argument that I am wrong in saying that the situation of these men removed them from the effect of our positive law, and I assume that the Consolidated Statutes have the power to penetrate five hundred feet of rock and to impose themselves upon these starving men huddled in their underground prison.

Now it is, of course, perfectly clear that these men did an act that violates the literal wording of the statute which declares that he who "shall willfully take the life of another" is a murderer. But one of the most ancient bits of legal wisdom is the saying that a man may break the letter of the law without breaking the law itself. Every proposition of positive law, whether contained in a statute or a judicial precedent, is to be interpreted reasonably, in the light of its evident purpose. * * *

The statute before us for interpretation has never been applied literally. Centuries ago it was established that a killing in self-defense is excused. There is nothing in the wording of the statute that suggests this exception. Various attempts have been made to reconcile the legal treatment of self-defense with the words of the statute, but in my opinion these are all merely ingenious sophistries. The truth is that the exception in favor of self-defense cannot be reconciled with the *words* of the statute, but only with its *purpose*.

The true reconciliation of the excuse of self-defense with the statute making it a crime to kill another is to be found in the following line of reasoning. One of the principal objects underlying any criminal legislation is that of deterring men from crime. Now it is apparent that if it were declared to be the law that a killing in self-defense is murder such a rule could not operate in a deterrent manner. A man whose life is threatened will repel his aggressor, whatever the law may say. Looking therefore to the broad purposes of criminal legislation, we may safely declare that this statute was not intended to apply to cases of self-defense. * * *

* * * [P]recisely the same reasoning is applicable to the case at bar. If in the future any group of men ever find themselves in the tragic predicament of these defendants, we may be sure that their decision whether to live or die will not be controlled by the contents of our criminal code. * * * The withdrawal of this situation from the effect of this statute is justified by precisely the same considerations that were applied by our predecessors in office centuries ago to the case of self-defense.

* * * The line of reasoning I have applied above raises no question of fidelity to enacted law, though it may possibly raise a question of the distinction between intelligent and unintelligent fidelity. No superior wants a servant who lacks the capacity to read between the lines. The stupidest housemaid knows that when she is told "to peel the soup and skim the potatoes" her mistress does not mean what she says. She also knows that when her master tells her to "drop everything and come running" he has overlooked the possibility that she is at the moment in the act of rescuing the baby from the rain barrel. Surely we have a right to expect the same modicum of intelligence from the judiciary. The

correction of obvious legislative errors or oversights is not to supplant the legislative will, but to make that will effective. * * *

TATTING, J. [This jurist responds to both arguments raised by Judge Foster. At what point, exactly, did the explorers find themselves back in a state of nature? Even if they were in a state of nature, by what authority or right can the Court resolve itself into a "Court of Nature"? Isn't the propounded code of nature a "topsy-turvy and odious" one? "It is a code in which the law of contracts is more fundamental than the law of murder." Would Whetmore have had a defense if he had shot his assailants as they set upon him? For these reasons, Judge Tatting cannot join Judge Foster's first reason. Nor can he join the second.]

* * * It is true that a statute should be applied in the light of its purpose, and that *one* of the purposes of criminal legislation is recognized to be deterrence. The difficulty is that other purposes are also ascribed to the law of crimes. It has been said that one of its objects is to provide an orderly outlet for the instinctive human demand for retribution. It has also been said that its object is the rehabilitation of the wrongdoer. Other theories have been propounded. Assuming that we must interpret a statute in the light of its purpose, what are we to do when it has many purposes or when its purposes are disputed?

[These other purposes provide a different explanation for self-defense as outside the murder prohibition. The statute requires a "willful" act, but the person who acts to repel a threat to life is not acting "willfully," according to at least one precedent, *Commonwealth v. Parry*. This purpose of the statute provides no justification for the explorers, who acted willfully. Moreover, the Court's decision in *Commonwealth v. Valjean* upheld the larceny conviction of a man who stole bread to prevent his own starvation.] If hunger cannot justify the theft of wholesome and natural food, how can it justify the killing and eating of a man? Again, if we look at the thing in terms of deterrence, is it likely that a man will starve to death to avoid a jail sentence for the theft of a loaf of bread? My brother's demonstrations would compel us to overrule *Commonwealth v. Valjean* and many other precedents that have been built on that case. * * *

There is still a further difficulty in my brother Foster's proposal to read an exception into the statute to favor this case * * *. What shall be the scope of this exception? Here the men cast lots and the victim was himself originally a party to the agreement. What would we have to decide if Whetmore had refused from the beginning to participate in the plan? Would a majority be permitted to overrule him? Or, suppose that no plan were adopted at all and the others simply conspired to bring about Whetmore's death, justifying their act by saying that he was in the weakest condition. Or again, that a plan of selection was followed but one based on a different justification than the one adopted here, as if the others were atheists and insisted that Whetmore should die because he was the only one who believed in an afterlife. These illustrations could be multiplied, but enough have been suggested to reveal what a quagmire of hidden difficulties my brother's reasoning contains. * * *

Since I have been wholly unable to resolve the doubts that beset me about the law of this case, I am with regret announcing a step that is, I believe, unprecedented in the history of this tribunal. I declare my withdrawal from the decision of this case.

KEEN, J. [This jurist insists that the Court put aside the issue, raised by the Chief Justice, of whether the Chief Executive should grant clemency. This is a "confusion of government functions," and judges should not intrude into this realm of the executive.]

The second question that I wish to put to one side is that of deciding whether what these men did was "right" or "wrong," "wicked" or "good." That is also a question that is irrelevant to the discharge of my office as a judge sworn to apply, not my conceptions of morality, but the law of the land. * * *

Whence arise all the difficulties of the case, then, and the necessity for so many pages of discussion about what ought to be so obvious? The difficulties, in whatever tortured form they may present themselves, all trace back to a single source, and that is a failure to distinguish the legal from the moral aspects of this case. To put it bluntly, my brothers do not like the fact that the written law requires the conviction of these defendants. Neither do I, but unlike my brothers I respect the obligations of an office that requires me to put my personal predilections out of my mind when I come to interpret and apply the law of this Commonwealth. * * *

[After a period in which the Commonwealth's judiciary often freely interpreted statutes,] we now have a clear-cut principle, which is the supremacy of the legislative branch of our government. From that principle flows the obligation of the judiciary to enforce faithfully the written law, and to interpret that law in accordance with its plain meaning without reference to our personal desires or our individual conceptions of justice. I am not concerned with the question whether the principle that forbids the judicial revision of statutes is right or wrong, desirable or undesirable; I observe merely that this principle has become a tacit premise underlying the whole of the legal and governmental order I am sworn to administer. * * *

My brother Foster's penchant for finding holes in statutes reminds one of the story told by an ancient author about the man who ate a pair of shoes. Asked how he liked them, he replied that the part he liked best was the holes. That is the way my brother feels about statutes; the more holes they have in them the better he likes them. In short, he doesn't like statutes.

One could not wish for a better case to illustrate the specious nature of this gap-filling process than the one before us. My brother thinks he knows exactly what was sought when men made murder a crime, and that was something he calls "deterrence." My brother Tatting has already shown how much is passed over in that interpretation. But I think the trouble goes deeper. I doubt very much whether our statute making murder a crime really has a "purpose" in any ordinary sense of the term. Primarily, such a statute reflects a deeply-felt human conviction that murder is wrong and that something should be done to the man who commits it. * * *

Now I know that the line of reasoning I have developed in this opinion will not be acceptable to those who look only to the immediate effects of a decision and ignore the long-run implications of an assumption by the judiciary of a power of dispensation. A hard decision is never a popular decision. * * * Hard cases may even have a certain moral value by bringing home to the people their own responsibilities toward the law that is ultimately their creation, and by reminding them that there is no principle of personal grace that can relieve the mistakes of their representatives.

Indeed, I will go farther and say that not only are the principles I have been expounding those which are soundest for our present conditions, but that we would have inherited a better legal system from our forefathers if those principles had been observed from the beginning. For example, with respect to the excuse of self-defense, if our courts had stood steadfast on the language of the statute the result would undoubtedly have been a legislative revision of it. Such a revision would have drawn on the assistance of natural philosophers and psychologists, and the resulting regulation of the matter would have had an understandable and rational basis, instead of the hodgepodge of verbalisms and metaphysical distinctions that have emerged from the judicial and professional treatment.

HANDY, J. * * * I never cease to wonder at my colleagues' ability to throw an obscuring curtain of legalisms about every issue presented to them for decision. * * *

* * * The problem before us is what we, as officers of the government, ought to do with these defendants. That is a question of practical wisdom to be exercised in a context, not of abstract theory, but of human realities. When the case is approached in this light, it becomes, I think, one of the easiest to decide that has ever been argued before this Court. * * *

I have never been able to make my brothers see that government is a human affair, and that men are ruled, not by words on paper or by abstract theories, but by other men. They are ruled well when their rulers understand the feelings and conceptions of the masses. They are ruled badly when that understanding is lacking. * * *

* * * I believe that all government officials, including judges, will do their jobs best if they treat forms and abstract concepts as instruments. We should take as our model, I think, the good administrator, who accommodates procedures and principles to the case at hand, selecting from among the available forms those most suited to reach the proper result.

The most obvious advantage of this method of government is that it permits us to go about our daily tasks with efficiency and common sense. My adherence to this philosophy has, however, deeper roots. I believe that it is only with the insight this philosophy gives that we can preserve the flexibility essential if we are to keep our actions in reasonable accord with the sentiments of those subject to our rule. More governments have been wrecked, and more human misery caused, by the lack of this accord between ruler and ruled than by any other factor that can be discerned in history. Once drive a sufficient wedge between the mass of people and those who direct their legal, political, and economic life, and our society is ruined. Then neither Foster's law of nature nor Keen's fidelity to written law will avail us anything.

* * * One of the great newspaper chains made a poll of public opinion on the question, "What do you think the Supreme Court should do with the Speluncean explorers?" About ninety per cent expressed a belief that the defendants should be pardoned or let off with a kind of token punishment. It is perfectly clear, then, how the public feels about the case. We could have known this without the poll, of course, on the basis of common sense, or even by observing that on this Court there are apparently four-and-a-half men, or ninety per cent, who share the common opinion.

This makes it obvious, not only what we should do, but what we must do if we are to preserve between ourselves and public opinion a reasonable and decent accord. Declaring these men innocent need not involve us in any undignified quibble or trick. No principle of statutory construction is required that is not consistent with the past practices of this Court. Certainly no layman would think that in letting these men off we had stretched the statute any more than our ancestors did when they created the excuse of self-defense. If a more detailed demonstration of the method of reconciling our decision with the statute is required, I should be content to rest on the arguments developed in the second and less visionary part of my brother Foster's opinion.

HENRY M. HART JR. AND ALBERT M. SACKS, THE LEGAL PROCESS: BASIC PROBLEMS IN THE MAKING AND APPLICATION OF LAW

pp. 1374–80 (William N. Eskridge Jr. & Philip P. Frickey eds., 1994) (tent. ed. 1958)*

NOTE ON THE RUDIMENTS OF STATUTORY INTERPRETATION

Consider the adequacy of the following summation:

A. The General Nature of the Task of Interpretation

The function of the court in interpreting a statute is to decide what meaning ought to be given to the directions of the statute in the respects relevant to the case before it. * * *

---

* Reprinted by permission of the editors of the materials.

B. The Mood in Which the Task Should Be Done

In trying to discharge this function the court should:

1. Respect the position of the legislature as the chief policy-determining agency of the society, subject only to the limitations of the constitution under which it exercises its powers; * * *

5. Be mindful of the nature of law and of the fact that every statute is a part of the law and partakes of the qualities of law, and particularly of the quality of striving for even-handed justice.

C. A Concise Statement of the Task

In interpreting a statute a court should:

1. Decide what purpose ought to be attributed to the statute and to any subordinate provision of it which may be involved; and then

2. Interpret the words of the statute immediately in question so as to carry out the purpose as best it can, making sure, however, that it does not give the words either—

(a) a meaning they will not bear, or

(b) a meaning which would violate any established policy of clear statement.

D. The Double Role of the Words as Guides to Interpretation

* * * When the words fit with all the relevant elements of their context to convey a single meaning, as applied to the matter at hand, the mind of the interpreter moves to a confident conclusion almost instantaneously * * *.

Interpretation requires a conscious effort when the words do not fit with their context to convey any single meaning. It is in such case that the words will be seen to play a double part, first, as a factor together with relevant elements of the context in the formulation of hypotheses about possible purposes, and, second, as a separately limiting factor in checking the hypotheses.

E. The Meaning the Words Will Bear

* * * The words of the statute are what the legislature has enacted as law, and all that it has the power to enact. Unenacted intentions or wishes cannot be given effect as law.

In deciding whether words will bear a particular meaning, a court needs to be linguistically wise and not naive. It needs to understand, especially, that meaning depends upon context. But language is a social institution. Humpty Dumpty was wrong when he said that you can make words mean whatever you want them to mean.

The language belongs to the whole society and not to the legislature in office for the time being. Courts on occasion can correct mistakes, as by inserting or striking out a negative, when it is completely clear from the context that a mistake has been made. But they cannot permit the legislative process, and all the other processes which depend upon the integrity of language, to be subverted by the misuse of words. * * *

* * * [T]he proposition that words must not be given a meaning they will not bear operates almost wholly to *prevent* rather than to *compel* expansion of the scope of statutes. The meaning of words can almost always be narrowed if the context seems to call for narrowing.

F.   Policies of Clear Statement

* * * Like the first requirement just considered that words must bear the meaning given them, these policies of clear statement may on occasion operate to defeat the actual, consciously held intention of particular legislators, or of the members of the legislature generally. * * * But the requirement should be thought of as constitutionally imposed. The policies have been judicially developed to promote objectives of the legal system which transcend the wishes of any particular session of the legislature. * * *

Two policies of clear statement call for particular mention.

The first of these * * * requires that words which mark the boundary between criminal and non-criminal conduct should speak with more than ordinary clearness. This policy has special force when the conduct on the safe side of the line is not, in the general understanding of the community, morally blameworthy.

The second forbids a court to understand the legislature as directing a departure from a generally prevailing principle or policy of the law unless it does so clearly. This policy has special force when the departure is so great as to raise a serious question of constitutional power. * * *

G.   The Attribution of Purpose

[Hart and Sacks emphasize the complexity of the task. A statute may have several purposes, each one may be of differing degrees of definiteness, and purpose includes both the immediate policy objective as well as "a larger and subtler purpose as to how the particular statute is to be fitted into the legal system as a whole."]

In determining the more immediate purpose which ought to be attributed to a statute * * * a court should try to put itself in imagination in the position of the legislature which enacted the measure.

The court, however, should not do this in the mood of a cynical political observer, taking account of all the short-run currents of political expedience that swirl around any legislative session.

It should assume, unless the contrary unmistakably appears, that the legislature was made up of reasonable persons pursuing reasonable purposes reasonably. * * *

[The court should follow the approach of *Heydon's Case.*] Why would reasonable men, confronted with the law as it was, have enacted this new law to replace it? * * *

The most reliable guides to an answer will be found in the instances of unquestioned application of the statute. Even in the case of a new statute there almost invariably *are* such instances, in which, because of the perfect fit of words and context, the meaning seems unmistakable.

Once these points of reference are established, they throw a double light. The purposes necessarily implied in them illuminate facets of the general purpose. At the same time they provide a basis for reasoning by analogy to the disputed application in hand. * * * What is crucial here is the realization that law is being made, and that law is not supposed to be irrational. * * *

[Hart and Sacks urge that "the whole context of the statute" should be examined, including the "state of the law" both before and after enactment, "general public knowledge" of the mischief to be remedied, and published legislative history as it sheds light on the statute's general purpose.]

The judicial, administrative, and popular construction of a statute, subsequent to its enactment, are all relevant in attributing a purpose to it.

The court's own prior interpretations of a statute in related applications should be accepted, on the principle of *stare decisis*, unless they are manifestly out of accord with other indications of purpose. * * *

H. Interpreting the Words to Carry Out the Purpose

* * * The main burden of the [interpretive] task should be carried by the institution (court or administrative agency) which has the first-line responsibility for applying the statute authoritatively.

This agency should give sympathetic attention to indications in the legislative history of the lines of contemplated growth, if the history is available. It should give weight to popular construction of self-operating elements of the statute, if that is uniform. Primarily, it should strive to develop a coherent and reasoned pattern of applications intelligibly related to the general purpose. * * *

An interpretation by an administrative agency charged with first-line responsibility for the authoritative application of the statute should be accepted by the court as conclusive, if it is consistent with the purpose properly to be attributed to the statute, and if it has been arrived at with regard to the factors which should be taken into account in elaborating it.

PROBLEM 2–2

Legal Process Theory as Applied

(A) If they were to join one of the opinions in *Speluncean Explorers*, which ones would the following thinkers have joined, and why: (i) Justice Holmes; (ii) Professor Radin; (iii) Professors Hart and Sacks. See William N. Eskridge Jr., The Case of the Speluncean Explorers: *Twentieth Century Statutory Interpretation in a Nutshell*, 61 Geo. Wash. L. Rev. 1731 (1993).

(B) A British statute provides criminal penalties for a person who willfully, fraudulently, and with intent to affect the result in an election "personate[s] any person entitled to vote at such election." The defendant, Whiteley, is charged with having "personated" Marston, a person who had been entitled to vote at an election of guardians for the township of Bradford; Marston was a ratepayer listed in the proper book and was authorized to vote at the election. Marston had died before the election, and Whiteley delivered a vote ostensibly signed by Marston to the proper voting personnel. The dictionary defines "personate" as meaning "to act or play the part of a character in a drama or the like." There is no relevant legislative history.

How would Hart and Sacks decide such a case? Before you answer, try their suggestion of figuring out the statute's purpose by posing various situations, starting with the "core" of the statutory policy and radiating out with variations. Compare *The Legal Process* 1116–26 (1994 ed.), with *Whiteley v. Chappell*, [1868] L.R. 4 Q.B. 147.

(C) Return to *Weber* in Chapter 1. How would Professors Hart and Sacks have decided that case? How would their opinion have differed from those written in the case?

B. IMPLICATIONS OF AND DEBATES WITHIN LEGAL PROCESS THEORY, 1950s–80s

The legal process methodology was the dominant mode for thinking about statutes for a generation and, in fact, remains highly relevant to issues of statutory interpretation.[a] At the very same time Lon Fuller, Henry Hart, and other scholars were crystallizing their purposive theory, it was being written into the U.S. Reports. Consider the analysis of Justice Stanley Reed (President Franklin Roosevelt's former Solicitor General) in *United States v. American Trucking Associations*, 310 U.S. 534, 543 (1940):

> There is, of course, no more persuasive evidence of the purpose of a statute than the words by which the legislature undertook to give expression to its wishes. Often these words are sufficient in and of themselves to determine the purpose of the legislation. In such cases we have followed their plain meaning. When that meaning has led to absurd or futile results, however, this Court has looked beyond the words to the purpose of the Act. Frequently, however, even when the plain meaning did not produce absurd results but merely an unreasonable one "plainly at variance with the policy of the legislation as a whole" this Court has followed that purpose, rather than the literal words. When aid to construction of the meaning of words, as used in the statute, is available, there certainly can be no "rule of law" which forbids its use, however clear the words may appear on "superficial examination."

The Supreme Court in the 1950s and 1960s generally followed this approach, but not without some debate as to how far to carry out purposive analysis. *Schwegmann Bros. v. Calvert Distillers Corp.*, 341 U.S. 384 (1951), for example, contained an excellent debate among the Justices

---

a. On the robustness of legal process thought for current theorizing, see, e.g., Stephen Breyer, *Making Our Democracy Work: A Judge's View* (2010); Daniel B. Rodriguez, *The Substance of the New Legal Process*, 77 Calif. L. Rev. 919 (1989) (book review); Edward L. Rubin, *Legal Reasoning, Legal Process and the Judiciary as an Institution*, 85 Calif. L. Rev. 265 (1997); Peter L. Strauss, *On Resegregating the Worlds of Statute and Common Law*, 1994 Sup. Ct. Rev. 429. See also William N. Eskridge Jr. & Philip P. Frickey, *The Supreme Court, 1993 Term—Foreword: Law as Equilibrium*, 108 Harv. L. Rev. 26, 27 (1994) (alumni of the legal process class were a majority of the Court in 1994, and still number four in 2011).

as to whether the Court's responsibility to apply the statute's purpose (as Justice Douglas' plurality opinion did) could trump the original legislative expectations (Justice Frankfurter's dissenting opinion argued not). Justice Jackson's influential concurring opinion relied solely on the statutory text: because its meaning was plain, he did not care much about the original legislative intent.

As the debate in *Schwegmann* illustrated and the Speluncean Explorers essay anticipated, the two generations of judges and lawyers who have deployed legal process arguments have followed more than one path. Oversimplifying somewhat, one can identify two contesting strains within legal process thinking that have often diverged into competing schools of thought.[b] One strain, represented by Judge Foster in Speluncean Explorers, emphasizes statutory purposes and sees judges and agencies as helpful partners as well as normative updaters in the ongoing statutory enterprise. The other strain, represented by Judge Keen, emphasizes the rule-of-law virtues in following statutory plain meanings and the greater institutional competence of the legislature to make and update public policy. See how these legal process debates play out in three kinds of cases: When, if ever, should judges or agencies correct what they consider to be legislative "mistakes"? Can courts or agencies "update" statutes or read them "dynamically"? To what extent should judges "bend" statutes in light of larger public values?

1. Correcting Legislative "Mistakes"?

SHINE v. SHINE

United States Court of Appeals, First Circuit, 1986
802 F.2d 583

Before COFFIN, BOWNES and BREYER, CIRCUIT JUDGES.

BOWNES, CIRCUIT JUDGE. * * *

The plaintiff, Marguerite Shine, and the defendant, Louis Shine, were married in the District of Columbia on September 20, 1969. They did not have any children and, on October 30, 1972, they divided their property and separated without making any agreement regarding support. In December of 1972, plaintiff commenced an action for separate maintenance from defendant in the Superior Court of the District of Columbia where defendant was a resident. The Superior Court issued an order requiring defendant to pay $250 per month to plaintiff beginning in April 1973. In 1975, plaintiff, then a resident of Virginia, was granted a decree of divorce from defendant by the Circuit Court of Fairfax County, Virginia. The decree made no provision for alimony and support. [Marguerite later secured a judgment requiring Louis to pay his support arrearage. Louis still did not pay, and Marguerite brought a second lawsuit, which was stayed when Louis filed for bankruptcy.]

---

b. This is the argument of William N. Eskridge Jr. & Gary Peller, *The New Public Law Movement: Moderation as a Postmodern Cultural Form*, 89 Mich. L. Rev. 707 (1991).

Plaintiff then filed a complaint in the United States Bankruptcy Court for the District of New Hampshire seeking to have the support obligation declared nondischargeable under 11 U.S.C. § 523(a)(5) (1978). Section 523(a)(5) excepted from discharge any debt "to a spouse, former spouse, or child of the debtor, for alimony to, maintenance for, or support of such spouse or child, in connection with a separation agreement, divorce decree, or property settlement agreement * * *." The Bankruptcy Court initially held that the debt was not dischargeable because it "relates to the oral separation agreement between the parties." *In re Shine*, 43 B.R. 686, 688 (Bankr.D.N.H.1984). Upon motion for reconsideration, however, it held that the debt was dischargeable because it was not created by a "separation agreement *which itself* embodies an agreed arrangement between the parties for the obligation to make support payments." Upon appeal, the district court held that the debt was not dischargeable because "to allow the defendant's debt to be discharged would be contrary to Congressional intent and public policy." Defendant has appealed. [The courts are divided on the issue whether child or spousal support obligations ordered by a court independent of a divorce proceeding or formal agreement are dischargeable.]

These conflicting interpretations of the statute derive from the two established public policies in this area. The general bankruptcy rule of construing exceptions to discharge against the creditor and in favor of the debtor, *Gleason v. Thaw*, 236 U.S. 558, 562 (1915), supports a narrow construction of the statute. This general rule implements "[t]he overriding purpose of the bankruptcy laws * * * to provide the bankrupt with comprehensive, much needed relief from the burden of his indebtedness by releasing him from virtually all his debts." On the other hand, the longstanding policy of excepting spousal and child support from discharge in bankruptcy supports a more liberal construction:

> The bankruptcy law should receive such an interpretation as will effectuate its beneficent purposes and not make it an instrument to deprive dependent wife and children of the support and maintenance due them from the husband and father, which it has ever been the purpose of the law to enforce. * * * Unless positively required by direct enactment the courts should not presume a design upon the part of Congress in relieving the unfortunate debtor to make the law a means of avoiding enforcement of the obligation, moral and legal, devolved upon the husband to support his wife and to maintain and educate his children.

Wetmore v. Markoe, 196 U.S. 68, 77 (1904).

The exception from discharge for alimony and payments for maintenance and support has long been an accepted part of bankruptcy law. Even prior to the 1903 Amendment to § 17 of the 1898 Bankruptcy Act, which explicitly incorporated this exception, the majority of courts held that such payments constituted a nondischargeable "duty" rather than a provable "debt." In *Audubon v. Shufeldt*, 181 U.S. 575 (1901), the

Supreme Court found this exception to be implied in the 1898 Act, which discharged all debts "founded * * * upon a contract, expressed or implied," Act of July 1, 1898, ch. 541, § 63(4), 30 Stat. 544, 563:

> Alimony does not arise from any business transaction but from the relation of marriage. It is not founded on a contract, express or implied, but on the natural and legal duty of the husband to support the wife. The general obligation to support is made specific by the decree of the Court of appropriate jurisdiction. * * * But its obligation in that respect does not affect its nature.

And in *Wetmore*, the Court found that the 1903 Amendment explicitly including the exception was "declaratory of the true meaning and sense of the statute," rather than indicating the exception's absence prior to 1903.

Litigation arose under amended § 17 concerning the definition of "alimony." Cases were decided on the basis of whether the payments in question constituted genuine "alimony" or, rather, dischargeable "property settlements." In making this determination courts looked at the substance, rather than the formal designation, of the payments. [Citing cases.]

Under the interpretation of the statute urged by the appellant, the 1978 Amendment would be viewed as reversing this long-standing differentiation between property settlements and alimony or payments for maintenance and support. Under appellant's interpretation, property settlements, traditionally dischargeable, would have become nondischargeable, while alimony and payments for maintenance and support, traditionally nondischargeable, would have been limited by a strictly construed "in connection" clause. We, therefore, examine the history of the 1978 Amendment to determine whether such a reversal was intended by Congress.

In 1970, the Commission on the Bankruptcy Laws of the United States was charged with recommending changes in the statute. Act of July 24, 1970, Pub.L. No. 91–354, 84 Stat. 468. The Commission proposed amending § 17(a)(7) to make nondischargeable "any liability to a spouse or child for maintenance or support, for alimony due or to become due, or under a property settlement in connection with a separation agreement or divorce decree." *Report of the Commission*, H.R. Doc. No. 93–137, 93d Cong., 1st Sess. (1973)[.] The Commission's proposal left untouched the existing broad exemption for *any* liability for maintenance or support. * * * The Commission intended to expand nondischargeable support debts beyond the support, maintenance and alimony obligations which had traditionally been nondischargeable. The proposal included property settlements in divorce or separation agreements which were in the nature of support but which did not take the form of periodic payments. The Commission did not intend to *limit* the nondischargeability of the traditionally protected categories. It sought, rather, to broaden the bankruptcy law's protection of the families of the bankrupt spouse in accordance with changing times.

The version of the Amendment that originally passed the House of Representatives, H.R. 8200, retained the traditional exception to dischargeability:

(a) A discharge * * * does not discharge an individual debtor from any debt—

* * *

(5) to a spouse, former spouse, or child of the debtor, for alimony to, maintenance for, or support of such spouse or child * * *.

H.R. 8200, § 523, 95th Cong., 1st Sess., U.S. Code Cong. & Admin. News 1978, p. 5787 (1977).

In the Senate, the original version of the Amendment substantially repeated the Commission's language, making nondischargeable "any liability to a spouse or child for maintenance or support, or for alimony due or to become due, or under a property settlement in connection with a separation agreement or divorce decree * * *." S. 2266, 95th Cong., 1st Sess. (1977). When it was reported out of committee, the Amendment read:

(a) A discharge * * * does not discharge an individual debtor from * * *—

* * *

(6) any liability to a spouse or child for maintenance or support, or for alimony due or to become due, in connection with a separation agreement or divorce decree.

S. 2266, § 523, 95th Cong., 2d Sess. (1978).

The final text of the bill was an amalgam of the Commission, House and Senate versions. The first part of the new § 523(a)(5) derived from the House language, while the "in connection" clause combines the wording of the House and Senate. The result, if construed narrowly, could convey a meaning not intended by anyone.

This final version, produced in the "harried and hurried atmosphere" in which the bill was finally enacted [at the eleventh-plus hour of the Congress ending in October 1978], should not be read to effect a reversal of the long-standing principles governing this area. Such a reversal would surely have been noted in the congressional discussions. Yet, neither the House nor Senate Committee Reports accompanying the final version make any reference to a limitation upon support debts considered nondischargeable. The Senate Report does not even mention the "in connection" language in its discussion of the section nor does it suggest that any kind of new limitation had been imposed. S.Rep. No. 989, 95th Cong., 2d Sess. 79, *reprinted in* 1978 U.S. Code Cong. & Ad. News 5787, 5865. The House Report follows the Senate Report in its general discussion, H.R.Rep. No. 595, 95th Cong., 2d Sess. 364, *reprinted in* 1978 U.S. Code Cong. & Ad. News 5963, 6320. In its section-by-section discussion of § 523(a)(5), the

House Report merely restates the "in connection" language without explaining any effect it might have on dischargeability. *Id.* at 6454.

In 1984, the statute was amended again, clearly making nondischargeable the kind of court-ordered debts involved in this case. Spousal or child support debts incurred "in connection with a separation agreement, divorce decree, or other order of a court of record or property settlement agreement" are now nondischargeable. 11 U.S.C. § 523(a)(5) (Supp. II) (as amended by the Bankruptcy Amendments and Federal Judgeship Act of 1984, Pub.L. 98–353, effective July 10, 1984). [The amendment was not retroactive and so did not apply to the current controversy.] This Amendment should not be read as proof of a contrary state of the law from 1978 through 1984. Rather, as the Supreme Court, in *Wetmore*, analogously noted in relation to the 1903 Amendment, it simply declares and clarifies the "true meaning and sense" of the law, allowing it to "effectuate its beneficent purposes."

After this examination of the legislative history of § 523, as well as of the established principles in this area, we cannot agree with the Bankruptcy Court's view of the requirements for nondischargeability under the 1978 statute. Congressional policy in this area has always been to ensure that genuine support obligations would not be discharged. Interpreting the statute to require the test proposed would violate the principle that in bankruptcy law, "substance will not give way to form * * * technical considerations will not prevent substantial justice from being done." *Pepper v. Litton*, 308 U.S. 295, 305 (1939). While the wording of the statute may have given rise to some confusion, "[t]he result of an obvious mistake should not be enforced, particularly when it 'overrides common sense and evident statutory purpose.'" *In re Adamo*, 619 F.2d 216, 222 (2d Cir. 1980), *cert. denied*, 449 U.S. 843 (1980) (quoting *United States v. Brown*, 333 U.S. 18, 26 (1948)).

We hold, therefore, that this support obligation is not dischargeable in bankruptcy. * * *

NOTE ON JUDICIAL CORRECTION OF LEGISLATIVE MISTAKES

Hart and Sacks opined that "[c]ourts on occasion can correct mistakes, as by inserting or striking out a negative, when it is completely clear from the context that a mistake has been made. But they cannot permit the legislative process, and all the other processes which depend upon the integrity of language, to be subverted by the misuse of words." *The Legal Process* 1375 (Eskridge & Frickey eds. 1994). Is *Shine* correctly decided under this precept? There are cases in which courts have disregarded, eliminated, transposed, or inserted words in a statute when it is clear that a drafting error or other mistake was made, or where an absurd interpretation would otherwise result. See 2A Sutherland, *Statutes and Statutory Construction*, §§ 47.35–.38 (5th ed. 1992).[c] Is *Shine* really a "scrivener's error" case? Would the contrary result

---

c. See also Michael Fried, *A Theory of Scrivener's Error*, 52 Rutgers L. Rev. 589 (2000) (Constitution allows courts to deviate from words enacted by legislature and signed by executive be "absurd"? (Hint: it appears that the statute contained a drafting mistake. See if you can figure out where that occurred.)

Consider another example. The district court entered an order denying remand back to state court of a lawsuit that had been removed by the defendant to federal court. 28 U.S.C. § 1453(c)(1) requires that any appeal from such an order must be made "not *less* than 7 days after entry of the order." Was there no time limit on appeals? The Ninth Circuit held this was a scrivener's error and interpreted the statute to require an appeal to be filed "not *more* than 7 days after entry of the order." *Amalgamated Transit Union Local 1309 v. Laidlaw Transit Servs., Inc.*, 435 F.3d 1140 (9th Cir. 2006). Dissenting from the full court's denial of en banc review, 448 F.3d 1092 (2006), Judge Bybee (joined by Judges Kozinski, O'Scannlain, Rymer, Callahan, and Bea) rejected the panel's rewrite of a statute. This kind of judging "is a trap for citizens (and their lawyers) who can no longer trust the statute as written to mean what it plainly says." Also, "[w]hen courts turn the meaning of statutes up-side-down, Congress must legislate defensively, not by enacting statutes in the plainest possible language, but by enacting statutes in the language that it predicts the courts will interpret to effectuate its intentions." 448 F.3d at 1100. For a response to these kinds of arguments, see Siegel, *Statutory Drafting Errors, supra* note c, at 333–44.

Shine noted that in 1984 Congress amended the statute *prospectively* to correct the problem in that case. (Recall the same phenomenon in *Holy Trinity*, though the Court did not note it.) Which way does that cut? Does it suggest that Congress can fix its own mistakes or oversights, and thus that courts ought not roam freely about the United States Code correcting legislative imprudence? Had there been no 1984 amendment, would it be easier or harder for you to agree with *Shine*? The effect of *Shine* is to make the 1984 amendment retroactive. Should this be a concern?

If a client brought you the *Shine* problem, what would you have advised? Would you have looked just at the United States Code, and if so, would you have simply concluded that the support obligation was dischargeable? Might the "need" for legal certainty and for the availability of low-cost, accurate legal advice militate against the approach of *Shine*? (Recall the Bybee critique in *Laidlaw*.) Consider these and any other objections you might have to *Shine*'s implicit use of the "golden rule" (avoiding absurd results) in light of the following case.

United States v. Locke, 471 U.S. 84 (1985). The Federal Land Policy and Management Act (FLPMA), Pub. L. 94–579, 90 Stat. 2743, codified at 43 U.S.C. §§ 1701–1784 (1982), provided that holders of certain mining claims to federal land must, "prior to December 31" of every year, file certain documents with state officials and the federal Bureau of Land Management (BLM) or lose their claims. *Id.* § 1744. Simply put, this is the quintessential trap for the unwary, since it seems wholly illogical to require someone to file something, under severe penalty for default, the day *before* the last day of the year.

that are absurd and can be easily fixed); Jonathan R. Siegel, *What Statutory Drafting Errors Teach Us About Statutory Interpretation*, 69 Geo. Wash. L. Rev. 309 (2001) (arguing that statutory drafting errors, which show up with some frequency, create intractable problems for strict textualists and highlight some advantages for more contextualist approaches).

The Locke family had been exercising rights to mine gravel on federal land since the 1950s. Knowing they were required to file papers in order to retain these rights, they sent their daughter to the nearest BLM office, which told her that claims had to be filed by December 31. The Lockes filed on that date, and the BLM rejected the papers on the ground that they were too late.

Justice Marshall, for the Court, agreed with the BLM that the Lockes were out of luck: "While we will not allow a literal reading of a statute to produce a result 'demonstrably at odds with the intentions of its drafters,' with respect to filing deadlines a literal reading of Congress' words is generally the only proper reading of those words. To attempt to decide whether some date other than the one set out in the statute is the date actually 'intended' by Congress is to set sail on an aimless journey, for the purpose of a filing deadline would be just as well served by nearly any date a court might choose as by the date Congress has in fact set out in the statute. * * * [N]othing in the legislative history suggests why Congress chose December 30 over December 31, [b]ut '[d]eadlines are inherently arbitrary,' while fixed dates 'are often essential to accomplish necessary results.' " * * *

Justice Marshall continued: "[W]e are not insensitive to the problems posed by congressional reliance on the words 'prior to December 31.' But the fact that Congress might have acted with greater clarity or foresight does not give courts a *carte blanche* to redraft statutes in an effort to achieve that which Congress is perceived to have failed to do. 'There is a basic difference between filling a gap left by Congress' silence and rewriting rules that Congress has affirmatively and specifically enacted.' *Mobil Oil Corp. v. Higginbotham*, 436 U.S. 618, 625 (1978). * * * [D]eference to the supremacy of the legislature, as well as recognition that congressmen typically vote on the language of a bill, generally requires us to assume that 'the legislative purpose is expressed by the ordinary meaning of the words used.' * * * The phrase 'prior to' may be clumsy, but its meaning is clear."

Justice Stevens, joined by **Justice Brennan**, dissented. In part, he argued: (1) FLPMA contained obvious drafting errors, which "should cause us to pause before concluding that Congress commanded blind allegiance to the remainder of the literal text" of the statute; (2) the BLM's implementing regulations do not repeat the statutory language, but rather state that filing must be accomplished "on or before December 30 of each year," suggesting that the BLM itself recognized that the statutory language was unclear; (3) indeed, the BLM once made the same mistake as the claimholders in *Locke*, for the agency had issued an information pamphlet that stated that documents must be filed "on or before December 31 of each [year]," demonstrating again that the statutory language is not "plain." Had the BLM issued regulations allowing filings on December 31, the Court surely would have upheld them, which suggests the anomaly that the agency "has more power to interpret an awkwardly drafted statute in an enlightened manner consistent with Congress' intent than does this Court." Justice Stevens continued: "The statutory scheme requires periodic filings on a calendar-year basis. The end of the calendar year is, of course, correctly described either as 'prior to the close of business on December 31,' or 'on or before December 31,' but it is surely understandable that the author of [this statute] might inadvertently use the words 'prior to December 31' when he meant to refer to the end of the calendar year. * * * That it was in fact an error seems rather clear to me because no one has suggested any rational basis for omitting just one day from the period in which an annual filing may be made, and I would not presume that Congress deliberately created a trap for the unwary by such an omission." The dissent concluded: "I have no doubt that Congress would have chosen to adopt a construction of the statute that filing take place by the end of the calendar year if its attention had been focused on this precise issue." Do you agree?

Query: How would Hart and Sacks have decided *Locke*? Can you think of a policy reason for requiring filing before December 31? Think hard, for this is not an impossible task. Suppose that the Lockes had shown up at the BLM at 11:00 p.m. on December 30, "before December 31," but after the BLM had closed for the day. Would they have satisfied the statute as interpreted by the Court? Is this example at all similar to the facts of *Locke*? To the example of the ordinance governing pharmacy closing mentioned at the outset of this chapter?

2. Statutory Evolution in Light of Changed Circumstances

William N. Eskridge Jr., *Dynamic Statutory Interpretation* 125–28 (1994).* Interpretation can be viewed as an honest effort by an "agent" to apply the "principal's" directive to unforeseen circumstances. (When circumstances were foreseen and provided for by the principal, it might be said that there is no "interpretive" effort needed.) The dynamic nature of interpretation arises, in large part, out of the agent's need for practical accommodation of the directive to new circumstances.[d] Consider the following homely example, adapted from Francis Lieber's famous "fetch me the soup meat" hypothetical.

" * * * Williams, the head of the household, retains Diamond as a relational agent to run the household while Williams is away on business. The contract is detailed, setting forth Diamond's duties to care for Williams' two children, maintain the house, prepare the meals, and do the shopping on a weekly basis. One of the more specific directives is that Diamond fetch five pounds of soup meat every Monday (the regular shopping day), so that he can prepare enough soup for the entire week. Diamond knows from talking to Williams that by 'soup meat' she means a certain type of nutritious beef that is sold at several local stores. When Williams leaves, Diamond has no doubt as to what he is supposed to do. But over time his interpretation of the directive will change if the social, legal, and constitutional context changes so as to affect important assumptions made in Williams' original directive.

---

* Reprinted by permission of the publishers, Harvard University Press, Copyright © 1994 by the President and Fellows of Harvard College.

d. See also Stephen Breyer, *Active Liberty: Interpreting Our Democratic Constitution* (2005); Richard A. Posner, *The Problems of Jurisprudence* ch. 7 (1990); Daniel A. Farber, *Legislative Deals and Statutory Bequests*, 75 Minn. L. Rev. 667 (1991); Philip P. Frickey, *Congressional Intent, Practical Reasoning, and the Dynamic Nature of Federal Indian Law*, 78 Calif. L. Rev. 1137 (1990); Lawrence Lessig, *Fidelity in Translation*, 71 Tex. L. Rev. 1165 (1993).

"*Changes in Social Context.* There are a number of changes in the world that would justify Diamond's deviation from the directive that he fetch five pounds of soup meat each Monday. For example, suppose Diamond goes to town one Monday and discovers that none of the stores has the precise kind of soup meat he knows Williams had in mind when she gave the order. Should he drive miles to other towns in search of the proper soup meat? Not necessarily. It might be reasonable for him to purchase a suitable alternative in town, especially if it appears in his judgment to be just as good for the children. One can imagine many practical reasons why, in a given week, Diamond should not follow the apparent command. The reasons for deviating are akin to the interpretive creation of 'exceptions' to a statute's broad mandate based on the interpreter's judgment about the statute's goals and the extent to which other goals should be sacrificed. [Recall Justice Brewer's opinion in *Holy Trinity Church* and Justice Brennan's opinion in *Weber.*]

"As the reasons multiply over time, one can imagine changed circumstances that effectively nullify Williams' directive altogether[.] Suppose Diamond discovers that one of the children has an allergy to soup meat. That child can continue to eat soup, but not with meat in it. Because Diamond realizes that one of the reasons Williams directed him to fetch soup meat every Monday was to ensure the good health and nourishment of the children, and because he believes that Williams would not want him to waste money on uneaten soup meat, he henceforth purchases only three pounds of soup meat per week. If both children are allergic to the soup meat, and Diamond does not care for the soup meat himself, he might be justified in entirely forgoing his directive to fetch it. Although he would be violating the original specific intent as well as the plain meaning of Williams's orders, Diamond could argue that his actions are consistent with her general intent that he act to protect the children's health and with her meta-intent that Diamond adapt specific directives to that end.

"*New Legal Rules and Policies.* The agent might receive inconsistent directives over time. Suppose that two months after Williams embarks on her trip, she reads in a 'Wellness Letter' that if children do not eat healthy foods, they will have cholesterol problems later in life. She sends Diamond a letter instructing him to place the children on a low-cholesterol diet, which should include Wendy's Bran Muffins and fresh apples. As a faithful relational agent, Diamond complies. He also reads up on the cholesterol literature, including the 'Wellness Letter,' and discovers that soup meat is high in cholesterol. He discontinues the weekly fetching of soup meat and fetches chicken instead because it is lower in cholesterol. Diamond's action is akin to a court's reconciliation of conflicting statutory mandates, in which one of the statutes often is given a narrowing interpretation to accommodate the policies of a later statute. * * *

"Changed circumstances might further alter Diamond's interpretation of Williams's inconsistent directives. Weeks after he has substituted chicken for soup meat, Diamond learns from the 'Wellness Letter' that Wendy's Bran Muffins actually do not help lower cholesterol, and that they have been found to cause cancer in rats. Furthermore, Diamond discovers that 50 percent of the apples sold in his region have a dangerous chemical on them. Diamond thereupon switches from Wendy's Bran Muffins to Richard's Bran Muffins, recommended by the 'Wellness Letter,' and from fresh apples to fresh oranges. Thus, not only has Diamond overthrown Williams' earlier directive on soup meat because of the new policy in her latter directive, but he has also altered her specific choice of low-cholesterol foods in the latter directive!

"New Meta–Policies. The relational agent's interpretation of his orders may well be influenced over time by changing meta-policies. The new meta-policies may be endogenous or exogenous. Endogenous meta-policies are those generated from the principal herself and are just a more dramatic form of inconsistent directives. Suppose that, after several months, Williams writes to Diamond that financial reversals impel her to cut back on household expenses. Food costs must thereafter be limited to $100 per week. Although he has long been directed to fetch soup meat every Monday, and there are other ways to economize, Diamond cuts back on soup meat, in part because it is the most expensive item on the shopping list. This is akin to a court's modifying an original statutory policy to take account of supervening statutory policies.

"Exogenous meta-policies are those generated from an authority greater than the principal. Suppose that Diamond has an unlimited food budget and no health concerns about soup meat, yet he stops fetching it on a weekly basis because the town is in a crisis period and meat of all sorts is being rationed; hence, Diamond could not lawfully fetch five pounds of soup meat per week. This is akin to a court construing a statute narrowly to avoid constitutional problems based on the legislature's meta-intent not to pass statutes of questionable constitutionality.

"In all of these hypotheticals Diamond, our relational agent, has interpreted Williams's soup meat directive dynamically. Quite dynamically, in fact, because in most of the variations Diamond created substantial exceptions to or even negated the original specific meaning of the directive. Notwithstanding his dynamic interpretation of the directive, I believe that Diamond has been nothing but an honest agent."

Query: Consider how Eskridge's theory of changed circumstances could explain (and defend) the result in *Weber* (Chapter 1, § 3). Does it have any bearing on *Holy Trinity*, where the Court was construing a more recent statute? Is it a persuasive justification for dynamic readings of laws in the following state cases? If so, what "circumstances" have "changed," and why do any such changes support interpretations that seem to bend statutory language, perhaps beyond its breaking point?

IN THE MATTER OF JACOB
New York Court of Appeals, 1995
86 N.Y.2d 651, 636 N.Y.S.2d 716, 660 N.E.2d 397

KAYE, C.J. [delivered the opinion for the Court.]

[The appeal involved two petitions for adoption. In the *Jacob* case, the cohabiting boyfriend, Stephen T.K., of the child's biological mother, Roseanne M.A., moved to adopt Jacob. In the *Dana* case, the cohabiting female partner, G.M., of the child's biological mother, P.I., petitioned to adopt Dana. In both cases, the family courts denied the petitions as not falling within New York's adoption statute. The Court of Appeals, by a 4–3 vote, reversed.]

[S]ince adoption in this State is "solely the creature of . . . statute," the adoption statute must be strictly construed. What is to be construed strictly and applied rigorously in this sensitive area of the law, however, is legislative purpose as well as legislative language. Thus, the adoption statute must be applied in harmony with the humanitarian principle that adoption is a means of securing the best possible home for a child. * * *

This policy would certainly be advanced in situations like those presented here by allowing the two adults who actually function as a child's parents to become the child's legal parents. The advantages which would result from such an adoption include Social Security and life insurance benefits in the event of a parent's death or disability, the right to sue for the wrongful death of a parent, the right to inherit under rules of intestacy and eligibility for coverage under both parents' health insurance policies. In addition, granting a second parent adoption further ensures that two adults are legally entitled to make medical decisions for the child in case of emergency and are under a legal obligation for the child's economic support *(see,* Domestic Relations Law § 32).

Even more important, however, is the emotional security of knowing that in the event of the biological parent's death or disability, the other parent will have presumptive custody, and the children's relationship with their parents, siblings and other relatives will continue should the coparents separate. Indeed, viewed from the children's perspective, permitting the adoptions allows the children to achieve a measure of permanency with both parent figures * * *.

A second, related point of overriding significance is that the various sections comprising New York's adoption statute today represent a complex and not entirely reconcilable patchwork. Amended innumerable times since its passage in 1873, the adoption statute was last consolidated nearly 60 years ago, in 1938 (L. 1938, ch. 606). Thus, after decades of piecemeal amendment upon amendment, the statute today contains language from the 1870's alongside language from the 1990's. * * *

Despite ambiguity in other sections, one thing is clear: section 110 allows appellants to become adoptive parents. Domestic Relations Law § 110, entitled "Who May Adopt," provides that an "adult unmarried person or an adult husband and his adult wife together may adopt another person" (Domestic Relations Law § 110). Under this language, both appellant G. M. in *Matter of Dana* and appellant Stephen T.K. in *Matter of Jacob,* as adult unmarried persons, have standing to adopt and appellants are correct that the Court's analysis of section 110 could appropriately end here. [Although Jacob's adoption was a joint petition, his mother already enjoyed parental rights, and so only Stephen T.K.'s rights were really at stake in the petition. She faulted the dissenting opinion for reading too much into the word "together."]

The conclusion that appellants have standing to adopt is also supported by the history of section 110. The pattern of amendments since the end of World War II evidences a successive expansion of the categories of persons entitled to adopt regardless of their marital status or sexual orientation. [Section 110 was expanded in 1951 to allow adoptions by minors and in 1984 to allow adoptions by adults not yet divorced but living apart from their spouses pursuant to separation agreements.] Supporting [the 1984] amendment was New York's "strong policy of assuring that as many children as possible are adopted into suitable family situations" (Bill Jacket, L. 1984, ch. 218, Mem. of Dept. of Social Services, at 2 [June 19, 1984]). * * *

These amendments reflect some of the fundamental changes that have taken place in the makeup of the family. Today, for example, at least 1.2 of the 3.5 million American households which consist of an unmarried adult couple have children under 15 years old, more than a six-fold increase from 1970 (see, Current Population Reports, Population Characteristics, U.S. Bur. of Census, Marital Status & Living Arrangements, P20–478, at IX [1993]). Yet further recognition of this transformation is evidenced by the fact that unlike the States of New Hampshire and Florida (N.H.Rev.Stat.Annot. § 170–B:4; Fla.Stat.Ann. § 63.042[3]), New York does not prohibit adoption by homosexuals. Indeed, as noted earlier, an administrative regulation is in place in this State forbidding the denial of an agency adoption based solely on the petitioner's sexual orientation (18 NYCRR 421.16[h][2]). * * *

Appellants having standing to adopt pursuant to Domestic Relations Law § 110, the other statutory obstacle relied upon by the lower courts in denying the petitions is the provision that "[a]fter the making of an order of adoption the natural parents of the adoptive child shall be relieved of all parental duties toward and of all responsibilities for and shall have no rights over such adoptive child or to his property by descent or succession" (Domestic Relations Law § 117[1][a]). Literal application of this language would effectively prevent these adoptions since it would require the termination of the biological mothers' rights upon adoption thereby placing appellants in the "Catch–22" of having to choose one of two coparents as the child's only legal parent. * * *

Both the title of section 117 ("Effect of adoption") and its opening phrase ("After the making of an order of adoption") suggest that the section has nothing to do with the standing of an individual to adopt, an issue treated exclusively in section 110. Rather, section 117 addresses the legal effect of an adoption on the parties and their property. [This reading of section 117 is directed by the Court's precedents and commentary on the section, as well as the section's textual focus on estate law.]

[E]ven though the language of section 117 still has the effect of terminating a biological parent's rights in the majority of adoptions between strangers—where there is a need to prevent unwanted intrusion by the child's former biological relatives to promote the stability of the new adoptive family—the cases before us are entirely different. As we recognized in *Matter of Seaman* (78 N.Y.2d 451, 461), "complete severance of the natural relationship is not necessary when the adopted person remains within the natural family unit as a result of an intrafamily adoption." [The legislature has recognized this principle by amending section 117 to allow adoptions by stepparents and to allow adoptive parents in some circumstances to agree to a continuing relationship between the child and her or his biological parents. The latter amendment, allowing "open adoptions," overrode a Court of Appeals decision construing the adoption law too narrowly.]

Given the above, it is plain that an interpretation of section 117 that would limit the number of beneficial intrafamily adoptions cannot be reconciled with the legislative intent to authorize open adoptions and adoptions by minors. The coexistence of the statute's seemingly automatic termination language along with these more recent enactments creates a statutory puzzle not susceptible of ready resolution. * * *

"Where the language of a statute is susceptible of two constructions, the courts will adopt that which avoids injustice, hardship, constitutional doubts or other objectionable results" (*Kauffman & Sons Saddlery Co. v Miller*, 298 N.Y. 38, 44 [Fuld, J.]; *see also*, McKinney's Cons. Laws of N.Y., Book 1, Statutes § 150). Given that section 117 is open to two differing interpretations as to whether it automatically terminates parental rights in all cases, a construction of the section that would deny children like Jacob and Dana the opportunity of having their two de facto parents become their legal parents, based solely on their biological mother's sexual orientation or marital status, would not only be unjust under the circumstances, but also might raise constitutional concerns in light of the adoption statute's historically consistent purpose—the best interests of the child. (*See, e.g., Gomez v Perez*, 409 U.S. 535, 538 [Equal Protection Clause prevents unequal treatment of children whose parents are unmarried]; *Plyler v Doe*, 457 U.S. 202, 220 [State may not direct the onus of parent's perceived "misconduct against his (or her) children"]; *Matter of Burns v Miller Constr.*, 55 N.Y.2d 501, 507–510 [New York statute requiring child born out of wedlock to prove "acknowledgment" by deceased parent did not further legitimate State interest].

These concerns are particularly weighty in *Matter of Dana*. Even if the Court were to rule against him on this appeal, the male petitioner in *Matter of Jacob* could still adopt by marrying Jacob's mother. Dana, however, would be irrevocably deprived of the benefits and entitlements of having as her legal parents the two individuals who have already assumed that role in her life, simply as a consequence of her mother's sexual orientation.

Any proffered justification for rejecting these petitions based on a governmental policy disapproving of homosexuality or encouraging marriage would not apply. * * * New York has not adopted a policy disfavoring adoption by either single persons or homosexuals. In fact, the most recent legislative document relating to the subject urges courts to construe section 117 in precisely the manner we have as it cautions against discrimination against "nonmarital children" and "unwed parents". An interpretation of the statute that avoids such discrimination or hardship is all the more appropriate here where a contrary ruling could jeopardize the legal status of the many New York children whose adoptions by second parents have already taken place (*e.g., Matter of Camilla,* 163 Misc. 2d 272; *Matter of Evan,* 153 Misc. 2d 844; *Matter of A.J.J.,* 108 Misc. 2d 657). * * *

BELLACOSA, J., dissenting. JUDGES SIMONS, TITONE and I respectfully dissent and vote to affirm in each case. * * *

Although adoption has been practiced since ancient times, the authorization for this unique relationship derives solely from legislation. It has no common-law roots or evolution. Therefore, our Court has approved the proposition that the statutory adoption charter exclusively controls. [Judge Bellacosa also emphasized that the "transcendent societal goal in the field of domestic relations is to stabilize family relationships, particularly parent-child bonds. That State interest promotes permanency planning and provides protection for an adopted child's legally secure familial placement." The state has chosen not to recognize common-law marriages or "lesbian marriages."]

Domestic Relations Law § 110, entitled "Who May Adopt," provides at its outset that *"an adult unmarried person or an adult husband and his adult wife together* may adopt another person" (emphasis added). Married aspirants are directed to apply "together", i.e., jointly, as spouses, except under circumstances not applicable in these cases. [Appellant G.M., the lesbian co-parent in *Dana,* meets this requirement, but appellants Stephen T.K. and Roseanne M.A., the unmarried cohabitants in *Jacob,* do not.]

The legislative history of adoption laws over the last century also reveals a dynamic process with an evolving set of limitations. The original version enacted in 1873 provided: "Any minor child may be adopted *by any adult*" (L. 1873, ch 830 [emphasis added]). In 1896, the Legislature cut back by stating that "[a]n adult unmarried person, or an adult husband or wife, or an adult husband and his adult wife together, may adopt a minor" (L. 1896, ch. 272, § 60; *see also,* L. 1915, ch. 352; L. 1917, ch. 149). This language was further restricted, in 1920, when the Legislature omitted from the statute the language "or an adult husband or wife" (*see,* L. 1920, ch. 433). Since enactment of the 1920 amendment, the statute has provided that "[a]n adult unmarried person or an adult husband and his adult wife *together* may adopt" (Domestic Relations Law § 110 [emphasis added]). The words chosen by the Legislature demonstrate its conclusion that a stable familial entity is provided by either a one-parent family or a two-parent family when the concentric interrelationships enjoy a legal bond. The statute demonstrates that the Legislature, by express will and words, concluded that households that lack legally recognized bonds suffer a relatively greater risk to the stability needed for adopted children and families, because individuals can walk out of these relationships with impunity and unknown legal consequences. * * *

Domestic Relations Law § 117 provides: "After the making of an order of adoption the natural parents of the adoptive child *shall be relieved of all parental duties toward and of all responsibilities for and* shall have no rights over such adoptive child *or* to his [or her] property by descent or succession" (emphasis added). The plain and overarching language and punctuation of section 117 cannot be judicially blinked, repealed or rendered obsolete by interpretation. [Judge Bellacosa cited precedent where the Court of Appeals had refused to read equitable exceptions into the plain language of section 117 to ameliorate its harsh application.]

A careful examination of the Legislature's unaltered intent based on the entire history of the statute reveals the original purpose of section 117 was to enfold adoptees within the exclusive embrace of their new families and to sever all relational aspects with the former family. That goal still applies and especially to the lifetime and lifelong relationships of the affected individuals, not just to the effect of dying intestate.

[Judge Bellacosa faulted the majority's concern that the statute be construed to avoid constitutional problems because (1) that concern had not been briefed or even mentioned by appellants, nor did the Attorney General have an opportunity to present the state's views, (2) the presumption of constitutionality augurs against vague and speculative doubts about a statute's constitutionality, and (3) such a concern could not override the plain meaning of the statute.] Ambiguity cannot directly or indirectly create or substitute for the lack of statutory authorization to adopt. These adoption statutes are luminously clear on one unassailable feature: no express legislative authorization is discernible for what is, nevertheless, permitted by the holdings today. Nor do the statutes anywhere speak of de facto, functional or second parent adoptions. Frankly, if the Legislature had intended to alter the definitions and interplay of its plenary, detailed adoption blueprint to cover the circumstances as presented here, it has had ample and repeated opportunities, means and words to effectuate such purpose plainly and definitively as a matter of notice, guidance, stability and reliability. It has done so before *(see, e.g.,* L. 1984, ch. 218 [permitting adoption by adults not yet divorced]; L. 1951, ch. 211 [permitting adoption by a minor]).

Because the Legislature did not do so here, neither should this Court in this manner. Cobbling law together out of interpretative ambiguity that transforms fundamental, societally recognized relationships and substantive principles is neither sound statutory construction nor justifiable lawmaking. * * *

Li v. Yellow Cab of California, 13 Cal. 3d 804, 119 Cal. Rptr. 858, 532 P.2d 1226 (Cal. 1975). Although the doctrine of contributory negligence (barring all recovery to a tort plaintiff whose own negligence contributes in any way to her or his injury) is of judicial origin, see *Butterfield v. Forrester* (1809) 103 Eng. Rep. 926 (K.B.), the California Supreme Court had long construed section 1714 of the Civil Code (1872) to have codified the doctrine as it stood at that date. Section 1714 provided: "Everyone is responsible, not only for the result of his willful acts, but also for an injury occasioned to another by his want of ordinary care or skill in the management of his property or person, *except so far as the latter has, willfully or by want of ordinary care, brought the injury upon himself.* The extent of liability in such cases is defined by the Title on Compensatory Relief" (emphasis added). Although the statutory language might easily be read to adopt a rule of comparative negligence (where the plaintiff's recovery is reduced according to her or his negligence but not eliminated entirely), the California Supreme Court, in an opinion by **Justice Sullivan**, reaffirmed that the 1872 code had originally codified the rule of contributory negligence.[e] Nonetheless, the Court ruled that section 1714 should be reinterpreted to codify a rule of comparative negligence—the modern trend in other states (where it had mostly been adopted by statute rather than by judicial decision) and a practice that was apparently being informally followed by many juries in California and elsewhere.

The Court justified this updating, first, by reference to the flexible rules of construction the court has traditionally applied to the code. "The Civil Code was not designed to embody the whole law of private and civil relations, rights and duties; it is incomplete and partial; and except in those instances where its language clearly and unequivocally discloses an intention to depart from, alter, or abrogate the common-law rule concerning a particular subject matter, a section of the Code purporting to embody such doctrine or rule will be construed in light of common-law decisions on the same subject." *Estate of Elizalde* (1920) 188 P. 560, 562. Indeed, the Code itself said, "The rule of the common law, that statutes in derogation thereof are to be strictly construed, has no application to this

---

e. Justice Sullivan noted that comparative negligence was virtually unheard of in American law in 1872 and relied on the Code Commissioners' Note that appeared immediately following section 1714 in the 1872 code. That note provided in full as follows: "Code La., § 2295; Code Napoleon, § 1383; Austin vs. Hudson River R.R. Co., 25 N.Y., p. 334; Jones vs. Bird, 5 B. & Ald., p. 837; Dodd vs. Holmes, 1 Ad. & El., p. 493. *This section modifies the law heretofore existing.—* See 20 N.Y., p. 67; 10 M. & W., p. 546; 5 C.B. (N.S.), p. 573. This class of obligations imposed by law seems to be laid down in the case of Baxter vs. Roberts, July Term, 1872, Sup.Ct. Cal. Roberts employed Baxter to perform a service which he (Roberts) knew to be perilous, without giving Baxter any notice of its perilous character; Baxter was injured. Held: that Roberts was responsible in damages for the injury which Baxter sustained. (See facts of case.)" (1 Annot. Civ. Code (Haymond & Burch 1874 Ed.) p. 519; italics added.) The Court unanimously construed this reference to be a legislative recognition of contributory negligence, as modified to incorporate the common-law exception of "last clear chance" (which explains the statute's "except so far as" clause).

Code. The Code establishes the law of this State respecting the subjects to which it relates, and its provisions are to be liberally construed with a view to effect its objects and to promote justice." Civ. Code [1872] § 4. Also, "[t]he provisions of this Code, so far as they are substantially the same as existing statutes or the common law, must be construed as *continuations* thereof, and not as new enactments." *Id.* § 5; emphasis added.

The Court further explained that its precedents had developed section 1714 in a common-law way. "For example, the statute by its express language speaks of causation only in terms of actual cause or cause in fact ('Every one is responsible * * * for an injury occasioned to another by his want of ordinary care.'), but this has not prevented active judicial development of the twin concepts of proximate causation and duty of care. Conversely, the presence of this statutory language has not hindered the development of rules which, in certain limited circumstances, permit a finding of liability *in the absence* of direct evidence establishing the defendant's negligence as the actual cause of damage. (See *Summers v. Tice* (1948) 199 P.2d 1, 5; *Ybarra v. Spangard* (1944) 154 P.2d 687.) By the same token we do not believe that the general language of section 1714 dealing with defensive considerations should be construed so as to stifle the orderly evolution of such considerations in light of emerging techniques and concepts. On the contrary we conclude that the rule of liberal construction made applicable to the code by its own terms (Civ. Code, § 4, discussed [above]) together with the Code's peculiar character as a continuation of the common law (see Civ. Code, § 5, also discussed [above]) permit if not require that section 1714 be interpreted so as to give dynamic expression to the fundamental precepts which it summarizes.

"The aforementioned precepts are basically two. The first is that one whose negligence has caused damage to another should be liable therefor. The second is that one whose negligence has contributed to his own injury should not be permitted to cast the burden of liability upon another." The legislature used what common law resources that existed in 1872 (namely, contributory negligence, with a last clear chance defense) to balance these precepts. By 1975, the common law had developed a more equitable way to balance them, namely, comparative negligence. Now that such a doctrine has been developed, and adopted in most other states, the court ruled that it should be read into section 1714.

Justice Clark dissented. "First, the majority's decision deviates from settled rules of statutory construction. A cardinal rule of construction is to effect the intent of the Legislature," which the court concededly violated. "The majority decision also departs significantly from the recognized limitation upon judicial action—encroaching on the powers constitutionally entrusted to the Legislature.... The majority's altering the meaning of section 1714, notwithstanding the original intent of the framers and the century-old judicial interpretation of the statute, represents no less than amendment by judicial fiat." Although society has changed, the proper process to update the statute is through legislative, not judicial, amendment.

NOTES ON *JACOB*, *LI*, AND DYNAMIC READINGS OF STATE CODES

1. *Common Law Judges Interpreting Civil Codes.* Statutory interpretation of a provision (like § 1714) in a comprehensive civil (or other) code is in some ways different from interpretation of a provision in a less integrated statutory scheme.[f] Recall our mention in Chapter 6, § 1 of civil law versus common law approaches to statutes—especially the code concept of the "equity of a statute," which encourages reasoning from one statute to another. The *Li* case points out another peculiarly code concept—that the statute itself will set forth rules of interpretation. The Italian Civil Code, for example, provides:

> In interpreting the statute, no other meaning can be attributed to it than that made clear by the actual significance of the words * * * and by the intention of the legislature.

> If a controversy cannot be decided by a precise provision, consideration is given to provisions that regulate similar cases or analogous matters; if the case still remains in doubt, it is decided according to the general principles of the legal order of the state.

Note the similarities between this formulation and that of Hart and Sacks' general theory of statutory interpretation—and of the approach followed by Chief Judge Kaye in *Jacob*.

Likewise, the California Civil Code provisions quoted by the *Li* Court arguably mandate a "liberal" construction of the Code. Section 3510 of the California Civil Code also enacted in 1872 (not cited by the Court) is perhaps most pertinent to the Court's reworking of § 1714: "When the reason of a rule ceases, so should the rule itself." The leading commentator on the California Code, John Norton Pomeroy, argued that the Code provisions should be treated like common law precedents, to be expanded or modified as times changed. Pomeroy, *The True Method of Interpreting the Civil Code*, 4 West Coast Rptr. 109–10 (1884). *Li* seems to follow the Pomeroy precept.

Another way of understanding the dynamic interpretations in *Li* and *Jacob* is through the lens of common law judging. In contrast to federal courts, which are courts of strictly limited jurisdiction having little if any lawmaking authority, see Thomas A. Merrill, *The Common Law Powers of Federal Courts*, 52 U. Chi. L. Rev. 1, 32–35 (1985), state judiciaries are common law courts, with inherent lawmaking authority. Their common law authority to make law vests state judges with greater legitimacy as well as competence to update statutes to reflect new circumstances. See Chief Judge Judith S. Kaye, *State Courts at the Dawn of a New Century: Common Law Courts Reading Statutes and Constitutions*, 70 N.Y.U. L. Rev. 1 (1995). Additionally, most state court judges do not serve for life, and many are either

---

f. On statutory interpretation of civil law codes, see John Henry Merryman, *The Civil Law Tradition* 40–49 (1969); *Interpreting Statutes: A Comparative Study* (Neil MacCormick & Robert S. Summers eds. 1991); Konrad Zweigert & Hans–Jurgen Puttfarken, *Statutory Interpretation— Civilian Style in Civilian Methodology*, 44 Tul. L. Rev. 673 (1970).

initially elected by the voters or subject to retention elections. As a result, such judges are also more democratically accountable, and their accountability might give them greater freedom (a freedom which we should expect such judges to exercise cautiously). Do these rationales justify Chief Judge Kaye's significant recasting of the adoption statute in *Jacob*? Would her rationales be a better justification for *Li*, which involved a common law area (torts), an open-textured statute, and judges subject to retention elections?

2. *Reversing the Burden of Legislative Inertia as a Justification for Judicial Recognition of Second–Parent Adoptions.* The changed circumstance in *Jacob* is somewhat different from the one in *Li*. When New York passed its adoption law, the idea of two women raising a child in a "lesbian" household would have been inconceivable; the legislators in 1872 would have had the women arrested for violating the state sodomy law. By 1995, New York had judicially invalidated its sodomy law, and lesbian unions with children were not unusual. Like most other states, New York had amended its adoption law to accommodate "second-parent adoptions," but those did not include female couples whose unions were not recognized as "marriages" by the state.[g] (Section 117 allowed adoption only if the biological mother gave up her rights; the legislature had relaxed this rule for stepparent adoptions, but not second parents of the same sex.)

This legislative failure may have been due to ambivalence about lesbian and gay families—and so the New York Court of Appeals' willingness to update the statute may have been a move to *reverse the burden of legislative inertia* in these cases: second parents presumptively can adopt, until the legislature overrides that interpretation. Most state supreme courts in gay-tolerant states have followed Chief Judge Kaye's dynamic reading of state adoption statutes,[h] but some have gone the other way,[i] and some states have allowed joint lesbian or gay parenting through legislation recognizing their civil unions (Connecticut, New Jersey, Vermont) or domestic partnerships (California, Oregon, and Washington).

Is this kind of political burden-shifting justifiable—or is it yet another example of hated "judicial activism"? Drawing from representation-reinforcing theories of judicial review, Eskridge, *Dynamic Statutory Interpretation* ch. 5, argues that reversing the burden of inertia is particularly justified when the political process has traditionally been hostile to a minority group. Not only does this kind of judicial updating level the playing field a little, but it places the burden on political groups that are actually able to attract the legislature's attention. If the will of the people is to deny lesbian and gay

---

g. See Nancy D. Polikoff, *This Child Does Have Two Mothers: Redefining Parenthood To Meet the Needs of Children in Lesbian–Mother and Other Nontraditional Families*, 78 Geo. L.J. 459 (1990).

h. See *Sharon S. v. Superior Court*, 31 Cal.4th 417 (2003); *In re Hart*, 806 A.2d 1179 (Del. Fam. Ct. 2001); *In re M.M.D. and B.H.M.*, 662 A.2d 837 (D.C. 1995); *Petition of K.M. and D.M.*, 653 N.E.2d 888 (Ill. App. 1995); *Adoption of K.S.P.*, 804 N.E.2d 1253 (Ind. App. 2004); *Adoption of Tammy*, 619 N.E.2d 315 (Mass. 1993); *Adoptions of B.L.V.B. and E.L.V.B.*, 628 A.2d 1271 (Vt. 1993).

i. See *Adoption of Baby Z*, 724 A.2d 1035 (Conn. 1999); *Adoption of Luke*, 640 N.W.2d 374 (Neb. 2002); *Adoption of Jane Doe*, 719 N.E.2d 1071 (Ohio App. 1998); *In re Angel Lace M.*, 516 N.W.2d 678 (Wis. 1994). Wisconsin recognized de facto parentage, which is functionally similar to second-parent adoptions. See *In re Custody of H.S.H.–K.*, 533 N.W.2d 419 (Wis. 1995).

parents these rights, a decision granting relief in *Jacob* will probably be overridden in short order. (The converse case will not be: minorities traditionally disadvantaged in the political process find it doubly hard to persuade the legislature to do anything for them, because legislators fear backlash.)

Moreover, reversing the burden of inertia gives the persecuted minority an opportunity to falsify stereotypes—in this case, the stereotype of gay people as incapable of forming families or, indeed, as anti-family or even predatory. By allowing lesbian and gay couples to adopt children, Chief Judge Kaye was giving New Yorkers an opportunity to see that lesbian and gay families can be nurturing and productive. Not only did the New York Legislature not rebuke Chief Judge Kaye, but years of lesbian and gay family formation helped persuade the Legislature in 2011 to amend its family law code to recognize same-sex marriages.

3. *The Female Juror Cases, a Classic Example of Judicial Updating.* State statutes have often provided that juries are to be selected from a list of the qualified "electors" (i.e., voters) of the jurisdiction. Both the legislatures of Pennsylvania and Illinois adopted such statutes at a time when women were not allowed to vote in either state. After the ratification of the Nineteenth Amendment to the United States Constitution, which guaranteed women the right to vote, were women eligible to serve as jurors in these states by virtue of these statutes?

In *Commonwealth v. Maxwell*, 114 A. 825, 829 (Pa. 1921), the Supreme Court of Pennsylvania held that women were qualified to serve on juries:

> We then have the act of 1867, constitutionally providing that the jury commissioners are required to select "from the whole qualified electors of the respective county * * * persons, to serve as jurors in the several courts of such county," and the Nineteenth Amendment to the federal Constitution, putting women in the body of electors. * * *

> "Statutes framed in general terms apply to new cases that arise, and to new subjects that are created from time to time, and which come within their general scope and policy. It is a rule of statutory construction that legislative enactments in general and comprehensive terms, prospective in operation, apply alike to all persons, subjects, and business within their general purview and scope coming into existence subsequent to their passage." 25 Ruling Case Law, 778.

But in *People ex rel. Fyfe v. Barnett*, 150 N.E. 290, 292 (Ill. 1925), the Supreme Court of Illinois reached the opposite result:

> At the time of the passage by the Legislature of the act above mentioned, providing for the appointment of a jury commission and the making of jury lists, the words "voters" and "electors" were not ambiguous terms. They had a well-defined and settled meaning. [The Illinois Constitution of 1870 limited the franchise to "male citizen[s] of the United States, above the age of twenty-one."]

> The legislative intent that controls in the construction of a statute has reference to the Legislature which passed the given act. 25 R.C.L. 1029. Applying the rules of construction herein mentioned, it is evident that when the Legislature enacted the law in question, which provided for the

appointment of jury commissioners in counties having more than 250,000 inhabitants and imposing upon them the duty of making a jury list, using the words "shall prepare a list of all electors between the ages of twenty-one and sixty years, possessing the necessary legal qualifications for jury duty, to be known as the jury list," it was intended to use the words "electors" and "elector" as the same were then defined by the Constitution and laws of the state of Illinois. At that time the Legislature did not intend that the name of any women should be placed on the jury list, and must be held to have intended that the list should be composed of the names of male persons, only. In interpreting a statute, the question is what the words used therein meant to those using them. 25 R.C.L. 1029. The word "electors," in the statute here in question, meant male persons, only, to the legislators who used it. We must therefore hold that the word "electors," as used in the statute, means male persons, only, and that the petitioner was not entitled to have her name replaced upon the jury list of Cook County.

Accord *Commonwealth v. Welosky*, 177 N.E. 656 (Mass. 1931).

Hart and Sacks' *The Legal Process* 1172–85 (1994 ed.) discussed these cases. Their critical questions suggest several reasons why a court might interpret a statute beyond or against the original legislative intent (as the courts did in *Jacob* and in *Li*).

(a) Consider how these courts addressed the issue of legislative intent. Is the question whether the legislature that enacted the jury-selection statute had a specific intent concerning women as jurors? What is the likelihood that there was such a specific intent? Or is the question whether the legislature intended the term "elector" to be frozen in the meaning given it by voter-qualification statutes in effect when the jury selection statutes were first enacted, or to vary as voter qualifications changed over time?

(b) What was the purpose of the juror-qualification statutes? Would that purpose be better served by interpreting "elector" as frozen to the factual setting prior to the ratification of the Nineteenth Amendment, or alternatively as embodying later developments? If the legislature had known that the Nineteenth Amendment was going to be adopted, wouldn't its members have wanted its juror statutes to conform to the expanded concept of citizenship represented by that Amendment?

(c) Should the court avoid an "irrational pattern of particular applications" of the statute? Hart and Sacks, *The Legal Process*, at 1125. Doesn't a court have an obligation to enhance law's overall "coherence," rather than recognizing inconsistent rules? Shouldn't the court be reluctant to interpret the juror-selection statutes in a way that runs against a fundamental legal principle or policy? Would the exclusion of women from juries have been unconstitutional when Hart and Sacks were writing? See *Hoyt v. Florida*, 368 U.S. 57 (1961) (not unconstitutional). If so, or even if the issue just raised difficult constitutional questions, wouldn't that provide a justification for construing the open-textured statute to include women? Consider these points as you read the cases in the next section.

3. Coherence With Public Norms

Public Citizen v. United States Department of Justice, 491 U.S. 440 (1989). The question was whether the Standing Committee on the Federal Judiciary of the American Bar Association (ABA) was subject to the Federal Advisory Committee Act (FACA), 5 U.S.C. § 1 et seq., which imposes disclosure and open meeting requirements on a federal "advisory committee." The statute defines "advisory committee" as, among other things, any committee "established or utilized by the President [or] by one or more agencies, in the interest of obtaining advice or recommendations for the President." The President, through the Justice Department, routinely seeks the advice of the ABA committee concerning the qualifications of potential federal judicial nominees. **Justice Brennan**'s majority opinion declined to hold that the ABA committee was within the statute's scope. He invoked *Holy Trinity Church* to escape the apparent meaning of "utilize," and after a lengthy evaluation of the legislative history concluded that "utilize" had been added late in the legislative process "simply to clarify that FACA applies to advisory committees established by the Federal Government in a generous sense of that term"—that is, in addition to groups formally established by the federal government, to groups formed indirectly by quasi-public organizations, such as the National Academy of Sciences, that are used and officially recognized as advisory to the executive branch.

Justice Kennedy, joined by Chief Justice Rehnquist and Justice O'Connor, concurred only in the judgment. (Justice Scalia did not participate in this case.) "Where the language of a statute is clear in its application, the normal rule is that we are bound by it. There is, of course, a legitimate exception to this rule, which the Court invokes, citing *Holy Trinity Church*, and with which I have no quarrel. Where the plain language of the statute would lead to 'patently absurd consequences' that 'Congress could not *possibly* have intended,' we need not apply the language in such a fashion. When used in a proper manner, this narrow exception to our normal rule of statutory construction does not intrude upon the lawmaking powers of Congress, but rather demonstrates a respect for the coequal Legislative Branch, which we assume would not act in an absurd way.

"This exception remains a legitimate tool of the judiciary, however, only as long as the Court acts with self-discipline by limiting the exception to situations where the result of applying the plain language would be, in a genuine sense, absurd, *i.e.*, where it is quite impossible that Congress could have intended the result, and where the alleged absurdity is so clear as to be obvious to most anyone. * * * In today's opinion, however, the Court disregards the plain language of the statute not because its application would be patently absurd, but rather because, on the basis of its view of the legislative history, the Court is 'fairly confident' that 'FACA should [not] be construed to apply to the ABA Committee.' I believe the Court's loose invocation of the 'absurd result' canon of statutory construction creates too great a risk that the Court is exercising its own 'WILL instead of JUDGMENT,' with the consequence of 'substituti[ng] [its own] plea-sure to that of the legislative body.' The Federalist No. 78 (A. Hamilton).'' Kennedy argued that it would not at all be ''absurd'' to apply the FACA to ABA committees and then concluded:

''Unable to show that an application of FACA according to the plain meaning of its terms would be absurd, the Court turns instead to the task of demonstrating that a straightforward reading of the statute would be inconsistent with the congressional purposes that lay behind its passage. To the student of statutory construction, this move is a familiar one. It is, as the Court identifies it, the classic *Holy Trinity* argument. '[A] thing may be within the letter of the statute and yet not within the statute, because not within its spirit, nor within the intention of its makers.' *Holy Trinity.* I cannot embrace this principle. Where it is clear that the unambiguous language of a statute embraces certain conduct, and it would not be patently absurd to apply the statute to such conduct, it does not foster a democratic exegesis for this Court to rummage through unautho-ritative materials to consult the spirit of the legislation in order to discover an alternative interpretation of the statute with which the Court is more comfortable. It comes as a surprise to no one that the result of the Court's lengthy journey through the legislative history is the discovery of a congressional intent not to include the activities of the ABA Committee within the coverage of FACA. The problem with spirits is that they tend to reflect less the views of the world whence they come than the views of those who seek their advice.

''Lest anyone think that my objection to the use of the *Holy Trinity* doctrine is a mere point of interpretive purity divorced from more prac-tical considerations, I should pause for a moment to recall the unhappy genesis of that doctrine and its unwelcome potential. * * * The central support for the Court's ultimate conclusion [in *Holy Trinity*] that Con-gress did not intend the law to cover Christian ministers is its lengthy review of the 'mass of organic utterances' establishing that 'this is a Christian nation,' and which were taken to prove that it could not 'be believed that a Congress of the United States intended to make it a misdemeanor for a church of this country to contract for the services of a Christian minister residing in another nation.' I should think the potential of this doctrine to allow judges to substitute their personal predilections for the will of the Congress is so self-evident from the case which spawned it as to require no further discussion of its susceptibility to abuse.''

STATE OF NEW JERSEY v. 1979 PONTIAC TRANS AM ETC.

New Jersey Supreme Court, 1985
487 A.2d 722, 98 N.J. 474

Opinion of POLLOCK, J. * * *

[On July 25, 1982, Orlando Figueroa and a companion were driving home from the shore in his father's Pontiac. Inebriated, the young men confiscated the "T-roof" of a Corvette and drove off with it. The police tracked down the youths and reclaimed the T-roof. Pursuant to N.J.S.A. 2C:64–3, the county moved to confiscate the father's Pontiac, and the courts granted the motion.]

[F]orfeiture refers to the divestiture without compensation of title to property used to further criminal activity. Statutes authorizing forfeiture stem from ancient religious beliefs that religious expiation was required of a chattel that caused a person's death. *Calero–Toledo v. Pearson Yacht Leasing Co.*, 416 U.S. 663, 680–81 (1974) (*Calero–Toledo*). * * *

Modern forfeiture statutes are supported by more contemporary considerations than those that originally gave rise to forfeiture. At present, forfeiture proceedings are often viewed as the only adequate means to protect against a particular offense, *e.g.*, the forfeiture of a still may be the only way to prevent the continued illegal distillation of alcohol. Consistent with that viewpoint, the New Jersey Organized Crime Task Force proposed the use of forfeiture as a civil remedy to combat organized crime. In addition, forfeiture is regarded as a means of encouraging owners to be more responsible in lending their personal property. Ultimately, forfeiture statutes are justifiable to the extent that they are a legitimate exercise of the police power.

Despite their utility to law enforcement officials, forfeitures remain disfavored in the law. One problem is that forfeitures result in the taking of private property for public use without compensation to the owner. The United States Supreme Court has recognized this problem under the fifth amendment of the United States Constitution, *U.S. v. U.S. Coin & Currency*, 401 U.S. [715,] 720–21; similar concerns arise under article 1, paragraph 20 of the New Jersey Constitution. Accordingly, New Jersey courts have required that forfeiture statutes be strictly construed "and in a manner as favorable to the person whose property is to be seized as is consistent with the fair principles of interpretation." *State v. One (1) Ford Van Econoline*, 154 N.J. Super. at 331–32.

In defining property subject to forfeiture, N.J.S.A. 2C:64–1 establishes two broad categories: (1) prima facie contraband, such as unlawfully possessed controlled dangerous substances and firearms, and (2) other kinds of property, such as conveyances "utilized in furtherance of an unlawful activity * * *." As originally enacted, N.J.S.A. 2C:64–1 applied only to "the defendant's interest" in the forfeited property. In 1981, however, the statute was broadened to apply to "any interest" that falls within the statutory definition of property subject to forfeiture. * * *

As a result of the 1981 amendment, that statute now provides:

No forfeiture under this chapter shall affect the rights of any lessor or any person holding a perfected security interest in property subject to seizure unless it shall appear that such person had knowledge of or consented to any act or omission upon which the right of forfeiture is based. Such rights are only to the extent of interest in the seized property and at the option of the entity funding the prosecuting agency involved may be extinguished by appropriate payment. * * *

Because forfeitures are not generally favored in the law, provisions relieving owners from the application of forfeiture statutes are liberally construed. Consistent with that perspective, we construe N.J.S.A. 2C:64–5 to exempt not only lessors and lienholders but also innocent owners who can prove that they were "uninvolved in and unaware of the wrongful activity, [and] that [they] had done all that reasonably could be expected to prevent the proscribed use of [their] property." *Calero–Toledo*, 416 U.S. at 689. As to these owners, it "would be difficult to conclude that forfeiture served legitimate purposes and was not unduly oppressive." *Id.* at 690. A stricter interpretation of the statute would run afoul of constitutional prohibitions against taking property without due process. *Id.*

In *Calero–Toledo*, the Court upheld the constitutionality of Puerto Rico's forfeiture statute as applied to an innocent lessor whose yacht was seized by the Puerto Rican government after the lessee was arrested for possession of marijuana. [The Court found that the lessor had not done all it reasonably could have done to prevent the illegal use of its vessel. In dicta, the Court said a forfeiture law would be unduly oppressive if applied to those owners who had not consented to and were unaware of the unlawful use of their property, provided they had done all that reasonably could be expected to prevent that use.]

Following the lead of the United States Supreme Court, we construe N.J.S.A. 2C:64–1 and–5 to exclude innocent owners who did not consent to or know of the illegal use of their property and who did all that reasonably could be expected to prevent that use. Thus construed, the statute survives the constitutional attack that it constitutes an unlawful taking of property without just compensation. See *Town Tobacconist v. Kimmelman*, 94 N.J. 85, 104 (1983) ("judicial surgery" used to save from constitutional attack the statutory definition of drug paraphernalia).

Reading into the statute an exemption for innocent owners who use due care to prevent unlawful use of their property is consistent with the legislative intent as expressed elsewhere in the statute. For example, N.J.S.A. 2C:64–2 provides that the forfeiture of *prima facie* contraband, such as controlled dangerous substances, is subject to the rights of owners. Because the Legislature acknowledged that the forfeiture of an item such as drugs was subject to rights of owners, it is reasonable to assume that the Legislature intended to provide a similar exemption for property that is not *prima facie* contraband. Furthermore, N.J.S.A. 2C:64–8 gives innocent owners up to three years to file a claim, if with due diligence they could not have discovered the seizure of the contraband. By restricting relief under N.J.S.A. 2C:64–8 to owners unaware of the unlawful use of the property, the Legislature apparently recognized that knowledge was relevant to forfeiture. * * *

Postscript. The U.S. Supreme Court (5–4) subsequently upheld the application of a state forfeiture law to an automobile half-owned by an innocent third party. *Bennis v. Michigan*, 516 U.S. 442 (1996). The Court characterized the quoted *Calero–Toledo* language as "obiter dictum" and abrogated it. The Court held that the innocence of the co-owner made no constitutional difference. Should the New Jersey Supreme Court now revisit its statutory interpretation in the *Trans Am* case?

NOTES ON PUBLIC CITIZEN, TRANS AM, AND COHERENCE-BASED JUSTIFICATIONS FOR "JUDICIAL SURGERY"

1. *Legal Process Theory and Judicial Surgery.* Neither *Public Citizen* nor *Trans Am* is easily justified by the purpose of the statute, the usual legal process move when judges are reading exceptions into a statutory text (recall *Weber* or the first part of *Holy Trinity*). Although the author of the New Jersey opinion has analogized this kind of "judicial surgery" to the limited discretion afforded a musician interpreting a piece of music, Stewart G. Pollock, *The Art of Judging*, 71 N.Y.U. L. Rev. 591, 601–02 (1996), the strong arm given the statutory language makes the case look more like an exercise in "spurious interpretation," to use Roscoe Pound's terminology. Both Courts ultimately justify their exceedingly narrow readings by reference to larger public norms, like the second part of *Holy Trinity*. But the concurring Justices in *Public Citizen* excoriate the Court for this move, and the Christian Nation portions of *Holy Trinity* are surely controversial today even under a normativist approach. Can this methodology be defended under legal process assumptions?

One way to defend this approach is to say that it is properly respectful of the legislature: courts and agencies should assume that the legislature intends to adopt constitutional laws, and if new constitutional norms raise troubles for statutes, courts should trim the statutes back a little—so long as the "judicial surgery" is not too radical and does not undermine the statutory goal. Can that be said of the surgery performed in *Public Citizen* and *Trans Am*?

Another way to defend this approach is by charging judges with a duty to make the law coherent. This is the basis for Hart and Sacks' maxim that "forbids a court to understand a legislature as directing a departure from a generally prevailing principle or policy of the law unless it does so clearly. This policy has special force when the departure is so great as to raise a serious question of constitutional power." *The Legal Process* 1377. Public norms, especially constitutional ones, have a "gravitational" pull on statutes. See William N. Eskridge Jr., *Public Values in Statutory Interpretation*, 137 U. Pa. L. Rev. 1007 (1989).

A final way to view these cases is to understand the role of judges as openly critical and normative. This does not sound like a legal process mode of thinking, but two leading process writers have developed precisely that idea. As you read the following notes, consider the separation of powers and majoritarian difficulties with each theory.

2. *Lon Fuller's Theory of the Repeatedly Retold Anecdote.* In his book, *Law in Quest of Itself* 8–9 (1940), Lon L. Fuller contested the positivist claim

that fact is wholly independent of value—and interpretation independent of norms:

> If I attempt to retell a funny story which I have heard, the story as I tell it will be the product of two forces: (1) the story as I heard it ... [and] (2) my conception of the point of the story, in other words, my notion of the story *as it ought to be* ... If the story as I heard it was, in my opinion, badly told, I am guided largely by my conception of the story as it ought to be ... On the other hand, if I had the story from a master raconteur, I may exert myself to reproduce his exact words ... These two forces, then, supplement one another in shaping the story as I tell it. It is the product of the *is* and the *ought* working together ... The two are inextricably interwoven, to the point where we can say that "the story" as an entity really embraces both of them. Indeed, if we look at the story across time, its reality becomes even more complex. The "point" of the story, which furnishes its essential unity, may in the course of retelling be changed. As it is brought out more clearly through the skill of successive tellers it becomes a new point; at some indefinable juncture the story has been so improved that it has become a new story. In a sense, then, the thing we call "the story" is not something that is, but something that becomes; it is not a hard chunk of reality, but a fluid process, which is as much directed by men's creative impulses, by their conception of the story as it ought to be, as it is by the original even which unlocked those impulses. The *ought* here is just as real, as a part of human experience, as the *is*, and the line between the two melts away in the common stream of telling and retelling into which they both flow.

"Exactly the same thing may be said of a statute or a decision," Fuller continues. "The statute or decision is not a segment of being, but, like the anecdote, a process of becoming." *Id.* at 9–10.

Fuller's justification for this way of approaching law is not its inevitability, however. Rather, he maintains that the interconnection between law and morality is a good thing. The main argument is one of coherence. Because the "bulk of human relations find their regulation outside the field of positive law," a continuous interpenetration of law and social morality creates a more seamless web of interconnected rights and duties. *Id.* at 11–12. Fuller emphasized that such interconnection was necessary to the efficacy of law; without a link with changing social mores, law would not be able to achieve its goals or, worse, would lose the respect of the citizenry. See Lon L. Fuller, *Human Interaction and the Law*, in *The Principles of Social Order: The Selected Essays of Lon L. Fuller* 211–46 (Kenneth Winston ed. 1981).

Does Fuller's theory provide a good justification for the textual strongarming in the *Trans Am* and *Public Citizen* cases? Consider a later version of his theory, discussed in the next note.

3. *"Chain Novels" and Dworkin's Theory of Law as Integrity.* Many legal scholars have followed Fuller's lead and have explored his idea that law is interpretive in some of the same ways that stories are.[j] The most influential

---

j. For uses of hermeneutics in statutory interpretation, see William N. Eskridge Jr., *Gadamer/Statutory Interpretation*, 90 Colum. L. Rev. 609 (1990); Francis J. Mootz III, *The Ontological Basis of Legal Hermeneutics: A Proposed Model of Inquiry Based on the Work of Gadamer,* of the post-Fuller theories is Ronald Dworkin's idea that law is an interpretive enterprise that seeks to "show it as the best work of art it can be." *Law as Interpretation*, 60 Tex. L. Rev. 527 (1982). Dworkin explains his vision of interpretation by reference to the idea of a "chain novel," *id*. at 541–43:

> * * * Suppose that a group of novelists is engaged for a particular project and that they draw lots to determine the order of play. The lowest number writes the opening chapter of a novel, which he or she then sends to the next number, with the understanding that he is adding a chapter to that novel rather than beginning a new one, and then sends the two chapters to the next number, and so on. Now every novelist but the first has the dual responsibilities of interpreting and creating because each must read all that has gone before in order to establish, in the interpretivist sense, what the novel so far created is. He or she must decide what the characters are "really" like; what motives in fact guide them; what the point or theme of the developing novel is; how far some literary device or figure, consciously, or unconsciously used, contributes to these, and whether it should be extended or refined or trimmed or dropped in order to send the novel further in one direction rather than another. This must be interpretation in a non-intention-bound style because, at least for all novelists after the second, there is no single author whose intentions any interpreter can, by the rules of the project, regard as decisive. * * *

> Deciding hard cases at law is rather like this strange literary exercise. The similarity is most evident when judges consider and decide common-law cases; that is, when no statute figures centrally in the legal issue, and the argument turns on which rules or principles of law "underlie" the related decisions of other judges in the past. Each judge is then like a novelist in the chain. He or she must read through what other judges in the past have written not simply to discover what these judges have said, or their state of mind when they said it, but to reach an opinion about what these judges have collectively *done*, in the way that each of our novelists formed an opinion about the collective novel so far written.

In *Law's Empire* 313 (1986), Dworkin describes how the chain novel tells judges to interpret statutes:

> He will treat Congress as an author earlier than himself in the chain of law, though an author with special powers and responsibilities different from his own [as a judge], and he will see his own role as fundamentally the creative one of a partner continuing to develop, in what he believes is the best way, the statutory scheme Congress began. He will ask himself which reading of the act * * * shows the political history including and surrounding that statute in the better light. His view of how the statute should be read will in part depend on what certain congressmen said when debating it. But it will also depend on the best answer to political questions: how far Congress should defer to public opinion in matters of this sort, for example * * *.

Habermas, and Ricoeur, 68 B.U. L. Rev. 523 (1988); Dennis M. Patterson, *Wittgenstein and the Code: A Theory of Good Faith Performance and Enforcement under Article Nine*, 137 U. Pa. L. Rev. 335 (1988). On the connection between theories of statutory interpretation and philosophical postmodernism, see Peter C. Schanck, *Understanding Postmodern Thought and Its Implications for Statutory Interpretation*, 65 S. Cal. L. Rev. 2505 (1992).

On the application of his theory to *Weber*, see Dworkin, *How to Read the Civil Rights Act*, in Dworkin, *A Matter of Principle* (1985). How would Dworkin's theory apply to the *Trans Am* and *Public Citizen* cases?

C.   CONCERNS ABOUT LEGAL PROCESS THEORY, 1970s–80s

Legal process theory came into focus around the time of World War II. This was a period of relative consensus in America, sustained economic growth, and burgeoning optimism about government's ability to foster economic growth by solving market failures and creating opportunities. After the mid–1960s, America was a different society, as consensus collapsed on fundamental issues of war, family, and citizenship; economic growth faltered and oil price shocks introduced stagflation; and government came to be perceived as problematic, often even as a drain on society's productivity. These developments raised inevitable questions about statutory methodology, such as the ones that follow.

1. *The Need for a More Realistic View of the Legislative Process?* Recall our discussion of theories of legislatures in Chapter 1, § 2. One lesson of "public choice" theories is that legislators are not entirely "reasonable," as Hart and Sacks assume, and are often acting to extract "rents" for their constituents and supportive interest groups. Moreover, even reasonable legislators will disagree, and the resulting statutes may be compromises more than easily understood purposive enactments. Some law and economics scholars have argued from such theories that Hart and Sacks' purposive approach should therefore be reined back toward something like Pound's imaginative reconstruction. See Richard A. Posner, *The Federal Courts: Crisis and Reform* 286–93 (1985).

On the other hand, Hart and Sacks never claimed their "reasonable legislator" approach actually describes the legislature; they only said that courts should "attribute" purposes to the legislature, suggesting that theirs is a normative-based rather than a descriptive-based theory of interpretation. Why should ambiguous interest-group deals be enforced by courts if they do not serve a larger public purpose? See Jonathan R. Macey, *Promoting Public–Regarding Legislation Through Statutory Interpretation: An Interest Group Model*, 86 Colum. L. Rev. 223 (1986), who argues that rent-seeking legislators should be held to their stated public-regarding justifications.

2. *Does the Hart and Sacks Approach Submerge Substantive Issues Too Much?* Both pragmatic and critical scholars criticize legal process theory for suppressing useful substantive discussion. Judge Posner, for example, openly inquires about the practical consequences of different interpretations. See, e.g., Richard A. Posner, *How Judges Think* ch. 5 (2008), and *The Problems of Jurisprudence* (1990). His practice is to figure out what is the most reasonable statutory interpretation, as applied to the facts before him, and then see if statutory text, history, and precedent foreclose the best option. This sounds a lot like Hart and Sacks, but

Posner would say that he adds empirical data and systematic economic thinking that Hart and Sacks did not emphasize. Why not introduce rigorous, empirically based economic analysis into decisionmaking?

Critical scholars argue that legal process judges are making unarticulated value choices under the auspices of neutral craft. Allan Hutchinson and Derek Morgan, in *The Semiology of Statutes*, 21 Harv. J. Legis. 583, 593–94 (1984) (book review), state:

> While there has been a judicial capitulation to the supremacy of Parliament, that surrender is to a command to be obeyed begrudgingly according to its letter. Otherwise, it is of little consequence. For the courts, the triumph of statute over common law is a pyrrhic victory. But this betrays the ideological superstructure of adjudication. Words do not interpret themselves. A sentence will never mean exactly the same thing to any two different people or even the same thing to one person on different occasions. Meaning is shaped by the apperceptive mass of understanding and background that an individual brings to bear on the external fact of a sound or series of marks. As words lack "self-evident reference," purpose and context are ultimately major determinants of meaning. However, as the expression of legislative intent is always more or less incomplete, it is doubtful whether any impartial method of adjudication can be fashioned in a liberal society.
> * * *
>
> The necessity of engaging in such invention requires the courts to make substantive political decisions, the very decisions that semantic, historical or counter-factual approaches *claim* to avoid. No one single "construction" is inevitable or natural. Construction means choice. And choice confers power. Of course, this is not to suggest that judicial creativity breeds constitutional anarchy. Communities of interpretation have their own bonding mechanisms, a mixture of moral values and social customs. Interpretation is inextricably bound up with values and it is nowhere seriously suggested the values do not carry ideological underpinnings. The lesson to be gathered from this realization is quite simple. Courts that shield themselves behind descriptions of law as clear, predetermined and objective norms against which they pitch their neutral decisions are worthy of suspicion. * * *

On this understanding, a virtue of Justice Brewer's opinion in *Holy Trinity Church* is that it was candid about the values it was implementing (the Christian nation idea). Hart and Sacks' approach would likely generate the same result in the hands of a Justice Brewer, but perhaps a less candid discussion. Recall, too, Judge Handy's opinion in the Case of the Speluncean Explorers.

3. *The Appeal of Formalism.* Among judges, the most telling criticism of the legal process approach to statutory interpretation is that it neglects the virtues of a more formalist approach. Even contextualists might concede the attractions of the plain meaning rule, very ably defend-

ed by Judge Keen in Speluncean Explorers. First, it is arguably more consistent with the structure of the U.S. Constitution (and most state constitutions), which vests political power with the legislative and executive branches and only the judicial power with the courts, and which creates formal barriers to lawmaking that are disregarded when courts make new law. See John F. Manning, *Textualism as a Nondelegation Doctrine*, 97 Colum. L. Rev. 673 (1997). Second, and entirely within the legal process tradition, it can be argued that applying statutory plain meanings is more within the "judicial competence" than making policy or even scanning through legislative history to figure out whether the legislature "really meant" the apparent meaning of its statutory words. See Adrian Vermeule, *Legislative History and the Limits of Judicial Competence: The Untold Story of* Holy Trinity Church, 50 Stan. L. Rev. 1833 (1998).

Third, and in our view most powerfully, the ordinary meaning of statutory language is the common understanding of what the "rule of law" is. See Antonin Scalia, *The Rule of Law as a Law of Rules*, 56 U. Chi. L. Rev. 1175 (1989). Citizens ought to be able to open up the statute books and find out what the law requires of them. Once law is understood by the cognoscenti as purposes, spirits, and collective intents, the citizenry might lose faith in the externality of law—the objectivity of legal reasoning which provides us with some assurance that our problems are susceptible of the same rules as those of our neighbor (even if she is a rich and influential neighbor). The changes in American society since the 1960s make an external vision of the rule of law even more important than before. In a society where so many values are open to contest, language may be the main thing we share in common. In a society where "the pie" is not expanding and the economy is stagnant, dividing the pie by an objective criterion becomes ever more critical.

A less complicated approach may also be more democracy-enhancing, because it places responsibility for updating statutes on the shoulders of the people and their legislators, rather than their unelected (federal and some state) or not-often-elected (most state) judges. Recall Judge Keen's argument that hard cases generating inequitable results should trigger a popular outrage that changes statutes more usefully and more democratically than judicial updating through a Hart-and-Sacks purpose approach. As potential examples of this phenomenon, consider the following cases.

TVA v. HILL
United States Supreme Court, 1978
437 U.S. 153, 98 S.Ct. 2279, 57 L.Ed.2d 117

CHIEF JUSTICE BURGER delivered the opinion of the Court.

[The Endangered Species Act of 1973, 87 Stat. 884, codified as amended at 16 U.S.C. § 1531 *et seq.*, authorized the Secretary of the Interior to declare species of animal life "endangered" and, upon such designation, triggered various protections for such species. Section 7 of the

Act specified that all "Federal departments and agencies shall, * * * with the assistance of the Secretary, utilize their authorities in furtherance of the purposes of [the] Act by carrying out programs for the conservation of endangered species * * * and by taking such action necessary to insure that actions authorized, funded, or carried out by them do not jeopardize the continued existence of such endangered species and threatened species or result in the destruction or modification of habitat of such species which is determined by the Secretary * * * to be critical." 16 U.S.C. § 1536 (1976).

[Pursuant to the statute, the Secretary declared the snail darter (*Percina tanasi*) an endangered species and designated a portion of the Little Tennessee River as the only remaining natural habitat of the snail darter. That part of the river, however, would be flooded by operation of the Tellico Dam, a $100 million Tennessee Valley Authority (TVA) project that was under way in 1973 and was almost completed by 1976, when environmentalists sought an injunction against the dam's operation. The district court denied relief. It found that the dam would destroy the snail darter's critical habitat, but it noted that Congress, though fully aware of the snail darter problem, had continued to fund the Tellico Dam after 1973. The court concluded that the Act did not justify an injunction against a project initiated before enactment. The court of appeals reversed and ordered the lower court to enjoin completion of the dam.]

One would be hard pressed to find a statutory provision whose terms were any plainer than those in § 7 of the Endangered Species Act. Its very words affirmatively command all federal agencies "to *insure* that actions *authorized, funded, or carried out* by them do not *jeopardize* the continued existence" of an endangered species or *"result* in the destruction or modification of habitat of such species. . . ." 16 U.S.C. § 1536 (1976 ed.). (Emphasis added.) This language admits of no exception. Nonetheless, petitioner urges, as do the dissenters, that the Act cannot reasonably be interpreted as applying to a federal project which was well under way when Congress passed the Endangered Species Act of 1973. To sustain that position, however, we would be forced to ignore the ordinary meaning of plain language. It has not been shown, for example, how TVA can close the gates of the Tellico Dam without "carrying out" an action that has been "authorized" and "funded" by a federal agency. Nor can we understand how such action will *"insure"* that the snail darter's habitat is not disrupted. * * *

Concededly, this view of the Act will produce results requiring the sacrifice of the anticipated benefits of the project and of many millions of dollars in public funds. But examination of the language, history, and structure of the legislation under review here indicates beyond doubt that Congress intended endangered species to be afforded the highest of priorities.

[Chief Justice Burger examined statutes enacted in 1966 and 1969, which sought to discourage the taking of endangered species. Congressional hearings in 1973 revealed that strategies of encouragement had not abated the "pace of disappearance of species," which appeared to be "accelerating." H.R. Rep. No. 93–412, p. 4 (1973). The dominant theme of the hearings and debates on the 1973 Act was "the overriding need to devote whatever effort and resources were necessary to avoid further diminution of national and worldwide wildlife resources." George Cameron Coggins, *Conserving Wildlife Resources: An Overview of the Endangered Species Act of 1973*, 51 Notre Dame L. Rev. 315, 321 (1975). Congressional committees expressed the "incalculable" value of lost species.]

Section 7 of the Act * * * provides a particularly good gauge of congressional intent. As we have seen, this provision had its genesis in the Endangered Species Act of 1966, but that legislation qualified the obligation of federal agencies by stating that they should seek to preserve endangered species only *"insofar as is practicable and consistent with their primary purposes . . . ."* Likewise, every bill introduced in 1973 contained a qualification similar to that found in the earlier statutes. * * * This type of language did not go unnoticed by those advocating strong endangered species legislation. A representative of the Sierra Club, for example, attacked the use of the phrase "consistent with the primary purpose" in proposed H.R. 4758, cautioning that the qualification "could be construed to be a declaration of congressional policy that other agency purposes are necessarily more important than protection of endangered species and would always prevail if conflict were to occur."

What is very significant in this sequence is that the final version of the 1973 Act carefully omitted all of the reservations described above. [The Senate bill contained a practicability reservation; the House bill had no qualifications. The Conference Committee rejected the Senate version of § 7 and adopted the House language. Explaining the Conference action, Representative Dingell pointed out that under existing law the Secretary of Defense has discretion to ignore dangers its bombing missions posed to the near-extinct whooping crane. "[O]nce the bill is enacted, [the Secretary of Defense] *would be required to take the proper steps*." Another example was the declining population of grizzly bears, whose habitats would have to be protected by the Department of Agriculture. "The purposes of the bill included the conservation of the species and of the ecosystems upon which they depend, and every agency of government is committed to see that those purposes are carried out. The agencies of Government can no longer plead that they can do nothing about it. *They can and they must. The law is clear*." 119 Cong. Rec. 42913 (emphasis added by the Chief Justice).]

It is against this legislative background that we must measure TVA's claim that the Act was not intended to stop operation of a project which, like Tellico Dam, was near completion when an endangered species was discovered in its path. While there is no discussion of precisely this problem, the totality of congressional action makes it abundantly clear that the result we reach today is wholly in accord with both the words of the statute and the intent of Congress. The plain intent of Congress in enacting this statute was to halt and reverse the trend toward species extinction, whatever the cost. This is reflected not only in the stated provisions of the Act, but in literally every section of the statute. All persons, including federal agencies, are specifically instructed not to "take" endangered species, meaning that no one is "to harass, harm, pursue, hunt, shoot, wound, kill, trap, capture, or collect" such life forms. 16 U.S.C. §§ 1532(14), 1538(a)(1)(B) (1976 ed.). * * *

[TVA also argued that Congress's continued funding of the Dam reflected a congressional judgment, embodied in appropriations statutes, that the Dam not be shut down. Appropriations committees were aware of the effect of the Dam on the snail darter.] There is nothing in the appropriations measures, as passed, which states that the Tellico Project was to be completed irrespective of the requirements of the Endangered Species Act. * * * To find a repeal of the Endangered Species Act under these circumstances would surely do violence to the " 'cardinal rule . . . that repeals by implication are not favored.' " *Morton v. Mancari*, 417 U.S. 535, 549 (1974), quoting *Posadas v. National City Bank*, 296 U.S. 497, 503 (1936). * * *

The doctrine disfavoring repeals by implication "applies with full vigor when . . . the subsequent legislation is an *appropriations* measure." *Committee for Nuclear Responsibility v. Seaborg*, 463 F.2d 783, 785 (D.C. Cir. 1971). This is perhaps an understatement since it would be more accurate to say that the policy applies with even *greater* force when the claimed repeal rests solely with an Appropriations Act. * * * When voting on appropriations measures, legislators are entitled to operate under the assumption that the funds will be devoted to purposes which are lawful and not for any purpose forbidden. [The Chief Justice also pointed to House Rule XX(2), which forbids amendments to appropriations bills which seeks to "chang[e] existing law." See also Senate Rule 16.4.] Thus, to sustain petitioner's position, we would be obliged to assume that Congress meant to repeal *pro tanto* § 7 of the Act by means of a procedure expressly prohibited under the rules of Congress.

[Chief Justice Burger rejected TVA's urging the Court to balance the harms of shutting down the dam against the dangers to the snail darter. Not only did the Court not consider itself competent to calibrate such a balance, but Congress had already made the judgment that no cost was too high to allow the federal government to imperil a species.] [I]n our constitutional system the commitment to the separation of powers is too fundamental for us to pre-empt congressional action by judicially decreeing what accords with "common sense and the public weal." Our Constitution vests such responsibilities in the political branches.

[JUSTICE POWELL's dissenting opinion, joined by Justice Blackmun, argued that the Court's opinion "disregards 12 years of consistently expressed congressional intent to complete the Tellico Project" and is "an extreme example of a literalist construction, not required by the language of the Act and adopted without regard to its manifest purpose." Citing *Holy Trinity Church*, Justice Powell contended that the Court ought not read the broad language of § 7 so sweepingly and, instead, ought to narrow the language so as to avoid "absurd results." He would have construed the "actions" governed by § 7 to be only those taken *after* 1973, when the statute was enacted.]

[JUSTICE REHNQUIST dissented on the ground that the legitimate debate over the statute's meaning properly informed the district court's decision not to enjoin work on the dam.]

GRIFFIN v. OCEANIC CONTRACTORS, INC.

Supreme Court of the United States, 1982
458 U.S. 564, 102 S.Ct. 3245, 73 L.Ed.2d 973

JUSTICE REHNQUIST delivered the opinion of the Court.

[In February 1976, Danny Griffin contracted to work as a senior pipeline welder on board vessels operated by respondent in the North Sea. The contract specified that petitioner's employment would extend "until December 15, 1976 or until Oceanic's 1976 pipeline committal in the North Sea is fulfilled, whichever shall occur first." The contract also provided that if Griffin quit the job prior to its termination date, or if his services were terminated for cause, he would be charged with the cost of transportation back to the United States. Oceanic reserved the right to withhold $137.50 from each of petitioner's first four paychecks "as a cash deposit for the payment of your return transportation in the event you should become obligated for its payment." On April 1, 1976, Griffin suffered an injury while working on the deck of the vessel readying it for sea. Oceanic refused to take responsibility for the injury or to furnish transportation back to the United States, and continued to retain $412.50 in earned wages that had been deducted from Griffin's first three paychecks for that purpose. He returned to the United States and on May 5, began working as a welder for another company operating in the North Sea.

[In 1978 Griffin brought suit against respondent under the Jones Act, § 20, 38 Stat. 1185, as amended, 46 U.S.C. § 688, and under general maritime law, seeking damages for respondent's failure to pay maintenance, cure, unearned wages, repatriation expenses, and the value of certain personal effects lost on board respondent's vessel. He also sought penalty wages under Rev. Stat. § 4529, as amended, 46 U.S.C. § 596, for respondent's failure to pay over the $412.50 in earned wages allegedly due upon discharge. The District Court found for Griffin and awarded damages totaling $23,670.40.]

In assessing penalty wages under 46 U.S.C. § 596, the court held that "[t]he period during which the penalty runs is to be determined by the sound discretion of the district court and depends on the equities of the case." It determined that the appropriate period for imposition of the penalty was from the date of discharge, April 1, 1976, through the date of petitioner's reemployment, May 5, 1976, a period of 34 days. Applying the statute, it computed a penalty of $6,881.60. Petitioner appealed the award of damages as inadequate. [The Fifth Circuit affirmed the district court judgment. The Supreme Court reversed and ruled that Oceanic owed Griffin more than $302,000 in penalty wages.]

[II.A] The language of the statute first obligates the master or owner of any vessel making coasting or foreign voyages to pay every seaman the balance of his unpaid wages within specified periods after his discharge.[6] It then provides:

> "Every master or owner who refuses or neglects to make payments in the manner hereinbefore mentioned without sufficient cause shall pay to the seaman a sum equal to two days' pay for each and every day during which payment is delayed beyond the respective periods * * *."

The statute in straightforward terms provides for the payment of double wages, depending upon the satisfaction of two conditions. First, the master or owner must have refused or failed to pay the seaman his wages within the periods specified. Second, this failure or refusal must be "without sufficient cause." Once these conditions are satisfied, however, the unadorned language of the statute dictates that the master or owner "*shall pay* to the seaman" the sums specified "*for each and every day* during which payment is delayed." The words chosen by Congress, given their plain meaning, leave no room for the exercise of discretion either in deciding whether to exact payment or in choosing the period of days by which the payment is to be calculated. As this Court described the statute many years ago, it "affords a definite and reasonable procedure by which the seaman may establish his right to recover double pay where his wages are unreasonably withheld." Our task is to give effect to the will of Congress, and where its will has been expressed in reasonably plain terms, "that language must ordinarily be regarded as conclusive." *Consumer Product Safety Comm'n v. GTE Sylvania, Inc.*, 447 U.S. 102, 108 (1980).

The District Court found that respondent had refused to pay petitioner the balance of his earned wages promptly after discharge, and that its refusal was "without sufficient cause." Respondent challenges neither of these findings. Although the two statutory conditions were satisfied,

---

6. The statute reads in full:

"The master or owner of any vessel making coasting voyages shall pay to every seaman his wages within two days after the termination of the agreement under which he was shipped, or at the time such seaman is discharged, whichever first happens; and in case of vessels making foreign voyages, or from a port on the Atlantic to a port on the Pacific, or vice versa, within twenty-four hours after the cargo has been discharged, or within four days after the seaman has been discharged, whichever first happens; and in all cases the seaman shall be entitled to be paid at the time of his discharge on account of wages a sum equal to one-third part of the balance due him. Every master or owner who refuses or neglects to make payment in the manner hereinbefore mentioned without sufficient cause shall pay to the seaman a sum equal to two days' pay for each and every day during which payment is delayed beyond the respective periods, which sum shall be recoverable as wages in any claim made before the court; but this section shall not apply to masters or owners of any vessel the seamen of which are entitled to share in the profits of the cruise or voyage. This section shall not apply to fishing or whaling vessels or yachts."

however, the District Court obviously did not assess double wages "for each and every day" during which payment was delayed, but instead limited the assessment to the period of petitioner's unemployment. Nothing in the language of the statute vests the courts with the discretion to set such a limitation.

[B] Nevertheless, respondent urges that the legislative purpose of the statute is best served by construing it to permit some choice in determining the length of the penalty period. In respondent's view, the purpose of the statute is essentially remedial and compensatory, and thus it should not be interpreted literally to produce a monetary award that is so far in excess of any equitable remedy as to be punitive.

Respondent, however, is unable to support this view of legislative purpose by reference to the terms of the statute. "There is, of course, no more persuasive evidence of the purpose of a statute than the words by which the legislature undertook to give expression to its wishes." *United States v. American Trucking Assns., Inc.*, 310 U.S. 534, 543 (1940). Nevertheless, in rare cases the literal application of a statute will produce a result demonstrably at odds with the intentions of its drafters, and those intentions must be controlling. We have reserved "some 'scope for adopting a restricted rather than a literal or usual meaning of its words where acceptance of that meaning * * * would thwart the obvious purpose of the statute.'" *Commissioner v. Brown*, 380 U.S. 563, 571 (1965) (quoting *Helvering v. Hammel*, 311 U.S. 504, 510–511 (1941)). This, however, is not the exceptional case.

As the Court recognized in *Collie v. Fergusson*, 281 U.S. 52 (1930), the "evident purpose" of the statute is "to secure prompt payment of seamen's wages * * * and thus to protect them from the harsh consequences of arbitrary and unscrupulous action of their employers, to which, as a class, they are peculiarly exposed." This was to be accomplished "by the imposition of a liability which is not exclusively compensatory, but designed to prevent, by its coercive effect, arbitrary refusals to pay wages, and to induce prompt payment when payment is possible." Thus, although the sure purpose of the statute is remedial, Congress has chosen to secure that purpose through the use of potentially punitive sanctions designed to deter negligent or arbitrary delays in payment.

The legislative history of the statute leaves little if any doubt that this understanding is correct. The law owes its origins to the Act of July 20, 1790, ch. 29, § 6, 1 Stat. 133, passed by the First Congress. Although the statute as originally enacted gave every seaman the right to collect the wages due under his contract "as soon as the voyage is ended," it did not provide for the recovery of additional sums to encourage compliance. Such a provision was added by the Shipping Commissioners Act of 1872, ch. 322, § 35, 17 Stat. 269, which provided for the payment of "a sum not exceeding the amount of two days' pay for each of the days, not exceeding ten days, during which payment is delayed." The Act of 1872 obviously established a ceiling of 10 days on the period during which the penalty could be assessed and, by use of the words "not exceeding," left the courts with discretion to choose an appropriate penalty within that period.

Congress amended the law again in 1898. As amended, it read in relevant part:

> "Every master or owner who refuses or neglects to make payment in manner hereinbefore mentioned without sufficient cause shall pay to the seaman a sum equal to one day's pay for each and every day during which payment is delayed beyond the respective periods." Act of Dec. 21, 1898, ch. 28, § 4, 30 Stat. 756.

The amending legislation thus effected two changes: first, it removed the discretion theretofore existing by which courts might award less than an amount calculated on the basis of each day during which payment was delayed, and, second, it removed the 10–day ceiling which theretofore limited the number of days upon which an award might be calculated. The accompanying Committee Reports identify the purpose of the legislation as "the amelioration of the condition of the American seamen," and characterize the amended wage penalty in particular as "designed to secure the promptest possible payment of wages." H.R.Rep. No. 1657, 55th Cong., 2d Sess., 2, 3 (1898). See also S.Rep. No. 832, 54th Cong., 1st Sess., 2 (1896). Nothing in the legislative history of the 1898 Act suggests that Congress intended to do anything other than what the Act's enacted language plainly demonstrates: to strengthen the deterrent effect of the statute by removing the courts' latitude in assessing the wage penalty.

The statute was amended for the last time in 1915 to increase further the severity of the penalty by doubling the wages due for each day during which payment of earned wages was delayed. Seamen's Act of 1915, ch. 153, § 3, 38 Stat. 1164. There is no suggestion in the Committee Reports or in the floor debates that, in so doing, Congress intended to reinvest the courts with the discretion it had removed in the Act of 1898. Resort to the legislative history, therefore, merely confirms that Congress intended the statute to mean exactly what its plain language says.

[III] Respondent argues, however, that a literal construction of the statute in this case would produce an absurd and unjust result which Congress could not have intended. The District Court found that the daily wage to be used in computing the penalty was $101.20. If the statute is applied literally, petitioner would receive twice this amount for each day after his discharge until September 17, 1980, when respondent satisfied the District Court's judgment.[9] Petitioner would receive over $300,000 simply because respondent improperly withheld $412.50 in wages. In respondent's view, Congress could not have intended seamen to receive windfalls of this nature without regard to the equities of the case.

---

9. Respondent assumes that the penalty would run until September 17, 1980, since that was the date on which it finally paid petitioner the $412.50. Brief for Respondent 17. Petitioner, on the other hand, apparently assumes that the penalty period expired on May 6, 1980, the date of the District Court's judgment. Brief for Petitioner 19. Under our construction of the statute, the District Court's entry of judgment will not toll the running of the penalty period unless delays beyond that date are explained by sufficient cause. * * *

It is true that interpretations of a statute which would produce absurd results are to be avoided if alternative interpretations consistent with the legislative purpose are available. See *United States v. American Trucking Assns., Inc.*, 310 U.S., at 542–543; *Haggar Co. v. Helvering*, 308 U.S. 389, 394 (1940). In refusing to nullify statutes, however hard or unexpected the particular effect, this Court has said:

> "Laws enacted with good intention, when put to the test, frequently, and to the surprise of the law maker himself, turn out to be mischievous, absurd or otherwise objectionable. But in such case the remedy lies with the law making authority, and not with the courts." *Crooks v. Harrelson*, 282 U.S. 55, 60 (1930).

It is highly probable that respondent is correct in its contention that a recovery in excess of $300,000 in this case greatly exceeds any actual injury suffered by petitioner as a result of respondent's delay in paying his wages. But this Court has previously recognized that awards made under this statute were not intended to be merely compensatory:

> "We think the use of this language indicates a purpose to protect seamen from delayed payments of wages by the imposition of a liability which is not exclusively compensatory, but designed to prevent, by its coercive effect, arbitrary refusals to pay wages, and to induce prompt payment when payment is possible." *Collie v. Fergusson*, 281 U.S., at 55–56.

It is in the nature of punitive remedies to authorize awards that may be out of proportion to actual injury; such remedies typically are established to deter particular conduct, and the legislature not infrequently finds that harsh consequences must be visited upon those whose conduct it would deter. It is probably true that Congress did not precisely envision the grossness of the difference in this case between the actual wages withheld and the amount of the award required by the statute. But it might equally well be said that Congress did not precisely envision the trebled amount of some damages awards in private antitrust actions, see *Reiter v. Sonotone Corp.*, 442 U.S. 330, 344–345 (1979), or that, because it enacted the Endangered Species Act, "the survival of a relatively small number of three-inch fish * * * would require the permanent halting of a virtually completed dam for which Congress ha[d] expended more than $1 million," *TVA v. Hill*, 437 U.S. 153, 172 (1978). It is enough that Congress intended that the language it enacted would be applied as we have applied it. The remedy for any dissatisfaction with the results in particular cases lies with Congress and not with this Court. Congress may amend the statute; we may not. * * *

JUSTICE STEVENS, with whom JUSTICE BLACKMUN joins, dissenting.

In final analysis, any question of statutory construction requires the judge to decide how the legislature intended its enactment to apply to the case at hand. The language of the statute is usually sufficient to answer that question, but "the reports are full of cases" in which the will of the legislature is not reflected in a literal reading of the words it has chosen.[1] In my opinion this is such a case. * * *

[II.A] In fixing the amount of the award of double wages, the District Court in this case may have reasoned that respondent had sufficient cause for its delay in paying the earned wages after petitioner obtained employment with another shipmaster, but that there was not sufficient cause for its failure to make payment before that time. Although this reasoning conflicts with a literal reading of § 596, it is perfectly consistent with this Court's contemporary construction of the statute in *Pacific Mail S.S. Co. v. Schmidt*, 241 U.S. 245 (1916). The teaching of Justice Holmes' opinion for the Court in that case is that the wrongful character of the initial refusal to pay does not mean that all subsequent delay in payment is also "without sufficient cause" within the meaning of the statute.

The controversy in *Pacific Mail* arose in 1913, when the statute provided that the sum recoverable as wages was measured by one day's pay, rather than double that amount, for each day that the wages were withheld without sufficient cause; the statute was otherwise exactly as it is today. The seaman was discharged on October 1, 1913, but $30.33 was withheld from his wages because he was believed responsible for the loss of some silverware. He filed an action on October 20, 1913, and on November 5, 1913, obtained a judgment for his wages and an additional sum of $151.59, representing the sum recoverable as wages for the period between October 1 and November 5, 1913. The District Court's decree established the proposition that the vessel owner's defenses did not constitute sufficient cause for refusing to pay the wages and requiring the seaman to sue to recover them.

The vessel owner prosecuted an unsuccessful appeal. The Court of Appeals not only affirmed the decision of the District Court, but also added an additional recovery of daily wages for the period between the entry of the original judgment on November 5 and the actual payment of the disputed wages. The Court of Appeals thus read the statute literally and ordered the result that the District Court's finding seemed to dictate. This Court, however, set aside the additional recovery, reaching a conclusion that cannot be reconciled with a wooden, literal reading of the statute. Concurrent findings of the District Court and the Court of Appeals established that the refusal to make the wage payment when due was without sufficient cause. Justice Holmes and his Brethren accepted that finding for purposes of decision, but reasoned that there was sufficient cause for the owner's decision to appeal and his refusal to pay while the appeal was pending.

The curious character of this Court's conclusion that reasons insufficient to justify the refusal to pay before the trial court's decision somehow became sufficient to justify a subsequent refusal to pay is not the most

---

1. It is a familiar rule, that a thing may be within the letter of the statute and yet not within the statute, because not within its spirit, nor within the intention of its makers. This has been often asserted, and the reports are full of cases illustrating its application. * * * *Holy Trinity Church.*

significant point to Justice Holmes' opinion. The case is primarily significant because its holding cannot be squared with a literal reading of the statute. Even though the initial refusal is without sufficient cause, statutory wages are not necessarily recoverable for the entire period until payment is made either to the seaman or to a stakeholder. A subsequent event—even though not expressly mentioned in the statute itself—may foreshorten the recovery period.

In *Pacific Mail* the subsequent event was the vessel owner's decision to appeal. The finding that that event provided sufficient cause for the delay after November 5, 1913, was made *sua sponte* by this Court. In this case the subsequent event was the reemployment of petitioner in a comparable job on May 5, 1976. The finding that that event—coupled with the failure to make any additional demand for almost two years thereafter—was sufficient cause for the delay after May 5, 1976, was made by the District Court. It is true that the judge did not expressly frame his decision in these terms, but his actual decision fits precisely the mold established by *Pacific Mail*. Both cases give a flexible reading to the "sufficient cause" language in the statute. They differ with respect to the nature of the subsequent event but not with respect to their departure from the statutory text. [Justice Stevens also cited *Collie v. Fergusson*, 281 U.S. 52 (1930), in which the Court refused to read the statute to penalize an employer for failing to pay wages because of its financial difficulties. The conclusions reached by Justice Stevens's analysis "dispel any notion that the statute means exactly what it says." Indeed, the same flexibility shown by the Supreme Court in *Collie* also characterized the lower federal courts' treatment of the statute from 1896 to 1966.]

[III] The construction permitting the district court to exercise some discretion in tailoring the double-wage award to the particular equities of the case is just as consistent with the legislative history of § 596 as the Court's new literal approach to this statute. In 1872, when Congress authorized the recovery of additional wages by seamen who were not paid within five days of their discharge, it used the word "shall" to make it clear that such a recovery must be awarded, but it allowed the district courts a limited discretion in setting the amount of such recovery.[17] The judge's discretion as to amount was limited in two ways: (1) the statutory wage rate could not be more than double the amount of the seaman's daily wage; and (2) the period for which the statutory wage could be awarded could not exceed 10 days.

Subsequent amendments to the statute did not remove the requirement that some recovery "shall" be awarded, but did modify both of the limits on the judge's discretion. With respect to the wage rate, Congress

---

17. The 1872 version of § 596 provided in pertinent part:

"[E]very master or owner who neglects or refuses to make payment [of a seaman's earned wages within five days after the seaman's discharge] without sufficient cause shall pay to the seaman a sum not exceeding the amount of two days' pay for each of the days, not exceeding ten days, during which payment is delayed beyond the [five-day period]; and such sum shall be recoverable as wages in any claim made before the court * * *." Act of June 7, 1872, ch. 322, § 35, 17 Stat. 269.

first specified that it should equal the daily rate—rather than double the daily rate—and later specified that the rate should be the double rate.[18] With respect to the period for which the statutory wage was payable, the 1898 amendment simply removed the 10–day limit. This amendment is subject to two different interpretations, one that would represent a rather unremarkable change and the other that would be both drastic and dramatic.

The unremarkable change would amount to nothing more than a removal of the narrow 10–day limit on the scope of the judge's discretion. The word "shall" would continue to do nothing more than require some recovery in an amount to be fixed by the judge, but in recognition of the reality that seamen might be stranded for more than 10 days, the recovery period could extend beyond 10 days. This sort of unremarkable change is consistent with the purpose of the statute, as well as with a legislative history that fails to make any comment on its significance. As Justice Rehnquist has perceptively observed in another context, the fact that the dog did not bark can itself be significant.[20]

The Court's construction of the amendment is, however, both drastic and dramatic. Instead of effecting a modest enlargement of the judge's discretion to do justice in these cases, the Court's construction effects a complete prohibition of judicial discretion. Instead of permitting recoveries for a period somewhat longer than 10 days, the amendment is construed as a command that even when the unresolved dispute persists for two or three years without any special hardship to the seaman, an automatic recovery must be ordered for the entire period regardless of the equitable considerations that may arise after the shipmaster's initial mistake has been made. Such a major change in both the potential amount of the statutory recovery and the character of the judge's authority would normally be explained in the committee reports or the debates if it had been intended. * * *

NOTES ON HILL, GRIFFIN, AND THE REVIVAL OF THE PLAIN MEANING RULE

1. *The Legislative Response in* Griffin *and in* TVA v. Hill. Chief Justice Burger's opinion in *TVA v. Hill* had an immediate legislative response. The Endangered Species Act Amendments of 1978, Pub. L. No. 95–632, § 7, 92 Stat. 3751, 3752–60 (1978), established an administrative mechanism for granting exemptions to the Act. When administrators revealed reluctance to

---

18. The 1898 version of § 596 provided in pertinent part:

"Every master or owner who refuses or neglects to make payment [of a seaman's earned wages within four days of the seaman's discharge] without sufficient cause shall pay to the seaman a sum equal to one day's pay for each and every day during which payment is delayed beyond the [four-day period], which sum shall be recoverable as wages in any claim made before the court * * *." Act of Dec. 21, 1898, § 4, 30 Stat. 756.

The 1915 amendment substituted "two days' pay" for "one day's pay." See Act of Mar. 4, 1915, § 3, 38 Stat. 1164–1165.

20. *Harrison v. PPG Industries, Inc.,* 446 U.S. 578, 602 (1980) (dissenting opinion); cf. A. Conan Doyle, Silver Blaze, in The Complete Sherlock Holmes 383 (1938).

apply this process to save the Tellico Dam, that project was specifically exempted by Congress in Pub. L. No. 96–69, tit. IV, 93 Stat. 437, 449 (1979). For an analysis of the complicated politics of the override process in this case, see Elizabeth Garrett, *The Story of* TVA v. Hill: *Congress Has the Last Word*, in *Statutory Interpretation Stories* 58–90 (Eskridge, Frickey & Garrett eds. 2011).

Justice Rehnquist's argument for deferring to Congress to change the statute in *Griffin* had a very different legislative response. In 1983, Congress revised much of 46 U.S.C. through Pub. L. No. 98–89. Section 596 was repealed and replaced in part by 46 U.S.C. § 10313(g). The new provision says: "When payment is not made as provided [by the statute] without sufficient cause, the master or owner shall pay to the seaman 2 days' wages for each day payment is delayed." See also *id.* § 10504(c). Obviously, Congress did not change the language important to the Court's result in *Griffin*. Can you speculate why not?

2. *The Supreme Court's Revival of the Plain Meaning Rule, 1976–86.* Although most commentators of the Burger Court's statutory opinions assumed that the Court was no more interested in the plain meaning rule than the Warren Court had been, e.g., Judge Patricia Wald, *Some Observations on the Use of Legislative History in the 1981 Supreme Court Term*, 68 Iowa L. Rev. 195, 195, 199 (1983), one commentator astutely observed that *Griffin's* literalism was more characteristic of the Burger Court's statutory interpretation than the legal process purpose approach was. See Richard H. Pildes, Note, *Intent, Clear Statements and the Common Law: Statutory Interpretation in the Supreme Court*, 95 Harv. L. Rev. 892 (1982).

On the one hand, *Hill* and similar cases suggest that the Burger Court would sometimes find the bare language of a statute determinative and would apply it stringently, even if it yielded unreasonable results. See, e.g., *Board of Governors of the Federal Reserve System v. Dimension Financial Corp.*, 474 U.S. 361 (1986); *United Air Lines v. McMann*, 434 U.S. 192 (1977). On the other hand, the Burger Court followed a rather "soft" version of the plain meaning rule, for it typically (as it did in *Hill* and *Griffin*) attempted to justify harsh results in light of the legislative history and purposes of the statute. See *CPSC v. GTE Sylvania*, 447 U.S. 102 (1980). Indeed, passages in *Griffin* can be read for the proposition that legislative intent controls interpretation, and that the primacy of statutory text is simply because it provides the best evidence of legislative intent. Moreover, sometimes the Burger Court went beyond even this understanding and interpreted statutes contrary to their apparent plain meaning, but consistent with their purposes and policies. See, e.g., *FDIC v. Philadelphia Gear Corp.*, 476 U.S. 426 (1986); *Midlantic Nat'l Bank v. New Jersey Dept. of Environmental Protection*, 474 U.S. 494 (1986).

3. *What Is a "Plain Meaning"?* An important issue underlying both *TVA* and *Griffin*, but not seriously examined by the Court's opinions, is what suggests to a judge that there is a "plain meaning" for a statutory provision? The obvious answer to that question is that a statute has a plain meaning if there is only one reasonable interpretation that an ordinary speaker/reader of English would take from the text. One might put it as Hart and Sacks did: there is one plain meaning if any other interpretation would impose on the

statutory words a meaning they will not bear. E.g., *Rapanos v. United States*, 547 U.S. 715, 731–32 (2006) (Scalia, J., plurality opinion) (asserting plain meaning in precisely those terms). Do § 7 of the ESA (*TVA*) and § 596 (*Griffin*) both have plain meanings under this formulation?

The dissenting opinions in both cases can be read to argue that there is no single plain meaning when the literal meaning is so unreasonable. Thus, if I tell a subordinate to "drop everything and come here immediately," the plain meaning of my command does not require him or her to drop a $100,000 vase or arise immediately from the bathroom. The Court in both *TVA* and *Griffin* seems to concede that possibility, by checking the legislative history to make sure its reading is not unreasonable in light of the statutory purposes. (In both instances, the Court finds evidence that Congress's purpose supported the literal meaning. Why did this not satisfy the dissenters?)

Plain meaning analysis does not necessarily stop with ordinary meaning. See Miranda Oshige McGowan, *Do as I Do, Not as I Say: An Empirical Investigation of Justice Scalia's Ordinary Meaning Method of Statutory Interpretation,* 78 Miss. L.J. 129 (2008) (comparing Justice Scalia's textualist approach with that of the Court as a whole). A statute may have a "plain meaning" that would be unavailable to ordinary readers when legal authorities impose a specialized meaning on a term or phrase. Thus, a plain meaning might be different from an ordinary meaning when (a) Congress has defined the term in the statute; (b) the term has been authoritatively construed by the Court, or perhaps even just by the specialized community to which the statute applies (or experts testifying about that); or (c) the ordinary meaning is inconsistent with the whole act or with the way Congress has used the term in other statutes. See *Rapanos* (applying those exceptions).

One of these special exceptions to the presumption in favor of ordinary meaning applied in *Griffin*: the Supreme Court *had* authoritatively construed the statutory terms in *Pacific Mail*, to cut off the running of the double wages ticker when the district court entered judgment. In footnote 9, Justice Rehnquist (or some aggressive law clerk) overruled the holding of *Pacific Mail*, without even mentioning the precedent. This is bizarre as well as anti-textualist, for the *Pacific Mail* cutoff is justified by the law of judgments: all damages are "merged" into a trial court's judgment, hence the cutting of double wages by Justice Holmes. Is there any justification for the Court's footnote-overrule?

In *Griffin,* Justice Stevens propounded another source of context: *statutory history*, namely, the formal evolution in the actual terms of the statute, as it is amended over time. Stevens demonstrates that Congress's editing of the double wages law in the two generations after the Civil War rested upon the assumption that there would be a short time between injury (the ship abandons the seaman) and lawsuit and judgment (any judgment for penalty wages would merge with the judgment). See *Pacific Mail*, where the whole matter was wrapped up in months. How would Justice Rehnquist respond to Justice Stevens?

NOTE ON THE PLAIN MEANING RULE IN STATE COURTS

In general, the plain meaning rule had greater staying power at the state level. Through most of the twentieth century, state courts were more likely to resolve issues of statutory interpretation merely by construing the apparent meaning of the statutory language, with attention to textual canons of statutory construction but without *any* examination of the statute's purpose or legislative history. See, e.g., *Bishop v. Linkway Stores, Inc.*, 655 S.W.2d 426 (Ark. 1983). The two most frequently mentioned reasons for state court textualism are the dearth of legislative history materials available for state statutes and a more restrained methodology practiced by many state judges, especially those who are elected by the people or subject to retention elections to remain in office.

This textualist practice changed during the post-World War II era in most states. For example, California courts often eschewed a plain meaning approach. See, e.g., *People v. Hallner*, 277 P.2d 393 (Cal. 1954); *McKeag v. Board of Pension Comm'rs of Los Angeles*, 132 P.2d 198 (Cal. 1942). The California Supreme Court has often used a contextual approach to interpret legislation broadly to promote liberal social policy and fairness. For instance, *County of San Diego v. Muniz*, 583 P.2d 109 (Cal. 1978), involved a statute requiring former or present welfare recipients to reimburse the state if the person "acquires property." The Supreme Court construed "property" *not* to include wages, because deprivation of wages would undermine the overall goal of the welfare law to assist recipients in becoming self-supporting and would be unfair and oppressive.

Other states have looked beyond the plain language of state statutes more and more. Written or published legislative histories of state statutes are now more readily available than at any previous point in American history, and they have wider availability now that more of the materials can be found on the internet. See Brian Barnes, *The Transformation of State Statutory Interpretation* (Yale Law School, Seminar Paper, May 10, 2010) (documenting dramatic increase in availability of legislative materials through a state-by-state survey). This phenomenon (increased availability) has given rise to a growing body of scholarship analyzing state court use of state legislative history. See generally Abbe R. Gluck, *States as Laboratories of Statutory Interpretation: Methodological Consensus and the New Modified Textualism*, 117 Yale L.J. 1750 (2010).[k]

---

k. For leading scholarship tracing the decline of the plain meaning rule, and concomitant rise of the use of legislative history, by courts in particular states, see Shirley Schlanger Abrahamson & Robert L. Hughes, *Shall We Dance? Steps for Legislators and Judges in Statutory Interpretation*, 75 Minn. L. Rev. 1045 (1991); Kenneth R. Dortzbach, *Legislative History: The Philosophies of Justices Scalia and Breyer and the Use of Legislative History by the Wisconsin State Courts*, 80 Marq. L. Rev. 161 (1996); Judith S. Kaye, *Things Judges Do: State Statutory Interpretation*, 13 Touro L. Rev. 595 (1997); Jack Landau, *Some Observations About Statutory Construction in Oregon*, 32 Willamette L. Rev. 1 (1996); Eric Lane, *How To Read a Statute in New York: A Response to Judge Kaye and Some More*, 28 Hofstra L. Rev. 85 (1999); William D. Popkin, *Statutory Interpretation in State Courts—A Study of Indiana Opinions*, 24 Ind. L. Rev. 1155 (1991); Adam Yoffie, *From Poritz to Rabner: The New Jersey Supreme Court's Statutory Jurisprudence, 2000–2009*, 35 Seton Hall Legis. J. 302 (2011); Matthew Hertko, Note, *Statutory*

SECTION 3. CURRENT DEBATES IN STATUTORY INTERPRETATION

In this final section we survey the debates over appropriate method concerning statutory interpretation that began in the 1980s. The primary debate has involved the challenge of the "new textualism" against more traditional approaches relying on legislative purpose and intent. We introduce the new textualism in Part A. Part B considers the ramifications of economic approaches to statutory interpretation, and Part C does the same for pragmatic and critical approaches.

A. THE NEW TEXTUALISM

In the 1980s, a group of judges and executive officials developed a more constrained version of the plain meaning rule than that followed in cases like *Griffin* and *TVA v. Hill*. For example, Judge Frank Easterbrook's *Statutes' Domains*, 50 U. Chi. L. Rev. 533 (1983), insisted that courts have no authority even to apply a statute to a problem unless the statute's language clearly targets that problem. Judge Easterbrook's *Legal Interpretation and the Power of the Judiciary*, 7 Harv. J.L. & Pub. Pol'y 87 (1984), argued that courts interpreting statutes have no business figuring out legislative intent, which is an incoherent concept, largely for the reasons suggested in 1930 by Professor Radin, but updated to reflect modern public choice theory. Judge Antonin Scalia delivered a series of speeches in 1985–86, urging courts to abandon virtually any reference to legislative history, especially the committee reports referred to in *Griffin* and *TVA v. Hill*. The Department of Justice's Office of Legal Policy endorsed and developed these views in a document drafted by Stephen J. Markman, *Using and Misusing Legislative History: A Re-Evaluation of the Status of Legislative History in Statutory Interpretation* (1989).

What we call "the new textualism"[a] is an approach to statutory interpretation developed by these judges and scholars. Although its proponents draw from legal process theory for their own purposes, their approach to statutory interpretation differs from that supported by Professors Hart, Sacks, and Fuller. Also, new textualist construction is different from the "soft" plain meaning rule of *TVA v. Hill* and *Griffin*, as suggested by the exchanges in the cases that follow.

Interpretation in Illinois: Abandoning the Plain Meaning Rule for an Extratextual Approach, 2005 U. Ill. L. Rev. 377.

a. See William N. Eskridge Jr., *The New Textualism*, 37 UCLA L. Rev. 621 (1990); Jonathan T. Molot, *The Rise and Fall of Textualism*, 106 Colum. L. Rev. 1 (2006); Judge Patricia M. Wald, *The Sizzling Sleeper: The Use of Legislative History in Construing Statutes in the 1988–89 Term of the United States Supreme Court*, 39 Am. U. L. Rev. 277 (1990); Nicholas S. Zeppos, *Justice Scalia's Textualism and the "New" New Legal Process*, 12 Cardozo L. Rev. 1597 (1991). For a short overview placing textualism in context with prior theories, see Philip P. Frickey, *From the Big Sleep to the Big Heat: The Revival of Theory in Statutory Interpretation*, 77 Minn. L. Rev. 241 (1992).

GREEN v. BOCK LAUNDRY MACHINE COMPANY

Supreme Court of the United States, 1989
490 U.S. 504, 109 S.Ct. 1981, 104 L.Ed.2d 557

JUSTICE STEVENS delivered the opinion of the Court.

[Paul Green, a county prisoner working at a car wash on a work-release program, reached inside a large dryer to stop it and had his arm torn off. At trial in his product liability action against the machine's manufacturer, he testified that he had been inadequately instructed about the machine's operation and dangerousness. Green admitted that he had been convicted of burglary and of conspiracy to commit burglary, both felonies, and those convictions were used by defendant to impeach his credibility. The jury returned a verdict for Bock Laundry. The Court of Appeals affirmed, rejecting Green's argument that the district court erred by denying his pretrial motion to exclude the impeaching evidence.]

[Criticism of automatic admissibility of prior felony convictions to impeach civil witnesses, particularly civil plaintiffs, has been "longstanding and widespread."] Our task in deciding this case, however, is not to fashion the rule we deem desirable but to identify the rule that Congress fashioned. * * *

[I] Federal Rule of Evidence 609(a) provides:

"General Rule. For the purpose of attacking the credibility of a witness, evidence that the witness has been convicted of a crime shall be admitted if elicited from the witness or established by public record during cross-examination but only if the crime (1) was punishable by death or imprisonment in excess of one year under the law under which the witness was convicted, and the court determines that the probative value of admitting this evidence outweighs its prejudicial effect to the defendant, or (2) involved dishonesty or false statement, regardless of the punishment."

By its terms the Rule requires a judge to allow impeachment of any witness with prior convictions for felonies not involving dishonesty "only if" the probativeness of the evidence is greater than its prejudice "to the defendant." It follows that impeaching evidence detrimental to the prosecution in a criminal case "shall be admitted" without any such balancing.

The Rule's plain language commands weighing of prejudice to a defendant in a civil trial as well as in a criminal trial. But that literal reading would compel an odd result in a case like this. Assuming that all impeaching evidence has at least minimal probative value, and given that the evidence of plaintiff Green's convictions had some prejudicial effect on his case—but surely none on defendant Bock's—balancing according to the strict language of Rule 609(a)(1) inevitably leads to the conclusion that the evidence was admissible. In fact, under this construction of the Rule, impeachment detrimental to a civil plaintiff always would have to be admitted.

No matter how plain the text of the Rule may be, we cannot accept an interpretation that would deny a civil plaintiff the same right to impeach an adversary's testimony that it grants to a civil defendant. The Sixth Amendment to the Constitution guarantees a criminal defendant certain fair trial rights not enjoyed by the prosecution, while the Fifth Amendment lets the accused choose not to testify at trial. In contrast, civil litigants in federal court share equally the protections of the Fifth Amendment's Due Process Clause. Given liberal federal discovery rules, the inapplicability of the Fifth Amendment's protection against self-incrimination, and the need to prove their case, civil litigants almost always must testify in depositions or at trial. Denomination as a civil defendant or plaintiff, moreover, is often happenstance based on which party filed first or on the nature of the suit. Evidence that a litigant or his witness is a convicted felon tends to shift a jury's focus from the worthiness of the litigant's position to the moral worth of the litigant himself. It is unfathomable why a civil plaintiff—but not a civil defendant—should be subjected to this risk. Thus we agree with the Seventh Circuit that as far as civil trials are concerned, Rule 609(a)(1) "can't mean what it says." *Campbell v. Greer*, 831 F.2d 700, 703 (1987) [Posner, J.].

Out of this agreement flow divergent courses, each turning on the meaning of "defendant." The word might be interpreted to encompass all witnesses, civil and criminal, parties or not. It might be read to connote any party offering a witness, in which event Rule 609(a)(1)'s balance would apply to civil, as well as criminal, cases. Finally, "defendant" may refer only to the defendant in a criminal case. These choices spawn a corollary question: must a judge allow prior felony impeachment of all civil witnesses as well as all criminal prosecution witnesses, or is Rule 609(a)(1) inapplicable to civil cases, in which event Rule 403 would authorize a judge to balance in such cases?* Because the plain text does not resolve these issues, we must examine the history leading to enactment of Rule 609 as law.

[II] At common law a person who had been convicted of a felony was not competent to testify as a witness. "[T]he disqualification arose as part of the punishment for the crime, only later being rationalized on the basis that such a person was unworthy of belief." 3 J. Weinstein & M. Berger, Weinstein's Evidence paragraph 609[02], p. 609–58 (1988)[.] As the law evolved, this absolute bar gradually was replaced by a rule that allowed such witnesses to testify in both civil and criminal cases, but also to be impeached by evidence of a prior felony conviction or a *crimen falsi* misdemeanor conviction. In the face of scholarly criticism of automatic admission of such impeaching evidence, some courts moved toward a more flexible approach.

[The American Law Institute's Model Code of Evidence and the ABA's proposed Uniform Rules of Evidence recommended that trial judges be given discretion to exclude evidence of prior convictions in appropriate

---

* *Editors' note*: Rule 403 provides that relevant evidence may be excluded "if its probative value is substantially outweighed by the danger of unfair prejudice, confusion of the issues, or misleading the jury, or by considerations of undue delay, waste of time, or needless presentation of cumulative evidence."

circumstances. In 1969, however, the Advisory Committee's proposed Rules of Evidence included Rule 6–09, which allowed all *crimen falsi* and felony convictions evidence without mention of judicial discretion. But the Committee's second draft Rule 609(a)] authorized the judge to exclude either felony or *crimen falsi* evidence upon determination that its probative value was "substantially outweighed by the danger of unfair prejudice." The Committee specified that its primary concern was prejudice to the witness-accused; the "risk of unfair prejudice to a party in the use of [convictions] to impeach the ordinary witness is so minimal as scarcely to be a subject of comment." Yet the text of the proposal was broad enough to allow a judge to protect not only criminal defendants, but also civil litigants and nonparty witnesses, from unfair prejudice.

[T]he Advisory Committee's revision of Rule 609(a) met resistance. The Department of Justice urged that the Committee supplant its proposal with the strict, amended version of the District Code. Senator McClellan objected to the adoption of the *Luck* doctrine and urged reinstatement of the earlier draft.

The Advisory Committee backed off. As Senator McClellan had requested, it submitted as its third and final draft the same strict version it had proposed in March 1969. * * * This Court forwarded the Advisory Committee's final draft to Congress on November 20, 1972.

The House of Representatives did not accept the Advisory Committee's final proposal. A Subcommittee of the Judiciary Committee recommended an amended version similar to the text of the present Rule 609(a), except that it avoided the current rule's ambiguous reference to prejudice to "the defendant." Rather, in prescribing weighing of admissibility of prior felony convictions, it used the same open-ended reference to "unfair prejudice" found in the Advisory Committee's second draft.

The House Judiciary Committee departed even further from the Advisory Committee's final recommendation, preparing a draft that did not allow impeachment by evidence of prior conviction unless the crime involved dishonesty or false statement. Motivating the change were concerns about the deterrent effect upon an accused who might wish to testify and the danger of unfair prejudice, "even upon a witness who was not the accused," from allowing impeachment by prior felony convictions regardless of their relation to the witness' veracity. H.R.Rep. No. 93–650, p. 11 (1973). Although the Committee Report focused on criminal defendants and did not mention civil litigants, its express concerns encompassed all nonaccused witnesses.

Representatives who advocated the automatic admissibility approach of the Advisory Committee's draft and those who favored the intermediate approach proposed by the Subcommittee both opposed the Committee's bill on the House floor. Four Members pointed out that the Rule applied in civil as well as criminal cases. The House voted to adopt the Rule as proposed by its Judiciary Committee.

The Senate Judiciary Committee proposed an intermediate path. For criminal defendants, it would have allowed impeachment only by *crimen falsi* evidence; for other witnesses, it also would have permitted prior felony evidence only if the trial judge found that probative value outweighed "prejudicial effect against the party offering that witness." This language thus required the exercise of discretion before prior felony convictions could be admitted in civil litigation. But the full Senate, prodded by Senator McClellan, reverted to the version that the Advisory Committee had submitted. See 120 Cong. Rec. 37076, 37083 (1974).

Conflict between the House bill, allowing impeachment only by *crimen falsi* evidence, and the Senate bill, embodying the Advisory Committee's automatic admissibility approach, was resolved by a Conference Committee. The conferees' compromise—enacted as Federal Rule of Evidence 609(a)(1)—authorizes impeachment by felony convictions, "but only if" the court determines that probative value outweighs "prejudicial effect to the defendant." The Conference Committee's Report makes it perfectly clear that the balance set forth in this draft, unlike the second Advisory Committee and the Senate Judiciary Committee versions, does not protect all nonparty witnesses:

> "The danger of prejudice to a witness other than the defendant (such as injury to the witness' reputation in his community) was considered and rejected by the Conference as an element to be weighed in determining admissibility. It was the judgment of the Conference that the danger of prejudice to a nondefendant witness is outweighed by the need for the trier of fact to have as much relevant evidence on the issue of credibility as possible." H.R.Conf.Rep. No. 93–1597, pp. 9–10 (1974).

Equally clear is the conferees' intention that the rule shield the accused, but not the prosecution, in a criminal case. Impeachment by convictions, the Committee Report stated, "should only be excluded where it presents a danger of improperly influencing the outcome of the trial by persuading the trier of fact to convict the defendant on the basis of his prior criminal record."

But this emphasis on the criminal context, in the Report's use of terms such as "defendant" and "to convict" and in individual conferees' explanations of the compromise,[26] raises some doubt over the Rule's

---

26. Representative Dennis, who had stressed in earlier debates that the Rule would apply to both civil and criminal cases, see 120 Cong. Rec. 2377 (1974), explained the benefits of the Rule for criminal defendants and made no reference to benefits for civil litigants when he said:

"[Y]ou can ask about all … felonies on cross examination, only if you can convince the court, and the burden is on the *government*, which is an important change in the law, that the probative value of the question is greater than the damage to the *defendant*; and that is damage or prejudice *to the defendant alone." Id.*, at 40894 (emphases supplied).

In the same debate Representative Hogan manifested awareness of the Rule's broad application. While supporting the compromise, he reiterated his preference for a rule

"that, for the purpose of attacking the credibility of a witness, *even if the witness happens to be the defendant in a criminal case*, evidence that he has been convicted of a crime is admissible pertinence to civil litigants. The discussions suggest that only two kinds of witnesses risk prejudice—the defendant who elects to testify in a criminal case and witnesses other than the defendant in the same kind of case. Nowhere is it acknowledged that undue prejudice to a civil litigant also may improperly influence a trial's outcome. Although this omission lends support to [an] opinion that "legislative oversight" caused exclusion of civil parties from Rule 609(a)(1)'s balance, a number of considerations persuade us that the Rule was meant to authorize a judge to weigh prejudice against no one other than a criminal defendant.

A party contending that legislative action changed settled law has the burden of showing that the legislature intended such a change. Cf. *Midlantic National Bank v. New Jersey Department of Environmental Protection*, 474 U.S. 494, 502 (1986). The weight of authority before Rule 609's adoption accorded with the Advisory Committee's final draft, admitting all felonies without exercise of judicial discretion in either civil or criminal cases. Departures from this general rule had occurred overtly by judicial interpretation, as in *Luck*, or in evidence codes, such as the Model Code and the Uniform Rules. Rule 609 itself explicitly adds safeguards circumscribing the common-law rule. The unsubstantiated assumption that legislative oversight produced Rule 609(a)(1)'s ambiguity respecting civil trials hardly demonstrates that Congress intended silently to overhaul the law of impeachment in the civil context.

To the extent various drafts of Rule 609 distinguished civil and criminal cases, moreover, they did so only to mitigate prejudice to criminal defendants. Any prejudice that convictions impeachment might cause witnesses other than the accused was deemed "so minimal as scarcely to be a subject of comment." Advisory Committee's Note, 51 F.R.D., at 392. Far from voicing concern lest such impeachment unjustly diminish a civil witness in the eyes of the jury, Representative Hogan declared that this evidence ought to be used to measure a witness' moral value.[27] Furthermore, Representative Dennis—who in advocating a Rule limiting impeachment to *crimen falsi* convictions had recognized the impeachment Rule's applicability to civil trials—not only debated the issue on the House floor, but also took part in the conference out of which Rule 609 emerged. See 120 Cong.Rec. 2377–2380, 39942, 40894–40895 (1974). These factors indicate that Rule 609(a)(1)'s textual limitation of the prejudice balance to criminal defendants resulted from deliberation, not oversight.

---

and may be used to challenge that witness' credibility if the crime is a felony or is a misdemeanor involving dishonesty of [sic] false statement." *Id.*, at 40895 (emphasis added).

27. "Suppose some governmental body instituted a civil action for damages, and the defendant called a witness who had been previously convicted of malicious destruction of public property. Under the committee's formulation, the convictions could not be used to impeach the witness' credibility since the crimes did not involve dishonesty or false statement. Yet, in the hypothetical case, as in any case in which the government was a party, justice would seem to me to require that the jury know that the witness had been carrying on some private war against society. Should a witness with an anti-social background be allowed to stand on the same basis of believability before juries as law-abiding citizens with unblemished records? I think not.... Personally I am more concerned about the moral worth of individuals capable of engaging in such outrageous acts as adversely reflecting on a witness' character than I am of thieves...." *Id.*, at 2376.

Had the conferees desired to protect other parties or witnesses, they could have done so easily. Presumably they had access to all of Rule 609's precursors, particularly the drafts prepared by the House Subcommittee and the Senate Judiciary Committee, both of which protected the civil litigant as well as the criminal defendant. Alternatively, the conferees could have amended their own draft to include other parties. They did not for the simple reason that they intended that only the accused in a criminal case should be protected from unfair prejudice by the balance set out in Rule 609(a)(1).

[Finally, the Court concluded that Rule 609, as the specific provision governing the facts of the case, controlled over the general balancing provisions of Rule 403. The Court affirmed the judgment for defendant.]

JUSTICE SCALIA, concurring in the judgment.

We are confronted here with a statute which, if interpreted literally, produces an absurd, and perhaps unconstitutional, result. Our task is to give some alternate meaning to the word "defendant" in Federal Rule of Evidence 609(a)(1) that avoids this consequence; and then to determine whether Rule 609(a)(1) excludes the operation of Federal Rule of Evidence 403.

I think it entirely appropriate to consult all public materials, including the background of Rule 609(a)(1) and the legislative history of its adoption, to verify that what seems to us an unthinkable disposition (civil defendants but not civil plaintiffs receive the benefit of weighing prejudice) was indeed unthought of, and thus to justify a departure from the ordinary meaning of the word "defendant" in the Rule. For that purpose, however, it would suffice to observe that counsel have not provided, nor have we discovered, a shred of evidence that anyone has ever proposed or assumed such a bizarre disposition. The Court's opinion, however, goes well beyond this. Approximately four-fifths of its substantive analysis is devoted to examining the evolution of Federal Rule of Evidence 609 * * * all with the evident purpose, not merely of confirming that the word "defendant" cannot have been meant literally, but of determining what, precisely, the Rule does mean.

I find no reason to believe that any more than a handful of the Members of Congress who enacted Rule 609 were aware of its interesting evolution from the 1942 Model Code; or that any more than a handful of them (if any) voted, with respect to their understanding of the word "defendant" and the relationship between Rule 609 and Rule 403, on the basis of the referenced statements in the Subcommittee, Committee, or Conference Committee Reports, or floor debates—statements so marginally relevant, to such minute details, in such relatively inconsequential legislation. The meaning of terms on the statute books ought to be determined, not on the basis of which meaning can be shown to have been understood by a larger handful of the Members of Congress; but rather on the basis of which meaning is (1) most in accord with context and ordinary usage, and thus most likely to have been understood by the *whole*

Congress which voted on the words of the statute (not to mention the citizens subject to it), and (2) most compatible with the surrounding body of law into which the provision must be integrated—a compatibility which, by a benign fiction, we assume Congress always has in mind. I would not permit any of the historical and legislative material discussed by the Court, or all of it combined, to lead me to a result different from the one that these factors suggest.

I would analyze this case, in brief, as follows:

(1) The word "defendant" in Rule 609(a)(1) cannot rationally (or perhaps even constitutionally) mean to provide the benefit of prejudice-weighing to civil defendants and not civil plaintiffs. Since petitioner has not produced, and we have not ourselves discovered, even a snippet of support for this absurd result, we may confidently assume that the word was not used (as it normally would be) to refer to all defendants and only all defendants.

(2) The available alternatives are to interpret "defendant" to mean (a) "civil plaintiff, civil defendant, prosecutor, and criminal defendant," (b) "civil plaintiff and defendant and criminal defendant," or (c) "criminal defendant." Quite obviously, the last does least violence to the text. It adds a qualification that the word "defendant" does not contain but, unlike the others, does not give the word a meaning ("plaintiff" or "prosecutor") it simply will not bear. The qualification it adds, moreover, is one that could understandably have been omitted by inadvertence—and sometimes is omitted in normal conversation ("I believe strongly in defendants' rights"). Finally, this last interpretation is consistent with the policy of the law in general and the Rules of Evidence in particular of providing special protection to defendants in criminal cases.*

(3) As well described by the Court, the "structure of the Rules" makes it clear that Rule 403 is not to be applied in addition to Rule 609(a)(1).

I am frankly not sure that, despite its lengthy discussion of ideological evolution and legislative history, the Court's reasons for both aspects of its decision are much different from mine. I respectfully decline to join that discussion, however, because it is natural for the bar to believe that the juridical importance of such material matches its prominence in our opinions—thus producing a legal culture in which, when counsel arguing before us assert that "Congress has said" something, they now frequently mean, by "Congress," a committee report; and in which it was not beyond the pale for a recent brief to say the following: "Unfortunately, the

---

* Acknowledging the statutory ambiguity, the dissent would read "defendant" to mean "any party" because, it says, this interpretation "extend[s] the protection of judicial supervision to a larger class of litigants" than the interpretation the majority and I favor, which "takes protection *away* from litigants." But neither side in this dispute can lay claim to generosity without begging the policy question whether judicial supervision is better than the automatic power to impeach. We could as well say—and with much more support in both prior law and this Court's own recommendation—that our reading "extend[s] the protection of [the right to impeach with prior felony convictions] to a larger class of litigants" than the dissent's interpretation, which "takes protection *away* from litigants."

legislative debates are not helpful. Thus, we turn to the other guidepost in this difficult area, statutory language." * * *

JUSTICE BLACKMUN, with whom JUSTICE BRENNAN and JUSTICE MARSHALL join, dissenting.

* * * The majority concludes that Rule 609(a)(1) cannot mean what it says on its face. I fully agree.

I fail to see, however, why we are required to solve this riddle of statutory interpretation by reading the inadvertent word "defendant" to mean "criminal defendant." I am persuaded that a better interpretation of the Rule would allow the trial court to consider the risk of prejudice faced by any party, not just a criminal defendant. Applying the balancing provisions of Rule 609(a)(1) to all parties would have prevented the admission of unnecessary and inflammatory evidence in this case and will prevent other similar unjust results until Rule 609(a) is repaired, as it must be. The result the Court reaches today, in contrast, endorses "the irrationality and unfairness" of denying the trial court the ability to weigh the risk of prejudice to any party before admitting evidence of a prior felony for purposes of impeachment.

The majority's lengthy recounting of the legislative history of Rule 609 demonstrates why almost all that history is entitled to very little weight. Because the proposed rule changed so often—and finally was enacted as a compromise between the House and the Senate—much of the commentary cited by the majority concerns versions different from the Rule Congress finally enacted.

The only item of legislative history that focuses on the Rule as enacted is the Report of the Conference Committee. Admittedly, language in the Report supports the majority's position: the Report mirrors the Rule in emphasizing the prejudicial effect on the defendant, and also uses the word "convict" to describe the potential outcome. But the Report's draftsmanship is no better than the Rule's, and the Report's plain language is no more reliable an indicator of Congress' intent than is the plain language of the Rule itself.

Because the slipshod drafting of Rule 609(a)(1) demonstrates that clarity of language was not the Conference's forte, I prefer to rely on the underlying reasoning of the Report, rather than on its unfortunate choice of words, in ascertaining the Rule's proper scope. The Report's treatment of the Rule's discretionary standard consists of a single paragraph. After noting that the Conference was concerned with prejudice to a defendant, the Report states:

> "The danger of prejudice to a witness other than the defendant (such as injury to the witness' reputation in the community) was considered and rejected by the Conference as an element to be weighed in determining admissibility. It was the judgment of the Conference that the danger of prejudice to a nondefendant witness is outweighed by the need for the trier of fact to have as much relevant evidence on the

issue of credibility as possible. Such evidence should only be excluded where it presents a danger of improperly influencing the outcome of the trial by persuading the trier of fact to convict the defendant on the basis of his prior criminal record."

The Report indicates that the Conference determined that any felony conviction has sufficient relevance to a witness' credibility to be admitted, even if the felony had nothing directly to do with truthfulness or honesty. In dealing with the question of undue prejudice, however, the Conference drew a line: it distinguished between two types of prejudice, only one of which it permitted the trial court to consider.

As the Conference observed, admitting a prior conviction will always "prejudice" a witness, who, of course, would prefer that the conviction not be revealed to the public. The Report makes clear, however, that this kind of prejudice to the witness' life outside the courtroom is not to be considered in the judicial balancing required by Rule 609(a)(1). Rather, the kind of prejudice the court is instructed to be concerned with is prejudice which "presents a danger of improperly influencing the outcome of the trial." Congress' solution to that kind of prejudice was to require judicial supervision: the conviction may be admitted only if "the court determines that the probative value of admitting this evidence outweighs its prejudicial effect to the defendant." Rule 609(a)(1).

Although the Conference expressed its concern in terms of the effect on a criminal defendant, the potential for prejudice to the outcome at trial exists in any type of litigation, whether criminal or civil, and threatens all parties to the litigation. The Report and the Rule are best read as expressing Congress' preference for judicial balancing whenever there is a chance that justice shall be denied a party because of the unduly prejudicial nature of a witness' past conviction for a crime that has no direct bearing on the witness' truthfulness. In short, the reasoning of the Report suggests that by "prejudice to the defendant," Congress meant "prejudice to a party," as opposed to the prejudicial effect of the revelation of a prior conviction to the witness' own reputation.

It may be correct, as Justice Scalia notes in his opinion concurring in the judgment, that interpreting "prejudicial effect to the defendant" to include only "prejudicial effect to [a] *criminal* defendant," and not prejudicial effect to other categories of litigants as well, does the "least violence to the text," if what we mean by "violence" is the interpolation of excess words or the deletion of existing words. But the reading endorsed by Justice Scalia and the majority does violence to the logic of the only rationale Members of Congress offered for the Rule they adopted.

Certainly the possibility that admission of a witness' past conviction will improperly determine the outcome at trial is troubling when the witness' testimony is in support of a criminal defendant. The potential, however, is no less real for other litigants. Unlike Justice Scalia, I do not approach the Rules of Evidence, which by their terms govern both civil and criminal proceedings, with the presumption that their general provisions should be read to "provid[e] special protection to defendants in criminal cases." Rather, the Rules themselves specify that they "shall be construed to secure fairness in administration ... to the end that the truth may be ascertained and proceedings justly determined" in *all* cases. Rule 102. The majority's result does not achieve that end. * * *

As I see it, therefore, our choice is between two interpretations of Rule 609(a)(1), neither of which is completely consistent with the Rule's plain language. The majority's interpretation takes protection *away* from litigants—*i.e.*, civil defendants—who would have every reason to believe themselves entitled to the judicial balancing offered by the Rule. The alternative interpretation—which I favor—also departs somewhat from plain language, but does so by *extending* the protection of judicial supervision to a larger class of litigants—*i.e.*, to all parties. Neither result is compelled by the statutory language or the legislative history, but for me the choice between them is an easy one. I find it proper, as a general matter and under the dictates of Rule 102, to construe the Rule so as to avoid "unnecessary hardship," see *Burnet v. Guggenheim*, 288 U.S. 280, 285 (1933), and to produce a sensible result. * * *

NOTES ON BOCK LAUNDRY AND DIFFERENT FOUNDATIONALIST THEORIES IN ACTION

1. *Does Textualism Work in* Bock Laundry? Note that, like the other eight Justices, textualist Justice Scalia *also* rewrote the statute, which has a perfectly "plain meaning" in this case: the felony convictions of civil plaintiffs can always be introduced to impeach them, but those of civil defendants are subject to a balancing test. Of course, such a plain meaning surely is unconstitutional, but in that event why doesn't the textualist simply invalidate Rule 609(a)(1) (at least as far as civil cases) and apply the Rule 403 default rule, which would probably exclude Green's conviction from evidence?

Justice Scalia disregarded plain meaning in this case because he believed that Rule 609(a)(1) was absurd as written, that the absurdity was unintended, and that an unintended absurdity justifies departure from plain meaning. This is itself significant. By creating an exception to textualism when a statute requires unintended "absurd" consequences, is Justice Scalia not conceding that following statutory text is not all that is going on in statutory interpretation, and that current interpretive values have a role to play in statutory interpretation? While Justice Scalia surely believes that plain meaning can only be sacrificed in the rare absurd-result case, why not sacrifice plain meaning when it directs an "unreasonable" result that was probably unintended by Congress?

Although Justice Scalia agreed to rewrite the statute in *Bock Laundry*, his opinion dismissed the dissenting opinion's rewrite in favor of the majority's rewrite:

> The available alternatives [for rewriting the rule] are to interpret "defendant" to mean (a) "civil plaintiff, civil defendant, prosecutor and criminal defendant," (b) "civil plaintiff and defendant and criminal defendant," or

(c) "criminal defendant." Quite obviously, the last does least violence to the text.

Is that so obvious? In essence, Justice Blackmun's dissent rewrote Rule 609(a)(1) to permit impeaching convictions only when "the court determines that the probative value of admitting this evidence outweighs its prejudicial effect to *a party*" (new language italicized). Does this do more "violence" to the text than Justice Scalia's rewrite to permit impeaching convictions only when "the court determines that the probative value of admitting this evidence outweighs its prejudicial effect to the *criminal* defendant"?

Indeed, from a purely textualist perspective, Justice Blackmun's rewrite may be a better version, because Justice Scalia's rewrite leaves the statute as chaotic as it was originally. Rewritten Rule 609(a)(1) still applies in a civil case like *Bock Laundry*, and Justice Scalia's version tells the judge to follow a strange rule: allow the witness to be impeached by his prior felony convictions, but only if its probative value outweighs its prejudice to the "criminal defendant." What criminal defendant? This is a civil case, after all. While the original Rule 609(a)(1) favored civil defendants over civil plaintiffs without apparent justification, it at least set forth a rule that could be applied by the district judge in a civil case. Under the pretense of doing "least violence" to the text, does Justice Scalia's rewrite deprive the judge of an intelligible rule?

In our view, the shortest way to rewrite Rule 609(a)(1) to reflect the understanding of the majority and of Justice Scalia *and* to have it make sense as a rule applicable to civil as well as criminal cases is something like the following: Allow a witness to be impeached by his prior criminal conviction "if the crime (1) was punishable by death or imprisonment in excess of one year under the law under which the witness was convicted, and, *in a criminal case*, the court determines that the probative value of admitting this evidence outweighs its prejudicial effect to the defendant" (new language italicized). Would this flunk Justice Scalia's test of doing "least violence" to the text?

2. *Does Imaginative Reconstruction Work Any Better?* Imaginative reconstruction also may be problematic in *Bock Laundry*, for the reasons suggested by Professor Radin and revived by the new textualists. Who can really tell what the median Member of Congress thought about this issue?

Recall that the House voted for a version of Rule 609(a) that would have given Green the benefit of a balancing test, and a similar version was voted out of the Senate Judiciary Committee. On the floor of the Senate, Senator McClellan proposed an amendment making all felony convictions admissible; his amendment failed by a 35–35 vote. 120 Cong. Rec. 37080 (1974). But on immediate motion for reconsideration, his amendment was adopted, 38–34, because a couple of new senators showed up and a couple changed their votes. *Id.* at 37083. The median senator was apparently (and ironically) Senator Ted Stevens (R–Alaska). He voted against the McClellan amendment, for reconsideration, for the McClellan amendment, and then for the final conference bill, which adopted the ambiguous compromise. Why did he vote this way? What was his "intent"?

In 2006, we posed these very questions to Senator Stevens, who was still representing Alaska in the Senate (several years later, he tragically died in an airplane accident). Senator Stevens told us that the voting pattern for him and several other senators was "confused" as a matter of logic, but not as a matter of political collegiality. "As a former U.S. Attorney I favored the House and Senate Judiciary Committees' version—but McClellan was a friend. He had traveled to Alaska with me—and Jackson and Stennis were sort of mentors. This was my sixth year in the Senate—I voted with McClellan to take his 'compromise' to conference."[b]

In any event, the Senate did vote for a much more limited version of Rule 609(a) than the House, and so the key question for imaginative reconstruction is: What was the conference committee "deal" that was struck on Rule 609(a)? And of course that's completely unclear as well, since the conference report doesn't even mention civil cases, and Senator Stevens does not recall any consensus on the matter when he and other senators passed the conference bill by voice vote. Justice Stevens finds great significance in the conference action, but only because of a judicially created canon of statutory construction. If the dog (here, Congress) doesn't bark, assume that "nothing happened"—no radical change was made in the fabric of the law (recall the dog-doesn't-bark canon). Thus, Justice Stevens's imaginative reconstruction boils down to the application of a judicial presumption! And one that seems flimsy at best, because the common law rule was in the process of collapsing— and did collapse within the federal system the year after *Bock Laundry*. See the next note.

3. *Why Did the Court Go Through This Exercise?* As Justice Stevens's opinion noted, there was a proposed change to Rule 609(a) pending when the Supreme Court interpreted the Rule in *Bock Laundry*.[c] In January 1990 (soon after the decision in *Bock Laundry*), the Supreme Court notified Congress that it had adopted an amendment to Federal Rule of Evidence 609 to take effect on December 1, 1990, unless Congress by statute disapproved it. As explained in the report of the advisory committee, the amendment "does not disturb the special balancing test for the criminal defendant who chooses to testify, but applies the general balancing test of Rule 403 to protect all other litigants against unfair impeachment of witnesses." (Rule 403 is quoted in the editors' footnote in the majority opinion in *Bock Laundry*.) The report noted that the advisory committee had approved the proposed amendment prior to *Bock Laundry*, but had held it pending the outcome of the case. Congress never disapproved the revised Rule 609(a), and it went into effect on December 1, 1990.

After this amendment, Rule 609 provided:

a.   General rule.—For purposes of attacking the credibility of a witness,

(1) evidence that a witness other than an accused has been convicted of a crime shall be admitted, subject to Rule 403, if the crime was punishable by death or imprisonment in excess of one year under the law under

---

b.   E-mail from Lily Stevens (Senator Stevens's daughter) to Philip Frickey (April 5, 2006) (incorporating an email that Senator Stevens authorized his daughter to forward to Professor Frickey).

c.   Pursuant to the Federal Rules Enabling Act, amendments to the Federal Rules of Evidence are proposed to the Supreme Court by an advisory committee established by the Judicial Conference of the United States. The Court then notifies Congress of the amendment, including any modifications made by the Court. After a waiting period, the amendment takes effect unless, in the interim, Congress has nullified it by statute.

which the witness was convicted, and evidence that an accused has been convicted of such a crime shall be admitted if the court determines that the probative value of admitting this evidence outweighs its prejudicial effect to the accused; and

(2) evidence that any witness has been convicted of a crime shall be admitted if it involved dishonesty or false statement, regardless of the punishment.

Under this rule, Paul Green would have gotten a new trial. Why did the Court not reach that result in *Bock Laundry*? If the Court was required to deny Green relief in *Bock Laundry*, why did it have the power to veto Congress's intent a year later?

Antonin Scalia, *A Matter of Interpretation* (1997).* In this published version of his Tanner Lectures delivered at Princeton University, Justice Antonin Scalia presents his *textualist* philosophy of legal interpretation. He contends that law students (brainwashed by the first-year indoctrination in common-law methodology) and law professors (who do the brainwashing) tend to approach statutory interpretation as an exercise in applying legal authorities to new factual settings in a manner which yields both a fair result in the case and works toward a just and efficient general rule. Such an equitable common-law approach is not appropriate for construing statutes in a democracy, Justice Scalia argues, because it is fundamentally anti-democratic (pp. 9–14). A theme of the Tanner Lectures is that the common law has its place, but in a democracy it is more important that judges be constrained by, and held to, the legislatively enacted statutory law, than that they do "justice" in the individual case.

Should the lodestar for statutory interpretation, then, be legislative *intent*? Most assuredly not! "It is the *law* that governs, not the intent of the lawgiver. That seems to me the essence of the famous American ideal set forth in the Massachusetts constitution: A government of laws, not of men. Men may intend what they will; but it is only the laws that they enact which bind us" (p. 17). Indeed, Justice Scalia argues that judges following a legislative-intent approach usually end up finding their own preferences in the statute, because "your best shot at figuring out what the legislature meant is to ask yourself what a wise and intelligent person *should* have meant; and that will surely bring you to the conclusion that the law means what you think it *ought* to mean—which is precisely how judges decide things under the common law" (p. 18). Note the implicit criticism of Hart and Sacks' theory, *supra*.

Justice Scalia then applies this critique to *Holy Trinity Church*. The Court interpreted the alien contract law contrary to its plain meaning because the Justices believed it inconsistent with legislative intent and purpose. Justice Scalia finds such an approach no more than invalid judicial lawmaking, although he would allow courts to correct scrivener's errors. "Well of course I think that the act was within the letter of the statute, and was therefore within the statute: end of case" (p. 20). "The text is the law, and it is the text which must be observed" (p. 22), says the author, citing Justice Holmes (quoted *supra*, pp. 709–10).

---

* Copyright © 1997 by Princeton University Press. Quotations reprinted by permission of Princeton University Press.

The apparent plain meaning of a statutory text must be the alpha and the omega in a judge's interpretation of a statute. The apparent plain meaning is that which an ordinary speaker of the English language—twin sibling to the common law's reasonable person—would draw from the statutory text. That is what textualism *is*. What it is *not*, according to Justice Scalia, is either "strict constructionism" (p. 23), which gives statutory words their stingiest ambit, nor "nihilism" (p. 24), which reads words to mean anything and everything. "A text should not be construed strictly, and it should not be construed leniently; it should be construed reasonably, to contain all that it fairly means" (p. 23).

Nor is textualism canonical, maintains Justice Scalia. The Tanner Lectures are skeptical of "presumptions and rules of construction that load the dice for or against a particular result" (p. 27), because they "increase the unpredictability, if not the arbitrariness of judicial decisions" (p. 28). "To the honest textualist, all of these preferential rules and presumptions are a lot of trouble," says Scalia (p. 28). On the other hand, canons such as the rule of lenity (ambiguous penal statutes should be construed in favor of the defendant) might have been "validated by sheer antiquity," and other canons (such as the requirement of a clear statement for congressional abrogation of state immunity) might be defensible as rule-of-thumb presumptions about normal meaning (p. 29).

Doctrinally, the most distinctive feature of Justice Scalia's legisprudence is an insistence that judges should almost never consult, and never rely on, the legislative history of a statute (pp. 29–37). Consistent with his concurring opinion in *Bock Laundry*, the Tanner Lectures identify several kinds of reasons for rejecting the relevance of legislative history. First, to the extent that legislative history is mined to determine legislative "intent," it must be rejected as a matter of constitutional principle. Legislative intent is not the proper goal for the statutory interpreter. This is a corollary of the rule of law: law must be objective and impersonal (the "government of laws"), not subjective and intentional ("and not of men"). This reason is related to Professor Radin's critique of legislative intent—and Justice Scalia's second objection to legislative history is very much an elaboration of Professor Radin's criticism two generations earlier.

Even if intent were a proper criterion and it were constitutional to consider the views of legislative subgroups, the debating history preceding statutory enactment would not be reliable evidence of such intent. For most issues, there was no collective understanding; if there were such an understanding, public statements would often point in different directions, as some representatives would find it in their interest to plant misleading evidence. Indeed, the more courts have relied on legislative history, the less reliable it has become! "In earlier days, it was at least genuine and not contrived—a real part of the legislation's *history*, in the sense that it was part of the *development* of the bill, part of the attempt to inform and persuade those who voted. Nowadays, however, when it is universally known and expected that judges will resort to floor debates and (especially) committee reports as authoritative expressions of 'legislative intent,' affecting the courts rather than informing the Congress has become the primary purpose of the exercise" (p. 34).

Justice Scalia also claims that legislators themselves do not read the committee reports (pp. 32–33). Critics respond that legislators do not read the statutes they enact, either. Justice Scalia replies that the claim to authority of the two sources is different: a committee report's (supposed) authority is bottomed on its being evidence of intent about the law, and so knowledge about its contents would seem critical; the statutory text, on the other hand, is law itself, whether or not anyone read or understood it before enactment (pp. 34–35).

In response to this reply, critics say that committee reports are authoritative evidence because of conventions by which Congress has delegated most of the detail work to committees, with the implication being that the committee product is presumptively the work of Congress. Unconstitutional! says Justice Scalia.[d] "The legislative power is the power to make laws, not the power to make legislators. It is nondelegable. Congress can no more authorize one committee to 'fill in the details' of a particular law in a binding fashion than it can authorize a committee to enact minor laws. * * * That is the very essence of the separation of powers [and Article I, Section 7, requiring bicameral approval and presentment to the President]. The only conceivable basis for considering committee reports authoritative, therefore, is that they are a genuine indication of the will of the entire house—which, as I have been at pains to explain, they assuredly are not" (p. 35).

Earlier thinkers—like Dean Pound and Professor Landis—had called for courts to consider legislative history, so that judges might be constrained by the legislators' preferences. This was a laudable impulse, Justice Scalia concedes, but it has not worked. Legislative history has augmented rather than ameliorated the discretion of the willful judge, and this is Justice Scalia's third major quarrel with the use of legislative history. "In any major piece of legislation, the legislative history is extensive, and there is something for everybody. As Judge Harold Leventhal used to say, the trick is to look over the heads of the crowd and pick out your friends" (p. 36).

NOTES ON THE NEW TEXTUALISM AS A THEORY OF INTERPRETATION

One might say that the new textualist approach demands that the statutory interpreter consider the text, the whole text, and nothing but the text. This description leaves many important issues unaddressed and may be an oversimplification. Consider the following nuances that have been flagged by scholars and by Justice Scalia himself.

1. *When Is Meaning Ambiguous?* Surely the obvious question for a textualist theory is this: When is the meaning "plain"? When is there ambiguity? The plain meaning is that which an ordinary speaker of the English language—twin sibling to the common law's reasonable person—

---

d. The following argument is supported and elaborated in detail by John F. Manning, *Textualism as a Nondelegation Doctrine*, 97 Colum. L. Rev. 673 (1997). But see Peter L. Strauss, *The Courts and the Congress: Should Judges Disdain Political History?*, 98 Colum. L. Rev. 242 (1998) (disagreeing with Manning and arguing in favor of the use of legislative history, particularly to discern statutory purpose). More broadly, Professor Strauss has contended that our common-law system legitimates judicial interpretive methods that range beyond textualism. See Peter L. Strauss, *The Common Law and Statutes*, 70 U. Colo. L. Rev. 225 (1999).

would draw from the statutory text. In another context, Justice Scalia has said that ordinary meaning requires judges to ask "whether you could use the word in that sense at a cocktail party without having people look at you funny." *Johnson v. United States*, 529 U.S. 694, 718 (2000) (Scalia, J., dissenting). Does a "cocktail party textualism" render statutory meaning too dependent on the perspective of the group a judge parties with?

Many words, phrases, and sentences can have more than one meaning to the ordinary speaker of the English language (fellow partiers will not "look at you funny"). Often Justice Scalia will still find a plain meaning, based on statutory context, including the whole act or even the entire U.S. Code. Thus, if Congress has used the same language elsewhere in the statute or even in other statutes, Justice Scalia will presume that the same language has the same ordinary meaning. E.g., *United Sav. Ass'n v. Timbers of Inwood Forest Assocs. Ltd.*, 484 U.S. 365, 371 (1988). Consider also his point in *Bock Laundry*, that the ordinary use of "defendant" typically assumes one is talking about a criminal defendant; that takes some edge off of Justice Scalia's willingness to give Rule 609(a)(1) a narrowing construction.

If a statute is genuinely ambiguous, one might wonder what a textualist should do. For Justice Scalia himself, the answer is to follow and reason from Supreme Court precedent construing open-textured laws like the Sherman Act *or* defer to reasonable agency interpretations of statutes *or* attribute a purpose to the statute and construe it according to such purpose. See Miranda Oshige McGowan, *Do as I Do, Not as I Say: An Empirical Investigation of Justice Scalia's Ordinary Meaning Method of Statutory Interpretation*, 78 Miss. L.J. 129 (2008). In an empirical analysis of Justice Scalia's dissents, Professor McGowan reports that the Justice followed something other than an "ordinary" or "plain" meaning in most cases and, instead, followed judicial or administrative implications of purpose as the lodestar for construing statutes. Her conclusion is that Justice Scalia's textualism (even in his dissents, less constrained by the process of collecting a majority) contains just as much judicial discretion and judgment as does the approach traditionally followed by the Court.

2. *Should the New Textualists Ever Examine Legislative History?* All of the new textualists reject the use of legislative history for its *authoritative value*: such materials have no legal authority. This is their strongest point, but it does not preclude consultation of legislative history for other kinds of reasons.

Notice that Justice Scalia was willing to have a law clerk examine the legislative history of the 1974 amendment—but simply to confirm that no one in Congress realized that rule 609(a)(1), as written, was going to have possibly unconstitutional consequences in civil cases. This might be the *confirmatory value* of legislative history. If legislative history can be examined to determine whether Members of Congress "intended" or "thought of" an absurd or probably unconstitutional interpretation, why not look at it to confirm the apparent plain meaning of a statute? See *Carr v. United States*, 130 S.Ct. 2229 (2010), where Justice Sotomayor deployed legislative history in precisely this way—but Justice Scalia refused to join that portion of her opinion.

Why shouldn't legislative history be consulted for its *linguistic value*—namely, as evidence of how language was used at the time of the statute's enactment? One would expect new textualists who follow "original meaning" to consider legislative history carefully, for the same kinds of reasons they consider *The Federalist Papers* in determining the "original meaning" of the language used in the Constitution, as amended. Such legislative history would take the edge off of Justice Scalia's bitter critique of *Holy Trinity*. Scholars have reported that the legislative debates used the terms "labor and service" to refer only to manual work, and never to pastoral or brain work.[e]

Also, should the new textualists ever consider legislative history as a means to understand the structure of a statute? In his analysis of Justice Scalia's blistering critique of *Holy Trinity*, William N. Eskridge Jr., *No Frills Textualism*, 119 Harv. L. Rev. 2041, 2065–70 (2006), argues that the legislative history indicates that §§ 1 and 4 of the Alien Contract Law were *in pari materia*, namely, they were intended to cover the same class of aliens. This suggests that the more general terms in § 1 (persons performing labor or service of any kind) might be limited to the more particular ones in § 4 (mechanics, artisans, and laborers). Justice Scalia's book never mentions § 4. Is there a possibility that he would consider legislative materials to reveal statutory structure?

3. *Should the New Textualists Recognize an Absurd Results Rule?* Justice Scalia's concurring opinion in *Bock Laundry* rests on the absurdity of following Rule 609(a)(1) as written. For other examples where Justice Scalia has emphasized absurdity as a guide to statutory text, see *Brown v. Plata*, 131 S.Ct. 1910, 1950–51 (2011) (Scalia, J., dissenting in part because the majority's interpretation of the statute is "absurd" and represents a "judicial travesty"); Jane S. Schacter, *Text or Consequences?*, 76 Brooklyn L. Rev. 1007 (2011) (collecting pre-*Plata* examples from Justice Scalia's opinions).

Recognizing an absurd results exception to the plain meaning rule has its risks: what is absurd to conservative Justice Scalia might be debatable or even reasonable to moderate conservatives such as Justice Kennedy and might be good policy to more liberal Justice Ginsburg. (Indeed, that was the case in *Brown v. Plata*, where five Justices approved an injunction requiring a state to reduce its prison population because it created cruel and unusual conditions for mentally and physically disabled inmates. The majority considered the injunction not only lawful but also necessary to correct constitutional violations—while the dissenters considered it legally "absurd" to protect prisoners against probable harm through a "structural" injunction.)

For this reason, leading textualist theorists argue that there should *not* be an "absurd results" exception to the plain meaning rule. See John C. Nagle, *Textualism's Exceptions*, Issues in Legal Scholarship: Dynamic Statutory Interpretation (2002): Article 15, available at http://www.bepress.com/ils/iss 3/art15; John F. Manning, *The Absurdity Doctrine*, 116 Harv. L. Rev. 2387 (2003). Their argument is that the normative rule of law advantages of

---

e. Carol Chomsky, *The Story of* Holy Trinity Church v. United States: *Spirit and History in Statutory Interpretation*, in *Statutory Interpretation Stories* 2, 15–23 (Eskridge, Frickey & Garrett eds. 2010); William N. Eskridge Jr., *Textualism, The Unknown Ideal?*, 96 Mich. L. Rev. 1509 (1998) (reviewing Scalia's book and examining the original meaning of "labor or service" in 1885).

textualism would be compromised by a subjective absurd-results exception: because "absurdity" is in the mind of the beholder, the law would lose some degree of predictability and objectivity. Should Justice Scalia abandon his support for the absurd results exception? For an argument that normative judgments pervade his statutory jurisprudence, see Schacter, *Text or Consequences, supra.*

PROBLEM 2–3

The New Textualism as Applied

From his book, we know that Justice Scalia would have dissented in *Holy Trinity Church.* There is little doubt he would have voted with the majority in *TVA* and *Griffin*—but he would have written the opinions differently or would not have joined the Court's discussion of legislative history in either case. Recall also the different approaches to Title VII in the dissenting opinions in *Weber* by Justice Rehnquist and *Johnson* by Justice Scalia (Chapter 1, § 3). How would Justice Scalia have voted in *Shine*? Given his *Bock Laundry* concurring opinion, craft Justice Scalia's opinion for *Shine.*

For a new issue, consider the Voting Rights Act of 1982, which invalidates state electoral districts or rules that have a disparate impact on racial minorities. For example, in the South, at-large elections were an effective way of excluding candidates of color from elected office, because the majority white electorate would vote against any such candidate. In 1980, the Supreme Court had ruled that § 2 did not police electoral arrangements that were race-neutral and not motivated by racial exclusionary motives (which are hard to prove). To enable minority voters to challenge electoral arrangements, like at-large elections, that were not race-based on their face but that had questionable race-based effects, § 2 was amended in 1982 to provide as follows:

(a) No voting qualification or prerequisite to voting or standard, practice, or procedure shall be imposed or applied by any State or political subdivision in a manner which results in a denial or abridgement of the right of any citizen of the United States to vote on account of race or color, or in contravention of the guarantees set forth in section 4(f)(2), as provided in subsection (b).

(b) A violation of subsection (a) is established if, based on the totality of circumstances, it is shown that the political processes leading to nomination or election in the State or political subdivision are not equally open to participation by members of a class of citizens protected by subsection (a) in that its members have less opportunity than other members of the electorate to participate in the political process and to elect representatives of their choice. The extent to which members of a protected class have been elected to office in the State or political subdivision is one circumstance which may be considered: *Provided,* That nothing in this section establishes a right to have members of a protected class elected in numbers equal to their proportion in the population.

Does § 2 apply to state elections for judges? (Unlike the federal system, judges are popularly elected in many states.) How would a new textualist analyze the foregoing statutory text? Is there a plain meaning? If not, how should ambiguities be resolved? Would it make a difference to you if you knew that § 2 was applied to judicial elections before the Voting Rights Act was amended in 1982? Jot down your answer now.

CHISOM v. ROEMER

Supreme Court of the United States, 1991
501 U.S. 380, 111 S.Ct. 2354, 115 L.Ed.2d 348

JUSTICE STEVENS delivered the opinion of the Court.

[Five of the seven members of the Louisiana Supreme Court are elected from single-member districts, each of which consists of a number of parishes (counties). The other two are elected from one multimember district. In three of the four parishes in this multimember district, more than three-fourths of the registered voters are white. In the fourth parish in the multimember district, Orleans Parish, which contains about half of the population of the multimember district and has about half the registered voters in the district, more than one-half of the registered voters are African American. A class of African American registered voters in Orleans Parish brought this action, contending that the use of the multimember district diluted the voting strength of the minority community in violation of section 2 of the Voting Rights Act, as amended in 1982. (For discussion of what minority vote dilution is and how section 5 and section 2 of the Voting Rights Act forbid minority vote dilution in some circumstances, see Chapter 2, § 1.) Under the controlling precedent in the Fifth Circuit, *League of United Latin American Citizens Council No. 4434 v. Clements*, 914 F.2d 620 (5th Cir. 1990) (en banc) ("*LULAC*"), section 2 was inapplicable to judicial elections.]

The text of § 2 * * * as originally enacted [in 1965] read as follows:

"SEC. 2. No voting qualification or prerequisite to voting, or standard, practice, or procedure shall be imposed or applied by any State or political subdivision to deny or abridge the right of any citizen of the United States to vote on account of race or color." * * *

At the time of the passage of the Voting Rights Act of 1965, § 2, unlike other provisions of the Act, did not provoke significant debate in Congress because it was viewed largely as a restatement of the Fifteenth Amendment. This Court took a similar view of § 2 in *Mobile v. Bolden*, 446 U.S. 55, 60–61 (1980). * * * Section 2 protected the right to vote, and it did so without making any distinctions or imposing any limitations as to which elections would fall within its purview. * * *

Justice Stewart's opinion for the plurality in *Mobile v. Bolden*, which held that there was no violation of either the Fifteenth Amendment or § 2 of the Voting Rights Act absent proof of intentional discrimination, served as the impetus for the 1982 amendment [to § 2]. * * *

Under the amended statute, proof of intent is no longer required to prove a § 2 violation. * * * The full text of § 2 as amended in 1982 reads as follows:

"SEC. 2. (a) No voting qualification or prerequisite to voting or standard, practice, or procedure shall be imposed or applied by any State or political subdivision in a manner which results in a denial or abridgement of the right of any citizen of the United States to vote on account of race or color, or in contravention of the guarantees set forth in section 4(f)(2), as provided in subsection (b).

"(b) A violation of subsection (a) is established if, based on the totality of circumstances, it is shown that the political processes leading to nomination or election in the State or political subdivision are not equally open to participation by members of a class of citizens protected by subsection (a) in that its members have less opportunity than other members of the electorate to participate in the political process and to elect representatives of their choice. The extent to which members of a protected class have been elected to office in the State or political subdivision is one circumstance which may be considered: *Provided*, That nothing in this section establishes a right to have members of a protected class elected in numbers equal to their proportion in the population."

The two purposes of the amendment are apparent from its text. Section 2(a) adopts a results test, thus providing that proof of discriminatory intent is no longer necessary to establish *any* violation of the section. Section 2(b) provides guidance about how the results test is to be applied.

Respondents contend, and the *LULAC* majority agreed, that Congress' choice of the word "representatives" in the phrase "have less opportunity than other members of the electorate to participate in the political process and to elect representatives of their choice" in section 2(b) is evidence of congressional intent to exclude vote dilution claims involving judicial elections from the coverage of § 2. We reject that construction because we are convinced that if Congress had such an intent, Congress would have made it explicit in the statute, or at least some of the Members would have identified or mentioned it at some point in the unusually extensive legislative history of the 1982 amendment.[23]
* * *

The *LULAC* majority assumed that § 2 provides two distinct types of protection for minority voters—it protects their opportunity "to participate in the political process" and their opportunity "to elect representatives of their choice." Although the majority interpreted "representatives" as a word of limitation, it assumed that the word eliminated judicial elections only from the latter protection, without affecting the former. In other words, a standard, practice, or procedure in a judicial election, such as a limit on the times that polls are open, which has a disparate impact

---

23. Congress' silence in this regard can be likened to the dog that did not bark. See A. Doyle, Silver Blaze, in The Complete Sherlock Holmes 335 (1927). Cf. *Harrison v. PPG Industries, Inc.,* 446 U.S. 578, 602 (1980) (Rehnquist, J., dissenting) ("In a case where the construction of legislative language such as this makes so sweeping and so relatively unorthodox a change as that made here, I think judges as well as detectives may take into consideration the fact that a watchdog did not bark in the night.").

on black voters' opportunity to cast their ballots under § 2, may be challenged even if a different practice that merely affects their opportunity to elect representatives of their choice to a judicial office may not. This reading of § 2, however, is foreclosed by the statutory text and by our prior cases.

Any abridgement of the opportunity of members of a protected class to participate in the political process inevitably impairs their ability to influence the outcome of an election. As the statute is written, however, the inability to elect representatives of their choice is not sufficient to establish a violation unless, under the totality of the circumstances, it can also be said that the members of the protected class have less opportunity to participate in the political process. The statute does not create two separate and distinct rights. Subsection (a) covers every application of a qualification, standard, practice, or procedure that results in a denial or abridgement of *"the right"* to vote. The singular form is also used in subsection (b) when referring to an injury to members of the protected class who have less "opportunity" than others "to participate in the political process *and* to elect representatives of their choice." 42 U.S.C. § 1973 (emphasis added). It would distort the plain meaning of the sentence to substitute the word "or" for the word "and." Such radical surgery would be required to separate the opportunity to participate from the opportunity to elect.

The statutory language is patterned after the language used by Justice White in his opinions for the Court in *White v. Regester*, 412 U.S. 755 (1973) and *Whitcomb v. Chavis*, 403 U.S. 124 (1971).* In both opinions, the Court identified the opportunity to participate and the opportunity to elect as inextricably linked. In *White v. Regester*, the Court described the connection as follows: "The plaintiffs' burden is to produce evidence . . . that its members had less opportunity than did other residents in the district to participate in the political processes *and* to elect legislators of their choice." (emphasis added). And earlier, in *Whitcomb v. Chavis*, the Court described the plaintiffs' burden as entailing a showing that they "had less opportunity than did other . . . residents to participate in the political processes *and* to elect legislators of their choice." (emphasis added).

The results test mandated by the 1982 amendment is applicable to all claims arising under § 2. If the word "representatives" did place a limit on the coverage of the Act for judicial elections, it would exclude all claims involving such elections from the protection of § 2. For all such claims must allege an abridgement of the opportunity to participate in the political process *and* to elect representatives of one's choice. * * *

Both respondents and the *LULAC* majority place their principal reliance on Congress' use [in § 2] of the word "representatives" instead of

---

* *Editors' note: White* and *Whitcomb* were pre-*Bolden* cases in which the Court had suggested that the Constitution prohibited electoral structures or rules that had racially discriminatory effects, even without a showing that the government action in question was rooted in intentional discrimination.

"legislators" in the phrase "to participate in the political process and to elect representatives of their choice." When Congress borrowed the phrase from *White v. Regester*, it replaced "legislators" with "representatives."[26] This substitution indicates, at the very least, that Congress intended the amendment to cover more than legislative elections. Respondents argue, and the majority agreed, that the term "representatives" was used to extend § 2 coverage to executive officials, but not to judges. We think, however, that the better reading of the word "representatives" describes the winners of representative, popular elections. If executive officers, such as prosecutors, sheriffs, state attorneys general, and state treasurers, can be considered "representatives" simply because they are chosen by popular election, then the same reasoning should apply to elected judges.

Respondents suggest that if Congress had intended to have the statute's prohibition against vote dilution apply to the election of judges, it would have used the word "candidates" instead of "representatives." But that confuses the ordinary meaning of the words. The word "representative" refers to someone who has prevailed in a popular election, whereas the word "candidate" refers to someone who is seeking an office. Thus, a candidate is nominated, not elected. When Congress used "candidate" in other parts of the statute, it did so precisely because it was referring to people who were aspirants for an office. See, e.g., 42 U.S.C. § 1971(b) ("any candidate for the office of President"), § 1971(e) ("candidates for public office"), § 1973i(c) ("any candidate for the office of President"), § 1973i(e)(2) ("any candidate for the office of President"), § 1973l(c) ("candidates for public or party office"), § 1973ff–2 ("In the case of the offices of President and Vice President, a vote for a named candidate"), § 1974 ("candidates for the office of President"), § 1974e ("candidates for the office of President").

The *LULAC* majority was, of course, entirely correct in observing that "judges need not be elected at all," and that ideally public opinion should be irrelevant to the judge's role because the judge is often called upon to disregard, or even to defy, popular sentiment. The Framers of the Constitution had a similar understanding of the judicial role, and as a consequence, they established that Article III judges would be appointed, rather than elected, and would be sheltered from public opinion by receiving life tenure and salary protection. Indeed, these views were generally shared by the States during the early years of the Republic. Louisiana, however, has chosen a different course. It has decided to elect its judges and to compel

---

26. The word "representatives" rather than "legislators" was included in Senator Robert Dole's compromise, which was designed to assuage the fears of those Senators who viewed the House's version, H.R. 3112, as an invitation for proportional representation and electoral quotas. Senator Dole explained that the compromise was intended both to embody the belief "that a voting practice or procedure which is discriminatory in result should not be allowed to stand, regardless of whether there exists a discriminatory purpose or intent" and to "delineat[e] what legal standard should apply under the results test and clarif[y] that it is not a mandate for proportional representation." Hearings on S. 53 et al. before the Subcommittee on the Constitution of the Senate Committee on the Judiciary, 97th Cong., 2d Sess., 60 (1982). Thus, the compromise was not intended to exclude any elections from the coverage of subsection (a), but simply to make clear that the results test does not require the proportional election of minority candidates in *any* election.

judicial candidates to vie for popular support just as other political candidates do.

The fundamental tension between the ideal character of the judicial office and the real world of electoral politics cannot be resolved by crediting judges with total indifference to the popular will while simultaneously requiring them to run for elected office. When each of several members of a court must be a resident of a separate district, and must be elected by the voters of that district, it seems both reasonable and realistic to characterize the winners as representatives of that district. * * * Louisiana could, of course, exclude its judiciary from the coverage of the Voting Rights Act by changing to a system in which judges are appointed, and in that way, it could enable its judges to be indifferent to popular opinion. The reasons why Louisiana has chosen otherwise are precisely the reasons why it is appropriate for § 2, as well as § 5, of the Voting Rights Act to continue to apply to its judicial elections.

The close connection between § 2 and § 5 further undermines respondents' view that judicial elections should not be covered under § 2. Section 5 requires certain States to submit changes in their voting procedures to the District Court of the District of Columbia or to the Attorney General for preclearance. Section 5 uses language similar to that of § 2 in defining prohibited practices: "any voting qualification or prerequisite to voting, or standard, practice, or procedure with respect to voting." This Court has already held that § 5 applies to judicial elections. *Clark v. Roemer*, 500 U.S. 646 (1991). If § 2 did not apply to judicial elections, a State covered by § 5 would be precluded from implementing a new voting procedure having discriminatory effects with respect to judicial elections, whereas a similarly discriminatory system already in place could not be challenged under § 2. It is unlikely that Congress intended such an anomalous result. * * *

Congress enacted the Voting Rights Act of 1965 for the broad remedial purpose of "rid[ding] the country of racial discrimination in voting." *South Carolina v. Katzenbach*, 383 U.S. 301, 315 (1966). In *Allen v. State Board of Elections*, 393 U.S. 544, 567 (1969), we said that the Act should be interpreted in a manner that provides "the broadest possible scope" in combatting racial discrimination. Congress amended the Act in 1982 in order to relieve plaintiffs of the burden of proving discriminatory intent, after a plurality of this Court had concluded that the original Act, like the Fifteenth Amendment, contained such a requirement. See *Mobile v. Bolden*. Thus, Congress made clear that a violation of § 2 could be established by proof of discriminatory results alone. It is difficult to believe that Congress, in an express effort to broaden the protection afforded by the Voting Rights Act, withdrew, without comment, an important category of elections from that protection. Today we reject such an anomalous view and hold that state judicial elections are included within the ambit of § 2 as amended.

The judgment of the Court of Appeals is reversed and the case is remanded for further proceedings consistent with this opinion.

JUSTICE SCALIA, with whom THE CHIEF JUSTICE and JUSTICE KENNEDY join, dissenting.

Section 2 of the Voting Rights Act is not some all-purpose weapon for well-intentioned judges to wield as they please in the battle against discrimination. It is a statute. I thought we had adopted a regular method for interpreting the meaning of language in a statute: first, find the ordinary meaning of the language in its textual context; and second, using established canons of construction, ask whether there is any clear indication that some permissible meaning other than the ordinary one applies. If not—and especially if a good reason for the ordinary meaning appears plain—we apply that ordinary meaning.

Today, however, the Court adopts a method quite out of accord with that usual practice. It begins not with what the statute says, but with an expectation about what the statute must mean absent particular phenomena (*"we are convinced* that if Congress had ... an intent [to exclude judges] Congress would have made it explicit in the statute, or at least some of the Members would have identified or mentioned it at some point in the unusually extensive legislative history"); and the Court then interprets the words of the statute to fulfill its expectation. Finding nothing in the legislative history affirming that judges were excluded from the coverage of § 2, the Court gives the phrase "to elect representatives" the quite extraordinary meaning that covers the election of judges.

As method, this is just backwards, and however much we may be attracted by the result it produces in a particular case, we should in every case resist it. Our job begins with a text that Congress has passed and the President has signed. We are to read the words of that text as any ordinary Member of Congress would have read them, see Holmes, The Theory of Legal Interpretation, 12 Harv. L. Rev. 417 (1899), and apply the meaning so determined. In my view, that reading reveals that § 2 extends to vote dilution claims for the elections of representatives only, and judges are not representatives.

* * * I agree with the Court that [original § 2], directed towards intentional discrimination, applied to all elections, for it clearly said so:

> "No voting qualification or prerequisite to voting, or standard, practice, or procedure shall be imposed or applied by any State or political subdivision to deny or abridge the right of any citizen of the United States to vote on account of race or color."

The 1982 amendments, however, radically transformed the Act. As currently written, the statute proscribes intentional discrimination only if it has a discriminatory effect, but proscribes practices with discriminatory effect whether or not intentional. This new "results" criterion provides a powerful, albeit sometimes blunt, weapon with which to attack even the most subtle forms of discrimination. The question we confront here is how broadly the new remedy applies. The foundation of the Court's analysis, the itinerary for its journey in the wrong direction, is the following statement: "It is difficult to believe that Congress, in an express effort to broaden the protection afforded by the Voting Rights Act, withdrew, without comment, an important category of elections from that protection." There are two things wrong with this. First is the notion that Congress cannot be credited with having achieved anything of major importance by simply saying it, in ordinary language, in the text of a statute, "without comment" in the legislative history. As the Court colorfully puts it, if the dog of legislative history has not barked nothing of great significance can have transpired. Apart from the questionable wisdom of assuming that dogs will bark when something important is happening, see 1 T. Livius, The History of Rome 411–413 (1892) (D. Spillan translation), we have forcefully and explicitly rejected the Conan Doyle approach to statutory construction in the past. See *Harrison v. PPG Industries, Inc.*, 446 U.S. 578, 592 (1980) ("In ascertaining the meaning of a statute, a court cannot, in the manner of Sherlock Holmes, pursue the theory of the dog that did not bark"). We are here to apply the statute, not legislative history, and certainly not the absence of legislative history. Statutes are the law though sleeping dogs lie.

The more important error in the Court's starting-point, however, is the assumption that the effect of excluding judges from the revised § 2 would be to "withdr[aw] . . . an important category of elections from [the] protection [of the Voting Rights Act]." There is absolutely no question here of *withdrawing* protection. Since the pre–1982 content of § 2 was coextensive with the Fifteenth Amendment, the entirety of that protection subsisted in the Constitution, and could be enforced through the other provisions of the Voting Rights Act. Nothing was lost from the prior coverage; *all* of the new "results" protection was an add-on. The issue is not, therefore, as the Court would have it, whether Congress has cut back on the coverage of the Voting Rights Act; the issue is how far it has extended it. Thus, even if a court's expectations were a proper basis for interpreting the text of a statute, while there would be reason to expect that Congress was not "withdrawing" protection, there is no particular reason to expect that the supplemental protection it provided was any more extensive than the text of the statute said.

[Justice Scalia agreed with the *LULAC* majority that section 2 created two separate rights for protected classes: (1) "to participate in the political process" and (2) "to elect representatives of their choice." On this reading, judicial elections are subject to the first right, but not the second because judges are not "representatives."] The Court, petitioners, and petitioners' *amici* have labored mightily to establish that there is *a* meaning of "representatives" that would include judges, and no doubt there is. But our job is not to scavenge the world of English usage to discover whether there is any possible meaning of "representatives" which suits our preconception that the statute includes judges; our job is to determine whether the *ordinary* meaning includes them, and if it does not, to ask whether there is any solid indication in the text or structure of the statute that something other than ordinary meaning was intended.

There is little doubt that the ordinary meaning of "representatives" does not include judges, see Webster's Second New International Dictionary 2114 (1950). The Court's feeble argument to the contrary is that "representatives" means those who "are chosen by popular election." On that hypothesis, the fan-elected members of the baseball All–Star teams are "representatives"—hardly a common, if even a permissible, usage. Surely the word "representative" connotes one who is not only *elected by* the people, but who also, at a minimum, *acts on behalf of* the people. Judges do that in a sense—but not in the ordinary sense. As the captions of the pleadings in some States still display, it is the prosecutor who represents "the People"; the judge represents the Law—which often requires him to rule against the People. It is precisely because we do not *ordinarily* conceive of judges as representatives that we held judges not within the Fourteenth Amendment's requirement of "one person, one vote." *Wells v. Edwards*, 347 F.Supp. 453 (MD La.1972), aff'd, 409 U.S. 1095 (1973). The point is not that a State could not make judges in some senses representative, or that all judges must be conceived of in the Article III mold, but rather, that giving "representatives" its ordinary meaning, the ordinary speaker in 1982 would not have applied the word to judges, see Holmes, The Theory of Legal Interpretation, 12 Harv. L. Rev. 417 (1899). It remains only to ask whether there is good indication that ordinary meaning does not apply. * * *

While the "plain statement" rule may not be applicable, there is assuredly nothing whatever that points in the opposite direction, indicating that the ordinary meaning here should *not* be applied. Far from that, in my view the ordinary meaning of "representatives" gives clear purpose to congressional action that otherwise would seem pointless. As an initial matter, it is evident that Congress paid particular attention to the scope of elections covered by the "to elect" language. As the Court suggests, that language for the most part tracked this Court's opinions in *White v. Regester* and *Whitcomb v. Chavis*, but the word "legislators" was not copied. Significantly, it was replaced not with the more general term "candidates" used repeatedly elsewhere in the Act, see, *e.g.*, 42 U.S.C. §§ 1971(b), (e); 1973i(c), 19731(c); 1973ff–2; 1974; 1974e, but with the term "representatives," which appears nowhere else in the Act (except as a proper noun referring to Members of the federal lower House, or designees of the Attorney General). The normal meaning of this term is broader than "legislators" (it includes, for example, school boards and city councils as well as senators and representatives) but narrower than "candidates."

The Court says that the seemingly significant refusal to use the term "candidate" and selection of the distinctive term "representative" are really inconsequential, because "candidate" could not have been used. According to the Court, since "candidate" refers to one who has been nominated but *not yet* elected, the phrase "to elect candidates" would be a contradiction in terms. The only flaw in this argument is that it is not true, as repeated usage of the formulation "to elect candidates" by this Court itself amply demonstrates. [Citing cases.] * * * In other words, far from being an impermissible choice, "candidates" would have been the natural choice, even if it had not been used repeatedly elsewhere in the statute. It is quite absurd to think that Congress went out of its way to replace that term with "representatives," in order to convey what "candidates" naturally suggests (*viz.*, coverage of *all* elections) and what "representatives" naturally does not.

A second consideration confirms that "representatives" in § 2 was meant in its ordinary sense. When given its ordinary meaning, it causes the statute to reproduce an established, eminently logical and perhaps practically indispensable limitation upon the availability of vote dilution claims. Whatever other requirements may be applicable to elections for "representatives" (in the sense of those who are not only elected by but act on behalf of the electorate), those elections, unlike elections for *all* office-holders, must be conducted in accordance with the equal-protection principle of "one person, one vote." And it so happens—more than coincidentally, I think—that in every case in which, prior to the amendment of § 2, we recognized the possibility of a vote dilution claim, the principle of "one person, one vote" was applicable. Indeed, it is the principle of "one person, one vote" that gives meaning to the concept of "dilution." One's vote is diluted if it is not, *as it should be*, of the same practical effect as everyone else's. Of course the mere fact that an election practice satisfies the constitutional requirement of "one person, one vote" does not establish that there has been no vote dilution for Voting Rights Act purposes, since that looks not merely to equality of individual votes but also to equality of minority blocs of votes. * * * But "one person, one vote" has been the premise and the necessary condition of a vote dilution claim, since it establishes the baseline for computing the voting strength that the minority bloc *ought* to have. As we have suggested, the first question in a dilution case is whether the "one person, one vote" standard is met, and if it is, the second is whether voting structures nonetheless operate to " 'minimize or cancel out the voting strength of racial or political elements of the voting population.' "

Well before Congress amended § 2, we had held that the principle of "one person, one vote" does not apply to the election of judges, *Wells v. Edwards*, 347 F.Supp. 453 (MD La. 1972), aff'd, 409 U.S. 1095 (1973). If Congress was (through use of the extremely inapt word "representatives") making vote dilution claims available with respect to the election of judges, it was, for the first time, extending that remedy to a context in which "one person, one vote" did not apply. *That* would have been a significant change in the law, and given the need to identify some other baseline for computing "dilution," *that* is a matter which those who believe in barking dogs should be astounded to find unmentioned in the legislative history. If "representatives" is given its normal meaning, on the other hand, there is no change in the law (except elimination of the intent requirement) and the silence is entirely understandable. * * *

Finally, the Court suggests that there is something "anomalous" about extending coverage under § 5 of the Voting Rights Act to the election of judges, while not extending coverage under § 2 to the same elections. This simply misconceives the different roles of § 2 and § 5. The latter requires certain jurisdictions to preclear changes in election methods before those changes are implemented; it is a means of assuring in advance the absence of all electoral illegality, not only that which violates the Voting Rights Act but that which violates the Constitution as well. In my view, judges *are* within the scope of § 2 for nondilution claims, and thus for those claims, § 5 preclearance would enforce the Voting Rights Act with respect to judges. Moreover, intentional discrimination in the election of judges, whatever its form, is constitutionally prohibited, and the preclearance provision of § 5 gives the government a method by which to prevent that. The scheme makes entire sense without the need to bring judges within the "to elect" provision. * * *

As I said at the outset, this case is about method. The Court transforms the meaning of § 2, not because the ordinary meaning is irrational, or inconsistent with other parts of the statute, see, *e.g.*, *Green v. Bock Laundry*; *Public Citizen v. Department of Justice* (Kennedy, J., concurring in the judgment), but because it does not fit the Court's conception of what Congress must have had in mind. When we adopt a method that psychoanalyzes Congress rather than reads its laws, when we employ a tinkerer's toolbox, we do great harm. Not only do we reach the wrong result with respect to the statute at hand, but we poison the well of future legislation, depriving legislators of the assurance that ordinary terms, used in an ordinary context, will be given a predictable meaning. Our highest responsibility in the field of statutory construction is to read the laws in a consistent way, giving Congress a sure means by which it may work the people's will. We have ignored that responsibility today. I respectfully dissent.

[The dissenting opinion of JUSTICE KENNEDY is omitted.]

WEST VIRGINIA UNIVERSITY HOSPITALS v. CASEY

Supreme Court of the United States, 1991
499 U.S. 83, 111 S.Ct. 1138, 113 L.Ed.2d 68.

JUSTICE SCALIA delivered the opinion of the Court.

[West Virginia University Hospitals (WVUH) prevailed in its lawsuit asserting its rights under the federal Medicaid statute. The Attorneys' Fees Awards Act of 1976, 42 U.S.C. § 1988, permits the award of "a reasonable attorney's fee" to prevailing plaintiffs in federal rights cases such as this one. The question was whether § 1988 authorizes the award to prevailing plaintiffs of fees for services rendered to their attorneys by experts.]

Title 28 § 1920 provides:

"A judge or clerk of any court of the United States may tax as costs the following:

"(1) Fees of the clerk and marshal;

"(2) Fees of the court reporter for all or any part of the stenographic transcript necessarily obtained for use in the case;

"(3) Fees and disbursements for printing and witnesses;

"(4) Fees for exemplification and copies of papers necessarily obtained for use in the case;

"(5) Docket fees under section 1923 of this title;

"(6) Compensation of court appointed experts, compensation of interpreters, and salaries, fees, expenses, and costs of special interpretation services under section 1828 of this title."

Title 28 U.S.C. § 1821(b) limits the witness fees authorized by § 1920(3) as follows: "A witness shall be paid an attendance fee of $30 per day for each day's attendance. A witness shall also be paid the attendance fee for the time necessarily occupied in going to and returning from the place of attendance...." In *Crawford Fitting Co. v. J.T. Gibbons, Inc.,* 482 U.S. 437 (1987), we held that these provisions define the full extent of a federal court's power to shift litigation costs absent express statutory authority to go further. "[W]hen," we said, "a prevailing party seeks reimbursement for fees paid to its own expert witnesses, a federal court is bound by the limits of § 1821(b), absent contract or explicit statutory authority to the contrary." *Id.* "We will not lightly infer that Congress has repealed §§ 1920 and 1821, either through [Federal Rule of Civil Procedure] 54(d) or any other provision not referring explicitly to witness fees."

As to the testimonial services of the hospital's experts, therefore, *Crawford Fitting* plainly requires, as a prerequisite to reimbursement, the identification of "explicit statutory authority." WVUH argues, however, that some of the expert fees it incurred in this case were unrelated to expert *testimony,* and that as to those fees the § 1821(b) limits, which apply only to witnesses in attendance at trial, are of no consequence. We agree with that, but there remains applicable the limitation of § 1920. *Crawford Fitting* said that we would not lightly find an implied repeal of § 1821 *or* of § 1920, which it held to be an express limitation upon the types of costs which, absent other authority, may be shifted by federal courts. None of the categories of expenses listed in § 1920 can reasonably be read to include fees for services rendered by an expert employed by a party in a nontestimonial advisory capacity. The question before us, then, is—with regard to both testimonial and nontestimonial expert fees— whether the term "attorney's fee" in § 1988 provides the "explicit statutory authority" required by *Crawford Fitting.*

The record of statutory usage demonstrates convincingly that attorney's fees and expert fees are regarded as separate elements of litigation cost. While some fee-shifting provisions, like § 1988, refer only to "attorney's fees," see, *e.g.,* Civil Rights Act of 1964, 42 U.S.C. § 2000e–5(k), many others explicitly shift expert witness fees *as well as* attorney's fees. In 1976, just over a week prior to the enactment of § 1988, Congress passed those provisions of the Toxic Substances Control Act, 15 U.S.C. §§ 2618(d), 2619(c)(2), which provide that a prevailing party may recover "the costs of suit and reasonable fees for attorneys *and expert witnesses.*" (Emphasis added.) Also in 1976, Congress amended the Consumer Product Safety Act, 15 U.S.C. §§ 2060(c), 2072(a), 2073, which as originally enacted in 1972 shifted to the losing party "cost[s] of suit, including a reasonable attorney's fee," see 86 Stat. 1226. In the 1976 amendment, Congress altered the fee-shifting provisions to their present form by adding a phrase shifting expert witness fees *in addition to* attorney's fees. See Pub.L. 94–284, § 10, 90 Stat. 506, 507. Two other significant Acts passed in 1976 contain similar phrasing: the Resource Conservation and Recovery Act of 1976, 42 U.S.C. § 6972(e) ("costs of litigation (including reasonable attorney and expert witness fees)"), and the Natural Gas Pipeline Safety Act Amendments of 1976, 49 U.S.C.App. § 1686(e) ("costs of suit, including reasonable attorney's fees and reasonable expert witnesses fees").

Congress enacted similarly phrased fee-shifting provisions in numerous statutes both before and after 1976. These statutes encompass diverse categories of legislation, including tax, administrative procedure, environmental protection, consumer protection, admiralty and navigation, utilities regulation, and, significantly, civil rights: The Equal Access to Justice Act (EAJA), the counterpart to § 1988 for violation of federal rights by federal employees, states that " 'fees and other expenses' [as shifted by § 2412(d)(1)(A)] includes the reasonable expenses of expert witnesses . . . and reasonable attorney fees." 28 U.S.C. § 2412(d)(2)(A). At least 34 statutes in 10 different titles of the United States Code explicitly shift attorney's fees *and* expert witness fees.

[Justice Scalia rejected WVUH's argument that pre–1976 practice supported the award of expert witness fees. To begin with, the cases where such fees were awarded almost always awarded attorneys' fees and costs separately from expert witness fees.] The laws that refer to fees for nontestimonial expert services are less common, but they establish a similar usage both before and after 1976: Such fees are referred to *in addition to* attorney's fees when a shift is intended. A provision of the Criminal Justice Act of 1964, 18 U.S.C. § 3006A(e), directs the court to reimburse appointed counsel for expert fees necessary to the defense of indigent criminal defendants—even though the immediately preceding provision, § 3006A(d), already directs that appointed defense counsel be paid a designated hourly rate plus "expenses reasonably incurred." WVUH's position must be that expert fees billed to a client through an attorney are "attorney's fees" because they are to be treated as part of the expenses of the attorney; but if this were normal usage, they would have been reimbursable under the Criminal Justice Act as "expenses reasonably incurred"—and subsection 3006A(e) would add nothing to the recoverable amount. The very heading of that subsection, "Services *other than* counsel" (emphasis added), acknowledges a distinction between services provided by the attorney himself and those provided to the attorney (or the client) by a nonlegal expert.

To the same effect is the 1980 EAJA, which provides: " 'fees and other expenses' [as shifted by § 2412(d)(1)(A)] includes the reasonable expenses of expert witnesses, *the reasonable cost of any study, analysis, engineering report, test, or project* which is found by the court to be necessary for the preparation of the party's case, and reasonable attorney fees." 28 U.S.C. § 2412(d)(2)(A) (emphasis added). If the reasonable cost of a "study" or "analysis"—which is but another way of describing nontestimonial expert services—is by common usage already included in the "attorney fees," again a significant and highly detailed part of the statute becomes redundant. The Administrative Procedure Act, 5 U.S.C. § 504(b)(1)(A) (added 1980), and the Tax Equity and Fiscal Responsibility Act of 1982, 26 U.S.C. § 7430(c)(1), contain similar language. Also reflecting the same usage are two railroad regulation statutes, the Regional Rail Reorganization Act of 1973, 45 U.S.C. §§ 726(f)(9) ("costs and expenses (including reasonable fees of accountants, experts, and attorneys) actually incurred"), and the Railroad Revitalization and Regulatory Reform Act of 1976, 45 U.S.C. § 854(g) ("costs and expenses (including fees of accountants, experts, and attorneys) actually and reasonably incurred").[5]

Prior to 1976, the leading fee-shifting statute was the Clayton Act, 38 Stat. 731, as amended, 15 U.S.C. § 15 (shifting "the cost of suit, including a reasonable attorney's fee"). As of 1976, four Circuits (six Circuits, if one includes summary affirmances of district court judgments) had held that this provision did not permit a shift of expert witness fees. No court had held otherwise. Also instructive is pre–1976 practice under the federal patent laws, which provided, 35 U.S.C. § 285, that "[t]he court in exceptional cases may award reasonable attorney fees to the prevailing party." Again, every court to consider the matter as of 1976 thought that this provision conveyed no authority to shift expert fees.

WVUH suggests that a distinctive meaning of "attorney's fees" should be adopted with respect to § 1988 because this statute was meant to overrule our decision in *Alyeska Pipeline Service Co. v. Wilderness Society,* 421 U.S. 240 (1975). As mentioned above, prior to 1975 many courts awarded expert fees and attorney's fees in certain circumstances pursuant to their equitable discretion. In *Alyeska,* we held that this discretion did not extend beyond a few exceptional circumstances long

---

5. WVUH cites a House Conference Committee Report from a statute passed in 1986, stating: "The conferees intend that the term 'attorneys' fees as part of the costs' include reasonable expenses and fees of expert witnesses and the reasonable costs of any test or evaluation which is found to be necessary for the preparation of the ... case." H.R.Conf.Rep. No. 99–687, p. 5 (1986) (discussing the Handicapped Children's Protection Act of 1986, 20 U.S.C. § 1415(e)(4)(B)). In our view this undercuts rather than supports WVUH's position: The specification would have been quite unnecessary if the ordinary meaning of the term included those elements. The statement is an apparent effort to *depart* from ordinary meaning and to define a term of art.

recognized by common law. Specifically, we rejected the so-called "private attorney general" doctrine recently created by some lower federal courts, which allowed equitable fee shifting to plaintiffs in certain types of civil rights litigation. WVUH argues that § 1988 was intended to restore the pre-*Alyeska* regime—and that, since expert fees were shifted then, they should be shifted now.

Both chronology and the remarks of sponsors of the bill that became § 1988 suggest that at least some members of Congress viewed it as a response to *Alyeska*. See, *e.g.,* S.Rep. No. 94–1011, pp. 4, 6 (1976). It is a considerable step, however, from this proposition to the conclusion the hospital would have us draw, namely, that § 1988 should be read as a reversal of *Alyeska* in all respects.

By its plain language and as unanimously construed in the courts, § 1988 is both broader and narrower than the pre-*Alyeska* regime. Before *Alyeska,* civil rights plaintiffs could recover fees pursuant to the private attorney general doctrine only if private enforcement was necessary to defend important rights benefiting large numbers of people, and cost barriers might otherwise preclude private suits. Section 1988 contains no similar limitation—so that in the present suit there is no question as to the propriety of shifting WVUH's *attorney's* fees, even though it is highly doubtful they could have been awarded under pre-*Alyeska* equitable theories. In other respects, however, § 1988 is not as broad as the former regime. It is limited, for example, to violations of specified civil rights statutes—which means that it would not have reversed the outcome of *Alyeska* itself, which involved not a civil rights statute but the National Environmental Policy Act of 1969, 42 U.S.C. § 4321 *et seq.* Since it is clear that, in many respects, § 1988 was not meant to return us precisely to the pre-*Alyeska* regime, the objective of achieving such a return is no reason to depart from the normal import of the text.

WVUH further argues that the congressional purpose in enacting § 1988 must prevail over the ordinary meaning of the statutory terms. It quotes, for example, the House Committee Report to the effect that "the judicial remedy [must be] full and complete," and the Senate Committee Report to the effect that "[c]itizens must have the opportunity to recover what it costs them to vindicate [civil] rights in court." As we have observed before, however, the purpose of a statute includes not only what it sets out to change, but also what it resolves to leave alone. See *Rodriguez v. United States,* 480 U.S. 522, 525–26 (1987). The best evidence of that purpose is the statutory text adopted by both Houses of Congress and submitted to the President. Where that contains a phrase that is unambiguous—that has a clearly accepted meaning in both legislative and judicial practice—we do not permit it to be expanded or contracted by the statements of individual legislators or committees during the course of the enactment process. Congress could easily have shifted "attorney's fees and expert witness fees," or "reasonable litigation expenses," as it did in contemporaneous statutes; it chose instead to enact more restrictive language, and we are bound by that restriction.

WVUH asserts that we have previously been guided by the "broad remedial purposes" of § 1988, rather than its text, in a context resolving an "analogous issue": In *Missouri v. Jenkins,* 491 U.S. 274, 285 (1989), we concluded that § 1988 permitted separately billed paralegal and law clerk time to be charged to the losing party. The trouble with this argument is that *Jenkins* did *not* involve an "analogous issue," insofar as the relevant considerations are concerned. The issue there was not, as WVUH contends, whether we would permit our perception of the "policy" of the statute to overcome its "plain language." It was not remotely plain in *Jenkins* that the phrase "attorney's fee" did not include charges for law clerk and paralegal services. Such services, like the services of "secretaries, messengers, librarians, janitors, and others whose labor contributes to the work product," had traditionally been included in calculation of the lawyers' hourly rates. Only recently had there arisen "the 'increasingly widespread custom of separately billing for [such] services.' " By contrast, there has never been, to our knowledge, a practice of including the cost of expert services within attorneys' hourly rates. * * *

WVUH's last contention is that, even if Congress plainly did not include expert fees in the fee-shifting provisions of § 1988, it would have done so had it thought about it. Most of the pre–§ 1988 statutes that explicitly shifted expert fees dealt with environmental litigation, where the necessity of expert advice was readily apparent; and when Congress later enacted the EAJA, the federal counterpart of § 1988, it explicitly included expert fees. Thus, the argument runs, the 94th Congress simply forgot; it is our duty to ask how they would have decided had they actually considered the question.

This argument profoundly mistakes our role. Where a statutory term presented to us for the first time is ambiguous, we construe it to contain that permissible meaning which fits most logically and comfortably into the body of both previously and subsequently enacted law. See 2 J. Sutherland, Statutory Construction § 5201 (3d F. Horack ed.1943). We do so not because that precise accommodative meaning is what the lawmakers must have had in mind (how could an earlier Congress know what a later Congress would enact?), but because it is our role to make sense rather than nonsense out of the *corpus juris.* But where, as here, the meaning of the term prevents such accommodation, it is not our function to eliminate clearly expressed inconsistency of policy and to treat alike subjects that different Congresses have chosen to treat differently. The facile attribution of congressional "forgetfulness" cannot justify such a usurpation. Where what is at issue is not a contradictory disposition within the same enactment, but merely a difference between the more parsimonious policy of an earlier enactment and the more generous policy of a later one, there is no more basis for saying that the earlier Congress forgot than for saying that the earlier Congress felt differently. In such circumstances, the attribution of forgetfulness rests in reality upon the judge's assessment that the later statute contains the *better* disposition. But that is not for judges to prescribe. We thus reject this last argument for the same reason that Justice Brandeis, writing for the Court, once rejected a similar (though less explicit) argument by the United States:

> "[The statute's] language is plain and unambiguous. What the Government asks is not a construction of a statute, but, in effect, an enlargement of it by the court, so that what was omitted, presumably by inadvertence, may be included within its scope. To supply omissions transcends the judicial function." *Iselin v. United States,* 270 U.S. 245, 250–51 (1926).[7]

For the foregoing reasons, we conclude that § 1988 conveys no authority to shift expert fees. When experts appear at trial, they are of course eligible for the fee provided by § 1920 and § 1821—which was allowed in the present case by the Court of Appeals.

JUSTICE MARSHALL, dissenting.

As Justice Stevens demonstrates, the Court uses the implements of literalism to wound, rather than to minister to, congressional intent in this case. That is a dangerous usurpation of congressional power when any statute is involved. It is troubling for special reasons, however, when the statute at issue is clearly designed to give access to the federal courts to persons and groups attempting to vindicate vital civil rights. A District Judge has ably put the point in an analogous context:

> "At issue here is much more than the simple question of how much [plaintiff's] attorneys should receive as attorney fees. At issue is . . . continued full and vigorous commitment to this Nation's lofty, but as yet unfulfilled, agenda to make the promises of this land available to all citizens, without regard to race or sex or other impermissible characteristic. There are at least two ways to undermine this commitment. The first is open and direct: a repeal of this Nation's antidiscrimination laws. The second is more indirect and, for this reason, somewhat insidious: to deny victims of discrimination a means for redress by creating an economic market in which attorneys cannot afford to represent them and take their cases to court." *Hidle v. Geneva County Bd. of Ed.,* 681 F.Supp. 752, 758–759 (MD Ala.1988) (awarding attorney's fees and expenses under Title VII of the Civil Rights Act of 1964).

JUSTICE STEVENS, joined by JUSTICE MARSHALL and JUSTICE BLACKMUN, dissenting.

Since the enactment of the Statute of Wills in 1540, careful draftsmen have authorized executors to pay the just debts of the decedent, including

---

7. WVUH at least asks us to guess the preferences of the *enacting* Congress. Justice Stevens apparently believes our role is to guess the desires of the *present* Congress, or of Congresses yet to be. "Only time will tell," he says, "whether the Court, with its literal reading of § 1988, has correctly interpreted the will of Congress." The implication is that today's holding will be proved wrong if Congress amends the law to conform with his dissent. We think not. The "will of Congress" we look to is not a will evolving from Session to Session, but a will expressed and fixed in a particular enactment. Otherwise, we would speak not of "interpreting" the law but of "intuiting" or "predicting" it. Our role is to say what the law, as hitherto enacted, *is;* not to forecast what the law, as amended, *will be.*

the fees and expenses of the attorney for the estate. Although the omission of such an express authorization in a will might indicate that the testator had thought it unnecessary, or that he had overlooked the point, the omission would surely not indicate a deliberate decision by the testator to forbid any compensation to his attorney.

In the early 1970's, Congress began to focus on the importance of public interest litigation, and since that time, it has enacted numerous fee-shifting statutes. In many of these statutes, which the majority cites at length, Congress has expressly authorized the recovery of expert witness fees as part of the costs of litigation. The question in this case is whether, notwithstanding the omission of such an express authorization in 42 U.S.C. § 1988, Congress intended to authorize such recovery when it provided for "a reasonable attorney's fee as part of the costs." In my view, just as the omission of express authorization in a will does not preclude compensation to an estate's attorney, the omission of express authorization for expert witness fees in a fee-shifting provision should not preclude the award of expert witness fees. We should look at the way in which the Court has interpreted the text of *this statute* in the past, as well as *this statute's* legislative history, to resolve the question before us, rather than looking at the text of the many other statutes that the majority cites in which Congress expressly recognized the need for compensating expert witnesses.

[I] Under either the broad view of "costs" typically assumed in the fee-shifting context or the broad view of "a reasonable attorney's fee" articulated by this Court, expert witness fees are a proper component of an award under § 1988. Because we are not interpreting these words for the first time, they should be evaluated in the context that this and other courts have already created.

The term "costs" has a different and broader meaning in fee-shifting statutes than it has in the cost statutes that apply to ordinary litigation. The cost bill in this case illustrates the point. Leaving aside the question of expert witness fees, the prevailing party sought reimbursement for $45,867 in disbursements, which plainly would not have been recoverable costs under 28 U.S.C. § 1920. These expenses, including such items as travel and long-distance telephone calls, were allowed by the District Court and were not even questioned by respondents. They were expenses that a retained lawyer would ordinarily bill to his or her client. They were accordingly considered proper "costs" in a case of this kind. * * *

[In *Missouri v. Jenkins,* 491 U.S. 274 (1989), the Court, over the solo dissent of Chief Justice Rehnquist, ruled that § 1988 covered paralegal expenses as part of the recoverable "costs," even though such expenses are not "costs" under § 1920.] In *Jenkins,* the Court acknowledged that the use of paralegals instead of attorneys reduced the cost of litigation, and " 'by reducing the spiraling cost of civil rights litigation, further[ed] the policies underlying civil rights statutes.' " If attorneys were forced to do the work that paralegals could just as easily perform under the supervision of an attorney, such as locating and interviewing witnesses or compiling statistical and financial data, then "it would not be surprising to see a greater amount of such work performed by attorneys themselves, thus increasing the overall cost of litigation."

This reasoning applies equally to other forms of specialized litigation support that a trial lawyer needs and that the client customarily pays for, either directly or indirectly. Although reliance on paralegals is a more recent development than the use of traditional expert witnesses, both paralegals and expert witnesses perform important tasks that save lawyers' time and enhance the quality of their work product. * * *

[II] The Senate Report on the Civil Rights Attorney's Fees Awards Act of 1976 explained that the purpose of the proposed amendment to 42 U.S.C. § 1988 was "to remedy anomalous gaps in our civil rights laws created by the United States Supreme Court's recent decision in *Alyeska Pipeline Service Co. v. Wilderness Society,* 421 U.S. 240 (1975), and to achieve consistency in our civil rights laws." S.Rep. No. 94–1011, p. 1 (1976), 1976 U.S.Code Cong. & Admin.News 5909. The Senate Committee on the Judiciary wanted to level the playing field so that private citizens, who might have little or no money, could still serve as "private attorneys general" and afford to bring actions, even against state or local bodies, to enforce the civil rights laws. The Committee acknowledged that "[i]f private citizens are to be able to assert their civil rights, and if those who violate the Nation's fundamental laws are not to proceed with impunity, then citizens must have the opportunity to recover *what it costs them* to vindicate these rights in court." *Id.* (emphasis added). According to the Committee, the bill would create "no startling new remedy," but would simply provide "the technical requirements" requested by the Supreme Court in *Alyeska,* so that courts could "continue the practice of awarding attorneys' fees which had been going on for years prior to the Court's May decision." *Id.*

To underscore its intention to return the courts to their pre-*Alyeska* practice of shifting fees in civil rights cases, the Senate Committee's Report cited with approval not only several cases in which fees had been shifted, but also all of the cases contained in Legal Fees, Hearings before the Subcommittee on Representation of Citizen Interests of the Senate Committee on the Judiciary, 93d Cong., 1st Sess., pt. 3, pp. 888–1024, 1060–1062 (1973). The cases collected in the 1973 Senate Hearings included many in which courts had permitted the shifting of costs, including expert witness fees. At the time when the Committee referred to these cases, though several were later reversed, it used them to make the point that prior to *Alyeska,* courts awarded attorney's fees and costs, including expert witness fees, in civil rights cases, and that they did so in order to encourage private citizens to bring such suits. It was to this pre- *Alyeska* regime, in which courts could award expert witness fees along with attorney's fees, that the Senate Committee intended to return through the passage of the fee-shifting amendment to § 1988. [The House Committee Report was to the same effect.]

The case before us today is precisely the type of public interest litigation that Congress intended to encourage by amending § 1988 to provide for fee shifting of a "reasonable attorney's fee as part of the costs." Petitioner, a tertiary medical center in West Virginia near the Pennsylvania border, provides services to a large number of Medicaid recipients throughout Pennsylvania. In January 1986, when the Pennsylvania Department of Public Welfare notified petitioner of its new Medicaid payment rates for Pennsylvania Medicaid recipients, petitioner believed them to be below the minimum standards for reimbursement specified by the Social Security Act. Petitioner successfully challenged the adequacy of the State's payment system under 42 U.S.C. § 1983.

This Court's determination today that petitioner must assume the cost of $104,133 in expert witness fees is at war with the congressional purpose of making the prevailing party whole. As we said in *Hensley v. Eckerhart,* 461 U.S. 424, 435 (1983), petitioner's recovery [under § 1988] should be "fully compensatory," or, as we expressed in *Jenkins,* petitioner's [§ 1988] recovery should be "comparable to what 'is traditional with attorneys compensated by a fee-paying client.' S.Rep. No. 94–1011, p. 6 (1976), * * *

[III] In recent years the Court has vacillated between a purely literal approach to the task of statutory interpretation and an approach that seeks guidance from historical context, legislative history, and prior cases identifying the purpose that motivated the legislation. * * *

On those occasions, however, when the Court has put on its thick grammarian's spectacles and ignored the available evidence of congressional purpose and the teaching of prior cases construing a statute, the congressional response has been dramatically different. It is no coincidence that the Court's literal reading of Title VII, which led to the conclusion that disparate treatment of pregnant and nonpregnant persons was not discrimination on the basis of sex, see *General Electric Co. v. Gilbert,* 429 U.S. 125 (1976), was repudiated by the 95th Congress; that its literal reading of the "continuous physical presence" requirement in § 244(a)(1) of the Immigration and Nationality Act, which led to the view that the statute did not permit even temporary or inadvertent absences from this country, see *INS v. Phinpathya,* 464 U.S. 183 (1984), was rebuffed by the 99th Congress; that its literal reading of the word "program" in Title IX of the Education Amendments of 1972, which led to the Court's gratuitous limit on the scope of the antidiscrimination provisions of Title IX, see *Grove City College v. Bell,* 465 U.S. 555 (1984), was rejected by the 100th Congress; or that its refusal to accept the teaching of earlier decisions in *Wards Cove Packing Co. v. Atonio,* 490 U.S. 642 (1989) (reformulating order of proof and weight of parties' burdens in disparate-impact cases), and *Patterson v. McLean Credit Union,* 491 U.S. 164 (1989) (limiting scope of 42 U.S.C. § 1981 to the making and enforcement of contracts), was overwhelmingly rejected by the 101st Congress, and its refusal to accept the widely held view of lower courts about the scope of fraud, see *McNally v. United States,* 483 U.S. 350 (1987) (limiting mail fraud to protection of property), was quickly corrected by the 100th Congress.

In the domain of statutory interpretation, Congress is the master. It obviously has the power to correct our mistakes, but we do the country a disservice when we needlessly ignore persuasive evidence of Congress' actual purpose and require it "to take the time to revisit the matter" [*Smith v. Robinson,* 468 U.S. 992, 1031 (1984) (Brennan, J., dissenting)] and to restate its purpose in more precise English whenever its work product suffers from an omission or inadvertent error. As Judge Learned Hand explained, statutes are likely to be imprecise.

> "All [legislators] have done is to write down certain words which they mean to apply generally to situations of that kind. To apply these literally may either pervert what was plainly their general meaning, or leave undisposed of what there is every reason to suppose they meant to provide for. Thus it is not enough for the judge just to use a dictionary. If he should do no more, he might come out with a result which every sensible man would recognize to be quite the opposite of what was really intended; which would contradict or leave unfulfilled its plain purpose." L. Hand, How Far Is a Judge Free in Rendering a Decision?, in The Spirit of Liberty 103, 106 (I. Dilliard ed.1952).

The Court concludes its opinion with the suggestion that disagreement with its textual analysis could only be based on the dissenters' preference for a "better" statute. It overlooks the possibility that a different view may be more faithful to Congress' command. The fact that Congress has consistently provided for the inclusion of expert witness fees in fee-shifting statutes when it considered the matter is a weak reed on which to rest the conclusion that the omission of such a provision represents a deliberate decision to forbid such awards. Only time will tell whether the Court, with its literal reading of § 1988, has correctly interpreted the will of Congress with respect to the issue it has resolved today.

NOTES ON CASEY, CHISOM, AND THE COURT'S TEXTUALIST TRAJECTORY

1. *The Rise of the New Textualism, 1987–95, and Its Relationship to the Plain Meaning Rule.* The Court's practice changed after Justice Scalia's appointment. After 1986, the Court's statutory opinions more often found a "plain meaning," less often examined legislative history to confirm the existence of a plain meaning, and relied less often on legislative history to interpret a statute against what the Court felt was its plain meaning. The Justices' opinions also have tended to be more dogmatic about whether there is any ambiguity in statutes; the Court was more likely to find a plain meaning in the 1990s than it was before 1986.[f] As in *Casey,* Justice Scalia's own opinions set forth and defend the precepts of the new textualism, often

---

f. See William N. Eskridge Jr., *Dynamic Statutory Interpretation* ch. 7 (1994); Lawrence M. Solan, *The Language of Judges* (1993); Thomas A. Merrill, *Textualism and the Future of the* Chevron *Doctrine*, 72 Wash. U. L. Q. 351 (1994).

with Justice Stevens in dissent (also as in *Casey*).[g]

The relationship between the new textualism and the old plain meaning rule is evident, but they are not the same thing. Justice Scalia's formulation of textualism at the beginning of his *Chisom* dissent, as well as his discussion in *A Matter of Interpretation*, stresses the "ordinary meaning" or "reasonable meaning" of statutory text. In his view, legislative history should never trump such ordinary meaning. In contrast, the old plain meaning rule, as exemplified by *Caminetti* (§ 1 of this chapter), operated as an exclusionary rule concerning the use of legislative history: if the statutory text was "plain," one could not consult legislative history; if the statutory text was ambiguous, legislative history was fair game. The softer approach to plain meaning in *TVA v. Hill* and *Griffin* was even less confining, stating merely that a statutory plain meaning was presumptively the interpretation to be given to the statute, but legislative history could be consulted to confirm that understanding (and in a rare case in which the legislative history conclusively demonstrated that the textual plain meaning was not the appropriate interpretation, the plain meaning could be jettisoned).

In the post–1986 (i.e., Scalia) period, "plain meaning" remains a deeply ambiguous term. Our sense is that courts that speak of "plain meaning" are usually positing that the statute is quite clear in a literal sense—much more than "ordinary meaning" connotes. What we understand Justice Scalia to mean by "plain meaning" is the best (most coherent) textual understanding that emerges after close textual analysis, which then makes the result in the case plain on his terms—not merely the relatively rare "plain meaning" that leaps off the page to the experienced judge. It is regrettable that in some cases—both federal and state—judges have used the term "plain meaning" loosely, sometimes to mean a textual interpretation that is pretty obvious on the face of the statute (say, 90/10 clear) and sometimes to mean something similar to Justice Scalia's expression of the best textual understanding that emerges from close analysis of statutory provisions that, at the outset, may have seemed ambiguous, confusing, or at least complicated. The former approach to plain meaning is akin to a pretty literal approach to the face of the statute; the latter approach of Justice Scalia sees statutory interpretation to be something like a word puzzle, capable of being solved in almost all cases with a best answer emerging.

Although the Court's practice was influenced by the new textualism in the first few years of Justice Scalia's membership, the Court never completely accepted its tenets. In *Wisconsin Public Intervenor v. Mortier*, 501 U.S. 597, 610 n.4 (1991), all of the other Justices joined a footnote explicitly rejecting Justice Scalia's insistence that legislative history is irrelevant to proper statutory interpretation. And, as in *Chisom* and *Bock Laundry*, the Court still considered legislative background to statutes and is open to understanding a statute from the perspective of the legislators who enacted it. Often such

---

g. In this era, Justice Scalia applied the new textualism in opinions for the Court in *MCI Telecommunications Corp. v. American Tel. & Tel. Co.*, 512 U.S. 218 (1994) (Stevens in dissent); *BFP v. Resolution Trust Corp.*, 511 U.S. 531 (1994) (Stevens joining Souter dissent); *United States v. Nordic Village*, 503 U.S. 30 (1992) (Stevens in dissent); *Sullivan v. Everhart*, 494 U.S. 83 (1990) (Stevens in dissent); *Finley v. United States*, 490 U.S. 545 (1989) (Stevens in dissent); *Chan v. Korean AirLines, Ltd.*, 490 U.S. 122 (1989) (Stevens joining Brennan dissent); *Pierce v. Underwood*, 487 U.S. 552 (1988) (unanimous Court).

decisions are written by Justices Stevens or Souter, with Justice Scalia dissenting, as in *Chisom*, or concurring only in the judgment, as in *Bock Laundry*.[h]

2. *1995 Onward.* According to Charles Tiefer, *The Reconceptualization of Legislative History in the Supreme Court*, 2000 Wis. L. Rev. 205, the new textualism is not only past its peak, but its strong claims were rejected by the Court in the 1990s.[i] Since 1995, the Court has often followed the approach pressed by Justice Breyer in *The Uses of Legislative History*, 65 S. Cal. L. Rev. 845 (1992) and by Justice Stevens in *Chisom* and his *Casey* dissent—what Professor Tiefer calls "institutional legislative history."

Under the institutional approach, the Court treats the legislative process as a group engaged in coordinated purposive action, in which the group relies on the guidance and judgment of subgroups (committees) and ratifies their publicly presented understandings when the group takes action (i.e., enacts statutes). Hence, statutory interpretation is neither an effort to imaginatively reconstruct a collective intent nor to divine the objective meaning the statutory text would have had when adopted, but instead is an effort to carry out the ongoing institutional project along the lines laid out in the public presentations of those institutional actors charged with developing the original statute. Note the close connection between the institutionalist approach espoused by Justices Stevens and Breyer, and the legal process theory of Professors Hart and Sacks.

3. *So Where Is the Court's Methodology Now?* The Supreme Court has not returned to the pre-Scalia days. Consider the following observations about where it is today. First, the text is now, more than it was 20 or 30 years ago, the central inquiry at the Supreme Court level and in other courts that are now following the Supreme Court's lead. A brief that starts off with, "The statute means thus-and-so because it says so in the committee report," is asking for trouble. Both advice and advocacy should start with the statutory text: "The statute means thus-and-so because that is its plain meaning," "because that is the meaning the structure of the statute supports," or "because this statute uses more narrow language than Congress purposefully used in other statutes."

Because the Court frequently uses the dictionary to provide meaning to key statutory terms,[j] the advocate should incorporate this methodology as

---

h. For cases in this era, see *Landgraf v. USI Film Products*, 511 U.S. 244 (1994) (Stevens opinion, Scalia concurring in the judgment); *American Red Cross v. S.G.*, 505 U.S. 247 (1992) (Souter opinion, Scalia dissent); *United States v. R.L.C.*, 503 U.S. 291 (1992) (Souter plurality opinion, Scalia concurring in the judgment); *Taylor v. United States*, 495 U.S. 575 (1990) (Blackmun opinion, Scalia concurring in the judgment); *Crandon v. United States*, 494 U.S. 152 (1990) (Stevens opinion, Scalia concurring only in the judgment); *Blanchard v. Bergeron*, 489 U.S. 87 (1989) (White opinion, Scalia concurring only in the judgment).

i. In addition, see James J. Brudney & Corey Ditslear, *The Decline and Fall of Legislative History? Patterns of Supreme Court Reliance in the Burger and Rehnquist Eras*, 89 Judicature 220 (2006); Jonathan T. Molot, *The Rise and Fall of Textualism*, 106 Colum. L. Rev. 1 (2006); Lawrence M. Solan, *Learning Our Limits: The Decline of Textualism in Statutory Cases*, 1997 Wis. L. Rev. 235, as well as Lawrence M. Solan, *The Language of Statutes* (2011).

j. See Ellen P. Aprill, *The Law of the Word: Dictionary Shopping in the Supreme Court*, 30 Ariz. St. L.J. 275 (1998); Lawrence M. Solan, *Finding Ordinary Meaning in the Dictionary*, in *Language and the Law* 255 (Marlyn Robinson ed. 2003); Samuel A. Thumma & Jeffrey L. Kirchmeier, *The Lexicon Has Become a Fortress: The United States Supreme Court's Use of* well. The lexicon has become a fortress, as Judge Thumma and Professor Kirchmeier have aptly observed. See Samuel A. Thumma & Jeffrey L. Kirchmeier, *The Lexicon Has Become a Fortress: The United States Supreme Court's Use of Dictionaries*, 47 Buff. L. Rev. 227 (1999). The effective advocate should understand there are many theoretical problems with relying upon dictionaries to support textualism—e.g., they are not part of the text of a statute and might seem even further removed from it than legislative history; they are not necessarily "objective"; they are necessarily conservative, in the sense of reflecting past English usage rather than emerging usage; although judges may consult them in the hope of avoiding contextual, purposive inquiries, dictionaries usually present several definitions of a term and suggest (frequently quite explicitly, in a preface) that only through considering the context of usage can the term be properly defined. Although this is chaotic theoretically, as a practical matter this opens the door for advocates to engage in "dictionary shopping," as well as "definition shopping" within any particular dictionary.[k] In this respect, consider Justice Scalia's conclusion in *Chisom*, based on a dictionary, that the customary usage of "representative" excludes elected judges. Consult your own dictionary, or several: Can you find a definition of "representative" that supports the majority's holding in *Chisom*?

Second, the "contextual" evidence the Court is interested in is now statutory more than just historical context. Arguments that your position is more consistent with other parts of the same statute are typically winning arguments. Similarly, as *Casey* indicates, the Court today goes beyond the "whole act" rule to something like a "whole code" rule, searching the United States Code for guidance on the usage of key statutory terms and phrases. For a recent example, consult *Arlington Central School District v. Murphy*, 548 U.S. 291 (2006), where the Court narrowly construed the fee-shifting provision of a 1986 education-rights statute following the same methodology as *Casey*, over strong contrary legislative history and a powerful argument based on the statutory structure (both developed by Justice Breyer's dissenting opinion).

Third, the Court will still look at contextual evidence and is very interested in the public law background of the statute. If a statute seems to require an odd result (as in *Bock Laundry*), the Court will interrogate the background materials to find out why. If a statute overrides judicial or agency decisions (as in *Chisom*), the Court will usually be responsive to Congress' concerns. When the Justices are themselves divided as to what the statute's "plain meaning" is, as in *Weber* (which the Rehnquist Court reaffirmed in

---

Dictionaries, 47 Buff. L. Rev. 227 (1999); Note, *Looking It Up: Dictionaries and Statutory Interpretation*, 107 Harv. L. Rev. 1437, 1438 (1994) (first noting this trend).

k. See Note, *Looking It Up*, *supra*, at 1447 (describing the wide range of dictionaries the Court has consulted). To avoid cherry-picking from the wide array of dictionary definitions often available for normatively freighted terms (like "discriminate" and "modify"), Justice Scalia has suggested that judges might follow the weight of dictionary definitions. See *MCI Telecommunications Corp. v. American Tel. & Tel. Co.*, 512 U.S. 218, 226–27, 228 n.3 (1994) (following "[v]irtually every dictionary" while rejecting the definition found in *Webster's Third*, which was published after the statute in question was enacted and in any event was less worthy of reliance because of "its portrayal of common error as proper usage"). In dissent, Justice Stevens disputed the weight of dictionary authority and concluded that, in any event, "[d]ictionaries can be useful aids in statutory interpretation, but they are no substitute for close analysis of what words mean as used in a particular statutory context." *Id.* at 240 (Stevens, J., dissenting).

Johnson v. Transportation Agency, both excerpted in Chapter 1, § 3), at least some of them will examine the statute's background to figure out how the typical legislator would have read the statute. For all of these reasons, it remains important to research and brief the legislative history thoroughly. The effective advocate will appreciate that the presence of such materials in the briefs may influence the outcome more than the opinion in the case will indicate.[1]

With these factors in mind, can you find a sensible way in which three Justices (White, O'Connor, Souter) were in the majority in *both Chisom* and *Casey*? Are the textual arguments equally strong in both cases? From the excerpts you have read, weigh the strength of the legislative history and the statutory purposes present in both cases as well, and in addition consider the subject matter and the current "stakes" involved in each case. Consider, also, the kind of legal coherence arguments suggested by legal process theory. The background norm in *Casey* was the "American rule," presuming against free-shifting unless there is affirmative legislative authorization. The background norm in *Chisom* was the repeated congressional commitment to federal monitoring of electoral rules in the south. In each case, the majority (including White, O'Connor, and Souter) did not think that the background norm had been rebutted by the congressional materials at hand.

Zuni Public School District No. 89 v. Department of Education, 550 U.S. 81 (2007). The federal Impact Aid Act, 108 Stat. 3749, provides financial assistance to local school districts whose ability to finance public school education is adversely affected by a federal presence. The statute prohibits a State from offsetting this federal aid by reducing state aid to a local district. So as not to interfere with a state program that seeks to equalize per-pupil expenditures, the statute contains an exception permitting a State to reduce its own local funding on account of the federal aid where the Secretary of Education finds that the state program "equalizes expenditures" among local school districts. 20 U.S.C. § 7709(b)(1). The Secretary is required to use a formula that compares the local school district with the greatest per-pupil expenditures in a State to the school district with the smallest per-pupil expenditures. If the former does not exceed the latter by more than 25 percent, the state program qualifies as one that "equalizes expenditures." In making this determination, the Secretary must "disregard [school districts] with per-pupil expenditures * * * above the 95th percentile or below the 5th percentile of such expenditures in the State." *Id.* § 7709(b)(2)(B)(i).

---

1. Consider the comments of Judge A. Raymond Randolph of the United States Court of Appeals for the District of Columbia Circuit, in *Dictionaries, Plain Meaning, and Context in Statutory Interpretation*, 17 Harv. J.L. & Pub. Pol'y 71, 76 (1994):

* * * Nearly every brief I see in cases involving issues of statutory construction contains a discourse on legislative history. This is a wise precaution on the part of appellate advocates. Counsel can never be sure that the court will find the words plain, and stop there. To be safe, in the event the court takes two steps instead of one, counsel must include a backup argument addressing the meaning of the statute in light of the legislative history. Judges read those briefs from cover to cover, or at least they are supposed to. I do. Somewhere during the reading, preliminary views begin to form. When the reading is done and the case has been analyzed and argued, how can it be said that the judge turned to the legislative history only after finding the statutory language ambiguous? The judge himself often cannot identify exactly when his perception of the words actually jelled. * * *

Department of Education regulations first promulgated more than 30 years ago provide that the Secretary will (1) create a list of school districts ranked in order of per-pupil expenditure; then (2) identify the relevant percentile cutoff point on that list based on a specific (95th or 5th) percentile of student population (essentially identifying those districts whose students account for the 5% of the State's total student population that lies at both the high and low ends of the spending distribution); and finally (3) compare the highest spending and lowest spending of the remaining school districts to see whether they satisfy the statute's requirement that the disparity between them not exceed 25%. Two New Mexico school districts challenged this method of calculation on the ground that it was inconsistent with the plain language of the "disregard" clause. According to the districts, the clause required the Department to disregard the bottom and top 5% of school districts by number (i.e., the top 5 and the bottom 5 if there were 100 districts)—and not to consider the districts' populations, as the Department was doing.

Justice Breyer's opinion for the Court ruled that the Department's method was permissible. First, it was consistent with the evolution of the statute. Congress first enacted an equalization law in 1974, which explicitly delegated to the Department authority to define the conditions under which equalization funds would be allowed. The Department issued regulations in 1976, essentially the same as those challenged. No one in Congress objected to those regulations, which the Department has administered them consistently. "The present statutory language originated in draft legislation that the Secretary himself sent to Congress in 1994. With one minor change (irrelevant to the present calculation controversy), Congress adopted that language without comment or clarification. No one at the time—no Member of Congress, no Department of Education official, no school district or State—expressed the view that this statutory language (which, after all, was supplied by the Secretary) was intended to require, or did require, the Secretary to change the Department's system of calculation, a system that the Department and school districts across the Nation had followed for nearly 20 years, without (as far as we are told) any adverse effect."

Second, the Department's approach was consistent with the purpose of the disregard clause, to exclude "outlier" districts from the calculation. The Department originally explained why it did not follow a number-of-school-districts approach: "In States with a small number of large districts, an exclusion based on percentage of school districts might exclude from the measure of disparity a substantial percentage of the pupil population in those States. Conversely, in States with large numbers of small districts, such an approach might exclude only an insignificant fraction of the pupil population and would not exclude anomalous characteristics." 41 Fed. Reg. 26,324 (1976).

Third, the Department's approach was not inconsistent with the statutory language, which Justice Breyer thought ambiguous in light of his survey of technical and general dictionaries. The statutory language ("percentile") signifies only that the Department must divide districts into a population with a top 5% and a bottom 5%, but does not tell the Department how those "5%" figures must be calculated. "No dictionary definition we have found suggests that there is any *single* logical, mathematical, or statistical link between, on the one hand, the characterizing data (used for ranking purposes) and, on the other hand, the nature of the relevant population or how that population might be weighted for purposes of determining a percentile cutoff." When Congress has wanted to limit agency discretion in making such percentile rankings, it has phrased statutory language more precisely. For example, in another education-related law, Congress referred to "the school at the 20th percentile in the State, *based on enrollment,* among all schools *ranked by the percentage of students at the proficient level.*" 20 U.S.C. § 6311(b)(2)(E)(ii) (emphasis supplied by Justice Breyer).

Justice Breyer drew further "reassurance from the fact that no group of statisticians, nor any individual statistician, has told us directly in briefs, or indirectly through citation, that the language before us cannot be read as we have read it. This circumstance is significant, for the statutory language is technical, and we are not statisticians. And the views of experts (or their absence) might help us understand (though not control our determination of) what Congress had in mind."

Justice Scalia's dissenting opinion (joined by Chief Justice Roberts and Justices Souter and Thomas) faulted the majority for starting its analysis with the history and evolution of the statute, rather than its text. In his view, this "cart-before-the-horse approach" was inconsistent with the primary lesson of "Statutory Interpretation 101." (Writing also for Justice Alito, **Justice Kennedy** wrote a concurring opinion stating that he would be alarmed if Justice Breyer's order of treatment became "systemic." Justice Scalia responded that such deviant practices should be nipped in the bud, lest they become "systemic.")

Justice Scalia castigated the majority for finding ambiguity in a statute having a plain meaning. "This is not a scary math problem," and judges "do not need the cadre of the Court's number-crunching *amici* to guide our way." "The question is: Whose per-pupil expenditures or revenues? Or, in the Court's terminology, what 'population' is assigned the 'characteristic' 'perpupil expenditure or revenue'? At first blush, second blush, or twenty-second blush, the answer is abundantly clear: local educational agencies. The statute requires the Secretary to 'disregard local educational agencies with' certain per-pupil figures above or below specified percentiles of those per-pupil figures. § 7709(b)(2)(B)(i). The attribute 'per-pupil expenditur[e] or revenu[e]' is assigned to LEAs [local educational agencies]—there is no mention of student population whatsoever. And thus under the statute, 'per-pupil expenditures or revenues' are to be arrayed using a population consisting of LEAs, so that percentiles are determined from a list of (in New Mexico) 89 per-pupil expenditures or revenues representing the 89 LEAs in the State. It is just that simple."

Concurring in the Court's opinion, **Justice Stevens** further opined that he would agree with the majority's interpretation in this case even if were inconsistent with statutory plain meaning. "There is no reason why we must confine ourselves to, or begin our analysis with, the statutory text if other tools of statutory construction provide better evidence of congressional intent with respect to the precise point at issue. As the Court's opinion demonstrates, this is a quintessential example of a case in which the statutory text was obviously enacted to adopt the rule that the Secretary administered both before and after the enactment of the rather confusing language found in 20 U.S.C. § 7709(b)(2)(B)(i). That text is sufficiently ambiguous to justify the Court's exegesis, but my own vote is the product of a more direct route to the Court's patently correct conclusion. This happens to be a case in which the legislative history is pellucidly clear and the statutory text is difficult to fathom.'' Justice Stevens justified his approach by reference to *Griffin*, where the Court followed statutory plain meaning consistent with its reading of the legislative history, and *Holy Trinity*, where it did not.

The latter reference sparked a further response from **Justice Scalia** (in a portion of his dissent joined by Chief Justice Roberts and Justice Thomas but not by Justice Souter). *Holy Trinity*, "that miraculous redeemer of lost causes," is a dangerous precedent. "Thus, what judges believe Congress 'meant' (apart from the text) has a disturbing but entirely unsurprising tendency to be whatever judges think Congress *must* have meant, *i.e., should* have meant. In *Church of the Holy Trinity*, every Justice on this Court disregarded the plain language of a statute that forbade the hiring of a clergyman from abroad because, after all (they thought), 'this is a Christian nation,' so Congress could not have meant what it said. Is there any reason to believe that those Justices were lacking that 'intellectua[l] honest[y]' that Justice Stevens 'presume[s]' all our judges possess? Intellectual honesty does not exclude a blinding intellectual bias. And even if it did, the system of judicial amendatory veto over texts duly adopted by Congress bears no resemblance to the system of lawmaking set forth in our Constitution."

Query: What does this recent dust-up among the Justices tell you about the Court's current practice? Specifically, what is the current status of legislative history? Statutory purpose? The plain meaning rule? *Holy Trinity*?

B. ECONOMIC THEORIES OF STATUTORY INTERPRETATION

Economic theory assumes that individuals are rational actors who seek to maximize their utilities through actions reasonably designed to do so. Institutions, too, may be rational actors, with their preferences usually determined by the views of the median senator, representative, or judge. Most purely economic theorizing is descriptive, helping us predict the behavior of groups of real people. Consider a simple example of how purely descriptive economic theorizing can enrich your thinking about statutory interpretation.

For most of us, law is prediction of the rules that interacting government institutions will apply to your facts. We ask the IRS, read the newspaper, call a government clerk, note the posted speed limit, or just absorb it by osmosis. Law as prediction also entails evolution through sequential institutional interaction.[m] Congress enacts statutes, agencies

---

m. The model that follows was developed in William N. Eskridge Jr. & John Ferejohn, *Politics, Interpretation, and the Rule of Law*, in *The Rule of Law: Nomos XXXVI* 265 (Ian Shapiro interpret and apply those statutes, the judiciary reviews agency actions and interpretations, and Congress periodically considers legislation updating the law or overriding errant interpretations. A consequence of this sequence is that each institution has trumping power. The agency can undo some legislative bargains by stingy enforcement, the Supreme Court can overturn the agency's application, and Congress can override the Court or the agency. Groups press for changes in the law by working the institution most favorable to their interests and then seeking to protect it against trumping by the next institution down the line.

Most of the time, law is in a *stable equilibrium*: none of the institutions wants to change the rule, in part because if any makes that effort it may be overridden by the next institution in the chain. As a weak political actor ("the least dangerous branch"), the Supreme Court usually locates and applies that political equilibrium on high-visibility issues of public law, as it did in the affirmative action cases (*Weber* and *Johnson*) in Chapter 1, § 3. On the other hand, the equilibrium is often potentially unstable: one actor may be able to change the rule without being overridden. This is what happened in *Griffin*, where the Supreme Court imposed its rule-of-law values on a statute that apparently was understood for decades to embody a less generous compensation rule—and the issue was too divisive (seafaring unions liking the Court's result, companies not) for Congress to override.

Political scientists and many law professors maintain that judges, especially Supreme Court Justices, also harbor substantive values that they read into statutes when they can.[n] *Casey* can be read as such an effort, in which the Court majority was tipping the scales strongly in favor the "American rule" (providing that prevailing plaintiffs do not recover their attorney's fees from losing defendants). Although Congress overrode *Casey* and other anti-fee-shifting decisions, the Court still relies on those anti-fee-shifting precedents when the Justices can reasonably expect no override. See *Arlington Central School Board of Education v. Murphy*, 548 U.S. 291 (2006) (narrowly interpreting fee-shifting law benefitting parents of disabled schoolchildren).

---

ed. 1993); William N. Eskridge Jr. & Philip P. Frickey, *The Supreme Court, 1993 Term—Foreword: Law as Equilibrium*, 108 Harv. L. Rev. 26 (1994). For a different interactive model attempting to explain why interpretive methodology changes over time, see Adrian Vermeule, *The Cycles of Statutory Interpretation*, 68 U. Chi. L. Rev. 149 (2001). Vermeule suggests that legislators and judges develop inconsistent expectations of each other and engage in sequential interaction to affect the other's behavior—for example, judges consult legislative history; legislators notice and abuse the process by skewing the legislative history to affect interpretation; judges notice and stop using legislative history; legislators notice and stop abusing it; judges then start consulting the legislative history because it seems uncontaminated.

n. Lee Epstein & Jack Knight, *The Choices Justices Make* (1998); James J. Brudney & Corey Ditslear, *Canons of Construction and the Elusive Quest for Neutral Reasoning*, 58 Vand. L. Rev. 1, 6 (2005) (excerpted in Chapter 3, § 3); Richard L. Revesz, *Environmental Regulation, Ideology, and the D.C. Circuit*, 83 Va. L. Rev. 1717 (1997); Jeffrey Segal & Albert Cover, *Ideological Values and the Votes of U.S. Supreme Court Justices*, 83 Am. Pol. Sci. Rev. 557 (1989); Jeffrey Segal, *Separation-of-Powers Games in the Positive Theory of Congress and Courts*, 91 Am. Pol. Sci. Rev. 28–43 (1997).

Some of these descriptive points, such as the political science view that judges mainly vote their substantive preferences, are controversial (but stubbornly resistant to refutation, we might add). You might maintain a healthy skepticism about the predictive claims of economics-based theories. In the hands of legal scholars and judges, economics-based thinking is more typically harnessed for some kind of normative point. In this part of the chapter, we shall explore three different kinds of normative contributions law and economics might make to statutory interpretation. They draw from economists' *ex ante* approach to rules, from public choice theory, and from cost-benefit analysis.

1. Ex Ante Approaches to the Debate Between Textualists and Contextualists

Most students, and many professors and judges, respond to "hard cases" from an *ex post* point of view: this result is unfair to or visits needless hardship upon a sympathetic claimant. From an economics point of view, hard cases make bad law because they invite *ex post* decisionmaking, where the judge creates rules and standards that are fair in the particular case—but often have excessive social costs for a society that then has to apply the rule in future interactions and lawsuits. In law generally, and statutory interpretation particularly, economic theory would valorize an *ex ante* perspective: evaluate a decision or rule based on whether it sets up a rule that will be good for the average case and provides proper incentives for the citizenry—and not because you like its result in a particular case. The same kind of thinking can apply to general theories. What could be more reasonable than Hart and Sacks's notion that interpreters should apply statutes to carry out admirable public-regarding purposes? Defending the Hart and Sacks approach from an *ex ante* perspective is Jonathan R. Macey, *Promoting Public–Regarding Legislation Through Statutory Interpretation: An Interest Group Model*, 86 Colum. L. Rev. 223 (1986). Macey argues that interpreting statutes to carry out their *announced* public-regarding purposes is a good way for judges to maintain a minimal level of honesty in the legislative process.

Pushing in a different direction, William Landes and Richard A. Posner once made an *ex ante* argument for applying original legislative intent in statutory cases, even when such application leads to harsh results. Landes & Posner, *The Independent Judiciary in an Interest–Group Perspective,* 18 J.L. & Econ. 875 (1976). They argued that judges must be faithful agents reconstructing original deals, not because that is required by the Constitution or the rule of law, but because any other rule would undermine the conditions under which statutes are enacted. *Ex ante,* such an originalist approach gives members of Congress and interest groups sufficient assurance that their deals will be enforced. To the extent that the enforcement of statutory deals is a good thing for our pluralist democracy, this is what judges ought to do. The Landes and Posner approach would consider legislative materials for whatever light they might shed on those deals.

Judge Frank Easterbrook (Posner's former academic and current court of appeals colleague) and Justice Scalia agree with Landes and Posner's *ex ante* way of thinking: the best approach to statutory interpretation is one that reassures citizens, interest groups, and legislators that statutory deals will be respected and enforced; this makes the operation of a pluralist representative government possible. Yet they reject Landes and Posner's application of this method and maintain that the best evidence of statutory deals is the statutory text, with legislative history likely to mislead.

Treating statutes as contract-like deals is controversial, e.g., Mark L. Movesian, *Are Statutes Really "Legislative Bargains"? The Failure of the Contract Analogy in Statutory Interpretation*, 76 N.C. L. Rev. 1145 (1998), but assume that this is an apt analogy. Consider how the different dealist theories play out in the following case.[o] Note how the approach Judge Posner takes here is somewhat different than the theory he developed with Landes and reiterated just five years before this case, in Richard A. Posner, *The Federal Courts: Crisis and Reform* 286–93 (1985).

UNITED STATES v. MARSHALL

United States Court of Appeals for the Seventh Circuit (en banc), 1990
908 F.2d 1312, aff'd sub nom. Chapman v. United States, 500 U.S. 453 (1991)

EASTERBROOK, CIRCUIT JUDGE.

* * * Stanley J. Marshall was convicted after a bench trial and sentenced to 20 years' imprisonment for conspiring to distribute, and distributing, more than ten grams of LSD, enough for 11,751 doses. Patrick Brumm, Richard L. Chapman, and John M. Schoenecker were convicted by a jury of selling ten sheets (1,000 doses) of paper containing LSD. Because the total weight of the paper and LSD was 5.7 grams, a five-year mandatory minimum applied. The district court sentenced Brumm to 60 months (the minimum), Schoenecker to 63 months, and Chapman to 96 months' imprisonment. All four defendants confine their arguments on appeal to questions concerning their sentences.

The three questions we must resolve are these: (1) Whether 21 U.S.C. § 841(b)(1)(A)(v) and (B)(v), which set mandatory minimum terms of imprisonment—five years for selling more than one gram of a "mixture or substance containing a detectable amount" of LSD, ten years for more than ten grams—exclude the weight of the carrier medium. (2) Whether the weight tables in the sentencing guidelines likewise exclude the weight of any carrier. (3) Whether the statute and the guidelines are unconstitutional to the extent their computations are based on anything other than the weight of the pure drug. * * *

---

o. Consistent with descriptive economic theory, Posner and Easterbrook, both law and economics "conservatives" appointed by President Reagan, vote the same way in the large majority of statutory cases, even if for different reasons. See Daniel A. Farber, *Do Theories of Statutory Interpretation Matter?*, 94 Nw. U. L. Rev. 1409 (2000). For a more general comparative examination of judicial practice with interpretive theories, see Frank B. Cross, *The Significance of Statutory Interpretive Methodologies*, 82 Notre Dame L. Rev. 1971 (2007).

According to the Sentencing Commission, the LSD in an average dose weighs 0.05 milligrams. Twenty thousand pure doses are a gram. But 0.05 mg is almost invisible, so LSD is distributed to retail customers in a carrier. Pure LSD is dissolved in a solvent such as alcohol and sprayed on paper or gelatin; alternatively the paper may be dipped in the solution. After the solvent evaporates, the paper or gel is cut into one-dose squares and sold by the square. Users swallow the squares or may drop them into a beverage, releasing the drug. Although the gelatin and paper are light, they weigh much more than the drug. Marshall's 11,751 doses weighed 113.32 grams; the LSD accounted for only 670.72 mg of this, not enough to activate the five-year mandatory minimum sentence, let alone the ten-year minimum. The ten sheets of blotter paper carrying the 1,000 doses Chapman and confederates sold weighed 5.7 grams; the LSD in the paper did not approach the one-gram threshold for a mandatory minimum sentence. This disparity between the weight of the pure LSD and the weight of LSD-plus-carrier underlies the defendants' arguments.

If the carrier counts in the weight of the "mixture or substance containing a detectable amount" of LSD, some odd things may happen. Weight in the hands of distributors may exceed that of manufacturers and wholesalers. Big fish then could receive paltry sentences or small fish draconian ones. Someone who sold 19, 999 doses of pure LSD (at 0.05 mg per dose) would escape the five-year mandatory minimum of § 841(b)(1)(B)(v) and be covered by § 841(b)(1)(C), which lacks a minimum term and has a maximum of "only" 20 years. Someone who sold a single hit of LSD dissolved in a tumbler of orange juice could be exposed to a ten-year mandatory minimum. Retailers could fall in or out of the mandatory terms depending not on the number of doses but on the medium: sugar cubes weigh more than paper, which weighs more than gelatin. One way to eliminate the possibility of such consequences is to say that the carrier is not a "mixture or substance containing a detectable amount" of the drug. Defendants ask us to do this.

Defendants' submission starts from the premise that the interaction of the statutory phrase "mixture or substance" with the distribution of LSD by the dose in a carrier creates a unique probability of surprise results. The premise may be unwarranted. The paper used to distribute LSD is light stuff, not the kind used to absorb ink. Chapman's 1,000 doses weighed about 0.16 ounces. More than 6,000 doses, even in blotter paper, weigh less than an ounce. Because the LSD in one dose weighs about 0.05 milligrams, the combination of LSD-plus-paper is about 110 times the weight of the LSD. The impregnated paper could be described as "0.9% LSD". * * *

This is by no means an unusual dilution rate for illegal drugs. Heroin sold on the street is 2% to 3% opiate and the rest filler. Sometimes the mixture is even more dilute, approaching the dilution rate for LSD in blotter paper. Heroin and crack cocaine, like LSD, are sold on the streets by the dose, although they are sold by weight higher in the distributional chain. * * *

It is not possible to construe the words of § 841 to make the penalty turn on the net weight of the drug rather than the gross weight of carrier and drug. The statute speaks of "mixture or substance containing a detectable amount" of a drug. "Detectable amount" is the opposite of "pure"; the point of the statute is that the "mixture" is not to be converted to an equivalent amount of pure drug.

The structure of the statute reinforces this conclusion. The 10–year minimum applies to any person who possesses, with intent to distribute, "100 grams or more of phencyclidine (PCP) or 1 kilogram or more of a mixture or substance containing a detectable amount of phencyclidine (PCP)", § 841(b)(1)(A)(iv). Congress distinguished the pure drug from a "mixture or substance containing a detectable amount of" it. All drugs other than PCP are governed exclusively by the "mixture or substance" language. Even brute force cannot turn that language into a reference to pure LSD. Congress used the same "mixture or substance" language to describe heroin, cocaine, amphetamines, and many other drugs that are sold after being cut—sometimes as much as LSD. There is no sound basis on which to treat the words "substance or mixture containing a detectable amount of", repeated verbatim for every drug mentioned in § 841 except PCP, as *different* things for LSD and cocaine although the language is identical, while treating the "mixture or substance" language as meaning the *same* as the reference to pure PCP in 21 U.S.C. § 841(b)(1)(A)(iv) and (B)(iv).

Although the "mixture or substance" language shows that the statute cannot be limited to pure LSD, it does not necessarily follow that blotter paper *is* a "mixture or substance containing" LSD. That phrase cannot include all "carriers". One gram of crystalline LSD in a heavy glass bottle is still only one gram of "statutory LSD". So is a gram of LSD being "carried" in a Boeing 747. How much mingling of the drug with something else is essential to form a "mixture or substance"? The legislative history is silent, but ordinary usage is indicative.

"Substance" may well refer to a chemical compound, or perhaps to a drug in a solvent. LSD does not react chemically with sugar, blotter paper, or gelatin, and none of these is a solvent. "Mixture" is more inclusive. Cocaine often is mixed with mannitol, quinine, or lactose. These white powders do not react, but it is common ground that a cocaine-mannitol mixture is a statutory "mixture".

LSD and blotter paper are not commingled in the same way as cocaine and lactose. What is the nature of their association? The possibility most favorable to defendants is that LSD sits on blotter paper as oil floats on water. Immiscible substances may fall outside the statutory definition of "mixture". The possibility does not assist defendants—not on this record, anyway. LSD is applied to paper in a solvent; after the solvent evaporates, a tiny quantity of LSD remains. Because the fibers absorb the alcohol, the LSD solidifies inside the paper rather than on it. You cannot pick a grain of LSD off the surface of the paper. Ordinary parlance calls the paper containing tiny crystals of LSD a mixture.

United States v. Rose, 881 F.2d 386 (7th Cir. 1989), like every other appellate decision that has addressed the question, concludes that the carrier medium for LSD, like the "cut" for heroin and cocaine, is a "mixture or substance containing a detectable amount" of the drug. Although a chemist might be able to offer evidence bearing on the question whether LSD and blotter paper "mix" any more fully than do oil and water, the record contains no such evidence. Without knowing more of the chemistry than this record reveals, we adhere to the unanimous conclusion of the other courts of appeals that blotter paper treated with LSD is a "mixture or substance containing a detectable quantity of" LSD.

Two reasons have been advanced to support a contrary conclusion: that statutes should be construed to avoid constitutional problems, and that some members of the sitting Congress are dissatisfied with basing penalties on the combined weight of LSD and carrier. Neither is persuasive.

A preference for giving statutes a constitutional meaning is a reason to construe, not to rewrite or "improve". * * * "[S]ubstance or mixture containing a detectable quantity" is not ambiguous. * * * Neither the rule of lenity nor the preference for avoiding constitutional adjudication justifies disregarding unambiguous language.

The canon about avoiding constitutional decisions, in particular, must be used with care, for it is a closer cousin to invalidation than to interpretation. It is a way to enforce the constitutional penumbra, and therefore an aspect of constitutional law proper. Constitutional decisions breed penumbras, which multiply questions. Treating each as justification to construe laws out of existence too greatly enlarges the judicial power. And heroic "construction" is unnecessary, given our conclusion [in discussion omitted here] that Congress possesses the constitutional power to set penalties on the basis of gross weight.

As for the pending legislation: subsequent debates are not a ground for avoiding the import of enactments. Although the views of a subsequent Congress are entitled to respect, ongoing debates do not represent the views of Congress. * * *

CUMMINGS, CIRCUIT JUDGE, with whom BAUER, CHIEF JUDGE, and WOOD, JR., CUDAHY, and POSNER, CIRCUIT JUDGES, join, dissenting.

[T]he United States District Court for the District of Columbia held that blotter paper was not a mixture or substance within the meaning of the statute. *United States v. Healy*, 729 F.Supp. 140 (D.D.C. 1990). The court relied not only on ordinary dictionary definitions of the words mixture and substance but also on a November 30, 1988, Sentencing Commission publication, entitled "Questions Most Frequently Asked About the Sentencing Guidelines," which states that the Commission has not taken a position on whether the blotter paper should be weighed. The conclusion that the Commission has not yet resolved this question is further supported by a Sentencing Commission Notice issued on March 3, 1989, which requested public comments on whether the Commission should exclude the weight of the carrier for sentencing purposes in LSD cases.[3]

The *Healy* court also stated that Congress could have intended the words "mixture or substance" to refer to the liquid in which the pure LSD is dissolved. Finally, the *Healy* court relied on a Guidelines table designed to provide a sentencing court with an equivalent weight for sentencing purposes in cases in which the number of doses distributed is known but the actual weight is unknown. The table provides that a dose of LSD weighs .05 milligrams. Guidelines § 2D1.1, Commentary, Drug Equivalency Tables. This weight closely approximates the weight of one dose of LSD without blotter paper, but is not an accurate reflection of one dose with blotter paper. * * *

Two subsequent pieces of legislative history * * * shed some light on this question. In a letter to Senator Joseph R. Biden, Jr., dated April 26, 1989, the Chairman of the Sentencing Commission, William W. Wilkens, Jr., noted the ambiguity in the statute as it is currently written:

> With respect to LSD, it is unclear whether Congress intended the carrier to be considered as a packaging material, or, since it is commonly consumed along with the illicit drug, as a dilutant ingredient in the drug mixture.... The Commission suggests that Congress may wish to further consider the LSD carrier issue in order to clarify legislative intent as to whether the weight of the carrier should or should not be considered in determining the quantity of LSD mixture for punishment purposes.

Presumably acting in response to this query, Senator Biden added to the Congressional Record for October 5, 1989, an analysis of one of a series of technical corrections to 21 U.S.C. § 841 that were under consideration by the Senate that day. This analysis states that the purpose of the particular correction at issue was to remove an unintended "inequity" from Section 841 caused by the decisions of some courts to include the weight of the blotter paper for sentencing purposes in LSD cases. According to Senator Biden, the correction "remedie[d] this inequity by removing the weight of the carrier from the calculation of the weight of the mixture or substance." This correction was adopted as part of Amendment No. 976 to S. 1711. 135 Cong.Rec. S12749 (daily ed. Oct. 5, 1989). The amended bill was passed by a unanimous vote of the Senate (*id.* at S12765) and is currently pending before the House.

Comments in more recent issues of the Congressional Record indicate that S. 1711 is not expected to pass the House of Representatives. See 136

---

3. The Commission has recently adopted several amendments and sent them to Congress for approval. Among these is an amendment to Application Note 11 to Guidelines Section 2D1.1. This amendment specifically states that the typical weight per dose of LSD that is given in the Weight Per Dose Table as .05 milligrams is the weight of the LSD alone and not of the LSD combined with any carrier. 55 Fed.Reg. 19197 (May 8, 1990). * * *

Cong.Rec. S943 (daily ed. Feb. 7, 1990). In the meantime, however, a second attempt to clarify Congress' intent in amending 21 U.S.C. § 841 to include the words mixture or substance has now been introduced in the Senate. On April 18, 1990, Senator Kennedy introduced an amendment to S. 1970 (a bill establishing constitutional procedures for the imposition of the death penalty) seeking to clarify the language of 21 U.S.C. § 841. That amendment, Amendment No. 1716, states:

> Section 841(b)(1) of title 21, United States Code, is amended by inserting the following new subsection at the end thereof: "(E) In determining the weight of a 'mixture or substance' under this section, the court shall not include the weight of the carrier upon which the controlled substance is placed, or by which it is transported."

136 Cong.Rec. S7069 (daily ed. May 24, 1990).

[Judge Cummings argued from this evidence that the draconian penalty scheme for LSD was simply a mistake never intended by Congress and that the Seventh Circuit should follow *Healy*.]

POSNER, CIRCUIT JUDGE, joined by BAUER, CHIEF JUDGE, and CUMMINGS, WOOD, JR., and CUDAHY, CIRCUIT JUDGES, dissenting.

* * * Based as it is on weight, [the § 841 sentencing scheme] works well for drugs that are sold by weight; and ordinarily the weight quoted to the buyer is the weight of the dilute form, although of course price will vary with purity. The dilute form is the product, and it is as natural to punish its purveyors according to the weight of the product as it is to punish moonshiners by the weight or volume of the moonshine they sell rather than by the weight of the alcohol contained in it. So, for example, under Florida law it is a felony to possess one or more gallons of moonshine, and a misdemeanor to possess less than one gallon, regardless of the alcoholic content. Fla.Stat. §§ 561.01, 562.451.

LSD, however, is sold to the consumer by the dose; it is not cut, diluted, or mixed with something else. Moreover, it is incredibly light. An average dose of LSD weighs .05 milligrams, which is less than two millionths of an ounce. To ingest something that small requires swallowing something much larger. Pure LSD in granular form is first diluted by being dissolved, usually in alcohol, and then a quantity of the solution containing one dose of LSD is sprayed or eyedropped on a sugar cube, or on a cube of gelatin, or, as in the cases before us, on an inch-square section of "blotter" paper. * * * After the solution is applied to the carrier medium, the alcohol or other solvent evaporates, leaving an invisible (and undiluted) spot of pure LSD on the cube or blotter paper. The consumer drops the cube or the piece of paper into a glass of water, or orange juice, or some other beverage, causing the LSD to dissolve in the beverage, which is then drunk. * * * [A] quart of orange juice containing one dose of LSD is not more, in any relevant sense, than a pint of juice containing the same one dose, and it would be loony to punish the purveyor of the quart more heavily than the purveyor of the pint. It would be like basing the punishment for selling cocaine on the combined weight of the cocaine and of the vehicle (plane, boat, automobile, or whatever) used to transport it or the syringe used to inject it or the pipe used to smoke it. The blotter paper, sugar cubes, etc. are the vehicles for conveying LSD to the consumer.

The weight of the carrier is vastly greater than that of the LSD, as well as irrelevant to its potency. There is no comparable disparity between the pure and the mixed form (if that is how we should regard LSD on blotter paper or other carrier medium) with respect to the other drugs in section 841, with the illuminating exception of PCP. There Congress specified alternative weights, for the drug itself and for the substance or mixture containing the drug. For example, the five-year minimum sentence for a seller of PCP requires the sale of either ten grams of the drug itself or one hundred grams of a substance or mixture containing the drug. 21 U.S.C. § 841(b)(1)(B)(iv).

Ten sheets of blotter paper, containing a thousand doses of LSD, weigh almost six grams. The LSD itself weighs less than a hundredth as much. If the thousand doses are on gelatin cubes instead of sheets of blotter paper, the total weight is less, but it is still more than two grams, which is forty times the weight of the LSD. In both cases, if the carrier plus the LSD constitutes the relevant "substance or mixture" (the crucial "if" in this case), the dealer is subject to the minimum mandatory sentence of five years. One of the defendants before us (Marshall) sold almost 12,000 doses of LSD on blotter paper. This subjected him to the ten-year minimum, and the Guidelines then took over and pushed him up to twenty years. Since it takes 20,000 doses of LSD to equal a gram, Marshall would not have been subject to even the five-year mandatory minimum had he sold the LSD in its pure form. And a dealer who sold fifteen times the number of doses as Marshall—180,000—would not be subject to the ten-year mandatory minimum sentence if he sold the drug in its pure form, because 180,000 doses is only nine grams.

At the other extreme, if Marshall were not a dealer at all but dropped a square of blotter paper containing a single dose of LSD into a glass of orange juice and sold it to a friend at cost (perhaps 35 cents), he would be subject to the ten-year minimum. The juice with LSD dissolved in it would be the statutory mixture or substance containing a detectable amount of the illegal drug and it would weigh more than ten grams (one ounce is about 35 grams, and the orange juice in a glass of orange juice weighs several ounces). So a person who sold one dose of LSD might be subject to the ten-year mandatory minimum sentence while a dealer who sold 199,999 doses in pure form would be subject only to the five-year minimum. Defendant Dean sold 198 doses, crowded onto one sheet of blotter paper: this subjected him to the five-year mandatory minimum, too, since the ensemble weighed slightly more than a gram. * * *

All this seems crazy but we must consider whether Congress might have had a reason for wanting to key the severity of punishment for selling LSD to the weight of the carrier rather than to the number of doses or to some reasonable proxy for dosage (as weight is, for many drugs). The only one suggested is that it might be costly to determine the weight of the LSD in the blotter paper, sugar cube, etc., because it is so light! That merely underscores the irrationality of basing the punishment for selling this drug on weight rather than on dosage. But in fact the weight is reported in every case I have seen, so apparently it can be determined readily enough; it *has* to be determined in any event, to permit a purity adjustment under the Guidelines. If the weight of the LSD is difficult to determine, the difficulty is easily overcome by basing punishment on the number of doses, which makes much more sense in any event. To base punishment on the weight of the carrier medium makes about as much sense as basing punishment on the weight of the defendant. * * *

This is a quilt the pattern whereof no one has been able to discern. The legislative history is silent, and since even the Justice Department cannot explain the why of the punishment scheme that it is defending, the most plausible inference is that Congress simply did not realize how LSD is sold. The inference is reinforced by the statutory treatment of PCP. * * *

[The] irrationality is magnified when we compare the sentences for people who sell other drugs prohibited by 21 U.S.C. § 841. Marshall, remember, sold fewer than 12,000 doses and was sentenced to twenty years. Twelve thousand doses sounds like a lot, but to receive a comparable sentence for selling heroin Marshall would have had to sell ten kilograms, which would yield between one and two million doses. To receive a comparable sentence for selling cocaine he would have had to sell fifty kilograms, which would yield anywhere from 325,000 to five million doses. While the corresponding weight is lower for crack—half a kilogram—this still translates into 50,000 doses. * * *

Well, what if anything can we judges do about this mess? The answer lies in the shadow of a jurisprudential disagreement that is not less important by virtue of being unavowed by most judges. It is the disagreement between the severely positivistic view that the content of law is exhausted in clear, explicit, and definite enactments by or under express delegation from legislatures, and the natural lawyer's or legal pragmatist's view that the practice of interpretation and the general terms of the Constitution (such as "equal protection of the laws") authorize judges to enrich positive law with the moral values and practical concerns of civilized society. Judges who in other respects have seemed quite similar, such as Holmes and Cardozo, have taken opposite sides of this issue. Neither approach is entirely satisfactory. The first buys political neutrality and a type of objectivity at the price of substantive injustice, while the second buys justice in the individual case at the price of considerable uncertainty and, not infrequently, judicial willfulness. It is no wonder that our legal system oscillates between the approaches. The positivist view, applied unflinchingly to this case, commands the affirmance of prison sentences that are exceptionally harsh by the standards of the modern

Western world, dictated by an accidental, unintended scheme of punishment nevertheless implied by the words (taken one by one) of the relevant enactments. The natural law or pragmatist view leads to a freer interpretation, one influenced by norms of equal treatment; and let us explore the interpretive possibilities here. One is to interpret "mixture or substance containing a detectable amount of [LSD]" to exclude the carrier medium—the blotter paper, sugar or gelatin cubes, and orange juice or other beverage. That is the course we rejected in *United States v. Rose, supra*, as have the other circuits. I wrote *Rose*, but I am no longer confident that its literal interpretation of the statute, under which the blotter paper, cubes, etc. are "substances" that "contain" LSD, is inevitable. The blotter paper, etc. are better viewed, I now think, as carriers, like the package in which a kilo of cocaine comes wrapped or the bottle in which a fifth of liquor is sold.

Interpreted to exclude the carrier, the punishment schedule for LSD would make perfectly good sense; it would not warp the statutory design. The comparison with heroin and cocaine is again illuminating. The statute imposes the five-year mandatory minimum sentence on anyone who sells a substance or mixture containing a hundred grams of heroin, equal to 10,000 to 20,000 doses. One gram of pure LSD, which also would trigger the five-year minimum, yields 20,000 doses. The comparable figures for cocaine are 3250 to 50,000 doses, placing LSD in about the middle. So Congress may have wanted to base punishment for the sale of LSD on the weight of the pure drug after all, using one and ten grams of the pure drug to trigger the five-year and ten-year minima (and corresponding maxima—twenty years and forty years). This interpretation leaves "substance or mixture containing" without a referent, so far as LSD is concerned. But we must remember that Congress used the identical term in each subsection that specifies the quantity of a drug that subjects the seller to the designated minimum and maximum punishments. In thus automatically including the same term in each subsection, Congress did not necessarily affirm that, for each and every drug covered by the statute, a substance or mixture containing the drug *must* be found.

The flexible interpretation that I am proposing is decisively strengthened by the constitutional objection to basing punishment of LSD offenders on the weight of the carrier medium rather than on the weight of the LSD. Courts often do interpretive handsprings to avoid having even to *decide* a constitutional question. In doing so they expand, very questionably in my view, the effective scope of the Constitution, creating a constitutional penumbra in which statutes wither, shrink, are deformed. A better case for flexible interpretation is presented when the alternative is to nullify Congress's action: when in other words there is not merely a constitutional question about, but a constitutional barrier to, the statute when interpreted literally. This is such a case.

[Judge Posner then argued that the sentencing scheme for LSD upheld by the majority violates the equal protection guarantee of the Fifth Amendment's due process clause, because of the "unequal treatment of

people equally situated." That even the Justice Department cannot formulate a rational basis for the distinctions it has drawn from § 841 in LSD
cases is persuasive evidence that Congress has to be sent back to the
drawing board.]

The literal interpretation adopted by the majority is not inevitable.
All interpretation is contextual. The words of the statute—interpreted
against a background that includes a constitutional norm of equal treatment, a (closely related) constitutional commitment to rationality, an
evident failure by both Congress and the Sentencing Commission to
consider how LSD is actually produced, distributed, and sold, and an
equally evident failure by the same two bodies to consider the interaction
between heavy mandatory minimum sentences and the Sentencing Guidelines—will bear an interpretation that distinguishes between the carrier
vehicle of the illegal drug and the substance or mixture containing a
detectable amount of the drug. The punishment of the crack dealer is not
determined by the weight of the glass tube in which he sells the crack; we
should not lightly attribute to Congress a purpose of punishing the dealer
in LSD according to the weight of the LSD carrier. We should not make
Congress's handiwork an embarrassment to the members of Congress and
to us.

NOTES ON THE *LSD* CASE AND *EX ANTE* THINKING

1. *Review: The New Textualism and Linguistic Meaning.* Judge Easterbrook's opinion in the LSD case is an excellent example of the distinctive
features of the new textualism: (a) focus on the text of the statute, including
not just the plain meaning of the provision at issue, but also how that
provision fits into the "whole statute"; (b) a rejection of, and some contempt
for, legislative history as a context for interpreting the statute; and (c) a
relatively black-and-white vision of what words mean. Note that judges on the
Seventh Circuit were in sharp disagreement about whether LSD on blotter
paper is a "mixture." Should the very fact of good-faith disagreement about
the law's plain meaning be evidence that the statute has no plain meaning (as
Professor Stephen Ross has long suggested)?

In affirming *Marshall*, the Justices of the Supreme Court were also
divided as to what "mixture" meant in the LSD sentencing law. See *Chapman
v. United States*, 500 U.S. 453 (1991). While Judge Easterbrook relied on
"ordinary usage" to define "mixture," Chief Justice Rehnquist's opinion for
the Supreme Court relied on a dictionary definition of mixture as "two
substances blended together so that the particles of one are diffused among
the particles of the other." Because the LSD "is diffused among the fibers of
the paper," the Chief Justice found a statutory plain meaning. This might be
called a denotative approach to plain meaning: apply the dictionary definition
and see if it fits.

Professional linguists don't necessarily approach meaning in this way.
They are willing to expand and contract meaning beyond its dictionary
denotations. Words reflect categories which are fuzzy at the margins; the
necessary and sufficient conditions for membership in the category are not

completely accessible to us before the fact. Law professor Lawrence M. Solan, who is also a Ph.D. linguist, in *When Judges Use the Dictionary*, 68 Am. Speech 50, 54–55 (1993), analyzes the *Marshall* case in this way:

> Calling the blotter paper impregnated with LSD a mixture seems odd for the same reason that it seems odd to call a pancake soaked with syrup *a pancake-syrup mixture*; or to call a wet towel *a water-cotton mixture*; or to call a towel that one has used to dry one's face during a tennis game *a cotton-sweat mixture*, or later, after the sweat has dried, *a cotton-salt mixture*. The last two I would call *a wet towel* and *a dirty towel*, respectively. In all of these examples, both substances have kept their character in a chemical sense, but one of the substances seems to have kept too much of its character for us to feel natural using the term *mixture*. * * *

> As an analytical matter, the Supreme Court in *Chapman* has erred by taking a concept that is fuzzy at the margins and substituting for it a definition that is subject to more refined application than the concept itself. * * *

If the new textualists cannot satisfy professional linguists with their insistence that a statute has a "plain meaning," what legitimacy does their approach offer? Recall that people's personal liberty (the terms of their incarceration) depended upon this semantic debate. On the other hand, is there some necessary reason why judicial and linguistic interpreters must agree on methodology?

2. *Liberty versus* Ex Ante *Thinking?* Judge Easterbrook's first major article on interpretation urged that statutes not be construed beyond the "domain" clearly demarcated by their texts. He defended this approach on the basis of a libertarian presumption akin to the standard Chicago School idea that most things should not be regulated by the state and should be left to the free operation of the market:

> Those who wrote and approved the Constitution thought that most social relations would be governed by private agreements, customs, and understandings, not resolved in the halls of government. There is still at least a presumption that people's arrangements prevail unless expressly displaced by legal doctrine. All things are permitted unless there is some contrary rule. It is easier for an agency to justify the revocation of rules (or simple nonregulation) than the creation of new rules.

Easterbrook, *Statutes' Domains*, 50 U. Chi. L. Rev. 533, 549–50 (1983). Note that the libertarian position in *Marshall* is the one taken by Judges Cummings and Posner, not that of Judge Easterbrook, who sends the defendants into confinement for a long period of time. (The same is true for a new textualist approach to *Holy Trinity*; as it involves an issue of criminal liability.)

Consider an *ex ante* counterargument: a textualism that yields harsh results, as in the LSD case, sends a signal to judges that they should be careful not to make policy—and to Congress that its statutes will be interpreted "as written," and that any updating or fixing will have to be done by the legislators themselves. If they adopt the "tough love" of the new textualism, as Judge Keen argued in Speluncean Explorers, courts will actually enhance democracy and legislative accountability. Everyone will know that Congress, alone, is responsible for statutory applications, and voters can act accordingly. (Justice Scalia suggests such an argument in his Tanner Lectures, *supra*, and in some judicial opinions.) A problem is that there is no evidence that such tough love will have any effect on Congress, and knowledgeable commentators are skeptical. Professor Brudney argues from the nature and structure of the politics of legislation that Congress cannot enact statutes with the degree of specification Justice Scalia would require. See James J. Brudney, *Congressional Commentary on Judicial Interpretations of Statutes: Idle Chatter or Telling Response?*, 93 Mich. L. Rev. 1 (1994). An implication of Brudney's idea is that the new textualism will sometimes have a likely libertarian effect (by reducing Congress' practical capacity to regulate), bringing us back to Judge Easterbrook's point in *Statute's Domain*. The problem is that legislative paralysis will also sometimes have an anti-libertarian effect—as in the LSD Case, when Congress could not correct what was apparently a drafting error, and Messrs. Marshall, Chapman et al. paid the price with more years in federal prison.

3. Ex Ante *Arguments for an Approach that Considers Fairness.* Judge Posner is not a bleeding-heart liberal—the classic *ex post* position—yet he voted to overturn the conviction. And he did so for reasons that go well beyond the original legislative intent approach he championed in the 1985 edition of *The Federal Courts.* Since 1990, Judge Posner has come completely out of the closet as a flexible pragmatic interpreter of statutes.[p]

There are some economic arguments for a more flexible approach than the one followed by the en banc majority. One is that a relentless textualism will undermine rather than cultivate the conditions for legislation: because deals will not be reasonably enforced, legislators will be more reluctant to make them; legislators might even lose confidence that the judiciary can be trusted to carry out statutes in a fair way. Another *ex ante* argument is that an unreasonable construction of the LSD law also undermines the overall legitimacy of our system of criminal justice (the small fries like Mr. Marshall are being treated really unfairly; many of those arrested are people of color), without any discernible offsetting benefit to criminal justice (such as increased deterrence). Congress has not shown enormous wisdom in this area, and if any institution is going to act responsibly it must be the judiciary.

PROBLEM 2–4

A New LSD Issue

In 1993, the Sentencing Commission revised the method for calculating the weight of LSD for Sentencing Guideline purposes. Abandoning its former approach of weighing the entire blotter paper containing LSD, the amended Guideline told courts to give each dose of LSD on a carrier medium a presumed weight of 0.4 mg. U.S. Sentencing Comm'n, U.S. Sentencing Guidelines Manual § 2D1.1(c), n. (H). The new method was retroactive.

---

p. Richard A. Posner, *The Problems of Jurisprudence* (1990); *Overcoming Law* (1995); and *How Judges Think* (2008). See also John F. Manning, *Statutory Pragmatism and Constitutional Structure*, 120 Harv. L. Rev. 1161 (2007) (evaluating Posner's approach from a textualist perspective).

Meirl Neal was sentenced to 192 months in prison for selling 11,456 doses of LSD on blotter paper. He moved to have his sentence reduced to between 70 and 87 months, the Guideline period for sale of 4.58 grams of LSD (11,456 times 0.4 mg). The Government argued that Neal should serve at least 120 months, because of the mandatory minimum sentence required by 21 U.S.C. § 841(b)(1)(A)(v), as interpreted in *Marshall/Chapman*. Neal argued that the blotter paper should now not be counted for purposes of the mandatory minimum, just as it is now not counted for purposes of setting the ordinary sentence. Should the courts have accepted Neal's argument and reduced his sentence? See *Neal v. United States*, 516 U.S. 284 (1996).

2. Advancing Public–Regarding Goals and Minimizing Rent–Seeking

Public choice theory is the application of economic principles to actions by the state. One conclusion reached by some public choice theorists, developed in Chapter 1, § 2, is that an interest-group-driven legislative process produces too few public-regarding statutes (i.e., those broadly distributing benefits as well as costs) and too many rent-seeking statutes (i.e., those distributing benefits to a small group, at the expense of the general public, and without an efficiency justification).

Frank Easterbrook, *The Supreme Court, 1983 Term—Foreword: The Court and the Economic System*, 98 Harv. L. Rev. 4, 14–15 (1984), suggested a general interpretive strategy for the judiciary to respond to this asymmetry:

> * * * There are two basic styles of statutory construction. In one the judge starts with the statute, attributes to it certain purposes (evils to be redressed), and then brings within the statute the class of activities that produce the same or similar objectionable results. The statute's reach goes on expanding so long as there are unredressed objectionable results. The judge interprets omissions and vague terms in the statute as evidence of want of time or foresight and fills in these gaps with more in the same vein. The maxim "Remedial statutes are to be liberally construed" sums up this approach.

> In the other approach the judge treats the statute as a contract. He first identifies the contracting parties and then seeks to discover what they resolved and what they left unresolved. For example, he may conclude that a statute regulating the price of fluid milk is a pact between milk producers and milk handlers designed to cut back output and raise price, to the benefit of both at the expense of consumers. A judge then implements the bargain as a faithful agent but without enthusiasm; asked to extend the scope of a back-room deal, he refuses unless the proof of the deal's scope is compelling. Omissions are evidence that no bargain was struck: some issues were left for the future, or perhaps one party was unwilling to pay the price of a resolution in its favor. Sometimes the compromise may be to toss an issue to the courts for resolution, but this too is a term of the bargain, to be demonstrated rather than presumed. What the parties

did not resolve, the court should not resolve either. The maxim "Statutes in derogation of the common law are to be strictly construed" sums up this approach.

These maxims are useless as guides to construction; every remedial statute is in derogation of the common law. Yet this hopeless conflict of maxims does not justify despair. The appropriate treatment of statutes depends on how they come to be and what they are for. A judge cannot set about rearranging economic relations on the basis of an ambiguous statute without first resolving a question about the nature of legislation. If statutes generally are designed to overcome "failures" in markets and to replace the calamities produced by unguided private conduct with the ordered rationality of the public sector, then it makes sense to use the remedial approach to the construction of statutes—or at least most of them. If, on the other hand, statutes often are designed to replace the outcomes of private transactions with monopolistic ones, to transfer the profits ("rents") of productive activity to a privileged few, then judges should take the beady-eyed contractual approach. The warehouseman does not deliver the grain without seeing the receipt, and so too with goodies dispensed by judges.

See also Jonathan R. Macey, *Promoting Public–Regarding Legislation Through Statutory Interpretation: An Interest Group Model*, 86 Colum. L. Rev. 223 (1986), who argues that public-interest statutes ought to be liberally interpreted by reference to their announced purposes. By raising the costs of rent-seeking, judges can contribute to the public welfare.

The Table below suggests the risks entailed in various kinds of statutes, together with counter-strategies courts could follow in applying those statutes. Consider the application of this kind of thinking to cases like *Weber*, the affirmative action case in Chapter 1, § 3, and to the cases in this chapter. For example, into which quadrant would the alien contract labor law of *Holy Trinity* fit? If quadrant one, the Court's stingy construction becomes less defensible—but there is good reason to think the law was purely rent-seeking: unions were seeking to restrict the supply of labor so as to bid up wages in certain occupations. Congress has the power to enact such laws, but the Court ought not apply them beyond the original statutory target.

Table of Interpretive Strategies for Different Kinds of Laws

[1] Distributed Benefit/Distributed Cost Laws (General Interest)	**[2] Distributed Benefit/Concentrated Cost Laws**
Danger: These laws are usually in the public interest, but the legislature will often fail to update them as society and the underlying problem change.	*Danger*: Regulated groups will tend to evade their statutory duties and press to "capture" the agency created to administer the law.
Response: Courts can expand the law to new situations and develop it in common law fashion, subject to the limits imposed by the statutory text.	*Response*: Courts can monitor agency enforcement and private compliance, and open up procedures to assure excluded groups are heard. Courts can press the agency to be faithful to the stated public-regarding goal of the law.
[3] Concentrated Benefit/Distributed Cost Laws (Rent–Seeking)	**[4] Concentrated Benefit/Concentrated Cost Laws**
Danger: Rent-seeking by special interest groups at the expense of the general public.	*Danger*: The statutory deal may grow unexpectedly lopsided over time.
Response: Courts ought to construe the law narrowly to minimize the unwarranted benefits. Hold the statute to its public-regarding justifications.	*Response*: Do not attempt much judicial updating, unless affected groups are not able to get the legislature's attention.

Source: William N. Eskridge Jr., *Politics Without Romance: Implications of Public Choice Theory for Statutory Interpretation*, 74 Va. L. Rev. 275, 325 (1988).

PEREZ v. WYETH LABORATORIES, INC.

New Jersey Supreme Court, 1999
161 N.J. 1, 734 A.2d 1245

O'HERN, J., writing for a majority of the Court.

[Norplant is an FDA-approved, reversible contraceptive that prevents pregnancy for up to five years. Wyeth began a massive advertising campaign for Norplant in 1991, which it directed at women rather than at their doctors. Wyeth advertised on television and in women's magazines. None of the advertisements warned of any dangers or side effects associated with Norplant, but rather praised its convenience and simplicity. In 1995, several women filed lawsuits in various New Jersey counties claiming injuries that resulted from their use of Norplant. Their principal claim was that Wyeth failed to warn adequately about the side effects associated with the contraceptive, including weight gain, headaches, dizziness, nausea, diarrhea, acne, vomiting, fatigue, facial hair growth, numbness in the arms and legs, irregular menstruation, hair loss, leg cramps, anxiety and nervousness, vision problems, anemia, mood swings and depression, high blood pressure, and removal complications that resulted in scarring.

[Perez sought a determination of whether the "learned intermediary" doctrine applied. This doctrine generally relieves a pharmaceutical manufacturer of an independent duty to warn the ultimate user of prescription drugs, so long as it has supplied the physician with information about a drug's dangerous propensities and risks. The assumption of the doctrine is that the doctor will play the key role in informing and counseling the patient about the risks. Holding the doctrine applicable by reason of the New Jersey Products Liability Act, N.J.S.A. 2A:58C–1 to–11, the trial court dismissed those plaintiffs' complaints, concluding that even when a manufacturer advertises directly to the public, and a woman is influenced by the advertising campaign, a physician nevertheless retains the duty to weigh the benefits and risks associated with a drug before deciding whether the drug is appropriate for the patient.]

Our medical-legal jurisprudence is based on images of health care that no longer exist. At an earlier time, medical advice was received in the doctor's office from a physician who most likely made house calls if needed. The patient usually paid a small sum of money to the doctor. Neighborhood pharmacists compounded prescribed medicines. Without being pejorative, it is safe to say that the prevailing attitude of law and medicine was that the "doctor knows best."

Pharmaceutical manufacturers never advertised their products to patients, but rather directed all sales efforts at physicians. In this comforting setting, the law created an exception to the traditional duty of manufacturers to warn consumers directly of risks associated with the product as long as they warned health-care providers of those risks.

For good or ill, that has all changed. Medical services are in large measure provided by managed care organizations. Medicines are purchased in the pharmacy department of supermarkets and often paid for by third-party providers. Drug manufacturers now directly advertise products to consumers on the radio, television, the Internet, billboards on public transportation, and in magazines.

[New Jersey has accepted the learned intermediary doctrine as a defense in tort suits against drug companies, e.g., *Niemiera v. Schneider*, 114 N.J. 550, 559, 555 A.2d 1112 (1989). In light of the recent trend of mass-marketing drugs directly to consumers, see Jon D. Hanson & Douglas A. Kysar, *Taking Behavioralism Seriously: Some Evidence of Market Manipulation*, 112 Harv. L. Rev. 1420, 1456 (1999), the court was faced with the question whether the learned intermediary doctrine should still apply to such drugs, like Norplant.]

[T]he New Jersey Products Liability Act provides:

An adequate product warning or instruction is one that a reasonably prudent person in the same or similar circumstances would have provided with respect to the danger and that communicates adequate information on the dangers and safe use of the product, taking into account the characteristics of, and the ordinary knowledge common to, the persons by whom the product is intended to be used, or in the case of prescription drugs, taking into account the characteristics of, and the ordinary knowledge common to, the prescribing physician. If the warning or instruction given in connection with a drug or device or food or food additive has been approved or prescribed by the federal Food and Drug Administration under the "Federal Food, Drug, and Cosmetic Act," 52 Stat. 1040, 21 U.S.C. § 301 et seq., . . . a rebuttable presumption shall arise that the warning or instruction is adequate. . . .

N.J.S.A. 2A:58C–4.

The Senate Judiciary Committee Statement that accompanied L. 1987, c. 197 recites: "The subsection contains a general definition of an adequate warning and a special definition for warnings that accompany prescription drugs, since, in the case of prescription drugs, the warning is owed to the physician." See N.J.S.A. 2A:58C–1 (providing the Committee Statement). At oral argument, counsel for Wyeth was candid to acknowledge that he could not "point to a sentence in the statute" that would make the learned intermediary doctrine applicable to the manufacturers' direct marketing of drugs, but rather relied on the Committee Statement. Although the statute provides a physician-based standard for determining the adequacy of the warning due to a physician, the statute does not legislate the boundaries of the doctrine. For example, the Act does not purport to repeal a holding such as *Davis v. Wyeth Labs*, [399 F.2d 121 (9th Cir. 1968)], which required that manufacturers directly warn patients in mass inoculation cases. Rather, the statute governs the content of an "adequate product warning," when required. As noted [above], in 1987, direct-to-consumer marketing of prescription drugs was in its beginning stages. The Committee Statement observes that "the warning is owed to the physician" because drugs were then marketed to the physician. We believe that the part of the provision establishing "a presumption that a warning or instruction is adequate on drug or food products if the warning has been approved or prescribed by the Food and Drug Administration," Committee Statement, *supra*, will provide the benchmark for this decision.

[The court ruled that the rationales for the learned intermediary doctrine—deference to physicians and the integrity of the doctor-patient relationship—did not apply when the drug company marketed directly to patients. Hence, the doctrine was not legally available as a defense in this case.]

POLLOCK, J., dissenting.

* * * The majority opinion sustains itself only by ignoring the plain language of an unambiguous statute, the New Jersey Products Liability Act, N.J.S.A. 2A:58C–1 to–7 (NJPLA), and by substituting its own policy preference for that of the Legislature. * * * I respectfully dissent. * * *

The majority finds ambiguity in the NJPLA, stating that "although the statute provides a physician-based standard for determining the adequacy of the warning due to a physician, the statute does not legislate the boundaries of the doctrine." According to the Senate Committee statement accompanying the NJPLA, however, a drug manufacturer's duty to warn is owed to the physician, not the consumer:

> A manufacturer or seller is not liable in a warning-defect case if an adequate warning is given when the product has left the control of the manufacturer or seller.... The subsection contains a general definition of an adequate warning and a special definition for warnings that accompany prescription drugs, since, in the case of prescription drugs, the warning is owed to the physician.

Senate Judiciary Committee, Statement to Senate Bill No. 2805 (L. 1987, c. 197), N.J.S.A. 2A:58C–1a.

The NJPLA provides that "committee statements that may be adopted or included in the legislative history of this act shall be consulted in the interpretation and construction of this act." N.J.S.A. 2A:58C–1a. Through that extraordinary mandate, the Legislature sought to preclude judicial circumvention of the plain meaning of the statute.

Today's decision demonstrates that the Legislature's efforts were unavailing. The majority has mischaracterized both the statute and the rationale for the learned intermediary doctrine. Contrary to the majority opinion, the statute directs that the warning is owed to the physician not "because drugs were then marketed to the physician," but because the physician is in the best position to make an individualized evaluation of the risks of drugs and warn the patient of those risks. The patient, moreover, cannot obtain the drugs without a prescription written by a physician.

Underlying the majority opinion is the assumption that the Legislature in 1987 could not have anticipated the mass-marketing of prescription drugs. That assumption, however, has no basis in the record. In fact, the drug companies and the Legislature, like the Federal Food and Drug Administration (FDA), were aware of such marketing. * * *

The majority's imposition of expanded duties on drug manufacturers contravenes the legislative history of the NJPLA. That history demonstrates that the statute was intended to strengthen the protections afforded manufacturers:

> It is important to recognize that this bill not only conforms New Jersey product liability law to the law of the majority of states but, in some instances, changes New Jersey law in favor of the manufacturer in a way that is not currently recognized by the law of the majority of states. Thus, the effect of the enactment of this bill would be to shift the status of the law of New Jersey on certain issues from its current position of being more favorable to the injured consumer than the majority of states to being more favorable to the manufacturer than the majority of states.

Passed Bill Memorandum to Governor Thomas H. Kean on S–2805, *supra*, at 3.

Judges, although they may disagree with a legislative policy, are bound to respect it. In adapting the common law to society's needs, this Court may not have favored manufacturers, including pharmaceutical companies, as enthusiastically as has the Legislature. The issue, however, is not whether the Court shares the Legislature's enthusiasm or even whether the majority would prefer to amend the common-law learned intermediary doctrine. Because of the enactment of the NJPLA, the issue is whether the majority should respect the learned intermediary doctrine as declared by the Legislature. * * *

NOTE ON THE NORPLANT CASE AND NARROW INTERPRETATIONS OF RENT-SEEKING STATUTES

Assume that the liability-waiver law is rent-seeking: How would the Table's analysis apply here? Presumably Judge Easterbrook would not apply his narrow interpretation rule, given the relative clarity of the statutory language. We are doubtful Judge Posner would go along either, as the legislative history supports the plain meaning. How about Professor Macey: Does his theory support the majority's result? Note that Justice Pollock, the author of the very dynamic opinion in *Trans Am*, dissented here. At what point should standard legal criteria trump an anti-rent-seeking rationale under economic theory?

A special case is presented by statutes regulating areas in which the common law has long been the baseline. Many law and economics scholars believe the common law is more efficient than other forms of law, because of the way it develops incrementally and relatively untainted by special interest pressure.[q] If this is true, relatively speaking, then courts might be particularly picky in applying exceptions to the common law that are pressed upon the legislative process by special interests—which is precisely the way the New Jersey Supreme Court seems to see the matter in *Perez*. The dissent sees the statute the same way but feels that it is too clearly written to support the narrowing construction. How do you arbitrate this kind of dispute? How clear does a rent-seeking statute have to be under the Easterbrook approach?

3. Institutional Cost–Benefit Analysis

Professor Neil K. Komesar argues, in *Imperfect Alternatives: Choosing Institutions in Law, Economics, and Public Policy* (1994), that allocation of public law decisionmaking duties should be the result of an institutional cost-benefit analysis, much like the Kaldor–Hicks concept of efficiency. (Under Kaldor–Hicks, a move is efficient if the overall benefits to society of such a move outweigh the overall costs.) Thus, he urges courts to reconsider their constitutional activism, in some areas at least, because it is not clear that the system-wide benefits of judge-made rules outweigh their costs. The benefits of judicial activism are limited by the structure of adjudication and the constrained resources of the court system. Costs of judicial activism include third-party expenses incurred in following new judicial rules, as well as the effects of judicial activism on other institutions, such as the legislature. Professor Komesar does not apply his

---

q. See, e.g., William Landes & Richard A. Posner, *Adjudication as a Private Good*, 8 J. Legal Stud. 235 (1979). But see George Priest, *The Common Law Process and the Selection of Efficient Rules*, 6 J. Legal Stud. 65 (1977).

institutional cost-benefit analysis to issues of statutory interpretation, but other scholars have done so.

A Komesarian skepticism about the institutional limits of courts has driven most statutory scholars to endorse the notion that it is agencies, rather than courts, that should do most of the work updating statutes to reflect new circumstances. E.g., William N. Eskridge Jr., *Dynamic Statutory Interpretation* ch. 5 (1994). Professional administrators have the expertise and at least some resources to follow changes in society and to adapt statutory policy so that new developments do not undermine the statutory goals. They are in a position to think about the statutory scheme holistically and to balance competing considerations in the context of the big regulatory picture. Agencies will tend to be much more responsive to current presidential and legislative policy preferences than to those of enacting Congresses. Edward L. Rubin, *Dynamic Statutory Interpretation in the Administrative State,* Issues in Legal Scholarship: Dynamic Statutory Interpretation (2002): Article 2, http://www.bepress.com/ils/iss3/art2, argues that agencies will interpret statutes even more dynamically than courts will, and that agency dynamism fuels ever more judicial dynamism in statutory interpretation. See also Edward L. Rubin, *Law and Legislation in the Administrative State,* 89 Colum. L. Rev. 369 (1989).

Going further than Rubin and Eskridge, Adrian Vermeule, *Judging Under Uncertainty: An Institutional Theory of Legal Interpretation* (2006), maintains that courts are completely incompetent to do anything but apply statutory plain meanings—and ought to defer to agencies in statutory interpretation unless the specific statutory language is clearly contrary to the agency's rule of law. The costs of such an approach, Vermeule argues, would be relatively small, because lawyers and officials would no longer "waste" their time reading legislative histories. The main benefit would be greater agency freedom to update statutes in light of new information.

Professor Jane S. Schacter, in *Accounting for Accountability in Dynamic Statutory Interpretation and Beyond*, Issues in Legal Scholarship: Dynamic Statutory Interpretation (2002): Article 5, http://www.bepress. com/ils/iss3/art5, poses a harder question for agency- or judge-driven dynamic statutory interpretation: Does it contribute to or undermine popular accountability?[r] As Professor Schacter puts it, dynamic statutory interpretation can cloud democratic accountability by allowing elected legislators to deny responsibility for policy choices they essentially refer to agencies and judges. Schacter concludes from the empirical literature that the accountability of Congress is beclouded with plenty of other problems:

---

[r] This is an important question that the Supreme Court has strongly pressed in its recent federalism decisions. State officials must make hard choices as to priorities—and they are accountable to the voters for unsatisfactory choices at election time. This political accountability is sacrificed whenever the federal government asserts authority over the state's political processes or hijacks part of the state budget for its own goals. For this reason, the Court has created new immunities preventing the federal government from burdening state officials with unwanted tasks, see *Printz v. United States*, 521 U.S. 898 (1997), or commandeering their legislatures for federal projects, see *New York v. United States*, 505 U.S. 144 (1992).

voters are not aware of the policies and laws adopted by their representatives; the interest groups that do follow the policies and laws carefully do not symmetrically reflect the wide array of interests in the voting population; and even the support of informed voters or groups rarely hinges on a specific policy proposal. Schacter concludes that the mechanisms of accountability, mainly elections, work best as mechanisms of representativeness. So long as voters understand the ideology and general character of the people they select to represent them, the system works fine—dynamic interpretation or not.

Evaluate the following case. Does an institutional cost-benefit analysis support the Court's approach? Does a textualist (Easterbrook), legislative intent (old Posner), or purposive (Eskridge, Macey, and newer Posner) approach support the majority? Or is the majority reading its own pro-business values into a public interest health-protective statute?

FDA v. BROWN & WILLIAMSON TOBACCO CORP.

Supreme Court of the United States, 2000.
529 U.S. 120, 120 S.Ct. 1291, 146 L.Ed.2d 121.

JUSTICE O'CONNOR delivered the opinion of the Court.

[The Food, Drug, and Cosmetic Act (FDCA), 21 U.S.C. § 301 et seq., grants the Food and Drug Administration (FDA) the authority to regulate, among other items, "drugs" and "devices," §§ 321(g)–(h), 393. In 1996, the FDA asserted jurisdiction to regulate tobacco products, concluding that, under the FDCA, nicotine is a "drug" and cigarettes and smokeless tobacco are "devices" that deliver nicotine to the body. Pursuant to this authority, the FDA promulgated regulations governing tobacco products' promotion, labeling, and accessibility to children and adolescents. The FDA found that tobacco use is the Nation's leading cause of premature death, resulting in more than 400,000 deaths annually, and that most adult smokers begin when they are minors. The regulations therefore aim to reduce tobacco use by minors so as to substantially reduce the prevalence of addiction in future generations, and thus the incidence of tobacco-related death and disease. Respondents, a group of tobacco manufacturers, retailers, and advertisers, filed this suit challenging the FDA's regulations. The Supreme Court held that Congress has not granted the FDA jurisdiction to regulate tobacco products.]

[II] In determining whether Congress has specifically addressed the question at issue, a reviewing court should not confine itself to examining a particular statutory provision in isolation. The meaning—or ambiguity—of certain words or phrases may only become evident when placed in context. See *Brown v. Gardner,* 513 U.S. 115, 118 (1994) ("Ambiguity is a creature not of definitional possibilities but of statutory context"). It is a "fundamental canon of statutory construction that the words of a statute must be read in their context and with a view to their place in the overall statutory scheme." *Davis v. Michigan Dept. of Treasury,* 489 U.S. 803, 809 (1989). A court must therefore interpret the statute "as a symmetrical and coherent regulatory scheme," *Gustafson v. Alloyd Co.*, 513 U.S. 561, 569 (1995), and "fit, if possible, all parts into an harmonious whole," *FTC v. Mandel Brothers, Inc.*, 359 U.S. 385, 389 (1959). Similarly, the meaning of one statute may be affected by other Acts, particularly where Congress has spoken subsequently and more specifically to the topic at hand. See *United States v. Estate of Romani*, 523 U.S. 517, 530–31 (1998); *United States v. Fausto*, 484 U.S. 439, 453 (1988). In addition, we must be guided to a degree by common sense as to the manner in which Congress is likely to delegate a policy decision of such economic and political magnitude to an administrative agency. * * *

[In Part IIA, Justice O'Connor concluded that the FDCA assumes that the FDA will refuse to approve unsafe drugs or devices and will remove them from the market as soon as it determines they are unsafe. E.g., 21 U.S.C. § 355(e)(1)–(3). Congress has enacted six statutes that require disclosure of information regarding tobacco products but do not ban their sale. E.g., 15 U.S.C. § 1331. Given the assumption of the FDCA, these statutes disallow the agency from finding that tobacco products fall within its health and safety regime. "A fundamental precept of the FDCA is that any product regulated by the FDA—but not banned—must be safe for its intended use. * * * Consequently, if tobacco products were within the FDA's jurisdiction, the Act would require the FDA to remove them from the market entirely. But a ban would contradict Congress' clear intent as expressed in its more recent, tobacco-specific legislation. The inescapable conclusion is that there is no room for tobacco products within the FDCA's regulatory scheme."]

[B] In determining whether Congress has spoken directly to the FDA's authority to regulate tobacco, we must also consider in greater detail the tobacco-specific legislation that Congress has enacted over the past 35 years. At the time a statute is enacted, it may have a range of plausible meanings. Over time, however, subsequent acts can shape or focus those meanings. The "classic judicial task of reconciling many laws enacted over time, and getting them to 'make sense' in combination, necessarily assumes that the implications of a statute may be altered by the implications of a later statute." *Fausto*. This is particularly so where the scope of the earlier statute is broad but the subsequent statutes more specifically address the topic at hand. As we recognized recently in *United States v. Estate of Romani*, "a specific policy embodied in a later federal statute should control our construction of the earlier statute, even though it has not been expressly amended."

Congress has enacted six separate pieces of legislation since 1965 addressing the problem of tobacco use and human health. Those statutes, among other things, require that health warnings appear on all packaging and in all print and outdoor advertisements, see 15 U.S.C. §§ 1331, 1333, 4402; prohibit the advertisement of tobacco products through "any medium of electronic communication" subject to regulation by the Federal Communications Commission (FCC), see §§ 1335, 4402(f); require the Secretary of Health and Human Services (HHS) to report every three years to Congress on research findings concerning "the addictive property of tobacco," 42 U.S.C. § 290aa–2(b)(2); and make States' receipt of certain federal block grants contingent on their making it unlawful "for any manufacturer, retailer, or distributor of tobacco products to sell or distribute any such product to any individual under the age of 18," § 300x–26(a)(1).

In adopting each statute, Congress has acted against the backdrop of the FDA's consistent and repeated statements that it lacked authority under the FDCA to regulate tobacco absent claims of therapeutic benefit by the manufacturer. In fact, on several occasions over this period, and after the health consequences of tobacco use and nicotine's pharmacological effects had become well known, Congress considered and rejected bills that would have granted the FDA such jurisdiction. Under these circumstances, it is evident that Congress' tobacco-specific statutes have effectively ratified the FDA's long-held position that it lacks jurisdiction under the FDCA to regulate tobacco products. Congress has created a distinct regulatory scheme to address the problem of tobacco and health, and that scheme, as presently constructed, precludes any role for the FDA.

[In 1964 congressional hearings responding to the Surgeon General's opinion that cigarette smoking is hazardous to one's health, FDA representatives testified that the agency did not have authority to regulate cigarettes or smoking under the FDCA. This was consistent with the position taken by the FDA's predecessor agency, the Bureau of Chemistry under the Pure Food & Drug Act of 1906.] And, as the FDA admits, there is no evidence in the text of the FDCA or its legislative history that Congress in 1938 even considered the applicability of the Act to tobacco products. Given the economic and political significance of the tobacco industry at the time, it is extremely unlikely that Congress could have intended to place tobacco within the ambit of the FDCA absent any discussion of the matter. * * *

Moreover, before enacting the FCLAA [Federal Cigarette Labeling and Advertising Act] in 1965, Congress considered and rejected several proposals to give the FDA the authority to regulate tobacco. In April 1963, Representative Udall introduced a bill "to amend the Federal Food, Drug, and Cosmetic Act so as to make that Act applicable to smoking products." H. R. 5973, 88th Cong., 1st Sess., 1. Two months later, Senator Moss introduced an identical bill in the Senate. S. 1682, 88th Cong., 1st Sess. (1963). In discussing his proposal on the Senate floor, Senator Moss explained that "this amendment simply places smoking products under FDA jurisdiction, along with foods, drugs, and cosmetics." 109 Cong. Rec. 10322 (1963). In December 1963, Representative Rhodes introduced another bill that would have amended the FDCA "by striking out 'food, drug, device, or cosmetic,' each place where it appears therein and inserting in lieu thereof 'food, drug, device, cosmetic, or smoking product.' " H. R. 9512, 88th Cong., 1st Sess., § 3 (1963). And in January 1965, five months before passage of the FCLAA, Representative Udall again introduced a bill to amend the FDCA "to make that Act applicable to smoking products." H. R. 2248, 89th Cong., 1st Sess., 1. None of these proposals became law.

Congress ultimately decided in 1965 to subject tobacco products to the less extensive regulatory scheme of the FCLAA, which created a "comprehensive Federal program to deal with cigarette labeling and advertising with respect to any relationship between smoking and health." Pub. L. 89–92, § 2, 79 Stat. 282. The FCLAA rejected any regulation of advertising, but it required the warning, "Caution: Cigarette Smoking May Be Hazardous to Your Health," to appear on all cigarette packages. *Id.*, § 4, 79 Stat. 283. In the Act's "Declaration of Policy," Congress stated that its objective was to balance the goals of ensuring that "the public may be adequately informed that cigarette smoking may be hazardous to health" and protecting "commerce and the national economy . . . to the maximum extent." *Id.*, § 2, 79 Stat. 282 (codified at 15 U.S.C. § 1331).

Not only did Congress reject the proposals to grant the FDA jurisdiction, but it explicitly preempted any other regulation of cigarette labeling: "No statement relating to smoking and health, other than the statement required by . . . this Act, shall be required on any cigarette package." *Id.*, § 5(a), 79 Stat. 283. The regulation of product labeling, however, is an integral aspect of the FDCA, both as it existed in 1965 and today. The labeling requirements currently imposed by the FDCA, which are essentially identical to those in force in 1965, require the FDA to regulate the labeling of drugs and devices to protect the safety of consumers. See 21 U.S.C. § 352; 21 U.S.C. § 352 (1964 ed. and Supp. IV). As discussed earlier, the Act requires that all products bear "adequate directions for use . . . as are necessary for the protection of users," 21 U.S.C. § 352(f)(1); 21 U.S.C. § 352(f)(1) (1964 ed.); requires that all products provide "adequate warnings against use in those pathological conditions or by children where its use may be dangerous to health," 21 U.S.C. § 352(f)(2); 21 U.S.C. § 352(f)(2) (1964 ed.); and deems a product misbranded "if it is dangerous to health when used in the dosage or manner, or with the frequency or duration prescribed, recommended, or suggested in the labeling thereof," 21 U.S.C. § 352(j); 21 U.S.C. § 352(j) (1964 ed.). In this sense, the FCLAA was—and remains—incompatible with FDA regulation of tobacco products. This is not to say that the FCLAA's preemption provision by itself necessarily foreclosed FDA jurisdiction. But it is an important factor in assessing whether Congress ratified the agency's position—that is, whether Congress adopted a regulatory approach to the problem of tobacco and health that contemplated no role for the FDA.
* * *

Four years later, after Congress had transferred the authority to regulate substances covered by the Hazardous Substances Act (HSA) from the FDA to the Consumer Products Safety Commission (CPSC), the American Public Health Association, joined by Senator Moss, petitioned the CPSC to regulate cigarettes yielding more than 21 milligrams of tar. After the CPSC determined that it lacked authority under the HSA to regulate cigarettes, a District Court held that the Act did, in fact, grant the CPSC such jurisdiction and ordered it to reexamine the petition. Before the CPSC could take any action, however, Congress mooted the issue by adopting legislation that eliminated the agency's authority to regulate "tobacco and tobacco products." Consumer Product Safety Commission Improvements Act of 1976, Pub. L. 94–284, § 3(c), 90 Stat. 503 (codified at 15 U.S.C. § 1261(f)(2)). Senator Moss acknowledged that the "legislation, in effect, reversed" the District Court's decision, 121 Cong. Rec. 23563 (1975), and the FDA later observed that the episode was "particularly indicative of the policy of Congress to limit the regulatory authority over cigarettes by Federal Agencies," Letter to Action on Smoking and Health (ASH) Executive Director Banzhaf from FDA Commissioner Goyan (Nov. 25, 1980), App. 59. A separate statement in the Senate Report underscored that the legislation's purpose was to "unmistakably reaffirm the clear mandate of the Congress that the basic regulation of tobacco and tobacco products is governed by the legislation dealing with the subject, . . . and that any further regulation in this sensitive and complex area must be reserved for specific Congressional action." S. Rep. No. 94–251, p. 43 (1975) (additional views of Sens. Hartke, Hollings, Ford, Stevens, and Beall).

[Justice O'Connor assembled an abundance of subsequent statutes regulating smoking and drew extensively from their legislative history the proposition that Congress was consistently following a disclosure strategy and rejecting broader regulations of cigarettes and smoking. At various points, the FDA or other observers reminded congressional committees holding hearings on the tobacco problem that the FDA could not regulate the drug. The FDA also, in 1977, denied a citizen petition asking it to regulate cigarettes, on the ground that "[t]he interpretation of the Act by FDA consistently has been that cigarettes are not a drug unless health claims are made by the vendors." When the citizen group challenged the agency, the government argued that Congress had "acquiesced" in the FDA's no-jurisdiction stance, and the D.C. Circuit affirmed on that ground. The HHS Assistant Secretary told a congressional committee in 1983 that smoking had horrible health effects but that Congress's early legislation deprived HHS of any authority to regulate those ill effects. Congress incrementally expanded its regulation of tobacco with statutes authorizing and funding anti-smoking educational campaigns in the 1980s.]

In 1988, the Surgeon General released a report summarizing the abundant scientific literature demonstrating that "cigarettes and other forms of tobacco are addicting," and that "nicotine is psychoactive" and "causes physical dependence characterized by a withdrawal syndrome that usually accompanies nicotine abstinence." 1988 Surgeon General's Report 14. The report further concluded that the "pharmacologic and behavioral processes that determine tobacco addiction are similar to those that determine addiction to drugs such as heroin and cocaine." *Id.*, at 15. In the same year, FDA Commissioner Young stated before Congress that "it doesn't look like it is possible to regulate tobacco under the Food, Drug and Cosmetic Act even though smoking, I think, has been widely recognized as being harmful to human health." [House Appropriations Subcomm. Hearing.] At the same hearing, the FDA's General Counsel testified that "what is fairly important in FDA law is whether a product has a therapeutic purpose," and "cigarettes themselves are not used for a therapeutic purpose as that concept is ordinarily understood." Between 1987 and 1989, Congress considered three more bills that would have amended the FDCA to grant the FDA jurisdiction to regulate tobacco products. See H. R. 3294, 100th Cong., 1st Sess. (1987); H. R. 1494, 101st Cong., 1st Sess. (1989); S. 769, 101st Cong., 1st Sess. (1989). As before, Congress rejected the proposals. In 1992, Congress instead adopted the Alcohol, Drug Abuse, and Mental Health Administration Reorganization Act, Pub. L. 102–321, § 202, 106 Stat. 394 (codified at 42 U.S.C. § 300x *et seq.*), which creates incentives for States to regulate the retail sale of tobacco products by making States' receipt of certain block grants contingent on their prohibiting the sale of tobacco products to minors.

Taken together, these actions by Congress over the past 35 years preclude an interpretation of the FDCA that grants the FDA jurisdiction to regulate tobacco products. We do not rely on Congress' failure to act—its consideration and rejection of bills that would have given the FDA this authority—in reaching this conclusion. Indeed, this is not a case of simple inaction by Congress that purportedly represents its acquiescence in an agency's position. To the contrary, Congress has enacted several statutes addressing the particular subject of tobacco and health, creating a distinct regulatory scheme for cigarettes and smokeless tobacco. In doing so, Congress has been aware of tobacco's health hazards and its pharmacological effects. It has also enacted this legislation against the background of the FDA repeatedly and consistently asserting that it lacks jurisdiction under the FDCA to regulate tobacco products as customarily marketed. Further, Congress has persistently acted to preclude a meaningful role for *any* administrative agency in making policy on the subject of tobacco and health. Moreover, the substance of Congress' regulatory scheme is, in an important respect, incompatible with FDA jurisdiction. Although the supervision of product labeling to protect consumer health is a substantial component of the FDA's regulation of drugs and devices, see 21 U.S.C. § 352 (1994 ed. and Supp. III), the FCLAA and the CSTHEA [Comprehensive Smokeless Tobacco Health Education Act] explicitly prohibit any federal agency from imposing any health-related labeling requirements on cigarettes or smokeless tobacco products, see 15 U. S C. §§ 1334(a), 4406(a). * * *

JUSTICE BREYER, joined by JUSTICE STEVENS, JUSTICE SOUTER, and JUSTICE GINSBURG, dissenting.

The Food and Drug Administration (FDA) has the authority to regulate "articles (other than food) intended to affect the structure or any function of the body. . . ." Federal Food, Drug and Cosmetic Act (FDCA), 21 U.S.C. § 321(g)(1)(C). Unlike the majority, I believe that tobacco products fit within this statutory language.

In its own interpretation, the majority nowhere denies the following two salient points. First, tobacco products (including cigarettes) fall within the scope of this statutory definition, read literally. Cigarettes achieve their mood-stabilizing effects through the interaction of the chemical nicotine and the cells of the central nervous system. Both cigarette manufacturers and smokers alike know of, and desire, that chemically induced result. Hence, cigarettes are "intended to affect" the body's "structure" and "function," in the literal sense of these words.

Second, the statute's basic purpose—the protection of public health—supports the inclusion of cigarettes within its scope. See *United States v. Article of Drug ... Bacto–Unidisk,* 394 U.S. 784, 798 (1969) (FDCA "is to be given *a liberal construction consistent with [its] overriding purpose to protect the public health*" (emphasis added)). Unregulated tobacco use causes "more than 400,000 people [to] die each year from tobacco-related illnesses, such as cancer, respiratory illnesses, and heart disease." 61 Fed. Reg. 44398 (1996). Indeed, tobacco products kill more people in this country every year "than ... AIDS, car accidents, alcohol, homicides, illegal drugs, suicides, and fires, *combined.*" *Ibid.* (emphasis added).

Despite the FDCA's literal language and general purpose (both of which support the FDA's finding that cigarettes come within its statutory authority), the majority nonetheless reads the statute as *excluding* tobacco products for two basic reasons:

(1) the FDCA does not "fit" the case of tobacco because the statute requires the FDA to prohibit dangerous drugs or devices (like cigarettes) outright, and the agency concedes that simply banning the sale of cigarettes is not a proper remedy; and

(2) Congress has enacted other statutes, which, when viewed in light of the FDA's long history of denying tobacco-related jurisdiction and considered together with Congress' failure explicitly to grant the agency tobacco-specific authority, demonstrate that Congress did not intend for the FDA to exercise jurisdiction over tobacco.

In my view, neither of these propositions is valid. Rather, the FDCA does not significantly limit the FDA's remedial alternatives. And the later statutes do not tell the FDA it cannot exercise jurisdiction, but simply leave FDA jurisdictional law where Congress found it. [C]f. Food and Drug Administration Modernization Act of 1997, 111 Stat. 2380 (codified at note following 21 U.S.C. § 321 (1994 ed., Supp. III)) (statute "shall" *not* "be construed to affect the question of whether" the FDA "has any authority to regulate any tobacco product").

The bulk of the opinion that follows will explain the basis for these latter conclusions. In short, I believe that the most important indicia of statutory meaning—language and purpose—along with the FDCA's legislative history (described briefly in Part I) are sufficient to establish that the FDA has authority to regulate tobacco. The statute-specific arguments against jurisdiction that the tobacco companies and the majority rely upon (discussed in Part II) are based on erroneous assumptions and, thus, do not defeat the jurisdiction-supporting thrust of the FDCA's language and purpose. The inferences that the majority draws from later legislative history are not persuasive, since (as I point out in Part III) one can just as easily infer from the later laws that Congress did not intend to affect the FDA's tobacco-related authority at all. And the fact that the FDA changed its mind about the scope of its own jurisdiction is legally insignificant because (as Part IV establishes) the agency's reasons for changing course are fully justified. [The FDA's stated reasons for not regulating were that it did not have evidence that the cigarette manufacturers "intended" for their product to have a medical effect; by the 1990s, there was ample evidence of such intent.]

In the majority's view, laws enacted since 1965 require us to deny jurisdiction, whatever the FDCA might mean in their absence. But why? Do those laws contain language barring FDA jurisdiction? The majority must concede that they do not. Do they contain provisions that are inconsistent with the FDA's exercise of jurisdiction? With one exception, the majority points to no such provision. Do they somehow repeal the principles of law * * * that otherwise would lead to the conclusion that the FDA has jurisdiction in this area? The companies themselves deny making any such claim. See Tr. of Oral Arg. 27 (denying reliance on doctrine of "partial repeal"). Perhaps the later laws "shape" and "focus" what the 1938 Congress meant a generation earlier. But this Court has warned against using the views of a later Congress to construe a statute enacted many years before. See *Pension Benefit Guaranty Corporation v. LTV Corp.,* 496 U.S. 633, 650 (1990) (later history is " 'a hazardous basis for inferring the intent of an earlier' Congress") (quoting *United States v. Price,* 361 U.S. 304, 313 (1960)). And, while the majority suggests that the subsequent history "controls our construction" of the FDCA, this Court expressly has held that such subsequent views are not "controlling." *Haynes v. United States,* 390 U.S. 85, 87–88 n.4 (1968). Regardless, the later statutes do not support the majority's conclusion. That is because, whatever individual Members of Congress after 1964 may have assumed about the FDA's jurisdiction, the laws they enacted did not embody any such "no jurisdiction" assumption. And one cannot automatically *infer* an antijurisdiction intent, as the majority does, for the later statutes are both (and similarly) consistent with quite a different congressional desire, namely, the intent to proceed without interfering with whatever authority the FDA otherwise may have possessed. As I demonstrate below, the subsequent legislative history is critically ambivalent, for it can be read *either* as (a) "ratifying" a no-jurisdiction assumption, *or* as (b) leaving the jurisdictional question just where Congress found it. And the fact that both inferences are "equally tenable," *Pension Benefit Guaranty Corp.,* prevents the majority from drawing from the later statutes the firm, antijurisdiction implication that it needs.

Consider, for example, Congress' failure to provide the FDA with express authority to regulate tobacco—a circumstance that the majority finds significant. In fact, Congress *both* failed to grant express authority to the FDA when the FDA denied it had jurisdiction over tobacco *and* failed to take that authority expressly away when the agency later asserted jurisdiction. See, *e.g.*, S. 1262, 104th Cong., 1st Sess., § 906 (1995) (failed bill seeking to amend FDCA to say that "nothing in this Act or any other Act shall provide the [FDA] with any authority to regulate in any manner tobacco or tobacco products"); see also H. R. 516, 105th Cong., 1st Sess., § 2 (1997) (similar); H. R. Res. 980, reprinted in 142 Cong. Rec. 5018 (1996) (Georgia legislators unsuccessfully requested that Congress "rescind any action giving the FDA authority" over tobacco); H. R. 2283, 104th Cong., 1st Sess. (1995) (failed bill "to prohibit the [FDA] regulation of the sale or use of tobacco"); H. R. 2414, 104th Cong., 1st Sess., § 2(a) (1995) (similar). Consequently, the defeat of various different proposed jurisdictional changes proves nothing. This history shows only that Congress could not muster the votes necessary either to grant or to deny the FDA the relevant authority. It neither favors nor disfavors the majority's position.

[We omit the remainder of Justice Breyer's lengthy opinion, but like Justice O'Connor's opinion it is worth reading in its entirety.]

NOTE ON THE *FDA* TOBACCO CASE AND THE SUPREME COURT AS A STRATEGIC ACTOR IN OUR POLITY

1. *Lawmaking as a Sequential Game.* This case might be an example of strategic behavior among legal institutions.[s] For years the FDA had known that tobacco was a deadly drug; one reason it did not move earlier was that it knew that any regulation would be overridden by Congress, where the tobacco companies were powerfully represented. President Clinton was a relatively anti-tobacco chief executive, who supported the regulatory moves of Dr. David Kessler, the FDA Administrator, to bring tobacco within the agency's health-protective regime. Unlike Presidents Bush and Reagan, Clinton would probably have vetoed a congressional effort to override the agency. Armed with that political knowledge—as well as the medical and "intent" knowledge emphasized in Justice Breyer's dissent—the agency moved to regulate.

The FDA's problem was that the tobacco industry might be able to mobilize the judiciary to override the agency even if Congress-with-the-President would not. Affirming the Fourth Circuit (filled with North Carolina and Virginia tobacco farms as well as GOP judges), the Supreme Court trumped the agency's initiative. Under the assumptions of rational choice theory, the Court might have been reluctant to act if it were likely to be overridden by Congress—but the Justices knew that would not happen, because relatively pro-tobacco Republicans controlled both houses of Congress in 2000. By reversing the default rule—from the FDA's regulation to the industry's nonregulation—the Court reversed the political outcome, and its resolution stuck until the Democrats secured control of both the Presidency and Congress in 2009. At that point, Congress vested the FDA with jurisdic-

---

s. The rich history is recounted and analyzed in Theodore W. Ruger, *The Story of* FDA v. Brown & Williamson: *The Norm of Agency Continuity*, in *Statutory Interpretation Stories* 334–65 (Eskridge, Frickey & Garrett eds. 2011).

tion over tobacco products, with some strings attached. From an institutionalist or legal process point of view, that resolution might have been optimal. From a tobacco point of view, it certainly was, as it gave the industry more time to adjust to the probability of regulation.

2. *The Judiciary as a Part of the Rent–Seeking Process?* The FDA Tobacco Case can be viewed as one kind of caution about economic theories of statutory interpretation, such as ours and Judge Easterbrook's, that urge the courts to press statutes away from rent-seeking. The courts can be part of the interest-group process. Groups press for the appointment of friendly lawyers or ideologically compatible law professors as judges and then use the judiciary to overturn at least some of their defeats in the political process. This is easier to accomplish by "have" groups, because judges tend to be libertarian, either as a matter of philosophy or practicality (it is much easier for the courts to slow things down than to require the state to act), and "have" groups are usually trying to protect their freedom of action against government regulation.[t]

So the FDA Tobacco Case can be viewed, in part, as an expression of the majority Justices' personal aversion to aggressive state regulation of private industry. The five Justices in the majority are the most conservative Republican Justices; the four dissenters include the only two Democrats on the Court, an Independent appointed by a Republican (Stevens), and a Republican who turned out to be more liberal than expected (Souter). The case can be viewed as a signal to the Clinton Administration that the Court will slap down new regulatory initiatives that are too ambitious. (Congress has shown itself unwilling to enact them; now the President and agencies cannot adopt them under prior authorizing statutes.) Is this assessment too harsh?

Opponents of the outcome in FDA Tobacco Case may view it as rent-seeking. For them, if ever the Court were to follow the Easterbrook idea of liberal construction of public-regarding statutes, it is this case, for there is little doubt that tobacco products represent rent-seeking of the worst sort: a special interest not only makes money at the expense of the public good, but at the expense of untold suffering and death. Moreover, the FDA's interpretation is consistent with, if not compelled by, the statutory text and purpose. How should supporters of the decision respond to these arguments? For an excellent analysis, see Richard A. Merrill, *The FDA May Not Regulate Tobacco Products as "Drugs" or "Medical Devices,"* 47 Duke L.J. 1071 (1998).

3. *The Rule of Law as a Judicial Preference.* There is another way of looking at the FDA Tobacco Case from an economic perspective. Whatever their political preferences, almost all federal judges carry or develop strong preferences for rule-of-law values, including predictability in the law, following orderly procedures, and acting only within authorized jurisdictional boundaries. From Justice O'Connor's point of view, the FDA Tobacco Case is a dramatic example of the power of the rule of law: these companies may be morally squalid, but regulation of moral squalor must still follow the proper procedures under the appropriate congressional authorization. As Professor

---

t. See also Mark Galanter, *Why the "Haves" Come Out Ahead: Speculations on the Limits of Legal Change*, 9 L. & Soc'y Rev. 95 (1974), which shows how Repeat–Player "Have" groups can deploy the litigation process to advance their goals even if judges are neutral or even hostile.

Merrill puts it, the 1965 statute confirmed a longstanding political *deal*, that the FDCA did not regulate tobacco products, which would be subject to warning and disclosure regimes instead (the FCLAA and subsequent laws). Everything Congress did after 1965 reflected and reaffirmed that deal—until the FDA unilaterally abrogated it in 1996. Merrill, *FDA May Not Regulate Tobacco Products,* 47 Duke L.J. at 1074–82.

In response, Justice Breyer's dissent argues that the statute's plain meaning (the rule of law's primary tool) and the Court's precedents (next-best tool) supported the agency. Thus, a "liberal" construction in this case was also a "literal" construction, for the statutory language includes tobacco and cigarettes. Justice O'Connor could respond that the FDA's assertion of jurisdiction to regulate tobacco products is inconsistent with the statutory structure, whereby dangerous drugs must be banned entirely. See Merrill, *FDA May Not Regulate Tobacco Products,* 47 Duke L.J. at 1082–86.

Justice O'Connor also apparently rests her opinion upon an equilibrium-based idea: the longstanding agreement that the FDA could not regulate smoking without fresh congressional authorization, and the reliance interests it generated, have created a stable "rule of law" not perfectly reflected in the statutory text. This kind of response would be inconsistent with the philosophy of two of the Justices in the majority, Scalia and Thomas. But they swallowed, without a textualist whimper, Justice O'Connor's lengthy recitation of evidence from legislative hearings, reports, and debates to show that even though no tobacco statute limited the FDA's jurisdiction, many of them were enacted under the assumption that the FDA did not have such jurisdiction. Why did Justice Scalia, in particular, not reject the Court's extensive reliance on legislative history and simply concur with the result for the structure-of-statute reasons set forth in Part II of the Court's opinion? One explanation is that Justice Scalia is not as dogmatic about editing other Justice's opinions when the result is ideologically congenial. Can you think of a more principled explanation in this case?

A further irony: Justice O'Connor (with Justices Scalia and Thomas going along) deploys the kind of "institutional legislative history" that Justices Breyer and Stevens have championed—with Breyer and Stevens themselves in dissent based in part on the plain meaning rule.

C. PRAGMATIC AND CRITICAL THEORIES OF STATUTORY INTERPRETATION

1. Introduction to Pragmatic Theory and the Funnel of Abstraction

In *How Judges Think* (2008), Judge Richard A. Posner broadly distinguishes between "legalistic" and "pragmatic" theories of statutory interpretation. Legalistic theories claim that law is an autonomous discipline that can reach neutral interpretations through application of plain meanings (assisted perhaps with dictionaries and linguists), following precedent, reasoning by analogy, and the like. Pragmatic theories, in contrast, openly admit that law is not (entirely) separate from politics and that interpretation carries with it discretion and policy choice. Hart and Sacks's purpose-based interpretation is, by this reading, pragmatic, and Posner's current approach, well-illustrated in the LSD Case above, is an updated or more sophisticated version of legal process theory. Similarly pragmatic is Justice Stephen Breyer, as illustrated in his opinion for the Court in *Zuni*, as well as his recent books, namely, *Active Liberty: Interpreting Our Democratic Constitution* (2005), and *Making Our Democracy Work: A Judge's View* (2010).

Another kind of *pragmatic* thinking focuses less on realistic consequences. Inspired by American pragmatic philosophers who rejected "foundationalist" thinking and urged multi-focal thinking, the following article reflects a practical approach to statutory interpretation that the authors believe best reflects what the Supreme Court (and most state courts) are actually doing in statutory cases.

William N. Eskridge Jr. and Philip P. Frickey, *Statutory Interpretation as Practical Reasoning*, 42 Stan. L. Rev. 321, 345–53 (1990). Professors Eskridge and Frickey criticize each of the leading "foundationalist" theories of interpretation—textualism, original intent, purpose—and find each wanting in the same ways. "[T]he leading foundationalist theories cannot redeem their claim to follow from the very nature of majoritarian democracy, that they do not yield objective and determinate answers, and that they cannot convincingly exclude other values, including current values. *Weber* [Chapter 1, § 3] [and] *Griffin* illustrate our theoretical critique and suggest that the Supreme Court does not follow any one of the foundationalist theories. We now suggest that these observations form the basis for a positive theory which refuses to privilege intention, purpose or text as the sole touchstone of interpretation, but which both explains the Supreme Court's practice in statutory interpretation and, at the same time, reflects the insights of modern theories of interpretation.

"First, statutory interpretation involves creative policymaking by judges and is not just the Court's figuring out the answer that was put 'in' the statute by the enacting legislature. An essential insight of hermeneutics is that interpretation is a dynamic process, and that the interpreter is inescapably situated historically. 'Every age has to understand a transmitted text in its own way,' says Gadamer [in *Truth and Method* 263 (1965):]

> The real meaning of a text, as it speaks to the interpreter, does not depend on the contingencies of the author and whom he originally wrote for. It certainly is not identical with them, for it is always partly determined also by the historical situation of the interpreter and hence by the totality of the objective course of history. * * *

"Hermeneutics suggests that the text lacks meaning *until* it is interpreted. Given the importance of the interpretive horizon, which itself changes over time, interpretation must not 'chase the phantom of an historical object.' A text, then, is not meaningful 'in itself,' apart from possible interpreters and their historical contexts. Nor is it meaningful apart from the task of the interpreter. Gadamer argues, following Aristotle, that one does not 'understand' a text in the abstract, without an 'application' of the text to a specific problem. American pragmatism, also influenced by Aristotle, complements this hermeneutic insight. Reasoning in human affairs does not seek abstract answers, but concretely useful results. Theories of reasoning, for [William James, in *Pragmatism* (1907)] are simply 'mental modes of *adaptation* to reality, rather than revelations or gnostic answers.'

"Consider *Weber* in this light. The interpretive process is creative, not mechanical. Viewed in the context of the complex goals of the Civil Rights Act and subsequent difficulties in implementation, making sense of the statute's command not to 'discriminate' requires much more than finding a meaning for the term. Even if the interpretive process were viewed as retrieving the answer Congress would have reached in 1964 (had it deliberated on the issue), the inquiry involves 'imaginative' work by the judge. These lessons of *Weber* are consistent with the insights of modern literary theory, historiography, and philosophy: There is no interpretation without an interpreter, and the interpreter will interact with the text or historical event. Just as the interpreter learns from the text and history, so too does she speak to it. What was decisive in *Weber*, surely to Justice Blackmun and probably to other Justices in the majority as well, was what the interpreters learned about the statute from considering the facts of the case: More than a decade after the statute was enacted there were only 2 percent blacks in the craft workforce, contrasted with 39 percent blacks in the overall workforce.

"Second, because this creation of statutory meaning is not a mechanical operation, it often involves the interpreter's choice among several competing answers. Although the interpreter's range of choices is somewhat constrained by the text, the statute's history, and the circumstances of its application, the actual choice will not be 'objectively' determinable; interpretation will often depend upon political and other assumptions held by judges. Under Gadamer's [analysis], interpretation seeks 'to make the law concrete in each specific case,' and '[t]he creative supplementing of the law that is involved is a task that is reserved to the judge.' As a practical matter, how could it be otherwise? Many statutes leave key terms ambiguous, often intentionally, and thereby delegate rulemaking authority to courts or agencies. Over time, these ambiguities and unanswered questions multiply, as society changes and background legal assumptions change with it. Hermeneutics suggests that as the interpreter's own background context—her 'tradition'—changes, so too will her interpretive choices. * * *

"Third, when statutory interpreters make these choices, they are normally not driven by any single value—adhering to majoritarian commands *or* encouraging private reliance on statutory texts *or* finding the best answer according to modern policy—but are instead driven by multiple values. Both hermeneutics and pragmatism emphasize the complex nature of human reasoning. When solving a problem, we tend to test different solutions, evaluating each against a range of values and beliefs we hold as important. The pragmatic idea that captures this concept is the 'web of beliefs' metaphor. We all accept a number of different values and propositions that, taken together, constitute a web of intertwined beliefs about, for example, the role of statutes in our public law. Each of us may accord different weight to the specific values, but almost no one excludes any of the important values altogether. Decisionmaking is, therefore, polycentric, and thus cannot be linear and purely deductive. Instead, it is spiral and inductive: We consider the consistency of the evidence for each value before reaching a final decision, and even then check our decision against the values we esteem the most. Given this web of beliefs and the spiral form of decisionmaking, an individual's reasoning will depend very much on the context of the case at hand, and specifically on the relative strength of each consideration.

"Consider *Griffin* from the perspective of the web metaphor. A Justice who is a thoroughgoing textualist would surely agree with the *Griffin* result, given the relative clarity of the statutory language. But so could an intentionalist Justice: Although there is no smoking gun in the legislative history, the legislative context and the strong statutory language suggest that Congress would probably have favored substantial punitive sanctions had it addressed the issue. And so could a purposivist Justice, because surely one major purpose of the statute was to deter employer misconduct, which the $302,000 award in *Griffin* would seem to do. Even a Justice concerned only with fair results might applaud the *Griffin* result. In fact, seven Justices of differing jurisprudential stripes formed the majority in *Griffin,* and Justice Rehnquist's opinion justified the result by arguing from the relatively clear statutory language, the original legislative intent, the overall statutory purpose, and (to some extent) the reasonableness of the interpretation. Whether ultimately correct, the opinion in *Griffin,* by its strategy of cumulative assessment and weighing of factors potentially relevant to interpretation, seems more persuasive than would any foundationalist avenue to the same result. * * *

"In addition to the web of beliefs idea, two other metaphors, one drawn from the pragmatist tradition and one drawn from the hermeneutical tradition, suggest more precisely how a practical reasoning approach would work. First, consider Peirce's contrast of the chain and the cable. A chain is no stronger than its weakest link, because if any of the singly connected links should break, so too will the chain. In contrast, a cable's strength relies not on that of individual threads, but upon their cumulative strength as they are woven together. Legal arguments are often constructed as chains, but they tend to be more successful when they are cable-like. The Court's opinion in *Griffin* draws its strength from this phenomenon: The text, one probable purpose, some legislative history, and current policy each lend some—even if not unequivocal—support to the result. Each thread standing alone is subject to quarrel and objection;

woven together, the threads persuaded both Justice Rehnquist *and* Justice Brennan, a not unimpressive achievement.

"In many cases of statutory interpretation, of course, the threads will not all run in the same direction. The cable metaphor suggests that in these cases the result will depend upon the strongest overall combination of threads. That, in turn, depends on which values the decisionmakers find most important, and on the strength of the arguments invoking each value. For most of the Supreme Court Justices, a persuasive textual argument is a stronger thread than an otherwise equally persuasive current policy or fairness argument, because of the reliance and legislative supremacy values implicated in following the clear statutory text. And a clear and convincing textual argument obviously counts more than one beclouded with doubts and ambiguities.

"Our model of practical reasoning in statutory interpretation is still not complete, for it lacks a dynamic element that is intrinsic to human reasoning in general, and interpretation in particular. The various arguments (the threads of our cable) do not exist in isolation; they interact with one another. A final metaphor that captures this interaction is the 'hermeneutical circle': A part can only be understood in the context of the whole, and the whole cannot be understood without analyzing its various parts. To interpret the statute in *Griffin,* for example, the interpreter will look at the text and the legislative history and the purpose and current values. But to evaluate the text, the interpreter will consider it in light of the whole enterprise, including the history, purpose, and current values. In other words, none of the interpretive threads can be viewed in isolation, and each will be evaluated in its relation to the other threads.

"Following Heidegger, Gadamer deploys the hermeneutical circle in a particularly interesting way, which roughly captures the dynamics of legal interpretation. Because we always approach texts from the perspective of our own historically situated horizon, we tend to project our 'preunderstandings' onto the text, viewed as a whole. That is essential to interpretation, because the preunderstandings are conditioned by tradition and, hence, help us link our horizon with that of the text. But the hermeneutical circle suggests that a true dialogue with the text requires the interpreter to reconsider her preunderstandings as she considers the specific evidence in the case, and then to formulate a new understanding, which in turn is subject to reconsideration. For Gadamer, the essential lesson of the circle metaphor is the hermeneutical attitude: 'A person trying to understand a text is prepared for it to tell him something.' The 'to and fro movement' involved in the hermeneutical circle is not just the interpreter's movement from a general view of the statute to the specific evidence and back again; rather, it requires her to test different understandings of the text in an ongoing effort to determine its proper interpretation.

"The positive metaphors of our analysis—the web of beliefs idea, the cable-versus-chain contrast, and the hermeneutical circle—suggest the contours of a practical reasoning model of statutory interpretation that roughly captures the Court's practice. Our model holds that an interpreter will look at a broad range of evidence—text, historical evidence, and the text's evolution—and thus form a preliminary view of the statute. The interpreter then develops that preliminary view by testing various possible interpretations against the multiple criteria of fidelity to the text, historical accuracy, and conformity to contemporary circumstances and values. Each criterion is relevant, yet none necessarily trumps the others. Thus while an apparently clear text, for example, will create insuperable doubts for a contrary interpretation if the other evidence reinforces it *(Griffin)*, an apparently clear text may yield if other considerations cut against it (* * * *Weber*). As the interpreter comes to accept an interpretation (perhaps a confirmation of her preliminary view), she considers a congeries of supporting arguments, which may buttress her view much 'like the legs of a chair and unlike the links of a chain.'

"This dialectical method of statutory interpretation, which is familiar to us all, can be schematized as follows:

A PRACTICAL REASONING MODEL OF STATUTORY INTERPRETATION

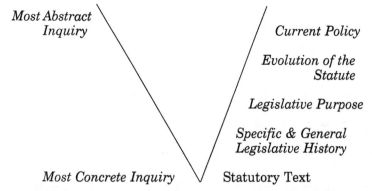

Most Abstract Inquiry

Current Policy

Evolution of the Statute

Legislative Purpose

Specific & General Legislative History

Most Concrete Inquiry   Statutory Text

" * * * [T]his model identifies the primary evidentiary inquiries in which the Court will engage. The model is, in crude imagery, a 'funnel of abstraction.' It is funnel-shaped for three reasons. First, the model suggests the hierarchy of sources that the Court has in fact assumed. For example, in formulating her preunderstanding of the statute *and* in testing it, the interpreter will value more highly a good argument based on the statutory text than a conflicting and equally strong argument based upon the statutory purpose. Second, the model suggests the degree of abstraction at each source. The sources at the bottom of the diagram involve more focused, concrete inquiries, typically with a more limited range of arguments. As the interpreter moves up the diagram, a broader range of arguments is available, partly because the inquiry is less concrete. Third, the model illustrates the pragmatistic and hermeneutical insights explained above: In formulating and testing her understanding of the statute, the interpreter will move up and down the diagram, evaluating and comparing the different considerations represented by each source of argumentation. * * * "

NOTE ON THE FUNNEL OF ABSTRACTION

On the whole, the funnel of abstraction is a descriptive theory of statutory interpretation: this is how the judicial (or administrative) mind goes about deciding statutory cases.[u] The features of the funnel that are most important are these: **First**, judges will consider a variety of factors, including statutory text and structure, but also statutory purpose, legislative history, authoritative precedents, practical applications of the statute, and current norms. The funnel theory is distinctive in the formal importance it attributes to *stare decisis* in statutory cases: Supreme Court precedents interpreting a particular statute, or words and phrases borrowed from other statutes (e.g., *Casey*), are always relevant and will be controlling if the statutory text is open-ended or vague. See also Miranda Oshige McGowan, *Do as I Do, Not as I Say: An Empirical Investigation of Justice Scalia's Ordinary Meaning Method of Statutory Interpretation*, 78 Miss. L.J. 129 (2008) (showing that even Justice Scalia ignores statutory text that he thinks delegates lawmaking authority to federal judges).

Second, the factors have varying legal force. They are hierarchical: a good text-based argument will trump a good legislative history or purpose argument, as in *Casey*. (*Chisom* would be distinguishable on the ground that the statutory text was ambiguous and statutory structure supported the majority.) This feature, by the way, is highly normative as well as descriptive. The funnel authors are textualists, like Justice Rehnquist in *Griffin*, for they start with the text but do not stop with the text (as Justice Scalia would have done in *Griffin*). **Third**, and most strongly unlike more formalist theories, the funnel of abstraction posits that the various factors will *interact* with one another. Thus, a textual "plain meaning" will not become firm in the judicial mind until *after* the judge has considered all the evidence; the "authority" of a precedent will not be conclusive until the judge has thought about its consistency with statutory text and purpose; the good judge will not be firm about the relevance of "norms" until she has processed the weight of the textual and historical factors. And so forth.

Think about how the funnel helps explain the decisions in this chapter, especially *Holy Trinity*, *Bock Laundry*, *Jacob*, *Li*, and *Chisom*, which openly follow the method, but also cases that don't seem to follow the method, like *Casey* and *Marshall*. Although Judge Easterbrook is not a "funnel judge," the judges who went along with his decision in *Marshall* might well have been— what might have been persuasive to them? Consider the debate among the Justices in *Brown & Williamson* as a debate about how to apply the funnel. How would the funnel apply to the issue raised by the Case of the Speluncean Explorers? Map out your analysis and then rethink it after you read the material that immediately follows. Next, take the reasoning and see if you can devise a more complicated model for understanding the courts' decisions. Finally, rethink the funnel from a normative perspective. What values should courts be pressing in statutory cases? The funnel assumes that the rule-of-law

---

u. For evidence suggesting that this diagram accurately displays the factors routinely taken into account in judicial opinions interpreting statutes, see Nicholas R. Zeppos, *The Use of Authority in Statutory Interpretation: An Empirical Analysis*, 70 Tex. L. Rev. 1073 (1992).

values (text, original intent, precedent) are the weightiest and that process
and substantive values are relevant but less weighty. Should the text be as
privileged as we assume it to be? Should it be as flexible as hermeneutics
suggests? And so on. See how your normative deliberation edits or changes
the funnel or your variation of it.

2. Critical Theories of Statutory Interpretation

Critical theory has not often found its way into the statutory interpretation literature, and critical scholars are unlikely to end up with judicial
positions, but it is not hard to imagine what critical theories of statutory
interpretation would look like.[v] Critical theory is typically deconstructive
but can be reconstructive as well.

Deconstruction, loosely put, opens up interpretive possibilities in
statutory texts, the opposite agenda of textualist theories. In the famous
Weber case (Chapter 1, § 3), Justice Brennan's deployment of section
703(j), which says the government cannot *require* race-based preferences
to offset workforce imbalances, was playfully ironic, as it showed how the
gaps in an anti-preference provision could support affirmative action
under Title VII. The playfulness was exercised with a serious undertone of
critique, however: Why should a provision put in to satisfy objectives of
white conservatives not be *read* from the perspective of people of color?
Brennan could, even more effectively, have made the same move with
discriminate: What does the word mean to the Gramercy blacks who had
been trying for a generation to break into the craft jobs? Indeed, white
opponents could be seen as making a deconstructive move themselves,
showing how the subjects arguably benefitting from centuries of slavery
and apartheid could now claim to be objects of *reverse discrimination*
when remediation for continuing segregation was adopted; this was particularly ironic in Weber's case, for he would not even have been eligible for
a craft position if it were not for the affirmative action training program,
which bypassed the older requirement of prior craft experience. The
potentially playful seriousness of Brennan's arguments and the irony of
Weber's position were lost on Justice Rehnquist, who cast Weber as a
victim and accused Brennan of Orwellian doublethink. Like Rehnquist in
Weber, Brewer in *Holy Trinity* (§ 1 of this chapter) was incapable of irony
or deconstruction (he can be said to have trumped the law with God, a
premodernist move), but his opinion can be defended by showing how
chaotic the statutory text was and, more deeply, how language could not
(or at least did not) capture what the sponsors of the bill were concerned
with regulating.

By revealing multiple possibilities, this method deconstructs the *rule
of law* itself. The common idea that "the rule of law is a law of rules"

---

v. By critical theory, we mean work that deconstructs statutory texts, typically in order to
show how reactionary readings are ideologically rather than objectively grounded. See, e.g., J.M.
Balkin, *Deconstructive Practice and Legal Theory*, 96 Yale L.J. 743 (1987); William N. Eskridge Jr.
& Gary Peller, *The New Public Law Movement: Moderation as a Postmodern Cultural Form*, 89
Mich. L. Rev. 707 (1991); Peter C. Schanck, *Understanding Postmodern Thought and Its
Implications for Statutory Interpretation*, 65 S. Cal. L. Rev. 2505 (1992).

assumes a hierarchy whereby the subject (interpreter) retrieves the answer from the object (text) to which she pays homage. But if interpretation depends critically on the perspective of the interpreter, even more than what the text says, then the hierarchy is flipped: the seemingly subordinate subject actually controls the meaning of the supposedly superior object. All the foregoing theories of statutory interpretation—textualist, intentionalist, purposivist, and even pragmatic—deny or suppress this flip of the rule in cases like *Weber* and *Holy Trinity*. From the critical perspective, everybody knows this goes on, and they all stonewall it. Do not expect Justices Scalia, Brennan, or even Blackmun to confess, as Judge (later Justice) Cardozo did several generations ago, that the hard work of judging is creative, for it happens when the conventional sources fail to provide interpretive closure. The strategy of the people in power whose work can be deconstructed is to ignore the critique or, if it cannot be ignored, to denounce it in eschatological terms as nihilist, or fascist, or even illiberal.

Critical theory can also be reconstructive, suggesting positive moves that interpreters could take in the face of pervasive indeterminacy. The statutory interpreter, especially judges given some degree of academic luxury by their life tenure, might become, perhaps episodically, a *counter-hegemonic* force in our polity, insisting that unspoken voices be considered. A critical approach to *Weber* would, with Blackmun, candidly admit the play within the text of Title VII and the assumption of the enacting Congress that colorblind employment decisions would lead to workforce integration. But rather than looking at the *Weber* dilemma only from the perspective of the displaced white employees (Rehnquist) or of the politically powerful unions and employers (Blackmun), the critic might have thought about the issue from the perspective of the people of color who, rather than Weber, got the opportunity to train for craft positions because of the Steelworkers/Kaiser program. Was it discrimination to help them? Was their lack of qualification (they had less seniority than Weber) a function of prior race-based policies? What doors did the training program open up for them? Was there disabling resentment against them by people who felt the Webers were cheated out of their rightful spots?

Holy Trinity looks even more different when viewed critically. Brewer's soliloquy about the United States as a Christian Nation was obviously very important to his resolution of the case, yet that norm seems more exclusionary than visionary today. The statute itself has more than a whiff of xenophobia and racism about it, patterned as it was on earlier Chinese exclusionary laws. Brewer's opinion can be defended as a narrowing construction of a broadly sweeping, somewhat hysterical piece of legislation. Curtailing such laws is traditionally something judges have done, often to their great credit, in this country. But Brewer's resolution also created a new injustice in the statute: the upper class, professional, brain-toiling imported "alien" can enter the country, and only the working-class manual laborers and servants (unless they were domestic servants, exempted by § 5) were found to be excluded by the law. By carving out a theoretically large exception for professionals, *Holy Trinity* made a morally questionable statute more squalid (by adding a new class-based discrimination) and more palatable to the political culture (by exempting acceptable aliens from the prohibition). A counterhegemonic approach to the case would have given less emphasis to the Christian Nation, and more to the Equal Nation.

Such an aggressively counterhegemonic judiciary can readily be criticized, not only for undermining the rule of law and disrespecting the democratic process, but also for kamikaze normative arrogance. Unhappily, judges are neither well-trained in moral philosophy nor necessarily especially virtuous people themselves, and Alexander Hamilton was right to call their office the "least dangerous branch" (*Federalist* No. 78). How can we expect such state functionaries, first, to transcend their own prejudices and empathize with the poor or the outcast; second, to translate that empathy into concrete statutory interpretations that have real-world bite; and, third, to pursue truly other-regarding moral theory in the face of political criticism and threats to the judicial office? On the other hand, pragmatists and even more formal theorists might be inspired by critical thinkers to shake up the status quo and kick some sacred cows more often, and to take a few calculated risks to do the right thing for the dispossessed of our society.

Consider the following excerpts from a symposium on the Case of the Speluncean Explorers, in which critical theorists added their own opinions to those of Judges Foster, Keen, and the others in Professor Fuller's leading article.

THE CASE OF THE SPELUNCEAN EXPLORERS: CONTEMPORARY PROCEEDINGS

61 Geo. Wash. U. L. Rev. 1754, 1755–63 (1993)*

NAOMI R. CAHN, J. * * * Although there can be no one feminist approach to statutory interpretation, the differing perspectives within feminism provide a basis for showing the dilemmas in a finding that the explorers violated, or did not violate, N.C.S.A. (N.S.) § 12–A. * * *

* * * The meaning of the language of the statute depends on who is reading the statute and where she places emphasis as to what different "plain meaning(s)" will emerge. Our statute requires that one "willfully take the life of another." This could mean that the explorers must have acted "willfully" in killing Roger Whetmore. * * * But perhaps they were "willfully" seeking to prolong their own lives rather than to take the life of Whetmore. * * * Is it a crime to seek to prolong life, regardless of the means? As liberal feminism suggests, the issue of individual choice is an important consideration. How were Whetmore's choices constructed? The record * * * does not give enough information about Roger Whetmore's "participation" in the decisionmaking process. The stories of the four

---

* Reprinted with the permission of *The George Washington Law Review* © 1993.

defendants are not available to us and may not have been available to the jury. * * * What is presented in the trial court as the "facts," and then what we, as judges, do with those "facts," is critical to our application of the law. The plain meaning of the statute cannot exist apart from the context in which the statute is applied. * * *

* * * We are all familiar with the work of Carol Gilligan, [*In a Different Voice* (1982),] who identified two different methods of moral reasoning: one based on an ethic of care, and one based on an ethic of justice. Within the ethic of care, reasoning draws on interconnections between people and seeks to minimize harms to others; for example, statutes should be interpreted in the light of their effect on people's interactions and mutual interdependence. Within the ethic of justice, reasoning is based on hierarchies of values, seeking to do what is morally (or legally) right; for example, people's interactions should be interpreted in the light of whether they comply with the law as written. Within an ethic of justice statutory *interpretation* becomes more of an exercise in statutory *application*. * * * Our judgments should integrate insights from the two different ethics, seeking to do justice yet respecting connections between people and recognizing that our own (sometimes shifting) perspectives construct this decision.

Reasoning constructed solely under an ethic of care might find none of the defendants guilty. They examined all the different options, talked amongst themselves, and agreed to a solution initially suggested by Roger Whetmore. Rather than all five people dying, only one person died: The collective good was served at the expense of one individual. * * * Power was exercised responsibly and compassionately, in consideration of the rights and interests of the community of explorers. The explorers willfully considered the lives of each other and the impacts of different solutions on their survival before Whetmore died.

[Justice Cahn suggests that the ethic of care might also support conviction, because Whetmore withdrew from the compact before the lots were cast; the other explorers' decision to enforce the compact destroyed their community and disregarded Whetmore's objections. Similarly, the ethic of justice might support either conviction (the defendants violated the letter of the law) or acquittal (the self-defense rationale).]

Thus, I would remand this case with directions to the jury and trial judge to consider the context in which this case arose and to encourage them to use their own emotions as a guide to interpreting the statute and to deciding the meaning of "willfully." While this call for context is not a call for unrestrained emotions and standardless discretion, it is an invitation to integrate emotions with the application of standards and to use our power responsibly, morally, and generously.

MARY I. COOMBS, J. * * * Feminist method requires us to consider the effect of various possible, technically plausible interpretations of § 12–A on homicides that do not take place in caves. For example, there are numerous cases in which women who have been subjected to domestic violence kill their abusers. Lower courts have struggled with these cases, examining both the appropriate interpretation of the self-defense exception to the statute and such evidentiary questions as the admissibility of expert testimony on battered women's syndrome. Our decision here is likely to affect those cases. For example, if the self-defense exception were inapplicable to the Spelunceans because they deliberated before they killed Whetmore rather than acting impulsively, as Justice Tatting suggests, it might also be inapplicable to a woman who has endured a long and escalating pattern of abuse, because her action is not sudden.

On the other hand, women are more frequently victims than perpetrators of violence. What if we were to interpret § 12–A, as Justice Foster proposes, to include an implicit exception whenever the defendant is undeterrable? Would we open the door to exculpation of men who kill their wives and lovers in uncontrollable jealous rages? * * * I feel obliged to interpret the statute in the light of justice. Yet, I lack sufficient information to know what justice requires and sufficient perspicacity to draft an exception certain to have no unforeseen and undesirable broader consequences. * * *

Am I, then, left to join my brother Tatting in utter ambivalence and failure of nerve? Perhaps, but I at least see a more judicious way to avoid a task we ought not to have been given. This case reaches us in this form only because the jury (led by a foreman both male and a lawyer) evaded its assigned task. * * * Under the Newgarth Constitution, however, every defendant is entitled to a trial by jury. Nothing in the record indicates that the defendants personally waived that right, which is too fundamental to be waivable by counsel alone. I would therefore find this case, in the form presented to us, procedurally defective and remand for a new trial. * * *

[DWIGHT L.] GREENE, J. * * * I vote to affirm the convictions of the defendants but reverse their death sentences and remand for further proceedings consistent with this opinion. In doing so, I expressly rely on some of my perspectives as a Melanoderm. As such, I generally favor expansive and contextual criminal adjudicatory processes by diverse juries, trial courts, and appellate courts. I believe that the Constitution of Newgarth requires some of this contextualization at sentencing. As developed below, however, there is no such contextual constraint on the predicate substantive, fact-finding process. As construed, many criminal laws are little more than automatic legal traps set for the less privileged. The privileged defendants in this case have been ensnared in one of these traps.

* * * Being Caucasoid confers many structural privileges in Newgarth. For example, Caucasoids can assume that the excess labor pool, three-quarters of which is Melanoderm, is available to them whenever they need it. Although the racial composition of the rescuers is not of record, we can assume that in this case, as in other similar rescue efforts,

many of the rescuers were Melanoderms. Ten lives were lost rescuing these Caucasoids from their recreational follies.

[Justice Greene analyzes the structure of the Newgarth murder statute. It was enacted to reduce jury discretion: If the jurors found the predicate facts, "willfully" taking someone's life, then death is the required penalty. He also noted that the Court heard few cases under this sort of statute. It was usually enforced against Melanoderms, especially those accused of killing Caucasoids; such defendants did not have the resources to appeal their convictions, and Newgarth was no longer willing to fund criminal appeals as a matter of individual right.]

* * * There can be no argument but that the killing of Whetmore was knowing, deliberate, and intentional. Thus, the question before this Court is whether a knowing, deliberate, and intentional killing to enhance the probabilities of the defendants' survival can be deemed not willful. * * *

If I were starting on a clean interpretive slate * * * I would allow a jury composed of diverse participants to consider whether the defendants' actions were directly influenced by exogenous social circumstances. The finders of fact could consider whether circumstances beyond the killers' control, a kind of social duress, mitigated the killing. * * * Based on precedent, however, I am precluded from adopting such an open-ended fact-finding process in this case. This Court has construed the word "willfully" in a manner that precludes factfinders from considering the influence of social circumstances.

The precedent to which I refer is obviously *Commonwealth v. Valjean.* In that case, a starving man was indicted for stealing a loaf of bread and offered his starving condition as a defense. * * * This Court affirmed that the social circumstances under which property is taken cannot be considered as negating a defendant's willfulness, even if the stolen property is the bread literally necessary to sustain life. This niggardly construction of willfulness controls the case now before the Court. * * *

[Justice Greene considers Justice Foster's argument that defendants had relapsed into a "state of nature," thereby enabling them to negotiate a new "social contract." Justice Greene questions whether Whetmore actually "consented" to this arrangement and whether consent is a defense to murder.]

Justice Foster's approach also reinforces an elitist perspective of contractarian social theory in our jurisprudence, which I reject. This approach provides options selectively under the criminal laws for the privileged while denying the same prerogatives to the unprivileged. Although the myth of an open society with transactions between and among freely contracting individuals is popular, it does not now reflect and never has reflected the reality of most people in Newgarth and certainly not that of Melanoderms. All contracts depend not only on the free will of the participants but also on their power within a real, not hypothetical social context. * * * [M]any Melanoderms and abandoned women and children live with inadequate education and in abject poverty, conditions they did not choose. These conditions, against which there is constant struggle, severely limit their power in social contracts. They are bound, nevertheless, by the laws of Newgarth.

Indeed, one could argue that in many of our ghettos conditions have deteriorated to a virtual state of nature "removed morally from the force of the legal order." Surely, this Court would be unwilling to excuse a group of Melanoderms from such a ghetto who formed their own social contract and imposed its outcomes on others within the community who dissented from that contract. Stated differently, assume Whetmore had been trapped in a ghetto during a riot with four nonrioting Melanoderms and food supplies were cut off. If these Melanoderms had used the same procedure used here to kill and eat Whetmore and then argued that their actions were in accord with their own social contract, such a specious argument would have been summarily rejected.

* * * In real life, as opposed to mythical states of nature, we are all limited in our ability to choose, and to contract, by social externalities [over which we have little or no control]. If the law is too constraining, then it must be changed for everyone. * * *

* * * [I]f the poor cannot be excused their poverty as sometimes necessitating the theft of the bread of life, then the privileged cannot be excused their killings to sustain their lives. The constraint imposed on the word "willfully" by *Valjean* limits the privileged just as it does the unprivileged. If social circumstances are irrelevant in deciding whether the actions of the poor are willful, then social circumstances are irrelevant in deciding whether the actions of the privileged are willful. These defendants have been trapped by laws designed to deny the unprivileged contextual review in efficient criminal justice machines. This is the legislative will in which this Court concurred in *Valjean*. So be it. * * *

NOTE ON CRITICAL RACE AND FEMINIST THEORIES AND STATUTORY INTERPRETATION

Critical feminist and race theories can have at least three different kinds of insights about statutory interpretation. One kind of insight asks about the possible effect of a law or of an interpretation on women or racial minorities. Critical theory would insist that the law take into account these perspectives and cannot be considered "neutral" and surely not "universal" if it is not responsive to a variety of perspectives. This is reflected most strongly in Mary Coombs' opinion.

Another kind of insight wonders whether legal premises are neutral, whether assumptions that are foundational to law might not reflect a partial viewpoint. This is reflected most strongly in Dwight Greene's opinion. When you originally read our excerpts from Lon Fuller's article, did you feel "empathy" for the explorers? Did you feel less empathy for the explorers after reading the Coombs and Greene opinions?

A third (but surely not final) kind of insight might be about legal reasoning itself. All three of the critical opinions urge that law be more "contextualized," focusing more on the particular facts and less on universal principles. Naomi Cahn's opinion draws upon "cultural feminism," which contrasts an ethic of care with an ethic of justice. Although the latter is associated with traditional legal discourse, cultural feminism posits that there is no reason for law not to follow the ethic of care. Among the insights suggested by an ethic of care is a "resistance to the question." The original Speluncean Justices all answer the question as though they had a binary choice: either affirm the convictions, or reverse them. All of our three new Speluncean Justices resist this binariness, and all three reconceptualize their alternatives (thereby avoiding the fate of Justice Tatting).

How would our critical panel (Justices Cahn, Coombs, and Greene) analyze the issue in *Holy Trinity Church? Locke? Weber?*

3. New and More Pragmatic Versions of Textualism

PORTLAND GENERAL ELECTRIC CO. v. BUREAU OF LABOR AND INDUSTRIES

Court of Appeals of Oregon, 1992
116 Or.App. 356, 842 P.2d 419

DE MUNIZ, J.

Petitioner seeks review of an order of the Commissioner of the Bureau of Labor and Industries (BOLI) that held that petitioner had engaged in an unlawful employment practice. ORS 659.360. It assigns error to BOLI's conclusion that an employee was entitled to use his accrued paid sick leave as parental leave, even though he was not "sick" within the definition of his employment agreement or company policy. We affirm.

The employee is a service inspector and a member of the International Brotherhood of Electrical Workers (IBEW). In March 1988, he requested 12 weeks of parental leave, composed of two weeks of accrued vacation leave, three days of accrued sick leave available for elective surgery and nine weeks and two days of other accrued sick leave. Petitioner denied the request, because the collective bargaining agreement in effect between petitioner and IBEW provides that sick leave is to be used only when an employee is actually sick or injured. Petitioner later granted the employee's amended request for 10 weeks of parental leave, which substituted seven weeks and two days unpaid leave for the nine weeks and two days paid sick leave.

BOLI's decision was based on ORS 659.360(3), which provides:

> "The employee seeking parental leave *shall be entitled to utilize any accrued* vacation leave, *sick leave* or other compensatory leave, paid or unpaid, *during the parental leave*. The employer may require the employee seeking parental leave to utilize any accrued leave during the parental leave unless otherwise provided by an agreement of the employer and the employee, by collective bargaining agreement or by employer policy." (Emphasis supplied.)

Petitioner argues that the emphasized language means that an employee may use paid sick leave during parental leave only if the employee is sick, as defined by the collective bargaining agreement. BOLI concluded that the employee's right to take that leave is not subject to the preconditions for use of sick leave contained in the collective bargaining agreement.

We begin with the language of the statute. It says that an employee "shall be entitled to utilize *any accrued * * * sick leave * * * during the parental leave.*" (Emphasis supplied.)

"Entitled to utilize" must mean "has a right to use." The only limit on that right to use sick leave during a parental leave is that the leave have accrued. Period. The provision simply says that, if the leave is accrued, the employee has a right to use it during the parental leave. That should be the end to a simple statutory question.

However, petitioner argues, and the dissenters agree, that the right to use paid sick leave during the parental leave is subject to the preconditions for use of the leave provided in the collective bargaining agreement. The easy answer to that contention is that the statute does not include that limitation, and we are not at liberty to add it. ORS 174.010. In addition, careful review of the statutory language, both in isolation and in context, leads inescapably to the conclusion that that interpretation is inconsistent with legislative intent.

The sole modifier before "vacation leave" and "sick leave" is "accrued." That modifier has a definite meaning in the employment context. As the *amicus* brief so ably explains, there is a difference between "accrued" leave, which is the maturation or vesting of the right to a benefit, usually based on completion of periods of employment; "eligibility" for leave or other benefits, which is the meeting of the threshold legal requirements, such as permanent employment versus temporary employment; and "entitlement" to use benefits, which is the result of fulfillment of preconditions to use, such as illness in the case of sick leave. By providing a single precondition for use of sick leave during parental leave, that the leave have *accrued*, the legislature did *not* limit the use of that leave to sick leave the employee would otherwise be entitled to use under a collective bargaining agreement.[5]

Furthermore, the contrast between the two sentences in subsection (3) makes it patently clear that the employee's right to use accrued sick leave is not otherwise limited by the collective bargaining agreement. The first sentence, which sets out the *employee*'s right to use accrued leave, does not refer to employment agreements:

> "The employee seeking parental leave *shall be entitled to utilize any accrued* vacation leave, *sick leave* or other compensatory leave, paid or unpaid, *during the parental leave.*" (Emphasis supplied.)

---

5. When the legislature intended collective bargaining agreements to govern in the Parental Leave Law, it specifically said so. [E.g., ORS 659.360(3) (second sentence), and .360(6) (quoted in text).]

In contrast, the second sentence says:

> "The employer may require the employee seeking parental leave to utilize any accrued leave during the parental leave *unless otherwise provided by an agreement of the employer and the employee, by collective bargaining agreement or by employer policy.*" (Emphasis supplied.)

Thus, the *employer's* right to require an employee to use accrued leave is specifically limited by any contrary agreement. When the legislature includes limiting language in one sentence of a subsection and excludes it in another, we can divine an intent that the limitation apply only as specified.

Our reading of ORS 659.360(3) comports with ORS 659.360(6):

> "The parental leave required by subsection (1) of this section is not required to be granted with pay unless so specified by agreement of the employer and employee, by collective bargaining agreement or by employer policy."

The subsection shows the distinction between a new kind of mandated leave, parental leave, and other types of leave that an employee may have accrued. Although parental leave *per se* need not be paid, an employee is entitled to use other types of leave, paid or unpaid, during the 12–week parental leave period. Subsection (6) makes clear that an employer need not provide a *new* type of *paid* leave in addition to the other types of leave already provided, unless required by an employment agreement. Regardless of the employment agreement, however, the employer must allow an employee a 12–week period for parental leave, which is unpaid unless the employee has accrued other paid leave *that the employee elects to take or that the employer requires the employee to take* during that period.

Finally, to the extent that there is any ambiguity, the legislative history supports BOLI's and our reading. The original draft of the bill provided that "[t]he leave required by subsection (1) of this Act may be unpaid leave or any other leave the employer and employe agree upon or any leave specified or allowed by any collective bargaining agreement." That language was changed to say: "The leave, with preference given to accumulated sick leave and vacation leave, required by subsection (1) of this section may be paid or unpaid leave or any other leave the employer and employee agree upon or any leave specified or allowed by any collective bargaining agreement." Finally, that subsection was changed and subsection (6) added, to read essentially as it now reads. Representative Kopetski explained that the final change was to clarify the meaning in the second version:

> "The second change is * * * to clarify, * * * to make certain that any sick leave, vacation leave, that that will run *concurrently* with the 12 weeks. *And so this 12 weeks is not added on to any vacation time or sick leave that the individual would have.*" Tape Recording, House

Committee on Labor, March 18, 1987, Tape 61, Side B. (Emphasis supplied.)

The language of the first draft allowed the leave to be unpaid *unless* otherwise agreed. Under the second draft language, the legislature indicated a preference for accumulated sick leave and vacation leave, *or* any other leave agreed on by the employer and employee. Clearly, it was anticipated that the employee would use accumulated sick and vacation leave during the parental leave, *i.e.*, concurrently with, rather than as a replacement for, the mandated leave. The changes in the final draft added the employer's right to *require* the employee to use that leave, if the employee did not elect to do so, in order to prevent extended absences beyond 12 weeks. It also clarified that the legislature did not intend a newly mandated paid parental leave, but that an employment agreement could provide for paid parental leave.

A careful reading of the Parental Leave Law persuades us that the legislature found a balance between the employee's need for time off to care for new family members during the critical first weeks and the employer's need for a stable work force. The law provides that an employee must be granted up to 12 weeks leave, if requested, and can elect to use any accrued leave, paid or unpaid, during that 12–week period. On the other hand, if the employee does not make the election to use accrued leave, the employer can force the employee to use the leave, subject to any agreement limiting that right. The purpose was to eliminate the danger that the employee might take 12 weeks of unpaid parental leave, during which time a replacement might need to be found, and then might seek to tack on a period thereafter in which the employee would use other accrued leave, necessitating additional replacement. The statutory scheme assures the employer that the employee is entitled to be gone 12 weeks at the maximum, and not 12 weeks in addition to any other accrued leave that the employee might be entitled to take.

The dissenters would rewrite the statute to say:

> "The employee seeking parental leave *may* use any accrued * * * sick leave * * * during the parental leave, *if the employee would be entitled otherwise to use that leave as specified in an agreement of the employer and the employee, a collective bargaining agreement or by employer policy*."

In other words, they would engraft the qualification contained in the second sentence of subsection (3) onto the first sentence. The statute imposes no such qualification; the legislature chose clear, strong, compulsory language to assure that accrued leave, paid or unpaid, would be available for employees' use during parental leave. The qualification that the dissents propose is not in the statute, and this court cannot rewrite legislation in accordance with a policy choice that it may think is appropriate. ORS 174.010. That policy choice is for the legislature, not for the courts. * * *

JOSEPH, C.J., dissenting (joined by two other Judges). * * *

* * * [The Court holds] that the accrued sick leave may be used *as* paid parental leave. The statute simply does not say that. It says that the accrued sick leave may be used *during* the parental leave. Nothing in the language of the statute even remotely suggests that accrued sick leave may be applied to a kind of leave other than the one for which it *has accrued* simply by reason of a happenstance that the employee is enjoying a different kind of leave while some of the accrued sick time remains. * * *

EDMONDS, J., dissenting (joined by CHIEF JUDGE JOSEPH).

I suggest that ORS 659.360(3) is, on its face, equally susceptible to the interpretations proposed by the majority and Chief Judge Joseph in his dissent. What persuades me that the legislature intended that the terms of a collective bargaining agreement control over the election of an employee are the previous drafts of the statute. There is a consistent thread in them that the legislature intended parental leave to be unpaid unless otherwise agreed by the employer and employee or unless controlled by a collective bargaining agreement. The collective bargaining agreement controls.

The majority concedes that the final draft was not intended to change the meaning of the statute but to clarify it so that the parental leave would not be added to any vacation or sick leave. That change created the ambiguity that is at the heart of the dispute over the meaning of the statute but did not change what the legislature intended. Both sentences in ORS 659.360(3) must be read together in the light of the legislative history. When that is done, it is apparent that BOLI erred when it held that petitioner had engaged in an unlawful employment practice when it adhered to the terms of the collective bargaining agreement.

PORTLAND GENERAL ELECTRIC CO. v. BUREAU OF LABOR AND INDUSTRIES

Supreme Court of Oregon, 1993
317 Or. 606, 859 P.2d 1143

VAN HOOMISSEN, J. * * *

[The Supreme Court of Oregon unanimously affirmed the Court of Appeals. Justice Van Hoomissen's opinion started with a statement of the interpretive approach Oregon courts are supposed to follow.] In interpreting a statute, the court's task is to discern the intent of the legislature. ORS 174.020. To do that, the court examines both the text and context of the statute. That is the first level of our analysis.

In this first level of analysis, the text of the statutory provision itself is the starting point for interpretation and is the best evidence of the legislature's intent. In trying to ascertain the meaning of a statutory provision, and thereby to inform the court's inquiry into legislative intent, the court considers rules of construction of the statutory text that bear directly on how to read the text. Some of those rules are mandated by statute, including, for example, the statutory enjoinder "not to insert what has been omitted, or to omit what has been inserted." ORS 174.010. Others are found in the case law, including, for example, the rule that words of common usage typically should be given their plain, natural, and ordinary meaning.

Also at the first level of analysis, the court considers the context of the statutory provision at issue, which includes other provisions of the same statute and other related statutes. Just as with the court's consideration of the text of a statute, the court utilizes rules of construction that bear directly on the interpretation of the statutory provision in context. Some of those rules are mandated by statute, including, for example, the principles that "where there are several provisions or particulars such construction is, if possible, to be adopted as will give effect to all," ORS 174.010, and that "a particular intent shall control a general one that is inconsistent with it," ORS 174.020. Other such rules of construction are found in case law, including, for example, the rules that use of a term in one section and not in another section of the same statute indicates a purposeful omission, and that use of the same term throughout a statute indicates that the term has the same meaning throughout the statute.

If the legislature's intent is clear from the above-described inquiry into text and context, further inquiry is unnecessary.

If, but only if, the intent of the legislature is not clear from the text and context inquiry, the court will then move to the second level, which is to consider legislative history to inform the court's inquiry into legislative intent. When the court reaches legislative history, it considers it along with text and context to determine whether all of those together make the legislative intent clear. If the legislative intent is clear, then the court's inquiry into legislative intent and the meaning of the statute is at an end and the court interprets the statute to have the meaning so determined.

If, after consideration of text, context, and legislative history, the intent of the legislature remains unclear, then the court may resort to general maxims of statutory construction to aid in resolving the remaining uncertainty. Although some of those maxims of statutory construction may be statutory, *see, e.g.,* ORS 174.030 (natural rights), others more commonly may be found in case law. Those include, for example, the maxim that, where no legislative history exists, the court will attempt to determine how the legislature would have intended the statute to be applied had it considered the issue. * * *

[Applying this structure to the issue on appeal, the Court went no further than step one.] Both of the sentences in ORS 659.360(3) are *empowerment* sentences. The second sentence *empowers* the employer to compel an employee taking parental leave "to utilize any accrued leave." Thus, if an employee has accrued leave, the employer could require the employee to utilize that accrued leave during the parental leave, "unless otherwise provided by an agreement of the employer and the employee, by collective bargaining agreement or by employer policy." ORS 659.360(3).

The reciprocal power, granted to the employee by the first sentence of ORS 659.360(3), permits the employee, at the employee's option, to do what the employer may require the employee to do. The employee may require the employer to let the employee "utilize" any accrued vacation leave, sick leave or other compensatory leave, paid or unpaid, during the parental leave. As noted, the first sentence of the statute does not contain any limitation on the employee's rights imposed under the provisions of a collective bargaining agreement.

In sum, the employer may *require* the employee seeking parental leave to utilize any accrued leave during parental leave, unless otherwise provided by an agreement of the employer and the employee, by collective bargaining agreement, or by employer policy, even if the employee is not on vacation or sick or does not wish to use accrued leave during the parental leave. Similarly, the employee may *require* the employer to let the employee utilize any accrued vacation leave, sick leave, or other compensatory leave, paid or unpaid during the parental leave, even if the employee is not on vacation or sick, and even if the employer does not want to do so. If the legislature had wanted to make the use of accrued leave during parental leave subject to any preconditions in an existing collective bargaining agreement, it easily could have done so by including in the first sentence of ORS 659.360(3) the same qualifying language that presently is found only in the second sentence of that subsection. The legislature knows how to include qualifying language in a statute when it wants to do so. It did not do so here. * * *

NOTE ON METHODOLOGICAL STARE DECISIS

An important feature of the Oregon Supreme Court's opinion is its effort to give *stare decisis* effect to methodological precedents like *PGE*. The House of Lords in the United Kingdom gives *stare decisis* effect to methodological precedents, and Sydney Foster argues that the U.S. Supreme Court should do the same. See Sydney Foster, *Should Courts Give* Stare Decisis *Effect to Statutory Interpretation Methodology?*, 96 Geo. L.J. 1863 (2008). Consider the values of *stare decisis*: judicial economy, predictability, and reliance interests. Foster argues that consistent treatment in matters of methodology would serve those interests—so courts should follow that practice.

On the other hand, are the reliance interests so strong in matters of methodological *stare decisis*? Is *stare decisis* as desirable or even workable for legal *standards* as they are for legal *rules*? Compare Foster, Stare Decisis *Effect*, 96 Geo. L.J. at 1901—05 (on the whole, yes), with Connor Raso & William N. Eskridge Jr., Chevron *as a Canon, Not a Precedent: An Empirical Analysis of What Motivates Justices in Agency Deference Cases*, 110 Colum. L. Rev. 1727 (2010) (on the whole, no).

Note, finally, that Oregon's *PGE* experiment in methodological *stare decisis* has been successful in some ways but not in others. The following article examines the *PGE* experiment, which has seen a few unexpected twists in the new millennium. Once you have read Professor Gluck's article, reflect on the debate between Sydney Foster and her critics. Also reflect on this question: Did the Oregon Supreme Court reach the right result in *PGE*? Or have the Justices strong-armed a statutory text to yield a liberal interpretation inconsistent with reliance interests? (We shall pose further questions in the notes following the Gluck article.)

Abbe R. Gluck, *The States as Laboratories of Statutory Interpretation: Methodological Consensus and the New Modified Textualism,* 119 Yale L.J. 1750 (2010).* "The vast majority of statutory interpretation theory is based on a strikingly small slice of American jurisprudence, the mere two percent of litigation that takes place in our federal courts—and, really, only the less-than-one percent of that litigation that the U.S. Supreme Court decides. The remaining ninety-eight percent of cases are heard in the netherworld of the American legal system, the state courts. And yet it would likely surprise most academics and many judges to learn that, while academics have spent the past decade speculating about the 'posttextualist era,' or the utility of congressionally legislated rules of interpretation, or the capacity of judges on multimember courts to agree on a single set of interpretive rules, many state courts have been engaging in real-world applications of precisely these concepts.

"Several state courts have implemented formalistic interpretive frameworks that govern all statutory questions. Methodological stare decisis—the practice of giving precedential effect to judicial statements about methodology—is generally absent from the jurisprudence of mainstream federal statutory interpretation, but appears to be a common feature of some states' statutory case law. Every state legislature in the nation has enacted certain rules of interpretation, which some state courts are, in an unexpected twist, flouting. * * * Justice Scalia's textualist statutory interpretation methodology has taken startlingly strong hold in some states, although in a form of which the Justice himself might not approve. Clearly, these developments are relevant to the mainstream debates about predictability and methodological choice, and yet federal scholars and jurists have hardly noticed them."

The state cases surveyed in Professor Gluck's article illustrate that the critical wars in statutory interpretation are far from over—and that the most interesting situs of those debates is in state rather than federal courts. Professor Gluck then provides an in-depth examination of the practice in five states, Oregon, Connecticut, Texas, Wisconsin and Michigan, where judges take methodological *stare decisis* seriously and have adopted approaches grappling with the challenges posed by the new textualism.

"Not incidentally, these state efforts also respond directly to the leading academic proposals advanced to make federal statutory interpretation more determinate. Legislated interpretive rules, suggested in one prominent proposal, do not appear to be the answer, given the number of courts already actively resisting them. The resulting interbranch power struggles, in turn, raise new questions about separation of powers in statutory interpretation, shifting the debate away from what has been the prevailing question—which methodology best respects the respective roles of court and legislature—to the entirely different question of which branch gets to choose it.

"Another path to determinacy, however, long thought remote, now seems more possible in light of the state experiences. These state supreme courts have exercised interpretive leadership: they have imposed, both on themselves and on their subordinate courts, controlling interpretive frameworks for all statutory questions. This is a powerful counter-paradigm to that of the U.S. Supreme Court, where persistent interpretive divides and a refusal to treat methodological statements as precedential have made interpretive consensus seem impossible. Indeed, methodology seems to be an entirely different animal in these state courts. In these states, it *is* possible for one judge to bind another judge's methodological choice. And in fact, federal judges, too, readily assent to this conception of methodology in other areas of law, like contract interpretation. Yet these principles have failed to translate to the federal statutory interpretation context, without much explanation of why statutory interpretation should be any different.

"The mainstream statutory interpretation scholarship, too, may be overstating the intractability of methodological divides and the 'softness' of interpretive methodology. Its near-exclusive focus on U.S. Supreme Court cases is the culprit: the Court's often-divisive statutory cases (and personalities) have become the theoretical paradigm. * * * In less politically charged cases, consistent methodological rules may make the interpretive process more predictable, performing a coordinating function for the many parties affected—legislators who must negotiate and draft statutes, citizens who must act and litigate under them, and lower courts that must interpret them. There also are important expressive and fairness values attendant to having judges agree in advance on the nature of the project and decide all litigants' cases using the same legal principles. The state cases challenge the prevailing theoretical resistance to these concepts and highlight the possibility that, even putting the Court aside, many lower courts (both state and federal) might be receptive to consistent methodological frameworks, and that, in fact, more courts than we realize already may be implementing them.

"Finally, the state cases also challenge prevailing assumptions about textualism, the text-centric methodology that, despite its significant impact on modern statutory interpretation, has failed to emerge as the dominant methodology in the U.S. Supreme Court's interpretive battles. Of late, debates have raged in the academy over whether a methodological compromise between textualists and purposivists is possible. The prognosis has been pessimistic, as most scholars have assumed that textualism is too rigid a methodology to be the basis of a broader consensus that also includes nontextualists and, alternatively, that the textualists themselves will not bend to meet other judges halfway. But in the states studied, textualism is more than merely alive and well; it is the *controlling* interpretive approach—the consensus methodology chosen by the courts. That said, this state textualism is clearly not identical to its federal model. It is instead, I argue, a compromise version of textualism, what might be called 'modified textualism,' a theory that retains the fundamental text-first formalism of traditional textualism and yet still appears multitextured enough to offer a middle way in the methodological wars. * * *

"Modified textualism has two salient differences from the original: it ranks interpretive tools in a clear order—textual analysis, then legislative history, then default judicial presumptions—and it includes legislative history in the hierarchy. The individual components here are not new. Many jurists (though it has been assumed, not many self-proclaimed textualists) employ such a text-plus-legislative history approach. But what is new is the 'tiering' concept and the order itself. The strict hierarchy emphasizes textual analysis (step one); limits the use of legislative history (only in step two, and only if textual analysis alone does not suffice); and dramatically reduces reliance on the oft-used policy presumptions, the 'substantive canons' of interpretation (only in step three, and only if all else fails).

"To be sure, some textualist purists might not consider this theory 'textualist' at all. Textualists generally have eschewed use of legislative history and do widely employ the substantive canons. Such a rush to judgment against modified textualism, however, would be a mistake. These state cases illustrate both that traditional textualist theory is capacious enough to accommodate this moderate heterogeneity and that, in fact, this accommodation may be textualism's best chance to accomplish its core theoretical goal of implementing a predictable, text-centric approach to interpretation.

"And because this methodology is the basis for broader agreement in the states studied, it also has implications for purposivism, the other dominant modern theory, and the broader literature about methodological compromise. Purposivists typically embrace a more flexible approach, an approach from which modified textualism's strict interpretive hierarchy is a departure. But, arguably, modified textualism offers purposivists what might be called a more 'disciplined' version of their current method—a way to legitimize the use of legislative history and concretize their approach so that it can be applied consistently, and repeatedly, by lower courts. It is intriguing to see at least some purposivist judges attracted to this structured approach—an approach that, unlike other compromise proposals advanced in the scholarship, still appeals to textualism on its own theoretical terms.

"The five states chosen for focused study—Oregon, Connecticut, Texas, Wisconsin and Michigan—were chosen following a preliminary review of state statutory interpretation across the highest courts of all fifty states and the District of Columbia, and they were selected because their interpretive moves were particularly explicit, both in terms of clearly identifiable interpretive developments underway and the extensive discussions, in the cases themselves, of those developments. My initial focus was on identifying courts with internal divides over methodological choice and states in which the legislatures had passed laws concerning interpretive rules. Texas and Connecticut were chosen once it became apparent that both states' courts, despite different methodological preferences, were engaged in similar dialogues with their legislatures over which branch controls the rules of interpretation. Michigan and Wisconsin were originally chosen because those states' supreme courts are internally divided and methodological choice is often heatedly debated in opinions. Oregon was chosen simply because of the surprise of identifying a sixteen-year controlling interpretive regime that has gone virtually unnoticed by the academy. My aims in state selection, moreover, did not include identifying methodological stare decisis, consensus regimes, or modified textualism. The state courts' convergences on those themes emerged, and subsequently became the focus of the Article, only after I had selected the states and completed a deeper analysis of their case law. The five states are also geographically and demographically diverse and employ different methods of judicial selection. * * *

"In 1993, the Oregon Supreme Court took the problem of interpretive choice into its own hands. In the watershed case, *Portland General Electric v. Bureau of Labor and Industries (PGE)*, the court unanimously announced a three-step methodology to control all future statutory interpretation questions. Even more notably, the new methodological regime stuck. The court not only applied the methodology 'religiously' in the sixteen years following its announcement, it did so without a single dissenting opinion from any member of that court arguing the methodology did not control as a matter of stare decisis. *PGE* 'is the single most frequently cited case decision in the state's history.' The announced methodology even remained controlling despite legislation enacted in 2001 aimed at overruling part of it. Indeed, it was not until April 2009—eight years after the legislation was enacted—that the Oregon court even was willing to consider whether the legislature could amend the court-imposed framework.

"The *PGE* case and its implications for interpretive indeterminacy have gone completely unnoticed outside of Oregon. The case and its progeny offer a perhaps unparalleled example of a judicially imposed, consistently applied interpretive regime for statutory cases that has remained in place unaltered for a sixteen-year period. For this reason, it is worth bracketing for a moment the Oregon Supreme Court's recent opinion concerning the legislative attempt to amend *PGE* (which muddies the waters somewhat), and examining in detail the three-step *PGE* test. * * *

"The Oregon Framework not only lists relevant interpretive factors, it orders and ranks them. As *PGE* held:

[1] In this first level of analysis, the text of the statutory provision itself is the starting point for interpretation.... In trying to ascertain the meaning of a statutory provision ... the court considers rules of construction of the statutory text that bear directly on how to read the text ... for example, the statutory enjoinder "not to insert what has been omitted, or to omit what has been inserted." ...

Also at the first level of analysis, the court considers the context of the statutory provision at issue, which includes other provisions of the same statute and other related statutes ...

[2] *If, but only if*, the intent of the legislature is not clear from the text and context inquiry, the court will then move to the second level, which is to consider legislative history.... If the legislative intent is clear, then the court's inquiry into legislative intent ... is at an end....

[3] If, after consideration of text, context, and legislative history, the intent of the legislature remains unclear, then the court may resort to general maxims of statutory construction to aid in resolving the remaining uncertainty.

"Although the *PGE* framework gives text precedence, it is decidedly different from Justice Scalia's textualism. *PGE*'s first, text-only, tier would certainly appeal to textualists. The Oregon Supreme Court made clear that the only interpretive rules permitted in this first step are the so-called 'textual' canons, which 'assist the statutory interpreter in deriving probable meaning from the four corners of the statutory text.' If the textual aids do not achieve clarity, however, the *PGE* framework mandates an antitextualist turn: legislative history is the second step of the inquiry. Only where ambiguity persists after consideration of text and legislative history, does the Oregon court allow for resort to all the remaining 'general maxims of statutory construction.'

"Textualists in Justice Scalia's vein would not look to legislative history in any event and often *do* consider the various substantive canons of interpretation that the Oregon court considers 'general maxims,' including the rule of lenity and the canon of constitutional avoidance. In contrast, Oregon has significantly diminished the importance of these canons by relegating them to the third tier of the *PGE* analysis. The *PGE* framework has caused the near-elimination of the rule of lenity and the canon of constitutional avoidance from Oregon Supreme Court cases. In addition, Oregon's highest court has expressly excluded from the 'level one' textual analysis the rule against absurdities. That rule has been the main escape valve for Scalia-style textualists, who invoke it to justify departure from clear statutory text if a literal reading would work absurd results. The Oregon Court's rationale for demoting the rule—'we would be rewriting a clear statute based solely on our conjecture that the legislature should not have intended a particular result'— echoes the main criticism that academics have levied at the textualist jurists on the federal side who still employ the canon, and also upends some academic assumptions that courts would never compromise on a text-based methodology without that escape valve.

"*PGE* also differs from purposivism or a more eclectic approach. The test's tiered hierarchy is strict: it prioritizes text over purpose in all situations, prohibits consultation of legislative history absent a threshold finding of ambiguity, and eschews an all-things-considered approach in favor of a formalized step-by-step process. Indeed, the Oregon Supreme Court devised the *PGE* regime at least partially in direct response to the uncertainty occasioned by the federal courts' eclectic approach.

"Three preliminary studies, including one conducted as part of this project, have collected data on how the *PGE* regime has been implemented since its installation. One clearly observable effect of the regime is that it has reduced the number of interpretive tools employed by the Oregon Supreme Court and so made it easier to predict which tools the court will rely on to decide cases. 'The court resolves the vast majority of statutory issues at level one, i.e., the text-based tier. Between 1993 and 1998, for example, out of 137 statutory interpretation cases, the court looked at legislative history only thirty-three times, finding it 'useless' in one third of those cases. It consequently reached tier three—nontextual canons—only eleven times during the same period. Even more strikingly, between 1999 and 2006, the court applied the *PGE* framework 150 times, and only reached tier two (legislative history) nine times. Not a single case during that period reached the other-maxims tier (tier three). And, in a study conducted as part of this project, across the thirty-five cases in which *PGE* was cited between 2006 and May 2009, legislative history was applied six times and a substantive canon only once

"Compare the five years before *PGE* was decided. There was no single approach: more than half of the cases resorted immediately to legislative history or policy analysis without prior consideration of text alone, and without the tiered hierarchy of sources that *PGE* later imposed. One justice called the pre-*PGE* period a 'legislative history free-for-all.'

"In contrast, under *PGE*, the court is fairly consistent with respect to which interpretive tools it relies upon. Over the four-and-a-half year period ending in May 2009, the following eight types of textual tools were used in roughly half of the cases: 'plain meaning,' dictionaries, state court precedents, close readings of statutory definition sections, analysis of related statutes, analysis of the contested term's place in the statutory scheme, historical evolution of the statute itself, and textual canons. With respect to the textual canons, the court applied the same eight canons repeatedly throughout the cases in which textual canons were used. The only additional tools used in more than three cases were rules of grammar (ten cases) and legislative history (nine cases), making the list of the eight types of tools described above the fairly complete universe of Oregon statutory interpretation principles. All but six of the opinions over the five-year period were unanimous.

"Moreover, all of the Oregon judges and justices agree that *PGE*'s application is mandatory. Even those Oregon judges who disagree with aspects of the framework, or the results dictated by it in particular cases, concede that they must use it. There are examples of cases in which legislative history likely would have dictated the opposite result, but the Oregon courts confined themselves to a different, text-based decision because of *PGE*. The framework survived the turnover of almost the entire state supreme court; only one justice who was on the court when *PGE* was decided remains. Litigants tailor their briefs to match the three-step regime. * * *

"While the idea of a single interpretive regime appears to have taken firm root in Oregon, what that regime should look like remains a live issue. In 2001, the Oregon legislature enacted a statute in direct response to *PGE*. The statute stated: 'A court may limit its consideration of legislative history to the information that the parties provide to the court. A court shall give the weight to the legislative history that the court considers to be appropriate.' Although on its face, the statute does not appear to contradict *PGE*, the legislative history (ironically) makes clear that the bill 'addresses the Oregon Supreme Court's three-level approach to statutory interpretation as announced in [*PGE*],' was enacted with the purpose of bringing legislative history into the first tier of analysis, and would 'allow a party to offer legislative history to the court to aid in its pursuit of the legislature's intent, regardless of whether the meaning of a statute is clear from its text and context.'

"For eight years, the Oregon Supreme Court refused to even acknowledge the possibility that the statute amended the *PGE* test. Instead, it ignored litigants' repeated requests that the supreme court apply it, and adhered to its three-step regime. As a result, the lower state courts consistently read the statute as in conflict with *PGE* and so refused to give the statute any effect. Every court to consider the issue—including the Ninth Circuit—assumed that *PGE* controlled and so refused to even consider legislative history in Oregon cases if the text was clear.

"All the more puzzling, then, is what happened next. In a case decided in April 2009, *Gaines v. State,* the Oregon Supreme Court unexpectedly requested briefing on the relevance of the statute. The ensuing decision—even as the opinion insists that *PGE* still governs—contains confusing language about when the court will now consider legislative history. The court held that *PGE*'s text-only first step remains the same but that the parties are free to 'proffer' legislative history, and that the court will consult it regardless of ambiguity, but only 'where that legislative history appears useful.' The court also held, however, that even clear contradictory evidence of purpose will not trump plain text. The opinion left many open questions, and it is too soon to predict its lasting effect, but one immediate effect is remarkable: fifteen of the sixteen Oregon Supreme Court cases that since have cited *Gaines* looked to legislative history—a dramatic turnaround from the near-disappearance of legislative history use in the state under *PGE*. * * *

"The *PGE* test might prove to be an enduring framework or only a sixteen-year experiment. But, either way, the Oregon Supreme Court's experience with it refutes the claim, made in the mainstream scholarship, that methodological consensus is impossible. What the court did was more than just articulate a preferred standard; it applied it in virtually all statutory cases. What's more, it appears to have applied it with a fair degree of consistency, creating a small and predictable universe of interpretive tools, producing very few intracourt fights about whether cases are to be decided at step one, two, or three, and giving rise to apparently not a single dissenting or concurring opinion claiming the court was manipulating its methodological framework to reach preferred results. Indeed, although *Gaines* may ultimately change what the controlling framework looks like, it will not change the more important development from a theoretical standpoint, namely, that the Oregon Supreme Court remains committed to having a single approach for all statutory questions and treats its methodological statements as binding precedents."

Professor Gluck examines the different experiments in **Texas**, where the Supreme Court has applied a strict plain meaning rule and excluded legislative history unless the statute is ambiguous (substantially ignoring a statute requiring consideration of legislative history and purpose in all cases); **Connecticut**, where the Supreme Court has rejected the plain meaning rule, see *State v. Courchesne,* 816 A.2d 562 (Ct. 2003), and has usually ignored a state statute seeking to re-impose the plain meaning rule; **Wisconsin**, where the Supreme Court has established a precedential regime centered around a plain meaning rule, see *Kalal v. Circuit Court,* 681 N.W.2d 110 (Wis. 2004), but one that continues to be challenged from time to time; and **Michigan**, a similar story as Wisconsin.

Quo Vadis, Textualism? Some Theoretical Notes

1. *A Modified Textualism.* Professor Gluck's article celebrates *PGE* as a "modified textualism" that has greater appeal and more hope to create a stable equilibrium than Justice Scalia's new textualism. Note three differences between Oregon's approach and Justice Scalia's approach:

(A) *Legislative History.* The Oregon model retains a role for legislative history, anathema to Justice Scalia. Indeed, the role is bigger than the Oregon

Supreme Court openly acknowledges. Any lawyer writing an appellate brief in Oregon must research legislative history and report anything that she believes is relevant and helpful to the case. (If counsel is 100% "certain" that the statute has a plain meaning, she might ignore it. But many a lawyer has been "certain" that one argument will prevail, thereby neglecting other arguments, and discovered with dismay that the judges did not agree. This kind of "certainty" may constitute "malpractice.") And if judges are reading the legislative history (via the appellate briefs), is it not apparent that any judgment about "plain meaning" is one that will consider the meaning legislators thought they were writing into the statute?

The news is even worse for the new textualism at the state level. In an unpublished paper, Yale law student Brian Barnes has empirically demonstrated that, at the state level, much more legislative history is publicly available now than ten years ago (and more was available ten years ago than twenty years ago), and much is available online. The greater *accessibility* of legislative history drives more briefing of legislative history by lawyers and, ultimately, greater judicial reliance on legislative history. See Brian Barnes, *The Transformation of State Statutory Interpretation* (Yale Law School, Seminar Paper, May 10, 2010). Barnes's analysis suggests that the big development in state statutory interpretation is neither textualism nor *stare decisis*, but rather the steadily increasing availability and judicial deployment of legislative history.

(B) *Substantive Canons of Statutory Construction.* The *PGE* approach preserves a potentially important role for substantive canons of statutory construction. Although Professor Gluck notes that the Oregon Supreme Court has excluded the presumption against absurd results from Step 1, it may be available at Step 3. Perhaps, after *Gaines*, this substantive canon might gravitate upwards in the Court's list. Step 3 surely includes the major substantive canons—including the notions of interpreting statutes to carry out their purposes, to avoid constitutional problems, and to impose criminal liability only where the legislature has clearly targeted the defendant's conduct.

(C) *Liberal Textualism.* It is hard for us to imagine that Justice Scalia would have gone along with the Oregon Supreme Court in *PGE,* largely because the result is so pro-union and imposes new costs upon employers. Justice Scalia could dissent by invoking textualist premises. The collective bargaining agreement says an employee *cannot* take *paid* sick leave unless she/he is actually sick; ORS 659.360(6) says that parental leave need *not* be *paid* unless the collective bargaining (or some other) agreement provides for it; ORS 659.360(3) says *nothing* about whether sick leave invoked by the employee for use as parental leave must be *paid* (the sick or other compensatory leave can be either "paid" or "unpaid"). Yet the Oregon Supreme Court says that ORS 659.360(3) requires the employer to pay for most of the parental leave under the aegis of accrued sick leave, even though the collective bargaining agreement says this does not qualify as paid leave. The state parental leave statute is transformed from one where the state guarantees 12 weeks of *unpaid* leave into a statute where the state guarantees 12 weeks of largely *paid* leave. Can the language of the first sentence of ORS 659.360(3) carry the weight of this transformation? Has the Oregon Supreme Court sacrificed judicial neutrality through this exercise in dynamic textualism?

2. *No Frills Textualism.* At *PGE* Step 1, the Oregon Supreme Court says that judges should look at the structure of the statute as well as its plain meaning; when the statute is ambiguous, judges are supposed to consult legislative history (Step 2) and substantive canons (Step 3). Justice Scalia's new textualism would eliminate Step 2. His former law clerk, Professor Adrian Vermeule, argues for a much more parsimonious textualism in *Judging Under Uncertainty* (2006). Professor Vermeule's normative baseline is an institutional cost-benefit calculus: *ex ante*, what method of statutory interpretation will minimize institutional costs, especially errors? His judgment is that judges applying the traditional, multi-factored approach make a lot of mistakes and impose huge research costs on lawyers and their clients.

In his view, institutional costs would be lower—for both judges and for parties—if the Supreme Court trimmed away the least useful sources of statutory meaning, not only legislative history, but also arguments from statutory structure. Fewer mistakes would be made if courts deferred to agencies that understand the statute and can fill in legal gaps with expert judgments. Hence, what we have dubbed a *no frills textualism,* Professor Vermeule's approach would exclude "related statutes" from statutory meaning and would consider only the "directly dispositive clauses or provisions at hand," apparently excluding most whole act analysis. Although resort to linguistic canons and some substantive canons is, concededly, inevitable (page 200), Professor Vermeule says that agencies, not courts, should pick the canonical default rules in a systematic way before the case arises (page 201).

How would Professor Vermeule's theory apply to *PGE*? What provisions in the labor statute would be the "directly dispositive clauses or provisions at hand"? How should the interpreter view them? If there were ambiguity (is there?), Professor Vermeule would say that BOLI (the agency litigant) should identify the canons that should govern. Assume that BOLI identified as an important canon the notion that statutes should be interpreted to carry out their liberal, pro-employee purposes. (This is quite plausible given BOLI's decision in *PGE*.) Should BOLI be able to bootstrap its pro-employee stance in this way—and make it binding on courts? Does its application to *PGE* suggest that Professor Vermeule's theory would be easy to apply?

3. *Funnel of Abstraction Textualism.* Another kind of textualist theory is the Eskridge and Frickey "Funnel of Abstraction." The Funnel is a textualist theory, because it not only starts with the statutory text (including the statutory structure) but considers text the weightiest factor: when it is clear, the text trumps legislative history, statutory purpose, and agency interpretations. The Funnel is a softer textualist theory, however: Professors Eskridge and Frickey never stop with the text and urge interpreters to consult other sources to make sure the text is really as "clear" as they view it on first impression *and* invite judges to adjust relatively clear texts when legislative history, statutory purpose, and public norms press strongly in the other direction.

How would a judge applying the Funnel of Abstraction decide *PGE*? (To answer this question, you must examine the Oregon Court of Appeals decision as well as the Oregon Supreme Court decision in *PGE*.) By the way, Professors Eskridge and Frickey believe that the *PGE* three-tiered approach is a simpler version of the Funnel. The main articulated difference is that the *PGE* Mini–Funnel requires "ambiguity" for the interpreter to travel up the Funnel—but Eskridge and Frickey observe that any judicial judgment about plain meaning (Step 1 of *PGE*) would be made *only* after the judge has read what the briefs have to say about drafting history, legislative history and purpose, and applicable canons, and so the Funnel factors sneak into the judge's deliberation. The Oregon Supreme Court has, in *Gaines*, opened the door for this more openly. So should state courts adopt the Funnel? Would that serve the *stare decisis* interests that Professor Gluck celebrates?

A TRANSITIONAL NOTE

The foregoing historical and theoretical introduction to statutory interpretation can, we admit, be a bit overwhelming. Between the various theories and the strong critiques that can be lodged against each of them, keeping track of everything can be difficult, and finding one's own moorings about which approach to prefer can be daunting indeed. We offer this discussion to review what we have seen and to provide a transition to the remaining, largely doctrinal, chapters in the book.

When we think of a legal theory, we often suppose a rule or method that one follows to deduce the answer to a question. In this chapter, we examined three such deductive theories. Textualism, or plain meaning, posits that the court's role is to give the statutory text its plain or best meaning. Intentionalism posits that the court's role is to give the statute the meaning most consistent with the intentions of the enacting legislature. Purposivism (admittedly, an awkward term) posits that the court's role is to attribute to the statute the meaning most consistent with the general reasons why the enacting legislature believed the statute should be adopted. Another way to articulate purposivism is to recall the "mischief approach" of *Heydon's Case, supra*, under which the court first identifies the mischief in the prior law that the legislature wished to remedy and then interprets the statute to promote that remedial purpose. Much of the history of American statutory interpretation has involved the elaboration of the fine points of these theories (e.g., the old "plain meaning" approach versus the new textualism) and the competition among them for the hearts and opinions of judges.

Recently, several commentators have proposed less deductive methods of attributing meaning to statutes. These approaches, sometimes labeled "dynamic interpretation" or "practical reasoning," are inspired by hermeneutics, the study of interpretation in general. They all see statutory interpretation as essentially a practical, rather than primarily a theoretical or deductive, inquiry. On this understanding, the interpreter's task is to mediate the important factors in a statutory case—statutory text, the original context in which the statute was adopted, and the context in which the interpreters currently find themselves—rather than privilege one or more of these factors to the exclusion of the remainder. As this chapter indicates, your casebook authors fall into this last camp. Nonetheless, we do not agree among ourselves on all matters of statutory interpretation, and we hope that you will feel free to disagree with us in any or all respects.

In assessing the utility of the theories introduced in this chapter, we suggest three approaches.

1. Begin by engaging in empirical analysis. Which theory best describes the way American judges actually interpret statutes? We realize that this is an impossible question to answer completely, in part because you have not seen anything approaching the whole universe of American case law interpreting statutes. It may be possible at this point, however, to answer a subsidiary question: Based on the cases in this chapter, does any one theory capture the universal judicial practice? If, based on the cases we have read, it seems doubtful that a working majority on the current Supreme Court follows any one theory religiously, does that suggest that attorneys will find it impossible to advise clients about the probabilities in a hard statutory case (that is, one where the theories would produce different answers)? Or will the attorney skilled in statutory analysis (that is, you, once you complete this course and eventually graduate from law school) have the capacity to provide appropriate advice and to write strong briefs on either side of a hard statutory case? Recall, again, the revealing comparisons that can be made between *Chisom* and *Casey* (review note 3 following those cases).

As the Eskridge and Frickey article on statutory interpretation as practical reasoning indicates, although we are not deductive theorists about statutory interpretation, we do believe theoretical inquiry is important in a statutory case. In our judgment, the hard cases are those in which the plausible competing theories conflict, and one role of theory (whether solely deductive or otherwise) is to develop a defensible, replicable model for resolving these conflicts. In this respect, some would say that even we are too theoretical. Some scholars, from the legal realists onward, have argued that judicial *decisionmaking*, as opposed to opinion writing, is barely theoretical at all.[w] We concede that judges reach decisions for a variety of reasons, and that

---

w. Robert Martineau, *Craft and Technique, Not Canons and Grand Theories: A Neo–Realist View of Statutory Interpretation*, 62 Geo. Wash. L. Rev. 1, 26 (1993):

There are several key elements to the appellate process that the statutory interpretation scholar should keep in mind. First, the positions that the parties take in their arguments to a court are purely result-oriented. Their lawyers make the arguments, textual or contextual, that support their position. Second, the judges' primary concern prior to the decision conference is understanding the facts and contentions of the parties. Third, the decision conference is devoted primarily to result, not to the approach to be taken in the opinion. Fourth, the law clerk, often the person with the principal responsibility for drafting an opinion to support the decision, is not present at the decision conference. The judge assigned the opinion-writing responsibility directs the law clerk concerning the result and may instruct the clerk about the approach to be taken in the draft opinion. Finally, the other judges on the panel play some part, but not a major role, in the opinion's development.

* * * [An appellate] opinion would justify the development of canons and grand theories of statutory construction if it either reflected the thought processes by which the judges reached the decision or was argued in the document submitted to the judges that persuaded them to decide the case in the way they did. In fact, the opinion is neither. It is, rather, a reasoned justification of the decision prepared after the decision is made. The principal purpose of the opinion is to make the decision appear consistent with the facts and the relevant statutory and judicial authority.

On whether theories and scholarship concerning statutory interpretation have affected judicial practice, see Gregory S. Crespi, *The Influence of a Decade of Statutory Interpretation Scholarship on Judicial Rulings: An Empirical Analysis*, 53 SMU L. Rev. 9 (2000) (identifying an explosion in pristine legal theory is not a high priority for many of them. We do reject the view, however, that theory makes no difference. Our view, expressed in the manner in which we have organized these materials, is that learning the craft of lawyering requires, among other things, the capacity to construct theoretical arguments persuasively within a given context. See Richard A. Posner, *The Problems of Jurisprudence* 100 (1990).

In concluding your empirical inquiry, consider whether context may affect the utility of a theory. For example, although none of us is a Scalia-type new textualist, as appellate judges we would give especially strong primacy to statutory text in some cases. Illustratively, the bankruptcy code is mammoth and complex, and none of us is much familiar with its complicated subject matter of secured financing, commercial transactions, and the like. To be sure, we might engage in flexible approaches to interpretation in uncomplicated bankruptcy cases involving obvious issues of justice, such as *Shine v. Shine.* In the complicated corporate bankruptcy case, however, we might pretty much stick with the statutory text, especially where no drafting error is apparent and policy arguments do not cut conclusively in either direction. We also might tend to defer to an interpreter with more expertise than ourselves, such as the specialized federal bankruptcy judges. Only after gaining greater familiarity and confidence with the bankruptcy code and the policy issues associated with it might we become more venturesome interpreters.[x]

2. Next, engage in normative analysis. What approach to statutory interpretation strikes you as the most attractive for the American legal system? Work hard to identify those values that lead you to this conclusion. What values ought to be important: Rule of law? Regularized decisionmaking by the institutions most competent to make each kind of decision? The best rule? If the last, what is the criterion for "best"? Efficiency? A conception of justice? (Whose—Rawls? Nozick?) Are all these values relevant? If so, how do you balance them?

In making your normative assessment, note that you do not escape empirical claims. For example, if textualism strikes you as the best approach because it is good to limit judicial discretion (a normative conclusion), you must assess criticisms of your conclusion from both empirical perspectives (e.g., textualism will not, in fact, operate to limit judicial discretion) and normative ones (e.g., handcuffing judges from reaching obviously just and right results in individual cases is wrong).

---

such scholarship over the past decade and increasing citation of several of these articles by judges, but speculating that the citations are included more to add academic flourish than to reflect influence upon actual decisionmaking); Daniel A. Farber, *Do Theories of Statutory Interpretation Matter? A Case Study*, 94 Nw. U. L. Rev. 1409 (2000) (finding only rare differences in outcome between Judges Posner and Easterbrook despite their differences in interpretive approach).

x. See generally Daniel J. Bussel, *Textualism's Failures: A Study of Overruled Bankruptcy Decisions*, 53 Vand. L. Rev. 887 (2000); Robert K. Rasmussen, *A Study of the Costs and Benefits of Textualism: The Supreme Court's Bankruptcy Cases*, 71 Wash. U. L.Q. 535 (1993). For the argument that statutes generally involve at least three interpretive communities (the policy community of specialists in government bureaucracies, the political community of elected officials, and the public) and that pragmatic interpreters should design their interpretive methodology in light of which community is the primary audience for the decision at hand, see William S. Blatt, *Interpretive Communities: The Missing Element in Statutory Interpretation*, 95 Nw. U. L. Rev. 629 (2001).

3. Finally, engage in doctrinal analysis. There is really no way to assess the utility of any approach to statutory interpretation without knowing the details of American legal doctrine. For example, textualism posits that legislative history should hardly ever be examined in the interpretive process. Is that consistent with the case law? Textualism—at least as articulated by Justice Scalia in his *Chisom* dissent—also posits that "established canons of statutory interpretation" should have a strong role in guiding the meaning of statutory text. What are these canons, and, in particular, how does one distinguish an "established" one from a mere pretender? Are the legal rules or presumptions found in the canons empirically supportable? Normatively attractive? Similar "micro-level" inquiries will enrich your perspectives on the other theories as well. Last, but hardly least important, it will be your knowledge of and capacity to use these doctrinal details that will determine much about your success as an attorney, at least if you (as do most attorneys) end up practicing in an area in which statutes and administrative regulations provide much of the law. It is to these doctrines that we turn in the next several chapters.

CHAPTER 3

CANONS OF STATUTORY INTERPRETATION

■ ■ ■

The previous chapter introduced you to the history of statutory interpretation in the United States and to the major theories that have been debated (textualism old and new, intentionalism and imaginative reconstruction, purposivism and dynamic theories). This chapter turns to the doctrines that underlie these theories. Specifically, we consider the accepted and evolving *canons of statutory construction*. The canons have been the bedrock of Anglo–American interpretation for centuries. Although they were de-emphasized in federal courts after the New Deal, the canons remained critically important at the state level and have made a federal comeback since the mid–1980s.

There are a good many rules of thumb for interpreting statutes. Called "maxims," "canons," or "principles" of construction, these rules are said to enable interpreters to draw inferences from the language, format, and subject matter of the statute. Most of the nineteenth century English and American treatises on statutory interpretation were organized around the canons, and the leading doctrinal compilation today (a descendant of an 1891 treatise) is an exhaustive canon-by-canon tour. Sutherland, *Statutes and Statutory Construction* (Norman J. Singer and J.D. Shambie Singer eds., 7th ed., 2007–2012) (hereinafter referred to as Sutherland).[a] State legislatures have codified the traditional canons in their state codes. E.g., Minn. Stat. ch. 645; Pennsylvania Statutory Construction Act, 1 Pa. Consol. Stat. §§ 1921–1928 (hereinafter "Pa. Stat. Constr. Act"). See also 1 U.S.C. §§ 1–7 (codification of word-meaning canons); Jacob Scott, *Codified Canons and the Common Law of Interpretation*, 98 Geo. L.J. 341 (2010) (systematic collection of legislatively codified canons in all 50 states and the District of Columbia).

---

a. Sutherland is the leading American treatise. Other valuable reference works include treatises in the United Kingdom, see P. St. J. Langan, *Maxwell on the Interpretation of Statutes* (12th ed. 1969) (reprinted 2010), and F.A.R. Bennion, *Bennion on Statutory Interpretation* (5th ed. 2008); Canada, see Ruth Sullivan, *Sullivan on the Construction of Statutes* (5th ed. 2008); Ruth Sullivan, *Statutory Interpretation* (2d ed. 2007); Australia, see Donald Gifford, *Statutory Interpretation* (1990), and D.C. Pearce & R.S. Geddes, *Statutory Interpretation in Australia* (4th ed. 1996); and South Africa, see G.E. Devenish, *Interpretation of Statutes* (1992). For a compendium surveying the practice in civil law countries as well, see *Interpreting Statutes: A Comparative Study* (D. Neil MacCormick & Robert S. Summers eds., 1991).

There are basically three kinds of canons. First are the *textual canons*, which set forth inferences that are usually drawn from the drafter's choice of words, their grammatical placement in sentences, and their relationship to other parts of the statute. These are sometimes called *intrinsic aids*, for they assist the statutory interpreter in deriving probable meaning from the four corners of the statutory text. Section 1 of this chapter sets forth many of these textual canons, with illustrations from state and federal cases.

A second genre consists of the *substantive canons*. These are presumptions about statutory meaning based upon substantive principles or policies drawn from the common law, other statutes, or the Constitution. An example is the "rule of lenity," which, based in part upon principles of fair notice, presumes that criminal statutes do not outlaw behavior unless the activity clearly comes within the sweep of the statutes. The substantive canons are explored in Section 2. (Chapter 4 will focus on the third group of maxims, the *reference canons*. These are sometimes called *extrinsic aids*. They are presumptive rules telling the interpreter what other materials— the common law, other statutes, legislative history, as well as agency interpretations—might be consulted to figure out what the statute means.)

Section 3 examines the theoretical debates over the textual and substantive canons and provides several practical problems with their usage. We start with the very practical problems raised by our version of the "vehicles in the park" statute.

PROBLEM 3–1

The No Vehicles in the Park Statute and Its Application

In the wake of an accident in which a motorcycle speeding through Pierre Trudeau Park ran over and killed an elderly gentleman, the City Council enacted the following statute in 1980:

Sec. 1.   The Council finds that vehicles create safety problems when they are operated in parks and further finds that the best solution is to ban any and all vehicles from all municipal parks.

Sec. 2.   No vehicles of any kind shall be allowed in any municipal park. Any person who brings or drives a vehicle into one of these parks shall be guilty of a misdemeanor, which may be punished by a fine not exceeding $500 or by a two-day incarceration in the municipal jail, or both.

Sec. 3.   "Vehicle" for purposes of this law means any mechanism for conveying a person from one place to another, including automobiles, trucks, motorcycles, and motor scooters. *Provided that*, bicycles shall be allowed in the park, so long as they are being pushed or carried and not ridden.

After a decade of spotty enforcement, a new constable adopts a strict, no-tolerance enforcement policy. In 1996, he arrests (a) a 13–year–old boy riding a skateboard through the park; (b) a mother pushing a baby carriage in the park; and (c) a 6–year–old girl riding her tricycle in the park. All three "perps" (and the parents of the child perps) challenge their arrests, on the ground that the statute does not apply to their conduct. How should the City Magistrate rule?

SECTION 1. TEXTUAL CANONS

The starting point of statutory interpretation is to *read* the statute carefully. A number of rules—based either on general notions of English composition or syntax or the structure of a statute—have been stated as guides for finding meaning from the words of the statute and nothing else. These are called "intrinsic aids" or "textual canons" of interpretation. They are normally invoked by courts as conventional benchmarks for figuring out whether a statute has a *plain meaning* or not. Some judicial rhetoric to the contrary, text-based canons are decidedly not hard-and-fast rules; they are at best presumptions and might be considered most like adages. See Lawrence M. Solan, *The Language of Judges* ch. 2 (1993) (linguistic analysis of several textual canons), as well as Solan, *The Language of Statutes* (2010). See also D. Neil MacCormick, *Argumentation and Interpretation in Law*, 6 Ratio Juris 16 (1993) (discussing linguistic arguments as a category of interpretive argument).

A. MAXIMS OF WORD MEANING AND ASSOCIATION

1. Ordinary Versus Technical Meaning of Words

Typically, courts will assume that the legislature uses words in their ordinary sense: What would these words convey to the "ordinary" or "reasonable" reader? To figure this out, judges may consult dictionaries,[b] but they will often just rely on their own linguistic experience or intuition to decide the most reasonable meaning of the words, given the context in which they are being used and applied. Ordinary meaning should be distinguished from literal meaning or strict construction; the latter connotes a narrow understanding of words used, while the former connotes the everyday understanding. Ordinary meaning should also be distinguished from plain meaning, which is the legal meaning a statute has in light of the provision's ordinary meaning, the statutory purpose and structure, and any specialized meaning the term has acquired over the years. See generally Miranda Oshige McGowan, *Do as I Do, Not as I Say: An Empirical Investigation of Justice Scalia's Ordinary Meaning Method of Statutory Interpretation*, 78 Miss. L.J. 129 (2008).

---

b. See Ellen S. Aprill, *The Law of the Word: Dictionary Shopping in the Supreme Court*, 30 Ariz. St. L.J. 275 (1998); Clark D. Cunningham et al., *Plain Meaning and Hard Cases*, 103 Yale L.J. 1561 (1994); Lawrence M. Solan, *When Judges Use the Dictionary*, 68 Am. Speech 50 (1993); Samuel A. Thumma & Jeffrey L. Kirchmeier, *The Lexicon Has Become a Fortress: The United States Supreme Court's Use of Dictionaries*, 47 Buff. L. Rev. 227 (1999); Note, *Looking It Up: Dictionaries and Statutory Interpretation*, 107 Harv. L. Rev. 1437 (1994); Rickie Sonpal, Note, *Old Dictionaries and New Textualists*, 71 Fordham L. Rev. 2177 (2003).

Linguists suggest that the interpreter start with the *prototypical* meaning of statutory words.[c] What is the core idea associated with a word or phrase? For example, this was the approach implicitly followed by Justice Brennan in *Weber*, the affirmative action case (Chapter 1, § 3). Although some dictionaries define "discriminate" broadly enough to include any kind of differentiation, the core or prototypical use of the word requires some invidious intent. Thus, we do not say we "discriminate" against pears if we prefer peaches, nor (according to Brennan) do we say we "discriminate" against a minority if we give him a helping hand to counterbalance what we believe is an inferior starting point because of preexisting prejudice or stereotyping. Ordinary meaning, therefore, might be associated with prototypical meaning. This idea usually supports cautious, or restrictive, readings of statutes. See, e.g., *Holy Trinity Church* (Chapter 2, § 1) (confining "labor or service of any kind" to manual work); *Canada (Attorney General) v. Mossop*, [1991] 1 F.C. 18, 34 (Fed. Ct.), aff'd, [1993] 1 S.C.R. 554 (Can. Sup. Ct.) (applying the "core meaning" of "family" to exclude same-sex partnerships).

What if the statute is an old one? In that event, judges sometimes consult dictionaries and other evidence from the era in which the statute was enacted. For example, the Supreme Court in *St. Francis College v. Al–Khazraji*, 481 U.S. 604 (1987), interpreted the Civil Rights Act of 1866 to apply to discrimination against a person of Arab ancestry. Defendant had argued that any discrimination against an ethnic Arab was not actionable, because the statute only required the same protections as are "enjoyed by white citizens" and Arabs are ethnographically Caucasian. The Court invoked nineteenth-century dictionaries and encyclopedias to demonstrate that defendant's conception of race was not the one held in the nineteenth century, which viewed different ethnic "stock" and family "lineage" as different "races." Thus, these sources referred to Finns, Greeks, Basques, Arabs, Norwegians, Jews, and Hungarians as identifiable "races." For another example, see *Cook County v. United States*, 538 U.S. 119, 132 (2003), interpreting the False Claims Act of 1863.

In addition to special meanings that words may have had historically, words often have meanings limited to parlance in a trade, academic discipline, or technical area. Where the statute itself deals with a technical, specialized subject, courts tend to adopt the specialized meaning of words used in the statute, unless that leads to an absurd result. For a hoary, and perhaps amusing, example of this maxim, see *Nix v. Hedden*, 149 U.S. 304, 305–07 (1893):

> This was an action, brought February 4, 1887, against the collector of the port of New York, to recover back duties, paid under protest, on tomatoes imported by the plaintiff from the West Indies in the spring of 1886, which the collector assessed under "Schedule G.—Provi-

---

c. See Lawrence M. Solan, *Learning Our Limits: The Decline of Textualism in Statutory Cases*, 1997 Wis. L. Rev. 235, 270–75 (explaining linguists' "prototype" theory and applying it to several statutory interpretation cases). See also Solan, *The Language of Statutes* (2011) (revised and updated version of the earlier article).

sions," of the Tariff Act of March 3, 1883, chap. 121, imposing a duty on "Vegetables in their natural state, or in salt or brine, not specially enumerated or provided for in this Act, ten per centum *ad valorem*"; and which the plaintiffs contended came within the clause in the free list of the same act. "Fruits, green, ripe or dried, not specially enumerated or provided for in this act." 22 Stat. 504, 519.

At the trial, the plaintiff's counsel, after reading in evidence definitions of the words "fruit" and "vegetables" from Webster's Dictionary, Worchester's Dictionary and the Imperial Dictionary, called two witnesses, who had been for thirty years in the business of selling fruit and vegetables, and asked them, after hearing these definitions, to say whether these words had "any special meaning in trade or commerce, different from those read."

One of the witnesses answered as follows: "Well, it does not classify all things there, but they are correct as far as they go. It does not take all kinds of fruit or vegetables; it takes a portion of them. I think the words 'fruit' and 'vegetable' have the same meaning in trade today that they had on March 1, 1883. I understand that the term 'fruit' is applied in trade only to such plants or parts of plants as contain the seeds. There are more vegetables than those in the enumeration given in Webster's Dictionary under the term 'vegetable,' as 'cabbage, cauliflower, turnips, potatoes, peas, beans, and the like,' probably covered by the words 'and the like.' "

The other witnesses testified: "I don't think the term 'fruit' or the term 'vegetables' had in March 1883, and prior thereto, any special meaning in trade and commerce in this country, different from that which I have read here from the dictionaries."

The plaintiff's counsel then read in evidence from the same dictionaries the definitions of the word "tomato."

The defendant's counsel then read in evidence from Webster's dictionary the definitions of the words "pea," "egg plant," "cucumber," "squash," and "pepper."

The plaintiff then read in evidence from Webster's and Worcester's dictionaries the definitions of "potato," "turnip," "parsnip," "cauliflower," "cabbage," "carrot," and "bean."

No other evidence was offered by either party. The court, upon the defendant's motion, directed a verdict for him, which was returned, and judgment rendered therein. The plaintiffs duly excepted to the instruction, and sued out this writ of error. * * *

There being no evidence that the words "fruit" and "vegetables" have acquired any special meaning in trade or commerce, they must receive their ordinary meaning. Of that meaning the court is bound to take judicial notice, as it does in regard to all words in our own tongue; and upon such a question dictionaries are admitted, not as evidence, but only as aids to the memory and understanding of the court.

Botanically speaking, tomatoes are the fruit of a vine, just as are cucumbers, squashes, beans and peas. But in the common language of the people, whether sellers or consumers of provisions, all these are vegetables, which are grown in kitchen gardens, and which, whether eaten cooked or raw, are, like potatoes, carrots, parsnips, turnips, beets, cauliflower, cabbage, celery and lettuce, usually served at dinner in, with, or after the soup, fish or meats which constitute the principal part of the repast, and not, like fruits generally, as dessert.

The attempt to class tomatoes as fruit is not unlike a recent attempt to class beans as seeds, of which Mr. Justice Bradley, speaking for this court, said: "We do not see why they should be classified as seeds, any more than walnuts should be so classified. Both are seeds in the language of botany or natural history, but not in commerce nor in common parlance. On the other hand, in speaking generally of provisions, beans may well be included under the term 'vegetables.' As an article of food on our tables, whether baked or boiled, or forming the basis of soup, they are used as a vegetable, as well as when ripe as when green. This is the principal use to which they are put. Beyond the common knowledge which we have on this subject, very little evidence is necessary, or can be produced." *Robertson v. Salomon*, 130 U.S. 412, 414 (1889).

See also *Zuni Pub. Sch. Dist. v. Department of Educ.*, 550 U.S. 81, 88 (2007), deferring to the experts when construing technical statutory language for determining whether a state aid program "equalizes expenditures."

A fundamental maxim is this: "Where Congress uses terms that have accumulated settled meaning under either equity or the common law, a court must infer, unless the statute otherwise dictates, that Congress means to incorporate the established meaning of these terms." *NLRB v. Amax Coal Co.*, 453 U.S. 322, 329 (1981); accord, *Scheidler v. NOW*, 537 U.S. 393, 402 (2003); *United States v. Wells*, 519 U.S. 482, 491 (1997); *Morissette v. United States*, 342 U.S. 246, 250 (1952) (leading case). Compare *Jodrey Estate v. Nova Scotia*, [1980] 2 S.C.R. 774 (Can. Sup. Ct.) (reflecting the Canadian preference for following ordinary rather than technical meanings). If the technical term originates outside the legal domain, American courts start with the presumption that "where Congress has used technical words or terms of art, it (is) proper to explain them by reference to the art or science to which they (are) appropriate." *Corning Glass Works v. Brennan*, 417 U.S. 188, 201 (1974).

An illustrative case is *Buckhannon Bd. & Care Home, Inc. v. West Virginia Dep't of Health and Human Res.*, 532 U.S. 598 (2001). Buckhannon operated an assisted living residential home for seniors in West Virginia. In 1996, state officials issued orders requiring Buckhannon to cease operating and to relocate its residents because some of the residents could not reach fire exits unassisted, in violation of state "self-preserva-tion" regulations. Buckhannon then commenced a lawsuit against the state agency, arguing that the regulations ran counter to the federal Fair Housing Amendments Act (FHAA) and the Americans with Disabilities Act (ADA). Within a month after Buckhannon survived the agency's motion for summary judgment, the West Virginia legislature repealed the state "self-preservation" regulations. The defendant agency successfully moved to dismiss the case as moot, and Buckhannon sought an award of attorney's fees as the "prevailing party" under both the FHAA and ADA. Invoking the *Morissette* rule, a divided Court ruled that "prevailing party" was a legal term of art, which according to *Black's Law Dictionary* (apparently the go-to source for terms of art) did not include parties that did not secure formal victories in litigation.

Four dissenting Justices assailed the majority's result. Because Buck-hannon had been successful in forcing the state to abandon its self-preservation regulations, he was "prevailing" in ordinary parlance. The legislative history for the fee awards law explicitly and repeatedly noted that prevailing party included parties who won what they were suing for, even if they were not awarded the relief in a formal court order. Indeed, all twelve of the courts of appeals had ruled, before 1994, that prevailing party included litigants like Buckhannon. (After the Supreme Court sent contrary signals, some of the courts of appeals shifted their views, but most stuck with the earlier consensus.)

2. Noscitur a Sociis and Ejusdem Generis

Words are social creatures: they travel in packs. Several canons suggest permissible inferences from the company that words keep. *"Nosci-tur a sociis"* translates as "[i]t is known from its associates." Light may be shed on the meaning of an ambiguous word by reference to words associated with it. "Thus, when two or more words are grouped together, and ordinarily have a similar meaning, but are not equally comprehensive, the general word will be limited and qualified by the special word." 2A Sutherland § 47.16; see P. St. J. Langan, *Maxwell on the Interpretation of Statutes* 289–93 (12th ed. 1969) (reprinted 2010) (hereinafter cited as Maxwell). For example, in *Jarecki v. G. D. Searle & Co.*, 367 U.S. 303 (1961), a federal income tax statute allowed allocation to other years of income "resulting from exploration, discovery, or prospecting." A drug manufacturer and a camera manufacturer argued that they should be allowed to take advantage of the allocation statute with respect to income from the sale of patented products because by definition such a product resulted from a "discovery." The Court disagreed. When interpreted in light of the associated words "exploration" and "prospecting," the term "discovery" meant only the discovery of mineral resources. See also *Gutierrez v. Ada*, 528 U.S. 250 (2000) (repeated statutory iteration of "any election" in connection with Governor and Lieutenant Governor suggests that the context is limited to those two elections only).

"*Ejusdem generis,*" a sibling of *noscitur a sociis*, translates as "[o]f the same kind, class, or nature." "Where general words follow specific words in a statutory enumeration, the general words are construed to embrace only objects similar in nature to those objects enumerated by the preceding specific words. Where the opposite sequence is found, i.e., specific words following general ones, the doctrine is equally applicable, and restricts application of the general term to things that are similar to those enumerated." 2A Sutherland § 47.17. The purpose of this rule is to give effect to all the words—the particular words indicate the class and the general words extend the provisions of the statute to everything else in the class (even though not enumerated by the specific words). See also *AT & T v. Iowa Util. Bd.*, 525 U.S. 366, 408 (1999) (Thomas, J., dissenting in part); *Norfolk & Western Ry. Co. v. American Train Dispatchers Ass'n*, 499 U.S. 117, 129 (1991).

An example of the application of this canon is *Heathman v. Giles*, 374 P.2d 839 (Utah 1962). In that case, plaintiff brought an action for false arrest, malicious prosecution, and other torts against a prosecutor and deputy prosecutors. The trial court had dismissed the action because the plaintiff had failed to file a bond for the payment of any costs and attorneys' fees that might be awarded to defendants. The trial court relied upon a statute that required such a bond in actions brought against "any sheriff, constable, peace officer, state road officer, or any other person charged with the duty of enforcement of the criminal laws of this state * * * when such action arises out of, or in the course of the performance of his duty." The Supreme Court of Utah reversed, holding that the defendants were not "other persons charged with the duty of enforcement of the criminal laws" for purposes of this statute. The "other person" language, the court concluded, must be limited to persons of the "same class as those expressly mentioned." The court noted that the specified officers identified (*id.* at 840):

> are all badge-carrying officers * * * in the front line of law enforcement * * * who are charged with the duty of seeking out persons suspected of crime; and of making arrests and taking them into custody. In the nature of their duties they often must accost persons who are unknown to them; and sometimes those who may be dangerous characters. They are therefore required to take various risks, including that of being mistaken. It seems so plain that it is unnecessary to dwell on the matter that defendants as prosecuting attorneys, although "charged with the duty of enforcement of criminal laws," are officers of such a significantly different character that they are not within the class for whom the protections of this statute was intended. * * *

See also *Hodgerney v. Baker*, 88 N.E.2d 625 (Mass. 1949) (automobile not covered by ordinance forbidding the placing of "dirt, rubbish, wood, timber, or other material of any kind" tending to obstruct the streets).

Section 1 of the Federal Arbitration Act of 1926 excludes from coverage "contracts of employment of seamen, railroad employees, or any other class of workers engaged in foreign or interstate commerce." 9 U.S.C. § 1. The issue in *Circuit City Stores, Inc. v. Adams*, 532 U.S. 105 (2001), was whether the exclusion was limited to contracts involving *transportation* but not other kinds of employment contracts. Workers suing their employers generally want a court, not an arbitrator, especially for discrimination claims such as those in *Circuit City*. So the plaintiff argued that his job at a retail store, obviously engaged in "interstate commerce," fell within the exclusion: Congress, he argued, meant to exclude employment contracts generally, and used language tied to the jurisdictional basis of the FAA, the Commerce Clause. The Supreme Court rejected that reading, on the ground that *ejusdem generis* suggested that Congress meant the exclusion to be limited to contracts "like" those involving seamen and railroad workers—namely, transportation contracts.

Noscitur a sociis and *ejusdem generis*, like the other canons, are just aids to meaning, not ironclad rules. Thus, they have no value if the statute evidences a meaning contrary to their presumptions. See *United States v. Turkette*, 452 U.S. 576, 581 (1981). Dissenting in *Circuit City*, Justice Souter argued that the legislative purpose and specific history rebutted any presumption created by *ejusdem generis*. Both labor unions petitioning Congress for an exemption and Secretary of Commerce Herbert Hoover, the primary architect of the law, endorsed the broader view of the exclusion. (The Court found the statute sufficiently clear and rejected this evidence.)

Deployment of *ejusdem generis* involves a judgment—often a debatable one—about what it is that makes the items in the series "similar." The *Circuit City* Court found that the common denominator was "transportation contracts," while the dissenters found it to be "employment contracts within Congress's Commerce Clause power." For another example of such a debatable judgment, compare Justice Alito's opinion for the Court in *James v. United States*, 550 U.S. 192, 198–99 (2007) (holding that "attempted burglary" is a crime that "otherwise involves conduct that presents a serious risk of physical injury to another"), with Justice Scalia's dissenting characterization, *id.* at 215–16. See 2A Sutherland § 47.17–.22 (discussing *ejusdem generis* and qualifications to its use); Maxwell 303–06 (similar).

3. Expressio Unius

Words omitted may be just as significant as words set forth. The maxim "*expressio* [or *inclusio*] *unius est exclusio alterius*" means "expression [or inclusion] of one thing indicates exclusion of the other." The notion is one of negative implication: the enumeration of certain things in a statute suggests that the legislature had no intent of including things not listed or embraced. "When a statute limits a thing to be done in a particular mode, it includes a negative of any other mode." *Raleigh & Galston R.R. Co. v. Reid*, 80 U.S. 269 ,13 Wall. 269, 270 (1872); see *Tate v.*

Ogg, 195 S.E. 496 (Va. 1938) (statute covering "any horse, mule, cattle, hog, sheep or goat" did not cover turkeys); Sutherland § 47.25 (discussing the limitations of the canon); Maxwell 293–97 (similar).

As *Holy Trinity Church* (Chapter 2, § 1) illustrates, courts feel free to refuse to apply the maxim when they believe it would lead to a result Congress did not intend.[d] One basic problem is that this canon, like many of the others, assumes that the legislature thinks through statutory language carefully, considering every possible variation. This is clearly not true, for the legislature often omits things because no one thinks about them or everyone assumes that courts will fill in gaps. See Richard A. Posner, *The Federal Courts: Crisis and Reform* 282 (1985). Some judges have suggested that the maxim is unreliable and should be invoked with caution because "it stands on the faulty premise that all possible alternative or supplemental provisions were necessarily considered and rejected by the [legislature]." *National Petroleum Refiners Ass'n v. FTC*, 482 F.2d 672, 676 (D.C. Cir. 1973); see also *Herman & MacLean v. Huddleston*, 459 U.S. 375, 388 (1983); *Director, Etc. v. Bethlehem Mines Corp.*, 669 F.2d 187 (4th Cir. 1982); *Gattis v. Chavez*, 413 F.Supp. 33 (D.S.C. 1976).

Another way of looking at this issue is to consider context, including normative context. If Mother tells Sally, "Don't hit, kick, or bite your sister Anne," Sally is *not* authorized by *expressio unius* to "pinch" her little sister. The reason is that the normative baseline (discerned from prior practice or just family culture) is "no harming sister," and the directive was an expression of such a baseline that ought to be broadly applied and not easily overridden. Contrariwise, where the directive in question is a departure from the normative baseline, the canon ought to have greater force. For example, if Mother tells Sally, "You may have a cookie and a scoop of ice cream," Sally has implicitly been forbidden to snap up that candy bar lying on the kitchen table. For cases where normative statutory baselines augured against application of *expressio unius*, see, e.g., *Marrama v. Citizens Bank of Mass.*, 549 U.S. 365, 374–75 (2007) (Stevens, J.); *Christensen v. Harris County*, 529 U.S. 576, 583–84 (2000) (Thomas, J.).

But consider *Chan v. Korean Air Lines*, 490 U.S. 122 (1989), where the Supreme Court held that international air carriers do not lose their Warsaw Convention limitation on damages arising out of passenger injury or death when they fail to provide the passenger with the requisite notice of limitation on her ticket. Article 3(1) of the Convention requires such notice, and article 3(2) provides that if the carrier fails to deliver a ticket to the passenger it cannot avail itself of the Convention's liability limits. Although many lower courts had interpreted article 3(2) to include situations where the passenger received a ticket, but without the requisite notice, the Court, in an opinion by Justice Scalia, held to the contrary.

---

d. In that case, the statute that prohibited bringing into the United States an alien for employment exempted certain persons such as lecturers and domestic servants. Had the Court followed *expressio unius*, it would have held that the listed exceptions were the only ones not covered by the prohibition, and therefore that the church had violated the statute.

Justice Scalia's key argument was that other sections of the Convention provide parallel rules for limiting carrier liability and providing notice thereof, for baggage checks (article 4) and cargo waybills (article 9). The various sections are identical in their notice requirements, but not in their remedies. Article 3 (passenger injury) provides no remedy explicitly covering insufficient notice, while articles 4 and 9 explicitly waive liability limits for the carrier's failure to include the required notice in the documents given to the consumer. By negative implication, Scalia construed article 3 not to have the remedy that had been clearly provided in the other articles.

The dissenting opinion argued from the Convention's negotiating history that the lack of a similar remedy in article 3(2) was probably inadvertent. Justice Scalia considered such evidence inadmissible. If such evidence were admissible, would it persuade you that Justice Scalia's invocation of *expressio unius* was too hasty? Note that fellow textualist Judge Easterbrook considers *expressio unius* arguments question-begging and unreliable. See *In re American Reserve Corp.*, 840 F.2d 487, 492 (7th Cir. 1988). But at the Supreme Court level, arguments drawn from the *expressio unius* concept have had an enduring appeal.[e]

B.   GRAMMAR CANONS

Although "justice should not be the hand maiden of grammar," *Value Oil Co. v. Irvington*, 377 A.2d 1225, 1231 (N.J. Super. 1977), the legislature is presumed to know and follow basic conventions of grammar and syntax. See Maxwell 28. Like the canons discussed above, the following are more rules of thumb than commands.

1.   Punctuation Rules

"The punctuation canon in America * * * has assumed at least three forms: (1) adhering to the strict English rule that punctuation forms no part of the statute; (2) allowing punctuation as an aid in statutory construction; and (3) looking on punctuation as a less-than-desirable, last-ditch alternative aid in statutory construction. The last approach * * * seems to have prevailed as the majority rule." Ray Marcin, *Punctuation and the Interpretation of Statutes*, 9 Conn. L. Rev. 227, 240 (1977). The English rule noted by Marcin was adopted because "[a]t one time * * * punctuation [was] inserted by a clerk after the statute had been enacted by Parliament." U.S. legislatures (at both state and federal levels) generally consider and pass bills whose punctuation is not changed after enactment. 2A Sutherland § 47.15, argues that "an act should be read as punctuated unless there is some reason to do otherwise," such as an

---

e. For deployment of *inclusio unius* arguments by a variety of Justices, see *Hinck v. United States,* 550 U.S. 501, 506 (2007) (Roberts, C.J.); *TRW, Inc. v. Andrews*, 534 U.S. 19 (2001) (Ginsburg, J.); *Solid Waste Agency v. Army Corps of Eng'rs*, 531 U.S. 159 (2001) (Rehnquist, C.J.); *City of Chicago v. Environmental Defense Fund*, 511 U.S. 328 (1994) (Scalia, J.,); *Key Tronic Corp. v. United States*, 511 U.S. 809, 818–19 (1994) (Stevens, J.); *United States v. Smith*, 499 U.S. 160 (1991) (Marshall, J.).

indication that such a reading would defeat the apparent intent of the legislature. "This is especially true where a statute has been repeatedly reenacted with the same punctuation, or has been the subject of numerous amendments without alteration of punctuation." See also Pa. Stat. Constr. Act § 1923(b): "In no case shall the punctuation of a statute control or affect the intention of the General Assembly in the enactment thereof but punctuation may be used in aid in the construction thereof * * *."

Consider *Tyrrell v. New York*, 53 N.E. 1111 (N.Y. 1899). A state statute provided that the salaries for persons employed as street cleaners "shall not exceed the following: * * * of the section foremen, one thousand dollars each; * * * of the hostlers, seven hundred and twenty dollars each, and extra pay for work on Sundays." (A "hostler" is someone who tends the horses in the stables.) The court ruled that a foreman was not entitled to extra pay for work on Sundays (*id.* at 1112):

> The punctuation of this statute is of material aid in learning the intention of the legislature. While an act of parliament is enacted as read, and the original rolls contain no marks of punctuation, a statute of this state is enacted as read and printed, so that the punctuation is a part of the act as passed, and appears in the roll when filed with the secretary of state.

The punctuation canon has *not* played a major role in the legisprudence of the U.S. Supreme Court. The Court found the punctuation rule decisive in *United States v. Ron Pair Enterprises, Inc.*, 489 U.S. 235 (1989), but otherwise this canon is rarely controlling. In *United States National Bank v. Independent Insurance Agents*, 508 U.S. 439 (1993), the Court in effect repunctuated a statute after concluding that a scrivener's error had occurred.

2. Referential and Qualifying Words: The Rule of the Last Antecedent

Referential and qualifying words or phrases refer only to the last antecedent, unless contrary to the apparent legislative intent derived from the sense of the entire enactment. E.g., *Jama v. Immigration & Customs Enforcement*, 543 U.S. 335 (2005). For example, in a statute providing that "the limitation of an action will not be extended beyond six years of the act or omission of alleged malpractice by a nondiscovery thereof," the "thereof" refers to the "act or omission of alleged malpractice." *Anderson v. Shook*, 333 N.W.2d 708 (N.D. 1983). Similarly, a proviso applies only to the provision, clause, or word immediately preceding it.

Consider this recent example. The Social Security Act's disability benefits program is available to a worker whose "physical or mental impairment or impairments are of such severity that he is not only unable to do his previous work but cannot, considering his age, education, and work experience, engage in any other kind of substantial gainful work which exists in the national economy." 42 U.S.C. § 423(d)(2)(A). Pauline

Thomas was an elevator operator until that job was eliminated from the economy; she claimed to be disabled from other jobs in the economy. The Third Circuit ruled that she was disabled, rejecting the agency's argument that she could still do "[her] previous work." In his opinion for the court of appeals, then-Judge Alito reasoned that "previous work" (like "any other kind of substantial gainful work") had to exist "in the national economy," but the Supreme Court unanimously reversed, based upon the rule of the last antecedent. Only the "other kind" of work—and *not* the "previous work"—had to exist in the national economy. *Barnhart v. Thomas*, 540 U.S. 20, 26 (2003).[f]

The last antecedent rule can be trumped by the punctuation rule. "Evidence that a qualifying phrase is supposed to apply to all antecedents instead of only to the immediately preceding one may be found in the fact that it is separated from the antecedents by a comma." 2A Sutherland § 47.33. Thus, if the statutory definition in *Thomas* had included a comma before "exists in the national economy," Pauline Thomas would have had a better chance of success at a textually oriented Supreme Court. See also *In re Associated Commercial Protectors Ltd. v. Mason*, [1970] 13 D.L.R.3d 643 (Manitoba Q.B.), aff'd, 16 D.L.R.3d 478 (C.A.) (reading intent requirement in criminal statute to all antecedent acts, because of comma).

The last antecedent rule can also be negated by other statutory context. In *City of Corsicana v. Willmann*, 216 S.W.2d 175 (Tex. 1949), the court declined to follow this rule to interpret the following statute:

> The said limits of the City of Corsicana may be extended so as to take in other territory, by ordinance duly passed by the Commission, in the manner and form as prescribed by the general laws of the State of Texas.

The court held that "in the manner * * * " modified "limits * * * may be extended," rather than "by ordinance passed * * *," because the general laws of the state had nothing to say about the manner or form by which municipalities adopt ordinances. Some courts have developed an "across the board rule" which is a special exception to the last antecedent rule: "[W]hen a clause follows several words in a statute and is applicable as much to the first word as to the others in the list, the clause should be applied to all of the words which preceded it." *Board of Trustees v. Judge*, 123 Cal.Rptr. 830, 834 (App. 1975).

---

f. In his court of appeals opinion, Judge Alito did not dispute that "which exists in the national economy" modified "any other kind of substantial gainful work," the last antecedent point. Alito's argument was that by using "*any other* kind of work," Congress was demanding a parallelism between these other jobs which exist in the national economy and the applicant's "previous work." The Supreme Court responded: "Consider, for example, the case of parents who, before leaving their teenage son alone in the house for the weekend, warn him, 'You will be punished if you throw a party or engage in any other activity that damages the house.' If the son nevertheless throws a party and is caught, he should hardly be able to avoid punishment by arguing that the house was not damaged. The parents proscribed (1) a party, and (2) any other activity that damages the house." Is this a persuasive answer to Judge Alito?

3. Conjunctive and Disjunctive Connectors: The And versus Or Rule

The nature of the conjunctions connecting different words or phrases may be significant. Terms connected by the disjunctive "or" are often read to have separate meanings and significance. For instance, 18 U.S.C. § 2114 (1988) prohibits assault with intent to rob "any person having lawful charge, control, or custody of any mail matter or of any money or other property of the United States." The issue in *Garcia v. United States*, 469 U.S. 70 (1984), was whether § 2114 applies to robbery of a Secret Service agent of his "flash money" (to be used to buy counterfeit currency from perpetrators). Petitioners argued that § 2114 only covered robbery of mail carriers, and that may have been the original focus of the statute. But the Court found the plain meaning clear: by separating "mail matter," "money," and "other property" with "or" (rather than "and"), Congress meant to include each of the three as an object of the statute and *not* to limit the statute to robbery of money and property in the custody of postal carriers. Why doesn't the *ejusdem generis* rule dictate the opposite result in *Garcia*? See *Schreiber v. Burlington Northern, Inc.*, 472 U.S. 1, 7–8 (1985) (interpreting "fraudulent, deceptive, or manipulative" language of Securities Act § 14(e) as all aimed at same thing: failures to disclose).

Linguists complicate the matter with these further observations: (1) The word "or" technically means "and/or" (a locution gaining in popularity). When I say "I want this or that," I might be saying I want either one item or the other, but I might also be saying I want both items. (2) In ordinary usage, people often use the two conjunctions interchangeably. "I want this and that" might signify that I want both items, or that I want only one. (3) De Morgan's Rules state that when preceded by a negative the logic is as follows:

Not (A *and* B) means Not A *or* Not B.

Not (A *or* B) means Not A *and* Not B.

See Solan, *Language of Judges*, 45–49. Professor Solan observes that courts do not always follow this logic, and typically for good reason.

The Comprehensive Crime Control Act of 1984 permits the United States to seize property used to commit crimes related to drug dealing. Under § 881(a)(7) such "real property" cannot be seized if the owner can establish (as an affirmative defense) that the criminal activity was "committed or omitted without the knowledge *or* consent of that owner." Can an owner prevail if he can only show lack of consent? Or does the owner also have to show lack of knowledge? If "without" has a negative connotation (which Solan and we think it does), De Morgan's Rules suggest that the defense requires both lack of knowledge (Not A) *and* lack of consent (Not B). But the Second Circuit held that the property owner could defend if he or she could show lack of consent, but only if the owner had taken reasonable steps to prevent illicit use of the property once the owner knew of such use. *United States v. 141st Street Corp.*, 911 F.2d 870, 878 (2d Cir. 1990). Solan says that this is an appropriate interpretation, notwithstanding De Morgan's Rules. Do you agree?

4. Mandatory versus Discretionary Language: The May versus Shall Rule

When a statute uses mandatory language ("shall" rather than "may"), courts often interpret the statute to exclude discretion to take account of equitable or policy factors. See *Escondido Mut. Water Co. v. LaJolla Indians*, 466 U.S. 765 (1984); *Dunlop v. Bachowski*, 421 U.S. 560 (1975). On the other hand, ordinary usage does sometimes consider "may" and "shall" interchangeable. "You may help Mother" may be either permissive or directive, depending upon the circumstances.

The statute in *In re Cartmell's Estate*, 138 A.2d 588 (Vt. 1958), provided that probate matters of law are to be tried by a court, and "if a question of fact is to be decided, issue *may* be joined thereon under the direction of the court and a trial had by jury unless waived * * *." The trial court had denied a jury trial, over objections. The appeals court reversed: "The word 'may' can be construed as 'shall' or 'must' when such was the legislative intention." The court, correctly, assumed that "may" applied both to the phrase "be joined * * * court" and to "trial had by jury." Solan, *Language of Judges*, 46–48. Compare *Lopez v. Davis*, 531 U.S. 230 (2001) (a law providing that the sentence of a nonviolent offender "may be reduced" by the Bureau of Prisons vested discretion with the Bureau not only to deny or grant this benefit to specific nonviolent offenders, but also to create a new category of nonviolent offenders (those whose crime involved a firearm) who could not receive the benefit of its discretion).

5. Singular and Plural Numbers; Male and Female Pronouns

One grammar rule that is *not* often followed by statutory interpreters is the difference between singular and plural nouns. "In determining the meaning of any act or resolution of Congress, unless the context otherwise indicates, words importing the singular include and apply to several persons, parties, or things; words importing the plural include the singular * * *." 1 U.S.C. § 1 (the federal "Dictionary Act"); accord, Interpretation Act of 1889, § 1(1)(b) (U.K.). Many states have analogous provisions. For example, the N.Y. Gen. Constr. Law § 35 (McKinney) provides: "Words in the singular number include the plural, and in the plural number include the singular." Like other rules of construction, however, New York courts will not consider this one decisive where it seems contrary to the apparent legislative purpose or intent. See, e.g., *Moynahan v. New York*, 98 N.E. 482 (N.Y. 1912).

A grammar rule even less often followed is the pronoun gender rule, to wit: he means a male referent, she a female referent. Because most statutes were drafted in eras when the main legal actors who counted were men, the modern presumption is that the male pronoun includes the female. 1 U.S.C. § 1; Interpretation Act § 1(1)(a). Interestingly, the federal Dictionary Act, 1 U.S.C. § 1, does not say that the female pronoun includes the male.

6. The Golden Rule (Against Absurdity)—and the Nietzsche Rule

English-speaking jurisdictions have a few catch-all rules providing a mental check for the technical process of word-parsing and grammar-crunching. The *golden rule* is that interpreters should "adhere to the ordinary meaning of the words used, and to the grammatical construction, unless that * * * leads to any manifest absurdity or repugnance, in which case the language may be varied or modified, so as to avoid such inconvenience, but no further." *Becke v. Smith*, 150 Eng. Rep. 724, 726 (U.K. Exch. 1836). (See also Hart & Sacks' excerpts from old British cases in Chapter 2, § 1.) For example, an early admiralty statute required purchasers of a vessel to register it immediately and barred them from receiving favorable duty treatment until they did so. In *United States v. Willings*, 8 U.S. 48 (1807), Chief Justice Marshall allowed favorable duty treatment for purchasers who had bought the vessel at sea and therefore could not have registered the purchase until their return. A strict application of the statute under those circumstances would have been manifestly unreasonable, the Chief Justice reasoned.

The golden rule is, in short, an *absurd results* exception to the plain meaning rule. In *Thomas*, the court of appeals thought it absurd for the government to consider the applicant not disabled from working her previous job when it no longer existed. Writing for the Supreme Court, Justice Scalia disagreed. A claimant who is concededly able to do her previous job is *probably* able to perform a job *somewhere* in the national economy. Hence, the agency's position was at most stingy, but by no means an absurd proof rule for a program with limited resources. (Recall that Pauline Thomas was an elevator operator in a community where those positions disappeared. We wonder whether the Supreme Court's judgment that she was not "disabled" from all productive work, was influenced by the fact that the Supreme Court elevators are staffed by operators like Pauline Thomas.)

Relatedly, courts should be willing to revise *scrivener's errors*—obvious mistakes in the transcription of statutes into the law books. See, e.g., *Lamie v. United States Trustee*, 540 U.S. 526, 530–31 (2004) (Court rewrites Bankruptcy Act to fix drafting error); *Green v. Bock Laundry* (Chapter 2, § 3) (all Justices agreeing to rewrite statute to correct an absurd provision that must have been the result of a scrivener's error); *Schooner Paulina's Cargo v. United States*, 11 U.S. 52, 67–68 (1812) (Marshall, C.J., revising statute to clean up scrivener's error).

The golden rule and its corollaries are now subject to academic debate. Although Justice Scalia recognized an absurd results exception to the plain meaning rule in *Bock Laundry* (concurring opinion), scholars of various persuasions maintain that an absurd results exception to plain meaning is inconsistent with the premises of the new textualism.[g] In *Zuni*

---

g. E.g., William N. Eskridge Jr., *Textualism, The Unknown Ideal?*, 96 Mich. L. Rev. 1509 (1998) (criticizing the new textualism for this inconsistency); John F. Manning, *The Absurdity*

Pub. Sch. Dist. v. Department of Educ., 550 U.S. 81, 104–07 (2007) (Chapter 2, § 2), Justice Stevens's concurring opinion rested the absurd result exception upon notions of probable legislative intent: if a plain meaning interpretation is truly absurd, that is prima facie reason to think Congress did not intend it (absent evidence to the contrary, of course). Justice Scalia roundly denounced that approach, in absolute language suggesting that he may agree with critics that there should be no absurd result exception to the plain meaning rule. *Id.* at 108, 116–22 (Scalia, J., dissenting); John F. Manning, *The Absurdity Doctrine,* 116 Harv. L. Rev. 2387 (2003) (arguing that textualists should not recognize an absurdity exception to the plain meaning rule).

Friedrich Nietzsche admonished in *Mixed Opinions and Maxims* No. 137 (1879): "The worst readers are those who proceed like plundering soldiers: they pick up a few things they can use, soil and confuse the rest, and blaspheme the whole."[h] All the Justices would agree with this sentiment; indeed, both Stevens and Scalia invoke it in their *Zuni* debate. We read Nietzsche's lesson for the statutory interpreter to include the following: Be humble. Consider how other people use language. Be helpful to the project rather than hypertechnical.

C. THE WHOLE ACT RULE

Other rules or maxims of statutory interpretation are based upon the context within the statute of the relevant language. The Sutherland treatise identifies different approaches that have been used: interpretation of each section in isolation from the others; interpretation of all the sections of each part of a statute together; resolution of ambiguities based upon the purposes and goals set forth in the preamble to the statute; and interpretation of each section in the context of the whole enactment. The treatise endorses the "whole act rule" as "the most realistic in view of the fact that a legislature passes judgment upon the act as an entity, not giving one portion of the act any greater authority than another. Thus any attempt to segregate any portion or exclude any other portion from consideration is almost certain to distort the legislative intent." 2A Sutherland § 47.02; accord, *Bishop v. Linkway Stores, Inc.,* 655 S.W.2d 426 (Ark. 1983); Maxwell 47–64 (English background and current application of the whole act rule).

From its earliest cases, the U.S. Supreme Court has followed the whole act rule in construing statutes. E.g., *United States v. Fisher,* 6 U.S.

Doctrine, 116 Harv. L. Rev. 2387 (2003) (agreeing with Eskridge and urging textualists to abandon the absurd results canon); John Nagle, *Textualism's Exceptions,* Issues in Legal Scholarship (Nov. 2002), www.bepress.com/ils/iss3/art5 (same). But see Jane S. Schacter, *Text or Consequences?,* 76 Brooklyn L. Rev. 1007 (2011) (demonstrating that Justice Scalia is thoroughly normative in statutory interpretation and repeatedly demands that judges avoid absurd or even unreasonable interpretations).

h.   Friedrich Nietzsche, *On the Genealogy of Morals (and Other Works)* 175 (Walter Kaufman trans. and ed., 1967). David Krentel, Georgetown University Law Center, Class of 1995, brought this maxim to our attention.

(2 Cranch) 358 (1805); *Priestman v. United States*, 4 U.S. (Dall.) 28 (1800) (per curiam). "Statutory interpretation * * * is a holistic endeavor. A provision that may seem ambiguous in isolation is often clarified by the remainder of the statutory scheme—because the same terminology is used elsewhere in a context that makes its meaning clear, or because only one of the permissible meanings produces a substantive effect that is compatible with the rest of the law." *United Savings Ass'n of Texas v. Timbers of Inwood Forest Assocs.*, 484 U.S. 365, 371 (1988). "When interpreting a statute, the court will not look merely to a particular clause in which general words may be used, but will take in connection with it the whole statute * * * and the objects and policy of the law, as indicated by its various provisions, and give to it such a construction as will carry into execution the will of the legislature." *Kokoszka v. Belford*, 417 U.S. 642, 650 (1974); see also *Doe v. Chao*, 540 U.S. 614 (2004) (considering uncodified parts of the "whole act"). A critical assumption of the whole act approach is *coherence*: the interpreter presumes that the legislature drafted the statute as a document that is internally consistent in its use of language and in the way its provisions work together.[i] Note similarities to interpretation of contracts and sacred texts like the Bible.

The presumption of coherence is an unrealistic one: the legislature does not always approach statute-drafting the way God is thought to have dictated the Bible. Instead, statutes are often assembled the way Christmas trees are decorated, with ornaments being added or subtracted willy nilly, and at the last minute, just to satisfy enough interest groups and legislators to gain the majorities needed to get through various legislative vetogates (recall Chapter 1, § 2). Staff and drafting offices are supposed to clean up legislation to make it appropriate for inclusion in the code, but even the best drafters cannot always meld all the deals into a coherent whole. Nonetheless, courts all over the world operate under the coherence assumption. Can you think of a normative defense of it?

Consider some corollaries to the whole act rule. (Section 3 of this chapter takes you further to a "whole code rule": interpreters must consider the provision in light of the whole code as well as the whole statute.)

1. Titles

Because Parliament's clerks, rather than Parliament, provided the titles of acts, the traditional English rule has been that the title could not be used for interpretive purposes. Thus, if the statute in Problem 3–1 had the title, "An Act to Prohibit Motorized Vehicles from the Park," English courts would have ignored this evidence of the statute's ambit. (The

---

i. See, e.g., *Ledbetter v. Goodyear Tire & Rubber Co.*, 550 U.S. 618 (2007); *Gonzales v. Oregon*, 546 U.S. 243 (2006); *Conroy v. Aniskoff*, 507 U.S. 511 (1993); *King v. St. Vincent's Hosp.*, 502 U.S. 215 (1991); see also *Canada Sugar Refining Co. v. Regina*, [1898] A.C. 735, 741 (U.K. House of Lords) (Davey, J.) (every clause of a law should be "construed with reference to the context and other clauses of the Act, so as, so far as possible, to make a consistent enactment of the whole statute"); *Greenshields v. Regina*, [1958] S.C.R. 216, 225 (Can. Sup. Ct.) ("a section or enactment must be construed as a whole, each portion throwing light, if need be, on the rest").

foregoing, by the way, is the *long title* of the statute; a *short title* would be something like the "The Motor Vehicles in the Park Act.") This is no longer the practice in most English-speaking jurisdictions, for the long title, and often a short title as well, are part of the legislative bill from the very beginning. In the United States, most state constitutions require the legislated enactment to have a title that gives accurate notice of the contents of the law.

As legislative practice has changed, so has the interpretive rule. According to 2A Sutherland 140, the "title cannot control the plain words of the statute" but "[i]n case of ambiguity the court may consider the title to resolve uncertainty in the purview [the body] of the act or for the correction of obvious errors." See also Maxwell 3–6 (long title but probably not short title may be used to resolve ambiguities).

The U.S. Supreme Court in *Holy Trinity Church* (Chapter 2, § 1) considered the statute's long title as cogent evidence of its purpose and indeed reworked the statutory provision to be consistent with it. See also *Committee for the Commonwealth of Can. v. Canada*, [1991] 1 S.C.R. 139, 162–63 (Can. Sup. Ct.) (considering both long and short titles to determine that the ambit of a law prohibiting advertising and soliciting in airports did not extend to political advertising or soliciting). Generally, today's Supreme Court does not rely on statutory titles as important evidence of statutory meaning, though Justices will sometimes quote the title as marginally relevant context. E.g., *Porter v. Nussle*, 534 U.S. 516, 524 (2002).

2. Preambles and Purpose Clauses

The traditional English rule gave great weight to statutory preambles,[j] because they were considered the best source for determining statutory purpose. The modern rule is more modest. American courts following the whole act approach have declined to give the preamble any greater weight than other parts of the statute (the title, purview, individual sections). "Thus the settled principle of law is that the preamble cannot control the enacting part of the statute in cases where the enacting part is expressed in clear, unambiguous terms" but "may be resorted to help discover the intention of the law maker." 2A Sutherland § 47.04; accord, *Attorney General v. Prince Ernest Augustus of Hanover*, [1957] A.C. 436, 467 (U.K. House of Lords) (preamble may be of some aid in discerning statutory purpose but tells the interpreter little about precisely how far the legislature has directed people to conform their activities to that goal); Maxwell 6–9 (examples of judicial use of preambles).

On the other hand, to the extent that the interpreter is able to find ambiguity and follows the Hart and Sacks purpose/context approach to statutory interpretation (Chapter 2, § 2), the preamble will be a particularly valuable contribution to the interpretive task. The Canadian Su-

---

j. A *preamble* sets out the important facts or considerations that gave rise to the legislation. A *purpose clause* sets out the objectives the legislation seeks to achieve or the problems it tries to solve. In text, we shall refer to both as preambles.

preme Court, for example, vigorously relies on statutory preambles for this reason. In *Rawluk v. Rawluk*, [1990] 1 S.C.R. 70 (Can. Sup. Ct.), the issue was whether Ontario's Family Law Act precluded divorcing spouses from invoking the common law remedy of constructive trust, to assure equitable distribution of the marital property. Justice Cory's opinion for the Court looked to the preamble, which recognized that marriage is a "form of partnership" and sought an "orderly and equitable settlement of the affairs of the spouses" upon their decision to divorce. "These fundamental objectives are furthered by the use of the constructive trust remedy in appropriate circumstances. It provides a measure of individualized justice and fairness which is essential for the protection of marriage as a partnership of equals. Thus the preamble itself is sufficient to warrant the retention and application of this remedy." *Id.* at 90.[k]

A preamble played a key interpretive role in *Sutton v. United Airlines, Inc.*, 527 U.S. 471 (1999). The Americans with Disabilities Act (ADA) prohibits job discrimination against people with disabilities. The airline had refused to consider hiring Karen Sutton and Kimberly Hinton as pilots because of their eyesight, which was severely myopic. The airline argued that the two women (twins) were not persons with a disability under the statute. Because poor eyesight could be completely corrected by eyeglasses, Sutton, Hinton, and other myopics did not have a "physical or mental impairment that substantially limits one or more ... major life activities." 42 U.S.C. § 12102(2)(C). This was an ironic construction of the ADA, for it would allow the airline to refuse to hire the sisters because of an impairment that the airline conceded was correctable. Yet the Supreme Court agreed, in part because the ADA's preamble found that 43 million people in the U.S. had disabilities, 42 U.S.C. § 12101(a)(1)—a far smaller number than people with poor enough vision to justify eyeglasses. *Id.* at 484–86; see *id.* at 494–95 (Ginsburg, J., concurring especially for this reason).

3. Provisos

Provisos restrict the effect of statutory provisions or create exceptions to general statutory rules. They typically follow the provision being restricted or excepted, and start with: " * * *. *Provided that* * * *." If there is doubt about the interpretation of a proviso, it is supposed to be strictly (narrowly) construed. "The reason for this is that the legislative purpose set forth in the purview of an enactment is assumed to express the legislative policy, and only those subjects expressly exempted by the proviso should be freed from the operation of the statute." 2A Sutherland § 47.08. We do not detect much interest in the proviso rule among recent Supreme Court Justices.

---

k. See also *LeBlanc v. LeBlanc*, [1988] 1 S.C.R. 217, 221–22 (Can. Sup. Ct.) (statute should be construed in light of general principles set out in preamble); *Regina v. V.T.*, [1992] 1 S.C.R. 749, 765, 770 (Can. Sup. Ct.) (L'Heureux–Dubé, J.) (stating that although preambles carry the same force as other provisions of the statute, generalized preamble statements will not trump longstanding principles of criminal procedure).

4. The Rule to Avoid Redundancy

Under the whole act rule, the presumption is that every word and phrase adds something to the statutory command. Accordingly, it is a "cardinal rule of statutory interpretation that no provision should be construed to be entirely redundant." *Kungys v. United States*, 485 U.S. 759, 778 (1988) (plurality opinion by Scalia, J.); see, e.g., *Circuit City Stores, Inc. v. Adams*, 532 U.S. 105 (2001); *United States v. Alaska*, 521 U.S. 1 (1997); *Walters v. Metropolitan Educ. Enters., Inc.*, 519 U.S. 202 (1997); *Rake v. Wade*, 508 U.S. 464 (1993); *Colautti v. Franklin*, 439 U.S. 379, 392 (1979). "A construction which would leave without effect any part of the language of a statute will normally be rejected." Maxwell 36.

For example, the issue in *Western Union Telegraph Co. v. Lenroot*, 323 U.S. 490 (1945), was whether the Fair Labor Standards Act prohibition against child labor applied to telegraph messengers. The prohibition reached any shipment of "goods" in interstate commerce, and "goods" were defined as "wares, products, commodities, merchandise, and articles or subjects of commerce of any character." The telegraph company argued that its service was intangible and therefore not a "good." Both Judge Learned Hand for the Court of Appeals and Justice Robert Jackson for the Supreme Court held that telegraph services were "subjects of commerce." Hand suggested that if the definition were read to include only tangible things, the term "subjects," which had been added by a special Senate amendment to "articles of commerce of any character," would add nothing to the statute.

The rule against redundancy is more at odds with the legislative drafting process than most of the other whole act rules, as words and phrases are added to important legislation right up to the last minute. Thus, the Court in *Gutierrez v. Ada*, 528 U.S. 250 (2000), declined to follow the rule against redundancy when other textual canons and common sense cut the other way. "But as one rule of construction among many, albeit an important one, the rule against redundancy does not necessarily have the strength to turn a tide of good cause to come out the other way."

Nonetheless, the rule against redundancy plays a more important role in Supreme Court opinions in the new millennium than it did in the old. *Circuit City* is but one example. Responding to Justice Souter's textual argument that "seamen, railroad employees, or any other class of workers engaged in foreign or interstate commerce" included all contract employees, Justice Kennedy's *Circuit City* opinion fell back on the rule against surplusage: "there would be no need for Congress to use the phrases 'seamen' and 'railroad employees' if these same classes of workers were subsumed within the meaning of the 'engaged in ... commerce' residual clause."

5. Presumption of Consistent Usage—and of Meaningful Variation

Under the holistic assumptions of the whole act rule, it is "reasonable to presume that the same meaning is implied by the use of the same expression in every part of the Act." Maxwell 278. Similarly, where a statutory word has been used in other statutes dealing with the same subject matter and has a settled meaning in those statutes, interpreters will presumptively follow the settled meaning. See Chapter 4, § 3. Although this is viewed as a weak presumption in most English-speaking countries, it has emerged as a stronger one in the United States, where it is presumed that "identical words used in different parts of the same act are intended to have the same meaning." *Sullivan v. Stroop*, 496 U.S. 478, 484 (1990), followed in, e.g., *Powerex Corp. v. Reliant Energy Servs., Inc.*, 551 U.S. 224 (2007); *Commissioner v. Lundy*, 516 U.S. 235, 249–50 (1996); *Gustafson v. Alloyd Co.*, 513 U.S. 561, 570 (1995). But see *Dewsnup v. Timm*, 502 U.S. 410, 417 & n.3 (1992) (finding such argument unilluminating).

The Equal Access to Justice Act, 28 U.S.C. § 2412(d)(1)(A), provides that a party prevailing in a lawsuit against the United States should be awarded attorney's fees "unless the court finds that the position of the United States was substantially justified or that special circumstances make an award unjust." The prevailing private party argued that the government had to pay unless its position was "justified to a high degree." The Supreme Court in *Pierce v. Underwood*, 487 U.S. 552 (1988), found this a plausible construction of the words but accepted the government's interpretation, that it could avoid counsel fees if its position were reasonable, or "justified in the main." Justice Scalia's opinion found a plain meaning, because the term "substantially justified" is used elsewhere in the U.S. Code and in the Federal Rules of Civil Procedure, especially Rule 37. Courts had never interpreted the term to require a higher degree of justification, and Justice Scalia accepted that as dispositive.

"From the general presumption that the same expression is presumed to be used in the same sense throughout an Act or a series of cognate Acts, there follows the further presumption that a change of wording denotes a change in meaning." Maxwell 282; cf. *id.* at 286 (but this is a weak presumption). The leading American case for this presumption of meaningful variation is Chief Justice Marshall's opinion in *United States v. Fisher*, 6 U.S. 358, 388–97 (1805). A statute whose first four sections regulated the relationship between the United States and "receivers of public monies" had a fifth section which said that "where any revenue officer, or other person[,] hereafter becoming indebted to the United States ... shall become insolvent, ... the debt due to the United States shall be first satisfied." A competing creditor argued that § 5 should have been limited to receivers of public moneys, like §§ 1–4 and the title of the law, but Marshall found no reason to think that Congress intended a narrower ambit for § 5 and so read it without the limitation. Accord, *Lawrence v. Florida*, 549 U.S. 327 (2007); *Hamdan v. Rumsfeld*, 548 U.S. 557 (2006).

Variation in terminology ought to have less force when one statute is adopted at a different time than another. E.g., *Gutierrez v. Ada*, 528 U.S. 250 (2000) (declining to apply a rule of meaningful variation when a later amendment used different terminology from the provision at issue). But when Congress changes a statute when reenacting it, the rule has renewed bite, as in *Osborn v. Bank of the United States*, 22 U.S. (9 Wheat.) 738, 817–18 (1824). The statute creating the first Bank of the United States contained a provision allowing the Bank to "sue and be sued * * * in Courts of record." The Supreme Court in 1810 construed that provision to afford no basis for federal jurisdiction in lawsuits involving the Bank. When the second Bank was established in 1816, the "sue and be sued" provision was changed to allow suits "in all State Courts having competent jurisdiction, and in any Circuit Court of the United States." Chief Justice Marshall construed the new language—pointedly expanding the language which was the focus of the earlier case—to be a congressional vesting of jurisdiction in circuit courts to hear lawsuits where the bank was a party. See also *Chisom v. Roemer* (Chapter 2, § 3) (1982 amendments to the Voting Rights Act abandoned the general language defining the ambit of § 2 and added a more specific term ["representatives"], which the dissenting opinion maintained was a deliberate narrowing of the provision's coverage).

A wedding of *expressio unius* and consistent usage is the rule that "[w]here Congress includes particular language in one section of a statute but omits it in another ..., it is generally presumed that Congress acts intentionally and purposely in the disparate inclusion or exclusion." *Keene Corp. v. United States*, 508 U.S. 200, 208 (1993); accord, *Arlington Cent. Sch. Dist. Bd. of Educ. v. Murphy*, 548 U.S. 291, 299–302 (2006); *Gozlon-Peretz v. United States*, 498 U.S. 395, 404–05 (1991). The Court refined this canon in *Field v. Mans*, 516 U.S. 59, 67–76 (1995), where it held this negative implication rule was inapplicable when there was a reasonable explanation for the variation. "The more apparently deliberate the contrast, the stronger the inference, as applied, for example, to contrasting statutory sections originally enacted simultaneously in relevant respects. * * * The rule is weakest when it suggests results strangely at odds with other textual pointers, like the common-law language at work in the [bankruptcy] statute here." *Id.* at 75–76.

The Court vigorously debated use of this canon in *Lindh v. Murphy*, 521 U.S. 320 (1997). Chapter 154 of the Antiterrorism and Effective Death Penalty Act created new rules restricting prisoner access to the courts to challenge their sentences in death penalty cases; chapter 154 was by its terms applicable to pending cases. Chapter 153 applied to noncapital cases and had no provision one way or the other. Justice Souter's opinion for the Court reasoned by negative implication that Congress meant the new rules not be applicable to pending noncapital cases. Chief Justice Rehnquist's dissenting opinion objected that this was not sensible, because it treated capital defendants more harshly than noncapital defendants. He argued that the Act should be construed to apply to all pending cases.

6. Rule Against Interpreting a Provision in Derogation of Other Provisions

An important corollary of the whole act rule is that one provision of a statute should not be interpreted in such a way as to derogate from other provisions of the statute (to the extent this is possible). An interpretation of provision 1 might derogate from other parts of the statute in one or more of the following ways:

- *Operational conflict.* As interpreted, provision 1's operation conflicts with that of provision 2. For example, a citizen cannot obey provision 1 without violating provision 2.

- *Philosophical tension.* As interpreted, provision 1 is in tension with an assumption of provision 2. For example, provision 2 might reflect a legislative compromise inconsistent with a broad reading of provision 1.

- *Structural derogation.* Sharing elements of both operational conflict and philosophical tension, provision 1's interpretation might be at odds with the overall structure of the statute. Thus, provisions 2 and 3 might reflect a legislative policy that certain kinds of violations be handled administratively rather than judicially, which a broad view of judicially enforceable provision 1 might undermine.

For an example of cross-cutting derogations, see *Robinson v. Shell Oil Co.,* 519 U.S. 337, 345–46 (1997). To see these ideas in action, consider the following case, where both the majority and dissenting opinions relied on the anti-derogation canon, as well as other textualist maxims.

BABBITT v. SWEET HOME CHAPTER OF COMMUNITIES FOR A GREAT OREGON

Supreme Court of the United States, 1995
515 U.S. 687, 115 S.Ct. 2407, 132 L.Ed.2d 597

Justice Stevens delivered the opinion of the Court.

The Endangered Species Act of 1973 (ESA or Act), 87 Stat. 884, 16 U.S.C. § 1531 (1988 ed. and Supp. V), contains a variety of protections designed to save from extinction species that the Secretary of the Interior designates as endangered or threatened. Section 9 of the Act makes it unlawful for any person to "take" any endangered or threatened species. The Secretary has promulgated a regulation that defines the statute's prohibition on takings to include "significant habitat modification or degradation where it actually kills or injures wildlife." This case presents the question whether the Secretary exceeded his authority under the Act by promulgating that regulation.

Section 9(a)(1) of the Act provides the following protection for endangered species:

Except as provided in sections 1535(g)(2) and 1539 of this title, with respect to any endangered species of fish or wildlife listed pursuant to section 1533 of this title it is unlawful for any person subject to the jurisdiction of the United States to—

(B) take any such species within the United States or the territorial sea of the United States. [16 U.S.C. § 1538(a)(1).]

Section 3(19) of the Act defines the statutory term "take":

> The term "take" means to harass, harm, pursue, hunt, shoot, wound, kill, trap, capture, or collect, or to attempt to engage in any such conduct. [16 U.S.C. § 1532(19).]

The Act does not further define the terms it uses to define "take." The Interior Department regulations that implement the statute, however, define the statutory term "harm":

> *Harm* in the definition of "take" in the Act means an act which actually kills or injures wildlife. Such act may include significant habitat modification or degradation where it actually kills or injures wildlife by significantly impairing essential behavioral patterns, including breeding, feeding, or sheltering. [50 CFR § 17.3 (1994).]

This regulation has been in place since 1975.

A limitation on the § 9 "take" prohibition appears in § 10(a)(1)(B) of the Act, which Congress added by amendment in 1982. That section authorizes the Secretary to grant a permit for any taking otherwise prohibited by § 9(a)(1)(B) "if such taking is incidental to, and not the purpose of, the carrying out of an otherwise lawful activity." 16 U.S.C. § 1539(a)(1)(B).

In addition to the prohibition on takings, the Act provides several other protections for endangered species. Section 4, 16 U.S.C. § 1533, commands the Secretary to identify species of fish or wildlife that are in danger of extinction and to publish from time to time lists of all species he determines to be endangered or threatened. Section 5, 16 U.S.C. § 1534, authorizes the Secretary, in cooperation with the States, see § 1535, to acquire land to aid in preserving such species. Section 7 requires federal agencies to ensure that none of their activities, including the granting of licenses and permits, will jeopardize the continued existence of endangered species "or result in the destruction or adverse modification of habitat of such species which is determined by the Secretary . . . to be critical." 16 U.S.C. § 1536(a)(2).

[A group of small landowners, logging companies, and families dependent on the forest products industries and organizations that represent their interests brought this action to challenge the Secretary's definition of *harm* to include habitat modification and degradation. They specifically objected to the application of the regulation to protect the red-cockaded woodpecker and the spotted owl by prohibiting changes in their natural habitat that would have the effect of injuring or killing those animals. The court of appeals agreed with respondents' challenge, but the Supreme Court reversed.]

The text of the Act provides three reasons for concluding that the Secretary's interpretation is reasonable. First, an ordinary understanding of the word "harm" supports it. The dictionary definition of the verb form of "harm" is "to cause hurt or damage to: injure." Webster's Third New International Dictionary 1034 (1966). In the context of the ESA, that definition naturally encompasses habitat modification that results in actual injury or death to members of an endangered or threatened species.

Respondents argue that the Secretary should have limited the purview of "harm" to direct applications of force against protected species, but the dictionary definition does not include the word "directly" or suggest in any way that only direct or willful action that leads to injury constitutes "harm." Moreover, unless the statutory term "harm" encompasses indirect as well as direct injuries, the word has no meaning that does not duplicate the meaning of other words that § 3 uses to define "take." A reluctance to treat statutory terms as surplusage supports the reasonableness of the Secretary's interpretation.

Second, the broad purpose of the ESA supports the Secretary's decision to extend protection against activities that cause the precise harms Congress enacted the statute to avoid. In *TVA v. Hill*, 437 U.S. 153 (1978) [Chapter 2, § 2C], we described the Act as "the most comprehensive legislation for the preservation of endangered species ever enacted by any nation." Whereas predecessor statutes enacted in 1966 and 1969 had not contained any sweeping prohibition against the taking of endangered species except on federal lands, the 1973 Act applied to all land in the United States and to the Nation's territorial seas. As stated in § 2 of the Act, among its central purposes is "to provide a means whereby the ecosystems upon which endangered species and threatened species depend may be conserved...."

In *Hill*, we construed § 7 as precluding the completion of the Tellico Dam because of its predicted impact on the survival of the snail darter. Both our holding and the language in our opinion stressed the importance of the statutory policy. "The plain intent of Congress in enacting this statute," we recognized, "was to halt and reverse the trend toward species extinction, whatever the cost. This is reflected not only in the stated policies of the Act, but in literally every section of the statute." Although the § 9 "take" prohibition was not at issue in *Hill*, we took note of that prohibition, placing particular emphasis on the Secretary's inclusion of habitat modification in his definition of "harm." In light of that provision for habitat protection, we could "not understand how TVA intends to operate Tellico Dam without 'harming' the snail darter." Congress' intent to provide comprehensive protection for endangered and threatened species supports the permissibility of the Secretary's "harm" regulation.
* * *

Third, the fact that Congress in 1982 authorized the Secretary to issue permits for takings that § 9(a)(1)(B) would otherwise prohibit, "if such taking is incidental to, and not the purpose of, the carrying out of an otherwise lawful activity," 16 U.S.C. § 1539(a)(1)(B), strongly suggests that Congress understood § 9(a)(1)(B) to prohibit indirect as well as deliberate takings. The permit process requires the applicant to prepare a "conservation plan" that specifies how he intends to "minimize and mitigate" the "impact" of his activity on endangered and threatened species, 16 U.S.C. § 1539(a)(2)(A), making clear that Congress had in mind foreseeable rather than merely accidental effects on listed species. No one could seriously request an "incidental" take permit to avert § 9 liability for direct, deliberate action against a member of an endangered or threatened species, but respondents would read "harm" so narrowly that the permit procedure would have little more than that absurd purpose. "When Congress acts to amend a statute, we presume it intends its amendment to have real and substantial effect." Congress' addition of the § 10 permit provision supports the Secretary's conclusion that activities not intended to harm an endangered species, such as habitat modification, may constitute unlawful takings under the ESA unless the Secretary permits them.

[The court of appeals had come to a contrary conclusion on the basis of the *noscitur a sociis* canon: the surrounding words—such as pursue, hunt, shoot—connoted application of force directed at a particular animal. But other words, such as harass, do not so connote, and the lower court's construction would effectively write *harm* out of the statute entirely.]

We need not decide whether the statutory definition of "take" compels the Secretary's interpretation of "harm," because our conclusions that Congress did not unambiguously manifest its intent to adopt respondents' view and that the Secretary's interpretation is reasonable suffice to decide this case. See generally *Chevron, U.S.A., Inc. v. Natural Resources Defense Council* [Chapter 6, § 3]. The latitude the ESA gives the Secretary in enforcing the statute, together with the degree of regulatory expertise necessary to its enforcement, establishes that we owe some degree of deference to the Secretary's reasonable interpretation. See Breyer, *Judicial Review of Questions of Law and Policy*, 38 Admin. L. Rev. 363, 373 (1986). [Justice Stevens also rejected application of the rule of lenity, see § 2B1 below. Although there is a separate criminal sanction for "knowing" violations of the ESA, the Court has never applied the rule of lenity to review agency rules implementing a civil statute that has parallel criminal sanctions.]

Our conclusion that the Secretary's definition of "harm" rests on a permissible construction of the ESA gains further support from the legislative history of the statute. The Committee Reports accompanying the bills that became the ESA do not specifically discuss the meaning of "harm," but they make clear that Congress intended "take" to apply broadly to cover indirect as well as purposeful actions. The Senate Report stressed that " '[t]ake' is defined . . . in the broadest possible manner to include every conceivable way in which a person can 'take' or attempt to 'take' any fish or wildlife." S. Rep. No. 93–307, p. 7 (1973). The House Report stated that "the broadest possible terms" were used to define restrictions on takings. H.R. Rep. No. 93–412, p. 15 (1973). The House Report underscored the breadth of the "take" definition by noting that it included "harassment, *whether intentional or not*." *Id.*, at 11 (emphasis added). The Report explained that the definition "would allow, for example, the Secretary to regulate or prohibit the activities of birdwatchers where the effect of those activities might disturb the birds and make it difficult for them to hatch or raise their young." *Ibid.* * * *

The definition of "take" that originally appeared in S. 1983 differed from the definition as ultimately enacted in [this] significant respect: It included "the destruction, modification, or curtailment of [the] habitat or range" of fish and wildlife. Respondents make much of the fact that the Commerce Committee removed this phrase from the "take" definition before S. 1983 went to the floor. See 119 Cong. Rec. 25663 (1973). We do not find that fact especially significant. The legislative materials contain no indication why the habitat protection provision was deleted. That provision differed greatly from the regulation at issue today. Most notably, the habitat protection in S. 1983 would have applied far more broadly than the regulation does because it made adverse habitat modification a categorical violation of the "take" prohibition, unbounded by the regulation's limitation to habitat modifications that actually kill or injure wildlife. The S. 1983 language also failed to qualify "modification" with the regulation's limiting adjective "significant." We do not believe the Senate's unelaborated disavowal of the provision in S. 1983 undermines the reasonableness of the more moderate habitat protection in the Secretary's "harm" regulation. [In footnote 19, Justice Stevens rejected the argument that statements by Senate and House sponsors supported the idea that the § 5 land acquisition provision and not § 9 was expected to be the ESA's remedy for habitat modification.]

The history of the 1982 amendment that gave the Secretary authority to grant permits for "incidental" takings provides further support for his reading of the Act. The House Report expressly states that "[b]y use of the word 'incidental' the Committee intends to cover situations in which it is known that a taking will occur if the other activity is engaged in but such taking is incidental to, and not the purpose of, the activity." H.R. Rep. No. 97–567, p. 31 (1982). This reference to the foreseeability of incidental takings undermines respondents' argument that the 1982 amendment covered only accidental killings of endangered and threatened animals that might occur in the course of hunting or trapping other animals. Indeed, Congress had habitat modification directly in mind: Both the Senate Report and the House Conference Report identified as the model for the permit process a cooperative state-federal response to a case in California where a development project threatened incidental harm to a species of endangered butterfly by modification of its habitat. See S. Rep. No. 97–418, p. 10 (1982); H.R. Conf. Rep. No. 97–835, pp. 30–32 (1982). Thus, Congress in 1982 focused squarely on the aspect of the "harm" regulation at issue in this litigation. Congress' implementation of a permit program is consistent with the Secretary's interpretation of the term "harm." * * *

JUSTICE SCALIA, with whom THE CHIEF JUSTICE [REHNQUIST] and JUSTICE THOMAS join, dissenting.

I think it unmistakably clear that the legislation at issue here (1) forbade the hunting and killing of endangered animals, and (2) provided federal lands and federal funds for the acquisition of private lands, to preserve the habitat of endangered animals. The Court's holding that the hunting and killing prohibition incidentally preserves habitat on private lands imposes unfairness to the point of financial ruin—not just upon the rich, but upon the simplest farmer who finds his land conscripted to national zoological use. I respectfully dissent.

[Justice Scalia objected to three features of the regulation, which, as he saw it, (1) failed to consider whether death or injury to wildlife is an intentional or even foreseeable effect of a habitat modification; (2) covered omissions as well as acts; and (3) considered injuries to future as well as present animal populations, and not just specific animals.] *None* of these three features of the regulation can be found in the statutory provisions supposed to authorize it. The term "harm" in § 1532(19) has no legal force of its own. An indictment or civil complaint that charged the defendant with "harming" an animal protected under the Act would be dismissed as defective, for the only *operative* term in the statute is to "take." If "take" were not elsewhere defined in the Act, none could dispute what it means, for the term is as old as the law itself. To "take," when applied to wild animals, means to reduce those animals, by killing or capturing, to human control. [Citing dictionaries, cases, and Blackstone.] This is just the sense in which "take" is used elsewhere in federal legislation and treaty. See, e.g., Migratory Bird Treaty Act, 16 U.S.C. § 703 (1988 ed., Supp. V) (no person may "pursue, hunt, take, capture, kill, [or] attempt to take, capture, or kill" any migratory bird); Agreement on the Conservation of Polar Bears, Nov. 15, 1973, Art. I, 27 U.S.T. 3918, 3921, T.I.A.S. No. 8409 (defining "taking" as "hunting, killing and capturing"). And that meaning fits neatly with the rest of § 1538(a)(1), which makes it unlawful not only to take protected species, but also to import or export them (§ 1538(a)(1)(A)); to possess, sell, deliver, carry, transport, or ship any taken species (§ 1538(a)(1)(D)); and to transport, sell, or offer to sell them in interstate or foreign commerce (§§ 1538(a)(1)(E), (F)). The taking prohibition, in other words, is only part of the regulatory plan of § 1538(a)(1), which covers all the stages of the process by which protected wildlife is reduced to man's dominion and made the object of profit. It is obvious that "take" in this sense—a term of art deeply embedded in the statutory and common law concerning wildlife—describes a class of acts (not omissions) done directly and intentionally (not indirectly and by accident) to particular animals (not populations of animals).

[Although "harm" has a range of meaning, the most likely in this statutory context is one that focuses on specific and intentional harming.] "Harm" is merely one of 10 prohibitory words in § 1532(19), and the other 9 fit the ordinary meaning of "take" perfectly. To "harass, pursue, hunt, shoot, wound, kill, trap, capture, or collect" are all affirmative acts (the provision itself describes them as "conduct," see § 1532(19)) which are directed immediately and intentionally against a particular animal—not acts or omissions that indirectly and accidentally cause injury to a population of animals. * * * What the nine other words in § 1532(19) have in common—and share with the narrower meaning of "harm" described above, but not with the Secretary's ruthless dilation of the word—is the sense of affirmative conduct intentionally directed against a particular animal or animals.

I am not the first to notice this fact, or to draw the conclusion that it compels. In 1981 the Solicitor of the Fish and Wildlife Service delivered a legal opinion on § 1532(19) that is in complete agreement with my reading:

> The Act's definition of "take" contains a list of actions that illustrate the intended scope of the term. . . . With the possible exception of "harm," these terms all represent forms of conduct that are directed against and likely to injure or kill *individual* wildlife. Under the principle of statutory construction, *ejusdem generis*, . . . the term "harm" should be interpreted to include only those actions that are directed against, and likely to injure or kill, individual wildlife. [Memorandum of April 17, 1981 (emphasis in original).]

I would call it *noscitur a sociis*, but the principle is much the same: The fact that "several items in a list share an attribute counsels in favor of interpreting the other items as possessing that attribute as well." * * * [Moreover,] the Court's contention that "harm" in the narrow sense adds nothing to the other words underestimates the ingenuity of our own species in a way that Congress did not. To feed an animal poison, to spray it with mace, to chop down the very tree in which it is nesting, or even to destroy its entire habitat in order to take it (as by draining a pond to get at a turtle), might neither wound nor kill, but would directly and intentionally harm.

The penalty provisions of the Act counsel this interpretation as well. Any person who "knowingly" violates § 1538(a)(1)(B) is subject to criminal penalties under § 1540(b)(1) and civil penalties under § 1540(a)(1); moreover, under the latter section, any person "who otherwise violates" the taking prohibition (i.e., violates it unknowingly) may be assessed a civil penalty of $500 for each violation, with the stricture that "[e]ach such violation shall be a separate offense." This last provision should be clear warning that the regulation is in error, for when combined with the regulation it produces a result that no legislature could reasonably be thought to have intended: A large number of routine private activities—for example, farming, ranching, roadbuilding, construction and logging—are subjected to strict-liability penalties when they fortuitously injure protected wildlife, no matter how remote the chain of causation and no matter how difficult to foresee (or to disprove) the "injury" may be (e.g., an "impairment" of breeding). * * *

So far I have discussed only the immediate statutory text bearing on the regulation. But the definition of "take" in § 1532(19) applies "[f]or the purposes of this chapter," that is, it governs the meaning of the word *as used everywhere in the Act.* Thus, the Secretary's interpretation of "harm" is wrong if it does not fit with the use of "take" throughout the Act. And it does not. In § 1540(e)(4)(B), for example, Congress provided for the forfeiture of "[a]ll guns, traps, nets, and other equipment ... used to aid the taking, possessing, selling, [etc.]" of protected animals. This listing plainly relates to "taking" in the ordinary sense. If environmental modification were part (and necessarily a major part) of taking, as the Secretary maintains, one would have expected the list to include "plows, bulldozers, and backhoes." * * * The Act is full of like examples. See, e.g., § 1538(a)(1)(D) (prohibiting possession, sale, and transport of "species taken in violation" of the Act). "[I]f the Act is to be interpreted as a symmetrical and coherent regulatory scheme, one in which the operative words have a consistent meaning throughout," *Gustafson v. Alloyd Co.,* 513 U.S. 561, 569 (1995), the regulation must fall.

The broader structure of the Act confirms the unreasonableness of the regulation. Section 1536 provides:

> Each Federal agency shall ... insure that any action authorized, funded, or carried out by such agency ... is not likely to jeopardize the continued existence of any endangered species or threatened species or *result in the destruction or adverse modification of habitat* of such species which is determined by the Secretary ... to be critical. [16 U.S.C. § 1536(a)(2) (emphasis added).]

The Act defines "critical habitat" as habitat that is "essential to the conservation of the species," §§ 1532(5)(A)(i), (A)(ii), with "conservation" in turn defined as the use of methods necessary to bring listed species "to the point at which the measures provided pursuant to this chapter are no longer necessary." § 1532(3).

These provisions have a double significance. Even if §§ 1536(a)(2) and 1538(a)(1)(B) were totally independent prohibitions—the former applying only to federal agencies and their licensees, the latter only to private parties—Congress's explicit prohibition of habitat modification in the one section would bar the inference of an implicit prohibition of habitat modification in the other section. "[W]here Congress includes particular language in one section of a statute but omits it in another ..., it is generally presumed that Congress acts intentionally and purposely in the disparate inclusion or exclusion." *Keene Corp. v. United States,* 508 U.S. 200, 208 (1993). And that presumption against implicit prohibition would be even stronger where the one section which uses the language carefully defines and limits its application. That is to say, it would be passing strange for Congress carefully to define "critical habitat" as used in § 1536(a)(2), but leave it to the Secretary to evaluate, willy-nilly, impermissible "habitat modification" (under the guise of "harm") in § 1538(a)(1)(B).

In fact, however, §§ 1536(a)(2) and 1538(a)(1)(B) do *not* operate in separate realms; federal agencies are subject to *both*, because the "person[s]" forbidden to take protected species under § 1538 include agencies and departments of the Federal Government. See § 1532(13). This means that the "harm" regulation also contradicts another principle of interpretation: that statutes should be read so far as possible to give independent effect to all their provisions. See *Ratzlaf v. United States*, 510 U.S. 135, 140–41 (1994). By defining "harm" in the definition of "take" in § 1538(a)(1)(B) to include significant habitat modification that injures populations of wildlife, the regulation makes the habitat-modification restriction in § 1536(a)(2) almost wholly superfluous. As "critical habitat" is habitat "essential to the conservation of the species," adverse modification of "critical" habitat by a federal agency would also constitute habitat modification that injures a population of wildlife.

The Court makes * * * other arguments. First, "the broad purpose of the [Act] supports the Secretary's decision to extend protection against activities that cause the precise harms Congress enacted the statute to avoid." I thought we had renounced the vice of "simplistically ... assum[ing] that *whatever* furthers the statute's primary objective must be the law." *Rodriguez v. United States*, 480 U.S. 522, 526 (1987) (*per curiam*) (emphasis in original). Deduction from the "broad purpose" of a statute begs the question if it is used to decide by what *means* (and hence to what *length*) Congress pursued that purpose; to get the right answer to that question there is no substitute for the hard job (or in this case, the quite simple one) of reading the whole text. "The Act must do everything necessary to achieve its broad purpose" is the slogan of the enthusiast, not the analytical tool of the arbiter.

Second, the Court maintains that the legislative history of the 1973 Act supports the Secretary's definition. Even if legislative history were a legitimate and reliable tool of interpretation (which I shall assume in order to rebut the Court's claim); and even if it could appropriately be resorted to when the enacted text is as clear as this, but see *Chicago v. Environmental Defense Fund*, 511 U.S. 328, 337 (1994); here it shows quite the opposite of what the Court says. I shall not pause to discuss the Court's reliance on such statements in the Committee Reports as " '[t]ake' is defined ... in the broadest possible manner to include every conceivable way in which a person can 'take' or attempt to 'take' any fish or wildlife." [S. Rep. No. 93–307, p. 7 (1973)]. This sort of empty flourish—to the effect that "this statute means what it means all the way"—counts for little even when enacted into the law itself. See *Reves v. Ernst & Young*, 507 U.S. 170, 183–84 (1993).

Much of the Court's discussion of legislative history is devoted to two items: first, the Senate floor manager's introduction of an amendment that added the word "harm" to the definition of "take," with the observation that (along with other amendments) it would " 'help to achieve the purposes of the bill' "; second, the relevant Committee's removal from the definition of a provision stating that "take" includes " 'the destruction, modification or curtailment of [the] habitat or range' " of fish and wildlife. The Court inflates the first and belittles the second, even though the second is on its face far more pertinent. But this elaborate inference from various pre-enactment actions and inactions is quite unnecessary, since we have direct evidence of what those who brought the legislation to the floor thought it meant—evidence as solid as any ever to be found in legislative history, but which the Court banishes to a footnote.

Both the Senate and House floor managers of the bill explained it in terms which leave no doubt that the problem of habitat destruction on private lands was to be solved principally by the land acquisition program of § 1534, while § 1538 solved a different problem altogether—the problem of takings. Senator Tunney stated:

> *Through [the] land acquisition provisions, we will be able to conserve habitats necessary to protect fish and wildlife from further destruction.*
>
> Although most endangered species are threatened primarily by the destruction of their natural habitats, a significant portion of these animals are subject to *predation by man for commercial, sport, consumption, or other purposes.* The provisions of [the bill] would prohibit the commerce in or the importation, exportation, or taking of endangered species. . . . [119 Cong. Rec. 25669 (1973) (emphasis added).]

The House floor manager, Representative Sullivan, put the same thought in this way:

> [T]he principal threat to animals stems from destruction of their habitat. . . . *[The bill] will meet this problem by providing funds for acquisition of critical habitat.* . . . It will also enable the Department of Agriculture to cooperate with willing landowners who desire to assist in the protection of endangered species, *but who are understandably unwilling to do so at excessive cost to themselves.* Another hazard to endangered species arises from those who would *capture or kill them for pleasure or profit.* There is no way that the Congress can make it less pleasurable for a person to take an animal, but we can certainly make it less profitable for them to do so. [*Id.*, at 30162 (emphasis added).]

Habitat modification and takings, in other words, were viewed as different problems, addressed by different provisions of the Act. [Justice Scalia argued that these statements destroy the Court's legislative history case and that the Court has no response.]

Third, the Court seeks support from a provision that was added to the Act in 1982, the year after the Secretary promulgated the current regulation. The provision states:

> [T]he Secretary may permit, under such terms and conditions as he shall prescribe—
>
> . . . .

> any taking otherwise prohibited by section 1538(a)(1)(B) ... if such taking is incidental to, and not the purpose of, the carrying out of an otherwise lawful activity. [16 U.S.C. § 1539(a)(1)(B).]

This provision does not, of course, implicate our doctrine that reenactment of a statutory provision ratifies an extant judicial or administrative interpretation, for neither the taking prohibition in § 1538(a)(1)(B) nor the definition in § 1532(19) was reenacted. The Court claims, however, that the provision "strongly suggests that Congress understood [§ 1538(a)(1)(B)] to prohibit indirect as well as deliberate takings." That would be a valid inference if habitat modification were the only substantial "otherwise lawful activity" that might incidentally and nonpurposefully cause a prohibited "taking." Of course it is not. This provision applies to the many otherwise lawful takings that incidentally take a protected species—as when fishing for unprotected salmon also takes an endangered species of salmon. * * *

This is enough to show, in my view, that the 1982 permit provision does not support the regulation. I must acknowledge that the Senate Committee Report on this provision, and the House Conference Committee Report, clearly contemplate that it will enable the Secretary to permit environmental modification. But the *text* of the amendment cannot possibly bear that asserted meaning, when placed within the context of an Act that must be interpreted (as we have seen) not to prohibit private environmental modification. The neutral language of the amendment cannot possibly alter that interpretation, nor can its legislative history be summoned forth to contradict, rather than clarify, what is in its totality an unambiguous statutory text. There is little fear, of course, that giving no effect to the relevant portions of the Committee Reports will frustrate the real-life expectations of a majority of the Members of Congress. If they read and relied on such tedious detail on such an obscure point (it was not, after all, presented as a revision of the statute's prohibitory scope, but as a discretionary-waiver provision) the Republic would be in grave peril. * * *

[JUSTICE O'CONNOR wrote a separate concurring opinion, responding to some of Justice Scalia's concerns. "[T]he regulation's application is limited by ordinary principles of proximate causation, which introduce notions of foreseeability." For example, she disapproved of an application of the statute where the grazing of sheep was found to be a "taking" of palila birds, as the sheep destroyed seedlings which would have grown into trees needed by the bird for nesting. The chain of causation is simply too attenuated, Justice O'Connor concluded. Justice Scalia responded that this was Justice O'Connor's gloss on the statute, not the agency's. He chided his colleague for trying to have it both ways—deferring to the agency under *Chevron* (see Chapter 6, § 3) but then rewriting the regulation to suit her fancy. Justice Scalia concluded: "We defer to reasonable agency interpretations of ambiguous statutes precisely in order that agencies, rather than courts, may exercise policymaking discretion in the interstices of statutes. See *Chevron*, 467 U.S. at 843–45. Just as courts may not exercise an agency's power to adjudicate, and so may not affirm an agency order on discretionary grounds the agency has not advanced, so also this Court may not exercise the Secretary's power to regulate, and so may not uphold a regulation by adding to it even the most reasonable of elements it does not contain.''\]

NOTES ON SWEET HOME AND THE WHOLE ACT RULE

1. *The Debate in* Sweet Home. Notice, first, how many of the canons are relevant to the Justices' deliberations about the plain meaning of the text in this case: the ordinary meaning rule, and its corollaries regarding dictionaries and technical meaning; *noscitur a sociis* and (possibly) *ejusdem generis*; *expressio* (or *inclusio*) *unius* and other rules of negative implication; the rule against redundancy; the rule of consistent usage and of significant variation; and the anti-derogation rule. Notice also how the anti-derogation rule figures centrally in both majority and dissenting opinions. Justice Scalia emphasizes the structural conflict between Congress's asserted allocation of responsibilities in §§ 5 and 7 and the majority's broad interpretation of § 9; Justice Stevens emphasizes the philosophical and structural conflict between a narrow reading of § 9 and the statutory scheme established in § 10.

A problem immediately apparent from this case is that different canons cut in different directions. How can one resolve conflicting canonical signals? One way to resolve the conflict is resort to the statutory purpose, but that may only generalize the disagreement. The dissenters' sarcasm suggests the possibility that they were not sympathetic to the statutory goals of biodiversity. Note their alarm that the "simplest farmer" finds his land "conscripted to national zoological use." Does this reflect a neutral interpretation of the law? Is the Nietzsche rule possibly applicable here?

Another kind of tiebreaker could be this: Qualitatively speaking, which side has more canons in support of its position? Which side is able to create a more complete—or more elegant—case for its interpretation? We are particularly impressed with the dissenters' ability to weave together a wide array of canons to support their position. Should this assure their triumph? If so, why did their usual ally, Justice O'Connor, jump ship? She might have been influenced by a third tiebreaker: the *political equilibrium* favored the agency (remember that she authored the Court's opinion in the FDA Tobacco Case, Chapter 2, § 3B). Indeed, the agency itself reflected the prevailing political consensus in this case, perhaps justifying the Court's deferring to its rule. See Chapter 6, § 3.

2. *Criticism of the Whole Act Rule.* Both the majority and the dissent in *Sweet Home* applied the whole act rule, reflecting its acceptance by most judges. Yet the whole act rule rests upon some heroic assumptions: it imputes "omniscience" to the legislature, and it assumes that a statute is written as a whole, internally coherent document (like a short story). These are faulty assumptions. "The conditions under which legislators work are not conducive to careful, farsighted, and parsimonious drafting. Nor does great care guarantee economy of language; a statute that is the product of compromise may contain redundant language as a by-product of the strains of the negotiating

process." Richard A. Posner, *The Federal Courts: Crisis and Reform* 281 (1985). More generally, the normative role of legislatures is to reflect the complexity of our pluralistic democracy—and pluralism also cuts against the assumption of legislative consistency. See Andrei Marmor, *Should We Value Legislative Integrity?*, in *The Least Examined Branch: The Role of Legislatures in the Constitutional State* 125–38 (Richard W. Bauman & Tsvi Kahana eds. 2006).

Although the U.S. Supreme Court regularly invokes the whole act rule, several of its Justices have recognized that the arrangement and phraseology of different statutory provisions is often "the consequence of a legislative *accident*, perhaps caused by nothing more than the unfortunate fact that Congress is too busy to do all of its work as carefully as it should." *Delaware Tribal Bus. Comm. v. Weeks*, 430 U.S. 73, 97 (1977) (Stevens, J., dissenting) (emphasis in original), quoted in *Mountain States Tel. & Tel. v. Pueblo of Santa Ana*, 472 U.S. 237, 255 (1985) (Brennan, J., dissenting). Note that this latter point is a critique of the canons generally. Even if Justice Stevens were correct descriptively, the whole act rule might be prescriptively correct. Think about both descriptive and prescriptive issues in connection with the case described in the next paragraph.

3. *A Case of Haphazard Drafting. Sorenson v. Secretary of the Treasury*, 475 U.S. 851 (1986), involved interpretation of the Omnibus Budget Reconciliation Act of 1981 (OBRA), Pub. L. No. 97–35, § 2331, 95 Stat. 860. The Act added provisions to the Social Security Act and the Internal Revenue Code to provide for "interception" of tax refunds for the benefit of state agencies which had been assigned child-support rights. Thus when a taxpayer is in arrears for his or her child support payments, and when the former spouse assigns them to a state (welfare) agency as a condition of receiving public assistance, the state can notify the IRS. The IRS will then give the state's recoupment claim priority over the taxpayer's claim for refunds of overpayment of federal income taxes. The issue in *Sorenson* was whether the "overpayment" which is subject to the recoupment claim includes refunds resulting from an earned-income credit. The Supreme Court held that it was. Section 6402(c), added by OBRA, provides that "*any* overpayment to be refunded * * * shall be reduced by the amount of any past-due support" (emphasis added). Section 6402(b), which was already in the Code, provides that if an earned-income credit exceeds taxpayer's tax liability, the excess amount is "considered an overpayment." Given the whole act rule that terms used in different parts of the statute should presumptively have the same meaning, the result follows.

But Justice Stevens's dissenting opinion pointed out the policy anomalies of the Court's result. The Earned Income Credit Program was created by Congress in 1975 to help keep low-income families off welfare: (1) social security taxes were assessed against earned income but not against welfare payments; (2) as a result, $500 a month in welfare meant more money in the pocket than $500 a month in earned income; (3) to redress this disincentive to work, Congress created a fully refundable credit for low income workers. Applying the OBRA recoupment scheme (one of the obscure goodies given to states in the 1981 reconciliation bill) to penalize low-income families is an accidental consequence of the statute's drafting; nothing in the legislative history supports any legislative desire to curtail the Earned Income Credit Program.

The Court's response to Justice Stevens was that "it defies belief that Congress was unaware" of the impact of the Intercept Program on the Earned Income Credit Program. Justice Stevens riposted: "With all due respect to the Court and to our hard working neighbors in the Congress, I think it 'defies belief' to assume that a substantial number of legislators were sufficiently familiar with OBRA to realize that somewhere in that vast piece of hurriedly enacted legislation there was a provision that changed the 6–year–old Earned Income Credit Program." In footnote 2, Justice Stevens quoted the following passage from N.Y. Times, July 1, 1981, p. A16, col. 1:

> Smoking a big cigar, the Speaker [of the House of Representatives] got angry again over the slap-dash quality of the bill [that became OBRA], with parts of it photocopied from memorandums, other parts handwritten at the last minute, and some final sections hastily crossed out in whorls of pencil marks. * * *

> But then he smiled, too, noting such cryptic and accidental entries in the bill as a name and phone number—"Ruth Seymour, 225–4844"—standing alone as if it were a special appropriation item.

There is a larger point to be drawn from Justice Stevens's criticisms. In the last generation, Congress has done an increasing amount of its work through gigantic and complex omnibus proposals. Doesn't the majority's approach in *Sorenson* ignore the realities of drafting and enacting a budget reconciliation bill—often in the days or even hours before congressional recess, with provisions added and dropped at the last minute in the conference room? In light of this new operation of the legislative process, should federal courts rethink at least some of the canons of construction? Should there be special canons, or at least practices, for construing omnibus reconciliation legislation like that in *Sorenson*? For a proposal that such omnibus bills be approached cautiously, see Seth Grossman, *Tricameral Legislating: Statutory Interpretation in an Era of Conference Committee Ascendancy*, 9 N.Y.U. J. Legis. & Pub. Pol'y 251 (2006).

SECTION 2. SUBSTANTIVE CANONS

Most of the canons discussed in the previous part are linguistic or syntactic guidelines that are policy-neutral. Other canons represent substantive decisions, and hence their application is not policy-neutral. Traditionally, the main canons were directives to interpret different types of statutes "liberally" or "strictly." The old Anglo–American rule was that "remedial" statutes were to be liberally interpreted, while statutes in derogation of the common law were to be strictly interpreted. (But what remedial statute is not in derogation of the common law?)

More modern typologies of the liberal-versus-strict construction canons have emerged. Certain statutes (such as civil rights, securities, and antitrust statutes) are supposed to be liberally construed—in other words, applied expansively to new situations.[a] As Appendix B, reporting the Court's deployment of canons from the 1986 through the 2006 Terms, demonstrates, these liberal construction canons have not been often invoked by the Rehnquist and Roberts Courts. Other statutes are to be strictly construed—in other words, applied stingily. The rule of lenity, requiring strict construction of penal statutes, is the best example and is explored in some detail below. Strict construction of statutes, especially for quasi-constitutional reasons, has been highly popular in the Rehnquist and Roberts Courts.

One way to understand the remedial/strict construction distinction is suggested by linguists' theory of prototypes. Words in a statute construed strictly should presumptively not be read beyond their prototypical meanings, while words in other statutes can be read beyond such meanings if consistent with the statutory purpose. In *Sweet Home*, Justice Stevens read the statutory term *take* beyond its prototypical meaning, because he understood the statute as a remedial one that Congress wanted read broadly, while Justice Scalia refused to read the term beyond its prototypical meaning, perhaps because this was a statute invading vested property rights. Thus, even cases seeming to be nothing but word-crunching exercises can be understood as reflecting profoundly substantive policy determinations by judges.

Consider other canons reflecting substantive judgments about how broadly to read the statute's text:

- *Strict Construction of Statutes in Derogation of Sovereignty.* If a statute is written in general language, it is presumed that it only applies to private parties; governments and their agencies are presumptively not included unless the statute clearly says so. See *Nevada Dep't of Human Res. v. Hibbs*, 538 U.S. 721 (2003) (finding such clarity). This canon is based upon the old idea of sovereign immunity: the state cannot be sued or otherwise regulated without its consent. See 3 Sutherland § 62.01.[b]

---

a. The Supreme Court has invoked the liberal-construction maxim when interpreting civil rights legislation such as § 1983, see *Dennis v. Higgins*, 498 U.S. 439 (1991); *Gomez v. Toledo*, 446 U.S. 635 (1980); statutes providing benefits to seamen, *Cox v. Roth*, 348 U.S. 207 (1955), and to veterans, *King v. St. Vincent's Hosp.*, 502 U.S. 215, 221 n.9 (1991); and safety legislation such as the Occupational Safety and Health Act, *Whirlpool Corp. v. Marshall*, 445 U.S. 1 (1980). See generally William N. Eskridge Jr. & John Ferejohn, *A Republic of Statutes: The New American Constitution* ch. 1 (2010) (super-statutes whose policy or principle comes to be entrenched in the public culture over time will be interpreted liberally to advance their policies or principles, and expansively vis-a-vis more ordinary statutes; examples include the Sherman Act of 1890, see *id.* ch. 3; the Social Security Act of 1935, see *id.* ch. 4; the Voting Rights Act of 1965, see *id.* ch. 2; and the Endangered Species Act of 1973 (the law at issue in *Sweet Home*), see *id.* ch. 6).

b. Since the absolute immunity of the state has eroded substantially in the last thirty years, this presumption has lost much of its original justification. A better rationale for the rule may be that the sovereign needs few constraints upon its freedom of activity as it decides how best to serve the public interest (though this explanation may be a naive view of the way government works). In the United States this rule has quasi-constitutional dimensions, since the states retained their basic immunities when they joined the union, see U.S. Const. amends. X–XI, and the federal government enjoys supremacy over states and their regulation. *Id.* art. VI. In any event, many states have statutes rejecting this rule of strict construction. 3 Sutherland § 62.04. For example: "The term 'person' may be construed to include the United States, this state, or any

- *Strict Construction of Public Grants.* Similarly, public grants by the government to private parties are to be construed narrowly, that is, in favor of the government. Sometimes, this precept has been justified on the grounds that such grants were gratuitous or solicited by the grantee, but the canon has been invoked in the whole range of cases— from leases and contracts with the government, to statutes allowing compromise settlements with the government, to pension and compensation laws for public officials.[c]

- *Strict Construction of (Some) Revenue Provisions.* 3 Sutherland § 66.01, announces that "it is a settled rule that tax laws are to be strictly construed against the state and in favor of the taxpayer. Where there is reasonable doubt as to the meaning of a revenue statute, the doubt is resolved in favor of those taxed." See *Gould v. Gould*, 245 U.S. 151 (1917). Generations of taxpayers who have lost lawsuits against the Internal Revenue Service over fine points of statutory interpretation would dispute that generalization. See *United States v. Fior D'Italia*, 536 U.S. 238, 242–43 (2002) (presuming that IRS-generated tax assessments are correct). Courts are turning to more liberal construction because of the necessary public purpose implicated in the system of taxation, "and it is the duty of the courts to see that no one, by mere technicalities which do not affect his substantial rights, shall escape his fair proportion of the public expenses." *Atlantic City Transp. Co. v. Walsh*, 25 N.J. Misc. 483, 55 A.2d 652 (1947); see 3 Sutherland § 66.02. Under this new thinking, the *tax-imposing* provisions would not be strictly construed—but the *tax-exempting* provisions ought to be.[d]

A second way of formulating substantive canons is as presumptions or rules of thumb that cut across different types of statutes and statutory schemes. These represent policies that the Court will "presume" Congress intends to incorporate into statutes, but such presumptions are rebuttable ones. Presumptions will generally not trump a contrary statutory text, legislative history, or purpose. See *Astoria Fed. Sav. & Loan Ass'n v. Solimino*, 501 U.S. 104, 108 (1991). A presumption or rule of thumb can be treated as a starting point for discussion, a tiebreaker at the end of discussion, or just a balancing factor. The policies underlying interpretive

state or territory or any public or private corporation, as well as an individual." West's Rev. Code Wash. Ann. 1.16.080 (1961). These state rules, of course, are subject to the Supremacy Clause and may be invalid as regards the United States. E.g., *McCulloch v. Maryland*, 17 U.S. (4 Wheat.) 316 (1819).

c. 3 Sutherland § 63.4 posits that the main reason for this canon is a general tendency "to regard all such grants with extreme distrust, so that in all its dealings the government will not suffer loss." Yet the rule has not generally been applied when the grant is for a great public purpose, such as the land grants to railroads in return for their building the transcontinental railroad in the 1860s. E.g., *Leo Sheep Co. v. United States*, 440 U.S. 668, 682 (1979); *Platt v. Union Pac. R.R. Co.*, 99 U.S. (9 Otto) 48 (1878).

d. Public choice theory (Chapter 1, § 2) lends support to this suggestion. Rent-seeking interest groups can be expected to extract from the legislature special exemptions from the broad taxing provisions. Not only do these exemptions undermine the public fisc, but they tend to do so for already-advantaged groups, thereby making the income tax system much less progressive than it is advertised as being.

presumptions are derived by courts from the Constitution, federal statutes, and the common law. Some examples of substantive presumptions:

- Presumption against congressional diminishment of American Indian rights. See *Hagen v. Utah*, 510 U.S. 399 (1994); *Montana v. Blackfeet Tribe*, 471 U.S. 759 (1985).

- Presumption of Indian tribal immunity from state regulation. See *Bryan v. Itasca County*, 426 U.S. 373 (1976).

- Presumption that Congress does not intend to pass statutes which violate international law. See *Sosa v. Alvarez–Machain*, 542 U.S. 692 (2004); *Weinberger v. Rossi*, 456 U.S. 25, 32 (1982); *Murray v. The Charming Betsy*, 6 U.S. 64, 118, 2 Cranch 64 (1804).

- Presumption that Congress does not intend to pass statutes which violate treaty obligations. See *Hamdan v. Rumsfeld*, 548 U.S. 557 (2006).

- Presumption that Congress does not intend that statutes have extraterritorial application. See *Foley Bros. v. Filardo*, 336 U.S. 281 (1949).

- Presumption that Congress does not intend that substantive statutes be applied retroactively. See *Landgraf v. USI Film Prods.*, 511 U.S. 244 (1994).

- Presumption that Congress does not intend that federal regulation unnecessarily intrude into traditional state responsibilities (any more than is necessary to subserve national objectives). See *Rush Prudential HMO v. Moran*, 536 U.S. 355 (2002); *Cipollone v. Liggett Group, Inc.*, 505 U.S. 504 (1992); *Ray v. Atlantic Richfield Co.*, 435 U.S. 151, 157 (1978).

- Presumption that Congress will not withdraw the courts' traditional equitable discretion. See *Weinberger v. Romero–Barcelo*, 456 U.S. 305, 320 (1982); *Hecht Co. v. Bowles*, 321 U.S. 321, 330 (1944).

- Presumption that Congress will not withdraw all remedies or judicial avenues of relief when it recognizes a statutory right. See *South Carolina v. Regan*, 465 U.S. 367 (1984).

- Presumption of judicial review. See *Demore v. Kim*, 538 U.S. 510 (2003); *Dunlop v. Bachowski*, 421 U.S. 560 (1975); *Abbott Labs. v. Gardner*, 387 U.S. 136 (1967).

- Presumption against derogation of the President's traditional powers. See *Department of Navy v. Egan*, 484 U.S. 518, 527 (1988); *Haig v. Agee*, 453 U.S. 280 (1981).

A third way of formulating substantive canons is as *clear statement rules*, which are presumptions that can only be rebutted only by clear language in the text of the statute. See *Solimino*, 501 U.S. at 108–09 (contrasting presumptions and clear statement rules). Clear statement rules have been developed by the Supreme Court as expressions of quasi-constitutional values. For example, Congress cannot impose liability and process directly against the states unless the statutory text clearly says so (see § 2B below).

There is some mobility in the Court's articulation of these substantive canons. For example, in *EEOC v. Arabian Am. Oil Co.*, 499 U.S. 244, 258–59 (1991), a majority of the Court transformed the old *Foley Brothers* presumption against extraterritorial application (of Title VII in that case) into a clear statement rule, requiring explicit statutory language in order for a law to apply outside the United States. Justice Marshall's dissenting opinion objected to the Court's transformation. *Id.* at 263. Note here how the general rule that civil rights laws, like Title VII, should be liberally construed was itself trumped by the more specific canon against extraterritorial regulation.

As suggested above, substantive canons may vary in their impact upon interpretation, and it is critical to identify how a court is using a canon. By way of review, consider three possibilities alluded to above. First, sometimes courts will treat a substantive canon as merely a *tiebreaker* that affects the outcome only if, at the end of the basic interpretive process, the court is left unable to choose between the two competing interpretations put forward by the parties. Second, courts might treat substantive canons as *presumptions* that, at the beginning of the interpretive process, set up a presumptive outcome, which can be overcome by persuasive support for the contrary interpretation. Typically, the party attempting to overcome the presumption may use any potential evidence of statutory meaning (e.g., statutory text, legislative history, statutory purposes, policy arguments, and so on) to rebut the presumption. On this understanding, a presumption simply adds weight to one side of the balancing process captured by eclectic statutory interpretation. Third, courts may treat substantive canons as *clear statement rules*, which purport to compel a particular interpretive outcome unless there is a clear statement to the contrary. We shall call those canons "clear statement rules" when they may be overcome by clear statutory language and those canons "super-strong clear statement rules" when they may be overcome only by extremely clear statutory text (where the "clear statement" is, in effect, a targeted statement of textual meaning). Keep a sharp eye on which of these approaches is used to implement the canons that are discussed in the remainder of this part.

A. THE RULE OF LENITY IN CRIMINAL CASES

One of the hoariest canons of statutory interpretation states that laws whose purpose is to punish (usually by fine or imprisonment) must be construed strictly. This is called the "rule of lenity" in construing penal statutes: If the punitive statute does not clearly outlaw private conduct, the private actor cannot be penalized. While criminal statutes are the most obvious and common type of penal law, many civil statutes have been so classified by at least some jurisdictions; recall Justice Scalia's invocation of this idea in *Sweet Home.*[e]

What is the purpose of the rule of lenity? In England, courts have long used this canon vigorously for humanitarian reasons "when the number of capital offences was still very large, when it was still punishable with death to cut down a cherry-tree." Maxwell 238. Early practice in this country was ambivalent about the rule of lenity: State and federal courts sometimes invoked it, but in early prosecutions for public insurrections and seditious libel, federal judges in particular showed no lenity; the Marshall Court, however, firmly established the rule of lenity in American legisprudence. Especially as penalties have been ameliorated, other kinds of reasons have been invoked to justify the rule of lenity. See generally Lawrence M. Solan, *Law, Language, and Lenity*, 40 Wm. & Mary L. Rev. 57 (1998).

For years, the leading justification has been *fair notice*. The state may not impose penalties upon people without clearly warning them about unlawful conduct and its consequences. A classic reference for this rationalization is *McBoyle v. United States*, 283 U.S. 25 (1931). A 1919 federal statute prohibited the transportation of stolen *motor vehicles* in interstate commerce. The law defined motor vehicle to "include an automobile, automobile truck, automobile wagon, motor cycle, or any other self-propelled vehicle not designed for running on rails." The issue in the case was whether defendant's transportation of a stolen airplane fell within the statute. Because *airplane* was not within the popular (or what linguists today call the prototypical) meaning of *motor vehicle*, Justice Oliver Wendell Holmes's opinion for the Court held that it did not. He justified lenity on grounds of notice:

> Although it is not likely that a criminal will carefully consider the text of the law before he murders or steals, it is reasonable that a fair warning should be given to the world in language that the common world will understand, of what the law intends to do if a certain line is passed. To make the warning fair, so far as possible the line should be clear. When a rule of conduct is laid down in words that evoke in the common mind only the picture of the vehicles moving on land, the statute should not be extended to aircraft, simply because it may seem to us that a similar policy applies, or upon the speculation that if the legislature had thought of it, very likely broader words would have been used.

Accord, *United States v. Lanier*, 520 U.S. 259, 265–66 (1997) (excellent elaboration of *McBoyle* and the various fair warning doctrines).

Under a fair warning rationalization, the rule of lenity is most appropriately applied to criminal statutes that create offenses that are

---

e. Among the statutes to which this canon has been applied are (i) statutes whose penalties include forfeiture; (ii) statutes providing for "extra" damages beyond those needed to make the complainant whole, including punitive damages, treble damages, attorneys' fees, penalty interest (often part of the remedy under usury laws); (iii) statutes permitting revocation of a professional license or disbarment of lawyers; (iv) statutes against extortion or discrimination; (v) statutes declaring certain acts to be per se negligence; and (vi) others. See 3 Sutherland § 59.02.

malum prohibitum (bad only because they are prohibited) rather than *malum in se* (bad by their very nature). Oliver Wendell Holmes Jr., *The Common Law* 50 (1881); J. Willard Hurst, *Dealing with Statutes* 64–65 (1982). Thus, a law criminalizing homicide doesn't have to be as clear in all respects as a law criminalizing hunting and fishing without a license from the state. But can this precept explain *McBoyle*? Or *Regina v. Harris*, 173 Eng. Rep. 198 (Cent. Crim. Ct. 1836), in which an English court held that one who bit off the end of the nose of another was not guilty of violating a statute punishing anyone "who shall unlawfully and maliciously stab, cut, or wound any person" because the statute reached only wounds inflicted by an instrument. In both those cases—and many others—defendants engaging in unquestionably squalid behavior got the benefit of the rule.

A justification related to fair notice might be the Anglo–American emphasis on mens rea as a presumptive requirement for criminal penalties. Although ignorance of the law is no defense to a crime, the inability of the reasonable defendant to know that his actions are criminal undermines the justice of inferring a criminal intent in some cases. It also suggests a corollary of the rule of lenity, namely, the presumption that criminal statutes carry with them a mens rea, or intentionality, requirement.

A dramatic illustration of the rule of lenity and its corollary is *Ratzlaf v. United States*, 510 U.S. 135 (1994), which construed the Money Laundering Control Act of 1986. Prior law required banks to report cash transactions in excess of $10,000; to prevent people from "structuring" their transactions to avoid the reports, the 1986 law made it illegal to make lower deposits for the purpose of evading the reporting requirements. The Court interpreted the statute to require *double scienter*: not only must the government prove that defendants Waldemar and Loretta Ratzlaf intended to evade the bank reporting law, but also that they knew about and intended to evade the anti-structuring law as well.[f] Justice Ginsburg's opinion for the Court emphasized that there were many benign reasons people would want to structure their transactions to avoid bank reporting requirements, including fear of burglary and a desire to secrete assets from a spouse or tax inspectors. According to Justice Ginsburg, "structuring is not inevitably nefarious." *Id.* at 144. Four dissenting Justices argued that a double scienter requirement was not justified by the statutory language, would render the statute a nullity, and focused on unduly extreme cases.

A third justification for the rule of lenity was originally suggested by Chief Justice John Marshall in *United States v. Wiltberger*, 18 U.S. 76, 92

---

f. The Supreme Court similarly read special scienter requirements into a statute making it a crime to possess a "machine gun," *Staples v. United States*, 511 U.S. 600 (1994) (government must prove defendant knew the gun was a machine gun), or to distribute images of minors engaged in sexually explicit conduct, *United States v. X–Citement Video, Inc.*, 513 U.S. 64 (1994) (government must prove defendant knew the performer was actually a minor). See also *Cheek v. United States*, 498 U.S. 192 (1991) (taxpayer's honest but unreasonable belief that he did not have to pay taxes was a valid defense to a charge of willful failure to pay taxes).

(1820): separation of powers. After much debate, the Marshall Court adopted the proposition that Congress cannot delegate to judges and prosecutors power to make common law crimes, because the moral condemnation inherent in crimes ought only to be delivered by the popularly elected legislature. If the legislature alone has the authority to define crimes, it is inappropriate for judges to elaborate on criminal statutes so as to expand them beyond the clear import of their directive words adopted by the legislature. There is also a separation of powers concern that judicial expansion of criminal statutes, common law style, risks expanding prosecutorial discretion beyond that contemplated by the legislature. See Herbert Packer, *The Limits of the Criminal Sanction* 79–96 (1968).

Notwithstanding the antiquity and multiple rationales for the rule of lenity, it has fallen into decline since the New Deal. See generally Francis Allen, *The Erosion of Legality in American Criminal Justice: Some Latter-Day Adventures of the* Nulla Poena *Principle*, 29 Ariz. L. Rev. 385 (1987). As many as twenty-eight states have abolished or even reversed the rule of lenity by statute.[g] Typical is Arizona Penal Code § 13–104, added in 1977: "The general rule that a penal statute is to be strictly construed does not apply to this title, but the provisions herein must be construed according to the fair meaning of their terms to promote justice and effect the objects of the law." The primary explanation for these anti-lenity statutes is that state legislatures in the late twentieth century were prone to invoke the criminal sanction liberally, and did not want judges obstructing such an expansion. If this rationale holds up, does that provide a reason *favoring* the rule of lenity? Do the rule's constitutional overtones trump such statutes under some circumstances? Cf. *State v. Pena*, 683 P.2d 744, 748–49 (Ariz. App.), aff'd, 683 P.2d 743 (Ariz. 1984) (applying rule of lenity notwithstanding the legislative abrogation).

Criticism of the rule of lenity has not been limited to legislators, however. Professor Dan Kahan, *Lenity and Federal Common Law Crimes*, 1994 Sup. Ct. Rev. 345, maintains that the nondelegation reason is the only coherent justification for the rule of lenity, at least for federal criminal statutes, but further argues that the rule of lenity should be abolished as a canon of construction. The polity would be better off without the rule of lenity. Accord, John C. Jeffries Jr., *Legality, Vagueness, and the Construction of Penal Statutes*, 71 Va. L. Rev. 189, 189 (1985). Normal interpretation of criminal statutes, without a judicial thumb on either side of the scale, would promote a more orderly and less costly development of criminal law (common law style, the way commercial law has developed, for example), without much in the way of unfairness, especially if the Department of Justice cleared up ambiguities by authoritative interpretations of federal criminal statutes. Consider this thesis in light of the following cases. Is there a coherent rationale for the

---

g. See Robert Yablon, "Lenity Without Strict Construction: Matching the Rule to Its Purposes" (Yale Law School SAW 2006) (collecting state statutes).

rule of lenity? Does it serve useful purposes? Or does it impose needless costs on the system?

MUSCARELLO v. UNITED STATES

Supreme Court of the United States, 1998
524 U.S. 125, 118 S.Ct. 1911, 141 L.Ed.2d 111

JUSTICE BREYER delivered the opinion of the Court.

[Section 924(c)(1) of 18 U.S.C. provides that "[w]hoever, during and in relation to any crime of violence or drug trafficking crime * * * uses or carries a firearm, shall, in addition to the punishment provided for such crime of violence or drug trafficking crime, be sentenced to imprisonment for five years[.]" The practical consequence of this provision is that someone who possessed a gun at the time of a drug offense gets a mandatory additional five-year sentence if § 924(c)(1) was violated; if that provision was not violated, the possession of the gun would be taken into account under the federal sentencing guidelines and would add some time to the sentence (perhaps a 30–40% enhancement) unless the gun was clearly not involved in the drug offense. Apparently it is almost always in the interest of the defendant to be subjected to the sentencing guidelines in this way rather than receive the mandatory additional sentence provided by § 924(c)(1). Accordingly, there has been much litigation concerning what the government must show beyond the mere possession of a gun during a drug offense to satisfy § 924(c)(1).

[In *Smith v. United States*, 508 U.S. 223 (1993), the Court held that, when a person traded a gun for drugs, he "used" the gun in violation of § 924(c)(1). Justice Scalia's dissenting opinion contended that the ordinary meaning of § 924(c)(1), read in context, is that "uses a firearm" means "uses the firearm as a weapon," and that in any event the issue was sufficiently doubtful for the rule of lenity to control the outcome in favor of the defendant. In *Bailey v. United States*, 516 U.S. 137 (1995), a unanimous Court held that the "use" element requires active employment of the firearm by the defendant, such that it did not apply to a defendant who had a gun in the trunk of his car in which illegal drugs were found or to a defendant who had a gun locked in a trunk in a closet in a bedroom where illegal drugs were stored.

[Muscarello unlawfully sold marijuana from his truck and confessed that he "carried" a gun in the truck's locked glove compartment " 'for protection in relation' to the drug offense." In a companion case, Donald Cleveland and Enrique Gray–Santana were arrested for stealing and dealing drugs; they had bags of guns in the locked trunk of their car at the scene. The issue was whether these defendants had "carrie[d]" a firearm within the meaning of § 924(c)(1).]

We begin with the statute's language. The parties vigorously contest the ordinary English meaning of the phrase "carries a firearm." Because they essentially agree that Congress intended the phrase to convey its ordinary, and not some special legal, meaning, and because they argue the linguistic point at length, we too have looked into the matter in more than usual depth. Although the word "carry" has many different meanings, only two are relevant here. When one uses the word in the first, or primary, meaning, one can, as a matter of ordinary English, "carry firearms" in a wagon, car, truck, or other vehicle that one accompanies. When one uses the word in a different, rather special, way, to mean, for example, "bearing" or (in slang) "packing" (as in "packing a gun"), the matter is less clear. But, for reasons we shall set out below, we believe Congress intended to use the word in its primary sense and not in this latter, special way.

Consider first the word's primary meaning. The Oxford English Dictionary gives as its *first* definition "convey, originally by cart or wagon, hence in any vehicle, by ship, on horseback, etc." 2 Oxford English Dictionary 919 (2d ed. 1989); see also Webster's Third New International Dictionary 343 (1986) (*first* definition: "move while supporting (*as in a vehicle* or in one's hands or arms)"); The Random House Dictionary of the English Language Unabridged 319 (2d ed. 1987) (*first* definition: "to take or support from one place to another; convey; transport").

The origin of the word "carries" explains why the first, or basic, meaning of the word "carry" includes conveyance in a vehicle. See The Barnhart Dictionary of Etymology 146 (1988) (tracing the word from Latin "carum," which means "car" or "cart"); 2 Oxford English Dictionary, *supra*, at 919 (tracing the word from Old French "carier" and the late Latin "carricare," which meant to "convey in a car") * * *.

The greatest of writers have used the word with this meaning. See, e.g., the King James Bible, 2 Kings 9:28 ("[H]is servants carried him in a chariot to Jerusalem"); *id.*, Isaiah 30:6 ("[T]hey will carry their riches upon the shoulders of young asses"). Robinson Crusoe says, "[w]ith my boat, I carry'd away every Thing." D. Defoe, Robinson Crusoe 174 (J. Crowley ed. 1972). And the owners of Queequeg's ship, Melville writes, "had lent him a [wheelbarrow], in which to carry his heavy chest to his boardinghouse." H. Melville, Moby Dick 43 (U. Chicago 1952). This Court, too, has spoken of the "carrying" of drugs in a car or in its "trunk." [Citations omitted.]

These examples do not speak directly about carrying guns. But there is nothing linguistically special about the fact that weapons, rather than drugs, are being carried. * * * And, to make certain that there is no special ordinary English restriction (unmentioned in dictionaries) upon the use of "carry" in respect to guns, we have surveyed modern press usage, albeit crudely, by searching computerized newspaper data bases—both the New York Times data base in Lexis/Nexis, and the "US News" data base in Westlaw. We looked for sentences in which the words "carry," "vehicle," and "weapon" (or variations thereof) all appear. We found thousands of such sentences, and random sampling suggests that many, perhaps more than one third, are sentences used to convey the meaning at issue here, *i.e.*, the carrying of guns in a car. [Justice Breyer gave several examples of such newspaper stories.]

Now consider a different, somewhat special meaning of the word "carry"—a meaning upon which the linguistic arguments of petitioners and the dissent must rest. The Oxford English Dictionary's *twenty-sixth* definition of "carry" is "bear, wear, hold up, or sustain, as one moves about; habitually to bear about with one." Webster's [Third New International Dictionary] defines "carry" as "to move while supporting," not just in a vehicle, but also "in one's hands or arms." And Black's Law Dictionary defines the entire phrase "carry arms or weapons" as "[t]o wear, bear or carry them upon the person or in the clothing or in a pocket, for the purpose of use, or for the purpose of being armed and ready for offensive or defensive action in case of a conflict with another person."

These special definitions, however, do not purport to *limit* the "carrying of arms" to the circumstances they describe. No one doubts that one who bears arms on his person "carries a weapon." But to say that is not to deny that one may also "carry a weapon" tied to the saddle of a horse or placed in a bag in a car.

Nor is there any linguistic reason to think that Congress intended to limit the word "carries" in the statute to any of these special definitions. To the contrary, all these special definitions embody a form of an important, but secondary, meaning of "carry," a meaning that suggests support rather than movement or transportation, as when, for example, a column "carries" the weight of an arch. 2 Oxford English Dictionary, *supra*, at 919, 921. In this sense a gangster might "carry" a gun (in colloquial language, he might "pack a gun") even though he does not move from his chair. It is difficult to believe, however, that Congress intended to limit the statutory word to this definition—imposing special punishment upon the comatose gangster while ignoring drug lords who drive to a sale carrying an arsenal of weapons in their van.

We recognize, as the dissent emphasizes, that the word "carry" has other meanings as well. But those other meanings, (e.g., "carry all he knew," "carries no colours") are not relevant here. And the fact that speakers often do *not* add to the phrase "carry a gun" the words "in a car" is of no greater relevance here than the fact that millions of Americans did *not* see Muscarello carry a gun in his car. The relevant linguistic facts are that the word "carry" in its ordinary sense includes carrying in a car and that the word, used in its ordinary sense, keeps the same meaning whether one carries a gun, a suitcase, or a banana. * * *

We now explore more deeply the purely legal question of whether Congress intended to use the word "carry" in its ordinary sense, or whether it intended to limit the scope of the phrase to instances in which a gun is carried "on the person." We conclude that neither the statute's basic purpose nor its legislative history support circumscribing the scope of the word "carry" by applying an "on the person" limitation.

This Court has described the statute's basic purpose broadly, as an effort to combat the "dangerous combination" of "drugs and guns." *Smith v. United States*, 508 U.S. 223, 240 (1993). And the provision's chief legislative sponsor has said that the provision seeks "to persuade the man who is tempted to commit a Federal felony to leave his gun at home." 114 Cong. Rec. 22231 (1968) (Rep. Poff); see *Busic v. United States*, 446 U.S. 398, 405 (1980) (describing Poff's comments as "crucial material" in interpreting the purpose of § 924(c)); *Simpson v. United States*, 435 U.S. 6, 13–14 (1978) (concluding that Poff's comments are "clearly probative" and "certainly entitled to weight"); see also 114 Cong. Rec. 22243–22244 (statutes would apply to "the man who goes out taking a gun to commit a crime") (Rep. Hunt); *id.*, at 22244 ("Of course, what we are trying to do by these penalties is to persuade the criminal to leave his gun at home") (Rep. Randall); *id.*, at 22236 ("We are concerned . . . with having the criminal leave his gun at home") (Rep. Meskill).

From the perspective of any such purpose (persuading a criminal "to leave his gun at home") what sense would it make for this statute to penalize one who walks with a gun in a bag to the site of a drug sale, but to ignore a similar individual who, like defendant Gray–Santana, travels to a similar site with a similar gun in a similar bag, but instead of walking, drives there with the gun in his car? How persuasive is a punishment that is without effect until a drug dealer who has brought his gun to a sale (indeed has it available for use) actually takes it from the trunk (or unlocks the glove compartment) of his car? It is difficult to say that, considered as a class, those who prepare, say, to sell drugs by placing guns in their cars are less dangerous, or less deserving of punishment, than those who carry handguns on their person.

We have found no significant indication elsewhere in the legislative history of any more narrowly focused relevant purpose. * * * One legislator indicates that the statute responds in part to the concerns of law enforcement personnel, who had urged that "carrying short firearms in motor vehicles be classified as carrying such weapons concealed." *Id.*, at 22242 (Rep. May). Another criticizes a version of the proposed statute by suggesting it might apply to drunken driving, and gives as an example a drunken driver who has a "gun in his car." *Id.*, at 21792 (Rep. Yates). Others describe the statute as criminalizing gun "possession"—a term that could stretch beyond both the "use" of a gun and the carrying of a gun on the person. See *id.*, at 21793 (Rep. Casey); *id.*, at 22236 (Rep. Meskill); *id.*, at 30584 (Rep. Collier); *id.*, at 30585 (Rep. Skubitz).

We are not convinced by petitioners' remaining arguments[.] First, they say that our definition of "carry" makes it the equivalent of "transport." Yet, Congress elsewhere in related statutes used the word "transport" deliberately to signify a different, and broader, statutory coverage. The immediately preceding statutory subsection, for example, imposes a different set of penalties on one who, with an intent to commit a crime, "ships, transports, or receives a firearm" in interstate commerce. 18 U.S.C. § 924(b). Moreover, § 926A specifically "entitle[s]" a person "not otherwise prohibited ... from transporting, shipping, or receiving a firearm" to "transport a firearm ... from any place where he may lawfully possess and carry" it to "any other place" where he may do so. Why, petitioners ask, would Congress have used the word "transport," or used both "carry" and "transport" in the same provision, if it had intended to obliterate the distinction between the two?

The short answer is that our definition does not equate "carry" and "transport." "Carry" implies personal agency and some degree of possession, whereas "transport" does not have such a limited connotation and, in addition, implies the movement of goods in bulk over great distances. See Webster's Third New International Dictionary 343 (noting that "carry" means "moving to a location some distance away while supporting or maintaining off the ground" and "is a natural word to use in ref. to cargoes and loads on trucks, wagons, planes, ships, or even beasts of burden," while "transport refers to carriage in bulk or number over an appreciable distance and, typically, by a customary or usual carrier agency"); see also Webster's Dictionary of Synonyms 141 (1942). If Smith, for example, calls a parcel delivery service, which sends a truck to Smith's house to pick up Smith's package and take it to Los Angeles, one might say that Smith has shipped the package and the parcel delivery service has transported the package. But only the truck driver has "carried" the package in the sense of "carry" that we believe Congress intended. Therefore, "transport" is a broader category that includes "carry" but also encompasses other activity.

The dissent refers to § 926A and to another statute where Congress used the word "transport" rather than "carry" to describe the movement of firearms. 18 U.S.C. § 925(a)(2)(B). According to the dissent, had Congress intended "carry" to have the meaning we give it, Congress would not have needed to use a different word in these provisions. But as we have discussed above, we believe the word "transport" is broader than the word "carry."

And, if Congress intended "carry" to have the limited definition the dissent contends, it would have been quite unnecessary to add the proviso in § 926A requiring a person, to be exempt from penalties, to store her firearm in a locked container not immediately accessible. See § 926A (exempting from criminal penalties one who transports a firearm from a place where "he may lawfully possess and carry such firearm" but not exempting the "transportation" of a firearm if it is "readily accessible or is directly accessible from the passenger compartment of transporting vehicle"). The statute simply could have said that such a person may not "carry" a firearm. But, of course, Congress did not say this because that is not what "carry" means.

As we interpret the statutory scheme, it makes sense. Congress has imposed a variable penalty with no mandatory minimum sentence upon a person who "transports" (or "ships" or "receives") a firearm knowing it will be used to commit any "offense punishable by imprisonment for

[more than] ... one year," § 924(b), and it has imposed a 5–year mandatory minimum sentence upon one who "carries" a firearm "during and in
relation to" a "drug trafficking crime," § 924(c). The first subsection
imposes a less strict sentencing regime upon one who, say, ships firearms
by mail for use in a crime elsewhere; the latter subsection imposes a
mandatory sentence upon one who, say, brings a weapon with him (on his
person or in his car) to the site of a drug sale.

Second, petitioners point out that, in *Bailey v. United States*, we
considered the related phrase "uses ... a firearm" found in the same
statutory provision now before us. We construed the term "use" narrowly,
limiting its application to the "active employment" of a firearm. Petitioners argue that it would be anomalous to construe broadly the word
"carries," its statutory next-door neighbor.

In *Bailey*, however, we limited "use" of a firearm to "active employment" in part because we assumed "that Congress ... intended each term
to have a particular, non-superfluous meaning." A broader interpretation
of "use," we said, would have swallowed up the term "carry." But "carry"
as we interpret that word does not swallow up the term "use." "Use"
retains the same independent meaning we found for it in *Bailey*, where we
provided examples involving the displaying or the bartering of a gun.
"Carry" also retains an independent meaning, for, under *Bailey*, carrying
a gun in a car does not necessarily involve the gun's "active employment."
More importantly, having construed "use" narrowly in *Bailey*, we cannot
also construe "carry" narrowly without undercutting the statute's basic
objective. For the narrow interpretation would remove the act of carrying
a gun in a car entirely from the statute's reach, leaving a gap in coverage
that we do not believe Congress intended.

Third, petitioners say that our reading of the statute would extend its
coverage to passengers on buses, trains, or ships, who have placed a
firearm, say, in checked luggage. To extend this statute so far, they argue,
is unfair, going well beyond what Congress likely would have thought
possible. They add that some lower courts, thinking approximately the
same, have limited the scope of "carries" to instances where a gun in a car
is immediately accessible, thereby most likely excluding from coverage a
gun carried in a car's trunk or locked glove compartment. * * *

In our view, this argument does not take adequate account of other
limiting words in the statute—words that make the statute applicable only
where a defendant "carries" a gun *both* "during *and* in relation to" a drug
crime. § 924(c)(1) (emphasis added). Congress added these words in part
to prevent prosecution where guns "played" no part in the crime. See S.
Rep. No. 98–225, at 314, n.10.

Once one takes account of the words "during" and "in relation to," it
no longer seems beyond Congress' likely intent, or otherwise unfair, to
interpret the statute as we have done. If one carries a gun in a car
"during" and "in relation to" a drug sale, for example, the fact that the
gun is carried in the car's trunk or locked glove compartment seems not

only logically difficult to distinguish from the immediately accessible gun, but also beside the point.

At the same time, the narrow interpretation creates its own anomalies. The statute, for example, defines "firearm" to include a "bomb," "grenade," "rocket having a propellant charge of more than four ounces," or "missile having an explosive or incendiary charge of more than one-quarter ounce," where such device is "explosive," "incendiary," or delivers "poison gas." 18 U.S.C. § 921(a)(4)(A). On petitioners' reading, the "carry" provision would not apply to instances where drug lords, engaged in a major transaction, took with them "firearms" such as these, which most likely could not be carried on the person.

Fourth, petitioners argue that we should construe the word "carry" to mean "immediately accessible." * * * That interpretation, however, is difficult to square with the statute's language, for one "carries" a gun in the glove compartment whether or not that glove compartment is locked. Nothing in the statute's history suggests that Congress intended that limitation. And, for reasons pointed out above, we believe that the words "during" and "in relation to" will limit the statute's application to the harms that Congress foresaw.

Finally, petitioners and the dissent invoke the "rule of lenity." The simple existence of some statutory ambiguity, however, is not sufficient to warrant application of that rule, for most statutes are ambiguous to some degree. " 'The rule of lenity applies only if, "after seizing everything from which aid can be derived," . . . we can make "no more than a guess as to what Congress intended." ' " *United States v. Wells*, 519 U.S. 482,499 (1997) [quoting earlier cases]. To invoke the rule, we must conclude that there is a " 'grievous ambiguity or uncertainty' in the statute." *Staples v. United States*, 511 U.S. 600, 619 n.17 (1994) (quoting *Chapman v. United States*) [Chapter 2, § 3B]. Certainly, our decision today is based on much more than a "guess as to what Congress intended," and there is no "grievous ambiguity" here. The problem of statutory interpretation [in this case] is indeed no different from that in many of the criminal cases that confront us. Yet, this Court has never held that the rule of lenity automatically permits a defendant to win. [Affirmed.]

JUSTICE GINSBURG, with whom THE CHIEF JUSTICE [REHNQUIST], JUSTICE SCALIA, and JUSTICE SOUTER join, dissenting.

[Justice Ginsburg explained that defendants' gun possession would have adverse consequences even if § 924(c)(1) were held to be inapplicable. For example, the federal sentencing guidelines provided Muscarello a 6–12 month presumptive sentence for his involvement in the distribution of 3.6 kilograms of marijuana. The "two-level enhancement" under the guidelines for possession of a gun would increase the sentencing range to 10–16 months. If, instead, as the majority held, Muscarello violated § 924(c)(1), his sentence would reflect the underlying drug offense (6–12 months) *plus* the five-year mandatory additional sentence provided by § 924(c)(1).]

* * * Unlike the Court, I do not think dictionaries, surveys of press reports, or the Bible[4] tell us, dispositively, what "carries" means embedded in § 924(c)(1). On definitions, "carry" in legal formulations could mean, *inter alia*, transport, possess, have in stock, prolong (carry over), be infectious, or wear or bear on one's person.[5] At issue here is not "carries" at large but "carries a firearm." The Court's computer search of newspapers is revealing in this light. Carrying guns in a car showed up as the meaning "perhaps more than one third" of the time. One is left to wonder what meaning showed up some two thirds of the time. Surely a most familiar meaning is, as the Constitution's Second Amendment ("keep and *bear* Arms") (emphasis added) and Black's Law Dictionary, at 214, indicate: "wear, bear, or carry ... upon the person or in the clothing or in a pocket, for the purpose ... of being armed and ready for offensive or defensive action in a case of conflict with another person."

On lessons from literature, a scan of Bartlett's and other quotation collections shows how highly selective the Court's choices are. If "[t]he greatest of writers" have used "carry" to mean convey or transport in a vehicle, so have they used the hydra-headed word to mean, *inter alia*, carry in one's hand, arms, head, heart, or soul, sans vehicle. [Justice Ginsburg quoted Isaiah 40:11, poems by Oliver Goldsmith and Rudyard Kipling, and Theodore Roosevelt's famous advice to "[s]peak softly and carry a big stick."][6]

These and the Court's lexicological sources demonstrate vividly that "carry" is a word commonly used to convey various messages. Such references, given their variety, are not reliable indicators of what Congress meant, in § 924(c)(1), by "carries a firearm."

Noting the paradoxical statement, " 'I *use* a gun to protect my house, but I've never had to *use* it,' " the Court in *Bailey* emphasized the importance of context—the statutory context. Just as "uses" was read to mean not simply "possession," but "active employment," so "carries," correspondingly, is properly read to signal the most dangerous cases—the gun at hand, ready for use as a weapon. It is reasonable to comprehend Congress as having provided mandatory minimums for the most life-

---

4. The translator of the Good Book, it appears, bore responsibility for determining whether the servants of Ahaziah "carried" his corpse to Jerusalem. Compare [majority opinion] with, e.g., The New English Bible, 2 *Kings* 9:28 ("His servants *conveyed* his body to Jerusalem."); Saint Joseph Edition of the New American Bible ("His servants *brought* him in a chariot to Jerusalem."); Tanakh: The Holy Scriptures ("His servants *conveyed* him in a chariot to Jerusalem."); see also *id.*, *Isaiah* 30:6 ("They *convey* their wealth on the backs of asses."); The New Jerusalem Bible ("[T]hey *bear* their riches on donkeys' backs.") (emphasis added in all quotations).

5. The dictionary to which this Court referred in *Bailey v. United States* contains 32 discrete definitions of "carry," including "[t]o make good or valid," "to bear the aspect of," and even "[t]o bear (a hawk) on the fist." See Webster's New International Dictionary of English Language 412 (2d ed. 1949).

6. Popular films and television productions provide corroborative illustrations. * * * [I]n the television series "M*A*S*H," Hawkeye Pierce (played by Alan Alda) presciently proclaims: "I will not carry a gun.... I'll carry your books, I'll carry a torch, I'll carry a tune, I'll carry on, carry over, carry forward, Cary Grant, cash and carry, carry me back to Old Virginia, I'll even 'hari-kari' if you show me how, but I will not carry a gun!" See http://www.geocities.com/Hollywood/8915/mashquotes.html.

jeopardizing gun-connection cases (guns in or at the defendant's hand when committing an offense), leaving other, less imminently threatening, situations for the more flexible guidelines regime. As the Ninth Circuit suggested, it is not apparent why possession of a gun in a drug dealer's moving vehicle would be thought more dangerous than gun possession on premises where drugs are sold: "A drug dealer who packs heat is more likely to hurt someone or provoke someone else to violence. A gun in a bag under a tarp in a truck bed [or in a bedroom closet] poses substantially less risk." *United States v. Foster*, 133 F.3d 704, 707 (1998) (en banc).

For indicators from Congress itself, it is appropriate to consider word usage in other provisions of Title 18's chapter on "Firearms." The Court, however, does not derive from the statutory complex at issue its thesis that " '[c]arry' implies personal agency and some degree of possession, whereas 'transport' does not have such a limited connotation and, in addition, implies the movement of goods in bulk over great distances." [Quoting majority opinion.] Looking to provisions Congress enacted, one finds that the Legislature did not acknowledge or routinely adhere to the distinction the Court advances today; instead, Congress sometimes employed "transports" when, according to the Court, "carries" was the right word to use.

Section 925(a)(2)(B), for example, provides that no criminal sanction shall attend "the transportation of [a] firearm or ammunition carried out to enable a person, who lawfully received such firearm or ammunition from the Secretary of the Army, to engage in military training or in competitions." The full text of § 926A, rather than the truncated version the Court presents, is also telling:

> Notwithstanding any other provision of any law or any rule or regulation of a State or any political subdivision thereof, any person who is not otherwise prohibited by this chapter from transporting, shipping, or receiving a firearm shall be entitled to transport a firearm for any lawful purpose from any place where he may lawfully possess and carry such firearm to any other place where he may lawfully possess and carry such firearm if, during such transportation the firearm is unloaded, and neither the firearm nor any ammunition being transported is readily accessible or is directly accessible from the passenger compartment of such transporting vehicle: *Provided,* That in the case of a vehicle without a compartment separate from the driver's compartment the firearm or ammunition shall be contained in a locked container other than the glove compartment or console.

In describing when and how a person may travel in a vehicle that contains his firearm without violating the law, §§ 925(a)(2)(B) and 926A use "transport," not "carry," to "impl[y] personal agency and some degree of possession." [Again quoting majority opinion.][10]

---

10. The Court asserts that " 'transport' is a broader category that includes 'carry' but encompasses other activity." "Carry," however, is not merely a subset of "transport." A person

Reading "carries" in § 924(c)(1) to mean "on or about [one's] person" is fully compatible with these and other "Firearms" statutes. For example, under § 925(a)(2)(B), one could carry his gun to a car, transport it to the shooting competition, and use it to shoot targets. Under the conditions of § 926A, one could transport her gun in a car, but under no circumstances could the gun be readily accessible while she travels in the car. "[C]ourts normally try to read language in different, but related, statutes, so as best to reconcile those statutes, in light of their purposes and of common sense." [*United States v. McFadden*, 13 F.3d 463, 467 (1st Cir. 1994) (Breyer, C.J., dissenting).] So reading the "Firearms" statutes, I would not extend the word "carries" in § 924(c)(1) to mean transports out of hand's reach in a vehicle.[12]

Section 924(c)(1), as the foregoing discussion details, is not decisively clear one way or another. The sharp division in the Court on the proper reading of the measure confirms, "[a]t the very least, . . . that the issue is subject to some doubt. Under these circumstances, we adhere to the familiar rule that, 'where there is ambiguity in a criminal statute, doubts are resolved in favor of the defendant.' " *Adamo Wrecking Co. v. United States*, 434 U.S. 275, 284–285 (1978); see *United States v. Granderson*, 511 U.S. 39, 54 (1994) ("[W]here text, structure, and history fail to establish that the Government's position is unambiguously correct—we apply the rule of lenity and resolve the ambiguity in [the defendant's] favor."). "Carry" bears many meanings, as the Court and the "Firearms" statutes demonstrate.[13] The narrower "on or about [one's] person" interpretation

---

seated at a desk with a gun in hand or pocket is carrying the gun, but is not transporting it. Yes, the words "carry" and "transport" often can be employed interchangeably, as can the words "carry" and "use." But in *Bailey*, this Court settled on constructions that gave "carry" and "use" independent meanings. Without doubt, Congress is alert to the discrete meanings of "transport" and "carry" in the context of vehicles, as the Legislature's placement of each word in § 926A illustrates. The narrower reading of "carry" preserves discrete meanings for the two words, while in the context of vehicles the Court's interpretation of "carry" is altogether synonymous with "transport." Tellingly, when referring to firearms traveling in vehicles, the "Firearms" statutes routinely use a form of "transport"; they never use a form of "carry."

12. The Court places undue reliance on Representative Poff's statement that § 924(c)(1) seeks " 'to persuade the man who is tempted to commit a Federal felony to leave his gun at home.' " See [majority opinion] (quoting 114 Cong. Rec. 22231 (1968)). As the Government argued in its brief to this Court in *Bailey*:

In making that statement, Representative Poff was not referring to the "carries" prong of the original Section 924(c). As originally enacted, the "carries" prong of the statute prohibited only the "unlawful" carrying of a firearm while committing an offense. The statute would thus not have applied to an individual who, for instance, had a permit for carrying a gun and carried it with him when committing an offense, and it would have had no force in "persuading" such an individual "to leave his gun at home." Instead, Representative Poff was referring to the "uses" prong of the original Section 924(c). [Quoting U.S. Brief in *Bailey*.]

Representative Poff's next sentence confirms that he was speaking of "uses," not "carries": "Any person should understand that if he *uses* his gun and is caught and convicted, he is going to jail." 114 Cong. Rec., at 22231 (emphasis added).

13. Any doubt on that score is dispelled by examining the provisions in the "Firearms" chapter, in addition to § 924(c)(1), that include a form of the word "carry": 18 U.S.C. § 922(a)(5) ("*carry out* a bequest"); §§ 922(s)(6)(B)(ii), (iii) ("*carry out* this subsection"); § 922(u) ("*carry away* [a firearm]"); 18 U.S.C.A. § 924(a)(6)(B)(ii) (Supp.1998) ("*carry* or otherwise possess or discharge or otherwise use [a] handgun"); 18 U.S.C. § 924(e)(2)(B) ("*carrying* of a firearm"); § 925(a)(2) ("*carried out* to enable a person"); § 926(a) ("*carry out* the provisions of this chapter"); § 926A ("lawfully possess and *carry* such firearm to any other place where he may is hardly implausible nor at odds with an accepted meaning of "carries a firearm."

Overlooking that there will be an enhanced sentence for the gun-possessing drug dealer in any event, the Court asks rhetorically: "How persuasive is a punishment that is without effect until a drug dealer who has brought his gun to a sale (indeed has it available for use) actually takes it from the trunk (or unlocks the glove compartment) of his car?" Correspondingly, the Court defines "carries a firearm" to cover "a person who knowingly possesses and conveys firearms [anyplace] in a vehicle . . . which the person accompanies." Congress, however, hardly lacks compe-tence to select the words "possesses" or "conveys" when that is what the Legislature means.[14] Notably in view of the Legislature's capacity to speak plainly, and of overriding concern, the Court's inquiry pays scant atten-tion to a core reason for the rule of lenity: "[B]ecause of the seriousness of criminal penalties, and because criminal punishment usually represents the moral condemnation of the community, legislatures and not courts should define criminal activity. This policy embodies 'the instinctive distaste against men languishing in prison unless the lawmaker has clearly said they should.' " *United States v. Bass* (quoting H. Friendly, Mr. Justice Frankfurter and the Reading of Statutes, in Benchmarks 196, 209 (1967)). * * *

Postscript: Soon after the Court's opinion in *Muscarello*, Congress overrode *Bailey* in Pub. L. No. 105–386, 112 Stat. 3469 (1998). The new law amended 18 U.S.C. § 924(c)(1), to trigger the sentence-enhancement provisions where the defendant possesses a firearm "in furtherance of" one of the predicate offenses. An additional enhancement is triggered if the firearm is "brandished," and a yet-higher one if it is "discharged." Brandish is defined in new § 924(c)(4): "to display all or part of the firearm, or otherwise to make the presence of the firearm known to another person, regardless of whether the firearm is directly visible to that person." Does this new statute lend support to the majority's ap-proach in *Muscarello*?

McNally v. United States, 483 U.S. 350 (1987). The federal mail fraud statute, 18 U.S.C. § 1341, provides that "[w]hoever, having devised or intending to devise any scheme or artifice to defraud, or for obtaining money or property by means of false or fraudulent pretenses, representa-tions, or promises, * * * for the purpose of executing such scheme or artifice or attempting to do so [uses the mails or causes them to be used,] shall be fined not more than $1,000 or imprisoned not more than five

---

lawfully possess and *carry* such firearm"); § 929(a)(1) ("uses or *carries* a firearm and is in possession of armor piercing ammunition"); § 930(d)(3) ("lawful *carrying* of firearms . . . in a Federal facility incident to hunting or other lawful purposes") (emphasis added in all quotations).

14. See, e.g., 18 U.S.C.A. § 924(a)(6)(B)(ii) (Supp.1998) ("if the person sold . . . a handgun . . . to a juvenile knowing . . . that the juvenile intended to *carry or otherwise possess* . . . the handgun . . . in the commission of a crime of violence"); 18 U.S.C. § 926A ("may lawfully *possess and carry* such firearm to any other place where he may lawfully *possess and carry* such firearm"); § 929(a)(1) ("uses or *carries a firearm and is in possession* of armor piercing ammunition"); § 2277 ("*brings, carries, or possesses* any dangerous weapon") (emphasis added in all quotations).

years, or both." The lower courts upheld the convictions of several public officials and one private party activist who made a deal with an insurance company, whereby the state would send business to the company, which in turn would send some of the commissions to other companies designated by the conspirators, including one company they owned. The record apparently did not demonstrate that the state had lost any money by virtue of this kickback scheme. The Court, in an opinion by **Justice White**, reversed the lower courts' interpretation of § 1341, concluding that the statute outlawed only those "frauds on the public" that result in a tangible loss to the public.

"As first enacted in 1872, as part of a recodification of the postal laws, the statute contained a general proscription against using the mails to initiate correspondence in furtherance of 'any scheme or artifice to defraud.' The sponsor of the recodification stated, in apparent reference to the antifraud provision, that measures were needed 'to prevent the frauds which are mostly gotten up in the large cities ... by thieves, forgers, and rapscallions generally, for the purpose of deceiving and fleecing the innocent people in the country.' Insofar as the sparse legislative history reveals anything, it indicates that the original impetus behind the mail fraud statute was to protect the people from schemes to deprive them of their money or property. * * *

"As the Court long ago stated, * * * the words 'to defraud' commonly refer 'to wronging one in his property rights by dishonest methods or schemes,' and 'usually signify the deprivation of something of value by trick, deceit, chicane or overreaching.' *Hammerschmidt v. United States*, 265 U.S. 182, 188 (1924). [Congress's adding the phrase "or for obtaining money or property" in] 1909 does not indicate that Congress was departing from this common understanding. As we see it, adding the second phrase simply made it unmistakable that the statute reached false promises and misrepresentations as to the future as well as other frauds involving money or property.

"We believe that Congress' intent in passing the mail fraud statute was to prevent the use of the mails in furtherance of such schemes. The Court has often stated that when there are two rational readings of a criminal statute, one harsher than the other, we are to choose the harsher only when Congress has spoken in clear and definite language. * * * Rather than construe the statute in a manner that leaves its outer boundaries ambiguous and involves the Federal Government in setting standards of disclosure and good government for local and state officials, we read § 1341 as limited in scope to the protection of property rights. If Congress desires to go further, it must speak more clearly than it has."

Justice Stevens, in dissent, relied on the plain meaning of the statute, which prohibits the use of the United States mails for the purpose of executing "[1] *any* scheme or artifice to defraud, [2] *or* for obtaining money or property by means of false or fraudulent pretenses, representations, or promises, [3] *or* to sell, dispose of, loan, exchange, alter, give away, distribute, supply, or furnish or procure for unlawful use any counterfeit or spurious coin, obligation, security, or other article, or anything represented to be or intimated or held out to be such counterfeit or spurious article ...'' 18 U.S.C. § 1341 (emphasis and brackets added).

"As the language makes clear, each of these restrictions is independent. One can violate the second clause—obtaining money or property by false pretenses—even though one does not violate the third clause—counterfeiting. Similarly, one can violate the first clause—devising a scheme or artifice to defraud—without violating the counterfeiting provision. Until today it was also obvious that one could violate the first clause by devising a scheme or artifice to defraud, even though one did not violate the second clause by seeking to obtain money or property from his victim through false pretenses. Every court to consider the matter had so held. Yet, today, the Court, for all practical purposes, rejects this long-standing construction of the statute by imposing a requirement that a scheme or artifice to defraud does not violate the statute unless its purpose is to defraud someone of money or property. I am at a loss to understand the source or justification for this holding. Certainly no canon of statutory construction requires us to ignore the plain language of the provision.

"In considering the scope of the mail fraud statute it is essential to remember Congress's purpose in enacting it. Congress sought to protect the integrity of the United States mails by not allowing them to be used as 'instruments of crime.' *United States v. Brewer*, 528 F.2d 492, 498 (4th Cir. 1975). 'The focus of the statute is upon the misuse of the Postal Service, not the regulation of state affairs, and Congress clearly has the authority to regulate such misuse of the mails.' *United States v. States*, 488 F.2d 761, 767 (8th Cir. 1973), cert. denied, 417 U.S. 909 (1974). Once this purpose is considered, it becomes clear that the construction the Court adopts today is senseless. Can it be that Congress sought to purge the mails of schemes to defraud citizens of money but was willing to tolerate schemes to defraud citizens of their right to an honest government, or to unbiased public officials? Is it at all rational to assume that Congress wanted to ensure that the mails not be used for petty crimes, but did not prohibit election fraud accomplished through mailing fictitious ballots? Given Congress' 'broad purpose,' I 'find it difficult to believe, absent some indication in the statute itself or the legislative history, that Congress would have undercut sharply that purpose by hobbling federal prosecutors in their effort to combat' use of the mails for fraudulent schemes.''

Postscript: Justice White's memorandum to the Conference, in which he circulated his opinion, expressed reservations about the broad holding but concluded: "But it is not rare that Opinions of the Court are no more persuasive than an opinion on the other side would have been. Of course, the saving grace in Statutory Construction cases is that Congress may have its way if it does not like the product of our work."[h] In 1988, Congress adopted 18 U.S.C. § 1346, which provides that for purposes of the mail fraud statute " 'scheme or artifice to defraud' includes a scheme or artifice to deprive another of the intangible right of honest services." The statute's legislative history indicates that it was meant to override *McNally* and reinstate the "intangible rights" theory.

NOTES ON *MUSCARELLO, McNALLY, AND THE* SUPREME COURT'S *APPROACH TO CRIMINAL STATUTES*

1. *The Rule of Lenity Cuts Across Political Lines.* Note the peculiar—perhaps unprecedented—lineup of Justices on both sides of the issue in *Muscarello.* The lineup in *McNally* is almost as odd, with Justices Scalia and Brennan in the majority and Stevens and O'Connor in dissent. The reason for the odd lineups is that the rule of lenity appeals to both civil libertarians (like Brennan, Marshall, Ginsburg) and high formalists who are fans of the nondelegation argument (like Scalia and perhaps Ginsburg), while a more expansive application of criminal statutes appeals to both pragmatists who are willing to apply common-law reasoning to statutory cases (like Stevens, O'Connor, Breyer) and hard-liners against criminals (Thomas perhaps). This heterogeneity also makes the rule of lenity cases hard to predict. We were surprised to find Scalia with the nontextualist majority in *McNally* and Rehnquist (usually a hard-liner in criminal cases) with the lenient *Muscarello* dissent.

2. *The Supreme Court's Inconsistency in Applying the Rule of Lenity?* Can *McNally*, where the Court invoked lenity, and *Muscarello*, where it did not, be reconciled? The cases are similar: each involved broadly phrased federal statutes being applied to antisocial conduct. Some possible bases for distinction: (a) the statute was clearer in the firearms case; (b) Supreme Court precedent supported lenity in the mail fraud case but not the firearm case, where *Smith* had already construed "carry" in a broad way; or (c) the mail fraud case involved federal prosecution of state officials and so trenched on federalism values more deeply if broadly construed (as lower courts had been doing). Even if those distinctions work to distinguish *Muscarello* from *McNally*, they do not distinguish it from *Ratzlaf*, where a clear statute that had not been construed by the Court and was not being applied to state officials was nonetheless applied leniently—indeed, in a way that rendered the statute unenforceable.[i] However one resolves the distinction between *Muscarello* and *McNally*, there are plenty of Supreme Court cases going one way or the other.

---

h. The Thurgood Marshall Papers, Library of Congress (Madison Building), Box 423, Folder 3 (Court memoranda regarding *McNally*, Nos. 86–234 & 86–286). Indeed, Congress does often override the Court's statutory decisions, and when the Court applies the rule of lenity to protect federal criminal defendants, the Department of Justice has the best record in the land for obtaining overrides. William N. Eskridge Jr., *Overriding Supreme Court Statutory Interpretation Decisions*, 101 Yale L.J. 331 (1991). Is this a good justification for writing a weak opinion, though?

i. For students tough on crime, don't worry about the lenity in cases like *Ratzlaf*, for it was immediately overridden by Congress. See Pub. L. No. 103–325, § 411, 108 Stat. 2253 (1994). The most frequent legislative overrides come where the government loses criminal law cases. See Eskridge, *Overriding the Court, supra* (about 17% of the congressional overrides of Supreme

For example, the Court in *Chiarella v. United States*, 445 U.S. 222, 232–33 (1980), held that an employee of the printer for paperwork involved in corporate takeover bids, who read the materials he was printing and used that knowledge to purchase stock before the takeover announcement, did not commit securities fraud. While the anti-fraud rule[j] had long applied to corporate officers, their agents, and their "tipees," the Supreme Court refused to expand its application to the printer's employee, because "he was not their agent, he was not a fiduciary, he was not a person in whom the sellers had placed their trust and confidence." The Supreme Court said that affirming such a conviction would have to "recogniz[e] a general duty between all participants in market transactions to forego actions based on material, nonpublic information. * * * This should not be undertaken absent some explicit evidence of Congressional intent."

Although the Supreme Court in *Chiarella* and *McNally* invoked the rule of lenity, *Muscarello* better reflects Supreme Court practice. Since 1984, the Court has cited the rule of lenity in just over one-fourth of its cases interpreting criminal statutes. In more than 60% of the cases, the Court has agreed with the government's interpretation.[k] Although there are still cases where the Court applies the rule of lenity, e.g., *Arthur Andersen LLP v. United States*, 544 U.S. 696 (2005); *Cleveland v. United States*, 531 U.S. 12 (2000), it remains unclear whether the rule has a systematic effect. But see *Skilling v. United States*, below.

3. *Recent Rule of Lenity Developments: Sentencing, Legislative History, Civil Statutes.* For most of American history, the rule of lenity was applied only in the context of substantive criminal law, because sentencing was largely a matter of judicial discretion within well-defined statutory confines. *McNally* is an example. In the last 20 years, the law of sentencing has become more complex and less discretionary with judges—and the Supreme Court applied the rule of lenity to criminal sentencing in *United States v. R.L.C.*, 503 U.S. 291 (1992). See Phillip Spector, *The Sentencing Rule of Lenity*, 33 U. Toledo L. Rev. 511 (2002), who argues against application of the rule to sentencing statutes, on the ground that the notice, prosecutorial discretion, and nondelegation rationales do not apply nearly as strongly to sentencing laws as to those defining substantive crimes.

As in substantive criminal law cases, the Court will not invoke the rule of lenity in sentencing cases where the statutory directive is clear. See *Chapman v. United States*, 500 U.S. 453 (1991) (affirming the Easterbrook decision in *Marshall v. United States*, Chapter 2, § 3); *Gozlon–Peretz v. United States*, 498 U.S. 395 (1991). To the extent § 924, an enhancement statute, is viewed

---

Court statutory opinions, 1967–89, came in criminal law, all but two of the overrides being to expand liability where the Court had applied lenity).

j. Section 10(b) of the Securities Exchange Act of 1934, 15 U.S.C. § 78j(b) (1988), proscribes the use of "any manipulative or deceptive device or contrivance" in violation of SEC rules and "in connection with the purchase or sale of any security." Rule 10b–5 prohibits use of "any device, scheme or artifice to defraud" or any act or practice which would "operate as a fraud or deceit upon any person, in connection with the purchase or sale of any security." 17 C.F.R. § 240.10b–5 (1993).

k. See William N. Eskridge Jr. & Lauren E. Baer, *The Continuum of Deference: Supreme Court Treatment of Agency Statutory Interpretations from* Chevron *to* Hamdan, 96 Geo. L.J. 1083 (2008).

as a sentencing law, *Muscarello* illustrates the difficulty of figuring out when sentencing statutes are clear. (*Muscarello* and *Chapman* might be read to support Spector's argument that the rule of lenity ought not be applied to sentencing statutes.)

As to this point, there is debate within the Court whether legislative history can be considered. In *R.L.C.*, a plurality of Justices stated that the application of the rule of lenity is reserved "for those situations in which a reasonable doubt persists about the statute's intended scope even *after* resort to the language and structure, legislative history, and motivating policies of the statute." See also *Smith v. United States*, 508 U.S. 223 (1993). Justice Scalia, joined by Justices Kennedy and Thomas, objected in *R.L.C.* to the presence of legislative history and statutory policies in this inquiry. Note that Kennedy and Thomas joined the Court's opinion in *Muscarello*, which relied on legislative history.

The Court has sometimes ruled that the rule of lenity also applies when a civil-type remedy is applied to a defendant for conduct violating a criminal-type statute. Thus, in *Hughey v. United States*, 495 U.S. 411 (1990), the Court applied the rule of lenity to a statute requiring a criminal defendant to provide restitution. And in *Crandon v. United States*, 494 U.S. 152 (1990), the Court invoked the rule of lenity to protect a civil defendant, where the applicable standard of conduct was found in a criminal statute.

Skilling v. United States, 130 S.Ct. 2896 (2010). Founded in 1985, Enron Corporation swiftly became the seventh highest-revenue-grossing company in America. Jeffrey Skilling was Enron's chief executive officer for most of 2001. Less than four months after he resigned, Enron crashed into bankruptcy, and its stock plummeted in value. After an investigation uncovered a conspiracy to prop up Enron's stock prices by overstating the company's financial well-being, the federal government prosecuted dozens of Enron employees, culminating in prosecutions of Skilling and two other top executives. The indictment charged that these three defendants violated several federal criminal statutes when they allegedly engaged in a scheme to deceive investors about Enron's true financial performance by manipulating its publicly reported financial results and making false and misleading statements. Count 1 of the indictment charged Skilling with conspiracy to commit "honest-services" wire fraud, 18 U. S. C. §§ 371, 1343, 1346, by depriving Enron and its shareholders of the intangible right of his honest services. Skilling was convicted of these and other charges, and his conviction was upheld on appeal to the Fifth Circuit. (Section 1346 was Congress's response to *McNally*.)

The Supreme Court reversed Skilling's § 1346 conviction. **Justice Ginsburg**'s opinion for the Court on this issue (joined by Chief Justice Roberts and Justices Stevens, Breyer, Alito, and Sotomayor) interpreted § 1346 to be limited to schemes to defraud of honest services only where there have been bribes and kickbacks. Justice Ginsburg started with a review of pre–1987 mail and wire fraud prosecutions under §§ 1341 and 1343 that expanded "scheme to defraud" crimes to include losses of "honest services" and not just losses of tangible property. The leading case was *Shushan* v. *United States*, 117 F.2d 110 (5th Cir. 1941), which upheld the mail fraud prosecution of a public official who allegedly accepted bribes from entrepreneurs in exchange for urging city action beneficial to the bribe payers. "A scheme to get a public contract on more favorable terms than would likely be got otherwise by bribing a public official," the court observed, "would not only be a plan to commit the crime of bribery, but would also be a scheme to defraud the public." By 1987, every federal court of appeals had accepted the "honest services" interpretation of the mail (§ 1341) and wire (§ 1343) fraud statutes, usually in cases that involved bribes or kickbacks.

In *McNally*, the Supreme Court stopped the lower court development of the intangible rights doctrine "in its tracks"—and Congress "responded swiftly," with new § 1346. Skilling argued that the swift response was too vague to satisfy the Due Process Clause, however. "To satisfy due process, 'a penal statute [must] define the criminal offense [1] with sufficient definiteness that ordinary people can understand what conduct is prohibited and [2] in a manner that does not encourage arbitrary and discriminatory enforcement.' *Kolender* v. *Lawson*, 461 U.S. 352, 357 (1983)." Skilling claimed that § 1346 does not clearly define what behavior it prohibits and its "standardless sweep allows policemen, prosecutors, and juries to pursue their personal predilections," and sought a judgment invalidating the statute.

"In urging invalidation of § 1346, Skilling swims against our case law's current, which requires us, if we can, to construe, not condemn, Congress' enactments." No court of appeals had ruled that § 1346 was void for vagueness, and the Supreme Court agreed that the better path was a narrowing construction. "First, we look to the doctrine developed in pre-*McNally* cases in an endeavor to ascertain the meaning of the phrase 'the intangible right of honest services.' Second, to preserve what Congress certainly intended the statute to cover, we pare that body of precedent down to its core: In the main, the pre-*McNally* cases involved fraudulent schemes to deprive another of honest services through bribes or kickbacks supplied by a third party who had not been deceived. Confined to these paramount applications, § 1346 presents no vagueness problem."

Based upon constitutional vagueness concerns and the rule of lenity in criminal cases, Justice Ginsburg rejected the government's suggestion that § 1346 also include cases where there is "undisclosed self-dealing by a public official or private employee—*i.e.*, the taking of official action by the employee that furthers his own undisclosed financial interests while purporting to act in the interests of those to whom he owes a fiduciary duty." Because Skilling's alleged misbehavior did not include charges that he received bribes or kickbacks, Justice Ginsburg reversed his § 1346 conviction and remanded to the lower courts to determine whether the other convictions could stand.

Justice Scalia (joined by Justices Thomas and Kennedy) concurred in the Court's judgment but would have declared § 1346 void for vagueness. He viewed the Court's surgery on § 1346 to be "not interpretation but invention," the equivalent of judicial crafting of a common law crime, which our nation's constitutional culture has long abjured. *E.g.*, *United States v. Hudson*, 7 Cranch 32, 34 (1812). Additionally, Justice Scalia wondered what rewritten/narrowed § 1346 now covered: Does it apply to private officials, such as Skilling, at all? What would constitute a "bribe" or "kickback" (terms that do not appear in the statute but that are now interpolated into it by the majority) in future cases?

PROBLEM 3–2

The Case of the Fraudulent Insurance Schemers

John Able is the state Commissioner of Insurance, who decides what insurance companies will receive contracts to insure certain state activities and buildings. Kim Bumble heads the Squalid Insurance Company, which wants to secure contracting rights to insure all state buildings associated with public education. Pat Cain is a leader of the Cut–Taxes Party, which has won control of the state legislature and just elected a governor in the state. Able switches parties to become a Cut–Taxer. In the process, Able, Bumble, and Cain enter into an agreement whereby Able would funnel all state education insurance contracts to Squalid Insurance, which would then pay $100,000 per year to a company partly owned by Able and would contribute $500,000 a year to the Cut–Taxes Party.

Federal investigators uncover this scheme, and prosecutors indict Able, Bumble, and Cain for violating § 1346. Each defendant argues that the statute does not apply to him or her after *Skilling*. Should any of the defendants prevail? Which one(s)?

People v. Davis, 15 Cal.4th 1096, 938 P.2d 938, 64 Cal. Rptr. 2d 879 (1997). Defendant Robert Vonroski Davis was charged with one count of murder and one count of attempted murder. In addition, three prior convictions were alleged under a "three-strikes law," § 667(b)–(i) of the Penal Code: a 1990 juvenile adjudication of felony assault; a 1991 juvenile adjudication of residential burglary; and a 1993 adult robbery conviction. The trial court granted Davis's motion that the two juvenile adjudications did not count as strikes. Davis was convicted of murder and attempted murder, and the judge sentenced him to thirty-five years to life, with a consecutive term of life plus five years. The court of appeal affirmed the conviction and reversed the trial court's order striking the prior juvenile adjudication for felony assault.

In general, the three-strikes legislation provides longer sentences for certain prior serious or violent felonies popularly denoted "strikes." A "two strike" case involves one prior qualifying felony; a "three strike" case involves two or more prior qualifying felonies. The statute's purpose is to provide greater punishment for recidivists (§ 667(b)). Section 667(d)(3) lists the requirements for a prior juvenile adjudication to qualify as a "strike":

(3) A prior juvenile adjudication shall constitute a prior felony conviction for purposes of sentence enhancement if:

(A) The juvenile was 16 years of age or older at the time he or she committed the prior offense.

(B) The prior offense is listed in Section 707(b) of the Welfare and Institutions Code or described in paragraph (1) [California prior serious or violent felony convictions] or (2) [other jurisdiction prior serious or violent felony convictions] as a felony.

(C) The juvenile was found to be a fit and proper subject to be dealt with under the juvenile court law.

(D) The juvenile was adjudged a ward of the juvenile court within the meaning of Section 602 of the Welfare and Institutions Code because the person committed an offense listed in Section 707(b) of the Welfare and Institutions Code. * * *

Defendant contended that § 667(d)(3)(C) required an express finding of fitness is required; the court majority, in an opinion by **Justice Brown**, disagreed and affirmed the trial judge's determination to count the juvenile convictions as strikes.

Under Welfare and Institutions Code § 602, "Any person who is under the age of 18 years when he violates any law of this state or of the United States or any ordinance of any city or county of this state defining crime other than an ordinance establishing a curfew based solely on age, is within the jurisdiction of the juvenile court, which may adjudge such person to be a ward of the court." A petition under this section "is the equivalent of a complaint in the adult court." The prosecutor may, however, also file a petition under Welfare and Institutions Code § 707 seeking a determination that the minor is unfit for treatment in the juvenile court system. When the juvenile is charged with a serious crime, and a § 707 petition is filed, the minor is "presumed to be not a fit and proper subject to be dealt with under the juvenile court law unless the juvenile court concludes ... that the minor would be amenable to the care, treatment, and training program available through the facilities of the juvenile court based upon an evaluation of" various criteria. If the juvenile court makes a finding of fitness, it makes "[a] determination that the minor is a fit and proper subject to be dealt with under the juvenile court law ...." (§ 707(c))

"As the Court of Appeal recognized, '[p]roceedings under section 602 with the resulting adjudication of wardship and treatment of the minor under the jurisdiction of the juvenile court constitute[ ] an implied finding that the minor is a "fit and proper subject to be dealt with under the juvenile court law." ' " By its terms, subdivision (d)(3)(C) requires a finding, not an express finding, of fitness. * * * Indeed, if subdivision (d)(3)(C) were construed to require an express finding of fitness, this would so severely limit those juvenile adjudications that would qualify as 'strikes,' that such a result would seem to be at odds with the intent of section 667(b)–(i).

"Finally, a conclusion that subdivision (d)(3)(C) requires an express finding of fitness would evoke questions regarding the statute's constitutional validity. The difference in punishment that two otherwise similarly situated defendants would receive would depend solely on an *unsuccessful* motion for a determination that the minor is unfit for treatment in the juvenile court system. An express finding requirement would be analogous to a statute that set the punishment for a manslaughter conviction at five years if the prosecution originally charged the case as manslaughter, but ten years if the prosecution originally charged the case as murder and the defendant was convicted of the lesser charge of manslaughter. Such a statute would arguably be open to a variety of constitutional challenges such as equal protection, due process, and separation of powers. We see no basis for concluding that the Legislature made such an arguably irrational distinction here.

"Defendant asserts that concluding an implied finding satisfies subdivision (d)(3)(C) renders that subdivision superfluous. He essentially argues that subdivision (d)(3)(C) would then apply to anyone tried in juvenile, as opposed to adult court, and subdivision (d)(3) already expressly applies to prior juvenile adjudications. However, the presence of some duplication in a multiprong statutory test does not automatically render it meaningless. * * * For the reasons set forth above, we conclude the more reasonable interpretation is that an implied finding of fitness satisfies subdivision (d)(3)(C). The trial court therefore erred in striking defendant's prior juvenile adjudications for felony assault and residential burglary on this ground. * * *

Justice Mosk (joined by Justice Werdegar) dissented, on the ground that § 667(d)(3)(C) clearly required a finding of fitness, end of analysis. "[T]he majority's argument comes close to passing on the wisdom of the requirement of a finding of fitness contained in section 667(d)(3)(C). That would be impermissible. But, contrary to the majority, we can surely conclude that it is not 'irrational.' For we may deem it a kind of screening device, separating classes of juveniles—those as to whom a doubt about fitness had been raised (albeit subsequently resolved), and those as to whom such a doubt had not."

Moreover, the majority's interpretation makes the statute too harsh. "The substantive scope of possible strikes for prior juvenile adjudications is broader than that for prior felony convictions properly so called. The latter comprises 'violent' and 'serious' California felonies and certain out-of-state felonies. The former, by contrast, embraces those same felonies and also reaches beyond to Welfare and Institutions Code section 707(b) offenses, which cover such otherwise uncovered crimes as bribery of a witness [Welf. & Inst. Code, § 707(b)(19)]. Consequently, some offenses committed by a juvenile are possible strikes, but the same ones committed by an adult are not. Such a result is harsh and hard to justify. A limitation like that referred to might have a mitigating effect."

Justice Kennard also dissented. In response to the majority's concern that Davis's interpretation would render the statutory scheme irrational as to juveniles, she offered the following explanation: "Some 16–year–old delinquents are already dangerous, violent criminals. But there may be others whose acts reflect youthful immaturity rather than a commitment to crime. Perhaps it was a concern not to subject juvenile offenders in the latter category to the harsh penalties of the new Three Strikes law that led the Legislature, which had never before permitted juvenile adjudications to be used in adult court for purposes of enhancement, to include within the class of 'strikes' only those crimes that, in the prosecutor's view, were so serious as to require trying the minor as an adult."

Like Justice Mosk, Justice Kennard invoked the plain meaning of § 667 and, further, rebuked the court for adopting an interpretation that rendered § 667(d)(3)(C) surplusage. Because the statute has a plain meaning, the rule to avoid constitutional difficulties cannot be invoked, as the majority sought to do, see *People v. Anderson*, 43 Cal.3d 1104, 1146, 240 Cal.Rptr. 585, 742 P.2d 1306 (1987), and any general equal protection or due process problems with the literal interpretation are premature. She concluded her dissent with this:

"We are all concerned about the epidemic of violent crime in our society. The Three Strikes law that the Legislature enacted in March 1994 and that we construe today (§ 667[b]–[i]) reflects a toughening public attitude towards repeat offenders. That attitude is also reflected in the nearly identical Three Strikes initiative that was overwhelmingly passed by the voters just eight months later. (§ 1170.12.)

"A court construing a statute, however, can never be guided by public sentiment alone. Here, in construing the Three Strikes law, it is not enough to say that because the Legislature and the electorate wished to impose tougher penalties on repeat violent offenders, we should therefore give that enactment the harshest possible construction. Judges are constrained by the law. For the sake of the predictability and stability of the law, our guideposts in interpreting the Three Strikes law must be the usual principles of statutory construction that apply in every case, not our projections of the hopes and fears that led to the statute's enactment. In the words of United States Supreme Court Justice Felix Frankfurter: 'For judicial construction to stick close to what the legislation says and not draw prodigally upon unformulated purposes or directions makes for careful draftsmanship and for legislative responsibility.... Judicial expansion of meaning beyond the limits indicated is reprehensible because it encourages slipshodness in draftsmanship and irresponsibility in legislation. It also enlists too heavily the private ... views of judges.' (Frankfurter, *Foreword, Symposium on Statutory Construction* [1950] 3 Vand. L. Rev. 365, 367–368.)"

NOTE ON DAVIS AND STATE CRIMINAL CODE CONSTRUCTIONS

What is most "striking" about *Davis* is that the court contravened clear statutory wording to extend a highly punitive statute to a defendant—an inversion of the rule of lenity. Yet the California Supreme Court has ruled that it will "construe a penal statute as favorably to the defendant as its language and the circumstances of its application may reasonably permit." *People v. Garcia*, 87 Cal.Rptr.2d 114, 120, 980 P.2d 829 (1999). What is going on? Consider some possible theories for the Court's sacrifice of the lenity principle.

First, California Penal Code § 4 revokes the rule of lenity and provides that penal statutes are to be construed according to "the fair import of their terms, with a view to effect its objects and to promote justice." How can § 4 be squared with *Garcia*? The most obvious answer is that the California courts consider the rule of lenity constitutionally required (and § 4 is therefore unconstitutional), but then *Davis* becomes even more of a mystery. Perhaps the rule of lenity, per *Garcia*, does not apply to sentencing laws, as Spector argues in *Sentencing Rule of Lenity*. Or perhaps the rule of lenity is dead as a rule of strict construction, but its underlying quasi-constitutional concerns survive. Consider the suggestion that state and federal judges in fact interpret vague criminal statutes in ways that (1) avoid criminalizing ordinary, day-to-day conduct, (2) that prevent prosecutors from exercising excessive discretion, and (3) that help rationalize statutory schemes—but without recognizing a general rule of strict construction in *all* criminal cases.[1] Might *Skilling* be an example of this phenomenon?

Second, such an emphasis on having an overall rational scheme of crimes and punishments might help explain *Davis*, where the rationality principle might support the prosecutor. The majority wonders what conceivable reason the legislature would have had to count as strikes only those juvenile convictions where a prosecutor had sought adult treatment and the judge had ruled against it. This puzzle mobilizes not only the golden rule against absurd results, but also Hart and Sacks's notion that every statutory distinction must rest on an articulable reason or principle.

Third, the majority felt there were constitutional problems raised by a literal reading of § 667(d)(3)(C). As to that last problem, consider the following discussion.

B.   INTERPRETATION TO AVOID CONSTITUTIONAL PROBLEMS

One justification for the rule of lenity arises from the constitutional notion that a legislature cannot penalize people who are wholly passive and unaware of any wrongdoing, based upon a vague criminal prohibition. See *Lambert v. California*, 355 U.S. 225 (1957); *Papachristou v. Jacksonville*, 405 U.S. 156 (1972). Assuming that the legislature is loathe to come close to enacting unconstitutional criminal statutes, courts will construe criminal penalties narrowly enough so that there is no question of the statute's constitutionality, as construed. Penal statutes, of course, are not the only ones that may venture close to the precipice beyond which a statute will fall athwart the Constitution, and the Supreme Court from time to time interprets non-penal statutes restrictively to avoid constitutional problems. Like the rule of lenity, this canon of construction has both defenders and detractors. Consider the following cases and the notes that follow.

United States v. Witkovich, 353 U.S. 194 (1957). Witkovich was indicted under § 242(d) of the Immigration and Nationality Act of 1952, 66 Stat. 163, 208, on the charge that, as an alien against whom a final order of deportation had been outstanding for more than six months, he had willfully failed to give information to the Immigration and Naturalization Service (INS) as required by that section. Appellee moved to dismiss the indictment on the grounds that it failed to state an offense within the statute and in the alternative, if it did so, that the statute was unconstitutional.

Section 242(d) provided for criminal penalties under the following circumstances:

---

1. The idea in text came from Robert Yablon (Yale Law School, Class of 2006). Yablon came up with this idea through a systematic examination of cases in Ohio, one of three states that have codified the rule of lenity rather than revoking it.

Any alien, against whom a final order of deportation * * * has been outstanding for more than six months, shall, pending eventual deportation, be subject to supervision under regulations prescribed by the Attorney General. Such regulations shall include provisions which will require any alien subject to supervision (1) to appear from time to time before an immigration officer for identification; (2) to submit, if necessary, to medical and psychiatric examination at the expense of the United States; (3) to give information under oath as to his nationality, circumstances, habits, associations, and activities, and such other information, whether or not related to the foregoing, as the Attorney General may deem fit and proper; and (4) to conform to such reasonable written restrictions on his conduct or activities as are prescribed by the Attorney General in his case. * * *

The Department of Justice used this statutory authority as the basis for asking Witkovich dozens of questions about his political activities, his association with the Slovene National Benefit Society and other groups, and even his social activities.[m] He was held criminally liable when he refused to answer. In an opinion by **Justice Frankfurter**, the Supreme Court ruled that the Department's questions were not authorized by § 242(d).

"The language of § 242(d)(3), if read in isolation and literally, appears to confer upon the Attorney General unbounded authority to require whatever information he deems desirable of aliens whose deportation has not been effected within six months after it has been commanded. The Government itself shrinks from standing on the breadth of these words. But once the tyranny of literalness is rejected, all relevant considerations for giving a rational content to the words become operative. A restrictive meaning for what appear to be plain words may be indicated by the Act as a whole, by the persuasive gloss of legislative history or by the rule of constitutional adjudication, relied on by the District Court, that such a restrictive meaning must be given if a broader meaning would generate constitutional doubts.

"The preoccupation of the entire subsection of which clause (3) is a part is certainly with availability for deportation. Clause (1) requires the alien's periodic appearance for the purpose of identification, and clause (2) dealing with medical and psychiatric examination, when necessary, clearly is directed to the same end; and the 'reasonable written restrictions on [the alien's] conduct or activities' authorized by clause (4) have an implied

---

m.   [Eds.] Some of the questions included the following:

"(n) Q. Have you addressed any lodges of the Slovene National Benefit Society requesting their aid in your case, since the order of deportation was entered June 25, 1953?"

"(r) Q. Have you attended any movies since your order of supervision was entered at the Cinema Annex, 3210 West Madison Street, Chicago?"

"(s) Q. Are you acquainted with an individual named Irving Franklin?"

"(t) Q. Are you now a member of the Communist Party of U.S.A.?" * * *

"(v) Q. Are you now or have you ever been a member of the United Committee of South Slavic Americans?"

scope to be gathered from the subject matter, *i. e.*, the object of the statute as a whole. Moreover, this limitation of 'reasonableness' imposed by clause (4) upon the Attorney General's power to restrict suggests that, if we are to harmonize the various provisions of the section, the same limitation must also be read into the Attorney General's seemingly limitless power to question under clause (3). For, assuredly, Congress did not authorize that official to elicit information that could not serve as a basis for confining an alien's activities. Nowhere in § 242(d) is there any suggestion of a power of broad supervision like unto that over a probationer. When Congress did want to deal with the far-flung interest of national security or the general undesirable conduct of aliens, it gave clear indication of this purpose, as in § 242(e). In providing for the release of aliens convicted of wilful failure to depart, that subsection specifically requires courts to inquire into both the effect of the alien's release upon national security and the likelihood of his continued undesirable conduct."

Justice Frankfurter also relied on the explanation for § 242(d)'s interrogation provisions by the Senate Judiciary Committee, where they originated. Contrasting its own approach with that of the House, which would have allowed detention, the Senate Committee said: " 'This provision in the bill as it passed the House of Representatives appears to present a constitutional question.' This history, although suggesting a desire to exercise continuing control over the activities as well as the availability of aliens whose deportation had been ordered but not effected, shows a strong congressional unwillingness to enact legislation that may subject the Attorney General's supervisory powers to constitutional challenge."

"Acceptance of the interpretation of § 242(d) urged by the Government would raise doubts as to the statute's validity. By construing the Act to confer power on the Attorney General and his agents to inquire into matters that go beyond assuring an alien's availability for deportation we would, at the very least, open up the question of the extent to which an administrative officer may inhibit deportable aliens from renewing activities that subjected them to deportation. This is not *Carlson v. Landon*, [342 U.S. 524 (1952),] where the question was whether an alien could be detained during the customarily brief period pending determination of deportability. Contrariwise, and as the Senate and House Committees recognized in passing on § 242(d), supervision of the undeportable alien may be a lifetime problem. In these circumstances, issues touching liberties that the Constitution safeguards, even for an alien 'person,' would fairly be raised on the Government's view of the statute.

"The path of constitutional concern in this situation is clear.

'When the validity of an act of the Congress is drawn in question, and even if a serious doubt of constitutionality is raised, it is a cardinal principle that this Court will first ascertain whether a construction of the statute is fairly possible by which the question may be avoided.' "
Crowell v. Benson, 285 U.S. 22, 62.

See also cases cited in the concurring opinion of Mr. Justice Brandeis in *Ashwander v. Tennessee Valley Authority*, 297 U.S. 288, 348 note 8. * * *

"Section 242(d) is part of a legislative scheme designed to govern and to expedite the deportation of undesirable aliens, and clause (3) must be placed in the context of that scheme. As the District Court held and as our own examination of the Act confirms, it is a permissible and therefore an appropriate construction to limit the statute to authorizing all questions reasonably calculated to keep the Attorney General advised regarding the continued availability for departure of aliens whose deportation is overdue."

In dissent, **Justice Clark** (joined only by Justice Burton) argued that the Court's interpretation was completely inconsistent with the statute's clear language, as well as the national security reasons Congress gave the Attorney General such broad authority. Under the INA, *all* aliens are under the supervision of the Department of Justice, with duties to register, be finger-printed, and to report regularly to the Department. Section 242(d) was added because Congress felt that deportable aliens were more likely to engage in subversive activities and therefore required more particularized supervision.

"We believe that the purpose of the Act was to prevent a deportable alien from using the period of his further residence for the continuation of subversive, criminal, immoral, or other undesirable activities which formed the basis of his ordered deportation. * * * Several thousand alien Communists who have been finally ordered deported will from now on, due to the Court's decision today, be under virtually no statutory supervision. Still they will, in all probability, remain among us for neither they nor the countries of which they are nationals wish them to leave. To their countries they are potential agents. The House Committee on the Judiciary recognized this danger in its report on facilitating the deportation of aliens. Case histories set out in this report indicate that aliens ordered deported were refused visas by their native countries so that they might remain in the United States and carry on the very activities for which they were ordered deported."

Justice Clark found the Court's "constitutional problems" completely baffling. Congress has plenary authority over aliens, which the Court in *Carlson v. Landon* invoked as a basis for detaining deportable aliens. Thus, it was hard to see how the Attorney General's reading of the statute raised constitutional problems; if anything, the Court's reading of the statute was problematic. "In this respect the construction places an alien who has been under a final order of deportation for more than six months in a more favorable position than one who is under no order at all. Other aliens are obliged to report to the Attorney General when called upon to do so. Indeed, they must testify or claim their privilege. No privilege was claimed here. The Congress could not have intended the anomalous result reached today, one which is entirely foreign to its over-all plan of control over resident aliens."

NATIONAL LABOR RELATIONS BOARD
v. CATHOLIC BISHOP OF CHICAGO

Supreme Court of the United States, 1979
440 U.S. 490, 99 S.Ct. 1313, 59 L.Ed.2d 533

THE CHIEF JUSTICE [BURGER] delivered the opinion for the Court.

[The National Labor Relations Board (NLRB) exercised jurisdiction over lay faculty members at two groups of Roman Catholic high schools, certified unions as bargaining agents for the teachers, and ordered the schools to cease and desist their refusals to bargain with these unions. The NLRB asserted jurisdiction based on its policy of declining jurisdiction only when schools are "completely religious," not "religiously associated." The NLRB found that the schools in the instant case were in the latter category, since secular as well as religious topics were taught in the schools.

[The Court of Appeals denied enforcement of the NLRB order, and the Supreme Court affirmed. The Court first held that the NLRB distinction between schools that were "completely religious" and those that were "religiously associated" was not a workable guide for the exercise of the NLRB's discretionary jurisdiction. Recognizing that rejection of this distinction meant that the Board could extend its jurisdiction to all church-operated schools, the Court stated that the Free Exercise and Establishment Clauses of the First Amendment might preclude such an exercise of jurisdiction.]

Although the respondents press their claims under the Religion Clauses, the question we consider first is whether Congress intended the Board to have jurisdiction over teachers in church-operated schools. In a number of cases the Court has heeded the essence of Mr. Chief Justice Marshall's admonition in *Murray v. The Charming Betsy*, 2 Cranch 64, 118 (1804), by holding that an Act of Congress ought not be construed to violate the Constitution if any other possible construction remains available. Moreover, the Court has followed this policy in the interpretation of the Act now before us and related statutes.

In *Machinists v. Street*, 367 U.S. 740 (1961), for example, the Court considered claims that serious First Amendment questions would arise if the Railway Labor Act were construed to allow compulsory union dues to be used to support political candidates or causes not approved by some members. The Court looked to the language of the Act and the legislative history and concluded that they did not permit union dues to be used for such political purposes, thus avoiding "serious doubt of [the Act's] constitutionality." * * *

The values enshrined in the First Amendment plainly rank high "in the scale of our national values." In keeping with the Court's prudential policy it is incumbent on us to determine whether the Board's exercise of its jurisdiction here would give rise to serious constitutional questions. If so, we must first identify "the affirmative intention of the Congress clearly expressed" before concluding that the Act grants jurisdiction. [Quoting *McCulloch v. Sociedad Nacional de Marineros de Honduras*, 372 U.S. 10 (1963).]

In recent decisions involving aid to parochial schools we have recognized the critical and unique role of the teacher in fulfilling the mission of a church-operated school. What was said of the schools in *Lemon v. Kurtzman*, 403 U.S. 602, 617 (1971), is true of the schools in this case: "Religious authority necessarily pervades the school system." The key role played by teachers in such a school system has been the predicate for our conclusions that governmental aid channeled through teachers creates an impermissible risk of excessive governmental entanglement in the affairs of the church-operated schools. * * *

Only recently we again noted the importance of the teacher's function in a church school: "Whether the subject is 'remedial reading,' 'advanced reading,' or simply 'reading,' a teacher remains a teacher, and the danger that religious doctrine will become intertwined with secular instruction persists." *Meek v. Pittenger*, 421 U.S. 349, 370 (1975). Good intentions by government—or third parties—can surely no more avoid entanglement with the religious mission of the school in the setting of mandatory collective bargaining than in the well-motivated legislative efforts consented to by the church-operated schools which we found unacceptable in *Lemon* [and *Meek.*]

The Board argues that it can avoid excessive entanglement since it will resolve only factual issues such as whether an anti-union animus motivated an employer's action. But at this stage of our consideration we are not compelled to determine whether the entanglement is excessive as we would were we considering the constitutional issue. Rather, we make a narrow inquiry whether the exercise of the Board's jurisdiction presents a significant risk that the First Amendment will be infringed.

Moreover, it is already clear that the Board's actions will go beyond resolving factual issues. The Court of Appeals' opinion refers to charges of unfair labor practices filed against religious schools. The court observed that in those cases the schools had responded that their challenged actions were mandated by their religious creeds. The resolution of such charges by the Board, in many instances, will necessarily involve inquiry into the good faith of the position asserted by the clergy-administrators and its relationship to the school's religious mission. It is not only the conclusions that may be reached by the Board which may impinge on rights guaranteed by the Religion Clauses, but also the very process of inquiry leading to findings and conclusions.

The Board's exercise of jurisdiction will have at least one other impact on church-operated schools. The Board will be called upon to decide what are "terms and conditions of employment" and therefore mandatory subjects of bargaining. See 29 U.S.C. § 158(d). Although the Board has not interpreted that phrase as it relates to educational institutions, similar state provisions provide insight into the effect of mandatory bargaining. The Oregon Court of Appeals noted that "nearly everything that goes on in the schools affects teachers and is therefore arguably a 'condition of employment.'" *Springfield Education Assn. v. Springfield School Dist. No. 19*, 547 P.2d 647, 650 (Or. App. 1976). [The introduction of the mandatory bargaining process itself represents an encroachment by the government into the autonomy of the school's management, which in these cases is pursuing religious purposes that will be compromised.]

The church-teacher relationship in a church-operated school differs from the employment relationship in a public or other nonreligious school. We see no escape from conflicts flowing from the Board's exercise of jurisdiction over teachers in church-operated schools and the consequent serious First Amendment questions that would follow. We therefore turn to an examination of the National Labor Relations Act to decide whether it must be read to confer jurisdiction that would in turn require a decision on the constitutional claims raised by respondents.

There is no clear expression of an affirmative intention of Congress that teachers in church-operated schools should be covered by the Act. Admittedly, Congress defined the Board's jurisdiction in very broad terms; we must therefore examine the legislative history of the Act to determine whether Congress contemplated that the grant of jurisdiction would include teachers in such schools.

In enacting the National Labor Relations Act in 1935, Congress sought to protect the right of American workers to bargain collectively. The concern that was repeated throughout the debates was the need to assure workers the right to organize to counterbalance the collective activities of employers which had been authorized by the National Industrial Recovery Act. But congressional attention focused on employment in private industry and on industrial recovery. See, *e.g.*, 79 Cong. Rec. 7573 (1935) (remarks of Sen. Wagner).

Our examination of the statute and its legislative history indicates that Congress simply gave no consideration to church-operated schools. It is not without significance, however, that the Senate Committee on Education and Labor chose a college professor's dispute with the college as an example of employer-employee relations *not* covered by the Act. S. Rep. No. 573, 74th Cong., 1st Sess., 7 (1935).

Congress' next major consideration of the jurisdiction of the Board came during the passage of the Labor Management Relations Act of 1947—the Taft–Hartley Act. In that Act Congress amended the definition of "employer" in § 2 of the original Act to exclude nonprofit hospitals. 61 Stat. 137, 29 U.S.C. § 152(2) (1970 ed.). There was some discussion of the scope of the Board's jurisdiction but the consensus was that nonprofit institutions in general did not fall within the Board's jurisdiction because they did not affect commerce. [Citing various portions of legislative history.]

The most recent significant amendment to the Act was passed in 1974, removing the exemption of nonprofit hospitals. Pub. L. 93–360, 88 Stat. 395. The Board relies upon that amendment as showing that Congress approved the Board's exercise of jurisdiction over church-operated schools. A close examination of that legislative history, however, reveals nothing to indicate an affirmative intention that such schools be within the Board's jurisdiction. Since the Board did not assert jurisdiction over teachers in a church-operated school until after the 1974 amendment, nothing in the history of the amendment can be read as reflecting Congress' tacit approval of the Board's action.

During the debate there were expressions of concern about the effect of the bill on employees of religious hospitals whose religious beliefs would not permit them to join a union. 120 Cong. Rec. 12946, 16914 (1974). The result of those concerns was an amendment which reflects congressional sensitivity to First Amendment guarantees:

> "Any employee of a health care institution who is a member of and adheres to established and traditional tenets or teachings of a bona fide religion, body, or sect which has historically held conscientious objections to joining or financially supporting labor organizations shall not be required to join or financially support any labor organization as a condition of employment; except that such employee may be required, in lieu of periodic dues and initiation fees, to pay sums equal to such dues and initiation fees to a nonreligious charitable fund exempt from taxation under section 501(c)(3) of title 26, chosen by such employee from a list of at least three such funds, designated in a contract between such institution and a labor organization, or if the contract fails to designate such funds, then to any such fund chosen by the employee." 29 U.S.C. § 169.

The absence of an "affirmative intention of the Congress clearly expressed" fortifies our conclusion that Congress did not contemplate that the Board would require church-operated schools to grant recognition to unions as bargaining agents for their teachers.

The Board relies heavily upon *Associated Press v. NLRB*, 301 U.S. 103 (1937). There the Court held that the First Amendment was no bar to the application of the Act to the Associated Press, an organization engaged in collecting information and news throughout the world and distributing it to its members. Perceiving nothing to suggest that application of the Act would infringe First Amendment guarantees of press freedoms, the Court sustained Board jurisdiction. Here, on the contrary, the record affords abundant evidence that the Board's exercise of jurisdiction over teachers in church-operated schools would implicate the guarantees of the Religion Clauses.

Accordingly, in the absence of a clear expression of Congress' intent to bring teachers in church-operated schools within the jurisdiction of the Board, we decline to construe the Act in a manner that could in turn call upon the Court to resolve difficult and sensitive questions arising out of the guarantees of the First Amendment Religion Clauses. [*Affirmed.*]

MR. JUSTICE BRENNAN, with whom MR. JUSTICE WHITE, MR. JUSTICE MARSHALL, and MR. JUSTICE BLACKMUN join, dissenting.

* * * The general principle of construing statutes to avoid unnecessary constitutional decisions is a well-settled and salutary one. The governing canon, however, is *not* that expressed by the Court today. The Court requires that there be a "clear expression of an affirmative intention of Congress" before it will bring within the coverage of a broadly worded regulatory statute certain persons whose coverage might raise constitutional questions. But those familiar with the legislative process know that explicit expressions of congressional intent in such broadly inclusive statutes are not commonplace. Thus, by strictly or loosely applying its requirement, the Court can virtually remake congressional enactments. * * *

The settled canon for construing statutes wherein constitutional questions may lurk was stated in *Machinists v. Street*, 367 U.S. 740 (1961), cited by the Court, *ante*:

> " 'When the validity of an act of the Congress is drawn in question, and even if a serious doubt of constitutionality is raised, it is a cardinal principle that this Court will first ascertain whether a construction of the statute is *fairly possible* by which the question may be avoided.' *Crowell v. Benson*, 285 U.S. 22, 62." *Id.*, at 749–750 (emphasis added).

This limitation to constructions that are "fairly possible" and "reasonable" acts as a brake against wholesale judicial dismemberment of congressional enactments. It confines the judiciary to its proper role in construing statutes, which is to interpret them so as to give effect to congressional intention. The Court's new "affirmative expression" rule releases that brake.

The interpretation of the National Labor Relations Act announced by the Court today is not "fairly possible." The Act's wording, its legislative history, and the Court's own precedents leave "the intention of the Congress * * * revealed too distinctly to permit us to ignore it because of mere misgivings as to power." Section 2(2) of the Act, 29 U.S.C. § 152(2), defines "employer" as:

> " * * * any person acting as an agent of an employer, directly or indirectly, *but shall not include* the United States or any wholly owned Government corporation, or any Federal Reserve Bank, or any State or political subdivision thereof, or any person subject to the Railway Labor Act, as amended from time to time, or any labor organization (other than when acting as an employer), or anyone acting in the capacity of officer or agent of such labor organization." (Emphasis added.)

Thus, the Act covers all employers not within the eight express exceptions. The Court today substitutes amendment for construction to insert one more exception—for church-operated schools. This is a particularly transparent violation of the judicial role: The legislative history reveals that Congress itself considered and rejected a very similar amendment.

[The 1935 Act could not have been written more broadly, and the NLRB rejected efforts to except nonprofit employers from its reach.] The Hartley bill, which passed the House of Representatives in 1947, would have provided the exception the Court today writes into the statute:

> "The term 'employer' * * * shall not include * * * any corporation, community chest, fund, or foundation organized and operated exclusively for *religious*, charitable, scientific, literary, or *educational* purposes, * * * no part of the net earnings of which inures to the benefit of any private shareholder or individual * * *." (Emphasis added.) H.R. 3020, 80th Cong., 1st Sess., § 2(2) (Apr. 18, 1947).

But the proposed exception was not enacted. The bill reported by the Senate Committee on Labor and Public Welfare did not contain the Hartley exception. Instead, the Senate proposed an exception limited to nonprofit hospitals, and passed the bill in that form. The Senate version was accepted by the House in conference, thus limiting the exception for nonprofit employers to nonprofit hospitals.

Even that limited exemption was ultimately repealed in 1974. In doing so, Congress confirmed the view of the Act expressed here: that it was intended to cover all employers—including nonprofit employers— unless expressly excluded, and that the 1947 amendment excluded only nonprofit hospitals. See H.R. Rep. No. 93–1051, p. 4 (1974); 120 Cong. Rec. 12938 (1974) (Senator Williams); 120 Cong. Rec. 16900 (1974) (Rep. Ashbrook). Moreover, it is significant that in considering the 1974 amendments, the Senate expressly rejected an amendment proposed by Senator Ervin that was analogous to the one the Court today creates—an amendment to exempt nonprofit hospitals operated by religious groups. Senator Cranston, floor manager of the Senate Committee bill and primary opponent of the proposed religious exception, explained:

> "[S]uch an exception for religiously affiliated hospitals would seriously erode *the existing national policy which holds religiously affiliated institutions generally such as* proprietary nursing homes, residential communities, and *educational facilities to the same standards as their nonsectarian counterparts.*" 120 Cong. Rec. 12957 (1974) (emphasis added).

See also *ibid.* (Sen. Javits); 120 Cong. Rec. 12957 (1974) (Sen. Williams).

In construing the Board's jurisdiction to exclude church-operated schools, therefore, the Court today is faithful to neither the statute's language nor its history. Moreover, it is also untrue to its own precedents. "This Court has consistently declared that in passing the National Labor Relations Act, Congress intended to and did vest in the Board the fullest *jurisdictional* breadth constitutionally permissible under the Commerce Clause." *NLRB v. Reliance Fuel Oil Corp.*, 371 U.S. 224, 226 (1963) (emphasis in original). As long as an employer is within the reach of Congress' power under the Commerce Clause—and no one doubts that respondents are—the Court has held him to be covered by the Act regardless of the nature of his activity. Indeed, *Associated Press v. NLRB*, 301 U.S. 103 (1937), construed the Act to cover editorial employees of a nonprofit news-gathering organization despite a claim—precisely parallel to that made here—that their inclusion rendered the Act in violation of the First Amendment. Today's opinion is simply unable to explain the grounds that distinguish that case from this one.

Thus, the available authority indicates that Congress intended to include—not exclude—lay teachers of church-operated schools. The Court does not counter this with evidence that Congress *did* intend an exception it never stated. Instead, despite the legislative history to the contrary, it construes the Act as excluding lay teachers only because Congress did not state explicitly that they were covered. In Mr. Justice Cardozo's words, this presses "avoidance of a difficulty * * * to the point of disingenuous evasion." *Moore Ice Cream Co. v. Rose*, 289 U.S., at 379.[11]

NOTES ON THE *"AVOIDANCE CANON"*

1. *Different Ways of Framing the Avoidance Canon.* As the debate in *Catholic Bishop* indicates, there are several ways to express this canon.[n] When one interpretation of an ambiguous statute would be unconstitutional, choose another one that would pass constitutional muster. *Murray v. The Schooner Charming Betsy*, 6 U.S. (2 Cranch) 64 (1804) (expressing what scholars call "classic" avoidance). When one interpretation would raise serious constitutional problems, choose the one that would not. *United States ex rel. Attorney General v. Delaware & Hudson Co.*, 213 U.S. 366 (1909) (which Professor Nagle dubs the "modern" avoidance doctrine); cf. *Ex parte Bollman*, 8 U.S. (4 Cranch) 75 (1807). When one interpretation presents constitutional difficulties, do not impose it unless there has been an affirmative indication from Congress that it is required. *McCulloch v. Sociedad Nacional de Marineros de Honduras*, 372 U.S. 10 (1963).

---

11. Not even the Court's redrafting of the statute causes all First Amendment problems to disappear. The Court's opinion implies limitation of its exception to church-operated schools. That limitation is doubtless necessary since this Court has already rejected a more general exception for nonprofit organizations. See *Polish National Alliance v. NLRB*, 322 U.S. 643 (1944). But such an exemption, available only to church-operated schools, generates a possible Establishment Clause *question* of its own. *Walz v. Tax Comm'n*, 397 U.S. 664 (1970), does not put that question to rest, for in upholding the property tax exemption for churches there at issue, we emphasized that New York had "not singled out * * * churches as such; rather, it has granted exemption to all houses of religious worship within a broad class of property owned by nonprofit, quasi-public corporations * * *." Like the Court, "at this stage of [my] consideration [I am] not compelled to determine whether the [Establishment Clause problem] is [as significant] as [I] would were [I] considering the constitutional issue." It is enough to observe that no matter which way the Court turns in interpreting the Act, it cannot avoid constitutional questions.

n. For useful introductions, see Trevor Morrison, *Constitutional Avoidance in the Executive Branch*, 106 Colum. L. Rev. 1189 (2006); John Copeland Nagle, Delaware & Hudson *Revisited*, 72 Notre Dame L. Rev. 1495 (1997); Adrian Vermeule, *Saving Constructions*, 85 Geo. L.J. 1945 (1997).

The most aggressive way of framing the avoidance canon is *McCulloch*, which Chief Justice Burger invokes in *Catholic Bishop*. The dissenters assail the Chief Justice for this, and the *McCulloch* language is rarely applied today. But neither is the *Charming Betsy* language. Generally, the avoidance canon today follows the *Delaware & Hudson* language, the modern version of the avoidance doctrine. Much of *Catholic Bishop* applies that language, and Justice Frankfurter's opinion in *Witkovich* clearly follows it and cites *Crowell v. Benson*, a leading case for that language.

There are many differences between *Witkovich* and *Catholic Bishop* (such as the ideology of the Court splits: "liberals" win in the earlier case, "conservatives" in the later one), but one similarity is striking: standard rule of law sources seem to cut *against* use of the avoidance canon, even suggesting that there was not really any statutory "ambiguity" to be resolved, yet the Court in both cases invoked the canon and effectively trumped the statutory plain meaning. Dissenting Justices in both cases made persuasive arguments that the statutes in question clearly supported the government's broad interpretations, as did key congressional committees (*Witkovich*) and sponsors (*Catholic Bishop*), and that the government's interpretation in both cases was clearly constitutional. Do you disagree with this characterization? If not, you have a mystery on your hands. Neither Chief Justice Burger nor Justice Frankfurter was known as a wild judicial activist in his era—yet each wrote opinions that are hard to justify as a matter of standard rule of law sources. What is going on?

2. *Values Underlying the Avoidance Canon*. There are a number of values the avoidance doctrine might serve, such as avoiding unnecessary constitutional holdings or advisory opinions by the Court. Consider three potentially important values. First, it may be a rule of thumb for ascertaining legislative intent. The avoidance interpreter assumes that the legislature would *not* have wanted to press constitutional limits. Fred Schauer, *Ashwander Revisited*, 1995 Sup. Ct. Rev. 71, finds such an implicit legislative intent theory most implausible. The assumption rests upon no evidence of actual legislative intent. In the average case, why shouldn't the enacting legislature prefer that its work product be given full force—and if it's unconstitutional the Court should say so openly so that there can be a full-blown constitutional controversy? See Jerry Mashaw, *Greed, Chaos, and Governance: Using Public Choice Theory To Improve Public Law* 105 (1997). Consider *Witkovich*: Is it plausible that Congress would have wanted the Court to trim back the statute in the way that it did? How about *Catholic Bishop*?

A second value of the avoidance canon is that it might provide a low-salience mechanism for giving effect to what Larry Sager calls "underenforced constitutional norms."[o] *Witkovich* exemplifies this idea. Judges are loathe to strike down immigration statutes, because of either the plenary powers idea or institutional competence concerns. But decisions like *Witkovich* are quite

---

o. William N. Eskridge Jr. & Philip P. Frickey, *Quasi–Constitutional Law: Clear Statement Rules as Constitutional Lawmaking*, 45 Vand. L. Rev. 593 (1992), drawing from Lawrence Sager, *Fair Measure: The Legal Status of Underenforced Constitutional Norms*, 91 Harv. L. Rev. 1212 (1978); see also Neal Katyal, *Judges as Advicegivers*, 50 Stan. L. Rev. 1709 (1998); Ronald Krotoszynski, Jr., *Constitutional Flares: On Judges, Legislatures, and Dialogue*, 83 Minn. L. Rev. 1 (1998); Ernest A. Young, *Constitutional Avoidance, Resistance Norms, and the Preservation of Judicial Review*, 78 Tex. L. Rev. 1549, 1585–87 (2000).

common, for reasons Hiroshi Motomura has identified: unwilling to close off congressional options through constitutional review, judges will give effect to due process and free speech norms through narrowing constructions.[p] And so the norm is vindicated—but Congress can (re)assert a broader result after deliberation and debate over a statutory amendment that clearly overrides the norm-adhering interpretation.

Consider ways in which this idea might apply to *Catholic Bishop*. Labor law has been another area where the avoidance canon has been especially active in the Supreme Court's jurisprudence. See the cases discussed in *Catholic Bishop*, as well as more recent cases such as *Edward J. DeBartolo Corp. v. Florida Gulf Coast Building & Constr. Trades Council*, 485 U.S. 568, 575 (1988) (now a leading citation for the *Witkovich/Crowell* expression of the canon).

A third value for the avoidance canon is suggested by Professor Bickel's theory of the passive virtues.[q] One way that courts conserve their institutional capital is by techniques of avoidance. Standard techniques are for the Court to divest itself of constitutional cases whose resolution is premature by dismissing the complaint on procedural grounds such as standing, ripeness, etc. The avoidance canon represents a middle ground between pure passive virtues and constitutional invalidation. That middle ground allows the Court to slow down a political process that is moving too hastily and overriding human rights, but without incurring the full wrath of a political process that doesn't like to be thwarted. As one of us has argued, this theory best explains *Witkovich* and several other cases where the Warren Court impeded McCarthy era initiatives, but without creating a full-blown constitutional crisis.[r] How might this theory apply to *Catholic Bishop*, which was handed down a generation later, and by a more conservative majority?

3. *Criticisms of the Avoidance Canon.* Perhaps the leading critique of the avoidance canon remains Judge Henry Friendly, *Mr. Justice Frankfurter and the Reading of Statutes*, in *Benchmarks* 211–12 (1967):

> Although questioning the doctrine of construction to avoid constitutional doubts is rather like challenging Holy Writ, the rule has always seemed to me to have almost as many dangers as advantages. For one thing, it is one of those rules that courts apply when they want and conveniently forget when they don't—some, perhaps, would consider that to be a virtue. * * * Some considerations advanced in its favor, such as the awesome consequences of "a decree of unconstitutionality," overlook that if the Court finds the more likely construction to be unconstitutional, another means of rescue—the principle of construing to avoid unconstitu-

---

p. Hiroshi Motomura, *Immigration Law After a Century of Plenary Power: Phantom Constitutional Norms and Statutory Interpretation*, 100 Yale L.J. 545, 561–75 (1990). There are good recent examples of Professor Motomura's thesis, such as *Zadvydas v. Davis*, 533 U.S. 678, 696–99 (2001); *INS v. St. Cyr*, 533 U.S. 289 (2001).

q. Alexander M. Bickel, *The Least Dangerous Branch: The Supreme Court at the Bar of Politics* 156–69 (1962). Bickel's ideas about statutory interpretation are set forth in Alexander M. Bickel & Harry H. Wellington, *Legislative Purpose and the Judicial Process: The Lincoln Mills Case*, 71 Harv. L. Rev. 1 (1957).

r. Philip P. Frickey, *Getting from Joe to Gene (McCarthy): The Avoidance Canon, Legal Process Theory, and Narrowing Statutory Interpretations in the Early Warren Court*, 93 Calif. L. Rev. 397 (2005).

tionality—will be at hand. The strongest basis for the rule is thus that the Supreme Court ought not to indulge in what, if adverse, is likely to be only a constitutional advisory opinion. While there is force in this, the rule of "construing" to avoid constitutional doubts should, in my view, be confined to cases where the doubt is exceedingly real. Otherwise this rule, whether it be denominated one of statutory interpretation or, more accurately, of constitutional adjudication—still more accurately, of constitutional nonadjudication—is likely to become one of evisceration and tergiversation.

Judge Friendly's charge is that the avoidance canon will be an occasion for *stealth judicial activism*, which is both anti-democratic and unhealthy for the judiciary. Accord, Judge Richard A. Posner, *The Federal Courts: Crisis and Reform* 285 (1985); Lisa Kloppenberg, *Avoiding Constitutional Questions*, 35 B.C. L. Rev. 1003 (1994); John F. Manning, *The Nondelegation Doctrine as a Canon of Avoidance*, 2000 Sup. Ct. Rev. 223; John Copeland Nagle, Delaware & Hudson *Revisited*, 72 Notre Dame L. Rev. 1495 (1997).

A corollary to Judge Friendly's charge is that the avoidance canon will be applied unpredictably. Even in the immigration area, where it has made regular appearances in Supreme Court opinions, this charge has much weight. For an example of a case where there were stronger constitutional doubts and less clear statutory language than in *Witkovich*, yet the Court refused to apply this canon (or the rule of lenity, which was also applicable), see *Almendarez–Torres v. United States*, 523 U.S. 224 (1998). See also *Rust v. Sullivan*, 500 U.S. 173 (1991).

In evaluating the canon, get beyond *Witkovich*, where the Court was standing up to McCarthyism, and *Catholic Bishop*, where the Court was protecting religious freedom. Those might be constitutional values you find admirable. But consider application of the canon to constitutional values you find normatively unappealing, or just plain boring. For example, do you lose some enthusiasm for the canon after reading the following case?

Department of Commerce v. United States House of Representatives, 525 U.S. 316 (1999). Article I, § 2, cl. 3 of the Constitution apportions Representatives among the states "according to their respective Numbers" and requires that there be an "Enumeration" of the "Numbers" of people in the various states every ten years, "in such Manner as they [Congress] shall by Law direct." The Census Act, 13 U.S.C. § 1 et seq., delegates the responsibility for this endeavor to the Commerce Department, which for the 2000 census proposed to supplement its survey with statistical sampling techniques to cure what has been documented as an "undercount" of the population, especially of racial minorities and poor people. As revised in 1976, the statute says: "Except for the determination of population for purposes of apportionment of Representatives in Congress among the several States, the Secretary shall, if he considers it feasible, authorize the use of the statistical method known as 'sampling' in carrying out the provisions of this title." 13 U.S.C. § 195.

Section 195 is ambiguous. It might mean that the Secretary has no discretion regarding sampling (if feasible) for use in various federal programs relying on census data, but does have discretion regarding sampling for use in the apportionment of Representatives. It might also mean that the Secretary may use sampling (if feasible) for program purposes but not for apportionment purposes. **Justice O'Connor**'s opinion resolved the ambiguity by reference to a principle of continuity (Part IIIA of her opinion). Joined by a majority of Justices on this point, Justice O'Connor reasoned that, because the Census Bureau's practice, required by statute before 1976, was never to use sampling techniques for apportionment purposes, "there is only one plausible reading of the amended § 195: It prohibits the use of sampling in calculating the population for purposes of apportionment."

The principle of continuity, moreover, was supported by the legislative history of the 1976 revision. Speaking for herself and only two other Justices, Justice O'Connor reasoned (Part IIIB): "At no point during the debates over these amendments did a single Member of Congress suggest that the amendments would so fundamentally change the manner in which the Bureau could calculate the population for purposes of apportionment. * * * [I]t tests the limits of reason to suggest that despite such silence, Members of Congress voting for those amendments intended to enact what would arguably be the single most significant change in the method of conducting the decennial census since its inception." Speaking again for five Justices (Part IV), Justice O'Connor invoked the avoidance canon and interpreted the statute to avoid the question whether adjusting the apportionment of Representatives based on sampling would violate Article I, § 2, cl. 3.

Justice Scalia, speaking also for Chief Justice Rehnquist and Justices Kennedy and Thomas, concurred in the Court's judgment and in part of the O'Connor opinion. These Justices found it "unquestionably doubtful whether the constitutional requirement of an 'actual Enumeration' is satisfied by statistical sampling" and so urged that the Census Act be construed so "as to avoid serious constitutional doubt." Hence, they resolved the ambiguity in the statute the same way Justice O'Connor did.

Justice Breyer dissented, on the ground that § 195 was not implicated in the case at all: it only regulated instances where the Secretary could use sampling as a *substitute* for actual counting, while the current proposal was to use sampling as a *supplement* for actual counting. **Justice Stevens**, joined by Justices Souter and Ginsburg, also dissented, on the ground that the 1976 revision was an explicit authorization for the Secretary to use sampling techniques for apportionment purposes. Section 141(a), as rewritten in 1976, says: "The Secretary shall * * * take a decennial census of the population * * * in such form and content as he may determine, including the use of sampling procedures and special surveys." Because nothing in § 195 countermands the broad authorization in § 141(a), the statute cannot be read the way the Court majority insisted it be read. (Justice Stevens also defended the constitutionality of his reading, joined by all three of the other dissenting Justices.)

Is Justice Stevens right as to the plain meaning of the statute's text? If so, how can the new textualists not follow the approach laid out by Justice Kennedy in *Public Citizen* (Chapter 2, § 2B3): construe the law as written, and then strike it down if it contravenes the Constitution as written?

NOTE ON SEVERABILITY

When a provision in a statute is unconstitutional, should the court treat the remainder of the statute as good law, or declare the entire statute invalid? This is a question of *severability*. When the statute contains an express severability clause (instructing courts to save the remainder of the statute) or an express nonseverability clause, the issue would appear to be easy. Nonetheless, because such clauses are sometimes inserted as boilerplate in bills without much thought given to their effects, courts sometimes struggle with whether the clause should be given its full textual meaning if that seems inconsistent with the probable legislative intent concerning the particular severability issue.[s]

Often the statute is silent on the question. In that circumstance, "[u]nless it is evident that the Legislature would not have enacted those provisions which are within its power, independently of that which is not, the invalid part may be dropped if what is left is fully operative as a law." *Alaska Airlines v. Brock*, 480 U.S. 678, 684 (1987).

C. THE NEW FEDERALISM CANONS

The Supreme Court in the 1980s and early 1990s created or clarified "clear statement rules" that reflect constitutional norms of federalism.[t] See *Pennhurst State Sch. & Hosp. v. Halderman*, 451 U.S. 1 (1981) (conditions attached to federal funding for state programs must be clear); *Atascadero State Hosp. v. Scanlon*, 473 U.S. 234 (1985) (super-strong clear statement rule against congressional abrogation of state Eleventh Amendment immunity from suit in federal courts). The following case is the most dramatic example to date of the Court's activity in protecting state sovereignty through the use of canons.

As background, note that in *Maryland v. Wirtz*, 392 U.S. 183 (1968), the Court upheld the application of the Fair Labor Standards Act's minimum wage provisions to state hospital and school employees, rejecting the claim that the Constitution forbids such direct federal regulation of important state functions. Then, in *National League of Cities v. Usery*, 426 U.S. 833 (1976), by a 5–4 vote, the Court overruled *Wirtz* and refused to apply the FLSA's minimum wage and maximum hours provisions to many state and municipal employees. *National League of Cities* then met its own apparent demise in *Garcia v. San Antonio Metropolitan Transit Authority*, 469 U.S. 528 (1985), another 5–4 case, which explicitly overruled the nine-year-old precedent. As the next case demonstrates, what

---

s. For excellent critical analyses of the Court's severability jurisprudence, see Michael Shumsky, *Severability, Inseverability, and the Rule of Law*, 41 Harv. J. Legis. 227 (2004); Israel Friedman, Comment, *Inseverability Clauses in Statutes*, 64 U. Chi. L. Rev. 903 (1997).

t. Recall our terminology: a "clear statement rule" requires that a statute be interpreted a certain way unless the contrary interpretation is clearly required by statutory text; a "super-strong clear statement rule" requires that the statutory text target the issue unmistakably, especially through specific language. See generally William N. Eskridge Jr. & Philip P. Frickey, *Quasi–Constitutional Law: Clear Statement Rules as Constitutional Lawmaking*, 45 Vand. L. Rev. 593 (1992).

the Court taketh away as constitutional protection it can revive as canonical interpretive protection.

GREGORY v. ASHCROFT

Supreme Court of the United States, 1991
501 U.S. 452, 111 S.Ct. 2395, 115 L.Ed.2d 410

JUSTICE O'CONNOR delivered the opinion of the Court.

[It is a prima facie violation of the federal Age Discrimination in Employment Act (ADEA), 29 U.S.C. §§ 621–34, for an "employer" covered by the Act to specify a mandatory retirement age for "employees" over forty years of age who are covered by the Act. State and local governments are "employers" covered by the ADEA. In this case, the Missouri Constitution provided a mandatory retirement age of seventy for most state judges. Petitioners were state judges seeking to obtain a declaration that the mandatory retirement age violates the ADEA. The district court dismissed the action, concluding that the judges were "appointees on the policymaking level," a category of state officials excluded from the definition of "employees" covered by the Act. The Court of Appeals affirmed. What follows is Part II of Justice O'Connor's opinion.]

[IIA] As every schoolchild learns, our Constitution establishes a system of dual sovereignty between the States and the Federal Government. This Court also has recognized this fundamental principle. In *Tafflin v. Levitt*, 493 U.S. 455, 458 (1990), "[w]e beg[a]n with the axiom that, under our federal system, the States possess sovereignty concurrent with that of the Federal Government, subject only to limitations imposed by the Supremacy Clause." Over 120 years ago, the Court described the constitutional scheme of dual sovereigns:

> " '[T]he people of each State compose a State, having its own government, and endowed with all the functions essential to separate and independent existence,' ... '[W]ithout the States in union, there could be no such political body as the United States.' Not only, therefore, can there be no loss of separate and independent autonomy to the States, through their union under the Constitution, but it may be not unreasonably said that the preservation of the States, and the maintenance of their governments, are as much within the design and care of the Constitution as the preservation of the Union and the maintenance of the National government. The Constitution, in all its provisions, looks to an indestructible Union, composed of indestructible States." *Texas v. White*, 7 Wall. 700, 725 (1869), quoting *Lane County v. Oregon*, 7 Wall. 71, 76 (1869).

The Constitution created a Federal Government of limited powers. "The powers not delegated to the United States by the Constitution, nor prohibited by it to the States, are reserved to the States respectively, or to the people." U.S. Const., Amdt. 10. The States thus retain substantial sovereign authority under our constitutional system. As James Madison put it:

"The powers delegated by the proposed Constitution to the federal government are few and defined. Those which are to remain in the State governments are numerous and indefinite.... The powers reserved to the several States will extend to all the objects which, in the ordinary course of affairs, concern the lives, liberties, and properties of the people, and the internal order, improvement, and prosperity of the State." The Federalist No. 45, pp. 292–293 (C. Rossiter ed. 1961).

This federalist structure of joint sovereigns preserves to the people numerous advantages. It assures a decentralized government that will be more sensitive to the diverse needs of a heterogenous society; it increases opportunity for citizen involvement in democratic processes; it allows for more innovation and experimentation in government; and it makes government more responsive by putting the States in competition for a mobile citizenry.

Perhaps the principal benefit of the federalist system is a check on abuses of government power. "The 'constitutionally mandated balance of power' between the States and the Federal Government was adopted by the Framers to ensure the protection of 'our fundamental liberties.' " *Atascadero State Hospital v. Scanlon*, 473 U.S. 234, 242 (1985), quoting *Garcia v. San Antonio Metropolitan Transit Authority*, 469 U.S. 528, 572 (1985) (Powell, J., dissenting). Just as the separation and independence of the coordinate Branches of the Federal Government serves to prevent the accumulation of excessive power in any one Branch, a healthy balance of power between the States and the Federal Government will reduce the risk of tyranny and abuse from either front. Alexander Hamilton explained to the people of New York, perhaps optimistically, that the new federalist system would suppress completely "the attempts of the government to establish a tyranny":

"[I]n a confederacy the people, without exaggeration, may be said to be entirely the masters of their own fate. Power being almost always the rival of power, the general government will at all times stand ready to check usurpations of the state governments, and these will have the same disposition towards the general government. The people, by throwing themselves into either scale, will infallibly make it preponderate. If their rights are invaded by either, they can make use of the other as the instrument of redress." The Federalist No. 28, pp. 180–181 (C. Rossiter ed. 1961).

James Madison made much the same point:

"In a single republic, all the power surrendered by the people is submitted to the administration of a single government; and the usurpations are guarded against by a division of the government into distinct and separate departments. In the compound republic of America, the power surrendered by the people is first divided between two distinct governments, and then the portion allotted to each subdivided among distinct and separate departments. Hence a double security arises to the rights of the people. The different governments will control each other, at the same time that each will be controlled by itself." The Federalist No. 51, p. 323.

One fairly can dispute whether our federalist system has been quite as successful in checking government abuse as Hamilton promised, but there is no doubt about the design. If this "double security" is to be effective, there must be a proper balance between the States and the Federal Government. These twin powers will act as mutual restraints only if both are credible. In the tension between federal and state power lies the promise of liberty.

The Federal Government holds a decided advantage in this delicate balance: the Supremacy Clause. U.S. Const., Art. VI, cl. 2. As long as it is acting within the powers granted it under the Constitution, Congress may impose its will on the States. Congress may legislate in areas traditionally regulated by the States. This is an extraordinary power in a federalist system. It is a power that we must assume Congress does not exercise lightly.

The present case concerns a state constitutional provision through which the people of Missouri establish a qualification for those who sit as their judges. This provision goes beyond an area traditionally regulated by the States; it is a decision of the most fundamental sort for a sovereign entity. Through the structure of its government, and the character of those who exercise government authority, a State defines itself as a sovereign. * * *

Congressional interference with this decision of the people of Missouri, defining their constitutional officers, would upset the usual constitutional balance of federal and state powers. For this reason, "it is incumbent upon the federal courts to be certain of Congress' intent before finding that federal law overrides" this balance. *Atascadero*. We explained recently:

> "[I]f Congress intends to alter the 'usual constitutional balance between the States and the Federal Government,' it must make its intention to do so 'unmistakably clear in the language of the statute.' *Atascadero*; see also *Pennhurst State School and Hospital v. Halderman*, 465 U.S. 89, 99 (1984). *Atascadero* was an Eleventh Amendment case, but a similar approach is applied in other contexts. Congress should make its intention 'clear and manifest' if it intends to preempt the historic powers of the States.... 'In traditionally sensitive areas, such as legislation affecting the federal balance, the requirement of clear statement assures that the legislature has in fact faced, and intended to bring into issue, the critical matters involved in the judicial decision.' " *Will v. Michigan Dept. of State Police*, 491 U.S. 58, 65 (1989).

This plain statement rule is nothing more than an acknowledgment that the States retain substantial sovereign powers under our constitutional scheme, powers with which Congress does not readily interfere.

In a recent line of authority, we have acknowledged the unique nature of state decisions that "go to the heart of representative government." [Here Justice O'Connor referred to cases holding that, although state exclusion of aliens from public employment generally raises serious equal protection questions, the Court has created a "political function" exception and upheld state programs limiting to citizens employment in positions that are "intimately related to the process of democratic self-government."]

These cases stand in recognition of the authority of the people of the States to determine the qualifications of their most important government officials. It is an authority that lies at " 'the heart of representative government.' " It is a power reserved to the States under the Tenth Amendment and guaranteed them by that provision of the Constitution under which the United States "guarantee[s] to every State in this Union a Republican Form of Government." U.S. Const., Art. IV, § 4.

The authority of the people of the States to determine the qualifications of their government officials is, of course, not without limit. Other constitutional provisions, most notably the Fourteenth Amendment, proscribe certain qualifications; our review of citizenship requirements under the political-function exception is less exacting, but it is not absent. Here, we must decide what Congress did in extending the ADEA to the States, pursuant to its powers under the Commerce Clause. See *EEOC v. Wyoming*, 460 U.S. 226 (1983) (the extension of the ADEA to employment by state and local governments was a valid exercise of Congress' powers under the Commerce Clause). As against Congress' powers "[t]o regulate Commerce ... among the several States," U.S. Const., Art. I, § 8, cl. 3, the authority of the people of the States to determine the qualifications of their government officials may be inviolate.

We are constrained in our ability to consider the limits that the state-federal balance places on Congress' powers under the Commerce Clause. See *Garcia v. San Antonio Metropolitan Transit Authority* (declining to review limitations placed on Congress' Commerce Clause powers by our federal system). But there is no need to do so if we hold that the ADEA does not apply to state judges. Application of the plain statement rule thus may avoid a potential constitutional problem. Indeed, inasmuch as this Court in *Garcia* has left primarily to the political process the protection of the States against intrusive exercises of Congress' Commerce Clause powers, we must be absolutely certain that Congress intended such an exercise. "[T]o give the state-displacing weight of federal law to mere congressional *ambiguity* would evade the very procedure for lawmaking on which *Garcia* relied to protect states' interests." Lawrence Tribe, American Constitutional Law § 6–25, p. 480 (2d ed. 1988).

[IIB] In 1974, Congress extended the substantive provisions of the ADEA to include the States as employers. At the same time, Congress amended the definition of "employee" to exclude all elected and most high-ranking government officials. Under the Act, as amended:

"The term 'employee' means an individual employed by any employer
except that the term 'employee' shall not include any person elected
to public office in any State or political subdivision of any State by the
qualified voters thereof, or any person chosen by such officer to be on
such officer's personal staff, or an appointee on the policymaking level
or an immediate adviser with respect to the exercise of the constitutional or legal powers of the office." 29 U.S.C. § 630(f).

Governor Ashcroft contends that the § 630(f) exclusion of certain
public officials also excludes judges, like petitioners, who are appointed to
office by the Governor and are then subject to retention election. The
Governor points to two passages in § 630(f). First, he argues, these judges
are selected by an elected official and, because they make policy, are
"appointee[s] on the policymaking level."

Petitioners counter that judges merely resolve factual disputes and
decide questions of law; they do not make policy. Moreover, petitioners
point out that the policymaking-level exception is part of a trilogy, tied
closely to the elected-official exception. Thus, the Act excepts elected
officials and: (1) "any person chosen by such officer to be on such officer's
personal staff"; (2) "an appointee on the policymaking level"; and (3) "an
immediate advisor with respect to the constitutional or legal powers of the
office." Applying the maxim of statutory construction *noscitur a sociis*—
that a word is known by the company it keeps—petitioners argue that
since (1) and (3) refer only to those in close working relationships with
elected officials, so too must (2). Even if it can be said that judges may
make policy, petitioners contend, they do not do so at the behest of an
elected official.

Governor Ashcroft relies on the plain language of the statute: It
exempts persons appointed "at the policymaking level." [The Governor
argued that state judges make policy in making common law decisions and
exercising supervisory authority over the state bar. Moreover, state appellate judges have additional policymaking responsibilities: supervising inferior courts, establishing rules of procedure for the state courts, and
developing disciplinary rules for the bar.]

The Governor stresses judges' policymaking responsibilities, but it is
far from plain that the statutory exception requires that judges actually
make policy. The statute refers to appointees "on the policymaking level,"
not to appointees "who make policy." It may be sufficient that the
appointee is in a position requiring the exercise of discretion concerning
issues of public importance. This certainly describes the bench, regardless
of whether judges might be considered policymakers in the same sense as
the executive or legislature.

Nonetheless, "appointee at the policymaking level," particularly in
the context of the other exceptions that surround it, is an odd way for
Congress to exclude judges; a plain statement that judges are not "employees" would seem the most efficient phrasing. But in this case we are
not looking for a plain statement that judges are excluded. We will not

read the ADEA to cover state judges unless Congress has made it clear that judges are *included*. This does not mean that the Act must mention judges explicitly, though it does not. Rather, it must be plain to anyone reading the Act that it covers judges. In the context of a statute that plainly excludes most important state public officials, "appointee on the policymaking level" is sufficiently broad that we cannot conclude that the statute plainly covers appointed state judges. Therefore, it does not.

The ADEA plainly covers all state employees except those excluded by one of the exceptions. Where it is unambiguous that an employee does not fall within one of the exceptions, the Act states plainly and unequivocally that the employee is included. It is at least ambiguous whether a state judge is an "appointee on the policymaking level." * * *

[IIC] The extension of the ADEA to employment by state and local governments was a valid exercise of Congress' powers under the Commerce Clause. *EEOC v. Wyoming.* In *Wyoming*, we reserved the questions whether Congress might also have passed the ADEA extension pursuant to its powers under § 5 of the Fourteenth Amendment, and whether the extension would have been a valid exercise of that power. We noted, however, that the principles of federalism that constrain Congress' exercise of its Commerce Clause powers are attenuated when Congress acts pursuant to its powers to enforce the Civil War Amendments. This is because those "Amendments were specifically designed as an expansion of federal power and an intrusion on state sovereignty." One might argue, therefore, that if Congress passed the ADEA extension under its § 5 powers, the concerns about federal intrusion into state government that compel the result in this case might carry less weight.

By its terms, the Fourteenth Amendment contemplates interference with state authority: "No State shall ... deny to any person within its jurisdiction the equal protection of the laws." But this Court has never held that the Amendment may be applied in complete disregard for a State's constitutional powers. Rather, the Court has recognized that the States' power to define the qualifications of their officeholders has force even as against the proscriptions of the Fourteenth Amendment.

We return to the political-function cases. In *Sugarman* [*v. Dougall*, 413 U.S. 634 (1973)], the Court noted that "aliens as a class 'are a prime example of a "discrete and insular" minority * * * and that classifications based on alienage are 'subject to close judicial scrutiny.' " The *Sugarman* Court held that New York City had insufficient interest in preventing aliens from holding a broad category of public jobs to justify the blanket prohibition. At the same time, the Court established the rule that scrutiny under the Equal Protection Clause "will not be so demanding where we deal with matters resting firmly within a State's constitutional prerogatives." Later cases have reaffirmed this practice. See [cases concerning the "political-function" exception from strict scrutiny of state classifications disadvantaging aliens]. These cases demonstrate that the Fourteenth Amendment does not override all principles of federalism.

Of particular relevance here is *Pennhurst State School and Hospital v. Halderman*, 451 U.S. 1 (1981). The question in that case was whether Congress, in passing a section of the Developmentally Disabled Assistance and Bill of Rights Act, 42 U.S.C. § 6010 (1982 ed.), intended to place an obligation on the States to provide certain kinds of treatment to the disabled. Respondent Halderman argued that Congress passed § 6010 pursuant to § 5 of the Fourteenth Amendment, and therefore that it was mandatory on the States, regardless of whether they received federal funds. Petitioner and the United States, as respondent, argued that, in passing § 6010, Congress acted pursuant to its spending power alone. Consequently, § 6010 applied only to States accepting federal funds under the Act.

The Court was required to consider the "appropriate test for determining when Congress intends to enforce" the guarantees of the Fourteenth Amendment. We adopted a rule fully cognizant of the traditional power of the States: "Because such legislation imposes congressional policy on a State involuntarily, and because it often intrudes on traditional state authority, we should not quickly attribute to Congress an unstated intent to act under its authority to enforce the Fourteenth Amendment." Because Congress nowhere stated its intent to impose mandatory obligations on the States under its § 5 powers, we concluded that Congress did not do so.

The *Pennhurst* rule looks much like the plain statement rule we apply today. In *EEOC v. Wyoming*, the Court explained that *Pennhurst* established a rule of statutory construction to be applied where statutory intent is ambiguous. In light of the ADEA's clear exclusion of most important public officials, it is at least ambiguous whether Congress intended that appointed judges nonetheless be included. In the face of such ambiguity, we will not attribute to Congress an intent to intrude on state governmental functions regardless of whether Congress acted pursuant to its Commerce Clause powers or § 5 of the Fourteenth Amendment.

[The Court also held that the mandatory retirement requirement for judges did not violate the Equal Protection Clause of the Fourteenth Amendment, rejecting arguments that it was irrational to distinguish between judges who have reached age 70 and younger judges, and between judges 70 and over and other state employees of the same age who are not subject to mandatory retirement.]

JUSTICE WHITE, with whom JUSTICE STEVENS joins, concurring in part, dissenting in part, and concurring in the judgment.

[I] While acknowledging [the] principle of federal legislative supremacy, the majority nevertheless imposes upon Congress a "plain statement" requirement. The majority claims to derive this requirement from the plain statement approach developed in our Eleventh Amendment cases, see, *e.g.,* *Atascadero*, and applied two Terms ago in *Will*. The issue in those cases, however, was whether Congress intended a particular statute to extend to the States *at all*. In *Atascadero*, for example, the issue was whether States could be sued under § 504 of the Rehabilitation Act of 1973, 29 U.S.C. § 794. Similarly, the issue in *Will* was whether States could be sued under 42 U.S.C. § 1983. In the present case, by contrast, Congress has expressly extended the coverage of the ADEA to the States and their employees. Its intention to regulate age discrimination by States is thus "unmistakably clear in the language of the statute." *Atascadero*. The only dispute is over the precise details of the statute's application. We have never extended the plain statement approach that far, and the majority offers no compelling reason for doing so.

The majority also relies heavily on our cases addressing the constitutionality of state exclusion of aliens from public employment. In those cases, we held that although restrictions based on alienage ordinarily are subject to strict scrutiny under the Equal Protection Clause, the scrutiny will be less demanding for exclusion of aliens "from positions intimately related to the process of democratic self-government." This narrow "political function" exception to the strict scrutiny standard is based on the "State's historical power to exclude aliens from participation in its democratic political institutions." *Sugarman*.

It is difficult to see how the "political function" exception supports the majority's plain statement rule. First, the exception merely reflects a determination of the scope of the rights of aliens under the Equal Protection Clause. Reduced scrutiny is appropriate for certain political functions because "the right to govern is reserved to citizens." This conclusion in no way establishes a method for interpreting rights that are statutorily created by Congress, such as the protection from age discrimination in the ADEA. Second, it is one thing to limit *judicially-created* scrutiny, and it is quite another to fashion a restraint on *Congress'* legislative authority, as does the majority; the latter is both counter-majoritarian and an intrusion on a co-equal branch of the Federal Government. Finally, the majority does not explicitly restrict its rule to "functions that go to the heart of representative government," and may in fact be extending it much further to all "state governmental functions."

The majority's plain statement rule is not only unprecedented, it directly contravenes our decisions in *Garcia v. San Antonio Metropolitan Transit Authority* and *South Carolina v. Baker*, 485 U.S. 505 (1988). In those cases we made it clear "that States must find their protection from congressional regulation through the national political process, not through judicially defined spheres of unregulable state activity." We also rejected as "unsound in principle and unworkable in practice" any test for state immunity that requires a judicial determination of which state activities are "traditional," "integral," or "necessary." The majority disregards those decisions in its attempt to carve out areas of state activity that will receive special protection from federal legislation.

The majority's approach is also unsound because it will serve only to confuse the law. First, the majority fails to explain the scope of its rule. Is the rule limited to federal regulation of the qualifications of state officials?

Or does it apply more broadly to the regulation of any "state governmental functions"? [Quoting majority opinion.] Second, the majority does not explain its requirement that Congress' intent to regulate a particular state activity be "plain to anyone reading [the federal statute]." Does that mean that it is now improper to look to the purpose or history of a federal statute in determining the scope of the statute's limitations on state activities? If so, the majority's rule is completely inconsistent with our pre-emption jurisprudence. See, *e.g.*, *Hillsborough County v. Automated Medical Laboratories, Inc.*, 471 U.S. 707, 715 (1985) (pre-emption will be found where there is a "clear and manifest *purpose*" to displace state law) (emphasis added). The vagueness of the majority's rule undoubtedly will lead States to assert that various federal statutes no longer apply to a wide variety of State activities if Congress has not expressly referred to those activities in the statute. Congress, in turn, will be forced to draft long and detailed lists of which particular state functions it meant to regulate.

The imposition of such a burden on Congress is particularly out of place in the context of the ADEA. Congress already has stated that all "individual[s] employed by any employer" are protected by the ADEA unless they are expressly excluded by one of the exceptions in the definition of "employee." See 29 U.S.C. § 630(f). The majority, however, turns the statute on its head, holding that state judges are not protected by the ADEA because "Congress has [not] made it clear that judges are *included.*" * * *

The majority asserts that its plain statement rule is helpful in avoiding a "potential constitutional problem." It is far from clear, however, why there would be a constitutional problem if the ADEA applied to state judges, in light of our decisions in *Garcia* and *Baker*, discussed above. As long as "the national political *process* did not operate in a defective manner, the Tenth Amendment is not implicated." *Baker*. There is no claim in this case that the political process by which the ADEA was extended to state employees was inadequate to protect the States from being "unduly burden[ed]" by the Federal Government. In any event, as discussed below, a straightforward analysis of the ADEA's definition of "employee" reveals that the ADEA does not apply here. Thus, even if there were potential constitutional problems in extending the ADEA to state judges, the majority's proposed plain statement rule would not be necessary to avoid them in this case. Indeed, because this case can be decided purely on the basis of statutory interpretation, the majority's announcement of its plain statement rule, which purportedly is derived from constitutional principles, *violates* our general practice of avoiding the unnecessary resolution of constitutional issues.

My disagreement with the majority does not end with its unwarranted announcement of the plain statement rule. Even more disturbing is its treatment of Congress' power under § 5 of the Fourteenth Amendment. Section 5 provides that "[t]he Congress shall have power to enforce, by appropriate legislation, the provisions of this article." Despite that sweeping constitutional delegation of authority to Congress, the majority holds that its plain statement rule will apply with full force to legislation enacted to enforce the Fourteenth Amendment. The majority states: "In the face of ... ambiguity, we will not attribute to Congress an intent to intrude on state governmental functions *regardless of whether Congress acted pursuant to its Commerce Clause powers or § 5 of the Fourteenth Amendment.*" (Emphasis added).

The majority's failure to recognize the special status of legislation enacted pursuant to § 5 ignores that, unlike Congress' Commerce Clause power, "[w]hen Congress acts pursuant to § 5, not only is it exercising legislative authority that is plenary within the terms of the constitutional grant, it is exercising that authority under one section of a constitutional Amendment whose other sections by their own terms embody limitations on state authority." *Fitzpatrick v. Bitzer*, 427 U.S. 445, 456 (1976). Indeed, we have held that "principles of federalism that might otherwise be an obstacle to congressional authority are necessarily overridden by the power to enforce the Civil War Amendments 'by appropriate legislation.' Those Amendments were specifically designed as an expansion of federal power and an intrusion on state sovereignty."

The majority relies upon *Pennhurst State School and Hospital v. Halderman*, but that case does not support its approach. There, the Court merely stated that "we should not quickly attribute to Congress an unstated intent to act under its authority to enforce the Fourteenth Amendment." In other words, the *Pennhurst* presumption was designed only to answer the question whether a particular piece of legislation was enacted pursuant to § 5. That is very different from the majority's apparent holding that even when Congress *is* acting pursuant to § 5, it nevertheless must specify the precise details of its enactment.

The majority's departures from established precedent are even more disturbing when it is realized, as discussed below, that this case can be affirmed based on simple statutory construction.

[II] The statute at issue in this case is the ADEA's definition of "employee," which provides:

> "The term 'employee' means an individual employed by any employer except that the term 'employee' shall not include any person elected to public office in any State or political subdivision of any State by the qualified voters thereof, or any person chosen by such officer to be on such officer's personal staff, or an appointee on the policymaking level or an immediate adviser with respect to the exercise of the constitutional or legal powers of the office. The exemption set forth in the preceding sentence shall not include employees subject to the civil service laws of a State government, governmental agency, or political subdivision." 29 U.S.C. § 630(f).

A parsing of that definition reveals that it excludes from the definition of "employee" (and thus the coverage of the ADEA) four types of (non-civil service) state and local employees: (1) persons elected to public office; (2) the personal staff of elected officials; (3) persons appointed by elected officials to be on the policymaking level; and (4) the immediate advisers of elected officials with respect to the constitutional or legal powers of the officials' offices.

The question before us is whether petitioners fall within the third exception. * * * [I] conclude that petitioners are "on the policymaking level."

"Policy" is defined as "a definite course or method of action selected (as by a government, institution, group, or individual) from among alternatives and in the light of given conditions to guide and usu[ally] determine present and future decisions." Webster's Third New International Dictionary 1754 (1976). Applying that definition, it is clear that the decisionmaking engaged in by common-law judges, such as petitioners, places them "on the policymaking level." In resolving disputes, although judges do not operate with unconstrained discretion, they do choose "from among alternatives" and elaborate their choices in order "to guide and ... determine present and future decisions." * * *

Moreover, it should be remembered that the statutory exception refers to appointees "on the policymaking level," not "policymaking employees." Thus, whether or not judges actually *make* policy, they certainly are on the same *level* as policymaking officials in other branches of government and therefore are covered by the exception. * * *

Petitioners argue that the "appointee[s] on the policymaking level" exception should be construed to apply "only to persons who advise or work closely with the elected official that chose the appointee." In support of that claim, petitioners point out that the exception is "sandwiched" between the "personal staff" and "immediate adviser" exceptions in § 630(f), and thus should be read as covering only similar employees.

Petitioners' premise, however, does not prove their conclusion. It is true that the placement of the "appointee" exception between the "personal staff" and "immediate adviser" exceptions suggests a similarity among the three. But the most obvious similarity is simply that each of the three sets of employees are connected in some way with elected officials: the first and third sets have a certain working relationship with elected officials, while the second is *appointed* by elected officials. There is no textual support for concluding that the second set must *also* have a close working relationship with elected officials. Indeed, such a reading would tend to make the "appointee" exception superfluous since the "personal staff" and "immediate adviser" exceptions would seem to cover most appointees who are in a close working relationship with elected officials.

Petitioners seek to rely on legislative history, but it does not help their position. There is little legislative history discussing the definition of "employee" in the ADEA, so petitioners point to the legislative history of the identical definition in Title VII, 42 U.S.C. § 2000e(f). If anything, that history tends to confirm that the "appointee[s] on the policymaking level" exception was designed to exclude from the coverage of the ADEA all high-level appointments throughout state government structures, including judicial appointments. * * *

[The dissenting opinion of JUSTICE BLACKMUN, joined by JUSTICE MARSHALL, is omitted.]

NOTES ON GREGORY AND CLEAR STATEMENT RULES

1. *Contrasting Approaches.* As Justice O'Connor noted, there is a respectable textual argument that the ADEA exceptions do not apply to appointed judges, in part because of the *noscitur a sociis* canon. But note that every other potential source of statutory meaning points in the other direction. See Philip P. Frickey, *Lawnet: The Case of the Missing (Tenth) Amendment*, 75 Minn. L. Rev. 755 (1991).

Consider first the absurd-result exception to the plain meaning approach, which even textualists will sometimes apply.[u] On the face of it, the exceptions provision to the ADEA seems to take elected judges completely out of the statute (and thus they can be required to step down at age 70), but protects appointed judges against any retirement requirement. This seems absolutely backwards from any public-policy perspective: if superannuated judges are to remain in authority, presumably that judgment should be made by the voters on a judge-by-judge basis, not as a categorical decision made by Congress. Why would Congress want to hogtie states in this manner? On the other hand, does the "absurdity" here rise to the level called for by Justice Kennedy in his separate opinion in *Public Citizen* (Chapter 2, § 2)? Is the apparent distinction between elected and appointed judges so irrational as to raise a serious constitutional question that should be avoided through statutory interpretation (cf. *Catholic Bishop of Chicago*)?

Sources of statutory meaning available to nontextualists strongly cut against the apparent plain meaning of the ADEA exceptions provision as well. The legislative history, irrelevant to Justice O'Connor because of her application of a super-strong clear statement rule, supports excepting these judges from the statute, as explained in a portion of Justice White's separate opinion that we have deleted. The statutory purpose, again irrelevant to Justice O'Connor's approach, seems narrower than the plain meaning of the exception; at least as originally conceived, the ADEA was designed to protect workers from being replaced by younger employees who would accept lower pay, and had little to do with persons who possess guaranteed tenure and who would be replaced by persons receiving the same salary. From the standpoint of public values, as Justice O'Connor suggests, the people of the state ought to be able to choose how to structure important governmental positions. But this need not lead to the creation of a super-strong clear statement rule: any kind of canon (a presumption at the outset, a tiebreaker at the end, a factor to be weighed in the interpretive process) based on federalism would surely be sufficient to tip the case to the conclusion Justice O'Connor desired. Why

---

u. See McNollgast (short for Mathew McCubbins, Roger Noll & Barry Weingast), *Legislative Intent: The Use of Positive Political Theory in Statutory Interpretation*, 57 Law & Contemp. Probs. 3 (1994).

create the canonical equivalent of a nuclear weapon when a fly swatter would have been sufficient?

For a more recent debate among the Justices as to the application of the federalism canons in the context of the ADEA, compare *Kimel v. Florida Bd. of Regents*, 528 U.S. 62 (2000) (O'Connor, J., for the Court, finding that the ADEA does make it "unmistakably clear" that its remedial provision abrogates the states' Eleventh Amendment immunity from suit, but finding the abrogation unconstitutional), with *id.* at 99–109 (Thomas, J., dissenting in part) (arguing that the ADEA is not sufficiently clear in abrogating state Eleventh Amendment immunity). Does it matter which approach is taken? (Four dissenting Justices found statutory abrogation and believed it constitutional.)

2. *When Does the Canon Apply? What Does It Require?* As Justice White stressed, it is by no means clear what Congress must do to comply with the *Gregory* canon. Must Congress rely upon its legislative authority under § 5 of the Fourteenth Amendment, or may it rely upon its commerce power as well? To what kinds of state governmental operations does the canon apply? Note that in *Garcia* one justification for overruling *National League of Cities* was that the standard identified there for state immunity from federal regulation—the federal government could not "directly displace the States' freedom to structure integral operations in areas of traditional government functions"—proved too vague for any consistent application in the lower courts. Is the *Gregory* canon any clearer?

One would think that, at a minimum, the canon applies with full force to federal regulation of state judges. One would be wrong. In *Chisom v. Roemer* (Chapter 2, § 3), the majority of the Court applied section 2 of the Voting Rights Act to the election of state judges without any mention of the *Gregory* canon. *Chisom* and *Gregory* were decided *the same day*, and Justice O'Connor was in the majority in *Chisom* (and, of course, the author of *Gregory*)! Justice Scalia, dissenting in *Chisom*, began with his textualist approach, concluded that the key statutory term "representatives" did not include judges, and then asked whether any canon suggested a deviation from the textualist answer. He then had this to say:

> If the [*Gregory*] principle were applied here, we would have double reason to give "representatives" its ordinary meaning. It is true, however, that in *Gregory* interpreting the statute to include judges would have made them the only high-level state officials affected, whereas here the question is whether judges were excluded from a general imposition upon state elections that unquestionably exists; and in *Gregory* it was questionable whether Congress was invoking its powers under the Fourteenth Amendment (rather than merely the Commerce Clause), whereas here it is obvious. Perhaps those factors suffice to distinguish the two cases. Moreover, we tacitly rejected a "plain statement" rule as applied to unamended § 2 in *City of Rome v. United States*, 446 U.S. 156 (1980), though arguably that was before the rule had developed the significance it currently has. I am content to dispense with the "plain statement" rule in the present case[,] but it says something about the Court's approach to

today's decision that the possibility of applying that rule never crossed its mind.

Fairly read, is *Gregory* susceptible to the potential distinctions between it and *Chisom* that Justice Scalia suggests? If not, are the two cases simply irreconcilable?

3. *The Relationship of Textualism and Super–Strong Clear Statement Rules.* Under Justice Scalia's formula for textualism set forth in his dissenting opinion in *Chisom*, it is critical to know what the "established canons" are and how they operate. How can the *Gregory* canon be an "established" one, when in fact the case took what was at most a presumption in prior cases and transformed it into a super-strong clear statement rule? What is Justice Scalia doing in the *Gregory* majority? Why didn't he join Justice White's more textualist concurring opinion?

Critics could suggest that cases like *Gregory* demonstrate that textualism fails to live up to its promise of providing objective interpretive methods in the face of outcomes judges cannot tolerate. In other words, every human interpretive technique, including textualism, needs a "safety valve" of some sort. For liberals, the *Holy Trinity Church* "purpose trumps plain meaning" approach sometimes serves this purpose, as in *Weber*. For conservative textualists who care about federalism, the safety valve when textualism gets them boxed in, as in *Gregory*, is the creation of a super-strong clear statement rule that trumps the result suggested by ordinary meaning. Is it fair to say that *Gregory* undercuts the textualist principle of constraining judicial discretion in interpretation? Is it fair to go even further and suggest that *Gregory* and *Chisom*, when read together, undermine the very notion of predictability and coherence in interpretation?

Another concern about *Gregory* is whether the notion of deference to ultimate congressional determination is more illusion than reality. The congressional agenda is limited, access to it is skewed in a variety of ways (toward more powerful interests, toward the interests of the federal, state, and local governments, and so on), and it is far easier to kill a bill than to pass a bill. Thus, in many circumstances at least, the use of a super-strong clear statement rule may be as "countermajoritarian" as invalidating the statute outright.

Yet another concern is whether the use of such rules may actually encourage judicial activism because it seems far easier to use them than to do constitutional decisionmaking. Because a decision like *Gregory* is made at the interpretive rather than the constitutional level, the visibility of the decision is lower and the attention paid to it even inside the Court may be less. Contrast the reaction to *Gregory* (except in limited academic and states' rights circles, virtually nothing) to the reaction to a hypothetical overruling of *Garcia* and a return to *National League of Cities* (where the Court's disrespect for stare decisis and return to a regime already arguably demonstrated to be unworkable would surely cause considerable controversy).

Ultimately, probably the most important question about the new super-strong clear statement rules is normative. In *Gregory*, for example, should the Court be promoting the value of federalism so strongly, or should it defer more to the political process (Congress and the President) to protect the states? Can textualists provide any objective grounding for the values promoted by their super-strong clear statement rules? Consider these quandaries in light of the next case.

BFP v. Resolution Trust Corp., 511 U.S. 531 (1994), Section 548 of the Bankruptcy Code, 11 U.S.C. § 548, sets forth the powers of a trustee in bankruptcy to avoid "fraudulent transfers" made within a year of the debtor's bankruptcy. Section 548(a)(2)(A) permits avoidance if the trustee can establish (1) that the debtor had an interest in property; (2) that a transfer of that interest occurred within one year of the filing of the bankruptcy petition; (3) that the debtor was insolvent at the time of the transfer or became insolvent as a result thereof; and (4) that the debtor received "less than a reasonably equivalent value in exchange for such transfer." The debtor in this case (BFP) was a company formed to buy a house; the lender subsequently foreclosed on the mortgage to the house and sold it at a foreclosure sale for $433,000; BFP filed for federal bankruptcy and moved to set aside the sale on the ground that $433,000 did not represent the home's "reasonably equivalent value," which BFP estimated at $725,000.

Justice Scalia, for the majority of the Court, held that "reasonably equivalent value," in the context of a foreclosure sale in compliance with state law, meant whatever price the property fetched, however low. Justice Scalia reasoned that tests invoking "fair market value" have no applicability in the forced-sale context. " 'The market value of . . . a piece of property is the price which it might be expected to bring if offered for sale in a fair market; not the price which might be obtained on a sale at public auction or a sale forced by the necessities of the owner, but such a price as would be fixed by negotiation and mutual agreement, after ample time to find a purchaser, as between a vendor who is willing (but not compelled) to sell and a purchaser who desires to buy but is not compelled to take the particular . . . piece of property.' Black's Law Dictionary 971 (6th ed. 1990). In short, 'fair market value' presumes market conditions that, by definition, simply do not obtain in the context of a forced sale. An appraiser's reconstruction of 'fair market value' could show what similar property would be worth if it did not have to be sold within the time and manner strictures of state-prescribed foreclosure. But property that must be sold within those strictures is simply worth less."

Justice Souter, in dissent, objected that Justice Scalia's reading is at war with the "plain meaning" of the statutory text, which requires the trustee to evaluate the reasonableness of the transfer price, and the judicial inquiry is similar to other common law "reasonableness" ones. Moreover, Justice Souter observed, Justice Scalia's interpretation was considered and rejected by Congress in 1984, when it specifically extended § 548 to cover foreclosure sales.

Justice Scalia responded that the dissenters overlooked the extent to which a "reasonableness" inquiry would upset state foreclosure law. The purpose of foreclosure law is to establish procedures that will effect conveyance of property fairly and finally; any post hoc federal "reasonableness" inquiry would unsettle the finality of titles. "Absent an explicit statutory requirement to the contrary, we must assume the validity of this state-law regulatory background and take due account of its effect. 'The existence and force and function of established institutions of local government are always in the consciousness of lawmakers and, while their weight may vary, they may never be completely overlooked in the task of interpretation.' *Davies Warehouse Co. v. Bowles*, 321 U.S. 144, 154 (1944). Cf. *Gregory v. Ashcroft*."

Justice Scalia continued: "Federal statutes impinging upon important state interests 'cannot ... be construed without regard to the implications of our dual system of government.... [W]hen the Federal Government takes over ... local radiations in the vast network of our national economic enterprise and thereby radically readjusts the balance of state and national authority, those charged with the duty of legislating [must be] reasonably explicit.' F. Frankfurter, *Some Reflections on the Reading of Statutes*, 47 Colum. L. Rev. 527, 539–540 (1947). It is beyond question that an essential state interest is at issue here: we have said that 'the general welfare of society is involved in the security of the titles to real estate' and the power to ensure that security 'inheres in the very nature of [state] government.' *American Land Co. v. Zeiss*, 219 U.S. 47, 60 (1911). Nor is there any doubt that the interpretation urged by petitioner would have a profound effect upon that interest: the title of every piece of realty purchased at foreclosure would be under a federally created cloud. * * * To displace traditional State regulation in such a manner, the federal statutory purpose must be 'clear and manifest,' *English v. General Electric Co.*, 496 U.S. 72, 79 (1990). Cf. *Gregory v. Ashcroft*. Otherwise, the Bankruptcy Code will be construed to adopt, rather than to displace, preexisting state law."

Justice Souter sharply criticized Justice Scalia's reliance on *Gregory*, which involved direct federal regulation of state employment rather than federal preemption of state regulatory power over the private sector. Justice Souter argued that *Gregory* concerns were not implicated, since *Gregory* had limited its rule to federal intrusions on matters "essential to their [the states'] independence." Au contraire, insisted Justice Scalia, "[t]his ignores the fact that it is not state authority over debtor-creditor law in general that is at stake in this case, but the essential sovereign interest in the security and stability of title to land."

NOTES ON THE *GREGORY–BFP* RULE IN ACTION AND CRITICISMS OF THE NEW FEDERALISM CANONS

1. **BFP *in Action: the Predictability Problem*.** Was *BFP* a predictable application of *Gregory*? If the outcome is mostly supportable by the policies of avoiding undue judicial interference with real estate markets and promoting efficiency in bankruptcy proceedings, should the majority have explicitly relied upon these policies rather than used the *Gregory* canon? No party in *BFP* had even cited *Gregory*, nor did the Ninth Circuit, whose interpretation was affirmed in *BFP*.

Furthermore, it is far from clear how broadly *BFP* should be read. It might simply be an example of the presumption against federal preemption of traditional state regulatory regimes such as property, tort, *Cipollone v. Liggett Group, Inc.*, 505 U.S. 504 (1992), and family law. See *Rose v. Rose*, 481 U.S. 619, 635–36 (1987) (O'Connor, J., concurring). Or it might be a tougher clear statement rule when federal regulation threatens not only to preempt but also disrupt an area of traditional state regulation. Such arguments have been frequently made in recent years. Over Justice Scalia's objection, the Court was sympathetic to this argument in *Gonzales v. Oregon*, 546 U.S. 243 (2006), where the Department of Justice sought to preempt a state aid in dying law. Justice Scalia's plurality opinion in *Rapanos v. United States*, 547 U.S. 715, 737–38 (2006), followed *BFP* to overrule agency wetlands regulations that displaced large swaths of state property law. (*BFP* and *Rapanos*, read together, suggest that state property law regimes get more Supreme Court protection than tort regimes.)

2. *The Need for Super–Strong Rules Once the Court Gives Teeth to Previously Underenforced Constitutional Norms?* Does the *Gregory* rule add anything to the rule to avoid constitutional questions? Perhaps as a special application of the avoidance canon, *Gregory* might be defended on the ground that the Tenth Amendment was underenforced by the Supreme Court, which had rarely invalidated federal laws because they intruded into core state functions. (The Court in *National League of Cities* in 1976 had invalidated such a law, but *Garcia* overruled it.) After *Gregory*, the Court has invalidated several federal statutory provisions on the ground that they commandeered state officials in violation of the Tenth Amendment. See *Printz v. United States*, 521 U.S. 898 (1997); *New York v. United States*, 505 U.S. 144 (1992). If these cases augur an overruling or narrowing of *Garcia*, should the Court trim back its use of the *Gregory* rule? See also *Kimel v. Florida Bd. of Regents*, 528 U.S. 62 (2000) (Court finds clear statement in ADEA abrogating states' Eleventh Amendment immunity and then rules the abrogation unconstitutional).

The parallel to the avoidance canon suggests a further criticism of the *Gregory–BFP* rule: it is a kind of stealth constitutionalism.[v] If the Supreme Court had struck down the ADEA or Bankruptcy Act provisions as violations of the Tenth Amendment in these two cases, you can be sure that the *New York Times* would have given the cases front-page treatment; probably, a certain amount of controversy would have ensued. By announcing these results in statutory, rather than constitutional decisions, the Court avoided any serious public scrutiny or controversy (even Linda Greenhouse missed *BFP*). Was the Rehnquist Court in the 1990s behaving much like the Warren Court in the 1950s—so if you approve *Witkovich*, you might have to swallow *BFP*?

3. *The Problem of Congressional Reliance. Bait and Switch?* In Chapter 2, § 3C, we suggested that one important factor in assessing any theory of statutory interpretation is whether it is compatible with the assumptions about law held by other legal actors (the Congress, the President, attorneys, citizens). One way of criticizing the Court's creation of new super-strong clear statement rules is, then, to focus on the ways in which our political system has relied upon understandings that the Court is now unraveling through the use of these rules. The use of reliance arguments in statutory interpretation appeals not just to the traditional conservative idea of legislative supremacy,

---

v. See William N. Eskridge Jr. & Philip P. Frickey, *The Supreme Court, 1993 Term— Foreword: Law as Equilibrium*, 108 Harv. L. Rev. 4 (1994), criticizing *BFP* and related decisions as examples of stealth constitutionalism.

but also answers the Court's frequent riposte that legislative supremacy is not implicated unless something is clear on the face of the statute. Consider the following example.

The Education of the Handicapped Act (EHA) is a comprehensive statutory scheme to assure that disabled children may receive a free public education appropriate to their needs. The Act guarantees parental rights to participate in state planning of their children's educational needs and to challenge state plans they don't like. The statute imposes pervasive obligations on state and local governments, and it provides that "[a]ny party aggrieved by the findings and decision [made in the state or local administrative process] shall have the right to bring a civil action ... in any State court of competent jurisdiction or in a district court of the United States without regard to the amount in controversy." 20 U.S.C. § 1415(e)(2). EHA's sponsor made it clear "that a parent or guardian may present a complaint alleging that a State or local educational agency has refused to provide services to which a child may be entitled" and may sue state and local governments in state or federal court. 121 Cong. Rec. 37415 (1975).

When the EHA was enacted in 1975, the above-noted evidence would probably have sufficed to abrogate the states' Eleventh Amendment immunity from suit in federal court, pursuant to *Employees v. Missouri Dep't of Public Health & Welfare*, 411 U.S. 279 (1973) (general jurisdictional grant plus explicit legislative history would be sufficient to abrogate Eleventh Amendment immunity). In *Atascadero State Hospital v. Scanlon*, 473 U.S. 234 (1985), however, the Court changed the rule for congressional abrogation of Eleventh Amendment immunity: "Congress may abrogate the States' constitutionally secured immunity from suit in federal court only by making its intention unmistakably clear in the language of the statute." The Court held that the Rehabilitation Act of 1973, another statute protecting the disabled, did not abrogate states' immunity, because there was no clear textual indication of such abrogation.

Sensing that the rules had changed, and reacting to the Court's restrictive interpretation of the Rehabilitation Act, Congress in 1986 enacted the following: "A State shall not be immune under the Eleventh Amendment * * * from suit in Federal Court for a violation of [enumerated provisions of the Rehabilitation Act], or the provisions of any other Federal statute prohibiting discrimination by recipients of Federal financial assistance." The latter clause clearly covers the EHA. Then, in *Dellmuth v. Muth*, 491 U.S. 223 (1989), a case that arose before the 1986 amendment, the Court held that the EHA did not abrogate state immunity. The Court pointed to the 1986 statute as a good example of the drafting clarity needed to abrogate immunity, and held that there was no abrogation before 1986.

Poor Congress. It thought it had abrogated state immunity in 1975, and given precedent in 1975 it probably had done so. Then it reiterated its intent in 1986, but the new statute was used by the Court to confirm Congress's failure to abrogate in 1975. This might be amusing if important rights were not involved.[w] The matter might become even worse for Congress. Following

---

w. Congress immediately overrode *Dellmuth* in the Education of the Handicapped Act of 1990, Pub. L. No. 101–476, § 103, 104 Stat. 1103, 1106, again with complaints that its expectations had

Kimel, the Supreme Court in *Board of Trustees, Univ. of Ala. v. Garrett*, 531 U.S. 356 (2001), ruled that Congress had no power under the Fourteenth Amendment to abrogate the states' Eleventh Amendment immunity in the Americans with Disabilities Act. The Court reasoned that Congress had not found enough of a "history and pattern" of intentional discrimination against people with disabilities by the states themselves to justify the exercise of its enforcement power under the Fourteenth Amendment. Under *Garrett*, Congress's repeated efforts to render the states liable for violations of the EHA might ultimately fail on constitutional grounds.

In assessing the statutory interpretation developments, be certain first that you understand the force of the *Atascadero* clear statement rule: Not only does it require abrogation of state immunity in the statute's text, without regard to legislative history, but the abrogation must be explicit and really clear. E.g., *Hoffman v. Connecticut Dep't of Income Maintenance*, 492 U.S. 96 (1989); *Will v. Michigan Dep't of State Police*, 491 U.S. 58 (1989). Thus *Atascadero*, like *Gregory*, fits our definition of a "super-strong clear statement rule." Others that the Court has created include the toughened rule against waivers of federal sovereign immunity, *United States v. Nordic Village*, 503 U.S. 30 (1992); the toughened rule against extraterritorial application of federal statutes, *EEOC v. Arabian Am. Oil Co.*, 499 U.S. 244 (1991); the rule against congressional derogation of traditional presidential powers, *Japan Whaling Ass'n v. American Cetacean Society*, 478 U.S. 221 (1986); and the rule created in 1981 that congressional conditions of grants to the states be explicit and clear, *Pennhurst State Sch. and Hosp. v. Halderman*, 451 U.S. 1 (1981).

A recent bait-and-switch debate occurred under the *Pennhurst* rule. Congress in a 1986 statute provided for "reasonable attorneys' fees as part of the costs" to prevailing litigants (usually parents) in cases arising under the Individuals with Disabilities Education Act. In *Arlington Central School District Board of Education v. Murphy*, 548 U.S. 291 (2006), the Court invoked *Pennhurst* to require a more targeted statement in order to justify recovery of expert fees as part of an attorney's fees award. Dissenting Justices accused the Court of bait-and-switch: when Congress added the fees provision in 1986, it had every reason to believe—and the relevant committees expressed precisely such a belief—that the enacted language was sufficient to justify the award of expert witness fees. Such belief was undone by Supreme Court decisions handed down in 1987 and 1991 (see *Casey*, digested in Chapter 2, § 3A)—decisions which Congress immediately overrode in the Civil Rights Act of 1991. The *Murphy* Court not only ignored the 1991 override, but cited the earlier decisions as confirming evidence that there was a plain meaning that trumped Congress's expectations. (Congress's override only extended to job discrimination cases, and not IDEA cases.)

The *Murphy* dissenters had another argument the *Dellmuth* dissenters did not have. There was no dispute that the 1986 statute not only added a provision giving attorneys' fees and other costs to prevailing parents, but also charged the GAO with collecting fee data and analyzing "the range of such

---

been thwarted. It took Congress three statutes to effectuate a policy it thought had been effectuated in 1975.

fees, costs and expenses awarded in the actions and proceedings under such section, * * * and * * * *the number of hours spent by personnel, including attorneys and consultants."* (Emphasis added.) The legislative history confirmed that this section was written under Congress's assumption that the 1986 authorization included expert witness fees. Thus, the parents had an argument grounded in the whole act, as well as the legislative history. The Court found this whole act evidence insufficient to refute the conventional text-based evidence. The dissenters expressed astonishment that the majority did not concede there was at least ambiguity in the statute, given this dramatic evidence.

SECTION 3. DEBUNKING AND DEFENDING THE CANONS OF STATUTORY INTERPRETATION

KARL LLEWELLYN, REMARKS ON THE THEORY OF APPELLATE DECISION AND THE RULES OR CANONS ABOUT HOW STATUTES ARE TO BE CONSTRUED

3 Vand. L. Rev. 395, 401–06 (1950). Reprinted by permission.

When it comes to presenting a proposed construction in court, there is an accepted conventional vocabulary. As in argument over points of case-law, the accepted convention still, unhappily, requires discussion as if only one single correct meaning could exist. Hence there are two opposing canons on almost every point. An arranged selection is appended. Every lawyer must be familiar with them all: they are still needed tools of argument. At least as early as Fortescue the general picture was clear, on this, to any eye which would see.

Plainly, to make any canon take hold in a particular instance, the construction contended for must be sold, essentially, by means other than the use of the canon: The good sense of the situation and a *simple* construction of the available language to achieve that sense, *by tenable means, out of the statutory language.*

Canons of Construction

Statutory interpretation still speaks a diplomatic tongue. Here is some of the technical framework for maneuver.

Thrust	But	Parry
1. A statute cannot go beyond its text.		
		1. To effect its purpose a statute may be implemented beyond its text.
2. Statutes in derogation of the common law will not be extended by construction.		

Thrust	But	Parry
		2. Such acts will be liberally construed if their nature is remedial.
3. Statutes are to be read in the light of the common law and a statute affirming a common law rule is to be construed in accordance with the common law.		
		3. The common law gives way to a statute which is inconsistent with it and when a statute is designed as a revision of a whole body of law applicable to a given subject it supersedes the common law.
4. Where a foreign statute which has received construction has been adopted, previous construction is adopted too.		
		4. It may be rejected where there is conflict with the obvious meaning of the statute or where the foreign decisions are unsatisfactory in reasoning or where the foreign interpretation is not in harmony with the spirit or policy of the laws of the adopting state.
5. Where various states have already adopted the statute, the parent state is followed.		
		5. Where interpretations of other states are inharmonious, there is no such restraint.
6. Statutes in pari materia must be construed together.		
		6. A statute is not in pari materia if its scope and aim are distinct or where a legislative design to depart from the general purpose or policy of previous enactments may be apparent.
7. A statute imposing a new penalty or forfeiture, or a new liability or disability, or creating a new right of action will not be construed as having a retroactive effect.		
		7. Remedial statutes are to be liberally construed and if a retro-

Thrust	**But**	**Parry**

active interpretation will promote the ends of justice, they should receive such construction.

8. Where design has been distinctly stated no place is left for construction.

8. Courts have the power to inquire into real—as distinct from ostensible—purpose.

9. Definitions and rules of construction contained in an interpretation clause are part of the law and binding.

9. Definitions and rules of construction in a statute will not be extended beyond their necessary import nor allowed to defeat intention otherwise manifested.

10. A statutory provision requiring liberal construction does not mean disregard of unequivocal requirements of the statute.

10. Where a rule of construction is provided within the statute itself the rule should be applied.

11. Titles do not control meaning; preambles do not expand scope; section headings do not change language.

11. The title may be consulted as a guide when there is doubt or obscurity in the body; preambles may be consulted to determine rationale, and thus the true construction of terms; section headings may be looked upon as part of the statute itself.

12. If language is plain and unambiguous it must be given effect.

12. Not when literal interpretation would lead to absurd or mischievous consequences or thwart manifest purpose.

13. Words and phrases which have received judicial construction before enactment are to be

Thrust	**But**	**Parry**

understood according to that construction.

13.   Not if the statute clearly requires them to have a different meaning.

14.   After enactment, judicial decision upon interpretation of particular terms and phrases controls.

14.   Practical construction by executive officers is strong evidence of true meaning.

15.   Words are to be taken in their ordinary meaning unless they are technical terms or words of art.

15.   Popular words may bear a technical meaning and technical words may have a popular signification and they should be so construed as to agree with evident intention or to make the statute operative.

16.   Every word and clause must be given effect.

16.   If inadvertently inserted or if repugnant to the rest of the statute, they may be rejected as surplusage.

17.   The same language used repeatedly in the same connection is presumed to bear the same meaning throughout the statute.

17.   This presumption will be disregarded where it is necessary to assign different meanings to make the statute consistent.

18.   Words are to be interpreted according to the proper grammatical effect of their arrangement within the statute.

18.   Rules of grammar will be disregarded where strict adherence would defeat purpose.

19.   Exceptions not made cannot be read.

19.   The letter is only the "bark." Whatever is within the

Thrust	But	Parry
		reason of the law is within the law itself.
20. Expression of one thing excludes another.		
		20. The language may fairly comprehend many different cases where some only are expressly mentioned by way of example.
21. General terms are to receive a general construction.		
		21. They may be limited by specific terms with which they are associated or by the scope and purpose of the statute.
22. It is a general rule of construction that where general words follow an enumeration they are to be held as applying only to persons and things of the same general kind or class specifically mentioned (*ejusdem generis*).		
		22. General words must operate on something. Further, ejusdem generis is only an aid in getting the meaning and does not warrant confining the operations of a statute within narrower limits than were intended.
23. Qualifying or limiting words or clauses are to be referred to the next preceding antecedent.		
		23. Not when evident sense and meaning require a different construction.
24. Punctuation will govern when a statute is open to two constructions.		
		24. Punctuation marks will not control the plain and evident meaning of language.
25. It must be assumed that language has been chosen with due regard to grammatical propriety and is not interchangeable on mere conjecture.		
		25. "And" and "or" may be read interchangeably whenever

Thrust	But	Parry
		the change is necessary to give the statute sense and effect.
26. There is a distinction between words of permission and mandatory words.		
		26. Words imparting permission may be read as mandatory and words imparting command may be read as permissive when such construction is made necessary by evident intention or by the rights of the public.
27. A proviso qualifies the provision immediately preceding.		
		27. It may clearly be intended to have a wider scope.
28. When the enacting clause is general, a proviso is construed strictly.		
		28. Not when it is necessary to extend the proviso to persons or cases which come within its equity.

NOTES ON THE THEORETICAL WARFARE OVER CANONS OF STATUTORY INTERPRETATION

1. *Assault on the Citadel by Legal Realists and Critical Scholars.* Llewellyn's wonderful *tour de farce* is a justly celebrated exposure of the many faces of the canons of statutory construction, and it is representative of the legal realists' tendency to debunk legal formalisms. Their view was that nothing turned on them. Canons of construction, for example, "are useful only as facades, which for an occasional judge may add luster to an argument persuasive for other reasons." Frank Newman & Stanley Surrey, *Legislation—Cases and Materials* 654 (1955). Critical scholars of the 1970s and 1980s did not focus on the canons, but the perspective of many of them (intellectual heirs to the most skeptical realists) would go one step further. The canons are just part of the mystifying game that is played with legal logic, which is ultimately indeterminate. Critical scholars argue that legal reasoning can be oppressive by denying its own contingency, i.e., denying that there are other ways of looking at the situation. Perhaps the canons of construction might be deemed similarly oppressive, for they are part of the linguistic and logical pretense that the legislature goes about its work in a methodical, rational way and that judicial interpreters can scientifically discern the proper meaning through simple rules.

2. *Legal Process Defense of the Canons.* Conventional legal process thinkers have tended to defend at least some of the canons against the

mockery of the realists. For example, Henry M. Hart Jr. & Albert M. Sacks, *The Legal Process: Basic Problems in the Making and Application of Law* 1191 (Eskridge & Frickey eds., 1994) (tent. ed. 1958), responded to Llewellyn as follows:

> All this [skepticism], it is ventured, involves a misunderstanding of the function of the canons, and at bottom of the problem of interpretation itself. Of course, there are pairs of maxims susceptible of being invoked for opposing conclusions. Once it is understood that meaning depends upon context and that contexts vary, how could it be otherwise? Maxims should not be treated, any more than a dictionary, as saying what meaning a word or group of words *must* have in a given context. They simply answer the question whether a particular meaning is linguistically permissible, if the context warrants it. Is this not a useful function?

Professor Dickerson suggests that some of the canons "reflect the probabilities generated by normal usage or legislative behavior. These represent either (1) lexicographical judgments of how legislatures tend to use language and its syntactical patterns, or (2) descriptions of how legislatures tend to behave. They serve as useful presumptions of supposed actual legislative intent and are, therefore, modestly useful in carrying [out] legislative meaning." Reed Dickerson, *The Interpretation and Application of Statutes* 228 (1975).

3. *The Law & Economics Debate over the Canons.* The canons were subjected to sharp criticism by Judge Richard A. Posner in *Statutory Interpretation—In the Classroom and in the Courtroom*, 50 U. Chi. L. Rev. 800, 806–07 (1983). Judge Posner complains that "most of the canons are just wrong" in that (1) they do not reflect a code by which legislatures draft statutes, (2) they are not even common-sense guides to interpretation, (3) they do not operate to constrain the discretion of judges, and (4) they do not force legislatures to draft statutes with care. Judge Posner blasts one canon after another—from the plain meaning rule to *expressio unius* to the whole act rule—by showing that the canons rest on wholly unrealistic conceptions of the legislative process. For example, many of the canons erroneously assume legislative omniscience (*id.* at 811):

> Most canons of statutory construction go wrong not because they misconceive the nature of judicial interpretation or of the legislative or political process but because they impute omniscience to Congress. Omniscience is always an unrealistic assumption, and particularly so when one is dealing with the legislative process. The basic reason why statutes are so frequently ambiguous in application is not that they are poorly drafted—though many are—and not that the legislators failed to agree on just what they wanted to accomplish in the statute—though often they do fail—but that a statute necessarily is drafted in advance of, and with imperfect appreciation for the problems that will be encountered in, its application.

For a contrary position, Einer R. Elhauge, *Statutory Default Rules: How to Interpret Unclear Legislation* (2008), argues that many of the canons actually "minimize political dissatisfaction with statutory results." Congress, Elhauge suggests, is perfectly happy that the Court smooths over statutory potholes, integrates statutes with the larger legal terrain, and even sends some sensitive issues back for more work. Which is the more credible understanding of Congress? See generally Elizabeth Garrett, *Preferences, Laws, and Default Rules*, 122 Harv. L. Rev. 2104 (2009) (review of Professor Elhauge's book, subjecting its assumptions about Congress to critical scrutiny).

From an economic point of view, it may be better to view the canons *ex ante* rather than *ex post*. Under an *ex ante* perspective, it may not matter whether a canon reflects legislative realities. Instead, the question is this: Does the legal process, including the lawmaking process, work *better* with this set of rules than with another set or with no rules at all? The canons might also be defended from an economic point of view as an *interpretive regime* that affords greater predictability for statutory interpreters. See William N. Eskridge Jr. & John Ferejohn, *Politics, Interpretation, and the Rule of Law*, in *The Rule of Law* 265, 282–85 (Ian Shapiro ed., 1994), as well as Appendix B to this Casebook (a complex array of more than two hundred canons followed by the Rehnquist–Roberts Court), and Adrian Vermeule, *Interpretive Choice*, 75 N.Y.U. L. Rev. 74, 140–43 (2000), who argues that the Court should just pick a set of canons and stick with them. The problem with the canons as an interpretive regime is that the canons are not deployed in a completely predictable manner. (See the Brudney and Ditslear article, excerpted below, for some recent evidence along these lines.)

Also from an *ex ante* point of view, some of the canons can be understood as institutional default rules. The best example is the rule of lenity: when the Court interprets criminal statutes narrowly, Congress typically returns to the issue and often overrides the Court with a better-specified statutory crime. See William N. Eskridge Jr., *Overriding Supreme Court Statutory Interpretation Decisions*, 101 Yale L.J. 331 (1991), as well as our notes after *Muscarello* and *McNally*. This dovetails perfectly with the best justification for the rule of lenity, the nondelegation idea. Eskridge and Frickey, *Quasi–Constitutional Law, supra*, argue that the avoidance canon, the federalism canons, and separation of powers canons can also be understood as requiring Congress—and not agencies or judges—to deliberate and decide to press constitutional envelopes.

4. *Pragmatic Defenses of the Canons*. Geoffrey Miller, *Pragmatics and the Maxims of Interpretation*, 1990 Wis. L. Rev. 1179, presents a defense of many of the linguistic canons, showing them to be consistent with the teachings of (Gricean) philosophical linguistics. Gricean theory understands communication as a purposive, cooperative endeavor, and communicative precepts are means by which cooperation is facilitated. Thus, the canons might be understood as essential to the communicative process and therefore inevitable.

Perhaps the least ambitious defense of the canons is to posit that they are just a checklist of things to think about when approaching a statute. If context will guide interpretation of statutes whose language is ambiguous (and some whose language is not), then the canons may at least be a catalogue of contextual factors which might be investigated. *Expressio unius*, in this way, will stimulate an investigation into why the legislators did include only one thing and not the other. The rule of lenity will remind interpreters that penal laws require greater clarity and justification in their prohibitions, and that one should be aware of fairness problems in particular. The whole act maxim will suggest that other parts of the statute, including definitional provisions, be read for clues about how the drafters used certain words, phrases, and concepts. And so on.

Professor Mermin says that the canons of construction are similar to folksayings. Samuel Mermin, *Law and the Legal System: An Introduction* 264 (2d ed. 1982). Does "haste make waste" have any validity as a suggestion on how to live? What about "the early bird catches the worm," one obvious "parry" to this "thrust"? Or "nothing ventured, nothing gained" versus "discretion is the better part of valor"? Don't all of those sayings have some truth in them, depending upon the context? Do any of these sayings provide guidance in decisionmaking, or do they simply provide a *post hoc* explanation of why we made a certain decision? Judge Posner believes that the canons never contribute to judicial decisionmaking. Is this a decisive objection to them?

5. *Openly Normative Visions of the Canons.* Some scholars argue that the substantive canons represent a way for "public values" drawn from the Constitution, federal statutes, and the common law to play an important role in statutory interpretation. See William N. Eskridge Jr., *Public Values in Statutory Interpretation*, 137 U. Pa. L. Rev. 1007 (1989). Professor Cass R. Sunstein, *Interpreting Statutes in the Regulatory State*, 103 Harv. L. Rev. 405, 507–08 (1989), argues that the canons ought to be central to statutory interpretation and proposes a variety of "principles for the regulatory state":

Constitutional Principles

1. Avoiding constitutional invalidity/doubts

2. Federalism

3. Political accountability (nondelegation principle)

4. Political deliberation,* checks and balances,* antipathy to naked interest-group transfers**

5. Disadvantaged groups**

6. Hearing rights

7. Property and contract rights

8. Welfare rights**

9. Rule of law

Institutional Concerns

1. Narrow construction of appropriations statutes

2. Presumption in favor of judicial review

3. Presumption against implied exemptions from taxation

4. Presumption against implied repeals

5. Question of administrative discretion*

6. Cautious approach to legislative history

7. Ratification, acquiescence,* stare decisis, and post-enactment history*

Counteracting Statutory Failure

1. Presumption in favor of political accountability

2. Presumption against subversion of statute through collective action problems*

3. Presumption in favor of coordination and consistency

4. Presumption against obsolescence*

5. Narrow construction of procedural qualifications of substantive rights*

6. Understanding systemic effects of regulatory controls*

7. Presumption against irrationality and injustice*

8. Proportionality (against overzealous implementation)*

9. De minimis exceptions

10. Narrow construction of statutes embodying interest-group transfers (to counteract "deals")*

11. Broad construction of statutes protecting disadvantaged groups*

12. Broad construction of statutes protecting nonmarket values**

13. Avoiding private law principles**

Compare these with the canons the Rehnquist and Roberts Courts have actually deployed (Appendix B to this Casebook). We have placed an asterisk (*) by those of Sunstein's principles which enjoy little support in the current Court's assembly of canons. A double asterisk (**) means that we discern implicit rejection in recent cases. Note that most of Sunstein's canons fall into one of these categories. He would respond that the canons not already in the Court's lexicon *should* be, for normative reasons regarding their usefulness for the modern regulatory state. But how can those normative reasons be articulated to a skeptical audience?

David Shapiro, in *Continuity and Change in Statutory Interpretation*, 67 N.Y.U. L. Rev. 921, 925 (1992), has provided a different justification for the canons: they promote legal stability, in that they assume "that close questions of statutory interpretation should be resolved in favor of continuity and against change." A difficulty in assessing this claim is figuring out the relevant status quo: Does it consist of longstanding general assumptions in the legal community (embodied in many canons, particularly the substantive ones), or the specific legislative assumptions surrounding a particular statute, which may be undone if a canon controls statutory meaning? As the next note indicates, these competing definitions may create widely divergent conclusions about the dynamic or static impact of canons in interpretation. Shapiro concludes that promoting continuity rather than change is more often than not consistent with legislative purposes. This is also the position taken by Justice O'Connor's opinion in the Census Case, excerpted in the previous section.

Justice Scalia says, in *A Matter of Interpretation* 28–29 (1997), that "all of these preferential rules and presumptions are a lot of trouble," for "it is virtually impossible to expect uniformity and objectivity [in statutory interpretation] when there is added, on one or the other side of the balance, a thumb of indeterminate weight" like the rule of lenity or the canon to avoid constitutional difficulties. In light of his own reliance on all the canons he denigrates, this is a remarkable statement, which the Justice immediately qualifies:

> The rule of lenity is almost as old as the common law itself, so I suppose that is validated by sheer antiquity. * * * Some of the rules, perhaps, can be considered merely an exaggerated statement of what normal, no-thumb-on-the-scales interpretation would produce anyway. For example, since congressional elimination of state sovereign immunity is such an extraordinary act, one would normally expect it to be explicitly decreed rather than offhandedly implied—so something like a "clear statement" rule is merely normal interpretation. And the same, perhaps, with waiver of [federal] sovereign immunity.

Note how Scalia's defense is a broader version of Shapiro's rule of continuity. But it brings out a disturbing normative edge. For example, Congress has often legislated to exclude lesbians and gay men from ordinary legal entitlements, like marriage, military service, and immigration, and has rarely adopted any kind of law that protects lesbians and gay men from the pervasive violence or discrimination directed at them. Does that mean Justice Scalia would recognize a clear statement rule, "Unless Congress clearly expresses a sentiment that lesbians and gay men are included in statutory protections, the Court should presume that they are excluded"?

6. *Dynamic Canons and the Problem of Legislative Supremacy.* Catholic *Bishop* illustrates the way in which the canons can contribute to the dynamic evolution of statutes. The dissenters may have more accurately discerned the expectations of Congress, but the Court majority found that evidence insufficient to require the result that they found constitutionally questionable. The Court's creation of a series of new or strengthened clear statement rules in the last few decades has generated results in case after case that would have surprised the enacting Congresses. Recall *Dellmuth* and *Gregory.* Also compare *EEOC v. Arabian Am. Oil Co. (Aramco)*, 499 U.S. 244 (1991) (Court invokes a clear statement rule as basis for holding that Title VII does not apply extraterritorially, to U.S. company allegedly discriminating against U.S. employees in its foreign offices), with *id.* at 263–64 (Marshall, J., dissenting) (arguing that the Court's clear statement rule was much tougher than the traditional presumption against extraterritoriality).

James J. Brudney & Corey Ditslear, *Canons of Construction and the Elusive Quest for Neutral Reasoning*, 58 Vand. L. Rev. 1 (2005). This article is a more systematic approach to the canons than any previous work of scholarship. The authors (a labor law professor and a political scientist) collected 630 Supreme Court workplace-law decisions between 1969 and 2003 and coded them by result (pro-labor liberal and pro-business conservative) and mode of reasoning. Using multiple regression analyses that control for other variables, Brudney and Ditslear found that the Rehnquist Court relied on textual canons (such as *ejusdem generis*) much more, and legislative history much less, than the Burger Court had done. *Circuit City Stores, Inc. v. Adams*, 532 U.S. 105 (2001) (analyzed in § 1A of this chapter), exemplifies the Rehnquist Court's (and now the Roberts Court's) approach to labor cases.

More troubling is their finding that this methodological development is serving ideological purposes (pp. 53–69). As the authors summarize their findings (p. 6), "canon usage by justices identified as liberals tends to be linked to liberal outcomes, and canon reliance by conservative justices to be associated with conservative outcomes. We also found that canons are often invoked to justify conservative results in close cases—*i.e.*, those decided by a one-vote or two-vote margin. Indeed, closely divided cases in which the majority relies on substantive canons are more likely to reach conservative results than close cases where those canons are not invoked.

"In addition, we identified a subset of cases in which the majority relies on canons while the dissent invokes legislative history: these cases, almost all decided since 1988, have yielded overwhelmingly conservative results. Doctrinal analysis of illustrative decisions indicates that conservative members of the Rehnquist Court are using the canons in such contested cases to ignore— and thereby undermine—the demonstrable legislative preferences of Congress. Taken together, the association between canon reliance and outcomes among both conservative and liberal justices, the distinctly conservative influence associated with substantive canon reliance in close cases, and the recent tensions in contested cases between conservative majority opinions that rely on canons and liberal dissents that invoke legislative history, suggest that the canons are regularly used in an instrumental if not ideologically conscious manner." In subsequent work, Professor Brudney controls for other variables and finds that "liberal" (pro-labor) Justices vote more neutrally when they look at legislative history, while "conservative" (pro-business) Justices vote more conservatively when they ignore legislative history and find "plain meanings." See James J. Brudney, *Liberal Justices' Reliance on Legislative History: Principle, Strategy, and the Scalia Effect*, 29 Berkeley J. Emp. & Lab. L. 117 (2008).

Professors Brudney and Ditslear apply their empirical findings to the theoretical debate over the utility of the canons. Their conclusions are as follows. First, the authors (pp. 95–102) are skeptical that the canons form an interpretive regime which can provide an ordering mechanism for legislators and lawyers to make statutory interpretation more predictable. Aside from the fact that legislators do not rely on the canons when drafting statutes, see Victoria Nourse & Jane S. Schacter, *The Politics of Legislative Drafting: A Congressional Case Study*, 77 N.Y.U. L. Rev. 575 (2002), legislators and lawyers cannot rely on the canons in predicting how statutes will be applied, because the canons are deployed in such an ideological way by both liberal and conservative judges. A neutral observer who just read the statute and the legislative history in *Circuit City*, for example, would have expected the Court to read the labor exemption to the Arbitration Act much more expansively than the five-Justice majority in fact did. Brudney and Ditslear offer almost two dozen equally dramatic canon surprises from their dataset.

Second, and relatedly, Brudney and Ditslear's study (pp. 77–95) lends empirical support to relatively cynical accounts of the canons. Stephen Ross, *Where Have You Gone Karl Llewellyn? Should Congress Turn Its Lonely Eyes to You?*, 45 Vand. L. Rev. 561 (1992), and Edward L. Rubin, *Modern Canons, Loose Canons, and the Limits of Practical Reason*, 45 Vand. L. Rev. 579 (1992), maintain that Supreme Court Justices, and perhaps other judges, use the canons strategically, to justify judicial policy preferences or to frustrate legislative intent. The malleability noted by Professor Llewellyn not only undermines canonical predictability, but allows the canons to be manipulated by result-oriented jurists. Brudney and Ditslear say their evidence is consistent with, though does not conclusively prove, this claim.

Third, Brudney and Ditslear (pp. 70–77) found some support for the hypothesis, first advanced by Jonathan Macey and Geoffrey P. Miller, *The Canons of Construction and Judicial Preferences*, 45 Vand. L. Rev. 647 (1992), that the canons are substitutes for judicial expertise and can reduce error costs in areas (such as ERISA and the procedural complexities of Title VII) where judicial knowledge and preferences are low. E.g., *Adams Fruit Co. v. Barrett*, 494 U.S. 638 (1990) (*expressio unius* provides the ground for a conservative Court to allow, without dissent, a private right of action under a technical migrant workers' law). Brudney and Ditslear add that such cases may be more strongly influenced by legislative purpose analysis and, most important, agency views than by canon reliance. In short, there is a correlation between canon invocation and technical issues but not necessarily any causal link.

These conclusions suggest that in the most technical areas of law—such as bankruptcy, civil procedure, energy regulation, intellectual property, taxation, telecommunications—canon usage would be more important and less ideologically slanted than in labor law. In less technical and more normatively charged areas—such as civil rights, criminal law and procedure, freedom of information, perhaps federal land law—canon usage would be less frequent and more ideologically slanted.

PROBLEM 3–3

A Hobbs Act Problem

In 1972, the District of Columbia Metro Authority contracted with Pullman to purchase 745 subway cars. Frankly Unctuous, a D.C. superintendent of quality control, was specifically responsible for ensuring Pullman's compliance with contract specifications. Thus, if a component of one of the cars were defective upon Unctuous' inspection, he could force Pullman to replace or modify the part at its own expense. During the contract period (1972–78), Unctuous went on several excursions—to The Greenbrier in White Sulphur Springs, The Homestead in Hot Springs, and other resorts. The trips were paid for by Pullman, to the tune of an estimated $30,000. Unctuous was indicted for extortion under the Hobbs Act, 18 U.S.C. § 1951. At trial, Pullman project supervisor Ewell B. Surrey, who made the arrangements for the trips, testifies that Unctuous never demanded or solicited the excursions and that Pullman paid for them voluntarily, as a means of providing access to an official. "It was our normal course of business," he testifies. There is no testimony to the contrary. Both Unctuous and Surrey testify that Unctuous was a strict inspector and declared numerous components defective. Only once during the contract period was Pullman able to persuade Unctuous to change his mind.

The issue is whether this set of facts justifies prosecution of Unctuous under the Hobbs Act. The Hobbs Act reads as follows:

(a) Whoever in any way or degree obstructs, delays, or affects commerce or the movement of any article or commodity in commerce, by robbery or extortion or attempts or conspires so to do, or commits or threatens physical violence to any person or property in furtherance of a plan or purpose to do anything in violation of this section shall be fined not more than $10,000 or imprisoned not more than twenty years, or both.

(b) As used in this section—

(1) The term "robbery" means the unlawful taking or obtaining of personal property from the person or in the presence of another, against his will, by means of actual or threatened force, or violence, or fear of injury, immediate or future, to his person or property, or property in his custody or possession, or the person or property of a relative or member of his family or of anyone in his company at the time of the taking or obtaining.

(2) The term "extortion" means the obtaining of property from another, with his consent, induced by wrongful use of actual or threatened force, violence, or fear, or under color of official right.

Unctuous argues that he cannot be convicted under the Act, as he committed neither robbery nor extortion. Although he may have received things from Pullman, he did not "induce" Pullman to give him these things, as § 1951 (b)(2) requires. The Government responds: all the statute requires the prosecution to show for extortion is that (1) defendant obtained property of another with his consent (2) because of his official position, and (3) defendant knew the property was given him as a result of his official position. There is no requirement of inducement when a public official is accused of extortion, says the Government. Is such a reading grammatically plausible? (Hint: Consider the punctuation of § 1951(b)(2).) E.g., *United States v. Jannotti*, 673 F.2d 578 (3d Cir. 1982) (en banc), cert. denied, 457 U.S. 1106 (1982). The defendant argues that the statute does require a showing of "inducement." What is the grammatical basis for this argument?

Another interpretation of the Hobbs Act which the Government might suggest is that inducement is an element of the crime, but in the case of most public officials their acceptance of money from private parties who are under their authority is conclusively presumed to be induced by the officials if they knew the reason for the property transfer. Is this a sensible reading of the statute? Compare *United States v. Hedman*, 630 F.2d 1184, 1192–93 (7th Cir. 1980), cert. denied, 450 U.S. 965 (1981), with *United States v. O'Grady*, 742 F.2d 682 (2d Cir. 1984) (en banc). In the alternative, the Government argues that inducement (if a statutory requirement for conviction) can be established by demonstrating a pattern of repeated acceptances of substantial benefits by an official with discretionary power over the giver of those benefits. How should Unctuous respond to these alternative arguments? What canons might support his position?

Note on Legislated Canons of Statutory Interpretation

Sometimes the legislature attempts to direct the court in how to approach interpreting a particular statute. For example, a provision of the federal

Racketeer Influenced and Corrupt Organizations Act (RICO), 18 U.S.C. § 1961, which contains criminal sanctions, provides that "[t]he provisions of this title shall be liberally construed to effectuate its remedial purposes." Some constitutional objections to such a provision could conceivably be raised—the most straightforward would be that it violates the separation of powers because it invades the court's power to say what the law is—but leaving that problem aside, what should a court do with it? In *Russello v. United States*, 464 U.S. 16, 26–27 (1983), the Court cited the RICO provision as well as legislative history to support a broad construction of the statute. In contrast, in *Reves v. Ernst & Young*, 507 U.S. 170, 183–84 (1993), the Court said the following about the RICO clause:

> This clause obviously seeks to ensure that Congress' intent is not frustrated by an overly narrow reading of the statute, but it is not an invitation to apply RICO to new purposes that Congress never intended. Nor does the clause help us to determine what purposes Congress had in mind. Those must be gleaned from the statute through the normal means of interpretation. The clause "only serves as an aid for resolving an ambiguity; it is not to be used to beget one."

Does this approach leave any role for the interpretive clause at all?

Congress has also adopted the Dictionary Act, which codifies a few generic canons of statutory construction, such as the rules that singular terms include the plural, and male pronouns also include females. See 1 U.S.C. § 1 et seq. All 50 states and the District of Columbia have adopted more ambitious model interpretation acts providing legisled canons to guide judicial interpretation for all statutes. Chapter 645 of the Minnesota Statutes, for example, contains the following provisions:

645.16. LEGISLATIVE INTENT CONTROLS

The object of all interpretation and construction of laws is to ascertain and effectuate the intention of the legislature. Every law shall be construed, if possible, to give effect to all its provisions.

When the words of a law in their application to an existing situation are clear and free from all ambiguity, the letter of the law shall not be disregarded under the pretext of pursuing the spirit.

When the words of a law are not explicit, the intention of the legislature may be ascertained by considering, among other matters:

(1) The occasion and necessity for the law;

(2) The circumstances under which it was enacted;

(3) The mischief to be remedied;

(4) The object to be attained;

(5) The former law, if any, including other laws upon the same or similar subjects;

(6) The consequences of a particular interpretation;

(7) The contemporaneous legislative history; and

(8) Legislative and administrative interpretations of the statute.

645.17. PRESUMPTIONS IN ASCERTAINING LEGISLATIVE INTENT

In ascertaining the intention of the legislature the courts may be guided by the following presumptions:

(1) The legislature does not intend a result that is absurd, impossible of execution, or unreasonable;

(2) The legislature intends the entire statute to be effective and certain;

(3) The legislature does not intend to violate the constitution of the United States or of this state;

(4) When a court of last resort has construed the language of a law, the legislature in subsequent laws on the same subject matter intends the same construction to be placed upon such language; and

(5) The legislature intends to favor the public interest as against any private interest.

Notice that Minnesota's legislated canons provide (1) a general theory of statutory interpretation, (2) an indication of the sources judges should consult and when they might consult them, and (3) specific presumptions of statutory meaning.

In a comprehensive study, Jacob Scott, *Codified Canons and the Common Law of Interpretation*, 98 Geo. L.J. 341 (2010), collected and categorized the statutory canons for all 50 states and the District of Columbia. Scott then analyzed the patterns he found across the nationwide sample. Among the patterns he reported are the following:

• **Plain Meaning.** Fifteen legislatures, including that of Minnesota, have codified the plain meaning rule, but with explicit inclusion of exceptions for "absurd results" and/or "scrivener's errors" (Table 1, p. 357). Thirty-four legislatures have codified the dictionary canon and the canon that "ordinary usage" should normally be applied (Table 1). No legislature has codified *expressio unius*, and only two have codified *ejusdem generis* or *noscitur a sociis*.

• **Whole Act.** Thirty legislatures (including Minnesota's) have codified the whole act rule *and* the presumption of consistent usage of terms within a statute (Table 3, p. 368). Thirty-one have codified the rule against interpreting one provision in a way that is inconsistent with the structure of the statute (Table 3). Ten states (including Minnesota) have codified the rule against surplusage (Table 3).

• **Consistency Across Statutes.** Twenty-six states (including Minnesota) have codified the presumption that the same term should be interpreted consistently across different statutes (Table 6, p. 378). Fifteen states have codified the canon against implied repeals (Table 10, p. 397).

• **Legislative History.** Eleven states (including Minnesota) have codified the rule that legislative history "may" be considered under various circumstances; no state has legislated against consideration of legislative history (Table 7, p. 383). Like Minnesota's codification, most of these codifications require the statute to be ambiguous, but a few states (such as Texas) say legislative history can be consulted under any circumstances.

● **Constitutional Canons.** Six states (including Minnesota) have codified the avoidance canon; none has rejected it (Table 8, p. 388). Thirty-five states have codified the presumption of severability (Table 8). Twenty-four states have codified the presumption against statutory retroactivity (Table 9, p. 391).

● **Purposive Canons.** Like Minnesota, 21 other states have codified the canon that ambiguous statutes should be interpreted to carry out the legislative purpose (Table 10, p. 397). Nineteen state legislatures say that remedial statutes should be liberally construed, and 17 states say that all statutes should be liberally construed (Table 11, p. 402). Eleven states have codified the presumption that the legislature intends "reasonable" results (Table 11).

Scott argues from this exhaustive survey that there is a "common law" of canons of statutory construction—a common law to which legislatures and not just courts are contributing. He suggests that judges ought to be chary of deploying canons, such as *expressio unius* or *ejusdem generis*, that legislatures have uniformly failed to embrace. If statutory interpretation is supposed to be attentive to legislative intent, as most state legislatures and courts claim, is it not relevant that legislated canons never include *expressio unius* or *ejusdem generis* and overwhelmingly endorse the absurd results exception to plain meaning and the importance of legislative purpose in resolving statutory ambiguities?

Moreover, this survey might have some traction for general theories of statutory interpretation. Scott concludes from his survey that state legislatures are not friendly to the new textualism's methodology (Chapter 2, § 3A): Although legislatures endorse the plain meaning rule, they do so with allowance for a generous absurd result exception and tend to favor consultation of legislative history and statutory purpose. Conversely, Scott suggests that the pattern of codification lends legislative, and perhaps democratic, support and legitimacy to the pragmatic approach laid out in William N. Eskridge Jr. & Philip P. Frickey, *Statutory Interpretation as Practical Reasoning*, 42 Stan. L. Rev. 321 (1990) (Chapter 2, § 3B). How would a new textualist respond to this?

For an argument that Congress has and should exercise the authority to enact more ambitious federal rules of statutory interpretation (more like those of Minnesota and other states), see Nicholas Quinn Rosenkranz, *Federal Rules of Statutory Interpretation*, 115 Harv. L. Rev. 2085 (2002). For a critique and modification of this approach, see Adam Kiracofe, Note, *The Codified Canons of Statutory Construction: A Response and Proposal to Nicholas Rosenkranz's* Federal Rules of Statutory Interpretation, 84 B.U. L. Rev. 571 (2004). For a critique and counter-proposal suggesting that an organization like the American Law Institute formulate a restatement of statutory interpretation, see Gary O'Connor, *Restatement (First) of Statutory Interpretation*, 7 N.Y.U. J. Legis. & Pub. Pol'y 333 (2003–04).

CHAPTER 4

EXTRINSIC SOURCES FOR STATUTORY INTERPRETATION

■ ■ ■

Extrinsic aids for statutory interpretation are sources outside the text of the statute and its authoritative constructions by judges and agencies. Extrinsic sources include the common law (examined in Section 1 of this chapter), the legislative background of the statute (Section 2), and other statutes and their interpretation (Section 3). The traditional rule was that extrinsic aids should not be considered if the statute had a "plain meaning." But how can we be sure that the statute really has a plain meaning, without considering relevant context? For example, if the legislature uses a term such as "fraud," which had an established common law meaning at the time, shouldn't we consult extrinsic evidence just to figure out what the plain meaning might be? Or if legislative discussions reveal a specialized use of the term "fraud," shouldn't they be relevant?

The new textualists introduced in Chapter 2, § 3A believe that the common law and other statutes are usually admissible extrinsic evidence, but that legislative background or history is not. This position is examined more closely in § 2B of this chapter. The new textualist philosophy has had some influence on the Supreme Court and the lower federal courts. In contrast, state courts have in the last several decades become more likely to consider legislative history, because documentary legislative materials are more readily available than in the past.[a]

SECTION 1. THE COMMON LAW

The traditional rule in Anglo–American law was that statutes in derogation of the common law should be narrowly construed. This was the philosophy of Blackstone's *Commentaries*, which were pervasively influen-

---

a. For a comprehensive overview, see José R. Torres & Steve Windsor, *State Legislative Histories: A Select, Annotated Bibliography*, 85 Law Libr. J. 545 (1993). Our student Brian Barnes, Yale Law School, Class of 2010, in "The Transformation of State Statutory Interpretation" (Yale Law School Seminar Paper, May 4, 2010), documented the steadily increasing availability of floor debates, committee hearings, and pre-enactment analyses of bills by committee staff or the governor's office in most of the states. This greater availability will probably render legislative history increasingly important at the state level.

tial at the founding of our constitutional republic, and in the early Supreme Court, especially in admiralty cases.[b] As the Supreme Court later articulated the principle, "[n]o statute is to be construed as altering the common law, farther than its words import." *Shaw v. Railroad Co.*, 101 U.S. 557, 565 (1879). This canon reflected the foundational character of the common law as a regulatory regime. Any deviation from common-law rules needed special justification.

Such a rule has eroded in the modern regulatory statute, where statutes are the rule and common law the exception. For example, in *Isbrandtsen Co. v. Johnson*, 343 U.S. 779, 783 (1952), the Supreme Court held, in an admiralty proceeding by a seaman for wages earned, that the employer's common-law right to set off damages resulting from the seaman's dereliction of duty had been preempted by federal statute. The Court stated:

> Statutes which invade the common law or the general maritime law are to be read with a presumption favoring the retention of long-established and familiar principles, except when a statutory purpose to the contrary is evident. No rule of construction precludes giving a natural meaning to legislation like this that obviously is of a remedial, beneficial and amendatory character. It should be interpreted so as to effect its purpose. Marine legislation, at least since the Shipping Commissioners Act of June 7, 1872, 17 Stat. 262, should be construed to make effective its design to change the general maritime law so as to improve the lot of seamen.

Isbrandtsen noted, further, that federal statutes regulated virtually every aspect of a seaman's rights and duties, hence negating the force of the common law argument. This suggests another reason for the demise of the common law canon: statutes substantially occupy the field to regulate many areas of human activity, whereas in the nineteenth century (the heyday of the common law canon), statutory regulation was the exception.

Nonetheless, the common law remains an important extrinsic source for interpreting many statutes. As noted in Chapter 3, § 1, when the legislature deploys words with well-established common law meanings, courts will presume that those meanings are adopted by Congress. E.g., *Wallace v. Kato*, 549 U.S. 384, 387–88 (2007) (§ 1983); *Community for Creative Non–Violence v. Reid*, 490 U.S. 730, 739 (1989). Especially for older, more generally phrased statutes, the common law serves a broader "gap-filling" role. That is, for issues entirely unaddressed by the statute, the interpreter might presume that the legislature intended to adopt the established common law rule. Consider the following problem and then a

---

b. For our early history, see William N. Eskridge Jr., *All About Words: The Original Understandings of the "Judicial Power" in Statutory Interpretation, 1776–1806*, 101 Colum. L. Rev. 990 (2001). The best historical source for eighteenth century English thinking is David Lieberman, *The Province of Legislation Determined* 16–20, 28, 52–72 (1989) (discussing the proliferation of mangled statutes in eighteenth-century England and Blackstone's disdainful attitude toward them, with judges being the main salvation by protecting the common law against bad statutes).

case excerpt to see how important the common law still is for filling in gaps.

PROBLEM 4-1

Common Law Gap-filling Rules in a Civil Rights Statute

The Civil Rights Act of 1871, 17 Stat. 13, codified as amended at 42 U.S.C. § 1983, provides as follows:

Every person who, under color of any statute, ordinance, regulation, custom, or usage, of any State or Territory or the District of Columbia, subjects, or causes to be subjected, any citizen of the United States or other person within the jurisdiction thereof to the deprivation of any rights, privileges, or immunities secured by the Constitution and laws, shall be liable to the party injured in an action at law, suit in equity, or other proper proceeding for redress.

This statute was passed in 1871, as part of the Reconstruction effort to ensure newly freed slaves their rights as citizens.

Carl Doe, an official of the NAACP, organizes a boycott of stores in Tylertown, Mississippi, because the stores follow segregated practices. He also organizes a sit-in. The sheriff arrests Doe for breach of the peace, and state Judge Joyce Judicious orders Doe to cease any and all activity meant to disrupt Tylertown businesses. Doe points out that a long line of Supreme Court First Amendment precedents render such an order "lawless," and Judge Judicious holds Doe in contempt and sentences him to a day in jail. When Judge Judicious' order is overturned, Doe sues the sheriff and the judge under § 1983 for violating his First Amendment rights. The sheriff settles the case with Doe, but Judge Judicious argues judicial immunity.

Judge Judicious demonstrates that at common law judges were immune from lawsuits arising out of their judicial duties. The Supreme Court in *Bradley v. Fisher*, 80 U.S. (13 Wall.) 335 (1871), endorsed absolute judicial immunity to protect the integrity of judicial decisionmaking, which would be compromised if the judge were worried about being sued by the losers of lawsuits. Because Congress may be assumed not to disturb such a long-established rule of immunity, § 1983 should be interpreted to include this immunity, argues Judicious.

Doe disagrees and cites to the legislative background of § 1983. During Reconstruction, the South was marked by disorder and violence, especially against the newly emancipated black citizens. Often this violence was accomplished under color of state law—through lynchings, rigged trials, and official harassment of freed slaves. The Reconstruction Congress enacted the Civil Rights Act of 1866, 14 Stat. 27, to abate the violence. Section 2 of the 1866 Act provided criminal liability for any person who, under color of any law, deprived another of federal rights by reason of race. Most of the discussion of § 2 recognized that it would apply to state judges, for much of the oppression was conducted through state tribunals. A proposed amendment to exempt state judges from criminal liability failed. President Andrew Johnson vetoed the 1866 bill, in part because it would allow prosecution of state court judges.

Members of Congress objected to President Johnson's reason. "I answer it is better to invade the judicial power of the State than permit it to invade, strike down, and destroy the civil rights of citizens. A judicial power perverted to such uses should be speedily invaded," argued one representative. Congress passed the bill over the President's veto.

Another amendment not adopted in 1866 was Representative John Bingham's proposal to substitute a civil action for the criminal penalties of § 2. (The bill's sponsor said the law's beneficiaries could not afford civil suits.) Violence against African Americans continued in the South, and this proposal was renewed in 1871. After President Ulysses Grant informed Congress of the urgency of attacking the violence of Southern racists against blacks, Congress passed the Civil Rights Act of 1871, § 1 of which is the predecessor of § 1983. Representative Samuel Shellabarger, the main House sponsor of the 1871 bill, said on the floor of the House that § 2 of the 1866 Act was "the model" for § 1 of the 1871 bill. "[Section 2] provides a criminal proceeding in identically the same case as [§ 1] provides a civil remedy for, except that the deprivation under color of State law must, under the [1866 Act], have been on account of race, color, or former slavery." The Senate sponsor, Senator Edmunds, stated that § 1 was intended to carry out the principles of the 1866 Act. No one in Congress disputed the analogy.

There was little discussion of § 1 in Congress (most of the discussion focused on the criminal conspiracy provision of the 1871 bill). Opponents of § 1 stressed its invasion of judicial independence and cited to criminal prosecutions of judges under the 1866 Act. "By the first section, in certain cases, the judge of a State court, though acting under oath of office, is made liable to a suit in Federal court and subject to damages for his decision against a suitor," exclaimed an opponent of the 1871 bill. Although Representative Shellabarger often corrected opponents' mischaracterizations of his bill, he never disputed opponents' allegations that § 1 would render judges civilly liable. Supporters of the 1871 bill argued that in the South "courts are in many instances under the control of those who are wholly inimical to the impartial administration of law and equity" and that the criminal liability of the 1866 Act was not enough to stop those abuses of justice. The 1871 bill was passed overwhelmingly. This legislative background, argues Doe, shows that the 1871 Congress did *not* expect that § 1 would include the common law's judicial immunity doctrine.

Would the Supreme Court accept Judicious's argument that she is immune from § 1983 in this case? Compare *Pierson v. Ray*, 386 U.S. 547 (1967).

If the Court interprets § 1983 to include a rule of absolute judicial immunity against damages liability, based upon the common law doctrine of judicial immunity existing in 1871, should it extend similar immunity to prosecutors? Although prosecutorial immunity is grounded on the same integrity-of-the-judicial-process basis as judicial immunity, there was no American case granting prosecutors common law immunity until *Griffith v. Slinkard*, 44 N.E. 1001 (Ind. 1896), and prosecutorial was not widely accepted by American courts until the 1930s. How would the Supreme Court decide this case? Compare *Imbler v. Pachtman*, 424 U.S. 409 (1976).

Jot down your answers now, and consider a different kind of issue: For officials who can be sued for damages, what damages might be allowed? Under what circumstances can punitive damages be awarded, for example? Consider the following case.

SMITH v. WADE

Supreme Court of the United States, 1983
461 U.S. 30, 103 S.Ct. 1625, 75 L.Ed.2d 632

JUSTICE BRENNAN delivered the opinion of the Court.

[Wade, an inmate of a Missouri state prison, brought a § 1983 suit against Smith and four guards and correction officials. Wade alleged that he was assaulted by cellmates and that defendants did nothing even though they knew or ought to have known that such an assault was likely to occur. The trial judge instructed the jury that Wade could obtain punitive damages if defendants' conduct were in reckless disregard of, or indifferent to, Wade's safety. The jury found Smith liable for both compensatory and punitive damages, and the circuit court affirmed. The issue before the Court was whether punitive damages may be awarded in a § 1983 action based upon a finding of reckless or callous disregard of, or indifference to, plaintiff's rights, or, as Smith contended, only upon a finding that the defendant acted with "actual malicious intent."]

Section 1983 is derived from § 1 of the Civil Rights Act of 1871, 17 Stat. 13. It was intended to create "a species of tort liability" in favor of persons deprived of federally secured rights. *Carey v. Piphus*, 435 U.S. 247, 253 (1978); *Imbler v. Pachtman*, 424 U.S. 409, 417 (1976). We noted in *Carey* that there was little in the section's legislative history concerning the damages recoverable for this tort liability. In the absence of more specific guidance, we looked first to the common law of torts (both modern and as of 1871), with such modification or adaptation as might be necessary to carry out the purpose and policy of the statute. We have done the same in other contexts arising under § 1983, especially the recurring problem of common-law immunities.[2]

---

2. [Citing cases, including *Imbler* and *Pierson*, both of which imported common law immunities into § 1983.] Justice Rehnquist's dissent faults us for referring to modern tort decisions in construing § 1983. Its argument rests on the unstated and unsupported premise that Congress necessarily intended to freeze into permanent law whatever principles were current in 1871, rather than to incorporate applicable general legal principles as they evolve. The dissents are correct, of course, that when the language of the section and its legislative history provide no clear answer, we have found useful guidance in the law prevailing at the time when § 1983 was enacted; but it does not follow that that law is absolutely controlling or that current law is irrelevant. On the contrary, if the prevailing view on some point of general tort law had changed substantially in the intervening century (which is not the case here), we might be highly reluctant to assume that Congress intended to perpetuate a now-obsolete doctrine. See *Carey v. Piphus* ("[O]ver the centuries the common law of torts has developed a set of rules to implement the principle that a person should be compensated fairly for injuries caused by the violation of his legal rights. These rules, defining the elements of damages and the prerequisites for their recovery, provide the appropriate starting point for the inquiry under § 1983 as well.") (footnote omitted). Indeed, in *Imbler* we recognized a common-law immunity that first came into existence 25 years after § 1983 was enacted. Under the dissents' view, *Imbler* was wrongly decided.

[Smith conceded that punitive damages are available in a "proper" § 1983 action.] Smith argues, nonetheless, that this was not a "proper" case in which to award punitive damages. More particularly, he attacks the instruction that punitive damages could be awarded on a finding of reckless or callous disregard of or indifference to Wade's rights or safety. Instead, he contends that the proper test is one of actual malicious intent—"ill will, spite, or intent to injure." He offers two arguments for this position: first, that actual intent is the proper standard for punitive damages in all cases under § 1983; and second, that even if intent is not always required, it should be required here because the threshold for punitive damages should always be higher than that for liability in the first instance. We address these in turn.

[III] Smith does not argue that the common law, either in 1871 or now, required or requires a showing of actual malicious intent for recovery of punitive damages.

Perhaps not surprisingly, there was significant variation (both terminological and substantive) among American jurisdictions in the latter nineteenth century on the precise standard to be applied in awarding punitive damages—variation that was exacerbated by the ambiguity and slipperiness of such common terms as "malice" and "gross negligence."[8] Most of the confusion, however, seems to have been over the degree of negligence, recklessness, carelessness, or culpable indifference that should be required—not over whether actual intent was essential. On the contrary, the rule in a large majority of jurisdictions was that punitive damages (also called exemplary damages, vindictive damages, or smart money) could be awarded without a showing of actual ill will, spite, or intent to injure.

This Court so stated on several occasions, before and shortly after 1871. In *Philadelphia, W. & B.R. Co. v. Quigley*, 21 How. 202 (1859), a diversity libel suit, the Court held erroneous an instruction that authorized the jury to return a punitive award but gave the jury virtually no substantive guidance as to the proper threshold. We described the standard thus:

> "Whenever the injury complained of has been inflicted maliciously or wantonly, and with circumstances of contumely or indignity, the jury are not limited to the ascertainment of a simple compensation for the wrong committed against the aggrieved person. But the malice spoken of in this rule is not merely the doing of an unlawful or injurious act. The word implies that the act complained of was conceived in the spirit of mischief, *or of criminal indifference to civil obligations.*" *Id.* at 214. * * *

---

8. [Footnote 8 is 76 lines of the U.S. Reports, attacking Justice Rehnquist's assumption that in 1871 "malice," "wantonness," and "willfulness" all denoted ill will. Justice Brennan asserted that "[w]ith regard to 'malice' the assumption is dubious at best; with regard to 'wantonness' and 'willfulness,' it is just plain wrong."]

The large majority of state and lower federal courts were in agreement that punitive damages awards did not require a showing of actual malicious intent; they permitted punitive awards on variously stated standards of negligence, recklessness, or other culpable conduct short of actual malicious intent.[11]

The same rule applies today. The Restatement (Second) of Torts (1977), for example, states: "Punitive damages may be awarded for conduct that is outrageous, because of the defendant's evil motive *or his reckless indifference to the rights of others.*" *Id.*, § 908(2) (emphasis added); see also *id.*, Comment *b.* Most cases under state common law, although varying in their precise terminology, have adopted more or less the same rule, recognizing that punitive damages in tort cases may be awarded not only for actual intent to injure or evil motive, but also for recklessness, serious indifference to or disregard for the rights of others, or even gross negligence.[13]

The remaining question is whether the policies and purposes of § 1983 itself require a departure from the rules of tort common law. As a general matter, we discern no reason why a person whose federally guaranteed rights have been violated should be granted a more restrictive remedy than a person asserting an ordinary tort cause of action. Smith offers us no persuasive reason to the contrary.

Smith's argument, which he offers in several forms, is that an actual-intent standard is preferable to a recklessness standard because it is less vague. He points out that punitive damages, by their very nature, are not awarded to compensate the injured party. He concedes, of course, that deterrence of future egregious conduct is a primary purpose of both § 1983 and of punitive damages, see * * * Restatement (Second) of Torts § 908(1) (1979). But deterrence, he contends, cannot be achieved unless the standard of conduct sought to be deterred is stated with sufficient clarity to enable potential defendants to conform to the law and to avoid the proposed sanction. Recklessness or callous indifference, he argues, is too uncertain a standard to achieve deterrence rationally and fairly. A

---

11. * * * *Maysville & L.R. Co. v. Herrick*, 76 Ky. 122 (1877), held that the trial court correctly refused to instruct the jury that "willful or intentional wrong" was required to award punitive damages in a railroad accident case, remarking: "The absence of slight care in the management of a railroad station, or in keeping a railroad track in repair, is gross negligence; and to enable a passenger to recover punitive damages, in a case like this, it is not necessary to show the absence of all care, or 'reckless indifference to the safety of * * * passengers,' or 'intentional misconduct' on the part of the agents and officers of the company." *Id.*, at 127 (ellipsis in original). [Justice Brennan cited 30 cases in accord with this proposition.]

Justice Rehnquist's assertion that a "solid majority of jurisdictions" required actual malicious intent is simply untrue. In fact, there were fairly few jurisdictions that imposed such a requirement, and fewer yet that adhered to it consistently. Justice Rehnquist's attempt to establish this proposition with case citations does not offer him substantial support. Because the point is not of controlling significance, we will not tarry here to analyze his citations case-by-case or state-by-state, but will only summarize the main themes. [According to Justice Brennan, some of the dissenters' cases support the availability of punitive damages for recklessness, others are too equivocal to categorize, and others support the dissenters' interpretation only if one assumes that terms like "malice," "wantonness," and "criminal" always meant actual intent to injure.]

13. [Justice Brennan cited 33 recent state cases to support the proposition in text.]

prison guard, for example, can be expected to know whether he is acting with actual ill will or intent to injure, but not whether he is being reckless or callously indifferent.

Smith's argument, if valid, would apply to ordinary tort cases as easily as to § 1983 suits; hence, it hardly presents an argument for adopting a different rule under § 1983. In any event, the argument is unpersuasive. While, *arguendo*, an intent standard may be easier to understand and apply to particular situations than a recklessness standard, we are not persuaded that a recklessness standard is too vague to be fair or useful. In [*Milwaukee & St. Paul R. Co. v. Arms,* 91 U.S. (1 Otto) 489 (1876),] we adopted a recklessness standard rather than a gross negligence standard precisely because recklessness would better serve the need for adequate clarity and fair application. Almost a century later, in the First Amendment context, we held that punitive damages cannot be assessed for defamation in the absence of proof of "knowledge of falsity or reckless disregard for the truth." [*Gertz v. Robert Welch, Inc.,* 418 U.S. 323, 349 (1974).] Our concern in *Gertz* was that the threat of punitive damages, if not limited to especially egregious cases, might "inhibit the vigorous exercise of First Amendment freedoms"—a concern at least as pressing as any urged by Smith in this case. Yet we did not find it necessary to impose an actual-intent standard there. Just as Smith has not shown why § 1983 should give higher protection from punitive damages than ordinary tort law, he has not explained why it gives higher protection than we have demanded under the First Amendment.

More fundamentally, Smith's argument for certainty in the interest of deterrence overlooks the distinction between a standard for punitive damages and a standard of liability in the first instance. Smith seems to assume that prison guards and other state officials look mainly to the standard for punitive damages in shaping their conduct. We question the premise; we assume, and hope, that most officials are guided primarily by the underlying standards of federal substantive law—both out of devotion to duty, and in the interest of avoiding liability for compensatory damages. At any rate, the conscientious officer who desires clear guidance on how to do his job and avoid lawsuits can and should look to the standard for actionability in the first instance. The need for exceptional clarity in the standard for punitive damages arises only if one assumes that there are substantial numbers of officers who will not be deterred by compensatory damages; only such officers will seek to guide their conduct by the punitive damages standard. The presence of such officers constitutes a powerful argument *against* raising the threshold for punitive damages.

In this case, the jury was instructed to apply a high standard of constitutional right ("physical abuse of such base, inhumane and barbaric proportions as to shock the sensibilities"). It was also instructed, under the principle of qualified immunity, that Smith could not be held liable at all unless he was guilty of "a callous indifference or a thoughtless disregard for the consequences of [his] act or failure to act," or of "a flagrant or remarkably bad failure to protect" Wade. These instructions are not challenged in this Court, nor were they challenged on grounds of vagueness in the lower courts. Smith's contention that this recklessness standard is too vague to provide clear guidance and reasonable deterrence might more properly be reserved for a challenge seeking different standards of liability in the first instance. As for punitive damages, however, in the absence of any persuasive argument to the contrary based on the policies of § 1983, we are content to adopt the policy judgment of the common law—that reckless or callous disregard for the plaintiff's rights, as well as intentional violations of federal law, should be sufficient to trigger a jury's consideration of the appropriateness of punitive damages.

[Justice Brennan, finally, rejected Smith's last argument, that it was error for the court to describe the standard of punitive damages in terms similar to those of the basic liability under § 1983 (indifference to Wade's rights). Primary reliance was placed on the Restatement (Second) of Torts and the modern common law, which generally provide that where the standard for compensatory liability is as high or higher than the usual threshold for punitive damages, such damages may be given without requiring any extra showing.]

JUSTICE REHNQUIST, with whom THE CHIEF JUSTICE [BURGER] and JUSTICE POWELL join, dissenting.

The Court rejects a "wrongful intent" standard, instead requiring a plaintiff to show merely "reckless * * * indifference to the federally protected rights of others." The following justifications are offered by the Court for this result: first, the rule in "[m]ost cases [decided in the last 15 years] under state common law" is "more or less" equivalent to a recklessness standard; second, the Court asserts that a similar rule "prevail[ed] at the time when § 1983 was enacted"; and finally, there is an "absence of any persuasive argument" for not applying existing state tort rules to the federal statutory remedies available against state and local officials under § 1983. In my opinion none of these justifications, taken singly or together, supports the Court's result. First, the decisions of state courts in the last decade or so are all but irrelevant in determining the intent of the 42d Congress, and thus, the meaning of § 1983. Second, the Court's characterization of the common law rules prevailing when § 1983 was enacted is both oversimplified and misleading; in fact, the majority rule in 1871 seems to have been that some sort of "evil intent"— and not mere recklessness—was necessary to justify an award of punitive damages. Third, the Court's inability to distinguish a *state* court's award of punitive damages against a state officer from a *federal* court's analogous action under §§ 1983 and 1988 precludes it from adequately assessing the public policies implicated by its decision. Finally, the Court fails utterly to grapple with the cogent and persuasive criticisms that have been offered of punitive damages generally.

[Part I of Justice Rehnquist's dissenting opinion is a brief consideration of criticism of punitive damages. In light of this criticism, some states do not allow punitive damage awards, and others have required some sort of evil motive to justify punitive awards. This latter proposition is supported by footnote 3, which spends more than 120 lines analyzing nineteenth-century use of the terms "malice," "willfulness," and "wantonness." His overall point is that nineteenth-century thinkers reserved punitive awards for those who "subjectively" visited evil on their fellows, not those whose conduct was deemed to have failed an "objective" or recklessness standard.]

[II] At bottom, this case requires the Court to decide when a particular remedy is available under § 1983. Until today, the Court has adhered, with some fidelity, to the scarcely controversial principle that its proper role in interpreting § 1983 is determining what the 42d Congress intended. That § 1983 is to be interpreted according to this basic principle of statutory construction is clearly demonstrated by our many decisions relying upon the plain language of the section. The Court's opinion purports to pursue an inquiry into legislative intent, yet relies heavily upon state court decisions decided well after the 42d Congress adjourned. I find these cases unilluminating, at least in part because I am unprepared to attribute to the 42d Congress the truly extraordinary foresight that the Court seems to think it had. The reason our earlier decisions interpreting § 1983 have relied upon common law decisions is simple: members of the 42d Congress were lawyers, familiar with the law of their time. In resolving ambiguities in the enactments of that Congress, as with other Congresses, it is useful to consider the legal principles and rules that shaped the thinking of its Members. The decisions of state courts decided well after 1871, while of some academic interest, are largely irrelevant to what Members of the 42d Congress intended by way of a standard for punitive damages.

In an apparent attempt to justify its novel approach to discerning the intent of a body that deliberated more than a century ago, the Court makes passing reference to our decisions relating to common law immunities under § 1983. These decisions provide no support for the Court's analysis, since they all plainly evidence an attempt to discern the intent of the 42d Congress, albeit indirectly, by reference to the common law principles known to members of that body. * * * More recently, in *City of Newport v. Fact Concerts, Inc.*, 453 U.S. 247, 258 (1981), we said:

> It is by now well settled that the tort liability created by § 1983 cannot be understood in a historical vacuum * * *. One important assumption underlying the Court's decisions in this area is that members of the 42d Congress were familiar with common-law principles, including defenses previously recognized in ordinary tort litigation, and that they likely intended these common-law principles to obtain, absent specific provisions to the contrary.

Likewise, our other decisions with respect to common law immunities under § 1983 clearly reveal that our consideration of state common law rules is only a device to facilitate determination of Congressional intent.

Decisions from the 1970s, relied on by the Court, are almost completely irrelevant to this inquiry into legislative intent.

[III] The Court also purports to rely on decisions, handed down in the second half of the last century by this Court, in drawing up its rule that mere recklessness will support an award of punitive damages. In fact, these decisions unambiguously support an actual malice standard. The Court rests primarily on *Philadelphia, W. & B.R. Co. v. Quigley*, 21 How. 202 (1859), a diversity tort action against a railroad. There, we initially observed that in "certain actions of tort," punitive damages might be awarded, and then described those actions as "[w]henever the injury complained of has been inflicted maliciously or wantonly, and with circumstances of contumely or indignity." *Id.* at 214. * * * [I]t was relatively clear at the time that "malice" required a showing of actual ill will or intent to injure. Perhaps foreseeing future efforts to expand the rule, however, we hastened to specify the type of malice that would warrant punitive damages: "the malice spoken of in this rule is not merely the doing of an unlawful or injurious act. The word implies that the act complained of *was conceived in the spirit of mischief, or of criminal indifference to civil obligations.*" It would have been difficult to have more clearly expressed the "actual malice" standard. We explicitly rejected an "implied malice" formulation, and then mandated inquiry into the "spirit" in which a defendant's act was "conceived."

[Justice Rehnquist analyzed other nineteenth century Supreme Court decisions consistent with his reading of *Quigley*.] In *Lake Shore & Michigan Southern Railway Co. v. Prentice*, 147 U.S. 101 (1893), the Court considered whether punitive damages were properly awarded against a railroad in a diversity action. The Court noted that the law on the subject was "well-settled," and paraphrased the *Quigley* standard: The jury may award punitive damages "if the defendant has acted wantonly, or oppressively, or with such malice as implies a spirit of mischief or criminal indifference to civil obligations." Then, * * * the Court explained this formulation, observing that a *"guilty intention* on the part of the defendant is *required* in order to charge him with exemplary or punitive damages." *Ibid.* (emphasis added). * * *

In addition, the decisions rendered by state courts in the years preceding and immediately following the enactment of § 1983 attest to the fact that a solid majority of jurisdictions took the view that the standard for an award of punitive damages included a requirement of ill will. To be sure, a few jurisdictions followed a broader standard; a careful review of the decisions at the time uncovers a number of decisions that contain some reference to "recklessness." And equally clearly, in more recent years many courts have adopted a standard including "recklessness" as the minimal degree of culpability warranting punitive damages.

Most clear of all, however, is the fact that at about the time § 1983 was enacted a considerable number of the 37 States then belonging to the Union required some showing of wrongful intent before punitive damages could be awarded.[12] As the cases set out in the margin reveal, it is but a statement of the obvious that "evil motive" was the general standard for punitive damages in many states at the time of the 42d Congress. * * *

[IV] Even apart from this historical background, I am persuaded by a variety of additional factors that the 42d Congress intended a "wrongful intent" requirement. As mentioned above, punitive damages are not, and never have been, a favored remedy. In determining whether Congress, not bound by *stare decisis*, would have embraced this often-condemned doctrine, it is worth considering the judgment of one of the most respected commentators in the field regarding the desirability of a legislatively enacted punitive damages remedy: "It is probable that, in the framing of a model code of damages today for use in a country unhampered by legal tradition, the doctrine of exemplary damages would find no place." C. McCormick, Damages 276 (1935).

In deciding whether Congress heeded such advice, it is useful to consider the language of § 1983 itself—which should, of course, be the starting point for any inquiry into legislative intent. Section 1983 provides:

> "Every person who, under color of any statute, ordinance, regulation, custom, or usage of any State * * * subjects, or causes to be subjected, any citizen of the United States or other person within the jurisdiction thereof to the deprivation of any rights, privileges, or immunities secured by the Constitution and laws, shall be liable to the party *injured* in an action at law, suit in equity, or other proper proceeding *for redress*." (emphasis added).

Plainly, the statutory language itself provides absolutely no support for the cause of action for punitive damages that the Court reads into the provision. Indeed, it merely creates "liab[ility] to the party injured * * * for redress." "Redress" means "[r]eparation of, satisfaction or compensation for, a wrong sustained or the loss resulting from this." 8 Oxford English Dictionary 310 (1933). And, as the Court concedes, punitive damages are not "reparation" or "compensation"; their very purpose is to

---

12. See, e.g., *Roberts v. Heim*, 27 Ala. 678, 683 (1855) ("the law allows [punitive damages] whenever the trespass is committed in a rude, aggravating, or insulting manner, as malice may be inferred from these circumstances"); [citation of 76 state cases followed, most with quotations to illustrate Justice Rehnquist's position].

The Court's treatment of the law prevailing in 1871 relies principally upon state-court decisions from the 1880's and 1890's. These cases are admittedly somewhat more relevant to what the 42d Congress intended than the 20th-century cases cited by the Court; particularly if they explain prior decisions, these cases may reflect a well-settled understanding in a particular jurisdiction of the law regarding punitive damages. Yet, decisions handed down well after 1871 are considerably *less* probative of legislative intent than decisions rendered before or shortly subsequent to the enactment of § 1983: it requires no detailed discussion to demonstrate that a member of the 42d Congress would have been more influenced by a decision from 1870 than by one from the 1890's. Accordingly, the bulk of the cases cited by the Court must be ignored; they simply illustrate the historical shift in legal doctrine, pointed out in text, from an actual-intent standard to a recklessness standard. If the Court is serious in its attention to 19th-century law, analysis must focus on the common law as it stood at the time of the 42d Congress. Here, notwithstanding the Court's numerous attempts to explain why decisions do not mean what they plainly say, it remains clear that in a majority of jurisdictions, actual malice was required in order to recover punitive damages.

punish, not to compensate. If Congress meant to create a right to recover punitive damages, then it chose singularly inappropriate words: both the reference to injured parties and to redress suggests compensation, and not punishment.

Other statutes roughly contemporaneous with § 1983 illustrate that if Congress wanted to subject persons to a punitive damages remedy, it did so explicitly. For example, in § 59, 16 Stat. 207, Congress created express punitive damage remedies for various types of commercial misconduct. Likewise, the False Claims Act, § 15, 12 Stat. 698, provided a civil remedy of double damages and a $2,000 civil forfeiture penalty for certain misstatements to the Government. As one Court of Appeals has remarked, "Where Congress has intended [to create a right to punitive damages] it has found no difficulty in using language appropriate to that end." *United Mine Workers v. Patton*, 211 F.2d 742, 749 (CA4 1954). And yet, in § 1983 one searches in vain for some hint of such a remedy.

In the light of the foregoing indications, it is accurate to say that the foundation upon which the right to punitive damages under § 1983 rests is precarious, at the best. * * *

JUSTICE O'CONNOR, dissenting.

Although I agree with the result reached in Justice Rehnquist's dissent, I write separately because I cannot agree with the approach taken by either the Court or Justice Rehnquist. Both opinions engage in exhaustive, but ultimately unilluminating, exegesis of the common law of the availability of punitive damages in 1871. Although both the Court and Justice Rehnquist display admirable skills in legal research and analysis of great numbers of musty cases, the results do not significantly further the goal of the inquiry: to establish the intent of the 42d Congress. In interpreting § 1983, we have often looked to the common law as it existed in 1871, in the belief that, when Congress was silent on a point, it intended to adopt the principles of the common law with which it was familiar. This approach makes sense when there was a generally prevailing rule of common law, for then it is reasonable to assume that congressmen were familiar with that rule and imagined that it would cover the cause of action that they were creating. But when a significant split in authority existed, it strains credulity to argue that Congress simply assumed that one view rather than the other would govern. Particularly in a case like this one, in which those interpreting the common law of 1871 must resort to dictionaries in an attempt to translate the language of the late nineteenth century into terms that judges of the late twentieth century can understand, and in an area in which the courts of the earlier period frequently used inexact and contradictory language, we cannot safely infer anything about congressional intent from the divided contemporaneous judicial opinions. The battle of the string citations can have no winner.

Once it is established that the common law of 1871 provides us with no real guidance on this question, we should turn to the policies underlying § 1983 to determine which rule best accords with those policies. In *Fact Concerts*, we identified the purposes of § 1983 as preeminently to compensate victims of constitutional violations and to deter further violations. The conceded availability of compensatory damages, particularly when coupled with the availability of attorney's fees under § 1988, completely fulfills the goal of compensation, leaving only deterrence to be served by awards of punitive damages. We must then confront the close question whether a standard permitting an award of unlimited punitive damages on the basis of recklessness will chill public officials in the performance of their duties more than it will deter violations of the Constitution, and whether the availability of punitive damages for reckless violations of the Constitution in addition to attorney's fees will create an incentive to bring an ever-increasing flood of § 1983 claims, threatening the ability of the federal courts to handle those that are meritorious. Although I cannot concur in Justice Rehnquist's wholesale condemnation of awards of punitive damages in any context or with the suggestion that punitive damages should not be available even for intentional or malicious violations of constitutional rights, I do agree with the discussion in * * * his opinion of the special problems of permitting awards of punitive damages for the recklessness of public officials. Since awards of compensatory damages and attorney's fees already provide significant deterrence, I am persuaded that the policies counseling against awarding punitive damages for the recklessness of public officials outweigh the desirability of any incremental deterrent effect that such awards may have. Consequently, I dissent.

NOTES ON THE EVOLVING COMMON LAW AS A SOURCE FOR CONSTRUING STATUTES

1. *Interpretation and the Common Law.* Justice Brennan's opinion for the Court argues that the common law in 1871 supports punitive damages for reckless misconduct. Perhaps, but would the common law have permitted a prisoner to obtain such damages from his or her jailer in the circumstances of *Smith v. Wade*? Certainly not! See, e.g., *Moxley v. Roberts*, 43 S.W. 482 (Ky. 1897) (jailer not liable for beating of one prisoner by another unless he actually knew of the beating and failed to stop it); *Williams v. Adams*, 85 Mass. (3 Allen) 171 (1861). Why didn't Justice Brennan just rely on the modern common law, which does support his position?

Contrary to Justice Rehnquist's dissent, the Supreme Court sometimes looks to modern common law to fill in the gaps of § 1983. See *Imbler v. Pachtman*, 424 U.S. 409, 421–22 (1976) (rule of prosecutorial immunity, which was first recognized 25 years after § 1983 was enacted); *Carey v. Piphus*, 435 U.S. 247, 257–58 (1978) (modern law as the starting point for determining which injuries are to be compensated under § 1983). Do you suppose the Congress that adopted § 1983 in 1871 intended that the common law of that era was to supply binding answers to questions left open by the statute? Did the Congress intend or expect courts to develop § 1983 law over time by reference to contemporary developments, and thus that § 1983 might mean one thing in 1871 and quite another thing today?

Note this puzzle: Justices Brennan and Rehnquist looked at the same historical evidence yet came up with diametrically opposed conclusions about what the "common law" was in 1871. The initial, and cynical, impulse is to think that they were just manipulating the evidence to support the result each wanted. A less cynical view is that, in this case, each Justice was an amateur historian, but like professional historians, the Justices had to figure out which evidence was important, what to make of conflicting signals, and how to assimilate the evidence into an account. In this complicated task, isn't the perspective of the interpreter going to make a difference? Professional historians recognize this. Shouldn't the Justices recognize it as well? Indeed, this is a point suggested by Justice O'Connor's dissent.

2. *Common Law Statutes.* Going one step beyond Justice Brennan's approach, Judge Richard A. Posner has argued in *The Federal Courts: Crisis and Reform* (1985) that some statutes, such as § 1983 and the Sherman Act, are essentially "common law statutes." That is, briefly phrased statutes addressing an important societal problem may be the occasion for judicial evolution in the common law tradition, especially if the legislature does not amend the statutes. The legitimacy of judicial lawmaking to fill in the gaps to a statutory scheme is greatest when Congress has essentially delegated the gap-filling duties to judges by using common law terms. Does this suggest a defense of Justice Brennan's majority opinion?

Classic instances in which the Supreme Court has interpreted a simple and vague federal statute as evidencing a congressional intent that the federal courts are to resolve open questions by use of an essentially common law method include the antitrust prohibitions of the Sherman Act and § 301 of the Taft–Hartley Act, which gives federal district courts jurisdiction to hear suits for violation of collective bargaining agreements. See, e.g., *Textile Workers Union v. Lincoln Mills*, 353 U.S. 448 (1957) ("federal common law" under § 301). More recently, the Foreign Sovereign Immunities Act of 1976 (FSIA), 28 U.S.C. §§ 1331, 1602–1611 et al., sets forth guidelines for federal and state court treatment of the sovereign immunity defense by foreign states. The main exception to immunity is the "commercial activity" exception, id. § 1605(a)(2), but the Act gives no precise definition of commercial activity. The House Report asserts that "courts would have a great deal of latitude in determining what is a 'commercial activity' for purposes of this bill," and courts have taken that as a charter to apply the most current common law approaches to the issue. For a recent example applying common law property concepts to fill out the details of the FSIA, see *Permanent Mission of India to the United Nations v. City of New York*, 551 U.S. 193 (2007).

One corollary of the common law statute idea is that Supreme Court precedents interpreting them ought to have the normal *stare decisis* effect of common law precedents—and not the super-strong presumption of correctness that accompanies other statutory precedents (Chapter 1, § 3). See *Leegin Creative Leather Prods., Inc. v. PSKS, Inc.*, 551 U.S. 877 (2007) (precisely this justification for overruling a Sherman Act precedent); *State Oil Co. v. Khan*,

522 U.S. 3 (1997) (same); William N. Eskridge Jr., *Overruling Statutory Precedents*, 76 Geo. L.J. 1361 (1988). A number of Supreme Court decisions have overruled previous constructions of § 1983, essentially for common law reasons. E.g., *Monell v. Department of Social Servs.*, 436 U.S. 658 (1978). Most Supreme Court Justices in 2011 probably disagree with the *Smith v. Wade* approach to punitive damages. Should the Court feel free to overrule *Smith*? Are there reasons to exercise caution? Jot down your thoughts and read the next note.

3. *Recent Statutory Treatment of Punitive Damages in Civil Rights Cases.* The Civil Rights Act of 1991 amended Title VII to permit awards of punitive damages in cases of intentional discrimination. New 42 U.S.C. § 1981a(b)(1) allows such an award if the complainant can show that defendant engaged in such discrimination "with malice or with reckless indifference to the federally protected rights of an aggrieved individual." Carole Kolstad sues her employer for allegedly passing over her for promotion on the basis of her sex. She seeks punitive damages because the decisionmaker not only manipulated the rules to deny her the promotion, but also made repeated derogatory references to women. The trial court refuses to charge the jury that Kolstad may receive punitive damages; the judge rules that, to satisfy § 1981a(b)(1), the complainant must show "egregious" misconduct beyond that which would justify a finding of intentional discrimination. The appellate court affirms.

Following *Smith v. Wade*, the Supreme Court reversed the lower courts and interpreted the 1991 Act to allow punitive damages for reckless as well as egregious conduct. See *Kolstad v. American Dental Ass'n*, 527 U.S. 526 (1999). Should *Kolstad* augur against overruling *Smith v. Wade* in § 1983 cases—or does it now provide an *additional reason* to overrule? Under the whole code rule of meaningful variation (*Casey*, Chapter 2, § 3A), when Congress wants liberal punitive damage awards in civil rights statutes, it explicitly provides for such damages (the 1991 Act). Because § 1983 says nothing about punitive damages, should they be available at all?

How should the Court approach the separate issue of when an employer should be liable in punitive damages for unauthorized conduct on the part of its supervisors? What relevance should the common law of agency have in this inquiry? See *Burlington Indus., Inc. v. Ellerth*, 524 U.S. 742 (1998) (standards for employer liability for hostile work environment and quid pro quo sexual harassment by supervisors).

PROBLEM 4–2

The Common Law and the Hobbs Act, Revisited

Reconsider Problem 3–2, the application of the Hobbs Act to Frankly Unctuous, in light of the common law background uncovered by James Lindgren, *The Elusive Distinction Between Bribery and Extortion: From the Common Law to the Hobbs Act*, 35 UCLA L. Rev. 815 (1988). According to Lindgren, at common law extortion was committed by a public official who took "by colour of his office" money that was not due him for the performance of his official duties. 1 William Hawkins, *Pleas of the Crown* 316 (6th ed.

1787). Hence, a demand for the money (an "inducement") was not an element of the offense at common law. By including private efforts to extort, the Hobbs Act expanded the definition of "extortion" beyond that of the common law, but there is no indication in its legislative history that the Act sought to narrow the common law definition. There is reference in the legislative history that the terms "robbery and extortion" were "based on the New York law." The New York extortion statute applied to a public officer "who asks, or receives, or agrees to receive" unauthorized compensation. N.Y. Penal Code § 557 (1881). With this evidence in mind, how would you interpret the Hobbs Act now? See *Evans v. United States*, 504 U.S. 255 (1992).

What if Unctuous raises this further common law argument: The "under color of office" language itself imposes a requirement not found in the government's case against Unctuous. "At common law it was essential that the money or property be obtained under color of office, *that is, under the pretense that the officer was entitled thereto by virtue of his office.* The money or thing received must have been claimed or accepted by right of office, and the person paying must have yielded to official authority." 3 Ronald A. Anderson, *Wharton's Criminal Law and Procedure* § 1393, at 790–91 (1957) (emphasis added). Assume this is a correct characterization of the common law. Should the Court interpret the Hobbs Act to overturn Unctuous' conviction? See *Evans,* 504 U.S. at 278–87 (Thomas, J., dissenting).

SECTION 2. LEGISLATIVE BACKGROUND (HISTORY)

Statutory history is, in a broad sense, the entire circumstances of a statute's creation and evolution, a point illustrated by the *Leo Sheep* case below. The formal history of a statute's evolution is widely considered relevant to statutory interpretation, even in jurisdictions whose courts will not examine legislative debates. See, e.g., Donald Gifford, *Statutory Interpretation* 91–95 (1990) (using Australia as an example). The same is true for the United States, whose courts do generally examine legislative documents and debates. Thus, the Court in *United States v. Wells,* 519 U.S. 482 (1997), interpreted 18 U.S.C. § 1014, criminalizing false statements to federally insured banks, not to have a materiality requirement. Justice Souter's opinion for the Court relied on the formal history of federal criminal provisions regarding such statements. Section 1014 was a synthesis of thirteen different provisions, at least ten of which had no materiality requirements at the time. This background suggested that Congress did not expect § 1014 to have a materiality requirement.

In this country, the term *legislative history* is mostly used in a narrower sense, to refer to the internal legislative pre-history of a statute—the internal institutional progress of a bill to enactment and the deliberation accompanying that progress.[c] The record of that journey may be quite voluminous and often contains statements by all sorts of people— legislators, bureaucrats, citizens, experts—which support one or another

---

c. Otto Hetzel, Michael Libonati & Robert Williams, *Legislative Law and Process* 438 (2d ed. 1993), provide an excellent checklist of the materials that will constitute the "legislative history" of a law:

1. Floor debate.

interpretation of the statute. A preliminary issue is how to carry out legal research that will reveal all the components of a statute's legislative history.[d] Once the material is identified, the question turns to what stuff in this internal legislative history "counts" toward interpreting the statute, and how much weight each relevant component should receive. Parts B–E will explore judicial use (or misuse) of statements made in committee reports, statements in hearings and floor debates, statements by sponsors, and post-enactment statements by legislators and committees. Part F will ask whether interpretive meaning can be derived from things that are *not* said or done in the legislature.

As you read the following materials, consider the suggestion of Judge Patricia M. Wald, in *Some Observations on the Use of Legislative History in the 1981 Supreme Court Term*, 68 Iowa L. Rev. 195, 214 (1983), that "consistent and uniform rules for statutory construction and use of legislative materials are not being followed today. It sometimes seems that citing legislative history is still, as my late colleague Harold Leventhal once observed, akin to 'looking over a crowd and picking out your friends.'"[e]

---

2. Planned colloquy.

3. Prepared statements on submission of a bill, in committee hearings and at the time of floor debates.

4. Revised and amended statements.

5. Statements in committees by the relevant executive branch administrators.

6. Committee reports.

7. Transcripts of discussions at committee hearings.

8. Statements and submissions by interested persons, both local or state government and private parties.

9. Committee debates on "mark-up" of bills.

10. Conference committee reports.

11. Analysis of bills by legislative counsel.

12. Analysis of bills by relevant executive departments.

13. Amendments accepted or rejected.

14. Actions on and discussions about separate bills on the same topic, offered by each house, or in contrast to a similar composite bill.

15. Executive branch messages and proposals whether from the President, cabinet secretaries or from independent agencies.

16. Prior relevant administrative action or judicial decisions, with or without congressional acknowledgment.

17. Other subsequent or prior legislation, especially conflicting acts.

18. Recorded votes.

19. The status of the person speaking, *i.e.*, a sponsor, committee chairman, floor leader, etc.

20. Actions taken and reports, hearings and debates on prior related legislation.

d. Many law schools offer courses in advanced legal research, in which legislative history is one major topic. Consult the excellent website operated by the law library of the University of California at Berkeley: http://www.law.berkeley.edu/library/dynamic/guide.php?id=53 (federal legislative history research) and http://www.law.berkeley.edu/library/dynamic/guide.php?id=54 (California legislative history research) (both viewed January 1, 2012)

e. Judge Leventhal's quip, in somewhat different form, has now made its way into the Supreme Court reports. Justice Scalia has offered it as a justification for his new textualism:

Part A.   Circumstances Surrounding the Introduction and Consideration of Legislation

LEO SHEEP CO. v. UNITED STATES

Supreme Court of the United States, 1979
440 U.S. 668, 99 S.Ct. 1403, 59 L.Ed.2d 677

MR. JUSTICE REHNQUIST delivered the opinion of the Court.

This is one of those rare cases evoking episodes in this country's history that, if not forgotten, are remembered as dry facts and not as adventure. Admittedly the issue is mundane: Whether the Government has an implied easement to build a road across land that was originally granted to the Union Pacific Railroad under the Union Pacific Act of 1862—a grant that was part of a governmental scheme to subsidize the construction of the transcontinental railroad. But that issue is posed against the backdrop of a fascinating chapter in our history. As this Court noted in another case involving the Union Pacific Railroad, "courts, in construing a statute, may with propriety recur to the history of the times when it was passed; and this is frequently necessary, in order to ascertain the reason as well as the meaning of particular provisions in it." *United States v. Union Pacific R. Co.*, 91 U.S. 72, 79 (1875). In this spirit we relate the events underlying passage of the Union Pacific Act of 1862.

[I] The early 19th century—from the Louisiana Purchase in 1803 to the Gadsden Purchase in 1853—saw the acquisition of the territory we now regard as the American West. During those years, however, the area remained a largely untapped resource, for the settlers on the eastern seaboard of the United States did not keep pace with the rapidly expanding western frontier. A vaguely delineated area forbiddingly referred to as the "Great American Desert" can be found on more than one map published before 1850, embracing much of the United States' territory west of the Missouri River. As late as 1860, for example, the entire population of the State of Nebraska was less than 30,000 persons, which represented one person for every five square miles of land area within the State.

With the discovery of gold at Sutter's Mill in California in 1848, the California gold rush began and with it a sharp increase in settlement of the West. Those in the East with visions of instant wealth, however, confronted the unenviable choice among an arduous 4-month overland trek, risking yellow fever on a 35-day voyage via the Isthmus of Panama, and a better than 4-month voyage around Cape Horn. They obviously yearned for another alternative, and interest focused on the transcontinental railroad.

The idea of a transcontinental railroad predated the California gold rush. From the time that Asa Whitney had proposed a relatively practical

---

"Judge Harold Leventhal used to describe the use of legislative history as the equivalent of entering a crowded cocktail party and looking over the heads of the guests for one's friends." *Conroy v. Aniskoff*, 507 U.S. 511, 519 (1993) (Scalia, J., concurring in the judgment).

plan for its construction in 1844, it had, in the words of one of this century's leading historians of the era, "engaged the eager attention of promoters and politicians until dozens of schemes were in the air." The building of the railroad was not to be the unalloyed product of the free-enterprise system. There was indeed the inspiration of men like Thomas Durant and Leland Stanford and the perspiration of a generation of immigrants, but animating it all was the desire of the Federal Government that the West be settled. This desire was intensified by the need to provide a logistical link with California in the heat of the Civil War. That the venture was much too risky and much too expensive for private capital alone was evident in the years of fruitless exhortation; private investors would not move without tangible governmental inducement.

In the mid–19th century there was serious disagreement as to the forms that inducement could take. Mr. Justice Story, in his Commentaries on the Constitution, described one extant school of thought which argued that "internal improvements," such as railroads, were not within the enumerated constitutional powers of Congress. Under such a theory, the direct subsidy of a transcontinental railroad was constitutionally suspect—an uneasiness aggravated by President Andrew Jackson's 1830 veto of a bill appropriating funds to construct a road from Maysville to Lexington within the State of Kentucky.

The response to this constitutional "gray" area, and source of political controversy, was the "checkerboard" land-grant scheme. The Union Pacific Act of 1862 granted public land to the Union Pacific Railroad for each mile of track that it laid. Land surrounding the railway right-of-way was divided into "checkerboard" blocks. Odd-numbered lots were granted to the Union Pacific; even-numbered lots were reserved by the Government. As a result, Union Pacific land in the area of the right-of-way was usually surrounded by public land, and vice versa. The historical explanation for this peculiar disposition is that it was apparently an attempt to disarm the "internal improvement" opponents by establishing a grant scheme with "demonstrable" benefits. As one historian notes in describing an 1827 federal land grant intended to facilitate private construction of a road between Columbus and Sandusky, Ohio:

> "Though awkwardly stated, and not fully developed in the Act of 1827, this was the beginning of a practice to be followed in most future instances of granting land for the construction of specific internal improvements: donating alternate sections or one half of the land within a strip along the line of the project and reserving the other half for sale.... In later donations the price of the reserved sections was doubled so that it could be argued, as the *Congressional Globe* shows *ad infinitum*, that by giving half the land away and thereby making possible construction of the road, canal, or railroad, the government would recover from the reserved sections as much as it would have received from the whole." P. Gates, History of Public Land Law Development 345–346 (1968).

In 1850 this technique was first explicitly employed for the subsidization of a railroad when the Illinois delegation in Congress, which included Stephen A. Douglas, secured the enactment of a bill that granted public lands to aid the construction of the Illinois Central Railroad. The Illinois Central and proposed connecting lines to the south were granted nearly three million acres along rights of way through Illinois, Mississippi, and Alabama, and by the end of 1854 the main line of the Illinois Central from Chicago to Cairo, Ill., had been put into operation. Before this line was constructed, public lands had gone begging at the Government's minimum price; within a few years after its completion, the railroad had disposed of more than one million acres and was rapidly selling more at prices far above those at which land had been originally offered by the Government.

The "internal improvements" theory was not the only obstacle to a transcontinental railroad. In 1853 Congress had appropriated moneys and authorized Secretary of War Jefferson Davis to undertake surveys of various proposed routes for a transcontinental railroad. Congress was badly split along sectional lines on the appropriate location of the route— so badly split that Stephen A. Douglas, now a Senator from Illinois, in 1854 suggested the construction of a northern, central, and southern route, each with connecting branches in the East. That proposal, however, did not break the impasse.

The necessary impetus was provided by the Civil War. Senators and Representatives from those States which seceded from the Union were no longer present in Congress, and therefore the sectional overtones of the dispute as to routes largely disappeared. Although there were no major engagements during the Civil War in the area between the Missouri River and the west coast which would be covered by any transcontinental railroad, there were two minor engagements which doubtless made some impression upon Congress of the necessity for being able to transport readily men and materials into that area for military purposes. * * *

These engagements gave some immediacy to the comments of Congressman Edwards of New Hampshire during the debate on the Pacific Railroad bill:

> "If this Union is to be preserved, if we are successfully to combat the difficulties around us, if we are to crush out this rebellion against the lawful authority of the Government, and are to have an entire restoration, it becomes us, with statesmanlike prudence and sagacity, to look carefully into the future, and to guard in advance against all possible considerations which may threaten the dismemberment of the country hereafter." Cong. Globe, 37th Cong., 2d Sess., 1703 (1862).

As is often the case, war spurs technological development, and Congress enacted the Union Pacific Act in May 1862. Perhaps not coincidentally, the Homestead Act was passed the same month.

The Union Pacific Act specified a route west from the 100th meridian, between a site in the Platte River Valley near the cities of Kearney and

North Platte, Neb., to California. The original plan was for five eastern terminals located at various points on or near the Missouri River; but in fact Omaha was the only terminal built according to the plan.

The land grants made by the Union Pacific Act included all the odd-numbered lots within 10 miles on either side of the track. When the Union Pacific's original subscription drive for private investment proved a failure, the land grant was doubled by extending the checkerboard grants to 20 miles on either side of the track. Private investment was still sluggish, and construction did not begin until July 1865, three months after the cessation of Civil War hostilities.[13] Thus began a race with the Central Pacific Railroad, which was laying track eastward from Sacramento, for the Government land grants which went with each mile of track laid. The race culminated in the driving of the golden spike at Promontory, Utah, on May 10, 1869.

[II] This case is the modern legacy of these early grants. Petitioners, the Leo Sheep Co. and the Palm Livestock Co., are the Union Pacific Railroad's successors in fee to specific odd-numbered sections of land in Carbon County, Wyo. These sections lie to the east and south of the Seminoe Reservoir, an area that is used by the public for fishing and hunting. Because of the checkerboard configuration, it is physically impossible to enter the Seminoe Reservoir sector from this direction without some minimum physical intrusion upon private land. In the years immediately preceding this litigation, the Government had received complaints that private owners were denying access over their lands to the reservoir area or requiring the payment of access fees. After negotiation with these owners failed, the Government cleared a dirt road extending from a local county road to the reservoir across both public domain lands and fee lands of the Leo Sheep Co. It also erected signs inviting the public to use the road as a route to the reservoir.

Petitioners initiated this action pursuant to 28 U.S.C. § 2409a to quiet title against the United States. The District Court granted petitioners' motion for summary judgment, but was reversed on appeal by the Court of Appeals for the Tenth Circuit. The latter court concluded that when Congress granted land to the Union Pacific Railroad, it implicitly

---

13. Construction would not have begun then without the Crédit Mobilier, a limited-liability company that was essentially owned by the promoters and investors of the Union Pacific. One of these investors, Oakes Ames, a wealthy New England shovel maker, was a substantial investor in Crédit Mobilier and also a Member of Congress. Crédit Mobilier contracted with the Union Pacific to build portions of the road, and by 1866 several individuals were large investors in both corporations. Allegations of improper use of funds and bribery of Members of the House of Representatives led to the appointment of a special congressional investigatory committee that during 1872 and 1873 looked into the affairs of Crédit Mobilier. These investigations revealed improprieties on the part of more than one Member of Congress, and the committee recommended that Ames be expelled from Congress. The investigation also touched on the career of a future President. See M. Leech & H. Brown, The Garfield Orbit (1978).

In 1872 the House of Representatives enacted a resolution condemning the policy of granting subsidies of public lands to railroads. Cong. Globe, 42d Cong., 2d Sess., 1585 (1872); see *Great Northern R. Co. v. United States*, 315 U.S. 262, 273–274 (1942). Of course, the reaction of the public or of Congress a decade after the enactment of the Union Pacific Act to the conduct of those associated with the Union Pacific cannot influence our interpretation of that Act today.

reserved an easement to pass over the odd-numbered sections in order to reach the even-numbered sections that were held by the Government. Because this holding affects property rights in 150 million acres of land in the Western United States, we granted certiorari, and now reverse.

The Government does not claim that there is any express reservation of an easement in the Union Pacific Act that would authorize the construction of a public road on the Leo Sheep Co.'s property. Section 3 of the 1862 Act sets out a few specific reservations to the "checkerboard" grant. The grant was not to include land "sold, reserved, or otherwise disposed of by the United States," such as land to which there were homestead claims. Mineral lands were also excepted from the operation of the Act. Given the existence of such explicit exceptions, this Court has in the past refused to add to this list by divining some "implicit" congressional intent. In *Missouri, K. & T.R. Co. v. Kansas Pacific R. Co.*, 97 U.S. 491, 497 (1878), for example, this Court in an opinion by Mr. Justice Field noted that the intent of Congress in making the Union Pacific grants was clear: "It was to aid in the construction of the road by a gift of lands along its route, without reservation of rights, except such as were specifically mentioned * * *." The Court held that, although a railroad right-of-way under the grant may not have been located until years after 1862, by the clear terms of the Act only claims established prior to 1862 overrode the railroad grant; conflicting claims arising after that time could not be given effect. To overcome the lack of support in the Act itself, the Government here argues that the implicit reservation of the asserted easement is established by "settled rules of property law" and by the Unlawful Inclosures of Public Lands Act of 1885.

Where a private landowner conveys to another individual a portion of his lands in a certain area and retains the rest, it is presumed at common law that the grantor has reserved an easement to pass over the granted property if such passage is necessary to reach the retained property. These rights-of-way are referred to as "easements by necessity." There are two problems with the Government's reliance on that notion in this case. First of all, whatever right of passage a private landowner might have, it is not at all clear that it would include the right to construct a road for public access to a recreational area.[15] More importantly, the easement is not actually a matter of necessity in this case because the Government has the power of eminent domain. Jurisdictions have generally seen eminent domain and easements by necessity as alternative ways to effect the same

---

15. It is very unlikely that Congress in 1862 contemplated this type of intrusion, and it could not reasonably be maintained that failure to provide access to the public at large would render the Seminoe Reservoir land useless. Yet these are precisely the considerations that define the scope of easements by necessity. As one commentator relied on by the Government notes: "As the name implies, these easements are the product of situations where the usefulness of land is at stake. The scope of the resultant easement embodies the best judgment of the court as to what is reasonably essential to the land's use. * * * Changes in the dominant parcel's use exert some, but not a great influence, in determining the scope of such easements." 3 [R. Powell, Real Property ¶ 416 (1978).] See, e.g., *Higbee Fishing Club v. Atlantic City Electric Co.*, 78 N.J.Eq. 434, 79 A. 326 (1911) (footpath, not roadway, proper scope of easement where use of dominant estate as clubhouse could not have been contemplated by parties to original grant).

result. For example, the State of Wyoming no longer recognizes the common-law easement by necessity in cases involving landlocked estates. It provides instead for a procedure whereby the landlocked owner can have an access route condemned on his behalf upon payment of the necessary compensation to the owner of the servient estate. For similar reasons other state courts have held that the "easement by necessity" doctrine is not available to the sovereign.

The applicability of the doctrine of easement by necessity in this case is, therefore, somewhat strained, and ultimately of little significance. The pertinent inquiry in this case is the intent of Congress when it granted land to the Union Pacific in 1862. The 1862 Act specifically listed reservations to the grant, and we do not find the tenuous relevance of the common-law doctrine of ways of necessity sufficient to overcome the inference prompted by the omission of any reference to the reserved right asserted by the Government in this case. It is possible that Congress gave the problem of access little thought; but it is at least as likely that the thought which was given focused on negotiation, reciprocity consider-ations, and the power of eminent domain as obvious devices for ameliorat-ing disputes.[18] So both as matter of common-law doctrine and as a matter of construing congressional intent, we are unwilling to imply rights-of-way, with the substantial impact that such implication would have on property rights granted over 100 years ago, in the absence of a stronger case for their implication than the Government makes here.

The Government would have us decide this case on the basis of the familiar canon of construction that, when grants to federal lands are at issue, any doubts "are resolved for the Government not against it." *Andrus v. Charlestone Stone Products Co.*, 436 U.S. 604, 617 (1978). But this Court long ago declined to apply this canon in its full vigor to grants under the railroad Acts. In 1885 this Court observed:

---

18. The intimations that can be found in the Congressional Globe are that there was no commonly understood reservation by the Government of the right to enter upon granted lands and construct a public road. Representative Cradlebaugh of Nevada offered an amendment to what became the Union Pacific Act of 1862 that would have reserved the right to the public to enter granted land and prospect for valuable minerals upon the payment of adequate compensa-tion to the owner. The proposed amendment was defeated. The only Representative other than Cradlebaugh who spoke to it, Representative Sargent of California, stated:

"The amendment of the gentleman proposes to allow the public to enter upon the lands of any man, whether they be mineral lands or not, and prospect for gold and silver, and as compensation proposes some loose method of payment for the injuries inflicted. Now, sir, it may turn out that the man who thus commits the injuries may be utterly insolvent, not able to pay a dollar, and how is the owner of the property to be compensated for tearing down his dwellings, rooting up his orchards, and destroying his crops?" Cong. Globe, 37th Cong., 2d Sess., 1910 (1862).

In debates on an earlier Pacific Railroad bill it was explicitly suggested that there be "a reservation in every grant of land that [the Government] shall have a right to go through it, and take it at proper prices to be paid hereafter." The author of this proposal, Senator Simmons of Rhode Island, lamented the lack of such a reservation in the bill under consideration. Cong. Globe, 35th Cong., 2d Sess., 579 (1859). Apparently the intended purpose of this proposed reservation was to permit railroads to obtain rights-of-way through granted property at the Government's behest. Senator Simmons' comments are somewhat confused, but they certainly do not evince any prevailing assumption that the Government implicitly reserved a right-of-way through granted lands.

"The solution of [ownership] questions [involving the railroad grants] depends, of course, upon the construction given to the acts making the grants; and they are to receive such a construction as will carry out the intent of Congress, however difficult it might be to give full effect to the language used if the grants were by instruments of private conveyance. To ascertain that intent we must look to the condition of the country when the acts were passed, as well as to the purpose declared on their face, and read all parts of them together." *Winona & St. Peter R. Co. v. Barney*, 113 U.S. 618, 625 (1885).

[Justice Rehnquist then discussed the Unlawful Inclosures of Public Lands Act of 1885 and concluded that it was aimed at a different sort of problem: the use of fencing arrangements by cattlemen to deprive sheep-herders of access to grazing lands. The Court's opinion concluded with the observation that Congress in 1862 did not anticipate these problems.] The order of the day was the open range—barbed wire had not made its presence felt—and the type of incursions on private property necessary to reach public land was not such an interference that litigation would serve any motive other than spite. Congress obviously believed that when development came, it would occur in a parallel fashion on adjoining public and private lands and that the process of subdivision, organization of a polity, and the ordinary pressures of commercial and social intercourse would work itself into a pattern of access roads. * * * It is some testament to common sense that the present case is virtually unprecedented, and that in the 117 years since the grants were made, litigation over access questions generally has been rare.

Nonetheless, the present times are litigious ones and the 37th Congress did not anticipate our plight. Generations of land patents have issued without any express reservation of the right now claimed by the Government. Nor has a similar right been asserted before. When the Secretary of the Interior has discussed access rights, his discussion has been colored by the assumption that those rights had to be purchased. This Court has traditionally recognized the special need for certainty and predictability where land titles are concerned, and we are unwilling to upset settled expectations to accommodate some ill-defined power to construct public thoroughfares without compensation. The judgment of the Court of Appeals for the Tenth Circuit is accordingly

Reversed.

Mr. Justice White took no part in the consideration or decision of this case.

Notes on *Leo Sheep* and Legislative Context

1. *The Sweep versus the Reality of History.* Reading Justice Rehnquist's opinion, you can almost feel the wagon train moving you West. The first part of the opinion, the historical saga of the railroad project, strikes us as cogent and useful. The next part, the legal reasoning, strikes us as less so. The

unanimous Court is obviously following the "imaginative reconstruction" approach of Judge Hand and Dean Pound—putting oneself in the mindset of the 1862 Congress (see Chapter 2, § 1). But the Court's assertion that "[i]t is possible that Congress gave the problem of access little thought" strikes us as an understatement. Is there any evidence adduced by the Court that the 1862 Congress gave *any* thought to the access issue? And if Congress had given some thought, surely it would have wanted the government to have a reasonable right of access. Is the Court's assumption credible that "the thought which was given focused on negotiation, reciprocity considerations, and the power of eminent domain" as ways of obtaining access? Congress in 1866, for example, enacted a statute giving any person free and unrestricted access over the public domain. Right of Way Act, 14 Stat. 251 (1866). If the 1862 Congress had "assumed" that it could negotiate a trade of railroad access through public lands in return for state access through the railroad's lands, why would Congress have given away that bargaining chip in 1866? Why would Congress in 1862 want to use eminent domain—paying money— for access rights that it could retain by simple statutory fiat? Would the venture capitalists (or robber barons, if you prefer) have built the transcontinental railroad otherwise?

2. *The Flip Side of* Leo Sheep. Does the private grantee or its successor have an easement by necessity through the government's checkerboard squares? The leading discussion on this question argued that it does. Comment, *Easements by Way of Necessity Across Federal Lands*, 35 Wash. L. Rev. 105, 113–17 (1960). This remarkable student comment correctly anticipated the *Leo Sheep* result and reasoning but argued that the same result (no easement by necessity) should not occur for the converse situation. The common law objections in *Leo Sheep*—that easements by necessity are not created for recreational uses or for government entities which may obtain access through eminent domain—have no force when a private developer demands an easement through the government lands. Nor does the legislative policy argument work against the private grantee's easement, since private access would subserve the Congressional goal of developing the granted land as quickly as possible. Cf. *Utah v. Andrus*, 486 F.Supp. 995, 1002 (D. Utah 1979), *appeal dismissed per stip.*, Nos. 79–2307 & 79–2308 (10th Cir. Jan. 28 & Mar. 28, 1980) (holding that Congress conveyed permanent rights of access to Utah when it granted school trust lands to the State as a means of generating revenue). A contrary position was taken in an Opinion by Attorney General Civiletti. 43 Op. Att'y Gen. 26 (1980). The opinion determined that easements by necessity did not run against the government, unless that was an implied term of the granting statute. "[L]and grants generally are to be strictly construed. This rule must be balanced against the conflicting rule that in some situations certain types of land grants may deserve a more liberal construction because of the circumstances surrounding passage of the statutes in question. [*Leo Sheep.*] Absent express language to the contrary, however, a grant should not be construed to include broad rights to use retained Government property, particularly in the case of gratuitous grants."

Consider this policy argument: Not to infer an easement by necessity in the original grant would impel the United States and private grantees holding alternate checkerboard squares to cooperate. That is, if neither holder has an easement, each has an incentive to work out a reasonable deal with the other, or neither will be able to have meaningful access to its land. On the other hand, if the United States has no easement but the grantee does, the grantee has little incentive to reach a "fair" bargain with the United States, forcing the United States to pay a high price or go to the trouble and expense of condemning the easement through eminent domain. Once the Supreme Court has decided that the government does not have an easement, doesn't it make sense then to deny the easement for the private holders as well? (One might argue that the rule which would minimize transactions costs would be to give *both* the government and the private holders an easement, or give them both eminent domain power.)

3. *Subsequent Developments.* In any event, the context in which the *Leo Sheep* problem arose was vastly different from that in which the law was passed. A shift in statutory policy came in the late nineteenth century, to protect the nation's natural resources from the results of what was then perceived as excessively generous land grants earlier. See Roy Marvin Robbins, *Our Landed Heritage: The Public Domain, 1776–1970*, at 301–24 (1976). Thus after giving away more than 125 million acres of public land to the railroads, Congress discontinued the land grant policy in the 1890s. See Paul Wallace Gates, *History of Public Land Law Development* (1968). And in 1891, Congress passed a law authorizing the President to reserve forest lands from the public domain (thus taking them out of the coverage of the 1866 access law), Act of March 3, 1891, ch. 561, § 24, 26 Stat. 1103 (the Forest Reserve Act), and 20 million acres were thereby reserved by Presidential proclamation in 1897. Further reservations were made throughout the twentieth century, as federal policy decisively turned toward conserving what was becoming perceived as a scarce resource. The Wilderness Act of 1964, 78 Stat. 890, codified at 16 U.S.C. §§ 1131–1136 (1988), placed even greater restrictions on certain federal lands, and this leading Act was followed in the 1970s and 1980s by more wilderness designations by Congress. In 1976, Congress repealed the access law of 1866 and replaced it with Title V of the Federal Land Policy & Management Act of 1976, 90 Stat. 2744, 2776, codified at 43 U.S.C. §§ 1761–1770 (1988), which authorizes the Department of the Interior to grant rights of access through a discretionary system. Are these subsequent statutes and federal policies relevant to the issue of whether private grantees have an absolute right of access across federal checkerboard lands?

Part B. Committee Reports (An Introduction to the Great Legislative History Debate)

Most judges and scholars agree that committee reports should be considered as authoritative legislative history and should be given great weight (i.e., a statement in a committee report will usually count more than a statement by a single legislator). Justice Jackson, concurring in *Schwegmann Bros. v. Calvert Distillers Corp.*, 341 U.S. 384, 395 (1951), objected to the use of legislative materials to interpret statutes, but excepted committee reports from his quarrel. In the leading empirical examination, Jorge Carro & Andrew Brann, *The U.S. Supreme Court and the Use of Legislative Histories: A Statistical Analysis*, 22 Jurimeterics J. 294, 304 (1982), report that over a 40–year period, over 60% of the

Supreme Court's citations to legislative history were references to committee reports. For a more recent examination of Supreme Court practice, confirming the dominance of committee reports since 1982, see Frank B. Cross, *The Theory and Practice of Statutory Interpretation* (2008).

Committee reports appear particularly well-suited for the authoritative role they have played. Most legislation is essentially written in committee or subcommittee, and any collective statement by the members of that subgroup will represent the best-informed thought about what the proposed legislation is doing. Committee reports are also accessible documents, both in the sense of being easily located through legal research and of being easy to comprehend once found. They usually set forth the problem(s) requiring the proposed legislation, the general solution(s) posited by the bill, and a section-by-section summary of the provisions of the bill. The report of a conference committee (where the two legislative chambers have passed different forms of the same bill and must resolve their differences in conference) typically sets forth, for each provision, the version passed by each chamber and what the conference committee did with the provision (and sometimes also an explanation why it took the action it did).

There are, on the other hand, limitations on the usefulness of committee reports in giving meaning to ambiguous statutes. First, there is sometimes *no* committee report for a particular bill or an important provision in the bill, because it has been added as part of the floor debate. This is especially true of many of the civil rights bills. Recall from Chapter 1, § 1, that the sex discrimination provision in Title VII was added as a floor amendment in the House (and as something of a surprise to the bill's sponsors); hence, there is no discussion of that critical amendment in the House Judiciary Committee report. There was no committee report for the Act in the Senate, because the sponsors avoided sending the House bill to the Senate Judiciary Committee, chaired by anti-civil rights Senator James Eastland of Mississippi. Compare *Hishon v. King & Spalding*, 467 U.S. 69, 75 & n.7 (1984) (relying on Senate report for civil rights bill that was similar but never enacted). And there was no conference committee report, because the House rapidly acceded to the Senate's revisions, the sponsors knowing that further delays in the bill's enactment might prove fatal. See also *Local 82, Furniture & Piano Moving Union v. Crowley*, 467 U.S. 526 (1984) (interpreting the Landrum–Griffin Act, much of which was written on the House and Senate floor).

Second, the committee report is often as ambiguous as the statute. As a shorter, more compressed form of the statute, the committee report may even be misleading, as it leaves out important qualifications in its discussion of the proposed legislation or particular provisions. (The committee report is probably most useful as a statement of the goals and their relative importance in the statutory scheme, since most statutes do not carry with them statements of purpose.) Indeed, a striking feature of the committee report is that it is the end-product of the committee's consideration, and therefore comes at a stage of consensus. In many instances, the key point in the process is "mark-up" of the bill in committee or subcommittee, for it is there that the legislators make the critical choices and compromises and specifically reject proposed alternatives. See John Kernochan, *The Legislative Process* 25 (1981). Traditionally, there was no official record of mark-up sessions. As a consequence, what is often the most revealing collection of statements was often not available, or admissible, in the process of statutory interpretation. See Patricia M. Wald, in *Some Observations on the Use of Legislative History in the 1981 Supreme Court Term*, 68 Iowa L. Rev. 195, 202 (1983). In the last generation, however, committee mark-up sessions have become more open and often yield publicly available records. One might therefore expect to see more references to these sources by judges willing to consider legislative history. E.g., *Regan v. Wald*, 468 U.S. 222 (1984) (both majority and dissenting opinions relying on explanation accompanying House committee mark-up).

Third, when there is a committee report and the report contains relevant statements, one might be suspicious of the usefulness of those statements under some circumstances. Lobbyists and lawyers maneuver endlessly to persuade staff members (who write the committee reports) or their legislator bosses to throw in helpful language in the reports when insertion of similar language would be inappropriate or infeasible for the statute itself. "Smuggling in" helpful language through the legislative history is a time-tested practice.

In state legislatures, committee-generated documents can take a variety of forms, not all of which are published or are readily available to the public: (1) regular reports of standing committees or conference committees, like those produced in the U.S. Congress; (2) staff analysis of a pending bill, which is in many states the main document which is actually distributed to legislators; and (3) reports of special committees created to investigate and to resolve important problems expeditiously or to investigate problems, as well as reports of collections of experts (often "law revision commissions") who have drafted legislation adopted in the state. As *Li v. Yellow Cab Co.* (Chapter 2, § 2B) suggests, committee reports and similar documents are often used to interpret ambiguous statutes at the state level.

BLANCHARD v. BERGERON

Supreme Court of the United States, 1989
489 U.S. 87, 109 S.Ct. 939, 103 L.Ed.2d 67

JUSTICE WHITE delivered the opinion of the Court.

[A jury awarded Blanchard $5,000 in compensatory damages and $5,000 in punitive damages on his civil rights claim, under 42 U.S.C. § 1983, that he had been beaten by a sheriff's deputy. He sought attorney's fees under the 1976 Civil Rights Attorney's Fee Award Act, codified at 42 U.S.C. § 1988. The district court awarded $7,500 in fees. The Fifth Circuit, however, held that under its decision in *Johnson v. Georgia Highway Express, Inc.*, 488 F.2d 714 (5th Cir. 1974), the 40% contingency fee agreement Blanchard had entered into with his attorney set a ceiling on recoverable fees. Thus, the Fifth Circuit limited the fee award to $4,000 (40% of the $10,000 damages awarded).]

Section 1988 provides that the court, "in its discretion, may allow . . . a reasonable attorney's fee . . . ." The section does not provide a specific definition of "reasonable" fee, and the question is whether the award must be limited to the amount provided in a contingent fee agreement. The legislative history of the Act is instructive insofar as it tells us: "In computing the fee, counsel for prevailing parties should be paid, as is traditional with attorneys compensated by a fee-paying client, 'for all time reasonably expended on a matter.' " S.Rep. No. 94–1011, p. 6 (1976) (citing *Davis v. County of Los Angeles*, 8 EPD ¶ 9444 (CD Cal. 1974); and *Stanford Daily v. Zurcher*, 64 F.R.D. 680, 684 (ND Cal. 1974)).

In many past cases considering the award of attorney's fees under § 1988, we have turned our attention to *Johnson v. Georgia Highway Express, Inc.*, a case decided before the enactment of the Civil Rights Attorney's Fee Award Act of 1976. As we stated in *Hensley v. Eckerhart*, 461 U.S. 424, 429–431 (1983), *Johnson* provides guidance to Congress' intent because both the House and Senate Reports refer to the 12 factors set forth in *Johnson* for assessing the reasonableness of an attorney's fee award. The Senate Report, in particular, refers to three District Court decisions that "correctly applied" the 12 factors laid out in *Johnson*.

In the course of its discussion of the factors to be considered by a court in awarding attorney's fees, the *Johnson* court dealt with fee arrangements:

> " 'Whether or not [a litigant] agreed to pay a fee and in what amount is not decisive. Conceivably, a litigant might agree to pay his counsel a fixed dollar fee. This might be even more than the fee eventually allowed by the court. Or he might agree to pay his lawyer a percentage contingent fee that would be greater than the fee the court might ultimately set. Such arrangements should not determine the court's decision. The criterion for the court is not what the parties agree but what is reasonable.' "

Yet in the next sentence, *Johnson* says "In no event, however, should the litigant be awarded a fee greater than he is contractually bound to pay, if indeed the attorneys have contracted as to amount." This latter statement, never disowned in the Circuit, was the basis for the decision below. But we doubt that Congress embraced this aspect of *Johnson*, for it pointed to the three District Court cases in which the factors are "correctly applied." Those cases clarify that the fee arrangement is but a single factor and not determinative. In *Stanford Daily v. Zurcher*, [supra,] for example, the District Court considered a contingent-fee arrangement to be a factor, but not dispositive, in the calculation of a fee award. In *Davis v. County of Los Angeles, supra*, the court permitted a fee award to counsel in a public interest firm which otherwise would have been entitled to no fee. Finally, in *Swann v. Charlotte–Mecklenburg Board of Education*, 66

F.R.D. 483 (WDNC 1975), the court stated that reasonable fees should be granted regardless of the individual plaintiff's fee obligations. *Johnson*'s "List of 12" thus provides a useful catalog of the many factors to be considered in assessing the reasonableness of an award of attorney's fees; but the one factor at issue here, the attorney's private fee arrangement, standing alone, is not dispositive.

The *Johnson* contingency-fee factor is simply that, a factor. The presence of a pre-existing fee agreement may aid in determining reasonableness. " 'The fee quoted to the client or the percentage of the recovery agreed to is helpful in demonstrating that attorney's fee expectations when he accepted the case.' " *Pennsylvania v. Delaware Valley Citizens' Council for Clean Air*, 483 U.S. 711 (1987), quoting *Johnson*. But as we see it, a contingent-fee contract does not impose an automatic ceiling on an award of attorney's fees and to hold otherwise would be inconsistent with the statute and its policy and purpose.

As we understand § 1988's provision for allowing a "reasonable attorney's fee," it contemplates reasonable compensation, in light of all of the circumstances, for the time and effort expended by the attorney for the prevailing plaintiff, no more and no less. Should a fee agreement provide less than a reasonable fee calculated in this manner, the defendant should nevertheless be required to pay the higher amount. The defendant is not, however, required to pay the amount called for in a contingent-fee contract if it is more than a reasonable fee calculated in the usual way. It is true that the purpose of § 1988 was to make sure that competent counsel was available to civil rights plaintiffs, and it is of course arguable that if a plaintiff is able to secure an attorney on the basis of a contingent or other fee agreement, the purpose of the statute is served if the plaintiff is bound by his contract. On that basis, however, the plaintiff should recover nothing from the defendant, which would be plainly contrary to the statute. And Congress implemented its purpose by broadly requiring all defendants to pay a reasonable fee to all prevailing plaintiffs, if ordered to do so by the court. Thus it is that a plaintiff's recovery will not be reduced by what he must pay his counsel. Plaintiffs who can afford to hire their own lawyers, as well as impecunious litigants, may take advantage of this provision. And where there are lawyers or organizations that will take a plaintiff's case without compensation, that fact does not bar the award of a reasonable fee. All of this is consistent with and reflects our decisions in cases involving court-awarded attorney's fees.

Hensley v. Eckerhart, [*supra*,] directed lower courts to make an initial estimate of reasonable attorney's fees by applying prevailing billing rates to the hours reasonably expended on successful claims. And we have said repeatedly that "[t]he initial estimate of a reasonable attorney's fee is properly calculated by multiplying the number of hours reasonably expended on the litigation times a reasonable hourly rate." The courts may then adjust this lodestar calculation by other factors. We have never suggested that a different approach is to be followed in cases where the prevailing party and his (or her) attorney have executed a contingent-fee agreement. To the contrary, * * * we have adopted the lodestar approach as the centerpiece of attorney's fee awards. The *Johnson* factors may be relevant in adjusting the lodestar amount but no one factor is a substitute for multiplying reasonable billing rates by a reasonable estimation of the number of hours expended on the litigation. * * *

If a contingent-fee agreement were to govern as a strict limitation on the award of attorney's fees, an undesirable emphasis might be placed on the importance of the recovery of damages in civil rights litigation. The intention of Congress was to encourage successful civil rights litigation, not to create a special incentive to prove damages and shortchange efforts to seek effective injunctive or declaratory relief. Affirming the decision below would create an artificial disincentive for an attorney who enters into a contingent fee agreement, unsure of whether his client's claim sounded in state tort law or in federal civil rights, from fully exploring all possible avenues of relief. Section 1988 makes no distinction between actions for damages and suits for equitable relief. Congress has elected to encourage meritorious civil rights claims because of the benefits of such litigation for the named plaintiff and for society at large, irrespective of whether the action seeks monetary damages.

It should also be noted that we have not accepted the contention that fee awards in § 1983 damages cases should be modeled upon the contingent-fee arrangements used in personal injury litigation. "[W]e reject the notion that a civil rights action for damages constitutes nothing more than a private tort suit benefiting only the individual plaintiffs whose rights were violated. Unlike most private tort litigants, a civil rights plaintiff seeks to vindicate important civil and constitutional rights that cannot be valued solely in monetary terms."

Respondent cautions us that refusing to limit recovery to the amount of the contingency agreement will result in a "windfall" to attorneys who accept § 1983 actions. Yet the very nature of recovery under § 1988 is designed to prevent any such "windfall." Fee awards are to be reasonable, reasonable as to billing rates and reasonable as to the number of hours spent in advancing the successful claims. Accordingly, fee awards, properly calculated, by definition will represent the reasonable worth of the services rendered in vindication of a plaintiff's civil rights claim. It is central to the awarding of attorney's fees under § 1988 that the district court judge, in his or her good judgment, make the assessment of what is a reasonable fee under the circumstances of the case. The trial judge should not be limited by the contractual fee agreement between plaintiff and counsel. * * *

JUSTICE SCALIA, concurring in part and concurring in the judgment.

I * * * join the opinion of the Court except that portion which rests upon detailed analysis of the Fifth Circuit's opinion in *Johnson* and the District Court decisions in *Swann, Stanford Daily*, and *Davis*. The Court carefully examines those opinions, separating holding from dictum, much as a lower court would study our opinions in order to be faithful to our guidance. The justification for this role reversal is that the Senate and House Committee Reports on the Civil Rights Attorney's Fees Awards Act of 1976 referred approvingly to *Johnson*, and the Senate Report alone referred to the three District Court opinions as having "correctly applied" *Johnson*. The Court resolves the difficulty that *Johnson* contradicts the three District Court opinions on the precise point at issue here by concluding in effect that the analysis in *Johnson* was dictum, whereas in the three District Court opinions it was a holding. Despite the fact that the House Report referred *only* to *Johnson*, and made no mention of the District Court cases, the Court "doubt[s] that Congress embraced this aspect of *Johnson*, for it pointed to the three District Court cases in which the factors are 'correctly applied.' "

In my view Congress did no such thing. Congress is elected to enact statutes rather than point to cases, and its Members have better uses for their time than poring over District Court opinions. That the Court should refer to the citation of three District Court cases in a document issued by a single committee of a single house as the action *of Congress* displays the level of unreality that our unrestrained use of legislative history has attained. I am confident that only a small proportion of the Members of Congress read either one of the Committee Reports in question, even if (as is not always the case) the Reports happened to have been published before the vote; that very few of those who did read them set off for the nearest law library to check out what was actually said in the four cases at issue (or in the more than 50 other cases cited by the House and Senate Reports); and that *no* Member of Congress came to the judgment that the District Court cases would trump *Johnson* on the point at issue here because the latter was dictum. As anyone familiar with modern-day drafting of congressional committee reports is well aware, the references to the cases were inserted, at best by a committee staff member on his or her own initiative, and at worst by a committee staff member at the suggestion of a lawyer-lobbyist; and the purpose of those references was not primarily to inform the Members of Congress what the bill meant (for that end *Johnson* would not merely have been cited, but its 12 factors would have been described, which they were not), but rather to influence judicial construction. What a heady feeling it must be for a young staffer, to know that his or her citation of obscure district court cases can transform them into the law of the land, thereafter dutifully to be observed by the Supreme Court itself.

I decline to participate in this process. It is neither compatible with our judicial responsibility of assuring reasoned, consistent, and effective application of the statutes of the United States, nor conducive to a genuine effectuation of congressional intent, to give legislative force to each snippet of analysis, and even every case citation, in committee reports that are increasingly unreliable evidence of what the voting Members of Congress actually had in mind. By treating *Johnson* and the District Court trilogy as fully authoritative, the Court today expands what

I regard as our cases' excessive preoccupation with them—and with the 12–factor *Johnson* analysis in particular. * * * Except for the few passages to which I object, today's opinion admirably follows our more recent approach of seeking to develop an interpretation of the statute that is reasonable, consistent, and faithful to its apparent purpose, rather than to achieve obedient adherence to cases cited in the committee reports. I therefore join the balance of the opinion.

NOTE ON THE NEW TEXTUALIST CRITIQUE OF COMMITTEE REPORTS

1. *Judge Scalia's Attack on Committee Reports.* Justice Scalia believes that committee reports, in particular, are untrustworthy legislative history. His first effort to explain his position systematically, an unpublished speech delivered at various law schools while he was a judge on the D.C. Circuit, is summarized, quoted, and criticized in Daniel A. Farber & Philip P. Frickey, *Legislative Intent and Public Choice*, 74 Va. L. Rev. 423 (1988). Judge Scalia also set forth his doubts in a concurring opinion in *Hirschey v. FERC*, 777 F.2d 1, 7–8 (D.C. Cir. 1985):

> I frankly doubt that it is ever reasonable to assume that the details, as opposed to the broad outlines of purpose, set forth in a committee report come to the attention of, much less are approved by, the house which enacts the committee's bill. And I think it time for courts to become concerned about the fact that routine deference to the detail of committee reports, and the predictable expansion in that detail which routine deference has produced, are converting a system of judicial construction into a system of committee-staff prescription.

Note the similarity to his reason for not joining the Court's opinion in *Bergeron*. In a footnote at the end of the first sentence of the above quotation, Judge Scalia reported the following "illuminating exchange" in the Senate (*id.* at 7–8 n.1):

> Mr. ARMSTRONG. * * * My question, which may take [the Chairman of the Committee on Finance] by surprise, is this: Is it the intention of the chairman that the Internal Revenue Service and the Tax Court and other courts take guidance as to the intention of Congress from the committee report which accompanies this bill?
>
> Mr. DOLE. I would certainly hope so. * * *
>
> Mr. ARMSTRONG. Mr. President, will the Senator tell me whether or not he wrote the committee report?
>
> Mr. DOLE. Did I write the committee report?
>
> Mr. ARMSTRONG. Yes.
>
> Mr. DOLE. No; the Senator from Kansas did not write the committee report.
>
> Mr. ARMSTRONG. Did any Senator write the committee report?
>
> Mr. DOLE. I have to check.
>
> Mr. ARMSTRONG. Does the Senator know of any Senator who wrote the committee report?

Mr. DOLE. I might be able to identify one, but I would have to search. I was here all during the time it was written, I might say, and worked carefully with the staff as they worked. * * *

Mr. ARMSTRONG. Mr. President, has the Senator from Kansas, the chairman of the Finance Committee, read the committee report in its entirety?

Mr. DOLE. I am working on it. It is not a bestseller, but I am working on it.

Mr. ARMSTRONG. Mr. President, did members of the Finance Committee vote on the committee report?

Mr. DOLE. No.

Mr. ARMSTRONG. Mr. President, the reason I raise the issue is not perhaps apparent on the surface, and let me just state it: * * * The report itself is not considered by the Committee on Finance. It was not subject to amendment by the Committee on Finance. It is not subject to amendment now by the Senate. * * *

* * * If there were matter within this report which was disagreed to by the Senator from Colorado or even by a majority of all Senators, there would be no way for us to change the report. I could not offer an amendment tonight to amend the committee report.

* * * [F]or any jurist, administrator, bureaucrat, tax practitioner, or others who might chance upon the written record of this proceeding, let me just make the point that this is not the law, it was not voted on, it is not subject to amendment, and we should discipline ourselves to the task of expressing congressional intent in the statute.

The co-parent of the new textualism has been Judge Frank Easterbrook of the Seventh Circuit, the author of the textualist en banc opinion in *Marshall* (Chapter 2, § 3A). Another of his opinions, *In re Sinclair*, is the next case in this chapter.

2. *Justice Scalia Updates His Critique of Committee Reports.* Since he has been elevated to the Supreme Court, Justice Scalia has developed a more systematic critique of the Court's traditional use of legislative history. See *Green v. Bock Laundry Mach. Co.*, 490 U.S. 504 (1989) (Scalia, J., concurring in the judgment); Antonin Scalia, *A Matter of Interpretation* (1997) (both excerpted in Chapter 2, § 3A).[f] Justice Scalia's more systematic critique goes well beyond the cynicism of *Bergeron* and rests upon a constitutional interpretation of Article I, § 7. Statutory text is the alpha and the omega of statutory

---

f. Some of Justice Scalia's classic criticisms are found in *Zuni Pub. Sch. Dist. No. 89 v. United States Department of Educ.*, 550 U.S. 81, 116–22 (2007) (Scalia, J., dissenting); *Hamdan v. Rumsfeld*, 548 U.S. 557, 665–68 (2006) (Scalia, J., dissenting); *Koons Buick Pontiac GMC, Inc. v. Nigh*, 543 U.S. 50, 70–76 (2004) (Scalia, J., dissenting); *Crosby v. National Foreign Trade Council*, 530 U.S. 363 (2000) (Scalia, J., concurring in the judgment); *Thunder Basin Coal Co. v. Reich*, 510 U.S. 200, 219 (1994) (Scalia, J., concurring in part and in the judgment); *Conroy v. Aniskoff*, 507 U.S. 511, 519 (1993) (Scalia, J., concurring in the judgment); *United States v. Thompson/Center Arms Co.*, 504 U.S. 505, 521 (1992) (Scalia, J., concurring in the judgment); *Union Bank v. Wolas*, 502 U.S. 151, 163 (1991) (Scalia, J., concurring); *Wisconsin Public Intervenor v. Mortier*, 501 U.S. 597, 617–23 (1991) (Scalia, J., concurring in the judgment); *Sullivan v. Finkelstein*, 496 U.S. 617, 631–32 (1990) (Scalia, J., concurring in all of the Court's opinion except footnote 8); *Begier v. IRS*, 496 U.S. 53, 67–71 (1990) (Scalia, J., concurring in the judgment).

interpretation, because it is the only matter that is enacted as authoritative *law* under our constitutional rule of recognition (Article I, § 7).[g] Even if there were a coherent legislative "intent" (a matter Scalia disputes), it would have no authority as law under the Constitution. Like Judge Easterbrook, who developed the structural constitutional features of the new textualism at an earlier stage, Justice Scalia would be willing to examine legislative materials in the same manner he uses dictionaries—as evidence of how statutory language was used at the time.

3. *The Impact of the New Textualism in the Supreme Court.* Justice Scalia's critique has had an impact upon the Court's practice, which is now more cautious in its use of legislative history. It has had even more of an impact upon the arguments made by the Supreme Court Bar (especially the Solicitor General and others regularly arguing before the Court), who now emphasize and usually lead with their textual arguments and use legislative history to back up these contentions rather than as the touchstone of statutory meaning. And the new textualism has had an impact among the Justices (and perhaps beyond). The Rehnquist and Roberts Courts (1986 onward) have been less likely to rely heavily upon legislative history today than did the Burger Court (1969–1986). There are more decisions like *Circuit City Stores, Inc. v. Adams*, 532 U.S. 105 (2001) (Chapter 2, § 1A2) (where the majority refused to examine legislative materials) than *Babbitt v. Sweet Home Chapter*, 515 U.S. 687 (1995) (Chapter 2, § 1C) (where all the Justices, even Justice Scalia, relied on legislative materials), and there has been a general decline in the Court's invocation of legislative history since the pre-New Deal era.[h]

Nonetheless, the new textualism has not swept the field. Although Justice Scalia has picked up a great deal of academic support, the majority of the commentators are unpersuaded.[i] The Supreme Court still relies on committee

---

g. William N. Eskridge Jr., *The New Textualism*, 37 UCLA L. Rev. 621 (1990); John F. Manning, *Textualism as a Nondelegation Doctrine*, 97 Colum. L. Rev. 673 (1997); Jonathan T. Molot, *The Rise and Fall of Textualism*, 106 Colum. L. Rev. 1, 23–29 (2006).

h. E.g., James J. Brudney & Corey Ditslear, *The Decline and Fall of Legislative History? Patterns of Supreme Court Reliance in the Burger and Rehnquist Eras*, 89 Judicature 220 (2006); Michael H. Koby, *The Supreme Court's Declining Reliance on Legislative History: The Impact of Justice Scalia's Critique*, 36 Harv. J. Legis. 369 (1999). Because Justices Scalia and Thomas routinely refuse to join any majority opinion that relies upon legislative history, in any case in which their votes might be necessary to form a majority, the Justice drafting the opinion may strategically avoid reliance upon legislative history. See Thomas A. Merrill, *Textualism and the Future of the* Chevron *Doctrine*, 72 Wash. U. L.Q. 351 (1994).

i. Skeptical treatments include William N. Eskridge Jr., *Dynamic Statutory Interpretation* ch. 7 (1994); Stephen Breyer, *On the Uses of Legislative History in Interpreting Statutes*, 65 S. Cal. L. Rev. 845 (1992); George A. Costello, *Average Voting Members and Other "Benign Fictions": The Relative Reliability of Committee Reports, Floor Debates, and Other Sources of Legislative History*, 1990 Duke L.J. 39; William N. Eskridge Jr., *Textualism, The Unknown Ideal?*, 96 Mich. L. Rev. 1509 (1998); Daniel A. Farber & Philip P. Frickey, *Legislative Intent and Public Choice*, 74 Va. L. Rev. 423 (1988); Philip P. Frickey, *Revisiting the Revival of Theory in Statutory Interpretation: A Lecture in Honor of Irving Younger*, 84 Minn. L. Rev. 199 (1999); Abner J. Mikva & Eric Lane, *The Muzak of Justice Scalia's Revolutionary Call To Read Unclear Statutes Narrowly*, 53 SMU L. Rev. 121 (2000); Stephen F. Ross & Daniel Tranen, *The Modern Parol Evidence Rule and Its Implications for New Textualist Statutory Interpretation*, 87 Geo. L.J. 195 (1998); Peter L. Strauss, *The Common Law and Statutes*, 70 U. Colo. L. Rev. 225 (1999); Patricia M. Wald, *The Sizzling Sleeper: The Use of Legislative History in Construing Statutes in the 1988–89 Term of the United States Supreme Court*, 39 Am. U. L. Rev. 277 (1990); Nicholas S. Zeppos, *Justice Scalia's Textualism: The "New" New Legal Process*, 12 Cardozo L. Rev. 1597 (1991).

reports (even if less than before). Moreover, in *Wisconsin Public Intervenor v. Mortier*, 501 U.S. 597, 610 n.4 (1991), all of the other Justices joined in a footnote explicitly rejecting Justice Scalia's general position that legislative history is irrelevant to proper statutory interpretation. Especially after the appointment of Justice Breyer (a big fan of legislative history), the Supreme Court has continued to rely on legislative materials.[j] During the Roberts Court (2005 onward), the Court has continued to invoke legislative history with some regularity and to treat committee reports as the most reliable materials. But the Roberts Court has tended to invoke legislative history almost always as "confirming" the apparent meaning of statutory texts, and almost never as "rebutting" a textual plain meaning. See James J. Brudney, *Confirmatory Legislative History*, 76 Brooklyn L. Rev. 901 (2011).

IN RE SINCLAIR

United States Court of Appeals for the Seventh Circuit, 1989
870 F.2d 1340

EASTERBROOK, CIRCUIT JUDGE.

This case presents a conflict between a statute and its legislative history. The Sinclairs, who have a family farm, filed a bankruptcy petition in April 1985 under Chapter 11 of the Bankruptcy Act of 1978. In October 1986 Congress added Chapter 12, providing benefits for farmers, and the Sinclairs asked the bankruptcy court to convert their case from Chapter 11 to Chapter 12. The bankruptcy judge declined, and the district court affirmed. Each relied on § 302(c)(1) of the Bankruptcy Judges, United States Trustees, and Family Farmer Bankruptcy Act of 1986, Pub.L. 99–554, 100 Stat. 3088:

> The amendments made by subtitle B of title II shall not apply with respect to cases commenced under title 11 of the United States Code before the effective date of this Act.

The Sinclairs rely on the report of the Conference Committee, which inserted § 302(c)(1) into the bill:

> It is not intended that there be routine conversion of Chapter 11 and 13 cases, pending at the time of enactment, to Chapter 12. Instead, it

---

Treatments sympathetic to Justice Scalia's approach include Frank H. Easterbrook, *Textualism and the Dead Hand*, 66 Geo. Wash. L. Rev. 1119 (1998); Alex Kozinski, *Should Reading Legislative History Be an Impeachable Offense?*, 31 Suffolk U.L. Rev. 807 (1998); John F. Manning, *Textualism as a Nondelegation Doctrine*, 97 Colum. L. Rev. 673 (1997); Jonathan T. Molot, *The Rise and Fall of Textualism*, 106 Colum. L. Rev. 1, 23–29 (2006); Frederick Schauer, *Statutory Construction and the Coordinating Function of Plain Meaning*, 1990 Sup. Ct. Rev. 231; Kenneth W. Starr, *Observations About the Use of Legislative History*, 1987 Duke L.J. 371; Adrian Vermeule, *Legislative History and the Limits of Judicial Competence: The Untold Story of* Holy Trinity Church, 50 Stan. L. Rev. 1833 (1998). Going beyond Justice Scalia (by excluding whole act evidence as well as legislative history), is Adrian Vermeule, *Judging Under Uncertainty: An Institutional Theory of Legal Interpretation* (2006).

j. See Jane S. Schacter, *The Confounding Common Law Originalism in Recent Supreme Court Statutory Interpretation: Implications for the Legislative History Debate and Beyond*, 51 Stan. L. Rev. 1 (1998); Charles Tiefer, *The Reconceptualization of Legislative History in the Supreme Court*, 2000 Wis. L. Rev. 205. For a recent example, and indeed the most lavish recent deployment of legislative history by a majority opinion (written by O'Connor but joined without cavil by Scalia and Thomas), see *FDA v. Brown & Williamson Tobacco Co.*, 529 U.S. 120 (2000) (Chapter 2, § 3B).

is expected that courts will exercise their sound discretion in each case, in allowing conversions only where it is equitable to do so.

Chief among the factors the court should consider is whether there is a substantial likelihood of successful reorganization under Chapter 12.

Courts should also carefully scrutinize the actions already taken in pending cases in deciding whether, in their equitable discretion, to allow conversion. For example, the court may consider whether the petition was recently filed in another chapter with no further action taken. Such a case may warrant conversion to the new chapter. On the other hand, there may be cases where a reorganization plan has already been filed or confirmed. In cases where the parties have substantially relied on current law, availability [sic] to convert to the new chapter should be limited.

The statute says conversion is impossible; the report says that conversion is possible and describes the circumstances under which it should occur.

Which prevails in the event of conflict, the statute or its legislative history? The statute was enacted, the report just the staff's explanation. Congress votes on the text of the bill, and the President signed that text. Committee reports help courts understand the law, but this report contradicts rather than explains the text. So the statute must prevail. * * *

Yet the advice from the Supreme Court about how to deal with our situation seems scarcely more harmonious than the advice from the legislature. The reports teem with statements such as: "When we find the terms of a statute unambiguous, judicial inquiry is complete," *Rubin v. United States*, 449 U.S. 424, 430 (1981). See also, e.g., *United States v. Ron Pair Enterprises, Inc.*, 489 U.S. 235 (1989) ("where, as here, the statute's language is plain, 'the sole function of the courts is to enforce it according to its terms.'"); [Judge Easterbrook cited several other cases, including *United States v. Locke*, 471 U.S. 84 (1985) (Chapter 2, § 2B) and *TVA v. Hill*, 437 U.S. 153 (1978) (Chapter 2, § 2C)]. Less frequently, yet with equal conviction, the Court writes: "When aid to the construction of the meaning of words, as used in the statute, is available, there certainly can be no 'rule of law' which forbids its use, however clear the words may appear on 'superficial examination.'" *United States v. American Trucking Assoc., Inc.*, 310 U.S. 534, 543–44 (1940) (footnotes omitted), repeated in *Train v. Colorado Public Interest Research Group, Inc.*, 426 U.S. 1, 10 (1976). See also, e.g., * * * *Holy Trinity Church v. United States*, 143 U.S. 457 (1892) [Chapter 2, § 1]. Some cases boldly stake out a middle ground, saying, for example: "only the most extraordinary showing of contrary intentions from [the legislative history] would justify a limitation on the 'plain meaning' of the statutory language." *Garcia v. United States*, 469 U.S. 70, 75 (1984). See also, e.g., *Griffin v. Oceanic Contractors, Inc.*, 458 U.S. 564 (1982) [Chapter 2, § 2C] * * *. This implies that once in a blue moon the legislative history trumps the statute (as opposed to affording a basis for its interpretation) but does not help locate such strange astronomical phenomena. These lines of cases have coexisted for a century, and many cases contain statements associated with two or even all three of them, not recognizing the tension.

What's a court to do? The answer lies in distinguishing among uses of legislative history. An unadorned "plain meaning" approach to interpretation supposes that words have meanings divorced from their contexts—linguistic, structural, functional, social, historical. Language is a process of communication that works only when authors and readers share a set of rules and meanings. What "clearly" means one thing to a reader unacquainted with the circumstances of the utterance—including social conventions prevailing at the time of drafting—may mean something else to a reader with a different background. Legislation speaks across the decades, during which legal institutions and linguistic conventions change. To decode words one must frequently reconstruct the legal and political culture of the drafters. Legislative history may be invaluable in revealing the setting of the enactment and the assumptions its authors entertained about how their words would be understood. It may show, too, that words with a denotation "clear" to an outsider are terms of art, with an equally "clear" but different meaning to an insider. It may show too that the words leave gaps, for short phrases cannot address all human experience; understood in context, the words may leave to the executive and judicial branches the task of adding flesh to bones. These we take to be the points of cases such as *American Trucking* holding that judges may learn from the legislative history even when the text is "clear". Clarity depends on context, which legislative history may illuminate. The process is objective; the search is not for the contents of the authors' heads but for the rules of language they used.

Quite different is the claim that legislative intent is *the* basis of interpretation, that the text of the law is simply evidence of the real rule. In such a regimen legislative history is not a way to understand the text but is a more authentic, because more proximate, expression of legislators' will. One may say in reply that legislative history is a poor guide to legislators' intent because it is written by the staff rather than by members of Congress, because it is often losers' history ("If you can't get your proposal into the bill, at least write the legislative history to make it look as if you'd prevailed"), because it becomes a crutch ("There's no need for us to vote on the amendment if we can write a little legislative history"), because it complicates the task of execution and obedience (neither judges nor those whose conduct is supposed to be influenced by the law can know what to do without delving into legislative recesses, a costly and uncertain process). Often there is so much legislative history that a court can manipulate the meaning of a law by choosing which snippets to emphasize and by putting hypothetical questions—questions to be answered by inferences from speeches rather than by reference to the text, so that great discretion devolves on the (judicial) questioner. Sponsors of opinion polls know that a small change in the text of a question can lead to large differences in the answer. Legislative history offers willful judges an opportunity to pose questions and devise answers, with predictable divergence in results. These and related concerns have lead to skepticism about using legislative history to find legislative intent. E.g., *Blanchard v. Bergeron* (Scalia, J., concurring); [Judge Easterbrook cited several lower court opinions, including Judge Scalia's separate opinion in *Hirschey*]. These cautionary notes are well taken, but even if none were salient there would still be a hurdle to the sort of argument pressed in our case.

Statutes are law, not evidence of law. References to "intent" in judicial opinions do not imply that legislators' motives and beliefs, as opposed to their public acts, establish the norms to which all others must conform. "Original meaning" rather than "intent" frequently captures the interpretive task more precisely, reminding us that it is the work of the political branches (the "meaning") rather than of the courts that matters, and that their work acquires its meaning when enacted ("originally"). Revisionist history may be revelatory; revisionist judging is simply unfaithful to the enterprise. Justice Holmes made the point when denouncing a claim that judges should give weight to the intent of a document's authors:

> [A statute] does not disclose one meaning conclusively according to the laws of language. Thereupon we ask, not what this man meant, but what those words would mean in the mouth of a normal speaker of English, using them in the circumstances in which they were used .... But the normal speaker of English is merely a special variety, a literary form, so to speak, of our old friend the prudent man. He is external to the particular writer, and a reference to him as the criterion is simply another instance of the externality of the law .... We do not inquire what the legislature meant; we ask only what the statute means.

Oliver Wendell Holmes, *The Theory of Legal Interpretation*, 12 Harv. L. Rev. 417, 417–19 (1899), reprinted in Collected Legal Papers 204, 207 (1920). Or as Judge Friendly put things in a variation on Holmes's theme, a court must search for "what Congress meant by what it said, rather than for what it meant *simpliciter*." Henry J. Friendly, *Mr. Justice Frankfurter and the Reading of Statutes*, in Benchmarks 218–19 (1967).

An opinion poll revealing the wishes of Congress would not translate to legal rules. Desires become rules only after clearing procedural hurdles, designed to encourage deliberation and expose proposals (and arguments) to public view and recorded vote. Resort to "intent" as a device to short-circuit these has no more force than the opinion poll—less, because the legislative history is written by the staff of a single committee and not subject to a vote or veto. The Constitution establishes a complex of procedures, including presidential approval (or support by two-thirds of each house). It would demean the constitutionally prescribed method of legislating to suppose that its elaborate apparatus for deliberation on, amending, and approving a text is just a way to create some *evidence* about the law, while the *real* source of legal rules is the mental processes of legislators. We know from *INS v. Chadha*, 462 U.S. 919 (1983) [Chapter 6, § 2C], that the express disapproval of one house of Congress cannot change the law, largely because it removes the President from the process; it would therefore be surprising if "intents" subject to neither vote nor veto could be sources of law.

* * * If Congress were to reduce the rate of taxation on capital gains, "intending" that this stimulate economic growth and so yield more in tax revenue, the meaning of the law would be only that rates go down, not that revenue go up—a judge could not later rearrange rates to achieve the "intent" with respect to federal coffers. On the other hand, doubt about the meaning of a term found in the statute could well be resolved by harmonizing that provision with the structure of the rest of the law, understood in light of a contemporaneous explanation. In this sense legislative intent is a vital source of meaning even though it does not trump the text.

Concern about the source of law—is the statute law, or is it just evidence of the law?—lies behind statements such as: "[T]he language being plain, and not leading to absurd or wholly impracticable consequences, it is the sole evidence of the ultimate legislative intent." *Caminetti*. To treat the text as conclusive evidence of law is to treat it *as* law—which under the constitutional structure it is. Legislative history then may help a court discover but may not change the original meaning. *Pierce v. Underwood*, 487 U.S. 552 (1988). The "plain meaning" rule of *Caminetti* [Chapter 2, § 1] rests not on a silly belief that texts have timeless meanings divorced from their many contexts, not on the assumption that what is plain to one reader must be clear to any other (and identical to the plan of the writer), but on the constitutional allocation of powers. The political branches adopt texts through prescribed procedures; what ensues is the law. Legislative history may show the meaning of the texts—may show, indeed, that a text "plain" at first reading has a strikingly different meaning—but may not be used to show an "intent" at variance with the meaning of the text. *Caminetti* and *American Trucking* can comfortably coexist when so understood. This approach also supplies the underpinning for the belief that legislative history is "only admissible to solve doubt and not to create it", which punctuates the U.S. Reports. Legislative history helps us learn what Congress meant by what it said, but it is not a source of legal rules competing with those found in the U.S. Code.

Ours is now an easy case. Section 302(c)(1) of the statute has an ascertainable meaning, a meaning not absurd or inconsistent with the structure of the remaining provisions. It says that Chapter 11 cases pending on the date the law went into force may not be converted to Chapter 12. No legislative history suggests any other meaning. The committee report suggests, at best, a different intent. Perhaps a reader could infer that the committee planned to allow conversion but mistakenly voted for a different text. So two members of the committee have said since, calling § 302(c)(1) an oversight. See 133 Cong.Rec. S2273–76 (daily ed. Feb. 19, 1987) (Sen. Grassley), E544 (daily ed. Feb. 19, 1987) (Rep. Coelho). Not only the committee's remarks on conversion but also the omission of § 302(c)(1) from the section-by-section description of the bill suggest that whoever wrote the report (a staffer, not a Member of Congress) wanted § 302(c)(1) deleted and may have thought that had been accomplished. Still another possibility is that the Conference Committee meant to distinguish Chapter 11 from Chapter 13: to ban conversions from Chapter 11 (covered by § 302(c)(1)) but allow them from Chapter 13. On this reading the gaffe is the failure to delete the reference to Chapter 11 from the report, which could still stand as a treatment of conversions from Chapter 13.

Congress has done nothing to change § 302(c)(1), implying that the statement in the committee report may have been the error. It is easy to imagine opposing forces arriving at the conference armed with their own texts and legislative histories, and in the scramble at the end of session one version slipping into the bill and the other into the report. Whichever was the blunder, we know which one was enacted. What came out of conference, what was voted for by House and Senate, what was signed by the President, says that pending Chapter 11 cases may not be converted. Accordingly, pending Chapter 11 cases may not be converted.

NOTES ON *SINCLAIR* AND THE SEARCH FOR OBJECTIVITY IN STATUTORY INTERPRETATION

1. *Textual Evidence Judge Easterbrook Missed.* Judge Easterbrook cites § 302 of the 1986 statute, which seems to prevent conversion of the *Sinclair* proceeding. But the legislative history he cites is the Conference Committee language not of § 302, but of § 256(1), which amended 11 U.S.C. § 1112(d). Section 1112 is the provision of Chapter 11 that deals with conversions. As amended, it now reads:

> (d) The Court may convert a case under this chapter to a case under chapter 12 or 13 of this title only if—

> (1) the debtor requests such conversion;

> (2) the debtor has not been discharged under section 1141(d) of this title; and

> (3) if the debtor requests conversion to chapter 12 of this title, such conversion is equitable.

Is the statutory text clearly against conversion? It is only if § 256(1) is interpreted not to apply to pending proceedings.

In light of this evidence, construct an argument that *In re Sinclair* is wrongly decided.[k] We have brought this evidence to Judge Easterbrook's attention, and he responded that it would not change his thinking about this case, because the new textual evidence was not briefed by the parties and in

---

k. For an extraordinary discussion concerning broader jurisprudential issues lingering in the *Sinclair* case, see Paul F. Campos, *The Chaotic Pseudotext*, 94 Mich. L. Rev. 2178 (1996).

any event he was not persuaded that this new evidence created any statutory ambiguity. Does this additional information demonstrate ambiguity?

2. *Judicial Fears of the Mischievous Staffer.* An enduring image from Justice Scalia's *Bergeron* concurring opinion (and a standard trope in Scalia's speeches deriding legislative history) is the possibility that mischievous staffers will smuggle stuff into committee reports and thereby "trick" judges into bad interpretations that Congress did not "intend." Notice how staffers bent on mischief can do the same thing to statutory text. In *Sinclair*, Judge Easterbrook notes that several Members of Congress later said that a mistake somehow arose with respect to § 302(c)(1), the effective date provision, and that the Congress intended to allow conversion of pending farmer bankruptcy proceedings. There are at least three reasons to believe that this is accurate.

First, it is fishy that the Conference Report has no mention of § 302(c)(1). That the "dog didn't bark" in the Conference Report is odd in light of a second factor, the emergency nature of this law. The 1986 statute creating Chapter 12 was adopted during the most serious farm economic depression since the 1930s. Farmers had been going under left and right, and Congress decided to ameliorate their debt situation somewhat by adopting Chapter 12, which is more favorable to farmers than is the bankruptcy scheme of Chapter 11, which is available to all debtors. This purpose of the 1986 statute of "helping the farmers during this emergency" seems in stark conflict with the notion that only future cases could be converted to new Chapter 12. Moreover, § 1112(d) as amended allows conversion only in cases in which it would be equitable, thereby providing some measure of protection to creditors in pending proceedings. Finally, according to prevalent rumors in one segment of the bankruptcy bar, at the behest of lending interests a Senate staff member put § 302 into the bill, contrary to the apparent wishes of the sponsors and supporters of the 1986 statute. It appears that sponsors and supporters of the statute did not even notice § 302 until well after the statute had been adopted. This may shed new light on why § 302 was not discussed in the section-by-section description of the bill in the conference committee report. This rumor seems to turn on its head the complaint by new textualists that *legislative history* is unreliable because of potential shenanigans by legislative staff.[1]

3. *Objectivity in Statutory Interpretation: Empirical Evidence from the Supreme Court's Labor Cases.* Complementing the image of the mischievous staffer in Justice Scalia's pitch for the new textualism is the result-oriented judge who will look out over the legislative history crowd and pick out his friends. You might review the *big cases* in this Casebook, such as *Weber*, the affirmative action case in Chapter 1; *Holy Trinity* and the FDA Tobacco Case in Chapter 2; and *Sweet Home* in Chapter 3. In all these cases, Justices (including Scalia, in *Sweet Home*) invoke legislative history to support results that match those Justices' apparent ideologies—but in all the cases except *Holy Trinity* the Justices also invoke textual plain meaning in the same way.

---

1. On end-of-the-game strategic moves in the legislative process, see William H. Rodgers, Jr., *The Lesson of the Red Squirrel: Consensus and Betrayal in the Environmental Statutes*, 5 J. Contemp. Health L. & Pol. 161 (1989).

Properly phrased, the inquiry demanded by the new textualism's appeal to objectivity in judging is that a judge who looks at legislative history as well as text is *more likely* to read his or her ideological presuppositions into a statute than a judge who just looks at the text alone. There is no empirical evidence that this is the case—and now some evidence to the contrary. James J. Brudney, *Liberal Justices' Reliance on Legislative History: Principle, Strategy, and the Scalia Effect*, 29 Berkeley J. Emp. & Lab. L. 117 (2008), did a deeper empirical analysis of the authors' dataset of 578 Supreme Court labor cases (1969–2003). Analyzing the voting records of the eight Justices conventionally considered "liberal," Professor Brudney reached the following conclusions:

> [F]or the eight liberals, the relationship between pro-employee outcomes and legislative history usage is not significant. If anything, legislative history reliance is associated with a somewhat neutralizing set of results. When liberal Justices use legislative history as part of their majority reasoning, they do so to help justify more than half of their *pro-employer* opinions for the Court but just under one-half of their *pro-employee* outcomes. Further evidence of this moderating association is that majority opinions authored by liberal Justices reach liberal outcomes 30 percent more often than conservative results when *not* relying on legislative history, but the liberal-conservative outcome differential declines to 21 percent when the majority opinion's reasoning includes legislative history.

For the Justices considered "conservative," Brudney found that reliance on legislative history was correlated with slightly more conservative voting. In short, legislative history of labor statutes, most of which were enacted by liberal Congresses, supported employer-oriented deals reached in the legislative process—and sometimes persuaded liberals to sacrifice their pro-employee biases. (An example of this phenomenon is *Muscarello v. United States*, 524 U.S. 125 (1998) (Chapter 3, § 2A), where liberal Justice Breyer relied on legislative history to interpret ambiguous statutory language and impose a harsh sentence on gun-"carrying" defendants.) This is preliminary evidence *against* the judicial objectivity argument for textualism.

On the other hand, Professor Brudney also found that this moderating association has waned among the cohort of liberal Justices since Justice Scalia's appointment to the Court. The suggestion is that Justice Scalia's hard-hitting style has polarized the Court, pitting text-wielding conservatives against liberals clinging to legislative history. An example of this phenomenon is *Circuit City Stores, Inc. v. Adams*, 532 U.S. 105 (2001) (Chapter 3, § 1A2), where conservatives rejected legislative history and liberals relied on it. Has Judge Leventhal's quip become a self-fulfilling prophesy?

Carr v. United States, 130 S.Ct. 2229 (2010). The Sex Offender Registration and Notification Act of 2006 (SORNA) makes it a federal crime for any person (1) who "is required to register under [SORNA]," and (2) who "travels in interstate or foreign commerce," to (3) "knowingly fai[l] to register or update a registration," 18 U.S.C. § 2250(a). Before SORNA's enactment, Thomas Carr, a registered sex offender in Alabama, relocated to Indiana without complying with Indiana's registration requirements. The federal government charged Carr with violating SORNA. After the trial court rejected his constitutional (ex post facto) challenge to this indictment, Carr pleaded guilty. On appeal, he argued that the statute requires that the interstate travel (as well as the failure to register or update a registration) be accomplished *after* SORNA went into effect. The government argued that only the failure to register or update needs to be after the effective date.

Reversing the Seventh Circuit, **Justice Sotomayor**'s opinion for the Court interpreted SORNA to apply only if both the travel and the failure to register/update occurred after the statute went into effect. "By its terms, the first element of § 2250(a) can only be satisfied when a person 'is required to register *under the Sex Offender Registration and Notification Act.*' § 2250(a)(1) (emphasis added)." The implication of this requirement is that SORNA is applicable to the defendant when he engages in travel and failure to register/update.

Justice Sotomayor found this reading consistent with the second requirement—that the defendant "travels" in commerce. "That § 2250 sets forth the travel requirement in the present tense ('travels') rather than in the past or present perfect ('traveled' or 'has traveled') reinforces the conclusion that pre-enactment travel falls outside the statute's compass. Consistent with normal usage, we have frequently looked to Congress' choice of verb tense to ascertain a statute's temporal reach. [E.g.,] *Gwaltney of Smithfield, Ltd.* v. *Chesapeake Bay Foundation, Inc.*, 484 U.S. 49, 57 (1987) ('Congress could have phrased its requirement in language that looked to the past ..., but it did not choose this readily available option'). The Dictionary Act also ascribes significance to verb tense. It provides that, '[i]n determining the meaning of any Act of Congress, unless the context indicates otherwise[,] ... words used in the present tense include the future as well as the present.' 1 U.S.C. § 1. By implication, then, the Dictionary Act instructs that the present tense generally does not include the past. Accordingly, a statute that regulates a person who 'travels' is not readily understood to encompass a person whose only travel occurred before the statute took effect. Indeed, neither the Government nor the dissent identifies any instance in which this Court has construed a present-tense verb in a criminal law to reach pre-enactment conduct.

"The Government accepts that th[e] last element—a knowing failure to register or update a registration—must postdate SORNA's enactment. Had Congress intended pre-enactment conduct to satisfy the first two requirements of § 2250 but not the third, it presumably would have varied the verb tenses to convey this meaning. Indeed, numerous federal statutes use the past-perfect tense to describe one or more elements of a criminal offense when coverage of pre-enactment events is intended. See, e.g., 18 U.S.C. § 249(a)(2)(B)(iii) (Supp. 2010) (proscribing hate crimes in which 'the defendant employs a firearm, dangerous weapon, explosive or incendiary device, or other weapon that *has traveled* in interstate or foreign commerce' (emphasis added)); 18 U.S.C. § 922(g)(9) (2006 ed.) (proscribing firearm possession or transport by any person 'who *has been convicted*' of a felony or a misdemeanor crime of domestic violence) (emphasis added). The absence of similar phrasing here provides powerful evidence that§ 2250 targets only post-enactment travel.

"In a final effort to justify its position, the Government invokes one of SORNA's underlying purposes: to locate sex offenders who had failed to abide by their registration obligations. SORNA, the Government observes, was motivated at least in part by Congress' concern about these 'missing' sex offenders—a problem the House Committee on the Judiciary expressly linked to interstate travel: 'The most significant enforcement issue in the sex offender program is that over 100,000 sex offenders, or nearly one-fifth in the Nation[,] are 'missing,' meaning they have not complied with sex offender registration requirements. This typically occurs when the sex offender moves from one State to another." H.R. Rep. No. 109–218, pt. 1, p. 26 (2005). The goal of tracking down missing sex offenders, the Government maintains, 'is surely better served by making Section 2250 applicable to them in their new States of residence immediately than by waiting for them to travel in interstate commerce and fail to register yet again.' Brief for United States 23–24.

"The Government's argument confuses a general goal of SORNA with the specific purpose of § 2250. Section 2250 is not a stand-alone response to the problem of missing sex offenders; it is embedded in a broader statutory scheme enacted to address the deficiencies in prior law that had enabled sex offenders to slip through the cracks. Among its many provisions, SORNA instructs States to maintain sex-offender registries that compile an array of information about sex offenders, § 16914; to make this information publicly available online, § 16918; to share the information with other jurisdictions and with the Attorney General for inclusion in a comprehensive national sex-offender registry, §§ 16919–16921; and to 'provide a criminal penalty that includes a maximum term of imprisonment that is greater than 1 year for the failure of a sex offender to comply with the requirements of this subchapter,' § 16913(e). Sex offenders, in turn, are required to 'register, and keep the registration current, in each jurisdiction where the offender resides, where the offender is an employee, and where the offender is a student,' § 16913(a), and to appear in person periodically to 'allow the jurisdiction to take a current photograph, and verify the information in each registry in which that offender is required to be registered,' § 16916. By facilitating the collection of sex-offender information and its dissemination among jurisdictions, these provisions, not § 2250, stand at the center of Congress' effort to account for missing sex offenders.

"Knowing that Congress aimed to reduce the number of noncompliant sex offenders thus tells us little about the specific policy choice Congress made in enacting § 2250. While subjecting pre-SORNA travelers to punishment under § 2250 may well be consistent with the aim of finding missing sex offenders, a contrary construction in no way frustrates that broad goal.

"None of the legislative materials the Government cites as evidence of SORNA's purpose calls this reading into question. To the contrary, the report of the House Judiciary Committee suggests not only that a prohibition on post-enactment travel is consonant with Congress' goals, but also that it is the rule Congress in fact chose to adopt. As the Government acknowledges, the bill under consideration by the Committee contained a version of § 2250 that 'would not have reached pre-enactment interstate travel.' Brief for United States 24, n.9. This earlier version imposed federal criminal penalties on any person who 'receives a notice from an official that such person is required to register under [SORNA] and ... thereafter travels in interstate or foreign commerce, or enters or leaves Indian country.' H.R. Rep. No. 109–218, pt. 1, at 9. Yet this did not stop the Committee from describing its legislation as a solution to the problem of missing sex offenders. The Government identifies nothing in the legislative record to suggest that, in modifying this language during the course of the legislative process, Congress intended to alter the statute's temporal sweep.''

Justice Scalia concurred in all but this last portion of the Court's opinion, discussing SORNA's legislative history. "I do not join that part because only the text Congress voted on, and not unapproved statements made or comments written during its drafting and enactment process, is an authoritative indicator of the law. But even if those pre-enactment materials were relevant, it would be unnecessary to address them here. The Court's thorough discussion of text, context, and structure demonstrates that the meaning of 18 U.S.C. § 2250(a) is plain.''

Justice Alito (joined by Justices Thomas and Ginsburg) dissented. "A man convicted in State A for sexual abuse is released from custody in that State and then, after the enactment of SORNA, moves to State B and fails to register as required by State B law. Section 2250(a) makes this offender's failure to register in State B a federal crime because his interstate movement frustrates SORNA's registration requirements. Because this offender is convicted and then released from custody in State A, the State A authorities know of his presence in their State and are thus in a position to try to ensure that he remains registered. At the time of his release, they can ascertain where he intends to live, and they can make sure that he registers as required by state law. Thereafter, they can periodically check the address at which he is registered to confirm that he still resides there. And even if he moves without warning to some other address in the State, they can try to track him down. Once this offender leaves State A, however, the authorities in that State are severely limited in their ability to monitor his movements. And because the State B authorities have no notice of his entry into their State, they are at a great disadvantage in trying to enforce State B's registration law. Congress enacted § 2250(a) in order to punish and deter interstate movement that seriously undermines the enforcement of sex-offender-registration laws.

"The second case is the same as the first in all respects except that the sex offender travels from State A to State B before SORNA's enactment. In other words, the sex offender is convicted and later released in State A; prior to SORNA's enactment, he moves to State B; and then, after SORNA takes effects, he fails to register in State B, as SORNA requires.

"Is there any reason why Congress might have wanted to treat the second case any differently from the first?" Justice Alito thought not—nor did he think that the statutory text required or even supported what he considered an absurd result. The Court's argument, that § 2250(a) uses the present tense and that the "present" is the date the law was enacted, "flies in the face of the widely accepted modern legislative drafting convention that a law should *not* be read to speak as of the date of enactment. The United States

Senate Legislative Drafting Manual directly addresses this point: 'A legislative provision speaks as of any date on which it is read (*rather than as of when drafted, enacted, or put into effect*).' Senate Office of the Legislative Counsel, Legislative Drafting Manual § 103(a), p. 4 (1997) (emphasis added). The House Manual makes the same point: 'Your draft should be a movable feast— that is, it speaks as of whatever time it is being read (*rather than as of when drafted, enacted, or put into effect*).' House Legislative Counsel's Manual on Drafting Style, HLC No. 104–1, § 102(c), p. 2 (1995).

"In accordance with this convention, modern legislative drafting manuals teach that, except in unusual circumstances, all laws, including penal statutes, should be written in the present tense. The Senate Manual, *supra*, § 103(a), at 4, states: '[A]lways use the present tense unless the provision addresses only the past, the future, or a sequence of events that requires use of a different tense.' Similarly, the House Manual, *supra*, § 102(c), at 2, advises: 'STAY IN THE PRESENT.—Whenever possible, use the present tense (rather than the past or future).' Numerous state legislative drafting manuals and other similar handbooks hammer home this same point. [Justice Alito cited the drafting manuals used by nine different states.]

"Once it is recognized that § 2250(a) should not be read as speaking as of the date when SORNA went into effect, petitioner's argument about the use of the present tense collapses. In accordance with current drafting conventions, § 2250(a) speaks, not as of the time when the law went into effect, but as of the time when the first act necessary for conviction is committed. In the case of § 2250(a), that occurs when an individual is convicted of a qualifying sex offense, for it is that act that triggers the requirement to register under SORNA." Justice Alito challenged the majority Justices to "double check" their too-confident textual analysis against the legislative history and purpose of the law.

"SORNA was a response to a dangerous gap in the then existing sex-offender-registration laws. In the years prior to SORNA's enactment, the Nation had been shocked by cases in which children had been raped and murdered by persons who, unbeknownst to their neighbors or the police, were convicted sex offenders. In response, Congress and state legislatures passed laws requiring the registration of sex offenders. See *Smith* v. *Doe*, 538 U.S. 84, 89–90 (2003); Jacob Wetterling Crimes Against Children and Sexually Violent Offender Registration Act, Tit. 17, 108 Stat. 2038; Megan's Law, 110 Stat. 1345. Despite those efforts, by 2006 an estimated 100,000 convicted sex offenders—nearly one-fifth of the Nation's total sex-offender population— remained unregistered. H.R. Rep. No. 109–218, pt. 1, p. 26 (2005). The principal problem, a House Report determined, was that sex offenders commonly moved from one State to another and then failed to register in their new State of residence. *Ibid.* In other words, interstate travel was dangerously undermining the effectiveness of state sex-offender-registration laws.

"Interpreting § 2250(a)(2)(B) to reach only post-enactment travel severely impairs § 2250(a)'s effectiveness. As interpreted by the Court, § 2250(a) applies to a pre-SORNA sex offender only if that offender traveled in interstate commerce at some point *after* SORNA's enactment. As the examples discussed at the beginning of this opinion illustrate, however, there is no apparent reason why Congress would have wanted to impose such a require-ment. To the contrary, under the Court's interpretation, the many sex offenders who had managed to avoid pre-existing registration regimes, mainly by moving from one State to another before SORNA's enactment, are placed beyond the reach of the federal criminal laws. It surely better serves the enforcement of SORNA's registration requirements to apply § 2250(a) to all pre-SORNA sex offenders, regardless of whether their interstate travel oc-curred before or after the statute's enactment.

"The Court provides only a weak defense of the result its analysis produces. The Court suggests that enhanced information collection and shar-ing and state enforcement of registration laws were the sole weapons that Congress chose to wield in order to deal with those convicted sex offenders whose whereabouts were unknown when SORNA was passed. I see no basis for this conclusion. There can be no dispute that the enactment of § 2250(a) shows that Congress did not think these measures were sufficient to deal with persons who have qualifying sex-offense convictions and who move from State to State after SORNA's enactment. And in light of that congressional judg-ment, is there any plausible reason to think that Congress concluded that these same measures would be adequate for those with qualifying sex offense convictions who had already disappeared at the time of SORNA's enactment?"

NOTES ON THE SEX OFFENDER REGISTRATION CASE AND A NEW DIRECTION IN THE LEGISLATIVE HISTORY DEBATE

1. *The Court Continues to Discuss and Analyze Legislative History.* The Justices' debate in *Carr* provides a current snapshot of the Great Committee Report Debate within the Court, as of 2011. Since 2005, four new Justices have been confirmed (Roberts, Alito, Sotomayor, and Kagan), and *Carr* indicates that legislative history remains alive and well at the Supreme Court level—over the continued (indeed, renewed) objections of Justice Scalia.

The dissenting Justices (Thomas, Ginsburg, and Alito), spanning the political spectrum, rely centrally on legislative history to make their case against the Court's narrow construction of SORNA. It is significant that Justice Alito's dissent does not stop after it has made its logical and textual arguments—and that Justice Sotomayor's majority opinion (for an equally heterogeneous cluster of Roberts, Stevens, Kennedy, and Breyer) responds with her own sharp-eyed analysis of the legislative history.

Justice Scalia remains alone in his objections to the admissibility of legislative history. Why does he persist? What is the purpose of his solo concurring opinions objecting to legislative history arguments in majority opinions? Jot down your thoughts, and then consider the next note.

2. *But Legislative History Is Rarely Decisive at the Supreme Court.* If the Justices continue to discuss and analyze legislative history, they do not often give it decisive effect in their opinions. Speaking for the Court (and for Justice Scalia), Justice Sotomayor's opinion says that there is a plain meaning—and the legislative history materials are discussed mainly in response to Justice Alito's dissenting opinion. But Justice Alito himself starts with a textual

argument and seems to deploy legislative history mainly to confirm what he thinks the statute's plain meaning is.

Does Justice Scalia not have a point, that the Court's (and, for that matter, Justice Alito's) legal analysis would not change significantly if legislative history were discarded? Because the Justices cite and discuss legislative history, lawyers in federal court cases and even advising clients must research legislative history, which generates enormous social expense. Is that expense worth the value added by legislative history? How would Justice Sotomayor respond to these concerns? See James J. Brudney, *Confirmatory Legislative History*, 96 Brooklyn L. Rev. 901 (2011).

3. *A New Source of Textual Analysis: Legislative Drafting Manuals?* Justice Alito's textualist argument drawn from legislative drafting manuals caught *everyone* by surprise—the lawyers and law students working for Mr. Carr, the lawyers for the government (which had not briefed this issue), and legal academics (who had neglected this source of textual understanding). Why did his argument not garner more than three votes? Why did Justice Scalia not find it persuasive?

The element of surprise may have worked against Justice Alito. Just as the majority Justices may have been concerned with the retroactive application of a major penal statute to Mr. Carr, so they might have been worried that he should not lose the case based upon novel, unbriefed evidence of legislative practice. If this was a concern in *Carr*, however, it should *not* be a concern in future cases. The word is now out, that both the House and the Senate have drafting manuals that provide potentially important insights into how legislators understand, as a conventional matter, the textualist rules of the game. Moreover, both manuals are available online and so are easily available to lawyers and judges. The House Manual has long been online, at http://www.thecapitol.net/Research/images/HOLC.Manual.on.Drafting.Style. 1995.pdf. Although not previously online, the Senate Manual is now available at http://www.law.yale.edu/faculty/legislativematerials.htm.

An important student comment argues that textualists ought to pay attention to legislative drafting manuals. See B.J. Ard, Comment, *Interpreting by the Book: Legislative Drafting Manuals and Statutory Interpretation*, 120 Yale L.J. 185 (2010). Ard points out that one critique of the new textualism is that it represents a judicial bait-and-switch game on Congress. Legislators enact statutes under conventional assumptions that text-loving judges later ignore and even thwart. When the legislative assumptions are well-documented rules for drafting statutory *texts*, then the new textualism seems theoretically mistaken, and the good faith of its users might be questioned. Should Justice Scalia incorporate legislative drafting manuals in his arsenal now? (Ard believes that drafting manuals are not the textualist treasure trove that dictionaries are, but he does claim that new textualists need to consider them as well.)

If *Carr* stimulates a new cottage industry surveying legislative drafting manuals, might that not render textualist analysis even more complicated? The more sources textualists draw into their net, the more judges will be tempted to look out over the crowd and pick out their friends.

PEREZ v. WYETH LABORATORIES, INC.

Supreme Court of New Jersey, 1999
161 N.J. 1, 734 A.2d 1245

[Excerpted in Chapter 2, § 3B2]

NOTE ON THE NORPLANT CASE AND STATE COURT RELIANCE ON COMMITTEE AND BILL REPORTS[m]

The Norplant Case is an unusually apt one for consideration of legislative history, as the statute itself contained a reference to the committee report.[n] Moreover, **New Jersey** is one of about a dozen states that have regular reports from standing committees to accompany legislation, and it is one of about eight states to make committee reports for recent legislation available online. Traditionally, New Jersey state judges have been among the most willing to rely on legislative history to construe statutes; judges in that state sometimes consider committee reports whether or not the statute's text is ambiguous. See, e.g., *State v. Fleischman,* 917 A.2d 722, 730 n.4 (N.J. 2007) (interpreting the creation of textual ambiguity by committee report and whole act, triggering rule of lenity); *State v. Hoffman,* 695 A.2d 236 (N.J. 1997); *Wingate v. Estate of Ryan,* 693 A.2d 457 (N.J. 1997); N.J. Stat. § 40:41A–1 et seq. But see *New Jersey Civ. Serv. Ass'n v. State,* 443 A.2d 1070 (N.J. 1982) (asserting that committee reports may not trump clear words of statute).

As in other states, the methodological lay-of-the-land in New Jersey is subject to challenge and possible change; Governor Chris Christie, elected in 2009, theoretically will have a chance to appoint four new justices, a majority of the court, and has vowed to appoint strict textualists in the mold of Justice Scalia. Should Governor Christie cite the Norplant Case as an example of contextualist interpretation gone awry? Or should he consider Justice Pollock's dissent (relying on the committee report and other legislative materials) to be the best approach to the issues in the Norplant Case?

For recent examples of state appellate courts' reliance on committee reports, see *People v. Gonzalez,* 184 P.3d 702 (**Cal.** 2008); *Aiken v. United States,* 956 A.2d 33, 43–44 (**D.C.** 2008); *State v. Woodfall,* 206 P.3d 841, 847–50 (**Haw.** 2009); *State v. Dohlman,* 725 N.W.2d 428, 432 (**Iowa** 2006); *Risdall v. Brown–Wilbert, Inc.,* 753 N.W.2d 723, 730 & n.6 (**Minn.** 2008); *State v. Neesley,* 239 S.W.3d 780, 785–86 (**Tex.** Crim. App. 2007).

In many other states a "bill report" is prepared by the committee staff after a bill is voted out of committee, but it is not necessarily reviewed by the committee or even its chair. The bill report typically contains a background statement, a summary of the bill's provisions, changes made by the committee, a list of the proponents and opponents who testified before the committee,

---

m. Maame Ewusi–Mensah (Yale Law School Class of 2001) provided the research background and first draft of this Note.

n. Compare Jonathan R. Siegel, *The Use of Legislative History in a System of Separated Powers,* 53 Vand. L. Rev. 1457 (2000) (statutory incorporation by reference to legislative history removes separation-of-powers objection) with John F. Manning, *Putting Legislative History to a Vote: A Response to Professor Siegel,* 53 Vand. L. Rev. 1529 (2000) (taking the contrary position).

and the pro and con arguments. Courts have traditionally discounted such sources. In *Gates v. Jensen*, 595 P.2d 919 (**Wash.** 1979), for example, the court failed to mention a bill report which explained the ambit of a statutory override of the court's prior decisions imposing a rather strict standard of care in medical malpractice actions. Dissenting justices argued from the bill report that the override went further than the majority was willing to take it.

The current trend among the states is to consider bill reports as weak but admissible evidence of legislative intent. The Supreme Court of **Florida** has deemed bill reports "one touchstone of the legislative will." *White v. State*, 714 So.2d 440, 443 n.5 (1998); see also *State v. Jefferson*, 758 So.2d 661, 665–66 (**Fla.** 2000); accord. *People v. Ramirez*, 201 P.3d 466, 470 (**Cal.** 2009) and *In re Derrick B.*, 139 P.3d 485 (**Cal.** 2006); *Kramer v. Liberty Prop. Trust*, 968 A.2d 120 (**Md.** 2009); *Fournier v. Elliott*, 966 A.2d 410 (**Me.** 2009); *Kern v. Blethen–Coluni*, 612 N.W.2d 838 (**Mich.** App. 2000); *Krupa v. State*, 286 S.W.3d 74, (**Tex.** App. 2009); *Cosmopolitan Engr'g Group, Inc. v. Ondeo Degremont, Inc.*, 149 P.3d 666, 672–73 (**Wash.** 2006).

In **New York**, the governor's staff compiles a "bill jacket" (the New York term) to assist the governor in her or his decision whether to veto a bill the legislature has passed. Containing analyses from legislative sponsors as well as interested agencies and private parties, bill jackets are often treasure troves of legislative background materials and legal arguments. Similar reports, called "governor's bill files," can be found in public archives for California, Massachusetts, Oregon, Utah, Washington, and perhaps other states. E.g., *Ramirez*, 201 P.3d at 471–72 (relying on sponsor's letter to file compiled for governor in **California**).

In addition to committee reports and bill reports, state legislative history can include a number of other reports compiled by official sources before statutes are enacted. In her dissenting opinion in *State ex rel. Kalal v. Circuit Ct., Dane Cnty.*, 681 N.W.2d 110, 125–26 (**Wis.** 2004), Chief Justice Shirley Abrahamson listed other sources her court had traditionally considered, including not just legislative committee reports, but also legislative reference bureau drafting files and prefatory notes for bills, governor's study commission reports, judicial council notes, joint legislative council notes, and governor's veto messages. **Wisconsin**'s Supreme Court still routinely relies on such materials. E.g., *State v. Duchow*, 749 N.W.2d 913 (Wis. 2008) (using legislative reference bureau's drafting file); *State v. Grunke*, 738 N.W.2d 137, 142 (Wis.App. 2007) (same). See also *Price v. Thomas Built Buses, Inc.*, 260 S.W.3d 300, 305–06 (**Ark.** 2007) (resolving ambiguity by reference to legislative council report); *Jones v. Lodge*, 177 P.3d 232, 240–43 (**Cal.** 2008) (relying on legislative counsel's digest summarizing bills, as well as committee report and agency bill analysis); *People v. Garson*, 848 N.E.2d 1264 (**N.Y.** 2006) (noting reliance on commission staff notes); *McKinney v. Richitelli*, 586 S.E.2d 258, 263 (**N.C.** 2003) (using report of general statutes commission).

In at least one state, there has been serious debate as to what kinds of legislative materials might be admissible. An important decision is *People v. Gardner*, 753 N.W.2d 78, 89 (**Mich.** 2008), where a divided **Michigan** Supreme Court ruled that legislative materials could only be considered when the statute is ambiguous *and* that only certain legislative materials should be admissible. *Admissible* materials included the statutory history and evidence of proposals rejected by one chamber or the other. *Inadmissible* materials, even when the statute is ambiguous, included committee reports, staff analyses of bills, and floor speeches by sponsors and other legislators. In 2008, the textualist chief justice was turned out of office by the voters, but in 2010 a new conservative, and probably textualist, justice was voted onto the court. No one knows where the Michigan Supreme Court is headed.

Consideration of committee and bill reports is hardly a monopoly of large-population states. Practices similar to those in the previous paragraphs can be found in **Alaska**, see, e.g., *Gossman v. Greatland Directional Drilling, Inc.*, 973 P.2d 93 (Alaska 1999); **Arizona**, see, e.g., *O'Malley Lumber Co. v. Riley*, 613 P.2d 629 (Ariz. App. 1980); **Connecticut**, see, e.g., *Burke v. Fleet Nat'l Bank*, 742 A.2d 293 (Conn. 1999); *State v. Ledbetter*, 692 A.2d 713 (Conn. 1997); **Oregon**, see, e.g., *State v. Laemoa*, 533 P.2d 370 (Or. App. 1975).

Some states have no high-court authorization for considering committee reports but may be open to the practice in cases yet to be decided. Although its judges will discuss "statutory history" (the formal evolution of the statute, as amended over time), appellate courts in **Missouri**, **Virginia**, and **Georgia** do not cite to legislative history. E.g., *Sikes v. State*, 485 S.E.2d 206, 211 (Ga. 1997); *State v. Premium Standard Farms, Inc.*, 100 S.W.3d 157 (Mo. App. 2003). Many smaller states have no readily available legislative history, and there are too few reported decisions to discern a hard-and-fast rule for lawyer use of legislative history. E.g., **Rhode Island**, *Such v. State*, 950 A.2d 1150, 1158–59 (2008); **Wyoming**, *Moncrief v. Harvey,* 816 P.2d 97, 111–12 (1991) (Urbigkit, J., dissenting). Finally, legislative history at the state level is more accessible than it was a generation ago. See William H. Manz, *Guide to State Legislative and Administrative Materials* (7th ed. 2008). Indeed, judges are sometimes even encouraging counsel to research it. In *Dillehey v. State*, 815 S.W.2d 623 (**Tex.** Crim. App. 1991), the appeals court not only relied on legislative history but, in an appendix to the court's opinion, provided counsel in future cases with a roadmap for researching legislative history in Texas. Increasingly, state legislative history is online. Some state supreme courts provide guides to researching legislative history on their websites. See, e.g., the Washington Supreme Court's website, www.courts.wa.gov/library/legis. cfm (last visited June 20, 2010).

Part C. *Statements by Sponsors or Drafters of Legislation*

Next to committee reports, the most persuasive legislative materials are explanations of statutory meanings, and compromises reached to achieve enactment, by the sponsors and floor managers of the legislation. Recall that Senator Humphrey and the other primary sponsors of the Civil Rights Act of 1964 were primary sources of legislative history on both sides of the affirmative action debate in *United Steelworkers v. Weber* (Chapter 1, § 3). Because there was no Senate Report for that legislation, the sponsors' statements were most reliable. Recall that even Justice Scalia relied on a sponsor's explanation as key evidence for his dissent in *Sweet Home v. Babbitt* (Chapter 3, § 1C).

As the availability of legislative history for state statutes has dramatically increased, state courts, too, are relying on statements of sponsors to interpret statutes. See, e.g., *Commonwealth v. Ahlborn*, 626 A.2d 1265 (Pa. 1993) (relying on explanation of clarifying amendment, acquiesced in by the committee chair, as useful evidence of legislative intent); *Dillehey v. State*, 815 S.W.2d 623 (Tex. Crim. App. 1991) (relying on colloquy and providing counsel with roadmap for researching legislative history in Texas). On the other hand, statements by ordinary legislators are rarely given much, if any, weight. See *Murphy v. Kenneth Cole Productions, Inc.*, 40 Cal. 4th 1094, 155 P.3d 284 (2007) ("we do not consider the motives or understandings of individual legislators, including the bill's author"); *Quelimane Co. v. Stewart Title Guar. Co.*, 960 P.2d 513 (Cal. 1998).

The statements by sponsors are given such deference in part because the sponsors are the most knowledgeable legislators about the proposed bill and in part because their representations about the purposes and effects of the proposal are relied upon by other legislators. This approach is not without its detractors, however. Sponsors or their friends might have incentives to distort the legislative history through "planned colloquies." Congressman William Moorhead, in *A Congressman Looks at the Planned Colloquy and Its Effect in the Interpretation of Statutes*, 45 A.B.A.J. 1314, 1314 (1959), observed that members of Congress are aware that courts will look to the record of floor debates, especially statements by sponsors of legislation, and that "by the use of the 'friendly colloquy', two [legislators] may be able to legislate more effectively than all of Congress." He continued:

> Many if not most bills are controversial to some degree, and often it may be desirable when drafting a bill to couch provisions in innocuous language in order to minimize possible objections during committee consideration. Naturally, however, the proponents of a particular viewpoint would like to insure that their interpretation be the accepted one. The friendly colloquy on the floor during debate can serve well in this situation. Acquiescence by the committee [chair] in a stated intent will very likely be relied upon by the courts in the absence of objection or other reliable evidence of an opposite intent.

Note the similarity between this bit of realism about colloquies and the Armstrong–Dole exchange about committee reports (Note 1 after *Bergeron*).

Political scientists tend to discount this kind of evidence, because sponsors who distort the deals reached to achieve statutory enactments will not be trusted in future legislative deals. Moreover, judges have shown themselves increasingly sophisticated in handling such evidence. For a recent example, Justice Stevens interpreted the Detainee Treatment Act of 2005 to be not retroactive in *Hamdan v. Rumsfeld*, 548 U.S. 557 (2006) (Chapter 6, § 3B6). He relied on the statement of Senator Carl Levin, one of the sponsors, and discounted statements by two other sponsors (Senators John Kyl and Lindsay Graham) whose remarks were apparently inserted into the Congressional Record *after the fact. Id.* at 2766–67 n.10. Characteristically, Justice Scalia objected that the majority's editing of the legislative history was not only selective, but illustrated the general unreliability of such materials. *Id.* at 2825–27 (Scalia, J., dissenting).

Speaking of Justice Scalia, when he was a judge on the D.C. Circuit, one of his arguments against judicial use of legislative history was that the United Kingdom's House of Lords had long excluded its use.[o] He lost that argument in the case that follows—where the House of Lords found the statutory explication by the parliamentary floor manager not only decisive evidence, but evidence that flipped everyone's reading of the statute's "plain meaning."

PEPPER v. HART

House of Lords for the United Kingdom, 1992
[1992] 3 W.L.R. 1032, [1993] 1 All E.R. 42

[Malvern College allowed employees to send their children to the school for 20% of the fees paid by other parents. The employees and the tax collector agreed that this kind of fringe benefit was subject to income taxation, but disagreed on how to measure the benefit. The statute in question, § 63 of the Finance Act of 1976, defined "cash equivalent of the benefit," which was the measure of taxable benefit, as follows:

(1) The cash equivalent of any benefit chargeable to tax under section 61 above is an amount equal to the cost of the benefit, less so much (if any) of it as is made good by the employee to those providing the benefit.

(2) Subject to the following subsections, the cost of a benefit is the amount of any expense incurred in or in connection with its provision, and (here and in those subsections) includes a proper proportion of any expense relating partly to the benefit and partly to other matters.

Because the school in question had not been able to fill all its seats, its marginal costs in providing education to these children were minimal (involving a few items of equipment and food) and amounted to less than the fees paid by the employees. Accordingly, the employees argued that they had received no actual income at all, because the fringe benefit they received, measured as the (marginal) expense incurred by their employer, was less than the fees they had paid. The tax collector disagreed, arguing that the "expense incurred" should be average cost per pupil incurred by the school. When this case made its way to the Law Lords on appeal, they initially voted 4–1 in favor of the tax collector. On rehearing, when they were urged to consider the legislative history, the Law Lords expanded the appellate panel, which then reached the opposite result. In a landmark

---

o. This argument was made in then-Judge Scalia's standard speech against legislative history, a copy of which was obtained and distributed by the *Virginia Law Review* and is analyzed in Daniel A. Farber & Philip P. Frickey, *Legislative Intent and Public Choice*, 74 Va. L. Rev. 423, 440–43 (1988).

ruling under English law, the expanded panel abandoned the rule that British courts may not consult legislative history.]

LORD MACKAY OF CLASHFERN [LORD CHANCELLOR].

* * * The benefit which the taxpayers in this case received was the placing of their children in surplus places at the college, if as a matter of discretion the college agreed to do so. * * * They were in a similar position to the person coming along on a standby basis for an airline seat as against the passenger paying a full fare, and without the full rights of a standby passenger, in the sense that the decision whether or not to accommodate them in the college was entirely discretionary. If one regards the benefit in this light I cannot see that the cost incurred in, or in connection with, the provision of the benefit, can properly be held to include the cost incurred, in any event, in providing education to fee-paying pupils at the school who were there as a right in return for the fees paid in respect of them. * * * Although the later words of section 63(2) * * * provide that the expense incurred in, or in connection with, the provision of a benefit includes a proper proportion of any expense relating partly to the benefit and partly to other matters, I consider that the expenses incurred in provision of places for fee-paying pupils were wholly incurred in order to provide those places. * * * I conclude that looking at the matter from the point of view of expense incurred and not from the point of view of loss to the employer no expense could be regarded as having been incurred as a result of the decision of the authorities of the college to provide this particular benefit to the taxpayer.

Notwithstanding the views that have found favour with others I consider this to be a reasonable construction of the statutory provisions and I am comforted in the fact that, apart from an attempt to tax airline employees, which was taken to the Special Commissioners who decided in favour of the taxpayer, this has been the practice of the Inland Revenue in applying the relevant words where they have occurred in the Income Tax Acts for so long as they have been in force, until they initiated the present cases.

At the very least it appears to me that the manner in which I have construed the relevant provisions in their application to the facts in this appeal is a possible construction and that any ambiguity there should be resolved in favour of the taxpayer.

For these reasons I would allow these appeals. I should perhaps add that I was not a member of the committee who heard these appeals in the first hearing * * *.

But much wider issues than the construction of the Finance Act 1976 have been raised in these appeals and for the first time this House has been asked to consider a detailed argument on the extent to which reference can properly be made before a court of law in the United Kingdom to proceedings in Parliament recorded in Hansard.

For the appellant [taxpayers] Mr. Lester submits that it should now be appropriate for the courts to look at Hansard in order to ascertain the intention of the legislators as expressed in the proceedings on the Bill which has then been enacted in the statutory words requiring to be construed. This submission appears to me to suggest a way of making more effective proceedings in Parliament by allowing the court to consider what has been said in Parliament as an aid to resolving an ambiguity which may well have become apparent only as a result of the attempt to apply the enacted words to a particular case. * * *

The principal difficulty I have on this aspect of the case is that in Mr. Lester's submission reference to Parliamentary material as an aid to interpretation of a statutory provision should be allowed only with leave of the court and where the court is satisfied that such a reference is justifiable:

(a) to confirm the meaning of a provision as conveyed by the text, its object and purpose;

(b) to determine a meaning where the provision is ambiguous or obscure; or

(c) to determine the meaning where the ordinary meaning is manifestly absurd or unreasonable.

I believe that practically every question of *statutory* construction that comes before the courts will involve an argument that the case falls under one or more of these three heads. It follows that the parties' legal advisors will require to study Hansard [the official collection of parliamentary debates] in practically every such case to see whether or not there is any help to be gained from it. I believe this is an objection of real substance. It is a practical objection not one of principle * * *. Such an approach appears to me to involve the possibility at least of an immense increase in the cost of litigation in which statutory construction is involved. * * * [T]he Law Commission and the Scottish Law Commission, in their joint report on *The Interpretation of Statutes* (1969) (Law Com. no. 21) (Scot. Law Com. no. 11) and the Renton Committee Report on *The Preparation of Legislation* ((1975) Cmnd. 6053), advised against a relaxation on the practical grounds to which I have referred. * * *

[We omit the separate opinions of LORD BRIDGE OF HARWICH, LORD GRIFFITHS, LORD OLIVER OF AYLMERTON, LORD KEITH OF KINKEL, and LORD ACKNER. With varying degrees of enthusiasm, all five agreed with the following opinion by LORD BROWNE-WILKINSON. Lords Bridge and Oliver had voted in the first hearing to dismiss the appeal, but the Hansard materials impelled them to change their votes. Finding the statute ambiguous, Lord Griffiths had voted with the taxpayer in the first hearing.]

LORD BROWNE-WILKINSON. * * *

* * * [I]t is necessary first to refer to the legislation affecting the taxation of benefits in kind before 1975. Under the Finance Act 1948, section 39(1), directors and employees of bodies corporate earning more

than £2,000 per annum were taxed under Schedule E on certain benefits in kind. The amount charged was the expense incurred by the body corporate "in or in connection with the provision" of the benefit in kind. By section 39(6) it was provided that references to expenses "incurred in or in connection with any matter includes a reference to a proper proportion of any expense incurred partly in or in connection with that matter." Employment by a school or charitable organisation was expressly excluded from the charge: sections 41(5) and 44. These provisions were re-enacted in the Income and Corporation Taxes Act 1970.

Those provisions covered in-house benefits as well as external benefits. We were told that after 1948 the Revenue sought to tax at least two categories of employees in receipt of in-house benefits. Higher-paid employees of the railways enjoy free or concessionary travel on the railways. The Revenue reached an agreement that such employees should be taxed on 20% (later 25%) of the full fare. Airline employees also enjoy concessionary travel. We were told that in the 1960s the Revenue sought to tax such employees on that benefit on the basis of the average cost to the airline of providing a seat, not merely on the marginal cost. The tax commissioners rejected such claim: the Revenue did not appeal. Therefore in practice from 1948 to 1975 the Revenue did not seek to extract tax on the basis of the average cost to the employer of providing in-house benefits.

In 1975 the government proposed a new tax on vouchers provided by an employer to his employees which could be exchanged for goods or services. Clause 33(1) of the Finance (No. 2) Bill 1975 provided that the employee was to be treated, on receipt of a voucher, as having received an emolument from his employment of an amount "equal to the expense incurred by the person providing the voucher in or in connection with the provision of the voucher and the money, goods or services for which it is capable of being exchanged." The statutory wording of the Bill was therefore similar to that in the Act of 1948 and in section 63(2) of the Finance Act 1976. On 1 July 1975 in the Standing Committee on the Bill (Standing Committee H), the Financial Secretary was asked about the impact of the clause on railwaymen. He gave the following answer:

> "Similarly, the railwayman travelling on his normal voucher will not be taxable either. The clause deals with the situation where a number of firms produce incentives of various kinds. In one or two instances, there is likely to be some liability concerning rail vouchers of a special kind, but in general, the position is as I have said and they will not be taxable."

He was then asked to explain why they would not be taxable and replied:

> "Perhaps I can make clear why there is no taxable benefit in kind, because the provision of the service that he provides falls upon the employer. Clearly, the railways will run in precisely the same way whether the railwaymen use this facility or not, so there is no extra

charge to the Railways Board itself therefore there would be no taxable benefits." * * *

The Finance Bill 1976 sought to make a general revision of the taxation of benefits in kind. The existing legislation on fringe benefits was to be repealed. Clause 52 of the Bill as introduced eventually became section 61 of the Act of 1976 and imposed a charge to tax on benefits in kind for higher-paid employees, i.e., those paid more than £5,000 per annum. Clause 54 of the Bill eventually became section 63 of the Act of 1976. As introduced, clause 54(1) provided that the cash equivalent of any benefit was to be an amount equal to "the cost of the benefit." Clause 54(2) provided that, except as provided in later subsections "the cost of a benefit is the amount of any expense incurred in or in connection with its provision." Crucially, clause 54(4) of the Bill sought to tax in-house benefits on a different basis from that applicable to external benefits. It provided that the cost of a benefit consisting of the provision of any service or facility which was also provided to the public (i.e., in-house benefits) should be the price which the public paid for such facility or service. Employees of schools were not excluded from the new charge.

Thus if the 1976 Bill had gone through as introduced, railway and airline employees would have been treated as receiving benefits in kind from concessionary travel equal to the open market cost of tickets and schoolmasters would have been taxed for concessionary education on the amount of the normal school fees.

After second reading, clause 52 of the Bill was committed to a committee of the whole House and clause 54 to Standing Committee E. On 17 May 1976, the House considered clause 52 and strong representations were made about the impact of clause 52 on airline and railway employees. At the start of the meeting of Standing Committee E on 17 June 1976 (before clause 54 was being discussed) the Financial Secretary to the Treasury, Mr. Robert Sheldon, made an announcement (Hansard, columns 893–895) in the following terms:

"The next point I wish to make concerns services and deals with the position of employees of organisations, bodies, or firms which provide services, where the employee is in receipt of those services free or at a reduced rate. Under Clause 54(4) the taxable benefit is to be based on the arm's length price of the benefit received. At present the benefit is valued on the cost to the employer. Representations have been made concerning airline travel and railway employees.... It was never intended that the benefit received by the airline employee would be the fare paid by the ordinary passenger. The benefit to him would never be as high as that, because of certain disadvantages that the employee has. Similar considerations, although of a different kind, apply to railway employees. I have had many interviews, discussions and meetings on this matter and I have decided to withdraw Clause 54(4). I thought I would mention this at the outset because so many details, which would normally be left until we reached that particular stage, will be discussed with earlier parts of the legislation. I shall give some reasons which weigh heavily in favour of the withdrawal of this provision. The first is the large difference between the cost of providing some services and the amount of benefit which under the Bill would be held to be received. There are a number of cases of this kind, and I would point out that air and rail journeys are only two of a number of service benefits which have a number of problems attached to them. But there is a large difference between the cost of the benefit to the employer and the value of that benefit as assessed. It could lead to unjustifiable situations resulting in a great number of injustices and I do not think we should continue with it. . . .

"The second reason for withdrawing Clause 54(4) is that these services would tend to be much less used. The problem would then arise for those who had advocated the continuation of this legislation that neither the employer nor the employee nor the Revenue would benefit from the lesser use of these services. This factor also weighed with me. The third reason is the difficulty of enforcement and administration which both give rise to certain problems. Finally, it was possible to withdraw this part of the legislation as the services cover not only a more difficult area, but a quite distinct area of these provisions, without having repercussions on some of the other areas. . . .

"A member: I, too, have talked to many airline employees about this matter, and I am not completely clear as to the purport of my Hon. Friend's remarks. Is he saying that these benefits will remain taxable but that the equivalent cost of the benefit will be calculated on some different basis? Or is he saying that these benefits will not be taxable at all?

"Financial Secretary: The existing law which applies to the taxation of some of these benefits will be retained. The position will subsequently be unchanged from what it is now before the introduction of this legislation."

[His Lordship quoted several further references where the Financial Secretary insisted that the government's intent was not to change the tax treatment previously afforded to railway and airline employees; they would and should be allowed to receive free travel and be assessed only for the extra cost to the employer.]

Simultaneously with the announcement to the standing committee, a press release was issued announcing the withdrawal of clause 54(4). It referred to the same matters as the Financial Secretary had stated to the Committee and concluded:

"The effect of deleting this subclause will be to continue the present basis of taxation of services, namely the cost to the employer of providing the service."

The point was further debated in committee on 22 June 1976. A member is reported as saying, at column 1013, that

> "Like many others, I welcome the concession that has been made to leave out the airline staff and the railway employees and all the others that are left out by the dropping of clause 54(4)."

Another member, after referring to the particular reference in the Financial Secretary's statement to airline and railway employees, asked (at col 1023) whether the same distinction applied to services provided by hotel companies to their employees—that is, to rooms which are freely available for the general public in hotels being offered at a concessionary rate to employees of the hotel group. In response, the Financial Secretary said (at col 1024) of the position of such employees:

> "The position is, as he probably expected, the same as that which, following my announcement last week about the withdrawal of Clause 54(4), applies to other employees in service industries; the benefit is the cost to the employer. It is a good illustration of one of the reasons why I withdrew this subsection, in that the cost to the employer in this instance could be much less than the arm's length cost to the outside person taking advantage of such a service." (Column 1024.)
> * * *

The very question which is the subject matter of the present appeal was also raised. A member said, at columns 1091–1092:

> "I should be grateful for the Financial Secretary's guidance on these two points.... The second matter applies particularly to private sector, fee-paying schools where, as the Financial Secretary knows, there is often an arrangement for the children of staff in these schools to be taught at less than the commercial fee in other schools. I take it that because of the deletion of Clause 54(4) that is not now caught. Perhaps these examples will help to clarify the extent to which the Government amendment goes."

The Financial Secretary responded to this question as follows:

> "He mentioned the children of teachers. The removal of clause 54(4) will affect the position of a child of one of the teachers at the child's school, because now the benefit will be assessed on the cost to the employer, which would be very small indeed in this case." (Column 1098.)

Thereafter, clause 54 was not the subject of further debate and passed into law as it now stands as section 63 of the Act. * * *

Under present law, there is a general rule that reference to Parliamentary material as an aid to statutory construction is not permissible ("the exclusionary rule") * * *. The exclusionary rule was probably first stated by Willes J. in *Millar v. Taylor* (1769) 4 Burr. 2303, 2332. [Lord Browne–Wilkinson provided a brief history of the exclusionary rule and possible loopholes as well as criticisms that developed over time.]

My Lords, I have come to the conclusion that, as a matter of law, there are sound reasons for making a limited modification to the existing rule (subject to strict safeguards) unless there are constitutional or practical reasons which outweigh them. In my judgment, subject to the questions of the privileges of the House of Commons, reference to Parliamentary material should be permitted as an aid to the construction of legislation which is ambiguous or obscure or the literal meaning of which leads to an absurdity. Even in such cases references in court to Parliamentary material should only be permitted where such material clearly discloses the mischief aimed at or the legislative intention lying behind the ambiguous or obscure words. In the case of statements made in Parliament, as at present advised I cannot foresee that any statement other than the statement of the minister or other promoter of the Bill is likely to meet these criteria.

I accept Mr. Lester's submissions [for the taxpayers], but my main reason for reaching this conclusion is based on principle. Statute law consists of the words that Parliament has enacted. It is for the courts to construe those words and it is the court's duty in so doing to give effect to the intention of Parliament in using those words. It is an inescapable fact that, despite all the care taken in passing legislation, some statutory provisions when applied to the circumstances under consideration in any specific case are found to be ambiguous. One of the reasons for such ambiguity is that the members of the legislature in enacting the statutory provision may have been told what result those words are intended to achieve. Faced with a given set of words which are capable of conveying that meaning it is not surprising if the words are accepted as having that meaning. Parliament never intends to enact an ambiguity. Contrast with that the position of the courts. The courts are faced simply with a set of words which are in fact capable of bearing two meanings. The courts are ignorant of the underlying Parliamentary purpose. Unless something in other parts of the legislation discloses such purpose, the courts are forced to adopt one of the two possible meanings using highly technical rules of construction. In many, I suspect most, cases references to Parliamentary materials will not throw any light on the matter. But in a few cases it may emerge that the very question was considered by Parliament in passing the legislation. Why in such a case should the courts blind themselves to a clear indication of what Parliament intended in using those words? The court cannot attach a meaning to words which they cannot bear, but if the words are capable of bearing more than one meaning why should not Parliament's true intention be enforced rather than thwarted?

A number of other factors support this view. As I have said, the courts can now look at white papers and official reports for the purpose of finding the "mischief" sought to be corrected, although not at draft clauses or proposals for the remedying of such mischief. A ministerial statement made in Parliament is an equally authoritative source of such information: why should the courts be cut off from this source of information as to the mischief aimed at? In any event, the distinction between looking at reports to identify the mischief aimed at but not to find the intention of Parliament in enacting the legislation is highly artificial. Take the normal Law Commission Report which analyses the problem and then annexes a draft Bill to remedy it. It is now permissible to look at the report to find the mischief and at the draft Bill to see that a provision in the draft was *not* included in the legislation enacted. There can be no logical distinction between that case and looking at the draft Bill to see that the statute as enacted reproduced, often in the same words, the provision in the Law Commission's draft. Given the purposive approach to construction now adopted by the courts in order to give effect to the true intentions of the legislature, the fine distinctions between looking for the mischief and looking for the intention in using words to provide the remedy are technical and inappropriate. Clear and unambiguous statements made by ministers in Parliament are as much the background to the enactment of legislation as white papers and Parliamentary reports.

The decision in *Pickstone v. Freemans Plc.* [1989] A.C. 66 which authorises the court to look at ministerial statements made in introducing regulations which could not be amended by Parliament is logically indistinguishable from such statements made in introducing a statutory provision which, though capable of amendment, was not in fact amended. * * *

Text books often include reference to explanations of legislation given by a minister in Parliament, as a result of which lawyers advise their clients taking account of such statements and judges when construing the legislation come to know of them. In addition, a number of distinguished judges have admitted to breaching the exclusionary rule and looking at Hansard in order to seek the intention of Parliament. When this happens, the parties do not know and have no opportunity to address the judge on the matter. A vivid example of this occurred in the *Hadmor* case [1983] 1 A.C. 191 where Lord Denning in the Court of Appeal relied on his own researches into Hansard in reaching his conclusions: in the House of Lords, counsel protested that there were other passages to which he would have wished to draw the court's attention had he known that Lord Denning was looking at Hansard: see the *Hadmor* case at p. 233. It cannot be right for such information to be available, by a sidewind, for the court but the parties be prevented from presenting their arguments on such material. * * *

It is said that Parliamentary materials are not readily available to, and understandable by, the citizen and his lawyers who should be entitled to rely on the words of Parliament alone to discover his position. It is undoubtedly true that Hansard and particularly records of Committee debates are not widely held by libraries outside London and that the lack of satisfactory indexing of Committee stages makes it difficult to trace the passage of a clause after it is redrafted or renumbered. But such practical difficulties can easily be overstated. It is possible to obtain Parliamentary materials and it is possible to trace the history. The problem is one of expense and effort in doing so, not the availability of the material. In considering the right of the individual to know the law by simply looking at legislation, it is a fallacy to start from the position that all legislation is available in a readily understandable form in any event: the very large number of statutory instruments made every year are not available in an indexed form for well over a year after they have been passed. Yet, the practitioner manages to deal with the problem albeit at considerable expense. Moreover, experience in New Zealand and Australia (where the strict rule has been relaxed for some years) has not shown that the non-availability of materials has raised these practical problems.

Next, it is said that lawyers and judges are not familiar with Parliamentary procedures and will therefore have difficulty in giving proper weight to the Parliamentary materials. Although, of course, lawyers do not have the same experience of these matters as members of the legislature, they are not wholly ignorant of them. If, as I think, significance should only be attached to the clear statements made by a minister or other promoter of the Bill, the difficulty of knowing what weight to attach to such statements is not overwhelming. In the present case, there were numerous statements of view by members in the course of the debate which plainly do not throw any light on the true construction of section 63. What is persuasive in this case is a consistent series of answers given by the minister, after opportunities for taking advice from his officials, all of which point the same way and which were not withdrawn or varied prior to the enactment of the Bill.

Then it is said that court time will be taken up by considering a mass of Parliamentary material and long arguments about its significance, thereby increasing the expense of litigation. In my judgment, though the introduction of further admissible material will inevitably involve some increase in the use of time, this will not be significant as long as courts insist that Parliamentary material should only be introduced in the limited cases I have mentioned and where such material contains a clear indication from the minister of the mischief aimed at, or the nature of the cure intended, by the legislation. Attempts to introduce material which does not satisfy those tests should be met by orders for costs made against those who have improperly introduced the material. Experience in the United States of America, where legislative history has for many years been much more generally admissible than I am now suggesting, shows how important it is to maintain strict control over the use of such material. That position is to be contrasted with what has happened in New Zealand and Australia (which have relaxed the rule to approximately the extent that I favour): there is no evidence of any complaints of this nature coming from those countries.

There is one further practical objection which, in my view, has real substance. If the rule is relaxed legal advisers faced with an ambiguous statutory provision may feel that they have to research the materials to see whether they yield the crock of gold, i.e., a clear indication of Parliament's intentions. In very many cases the crock of gold will not be discovered and the expenditure on the research wasted. This is a real objection to changing the rule. However, again it is easy to overestimate the cost of such research: if a reading of Hansard shows that there is nothing of significance said by the minister in relation to the clause in question, further research will become pointless.

In sum, I do not think that the practical difficulties arising from a limited relaxation of the rule are sufficient to outweigh the basic need for the courts to give effect to the words enacted by Parliament in the sense that they were intended by Parliament to bear. Courts are frequently criticised for their failure to do that. This failure is due not to cussedness but to ignorance of what Parliament intended by the obscure words of the legislation. The courts should not deny themselves the light which Parliamentary materials may shed on the meaning of the words Parliament has used and thereby risk subjecting the individual to a law which Parliament never intended to enact.

[The last section of his Lordship's opinion discussed the "constitutional" issue whether adverting to Hansard is a "questioning" of the freedom of parliamentary speech and debate that is prohibited by article 9 of the Bill of Rights of 1688. His Lordship interpreted article 9 much like the U.S. Constitution's Speech and Debate Clause (see Chapter 3, § 2) and found it inapplicable.]

The Attorney General raised a further constitutional point, namely, that for the court to use Parliamentary material in construing legislation would be to confuse the respective roles of Parliament as the maker of law and the courts as the interpreter. I am not impressed by this argument. The law, as I have said, is to be found in the words in which Parliament has enacted. It is for the courts to interpret those words so as to give effect to that purpose. The question is whether, in addition to other aids to the construction of statutory words, the courts should have regard to a further source. Recourse is already had to white papers and official reports not because they determine the meaning of the statutory words but because they assist the court to make its own determination. I can see no constitutional impropriety in this. * * *

I therefore reach the conclusion, subject to any question of Parliamentary privilege, that the exclusionary rule should be relaxed so as to permit reference to Parliamentary materials where:

(a) legislation is ambiguous or obscure, or leads to an absurdity;

(b) the material relied on consists of one or more statements by a minister or other promoter of the Bill together if necessary with such other Parliamentary material as is necessary to understand such statements and their effect;

(c) the statements relied on are clear.

[In the present case, the statute was ambiguous and the Hansard materials clearly resolved the ambiguity in favor of the taxpayers.]

The question then arises whether it is right to attribute to Parliament as a whole the same intention as that repeatedly voiced by the Financial Secretary. In my judgment it is. It is clear from reading Hansard that the committee was repeatedly asking for guidance as to the effect of the legislation once subclause (4) of clause 54 was abandoned. That Parliament relied on the ministerial statements is shown by the fact that the matter was never raised again after the discussions in committee, that amendments were consequentially withdrawn and that no relevant amendment was made which could affect the correctness of the minister's statement. * * *

Having once looked at what was said in Parliament, it is difficult to put it out of mind. I have the advantage that, after the first hearing and before seeing the Parliamentary materials, I had reached the conclusion, in agreement with Vinelott J. and the Court of Appeal, that the Revenue's submissions were correct. If it is not permissible to take into account what was said by the Financial Secretary, I remain of the same view. * * *

Notes on Pepper and the Demise of the Exclusionary Rule

1. *The Abandonment of the Exclusionary Rule in English–Speaking Countries.* In the United Kingdom, *Pepper v. Hart* created quite a stir, and unleashed a fair amount of interest in legislative history by lower courts and, to a lesser extent, the House of Lords. An excellent survey by James J. Brudney, *The Story of* Pepper v. Hart: *Examining Legislative History Across the Pond,* in *Statutory Interpretation Stories* 258, 285–90 (Eskridge, Frickey & Garrett eds. 2011), demonstrates that much of the Lords' reliance on Hansard cites to minister (floor manager) explanations and *not* to committee reports, which are not routinely generated in Parliament. On the other hand, Professor Brudney found that during the post-*Pepper* period, the Lords have greatly increased their references to government white papers and commission reports, background documents with some similarity to our committee reports. *Id.* at 279–85. In short, the Lords are explicitly considering a lot more background materials than they did twenty years ago.

Although the Law Lords remain divided over the wisdom of *Pepper*, a majority of them are committed to this new course of action, within limits that have yet to be determined once and for all.[p] In *Regina (Jackson) v. Attorney General*, [2005] H.L. 56, [2005] All E.R. 1253, for example, the Lords unanimously upheld the famous Hunting Act, which deployed a 1911 statute to override House of Lords opposition to a popular measure. Lord Bingham's lead opinion rejected the relevance of Hansard as authoritative evidence of parliamentary "intent" but relied on the debates (including eight rejected proposals) to confirm the meaning of words Parliament used in the 1911 statute. Lord Nicholls's speech relied even more extensively on Hansard, as confirmation of what he and the other Lords considered the apparent mean-

---

p. For example, Lord Millett, *Construing Statutes*, 20 Stat. L. Rev. 107 (1999), maintained that *Pepper* was a mistake and that the Lords should return to their previous practice of relying exclusively on statutory text. Lord Hoffmann praised *Pepper* for opening up probative evidence of legislative intent (and for discouraging government ministers from making promises to Parliament that they might later renounce) but was skeptical that the costs of extra research were worth these benefits. *The Intolerable Wrestle With Words and Meanings*, 114 S. Afr. L.J. 656, 669 (1997); see also *Robinson v. Secretary of State for Northern Ireland*, [2002] H.L. 32, 20–41, [2002] All E.R.(D) 364 (Lord Hoffmann, repeating his lament that *Pepper* generated large research costs, with scant benefit).

ing of the text. Lord Steyn objected to any use of Hansard in these circumstances.

The House of Lords' decision has had echoes throughout the Commonwealth countries. The leading Canadian treatise states: "Since the 1980s the [exclusionary] rule has been eroding at a rapid rate. Some courts have ignored it while other courts have carved out significant exceptions and qualifications. * * * The exclusionary rule in its traditional form is clearly dead." *Driedger* 486. See also David Duff, *Interpreting the Income Tax Act*, 47 Can. Tax. J. 471 & 741 (1999) (two-part article on use of legislative history in tax cases). The exclusionary rule had previously been abandoned in the United States, see *Holy Trinity Church v. United States* (Chapter 2, § 1); Australia, see Commonwealth Acts Interpretation Act § 15AB; and other Commonwealth countries. Many civil-law countries still follow such a rule or practice, however.

2. *When Should Legislative Materials Be Admissible? The Potato Chip Problem.* The key opinion is that of Lord Browne–Wilkinson, who admits legislative materials, but only in limited circumstances. But how should we characterize the holding of the case? This is more difficult than appears on first glance.

(a) *Sponsor Statements May Be Consulted When the Statute Is Ambiguous.* This appears to be the holding as articulated by Lord Browne–Wilkinson, and the U.S. Supreme Court sometimes says it follows a similar rule. See, e.g., *Director, OWCP v. Greenwich Collieries*, 512 U.S. 267 (1994). But does this precept explain the decision in this case? The first committee of Law Lords found the statute unambiguous against the taxpayer; on the original panel, only Lord Griffith found ambiguity. Lord Chancellor Mackay found ambiguity on rehearing and voted for the taxpayer on that ground, but only Lord Griffith agreed with him. Other Lords, including Browne–Wilkinson, found ambiguity only after they consulted the Hansard materials.

(b) *Hansard Materials May Be Consulted to Confirm Statutory Plain Meaning.* The narrowest interpretation of *Pepper*, embraced by Lord Steyn and others, is that Hansard materials can only be introduced for textualist reasons, namely, to suggest or confirm standard usage of statutory terms and the plain meaning they have to reasonable speakers of the English language.

(c) *Hansard May Be Invoked to Clear Up Any Statutory Matters.* In the aftermath of *Pepper*, some Law Lords used the decision as a Magna Carta for browsing parliamentary debates for what they were worth, essentially ignoring Lord Browne–Wilkinson's suggested limits. See David Miers, *Taxing Perks and Interpreting Statutes:* Pepper v. Hart, 56 Mod. L. Rev. 695, 705–06 (1993). Few Lords in the new millennium openly endorse this position, and there are procedural hurdles in place,[q] but there is some indication that some lower court judges are running wild with legislative materials. Should this have been expected?

---

q. The Lords directed that financial sanctions would be visited upon a party who relied on Hansard in a case that did not meet the three requirements of Lord Browne–Wilkinson's opinion. Also, the Lords issued a Practice Directive in 1994 (reaffirmed in 1999 and 2002) which required parties intending to invoke Hansard to give prior notice, including copies of the pages in Hansard and the argument to be made from it. Brudney, *Story of* Pepper v. Hart, *supra.*

Aside from the precise limits suggested in this case, consider a *potato chip theory*, suggested by the U.S. history after *Holy Trinity*: once a court starts looking at the "best" legislative history, like committee reports and sponsor statements, other kinds of history will get smuggled in, on the ground that they provide "context" for understanding the committee reports (which of course provide "context" for understanding the text). Before long, everything becomes relevant and might be considered "for what it is worth" (the trend in modern evidence law, by the way). Just as you can never eat just one potato chip, you can never admit just one bit of legislative history. It might take decades for the potato chip process to develop, but the theory is that Hansard reliance will grow by fits and starts until there is some kind of crisis that pushes in the other direction.

3. *Relevance for the U.S. Debate?* Should *Pepper* suggest to the new textualists that they should adopt a more moderate skepticism about legislative materials?[r] If you were Justice Scalia, how would you have voted in *Pepper*? (Hint: Consider the *evolution* of the treatment of in-house benefits, from 1948 to 1993, nicely laid out in Lord Browne–Wilkinson's opinion. You can be a textualist and consider the formal evolution of the statutory scheme, as the U.S. Supreme Court did in *Leo Sheep*. What argument might a textualist draw from that?)

Professor Brudney argues that the U.S. Supreme Court should conclude from the Mother Country's post-*Pepper* practice that the most fruitful debates focus not on the tired admissibility debate, but rather on the circumstances under which legislative history would be useful. "[S]hould legislative history be regarded as presumptively more valuable to help resolve textual ambiguities that stem from lack of foresight rather than lack of political consensus? Is legislative history accompanying omnibus bills generally less suitable for judicial use because congressional deals on such a grand scale are simply indecipherable? Should legislative history in certain subject areas be presumed to have less weight where the law is administered primarily by a federal agency rather than private parties, or where the statutory text tends to be detailed and technical rather than open-ended and of more general public interest?" James J. Brudney, *Below the Surface: Comparative Legislative History Usage by the Law Lords and the Supreme Court*, 85 Wash. U.L. Rev. 1 (2007). Apply these questions to the next case.

NOTE ON STATE COURT RELIANCE ON SPONSOR'S STATEMENTS

Like the U.K. House of Lords, and unlike the U.S. Supreme Court, state supreme courts in this country rely more heavily on the statements of legislative sponsors than on committee or bill reports as the sources for illumination about legislative expectations. A large majority of states make available to the public transcripts of legislative floor debates and of committee hearings. Much of the floor debate consists of statements by the sponsor or floor manager presenting the case for the proposed legislation, responding to objections made by opponents, and answering questions posed by colleagues.

---

r. This is the judgment offered by Brudney, *Story of* Pepper, *supra*, who argues that legislative history should be freely *admissible*, and objections should go to the *weight* attached to it.

Committee chairs (who are usually later the floor managers) play a large role in committee hearings, making speeches, questioning witnesses, and explaining proposed legislation. Because the sponsor/floor manager is usually the most knowledgeable legislator on topics relating to the proposed legislation and usually represents the coalition pushing for the legislation, his or her statements are much more probative than those of other legislators. Recall, for example, the Oregon Court of Appeals decision in *PGE* (Chapter 2, § 3C), where the dissenting judges relied on the explanation by the committee chair.

For examples of recent state supreme court decisions relying on statements by legislative sponsors or floor managers, see *State v. Batts*, 195 P.3d 144, 151–52 (**Alaska** App. 2008) (finding sponsor's explanation as critical evidence of statutory meaning); *Carter v. California Dep't of Veterans Affairs*, 135 P.3d 637, 646–47 (**Cal.** 2006) (treating sponsor's memo as authoritative but finding that it does not answer the issue before the court); *CLPF–Parkridge One, L.P. v. Harwell Invs, Inc.*, 105 P.3d 658, 664–65 (**Colo.** 2005) (relying entirely on legislative history to interpret law); *People v. Collins*, 824 N.E.2d 262, 267 (**Ill.** 2005); *State v. Allen*, 708 N.W.2d 361, 366–67 (**Iowa** 2006); *Rural Water Dist. #2 v. City of Louisburg*, 207 P.3d 1055 (**Kan.** 2009) (invoking post-enactment letter from sponsor to support plain meaning); *Stockman Bank of Mont. v. Mon–Kota, Inc.*, 180 P.3d 1125 (**Mont.** 2008); *Chanos v. Nevada Tax Comm'n*, 181 P.3d 675, 680 & n.17 (**Nev.** 2008); *State v. Mayes*, 186 P.3d 293, 297–98 (**Or.** App. 2008) (relying on evidence from drafter as well as sponsor); *Stewart Title Guar. Co. v. State Tax Assessor*, 963 A.2d 169, 178–79 (**Me.** 2009) (resolving ambiguity by reference to statutory history as explained by sponsor); *Kramer v. Liberty Prop. Trust*, 968 A.2d 120 (**Md.** 2009) (sponsor's statement confirms plain meaning); *Commonwealth v. Ahlborn*, 626 A.2d 1265 (**Pa.** 1993); *Lawrence County Educ. Ass'n v. Lawrence County Bd. of Educ.*, 244 S.W.3d 302, 312 (**Tenn.** 2007); *Department of Corrections v. Human Rights Comm'n*, 917 A.2d 451, 453 (**Vt.** 2006).

Like the U.S. Supreme Court, state supreme courts will not credit stray statements by legislators who are probably not speaking for the enacting coalition. See, e.g., *Wright v. Home Depot U.S.A., Inc.*, 142 P.3d 265, 275 n.8 (**Haw.** 2006). Likewise, state courts (like federal courts) will not credit post-hoc affidavits by the sponsors or floor managers of enacted bills, because the post-hoc nature of such evidence deprives it of reliability. Efforts to invoke after-the-fact legislator affidavits often occur (and are usually rebuffed) in states where there is not (at the time) much publicly available legislative material. See, e.g., *Tomei v. Sharp*, 902 A.2d 757, 769 n.41 (**Del.** Super. 2006); *Utility Center, Inc. v. City of Fort Wayne*, 868 N.E.2d 453, 459–60 (**Ind.** 2007); *DIRECTV, Inc. v. Levin*, 907 N.E.2d 1242, 1253 (**Ohio** App. 2009); *LaPlante v. Honda North Am., Inc.*, 697 A.2d 625, 628–29 (**R.I.** 1997); *Kennedy v. South Carolina Ret. Sys.*, 549 S.E.2d 243, 247 & n.4, 250–51 (**S.C.** 2001); *Phillips v. Larry's Drive–In Pharmacy, Inc.*, 647 S.E.2d 920, 924–26 (**W.Va.** 2007).

KOSAK v. UNITED STATES

Supreme Court of the United States, 1984
465 U.S. 848, 104 S.Ct. 1519, 79 L.Ed.2d 860

JUSTICE MARSHALL delivered the opinion of the Court.

[While a serviceman stationed in Guam, Kosak assembled a large collection of art. When he was transferred from Guam to Philadelphia, he brought his art collection with him. He was subsequently charged with smuggling the collection into this country, but he was acquitted by a jury. The Customs Service then notified Kosak that the seized objects were subject to civil forfeiture under 19 U.S.C. § 1592 (1976), which at the time permitted confiscation of goods brought into the United States "by means of any false statement." Although the Customs Service returned the art, Kosak claimed that some of the objects were damaged and filed suit for $12,000 pursuant to the Federal Tort Claims Act, 28 U.S.C. §§ 1346(b), 2671–2680.]

The Federal Tort Claims Act, enacted in 1946, provides generally that the United States shall be liable, to the same extent as a private party, "for injury or loss of property, or personal injury or death caused by the negligent or wrongful act or omission of any employee of the Government while acting within the scope of his office or employment." 28 U.S.C. § 1346(b); see also 28 U.S.C. § 2674. The Act's broad waiver of sovereign immunity is, however, subject to 13 enumerated exceptions. 28 U.S.C. §§ 2680(a)–(f), (h)–(n). One of those exceptions, § 2680(c), exempts from the coverage of the statute "[a]ny claim arising in respect of * * * the detention of any goods or merchandise by any officer of customs * * *."[6] Petitioner asks us to construe the foregoing language to cover only claims "for damage caused by the detention itself and not for the negligent * * * destruction of property while it is in the possession of the customs service." By "damage caused by the detention itself," petitioner appears to mean harms attributable to an illegal detention, such as a decline in the economic value of detained goods (either because of depreciation or because of a drop in the price the goods will fetch), injury resulting from deprivation of the ability to make use of the goods during the period of detention, or consequential damages resulting from lack of access to the goods. The Government asks us to read the exception to cover all injuries to property sustained during its detention by customs officials.

The starting point of our analysis of these competing interpretations must, of course, be the language of § 2680(c). * * * At first blush, the

---

6. The full text of § 2680(c) provides:

"The provisions of [28 U.S.C. §§ 2671–2679] and § 1346(b) of this title shall not apply to—
* * *

(c) Any claim arising in respect of the assessment or collection of any tax or customs duty, or the detention of any goods or merchandise by any officer of customs or excise or any other law-enforcement officer."

We have no occasion in this case to decide what kinds of "law-enforcement officer[s]," other than customs officials, are covered by the exception.

statutory language certainly appears expansive enough to support the Government's construction; the encompassing phrase, "arising in respect of," seems to sweep within the exception all injuries associated in any way with the "detention" of goods. It must be admitted that this initial reading is not ineluctable; as Judge Weis, dissenting in the Court of Appeals, pointed out, it is possible (with some effort) to read the phrase "in respect of" as the equivalent of "as regards" and thereby to infer that "the statutory exception is directed to the fact of detention itself, and that alone." But we think that the fairest interpretation of the crucial portion of the provision is the one that first springs to mind: "any claim arising in respect of" the detention of goods means any claim "arising out of" the detention of goods, and includes a claim resulting from negligent handling or storage of detained property. * * *

The legislative history of § 2680(c), though meager, supports the interpretation of the provision that we have derived from its language and context. Two specific aspects of the evolution of the provision are telling. First, the person who almost certainly drafted the language under consideration clearly thought that it covered injury to detained property caused by the negligence of customs officials. It appears that the portion of § 2680(c) pertaining to the detention of goods was first written by Judge Alexander Holtzoff, one of the major figures in the development of the Tort Claims Act. In his Report explicating his proposals, Judge Holtzoff explained:

> "[The proposed provision would exempt from the coverage of the Act] [c]laims arising in respect of the assessment or collection of any tax or customs duty. This exception appears in all previous drafts. It is expanded, however, so as to include immunity from liability in respect of *loss in connection with the detention of goods or merchandise* by any officer of customs or excise. The additional proviso has special reference to the detention of imported goods in appraisers' warehouses or customs houses, as well as seizures by law enforcement officials, internal revenue officers, and the like." A. Holtzoff, Report on Proposed Federal Tort Claims Bill 16 (1931) (Holtzoff Report) (emphasis added).[12]

Though it cannot be definitively established that Congress relied upon Judge Holtzoff's report, it is significant that the apparent draftsman of the crucial portion of § 2680(c) believed that it would bar a suit of the sort brought by petitioner.[13]

---

12. Judge Holtzoff went on to explain that "[t]his provision is suggested in the proposed draft of the bill submitted by the Crown Proceedings Committee in England in 1927 * * *." Holtzoff Report at 16. The relevant portion of the bill to which Holtzoff referred was even more explicit:

"No proceedings shall lie under this section—* * *

(c) for or in respect of the loss of or any deterioration or damage occasioned to, or any delay in the release of, any goods or merchandise by reason of anything done or omitted to be done by any officer of customs and excise acting as such * * *."

Report of Crown Proceedings Committee § 11(5)(c), pp. 17–18 (Apr. 1927). (It appears that this bill was never enacted into law in England.)

13. Mr. Holtzoff wrote his report while serving as Special Assistant to the Attorney General. He had been "assigned by Attorney General Mitchell to the special task of co-ordinating the views

Second, the Congressional committees that submitted Reports on the various bills that ultimately became the Tort Claims Act suggested that the provision that was to become § 2680(c), like the other exceptions from the waiver of sovereign immunity, covered claims "arising out of" the designated conduct. Thus, for example, the House Judiciary Committee described the proposed exceptions as follows:

> "These exemptions cover claims arising out of the loss or miscarriage of postal matter; the assessment or collection of taxes or assessments; the detention of goods by customs officers; admiralty and maritime torts; deliberate torts such as assault and battery; and others." H.R. Rep. No. 1287, 79th Cong., 1st Sess., 6 (1945).

The Committees' casual use of the words, "arising out of," with reference to the exemption of claims pertaining to the detention of goods substantially undermines petitioner's contention that the phrase, "in respect of," was designed to limit the sorts of suits covered by the provision.

[Justice Marshall further concluded that this interpretation accords with the purposes of the statute: ensuring that certain governmental activities not be disrupted by the threat of damage suits; avoiding exposure for fraudulent or excessive claims; and not extending the coverage of the Act to suits for which adequate remedies were already available. Allowing suits against the government in cases such as this one might impair the efficiency of Customs' operations, reasoned Justice Marshall. Additionally, even at common law property owners had (and retain) a right to sue individual customs officers who damage their goods.]

Petitioner and some commentators argue that § 2680(c) should not be construed in a fashion that denies an effectual remedy to many persons whose property is damaged through the tortious conduct of customs officials. That contention has force, but it is properly addressed to Congress, not to this Court. The language of the statute as it was written leaves us no choice but to affirm the judgment of the Court of Appeals that the Tort Claims Act does not cover suits alleging that customs officials injured property that had been detained by the Customs Service.

Justice Stevens, dissenting.

The Government's construction of 28 U.S.C. § 2680(c) is not the one that "first springs" to my mind. Rather, I read the exception for claims arising "in respect of * * * the detention of any goods" as expressing Congress' intent to preclude liability attributable to the temporary inter-

---

of the Government departments" regarding the proper scope of a tort claims statute. See Borchard, *The Federal Tort Claims Bill*, 1 U.Chi.L.Rev. 1, n. 2 (1933). Holtzoff submitted his report, in which his draft bill was contained, to Assistant Attorney General Rugg, who in turn transmitted it to the General Accounting Office of the Comptroller General. Insofar as Holtzoff's report embodied the views of the Executive Department at that stage of the debates over the tort claims bill, it is likely that, at some point, the report was brought to the attention of the Congressmen considering the bill. We agree with the dissent that, because the report was never introduced into the public record, the ideas expressed therein should not be given great weight in determining the intent of the legislature. But, in the absence of any direct evidence regarding how members of Congress understood the provision that became § 2680(c), it seems to us senseless to ignore entirely the views of its draftsman.

ference with the owner's possession of his goods, as opposed to liability for physical damage to his goods. That seems to me to be the normal reading of the statutory language that Congress employed, and the one that most Members of Congress voting on the proposal would have given it. Moreover, my reading, unlike the Court's, is supported by an examination of the language used in other exceptions. Congress did not use the words "arising out of" in § 2680(c) but did use those words in three other subsections of the same section of the Act. See §§ 2680(b), (e) and (h). Absent persuasive evidence to the contrary, we should assume that when Congress uses different language in a series of similar provisions, it intends to express a different intention. * * *

In the entire 15 year history preceding the enactment of the Tort Claims Act in 1946, the Court finds only two "clues" that it believes shed any light on the meaning of § 2680(c). The first—the so-called "Holtzoff Report"—is nothing but an internal Justice Department working paper prepared in 1931 and never even mentioned in the legislative history of the 1946 Act. There is no indication that any Congressman ever heard of the document or knew that it even existed. The position of the majority— that it is "significant" that the "apparent draftsman" of the relevant language himself "believed that it would bar a suit of the sort brought by petitioner"—is manifestly ill-advised. The intent of a lobbyist—no matter how public spirited he may have been—should not be attributed to the Congress without positive evidence that elected legislators were aware of and shared the lobbyist's intent.

Unless we know more about the collective legislative purpose than can be gleaned from an internal document prepared by a person who was seeking legislative action, we should be guided by the sensible statement that "in construing a statute * * * the worst person to construe it is the person who is responsible for its drafting. He is very much disposed to confuse what he intended to do with the effect of the language which in fact has been employed." *Hilder v. Dexter*, [1902] A.C. 474, 477 (Halsbury, L.C., abstaining).[2] If the draftsman of the language in question intended it to cover such cases as this one, he failed.

---

2. The majority's analysis, it should be observed, puts the cart before the horse.

"The essence of bill drafting is placing a legislative proposal in the proper legal phraseology and form to achieve congressional intent. It is primarily a task of legal analysis and research rather than of composition * * *. Framing the legal language to embody congressional purpose is not as difficult as ascertaining what that purpose is in its entirety. While a committee (or an individual member of Congress, as the case may be) is in the process of working out what it wants to do, the legislative counsel assist it by explaining the effect of alternative proposals. Even after the committee (or Congressman) has settled upon the major outlines of a measure, subsidiary policy questions seem to unfold endlessly. The legislative counsel must point up all of those for the committee (or Congressman) to decide. To accomplish that, the legislative counsel must envisage the broad application of the proposed law in all of its ramifications." K. Kofmehl, Professional Staffs of Congress 189 (3d ed. 1977) (footnote omitted).

Many bills are of course initially drafted in the Executive Branch. After today's decision, we can anticipate executive agencies searching long dormant files for documents similar to the Holtzoff Report. We can also anticipate that private parties will attempt to capitalize on this new reservoir of "legislative" history as well, through discovery and perhaps the Freedom of Information Act. In light of the Government's reliance on the Holtzoff Report, presumably it will not assert that this kind of material is privileged when private parties are in search of "legislative" intent.

The second "clue" relied upon by the majority consists of a brief summary in the House Committee Report which casually uses the prepositional phrase "arising out of" to introduce a truncated list of the exceptions. But the "casual" use of the latter phrase in the Committee Report is as understandable as it is insignificant. It is nothing more than an introduction. In such an introduction, precision of meaning is naturally and knowingly sacrificed in the interest of brevity. * * *

NOTES ON *KOSAK* AND THE VIEWS OF *NONLEGISLATOR DRAFTERS*

1. *Statements of Nonlegislative Drafters.* The majority opinion in *Kosak* realistically recognizes that much legislation is drafted by nonlegislators—executive officials and interest groups, mainly. But why should the views of a nonlegislator count—especially if the Court deems its inquiry as a search for the "intent" of *Congress*? Moreover, Holtzoff's memorandum was not "public." Distinguish between the testimony at congressional hearings by Holtzoff, in which Members of Congress could disagree with him (either then or during subsequent floor debate),[s] and his Department of Justice memorandum, which was written before the bill was acted upon even by a committee and which may have represented only his (and not even the Department's) point of view. Why should the latter be entitled to any consideration at all? Are there other ways of thinking about statutory interpretation which make Judge Holtzoff's statement relevant? (Hint: maybe, like a good commentary in a treatise or a law review article, it makes the most sense of the legislation.) See generally Alison Giles, Note, *The Value of Nonlegislators' Contributions to Legislative History*, 79 Geo. L.J. 359 (1991).

Notwithstanding these objections, the Supreme Court or individual Justices have occasionally relied on statements by public, nonlegislative officials who draft or promote statutes. See, e.g., *Circuit City Stores, Inc. v. Adams*, 532 U.S. 105, 128–29 (2001) (Stevens, J., dissenting) (relying on defense of statute by Secretary of Commerce, while majority does not address this argument because of the plain meaning rule); *Negonsott v. Samuels*, 507 U.S. 99, 106–09 (1993); *Gollust v. Mendell*, 501 U.S. 115, 125 & n.7 (1991); *Howe v. Smith*, 452 U.S. 473, 485 (1981); *Monroe v. Standard Oil Co.*, 452 U.S. 549, 558–59 (1981). Note, however, that (as in *Kosak*) the Court will not rely on these statements as the most probative—and certainly not the *only*—evidence of statutory meaning. There are very few state cases; almost all of them either reject or denigrate such evidence. E.g., *Hayes v. Continental Ins. Co.*, 872 P.2d 668 (Ariz. 1994).

2. *Statements of Private Drafters.* At least Holtzoff was a public servant. Should the Court consider authoritative the statements of interest groups which draft and press for legislation? In some instances the Court or some Justices have considered testimony about legislation by private groups or

---

Finally, the language in some bills is initially drafted by private lobbyists. One doubts that the majority would find "significant" the intention of such a draftsman when that intention was not shared with the Congress.

s. Ironically, when Holtzoff's public testimony was relevant to an issue of interpretation, the Court ignored it. Compare *Sheridan v. United States*, 487 U.S. 392 (1988) (opinion of the Court), with *id.* at 410 (O'Connor, J., dissenting).

individuals who drafted or commented on the legislation. See, e.g., *Circuit City Stores*, 532 U.S. at 127 (Stevens, J., dissenting) (relying on explanation by ABA committee that originated the statute); *Gustafson v. Alloyd Co.*, 513 U.S. 561 (1995) (relying on statement by Professor Landis, submitted as part of legislative deliberations, as support for Court's text-based interpretation); *Jefferson County Pharmaceutical Assoc. v. Abbott Labs*, 460 U.S. 150, 159–62 (1983) (relying upon explanation of lobbyist who was principal drafter of the statute in question); *NLRB v. Robbins Tire & Rubber Co.*, 437 U.S. 214, 230–32 (1978) (relying on explanation of ABA Administrative Law Division, which had originally proposed the statutory amendment in question during Senate hearings). See also *Group Life & Health Inc. Co. v. Royal Drug Co.*, 440 U.S. 205 (1979); *Southland Corp. v. Keating*, 465 U.S. 1, 26–29 (1984) (O'Connor, J., dissenting).

3. *The New Textualist Approach to* Kosak. Justice Stevens's dissent reflects a textualist approach to *Kosak*. Would Justice Scalia (not on the Court in 1984) agree with Stevens's interpretation? You might think so, except that Scalia recognizes a new super-strong clear statement rule presuming against waivers of federal sovereign immunity. See *United States v. Nordic Village, Inc.*, 503 U.S. 30 (1992) (opinion for the Court by Scalia, with Stevens in dissent). A corollary of that rule would be to construe waivers (such as the Federal Tort Claims Act) very narrowly or, correlatively, to construe reservations to such waivers (such as the § 2680 exceptions to the waiver) broadly. In that event, a new textualist could agree with the result reached by Justice Marshall.

Nordic Village reflects one of the criticisms of the new textualism: by removing or deemphasizing legislative history (created by and reflecting the norms of legislators), textualist judges put more emphasis on the famously malleable substantive canons of statutory construction (created by and reflecting the norms of judges). In *Matter of Interpretation* (1997), Justice Scalia defends the *Nordic Village* super-strong clear statement rule as reflecting the likely "intent" of most legislators. Yet the Justice cites no evidence for this belief, nor for the further proposition that legislators "intend" to make federal sovereign immunity (a common law concept perpetuated by judges like Scalia) as hard to rebut as the Court treated it in *Nordic Village*.

Part D.   Legislative Deliberation: Hearings, Floor Debate, Rejected Proposals, and Dogs That Do Not Bark

Compared to statements in committee reports, statements made during committee hearings and floor debates have traditionally received less weight in evaluating legislative intent. If the statement was made by a sponsor or informed supporter of the bill, courts might credit it as a reliable indication of legislative intent—as did the Supreme Court majority and dissenting opinions in *Weber* or as the House of Lords did in *Pepper v. Hart*. The conventional wisdom is that what is said in hearings and floor debates is usually of little value, except for confirmatory purposes. Reed Dickerson, *Statutory Interpretation: Dipping into Legislative History*, 11 Hofstra L. Rev. 1125, 1131–32 (1983).

Reflecting on the Burger Court's practice, Judge Wald, *Legislative History in the 1981 Term, supra*, at 202, opined that "[t]he hornbook rule that hearings are relevant only as background to show the purpose of the statute no longer holds. In many cases, the best explanation of what the legislation is about comes from the executive department or outside witnesses at the hearings." Indeed, since proposed legislation is frequently drafted by the executive department or by private interest groups, their statements and explanations at hearings might be the only truly informed explanation of the structure and operation of the statute. E.g., *Gustafson v. Alloyd Co.*, 513 U.S. 561 (1995) (testimony of academic expert commenting on interest group arguments made during congressional deliberations); *Lowe v. SEC*, 472 U.S. 181, 195–99 (1985) (testimony of industry witnesses at hearings); *Trbovich v. United Mine Workers of America*, 404 U.S. 528 (1972) (Senate hearing testimony by Senator John Kennedy, the sponsor, and Professor Archibald Cox, primary drafter of the proposed legislation). Now that many states record committee hearings, and still others provide staff summaries of statements made in them, state courts are coming to rely on statements made in those hearings.[t]

Potentially relevant for similar reasons are presidential statements initiating or issued during congressional deliberations, especially when the President has been a prime mover behind a piece of legislation, as he was with the Civil Rights Act of 1964 and the Voting Rights Act of 1965. Thus, presidential transmittal letters or speeches advocating legislation have sometimes been considered useful legislative history, e.g., *NLRB v. Local 103, Int'l Ass'n of Bridge Workers*, 434 U.S. 335, 347 n.9 (1978); *Connell Construction Co. v. Plumbers & Steamfitters Local 100*, 421 U.S. 616, 629 n.8 (1975); *Western Union Telegraph Co. v. Lenroot*, 323 U.S. 490, 492 (1945). See generally Note, *The First Word: The President's Place in "Legislative History,"* 89 Mich. L. Rev. 399 (1990).

In a like spirit, Justices sometimes rely on floor debates, including exchanges between supporters and opponents. Although statements by legislators about bills they oppose are not reliable, see *NLRB v. Fruit & Vegetable Packers*, 377 U.S. 58, 66 (1964), exchanges with supporters may sharpen the precise deals that have been reached. An interesting illustration is *BankAmerica v. United States*, 462 U.S. 122 (1983), where the Court interpreted the Clayton Act's general bar to interlocking corporate

---

t. For state cases relying on statements in hearings, see, e.g., *Pacific Bell v. California State and Consumer Services Agency*, 275 Cal. Rptr. 62, 67–68 (Cal. App. 1990) (testimony in committee hearings); *People v. Luciano*, 662 P.2d 480, 482 n.4 (Colo. 1983) (recordings of Senate and House committee hearings); *In re Sheldon G.*, 583 A.2d 112, 116 & n.6 (Conn. 1990) (testimony in committee hearings); *Jackson v. Kansas City*, 235 Kan. 278, 680 P.2d 877 (1984) (statements in committee hearings); *First Nat'l Bank of Deerwood v. Gregg*, 556 N.W.2d 214 (Minn. 1996) (tape-recorded hearings); *Wiseman v. Keller*, 358 N.W.2d 768 (Neb. 1984) (judiciary committee hearing); *Linlee Enters., Inc. v. State*, 445 A.2d 1130, 1131 (N.H. 1982) (House committee hearing and subcommittee report); *Dickinson v. Fund for Support of Free Public Schools*, 469 A.2d 1 (N.J. 1983) (statements made in subcommittee and committee hearings); *Sager v. McClenden*, 672 P.2d 697 (Ore. 1983) (minutes of committee hearings). A number of states have ruled that legislator statements during committee hearings cannot be the basis for the court's finding of legislative intent. See *State v. Miranda*, 715 A.2d 680 (Conn. 1998).

directorates to be inapplicable to bank-nonbank interlocks.[u] Chief Justice Burger's opinion for the Court relied on the plain meaning of the statutory provision, the structure of the statute, the longstanding interpretation by the relevant regulatory agencies and subcommittees, and the legislative history. The theme of the legislative history was that many progressives wanted to prohibit bank-nonbank interlocks, and at various points in the process criticized the general provision in the proposed legislation for not barring them.

The clinching evidence in *BankAmerica* was a colloquy among two supporters and an opponent at the close of the House debate. The opponent, Representative Mann, raised a point of order, that the House conferees had improperly agreed to a conference bill that cut back both Senate and House bills, which he construed as having regulated *all* bank interlocks. The supporters, Representatives Sherley and Webb, admonished Mann and asserted that the general catchall bar never applied to banks, and the final version of the bill only regulated bank-bank interlocks in a special provision. The Chief Justice believed that these representations by supporters of the legislation were persuasive—and their cogency was confirmed when the Speaker overruled Mann's point of order, apparently on the ground that the House conferees had not betrayed the earlier deal.

BankAmerica is perhaps an unusual case, because the key colloquy occurred at the very end of the legislative debate and spoke directly, and dramatically, to the issue before the Court. In *Weber*, by way of contrast, Justice Brennan's majority opinion responded that all of Justice Rehnquist's parade of quotes critical of racial quotas were uttered before Title VII achieved its final form, laden with compromises, including § 703(j) (which Brennan found critical to his judgment that Congress was tolerant of *voluntary* affirmative action). "To permit what we regard as clear statutory language to be materially altered by such colloquies, which often take place before the bill has achieved its final form, would open the door to the inadvertent, or perhaps even planned, undermining of the language actually voted on by Congress * * *." *Regan v. Wald*, 468 U.S. 222, 237–42 (1984).

Because legislative history has become much more controversial, among federal judges at least, one might expect that references to congressional hearings and floor debates would dry up at the Supreme Court level. This has *not* been the case, as the following opinions and notes will reflect. The first two cases present a recurring issue: What to make of the *rejection* of legislative proposals in committee, on the floor of either chamber, in conference committee, and so forth? The third case brings

---

u. The fourth paragraph of Clayton Act § 8, 15 U.S.C. § 19, reads: "No person at the same time shall be a director in *any two or more corporations*, any one of which has capital, surplus, and undivided profits aggregating more than $1,000,000, engaged in whole or in part in commerce, *other than banks, banking associations, trust companies, and common carriers* subject to the Act to regulate commerce * * *." The second paragraph prohibits bank-bank interlocks.

together a host of legislative sources and the famous "dog that doesn't bark" canon.

Food & Drug Administration v. Brown & Williamson Tobacco Co., 529 U.S. 120 (2000). This case is excerpted in Chapter 2, § 3B3. Focus on **Justice O'Connor**'s opinion for the Court and its lavish references to subcommittee hearings where FDA officials disclaimed jurisdiction over tobacco products, from which Justice O'Connor concluded that "Congress" had acquiesced in the agency's interpretation of the FDCA. Notice that Justice Scalia joined every bit of Justice O'Connor's extensive analysis of legislative materials. Contrast the following case, where Justice Scalia wrote the opinion for the Court.

Rapanos v. United States, 547 U.S. 715 (2006). The Federal Water Pollution Control Act Amendments of 1972 prohibit the discharge of pollutants into the nation's waters, excepting only discharges allowed in the Act. Section 404, administered by the Army Corps of Engineers, allows only administratively permitted discharge of dredge or fill into "navigable waters," which the statute defines as "waters of the United States, including the territorial seas." 33 U.S.C. § 1362(7). This statutory language reflected the *rejection* in Conference Committee of including the term "navigable" in § 1362(7)'s definition. "The Conferees fully intend that the term 'navigable waters' be given the broadest possible constitutional interpretation."

Under pressure from the EPA, the House, and the judiciary, the Army Corps adopted regulations in 1975 (finalized in 1977) defining "navigable waters" to include "wetlands" that are "adjacent" to (1) navigable waters as traditionally defined, (2) tributaries (including channels that are only episodically conduits of water) of navigable waters, and (3) interstate waters, whether or not navigable, and their tributaries. In addition, isolated wetlands are included if their degradation could affect interstate commerce.

The 1975 regulations were the subject of extensive committee hearings in both the House and Senate. Critics of the Corps's permit program attempted to insert limitations on the Corps's § 404 jurisdiction into the proposed 1977 clean water legislation. The House bill as reported out of committee proposed a redefinition of "navigable waters" that would have limited the Corps's authority under § 404 to waters navigable in fact and their adjacent wetlands (defined as wetlands periodically inundated by contiguous navigable waters). H.R. 3199, 95th Cong., 1st Sess., § 16 (1977). The bill reported by the Senate Committee on Environment and Public Works, by contrast, contained no redefinition of the scope of the "navigable waters" covered by § 404, and dealt with the perceived problem of over-regulation by exempting certain activities (primarily agricultural) from the permit requirement and by providing for assumption of some of the Corps's regulatory duties by federally approved state programs. S. 1952, 95th Cong., 1st Sess., § 49(b) (1977).

On the floor of the Senate, Senator Bentsen (D–Tex.) proposed an amendment to limit the scope of "navigable waters" along the lines set forth in the House bill. 123 Cong. Rec. 26,710–26,711 (1977). Reflecting the majority viewpoint, Senator Baker (R–Tenn.) endorsed the Corps's regulations, because "comprehensive coverage of this program is essential for the protection of the aquatic environment." *Id.* at 26,718. Other Senators (and Representatives) made similar comments. After extensive debate, the Senate rejected that amendment, 123 Cong. Rec. 26,728 (1977), as did the Conference Committee reconciling the two versions of the Clean Water Act of 1977, 91 Stat. 1566.

The Supreme Court ruled in *United States v. Riverside Bayview Homes, Inc.*, 474 U.S. 121 (1985), that the Corps's regulation of a wetland that was adjacent to a navigable creek was a permissible construction of the statute. A unanimous Court ruled that "navigable waters of the United States" could include "wetlands that are not the result of flooding or permeation by water having its source in adjacent bodies of open water. The Corps has concluded that wetlands may affect the water quality of adjacent lakes, rivers, and streams even when the waters of those bodies do not actually inundate the wetlands. For example, wetlands that are not flooded by adjacent waters may still tend to drain into those waters. In such circumstances, the Corps has concluded that wetlands may serve to filter and purify water draining into adjacent bodies of water, and to slow the flow of surface runoff into lakes, rivers, and streams and thus prevent flooding and erosion. In addition, adjacent wetlands may 'serve significant natural biological functions, including food chain production, general habitat, and nesting, spawning, rearing and resting sites for aquatic ... species.'" The key evidence supporting the Corps's very broad definition was Congress's rejection of proposals to limit the Corps's jurisdiction in 1977 and the congressional discussions supporting the Corps' 1977 regulations (described above).

After *Bayview*, the Corps expanded its regulation to create a "Migratory Bird Rule," extending its wetlands jurisdiction to waters "[w]hich are or would be used as habitat" by migratory birds. The Supreme Court in *Solid Waste Agency v. Army Corps of Engineers*, 531 U.S. 159 (2001), invalidated this rule as inconsistent with the statutory definition. Chief Justice Rehnquist's opinion for the Court also invoked the avoidance doctrine, because the rule pressed against, and perhaps beyond, Congress's Commerce Clause authority.

Over the objection of four dissenting Justices (Stevens, Souter, Ginsburg, and Breyer), the *Solid Waste* Court rejected the Corps's argument that Congress in 1977 had "acquiesced" in its broad understanding of wetlands jurisdiction. Because the Migratory Bird Rule did not appear in the Corps' regulations until 1986, Chief Justice Rehnquist felt that Congress's actions in 1977 could not have ratified that interpretation. Justice Stevens's dissenting opinion took a broader view of Congress's 1977 action. When the Senate voted down the Bentsen Amendment and the Conference Committee rejected the House bill in 1977, Congress was not just rejecting a technical adjustment to the Corps' jurisdiction, but it was rejecting the understanding of the Corps's jurisdiction as founded on protecting *navigability* and embracing the new conception of jurisdiction as founded on protecting hydrological ecosystems. The majority declined to read Congress's actions so broadly.

In 1989, John Rapanos backfilled wetlands on a parcel of land in Michigan; the nearest body of traditionally navigable waters was 11 to 20 miles away. The Corps asserted jurisdiction over the land and prosecuted civil and criminal charges against Rapanos, who essentially ignored the government's warnings. The Corps's justification was that Rapanos's wetland was adjacent to a "tributary" of a navigable waterway. At trial, expert witnesses testified that Rapanos's wetlands were connected by drains to various navigable rivers and were critical to flood prevention in the aquatic ecosystem of the region. The Corps relied on *Bayview* and the 1977 Clean Water Act described above.

Writing for Chief Justice Roberts and Justices Thomas and Alito, **Justice Scalia**'s plurality opinion distinguished *Bayview*, where the wetlands were adjacent to a navigable creek, rather than the non-navigable drainage in Rapanos's case. Because "navigable waters" is defined very broadly in the CWA, Justice Scalia reasoned that the term could *not* be limited to the traditional (and narrow) understanding. But there must be *some* limit, and a survey of dictionaries suggested that *waters* must be limited to "continuously present, fixed bodies of water, as opposed to ordinarily dry channels through which water occasionally or intermittently flows." Justice Scalia's definition excluded "transitory puddles or ephemeral flows of water." This somewhat narrower understanding is reinforced by the fact that the statute's separate category of *point sources* clearly includes intermittent water flows.

Moreover, a narrower definition is consistent with the "policy of Congress to recognize, preserve, and protect the primary responsibilities and rights of the States to prevent, reduce, and eliminate pollution, [and] to plan the development and use * * * of land and water resources." § 1251(b). The Corps's expansive definition would eliminate "virtually all" state and local planning by bringing all decisions under a national authority, what Justice Scalia refers to as an "enlightened despot." The *BFP* canon (Chapter 3, § 2C) closed the matter for the plurality: "We ordinarily expect a 'clear and manifest' statement from Congress to authorize an unprecedented intrusion into traditional state authority. *BFP.* The phrase 'the waters of the United States' hardly qualifies." Likewise, the Corps' definition stretches the statute potentially beyond Congress's Commerce Clause authority and so mobilizes the avoidance canon.

Justice Scalia dismissed the Corps's argument (adopted by the dissenting opinion filed by **Justice Stevens**) that the rejected proposals in 1977 constituted legislative adoption of the Corps' broad definition. "Congress takes no governmental action except by legislation. What the dissent refers to as 'Congress' deliberate acquiescence' should more appropriately be called Congress' failure to express any opinion. We have no idea whether the Members' failure to act in 1977 was attributable to their belief that the Corps' regulations were correct, or rather to their belief that the courts would eliminate any excesses, or indeed simply to their unwillingness to confront the environmental lobby. * * * '[Absent] such *overwhelming evidence* of acquiescence, we are loath to replace the plain text and original understanding of a statute with an amended agency interpretation.' *Solid Waste* (emphasis added).

" * * * [T]he dissent claims nothing more than that Congress 'conducted extensive debates about the Corps' regulatory jurisdiction over wetlands [and] rejected efforts to limit that jurisdiction. . . .' In fact, even that vague description goes too far. As recounted in *Riverside Bayview*, the 1977 debates concerned a proposal to 'limi[t] the Corps' authority under [§ 1344] to waters navigable in fact and their adjacent wetlands (defined as wetlands periodically inundated by contiguous navigable waters).' In rejecting this proposal, Congress merely failed to enact a limitation of 'waters' to include only navigable-in-fact waters—an interpretation we affirmatively reject today—and a definition of wetlands based on 'periodi[c] inundat[ion]' that appears almost nowhere in the briefs or opinions of those cases. No plausible interpretation of this legislative inaction can construe it as an implied endorsement of every jot and tittle of the Corps' 1977 regulations."

Concurring only in the result, but providing the needed fifth vote, **Justice Kennedy** followed the test announced in *Solid Waste*: To constitute *navigable waters* under the CWA, a wetland must possess a "significant nexus" to waters that are or were navigable in fact or that could reasonably be made navigable. *Solid Waste,* 531 U.S. at 167, 172. Because the lower court also did not follow this approach, Justice Kennedy voted to reverse and remand, and presumably the lower court on remand would have to apply the *Solid Waste* nexus standard, and not the more restrictive approach developed by Justice Scalia.

Justice Kennedy found the *Solid Waste* standard supportable by reference to the same dictionaries, statutory text and structure, balanced purpose, and common sense that Justice Scalia claimed for his approach— and with an additional bonus that the *Solid Waste* standard was supported by *stare decisis*, which is supposed to be super-strong in statutory cases. Justice Kennedy did not address the rejected proposal argument, probably because (unlike the dissenters) he joined the Court's discussion of it in *Solid Waste*.

NOTE ON REJECTED PROPOSALS AS EVIDENCE OF STATUTORY MEANING

Justice O'Connor's opinion in the FDA Tobacco Case is the most lavish deployment in the Court's history of what might be called the *rejected proposal rule*, that interpreters should be reluctant to read statutes broadly when a committee, a chamber, or a conference committee rejected language explicitly encoding that broad policy. *Bayview* reflects this presumption as well. See also, e.g., *Hamdan v. Rumsfeld,* 548 U.S. 557 (2006); *United States v. Yermian,* 468 U.S. 63 (1984) (relying on congressional adoption of broadening language of false swearing statute, 18 U.S.C. § 1001, after earlier bill was vetoed by President). Yet similar rejected proposal arguments were not persuasive to Court majorities in *Rapanos* and *Solid Waste.* How would you distinguish those cases? Or should they be signals that the Supreme Court should no longer follow a rejected proposal rule?

Commentators have been wary, because the range of reasons for rejecting a proposed amendment varies so widely. "It may be rejected by some legislators because they disagree with its substance (but not necessarily the same substance). On the other hand, those who agree with the substance may nevertheless vote against it as a spurious or unnecessary attempt to clarify. Simple non-action, being consistent with many explanations in circumstances not calling for consensus, has no probative value for any purpose." Dickerson, *supra,* at 1133; accord. *Solid Waste* (majority opinion's response to the dissenters); *Pattern Makers' League of North Am. v. NLRB,* 473 U.S. 95 (1985); William N. Eskridge Jr., *Interpreting Legislative Inaction,* 87 Mich. L. Rev. 67 (1988) (collecting cases using and declining to use the rejected proposal rule); Wald, *Legislative History in the 1981 Term, supra,* at 202.

A broader point links Justice O'Connor's opinion for the Court in FDA Tobacco and Justice Stevens's dissenting opinions in *Solid Waste* and *Rapanos.* Both Justices find in the legislative deliberations evidence that Congress has both accepted and relied upon well-grounded agency policy stances as regards their regulatory mandate. In the FDA Tobacco Case, there seems to have been a political consensus that the FDA did not have jurisdiction over tobacco products, and in the Wetlands Cases there seems to have been a similar consensus that the Corps has broad jurisdiction to protect hydrological ecosystems. Why did one consensus fail to move the Court while the other did move the Court? Consider not only the political preferences of the Justices, but also the Court's traditional role as braking or slowing down political actors.

MONTANA WILDERNESS ASSOCIATION v. UNITED STATES FOREST SERVICE

United States Court of Appeals for the Ninth Circuit, May 14, 1981
Docket No. 80–3374

NORRIS, CIRCUIT JUDGE:

This appeal raises fundamental questions concerning the conflict between the ability of the executive branch of the federal government to manage public lands and the access rights of persons whose property is surrounded by those lands. Environmentalists and a neighboring property owner seek to block construction by Burlington Northern of roads over parts of the Gallatin National Forest. They appeal from a partial summary judgment in the district court granting Burlington Northern a right of access to its totally enclosed timber lands. The district court held that Burlington Northern has an easement by necessity or, alternatively, an

implied easement under the Northern Pacific Land Grant of 1864. The
defendants argue that the Alaska National Interest Lands Act of 1980,
passed subsequent to the district court's decision, also grants Burlington
Northern assured access to its land. The appellants contend that the
doctrine of easement by necessity does not apply to the sovereign, that
there was no implied easement conveyed by the 1864 land grant, and that
the access provisions of the Alaska Lands Act do not apply to land outside
the state of Alaska. We conclude that the appellants are correct on all
three issues. We therefore reverse the partial summary judgment and
remand the case for further proceedings.

Defendant-appellee Burlington Northern, Inc. owns timber land located within the Gallatin National Forest southwest of Bozeman, Montana.
This land was originally acquired by its predecessor, the Northern Pacific
Railroad, under the Northern Pacific Land Grant Act of 1864, 13 Stat.
365. The Act granted odd-numbered square sections of land to the
railroad, which, with the even-numbered sections retained by the United
States, formed a checkerboard pattern.

To harvest its timber, Burlington Northern in 1979 acquired a permit
from defendant-appellee United States Forest Service, allowing it to
construct an access road across national forest land. The proposed roads
would cross the Buck Creek and Yellow Mules drainages, which are
protected by the Montana Wilderness Study Act of 1977, Pub. L. 95–150,
91 Stat. 1243, as potential wilderness areas. The proposed logging and
road-building will arguably disqualify the areas as wilderness under the
Act. * * *

Appellees contend that the recently enacted Alaska National Interest
Lands Conservation Act (Alaska Lands Act), Pub. L. No. 96–487, 94 Stat.
2371 (1980), establishes an independent basis for affirming the judgment
of the district court. They argue that § 1323(a) of the Act requires that
the Secretary of Agriculture provide access to Burlington Northern for its
enclosed land. Upon examination of the statute and the legislative history,
we do not find this interpretation of the Alaska Lands Act convincing.

Section 1323 is a part of the administrative provisions, Title XIII, of
the Alaska Lands Act. Appellees argue that it is the only section of the Act
which applies to the entire country; appellants argue that, like the rest of
the Act, it applies only to Alaska. Section 1323 reads as follows:

Sec. 1323. (a) Notwithstanding any other provision of law, and
subject to such terms and conditions as the Secretary of Agriculture
may prescribe, the Secretary shall provide such access to nonfederally
owned land within the boundaries of the National Forest System as
the Secretary deems adequate to secure to the owner the reasonable
use and enjoyment thereof: *Provided,* That such owner comply with
rules and regulations applicable to ingress and egress to or from the
National Forest System.

(b) Notwithstanding any other provision of law, and subject to
such terms and conditions as the Secretary of the Interior may

prescribe, the Secretary shall provide such access to nonfederally owned land surrounded by public lands managed by the Secretary under the Federal Land Policy and Management Act of 1976 (43 U.S.C. 1701–82) as the Secretary deems adequate to secure to the owner the responsible use and enjoyment thereof: *Provided*, That such owner comply with rules and regulations applicable to access across public lands.

This section provides for access to nonfederally-owned lands surrounded by certain kinds of federal lands. Subsection (b) deals with access to nonfederal lands "surrounded by public lands managed by the Secretary [of the Interior]." Section 102(3) of the Act defines "public lands" as certain lands "situated in Alaska." Subsection (b) is therefore limited by its terms to Alaska.

Subsection (a) deals with access to nonfederally-owned lands "within the boundaries of the National Forest System." The term "National Forest System" as used in § 1323(a) is to be interpreted as being limited to national forests in Alaska or as including the entire United States.

The parties have not directed us to, nor has our research disclosed, an established or generally accepted meaning for the term "National Forest System." The United States Code contains no statutory definitions for it. We find no record of Congressional use of the term prior to the enactment of the Federal Land Policy and Management Act of 1976. The term "National Forest System" appears in that Act but is nowhere defined; from the context, however, it is apparent that it is used there to refer to national forests anywhere in the United States. See 43 U.S.C. §§ 1701, *et seq*. The same Act also uses the term "public lands" and defines it as meaning lands "owned by the United States within the several States," clearly a definition different from that given the same term in the Alaska Lands Act.

We therefore perceive no basis for assuming that Congress necessarily used the term "National Forest System" in the Alaska Lands Act to refer to national forests in the United States generally. We think that in this context the meaning of the term is ambiguous and therefore look to other indicia.

The Act itself provides some help. Title V of the Act is entitled "National Forest System." Section 501(a) states: "The following units of the National Forest System are hereby expanded * * *." This language shows that Congress used the term "National Forest System" in this Act in a context which refers to and deals with national forests in Alaska. It is not unreasonable to read Section 1323(a) as referring to the "National Forest System" in the context in which it is used in Title V of the Act, rather than to all national forests in the United States.

As the parties agreed at oral argument, moreover, § 1323(b) is *in pari materia* with § 1323(a). The two subsections are placed together in the same section, and use not only a parallel structure but many of the same words and phrases. The natural interpretation is that they were meant to have the same effect, one on lands controlled by the Secretary of Agriculture, the other on lands controlled by the Secretary of the Interior. Since § 1323(b), by the definition of public lands in § 102(3), applies only to Alaskan land, a strong presumption arises that § 1323(a) was meant to apply only to Alaska as well.

That interpretation is confirmed by a review of the entire Act which discloses no other provision having nation-wide application.[4] To attach such a sweeping effect to this obscure and seemingly minor provision of the Act would seem incongruous under the circumstances. We therefore conclude that the language of the Act supports the interpretation that § 1323(a) applies only to national forests in Alaska. Bearing in mind that "[a]bsent a clearly expressed legislative intent to the contrary, [the statutory] language must ordinarily be regarded as conclusive," *Consumer Product Safety Commission v. GTE Sylvania*, 447 U.S. 102, 108 (1980), we turn to the legislative history.

Section 1323 was added to the Alaska Lands Bill by the Senate Committee on Energy and Natural Resources in its amendment to H.R. 39, originally passed by the House. S. Rep. No. 96–413, 96th Cong. 1st Sess. (1979). It was incorporated in the Tsongas substitute bill which replaced by amendment the Energy Committee's proposed bill, 126 Cong. Rec. S11099, S11140 (daily ed. Aug. 18, 1980). The Tsongas substitute bill was passed by the Senate, 126 Cong. Rec. S11193 (daily ed. Aug. 19, 1980), and House, 126 Cong. Rec. H10552 (daily ed. Nov. 12, 1980), and became law on December 1, 1980, 94 Stat. 2371.

Section 1323 is mentioned only twice in the Senate materials. The Energy Committee report discussed it in its section-by-section analysis, S. Rep. No. 96–413 at 310, and Senator Melcher, the author of the section, discussed it on the floor of the Senate, 126 Cong. Rec. S14770–71 (daily ed. Nov. 20, 1980). The remarks of Senator Melcher, however, were made on November 20th, eight days after Congress passed H.R. 39. His remarks clearly demonstrate that his personal understanding of the section is that it applies nationwide, but because they are the remarks of but one senator made subsequent to the passage of the bill they do not provide a reliable indication of the understanding of the Senate as a whole.

---

4. The appellees concede that no other section of the Act applies nationwide. They argue, however, that because another provision of the Act, § 1110(b), gives access rights to all Alaskan inholders, § 1323(a) is superfluous unless it is interpreted to apply to the entire country. Section 1110(b), they argue, like § 1323(b), applies only to Alaska because it uses terms, "public lands" and "conservation system unit," which are defined to include only Alaskan land.

The flaw in appellee's argument is that however § 1323(a) is interpreted, § 1110(b) essentially duplicates the protection given Alaskan lands by § 1323 as a whole. Section 1110(b) overlaps § 1323(b) just as much as it overlaps § 1323(a). If, as appellees claim, § 1110(b) gives access to all Alaskan inholders and § 1323(a) gives access to holders of land surrounded by land administered by the Secretary of Agriculture, the inclusion of § 1323(b) in the Act makes no sense at all. Section 1323(b), after all, gives access to holders of Alaskan land surrounded by land administered by the Secretary of the Interior. Under this view, not only is § 1323(b) superfluous in light of § 1110(b), it is paired with a provision, § 1323(a), of parallel structure but widely different scope. We do not see how the existence of § 1110(b) gives much support to the appellees' position.

Although the appellees contend that the language of the Energy Committee report makes perfectly clear the Committee's intent that § 1323 apply nationwide, we do not find their interpretation of the report's language persuasive:

> This section is designed to remove the uncertainties surrounding the status of the rights of the owners of non-Federal lands to gain access to such lands across Federal lands. It has been the Committee's understanding that such owners had the right of access to their lands subject to reasonable regulation by either, the Secretary of Agriculture in the case of national forests, or by the Secretary of the Interior in the case of public lands managed by the Bureau of Land Management under the Federal Land Policy and Management Act of 1976. However, a recent District Court decision in Utah (*Utah v. Andrus et al.*, C79–0037, October 1, 1979, D.C. Utah) has cast some doubt over the status of these rights. Furthermore, the Attorney General is currently reviewing the issue because of differing interpretations of the law by the Departments of Agriculture and the Interior. * * *
>
> The Committee amendment is designed to resolve any lingering legal questions by making it clear that non-Federal landowners have a right of access [across] National Forests and public land, subject, of course, to reasonable rules and regulations.

S. Rep. No. 96–413 at 310.

While the Committee's intent to guarantee access is clear, it is less than clear whether this provision was meant to guarantee access outside of Alaska. The problem raised in the first paragraph—the differing interpretations of the law of access—is not confined to Alaska, but the scope of the remedy as set forth in the last paragraph could be so confined. As with § 1323 itself, the report uses indiscriminately terms defined in the Act as applying only to Alaskan land ("public land") and terms not so defined ("National Forests").

The absence of any reference to Alaska is not of much import. The report's discussion of other access provisions such as § 1110 and § 1111, which all parties agree apply only to Alaska, fails to mention Alaska and is as ambiguous about whether § 1110 and § 1111 apply nationwide as is the discussion of § 1323. S. Rep. No. 96–413 at 299–300.

What we find most significant in the legislative history in the Senate is the same thing that Sherlock Holmes found to be crucial in solving the case of the Hound of the Baskervilles—the failure of the dog to bark. The Alaska Lands bill was discussed endlessly on the Senate floor. There are numerous occasions when one would expect a change in current laws of access of the magnitude of the appellees' proposed interpretation of § 1323 to be discussed, mentioned or at least alluded to. Yet we have not found in the Senate debates, and appellees have not called to our attention, one single suggestion that anything in the Alaska Land Bill would affect access rights in the rest of the country. In Senator Tsongas' long, detailed comparison of his substitute bill with the Energy Committee bill,

§ 1323 is not mentioned. 126 Cong. Rec. S11193 (daily ed. Aug. 19, 1980).[6] In discussion about the adequacy of the substitute bill's access provisions (which include § 1323) no mention is made of a change in the law of access for the rest of the country. 126 Cong. Rec. S11061–62 (daily ed. Aug. 18, 1980). We find it difficult to believe that the Senate would have contemplated and effected a profound change in the law of access across government land for the entire country without ever mentioning it.

The legislative history in the House, which considered and passed the Tsongas substitute bill after it was passed by the Senate, also presents an ambiguous picture of § 1323. On October 2, 1980, Representative Udall, chairman of the Committee on Interior and Insular Affairs which had joint responsibility for the bill, introduced an amendment one section of which was to "make clear that [the bill] applies only to Alaska." 127 Cong. Rec. 10376 (daily ed. October 2, 1980). This amendment was never adopted. Representative Udall subsequently declared in prepared remarks inserted into the Congressional Record that although the final version of the bill was "ambiguously drafted and not expressly limited to Alaskan lands, the House believes that, as with all the other provisions of the bill, the language of the section applies only to lands within the State of Alaska." 126 Cong. Rec. H10549 (daily ed. Nov. 12, 1980). Representative Weaver stated that the section granting access rights to inholders on national forest and BLM lands "apparently applies not only to Alaska but also to the entire United States." 126 Cong. Rec. H8638 (daily ed. September 9, 1980). Representative Sieberling inserted into the record a summary of proposed amendments, which refers to Section 1323 as the "nationwide access amendment." 126 Cong.Rec. H10350 (daily ed. October 2, 1980). Representative AuCoin stated that one of the flaws of the final bill is that it "grants private inholders carte blanche access across national forest and public lands nationwide." 126 Cong. Rec. H10529–30 (daily ed. Nov. 12, 1980).

Appellees rely heavily upon an exchange of letters between Representatives Sieberling and Weaver, chairmen of the subcommittees responsible for the bill (Public Lands of the Committee on Interior and Insular Affairs and Forest of the Committee on Agriculture), and the Attorney General's office. In their letter, the representatives express concern over § 1323, which they state applies nationwide, and ask for a clarification of how different the § 1323 access language is from existing access provisions. It is indeed clear from their letter that they believed that § 1323 applies nationwide.

Appellees argue, on the basis of the September 5, 1980 return letter from Assistant Attorney General Alan Parker, that the Department of Justice confirmed this interpretation of § 1323. We interpret the letter

---

6. Neither did Senator Tsongas remark on § 1323 when it was first proposed in the Energy Committee bill, even though in his statement in the Committee report he spends several pages criticizing the bill's overbroad provisions on access. [Citing Senate Report, additional views of Senators Metzenbaum and Tsongas.] Yet the extension of § 1323(a) to the entire country would certainly have a greater impact than the other measures he discusses.

differently. As we read the letter, the Assistant Attorney General assumed without analysis that the representatives' interpretation of § 1323 was correct, and proceeded to discuss in detail the effect of such a change in the law.

The exchanged letters are entitled to little weight. In general, off-the-record views of congressmen are not attributed to Congress as a whole. *See T.V.A. v. Hill*, 437 U.S. 153, 190–91 (1978). This is particularly true where, as here, there is no indication that the House as a whole was aware of the correspondence. *Id.* at 191–92.

In summary, the legislative history concerning § 1323 is surprisingly sparse. The report of the Senate committee which drafted the section is ambiguous. At times when the Senate could have been expected to comment on its intention to make a major change in current law, it did not. The only expression of intent that § 1323 apply nationwide came from a single senator eight days after the Alaska Lands Act was passed by Congress. In the House debates, three representatives suggested that § 1323 did apply nationwide, but the chairman of one of the responsible committees said it did not. Two chairmen of House subcommittees responsible for the bill did state in a letter to the Attorney General that they believed that § 1323 applied nationwide, but there is no indication that the contents of this letter were generally known by members of the House, and so the letter carries little weight in our analysis. We conclude that the ambiguous legislative history gives only slight support at best to the appellees' interpretation that § 1323 applies nationwide. It is not nearly sufficient to overcome the actual language of the statute, which we believe is more naturally read as applying only to Alaska.

Moreover, § 1323 as interpreted by the appellees would repeal by implication a portion of § 5(a) of the Wilderness Act, 16 U.S.C. § 1134(a). "It is, of course, a cardinal principle of statutory construction that repeals by implication are not favored," *Radzanower v. Touche Ross & Co.*, 426 U.S. 148, 154 (1976), and that "the intention of the legislature to repeal must be clear and manifest." *Posadas v. National City Bank*, 296 U.S. 497, 503 (1936). Here it is far from clear that the legislature intended that § 1323 apply nationwide. We hold that § 1323 of the Alaska National Interest Lands Conservation Act is limited in its application to the state of Alaska, and so has no relevance to this case. * * *

NOTES ON THE "CHECKERBOARD CASE" AND STATEMENTS DURING LEGISLATIVE DELIBERATION

1. *The Ninth Circuit's Use of Legislative History.* A textualist would likely agree with Judge Norris' analysis of the statutory text, and then would stop. Why should the judge proceed any further? When Judge Norris does, he causes himself some trouble. Note his strategy. Even though the opinion adduces no affirmative support in the legislative history for its view that § 1323(a) only applies to Alaska, Judge Norris isolates all the evidence to the contrary and seeks to neuter each piece of evidence in isolation, either by

demonstrating ambiguity or by denigrating the authority of the evidence. This technique—the "piecemeal critique"—is effective advocacy in response to a showing of a variety of evidence to the contrary, but shouldn't that evidence be allowed to have cumulative weight in assessing overall legislative intent? As you evaluate the following, consider whether an "intentionalist" interpreter would disagree with Judge Norris' outcome.

(a) *Committee Reports.* On first reading, the Senate Report in the Checkerboard Case may be ambiguous. But reread the quoted language of the Report. The Senate wants to avoid the problems raised by a federal district court decision in Utah and by the Attorney General's consideration (described in Note 2 after *Leo Sheep*). The Utah case (in the Tenth Circuit) is not controlling law in Alaska (in the Ninth Circuit). The Senate Report wants "to resolve *any* lingering legal questions by *making it clear* that non-Federal landowners have a right of access [across] National Forests" (emphasis added). While this Report is not 100% clear that § 1323(a) was meant to apply nationwide, isn't the more probable reading of the Report that Congress assumed that § 1323(a) would have nationwide application?

(b) *Statements of Sponsors and Committee Chairs.* Senator Melcher, the sponsor of the amendment adding § 1323(a), explicitly said that it applied nationwide. Judge Norris denigrates this clear evidence by saying that it was uttered after the bill was passed by Congress (but before it had been signed by the President). But he doesn't say that Representative Udall's statements, on which he relies, were inserted into the Congressional Record *after* the bill was passed. (Udall's remarks are reported in the *Record* for the day the bill was passed, but they are preceded by a "bullet" [●], which signifies that they were not spoken on the floor of the House but were inserted later.) Indeed, look at the dates of the Udall and Melcher statements. Why might Udall have abandoned any attempt to amend the statute to make it clearly apply only to Alaska and instead simply uttered a comment that the unamended version had the same impact? Why might Melcher have made his comment? Which is the more reliable?

Leaving strategic considerations aside, consider the roles of the key players. Melcher, the sponsor of § 1323(a), and Representatives Seiberling and Weaver, chairs of the relevant House subcommittees, interpreted § 1323(a) to apply nationwide, in statements made to their respective chambers. Udall, chair of the House Committee, interpreted it otherwise, in a statement inserted after the fact. Yet Judge Norris treats Udall's statements as roughly equal to those of Melcher, Seiberling, and Weaver in combination. Isn't this wrong, especially in light of the common view that greater weight should be accorded statements of *supporters* of a provision over statements of *opponents*? See also *Ernst & Ernst v. Hochfelder*, 425 U.S. 185, 204 n.24 (1976).

(c) *Dialogue with Bureaucrats.* The exchange of letters between Seiberling/Weaver and the Justice Department concerning the effect of the Melcher amendment is not unusual in Congress. It is quite common in state legislatures, where assistants to state attorneys general typically advise legislative committees about the probable legal effects of bills. Since Seiberling and Weaver were key House negotiators, and the House accepted the Melcher amendment in negotiations, isn't this exchange of letters more significant than Judge Norris was willing to admit? Compare this with *Lindahl v. Office of Personnel Management*, 470 U.S. 768, 785 n.17 (1985), where the Supreme Court relied heavily on letters from the OPM Director to the Chairs of the Senate and House Committees to interpret amendments to the Civil Service Retirement Act. Judge Wald, *Legislative History in the 1981 Term, supra*, at 202–03, noted in the early 1980s an increasing tendency of lawyers to use, and judges to cite, unpublished portions of the legislative history to support their interpretations of statutes. See *Borrell v. United States Int'l Communication Agency*, 682 F.2d 981, 988 (D.C. Cir. 1982).

2. *Evidence Judge Norris (and Everybody Else) Missed.* Judge Norris makes much of the fact that Senator Melcher's statement that § 1323 applies nationwide was made on the floor of the Senate after the bill was passed. But on July 29, 1980 (well before the bill passed the Senate), Senator Melcher sent a letter to every Senator, explaining that he was opposed to a portion of one of the amendments that would be offered when the Alaska Lands bill came before the Senate. The letter explained that Melcher's amendment was in response to the recent Department of Justice opinion (described in Note 2 following *Leo Sheep, supra*) indicating that private checkerboard landowners did not have an automatic right of access across government land; Melcher considered the Department of Justice view an innovation that disrupted prior understandings among property owners and federal lands administrators. The letter then said, with emphasis we have added:

> In the Alaskan Lands Bill, for Alaska only, specific access to state or private lands was explicitly guaranteed. In order to avoid any change in federal policy on this question, last October [1979] I introduced an amendment to that bill for continuing the historic policy of granting access to property inholders in all the rest of the Bureau of Land Management and National Forest lands. My amendment was accepted by the committee without objection and *it applies to landowners within federal lands (either in national forests or in public lands administered by the Bureau of Land Management) in all the rest of the states where such lands are located.* * * *

The letter warned that Amendment No. 1783, offered by Senators Tsongas and McGovern, would strike this committee amendment, and Melcher urged the other Senators to support his effort to preserve this national right of access provision.[v] Was Judge Norris wrong about the "deal" in Congress?

3. *The "Dog That Didn't Bark" Canon.* Although Judge Norris cited the wrong Sherlock Holmes story,[w] he is correct to say that the Supreme Court

---

v. The letter is reproduced in *Oversight on The Montana Wilderness Study Act: Hearing Before the Subcomm. on Public Lands and Reserved Water of the Senate Comm. on Energy and Natural Resources*, 97th Cong., 1st Sess. 53 (May 28, 1981). Senator Melcher represented that the letter was sent to every Senator. Id. at 12. One of our students in the Georgetown University Law Center, Class of 1990, came up with this "smoking gun" during class discussion. (Imagine our embarrassment that we didn't find this smoking gun when we worked on the case in private practice. This is one of the cases we have plundered from our experience as attorneys at the old Washington, D.C. law firm of Shea & Gardner [now absorbed into another law firm]. Apparently, it did not occur to us that anything relevant to the Alaska Act would be found in the legislative history of another act, the Montana Wilderness Study Act. *Should* that have occurred to us? Keep this question in mind when you read the next case.)

sometimes follows the *dog didn't bark* canon. That is, it may be significant that an intense congressional debate does not even mention an issue—suggesting that the statute contained no unusual departure from the status quo against which Congress was legislating. Thus, in a bill whose title and subject matter are all about Alaska, one would expect some special mention of a provision that adjusted important legal rights in the lower 49 states as well.

We have seen examples of it in *Zuni Public School District No. 89 v. Department of Education, Green v. Bock Laundry Machine Co.*, and *Chisom v. Roemer* (all reproduced in Chapter 2, § 3A). In *Chisom*, recall that Justice Scalia assailed this canon on the grounds that it is highly subjective and unreliable (how one characterizes the "status quo" drives the operation of the canon, and that judgment can be a matter of debate), as well as contrary to Justice Scalia's view (e.g., *Rapanos v. United States*, excerpted earlier in this § 2D) that Congress can proceed *only* through positive legislation adopted under Article I, § 7, and *never* through inaction, etc.

Part E.   Post–Enactment ("Subsequent") Legislative History

Statutes are often enacted and forgotten by the legislature. Sometimes, though, the legislature—or at least its members and committees—will continue to talk about the statute after enactment. Circumstances for post-enactment discussion include (1) proposals to amend the statute or to enact a new and related statute, including debate and hearings and committee reports on such proposals; (2) oversight hearings in response to agency and/or judicial implementation of the statute; and (3) efforts to "bend" interpretation of the statute. The statutory interpreter is torn between considering relevant evidence and avoiding strategic trickery. One way to set this balance would be to consider only "subsequent legislative history" that is tied to a subsequent statute enacted by the legislature. (The Supreme Court has not always limited itself in this way, as you will see in the notes after the following case.)

In the immediately preceding case, Judge Norris dismissed Senator Melcher's comment as mere subsequent legislative history. The following case is a later opinion on rehearing in the Checkerboard Case. Notice how Judge Norris' interpretation changed when he was confronted with different subsequent legislative history. Should he have changed his mind?

MONTANA WILDERNESS ASSOCIATION v. UNITED STATES FOREST SERVICE

United States Court of Appeals for the Ninth Circuit, 1981
655 F.2d 951, cert. denied, 455 U.S. 989

[After the May 1981 opinion, *supra*, which held that there was no easement created by the railroad land grant act of 1864 or the Alaska

---

w. In *Silver Blaze*, Sherlock Holmes solves the case of a murdered racehorse by observing that the dog in the barn did not bark when an intruder entered the barn to kill the horse; the deduction (elementary!) was that the killer was someone the dog knew well. In the *Hound of the Baskervilles*, which Judge Norris cites, the dog barked quite a lot and did not contribute to Holmes's solution of the mystery.

Lands Act of 1980, an intervening party defendant moved for reconsideration based upon yet another new statute, shedding light on the Alaska lands statute construed in the earlier opinion. In light of the new statute, the panel withdrew the May opinion and issued the instant opinion. Judge Norris, the author of the original panel opinion, also wrote the new one.]

The sole issue on appeal is whether Burlington Northern has a right of access across federal land to its inholdings of timberland. Appellees contend that the recently enacted Alaska National Interest Lands Conservation Act (Alaska Lands Act), Pub. L. No. 96–487, 94 Stat. 2371 (1980), establishes an independent basis for affirming the judgment of the district court. They argue that § 1323(a) of the Act requires that the Secretary of Agriculture provide access to Burlington Northern for its enclosed land.

Section 1323 is a part of the administrative provisions, Title XIII, of the Alaska Lands Act. Appellees argue that it is the only section of the Act which applies to the entire country; appellants argue that, like the rest of the Act, it applies only to Alaska. Section 1323 reads as follows:

> Sec. 1323. (a) Notwithstanding any other provision of law, and subject to such terms and conditions as the Secretary of Agriculture may prescribe, the Secretary shall provide such access to nonfederally owned land within the boundaries of the National Forest System as the Secretary deems adequate to secure to the owner the reasonable use and enjoyment thereof: *Provided*, That such owner comply with rules and regulations applicable to ingress and egress to or from the National Forest System.

> (b) Notwithstanding any other provision of law, and subject to such terms and conditions as the Secretary of the Interior may prescribe, the Secretary shall provide such access to nonfederally owned land surrounded by public lands managed by the Secretary under the Federal Land Policy and Management Act of 1976 (43 U.S.C. 1701–82) as the Secretary deems adequate to secure to the owner the responsible use and enjoyment thereof: *Provided*, That such owner comply with rules and regulations applicable to access across public lands.

This section provides for access to nonfederally-owned lands surrounded by certain kinds of federal lands. Subsection (b) deals with access to nonfederal lands "surrounded by public lands managed by the Secretary [of the Interior]." Section 102(3) of the Act defines "public lands" as certain lands "situated in Alaska." Subsection (b), therefore, is arguably limited by its terms to Alaska, though we do not find it necessary to settle that issue here. Our consideration of the scope of § 1323(a) proceeds under the assumption that § 1323(b) is limited to Alaska.

Subsection (a) deals with access to nonfederally-owned lands "within the boundaries of the National Forest System." The term "National Forest System" is not specifically defined in the Act.

The question before the court is whether the term "National Forest System" as used in § 1323(a) is to be interpreted as being limited to national forests in Alaska or as including the entire United States. We note at the outset that the bare language of § 1323(a) does not, when considered by itself, limit the provision of access to Alaskan land. We must look, however, to the context of the section to determine its meaning.

Elsewhere in the Act, Congress used the term "National Forest System" in a context which refers to and deals with national forests in Alaska. Title V of the Act is entitled "National Forest System." Section 501(a) states: "The following units of the National Forest System are hereby expanded * * *." It is not unreasonable to read Section 1323(a) as referring to the "National Forest System" in the context in which it is used in Title V of the Act, rather than to all national forests in the United States.

Congress did, however, supply us with a general definition of the term in another statute. Pub. Law 93–378, 88 Stat. 480 (1974). 16 U.S.C. § 1609(a) states *inter alia* that:

Congress declares that the National Forest System consists of units of federally owned forest, range, and related lands throughout the United States and its territories, united into a nationally significant system dedicated to the long-term benefit for present and future generations, and that it is the purpose of their section to include all such areas into one integral system. The 'National Forest System' shall include all national forest lands reserved or withdrawn from the public domain of the United States * * *.

Application of this definition to § 1323(a) would necessarily yield the conclusion that the section was intended to have nation-wide effect. This seems especially so when Congress uses the term "National Forest System" in § 1323(a) without limitation or qualification.

As the parties agreed at oral argument, however, § 1323(b) is *in pari materia* with § 1323(a). The two subsections are placed together in the same section, and use not only a parallel structure but many of the same words and phrases. The natural interpretation is that they were meant to have the same effect, one on lands controlled by the Secretary of Agriculture, the other on lands controlled by the Secretary of the Interior. Since we assume that § 1323(b), by definition of public lands in § 102(3), applies only to Alaskan land, we face a presumption that § 1323(a) was meant to apply to Alaska as well.

That interpretation is supported by a review of the entire Act which discloses no other provision having nation-wide application. We therefore conclude that the language of the Act provides tentative support for the view that § 1323(a) applies only to national forests in Alaska. Bearing in mind that "[a]bsent a clearly expressed legislative intent to the contrary, [the statutory] language must ordinarily be regarded as conclusive," *Consumer Product Safety Commission v. GTE Sylvania*, 447 U.S. 102, 108 (1980), we turn to the legislative history.

The legislative history concerning § 1323 is surprisingly sparse. The report of the Senate committee which drafted the section is ambiguous.[7] At times when the Senate could have been expected to comment on its intention to make a major change in current law, it did not. The only expression of intent that § 1323 apply nation-wide came from a single senator eight days after the Alaska Lands Act was passed by Congress.[8] In the House debates, three representatives suggested that § 1323 did apply nation-wide, but the chairman of one of the responsible committees said it did not.[9] Two chairmen of House subcommittees responsible for the bill

---

7. The Energy Committee report discussed it in its section-by-section analysis, S.Rep. No. 96–413 at 310. (The Committee analysis mixes up §§ 1323 and 1324. Thus, the analysis entitled § 1324 is really concerned with § 1323 and vice versa.) Although the appellees contend that the language of the Energy Committee report makes perfectly clear the Committee's intent that § 1323 apply nationwide, we do not find their interpretation of the report's language persuasive:

> This section is designed to remove the uncertainties surrounding the status of the rights of the owners of non-Federal lands to gain access to such lands across Federal lands. It has been the Committee's understanding that such owners had the right of access to their lands subject to reasonable regulation by either, the Secretary of Agriculture in the case of national forests, or by the Secretary of the Interior in the case of public lands managed by the Bureau of Land Management under the Federal Land Policy and Management Act of 1976. However, a recent District Court decision in Utah (*Utah v. Andrus et al.*, C79–0037, October 1, 1979, D.C. Utah) has cast some doubt over the status of these rights. Furthermore, the Attorney General is currently reviewing the issue because of differing interpretations of the law by the Departments of Agriculture and the Interior. * * *

> The Committee amendment is designed to resolve any lingering legal questions by making it clear that non-Federal landowners have a right of access [across] National Forests and public land, subject, of course, to reasonable rules and regulations.

S. Rep. No. 96–413 at 310.

While the Committee's intent to guarantee access is clear, it is less than clear whether this provision was meant to guarantee access outside of Alaska. The problem raised in the first paragraph—the differing interpretations of the law of access—is not confined to Alaska, but the scope of the remedy as set forth in the last paragraph could be so confined. As with § 1323 itself, the report uses indiscriminately terms defined in the Act as applying only to Alaskan land ("public land") and terms not so defined ("National Forests").

8. Senator Melcher, the author of the section, discussed it on the floor of the Senate, 126 Cong.Rec. S14770–71 (daily ed. Nov. 20, 1980). The remarks of Senator Melcher, however, were made on November 20th, eight days after Congress passed H.R. 39. His remarks clearly demonstrate that his personal understanding of the section is that it applies nation-wide, but because they are the remarks of but one senator made subsequent to the passage of the bill they do not provide a reliable indication of the understanding of the Senate as a whole.

9. On October 2, 1980, Representative Udall, chairman of the Committee on Interior and Insular Affairs which had joint responsibility for the bill, introduced an amendment one section of which was to "make clear that [the bill] applies only to Alaska." 127 Cong. Rec. 10376 (daily ed. October 2, 1980). This amendment was never adopted. Representative Udall subsequently declared in prepared remarks inserted into the Congressional Record that although the final version of the bill was "ambiguously drafted and not expressly limited to Alaskan lands, the House believes that, as with all the other provisions of the bill, the language of the section applies only to lands within the State of Alaska." 126 Cong. Rec. H10549 (daily ed. Nov. 12, 1980). Representative Weaver stated that the section granting access rights to inholders on national forest and BLM lands "apparently applies not only to Alaska but also to the entire United States." 126 Cong. Rec. H8638 (daily ed. September 9, 1980). Representative Sieberling inserted into the record a summary of proposed amendments, which refers to Section 1323 as the "nationwide access amendment." 126 Cong. Rec. H10350 (daily ed. October 2, 1980). Representadid state in a letter to the Attorney General that they believed that § 1323 applied nation-wide, but there is no indication that the contents of this letter were generally known by members of the House, and so the letter carries little weight in our analysis. All this gives only slight support at best to the appellees' interpretation that § 1323 applies nation-wide.

The appellees, however, have uncovered subsequent legislative history that, given the closeness of the issue, is decisive. Three weeks after Congress passed the Alaska Lands Act, a House–Senate Conference Committee considering the Colorado Wilderness Act interpreted § 1323 of the Alaska Lands Act as applying nation-wide:

> Section 7 of the Senate amendment contains a provision pertaining to access to non-Federally owned lands within national forest wilderness areas in Colorado. The House bill has no such provision.
>
> *The conferees agreed to delete the section because similar language has already passed Congress in Section 1323 of the Alaska National Interest Lands Conservation Act.*

H.R. Rep. No. 1521, 96th Cong., 2d Sess., 126 Cong. Rec. H11687 (daily ed. Dec. 3, 1980) (emphasis supplied).

This action was explained to both Houses during discussion of the Conference Report. *See* 126 Cong. Rec. S15571 (daily ed. Dec. 4, 1980) (remarks of Sen. Hart); *id.* at S15573 (remarks of Sen. Armstrong); *id.* at H11705 (daily ed. Dec. 3, 1980) (remarks of Rep. Johnson). Both houses then passed the Colorado Wilderness bill as it was reported by the Conference Committee.

Although a subsequent conference report is not entitled to the great weight given subsequent legislation, *Consumer Product Safety Commission v. GTE Sylvania*, 447 U.S. 102, 118 n.13 (1980), it is still entitled to significant weight, *Seatrain Shipbuilding Corp. v. Shell Oil Co.*, 444 U.S. 572 (1980), particularly where it is clear that the conferees had carefully considered the issue. The conferees, including Representatives Udall and Sieberling and Senator Melcher, had an intimate knowledge of the Alaska Lands Act.[11] Moreover, the Conference Committee's interpretation of § 1323 was the basis for their decision to leave out an access provision passed by one house. In these circumstances, the Conference Committee's interpretation is very persuasive. We conclude that it tips the balance decidedly in favor of the broader interpretation of § 1323.[12] We therefore

tive AuCoin stated that one of the flaws of the final bill is that it "grants private inholders carte blanche access across national forest and public lands nationwide." 126 Cong. Rec. H10529–30 (daily ed. Nov. 12, 1980).

11. The participation of Representative Udall is particularly noteworthy since he was the one congressman to proclaim in the legislative history of the Alaska Lands Act that § 1323 applied only to Alaska.

12. We recognize a facial problem or tension between § 1323(a) and a portion of § 5(a) of the Wilderness Act, 16 U.S.C. § 1134(a). We need not decide in this case whether there is repeal by implication. In passing, we note only that it is arguable that the two can stand together. § 1134(a) deals specifically with right of access "[i]n any case where State-owned or privately-owned land is completely surrounded by national forest lands *within areas designated by this chapter as wilderness * * *.*" (emphasis added). § 1323(a), on the other hand, deals with " * * *

hold that Burlington Northern has an assured right of access to its land pursuant to the nation-wide grant of access in § 1323. * * *

NOTES ON THE SECOND CHECKERBOARD OPINION AND THE USE OF POST-ENACTMENT STATEMENTS

1. *Should Subsequent Legislative History Ever Be Persuasive?* Is Judge Norris's reliance on subsequent legislative history persuasive? While the Supreme Court has said that subsequent statutes should inform interpretation of an earlier one, the Court has professed some skepticism about reliance on subsequent legislative statements. For example, in *Consumer Product Safety Comm'n v. GTE Sylvania*, 447 U.S. 102, 117–18 (1980), petitioners relied upon statements in a conference committee report concerning the 1976 amendments to the Consumer Product Safety Act that purported to interpret a section of the Act enacted in 1972 and not amended in 1976. The Court noted "the oft-repeated warning that 'the views of a subsequent Congress form a hazardous basis for inferring the intent of an earlier one.'" In a footnote, the Court further explained:

> Petitioners invoke the maxim that states: "Subsequent legislation declaring the intent of an earlier statute is entitled to great weight in statutory construction." With respect to subsequent *legislation*, however, Congress has proceeded formally through the legislative process. A mere statement in a conference report of such legislation as to what the Committee believes an earlier statute meant is obviously less weighty.

> The less formal types of subsequent legislative history provide an extremely hazardous basis for inferring the meaning of a congressional enactment.

But in a case decided the same Term, the Court adopted the interpretation of a 1936 statute set forth in a 1971 House committee report based on the theory that, "while the views of subsequent Congresses cannot override the unmistakable intent of the enacting one, * * * such views are entitled to significant weight, * * * and particularly so when the precise intent of the enacting Congress is obscure." *Seatrain Shipbuilding Corp. v. Shell Oil Co.*, 444 U.S. 572, 596 (1980).

Should "subsequent" legislative history *ever* be relevant to the statutory interpreter? Why was the subsequent history persuasive to Judge Norris, who was very skeptical of the argument that private landowners had an easement by necessity across government forest lands?

2. *The Checkerboard Problem, Subsequent Legislative History, and the New Textualism.* The policy consequences of Judge Norris's new opinion seem quite malign. The fairest rule for checkerboard cases would be to give a right

---

access to non-federally owned land within the boundaries of the National Forest System * * *." § 1134(a) is addressed specifically to an area designated as "wilderness," while § 1323(a) is addressed to National Forest System lands in general. In cases involving wilderness areas, the Secretary has the option of exchanging land of equal value so that the wilderness area may be preserved. Thus, § 1134(a) could be construed to apply in the specific case of a wilderness area, and § 1323(a) could be construed to apply in all other cases.

Whether or not they are in fact irreconcilable we leave to another case when the issue is squarely presented for review.

of reasonable access to both the government and the private holder, but this is precluded by *Leo Sheep, supra.* The second best rule, then, might be to deny rights of access to both parties, for their mutual dependence would probably lead to a deal approximating the best rule (but with more transactions costs). The worst rule is one in which one party has a right of access (*Montana Wilderness*) and the other does not (*Leo Sheep*). This does not create incentives to bargain and may force the government to pay extra money and high transactions costs to take the right of access through eminent domain.

Is this seemingly dysfunctional result compelled by § 1323(a)? Has Judge Norris persuaded you that Congress "intended" to deprive the treasury of this money, and impair wilderness lands as well? Has Judge Norris even persuaded himself that his first opinion was wrong? Perhaps Judge Norris lost heart when Representative Udall—his bulwark in the first opinion—abandoned his earlier view of § 1323(a). So what? Wasn't Udall posturing in the first place? If Congress is going to create such a dysfunctional rule, shouldn't courts require explicit *statutory* language? If your instinct is "yes," then you need to bring a canon of interpretation into play. Could any established substantive canon apply here?

Subsequent legislative history is surely of no use to the new textualists. If ordinary legislative history is, as Justice Scalia argues, often cooked up by congressional staff and lobbyists to try to slant interpretation after the fact, the possibility for abuse is worse with subsequent legislative history, because there is less congressional monitoring and correction of misleading statements after the statute has been passed. One effect of the new textualism has been to push the Supreme Court toward greater skepticism about the value of subsequent legislative history than the Court had shown in the 1970s and early 1980s. *Rapanos* and *Solid Waste* (discussed in § 2D above) illustrate this reluctance, as the Court in both cases was extremely reluctant to read the 1972 Water Act in light of proposals rejected by Congress in 1977.[x] But even the skeptical decisions say that the Court will consider subsequent legislative history if it is very persuasive and/or accompanied by an amendment to the statute. See *Mackey v. Lanier Collection Agency & Service*, 486 U.S. 825, 839–40 (1988).

The Court in *Gozlon–Peretz v. United States*, 498 U.S. 395 (1991), accepted a "public reliance" type of argument similar to the one accepted by Judge Norris in the Second Checkerboard opinion: When a subsequent Congress assumes one interpretation of an earlier statute and acts upon that assumption in enacting a new statute, the Court will consider that as evidence in favor of the assumed interpretation. See also Justice Scalia's opinion concurring in the judgment in *Franklin v. Gwinnett County Public Schools*

---

x. See *Massachusetts v. EPA*, 549 U.S. 497, 528–530 (2007); *Doe v. Chao*, 540 U.S. 614 (2004) (rejecting Privacy Act plaintiff's reliance on statutes in pari materia, when such statutes were enacted after the Privacy Act); *Central Bank of Denver N.A. v. First Interstate Bank of Denver N.A.*, 511 U.S. 164, 185–86 (1994) (ignoring congressional interpretations in 1983 and 1988 committee reports in interpreting 1934 statute); *Chapman v. United States*, 500 U.S. 453, 464 n.4 (1991), *aff'g Marshall v. United States* (Chapter 2, § 3A) (refusing even to consider subsequent legislative discussion as evidence of statutory ambiguity in criminal sentencing case); *Sullivan v. Finkelstein*, 496 U.S. 617, 628 n.8 (1990) (rejecting arguments based upon subsequent committee print and report; in this case, Scalia, J., concurred but refused to join note 8, because he thought it inappropriate even to discuss subsequent legislative history); *United States v. Monsanto*, 491 U.S. 600, 609–10 (1989) (disregarding postenactment statements of several legislators).

(Chapter 6, § 1B), arguing that the Court should generally be reluctant to imply causes of action to enforce federal statutes, but not when Congress has relied on that understanding in subsequent legislation. Compare this approach with *Public Employees Retirement System of Ohio v. Betts*, 492 U.S. 158, 167–68 (1989) (refusing to credit subsequent conference report's understanding of statutory meaning when Congress amended statute). See also the extensive use of such history, including references to discussions pertaining to bills never enacted into law, in *FDA v. Brown & Williamson Tobacco Corp.* (Chapter 2, § 3B3, and noted earlier in this section).

3. *Post–Enactment Testimony and Amicus Briefs by Legislators.* The second Checkerboard opinion is just one example of how the battle to create legislative meaning can continue after the statute is enacted. Two other techniques have been used. One is the use of affidavits and depositions by legislators, especially at the state level (where legislative history is not always readily available or elaborate enough to provide much guidance). Some states consider such testimony "inadmissible evidence" of "legislative intent" but are, nonetheless, sometimes moved by it. For example, the Washington Supreme Court in *City of Spokane v. State*, 89 P.2d 826 (Wash. 1939), refused to admit affidavits or depositions of the Governor, Speaker of the House, chairs of the relevant committees, 33 Senators and 68 Representatives in one legislature and 33 Senators and 70 Representatives in the next legislature. Nonetheless, the Court overruled its prior interpretation of the statute, effectively conforming to the views pressed in the affidavits and depositions. Compare this interpretation with *Western Air Lines v. Board of Equalization*, 480 U.S. 123, 130 n.* (1987) (refusing to consider affidavit from lobbyist involved in the enactment of the law in question).

Another method is a legislator amicus brief. The Supreme Court in *Blanchette v. Connecticut Gen. Ins. Corp.*, 419 U.S. 102 (1974), relied on the statements made at oral argument by Representative Brock Adams (D–Wash.), representing 36 Members of Congress, as evidence that the Act did not withdraw a Tucker Act remedy for just compensation. Nine key legislators (six Democrats, then the majority party in Congress, and three key Republicans) involved in the controlling legislation filed an amicus brief in *Rapanos*. Their brief provided a comprehensive examination of the evolution of wetlands regulation, from the Federal Water Pollution Control Act of 1948, through the transformational amendments in 1972 and concluding with the Clean Water Act of 1977. The theme of their brief was that the 1972 law "articulated one of the broadest ecosystem restoration and protection aspirations in all of environmental law." The mandate of the statute was for the EPA and the Army Corps to view the country as a collection of integrated hydrological ecosystems whose integrity was threatened—a threat that had dire consequences for flood control, safe drinking water, and damage to animal populations. The aggressive and comprehensive Corps regulations were affirmatively ratified by the 1977 statute. Although the *Rapanos* plurality rejected this analysis, it was adopted by the four dissenters and may have had an impact on Justice Kennedy, who followed its key points and whose cautious concurring opinion represented the holding of the Court.

NOTES ON PRESIDENTIAL SIGNING OR VETO STATEMENTS

1. *Presidents' Use of Signing Statements.* Throughout history, Presidents have made statements about the bills they sign into law, and sometimes those statements have addressed important policy-related issues of statutory meaning, along one of at least three dimensions: (1) discussions highlighting important features of legislation; (2) objections to the constitutionality of some part of a law, usually with an indication that the administration would apply the law more narrowly than it was written; or (3) an intention to apply a law in a particular way, based upon the executive department's interpretation of that statute. See Curtis A. Bradley & Eric A. Posner, *Presidential Signing Statements and Executive Power*, 23 Const. Comment. 307 (2006).

As Professors Bradley and Posner document, Presidents have long deployed signing statements to signal constitutional disagreements with Congress. In the last generation, Presidents have increasingly deployed signing statements to set forth their views that they will apply constitutionally questionable statutes narrowly or not at all. Such statements ordinarily appear in the Weekly Compilation of Presidential Documents, but beginning in 1986 the West Publishing Company has regularly included signing statements in its *United States Code Congressional and Administrative News* (USCCAN), which is the most readily accessible reference work for legislative history. Some members of the executive branch took the position that the President's statements are especially authoritative on issues of "legislative intent," perhaps trumping contrary statements of Senators and Representatives themselves.[y]

The Bush–Cheney Administration (2001–09) challenged or reinterpreted more than 800 statutory provisions, apparently more than the total number of provisions reinterpreted by all three of his immediate predecessors (Presidents Reagan, Bush, and Clinton). Bradley & Posner, *Presidential Signing Statements*, 324–25. For example, the Detainee Treatment Act of 2005 banned cruel, inhuman, or degrading treatment of detainees, such as those at Guantanamo Bay, Cuba. When signing this bill into law, President George W. Bush stated that the executive branch would construe the ban "in a manner consistent with the constitutional authority of the President to supervise the unitary executive branch and as Commander in Chief and consistent with the constitutional limitations on the judicial power." The administration itself engaged in fierce internal debates about how to interpret laws banning "torture" as well as "cruel, inhuman, or degrading treatment" of accused enemy combatants.

President Barack H. Obama issued to the heads of all executive departments and agencies a Memorandum on Presidential Signing Statements (March 9, 2009), available at http://www.gpo.gov/fdsys/pkg/DCPD–200900138/pdf/DCPD–200900138.pdf (viewed Jan. 1, 2012). The Memorandum started with the following general philosophy:

---

[y] *The New Republic*, 3 Nov. 1986, at 13–14. See also Memorandum from Samuel A. Alito, Jr., Deputy Assistant Attorney Gen., Office of Legal Counsel, to the Litigation Strategy Working Group (Feb. 5, 1986), available at http://www.archives.gov/news/samuel-alito/accession–060–89–269/Acc060–89–269–box6–SG–LSWG–AlitotoLSWG–Feb1986.pdf.

Constitutional signing statements should not be used to suggest that the President will disregard statutory requirements on the basis of policy disagreements. At the same time, such signing statements serve a legitimate function in our system, at least when based on well-founded constitutional objections. In appropriately limited circumstances, they represent an exercise of the President's constitutional obligation to take care that the laws be faithfully executed, and they promote a healthy dialogue between the executive branch and the Congress.

Accordingly, President Obama endorsed the prior presidential practice of using signing statements to articulate constitutional objections to provisions of statutes the President is signing, but cautioned that the President ought to respect the presumption of constitutionality that accompanies legislation adopted through the Article I, § 7 process. President Obama also endorsed the practice of using signing statements to announce narrowing constructions of such provisions, albeit "only if that construction is a legitimate one." Recall the avoidance canon discussed in Chapter 3, § 2B.

2. *Should Presidential Signing Statements Be Considered Persuasive of Statutory Meaning?* Attorney General Edward Meese and some subsequent commentators have maintained that presidential signing statements should "count" as evidence of statutory meaning, for the same reasons a committee report or a congressional sponsor's explanation might count. Academic commentators and the ABA have been reluctant to accept the argument that signing statements are authoritative, for the same reasons they are dubious about "subsequent legislative history"—it is unreliable evidence of the expectations of the enacting coalition, and there is too much opportunity for manipulation.[z] If an interpreter is a textualist, he or she would be suspicious of or uninterested in any such background material, whether originating in the Capitol or the White House. For more contextualist interpreters, problems of reliability are troubling: Congress cannot respond officially to the President's signing statement, whereas a misleading statement by a legislative sponsor can trigger all sorts of counterattacks (amendments to the bill, contrary statements by other Members, and so on). It is probably for these kinds of reasons that federal judges rarely mention presidential signing statements and almost never give them dispositive weight.[aa]

---

z. American Bar Association, Task Force on Presidential Signing Statements and the Separation of Powers Doctrine, Report with Recommendations (2006) (rejecting the aggressive use of signing statements); *Symposium: The Last Word? The Constitutional Implications of Presidential Signing Statements*, 16 Wm. & Mary Bill of Rts. J. 1–314 (2007) (presenting a variety of perspectives, almost all of them critical of signing statements as authoritative); Marc Graber & Kurt Wimmer, *Presidential Signing Statements as Interpretations of Legislative Intent: An Executive Aggrandizement of Power*, 24 Harv. J. Legis. 363 (1987); Christopher S. Kelley & Bryan W. Marshall, *Assessing Presidential Power: Signing Statements and Veto Threats as Coordinated Strategies*, 37 Am. Pol. Res. 508 (2009); Nicholas J. Leddy, Note, *Determining Due Deference: Examining When Courts Should Defer to Agency Use of Presidential Signing Statements*, 59 Admin. L. Rev. 869 (2008). See also Trevor W. Morrison, *Constitutional Avoidance in the Executive Branch*, 106 Colum. L. Rev. 1189 (2006), who argues against executive department reliance on the avoidance canon, which has been a mainstay of controversial presidential signing statements since the Reagan Administration.

aa. Among the few court of appeals decisions giving weight to signing statements, consider *United States v. Perlaza*, 439 F.3d 1149, 1163 (9th Cir. 2006) (Clinton signing statement confirms suggestion in conference report); *United States v. Gonzales*, 311 F.3d 440, 443 & n.2 (1st Cir. 2002) (similar); *United States v. Story*, 891 F.2d 988, 994 (2d Cir. 1989) (relying on a Reagan

On the other hand, for the same reasons that interpreters are usually interested in the views of the congressional sponsors, they might be interested in the views of the President, who effectively sponsors much major legislation and whose veto power (not to mention his status as chief of one of the two major political parties) gives him an important bargaining role in virtually all major legislation. See Charles Cameron, *Veto Bargaining: Presidents and the Politics of Negative Power* (2000); William N. Eskridge Jr. & John Ferejohn, *The Article I, Section 7 Game*, 80 Geo. L.J. 523 (1992). Such views provide useful policy or even linguistic context for understanding the statute, and they can be good evidence of where the political equilibrium lies. While the President might be tempted to negate deals made in Congress, the fact remains that Members can publicly denounce any such interpretation, as they have been doing, with increasing vigor. Because the President is a repeat player on Capitol Hill, he or she has some incentive not to lie about what deals were made. Moreover, as the official charged "to take care" that laws be "faithfully executed," U.S. Const. art. II, § 2, the President's interpretation might be entitled to considerable *deference*. See Elena Kagan, *Presidential Administration,* 114 Harv. L. Rev. 2245 (2001); Chapter 6, § 3C2 (examining the deference courts give to executive department interpretation of statutes).

Finally, from a more formal perspective, in assessing presidential signing statements it may be useful to retreat to a fundamental issue, whether the bill is ambiguous. If it is, and if the congressional history does not clear up the problem, there may be good reason for the President to state that he or she is signing it based on a certain interpretation of it, at least so long as that interpretation is reasonable. See Kagan, *Presidential Administration* (making this precise argument). In this circumstance, the President is not violating the text or legislative intent, and the President's good-faith interpretation may be a useful guide to courts and administrative agencies. On the other hand, if the bill, as supplemented by the legislative history, is pretty clear on a point, our constitutional system seems to give the President only two options—to acquiesce (by signing it or by allowing it to go into law without presidential signature) or to veto it—and not the option of attempting to skew it in some other direction. See Saikrishna Prakash, *Why the President Must Veto Unconstitutional Bills*, 16 Wm. & Mary Bill of Rts. J. 81 (2007). Although Congress may formally override a veto, it has no authoritative way to reject a signing statement (if the statute is already clear).

3. *Veto Statements.* Courts will sometimes rely on the President's veto statement. If Congress overrides the President's veto, then an interpreter might infer that Congress rejected the President's preferences. See *McDonald v. Santa Fe Trail Transportation Co.*, 427 U.S. 273, 295 & n.26 (1976); *Kennedy v. Mendoza–Martinez*, 372 U.S. 144, 178 & n.33 (1963); *United States v. CIO*, 335 U.S. 106, 138–39 (1948) (Rutledge, J., concurring in the result). If, instead, the bill is modified and enacted with the President's signature, the veto statement may provide a good understanding of the nature of the new bill. See *United States v. Yermian*, 468 U.S. 63, 72–75 (1984).

---

signing statement, among other factors, to resolve conflicting interpretations in the House and Senate legislative history).

In assessing whether the 1991 Civil Rights Act was retroactive, the Supreme Court in *Landgraf v. USI Film Prods.*, 511 U.S. 244, 255–57 (1994), considered President Bush's veto of the 1990 version of that legislation as relevant background. Specifically, Justice Stevens's opinion for the Court noted that the 1990 bill passed by Congress contained provisions making the congressional override of various Supreme Court decisions retroactive, thereby trumping the normal presumption that legislation is prospective only. President George H.W. Bush "briefly" objected to the retroactivity provisions in his veto message. After Congress in 1990 was unable to override his veto, Congress in 1991 developed a more moderate bill, designed to meet the President's objections. The 1991 bill (which became law) had no provisions whatsoever on retroactivity. Justice Stevens drew from this history the conclusion that Congress was aware of the presumption against retroactive legislation, tried to override it, and gave up on the effort when it met with presidential objection. Is this a cogent use of presidential veto statements? If yes, consider the following problem and see if you think it cogent as well.

PROBLEM 4–3

Presidential Signing Statement

Congressional outrage at media accounts of torture of non-American prisoners by American guards and interrogators led to the enactment, by large margins, of the Detainee Treatment Act of 2005, Pub. L. No. 109–148, Div. A, tit. X (2005). As noted above, the Act sets limits on torture that the executive branch resisted on grounds that they interfered with its authority to conduct the war on terror. For war-on-terror prisoners held at Guantanamo Bay, the Act also substituted for habeas corpus a special summary appeals process to the D.C. Circuit. When the Act was passed, in 2005, numerous Guantanamo detainees were already pursuing habeas relief in the federal courts. The question arose whether the Act applied to (and therefore required dismissal of) habeas cases filed by those detainees and pending on the date of enactment.

Section 1005(e) of the DTA amended 28 U.S.C. § 2241 (the federal habeas law) by adding at the end the following:

(e) Except as provided in section 1005 of the Detainee Treatment Act of 2005, no court, justice, or judge shall have jurisdiction to hear or consider—

(1) an application for a writ of habeas corpus filed by or on behalf of an alien detained by the Department of Defense at Guantanamo Bay, Cuba; or

(2) any other action against the United States or its agents relating to any aspect of the detention by the Department of Defense of an alien at Guantanamo Bay, Cuba, who—

(A) is currently in military custody; or

(B) has been determined by the United States Court of Appeals for the District of Columbia Circuit in accordance with the procedures set forth in section 1005(e) of the Detainee Treatment Act of 2005 to have been properly detained as an enemy combatant.

Section 1005(h)(1) provided that "this section shall take effect upon the date of the enactment of this Act." Section 1005(h)(2) said: "Paragraphs (2) and (3) of subsection (e) shall apply with respect to any claim whose review is governed by one of such paragraphs and that is pending on or after the date of the enactment of this Act."

The government invoked the canon in favor of applying statutes conferring or ousting jurisdiction immediately, *Landgraf v. USI Film Prods.*, 511 U.S. 244, 274 (1994), while the habeas claimants relied on the presumption against retroactive application of new statutes. Id. at 280. The claimants relied on statements by Senator Carl Levin, a Democratic sponsor, that the DTA would not apply to pending cases and objected to a proposal by Senator Lindsay Graham, a Republican sponsor, that would have made § 1005(e)(1) applicable to pending cases. The government responded with statements by Senators Graham and John Kyl, another Republican sponsor, that the Act as passed applied to pending Guantanamo cases.

The government also invoked President George W. Bush's signing statement, which said this: "[T]he executive branch shall construe section 1005 to preclude the Federal courts from exercising subject matter jurisdiction over any existing or future action, including applications for writs of habeas corpus, described in section 1005." See Presidential Statement on Signing the Department of Defense, Emergency Supplemental Appropriations to Address Hurricanes in the Gulf of Mexico, and Pandemic Influenza Act, 2006, 41 Weekly Comp. Pres. Doc. 1918 (Dec. 30, 2005).

This issue reached the Supreme Court, where the government argued that federal judges no longer had jurisdiction to adjudicate the Guantanamo habeas claims. What role, if any, should the President's signing statement have played in the Court's interpretation? How should textualist Justices Scalia and Thomas treat the signing statement? Justices Breyer and Stevens? In your view, what is the right interpretation? Compare *Hamdan v. Rumsfeld*, 548 U.S. 557, 575–84 (2006), with *id.* at 655–72 (dissenting opinion).

Part F. Legislative Inaction

What the legislature doesn't do may be as significant as what it does. Recall the dog didn't bark canon: when no one in the legislative discussions says that an important policy is being changed, a court should presume that no big changes are intended. This canon is related to the *canon of continuity* defended by David Shapiro, *Continuity and Change in Statutory Interpretation*, 67 N.Y.U. L. Rev. 921 (1992). Professor Shapiro maintains that the structure of American government suggests a constitutional bias against discontinuity in legal obligations and rights. Thus, in the absence of clear indications to the contrary, statutes should be construed to maintain established rules and practices.

You have already seen plenty of examples of judicial inferences (or not) from legislative inaction. There are three specific doctrines that relate to Congress's failure to do something, and it is useful to separate them out.[bb]

(a) *The Acquiescence Rule.* If Congress is aware of an authoritative agency or judicial interpretation of a statute and doesn't amend the statute, the Court has sometimes presumed that Congress has "acquiesced" in the interpretation's correctness. The acquiescence rule was followed by the Court to reaffirm its own prior interpretations of statutes in *Johnson v. Transportation Agency* and in *Flood v. Kuhn* (both reproduced in Chapter 1, § 3B). But the acquiescence rule can also support implicit congressional ratification of a uniform line of federal appellate interpretations or in a longstanding agency interpretation. E.g., *Zuni Pub. Sch. Dist. No. 89 v. Department of Educ.* (excerpted in Chapter 2, § 3A).

This rule is one that the new textualists find particularly abhorrent. E.g., *Johnson* (Scalia, J., dissenting). Absent overwhelming evidence of acquiescence, the *Solid Waste* Court announced that the Justices were loathe to replace the plain text and original understanding of a statute with an agency interpretation. *Solid Waste,* 531 U.S. at 172–73. Nonetheless, this doctrine is still invoked if there is concrete evidence Congress was aware of the longstanding interpretation and paid attention to the issue, as in the FDA Tobacco Case, where Justice Scalia himself signed onto dozens of pages of legislative history discussion. See also *Zuni Pub. Sch. Dist.* (Chapter 2, § 3A).[cc]

(b) *The Reenactment Rule.* If Congress reenacts a statute without making any material changes in its wording, the Court will often presume that Congress intends to incorporate authoritative agency and judicial interpretations of that language into the reenacted statute. The leading Supreme Court statement of this rule is found in *Lorillard v. Pons* (§ 3 of this chapter), which stated: "Congress is presumed to be aware of an administrative or judicial interpretation of a statute and to adopt that interpretation when it reenacts a statute without change." Like the acquiescence rule, the reenactment rule is much more likely to be invoked if the interpretation is a foundational one—that is, the interpretation is authoritative (namely, a leading Supreme Court case or the decision of the chief agency enforcing the law), settled, and likely to have yielded private and public reliance. See *Jama v. Immigration & Customs Enforcement,* 543 U.S. 335 (2005) (application of reenactment rule inappropriate because prior state of the law not well settled); *Fogerty v. Fantasy, Inc.,* 510 U.S. 517, 527–33 (1994) (same, and contrasting the well-settled stature of

---

bb. The account that follows is drawn from James J. Brudney, *Congressional Commentary on Judicial Interpretations of Statutes: Idle Chatter or Telling Response?*, 93 Mich. L. Rev. 1 (1994); William N. Eskridge Jr., *Interpreting Legislative Inaction*, 87 Mich. L. Rev. 67 (1988), which also contains appendices listing cases following or declining to follow these doctrines.

cc. See also *Evans v. United States,* 504 U.S. 255, 269 (1992) (assuming Congress had acquiesced in longstanding and highly visible interpretation of statute in lower courts); *United States v. Riverside Bayview Homes, Inc.,* 474 U.S. 121 (1985) (Conference Committee killed House effort to overrule Corps of Engineers' jurisdiction over "wetlands"); *Heckler v. Day,* 467 U.S. 104 (1984) (congressional hearings on disability benefit delays did not produce legislation to hurry agency along); *Guardians Ass'n v. Civil Serv. Comm'n,* 463 U.S. 582, 593 & n.14 (1983) (opinion of White, J.) (acquiescence in Title VI regulations).

Creedence Clearwater Revival "as one of the greatest American rock and roll bands of all time").

A dramatic invocation of the reenactment rule came in *Farragher v. City of Boca Raton*, 524 U.S. 775 (1998). The Court ruled that employers can be vicariously liable under Title VII for hostile work environments created or tolerated by supervisors, subject to a reasonableness defense. Justice Souter's opinion for the Court relied on the holding and reasoning in *Meritor Sav. Bank FSB v. Vinson*, 477 U.S. 57 (1986), which had greatly elaborated upon the spare language in Title VII that employers cannot "discriminate" because of sex by holding that "hostile environment sexual harassment" was prohibited. Dissenting Justices Thomas and Scalia objected that the Court's opinions were no more than "willful policymaking" in violation of the statute. Justice Souter responded that the holding and reasoning of *Meritor* were binding on the Court not only as a matter of *stare decisis*, but also because it had been ratified by Congress when it amended Title VII in 1991. See *Farragher*, 524 U.S. at 792. Although the 1991 Act overrode a number of Supreme Court interpretations of Title VII, it left *Meritor* intact, which Justice Souter deemed "conspicuous." He continued, "We thus have to assume that in expanding employers' potential liability under Title VII, Congress relied on our statements in *Meritor* about the limits of employer liability. To disregard those statements now * * * would be not only to disregard *stare decisis* in statutory interpretation, but to substitute our revised judgment about the proper allocation of the costs of harassment for Congress's considered decision on the subject." *Id.* at 804 n.4.

(c) *The Rejected Proposal Rule.* If Congress (in conference committee) or one chamber (on the floor) considers and rejects specific statutory language, the Court has often been reluctant to interpret the statute along the lines of the rejected language. The leading case is *Runyon v. McCrary*, 427 U.S. 160 (1976), where the Court reaffirmed a debatable precedent interpreting the Civil Rights Act of 1866, based in large part upon its perception that the Senate in 1971 had rejected attempts to override that interpretation. See also *FDA v. Brown & Williamson* (the FDA Tobacco Case reproduced in Chapter 2, § 3B3).

The *Solid Waste* Court expressed a skeptical view of this kind of evidence: " '[F]ailed legislative proposals are "a particularly dangerous ground on which to rest an interpretation of a prior statute." ' " *Central Bank of Denver N.A. v. First Interstate Bank of Denver N.A.*, 511 U.S. 164, 187 (1994). A bill can be proposed for any number of reasons, and it can be rejected for just as many others. The relationship between the actions and inactions of the 95th Congress and the intent of the 92d Congress in passing § 404(a) is also considerably attenuated. Because 'subsequent history is less illuminating than the contemporaneous evidence,' *Hagen v. Utah*, 510 U.S. 399, 420 (1994), respondents face a difficult task in overcoming the plain text and import of § 404(a)." *Solid Waste*, 531 U.S. at 169–70.

Consider these various doctrines in connection with the following case, which the FDA Tobacco Court relied on for its acquiescence argument.

BOB JONES UNIVERSITY v. UNITED STATES

Supreme Court of the United States, 1983
461 U.S. 574, 103 S.Ct. 2017, 76 L.Ed.2d 157

CHIEF JUSTICE BURGER delivered the opinion of the Court.

We granted certiorari to decide whether petitioners, nonprofit private schools that prescribe and enforce racially discriminatory admissions standards on the basis of religious doctrine, qualify as tax-exempt organizations under § 501(c)(3) of the Internal Revenue Code of 1954.

[I] Until 1970, the Internal Revenue Service granted tax-exempt status to private schools, without regard to their racial admissions policies, under § 501(c)(3) of the Internal Revenue Code, 26 U.S.C. § 501(c)(3),[6] and granted charitable deductions for contributions to such schools under § 170 of the Code, 26 U.S.C. § 170.[7]

On January 12, 1970, a three-judge District Court for the District of Columbia issued a preliminary injunction prohibiting the IRS from according tax-exempt status to private schools in Mississippi that discriminated as to admissions on the basis of race. *Green v. Kennedy*, 309 F. Supp. 1127, appeal dism'd *sub nom. Cannon v. Green*, 398 U.S. 956 (1970). Thereafter, in July 1970, the IRS concluded that it could "no longer legally justify allowing tax-exempt status [under § 501(c)(3)] to private schools which practice racial discrimination." IRS News Release July 7, 1970. At the same time, the IRS announced that it could not "treat gifts to such schools as charitable deductions for income tax purposes [under § 170]." By letter dated November 30, 1970, the IRS formally notified private schools, including those involved in this litigation, of this change in policy, "applicable to all private schools in the United States at all levels of education."

On June 30, 1971, the three-judge District Court issued its opinion on the merits of the Mississippi challenge. *Green v. Connally*, 330 F.Supp. 1150, summarily aff'd *sub nom. Coit v. Green*, 404 U.S. 997 (1971). That

---

6. Section 501(c)(3) lists the following organizations, which, pursuant to § 501(a), are exempt from taxation unless denied tax exemptions under other specified sections of the Code:

"Corporations, and any community chest, fund, or foundation, *organized and operated exclusively for religious, charitable*, scientific, testing for public safety, literary, *or educational purposes*, or to foster national or international amateur sports competition (but only if no part of its activities involves the provision of athletic facilities or equipment), or for the prevention of cruelty to children or animals, no part of the net earnings of which inures to the benefit of any private shareholder or individual, no substantial part of the activities of which is carrying on propaganda, or otherwise attempting, to influence legislation * * *, and which does not participate in, or intervene in (including the publishing or distributing of statements), any political campaign on behalf of any candidate for public office." (Emphasis added.)

7. Section 170(a) allows deductions for certain "charitable contributions." Section 170(c)(2)(B) includes within the definition of "charitable contribution" a contribution or gift to or for the use of a corporation "organized and operated exclusively for religious, charitable, scientific, literary, or educational purposes * * *."

court approved the IRS's amended construction of the Tax Code. The court also held that racially discriminatory private schools were not entitled to exemption under § 501(c)(3) and that donors were not entitled to deductions for contributions to such schools under § 170. The court permanently enjoined the Commissioner of Internal Revenue from approving tax-exempt status for any school in Mississippi that did not publicly maintain a policy of nondiscrimination.

The revised policy on discrimination was formalized in Revenue Ruling 71–447, 1971–2 Cum. Bull. 230:

> "Both the courts and the Internal Revenue Service have long recognized that the statutory requirement of being 'organized and operated exclusively for religious, charitable, * * * or educational purposes' was intended to express the basic common law concept [of 'charity']. * * * All charitable trusts, educational or otherwise, are subject to the requirement that the purpose of the trust may not be illegal or contrary to public policy."

Based on the "national policy to discourage racial discrimination in education," the IRS ruled that "a [private] school not having a racially nondiscriminatory policy as to students is not 'charitable' within the common law concepts reflected in sections 170 and 501(c)(3) of the Code."
* * *

[II.A] In Revenue Ruling 71–447, the IRS formalized the policy, first announced in 1970, that § 170 and § 501(c)(3) embrace the common-law "charity" concept. Under that view, to qualify for a tax exemption pursuant to § 501(c)(3), an institution must show, first, that it falls within one of the eight categories expressly set forth in that section, and second, that its activity is not contrary to settled public policy.

Section 501(c)(3) provides that "[c]orporations * * * organized and operated exclusively for religious, charitable * * * or educational purposes" are entitled to tax exemption. Petitioners argue that the plain language of the statute guarantees them tax-exempt status. They emphasize the absence of any language in the statute expressly requiring all exempt organizations to be "charitable" in the common-law sense, and they contend that the disjunctive "or" separating the categories in § 501(c)(3) precludes such a reading. Instead, they argue that if an institution falls within one or more of the specified categories it is automatically entitled to exemption, without regard to whether it also qualifies as "charitable." The Court of Appeals rejected that contention and concluded that petitioners' interpretation of the statute "tears section 501(c)(3) from its roots."

It is a well-established canon of statutory construction that a court should go beyond the literal language of a statute if reliance on that language would defeat the plain purpose of the statute. * * *

Section 501(c)(3) therefore must be analyzed and construed within the framework of the Internal Revenue Code and against the background of the congressional purposes. Such an examination reveals unmistakable evidence that, underlying all relevant parts of the Code, is the intent that entitlement to tax exemption depends on meeting certain common-law standards of charity—namely, that an institution seeking tax-exempt status must serve a public purpose and not be contrary to established public policy.

This "charitable" concept appears explicitly in § 170 of the Code. That section contains a list of organizations virtually identical to that contained in § 501(c)(3). It is apparent that Congress intended that list to have the same meaning in both sections.[10] In § 170, Congress used the list of organizations in defining the term "charitable contributions." On its face, therefore, § 170 reveals that Congress' intention was to provide tax benefits to organizations serving charitable purposes. The form of § 170 simply makes plain what common sense and history tell us: in enacting both § 170 and § 501(c)(3), Congress sought to provide tax benefits to charitable organizations, to encourage the development of private institutions that serve a useful public purpose or supplement or take the place of public institutions of the same kind.

Tax exemptions for certain institutions thought beneficial to the social order of the country as a whole, or to a particular community, are deeply rooted in our history, as in that of England. The origins of such exemptions lie in the special privileges that have long been extended to charitable trusts.[12]

More than a century ago, this Court announced the caveat that is critical in this case:

> "[I]t has now become an established principle of American law, that courts of chancery will sustain and protect * * * a gift * * * to public charitable uses, *provided the same is consistent with local laws and public policy * * *." Perin v. Carey,* 24 How. 465, 501 (1861) (emphasis added).

Soon after that, in 1877, the Court commented:

---

10. The predecessor of § 170 originally was enacted in 1917, as part of the War Revenue Act of 1917, ch. 63, § 1201(2), 40 Stat. 330, whereas the predecessor of § 501(c)(3) dates back to the income tax law of 1894, Act of Aug. 27, 1894, ch. 349, 28 Stat. 509. There are minor differences between the lists of organizations in the two sections. Nevertheless, the two sections are closely related; both seek to achieve the same basic goal of encouraging the development of certain organizations through the grant of tax benefits. The language of the two sections is in most respects identical, and the Commissioner and the courts consistently have applied many of the same standards in interpreting those sections. To the extent that § 170 "aids in ascertaining the meaning" of § 501(c)(3), therefore, it is "entitled to great weight," *United States v. Stewart,* 311 U.S. 60, 64–65 (1940).

12. The form and history of the charitable exemption and deduction sections of the various income tax Acts reveal that Congress was guided by the common law of charitable trusts. See Simon, *The Tax–Exempt Status of Racially Discriminatory Religious Schools,* 36 Tax L.Rev. 477, 485–489 (1981). Congress acknowledged as much in 1969. The House Report on the Tax Reform Act of 1969, Pub.L. 91–172, 83 Stat. 487, stated that the § 501(c)(3) exemption was available only to institutions that served "the specified charitable purposes," H.R.Rep. No. 91–413, pt. 1, p. 35 (1969), and described "charitable" as "a term that has been used in the law of trusts for hundreds of years." *Id.,* at 43. We need not consider whether Congress intended to incorporate into the Internal Revenue Code any aspects of charitable trust law other than the requirements of public benefit and a valid public purpose.

"A charitable use, *where neither law nor public policy forbids*, may be applied to almost any thing *that tends to promote the well-doing and well-being of social man." Ould v. Washington Hospital for Foundlings*, 95 U.S. 303, 311 (emphasis added). * * *

When the Government grants exemptions or allows deductions all taxpayers are affected; the very fact of the exemption or deduction for the donor means that other taxpayers can be said to be indirect and vicarious "donors." Charitable exemptions are justified on the basis that the exempt entity confers a public benefit—a benefit which the society or the community may not itself choose or be able to provide, or which supplements and advances the work of public institutions already supported by tax revenues. History buttresses logic to make clear that, to warrant exemption under § 501(c)(3), an institution must fall within a category specified in that section and must demonstrably serve and be in harmony with the public interest. The institution's purpose must not be so at odds with the common community conscience as to undermine any public benefit that might otherwise be conferred.

[II.B] We are bound to approach these questions with full awareness that determinations of public benefit and public policy are sensitive matters with serious implications for the institutions affected; a declaration that a given institution is not "charitable" should be made only where there can be no doubt that the activity involved is contrary to a fundamental public policy. But there can no longer be any doubt that racial discrimination in education violates deeply and widely accepted views of elementary justice. Prior to 1954, public education in many places still was conducted under the pall of *Plessy v. Ferguson*, 163 U.S. 537 (1896); racial segregation in primary and secondary education prevailed in many parts of the country.[20] This Court's decision in *Brown v. Board of Education*, 347 U.S. 483 (1954), signalled an end to that era. Over the past quarter of a century, every pronouncement of this Court and myriad Acts of Congress and Executive Orders attest a firm national policy to prohibit racial segregation and discrimination in public education.

An unbroken line of cases following *Brown v. Board of Education* establishes beyond doubt this Court's view that racial discrimination in education violates a most fundamental national public policy, as well as rights of individuals.

"The right of a student not to be segregated on racial grounds in schools * * * is indeed so fundamental and pervasive that it is

---

20. In 1894, when the first charitable exemption provision was enacted, racially segregated educational institutions would not have been regarded as against public policy. Yet contemporary standards must be considered in determining whether given activities provide a public benefit and are entitled to the charitable tax exemption. In *Walz v. Tax Comm'n*, 397 U.S. 664, 673 (1970), we observed: "Qualification for tax exemption is not perpetual or immutable; some tax-exempt groups lose that status when their activities take them outside the classification and new entities can come into being and qualify for exemption." Charitable trust law also makes clear that the definition of "charity" depends upon contemporary standards. See, e.g., Restatement (Second) of Trusts § 374, Comment *a* (1959).

embraced in the concept of due process of law." *Cooper v. Aaron*, 358 U.S. 1, 19 (1958).

In *Norwood v. Harrison*, 413 U.S. 455, 468–469 (1973), we dealt with a nonpublic institution:

> "[A] private school—even one that discriminates—fulfills an important educational function; *however, * * * [that] legitimate educational function cannot be isolated from discriminatory practices * * *. [D]iscriminatory treatment exerts a pervasive influence on the entire educational process.*" (Emphasis added.)

Congress, in Titles IV and VI of the Civil Rights Act of 1964, Pub.L. 88–352, 78 Stat. 241, 42 U.S.C. §§ 2000c et seq., 2000c–6, 2000d et seq., clearly expressed its agreement that racial discrimination in education violates a fundamental public policy. Other sections of that Act, and numerous enactments since then, testify to the public policy against racial discrimination. See, e.g., [the Voting Rights Act of 1965, Title VIII of the Civil Rights Act of 1968, the Emergency School Aid Acts of 1972 and 1978].

The Executive Branch has consistently placed its support behind eradication of racial discrimination. Several years before this Court's decision in *Brown v. Board of Education*, President Truman issued Executive Orders prohibiting racial discrimination in federal employment decisions, Exec. Order No. 9980, 3 CFR 720 (1943–1948 Comp.), and in classifications for the Selective Service, Exec. Order No. 9988, 3 CFR 726, 729 (1943–1948 Comp.). In 1957, President Eisenhower employed military forces to ensure compliance with federal standards in school desegregation programs. Exec. Order No. 10730, 3 CFR 389 (1954–1958 Comp.). And in 1962, President Kennedy announced:

> "[T]he granting of Federal assistance for * * * housing and related facilities from which Americans are excluded because of their race, color, creed, or national origin is unfair, unjust, and inconsistent with the public policy of the United States as manifested in its Constitution and laws." Exec. Order No. 11063, 3 CFR 652 (1959–1963 Comp.).

These are but a few of numerous Executive Orders over the past three decades demonstrating the commitment of the Executive Branch to the fundamental policy of eliminating racial discrimination.

Few social or political issues in our history have been more vigorously debated and more extensively ventilated than the issue of racial discrimination, particularly in education. Given the stress and anguish of the history of efforts to escape from the shackles of the "separate but equal" doctrine of *Plessy v. Ferguson*, it cannot be said that educational institutions that, for whatever reasons, practice racial discrimination, are institutions exercising "beneficial and stabilizing influences in community life," *Walz v. Tax Comm'n*, 397 U.S. 664, 673 (1970), or should be encouraged by having all taxpayers share in their support by way of special tax status.

There can thus be no question that the interpretation of § 170 and § 501(c)(3) announced by the IRS in 1970 was correct. That it may be seen as belated does not undermine its soundness. It would be wholly incompatible with the concepts underlying tax exemption to grant the benefit of tax-exempt status to racially discriminatory educational entities, which "exer[t] a pervasive influence on the entire educational process." *Norwood v. Harrison, supra.* Whatever may be the rationale for such private schools' policies, and however sincere the rationale may be, racial discrimination in education is contrary to public policy. Racially discriminatory educational institutions cannot be viewed as conferring a public benefit within the "charitable" concept discussed earlier, or within the congressional intent underlying § 170 and § 501(c)(3).

[II.C] [Chief Justice Burger rejected the argument that the IRS did not have the authority to issue the 1970 rule and that its longstanding prior policy could only be overturned by legislative amendment of the Code. He reasoned that the IRS had been given broad rulemaking power by Congress and, moreover, that the policy adopted by the IRS was fully consistent with national policy since *Brown* and the Civil Rights Act of 1964.]

[II.D] The actions of Congress since 1970 leave no doubt that the IRS reached the correct conclusion in exercising its authority. It is, of course, not unknown for independent agencies or the Executive Branch to misconstrue the intent of a statute; Congress can and often does correct such misconceptions, if the courts have not done so. Yet for a dozen years Congress has been made aware—acutely aware—of the IRS rulings of 1970 and 1971. As we noted earlier, few issues have been the subject of more vigorous and widespread debate and discussion in and out of Congress than those related to racial segregation in education. Sincere adherents advocating contrary views have ventilated the subject for well over three decades. Failure of Congress to modify the IRS rulings of 1970 and 1971, of which Congress was, by its own studies and by public discourse, constantly reminded, and Congress' awareness of the denial of tax-exempt status for racially discriminatory schools when enacting other and related legislation make out an unusually strong case of legislative acquiescence in and ratification by implication of the 1970 and 1971 rulings.

Ordinarily, and quite appropriately, courts are slow to attribute significance to the failure of Congress to act on particular legislation. We have observed that "unsuccessful attempts at legislation are not the best of guides to legislative intent." Here, however, we do not have an ordinary claim of legislative acquiescence. Only one month after the IRS announced its position in 1970, Congress held its first hearings on this precise issue. Equal Educational Opportunity: Hearings before the Senate Select Committee on Equal Educational Opportunity, 91st Cong., 2d Sess. 1991 (1970). Exhaustive hearings have been held on the issue at various times since then. These include hearings in February 1982, after we granted review in this case. Administration's Change in Federal Policy Regarding the Tax Status of Racially Discriminatory Private Schools: Hearing before the House Committee on Ways and Means, 97th Cong., 2d Sess. (1982).

Nonaction by Congress is not often a useful guide, but the nonaction here is significant. During the past 12 years there have been no fewer than 13 bills introduced to overturn the IRS interpretation of § 501(c)(3). Not one of these bills has emerged from any committee, although Congress has enacted numerous other amendments to § 501 during this same period, including an amendment to § 501(c)(3) itself. Tax Reform Act of 1976, Pub.L. 94–455, § 1313(a), 90 Stat. 1730. It is hardly conceivable that Congress—and in this setting, any Member of Congress—was not abundantly aware of what was going on. In view of its prolonged and acute awareness of so important an issue, Congress' failure to act on the bills proposed on this subject provides added support for concluding that Congress acquiesced in the IRS rulings of 1970 and 1971.

The evidence of congressional approval of the policy embodied in Revenue Ruling 71–447 goes well beyond the failure of Congress to act on legislative proposals. Congress affirmatively manifested its acquiescence in the IRS policy when it enacted the present § 501(i) of the Code, Act of Oct. 20, 1976, Pub.L. 94–568, 90 Stat. 2697. That provision denies tax-exempt status to social clubs whose charters or policy statements provide for "discrimination against any person on the basis of race, color, or religion." Both the House and Senate Committee Reports on that bill articulated the national policy against granting tax exemptions to racially discriminatory private clubs. S. Rep. No. 94–1318, p. 8 (1976); H.R. Rep. No. 94–1353, p. 8 (1976).

Even more significant is the fact that both Reports focus on this Court's affirmance of *Green v. Connally*, 330 F.Supp. 1150 (DC 1971), as having established that "discrimination on account of race is inconsistent with an *educational institution's* tax-exempt status." S. Rep. No. 94–1318 at 7–8, and n. 5; H.R. Rep. No. 94–1353 at 8, and n. 5 (emphasis added). These references in congressional Committee Reports on an enactment denying tax exemptions to racially discriminatory private social clubs cannot be read other than as indicating approval of the standards applied to racially discriminatory private schools by the IRS subsequent to 1970, and specifically of Revenue Ruling 71–447.[27]

---

27. Reliance is placed on scattered statements in floor debate by Congressmen critical of the IRS's adoption of Revenue Ruling 71–447. Those views did not prevail. That several Congressmen, expressing their individual views, argued that the IRS had no authority to take the action in question, is hardly a balance for the overwhelming evidence of congressional awareness of and acquiescence in the IRS rulings of 1970 and 1971. Petitioners also argue that the Ashbrook and Dornan Amendments to the Treasury, Postal Service, and General Government Appropriations Act of 1980, Pub.L. 96–74, §§ 103, 614, 615, 93 Stat. 559, 562, 576–577, reflect congressional opposition to the IRS policy formalized in Revenue Ruling 71–447. Those amendments, however, are directly concerned only with limiting more aggressive enforcement procedures proposed by the IRS in 1978 and 1979 and preventing the adoption of more stringent substantive standards. The Ashbrook Amendment, § 103 of the Act, applies only to procedures, guidelines, or measures adopted after August 22, 1978, and thus in no way affects the status of Revenue Ruling 71–447. In fact, both Congressman Dornan and Congressman Ashbrook explicitly stated that their amendments would have no effect on prior IRS policy, including Revenue Ruling 71–447, see 125 Cong.Rec. 18815 (1979) (Cong. Dornan: "[M]y amendment will not affect existing IRS rules which

[In Part III, Chief Justice Burger rejected the argument that the IRS ruling violated the Free Exercise Clause of the First Amendment, and in Part IV he rejected the argument that the IRS ruling was not properly applied to the petitioners.]

[The concurring opinion of JUSTICE POWELL is omitted.]

JUSTICE REHNQUIST, dissenting.

The Court points out that there is a strong national policy in this country against racial discrimination. To the extent that the Court states that Congress in furtherance of this policy could deny tax-exempt status to educational institutions that promote racial discrimination, I readily agree. But, unlike the Court, I am convinced that Congress simply has failed to take this action and, as this Court has said over and over again, regardless of our view on the propriety of Congress' failure to legislate we are not constitutionally empowered to act for it.

In approaching this statutory construction question the Court quite adeptly avoids the statute it is construing. This I am sure is no accident, for there is nothing in the language of § 501(c)(3) that supports the result obtained by the Court. Section 501(c)(3) provides tax-exempt status for:

"Corporations, and any community chest, fund, or foundation, organized and operated exclusively for religious, charitable, scientific, testing for public safety, literary, or educational purposes, or to foster national or international amateur sports competition (but only if no part of its activities involve the provision of athletic facilities or equipment), or for the prevention of cruelty to children or animals, no part of the net earnings of which inures to the benefit of any private shareholder or individual, no substantial part of the activities of which is carrying on propaganda, or otherwise attempting, to influence legislation (except as otherwise provided in subsection (h)), and which does not participate in, or intervene in (including the publishing or distributing of statements), any political campaign on behalf of any candidate for public office." 26 U.S.C. § 501(c)(3).

With undeniable clarity, Congress has explicitly defined the requirements for § 501(c)(3) status. An entity must be (1) a corporation, or community chest, fund, or foundation, (2) organized for one of the eight enumerated purposes, (3) operated on a nonprofit basis, and (4) free from involvement in lobbying activities and political campaigns. Nowhere is there to be found some additional, undefined public policy requirement.

The Court first seeks refuge from the obvious reading of § 501(c)(3) by turning to § 170 of the Internal Revenue Code, which provides a tax deduction for contributions made to § 501(c)(3) organizations. In setting forth the general rule, § 170 states:

IRS has used to revoke tax exemptions of white segregated academies under Revenue Ruling 71–447 * * *."); *id.*, at 18446 (Cong. Ashbrook: "My amendment very clearly indicates on its face that all the regulations in existence as of August 22, 1978, would not be touched"). These amendments therefore do not indicate Congressional rejection of Revenue Ruling 71–447 and the standards contained therein.

"There shall be allowed as a deduction any charitable contribution (as defined in subsection (c)) payment of which is made within the taxable year. A charitable contribution shall be allowable as a deduction only if verified under regulations prescribed by the Secretary." 26 U.S.C. § 170(a)(1).

The Court seizes the words "charitable contribution" and with little discussion concludes that "[o]n its face, therefore, § 170 reveals that Congress' intention was to provide tax benefits to organizations serving charitable purposes," intimating that this implies some unspecified common-law charitable trust requirement.

The Court would have been well advised to look to subsection (c) where, as § 170(a)(1) indicates, Congress has defined a "charitable contribution":

"For purposes of this section, the term 'charitable contribution' means a contribution or gift to or for the use of * * * [a] corporation, trust, or community chest, fund, or foundation * * * organized and operated exclusively for religious, charitable, scientific, literary, or educational purposes, or to foster national or international amateur sports competition (but only if no part of its activities involve the provision of athletic facilities or equipment), or for the prevention of cruelty to children or animals; * * * no part of the net earnings of which inures to the benefit of any private shareholder or individual; and * * * which is not disqualified for tax exemption under section 501(c)(3) by reason of attempting to influence legislation, and which does not participate in, or intervene in (including the publishing or distributing of statements), any political campaign on behalf of any candidate for public office." 26 U.S.C. § 170(c).

Plainly, § 170(c) simply tracks the requirements set forth in § 501(c)(3). Since § 170 is no more than a mirror of § 501(c)(3) and, as the Court points out, § 170 followed § 501(c)(3) by more than two decades, it is at best of little usefulness in finding the meaning of § 501(c)(3).

Making a more fruitful inquiry, the Court next turns to the legislative history of § 501(c)(3) and finds that Congress intended in that statute to offer a tax benefit to organizations that Congress believed were providing a public benefit. I certainly agree. But then the Court leaps to the conclusion that this history is proof Congress intended that an organization seeking § 501(c)(3) status "must fall within a category specified in that section *and must demonstrably serve and be in harmony with the public interest."* (Emphasis added). To the contrary, I think that the legislative history of § 501(c)(3) unmistakably makes clear that *Congress has decided* what organizations are serving a public purpose and providing a public benefit within the meaning of § 501(c)(3) and has clearly set forth in § 501(c)(3) the characteristics of such organizations. In fact, there are few examples which better illustrate Congress' effort to define and redefine the requirements of a legislative Act.

The first general income tax law was passed by Congress in the form of the Tariff Act of 1894. A provision of that Act provided an exemption for "corporations, companies, or associations organized and conducted solely for charitable, religious, or educational purposes." The income tax portion of the 1894 Act was held unconstitutional by this Court, see *Pollock v. Farmers' Loan & Trust Co.*, 158 U.S. 601 (1895), but a similar exemption appeared in the Tariff Act of 1909 which imposed a tax on corporate income. The 1909 Act provided an exemption for "any corporation or association organized and operated exclusively for religious, charitable, or educational purposes, no part of the net income of which inures to the benefit of any private stockholder or individual."

With the ratification of the Sixteenth Amendment, Congress again turned its attention to an individual income tax with the Tariff Act of 1913. And again, in the direct predecessor of § 501(c)(3), a tax exemption was provided for "any corporation or association organized and operated exclusively for religious, charitable, scientific, or educational purposes, no part of the net income of which inures to the benefit of any private stockholder or individual." In subsequent Acts Congress continued to broaden the list of exempt purposes. The Revenue Act of 1918 added an exemption for corporations or associations organized "for the prevention of cruelty to children or animals." The Revenue Act of 1921 expanded the groups to which the exemption applied to include "any community chest, fund, or foundation" and added "literary" endeavors to the list of exempt purposes. The exemption remained unchanged in the Revenue Acts of 1924, 1926, 1928, and 1932. In the Revenue Act of 1934 Congress added the requirement that no substantial part of the activities of any exempt organization can involve the carrying on of "propaganda" or "attempting to influence legislation." Again, the exemption was left unchanged by the Revenue Acts of 1936 and 1938.

The tax laws were overhauled by the Internal Revenue Code of 1939, but this exemption was left unchanged. When the 1939 Code was replaced with the Internal Revenue Code of 1954, the exemption was adopted in full in the present § 501(c)(3) with the addition of "testing for public safety" as an exempt purpose and an additional restriction that tax-exempt organizations could not "participate in, or intervene in (including the publishing or distributing of statements), any political campaign on behalf of any candidate for public office." Ch. 1, § 501(c)(3), 68A Stat. 163 (1954). Then in 1976 the statute was again amended adding to the purposes for which an exemption would be authorized, "to foster national or international amateur sports competition," provided the activities did not involve the provision of athletic facilities or equipment. Tax Reform Act of 1976, Pub. L. 94–455, § 1313(a), 90 Stat. 1730 (1976).

One way to read the opinion handed down by the Court today leads to the conclusion that this long and arduous refining process of § 501(c)(3) was certainly a waste of time, for when enacting the original 1894 statute Congress intended to adopt a common-law term of art, and intended that this term of art carry with it all of the common-law baggage which defines it. Such a view, however, leads also to the insupportable idea that Congress has spent almost a century adding illustrations simply to clarify an already defined common-law term. * * *

Perhaps recognizing the lack of support in the statute itself, or in its history, for the 1970 IRS change in interpretation, the Court finds that "[t]he actions of Congress since 1970 leave no doubt that the IRS reached the correct conclusion in exercising its authority," concluding that there is "an unusually strong case of legislative acquiescence in and ratification by implication of the 1970 and 1971 rulings." The Court relies first on several bills introduced to overturn the IRS interpretation of § 501(c)(3). But we have said before, and it is equally applicable here, that this type of congressional inaction is of virtually no weight in determining legislative intent. See *United States v. Wise*, 370 U.S. 405, 411 (1962); *Waterman S.S. Corp. v. United States*, 381 U.S. 252, 269 (1965). These bills and related hearings indicate little more than that a vigorous debate has existed in Congress concerning the new IRS position.

The Court next asserts that "Congress affirmatively manifested its acquiescence in the IRS policy when it enacted the present § 501(i) of the Code," a provision that "denies tax-exempt status to social clubs whose charters or policy statements provide for" racial discrimination. Quite to the contrary, it seems to me that in § 501(i) Congress showed that when it wants to add a requirement prohibiting racial discrimination to one of the tax-benefit provisions, it is fully aware of how to do it.

The Court intimates that the Ashbrook and Dornan Amendments also reflect an intent by Congress to acquiesce in the new IRS position. The amendments were passed to limit certain enforcement procedures proposed by the IRS in 1978 and 1979 for determining whether a school operated in a racially nondiscriminatory fashion. The Court points out that in proposing his amendment, Congressman Ashbrook stated: " 'My amendment very clearly indicates on its face that all the regulations in existence as of August 22, 1978, would not be touched.' " The Court fails to note that Congressman Ashbrook also said:

> "The IRS has no authority to create public policy * * *. So long as the Congress has not acted to set forth a national policy respecting denial of tax exemptions to private schools, it is improper for the IRS or any other branch of the Federal Government to seek denial of tax-exempt status * * *. There exists but a single responsibility which is proper for the Internal Revenue Service: To serve as tax collector." 125 Cong. Rec. 18444 (1979).

In the same debate, Congressman Grassley asserted: "Nobody argues that racial discrimination should receive preferred tax status in the United States. However, the IRS should not be making these decisions on the agency's own discretion. Congress should make these decisions." *Id.*, at 18448. The same debates are filled with other similar statements. While on the whole these debates do not show conclusively that Congress believed the IRS had exceeded its authority with the 1970 change in position, they likewise are far less than a showing of acquiescence in and ratification of the new position.

This Court continuously has been hesitant to find ratification through inaction. This is especially true where such a finding "would result in a construction of the statute which not only is at odds with the language of the section in question and the pattern of the statute taken as a whole, but also is extremely far reaching in terms of the virtually untrammeled and unreviewable power it would vest in a regulatory agency." *SEC v. Sloan*, 436 U.S. 103, 121 (1978). Few cases would call for more caution in finding ratification by acquiescence than the present ones. The new IRS interpretation is not only far less than a long-standing administrative policy, it is at odds with a position maintained by the IRS, and unquestioned by Congress, for several decades prior to 1970. The interpretation is unsupported by the statutory language, it is unsupported by legislative history, the interpretation has led to considerable controversy in and out of Congress, and the interpretation gives to the IRS a broad power which until now Congress had kept for itself. Where in addition to these circumstances Congress has shown time and time again that it is ready to enact positive legislation to change the Tax Code when it desires, this Court has no business finding that Congress has adopted the new IRS position by failing to enact legislation to reverse it.

I have no disagreement with the Court's finding that there is a strong national policy in this country opposed to racial discrimination. I agree with the Court that Congress has the power to further this policy by denying § 501(c)(3) status to organizations that practice racial discrimination. But as of yet Congress has failed to do so. Whatever the reasons for the failure, this Court should not legislate for Congress. * * *

NOTES ON BOB JONES AND THE "MEANING" OF LEGISLATIVE INACTION

1. *Criticisms of the Acquiescence Doctrine, Generally and in* Bob Jones. *Bob Jones* is now a leading citation for the acquiescence rule. That rule has, however, long been subject to criticism, see, e.g., Henry M. Hart Jr. & Albert M. Sacks, *The Legal Process* 1313–70 (Eskridge & Frickey eds., 1994) (tent. ed. 1958); John Grabow, *Congressional Silence and the Search for Legislative Intent: A Venture into "Speculative Unrealities,"* 64 B.U. L. Rev. 737 (1984), and several current Justices strongly object to it. Dissenting from the Court's reaffirmation of *Weber* in *Johnson* (see Chapter 1, § 3B), Justice Scalia rejected the majority's invocation of legislative acquiescence. For him, "vindication by congressional inaction is a canard," because congressional inaction has no formal significance under Article I as interpreted in *INS v. Chadha* (see Chapter 6, § 2C), and no functional significance given difficulties in figuring out why Congress did nothing. More recently, the Supreme Court has become much more reluctant to accept legislative acquiescence arguments. See, for example, *Patterson v. McLean Credit Union* (Chapter 1, § 3B), which rejected the dissenting opinion's reliance on legislative inaction (not only the acquiescence rule but also the reenactment and rejected proposal rules) as reason to reaffirm and expand the Court's decision in *Runyon v. McCrary*. Is

there any special reason for a skeptic such as Justice Scalia to apply the acquiescence rule in a case like *Bob Jones*, or is this just another "canard"?

Note *Bob Jones*'s inconsistent use of congressional inaction. The Court relies on the failure of Congress to overrule the 1971 revenue ruling: Congress, by doing nothing, acquiesced in the agency's action. The Court ignores the failure of Congress to overrule the IRS policy before 1971: that doesn't count, the Court seems to be saying. The Court ignores the repeated failure of Congress to enact statutes penalizing private education discrimination: Congress, by passing statutes which did not cover private schools, nonetheless disapproved of the private action. Is there any good reason to interpret congressional inaction as the Court does?

Justice Rehnquist is critical of the Court's reliance on legislative inaction in *Bob Jones* and, later when he was Chief Justice, in *Solid Waste Agency v. Army Corps of Engineers*, 531 U.S. 159 (2001) (discussed in § 2D of this chapter). Yet Justice Rehnquist frequently relied upon congressional inaction. See, e.g., *Weinberger v. Rossi*, 456 U.S. 25, 33 (1982) (Rehnquist, J.) (holding that unless Congress says otherwise, Court will presume that it acquiesces in executive agreements). See also *Haig v. Agee*, 453 U.S. 280 (1981) (Burger, C.J.) (asserting that absent intent to repudiate executive interpretation of the Passport Act, Congress is presumed to acquiesce in it). Are these foreign affairs cases more appropriate occasions for relying on legislative inaction than *Bob Jones* is?

2. *Reading Public Values into Statutes.* Mayer G. Freed and Daniel D. Polsby, in *Race, Religion & Public Policy*: Bob Jones University v. United States, 1983 Sup. Ct. Rev. 1, 5, object to Chief Justice Burger's reliance on general "public policy"—the Constitution, Title VI and other provisions of the Civil Rights Act—to rewrite § 501. None of the sources cited by Chief Justice Burger actually prohibited Bob Jones University's private race discrimination.[dd] Isn't there something anomalous about "expanding" these constitutional and statutory authorities beyond their well-defined ambit? As Olatunde Johnson points out, an earlier draft of the Chief Justice's opinion did note that federal law barred private schools from discriminating on the basis of race—but Burger dropped that highly relevant reference in the final opinion. See Olatunde Johnson, *The Story of* Bob Jones University v. United States: *Race, Religion, and Congress's Extraordinary Acquiescence*, in *Statutory Interpretation Stories* 126, 151 (Eskridge, Frickey & Garrett eds., 2011). See also that 42 U.S.C. § 1981, which the Supreme Court had interpreted to bar private schools from discriminating on the basis of race.

Moreover, Freed and Polsby argue that Chief Justice Burger's informal idea of "quasi-law" is inconsistent with the Chief Justice's strict, formalistic view of "law" in *INS v. Chadha* (Chapter 6, § 2C). Freed and Polsby believe that the world envisioned by the Chief Justice is "a manifold chock-full of law,

---

dd. Note that the discrimination practiced by Bob Jones University changed in the 1970s. Before 1973, Bob Jones excluded African Americans from admission. Starting in 1973, the university admitted African-American applicants who had been staff members for four years or more. After 1975, it admitted African-American students, but prohibited interracial marriages or dating. Johnson, *Story of* Bob Jones University, 141–42. Both the Court and the United States (which supported Bob Jones) treated discrimination on the basis of miscegenation as race discrimination.

either the law that was made by the actions of lawmakers or the law that was made by the lawmakers' nonaction. If there is any room at all in such a picture for private whim or liberty, it is not apparent where." Is this a fair statement of Chief Justice Burger's position? How can the Chief Justice justify his use of public policy?

Note that the Supreme Court sometimes refers to subsequent statutory developments in deciding cases. For other examples of the Court's willingness to extrapolate general public policy from a series of legislative enactments, see *Midlantic Nat'l Bank v. New Jersey Dep't of Envir. Prot.*, 474 U.S. 494 (1986), which reads policies of recent environmental laws into Bankruptcy Act, and *Toll v. Moreno*, 458 U.S. 1 (1982), which creates general federal policy from a series of international agreements.

3. *Public Values or Public Hypocrisy?* Freed and Polsby accuse Chief Justice Burger of not being sufficiently "positivist" (i.e., following the rules written by Congress). Another kind of criticism would accuse Chief Justice Burger of being insufficiently "normativist" (i.e., making the law the "best" one can).

Bob Jones reads like a very high-minded opinion: How can we as a society subsidize segregated schools? We cannot! That sounds great, a ringing reaffirmation of *Brown v. Board of Education* in a somewhat different setting. But the reality is more complicated, and a great deal less inspiring. See Johnson, *Story of* Bob Jones University (detailed account from which we now draw). The Carter Administration's IRS issued regulations in 1978–79 placing burdens on schools with low minority percentages to "prove" their nondiscrimination. Congress reacted with the Ashbrook Amendment to a 1980 appropriations statute, which effectively barred the IRS from implementing the new regulations. When *Bob Jones* was decided, IRS enforcement depended heavily on "self-reporting": Institutions which admitted to race discrimination were the only ones to lose their tax exemptions. In short, only those institutions that discriminated as a matter of principle—like Bob Jones—lost their tax exemption. Institutions that deceived the IRS (or themselves) did not. Is this a "public value"?

At the same time Bob Jones was suing to recover its tax-exempt status, African–American parents were suing the IRS to enforce the nondiscrimination rule. Judge Ruth Bader Ginsburg of the D.C. Circuit wrote an opinion favorable to the parents, but the Supreme Court reversed. A year after the Court decided *Bob Jones*, it held (by a slender 5–4 majority) that these parents lacked "standing" to sue the IRS, thereby failing to satisfy the Court's "case or controversy" requirement. *Allen v. Wright*, 468 U.S. 737 (1984). The grudging approach to standing taken in *Allen* is an ironic contrast to the expansive approach to the antidiscrimination principle taken in *Bob Jones*. The contrast is all the more striking when it is noted that there were significant justiciability problems in *Bob Jones* itself. While *Bob Jones* was pending on appeal to the Supreme Court, the Reagan Administration switched sides and announced that it agreed with Bob Jones and wanted to change the regulation back to its pre–1970 status. Since the two parties in *Bob Jones University v. United States* both agreed that Bob Jones should be exempt, there was under most conventional readings of the Court's precedents no "case or controversy": the case was moot. But the Court kept it alive by appointing William Coleman, a prominent Washington attorney and former Secretary of Transportation in the Ford Administration, "to brief and argue this case, as *amicus curiae*, in support of the judgments below." See 456 U.S. 922 (1982) (order of Court). And Coleman, who represented neither party, won the case!

After 1984, the IRS was left with few incentives to enforce *Bob Jones*: Congress in the Ashbrook Amendment had signaled that it didn't want vigorous enforcement, President Reagan had formally abandoned the policy until it was forced back upon him by the Supreme Court, and private citizens who might object to the virtual abandonment of the policy (such as African–American parents) were not easily able to get into court (while any segregated school that loses its exemption of course has standing to sue the IRS). Is this a scenario likely to promote "public values"? Consider, however, that Bob Jones University has in the new millennium not only revoked its race-discriminatory admissions policy, but also issued a public apology for the race discrimination it practiced for most of its history. See Johnson, *The Story of* Bob Jones University, 157.

NOTE ON POST-ENACTMENT ACQUIESCENCE AND "LAW AS EQUILIBRIUM"

In Chapter 2, § 3B3, we suggested that one way to think about law is that it is the result of the equilibrium of institutional forces, rather than the result of formal deduction from first premises. From this perspective, an important issue in *Bob Jones* was how clear the practical equilibrium was in the early 1980s on the question whether the federal government should indirectly support racially segregated schools through tax preferences. Once the IRS and the lower courts had coalesced around the anti-discrimination interpretation of the charitable exemption, and Congress had after extensive deliberation "approved" that policy in a meaningful way, then that policy was "law" in a very practical way (none of the three federal branches of government would change it) that should be apparent to such schools. When the Reagan Administration switched positions from that taken by the Nixon, Ford, and Carter Administrations, it was, under this perspective, changing the law, not returning the law to its "true" state, and therefore should have been allowed to do that only with the approval of Congress. The Court in *Bob Jones* recognized this practical reality and stabilized the law around its equilibrium point, leaving the Reagan Administration the option of seeking congressional authorization for reviving tax preferences for segregated schools. Is this a persuasive way to justify *Bob Jones*? You might want to apply a similar idea to the FDA Tobacco Case (Chapter 2, § 3B3) and to the Court's recent cutbacks on the Army Corps' wetlands regulations in *Solid Waste Agency v. Army Corps of Engineers*, 531 U.S. 159 (2001), and *United States v. Rapanos* (§ 2D of this chapter).[ee]

---

ee. *Solid Waste* (2001) and *Rapanos* (2006) were both handed down when the Republican Party controlled the Presidency, the House, and the Senate. After *Rapanos*, the Army Corps, under strong pressure from farmers, ranchers, mining companies, and the like, issued new wetlands regulations that cut back on the prior protections. This is ironic in the wake of the damage of New Orleans caused by Hurricane Katrina, because much of the Hurricane's force came from the loss of wetlands that had slowed down previous hurricanes.

Even if this explains *Bob Jones*, and even if you find it a good justification for the decision, this perspective leaves the Court a lot of room in which to affect the political balance, especially during periods of divided government when it is particularly hard for Congress to override the Court. An example is *Central Bank of Denver N.A. v. First Interstate Bank of Denver N.A.*, 511 U.S. 164 (1994). Justice Kennedy's majority opinion held that an action could not be brought alleging that defendant aided and abetted a violation of § 10(b) of the Securities Exchange Act of 1934, which prohibits securities fraud. In our judgment, this outcome upset a longstanding equilibrium to the contrary. *All* eleven federal courts of appeals that had considered the question had recognized a cause of action against aiders and abettors. Petitioner had asked the Court to address questions, such as the mens rea standard for aider and abettor liability, that also assumed that such a private right of action existed.

The Court sua sponte requested the parties to address the question whether the aiding and abetting action existed at all. Justice Kennedy's opinion stressed the plain meaning of § 10(b), which does not mention aiding and abetting liability. In dissent, Justice Stevens argued (1) that the majority had, in effect, engaged in "bait and switch" tactics (our term, not his) by applying the textualist interpretative approach to an old statute adopted by Congress in an era in which courts routinely elaborated upon rights of action, (2) that the majority had rejected a settled interpretation of law in terms of both judicial and administrative construction, which should be the province of Congress, not the Court, and (3) that actions of Congress since 1934 indicated congressional knowledge and approval of the implied right of action. One might add that, in light of this consensus, had a lawyer in the mid–to late–1980s informed Central Bank that it could *not* have been sued as an aider and abettor under § 10(b), that lawyer would have committed malpractice. (The certiorari petition filed by the lawyers for Central Bank did not even raise the question Justice Kennedy ultimately decided in Central Bank's favor.)

PROBLEM 4–3

Legislative History of the Immigration Exclusion for "Psychopaths"

In 1975, Clive Michael Boutilier, a citizen of Canada, is excluded from the United States by the Immigration and Naturalization Service (INS), based upon a report by the Public Health Service (PHS) that Boutilier has had sex with other men. The PHS and INS believe that Boutilier's "homosexual" activities require them to exclude him, based upon the immigration law's requirement excluding from admission into this country "[a]liens afflicted with psychopathic personality, epilepsy, or a mental defect." 8 U.S.C. § 1182(a)(4) (repealed in 1990). Boutilier takes his case to the Supreme Court, challenging his exclusion on the ground that medical affidavits submitted to the PHS indicated he was mentally healthy and not afflicted with "psychopathic personality" or the other listed disabilities. The PHS and INS admit that the exclusion was based solely on Boutilier's "homosexual" activities.

The government argues that Congress' intent when it enacted the immigration law in 1952 was to exclude "homosexuals" generally. The PHS observes that the American Psychiatric Association's *Diagnostic and Statisti-*

cal Manual: Mental Disorders 38–39 (1952), then characterized "homosexuality" as a "sociopathic personality disturbance." Based upon this medical understanding, the PHS drafted the "psychopathic personality" exclusion in 1952, which it represented to House and Senate committees as including "homosexuality." Committee reports for both chambers relied on the PHS' representations to say that "psychopathic personality" was "sufficiently broad to provide for the exclusion of homosexuals and sex perverts." S. Rep. No. 1137, 82d Cong., 2d Sess. 9 (1952); accord, H.R. Rep. No. 1365, 82d Cong., 2d Sess. 42–48 (1952). No one in Congress disputed this characterization.

Boutilier argues, in response, that the APA has abandoned its prior characterization of homosexuality and deleted it as a pathology in the 1973 edition of its manual. Especially in light of an emerging medical consensus that homosexuality is not a mental illness, Boutilier argues that the vague statutory term "psychopathic personality" is not precise enough to justify his exclusion. As to the legislative history, Boutilier observes that the original Senate bill excluded "homosexuals or sex perverts"; that language was dropped in favor of the PHS's term "psychopathic personality." Because Congress declined to exclude all "homosexuals," the Court should not bend the vague statute in that direction. And, besides, Boutilier himself is not "homosexual," but "bisexual" in orientation and conduct.

How would the Supreme Court rule on Boutilier's appeal? See *Boutilier v. INS*, 363 F.2d 488 (2d Cir. 1966), *aff'd*, 387 U.S. 118 (1967). How would a "new textualist" vote?

Now assume that in the early 1960s, a circuit court had accepted "the statute is too vague to cover 'homosexuals' " argument that we attributed to Boutilier. In 1965, Congress amended the exclusion to reach "[a]liens afflicted with psychopathic personality, *or sexual deviation*, or a mental defect" (new language emphasized). The committee reports establish that this amendment was intended to override the circuit court decision, on the ground that the decision had misconstrued the 1952 Congress's intent (relying on the PHS' representations) that the statutory exclusion "would encompass homosexuals and sex perverts." S. Rep. No. 748, 89th Cong., 1st Sess. 18 (1965). "To remove any doubt the Committee has specifically included the term 'sexual deviation' as a ground of exclusion in this bill." *Id.* at 19. If Boutilier had been excluded under this amended statute, is there any way the Court can avoid his exclusion? Compare *In re Longstaff*, 716 F.2d 1439 (5th Cir. 1983), with *Hill v. INS*, 714 F.2d 1470 (9th Cir. 1983).

SECTION 3. INTERPRETATION IN LIGHT OF OTHER STATUTES

"Statutory interpretation is a holistic endeavor," so that a provision "that may seem ambiguous in isolation is often clarified by" the greater consistency of one interpretation with "the rest of the law." *United Savings Ass'n of Texas v. Timbers of Inwood Forest Assocs.*, 484 U.S. 365, 371 (1988). See *West Virginia Univ. Hosp. v. Casey* (Chapter 2, § 3A), which interpreted one statute authorizing prevailing parties to recover attorney's fees by examining the text of many other such statutes. There are several reasons an interpreter might consider other statutes, and each is associated with a statutory interpretation canon or doctrine:

- *the in pari materia rule:* other statutes might use the same terminology or address the same issue as the statute being interpreted (Part A);

- *modeled or borrowed statute rule*: another statute might have been the template from which the statute in issue was designed (Part B),

- *presumption against implied repeals*: there might be a later statute possibly changing the implications of the statute being interpreted (Part C).

Note that the first two precepts are weaker versions of the rule that a word used several times in a statute is strongly presumed to have the same meaning every time it is used. See Chapter 3, § 1, and the debate in *Sweet Home.* The third precept is more complex, for it raises the possibility that statutes enacted at different times will be inconsistent with one another. How should interpreters figure out what law to apply when different statutes press in different directions? This conundrum vexed Judge Norris's two opinions in *Montana Wilderness, supra.* Part C will explore several different ways to reconcile apparently clashing statutes.

Part A.   Similar Statutes (The in Pari Materia Rule)

CARTLEDGE v. MILLER

United States District Court, Southern District of New York, 1978
457 F.Supp. 1146

WEINFELD, DISTRICT JUDGE.

This case involves the construction of the provisions of the Employee Retirement Income Security Act of 1974 ("ERISA") which prohibit the assignment or alienation of employees' pension benefits and thereby exempt such benefits from attachment or garnishment by creditors. The issue presented is whether there exists an implied exception to these "anti-assignment or alienation" provisions with respect to orders for the support of a wife and dependent children issued by a state court pursuant to statutory authority. Defendants Rockland County (New York) and the Rockland County Support Collection Unit have obtained a state court order garnishing the pension of George Allen Cozart in order to fulfill support obligations and arrears owed to his wife, defendant Vivian Cozart. Also named as a defendant is the Family Court Judge who issued the order. Plaintiffs, members of the Pension Plan Committee created under the Pension Agreement between Clevepak Corporation and the United Paperworkers International Union (the "Pension Committee"), bring this action to enjoin the enforcement of the state court order on the ground that such enforcement would violate ERISA. Finding that ERISA's anti-assignment or alienation provisions do not preclude the execution of validly issued court orders enforcing family support rights, this Court denies the injunction and dismisses the action upon the merits.

[George Cozart was ordered in 1958 to make support payments to his estranged wife, Vivian. By 1965, however, his chronic failure to make support payments led to his incarceration for contempt of court. In 1967, still in arrears, his wages were attached in part to pay $35 per week to support Vivian and the dependent children. Still, the arrearage increased (to over $5,000 by the time he retired in 1977). In 1977 the assignee of Vivian's support rights sued George for the debt and sought attachment of his pension, regulated by ERISA—but the garnishee argued that the attachment would violate ERISA's mandate that "benefits provided under the [pension] plan may not be assigned or alienated." I.R.C. § 401(a)(13), 26 U.S.C. § 401(a)(13) (1976); ERISA § 206(d)(1), 29 U.S.C. § 1056(d)(1) (1976).]

Finding and exercising jurisdiction, the Court considers the merits of plaintiff's complaint, which asserts that the attachment of George Cozart's pension to fulfill his support obligations is an invalid "assignment or alienation" under ERISA. Plaintiff's contention is based upon a literal and strict reading of that section to exempt pension benefits from any and every levy, garnishment, or attachment. So read, plaintiff may be correct, but, "[o]n the other hand, it is a commonplace that a literal interpretation of the words of a statute is not always a safe guide to its meaning" and should be "disregarded when it defeats the manifest purpose of the statute as a whole." Thus defendants argue that an exception to the exemption embodied in ERISA's anti-assignment or alienation provisions must be implied in order to secure enforcement of Cozart's obligations to support his dependents.

The anti-assignment or alienation sections of ERISA have been authoritatively interpreted to preclude "[a]ny direct or indirect arrangement (whether revocable or irrevocable) whereby a party acquires from a participant or beneficiary a right or interest enforceable against the plan in, or to, all or any part of a plan benefit payment which is, or may become, payable to the participant or beneficiary."[39] And Congress intended that ERISA's provisions would "supersede any and all State laws insofar as they may * * * relate to any employee benefit plan." [ERISA § 514(a), 29 U.S.C. § 1144(a).] These generalized proscriptions, however, are not sufficient to infer that Congress meant to preclude the ancient family law right of maintenance and support and the issuance of process to enforce that right.

As a fundamental principle of statutory interpretation, courts have presumed that the basic police powers of the States, particularly the regulation of domestic relations, are not superseded by federal legislation unless that was the clear and manifest purpose of Congress. An important and pervasive state law policy is to enforce the support rights of depen-

---

39.   Treas. Reg. § 1.401(a)–13(c)(1)(ii), *reported in* 43 Fed. Reg. 6942 (1978). The Internal Revenue Service's interpretation, always entitled to deference, finds support in the legislative history of ERISA. H.R. Conf. Rep. No. 93–1280, 93d Cong., 2d Sess. (1974) (for purposes of ERISA's anti-assignment or alienation provisions, "a garnishment or levy is not to be considered a voluntary assignment").

dent spouses and children, even when they require the attachment of assets or earnings normally inalienable or unassignable under state law. Consequently, the Supreme Court has held that "[u]nless positively required by direct enactment the courts should not presume a design upon the part of Congress in relieving the unfortunate debtor to make the law a means of avoiding enforcement of the obligation, moral and legal, devolved upon the husband to support his wife and to maintain and educate his children." [*Wetmore v. Markoe*, 196 U.S. 68, 77 (1904).]

The debates and reports on ERISA furnish little or no direction toward the precise issue: nothing contained therein suggests that the proscription against assignment or alienation was intended to include family support payments. Indeed, an overall congressional purpose not to interfere with the States' power to enforce family support obligations may be gleaned from judicial interpretation of exemption provisions in other federal statutes. Though not exactly in *pari passu*, they indicate a general congressional intent not to preclude enforcement of family support obligations. Provisions so interpreted include the exemption sections of the Social Security Act,[45] the Veterans Benefits Act,[46] and the Railway Retirement Act,[47] as well as the Bankruptcy Act's provision for discharge of prior obligations. [*Wetmore v. Markoe*.] The rationale behind such * * * interpretations of the will of Congress was aptly summarized by Judge, later Justice, Rutledge in *Schlaefer v. Schlaefer* [112 F.2d 177 (D.C. Cir. 1940)]: "[T]he usual purpose of exemptions is to relieve the person exempted from the pressure of claims hostile to his dependents' essential needs as well as his own personal ones, not to relieve him of familial obligations and destroy what may be the family's last and only security, short of public relief."

Moreover, the goals underlying ERISA support the reasoning of this common law presumption. Originally introduced in 1967, ERISA was meant "to prescribe legislative remedies for the various deficiencies exist-

---

45. Act of Aug. 14, 1935, § 207, 49 Stat. 624, *codified at* 42 U.S.C. § 407:

The right of any person to any future payment under this subchapter shall not be transferable or assignable, at law or in equity, and none of the moneys paid or payable or rights existing under this subchapter shall be subject to execution, levy, attachment, garnishment, or other legal process, or to the operation of any bankruptcy or insolvency law.

[Citations to cases interpreting § 207 to except support payments omitted.]

46. Act of Aug. 14, 1935, § 207, 49 Stat. 624, *codified at* 42 U.S.C. § 407:

The right of any person to any future payment under this subchapter shall not be transferable or assignable, at law or in equity, and none of the moneys paid or payable or rights existing under this subchapter shall be subject to execution, levy, attachment, garnishment, or other legal process, or to the operation of any bankruptcy or insolvency law.

[Citations to cases interpreting § 207 to except support payments omitted.]

47. Act of Aug. 29, 1935, § 12, 49 Stat. 973, *codified at* 45 U.S.C. § 231m:

Notwithstanding any other law of the United States, or of any State, territory, or the District of Columbia, no annuity or supplemental annuity shall be assignable or be subject to any tax or to garnishment, attachment, or other legal process under any circumstances whatsoever, nor shall the payment thereof be anticipated * * *.

This section has been interpreted to except support payments [citations omitted], and courts have frequently "anticipated" such payments when applicable against support obligations [citations omitted].

ing in the private pension plan systems," primarily relating to prior abuses in plan vesting, funding, termination, and fiduciary conduct. [S. Rep. No. 93–127, 93d Cong., 1st Sess. (1973).] In particular, Congress was solicitous of the "continued well-being and security of millions of employees *and their dependents* [who] are directly affected by these plans." [ERISA § 2(a), 29 U.S.C. § 1001(a) (emphasis added).] Rather than intending to undermine the family law rights of dependent spouses and children, the legislature was concerned that "employees and their beneficiaries"—the entire family—be protected by ERISA.[53]

Thus the conclusion is warranted that, like the previous congressional exemptions, ERISA's anti-assignment or alienation sections were included only "to protect a person and those dependent upon him from the claim of creditors," not to insulate a breadwinner from the valid support claims of spouse and offspring. This conclusion is buttressed by the *amicus* brief submitted on behalf of the Departments of Labor and the Treasury, which are charged with enforcement and interpretation of ERISA and whose interpretation of the Act, though not controlling, is entitled to great weight. The Government takes the position, which appears reasonable and correct, that "family support decrees were not intended to be within the scope of the anti-alienation provisions of ERISA." * * *

Postscript: In 1984, Congress amended § 256(d) to add an explicit statutory exception for (3) "qualified domestic relations orders." Pub. L. No. 98–397, 98 Stat. 1426 (1984), codified at 29 U.S.C. § 1056(d)(3). A qualified domestic relations order is "any judgment, decree, or order (including approval of a property settlement agreement) which relates to the provision of child support, alimony payments, or marital property rights to a spouse, former spouse, child, or other dependent of a participant, and is made pursuant to a State domestic relations law (including a community property law)," § 256(d)(3)(B)(ii) (new version), and meets various procedural and drafting requirements.

LORILLARD v. PONS

Supreme Court of the United States, 1978
434 U.S. 575, 98 S.Ct. 868, 55 L.Ed.2d 40

MR. JUSTICE MARSHALL delivered the opinion of the Court.

This case presents the question whether there is a right to a jury trial in private civil actions for lost wages under the Age Discrimination in Employment Act of 1967 (ADEA or Act), 81 Stat. 602, as amended, 88 Stat. 74, 29 U.S.C. § 621 *et seq.* (1970 ed. and Supp. V). * * *

---

53. ERISA § 2(c), 29 U.S.C. § 1001(c) (emphasis added):

It is hereby further declared to be the policy of this Act to protect interstate commerce, the Federal taxing power, and the interests of participants in private pension plans *and their beneficiaries* by improving the equitable character and the soundness of such plans * * *.

See also ERISA § 2(b), 29 U.S.C. § 1001(b) (similar language). Although ERISA § 3(8), 29 U.S.C. § 1002(8), defines "beneficiary" more narrowly, I take the term in its broader sense when it is used in the preamble, which was a general statement of the goals of the statute, not a technical recitation.

[I] The ADEA broadly prohibits arbitrary discrimination in the workplace based on age. Although the ADEA contains no provision expressly granting a right to jury trial, respondent nonetheless contends that the structure of the Act demonstrates a congressional intent to grant such a right. Alternatively, she argues that the Seventh Amendment requires that in a private action for lost wages under the ADEA, the parties must be given the option of having the case heard by a jury. We turn first to the statutory question since " 'it is a cardinal principle that this Court will first ascertain whether a construction of the statute is fairly possible by which the [constitutional] question may be avoided.' " Because we find the statutory issue dispositive, we need not address the constitutional issue.

The enforcement scheme for the statute is complex—the product of considerable attention during the legislative debates preceding passage of the Act. Several alternative proposals were considered by Congress. The Administration submitted a bill, modeled after §§ 10(c), (e) of the National Labor Relations Act, 29 U.S.C. §§ 160(c), (e), which would have granted power to the Secretary of Labor to issue cease-and-desist orders enforceable in the courts of appeals, but would not have granted a private right of action to aggrieved individuals, S. 830, H.R. 4221, 90th Cong., 1st Sess. (1967). Senator Javits introduced an alternative proposal to make discrimination based on age unlawful under the Fair Labor Standards Act (FLSA), 29 U.S.C. § 201 *et seq.*; the normal enforcement provisions of the FLSA, 29 U.S.C. § 216 *et seq.*, (1970 ed. and Supp. V), then would have been applicable, permitting suits by either the Secretary of Labor or the injured individual, S. 788, 90th Cong., 1st Sess. (1967). A third alternative that was considered would have adopted the statutory pattern of Title VII of the Civil Rights Act of 1964 and utilized the Equal Employment Opportunity Commission.

The bill that was ultimately enacted is something of a hybrid, reflecting, on the one hand, Congress' desire to use an existing statutory scheme and a bureaucracy with which employers and employees would be familiar and, on the other hand, its dissatisfaction with some elements of each of the preexisting schemes. Pursuant to § 7(b) of the Act, 29 U.S.C. § 626(b), violations of the ADEA generally are to be treated as violations of the FLSA. "Amounts owing * * * as a result of a violation" of the ADEA are to be treated as "unpaid minimum wages or unpaid overtime compensation" under the FLSA and the rights created by the ADEA are to be "enforced in accordance with the powers, remedies and procedures" of specified sections of the FLSA.

Following the model of the FLSA, the ADEA establishes two primary enforcement mechanisms. Under the FLSA provisions incorporated in § 7(b) of the ADEA, 29 U.S.C. § 626(b), the Secretary of Labor may bring suit on behalf of an aggrieved individual for injunctive and monetary relief. 29 U.S.C. §§ 216(c), 217 (1970 ed. and Supp. V). The incorporated FLSA provisions together with § 7(c) of the ADEA, 29 U.S.C. § 626(c), in addition, authorize private civil actions for "such legal or equitable relief as will effectuate the purposes of" the ADEA. Although not required by the FLSA, prior to the initiation of any ADEA action, an individual must give notice to the Secretary of Labor of his intention to sue in order that the Secretary can attempt to eliminate the alleged unlawful practice through informal methods. § 7(d), 29 U.S.C. § 626(d). After allowing the Secretary 60 days to conciliate the alleged unlawful practice, the individual may file suit. The right of the individual to sue on his own terminates, however, if the Secretary commences an action on his behalf. § 7(c), 29 U.S.C. § 626(c).

[II] Looking first to the procedural provisions of the statute, we find a significant indication of Congress' intent in its directive that the ADEA be enforced in accordance with the "powers, remedies, and *procedures*" of the FLSA. § 7(b), 29 U.S.C. § 626(b) (emphasis added). Long before Congress enacted the ADEA, it was well established that there was a right to a jury trial in private actions pursuant to the FLSA. Indeed, every court to consider the issue had so held. Congress is presumed to be aware of an administrative or judicial interpretation of a statute and to adopt that interpretation when it reenacts a statute without change. So too, where, as here, Congress adopts a new law incorporating sections of a prior law, Congress normally can be presumed to have had knowledge of the interpretation given to the incorporated law, at least insofar as it affects the new statute.

That presumption is particularly appropriate here since, in enacting the ADEA, Congress exhibited both a detailed knowledge of the FLSA provisions and their judicial interpretation and a willingness to depart from those provisions regarded as undesirable or inappropriate for incorporation. For example, in construing the enforcement sections of the FLSA, the courts had consistently declared that injunctive relief was not available in suits by private individuals but only in suits by the Secretary. Congress made plain its decision to follow a different course in the ADEA by expressly permitting "such * * * equitable relief as may be appropriate to effectuate the purposes of [the ADEA] including without limitation judgments compelling employment, reinstatement or promotion" "in *any* action brought to enforce" the Act. § 7(b), 29 U.S.C. § 626(b) (emphasis added). Similarly, while incorporating into the ADEA the FLSA provisions authorizing awards of liquidated damages, Congress altered the circumstances under which such awards would be available in ADEA actions by mandating that such damages be awarded only where the violation of the ADEA is willful.[8] Finally, Congress expressly declined to incorporate into the ADEA the criminal penalties established for violations of the FLSA.

---

8. By its terms, 29 U.S.C. § 216(b) requires that liquidated damages be awarded as a matter of right for violations of the FLSA. However, in response to its dissatisfaction with that judicial interpretation of the provision, Congress enacted the Portal-to-Portal Pay Act of 1947, 61 Stat. 84, which, *inter alia*, grants courts authority to deny or limit liquidated damages where the "employer shows to the satisfaction of the court that the act or omission giving rise to such action was in good faith and that he had reasonable grounds for believing that his act or omission was not a violation of" the FLSA, § 11, 29 U.S.C. § 260 (1970 ed., Supp. V). Although § 7(e) of the ADEA, 29 U.S.C. § 626(e), expressly incorporates §§ 6 and 10 of the Portal-to-Portal Pay Act, 29 U.S.C. §§ 255 and 259 (1970 ed. and Supp. V), the ADEA does not make any reference to § 11, 29 U.S.C. § 260 (1970 ed., Supp. V).

This selectivity that Congress exhibited in incorporating provisions and in modifying certain FLSA practices strongly suggests that but for those changes Congress expressly made, it intended to incorporate fully the remedies and procedures of the FLSA. Senator Javits, one of the floor managers of the bill, so indicated in describing the enforcement section which became part of the Act: "The enforcement techniques provided by [the ADEA] are directly analogous to those available under the Fair Labor Standards Act; in fact [the ADEA] incorporates by reference, to the greatest extent possible, the provisions of the [FLSA]." 113 Cong. Rec. 31254 (1967).[10] And by directing that actions for lost wages under the ADEA be treated as actions for unpaid minimum wages or overtime compensation under the FLSA, § 7(b), 29 U.S.C. § 626(b), Congress dictated that the jury trial right then available to enforce that FLSA liability would also be available in private actions under the ADEA.

This inference is buttressed by an examination of the language Congress chose to describe the available remedies under the ADEA. Section 7(b), 29 U.S.C. § 626(b), empowers a court to grant *"legal* or equitable relief" and § 7(c), 29 U.S.C. § 626(c), authorizes individuals to bring actions for *"legal* or equitable relief" (emphases added). The word "legal" is a term of art: In cases in which legal relief is available and legal rights are determined, the Seventh Amendment provides a right to jury trial. "[W]here words are employed in a statute which had at the time a well-known meaning at common law or in the law of this country they are presumed to have been used in that sense unless the context compels to the contrary." We can infer, therefore, that by providing specifically for "legal" relief, Congress knew the significance of the term "legal," and intended that there would be a jury trial on demand to "enforc[e] * * * liability for amounts deemed to be unpaid minimum wages or unpaid overtime compensation." § 7(b), 29 U.S.C. § 626(b).

Petitioner strives to find a contrary congressional intent by comparing the ADEA with Title VII of the Civil Rights Act of 1964, 42 U.S.C. § 2000e *et seq.* (1970 ed. and Supp. V), which petitioner maintains does not provide for jury trials. We, of course, intimate no view as to whether a jury trial is available under Title VII as a matter of either statutory or constitutional right. However, after examining the provisions of Title VII, we find petitioner's argument by analogy to Title VII unavailing. There are important similarities between the two statutes, to be sure, both in their aims—the elimination of discrimination from the workplace—and in their substantive prohibitions. In fact, the prohibitions of the ADEA were

10. Senator Javits made the only specific reference in the legislative history to a jury trial. He said:

"The whole test is somewhat like the test in an accident case—did the person use reasonable care. A jury will answer yes or no. The question here is: Was the individual discriminated against solely because of his age? The alleged discrimination must be proved and the burden of proof is upon the one who would assert that that was actually the case." 113 Cong.Rec. 31255 (1967).

It is difficult to tell whether Senator Javits was referring to the issue in ADEA cases or in accident cases when he said the jury will say yes or no.

derived *in haec verba* from Title VII.[12] But in deciding whether a statutory right to jury trial exists, it is the remedial and procedural provisions of the two laws that are crucial and there we find significant differences.

Looking first to the statutory language defining the relief available, we note that Congress specifically provided for both "legal or equitable relief" in the ADEA, but did not authorize "legal" relief in so many words under Title VII. Compare § 7(b), 29 U.S.C. § 626(b), with 42 U.S.C. § 2000e–5(g) (1970 ed., Supp. V). Similarly, the ADEA incorporates the FLSA provision that employers "shall be liable" for amounts deemed unpaid minimum wages or overtime compensation, while under Title VII, the availability of backpay is a matter of equitable discretion. Finally, rather than adopting the procedures of Title VII for ADEA actions, Congress rejected that course in favor of incorporating the FLSA procedures even while adopting Title VII's substantive prohibitions. Thus, even if petitioner is correct that Congress did not intend there to be jury trials under Title VII, that fact sheds no light on congressional intent under the ADEA. Petitioner's reliance on Title VII, therefore, is misplaced. * * * [*Affirmed.*]

NOTES ON CARTLEDGE, LORILLARD, AND REASONING FROM STATUTES IN PARI MATERIA

1. *Reasoning from One Statute to Another: What If There Are Several Statutory Analogies?* Both Judge Weinfeld in *Cartledge* and Justice Marshall in *Lorillard* rely on the interpretational history of similar statutes to justify their interpretations. Why do they consider this persuasive? Because Congress really and truly "intended" to incorporate all prior interpretations of similar statutes into a new statute? Because the other interpretations somehow represent "wise" public policy? Because the interpretational history of these other statutes represents a reasoned policy context which ought to affect the evolution of a related statute, so as to give greater coherence to the law? See *Bob Jones University v. United States* (reproduced in § 2F of this chapter).

Even if justified in general, this approach has its limitations. One is that there may be more than one statute *in pari materia*, and the statutes may have been interpreted differently. E.g., *Ledbetter v. Goodyear Tire & Rubber Corp.*, 550 U.S. 618 (2007), discussed in the note following this one. Or there may be several "similar" statutes, but none quite the same as the statute being interpreted. Thus, in *Lorillard*, the Supreme Court rejected the proposed analogy with Title VII. Are the Court's reasons persuasive? Why should an alleged victim of age discrimination get a jury trial (ADEA), when an alleged victim of sex discrimination (Title VII) apparently does not get one? (Congress eliminated this disparity when it provided for jury trials in Title VII cases by the Civil Rights Act of 1991.)

---

12. Title VII with respect to race, color, religion, sex, or national origin, and the ADEA with respect to age make it unlawful for an employer "to fail or refuse to hire or to discharge any individual," or otherwise to "discriminate against any individual with respect to his compensation, terms, conditions, or privileges of employment," on any of those bases. [Citing provisions of each statute.]

In 1974, Congress amended the ADEA to permit age discrimination lawsuits against the federal government. The enforcement provision says: "Any person aggrieved may bring a civil action in any Federal district court of competent jurisdiction for such legal or equitable relief as will effectuate the purposes of this Act." ADEA § 15(c), 29 U.S.C. § 633a(c). The Supreme Court held that § 15(c), unlike § 7, affords no jury trial right, finding the analogy to Title VII closer than the analogy to the FLSA. *Lehman v. Nakshian*, 453 U.S. 156 (1981). Is this consistent with *Lorillard*, upon which the four dissenting Justices relied? The majority responded that *Lorillard* is distinguishable (how?), the federal government is subject to jury trials only if it explicitly permits them (why?), and Congress in 1978 amended § 7(c) explicitly to allow ADEA jury trials but made no comparable amendment to § 15(c) (so what?).

2. *Different Statutes, Different Policies.* A second limitation on reasoning from one statute to another is that the new statute may embody policies or compromises subtly different from those in the similar statutes—if for no other reason than the different political context of the later statute. For example, the Supreme Court has interpreted Title VI of the Civil Rights Act of 1964 (prohibiting discrimination "under any program or activity receiving Federal financial assistance") to reach only instances of intentional discrimination. See *Guardians Ass'n v. Civil Serv. Comm'n of New York City*, 463 U.S. 582 (1983). Yet the Court in *Alexander v. Choate*, 469 U.S. 287, 294–99 (1985), was unwilling to limit § 504 of the Rehabilitation Act of 1973 (prohibiting discrimination or exclusion of any "qualified handicapped individual" "under any program or activity receiving Federal financial assistance") to instances of intentional discrimination. In dictum, the Court suggested that by 1973 national policy was more concerned with "disparate impact" discrimination than with the "intentional" discrimination that had been a focal point in 1964. Id. at 294–95 n.11. Ergo, the Court's interpretation of Title VI was not a helpful guide in its interpretation of § 504. Does this temporal dimension (evolving policy) help explain the result in *Lorillard*? See also *Webb v. Board of Ed. of Dyer County*, 471 U.S. 234 (1985) (rejecting analogy of Title VII attorney's fees provision as guide for interpreting 42 U.S.C. § 1988, because of different statutory schemes).

In *Ledbetter v. Goodyear Tire & Rubber Co.*, 550 U.S. 618 (2007), the Supreme Court strictly enforced the limitations period imposed by Title VII on plaintiffs bringing pay discrimination complaints to the EEOC. Under the Court's approach, an employee subjected to intentional race or sex discrimination in pay has to file a complaint with the EEOC soon after the illegal pay differential first shows up (and before many plaintiffs are even aware of the discrimination, because they do not know how much everyone else is paid). Ledbetter argued that the Court has allowed equitable tolling of Equal Pay Act (EPA) claims, a statutory analogy the Court rejected because EPA claims do not have to be brought before the EEOC first. The different statutory schemes required different interpretations of the limitations provisions. Indeed, the Court found a better analogy in the NLRA, also enforced by an agency. The Court had previously enforced that policy with similar strictness as it applied in *Ledbetter*. (Congress consequently repudiated *Ledbetter* in the first major statute enacted during the Obama Administration, in 2009.)

3. *The Possibility of Compromise.* A third limitation on reasoning from one statute to another is that it may undermine deliberative legislative compromises. Recall Judge Weinfeld's analysis of judge-created exceptions to anti-assignment and alienation provisions in four different federal statutes (see footnotes 45–48). Note that Congress at least once responded to the judicially created exceptions by codifying them in the statute, as Judge Weinfeld pointed out in footnote 48. If Congress in the past has been willing to put such an exception in the statute, why did it not do the same in ERISA? Why should courts continue to do Congress's drafting work? In 1974, more-over, Congress made provision for a limited exception for alimony and support payments, 42 U.S.C. § 659(a) (1988):

> Notwithstanding any other provision of law, * * * moneys (the entitle-ment to which is based upon remuneration for employment) due from, or payable by, the United States * * * to any individual * * * shall be subject * * * to legal process brought for the enforcement * * * of his legal obligations to provide child support or make alimony payments.

Does this codification support or undermine Judge Weinfeld's position? As our postscript to *Cartledge* indicates, Congress subsequently codified Judge Wein-feld's result through an explicit ERISA amendment. How does Congress's ability to revisit ERISA affect the interpretive issue before Judge Weinfeld? If such an issue arose again today, might today's more textualist Court reason that judges should simply apply § 256(d)(1) as written, and leave it to Congress to create exceptions?

Consider also *Ridgway v. Ridgway*, 454 U.S. 46 (1981). Richard Ridgway, a career sergeant in the U.S. Army, was granted a divorce from his wife April in 1977. The state divorce decree required Richard to keep in force then-existing life insurance policies for the benefit of the three children. Richard remarried and changed the beneficiary to his second wife, Donna, contrary to the divorce decree. When he died, both April and Donna claimed the proceeds to the life insurance—April relying on state law and Donna relying on the Servicemen's Group Life Insurance Act of 1965, 79 Stat. 880, codified as amended at 38 U.S.C. § 765 *et seq.* (1982). The Act provides comprehensive life insurance for members of the armed services, including Richard, and stipulates that the service person can designate the beneficiary, *id.* § 770(a), and that payment of insurance proceeds is not subject to attachment or "any legal or equitable process whatever." *Id.* § 770(g). The Supreme Court held that § 770(a) and (g) preempts state property decrees for support and alimony pursuant to a divorce. The Act's policy that the statutory benefits actually reach the designated beneficiary and that the insurance be operated on a national level clashes with state family law and supersedes it. See also *Hisquierdo v. Hisquierdo*, 439 U.S. 572, 584 (1979).

Three Justices dissented. Justice Stevens's dissenting opinion relied heavily on *Schlaefer v. Schlaefer*, the same case which Judge Weinfeld considered persuasive in *Cartledge*, and on the equitable argument that Richard's designation of Donna as his beneficiary violated his moral duty to support his children. Surely Congress would not have intended such a scandalous result, argued the dissenters. (What canine metaphor is apt here?) The majority in *Ridgway* responded that "[a] result of this kind, of course, may be avoided if Congress chooses to avoid it," but Congress has not so chosen. Does the *Ridgway* case undermine the cogency of Judge Weinfeld's opinion in *Cartledge*? Compare *Rose v. Rose,* 481 U.S. 619 (1987).

Part B.   *The Borrowed Statute Rule*

Reasoning from statutes *in pari materia* (similar statutes) has particular force when the statutes are all in the same jurisdiction. Indeed, sometimes, as *Lorillard* indicates, such statutes have a familial relationship because the drafting of a newer statute (e.g., the ADEA) was modeled on existing statutes in the same jurisdiction (e.g., the FLSA, Title VII). As *Lorillard* exemplifies, courts routinely assume that, unless there are strong indications to the contrary, the newer statute should be interpreted consistently with the older statutes upon which it was modeled.

Borrowed statutes are those adapted by one jurisdiction from another jurisdiction. For example, if West Virginia were to enact a pension regulation statute, it might "borrow" the language used in ERISA's anti-alienation and assignment provision or that used in a similar statute of another state. See Frank Horack Jr., *The Common Law of Legislation,* 23 Iowa L. Rev. 41 (1937) (noting that one legislature will copy a successful prior statute from another jurisdiction, following a process Horack called *"stare de statute"*). The issues of interpretation for borrowed statutes are subtly different from those concerning modeled statutes, in large part because the policies followed in one jurisdiction may be different from those followed in the original jurisdiction.

ZERBE v. STATE

Supreme Court of Alaska, 1978
578 P.2d 597

CONNOR, JUSTICE.

This appeal requires us to interpret those provisions of Alaska's government claims statute[1] which deal with claims which arise out of false imprisonment. Appellant's claim for damages against the state was dismissed by the trial court on the ground that it was barred by statute.

Stephen Zerbe's difficulties began when he was cited for driving an overweight truck. Zerbe's employer succeeded in having the complaint against Zerbe dismissed by informing the district attorney that the street on which Zerbe was driving was not a public street. Relying on the dismissal, Zerbe did not appear at the arraignment. An acting district judge who apparently had no knowledge that the complaint had been dismissed, issued a bench warrant for Zerbe's arrest. The bench warrant

---

1. AS 09.50.250 provides in pertinent part as follows:

"*Actionable claims against the state.* A person or corporation having a contract, quasi-contract, or tort claim against the state may bring an action against the state in the superior court. * * * However, no action may be brought under this section if the claim * * *

(3) arises out of assault, battery, false imprisonment, false arrest, malicious prosecution, abuse of process, libel, slander, misrepresentation, deceit, or interference with contract rights."

was served on Zerbe approximately five months later when Zerbe went to the police department to apply for a chauffeur's license.

Zerbe was taken to jail, and the guards apparently did not allow him to make any phone calls. As a result, Zerbe remained in custody for nine hours before he was able to post bail. Zerbe hired a lawyer and was successful in having the bench warrant quashed on grounds of the earlier dismissal. He then filed suit against the state, alleging that state employees were negligent in failing to properly inform the judge of the dismissal, and that jail personnel were negligent in failing to allow Zerbe to make a phone call to obtain bail.

Although the complaint was couched in terms of negligence, the state argued that plaintiff's cause of action arose out of false arrest and false imprisonment, and was, therefore, barred by AS 09.50.250.

The superior court, relying principally on federal cases interpreting similar language in the Federal Tort Claims Act (28 U.S.C. § 2680(h)), ruled that the gravamen of plaintiff's claim was "an improper arrest or imprisonment," and that Zerbe's claim was barred by the statute. This appeal followed.

Zerbe contends that the trial court erred in construing the complaint as alleging false arrest and false imprisonment, rather than common law negligence. Zerbe also challenges the constitutionality of Alaska's government claims statute. Because of our disposition of the first of appellant's points on appeal, we need not reach the constitutional question.

As there is no Alaska case law interpreting the statute here in question, we turn for guidance to federal cases construing the similar federal provisions.[2] There are numerous federal cases which have interpreted 28 U.S.C. § 2680(h), the provision which exempts the federal government from any liability for

"[a]ny claim arising out of assault, battery, false imprisonment, false arrest, malicious prosecution, abuse of process, libel, slander, misrepresentation, deceit, or interference with contract rights. * * * "

Three federal cases squarely support the state's contention that although the complaint is drafted in terms of negligence, it actually is a claim *arising out of* false imprisonment and false arrest. * * *

The state's strongest authority comes from *Duenges v. United States*, 114 F.Supp. 751 (S.D.N.Y. 1953), in which the plaintiff had been arrested and imprisoned for desertion from the army when, in fact, he had been honorably discharged. Plaintiff's complaint, like Zerbe's, alleged that the

---

2. *See State v. Abbott*, 498 P.2d 712, 717 (Alaska 1972). Appellant correctly notes that the federal tort claims statute has been amended so that claims arising out of false arrest or false imprisonment are not barred if the claim arises from acts or omissions of investigative or law enforcement officers of the United States government. Appellant infers that under the statute as amended, claims such as his would be allowed. The state disputes this point. In any event, Alaska's statute has not been amended in accordance with the changed federal statute, and none of the federal cases cited by the parties to this appeal deals with the statute as amended. Therefore, the federal statute is quoted as it read before amendment. That Congress chose to amend this statute recently does not shed much light on the case at bar.

government had negligently maintained its records, resulting in injuries to the plaintiff including loss of freedom, humiliation, fear, embarrassment, mental anguish, and loss of earnings. In granting the government's motion to dismiss, the court stated that

> " * * * the Government's negligence could become an actionable wrong only upon the event of resulting injury. The injuries alleged derive from a false arrest and imprisonment. In an action of negligence 'damage is of the very gist and essence of the plaintiff's cause.' Here, false arrest and imprisonment are of the very gist and essence of the plaintiff's cause. Section 2680(h) of 28 U.S.C. specifically excludes from the provisions of the Federal Tort Claims Act claims 'arising out of * * * false imprisonment [and] false arrest * * *.' This suit arises out of false imprisonment and false arrest within the meaning of that section, and consequently, it does not come within the scope of the Act."

It should be noted that all three of these cases were disposed of in short opinions without any detailed analysis or discussion of policy considerations. Some of the other federal cases cited in support of the state's position are reasoned in greater depth, yet they appear to be distinguishable on their facts from the case at bar.

Although the federal cases barring recovery under § 2680(h) are in the numerical majority, a number of federal courts have held for the plaintiff in situations similar to Zerbe's. We find this line of cases to be the better reasoned. * * *

The most persuasive authority in support of plaintiff's position comes from *Quinones v. United States*, 492 F.2d 1269 (3d Cir. 1974). Quinones alleged that the government's failure to use due care in maintaining his personnel records had resulted in damage to his reputation. The district court dismissed the complaint because defamation was excluded from the Federal Tort Claims Act by § 2680(h). The Third Circuit reversed, finding that although the resulting harm was defamation, the plaintiff's cause of action sounded in negligence. The court distinguished the two torts by showing that defamation requires malice, whereas negligence merely requires duty, breach, proximate and actual cause, and damage. The court stated that one civil remedy does not preempt another, and added that "[i]t is not the publication of the incorrect employment history and record that serves as the foundation of plaintiff's complaint; it is the method in which the defendant maintained the record of his employment that is being criticized."

We adopt the reasoning of the Third Circuit in the *Quinones* case, and hold that it was negligent record keeping, rather than false imprisonment, which caused Zerbe's injuries. Zerbe's suit is therefore not barred by the false imprisonment exception to Alaska's government claims statute, but instead ought to have been treated in the same manner as any other negligence case against the state.[6]

Today, when various branches of government collect and keep copious records concerning numerous aspects of the lives of ordinary citizens, we are unwilling to deny recourse to those hapless people whose lives are disrupted because of careless record keeping or poorly programmed computers. We see no justification for immunizing the government from the damaging consequences of its clerical employees' failure to exercise due care.

Reversed and Remanded.

Opinion On Petition for Rehearing [583 P.2d 845]

CONNOR, JUSTICE.

The State of Alaska petitions for rehearing on the ground that we have overlooked, failed to consider, or misconceived a controlling principle or proposition of law. It asserts that in the opinion which we handed down in this case we did not consider the principle that when a statute is adopted from another jurisdiction it is presumed that interpretations of that statute by courts of that jurisdiction are also adopted with it.

The state asserts that such cases as *Duenges v. United States*, 114 F.Supp. 751 (S.D.N.Y. 1953), *Klein v. United States*, 167 F.Supp. 410 (E.D.N.Y. 1958), *aff'd per curiam*, 268 F.2d 63 (2d Cir. 1959), and *United States v. Neustadt*, 366 U.S. 696 (1961), which interpret the federal act from which our own law was drawn, reach a result contrary to that which we reached in the case at bar. Therefore, it is urged, the case at bar was wrongly decided.

The state seeks to support its position by reference to our recent opinion in *Menard v. State*, 578 P.2d 966 (Alaska 1978), in which we resorted for guidance to the interpretations of our criminal assault statute by the Oregon Supreme Court prior to the statute's adoption as the law of Alaska. The state's petition then asserts that our failure to follow the doctrine concerning prior interpretations of adopted statutes results in "legal chaos," and that in determining Alaska law "predictions must be based on a 'result analysis' of decisions in this jurisdiction alone, presumably by ascertaining the trend of those decisions."

Thus, if the argument presented in the petition for rehearing is correct, this court has indulged in an indefensible interpretation of the Alaska tort claims act, and has issued two irreconcilable opinions on the same day.

---

6. This holding is consistent with previous decisions in which we have narrowly construed other exceptions to Alaska's government claims statute; e.g., *State v. Abbott*, 498 P.2d 712 (Alaska 1972) (narrowly construing AS 09.50.250(1), the discretionary state function exception); *State v. Stanley*, 506 P.2d 1284, 1291 (Alaska 1973) (negligence on the part of government employees "does not rise to the 'level of governmental policy decisions' to which the discretionary function immunity from suit applies.") *See also* Professor Van Alstyne's commentary in *California Government Tort Liability Supplement* § 5.63, at 24–25 (C.E.B. 1967), quoted in *Sullivan v. County of Los Angeles*, 527 P.2d 865, 872 (Cal. 1974).

The state's entire argument is built upon an erroneous major premise.

When a statute is adopted from another jurisdiction, it is not the interpretative decisions of all courts of that jurisdiction which are presumed to be adopted with the statute. As we have taken such pains to say in our earlier opinions, it is only the settled interpretations of the highest court of the other jurisdiction which are presumptively intended by the lawmaker to be adopted with the statute.

The cases of *Duenges v. United States, supra*, and *Klein v. United States, supra*, most certainly were not decisions of the sort which come within the presumption. It would be a curious, indeed irrational, doctrine under which we would somehow be hobbled indefinitely by the decisions of federal trial courts, rendered some years ago, in another part of the country. To our knowledge, no court has ever deemed itself so bound. The case of *United States v. Neustadt, supra*, to which the state alludes, concerns a different question than that presented in the case at bar. Because it is distinguishable it cannot come within the principle of adoptive construction.

It should be noted that the presumption is, in any event, not conclusive but merely a rule based on convenience and principles of *stare decisis*, whereby things once decided need not constantly be redetermined.

The rule is not invariably followed. It is conceivable, indeed likely, that if a precedent underlying an adopted statute were no longer vital or were poorly reasoned, we would decline to follow it. To do otherwise would represent mechanical jurisprudence of the worst kind.

Based as it is upon an untenable thesis, the petition for rehearing is devoid of merit, and it must be denied.

NOTE ON ZERBE AND INTERPRETATION OF BORROWED STATUTES

Four Justices of the U.S. Supreme Court rejected the *Zerbe* reading of § 2680(h) in *United States v. Shearer*, 473 U.S. 52 (1985). Vernon Shearer was kidnapped and murdered by a serviceman who had been previously convicted of manslaughter. Shearer's administratrix sued the government for negligent supervision of the murderer. Chief Justice Burger's opinion found two reasons why the lawsuit could not be maintained. The first was that § 2680(h) barred suit: any injury flowing from intentional torts committed by federal employees is excluded, even if a claim against the government can be framed in terms of negligence. "Section 2680(h) does not merely bar claims *for* assault or battery; in sweeping language it excludes any claim *arising out of* assault or battery." Four Justices joined this part of the opinion; four Justices joined only the second part, involving a judge-created exception to the FTCA for military activity; one Justice did not participate. Assume that Chief Justice Burger's interpretation had been accepted by the Court. Should the Alaska Supreme Court reconsider *Zerbe*?

Part C.   The Rule Against Implied Repeals

Not only similar statutes in the same jurisdiction and statutes copied from other jurisdictions, but also subsequent statutes in the same jurisdiction may be sources of guidance concerning the appropriate interpretation of a statute. The second opinion in *Montana Wilderness* is an example of how a similar, subsequently enacted statute may sometimes shed light on a prior statutory provision. In *Babbitt v. Sweet Home* (Chapter 3, § 1), the Court was persuaded to read a provision of the Endangered Species Act of 1973 broadly, in part to assure its consistency with a 1982 amendment to the law.

Recall our discussion of the Checkerboard Case in §§ 2D–E of this chapter. Both opinions in *Montana Wilderness* point to a clash between the Alaska Lands Act (as applied nationwide in the second opinion) and the Wilderness Act. How do judges resolve apparently conflicting statutes? Obviously, if the more recent statute expressly provides that it controls, the issue is easy. Similarly, if the newer statute contains a savings clause, which states that it does not alter existing law, the older statute controls. Unfortunately, most of the time the more recent statute says nothing on this question. Typically, courts do their best to reconcile the statutes, based on the presumption of whole code coherence. As the next case demonstrates, there is a longstanding canon in this area, which disfavors implied repeals.[a]

MORTON v. MANCARI

Supreme Court of the United States, 1974
417 U.S. 535, 94 S.Ct. 2474, 41 L.Ed.2d 290

MR. JUSTICE BLACKMUN delivered the opinion of the Court.

The Indian Reorganization Act of 1934, also known as the Wheeler–Howard Act, 48 Stat. 984, 25 U.S.C. § 461 *et seq.*, accords an employment preference for qualified Indians in the Bureau of Indian Affairs (BIA or Bureau). Appellees, non-Indian BIA employees, challenged this preference as contrary to the anti-discrimination provisions of the Equal Employment Opportunity Act of 1972, 86 Stat. 103, 42 U.S.C. § 2000e et seq. (1970 ed., Supp. II), and as violative of the Due Process Clause of the Fifth Amendment. * * *

[I] Section 12 of the Indian Reorganization Act, 48 Stat. 986, 25 U.S.C. § 472, provides:

"The Secretary of the Interior is directed to establish standards of health, age, character, experience, knowledge, and ability for Indians who may be appointed, without regard to civil-service laws, to the various positions maintained, now or hereafter, by the Indian Office,

---

a. See also *Hamdan v. Rumsfeld,* 548 U.S. 557, 593–95 (2006); *Granholm v. Heald,* 544 U.S. 460 (2005); *County of Yakima v. Confederated Tribes & Bands of Yakima Indian Nation,* 502 U.S. 251 (1992); *St. Martin Evangelical Lutheran Church v. South Dakota,* 451 U.S. 772, 788 (1981); *Watt v. Alaska,* 451 U.S. 259 (1981); *Radzanower v. Touche Ross & Co.,* 426 U.S. 148, 154 (1976).

in the administration of functions or services affecting any Indian tribe. Such qualified Indians shall hereafter have the preference to appointment to vacancies in any such positions."

In June 1972, pursuant to this provision, the Commissioner of Indian Affairs, with the approval of the Secretary of the Interior, issued a directive (Personnel Management Letter No. 72–12) stating that the BIA's policy would be to grant a preference to qualified Indians not only, as before, in the initial hiring stage, but also in the situation where an Indian and a non-Indian, both already employed by the BIA, were competing for a promotion within the Bureau. The record indicates that this policy was implemented immediately.

Shortly thereafter, appellees, who are non-Indian employees of the BIA at Albuquerque, instituted this class action, on behalf of themselves and other non-Indian employees similarly situated, in the United States District Court for the District of New Mexico, claiming that the "so-called 'Indian Preference Statutes' " were repealed by the 1972 Equal Employment Opportunity Act and deprived them of rights to property without due process of law, in violation of the Fifth Amendment. * * *

After a short trial focusing primarily on how the new policy, in fact, has been implemented, the District Court concluded that the Indian preference was implicitly repealed by § 11 of the Equal Employment Opportunity Act of 1972, Pub. L. 92–261, 86 Stat. 111, 42 U.S.C. § 2000e–16(a) (1970 ed., Supp. II), proscribing discrimination in most federal employment on the basis of race.[6] Having found that Congress repealed the preference, it was unnecessary for the District Court to pass on its constitutionality. The court permanently enjoined appellants "from implementing any policy in the Bureau of Indian Affairs which would hire, promote, or reassign any person in preference to another solely for the reason that such person is an Indian." * * *

[II] The federal policy of according some hiring preference to Indians in the Indian service dates at least as far back as 1834. Since that time, Congress repeatedly has enacted various preferences of the general type here at issue.[8] The purpose of these preferences, as variously expressed in

---

6. Section 2000e–16(a) reads:

"All personnel actions affecting employees or applicants for employment (except with regard to aliens employed outside the limits of the United States) in military departments as defined in section 102 of Title 5, in executive agencies (other than the General Accounting Office) as defined in section 105 of Title 5 (including employees and applicants for employment who are paid from nonappropriated funds), in the United States Postal Service and the Postal Rate Commission, in those units of the Government of the District of Columbia having positions in the competitive service, and in those units of the legislative and judicial branches of the Federal Government having positions in the competitive service, and in the Library of Congress shall be made free from any discrimination based on race, color, religion, sex, or national origin."

8. Act of May 17, 1882, § 6, 22 Stat. 88, and Act of July 4, 1884, § 6, 23 Stat. 97, 25 U.S.C. § 46 (employment of clerical, mechanical, and other help on reservations and about agencies); Act of Aug. 15, 1894, § 10, 28 Stat. 313, 25 U.S.C. § 44 (employment of herders, teamsters, and laborers, "and where practicable in all other employments" in the Indian service); Act of June 7, 1897, § 1, 30 Stat. 83, 25 U.S.C. § 274 (employment as matrons, farmers, and industrial teachers in Indian schools); Act of June 25, 1910, § 23, 36 Stat. 861, 25 U.S.C. § 47 (general preference as to Indian labor and products of Indian industry).

the legislative history, has been to give Indians a greater participation in their own self-government; to further the Government's trust obligation toward the Indian tribes[9]; and to reduce the negative effect of having non-Indians administer matters that affect Indian tribal life.

The preference directly at issue here was enacted as an important part of the sweeping Indian Reorganization Act of 1934. The overriding purpose of that particular Act was to establish machinery whereby Indian tribes would be able to assume a greater degree of self-government, both politically and economically. Congress was seeking to modify the then-existing situation whereby the primarily non-Indian-staffed BIA had plenary control, for all practical purposes, over the lives and destinies of the federally recognized Indian tribes. Initial congressional proposals would have diminished substantially the role of the BIA by turning over to federally chartered self-governing Indian communities many of the functions normally performed by the Bureau.[13] Committee sentiment, however, ran against such a radical change in the role of the BIA. The solution ultimately adopted was to strengthen tribal government while continuing the active role of the BIA, with the understanding that the Bureau would be more responsive to the interests of the people it was created to serve.

One of the primary means by which self-government would be fostered and the Bureau made more responsive was to increase the participation of tribal Indians in the BIA operations. In order to achieve this end, it was recognized that some kind of preference and exemption from otherwise prevailing civil service requirements was necessary.[16] Congressman Howard, the House sponsor, expressed the need for the preference:

> "The Indians have not only been thus deprived of civic rights and powers, but they have been largely deprived of the opportunity to enter the more important positions in the service of the very bureau which manages their affairs. Theoretically, the Indians have the right to qualify for the Federal civil service. In actual practice there has been no adequate program of training to qualify Indians to compete in these examinations, especially for technical and higher positions; and even if there were such training, the Indians would have to compete

---

9. A letter, contained in the House Report to the 1934 Act, from President F. D. Roosevelt to Congressman Howard states:

"We can and should, without further delay, extend to the Indian the fundamental rights of political liberty and local self-government and the opportunities of education and economic assistance that they require in order to attain a wholesome American life. This is but the obligation of honor of a powerful nation toward a people living among us and dependent upon our protection." H.R.Rep. No. 1804, 73d Cong., 2d Sess., 8 (1934).

13. Hearings on H.R. 7902, Readjustment of Indian Affairs, 73d Cong., 2d Sess., 1–7 (1934) (hereafter House Hearings).

16. "The bill admits qualified Indians to the position [*sic*] in their own service.

"Thirty-four years ago, in 1900, the number of Indians holding regular positions in the Indian Service, in proportion to the total of positions, was greater than it is today.

"The reason primarily is found in the application of the generalized civil service to the Indian Service, and the consequent exclusion of Indians from their own jobs." House Hearings 19 (memorandum dated Feb. 19, 1934, submitted by Commissioner Collier to the Senate and House Committees on Indian Affairs).

under existing law, on equal terms with multitudes of white applicants. * * * The various services on the Indian reservations are actually local rather than Federal services and are comparable to local municipal and county services, since they are dealing with purely local Indian problems. It should be possible for Indians with the requisite vocational and professional training to enter the service of their own people without the necessity of competing with white applicants for these positions. This bill permits them to do so." 78 Cong. Rec. 11729 (1934).

Congress was well aware that the proposed preference would result in employment disadvantages within the BIA for non-Indians.[17] Not only was this displacement unavoidable if room were to be made for Indians, but it was explicitly determined that gradual replacement of non-Indians with Indians within the Bureau was a desirable feature of the entire program for self-government.[18] Since 1934, the BIA has implemented the preference with a fair degree of success. The percentage of Indians employed in the Bureau rose from 34% in 1934 to 57% in 1972. This reversed the former downward trend, see n. 16, *supra*, and was due, clearly, to the presence of the 1934 Act. The Commissioner's extension of the preference in 1972 to promotions within the BIA was designed to bring more Indians into positions of responsibility and, in that regard, appears to be a logical extension of the congressional intent.

[III] It is against this background that we encounter the first issue in the present case: whether the Indian preference was repealed by the Equal Employment Opportunity Act of 1972. Title VII of the Civil Rights Act of 1964 was the first major piece of federal legislation prohibiting discrimination in *private* employment on the basis of "race, color, religion, sex, or national origin." 42 U.S.C. § 2000e–2(a). Significantly, §§ 701(b) and 703(i) of that Act explicitly exempted from its coverage the preferential employment of Indians by Indian tribes or by industries located on or near Indian reservations. 42 U.S.C. §§ 2000e(b) and 2000e–2(i).[19] This exemption reveals a clear congressional recognition, within the framework of Title VII, of the unique legal status of tribal and reservation-based

---

17. Congressman Carter, an opponent of the bill, placed in the Congressional Record the following observation by Commissioner Collier at the Committee hearings:

"[W]e must not blind ourselves to the fact that the effect of this bill if worked out would unquestionably be to replace white employees by Indian employees. I do not know how fast, but ultimately it ought to go very far indeed." 78 Cong. Rec. 11737 (1934).

18. "It should be possible for Indians to enter the service of their own people without running the gauntlet of competition with whites for these positions. Indian progress and ambition will be enormously strengthened as soon as we adopt the principle that the Indian Service shall gradually become, in fact as well as in name, an Indian service predominantly in the hands of educated and competent Indians." *Id.*, at 11731 (remarks of Cong. Howard).

19. Section 701(b) excludes "an Indian Tribe" from the Act's definition of "employer." Section 703(i) states:

"Nothing contained in this subchapter shall apply to any business or enterprise on or near an Indian reservation with respect to any publicly announced employment practice of such business or enterprise under which a preferential treatment is given to any individual because he is an Indian living on or near a reservation."

activities. The Senate sponsor, Senator Humphrey, stated on the floor by way of explanation:

> "This exemption is consistent with the Federal Government's policy of encouraging Indian employment and with the special legal position of Indians." 110 Cong. Rec. 12723 (1964).[20]

The 1964 Act did not specifically outlaw employment discrimination by the Federal Government. Yet the mechanism for enforcing longstanding Executive Orders forbidding Government discrimination had proved ineffective for the most part. In order to remedy this, Congress, by the 1972 Act, amended the 1964 Act and proscribed discrimination in most areas of federal employment. See n. 6, *supra*. In general, it may be said that the substantive anti-discrimination law embraced in Title VII was carried over and applied to the Federal Government. As stated in the House Report:

> "To correct this entrenched discrimination in the Federal service, it is necessary to insure the effective application of uniform, fair and strongly enforced policies. The present law and the proposed statute do not permit industry and labor organizations to be the judges of their own conduct in the area of employment discrimination. There is no reason why government agencies should not be treated similarly. * * * " H.R.Rep. No. 92–238, on H.R. 1746, pp. 24–25 (1971).

Nowhere in the legislative history of the 1972 Act, however, is there any mention of Indian preference.

Appellees assert * * * that since the 1972 Act proscribed racial discrimination in Government employment, the Act necessarily, albeit *sub silentio*, repealed the provision of the 1934 Act that called for the preference in the BIA of one racial group, Indians, over non-Indians:

> "When a conflict such as in this case, is present, the most recent law or Act should apply and the conflicting Preferences passed some 39 years earlier should be impliedly repealed." Brief for Appellees 7.

We disagree. For several reasons we conclude that Congress did not intend to repeal the Indian preference and that the District Court erred in holding that it was repealed.

First: There are the above-mentioned affirmative provisions in the 1964 Act excluding coverage of tribal employment and of preferential treatment by a business or enterprise on or near a reservation. These 1964 exemptions as to private employment indicate Congress' recognition of the longstanding federal policy of providing a unique legal status to Indians in matters concerning tribal or "on or near" reservation employment. The exemptions reveal a clear congressional sentiment that an Indian preference in the narrow context of tribal or reservation-related employment did not constitute racial discrimination of the type otherwise

---

20. Senator Mundt supported these exemptions on the Senate floor by claiming that they would allow Indians "to benefit from Indian preference programs now in operation or later to be instituted." 110 Cong.Rec. 13702 (1964).

proscribed. In extending the general anti-discrimination machinery to federal employment in 1972, Congress in no way modified these private employment preferences built into the 1964 Act, and they are still in effect. It would be anomalous to conclude that Congress intended to eliminate the longstanding statutory preferences in BIA employment, as being racially discriminatory, at the very same time it was reaffirming the right of tribal and reservation-related private employers to provide Indian preference. Appellees' assertion that Congress implicitly repealed the preference as racially discriminatory, while retaining the 1964 preferences, attributes to Congress irrationality and arbitrariness, an attribution we do not share.

Second: Three months after Congress passed the 1972 amendments, it enacted two *new* Indian preference laws. These were part of the Education Amendments of 1972, 86 Stat. 235, 20 U.S.C. §§ 887c(a) and (d), and § 1119a (1970 ed., Supp. II). The new laws explicitly require that Indians be given preference in Government programs for training teachers of Indian children. It is improbable, to say the least, that the same Congress which affirmatively approved and enacted these additional and similar Indian preferences was, at the same time, condemning the BIA preference as racially discriminatory. In the total absence of any manifestation of supportive intent, we are loathe to imply this improbable result.

Third: Indian preferences, for many years, have been treated as exceptions to Executive Orders forbidding Government employment discrimination. The 1972 extension of the Civil Rights Act to Government employment is in large part merely a codification of prior anti-discrimination Executive Orders that had proved ineffective because of inadequate enforcement machinery. There certainly was no indication that the substantive proscription against discrimination was intended to be any broader than that which previously existed. By codifying the existing anti-discrimination provisions, and by providing enforcement machinery for them, there is no reason to presume that Congress affirmatively intended to erase the preferences that previously had co-existed with broad anti-discrimination provisions in Executive Orders.

Fourth: Appellees encounter head-on the "cardinal rule * * * that repeals by implication are not favored." *Posadas v. National City Bank*, 296 U.S. 497, 503 (1936). They and the District Court read the congressional silence as effectuating a repeal by implication. There is nothing in the legislative history, however, that indicates affirmatively any congressional intent to repeal the 1934 preference. Indeed, as explained above, there is ample independent evidence that the legislative intent was to the contrary.

This is a prototypical case where an adjudication of repeal by implication is not appropriate. The preference is a longstanding, important component of the Government's Indian program. The anti-discrimination provision, aimed at alleviating minority discrimination in employment, obviously is designed to deal with an entirely different and, indeed, opposite problem. Any perceived conflict is thus more apparent than real.

In the absence of some affirmative showing of an intention to repeal, the only permissible justification for a repeal by implication is when the earlier and later statutes are irreconcilable. *Georgia v. Pennsylvania R. Co.*, 324 U.S. 439, 456–457 (1945). Clearly, this is not the case here. A provision aimed at furthering Indian self-government by according an employment preference within the BIA for qualified members of the governed group can readily coexist with a general rule prohibiting employment discrimination on the basis of race. Any other conclusion can be reached only by formalistic reasoning that ignores both the history and purposes of the preference and the unique legal relationship between the Federal Government and tribal Indians.

Furthermore, the Indian preference statute is a specific provision applying to a very specific situation. The 1972 Act, on the other hand, is of general application. Where there is no clear intention otherwise, a specific statute will not be controlled or nullified by a general one, regardless of the priority of enactment. See, e.g., *Bulova Watch Co. v. United States*, 365 U.S. 753, 758 (1961); *Rodgers v. United States*, 185 U.S. 83, 87–89 (1902).

The courts are not at liberty to pick and choose among congressional enactments, and when two statutes are capable of co-existence, it is the duty of the courts, absent a clearly expressed congressional intention to the contrary, to regard each as effective. "When there are two acts upon the same subject, the rule is to give effect to both if possible * * *. The intention of the legislature to repeal 'must be clear and manifest.' " *United States v. Borden Co.*, 308 U.S. 188, 198 (1939). In light of the factors indicating no repeal, we simply cannot conclude that Congress consciously abandoned its policy of furthering Indian self-government when it passed the 1972 amendments.

We therefore hold that the District Court erred in ruling that the Indian preference was repealed by the 1972 Act. * * *

Notes on *Mancari* and Interpretation in Light of Subsequent Statutes

1. *Repeals by Implication.* The canon that repeals by implication are disfavored is subject to the criticism that it naively assumes legislative omniscience—legislators and their staff members do not search the statute books to ensure that new legislation will interfere minimally with established legislation. And why should they? Shouldn't new legislative policy be applied to full effect, liberally supplanting outdated prior statutes? On the other hand, the canon against implied repeals might be defended, "not only to avoid misconstruction of the law effecting the putative repeal, but also to preserve the intent of later Congresses that have already enacted laws that are dependent on the continued applicability of the law whose implicit repeal is in question." *Smith v. Robinson*, 468 U.S. 992, 1026 (1984) (Brennan, J., dissenting).

As Judge Norris recognized in the Checkerboard Case (§ 2D–E of this chapter), *Mancari* is in tension with the Ninth Circuit's ultimate position in the Checkerboard Case: the Alaska Lands Act's access provision was found to repeal huge chunks of wilderness protection acts passed by Congress in the 1960s and 1970s. Why isn't the Checkerboard Case a much better case for *refusing* to allow repeals by implication?

2. *Applying the Canon in* Mancari. Figure out the best arguments against Justice Blackmun's reasons why no repeal by implication occurred in *Mancari*. Hint: As to the first, Congress showed itself able to exempt Indians from the operation of antidiscrimination laws in 1964; the absence of any express exemption in the 1972 Act, then, gives a strong *expressio unius* argument to plaintiffs. In addition, sticking to the first argument made by Justice Blackmun, isn't it quite different to exempt an Indian tribe or a private employer from the coverage of an employment discrimination statute, on the one hand, and to exempt the federal government, on the other? We think that the best arguments against Justice Blackmun's first three points are strong ones. If we are right, then the "repeal by implication" canon is crucial to the outcome of the case. As note 1 above suggests, that canon has some theoretical problems when it is stated broadly, as saying that repeals of *statutes* by implication are disfavored. Can the Blackmun result be saved by narrowing the canon to "repeals of *longstanding policies* are disfavored, especially where there is no collateral evidence (in other statutes, regulations, executive orders, authoritative committee reports, and the like) supporting the notion that the longstanding policy has been repudiated"? Does narrowing the canon in this way alleviate the general objections to it suggested in note 1 as well?

3. *Repeal of Treaties by Implication.* Treaties, like statutes, are the law of the land under the Supremacy Clause, U.S. Const., art. VI, and the Supreme Court has stated that "[a] treaty," like a statute, "will not be deemed to have been abrogated or modified by a later statute unless such purpose on the part of Congress has been clearly expressed." *Cook v. United States*, 288 U.S. 102, 120 (1933); see *Weinberger v. Rossi*, 456 U.S. 25 (1982). Consider the following problem. The United States in 1934 ratified the Warsaw Convention, which sets forth uniform rules governing air transportation. Article 22 sets a limit on carrier liability for lost cargo; the liability is expressed in terms of gold, a uniform international standard of value when the Convention was drafted in the 1920s. The United States suspended convertibility of the dollar for gold in 1971 and in 1978 passed a statute implementing an international agreement creating a new regime for international monetary cooperation. The federal agency charged with implementing the Warsaw Convention set the liability limits in 1978 at $9.07 per pound of lost cargo—the last figure it had used under the gold conversion approach before the 1978 statute. The Supreme Court in *TWA v. Franklin Mint Corp.*, 466 U.S. 243 (1984), rejected the Second Circuit's determination that the Warsaw Convention's liability limits were unenforceable as implicitly nullified by the 1978 statute, based upon the presumption against implied repeals. The Court noted that the presumption is potentially stronger in the case of treaties, because they usually have provisions requiring the U.S. to notify the

other country (or countries) party to the treaty if the U.S. is withdrawing from it.

BRANCH v. SMITH

Supreme Court of the United States, 2003
538 U.S. 254, 123 S.Ct. 1429, 155 L.Ed.2d 407

JUSTICE SCALIA announced the judgment of the Court and delivered the opinion of the Court with respect to Parts I, II, and III–A, and an opinion with respect to Parts III–B and IV, in which THE CHIEF JUSTICE [REHN-QUIST], JUSTICE KENNEDY, and JUSTICE GINSBURG join.

[The 2000 census caused Mississippi to lose one congressional seat. The state legislature failed to pass a new redistricting plan after the decennial census results were published in 2001. Beatrice Branch and others (state plaintiffs) filed suit in Mississippi state court, seeking a redistricting plan for the 2002 congressional elections. In November 2001, John Smith and others (federal plaintiffs) filed a similar action in federal court. The federal plaintiffs asked the court to order at-large elections pursuant to 2 U.S.C. § 2a(c)(5), or, alternatively, to devise its own redistricting plan. In December 2001, the state court adopted a redistricting plan, but the Department of Justice demanded more information before it would preclear the plan as required by the Voting Rights Act. Fearing that the state court plan would not be in place by March 1, 2002, the candidate qualification deadline, the federal court on February 26, 2002, enjoined use of the state court plan and directed that its own redistricting plan be used for the 2002 election. The state plaintiff's appealed this order. The Supreme Court ruled that the federal district court had properly enjoined enforcement of the state court redistricting plan. The main issue on appeal was whether the district court was also correct in drawing single-member, rather than at-large districts.]

[III.A] Article I, § 4, cl. 1, of the Constitution provides that the "Times, Places and Manner of holding Elections for Senators and Representatives, shall be prescribed in each State by the Legislature thereof...." It reserves to Congress, however, the power "at any time by Law [to] make or alter such Regulations, except as to the Places of chusing Senators." Pursuant to this authority, Congress in 1929 enacted the current statutory scheme governing apportionment of the House of Representatives. 2 U.S.C. §§ 2a(a), (b). In 1941, Congress added to those provisions a subsection addressing what is to be done pending redistricting:

> "Until a State is redistricted in the manner provided by the law thereof after any apportionment, the Representatives to which such State is entitled under such apportionment shall be elected in the following manner: (1) If there is no change in the number of Representatives, they shall be elected from the districts then prescribed by the law of such State, and if any of them are elected from the State at large they shall continue to be so elected; (2) if there is an increase in

the number of Representatives, such additional Representative or Representatives shall be elected from the State at large and the other Representatives from the districts then prescribed by the law of such State; (3) if there is a decrease in the number of Representatives but the number of districts in such State is equal to such decreased number of Representatives, they shall be elected from the districts then prescribed by the law of such State; (4) if there is a decrease in the number of Representatives but the number of districts in such State is less than such number of Representatives, the number of Representatives by which such number of districts is exceeded shall be elected from the State at large and the other Representatives from the districts then prescribed by the law of such State; or (5) if there is a decrease in the number of Representatives and the number of districts in such State exceeds such decreased number of Representatives, they shall be elected from the State at large." § 2a(c).

In 1967, 26 years after § 2a(c) was enacted, Congress adopted § 2c, which provides, as relevant here:

"In each State entitled in the Ninety-first Congress or in any subsequent Congress thereafter to more than one Representative under an apportionment made pursuant to the provisions of section 2a(a) of this title, there shall be established by law a number of districts equal to the number of Representatives to which such State is so entitled, and Representatives shall be elected only from districts so established, no district to elect more than one Representative...."

The tension between these two provisions is apparent: Section 2c requires States entitled to more than one Representative to elect their Representatives from single-member districts, rather than from multi-member districts or the State at large. Section 2a(c), however, requires multimember districts or at-large elections in certain situations; and with particular relevance to the present cases, in which Mississippi, by reason of the 2000 census, lost a congressional seat, § 2a(c)(5) requires at-large elections. Cross-appellants would reconcile the two provisions by interpreting the introductory phrase of § 2a(c) ("Until a State is redistricted in the manner provided by the law thereof after any apportionment") and the phrase "established by law" in § 2c to refer exclusively to *legislative* redistricting—so that § 2c tells the legislatures what to do (single-member districting) and § 2a(c) provides what will happen *absent* legislative action—in the present cases, the mandating of at-large elections.

The problem with this reconciliation of the provisions is that the limited role it assigns to § 2c (governing legislative apportionment but not judicial apportionment) is contradicted both by the historical context of § 2c's enactment and by the consistent understanding of all courts in the almost 40 years since that enactment. When Congress adopted § 2c in 1967, the immediate issue was precisely the involvement of the courts in fashioning electoral plans. The Voting Rights Act of 1965 had recently been enacted, assigning to the federal courts jurisdiction to involve themselves in elections. Even more significant, our decisions in [the one-person, one-vote cases] had ushered in a new era in which federal courts were overseeing efforts by badly malapportioned States to conform their congressional electoral districts to the constitutionally required one-person, one-vote standards. In a world in which the role of federal courts in redistricting disputes had been transformed from spectating to directing, the risk arose that judges forced to fashion remedies would simply order at-large elections.

At the time Congress enacted § 2c, at least six District Courts, two of them specifically invoking 2 U.S.C. § 2a(c)(5), had suggested that if the state legislature was unable to redistrict to correct malapportioned congressional districts, they would order the State's entire congressional delegation to be elected at large. * * * With all this threat of judicially imposed at-large elections, and (as far as we are aware) no threat of a legislatively imposed change to at-large elections, it is most unlikely that § 2c was directed solely at legislative reapportionment. [Indeed, lower courts have held as much.]

Of course the implausibility (given the circumstances of its enactment) that § 2c was meant to apply only to legislative reapportionment, and the unbroken unanimity of state and federal courts in opposition to that interpretation, would be of no consequence if the text of § 2c (and of § 2a(c)) unmistakably demanded that interpretation. But it does not. Indeed, it is more readily susceptible of the opposite interpretation.

The clause "there shall be established by law a number of districts equal to the number of Representatives to which such State is so entitled" could, to be sure, be so interpreted that the phrase "by law" refers only to legislative action. Its more common meaning, however, encompasses judicial decisions as well. * * *

In sum, § 2c is as readily enforced by courts as it is by state legislatures, and is just as binding on courts—federal or state—as it is on legislatures.

[III.B] Having determined that in enacting 2 U.S.C. § 2c, Congress mandated that States are to provide for the election of their Representatives from single-member districts, and that this mandate applies equally to courts remedying a state legislature's failure to redistrict constitutionally, we confront the remaining question: what to make of § 2a(c)? As observed earlier, the texts of § 2c and § 2a(c)(5) are in tension. Representatives cannot be "elected only from districts," § 2c, while being elected "at large," § 2a(c). Some of the courts confronted with this conflict have concluded that § 2c repeals § 2a(c) by implication. There is something to be said for that position—especially since paragraphs (1) through (4) of § 2a(c) have become (because of post-enactment decisions of this Court) in virtually all situations plainly unconstitutional. (The unlikely exception is the situation in which the decennial census makes no districting change constitutionally necessary.) Eighty percent of the section being a dead letter, why would Congress adhere to the flotsam of paragraph (5)?

We have repeatedly stated, however, that absent "a clearly expressed congressional intention," *Morton v. Mancari*, "repeals by implication are not favored." An implied repeal will only be found where provisions in two statutes are in "irreconcilable conflict," or where the latter act covers the whole subject of the earlier one and "is clearly intended as a substitute." So while there is a strong argument that § 2c was a substitute for § 2a(c), we think the better answer is that § 2a(c)—where what it prescribes is constitutional (as it is with regard to paragraph (5))—continues to apply.

Section 2a(c) is, of course, only *provisionally* applicable. It governs the manner of election for Representatives in any election held "[u]ntil a State is redistricted in the manner provided by the law thereof after any apportionment." That language clashes with § 2c only if it is interpreted to forbid judicial redistricting unless the state legislature has first acted. On that interpretation, whereas § 2c categorically instructs courts to redistrict, § 2a(c)(5) forbids them to do anything but order at-large elections unless the state legislature has acted. But there is of course no need for such an interpretation. "Until a State is redistricted" can certainly refer to redistricting by courts as well as by legislatures. Indeed, that interpretation would seem the preferable one even if it were not a necessary means of reconciling the two sections. Under prior versions of § 2a(c), its default or stopgap provisions were to be invoked for a State "until the *legislature* of such State ... [had] redistrict[ed] such State." Act of Jan. 16, 1901, ch. 93, § 4, 31 Stat. 734 (emphasis added); see Act of Feb. 7, 1891, ch. 116, § 4, 26 Stat. 736 ("until such State be redistricted as herein prescribed by the *legislature* of said State" (emphasis added)); Act of Feb. 25, 1882, ch. 20, § 3, 22 Stat. 6 ("shall be elected at large, unless the *Legislatures* of said States have provided or shall otherwise provide" (emphasis added)). These provisions are in stark contrast to the text of the current § 2a(c): "[u]ntil a State is redistricted in the manner provided by the law thereof."

If the more expansive (and more natural) interpretation of § 2a(c) is adopted, its condition can be met—and its demand for at-large elections suspended—by the very court that follows the command of § 2c. For when a court, state or federal, redistricts pursuant to § 2c, it necessarily does so "in the manner provided by [state] law." It must follow the "policies and preferences of the State, as expressed in statutory and constitutional provisions or in the reapportionment plans proposed by the state legislature," except, of course, when "adherence to state policy ... detract[s] from the requirements of the Federal Constitution." Federal constitutional prescriptions, and federal statutory commands such as that of § 2c, are appropriately regarded, for purposes of § 2a(c), as a part of the state election law.

Thus, § 2a(c) is inapplicable *unless* the state legislature, and state and federal courts, have all failed to redistrict pursuant to § 2c. How long is a court to await that redistricting before determining that § 2a(c) governs a forthcoming election? Until, we think, the election is so imminent that no entity competent to complete redistricting pursuant to state law (including the mandate of § 2c) is able to do so without disrupting the election process. Only then may § 2a(c)'s stopgap provisions be invoked. Thus, § 2a(c) cannot be properly applied—neither by a legislature nor a court—as long as it is feasible for federal courts to effect the redistricting mandated by § 2c. So interpreted, § 2a(c) continues to function as it always has, as a last-resort remedy to be applied when, on the eve of a congressional election, no constitutional redistricting plan exists and there is no time for either the State's legislature or the courts to develop one. * * *

[The concurring opinion of JUSTICE KENNEDY has been omitted.]

JUSTICE STEVENS, with whom JUSTICE SOUTER and JUSTICE BREYER join, concurring in part and concurring in the judgment.

[Justice Stevens agreed with Parts I–III.A of Justice Scalia's opinion and with his result. But Justice Stevens believed that the portion of that statute that is codified at 2 U.S.C. § 2c impliedly repealed § 2a(c).]

The question whether an Act of Congress has repealed an earlier federal statute is similar to the question whether it has pre-empted a state statute. When Congress clearly expresses its intent to repeal or to pre-empt, we must respect that expression. When it fails to do so expressly, the presumption against implied repeals, like the presumption against pre-emption, can be overcome in two situations: (1) if there is an irreconcilable conflict between the provisions in the two Acts; or (2) if the later Act was clearly intended to "cove[r] the whole subject of the earlier one."

As I read the 1967 statute it entirely prohibits States that have more than one congressional district from adopting either a multimember district or electing their Representatives in at-large elections, with one narrow exception that applied to the 1968 election in two States. After a rather long and contentious legislative process, Congress enacted this brief provision:

"AN ACT

"For the relief of Doctor Ricardo Vallejo Samala and to provide for congressional redistricting.

"*Be it enacted by the Senate and House of Representatives of the United States of America in Congress assembled*, That, for the purposes of the Immigration and Nationality Act, Doctor Ricardo Vallejo Samala shall be held and considered to have been lawfully admitted to the United States for permanent residence as of August 30, 1959.

"In each State entitled in the Ninety-first Congress or in any subsequent Congress thereafter to more than one Representative under an apportionment made pursuant to the provisions of subsection (a) of section 22 of the Act of June 18, 1929, entitled 'An Act to provide for apportionment of Representatives' (46 Stat. 26), as amended, there shall be established by law a number of districts equal to the number of Representatives to which such State is so entitled, *and Representatives shall be elected only from districts so established*, no district to elect more than one Representative (except that a State which is entitled to more than one Representative and which has in all previous elections elected its Representatives at Large may elect its Representatives at Large to the Ninety-first Congress)." Pub. L. 90–196, 81 Stat. 581 (emphasis added).

The second paragraph of this statute enacts a general rule prohibiting States with more than one congressional Representative from electing their Representatives to Congress in at-large elections. That the single exception to this congressional command applied only to Hawaii and New Mexico, and only to the 1968 election, emphasizes the fact that the Act applies to every other State and every other election. Thus, it unambiguously forbids elections that would otherwise have been authorized by § 2a(c)(5). It both creates an "irreconcilable conflict" with the 1941 law and it "covers the whole subject" of at-large congressional elections. Under either of the accepted standards for identifying implied repeals, it repealed the earlier federal statute. In addition, this statute pre-empts the Mississippi statute setting the default rule as at-large elections.

The first paragraph of the 1967 statute suggests an answer to the question of why Congress failed to enact an express repeal of the 1941 law when its intent seems so obvious. The statute that became law in December 1967 was the final gasp in a protracted legislative process that began on January 17, 1967, when Chairman Celler of the House Judiciary Committee introduced H.R. 2508, renewing efforts made in the preceding Congress to provide legislative standards responsive to this Court's holding in *Wesberry v. Sanders* that the one-person, one-vote principle applies to congressional elections. The bill introduced by Representative Celler in 1967 contained express language replacing § 2a(c) in its entirety. H.R. 2508, as introduced, had three principal components that are relevant to the implied repeal analysis. First, the bill required single-member district elections: "[T]here shall be established by law a number of districts equal to the number of Representatives to which such State is so entitled; and Representatives shall be elected only from districts so established, no district to elect more than one Representative." H.R. 2508, 90th Cong., 1st Sess., p. 2 (1967). Second, the bill limited gerrymandering, requiring each district to "at all times be composed of contiguous territory, in as compact form as practicable." Third, the bill required proportional representation: "[N]o district established in any State for the Ninetieth or any subsequent Congress shall contain a number of persons, excluding Indians not taxed, more than 15 per centum greater or less than the average obtained" by dividing the population by the number of Representatives.

This bill generated great controversy and discussion. Importantly for present purposes, however, only two of the three components were discussed in depth at all. At no point, either in any of the numerous Conference Reports or lengthy floor debates, does any disagreement regarding the language expressly repealing § 2a(c) or the single-member district requirement appear. Rather, the debate was confined to the gerrymandering requirement, the proportionality rule, and the scope and duration of the temporary exceptions to the broad prohibition against at-large elections.

The House Judiciary Committee amended the bill, limiting the proportional differences between districts in all States to not exceed 10 percent and creating an exception to the general rule for the 91st and 92d Congresses (1968 and 1970 elections) that allowed for "the States of Hawaii and New Mexico [to] continue to elect their Representatives at large" and for the proportional differences to be as large as 30 percent. The House then passed this amended bill. The Senate Judiciary Committee then amended this bill, striking Hawaii from the exception and allowing for 35 percent, rather than 30 percent, variation between districts during the 91st and 92d Congresses. The bill went to conference twice, and the conference recommended two sets of amendments. The first Conference Report, issued June 27, 1967, recommended striking any exception to the general rule and limiting proportional variation to 10 percent or less. After this compromise failed to pass either the House or the Senate, the conference then recommended a measure that was very similar to the second paragraph of the private bill eventually passed—a general rule requiring single-member districts with an exception, of unlimited duration, for Hawaii and New Mexico. Importantly, every version of the bill discussed in the House Report, the Senate Report, and both Conference Reports contained a provision expressly repealing § 2a(c). In spite of these several modifications, the bill, as recommended by the last conference, failed to pass either chamber.

The decision to attach what is now § 2c to the private bill reflected this deadlock. Indeed, proponents of this attachment remarked that they sought to take the uncontroversial components of the prior legislation to ensure that Congress would pass some legislation in response to *Wesberry v. Sanders* [one-person, one-vote requirement for the House of Representatives]. The absence of any discussion, debate, or reference to the provision expressly repealing § 2a(c) in the private bill prevents its omission from the final bill as being seen as a deliberate choice by Congress. Any fair reading of the history leading up to the passage of this bill demonstrates that all parties involved were operating under the belief that the changes they were debating would completely replace § 2a(c). * * *

The history of the 1967 statute, coupled with the plain language of its text, leads to only one conclusion—Congress impliedly repealed § 2a(c). It is far wiser to give effect to the manifest intent of Congress than, as the plurality attempts, to engage in tortured judicial legislation to preserve a remnant of an obsolete federal statute and an equally obsolete state statute. * * *

JUSTICE O'CONNOR, with whom JUSTICE THOMAS joins, concurring in part and dissenting in part.

[Justice O'Connor agreed with the plurality's somewhat reluctant conclusion that § 2c does not impliedly repeal § 2a(c)(5).] Here, it is quite easy to read §§ 2c and 2a(c) together. A natural statutory reading of § 2a(c) gives force to both §§ 2c and 2a(c): Section 2a(c) applies "[u]ntil a State is redistricted in the manner provided by the law thereof." Section 2c applies *after* a State has "redistricted in the manner provided by the law thereof."

As both the plurality and Justice Stevens recognize, an implied repeal can exist only if the "provisions in the two acts are in irreconcilable conflict" or if "the later act covers the whole subject of the earlier one and is clearly intended as a substitute." Indeed, " 'when two statutes are capable of co-existence, it is the duty of the courts . . . to regard each as effective.' " We have not found *any* implied repeal of a statute since 1975. And outside the antitrust context, we appear not to have found an implied repeal of a statute since 1917. Because it is not difficult to read §§ 2a(c) and 2c in a manner that gives force to both statutes, § 2c cannot impliedly repeal § 2a(c).

The previous versions of §§ 2c and 2a(c) confirm that an implied repeal does not exist here. Since 1882, versions of §§ 2c and 2a(c) have coexisted. Indeed, the 1882, 1891, 1901, and 1911 apportionment statutes all contained the single-member district requirement as well as the at-large default requirement. Compare Act of Feb. 25, 1882, ch. 20, § 3, 22 Stat. 6 ("[T]he number to which such State may be entitled . . . *shall be elected by Districts* . . ., no one District electing more than one Representative" (emphasis added)) with *ibid.* (". . . *shall be elected at large*, unless the Legislatures of said States have provided or shall otherwise provide before the time fixed by law for the next election of Representatives therein" (emphasis added)); Act of Feb. 7, 1891, ch. 116, § 3, 26 Stat. 735 ("[T]he number to which such State may be entitled . . . *shall be elected by districts*" and "[t]he *said districts shall be equal* to the number of Representatives to which such State may be entitled in Congress, no one district electing more than one Representative" (emphasis added)) with § 4, 26 Stat. 736 ("[S]uch additional Representative or Representatives *shall be elected by the State at large*" (emphasis added)); Act of Jan. 16, 1901, ch. 93, § 3, 31 Stat. 734 ("[T]he number to which such State may be entitled . . . *shall be elected by districts*" and "[t]he *said districts shall be equal* to the number of Representatives to which such State may be entitled in Congress, no one district electing more than one Representative" (emphasis added)) with § 4, 31 Stat. 734 ("[I]f the number hereby provided for shall in any State be less than it was before the change hereby made, then the whole number to such State hereby provided for *shall be elected at large*, unless the legislatures of said States have provided or shall otherwise provide before the time fixed by law for the next election of Representatives therein" (emphasis added)); Act of Aug. 8, 1911, ch. 5, § 3, 37 Stat. 14 ("[T]he Representatives . . . *shall be elected by districts*" and "[t]he *said districts shall be equal* to the number of Representatives to which such State may be entitled in Congress, no one district electing more than one Representative" (emphasis added)) with § 4, 37 Stat. 14 ("[S]uch additional Representative or Representatives *shall be elected by the State at large* ... until such State shall be redistricted in the manner provided by the laws thereof"). * * *

Given this history of the two provisions coexisting in the same statute, I would not hold that § 2c impliedly repeals § 2a(c). The two statutes are "capable of co-existence" because each covers a different subject matter. *Morton v. Mancari.* Section 2c was not intended to cover the whole subject of § 2a(c) and was not "clearly intended as a substitute" for § 2a(c). Section 2a(c) (requiring at-large elections) applies unless or until the State redistricts, and § 2c (requiring single-member districts) applies once the State has completed the redistricting process. * * *

Justice Stevens argues that Congress intended to " 'cove[r] the whole subject' " of at-large redistricting when it enacted § 2c in 1967. But the 1967 enactment of § 2c simply restored the prior balance between the at-large mandate and the single-member district mandate that had existed since 1882. To hold that an implied repeal exists, one would have to conclude that Congress repeatedly enacted two completely conflicting provisions in the same statute. The better reading is to give each provision a separate sphere of influence, with § 2a(c) applying until a "State is redistricted in the manner provided by the law thereof," and § 2c applying after the State is redistricted. Because the 1967 version of § 2c parallels the prior versions of § 2c, and because of the longstanding coexistence between the prior versions of §§ 2a(c) and 2c, Justice Stevens' argument that Congress " 'clearly intended' " § 2c " 'as a substitute' " for § 2a(c) is untenable.

Justice Stevens' strongest argument is that the legislative history indicates that "all parties involved were operating under the belief that the changes they were debating would completely replace § 2a(c)." Yet Justice Stevens acknowledges that Congress *could have* expressly repealed § 2a(c). Justice Stevens thinks the evidence that Congress tried to expressly repeal § 2a(c) four times cuts strongly in favor of an implied repeal here. But these four attempts to repeal § 2a(c) were unsuccessful. It is difficult to conclude that Congress can impliedly repeal a statute when it deliberately chose not to expressly repeal that statute. In this case, where the two provisions have co-existed historically, and where Congress explicitly rejected an express repeal of § 2a(c), I would not find an implied repeal of § 2a(c). * * *

[II.A] Although the plurality acknowledges that § 2a(c) remains in full force, it inexplicably adopts a reading of § 2a(c) that has no textual basis. Under § 2a(c)(5), the State must conduct at-large elections "[u]ntil a State is redistricted in the manner provided by the law thereof." Instead of simply reading the plain text of the statute, however, the plurality invents its own version of the text of § 2a(c). The plurality holds that "[u]ntil a State is redistricted ..." means "[u]ntil ... the election is so imminent that no entity competent to complete redistricting pursuant ... to the mandate of § 2c [ ] is able to do so without disrupting the election process." But such a reading is not faithful to the text of the statute. Like

Justice Stevens, I believe that the Court's interpretation of § 2a(c) is nothing more than "tortured judicial legislation." See also Scalia, *The Rule of Law as a Law of Rules*, 56 U. Chi. L. Rev. 1175, 1185 (1989) ("[W]hen one does not have a solid textual anchor or an established social norm from which to derive the general rule, its pronouncement appears uncomfortably like legislation"). * * *

Section 2a(c) contains *no* imminence requirement. It is not credible to say that "until a State is redistricted in the manner provided by the law thereof after any apportionment" means: "[u]ntil . . . the election is so imminent that no entity competent to complete redistricting pursuant to . . . the mandate of § 2c [ ] is able to do so without disrupting the election process." The plurality characterizes § 2a(c) as a "stopgap provisio[n]," but the text of § 2a(c) is not so limited. The plurality asks "[h]ow long is a court to await that redistricting before determining that § 2a(c) governs a forthcoming election?" Yet the text provides *no basis* for why the plurality would ask such a question. Indeed, the text tells us "how long" § 2a(c) should govern: "*until* a State is redistricted in the manner provided by the law thereof." (Emphasis added.) Under the plurality's reading, however, § 2a(c) would not apply even though § 2a(c) by its terms *should* apply, as the State has not yet "redistricted in the manner provided by the law thereof." The language of the statute cannot bear such a reading.

The dispositive question is what the text says it is: Has a State "redistricted in the manner provided by the law thereof"? 2 U.S.C. § 2a(c). "*Until* a State is redistricted in the manner provided by the law thereof after any apportionment," a court cannot draw single-member districts. (Emphasis added). The court must apply the terms of § 2a(c) and order at-large elections. If, however, the State is redistricted "in the manner provided by the law thereof," § 2c applies. Thus, *after* a State has been redistricted, if a court determines that the redistricting violates the Constitution or the Voting Rights Act, the correct remedy for such a violation is the § 2c procedure of drawing single-member districts that comport with federal statutory law and the Constitution. But "[u]ntil a State is redistricted in the manner provided by the law thereof," § 2a(c)(5) mandates that a court order at-large elections. In short, a court should enforce § 2a(c) *before* a "State is redistricted in the manner provided by the law thereof," and a court should enforce § 2c *after* a State has been "redistricted in the manner provided by the law thereof." * * *

NOTES ON BRANCH

1. *Holistic Textualism: When Has a Statute Been Implicitly Repealed? Implicitly Changed or Narrowed?* However you resolve this difficult case, there is much common ground among the Justices. To begin with, an implied repeal can exist only if the "provisions in the two acts are in irreconcilable conflict" or if "the later act covers the whole subject of the earlier one and is clearly intended as a substitute." Note the parallel to the approach the Court uses to determine whether a federal statute preempts state law. Like the

Mancari presumption, the Court starts with a presumption against federal preemption of state law, especially in such core areas as contract and property law. Recall Justice Scalia's opinion for the Court in *BFP* (Chapter 3, § 2C), which can be read as an example of the Court's reluctance to read federal statutes so broadly that they preempt fundamental portions of state property law.

Second, unlike the presumption against federal preemption of state law, the *Mancari* presumption against implied repeals is one that is rarely overcome. As Justice O'Connor suggests, the presumption has usually been litigated, and occasionally, rebutted in antitrust cases. Antitrust defendants often argue that post–1890 regulatory statutes create implicit exceptions to the Sherman Act. They usually lose with such arguments but have occasionally prevailed, e.g., *United States v. National Ass'n of Securities Dealers*, 422 U.S. 694 (1975). Outside of the antitrust context, it is almost unheard of for federal judges to declare that a recent federal law has implicitly repealed a previous one.

One reason for the former phenomenon is a third point: " 'when two statutes are capable of co-existence, it is the duty of the courts … to regard each as effective.' " Judges will usually strain to reconcile federal statutes seemingly at odds. What norms underlie that level of conciliatory commitment? Sometimes judges will go to great lengths and show considerable imagination in such efforts, as Justice Scalia does in *Branch*. Is his reconciliation a success? Does it amount to "judicial legislation," as Justice O'Connor charged? Compare Judge Norris's effort to reconcile his interpretation of the Alaska Lands Act with the Wilderness Act in the published opinion in the Checkerboard Case.

Perhaps a better way to understand Justice Scalia's plurality opinion is through the lens of holistic interpretation, illustrated by the majority and dissenting opinions in *Sweet Home*. While judges may strain against finding an implicit *repeal*, they more willingly find that a subsequent statute has had effects on earlier statutes. Section 2a(c)(5) had a wider ambit for application before 1967. When Congress added § 2c to the U.S. Code, its new textual material had the effect (whatever Congress's actual intent) of narrowing the application of § 2a(c)(5). This is normal textualism, Justice Scalia is saying in *Branch*, and he probably considers Justice O'Connor's "judicial legislation" charge galling for that reason.

So the plurality opinion in *Branch* might be understood as a lesson in holistic textualism. Read the whole code as coherently as you can. Later-added provisions can change the scope of pre-existing text, but the faithful textualist should try to understand the entire text in a way that best preserves its integrity. Unless simply impossible, every sentence and every provision should be read as doing some work and providing some guidance to the citizenry and its judges.

2. *The Relevance of Legislative History?* Notice that Justice Scalia invokes what we would call the *statutory history* of § 2c—the problem that apparently gave rise to the 1967 statute and its subsequent interpretation by lower courts. But, characteristically, he has no interest in the internal *legislative history* of § 2c, which is discussed in the concurring opinion. Can

you read these legislative materials without coming to the conclusion that, yes, Congress understood that § 2c did repeal § 2a(c)(5)? Do the materials provide support for the textual proposition, also stressed by Justice Stevens, that §§ 2a(c)(5) and 2c are irreconcilable? Recall *Pepper v. Hart* (§ 2C of this chapter). One way to read the House of Lords reversal in that case is that the extrinsic materials provided their Lordships with important context that helped them see the cogency of the pro-taxpayer reading of the statutory text. Could the legislative context surveyed by Justice Stevens serve this kind of textualist role? The plurality thinks not. Note that Justice Ginsburg joins the Scalia plurality rather than the Stevens concurring opinion.

As her opinion in the FDA Tobacco Case (Chapter 2, § 3B3) illustrates, Justice O'Connor is willing to look at cartloads of legislative history in appropriate circumstances. She objects to the Stevens reading of legislative history on the ground that Congress dropped the explicit preemption provision when it actually enacted the private bill containing § 2c. By negative implication, this supports the plurality's conclusion that § 2a(c)(5) was not repealed, she argues. "It is difficult to conclude that Congress can impliedly repeal a statute when it deliberately chose not to expressly repeal that statute." The adverb "deliberately" is a stretch. The point of Justice Stevens's legislative history discussion is that Congress, after repeated efforts, could not come to agreement on the other issues involved in the proposal and hastily passed the only part of it that was agreed upon (§ 2c). In the hurried and chaotic atmosphere of such last-minute maneuverings, the explicit repeal provision just got lost in the shuffle. Because § 2c was wholly uncontroversial, and no one objected to its entirely displacing § 2a(c), as earlier versions would have done, the likely inference is that the repealer provision was dropped without thought as to interpretive consequences. This is precisely the occasion where arguments from negative implication ought to have the least weight.

Reconsider the Great Legislative History debate discussed throughout Section 2 of this chapter. Does his refusal to consider legislative history lead Justice Scalia to a tortured and undemocratic interpretation of the statutes in play? Does the legislative history discussed by Justice Stevens really illuminate the debate, or does it only allow the Justices to pick out their friends?

3. *Underlying Norms?* Another angle for viewing *Branch* is constitutional and statutory voting rights. Southern states like Mississippi had traditionally denied people of color the right to vote across the board. Once federal judges and executive officials started enforcing the rights of African Americans to vote, southern states adopted other mechanisms to marginalize such voters, including race-based gerrymanders and at-large voting. In states that have a majority-white population and racially polarized voting, at-large districts will assure a whites-only congressional delegation. At-large districts are not per se unconstitutional, but they have been found invalid all over the south under the Constitution or (more typically) the Voting Rights Act, because they are either intended or have the effect (Voting Rights Act) of perpetuating minority under-representation.

The line of thought reflected in the previous paragraph was not the assumption of the Court or Congress in 1967, but was advanced in the 1980s. You can understand the alignment of Justices better in light of the norm against at-large districting in the south. The Justices most supportive of that norm (Stevens, Souter, Breyer) would displace § 2a(c)(5) entirely and let § 2c rule the field. The Justices less committed to that norm (Scalia, Rehnquist, Thomas, Kennedy, O'Connor) are willing to leave § 2a(c)(5) in place and allow at-large districts in some circumstances. Justice Ginsburg is the wild card, as she supports the norm but joins the Scalia plurality.

As noted above, § 2a(c)(5) is not unconstitutional, and applying it in *Branch* would probably not raise serious constitutional objections. But the at-large formula would not be acceptable to the Department of Justice under § 5 of the Voting Rights Act and would not likely be acceptable to a court under § 2 of that Act. So under a holistic understanding of the voting rights regime Congress has created since the 1960s, is there any appropriate room for § 2a(c)(5)?

CHAPTER 5

INTERPRETATION OF STATUTES CREATED BY POPULAR INITIATIVES

■ ■ ■

Thus far in our examination of statutory interpretation, we have focused on statutes enacted by the legislative process at the federal and state levels. Perhaps surprisingly, an increasing number of statutes are adopted in another manner—through a direct vote of We the People. About half the states allow voters to enact statutes and/or constitutional amendments through popular *initiatives*. Section 1 of this chapter will briefly introduce the student to the popular lawmaking process.

Should statutes adopted in this manner be interpreted according to the same precepts as statutes adopted through the legislative process? Most of the precepts examined in Chapters 1–4 of this casebook are applicable to the interpretation of popular initiatives. For example, the plain meaning rule is the baseline for statutes created by either the legislative or the initiative process. And judges applying the plain meaning rule will consider the ordinary meaning of the language enacted into law, coherence with the whole act and the legal landscape, and established inference-based canons such as *ejusdem generis*.

On the other hand, there are several debates distinctive to the interpretation of popular rather than legislated statutes. The great debate over extrinsic sources plays out differently in this context. Among academics, it is more controversial for judges to rely on the representations about an initiative-based statute by its proponent organization and its sponsors than it is for judges to rely on committee reports and sponsor statements associated with legislature-based statutes. Is this reluctance well-founded? If so, should judges develop canons of construction that are tailored to the interpretation of popular initiatives? These are the inquiries pursued in Section 2.

Section 3 will explore the distinctive normative issues associated with popular lawmaking. Among academics, there are many criticisms of popular lawmaking, and the Supreme Court has sometimes shown a willingness to review popular initiatives with more teeth than one suspects the Justices would have shown the same law had it been adopted through the legislative process. More strikingly, the Justices have engaged in odd, and uncharacteristic, moves when interpreting the meaning of popular initiatives that are being challenged as violations of the U.S. Constitution.

SECTION 1. INTRODUCTION TO POPULAR LAWMAKING

Doubts about the capacity of legislatures to address social problems, as well as fears that legislatures were often captured by powerful business interests and were subject to corruption, led the American populists (circa 1890) and their political successors, the progressives, to propose a "return of the government to the people." Two major methods of providing the populace with lawmaking authority that resulted are the initiative and the referendum. (A third, the recall of public officials, does not affect the requirements of the law the way initiatives and referenda do.)

The *initiative* is a method whereby a certain percentage of the electorate may petition to have a proposed statute or amendment to the state constitution put on the ballot for a vote of the electorate at large. The *direct initiative* refers to the method in which the issue goes on the ballot automatically after the requisite signatures of voters are collected. In contrast, under the format of the *indirect initiative*, upon the collection of the requisite signatures the proposed statute is submitted to the legislature, which is given a period of time in which to approve or disapprove the measure. If the legislature fails to pass the proposed statute, or if it adopts an amended version, the proposed statute in its original form is placed on the ballot, often along with any legislatively approved variation.

The *referendum* is a method whereby the electorate may approve or disapprove of a law proposed by or already enacted by the legislature. The *popular referendum* is a method under which, upon the collection of the requisite signatures, a law already passed by the legislature may be approved or rejected by the electorate. The *legislative referendum* is a format in which the legislature may place before the electorate a proposed law either for the voters' approval or disapproval (a "binding legislative referendum") or for their advice (an "advisory legislative referendum"). This chapter will *not* focus on the referendum, which is often accompanied by traditional legislative history. For an excellent treatment, see Ethan J. Lieb, *Interpreting Statutes Passed Through Referendums*, 7 Election L.J. 49 (2008).

The initiative and referendum have venerable historical roots, ultimately inspired by the practice in classical Athens of popular rather than purely representative democracy. In Switzerland, these practices date back to the Middle Ages, and since the middle of the nineteenth century many major laws have been adopted through direct democracy.[a] Their connec-

---

a. For an overview, see Philip L. Dubois & Floyd Feeney, *Lawmaking by Initiative: Issues, Options and Comparisons* 46–62 (1998); Jean–François Aubert, *Switzerland*, in *Referendums: A Comparative Study of Practice and Theory* 39–66 (David Butler & Austin Ranney eds. 1978).

tion with the New England town meeting is also apparent. In the United States, however, initiatives and referenda (as well as the recall) did not become widely adopted until the progressive era (circa 1900–1921). Newer states in the west were especially keen on the idea—but demand seems to keep growing. During the 1970's two states—Illinois in 1970 and Florida in 1978—adopted direct democracy, and in recent times ballot propositions have grown in importance and addressed such controversial subjects as tax or governmental spending limitations, fees for nonreturnable containers, and the death penalty. *See* David Magleby, *Direct Legislation* 5 (1984).

The basic idea of direct democracy is that elected representatives often "get in the way" of democracy, thwarting the adoption of popular measures. Legislatures can be slow to adopt measures enjoying great, and perhaps legitimate, popular support for a number of reasons: interest group pressure, legislator self-interest, or the inertia caused by the many vetogates in the legislative process. Direct democracy is a way to short-circuit these barriers. No one knows exactly how well direct democracy actually achieves this purpose, but the best empirical evidence suggests some effect. Comparing states with and without direct lawmaking, John G. Matsusaka reports in *For the Many or the Few: The Initiative, Public Policy, and American Democracy* (2004), that states enjoying direct democracy have during the last generation enjoyed significantly lower levels of public spending than states without initiatives. During the progressive era, in contrast, such states enjoyed significantly higher levels of spending, because voters wanted government to be more active than they do today. This is not the final word, but Professor Matsusaka's study is the most impressive empirical analysis so far. See also Elisabeth R. Gerber, *The Populist Paradox: Interest Group Influence and the Promise of Direct Democracy* 23–28 (1999) (demonstrating that the mere threat of an initiative can sometimes bestir the legislature to act).

Normatively, one might object that a direct popular vote is not likely to produce optimal public policy, however. Recall that most of the vetogates are in the legislative process for a reason. Indeed, direct democracy is in tension with the conception of representative government embraced by the Framers of the American Constitution. The contrast is evident in the writings of James Madison, who urged the adoption of a representational form of government rather than a more "democratic" form. Madison believed that a "republican" form of government was necessary to prevent a tyranny of the majority faction over the minority.[b]

On the other hand, the Madisonian concerns may be overstated—and it may be the case that representative government might actually work

---

b. For neo-Madisonian concerns along these lines, see, e.g., Thomas Cronin, *Direct Democracy: The Politics of Initiative, Referendum, and Recall* 7–37 (1999); Derrick A. Bell Jr., *The Referendum: Democracy's Barrier to Racial Equality*, 54 Wash. L. Rev. 1, 18 (1978); Philip P. Frickey, *The Communion of Strangers: Representative Government, Direct Democracy, and the Privatization of the Public Sphere*, 34 Willamette L. Rev. 421, 423–427 (1998); Barbara S. Gamble, *Putting Civil Rights to a Popular Vote*, 41 Am. J. Pol. Sci. 245 (1997); Marci A. Hamilton, *The People: The Least Accountable Branch*, 4 U. Chi. L. Sch. Roundtable 1 (1997).

better if some avenues of direct lawmaking were incorporated.[c] The early proponents of direct democracy saw it as a way to circumvent state legislators and political parties that would block governance reforms like the direct primary and anti-corruption laws. Many modern initiatives deal with electoral reforms such as changes in the primary system, lobbying and campaign finance laws, term limits for legislators, and less partisan redistricting commissions. The evidence that states with hybrid democracy design their representative institutions differently than states without any form of direct democracy, however, is mixed. States with vibrant initiative processes are more likely to have legislative term limits, tax and expenditure limitations, and supermajority voting requirements for tax increases, see Caroline J. Tolbert, *Changing Rules for State Legislatures: Direct Democracy and Governance Policies*, in *Citizens as Legislators: Direct Democracy in the United States* 171 (Shaun Bowler et al. eds., 1998). The presence of the initiative process has also driven the adoption of public financing for legislative elections and the creation of relatively neutral commissions to develop plans for legislative redistricting following decennial censuses. Nathaniel Persily & Melissa Thompson, *Regulating Democracy Through Democracy: The Use of Direct Legislation in Election Law Reform*, 78 S. Cal. L. Rev. 997 (2005); Michael Kang, *De–Rigging Elections: Direct Democracy and the Future of Redistricting Reform*, 84 U. Wash. L. Rev. 667 (2006).

As of 2011, twenty-four states and the District of Columbia allow for some sort of popular initiative,[d] and three additional states have popular referenda.[e] Recent years have seen an explosion in the number of ballot propositions, as well as an increase in their scope. Initiatives in recent years have addressed such disparate subjects as taxes and government spending, same-sex marriage and civil unions, drug sentencing, education policy, and other divisive social issues. What is more, the number of lawsuits requiring the courts to interpret the products of popular democracy have skyrocketed since 1990. See generally Kenneth P. Miller, *Direct Democracy and the Courts* (2009). Despite these developments, the courts have been slow to develop the tools of initiative interpretation. Indeed, unlike the interpretation of traditional, legislatively enacted statutes, which has been the subject of much heated debate in the courts and the academy, the judiciary has heretofore left relatively unexamined the methods of interpreting the products of direct democracy.

---

c. Compare Elizabeth Garrett, *Direct Democracy*, in *Research Handbook on Public Choice and Public Law* 137, 161–65 (Daniel A. Farber & Anne Joseph O'Connell eds., 2010), with Dennis F. Thompson, *The Role of Theorists and Citizens in* Just Elections: *A Response to Professors Cain, Garrett, and Sable,* 4 Election L.J. 153, 158–60 (2005).

d. See National Conference of State Legislatures, *Initiative, Referendum, and Recall*, available at http://ncsl.org/legislatures-elections/elections/initiative-referendum-and-recall-overview/aspx (visited May 21, 2011).

e. See Initiative & Referendum Institute, University of Southern California, Map of States with Popular Initiatives and Referenda, available at http://www.iandrinstitute.org/statewide_ir.htm (viewed Jan. 1, 2012).

SECTION 2. INTERPRETING POPULAR INITIATIVES: TEXT AND CONTEXT

Courts in initiative-friendly states like California, Washington, Oregon, and Arizona (which generate a majority of the initiatives in the country) have developed a standard methodology of initiative interpretation. In most cases in which the courts must interpret the language of a popular initiative, they purport to use the same tools that they use to interpret traditional statutes. As one California court put it, "[a] voter initiative . . . is construed using the familiar principles governing statutory construction." *People v. Duran*, 43 Cal. App. 4th Supp. 1, 2 (1995). Accord, Jane S. Schacter, *The Pursuit of "Popular Intent": Interpretive Dilemmas in Direct Democracy*, 105 Yale L.J. 107 (1995) (leading treatment, which demonstrates that most courts follow this kind of rhetoric).

Under this standard approach, the first step is to examine the plain meaning of the initiative. *See, e.g., People v. Superior Court (Pearson)*, 227 P.3d 858, 862 (Cal. 2010). The courts rely overwhelmingly on formal sources, namely, the text of the initiative, the relationship between the initiative's text and related legislation, and the standard text-based canons of statutory construction, including the whole act rule. If the language of an initiative is not ambiguous, the inquiry is supposed to stop there. *Id.* at 862. If the text admits of more than one reading, though, most courts will look to extrinsic sources, such as the official ballot materials, for guidance. See *Legislature v. Eu*, 816 P.2d 1309 (Cal. 1991); *Legislature v. Deukmejian*, 669 P.2d 17 (Cal. 1983).

In practice, the matter is not so simple, and the differences between lawmaking by popular vote and lawmaking by elected representatives have driven a growing academic debate regarding the precepts that should guide courts when they interpret initiatives. Consider a recent case, which allows us a chance both to revisit the textualism debates in the earlier chapters and to introduce you to the theories applicable to the products of direct democracy.

NATIONAL PRIDE AT WORK v. GOVERNOR OF MICHIGAN

Michigan Supreme Court, 2008.
481 Mich. 56, 748 N.W.2d 524.

MARKMAN, J., for the Court [joined by the CHIEF JUSTICE and three other Justices].

We granted leave to appeal to consider whether the marriage amendment, Const. 1963, art. 1, § 25, which states that "the union of one man and one woman in marriage shall be the only agreement recognized as a marriage or similar union for any purpose," prohibits public employers from providing health-insurance benefits to their employees' qualified same-sex domestic partners. Because we agree with the Court of Appeals that providing such benefits does violate the marriage amendment, we affirm its judgment. * * *

On March 16, 2005, in response to a state representative's request for an opinion regarding the marriage amendment's effect on the city of Kalamazoo's ability to provide same-sex domestic-partner health-insurance benefits to its employees, the Attorney General issued a formal opinion, concluding that the city's policy did violate the amendment. The Attorney General asserted that "Const. 1963, art. 1, § 25 prohibits state and local governmental entities from conferring benefits on their employees on the basis of a 'domestic partnership' agreement that is characterized by reference to the attributes of a marriage." OAG, 2005–2006, No. 7,171, p. 17 (March 16, 2005), 2005 Mich. Reg. 5, p. 35.

[Pursuant to the terms of its collective bargaining agreement with a public employees union, Kalamazoo's public policy entitled municipal employees to include their "domestic partners" in their health insurance coverage that came with their employment package. Married employees could include their legal spouses. Unmarried employees could include their domestic partners, so long as they met the following requirements:

1. the partners were of the same sex;

2. the partners were at least 18 years old and mentally competent to enter into a contract;

3. the partners shared a common residence and had done so for at least six (6) months;

4. the partners were unmarried and not related by blood closer than would prevent marriage;

5. the partners shared financial arrangements and daily living expenses related to their common welfare; and

6. the partners had filed a statement of termination of previous domestic partnership at least six (6) months prior to signing another Certification of Domestic Partnership.

The city required the employee and his or her domestic partner to sign a notarized certification of domestic partnership that affirmed these criteria. In addition, they were required to provide evidence of "mutual economic dependence," such as a joint lease or mortgage, and evidence of a "common legal residence," such as driver's licenses or voter's registrations. The city's official policy provided: "It is the intent of this program to provide insurance coverage and other benefits to domestic partners of the City of Kalamazoo identical to those provided to spouses of City employees." The declaratory judgment lawsuit also involved other domestic partnership benefits provided for the employees of other governmental entities, such as the University of Michigan.]

The primary objective in interpreting a constitutional provision is to determine the original meaning of the provision to the ratifiers, "we the people," at the time of ratification. * * * Thus, the primary objective of constitutional interpretation, not dissimilar to any other exercise in judicial interpretation, is to faithfully give meaning to the intent of those who enacted the law. This Court typically discerns the common understanding of constitutional text by applying each term's plain meaning at the time of ratification. *Wayne Co. v. Hathcock*, 684 N.W.2d 765 (Mich. 2004).

Plaintiffs argue that "the only thing that is prohibited by the [marriage] amendment is the recognition of a same-sex relationship as a marriage" and that the public employers here are not recognizing a domestic partnership "as a marriage." We respectfully disagree. First, the amendment prohibits the recognition of a domestic partnership "as a marriage or similar union . . . ." That is, it prohibits the recognition of a domestic partnership as a marriage or as a union that is similar to a marriage. Second, just because a public employer does not refer to, or otherwise characterize, a domestic partnership as a marriage or a union similar to a marriage does not mean that the employer is not recognizing a domestic partnership as a marriage or a union similar to a marriage.

The pertinent question is not whether public employers are recognizing a domestic partnership as a marriage or whether they have declared a domestic partnership to be a marriage or something similar to marriage; rather, it is whether the public employers are recognizing a domestic partnership as a union similar to a marriage. A "union" is "something formed by uniting two or more things; combination; . . . a number of persons, states, etc., joined or associated together for some common purpose." *Random House Webster's College Dictionary* (1991). Certainly, when two people join together for a common purpose and legal consequences arise from that relationship, i.e., a public entity accords legal significance to this relationship, a union may be said to be formed. When two people enter a domestic partnership, they join or associate together for a common purpose, and, under the domestic-partnership policies at issue here, legal consequences arise from that relationship in the form of health-insurance benefits. Therefore, a domestic partnership is most certainly a union.

The next question is whether a domestic partnership is similar to a marriage. Plaintiffs and the dissent argue that because the public employers here do not bestow upon a domestic partnership all the legal rights and responsibilities associated with marriage, the partnership is not similar to a marriage. Again, we respectfully disagree. "Similar" means "having a likeness or resemblance, [especially] in a general way; having qualities in common[.]" A union does not have to possess all the same legal rights and responsibilities that result from a marriage in order to constitute a union "similar" to that of marriage. If the marriage amendment were construed to prohibit only the recognition of a union that possesses legal rights and responsibilities identical to those that result from a marriage, the language "or similar union" would be rendered meaningless, and an interpretation that renders language meaningless must be avoided. Further, the dissimilarities identified by plaintiffs are not dissimilarities pertaining to the nature of the marital and domestic-partnership unions themselves, but are merely dissimilarities pertaining to the legal effects that are accorded these relationships. However, given that the marriage amendment prohibits the recognition of unions similar to marriage "for any purpose," the pertinent question is not whether these unions give rise to all the same legal effects; rather, it is whether these unions are being recognized as unions similar to marriage for any purpose.[7]

All the domestic-partnership policies at issue here require the partners to be of a certain sex, i.e., the same sex as the other partner. Similarly, Michigan law requires married persons to be of a certain sex, i.e., a different sex from the other. MCL 551.1 ("Marriage is inherently a unique relationship between a man and a woman."). In addition, each of the domestic-partnership policies at issue in this case requires that the partners not be closely related by blood. Similarly, Michigan law requires that married persons not be closely related by blood. MCL 551.3 and MCL 551.4. Although there are, of course, many different types of relationships in Michigan that are accorded legal significance—e.g., debtor-creditor, parent-child, landlord-tenant, attorney-client, employer-employee—marriages and domestic partnerships appear to be the only such relationships that are defined in terms of both gender and the lack of a close blood connection. As discussed earlier, "similar" means "having a likeness or resemblance, [especially] in a general way; having qualities in common[.]" *Random House Webster's College Dictionary* (1991). Marriages and domestic partnerships share two obviously important, and apparently unique (at least in combination), qualities in common.[14] Because marriages and domestic partnerships share these "similar" qualities, we believe that it can fairly be said that they "resembl[e]" one another "in a general way." Therefore, although marriages and domestic partnerships are by no means identical, they are similar. Because marriages and domestic partnerships are the only relationships in Michigan defined in terms of both gender and lack of a close blood connection, and, thus, have these core "qualities in common," we conclude that domestic partnerships are unions similar to marriage. * * *

---

7. Plaintiffs argue that the marriage amendment was adopted in response to *Baker v. State*, 744 A.2d 864 (Vt. 1999), in which the Vermont Supreme Court held that that state is constitutionally required to extend to same-sex couples a civil union all the same benefits and protections that are provided to married couples. Thus, plaintiffs contend that the amendment only prohibits the establishment of "civil unions" that confer the same rights and obligations as does a marriage. However, as explained earlier, a union does not have to confer all the same rights and obligations as does a marriage in order to be "similar" to a marriage. Moreover, it is no less plausible that the amendment was adopted in response to a series of judicial decisions holding that public employers can extend health-insurance benefits to employees' domestic partners. See, e.g., *Tyma v. Montgomery Co.*, 801 A.2d 148 (Md. 2002).

14. Although we believe that these are the core qualities that make marriages and domestic partnerships similar, these relationships are similar in other respects as well. For instance, marriages and domestic partnerships are relationships that only two people may enter into. In addition, persons involved in either marital or domestic-partnership relationships must undertake obligations of mutual support. * * * Further, both marital and domestic-partnership relationships require agreements or contracts as a precondition. Additionally, both marital and domestic-partnership relationships have a minimum age requirement. * * * Further, both marriages and domestic partnerships are relationships of an indefinite duration. That is, they are both ongoing relationships that continue until one of the parties takes affirmative action to terminate the relationship. Finally, it seems relevant that all but one of the domestic-partnership policies at issue here require the partners to share a common residence, a circumstance typically defining the marital relationship as well.

Plaintiffs and the dissent argue that Citizens for the Protection of Marriage, an organization responsible for placing the marriage amendment on the 2004 ballot and a primary supporter of this initiative during the ensuing campaign, published a brochure that indicated that the proposal would not preclude public employers from offering health-insurance benefits to their employees' domestic partners. However, such extrinsic evidence can hardly be used to contradict the unambiguous language of the constitution. * * *

In *Michigan Civil Rights Initiative v. Bd. of State Canvassers*, 475 Mich. 903, 903, 716 N.W.2d 590 (2006) (Markman, J., concurring), in which it was alleged that numerous petition signatures had been obtained in support of placing the Michigan Civil Rights Initiative (MCRI) on the ballot by circulators who misrepresented the MCRI, it was emphasized that "the signers of these petitions did not sign the oral representations made to them by circulators; rather, they signed written petitions that contained the actual language of the MCRI." Similarly, the voters here did not vote for or against any brochure produced by Citizens for the Protection of Marriage; rather, they voted for or against a ballot proposal that contained the actual language of the marriage amendment.[22]

In addition to the brochure, plaintiffs and the dissent rely on statements made by counsel for Citizens for the Protection of Marriage to the Board of State Canvassers in which he apparently asserted that the amendment would not prohibit public employers from providing health-insurance benefits to domestic partners. Whatever the accuracy of this characterization, it should bear little repeating that the people ultimately did not cast their votes to approve or disapprove counsel's, or any other person's, statements concerning the amendment; they voted to approve or disapprove the language of the amendment itself.

Moreover, given that the "Board of State Canvassers ... has the authority only to 'ascertain if the petitions have been signed by the requisite number of qualified and registered electors,'" *Michigan Civil Rights Initiative*, 475 Mich. at 903, 716 N.W.2d 590 (Markman, J., concurring), quoting MCL 168.476(1), we are not sure why the dissent places particular emphasis on the fact that this statement was made before the Board of State Canvassers.

Moreover, like the Citizens for the Protection of Marriage, the Michigan Civil Rights Commission issued a statement asserting:

---

22. As an aside, this brochure did not render a verdict on the instant controversy. Rather, it stated:

Marriage is a union between a husband and wife. Proposal 2 will keep it that way. This is not about rights or benefits or how people choose to live their life. This has to do with family, children and the way people are. It merely settles the question once and for all what marriage is—for families today and future generations.

We do not read this language as resolving that the marriage amendment would not prohibit domestic partners from obtaining health-insurance benefits. Moreover, statements made by other supporters of the amendment stated that partnership benefits would, in fact, be prohibited by the amendment. See amicus curiae brief of the American Family Association of Michigan, pp. 6–8.

If passed, Proposal 2 would result in fewer rights and benefits for unmarried couples, both same-sex and heterosexual, by banning civil unions and overturning existing domestic partnerships. Banning domestic partnerships would cause many Michigan families to lose benefits such as health and life insurance, pensions and hospital visitation rights.[23]

* * * [A]ll that can reasonably be discerned from the extrinsic evidence is this: before the adoption of the marriage amendment, there was public debate regarding its effect, and this debate focused in part on whether the amendment would affect domestic-partnership benefits. The people of this state then proceeded to the polls, they presumably assessed the actual language of the amendment in light of this debate, and a majority proceeded to vote in favor. The role of this Court is not to determine who said what about the amendment before it was ratified, or to speculate about how these statements may have influenced voters. Instead, our responsibility is, as it has always been in matters of constitutional interpretation, to determine the meaning of the amendment's actual language. * * *

MARILYN KELLY, J., joined by CAVANAUGH, J., dissenting.

First, the language of the amendment itself prohibits nothing more than the recognition of same-sex marriages or similar unions. It is a perversion of the amendment's language to conclude that, by voluntarily offering the benefits at issue, a public employer recognizes a union similar to marriage. Second, the circumstances surrounding the adoption of the amendment strongly suggest that Michigan voters did not intend to prohibit public employers from offering health-care benefits to their employees' same-sex partners. The majority decision does not represent "the law which the people have made, [but rather] some other law which

---

23. Other opponents made similar statements concerning the adverse consequences of the amendment. See, generally, amicus curiae brief of the American Family Association of Michigan, pp. 9–12. The dissent contends that "[i]t is reasonable to assume that the public relied heavily on the proponents of the amendment to explain its meaning and scope." We see no basis for this argument. Contrary to the dissent, it is no more likely that the voters relied on proponents' views rather than opponents' views of the amendment. Indeed, one might conceivably think that at least some of the people would be significantly more likely to rely on an assessment of the amendment from an official agency of the government than from a private organization with an obvious stake in the passage of the amendment. Similarly, it might be expected that at least some might be influenced by the characterizations of newspapers such as the Detroit Free Press, in which its political columnist stated in a question-answer format on September 13, 2004:

Q. What about employee benefits accorded to domestic partners and their dependents by some municipalities and public universities?

A. Proponents and opponents of the amendment say they would be prohibited to the extent they mimic benefits for married employees.

Because we cannot read voters' minds to determine whose views they relied on and whose they ignored—and because in the end this would not be relevant—we must look to the actual language of the amendment. The dissent inadvertently illustrates the principal infirmity of reliance upon legislative history, namely that it affords a judge essentially unchecked discretion to pick and choose among competing histories in order to select those that best support his own predilections. In relying on what she describes as the "wealth of extrinsic information available," the dissenting justice refers only to information supporting her own viewpoint, while disregarding the abundant "wealth of extrinsic information" that does not.

the words of the constitution may possibly be made to express." Accordingly, I dissent. * * *

As always, when interpreting the Michigan Constitution, this Court's "duty is to enforce the law which the people have made, and not some other law which the words of the constitution may possibly be made to express." The initial step in determining what law the people have made is to examine the specific language used. In so doing, "it is not to be supposed that [the people] have looked for any dark or abstruse meaning in the words employed, but rather that they have accepted them in the sense most obvious to the common understanding, and ratified the instrument in the belief that that was the sense designed to be conveyed." And, since our task is a search for intent, it is often necessary to "consider the circumstances surrounding the adoption of the provision and the purpose it is designed to accomplish.

Beginning in 1993 with the Hawaii Supreme Court case of *Baehr v. Lewin*, a number of state courts and state legislatures joined in a national discussion on the constitutionality of barring same-sex marriages. In *Baehr*, the court held that Hawaii's statute limiting marriage to one man and one woman was presumptively unconstitutional under the Hawaii Constitution. It held that the state had the burden of showing a compelling state interest in limiting marriage to male/female unions. Following *Baehr*, the Vermont Supreme Court issued a decision in 1999 ordering the state legislature to create a legal form that would afford same-sex couples a status similar to that of married couples. Then, in 2003, in the famous case of *Goodridge v. Dep't of Pub. Health*, the Massachusetts Supreme Judicial Court held that barring two people of the same sex from marrying violated the equal protection guarantees of the Massachusetts Constitution. That same year, the California Legislature granted registered domestic partners "the same rights, protections, and benefits . . . as are granted to and imposed upon spouses."

It was against this background that the Michigan Christian Citizens Alliance commenced an initiative to amend the Michigan Constitution to bar same-sex marriage. The alliance formed the Citizens for the Protection of Marriage committee (CPM) "in response to the debate taking place across the country over the definition of marriage." The committee's stated goal was to place the issue of same-sex marriage on the ballot so that Michigan voters would have the ultimate say in the matter.

During CPM's campaign, concerns arose regarding exactly what the amendment would prohibit. CPM attempted to address these concerns at an August 2004 public certification hearing before the Board of State Canvassers. Specifically, CPM addressed whether the amendment, which it had petitioned to place on the ballot, would bar public employers from providing benefits to their employees' same-sex domestic partners. CPM's representative, attorney Eric E. Doster, assured the board that it would not. Mr. Doster stated:

[T]here would certainly be nothing to preclude [a] public employer from extending [health-care] benefits, if they so chose, as a matter of contract between employer and employee, to say domestic dependent benefits ... [to any] person, and it could be your cat. So they certainly could extend it as a matter of contract. * * *

[A]n employer, as a matter of contract between employer and employee, can offer benefits to whomever the employer wants to. And if it wants to be my spouse, if it wants to be my domestic partner-however that's defined under the terms of your contract or my cat, the employer can do that. . . .

In its campaign to win over voters, CPM made a number of additional public statements that were consistent with Mr. Doster's testimony before the Board of State Canvassers. For example, Marlene Elwell, the campaign director for CPM, was quoted in *USA Today* as stating that "[t]his has nothing to do with taking benefits away. This is about marriage between a man and a woman." Similarly, CPM communications director Kristina Hemphill was quoted as stating that "[t]his Amendment has nothing to do with benefits. . . . It's just a diversion from the real issue."

CPM also made clear on its webpage that it was "not against anyone, [CPM is] for defining marriage as the union of one man and one woman. Period." Instead, CPM contended that its reason for proposing the amendment was its belief that "[n]o one has the right to redefine marriage, to change it for everyone else. Proposal 2 will keep things as they are and as they've been. And by amending Michigan's constitution, we can settle this question once and for all."

CPM even distributed a brochure that asserted that the amendment would not affect any employer health-benefit plan already in place. The brochure stated:

Proposal 2 is Only about Marriage

Marriage is a union between a husband and wife. Proposal 2 will keep it that way. This is not about rights or benefits or how people choose to live their life. This has to do with family, children and the way people are. It merely settles the question once and for all what marriage is-for families today and future generations.

It can be assumed that the clarifications offered by CPM, the organization that successfully petitioned to place the proposal on the ballot, carried considerable weight with the public. Its statements certainly encouraged voters who did not favor a wide-ranging ban to vote for what they were promised was a very specific ban on same-sex marriage.

And a poll conducted shortly before the election indicates that CPM's public position was in line with public opinion. The poll results indicated that, whereas the public was in favor of banning same-sex marriage, it was not opposed to employer programs granting benefits to same-sex domestic partners.

In an August 2004 poll of 705 likely voters, 50 percent of respondents favored the amendment while only 41 percent planned to vote against it. But 70 percent specifically disapproved of making domestic partnerships and civil unions illegal. Sixty-five percent disapproved of barring cities and counties from providing domestic-partner benefits. And 63 percent disapproved of prohibiting state universities from offering domestic-partner benefits.

Accordingly, the circumstances surrounding the adoption of the amendment indicate that the lead proponents of the amendment worked hard to convince voters to adopt it. CPM told voters that the "marriage amendment" would bar same-sex marriage but would not prohibit public employers from providing the benefits at issue. It is reasonable to conclude that these statements led the ratifiers to understand that the amendment's purpose was limited to preserving the traditional definition of marriage. And it seems that a majority of likely voters favored an amendment that would bar same-sex marriage but would go no further. Therefore, this Court's majority errs by holding that the amendment not only bars same-sex marriage but also prohibits the benefits at issue. The error of the majority decision is confirmed by examining the amendment's language.

The majority attempts to justify its disregard of the extrinsic sources available by concluding that the "marriage amendment" is unambiguous. As can be discerned by any reader of the amendment, the vague language used is ambiguous in regard to the resolution of the question presented by this case. Clearly, the amendment does not unambiguously state whether public employers are barred from providing health benefits to their employees' same-sex partners. It says nothing about these benefits. Accordingly, it is necessary to engage in judicial construction to resolve that question.

Since the amendment is ambiguous in regard to the proper resolution of the issue presented, I disagree with the majority's choice to ignore the extrinsic sources available. Because our goal is to discern the law that the people have made, when extrinsic sources exist that shed light on this intent, I believe it is essential to consider them. * * *

* * * [I]t is obvious that there are two separate elements to marriage: There is the private bond between two people, which the state recognizes by solemnifying the marriage. And there are the benefits, rights, and responsibilities that the state confers on individuals solely by virtue of their status of being married. Both elements are necessary and important components of marriage. Hence, for a union to be similar to marriage, it must mirror more than the manner in which the private bond is recognized. It must also carry with it comparable benefits, rights, and responsibilities.[50]

---

50. It is by relying exclusively on the personal commitments expressed in the domestic-partnership agreements that the majority determines that the benefit programs at issue violate the amendment. The majority attempts to justify its disregard of the legal incidents that flow

The employer benefit programs at issue do not grant same-sex couples the rights, responsibilities, or benefits of marriage. The most that can be said is that the programs provide health-insurance coverage to same-sex partners. But health coverage is not a benefit of marriage. Although many benefits are conferred on the basis of the status of being married, health benefits are not among them. Notably absent is any state or federal law granting health benefits to married couples. Instead, the health coverage at issue is a benefit of employment. And the fact that the coverage is conferred on the employee's significant other does not transform it into a benefit of marriage; the coverage is also conferred on other dependents, such as children.

But even if health coverage were a benefit of marriage, it is the only benefit afforded to the same-sex couples in this case. The same-sex couples are not granted any of the other rights, responsibilities, or benefits of marriage. It is an odd notion to find that a union that shares only one of the hundreds of benefits that a marriage provides is a union similar to marriage. It follows that the amendment is not violated because the employee-benefit programs do not constitute recognition of same-sex marriage or [a] similar union. * * *

Determining that the amendment does not prohibit public employers from providing health benefits to same-sex domestic partners is consistent with the purpose explicitly expressed in the amendment. The amendment's stated purpose is "[t]o secure and preserve the benefits of marriage for our society and for future generations of children[.]" As discussed earlier, the state is not required to provide health benefits to spouses. Therefore, it makes no sense to find that health benefits are benefits of marriage just because some public employers voluntarily provide those benefits to spouses. Instead, the health benefits at issue are benefits of employment. The amendment's stated purpose does not protect or restrict employment benefits. Therefore, barring public employers from providing the benefits at issue does nothing to further the purpose of the amendment. This is another fact that weighs in favor of my interpretation.

---

from the marital status by relying on the language "for any purpose." It concludes that, because of this language, a union can be similar to marriage even if it carries with it none of the rights, benefits, or responsibilities of marriage. This is preposterous. The language "for any purpose" does not modify the word "similar." It modifies the word "recognize": "the union of one man and one woman in marriage shall be the only agreement *recognized* as a marriage or similar union *for any purpose*." (Emphasis added.) Thus, it is error to conclude that the phrase "for any purpose" alters the word "similar." In any event, as already discussed, the word "similar" requires a comparison of essentials. Essential aspects of a marriage include the legal incidents that flow from it. Therefore, it is not I who misreads the meaning of the word "similar" but the majority. It distorts the amendment's language when it concludes that, in deciding whether a union is similar to marriage, the framers intended we consider solely the personal commitments expressed by individuals. The majority's holding contradicts the amendment's express purpose: "To secure and preserve the benefits of marriage for our society and for future generations of children. . . ." This language indicates that the amendment's drafters and ratifiers did not ignore the important-perhaps more important-rights, benefits, and responsibilities of marital status. Nor did they intend to equate the sacred benefits of marriage with the mundane benefits of employment.

The Attorney General makes much of the fact that the amendment uses the phrase "for any purpose." The Attorney General contends that, as long as one benefit is provided to same-sex couples in the same way that it is provided to married couples, the amendment is violated. The majority accepts this argument. The majority's interpretation of the amendment is problematic because it essentially reads the word "similar" out of the amendment. It construes the amendment to read: "the union of one man and one woman in marriage shall be the only agreement recognized as a marriage or union for any purpose."

NOTES ON THE MICHIGAN DOMESTIC PARTNERS CASE AND THE ADMISSIBILITY OF EXTRINSIC MATERIALS TO INTERPRET INITIATIVES

The Michigan Domestic Partners Case involves the interpretation of an initiative that amends the state constitution. (An initiative creating a new state statute would have had the same effect in this case, but the proponents were trying to head off state judicial recognition of same-sex marriage or "similar unions.") As Justice Markman says at the outset, and the dissenters agree, the Michigan Supreme Court follows the same precepts when it construes an initiative-based constitutional amendment as when it construes an initiative-based statute. This point can be generalized to other states, according to Jane S. Schacter, *The Pursuit of "Popular Intent": Interpretive Dilemmas in Direct Democracy*, 105 Yale L.J. 107 (1995). In that spirit, consider the interpretive issues posed by this case.

1. *Theoretically, What Is the Nature of the Interpretive Inquiry?* Both the majority and the dissent in the Michigan Domestic Partners Case say the inquiry is to discern the "intent" of We the People who voted in favor of adding the initiative language to the state constitution. The majority says the only way to figure out the voter's "intent" is through parsing the statutory language; the dissent says the language is ambiguous and looks to other kinds of evidence.

Notice, for starters, that this widely used rhetoric of "intent" is harder to apply to initiatives than to legislated statutes. Recall Max Radin's critique of legislative intent (Chapter 2, § 1). Are his points about the impossibility of aggregation cogent for initiative voters? Should this rhetoric be abandoned? How would the dissenters respond to the Radin critique? The majority might agree with Radin—but if they do, they should stop using the term "intent," yes? Or does it serve some public purpose?

2. *Was There a Plain Meaning?* The majority and dissent *also* agree that judges must apply a plain meaning if there is one—although they disagree about whether the initiative had a plain meaning that covered the Kalamazoo health benefit plan. There are a number of technical objections to the majority's extended effort to insist upon a plain meaning here. Recall that the text of the initiative provided that "the union of one man and one woman in marriage shall be the only agreement recognized as a marriage or similar union for any purpose."

First, what "agreement" was being recognized by Kalamazoo? That city did not require employees to have an "agreement" to be domestic partners;

instead, the city required the municipal employee and his or her partner to "certify" that they met the requirements quoted in Justice Markman's opinion. So was Kalamazoo recognizing an "agreement" as a marriage or similar union? Or was the city acting upon a "certification" signed by the employee and by the domestic partner? The city thought it was acting upon a certification rather than recognizing an agreement, but Justice Markman may have thought that the certification itself rested upon a presumed "agreement" of the domestic partners to form a household. Is a "presumed" agreement sufficient to find the "agreement" required by the terms of the initiative? Is there a single "plain meaning" here, or is there ambiguity?

Second, was Kalamazoo "recognizing" whatever it was that the majority thought to be an "agreement"? Marriages, civil unions, and many municipal domestic partnership laws create a registry where couples present themselves, secure an official authorization for their civil status (as married or partnered), and are recorded as such. The Kalamazoo policy was not a domestic partnership registry; it was an employment benefit, given out to employees who could make the certification. The majority saw this process as "recognition," but is it not also possible to say that official recognition comes only when there is an official registry? Is there a single "plain meaning" here, or is there ambiguity?

Third, if there was an "agreement" that was "recognized" by the city, was the city recognizing the partnership "as a marriage or similar union"? All seven Justices seem to agree that the city was not recognizing the partnerships as "marriages," so the issue in dispute is whether they were "similar unions." In 2004, civil *unions* were a legal term of art for the Vermont statute giving same-sex couples *all* of the same legal benefits and duties of marriage—but joining in a civil union was a far cry from asking for the Kalamazoo employment benefit. Indeed, as the dissenters argued, employment benefits (the only consequence of the domestic partnership status) are not among the hundreds of legal benefits and duties associated with marriage. Does the majority have a good response to the argument that "similar union" did not include domestic partner employment benefits? Is there a single "plain meaning" here, or is there ambiguity?

Consider a literary analogy to the majority's detailed argument that the employment benefit was "similar" to marriage. In Jane Austen's *Northanger Abbey* (1817), Henry Tilney is dancing with Catherine Morland. When a rival suitor tries to cut in, Henry compares the intrusion to an effort by an outsider to break up a marriage. Catherine expresses surprise: "But they are very different things!" In marriage, there is a lifetime commitment, she insists, while a dance is just a short interlude. Henry responds:

> "Taken in that light certainly, their resemblance is not striking; but I think I could place them in such a view.—You will allow, that in both, man has the advantage of choice, woman only the power of refusal; that in both, it is an engagement between man and woman, formed for the advantage of each; and that when once entered into, they belong exclusively to each other till the moment of its dissolution; that it is their duty, each to endeavour to give the other no cause for wishing that he or she had bestowed *themselves* elsewhere, and their best interest to keep their own imaginations from wandering towards the perfections of their

neighbours, or fancying that they should have been better off with anyone else. You will allow all this?"

Like the dissenters in the Michigan case, Catherine concedes there is an analogy, but that the differences are more striking. Like the majority in the Michigan case, Henry insists on the similarities. Is this not an example of how a reader can extract a variety of meanings from the same words?

Jane Austen provides a deeper lesson, however. She suggests that Henry is a motivated interpreter; he has an ulterior motive for treating a country dance like a marriage. He says:

"This disposition on your side is rather alarming. You totally disallow any similarity in the obligations; and may I not thence infer that your notions of the duties of the dancing state are not so strict as your partner might wish? Have I not reason to fear that if the gentleman who spoke to you just now were to return, or if any other gentleman were to address you, there would be nothing to restrain you from conversing with him as long as you chose?"

Edging closer toward the analogy to marriage, Catherine protests her disinterest in the interloper and affirms her devotion to Henry, who pronounces himself satisfied with her concession. (Read the novel to find out what happens to their relationship in the chapters following this exquisite exchange.)

3. *Ought the Concessions by the Initiative's Proponents Be Persuasive to the Court?* The main argument by the dissenters is adapted from Glen Straszewski, *The Bait-and-Switch in Direct Democracy*, 2006 Wis. L. Rev. 17–74. Professor Straszewski claims that these initiative proponents engaged in a bait-and-switch game, where during the campaign they denied their initiative would preempt domestic partnership benefits—only to take the opposite position once the initiative had been adopted. The professor argues that the formal proponents of an initiative should be treated as sponsors accountable for their representations to the electorate, especially ones that appeal to popular prejudices (for purposes of judicial review) or that claim a narrow effect of their proposals if enacted (for purposes of statutory interpretation). Glen Straszewski, *Rejecting the Myth of Popular Sovereignty and Applying an Agency Model to Direct Democracy*, 56 Vand. L. Rev. 395 (2003). Accord, Glenn Smith, *Solving the "Initiatory Construction" Puzzle (and Improving Direct Democracy) by Appropriate Refocusing on Sponsor Intent*, 78 U. Colo. L. Rev. 257 (2007), and D. Zachary Hudson, *Interpreting the Products of Direct Democracy*, 28 Yale L. & Pol'y Rev. 223, 224 (2009).

The majority has a number of answers. One is that there is a plain meaning, and so all these representations are not relevant. But if the proponents *themselves* said, repeatedly, that the plain meaning of the initiative would *not* cover domestic partnership employment benefits, is that not evidence of how a reasonable speaker of the English language *might* have understood these words and phrases? Cf. Shaun Bowler & Todd Donovan, *Do Voters Have a Cue? Television Advertisements as a Source of Information in Citizen–Initiated Referendum Campaigns*, 41 Eur. J. Pol. Res. 777, 781–82 (2002) (voters rely heavily on the ballot materials when deciding whether to support a popular initiative).

Moreover, the court, accurately, points out that opponents worried that the initiative would be broadly construed: Should *their* representations count just as much, and therefore cancel out the claims of the proponents? Do the dissenters have a cogent response to this argument?

The majority's final response is that concessions by the proponents are not binding upon We the People who voted for the initiative. But why not, especially when the proponents tell the electorate and the media that the text of their initiative does not cover something? Do the opinion polls cited by the dissenters not provide relevant evidence along these lines? The majority might respond that, contrary to some earlier suggestions such as the Bowler and Donovan study noted above, most voters are primarily informed by the language and description of the initiative in the ballot itself, and not by extrinsic materials. See Craig M. Burnett, Elizabeth Garrett & Matthew D. MacCubbins, *The Dilemma of Direct Democracy*, 9 Elect. L.J. 305 (2010) (empirical results supporting this conclusion).

There is another kind of reason why initiative proponents might not be treated the same as legislative sponsors: They are not repeat players.[f] Based upon an informal survey of popular initiatives in 2008 and 2010, it appears that most initiative-proposing organizations have never had an initiative on the ballot before. Because they are not repeat players who might lose valuable reputation for making misrepresentations during the initiative process, these institutions are not as accountable for their representations as legislators tend to be. Political scientists have concluded that legislators often engage in "cheap talk" (like the puffery of a used car sales person) that ought not be taken too seriously, but that when they make "promises" (commitments essential to carry out deals) interpreters ought to take notice, because legislators who are repeat players have reputation-based incentives to speak truthfully when other legislators are relying on their representations.[g] Such reputation-based incentives operate much less seriously for the one-time sponsors of initiatives than for repeat-player sponsors of legislation.

If you find this thesis cogent, does that mean that proponents ought not be held to their promises and representations? Consider the next note.

NOTE ON NORMATIVE CANONS FOR INTERPRETING INITIATIVES

Sensitive to the bait-and-switch problem Professor Glen Straszewski identifies, Professor Jane Schacter's leading article rejects an illusory and indeterminate inquiry into voter (or even proponents') "intent" and advocates a more openly normative stance toward interpreting initiatives. See Jane S. Schacter, *The Pursuit of "Popular Intent": Interpretive Dilemmas in Direct Democracy*, 105 Yale L.J. 107 (1995). For example, she proposes that ballot propositions disadvantaging groups subject to the hostility of the majority— such as antigay measures like the Michigan marriage initiative—should be

---

f. The idea in text was suggested to us by Jeffrey Love, Yale Law School, Class of 2012. Mr. Love also conducted the informal survey of recent initiatives referred to in the text.

g. See McNollGast [i.e., Matthew D. MacCubbins, Roger G. Noll, and Barry Weingast], *Legislative Intent: The Use of Positive Political Theory in Statutory Interpretation*, 57 L. & Contemp. Probs. 3 (1994); McNollGast, *Positive Canons: The Role of Legislative Bargains in Statutory Interpretation*, 80 Geo. L.J. 705 (1992).

interpreted narrowly. On the other hand, initiatives that break through self-interested legislative gridlocks and seek to enhance the legitimacy of government processes—such as campaign finance restrictions or perhaps term limits—might be interpreted more liberally.

One of us has attempted to develop a coherent interpretive regime for ballot measures. See Philip P. Frickey, *Interpretation on the Borderline: Constitution, Canons, Direct Democracy*, 1996 Ann. Surv. Am. L. 477. Professor Frickey's argument is premised on the notion that direct democracy is in tension with the federal constitutional principle of republican government. Because the Supreme Court has refused to invalidate state ballot measures on this ground, the voters must be given their due—and so ballot measures should be interpreted consistent with the plain meaning of their text and the obvious understandings of the voters concerning the core purposes of the measure. As to ambiguities, however, such measures should be interpreted narrowly, to limit their effects in displacing prior law enacted in republican fashion (i.e., by the legislature).

The Frickey theory is premised on the notion that republican lawmaking is an underenforced constitutional norm worthy of protection through canons of statutory interpretation, as the Supreme Court has done with another less underenforced constitutional norm, federalism (in *Gregory v. Ashcroft* and related cases, see Chapter 3, § 2C). In addition to privileging republican enactments, this approach suggests that longstanding substantive canons should be more strongly applied in the context of ballot propositions. For example, because the voters are less capable than a legislature in evaluating whether a proposal satisfies constitutional norms, ballot propositions should be subjected to a more aggressive canon concerning the avoidance of serious constitutional issues than would be applied to legislatively adopted laws.

In the Michigan Domestic Partners Case, the theories of Professors Schacter and Frickey would lend support to the dissenters. Given so many questions about the "plain meaning" of the anti-union measure, both professors would be loathe to apply it as expansively as the majority did. Other scholars and most judges argue against the Schacter and Frickey move, however. See Elizabeth Garrett, *Who Directs Direct Democracy?*, 4 U. Chi. L.Sch. Roundtable 17, 35 (1997); Jack L. Landau, *Interpreting Statutes Enacted by Initiative: An Assessment of Proposals To Apply Specialized Interpretive Rules*, 34 Willamette L. Rev. 487 (1998). In the Michigan Domestic Partners Case, the dissenters apply formal rules of construction to reject the majority's reading. Is it more effective to enforce "shadow norms" through ordinary rules of construction—or does that violate norms of judicial candor?

Consider these arguments in light of the following case.

Evangelatos v. Superior Court, 44 Cal. 3d 1188, 246 Cal. Rptr. 629, 753 P.2d 585 (1988). The voters of California approved Proposition 51, the "Fair Responsibility Act of 1986," which "modified the traditional, common law 'joint and several liability' doctrine [by] limiting an individual tortfeasor's liability for noneconomic damages to a proportion of such damages equal to the tortfeasor's own percentage of fault." Under the California Constitution, the measure took effect the day after the election. The proposition was silent on whether it applied to pending cases. A sharply divided California Supreme

Court held that the measure did not apply to causes of action that accrued prior to the effective date.

Justice Arguelles, for the majority, noted that it would have been simple enough for the proponents of the measure to have drafted it expressly to apply to pending cases and that they should have been on notice that, in the absence of a retroactivity provision, courts were likely to apply it only prospectively. The majority embraced a strong presumption against retroactivity, concluding that "in the absence of an express retroactivity provision, a statute will not be applied retroactively unless it is very clear from extrinsic sources that the Legislature or the voters must have intended a retroactive application." Compare *Landgraf v. USI Film Prods.*, 511 U.S. 244 (1994), a leading case for the presumption against retroactivity applied by the U.S. Supreme Court.

The majority then examined the textual and contextual evidence. It found nothing in the proposition's "findings and declaration of purpose" or in the ballot pamphlet distributed to the voters to indicate that the retroactivity question "was actually consciously considered during the enactment process." Absent clear evidence that the voters ought to have understood the initiative to have been retroactive, the presumption was far from rebutted. Justice Arguelles also worried that a retroactive application could interfere with the reasonable expectations of plaintiffs in pending cases (who might have decided whom to sue and not to sue based on the law existing at the time suit was filed) and could result in a windfall to insurance companies.

In dissent, **Justice Kaufman,** joined by two colleagues, disputed whether California precedents required such a strong canon against retroactivity and whether retroactivity would produce unfairness in pending cases or an insurance windfall. He argued that the presumption of prospectivity should apply " 'only after, considering *all pertinent factors*, it is determined that it is impossible to ascertain the legislative intent.' " Two pertinent factors, the history of the times and the perceived evils to be remedied by the measure, strongly supported retroactive application. Proposition 51, a tort reform measure, was a response to the widely perceived "liability crisis" facing government agencies and private businesses. Section 3 of Proposition 51 stated:

Findings and Declaration of Purpose

The People of the State of California find and declare as follows:

(a) The legal doctrine of joint and several liability, also known as "the deep pocket rule", has resulted in a system of inequity and injustice that has threatened financial bankruptcy of local governments, other public agencies, private individuals and businesses and has resulted in higher prices for goods and services to the public and in higher taxes to the taxpayers.

(b) Some governmental and private defendants are perceived to have substantial financial resources or insurance coverage and have thus been included in lawsuits even though there was little or no basis for finding them at fault. Under joint and several liability, if they are found to share even a fraction of the fault, they often are held financially liable for all the damage. The People—taxpayers and consumers alike—ultimately pay for these lawsuits in the form of higher taxes, higher prices and higher insurance premiums.

(c) Local governments have been forced to curtail some essential police, fire and other protections because of the soaring costs of lawsuits and insurance premiums.

Therefore, the People of the State of California declare that to remedy these inequities, defendants in tort actions shall be held financially liable in closer proportion to their degree of fault. To treat them differently is unfair and inequitable.

The People of the State of California further declare that reforms in the liability laws in tort actions are necessary and proper to avoid catastrophic economic consequences for state and local governmental bodies as well as private individuals and businesses.

Justice Kaufman concluded that, in light of both the text of § 3 and the spirit of the overall provision, "the inference is virtually inescapable that the electorate intended Proposition 51 to apply as soon and as broadly as possible. When the electorate voted to reform a system perceived as 'inequitable and unjust,' they obviously voted to change that system *now*, not in five or ten years when causes of action that accrued prior to Proposition 51 finally come to trial. * * * A crisis does not call for *future* action. It calls for action *now*, action across the board, action as broad and as comprehensive as the Constitution will allow. It is clear that the purposes of Proposition 51 will be fully served only if it is applied to all cases not tried prior to its effective date."

NOTE ON THE ANTI-RETROACTIVITY CANON, AS APPLIED TO INITIATIVES

Which approach to Proposition 51 makes the most sense: the canonical approach of the majority—which privileges legal continuity—or the purposive approach of the dissent, which applies to ballot measures the "mischief rule" in *Heydon's Case* (Chapter 2, § 1), an approach originally embraced in the context of legislative enactments?

Notice that the majority and the dissenters both apply the same rules of construction (including the anti-retroactivity canon) to initiatives that they would have applied to a statute adopted by the legislature. How would Professors Schacter, Straszewski, and Frickey decide this case, based upon their different theories?

How would you vote in *Evangelatos*? Jot down your answer, and then consider the most recent anti-retroactivity case decided by the California Supreme Court. In *Strauss v. Horton*, 207 P.3d 48 (Cal. 2009), the Court evaluated Proposition 8, an initiative which amended the state constitution to override the California Supreme Court's state constitutional recognition of same-sex marriages. A divided Court upheld Proposition 8 against state constitutional attack and then faced the issue: Did Proposition 8 retroactively preempt the same-sex marriages celebrated between June 2008 (when the Court's earlier decision required state recognition of same-sex marriages) and November 2008 (when the initiative passed and overrode the Court's decision)? Because neither the text nor the campaign for Proposition 8 gave any clear indication that it would terminate the earlier marriages, the Court *unanimously* ruled that the marriages survived, based upon the presumption against retroactivity.

This was a remarkable ruling in this respect. The Court's earlier recognition of same-sex marriages had been a 4–3 ruling—and the three dissenters from that ruling joined the four majority Justices in agreeing to recognize those June to November lesbian and gay marriages, based solely on the rule of law represented by the anti-retroactivity canon. Does this change your attitude about *Evangelatos*? The utility of a canons-based approach to interpreting initiatives? To interpreting statutes adopted by the legislature?

PROBLEM 5–1

Yet Another California Initiative Under Construction

In 1990, California voters adopted Proposition 140, "The Political Reform Act of 1990," which imposed term limits on state elected officials and limited expenditures funding the state legislature. You have been asked to provide advice to several former state legislators who fear that this measure imposes a lifetime ban on their ever seeking election to the legislature again. They are hoping that you will figure out a persuasive argument for construing the Proposition as allowing them to seek office again. In addition, they have asked you to investigate whether the Proposition might be invalidated as inconsistent with either the federal or state constitution.

Each registered voter in California is mailed an official voter pamphlet. The pamphlet contains the text of each ballot measure, an official summary of it, and arguments for and against it prepared by proponents and opponents. The California pamphlet for the November 1990 election contained the following:[h]

Proposition 140: Text of Proposed Law

This initiative measure is submitted to the people in accordance with the provisions of Article II, Section 8 of the Constitution.

This initiative measure expressly amends the Constitution by amending and combining sections thereof; therefore, new provisions proposed to be inserted or added are printed in *italic type* to indicate they are new.

Proposed Law

Section 1. This measure shall be known and may be cited as "The Political Reform Act of 1990."

Section 2. Section 1.5 is added to Article IV of the California Constitution, to read:

SEC 1.5. The people find and declare that the Founding Fathers established system of representative government based upon free, fair and

---

h. We are grateful to Professor Einer Elhauge, who served as counsel for the Secretary of State of California, and to Thomas Gede, Esquire, then the Special Assistant Attorney General of California, for providing these materials to us.

competitive elections. The increased concentration of political power in the hands of incumbent representatives has made our electoral system less free, less competitive and less representative.

The ability of legislators to serve unlimited number of terms, to establish their own retirement system, and to pay for staff and support services at state expense contribute heavily to the extremely high number of incumbents who are elected. These unfair incumbent advantages discourage qualified candidates from seeking public office and create a class of career politicians, instead of the citizen representatives envisioned by the Founding Fathers. these career politicians become representatives of the bureaucracy, rather than of the people whom they are elected to represent.

To restore a free and democratic system of fair elections, and to encourage qualified candidates to seek public office, the people find and declare that the powers of incumbency must be limited. Retirement benefits must be restricted, state-financed incumbent staff and support services limited, and limitations placed upon the number of terms which may be served.

SEC. 3.   Section 2 of Article IV of the California Constitution is amended to read:

SEC. 2. (a) The Senate has a membership of 40 Senators elected for 4–year terms, 20 to begin every 2 years. *No Senator may serve more than 2 terms.* The Assembly has a membership of 80 members elected for 2–year terms. *No member of the Assembly may serve more than 3 terms.* Their terms shall commence on the first Monday in December next following their election.

(b) Election of members of the Assembly shall be on the first Tuesday after the first Monday in November of even-numbered years unless otherwise prescribed by the Legislature. Senators shall be elected at the same time and place as members of the Assembly.

(c) A person is ineligible to be a member of the Legislature unless the person is an elector and has been a resident of the legislative district for one year, and a citizen of the United States and a resident of California for 3 years, immediately preceding the election.

(d) When a vacancy occurs in the Legislature, the Governor immediately shall hold an election to fill the vacancy.

SEC. 4.   Section 4.5 is added to Article IV of the California Constitution, to read:

SEC. 4.5.   Notwithstanding any other provision of this Constitution or existing law, a person elected to or serving in the Legislature on or after November 1, 1990, shall participate in the Federal Social Security (Retirement, Disability, Health Insurance) Program and the State shall pay only the employer's share of the contribution necessary to such participation. No other pension or retirement benefit shall accrue as a result of service in the Legislature, such service not being intended as a career occupation. This

Section shall not be construed to abrogate or diminish any vested pension or retirement benefit which may have accrued under an existing law to a person holding or having held office in the Legislature, but upon adoption of this Act no further entitlement to nor vesting in any existing program shall accrue to any such person, other than Social Security to the extent herein provided.

SEC. 5.   Section 7.5 is added to Article IV of the California Constitution to read:

SEC. 7.5.   In the fiscal year immediately following the adoption of this Act, the total aggregate expenditures of the Legislature for the compensation of members and employees of, and the operating expenses and equipment for, the Legislature may not exceed an amount equal to nine hundred fifty thousand dollars ($950,000) per member for that fiscal year or 80 percent of the amount of money expended for those purposes in the preceding fiscal year, whichever is less. For each fiscal year thereafter, the total aggregate expenditures may not exceed an amount equal to that expended for those purposes in the preceding fiscal year, adjusted and compounded by an amount equal to the percentage increase in the appropriations limit for the state established pursuant to Article XIII B.

SEC. 6.   Section 2 of Article V of the California Constitution is amended to read:

SEC. 2.   The Governor shall be elected every fourth year at the same time and places as members of the Assembly and hold office from the Monday after January 1 following the election until a successor qualifies. The Governor shall be an elector who has been a citizen of the United States and a resident of this State for 5 years immediately preceding the Governor's election. The Governor may hot hold other public office. *No Governor may serve more than 2 terms.*

SEC. 7.   Section 11 of Article V of the California Constitution is amended to read:

SEC. 11.   The Lieutenant Governor, Attorney General, Controller, Secretary of State, and Treasurer shall be elected at the same time and places and for the same term as the Governor. *No Lieutenant Governor, Attorney General, Controller, Secretary of State, or Treasurer may serve in the same office for more than 2 terms.*

SEC. 8.   Section 2 of Article IX of the California Constitution is amended to read:

SEC. 2.   A Superintendent of Public Instruction shall be elected by the qualified electors of the State at each gubernatorial election. The Superintendent of Public Instruction shall enter upon the duties of the office on the first Monday after the first day of January next succeeding each gubernatorial election. *No Superintendent of Public Instruction may serve more than 2 terms.*

SEC. 9. Section 17 of Article XIII of the California Constitution is amended to read:

SEC. 17. The Board of Equalization consists of 5 voting members: the Controller and 4 members elected for 4–year terms at gubernatorial elections. The state shall be divided into four Board of Equalization districts with the voters of each district electing one member. *No member may serve more than 2 terms.*

SEC. 10. Section 7 is added to Article XX of the California Constitution to read:

SEC. 7. The limitations on the number of terms prescribed by Section 2 of Article IV, Sections 2 and 11 of Article V, Section 2 of Article IX, and Section 17 of Article XIII apply only to terms to which persons are elected or appointed on or after November 6, 1990, except that an incumbent Senator whose office is not on the ballot for general election on that date may serve only one additional term. Those limitations shall not apply to any unexpired term to which a person is elected or appointed if the remainder of the term is less than half of the full term.

SEC. 11. Section 11 (d) is added to Article VII of the California Constitution to read:

SEC. 11. (a) The Legislators' Retirement System shall not pay any unmodified retirement allowance or its actuarial equivalent to any person who on or after January 1, 1987, entered for the first time any state office for which membership in the Legislators' Retirement System was elective or to any beneficiary or survivor of such a person, which exceeds the higher of (1) the salary receivable by the person currently serving in the office in which the retired person served, or (2) the highest salary that was received by the retired person while serving in that office.

(b) The Judges' Retirement System shall not pay any unmodified retirement allowance or its actuarial equivalent to any person who on or after January 1, entered for the first time any judicial office subject to the Judges' Retirement System or to any beneficiary or survivor of such a person, which exceeds the higher of (1) the salary receivable by the person currently serving in the judicial office in which the retired person served or (2) the highest salary that was received by the retired person while serving in that judicial office.

(c) The Legislature may define the terms used in this section.

(d) If any part of this measure or the application to any person or circumstance is held invalid, the invalidity shall not affect other provisions or applications which reasonably can be given effect without the invalid provision or application.

Official Title and Summary

LIMITS ON TERMS OF OFFICE, LEGISLATORS' RETIREMENT, LEGISLATIVE OPERATING COSTS. INITIATIVE CONSTITUTIONAL AMENDMENT

• Persons elected or appointed after November 5, 1990, holding offices of Governor, Lieutenant Governor, Attorney General, Controller, Secretary of State, Treasurer, Superintendent of Public Instruction, Board of Equalization members, and State Senators, limited to two terms; members of the Assembly limited to three terms.

• Requires legislators elected or serving after November 1, 1990, to participate in federal Social Security program; precludes accrual of other pension and retirement benefits resulting from legislative service, except vested rights.

• Limits expenditures of Legislature for compensation and operating costs and equipment, to specified amount.

Summary of Legislative Analyst's Estimate of Net State and Local Government Fiscal Impact

• The limitation on terms will have no fiscal effect.

• The restrictions on the legislative retirement benefits would reduce state costs by approximately $750,000 a year.

• To the extent that future legislators do not participate in the federal Social Security system, there would be unknown future savings to the state.

• Legislative expenditures in 1991–92 would be reduced by about 38 percent, or $70 million.

• In subsequent years, the measure would limit growth in these expenditures to the changes in the state's appropriations limit.

Analysis by the Legislative Analyst

Background

There are 132 elected state officials in California. This includes 120 legislators and 12 other state officials, including the Governor, Lieutenant Governor, and Attorney General. Currently, there is no limit on the number of terms that these officials can serve. Proposition 112, passed by the voters in June 1990, requires the annual salaries and benefits (excluding retirement) of these state officials to be set by a commission. Most of these officials participate in the federal Social Security system, and all have the option of participating in the Legislators' Retirement System. The vast majority of the 132 elected state officials participate in this retirement system. The system is supported by contributions from participating officials and the state.

Funding for the Legislature and its employees is included in the annual state budget. Before it becomes law, the budget must be approved by a two-thirds vote of the membership of both houses of the Legislature and must be signed by the Governor.

Proposal

This initiative makes three major changes to the California Constitution. First, it limits the number of terms that an elected state official can serve in the *same office* (the new office of Insurance Commissioner is not affected by this measure). Second, it prohibits legislators from earning state retirement benefits from their future service in the Legislature. Third, it limits the total amount of expenditures by the Legislature for salaries and operating expenses.

The specific provisions of this measure are:

Limits on the Terms of Elected State Officials

- The following state elected officials would be limited to no more than two four-year terms in the same office: Governor, Lieutenant Governor, Attorney General, Controller, Secretary of State, Superintendent of Public Instruction, Treasurer, members of the Board of Equalization, and State Senators.

- Members of the State Assembly would be limited to no more than three two-year terms in the same office.

- These limits apply to a state official who is elected on or after November 6, 1990. However, State Senators whose offices are *not* on the November 6, 1990 ballot may serve only one additional term.

Restrictions on Legislative Retirement Benefits

- This measure prohibits current and future legislators from earning state retirement benefits from their service in the Legislature on or after November 7, 1990. This restriction would not eliminate retirement benefits earned prior to that time.

- This measure requires a legislator serving in the Legislature on or after November 7, 1990 to participate in the federal Social Security system. (However, federal law may permit only current legislators who are presently participating in the federal Social Security system to continue to participate in the system. It may also prohibit future legislators from participating in the federal Society Security system.)

- This measure does not change the Social Security coverage or the state retirement benefits of other state elected officials such as the Governor, Lieutenant Governor, and Attorney General.

Limits on Expenditures by the Legislature

- This measure limits the amount of expenditures by the Legislature for salaries and operating expenses, beginning in the 1991–92 fiscal year.

• In 1991–92, these expenditures are limited to the *lower* of two amounts: (1) a total of $950,000 per Member or (2) 80 percent of the total amount of money expended in the previous year for these purposes. In future years, the measure limits expenditure growth to an amount equal to the percentage change in the state's appropriations limit.

Fiscal Effect

Limits on the Terms of Elected State Officials. This provision would not have any fiscal effect.

Restrictions on Legislative Retirement Benefits. The provision which prohibits current and future Members of the Legislature from earning state retirement benefits from legislative service on or after November 7, 1990 would reduce state costs by about $750,000 a year.

To the extent that future legislators do not participate in the federal Social Security system, the measure would result in unknown future savings to the state.

Limits on Expenditures by the Legislature. In 1991–92, expenditures by the Legislature would be reduced by about 38 percent, or $70 million. In subsequent years, this measure would limit growth in these expenditures to the changes in the state's appropriations limit.

Argument in Favor of Proposition 140

Proposition 140 will for the first time ever place a limit on the number of times a State official may serve in office.

A Yes Vote on Proposition 140 will reform a political system that has created a legislature of career politicians in California. It is a system that has given a tiny elite (only 120 people out of 30 million) almost limitless power over the lives of California's taxpayers and consumers.

Proposition 140, will limit State Senators to two terms (8 years); will limit Assembly members to three terms (6 years); and limit the Governor and other elected constitutional officers to two terms (8 years).

By reducing the amount they can spend on their personal office expenses, Proposition 140, will cut back on the 3,000 political staffers who serve the legislature in Sacramento. In the first year alone, according to the legislative analyst, it will save taxpayers $60 million.

Proposition 140, will end extravagant pensions for legislators. While most Californians have to depend on Social Security and their own savings, the legislative pension system often pays more than the legislator received while in office. In fact, 50 former officials receive $2,000.00 per month or more from the Legislative retirement fund.

Limiting Terms, will create more competitive elections, so good legislators will always have the opportunity to move up the ladder. Term limitation will end the ingrown, political nature of both houses—to the benefit of every man, woman and child in California.

Proposition 140, will remove the grip that vested interests have over the legislature and remove the huge political slush funds at the disposal of Senate and Assembly leaders.

Proposition 140 will put an end to the life-time legislators, who have developed cozy relationships with special interests. We all remember the saying, "Power corrupts and absolute power corrupts absolutely." But limit the terms of Legislative members, remove the Speaker's cronies, and we will also put an end to the Sacramento web of special favors and patronage.

Proposition 140 will end the reign of the Legislature's powerful officers—the Assembly Speaker (first elected a quarter of a century ago) and the Senate Leader (now into his third decade in the Legislature). Lobbyists and power brokers pay homage to these legislative dictators, for they control the fate of bills, parcel out money to the camp followers and hangers-on, and pull strings behind the scenes to decide election outcomes.

Incumbent legislators seldom lose. In the 1988 election, 100% of incumbent state senators and 96% of incumbent members of the assembly were re-elected. The British House of Lords—even the Soviet Legislature—has a higher turnover rate. Enough is Enough! It's time to put an end to a system that makes incumbents a special class of citizen and pays them a guaranteed annual wage from first election to the grave. Let's restore that form of government of citizens representing their fellow citizens.

VOTE YES ON PROPOSITION 140 TO *LIMIT STATE OFFICIALS TERM OF OFFICE!*

PETER E. SCHABARUM
Chairman, Los Angeles County Board of Supervisors

LEWIS K. UHLER
President, National Tax–Limitation Committee

J.G. FORD, JR.
President, Marin United Taxpayers Association

Rebuttal to Argument in Favor of Proposition 140

Proposition 140 is a proposal by a downtown Los Angeles politician to take away your right to choose your legislators. He has a history of taking away voting rights. He and two political cronies voted to spend $500,000.00 in tax dollars to hire a personal lawyer to defend him against

Voting Rights Act violations in Federal Court. Newspapers call it an "outrageous back room deal."

His "Big Bucks" friends, including high-priced lobbyists, have lined his pockets with campaign contributions to help control who *you* can vote for.

- IF 140 PASSES, LOBBYISTS COULD SUBSTITUTE THEIR OWN PAID EMPLOYEES FOR THE INDEPENDENT STAFF RESEARCHERS OF THE LEGISLATURE ELIMINATED BY THIS MEASURE.

- 140 MISLEADS YOU ABOUT THE SO–CALLED "HIGH" COST OF THE LEGISLATURE—THE COST IS LESS THAN 1/2 PENNY PER TAX DOLLAR.

- THE BIGGEST LIE IS THE FACT THAT THEY DON'T TELL YOU THAT 140 IS A *LIFETIME BAN*.

This is a blatant power grab by Los Angeles contributors and lobbyists who have been wining and dining "Mr. Downtown Los Angeles" in government for SEVEN TERMS—OVER TWENTY YEARS.

Practice what you preach, "Mr. Downtown Los Angeles," Peter Schabarum. Cut *your own* budget and limit *your own* terms. Don't be a piggy and take away the people's rights after you have fully eaten at the table.

There is no need for 140. The vast majority of the Legislature *already* serves less than 10 years.

That's *your* choice.

Keep it.

Stop Downtown Los Angeles' power grab.

Vote no on 140!

> ED FOGLIA
> *President, California Teachers Association*
>
> DAN TERRY
> *President, California Professional Firefighters*
>
> LINDA M. TANGREN
> *State Chair, California National Women's Political Caucus*

Argument Against Proposition 140

Proposition 140 claims to mandate term limits. But in fact, it limits our voting rights.

This measure takes away the cherished constitutional right to freely cast a ballot for candidates of our choice.

We are asked to forfeit *our* right to decide *who our* individual representatives will be.

PROPOSITION 140'S LIFETIME BAN

140 does *not* limit *consecutive* terms of office. Instead 140 says:

● After serving six years in the Assembly, individuals will be constitutionally *banned for life* from ever serving in the Assembly.

● After serving eight years in the Senate, individuals will be constitutionally *banned for life* from ever serving in the Senate.

● Similar lifetime bans will be imposed on the Superintendent of Public Instruction and other statewide offices.

There are no exceptions—not for merit, not for statewide emergencies, not for the overwhelming will of the people.

Once banned, always banned.

PROPOSITION 140 IS UNFAIR

It treats everyone—good and bad, competent and incompetent—the same.

No matter how good a job someone does in office, they will be *banned for life*.

You won't even be able to write-in their names on your ballot. If you do, your vote won't count.

That's just not fair.

LIMITS OUR RIGHT TO CHOOSE

The backers of 140 don't trust us, the people, to choose our elected officials. So instead of promoting thoughtful reforms that help us weed out bad legislators, they impose a lifetime ban that eliminates good legislators and bad ones alike at the expense of our constitutional rights.

No eligible citizen should be *permanently banned* for life from seeking any office in a free society. And we should not be *permanently banned* from voting freely for the candidate of our choice.

Resist the rhetoric. Proposition 140 is not about restricting the powers of incumbency. It's about taking away our powers to choose.

PHONY PENSION REFORM

Proposition 140's retirement provisions are also misdirected and counterproductive.

140 does not eliminate the real abuses: double and triple dipping—the practice of taking multiple pensions.

Instead it raises new barriers to public office by banning our future representatives from earning *any* retirement except their current social security.

140's retirement ban won't hurt rich candidates. It will hurt qualified, ordinary citizens who are not rich and have to work hard to prove economic security for themselves and their families.

PROPOSITION 140 GOES TOO FAR

It upsets our system of constitutional checks and balances, forcing our representatives to become even more dependent on entrenched bureaucrats and shrewd lobbyists.

If its proponents were sincere about political reform, they wouldn't have cluttered it with so many unworkable provisions.

VOTE NO ON PROPOSITION 140

STOP THIS RADICAL AND DANGEROUS SCHEME! PROTECT OUR CONSTITUTIONAL RIGHTS. VOTE NO ON PROPOSITION 140'S LIFETIME BAN.

DR. REGENE L. MITCHELL
President, Consumer Federation of California

LUCY BLAKE
Executive Director, California League of Conservation Voters

DAN TERRY
President, California Professional Firefighters

Rebuttal to Argument Against Proposition 140

Proposition 140 restores *true* democracy, gives you *real* choices of candidates, protects *your* rights to be represented by someone who knows and cares about *your* wishes. It opens up the political system so *everyone*— not just the entrenched career politicians—can participate.

Proposition 140 will bring new ideas, workable policies and fresh cleansing air to Sacramento. All are needed badly. A stench of greed, and vote-selling hangs over Sacramento because lifetime-in-office incumbents think it's *their* government, not yours.

Californians polled by the state's largest newspaper say "most politicians are for sale," and "taking bribes is a relatively common practice" among lawmakers. Proposition 140 cuts the ties between corrupting special interest money and long-term legislators.

Why don't more people vote? Because incumbents have rigged the system in their favor so much, elections are meaningless. Even the worst of legislators get reelected 98% of the time. Honest, ethical, *truly* representative people who want to run for office don't stand a chance.

Do career legislators *really* earn their guaranteed salaries, extravagant pensions, limousines, air travel and other luxury benefits? No. They use *your* money and *your* government to buy themselves power and guaranteed reelections.

Who really opposes Proposition 140? It isn't ordinary people who have to work for a living. It's incumbent legislators and their camp followers.

Beware of movie stars and celebrities in million-dollar TV ads, attacking Proposition 140. They're doing the dirty work for career politicians.

VOTE "YES!" ON PROPOSITION 140. ENOUGH, IS ENOUGH!

W. BRUCE LEE, II
Executive Director, California Business League

LEE A. PHELPS
Chairman, Alliance of California Taxpayers

ART PAGDAN, M.D.
National 1st V.P., Filipino–American Political Association

A final note from your casebook editors: As is customary in California, the November 1990 ballot did not reprint the text of Proposition 140 or any of the pro and con arguments. Instead, the voters were given this question:

> TERMS OF OFFICE. LEGISLATURE. INITIATIVE CONSTITUTIONAL AMENDMENT. Limits: terms of specified state elected officials, legislators' retirement, pensions. Legislature's operating costs [continued to describe the predicted financial impact of the proposal, as required by state law].
>
> Yes ___ No ___

The measure passed by a margin of 52.17% to 47.83%.

The question for the California Supreme Court is this: Does the initiative create a lifetime bar to a legislator serving more than the allotted time, or does it merely bar consecutive years of service? Break down the question in this way:

First, does the initiative have a "plain meaning" as applied to this issue?

Second, how do the extrinsic materials cut? If the initiative is ambiguous, do the materials we have provided cut decisively toward one interpretation? If so, why? Do these materials make you rethink whether there is a plain meaning?

Third, does it make a difference that the California Secretary of State files a brief arguing that the initiative only bars incumbents from serving too many consecutive years and does not constitute a lifetime bar? The Secretary of State administers the initiative process and coordinates the ballot materials filed by the proponents and opponents of the initiative.

When you have finished your analysis, compare your conclusions with the published judicial opinions. See *Bates v. Jones*, 131 F.3d 843 (9th Cir. 1997) (en banc), *cert. denied*, 523 U.S. 1021 (1998), vacating the panel opinion of *Jones v. Bates*, 127 F.3d 839 (9th Cir. 1997); *Legislature v. Eu*, 54 Cal.3d 492, 286 Cal.Rptr. 283, 816 P.2d 1309 (1991), *cert. denied*, 503 U.S. 919 (1992).

SECTION 3. CONSTITUTIONAL NORMS, THE AVOIDANCE CANON, AND INTERPRETING INITIATIVES

In Problem 5–1, your answer might be different if you have taken a course in the First Amendment and believe that there is a federal or state fundamental constitutional right for a voter to have as broad a choice of candidates as possible. The U.S. Supreme Court has never recognized such a right explicitly, and the en banc Ninth Circuit debated that precise issue in *Bates v. Jones*, 131 F.3d 843 (9th Cir. 1997). One group of judges believed such a fundamental right is implicit in the Court's First Amendment case law; the other group of judges believed that such a right has been implicitly rejected in the Court's precedents.

Should the avoidance canon (Chapter 3, § 2B) be applied more aggressively when judges are interpreting initiatives than when they are interpreting legislative enactments? The argument in favor of a super-avoidance canon is the following. Because they are more ad hoc, are often not drafted by experienced professional statute drafters, and frequently seem to target unpopular minorities, initiatives run into constitutional trouble from state or federal judges more often than do legislative enactments. See Kenneth P. Miller, *Direct Democracy and the Courts* (2009), and Kenneth P. Miller, *Courts as Watchdogs of the Washington State Initiative Process*, 24 Seattle U. L. Rev. 1053, 1085 n.12 (2001).

A wide array of legal scholars have urged the U.S. Supreme Court to scrutinize popular initiatives for equal protection violations more vigorously than the Court reviews ordinary statutes adopted by legislatures, on the ground that ballot campaigns are more prone to abuse.[a] Most of these scholars make the Madisonian point, that the representative process, with its vetogates, produces more deliberative statutes that are less likely to penalize minorities.

Other scholars reject or caution against this academic conventional wisdom—not because initiatives represent perfect lawmaking, but because there are serious problems with both legislative and popular lawmaking.[b] Initiatives are an intrinsically fair way for the voting population to focus on an issue that concerns them—and are often a better path to active citizen engagement in substantive issues. Public choice theory, for example, suggests that legislators have incentives not to confront or resolve

---

a. See, e.g., Julian Eule, *Judicial Review of Direct Democracy,* 99 Yale L.J. 1503 (1990); Sylvia Lazos Vargas, *Judicial Review of Initiatives and Referendums in which Majorities Vote on Minorities' Democratic Citizenship*, 60 Ohio St. L.J. 399 (1999); Lawrence Sager, *Insular Majorities Unabated:* Warth v. Seldin *and* City of Eastlake v. Forest City Enterprises, Inc., 91 Harv. L. Rev. 1373 (1978).

b. See, e.g., Richard Briffault, *Distrust of Democracy*, 63 Tex. L. Rev. 1347 (1985); Clayton Gillette, *Is Direct Democracy Anti-Democractic?*, 34 Willamette L. Rev. 609 (1998); Ethan J. Leib, *Can Direct Democracy be Made Deliberative?*, 54 Buff. L. Rev. 903 (2006); Mark Tushnet, *Fear of Voting: Differential Standards of Judicial Review of Direct Legislation*, 1996 NYU Ann. Surv. Am. L. 373.

conflictual issues. Moreover, the same kinds of questions raised against direct democracy—the inability of minorities to win, the lack of genuine deliberation, private interests winning over the common good—have been posed by public choice theorists criticizing representative democracy.

During the 1960s and 1970s, there were a series of state initiatives that had disparate effects on racial minorities—and the Supreme Court struck many of them down, even though similar legislated enactments might have passed constitutional muster. See, e.g., *Reitman v. Mulkey*, 387 U.S. 369 (1967), where the Court looked behind the formal rules created by a California initiative to find a retrogressive race-based discriminatory effect, which the Court struck down as a violation of equal protection. In the 1990s and the new millennium, there has been a proliferation of anti-gay initiatives, most of which were adopted by voters.[c]

Former Justice Hans Linde of the Oregon Supreme Court has argued that the history of antigay initiatives supports the conventional academic wisdom favoring heightened judicial review of initiatives targeting unpopular minorities. See Hans Linde, *When Initiative Lawmaking Is Not "Republican Government": The Campaign Against Homosexuality*, 72 Ore. L. Rev. 19 (1993). Consider Justice Linde's argument in light of the case that follows—and then focus on our notes to that case, which bring the discussion back around to the focus of this chapter.

ROMER v. EVANS

Supreme Court of the United States, 1996
517 U.S. 620, 116 S.Ct. 1620, 134 L.Ed.2d 855

JUSTICE KENNEDY delivered the opinion of the Court.

One century ago, the first Justice Harlan admonished this Court that the Constitution "neither knows nor tolerates classes among citizens." *Plessy v. Ferguson*, 163 U.S. 537, 559 (1896) (dissenting opinion). Unheeded then, those words now are understood to state a commitment to the law's neutrality where the rights of persons are at stake. The Equal Protection Clause enforces this principle and today requires us to hold invalid a provision of Colorado's Constitution.

[Aspen, Boulder, and Denver, Colorado adopted ordinances prohibiting private as well as public workplace, housing, and public accommodations discrimination on the basis of sexual orientation. Responding to these ordinances, in 1992 Colorado voters adopted a ballot proposal adding an Amendment 2 to the state constitution, which read:

---

c. Compare Barbara S. Gamble, *Putting Civil Rights to a Popular Vote*, 41 Am. J. Pol. Sci. 245 (1997) (from 1959–93, voters adopted 58% of ballot measures restricting civil rights, and almost four-fifths of the anti-gay measures placed before them), with Todd Donovan & Shaun Bowler, *Reforming the Republic: Democratic Institutions For the New America* 140–42 (2004) (finding a less impressive pass rate for anti-gay initiatives after 1993). On the intellectual history of anti-gay initiatives, see William N. Eskridge Jr., *Challenging the Apartheid of the Closet*, 25 Hofstra L. Rev. 817, 928–30 (1997); Jane S. Schacter, *The Gay Civil Rights Debate in the States: Decoding the Discourse of Equivalents*, 29 Harv. C.R.–C.L. L. Rev. 283 (1994).

Neither the State of Colorado, through any of its branches or departments, nor any of its agencies, political subdivisions, municipalities or school districts, shall enact, adopt or enforce any statute, regulation, ordinance or policy whereby homosexual, lesbian or bisexual orientation, conduct, practices or relationships shall constitute or otherwise be the basis of or entitle any person or class of persons to have or claim any minority status, quota preferences, protected status or claim of discrimination.]

The State's principal argument in defense of Amendment 2 is that it puts gays and lesbians in the same position as all other persons. So, the State says, the measure does no more than deny homosexuals special rights. This reading of the amendment's language is implausible. [The Colorado Supreme Court interpreted the amendment as repealing local protections for gay people and preventing further protections from being adopted unless the state constitution was first amended.]

Sweeping and comprehensive is the change in legal status effected by this law. So much is evident from the ordinances the Colorado Supreme Court declared would be void by operation of Amendment 2. Homosexuals, by state decree, are put in a solitary class with respect to transactions and relations in both the private and governmental spheres. The amendment withdraws from homosexuals, but no others, specific legal protection from the injuries caused by discrimination, and it forbids reinstatement of these laws and policies.

The change that Amendment 2 works in the legal status of gays and lesbians in the private sphere is far-reaching, both on its own terms and when considered in light of the structure and operation of modern antidiscrimination laws. [Justice Kennedy explained that the common law afforded no protection against discrimination by public accommodations because of race, sex, etc. The common law also placed few, if any, restrictions on employment discrimination. The Aspen, Boulder, and Denver ordinances are typical of antidiscrimination regulations adopted in hundreds of jurisdictions filling this gap in the common law. Additionally, those regulations, like others, prohibit discrimination on the basis of criteria that have not triggered constitutional strict scrutiny, including age, military status, marital status, pregnancy, parenthood, custody of a minor child, political affiliation, physical or mental disability of an individual or of his or her associates, and sexual orientation. The effect of Amendment 2 was to deprive gay people of those protections in public accommodations, housing, sale of real estate, insurance, health and welfare services, private education, and employment.]

Amendment 2's reach may not be limited to specific laws passed for the benefit of gays and lesbians. It is a fair, if not necessary, inference from the broad language of the amendment that it deprives gays and lesbians even of the protection of general laws and policies that prohibit arbitrary discrimination in governmental and private settings. See, *e.g.*, Colo. Rev. Stat. § 24–4–106(7) (1988) (agency action subject to judicial review under arbitrary and capricious standard); § 18–8–405 (making it a criminal offense for a public servant knowingly, arbitrarily or capriciously to refrain from performing a duty imposed on him by law); * * * 4 Colo. Code of Regulations 801–1, Policy 11–1 (1983) (prohibiting discrimination in state employment on grounds of specified traits or "other non-merit factor"). At some point in the systematic administration of these laws, an official must determine whether homosexuality is an arbitrary and, thus, forbidden basis for decision. Yet a decision to that effect would itself amount to a policy prohibiting discrimination on the basis of homosexuality, and so would appear to be no more valid under Amendment 2 than the specific prohibitions against discrimination the state court held invalid.

If this consequence follows from Amendment 2, as its broad language suggests, it would compound the constitutional difficulties the law creates. [The Colorado Supreme Court made the limited observation that the amendment is not intended to affect the many antidiscrimination laws protecting nonsuspect classes, *Romer II*, 882 P.2d at 1346, n.9, but the state court's construction left open the possibility of broader application. Justice Kennedy specifically rejected the view that Amendment 2's prohibition on specific legal protections did no more than deprive homosexuals of special rights.] We find nothing special in the protections Amendment 2 withholds. These are protections taken for granted by most people either because they already have them or do not need them; these are protections against exclusion from an almost limitless number of transactions and endeavors that constitute ordinary civic life in a free society. * * *

Amendment 2 fails, indeed defies, [rational basis] inquiry. First, the amendment has the peculiar property of imposing a broad and undifferentiated disability on a single named group, an exceptional and, as we shall explain, invalid form of legislation. Second, its sheer breadth is so discontinuous with the reasons offered for it that the amendment seems inexplicable by anything but animus toward the class that it affects; it lacks a rational relationship to legitimate state interests.

Taking the first point, even in the ordinary equal protection case calling for the most deferential of standards, we insist on knowing the relation between the classification adopted and the object to be attained. The search for the link between classification and objective gives substance to the Equal Protection Clause; it provides guidance and discipline for the legislature, which is entitled to know what sorts of laws it can pass; and it marks the limits of our own authority. In the ordinary case, a law will be sustained if it can be said to advance a legitimate government interest, even if the law seems unwise or works to the disadvantage of a particular group, or if the rationale for it seems tenuous. * * * By requiring that the classification bear a rational relationship to an independent and legitimate legislative end, we ensure that classifications are not drawn for the purpose of disadvantaging the group burdened by the law.

Amendment 2 confounds this normal process of judicial review. It is at once too narrow and too broad. It identifies persons by a single trait and then denies them protection across the board. The resulting disqualification of a class of persons from the right to seek specific protection from the law is unprecedented in our jurisprudence. The absence of precedent for Amendment 2 is itself instructive; "[d]iscriminations of an unusual character especially suggest careful consideration to determine whether they are obnoxious to the constitutional provision."

It is not within our constitutional tradition to enact laws of this sort. Central both to the idea of the rule of law and to our own Constitution's guarantee of equal protection is the principle that government and each of its parts remain open on impartial terms to all who seek its assistance. " 'Equal protection of the laws is not achieved through indiscriminate imposition of inequalities.' " *Sweatt v. Painter*, 339 U.S. 629, 635 (1950) (quoting *Shelley v. Kraemer*, 334 U.S. 1, 22 (1948)). Respect for this principle explains why laws singling out a certain class of citizens for disfavored legal status or general hardships are rare. A law declaring that in general it shall be more difficult for one group of citizens than for all others to seek aid from the government is itself a denial of equal protection of the laws in the most literal sense. * * *

A second and related point is that laws of the kind now before us raise the inevitable inference that the disadvantage imposed is born of animosity toward the class of persons affected. "[I]f the constitutional conception of 'equal protection of the laws' means anything, it must at the very least mean that a bare ... desire to harm a politically unpopular group cannot constitute a *legitimate* governmental interest." Even laws enacted for broad and ambitious purposes often can be explained by reference to legitimate public policies which justify the incidental disadvantages they impose on certain persons. Amendment 2, however, in making a general announcement that gays and lesbians shall not have any particular protections from the law, inflicts on them immediate, continuing, and real injuries that outrun and belie any legitimate justifications that may be claimed for it. We conclude that, in addition to the far-reaching deficiencies of Amendment 2 that we have noted, the principles it offends, in another sense, are conventional and venerable; a law must bear a rational relationship to a legitimate governmental purpose, and Amendment 2 does not.

The primary rationale the State offers for Amendment 2 is respect for other citizens' freedom of association, and in particular the liberties of landlords or employers who have personal or religious objections to homosexuality. Colorado also cites its interest in conserving resources to fight discrimination against other groups. The breadth of the Amendment is so far removed from these particular justifications that we find it impossible to credit them. We cannot say that Amendment 2 is directed to any identifiable legitimate purpose or discrete objective. It is a status-based enactment divorced from any factual context from which we could discern a relationship to legitimate state interests; it is a classification of persons undertaken for its own sake, something the Equal Protection

Clause does not permit. "[C]lass legislation ... [is] obnoxious to the prohibitions of the Fourteenth Amendment...." * * *

JUSTICE SCALIA, with whom THE CHIEF JUSTICE [REHNQUIST] and JUSTICE THOMAS join, dissenting.

The Court has mistaken a Kulturkampf for a fit of spite. The constitutional amendment before us here is not the manifestation of a " 'bare ... desire to harm' " homosexuals, but is rather a modest attempt by seemingly tolerant Coloradans to preserve traditional sexual mores against the efforts of a politically powerful minority to revise those mores through use of the laws. That objective, and the means chosen to achieve it, are not only unimpeachable under any constitutional doctrine hitherto pronounced (hence the opinion's heavy reliance upon principles of righteousness rather than judicial holdings); they have been specifically approved by the Congress of the United States and by this Court. * * *

[Justice Scalia criticized the Court for suggesting that Amendment 2 had a potentially broad impact upon gay people, for the Colorado Supreme Court authoritatively construed Amendment 2 "only to prevent the adoption of antidiscrimination laws intended to protect gays, lesbians, and bisexuals."] The amendment prohibits *special treatment* of homosexuals, and nothing more. It would not affect, for example, a requirement of state law that pensions be paid to all retiring state employees with a certain length of service; homosexual employees, as well as others, would be entitled to that benefit. But it would prevent the State or any municipality from making death-benefit payments to the "life partner" of a homosexual when it does not make such payments to the long-time roommate of a nonhomosexual employee. Or again, it does not affect the requirement of the State's general insurance laws that customers be afforded coverage without discrimination unrelated to anticipated risk. Thus, homosexuals could not be denied coverage, or charged a greater premium, with respect to auto collision insurance; but neither the State nor any municipality could require that distinctive health insurance risks associated with homosexuality (if there are any) be ignored.

Despite all of its hand wringing about the potential effect of Amendment 2 on general antidiscrimination laws, the Court's opinion ultimately does not dispute all this, but assumes it to be true. The only denial of equal treatment it contends homosexuals have suffered is this: They may not obtain *preferential* treatment without amending the state constitution. That is to say, the principle underlying the Court's opinion is that one who is accorded equal treatment under the laws, but cannot as readily as others obtain *preferential* treatment under the laws, has been denied equal protection of the laws. If merely stating this alleged "equal protection" violation does not suffice to refute it, our constitutional jurisprudence has achieved terminal silliness. * * *

* * * The Court's opinion contains grim, disapproving hints that Coloradans have been guilty of "animus" or "animosity" toward homosexuality, as though that has been established as un-American. Of course it is

our moral heritage that one should not hate any human being or class of human beings. But I had thought that one could consider certain conduct reprehensible—murder, for example, or polygamy, or cruelty to animals—and could exhibit even "animus" toward such conduct. Surely that is the only sort of "animus" at issue here: moral disapproval of homosexual conduct, the same sort of moral disapproval that produced the centuries-old criminal laws that we held constitutional in *Bowers*. The Colorado amendment does not, to speak entirely precisely, prohibit giving favored status to people who are *homosexuals*; they can be favored for many reasons—for example, because they are senior citizens or members of racial minorities. But it prohibits giving them favored status *because of their homosexual conduct*—that is, it prohibits favored status *for homosexuality*.

[Justice Scalia maintained that Colorado had, in fact, engaged in a measured response to homosexuality. The state in 1971 repealed its law making consensual sodomy a crime, but that repeal was not intended to connote an approval of homosexuality.] The problem (a problem, that is, for those who wish to retain social disapprobation of homosexuality) is that, because those who engage in homosexual conduct tend to reside in disproportionate numbers in certain communities, see Record, Exh. MMM, have high disposable income, see ibid.; App. 254 (affidavit of Prof. James Hunter), and, of course, care about homosexual-rights issues much more ardently than the public at large, they possess political power much greater than their numbers, both locally and statewide. Quite understandably, they devote this political power to achieving not merely a grudging social toleration, but full social acceptance, of homosexuality. * * *

That is where Amendment 2 came in. It sought to counter both the geographic concentration and the disproportionate political power of homosexuals by (1) resolving the controversy at the statewide level, and (2) making the election a single-issue contest for both sides. It put directly, to all the citizens of the State, the question: Should homosexuality be given special protection? They answered no. The Court today asserts that this most democratic of procedures is unconstitutional. Lacking any cases to establish that facially absurd proposition, it simply asserts that it *must* be unconstitutional, because it has never happened before. [This is completely false, says Justice Scalia. In the late nineteenth century, the federal government enacted a series of statutes singling out polygamists for special criminal, civil, and juridical treatment; the Court upheld all the legal disabilities, including one that disenfranchised not only polygamists, but also people who taught or counseled polygamy. *Davis v. Beason*, 133 U.S. 333 (1890). Although abstract advocacy cannot today be punished, *Beason* remains good for the proposition that disapproved status can be the basis for civil penalty.] Has the Court concluded that the perceived social harm of polygamy is a "legitimate concern of government," and the perceived social harm of homosexuality is not? * * *

NOTES ON THE COLORADO INITIATIVE CASE AND THE AVOIDANCE CANON

The Court's debate in *Romer* is now a staple for constitutional law courses, and we do not seek to revisit those debates here—but we do maintain that an underappreciated feature of the case is the different *interpretations* the majority and the dissent gave to Amendment 2. Those interpretations, in turn, illuminate different strategies that might be taken to constitutionally questionable initiatives.

1. *Did Amendment 2 Have a Plain Meaning?* Writing for the Court's leading contextualists (i.e., Justices Stevens and Breyer, big consumers of legislative history), Justice Kennedy found that Amendment 2 had a plain meaning that reflected broad hard-to-limit discriminatory potential to exclude gay citizens from basic state protections. Justice Scalia dismissed the possibility of such a plain meaning. There are not many cases where Stevens and Breyer find a plain meaning, while Scalia assumes ambiguity.

But is there not a plain meaning? Take a hypothetical. The head of a state agency learns that some of the state employees are harassing lesbian and gay coworkers, which is disrupting the workplace and producing great unhappiness among the gay staff. This is unacceptable, concludes the agency head, and she issues a memorandum to the staff barring them from discriminating against or harassing lesbian, gay, or bisexual coworkers. Has this memorandum violated Amendment 2? Justice Kennedy fears that it does; Justice Scalia is sure that it does not. Read the text of Amendment 2:

> Neither the State of Colorado, through any of its branches or departments, nor any of its agencies, political subdivisions, municipalities or school districts, shall enact, adopt or enforce any statute, regulation, ordinance or policy whereby homosexual, lesbian or bisexual orientation, conduct, practices or relationships shall constitute or otherwise be the basis of or entitle any person or class of persons to have or claim any minority status, quota preferences, protected status or claim of discrimination.

Did not one of the state "agencies * * * adopt * * * any * * * policy whereby homosexual, lesbian or bisexual orientation * * * shall constitute or otherwise be the basis of or entitle any person or class of persons to have or claim any * * * protected status or claim of discrimination"? Is there any way to avoid the conclusion that the "plain meaning" of Amendment 2 prevents the state agency from dealing with this problem? If that is the case, does it not take a lot of the sting out of Justice Scalia's outraged dissent?

2. *The Relevance of the Avoidance Canon.* But Justice Kennedy's majority opinion loses some of its sting if you consider the avoidance canon. The Colorado Supreme Court interpreted Amendment 2 as follows:

> "The immediate objective of Amendment 2 is, at a minimum, to repeal existing statutes, regulations, ordinances, and policies of state and local entities that barred discrimination based on sexual orientation. * * *

> "The 'ultimate effect' of Amendment 2 is to prohibit any governmental entity from adopting similar, or more protective statutes, regulations,

ordinances, or policies in the future unless the state constitution is first amended to permit such measures."

Romer, 854 P.2d, at 1284–1285 & n. 26. The state court's interpretation of Amendment 2 seems narrower than its plain meaning would have suggested. Thus, according to the state court, if there is a general anti-harassment law or rule, and the agency applies it to make sure lesbian and gay employees are not harassed, just as the agency applies it to make sure religious and racial minorities are not harassed, then there is no violation of Amendment 2. Is there a way to square this interpretation with the plain meaning of Amendment 2? (Hint: yes there is, so figure it out, please.)

This narrowing interpretation has several virtues, not least of which is that it was rendered by the Colorado Supreme Court, whose construction of the state initiative is supposed to be binding on the U.S. Supreme Court. Another virtue is that this interpretation finds substantial support in the ballot materials and the campaign supporting Amendment 2.[d] The supporters of Amendment 2 wanted to preempt existing and future municipal and gubernatorial protections for gay people against job and other forms of discrimination—which the proponents felt were "special rights" not justified by the same unjust treatment that supported anti-discrimination measures protecting women, racial minorities, the disabled, religious minorities, and the like. The ballot materials did not mention the possibility that Amendment 2 would preempt general anti-discrimination laws or permit state and local agencies to affirmatively discriminate against gay people.

Although Justice Scalia did not cite to the "legislative history" of Amendment 2, he nailed the public justifications set forth by its sponsors. Either Justice Scalia "peeked" at the legislative history or, more likely, understood intuitively what the traditionalists were trying to do when they devised and campaigned for voter ratification of Amendment 2. By the way, this suggests the utility of ballot materials developed by initiative sponsors. For judges who do *not* intuitively understand the worldview and goals of initiative supporters, the ballot materials provide needed normative context. They help judges understand the initiative's text *from the perspective* of those who supported the initiative. Is that not helpful?

Admittedly, Amendment 2 was very poorly drafted, without the assistance of the professional staff who work with the Colorado Legislature. If a little bit of judicial surgery can be performed on the language of the initiative, to make it correspond more closely to the purposes and announced expectations of the sponsors, why not do the surgery? One reason, of course, is that this makes the Scalia dissent in *Romer* look a lot like the Court's opinion in *Holy Trinity Church* (Chapter 2, § 1), which is Wrongness Incarnate according to Justice Scalia.

The fit with *Holy Trinity* becomes even closer in light of Justice Brewer's argument that a narrowing construction of the 1885 alien importation statute was needed to avoid conflict with the "Christian Nation" norm undergirding our polity. In modern terms, there might be a free exercise norm in the background: Do not be eager to apply a statute that makes it harder for

---

d. For the ballot materials, see William N. Eskridge Jr. & Nan D. Hunter, *Sexuality, Gender and the Law* app. 3 (3d ed. 2011).

citizens to create and operate faith-based institutions. See *Catholic Bishop of Chicago* (Chapter 3, § 2B). So, too, in *Romer* a narrowing construction might save Amendment 2 from conflict with core equal protection values. (For the record, Justice Scalia is a big fan of the avoidance canon, so this is a plausible reading of his dissenting opinion, except for the nice fit with *Holy Trinity*.)

As a normative matter, why shouldn't the avoidance canon be applied more aggressively to badly drafted initiatives?

3. *One Final Wrinkle.* There is another wrinkle that was emphasized by the American Bar Association's *amicus* brief in *Romer*. The ABA reminded the Court that the anti-discrimination ordinances targeted by Amendment 2 protected against discrimination because of sexual orientation generally, and not "homosexual" orientation specifically. Thus, Boulder's ordinance protected straight people from being denied employment at gay bookstores (for example) based on their sexual orientation. Such an application of Boulder's ordinance—to protect straight people—would be allowed by Amendment 2, while an application of Boulder's ordinance to protect gay people would not.

If this is right, Amendment 2 has produced a world only Humpty Dumpty could imagine: gay people—long objects of pervasive private prejudice and violence as well as state "Kulturkampfe" (which are, literally, campaigns to extinguish or domesticate a religious minority)—lose the anti-discrimination protections they need, while straight people—the group that has benefitted from state persecution and discrimination against gays—retain the protection that anti-discrimination laws afford. In other words, a neutral anti-discrimination law like Boulder's is transformed by Amendment 2 into a *special rights* law, but special rights for heterosexuals. Is this wacky enough to violate the Equal Protection Clause?

As a legal matter, how can Justice Scalia and other defenders of Amendment 2 respond to the ABA's devilish argument?

CHAPTER 6

IMPLEMENTATION AND INTERPRETATION OF STATUTES IN THE ADMINISTRATIVE STATE

■ ■ ■

Under the system of mutually encroaching government powers described in The Federalist No. 51 (James Madison), the legislature shares lawmaking power with the executive and the judiciary. As we have seen throughout this book, statutes are not the end of lawmaking, but are often only the beginning: Like judicial precedents and administrative decisions, they may be expanded beyond their terms, applied retroactively, and updated by courts and agencies in appropriate circumstances. We explore this theme—and the related theme of formalist versus realist reasoning in separation of powers problems—more systematically in this chapter.

There are a number of implementation choices available to the legislature. First, the legislature can authorize public enforcers to prosecute violators of the statute and exact some penalty from them (e.g., criminal laws). Second, the legislature can authorize victims of conduct violating the statute to sue the violators for damages and/or injunctive relief (e.g., the Uniform Commercial Code, most tort statutes). In these first two implementation choices, the legislature authorizes courts to adjudicate the enforcement lawsuits and to develop the standards and rules of the statute. Third, the legislature can delegate the development of standards and/or the adjudication of violations to a public administrative agency or a private group (e.g., federal securities laws, state licensing regulations). This last choice has been characteristic of the modern administrative state, whose history we trace in § 1 of this chapter.

Section 1 examines not only the implementation choices—private enforcement, public enforcement, agency enforcement, or a combination of the three—available to the legislature, but also the important legal issues related to these implementation choices. Is it legitimate for the legislature to delegate so much of its authority to agencies? At what point does delegation of *law-implementing* power essentially become abdication of *lawmaking* power? If Congress has vested enforcement of the statute in an agency or a prosecutor, do courts have the authority to *imply* a cause of action from the statute for private parties as well?

It would be irrational for Congress to delegate substantial lawmaking power to other officials, without retaining some (and perhaps a great deal of) control over the exercise of that power. Not surprisingly, Congress has sought to exercise that sort of control, and § 2 of this chapter briefly explores these mechanisms under the lenses of both political and constitutional theory. Among the mechanisms explored will be (1) legislative oversight and investigations of agency enforcement; (2) the legislative veto; (3) control over agency personnel; (4) judicial review; (5) the appropriations power; and (6) the original structuring of the agency. Constitutional problems limit the usefulness of the first three mechanisms; the last three mechanisms are perfectly constitutional but somewhat indirect (and therefore inefficacious) means of congressional control.

Building upon the previous two chapters and the automobile safety case study in this chapter, § 3 of this chapter lays out a theory of how agency approaches to statutory interpretation will systematically tend to be different from judicial approaches to statutory interpretation (the focus of Chapters 2–4). Compared to courts, agencies will emphasize statutory purpose more than plain meaning, current legislative and even presidential preferences more than historic preferences (i.e., "original meaning" of statutes), and flexible adaptation of the statute to new circumstances more than following precedent. In short, agencies will be more *dynamic* statutory interpreters than courts will be.

What does this insight mean for judicial consideration of agency statutory interpretations? Reflecting the traditional role of courts to "declare the law," many judges and commentators maintain that courts should overrule dynamic agency applications that are inconsistent with judges' reading of statutes, following the criteria laid out in Chapters 3–4. The Administrative Procedure Act, discussed in § 1, might be read this way. Reflecting the needs of the administrative state and the limited ability of judges to administer a vast legal interpretive regime, many judges and commentators have concluded that courts need to give agencies a lot of breathing room as they apply statutes. The U.S. Supreme Court's decision in *Chevron, U.S.A., Inc. v. Natural Resources Defense Council,* 467 U.S. 837 (1984), might be read this way. Most of § 3 will involve the Court's "continuum of deference" and the complicated, and often closeted, factors that drive judicial reactions to agency constructions.

SECTION 1. LAW IMPLEMENTATION IN THE ADMINISTRATIVE STATE

State and federal criminal laws are typically enforced exclusively by official prosecution of offenders. Many other statutes provide for both civil and criminal penalties that may be enforced by official actions filed in court. For example, the Justice Department may bring a civil lawsuit for an injunction under the Sherman Act to prevent or terminate violations of the Act, or it may refer discovered violations to a U.S. Attorney's Office for criminal prosecution, or both.

Since 1875, however, public enforcement has gradually been transformed from such a *prosecutorial model*, in which a government agency or department brings lawsuits against statutory violators and the adjudication and development of rules is accomplished by courts, to a *bureaucratic model*. Under the bureaucratic model, the government agency or department itself adjudicates the individual prosecutions or makes the rules, and the only role for courts is limited judicial review of what the administrators have done. In this section, we present a short history of the modern administrative state, the main constitutional problems that it presents, and its relationship to the primary common law enforcement device—the private cause of action.

A. A BRIEF HISTORY OF THE MODERN ADMINISTRATIVE STATE[a]

1. *Origins: Regulatory Police.* Wherever there is government, there is bureaucracy. Through most of the nineteenth century, the federal government created bureaucracies to deliver the mail, to fight the nation's wars and then to hand out pensions to veterans afterwards, to collect taxes and administer the nation's tariffs on imported goods, to regulate steamboats on the nation's waterways, to administer public lands, and to grant patents and licenses. See Mashaw, *Administrative Law in the Gilded Age*. Likewise, state and even municipal governments developed their own bureaucracies to build roads and canals, to provide communities with police and fire protection, to regulate public nuisances (including obscene displays and books), and so forth. See William Novak, *The People's Welfare: Law and Regulation in Nineteenth Century America* (1996).

There were twenty-five state railroad commissions in 1886, for example. The Supreme Court invalidated state railroad regulation under the Commerce Clause in *Wabash, St. Louis and Pac. Ry. v. Illinois*, 118 U.S. 557 (1886), which stimulated Congress to create a major new federal regulatory agency, the Interstate Commerce Commission (ICC), in 1887. Interstate Commerce Act of 1887, 24 Stat. 379. After the ICC's creation, federal agencies grew like weeds in a vacant lot. Congress established the Federal Trade Commission (FTC) in 1914 to enforce some of the antitrust laws and regulate unfair competition, the United States Shipping Board in 1916, the Federal Power Commission in 1920, and the Federal Radio Commission (predecessor to the Federal Communications Commission) in 1929. These commissions and the ICC were the first modern *independent federal agencies*, bureaucracies set up outside of the formal departments of

---

a. This history is drawn from Robert Rabin, *Federal Regulation in Historical Perspective*, 38 Stan. L. Rev. 1189 (1986), and from a series of articles by Professor Jerry L. Mashaw detailing the nineteenth century history of administrative law, starting with Mashaw, *Federal Administration and Administrative Law in the Gilded Age*, 119 Yale L.J. 1362 (2010).

the Executive Branch and with their own adjudicatory and rulemaking responsibilities.[b] See generally Geoffrey Miller, *Independent Agencies*, 1986 Sup. Ct. Rev. 41.

The philosophy behind the establishment of these agencies and bureaus by populist reformers in the 1880s and 1890s and progressives in the 1900s and 1910s was to "police" the excesses of businesses. The attitude of the judiciary, however, was often skeptical, as judges treated ICC and other agency determinations with little deference and refused to enforce well-justified agency requests. Nonetheless, the ICC managed to increase its statutory power in 1906 and 1910, when Congress granted the agency authority to regulate rates. Courts gradually came to defer to the agency, though they also required it to follow essential procedural safeguards (a trial-type hearing) in order to develop an administrative record that could be the basis for meaningful judicial review.[c] See, e.g., *ICC v. Louisville and Nashville Ry. Co.*, 227 U.S. 88, 93 (1913).

2. *The New Deal: Regulatory Planning and Market Management.* The Great Depression suggested that much more government direction was needed to correct market excesses and abuses. President Franklin Roosevelt's New Deal was a cluster of regulatory experiments—from the aspirations of comprehensive industrial planning in the National Industrial Recovery Act to the ambitious subsidy program of the Agricultural Adjustment Act. Most of these regulatory initiatives rejected the policing approach of the Populists and Progressives. The New Deal measures were more comprehensive and affirmative approaches to a market that was seen to be structurally unfair and unreliable.

The New Deal created an unprecedented array of new independent agencies and departmental bureaus. Some of them had brief lives. The National Industrial Recovery Act representing the New Deal's most ambitious effort at economic planning, was declared unconstitutional by the Supreme Court in *A.L.A. Schechter Poultry Corp. v. United States*, 295 U.S. 495 (1935). Other New Deal agencies have become part of our federal governance. The National Labor Relations Board (NLRB) was established as an independent agency to head off labor strife by adjudicating the existence of "unfair labor practices" by labor unions and management. The Securities and Exchange Commission (SEC) was established to prevent unstable capital markets by registering and regulating securities offerings according to the commands provided in the applicable statutes

---

b. At the same time Congress was creating independent agencies, it gave bureaus or divisions within the existing executive departments similar duties. The Patent Office had existed within the executive department since 1790, and what we now call U.S. Citizenship and Immigration Services was established within the Justice Department in 1882 to adjudicate immigration claims. The Secretary of Agriculture accumulated a great amount of adjudicatory responsibility as a result of the Pure Food and Drug Act of 1906, 34 Stat. 768; the Meat Inspection Act of 1906–07, 34 Stat. 674, 1260; the Cotton Futures Act and the Warehouse Act of 1916, 39 Stat. 453 & 486; and later statutes (for example, 42 Stat. 159).

c. See 3 Robert Himmelberg, *Growth of the Regulatory State, 1900–1917: State and Federal Regulation of Railroads and Other Enterprises* (1994). For an argument that most of these early statutes represented rent-seeking by regulated interests, see Gabriel Kolko, *The Triumph of Conservatism: A Reinterpretation of American History* (1963).

and SEC rules. By 1941 there were, by one count, nineteen separate lawmaking bureaus within the executive departments and twenty-two independent federal agencies. *Final Report of the Attorney General's Committee on Administrative Procedure* (1941).

As administrative agencies and bureaus proliferated, so did criticisms of them. But given the prevailing skepticism about the operation of free markets, criticism focused less on regulatory intervention and more on the processes by which administrators carried out their regulatory missions. Thus, critics complained that important property rights were being stripped away without proper procedural safeguards, such as trial-type hearing procedures and/or meaningful judicial review of the bureaucratic decision.[d] In 1945, the Attorney General endorsed legislation standardizing administrative procedure, and the Administrative Procedure Act (APA), 60 Stat. 237, codified as amended at 5 U.S.C. §§ 551–559, 701–706 *et al.*, was enacted in 1946.

On its face, the APA divides administrative decisions according to a *bipolar model*. Administrative decisions are treated as either *rules* or *orders*. Rules are like statutes, for they are "designed to implement, interpret, or prescribe law or policy." 5 U.S.C. § 551(4). Most rules are *informal*, but the procedure generating most informal rules is the more formal-sounding *notice-and-comment rulemaking*. In this process, the agency must publish notice of proposed rules in the Federal Register, followed by the opportunity for interested persons to submit comments, usually written, on the proposed rules. *Id.* § 553. See Cornelius Kerwin, *Rulemaking: How Government Agencies Write Law and Policy* (2d ed. 1999) (comprehensive description and analysis of notice-and-comment rulemaking); Peter L. Strauss, *The Rulemaking Continuum*, 41 Duke L.J. 1463 (1992) (the variety of rulemaking options).

Orders are like judicial decisions, for they constitute the "final disposition" of a controversy involving the statutory or agency rules. 5 U.S.C. § 551(6). Thus, the typical procedure for formal adjudicative orders is similar to trial in a court. If the enabling statute calls for decision "on the record after opportunity for agency hearing," *id.* §§ 554(a), 556(a), the agency must not only provide particularized notice to the affected person, but it must also allow him or her "to present his [or her] case or defense by oral or documentary evidence, to submit rebuttal evidence, and to conduct such cross-examination as may be required for a full and true disclosure of facts." *Id.* § 556(d). The agency's decision must be based on the trial-type record and supported by reliable, probative, and substantial evidence. *Id.* § 557.[e] Sections 554 and 556–557 mandate at least a partial

---

d. In 1938, the ABA Special Committee on Administrative Law issued a report scathingly denouncing the bureaucracy for malign "tendencies" to make decisions without hearings, to consider matters not in the record, to disregard jurisdictional limits, and to conflate legislative, prosecutorial, and adjudicative functions. Between 1938 and 1945, the ABA had such legislation introduced in every session of Congress.

e. The text sets forth the typical rulemaking and adjudication procedures. The APA has alternate procedures in each instance. Where the statute requires rulemaking decisions "on the record," §§ 556–557 set forth more detailed trial-like procedures. See *United States v. Florida* separation of functions between the prosecutorial staff and agency decisionmakers, particularly in formal adjudications. For example, formal adjudications are usually handled by *administrative law judges*, who have their own staff and are monitored and rewarded by the Civil Service Commission and not by the agency itself.

Sections 701–706 provide for judicial review of agency rules and orders. "Any person suffering legal wrong because of agency action, or adversely affected or aggrieved by agency action within the meaning of a relevant statute, is entitled to judicial review thereof," *id.* § 702, unless "(1) statutes preclude judicial review; or (2) agency action is committed to agency discretion by law." *Id.* § 701(a). In an action for judicial review, the court "shall" under § 706:

(1) compel agency action unlawfully withheld or unreasonably delayed; and

(2) hold unlawful and set aside agency action, findings, and conclusions found to be—

(A) arbitrary, capricious, an abuse of discretion, or otherwise not in accordance with law;

(B) contrary to constitutional right, power, privilege, or immunity;

(C) in excess of statutory jurisdiction, authority, or limitations, or short of statutory right;

(D) without observance of procedure required by law;

(E) unsupported by substantial evidence in a case subject to sections 556 and 557 of this title or otherwise reviewed on the record of an agency hearing provided by statute; or

(F) unwarranted by the facts to the extent that the facts are subject to trial de novo by the reviewing court.

The APA compromise was essentially designed to recognize the legislative and adjudicative roles of independent agencies and departmental bureaus (both of which are included in the APA definition of "agency," *id.* § 551(1)), but also to "rein in" the bureaucratic state with procedural safeguards and judicial review to prevent arbitrary or unlawful action. The APA's enactment broadly validated the bureaucratic revolution of the New Deal and ushered in a period of relative consensus in favor of agency lawmaking in the 1950s.

3. *The Public Interest Era: Deregulation and New Kinds of Regulation.* Scholars have worried that bureaucratic regulation of the economy is subject to bias and debilitation over time. Marver Bernstein, *Regulating Business by Independent Commission* (1955), for example, argued that agencies, like human beings, typically go through a "life cycle." The

East Coast Ry., 410 U.S. 224 (1973) (essentially requiring the magic words "on the record" to trigger the more burdensome formal rulemaking proceedings). The vast amount of agency work is done through informal mechanisms.

agency's *youth* is characterized by a crusading spirit engendered by its statutory mandate. The agency's *maturity* comes after it has lost much of its initial political support, but the agency understands the industry better and takes a less aggressive approach to regulating it, often becoming a "captive" of the regulated industry. *Senescence* comes when the agency grows not only less vital but also inflexible, a condition that may lead to some form of euthanasia. Later public choice scholars have been even less charitable in thinking about the typical agency biography than Bernstein was, characterizing agencies as captured from childhood by rent-seeking special interests.[f] The 1950s also saw the true beginnings of noneconomic regulatory activities stimulated first by the civil rights revolution, followed in the 1960s by the environmental movement.

These two developments inspired a new period of administrative law development in the 1960s and the 1970s. Bureaucracy became both more distrusted and better integrated into the great public interest movements of those decades. The regulatory emphasis had shifted from comprehensive direction of the economy to *command-and-control* statutes aimed at specific problems not traditionally thought of in market terms.

The Great Society was the linchpin of this shift. The Civil Rights Act of 1964, 78 Stat. 241, established an impressive range of bureaucratic sanctions for civil rights violations. For example, Titles III and IV of the Act authorized the Attorney General to file public lawsuits to desegregate public facilities and public education. Title VI provided for nondiscrimination in federally assisted programs. It was to be implemented by rules making federal grants, loans, or other financial assistance contingent upon the recipient's following nondiscriminatory policies.

Chapter 1 describes Title VII of the 1964 Act, which established the Equal Employment Opportunity Commission (EEOC) and charged it with rulemaking and adjudication of the very broad prohibition of employment discrimination. Though troubled with administrative problems over time, the EEOC served as a model for a new bureaucracy of conscience. Its intrusion into the affairs of corporations and state and local institutions helped broaden the concept of regulation. Government's agenda extended beyond the economic marketplace and toward concern for the creation of a "great society" in which racial, sexual, and ethnic equality would be recognized. Even many of the economic initiatives of the 1960s—the War on Poverty, Medicare, the Food Stamp Program—were aimed at different targets from traditional New Deal regulation. These programs, like Title VII, sought to help the poor and the disadvantaged, often without any attempted justification based upon systemic or isolated market failure.

The 1970s saw the societal-transformation approach to regulation expand to include consumer rights, public health and safety, and environmental purity as important agenda items. Just as the regulatory *agenda*

---

f. See, e.g., Anthony Downs, *Inside Bureaucracy* (1967); William Niskanen, *Bureaucracy and Representative Government* (1971); Sam Peltzman, *Toward a More General Theory of Regulation*, 19 J.L. & Econ. 211 (1976); George Stigler, *The Theory of Economic Regulation*, 2 Bell J. Econ. & Mgmt. Sci. 3 (1971).

was changing, so was the regulatory *mechanism*. Both authorized and encouraged by the new generation of regulatory statutes, United States agencies in the 1970s showed unprecedented interest in *rulemaking* rather than adjudication and less formal mechanisms.

The National Traffic and Motor Vehicle Safety Act of 1966, 80 Stat. 718 (1966), exemplified the new approach. This and other regulatory statutes of this period tended to have more specific mandates, to focus authority in a single administrator rather than a multi-member commission, to open up agencies to public input, and to focus agency action on the establishment of mandatory policy through general rules.[g] The agency rules themselves were different from what came before: rather than command-and-control models, agencies emphasized goals and limits, and left regulated institutions with choices about how to reach those goals and limits.

Closely following this new model was a wave of pollution control legislation, mainly the Clean Air Act Amendments of 1970 (CAA), 84 Stat. 1676, and the Federal Water Pollution Control Act Amendments of 1972, 86 Stat. 816. Congress established ambitious mandates to clean up our environment. Most of the directives were very general, with the details filled in by the Environmental Protection Agency (EPA). The National Environmental Policy Act of 1969 (NEPA), 83 Stat. 852, and other statutes directed all federal departments and agencies to consider environmental effects when decisions are made. The Occupational Health and Safety Act of 1970, 84 Stat. 1590, created the Occupational Health and Safety Administration and directed it to enforce more stringent standards of safety in the workplace. Several pieces of landmark legislation worked to redistribute resources to the less well-off in society; Congress enacted the Food Stamp Act, 1 U.S.C. § 2011 et seq., Head Start programs, Medicare, and Medicaid, and it expanded welfare programs substantially.

These statutes marked a significant change in economic regulation as well. First, they redefined market imperfection. The New Deal approach defined costs rather mechanically, in terms of lost output and distorted flows of resources. Things like pollution and injuries were treated as *externalities* borne for the most part by those receiving them. Regulation in the 1970s compelled businesses to consider these social costs and to do something about them. Second, the public interest legislation of the 1970s at least implicitly recognized and built upon perceived biases in the federal bureaucracy. Many reformers argued that even the few agencies and bureaus that were not essentially captured by their regulated interests were limited by their statutory mandate to consider only a few policy concerns, usually of a material and tangible nature. The regulatory structures created in the 1970s insisted that quality of life concerns be

---

g. Jerry L. Mashaw, *The Story of* Motor Vehicle Manufacturers Association of the U.S. v. State Farm Mutual Automobile Insurance Co.: *Law, Science, and Politics in the Administrative State*, in *Administrative Law Stories* 334, 339–42 (Peter L. Strauss ed., 2006) [hereinafter *The Story of* State Farm]; David Shapiro, *The Choice of Rulemaking or Adjudication in the Development of Administrative Policy*, 78 Harv. L. Rev. 921 (1965).

factored into the bureaucratic calculus (NEPA) and often provided very specific substantive guidelines and time deadlines for agencies to accomplish their regulatory goals (CAA).

Other developments have sought to open up agency decisionmaking. For example, the Freedom of Information Act, 5 U.S.C. § 552, was passed in 1966, 80 Stat. 250, and significantly amended in 1974, 88 Stat. 1561, to require federal agencies and departments to disclose documents and information to persons requesting them, subject to specific exemptions in the Act. The purpose of the Act was to encourage citizens to monitor government performance and publicize problems. See also the Privacy Act of 1974, 88 Stat. 1896, codified at 5 U.S.C. § 552a (protecting personal information from disclosure). The Government in the Sunshine Act of 1976, 90 Stat. 1241, codified at 5 U.S.C. § 552b, requires agencies headed by collegial bodies (e.g., FTC, SEC) to conduct their official business in public meetings, again subject to specific exemptions. Like the APA, these statutes were enacted to assure structures of agency decisionmaking that are responsive to the reasoned public interest. Indeed, this statutory liberalization in the 1970s was accompanied by more aggressive APA judicial review of agency decisions and procedures in the 1970s and 1980s, a phenomenon explored in § 2 of this chapter. See also Peter L. Strauss, *From Expertise to Politics: The Transformation of American Rulemaking*, 31 Wake Forest L. Rev. 745 (1996) (tracing developments in rulemaking and regulations over the past decades).

A Case Study
The National Traffic and Motor Vehicle Safety Act of 1966

As a result of charges by Ralph Nader and other policy entrepreneurs that automobiles were "unsafe at any speed," the issue of motor vehicle safety became a salient one on the national agenda. In a 1966 address to Congress, President Johnson declared that auto safety was a high priority issue for his administration. "The toll of Americans killed [on highways] since the introduction of the automobile is truly unbelievable. It is 1.5 million—more than all the combat deaths suffered in all wars." After numerous hearings, Congress enacted the National Traffic and Motor Vehicle Safety Act of 1966, Pub. L. No. 89–563, 80 Stat. 718, codified at 15 U.S.C. §§ 1381, 1391–1409, 1421–1425, which (together with the Highway Safety Act of 1966) created the National Traffic Safety Agency, later renamed the National Highway Traffic Safety Administration (NHTSA) within the new Department of Transportation.

Congress vested the agency with the authority to promulgate rules to establish "motor vehicle safety standards" that were "reasonable, practicable, and appropriate, * * * meet the need for motor vehicle safety, and * * * [were] stated in objective terms" (§ 1392). No one could sell or import into the United States motor vehicles or equipment not in conformity with these standards (15 U.S.C. § 1397). The penalty for selling or importing motor vehicles in violation of the § 1392 standards was $1,000 for each violation, to be assessed and possibly compromised by the Secretary of Transportation (§ 1398), as well as preliminary or final injunctive relief issued by a federal court at the behest of the United States (§ 1399). Additionally, a distributor or dealer in automobiles had a federal cause of action against a manufacturer or distributor, which sold it a vehicle or equipment not conforming to the standards and which failed to cure the problem through repurchase or replacement (§ 1400).

There was an exciting big idea underlying the 1966 Act. Prior efforts to effect auto safety, such as speed limits and drunk-driving sanctions, sought to *avoid accidents*. Epidemiologists noted that injuries and deaths were more proximately caused by the passenger's collision with parts of his own car, and not just the collisions of two cars. Hence, they proposed a second strategy for reducing death and injury: *redesign the automobile*. Mechanisms that hold the passenger in place (today's seatbelts and shoulder harnesses) or cushion the passenger from the chassis (today's airbags) could prevent injuries from the "second collision."

The auto safety law, passed without a single negative vote in Congress, had a fast start out of the gate but has run out of gas since then. According to Jerry L. Mashaw and David Harfst, *The Struggle for Auto Safety* (1990), the big problem has been the ability of the "Big Three" automakers (General Motors, Ford, Chrysler) to defeat or delay NHTSA's proposed regulations in judicial proceedings, executive department deliberations, and congressional oversight hearings. The upshot of these efforts has been that the agency has been unable to impose design changes that would save lives. According to Kevin McDonald, *Shifting Out of Park: Moving Auto Safety from Recalls to Reason* (2006), in contrast, the big problem has been neglect of human errors as the overwhelming cause of accidents and failure to attack accident-causing activities: tailgating, speeding, driving while drunk, and cell-phone use by drivers. Both McDonald and Mashaw–Harfst conclude that the NHTSA relies far too much on recalls as a method of regulation.

The auto industry was able to win cases which required NHTSA to prove that its regulations were practicable, *Paccar, Inc. v. NHTSA*, 573 F.2d 632 (9th Cir. 1978), but then made it hard for NHTSA to collect the data it needed to prove practicability. The auto industry also won favorable judicial decisions which required endless rounds of notice and discussion on even the most minute amendments to regulations. *Wagner Electric Corp. v. Volpe*, 466 F.2d 1013 (3d Cir. 1972). The courts were "inattentive to the opportunity costs of repeated cycles of notice and comment. With no apparent recognition of the potential for disruption it was creating, [*Wagner*] greatly complicated an increasingly unwieldy rulemaking process, legitimized opponents' dilatory tactics, and made information gathering much more difficult for the resource-strapped agency. * * * [N]ew rounds of notice and comment could go on for decades. All this in the name of procedural fairness to state agencies and consumer advocacy groups, who were about as common in agency rulemaking proceedings as Quakers at prize fights." Mashaw & Harfst, *Auto Safety*, 100.

The structure of American government arguably impeded the agency's ability to adopt strong directive regulations. Since safety regulation had traditionally been accomplished at the state rather than federal level, NHTSA was often required to postpone action until states had their opportunities to address problems. Separation of powers also made NHTSA's assignment burdensome, because it gave the agency too many bosses; it was accountable to both the President and the Congress, which in the 1970s had very different regulatory philosophies. Congress not only gave direction contrary to the President, but its members could not even agree with one another.

In the Motor Vehicle and Schoolbus Safety Amendments of 1974, Pub. L. No. 93–492, 88 Stat. 1477, Congress responded to some of the agency's concerns but also responded to concerns raised by the auto industry. Overall, the amendments made effective regulation more difficult, because the legislative coalition favoring strong highway safety measures (the coalition that had prevailed in 1966) was no longer able to control the legislative agenda or prevent raids on the agency's freedom. Thus, the 1974 Amendments imposed a legislative veto requirement on rules involving future passive restraints; under this provision, a vote of both houses of Congress could nullify any such regulation, without the President's signature. See § 2C of this chapter (discussing legislative vetoes which were later held to be unconstitutional). The 1974 Amendments also eliminated the agency's authority to adopt rules requiring an *interlock* between seat belts and a car's ignition, which prevented the car from starting unless belts were buckled. See Mashaw & Harfst, *Auto Safety,* ch. 7, for the history of the 1974 Amendments.

The disabilities recounted above eventually discouraged NHTSA from regulating auto safety though the adoption of motor vehicle safety rules, as the Act originally contemplated. This reality is particularly unfortunate because many of NHTSA's early standards, dealing with the interior of cars and manual safety belts, made significant contributions to safety, saved many lives, and cost relatively little money. Adapting to a legal and political culture that killed bold initiatives, NHTSA set its sights lower, focusing on the recall of cars with traditionally defined defects. The 1974 Amendments, in fact, expanded NHTSA's powers in this regard: upon notification of defects (§ 1413), the manufacturer had to provide an expeditious remedy (§ 1414), with federal courts available for enforcement of agency orders and with civil fines for violating the orders (§ 1415). The agency busied itself with the task of finding defects and requiring quick remedies. Recalls, which were originally not the primary purpose of the agency, statistically do little to contribute to auto safety, according to both McDonald and Mashaw–Harfst. We shall return to this agency and its problems throughout this chapter.

B. PRIVATE CAUSES OF ACTION IN THE BUREAUCRATIC STATE

The English common law considered private lawsuits the primary mode of enforcing both common law and statutes (even criminal statutes). The common law tradition of private enforcement, of course, is hardly moribund, and many statutes explicitly provide for enforcement by private lawsuits, unmediated by public enforcers. Examples include the Uniform Commercial Code, Title VII of the Civil Rights Act, and the Sherman Act and other antitrust statutes.

Several interesting conceptual questions are raised in connection with private law enforcement in the administrative state. One is whether the existence of agency enforcement may sometimes delay or preclude otherwise existing private lawsuits. Anomalously, the answer is that they can. The doctrine of "primary jurisdiction" applies to claims originally brought as court actions but in fact requiring "resolution of issues which, under a regulatory scheme, have been placed within the special competence of an administrative body; in such a case the judicial process is suspended pending referral of such issues to the administrative body for its views." *United States v. Western Pac. R.R. Co.*, 352 U.S. 59, 64 (1956). The policy reasons for referring such issues to an agency include preserving the uniformity and consistency of regulation and obtaining the insights of the agency, which has more experience and special insights into the market or issues being litigated. *Far East Conference v. United States*, 342 U.S. 570, 574–75 (1952). Is this traditional doctrine based upon concepts that retain current vitality?[h]

In some instances, the federal statutory scheme will be interpreted to strip individuals of their otherwise existing rights to sue. E.g., *Keogh v. Chicago and N.W. Ry.*, 260 U.S. 156 (1922) (interpreting the railroad-regulatory laws to that effect). Still, relatively comprehensive regulatory schemes do not necessarily represent an implicit desire by Congress to eliminate other causes of action under federal statutes or state law. In *Nader v. Allegheny Airlines, Inc.*, 426 U.S. 290 (1976), the Supreme Court held that the Federal Aviation Act did not preempt Ralph Nader's common law action for fraud and misrepresentation when the defendant airline "bumped" him from a flight to which he had a ticket. Should the Safety Act of 1966 close off state tort remedies for car owners injured because of safety defects in their vehicles? See 15 U.S.C. § 1420 (explicit provision preserving state consumer remedies, but added to Safety Act only in 1974).

The second question is the flip side of the first: Does a private party have a cause of action to enforce a statute even though the statute does

---

h. For example, in *Ricci v. Chicago Mercantile Exchange*, 409 U.S. 289 (1973), the Supreme Court affirmed a stay of an antitrust action pending proceedings before the Commodity Exchange Commission to determine whether the procedural rules of the local exchange had been followed in depriving plaintiff of his membership.

not explicitly set forth a private cause of action? Again, the answer is sometimes yes, and again this answer has changed in response to the Court's evolving understanding of the implications of the modern administrative state.

The Court's early cases simply followed the common law approach: interests Congress sought to protect or benefit through a statute presumptively had a cause of action to enforce the statute by seeking injunctive relief or damages. See *Texas & Pac. Ry. Co. v. Rigsby*, 241 U.S. 33 (1916). After the New Deal, the Court was pressed to justify implied causes of action in light of the primary responsibility given to agencies for enforcement of many of the new regulatory statutes. If Congress had established an agency and vested it with enforcement authority, and had not explicitly authorized private enforcement, shouldn't the *Rigsby* presumption be reversed? The Warren Court seemingly thought not. In its leading decision, *J.I. Case Co. v. Borak*, 377 U.S. 426 (1964), the Court held that § 14(a) of the Securities Exchange Act of 1934, 48 Stat. 895, codified at 15 U.S.C. § 78n(a), created an implied cause of action for private parties. As interpreted by the SEC, § 14(a) prohibits proponents of suggested corporate actions (in *Borak*, a merger) from promulgating false or misleading materials in connection with solicitation of shareholder proxies. The Court held that the Act's general authorization of federal court jurisdiction, in § 27, carried with it the creation of a cause of action for private parties. The Court explained that its interpretation was necessary to carry out the statute's purpose, "the protection of investors."

This rationale seems pretty simplistic, for it assumes that more enforcement is always better. What if Congress omitted a private cause of action from § 14 because it wanted a medium level of enforcement, carefully monitored by the SEC, which presumably could screen complaints and only pursue those that are most important and best supported by evidence? The Court responded to this argument with the observation, supported by the SEC itself, that the agency did not have enough staff to pore through the thousands of proxy statements submitted to it every year. "Private enforcement of the proxy rules provides a necessary supplement to Commission action." *Borak*, 377 U.S. at 432 (1964).

PROBLEM 6–1

Implied Right of Action for Violation of a NHTSA Standard

In 1971, Jane Doe sues General Motors (GM) in federal court, alleging that her Buick was in violation of a NHTSA standard and that the defect caused an accident, for which she seeks damages. Although the Act has no express cause of action for consumers like Doe, she relies on *Borak* and the Act's stated purpose, "to reduce traffic accidents" by establishing "motor vehicle safety standards." 15 U.S.C. § 1381. GM responds that the statutory scheme permits citizens to petition the agency to initiate investigations into alleged defects, with the implicit premise that citizen complaints should be channeled into the agency and not into courts.

Would a federal judge in 1971 find such an implied cause of action? See *Handy v. General Motors Corp.*, 518 F.2d 786 (9th Cir. 1975). Would it make a difference to you that Representative Eckhardt (D–Tex.) in 1974 urged Congress to recognize a private cause of action to challenge any NHTSA failure to proceed against an automotive defect? See 120 Cong. Rec. 27,807–08 (1974).

NOTE ON THE SUPREME COURT'S POST-BORAK PRACTICE: SHIFT FROM LEGISLATIVE PURPOSE TO LEGISLATIVE INTENT

Reconsider your answer to Problem 6–1 after *Cort v. Ash*, 422 U.S. 66 (1975). As in *Borak*, the plaintiff was a shareholder suing corporate directors for violating federal law. Unlike the earlier case, the federal statute in *Cort* was a criminal one, prohibiting corporations from contributing to presidential elections. 18 U.S.C. § 610. And unlike *Borak*, the Court did not find a private cause of action in order to effectuate the purpose of the statute. Justice Brennan's opinion in *Cort* announced the following approach (422 U.S. at 78):

> In determining whether a private remedy is implicit in a statute not expressly providing one, several factors are relevant. First, is the plaintiff "one of the class for whose *especial* benefit the statute was enacted," *Rigsby* (emphasis supplied [by the Court])—that is, does the statute create a federal right in favor of the plaintiff? Second, is there any indication of legislative intent, explicit or implicit, either to create such a remedy or to deny one? Third, is it consistent with the underlying purposes of the legislative scheme to imply such a remedy for the plaintiff? And finally, is the cause of action one traditionally relegated to state law, in an area basically the concern of the States, so that it would be inappropriate to infer a cause of action based solely on federal law?

Cort declined to imply a private cause of action, because criminal statutes are usually enacted for the benefit of the public generally and because the legislative history of § 610 suggested that protecting shareholders was, at best, a secondary concern of Congress. Does *Cort* change your answer in *Doe v. General Motors*?

Cort marks a watershed in the legisprudence of implied causes of action. Before *Cort*, private causes of action were usually implied; after *Cort*, they usually were not. For an exception, see *Cannon v. University of Chicago*, 441 U.S. 677 (1979), where the Court implied a private cause of action for violation of Title IX of the Education Amendments of 1972, 20 U.S.C. § 1681, which prohibits sex discrimination in educational programs receiving federal money. Dissenting in *Cannon*, Justice Powell mounted a powerful attack on the Court's practice. "Under Art. III, Congress alone has the responsibility for determining the jurisdiction of the lower federal courts. As the Legislative Branch, Congress also should determine when private parties are to be given causes of action under legislation it adopts. * * * When Congress chooses not to provide a private civil remedy, federal courts should not assume the legislative role of creating such a remedy and thereby enlarge their jurisdiction."

Writing for the Court in *Touche Ross & Co. v. Redington*, 442 U.S. 560 (1979), Justice Rehnquist opined that *Borak* and *Cort* were both obsolete and that the only test was whether Congress intended to create a cause of action. In *Thompson v. Thompson*, 484 U.S. 174 (1988), the Court held that the Parental Kidnapping Prevention Act did not create an implied cause of action in federal court to determine which of two conflicting state custody decrees is valid. Seven Justices joined Justice Marshall's opinion for the Court, which followed the *Cort/Cannon* analysis. The Court found persuasive the structure of the Act, which only worked to extend the Full Faith and Credit Clause to child custody determinations. Also, some specific legislative history suggested that the key legislative players assumed the statute would not create independent federal jurisdiction and would instead have its effect through state court proceedings following its dictates.

Justice Scalia concurred only in the *Thompson* judgment and sharply criticized any reference to *Cort* or *Cannon*. In his view, *Touche Ross* "effectively" overruled the four-factor test of *Cort* and established that the only relevant consideration in such cases is whether Congress intended to create a private cause of action. Justice Scalia then took up the position articulated by Justice Powell in *Cannon*, arguing that the Court has no authority to "imply" a cause of action not intended by Congress and that the Court should probably refuse to infer causes of action not explicitly created by Congress:

> An enactment by implication cannot realistically be regarded as the product of the difficult lawmaking process our Constitution has prescribed [in Article I, § 7]. It is at best dangerous to assume that all the necessary participants in the law-enactment process are acting upon the same unexpressed assumptions. And likewise dangerous to assume that, even with the utmost self-discipline, judges can prevent the implications they see from mirroring the policies they favor. * * *

> If we were to announce a flat rule that private rights of action will not be implied in statutes hereafter enacted, the risk that that course would occasionally frustrate genuine legislative intent would decrease from its current level of minimal to virtually zero. * * * I believe, moreover, that Congress would welcome the certainty that such a rule would produce. Surely conscientious legislators cannot relish the current situation, in which the existence or nonexistence of a private right of action depends upon which of the opposing legislative forces may have guessed right as to the implications the statute will be found to contain.

Thompson, 484 U.S. at 191–92. Consistent with Justice Scalia's critique, the Court has followed the *Touche Ross* skeptical approach (requiring positive evidence of congressional intent to create a private right of action) in most subsequent cases. E.g., *Gonzaga University v. Doe*, 536 U.S. 273 (2002) (no private right under the Family Education Rights and Privacy Act), and *Alexander v. Sandoval*, 532 U.S. 275 (2001) (no private right under Title VI's disparate impact regulations).

Franklin v. Gwinnett County Public Schools, 503 U.S. 60 (1992). The issue was whether the implied right of action created in *Cannon* permits claims for damages in Title IX cases. **Justice White** wrote the opinion for the Court upholding such a claim. The opinion reasoned that once a cause of action has been inferred by the Court, the Court presumes "the availability of all appropriate remedies unless Congress has expressly indicated otherwise." Significantly, the opinion relied on *Bell v. Hood*, 327 U.S. 678 (1946), and *Borak*, which some observers thought were no longer relevant in light of the Court's recent focus on legislative intent. See also *Virginia Bankshares, Inc. v. Sandberg*, 501 U.S. 1083 (1991), where the Court reaffirmed the *Borak* cause of action and defined its remedies more precisely.

Gwinnett County urged the Court to find no damages remedy, based upon separation of powers precepts similar to those argued by Justice Powell in *Cannon* and Justice Scalia in *Thompson*. Justice White not only rejected this argument, but countered that separation of powers supported damages relief:

> In making this argument, respondents misconceive the difference between a cause of action and a remedy. Unlike the finding of a cause of action, which authorizes a court to hear a case or controversy, the discretion to award appropriate relief involves no such increase in judicial power. Federal courts cannot reach out to award remedies when the Constitution or laws of the United States do not support a cause of action. Indeed, properly understood respondents' position invites us to abdicate our historic judicial authority to award appropriate relief in cases brought in our court system. It is well to recall that such authority historically has been thought necessary to provide an important safeguard against abuses of legislative and executive power, as well as to insure an independent judiciary. Moreover, selective abdication of the sort advocated here would harm separation of powers principles in another way, by giving judges the power to render inutile causes of action authorized by Congress through a decision that *no* remedy is available.

Justice Scalia, joined by Chief Justice Rehnquist and Justice Thomas, disputed the Court's analysis. He argued that "when the legislature says nothing about remedy in expressly creating a private right of action; perhaps even when it says nothing about remedy in creating a private right of action by clear textual implication; but not, I think, when it says nothing about remedy in a statute in which the courts divine a private right of action on the basis of 'contextual' evidence such as that in *Cannon*, which charged Congress with knowledge of a court of appeals' creation of a cause of action under a similarly worded statute." He further argued that implied rights of action created by earlier Courts, such as the Title IX right recognized in *Cannon*, need not be given broad readings. Justice Scalia nonetheless concurred in the Court's judgment, on the ground that subsequent civil rights statutes enacted in 1986 and 1987 obviously relied and built upon *Cannon*'s cause of action and the assumption that it included the traditional damages remedy.

Title IX Postscript. The debate among the Justices in *Franklin* continued in subsequent Title IX cases. In *Gebser v. Lago Vista*, 524 U.S. 274 (1998), the Court ruled that Title IX's implied cause of action for damages includes cases of teacher-student sexual harassment, but only when a school district official who has authority to institute corrective measures has actual notice of and is deliberately indifferent to the teacher's misconduct. Justice O'Connor's opinion for the Court rejected claimants' argument that the standards for Title IX relief ought to be the same as the standards for relief under Title VII for workplace sexual harassment. (Title VII, of course, provides an explicit cause of action for workplace sex discrimination; Title IX's cause of action has been implied.) Justice Stevens' dissenting opinion viewed this limitation as a retreat from *Franklin*, where the entire Court had viewed the implied cause of action as having been ratified by Congress.

The analysis changed in *Davis v. Monroe County Bd. of Educ.*, 526 U.S. 629 (1999), where the Court expanded the Title IX cause of action to include sexual harassment by other students under the supervision of the school system. Justice O'Connor's opinion for the Court deployed *Gebser* as a basis for limiting principles: the school board would only be liable when its official (such as a principal) had actual notice of and was deliberately indifferent to the peer harassment. In dissent, Justice Kennedy (joined by the Chief Justice and Justices Scalia and Thomas) vigorously attacked the judicial lawmaking involved in this case:

> The Court has encountered great difficulty in establishing standards for deciding when to imply a private cause of action under a federal statute which is silent on the subject. We try to conform the judicial judgment to the bounds of likely congressional purpose but, as we observed in *Gebser*, defining the scope of the private cause of action in general, and the damages remedy in particular, "inherently entails a degree of speculation, since it addresses an issue on which Congress has not specifically spoken."

> When the statute at issue is a Spending Clause statute [as Title IX is, but not the securities laws], this element of speculation is particularly troubling because it is in significant tension with the requirement that Spending Clause legislation give the States clear notice of the consequences of their acceptance of federal funds. Without doubt, the scope of potential damages liability is one of the most significant factors a school would consider in deciding whether to receive federal funds. Accordingly, the Court must not imply a private cause of action for damages unless it can demonstrate that the congressional purpose to create the implied cause of action is so manifest that the State, when accepting federal funds, had clear notice of the terms and conditions of its monetary liability.

Under this analysis, was *Cannon* not wrongly decided? How about *Franklin*, where the *Davis* dissenters went along with an extension of *Cannon*? Have they changed their minds? Are these decisions so wrong that they would have to be overruled?

PROBLEM 6–2

Implied Causes of Action Under the Court's New Approach

Recall *Doe v. General Motors* (Problem 6–1), in which a consumer injured in an accident allegedly caused by a defect violating one of the NHTSA's motor vehicle standards asserted a private right of action in damages against the manufacturer. Jane Doe retains her state law tort claims, pursuant to 15 U.S.C. § 1420. Based upon the newer Supreme Court's precedents described or excerpted above, how would a federal court rule on Doe's assertion of an implied cause of action? See *George Byers Sons, Inc. v. East Europe Import Export, Inc.*, 488 F.Supp. 574 (D. Md. 1980).

Consider a different statutory scheme. The Air Carriers Access Act of 1986 (ACAA), 49 U.S.C. App. § 1374(c), stated: "No air carrier may discriminate against any otherwise qualified handicapped individual, by reason of such handicap, in the provision of air transportation." (The current codification, with minor changes, is at 49 U.S.C. § 41705.) The Department of Transportation is charged with enforcing this Act through fines. The Department has rarely fined a carrier for violating the statute, and scholars believe the Department does little or nothing to enforce the law. See Nancy Eisenhauer, Comment, *Implied Causes of Action Under Federal Statutes: The Air Carriers Access Act of 1986*, 59 U. Chi. L. Rev. 1183 (1992).

Donna Roe is a quadriplegic who is scheduled to participate at an important conference on obstacles people with disabilities confront in the workplace. She purchased a ticket on an American Airlines flight, but the airline declined to let her travel, because of her disability. She missed the conference and sues for damages under the ACAA. Does she have an implied cause of action? See *Shinault v. American Airlines, Inc.*, 936 F.2d 796 (5th Cir. 1991); see also *Tallarico v. Trans World Airlines, Inc.*, 881 F.2d 566 (8th Cir. 1989); *Americans Disabled Accessible Public Transp. (ADAPT) v. Skywest Airlines, Inc.*, 762 F.Supp. 320 (D. Utah 1991).

C. THE NONDELEGATION DOCTRINE IN THE ADMINISTRATIVE STATE

The nondelegation doctrine posits that the legislature cannot delegate its inherent lawmaking powers to agencies without providing specific standards the bureaucracy shall apply in administering the delegation or, as Chief Justice Taft put it, laying down "an intelligible principle" to which the administrators must conform. *J.W. Hampton, Jr. & Co. v. United States*, 276 U.S. 394, 409 (1928). The doctrine reached the apex of its fame—or notoriety—when it was used by the Supreme Court to strike down most of the New Deal's National Industrial Recovery Act. *A.L.A. Schechter Poultry Corp. v. United States*, 295 U.S. 495 (1935). It has suffered a roller-coaster fate since the 1930s, however.

After President Franklin Roosevelt reconstituted the Supreme Court and the administrative state became an accepted part of our democracy, the nondelegation doctrine fell into constitutional disuse. In *Yakus v. United States*, 321 U.S. 414 (1944), the New Deal Court upheld a broad delegation of price control authority to the Office of Price Administration during World War II. The only "intelligible principle" in the statute was that prices be "fair and equitable"—and yet the Court sustained the delegation. "Only if we could say that there is an absence of standards for the guidance of the Administrator's action, so that it would be impossible in a proper proceeding to ascertain whether the will of Congress has been obeyed, would we be justified in overriding its choice of means for effecting its declared purpose." Recently, the Supreme Court upheld provisions of the Clean Air Act that a lower appellate court had struck down on delegation grounds; the Court found sufficient intelligible principles in the Act to guide the agency. *Whitman v. American Trucking Ass'ns, Inc.*, 531 U.S. 457 (2001) (noting how rarely the Court has struck a federal statute down on nondelegation grounds).

The Economic Stabilization Act of 1970, 84 Stat. 799, codified at 12 U.S.C. § 1904 note, did not even have a "fair and equitable" standard when it authorized the President "to issue such orders and regulations as he may deem appropriate to stabilize prices, rents, wages, and salaries at levels not less than those prevailing on May 25, 1970." Nonetheless, when President Nixon exercised that power to freeze prices and wages in Executive Order No. 11,615, 3 C.F.R. 602 (1971–1975), a special three-judge court rejected a nondelegation doctrine challenge. See *Amalgamated Meat Cutters & Butcher Workmen of N. Am. v. Connally*, 337 F.Supp. 737 (D.D.C. 1971) (three-judge court). Judge Leventhal constructed standards to guide presidential implementation of the Act from (1) its legislative history, which revealed the purposes of the law; (2) prior price control statutes, such as the one upheld in *Yakus*; and (3) judicial power to elaborate on implicit statutory terms, such as a "fairness and equitable" standard, enforceable through judicial review of the executive implementation decisions. In addition, the Court found that the agency's ability to act arbitrarily was blunted by a requirement that it promulgate additional standards to guide its actions taken under the statute. "This requirement, inherent in the Rule of Law and implicit in the Act, means that however broad the discretion of the Executive at the outset, the standard once developed limits the latitude of subsequent Executive action." *Amalgamated Meat Cutters*, 337 F.Supp. at 759. This period was the nadir of the nondelegation doctrine. Cf. *Mistretta v. United States*, 488 U.S. 361 (1989) (unanimously rejecting nondelegation challenge to Sentencing Commission; majority opinion suggests that doctrine might be limited to "giving narrow constructions to statutory delegations that might otherwise be thought to be unconstitutional").

Although no federal statute has been invalidated by the Supreme Court pursuant to the nondelegation doctrine since the 1930s, individual Justices have occasionally invoked the doctrine. See, e.g., *Zemel v. Rusk*, 381 U.S. 1, 20 (1965) (Black, J., dissenting); *Industrial Union Dep't, AFL–CIO v. American Petroleum Institute*, 448 U.S. 607, 685–86 (1980) (Rehnquist, J., dissenting); *American Textile Mfrs. Inst., Inc. v. Donovan*, 452 U.S. 490, 543 (1981) (Rehnquist, J., dissenting). Moreover, some state courts still enforce a nondelegation doctrine.

Notwithstanding the apparent demise of the nondelegation doctrine after *Schechter Poultry*, some scholars find the doctrine to be a useful concept and argue for its resurrection. Political scientist Theodore Lowi, in *The End of Liberalism: The Second Republic of the United States* (2d ed. 1979), argues that legislatures tend to avoid hard political choices by delegating virtually blanket authority to bureaucrats. Public choice theory, discussed in Chapter 1, § 2, reinforces Lowi's point. Public choice theorists posit that legislators' chief motivation is to achieve reelection. One effective method for achieving reelection is for legislators to spend most of their time doing things which their constituents find uncontroversial, such as casework helping constituents wind their way through the bureaucracy and pork barrel projects benefitting their districts. As to substantive legislation, the best strategy is usually to avoid positions that offend important electoral groups in the legislator's district. This can be done through ducking the issue entirely or, if that is impossible, delegating resolution of the most divisive issues to agencies. Following Lowi's argument, one can argue from a public choice perspective that the temptation to pass the substantive buck to agencies is as tempting as it is undemocratic (bureaucrats rather than legislators are making important policy choices) and counterproductive (the choices may be biased if the agency is captured and timid if the agency is not). See David Schoenbrod, *Power without Responsibility: How Congress Abuses the People Through Delegation* (1993).

Professor Mashaw disputes the pessimistic public choice perspective on the nondelegation doctrine, and he argues instead that broad delegations to administrative agencies can sometimes ensure better policymaking. See Jerry L. Mashaw, *Greed, Chaos, and Governance: Using Public Choice to Improve Public Law* 140–157 (1997). He demonstrates that broad delegations may actually reduce rent-seeking by interest groups because they inhibit vote-trading and deal-making. Once power has been delegated to an agency, lawmakers find it more difficult to offer bargains in that issue arena, and administrators cannot make tradeoffs on issues outside their jurisdiction. In fact, some laws that result from the most questionable interest group activity are often very specifically worded to guarantee that bargainers get the deals they struck. Professor Mashaw also argues that voters can often hold members of Congress accountable for broad delegations more easily than they can learn of specific deals found in the details of omnibus legislation. "No one has been able to demonstrate any systematic relationship between improving accountability, or enhancing the public welfare, or respecting the rule of law, and the specificity of legislation." Mashaw goes on to make the affirmative case for broad delegations, arguing that they take advantage of administrative expertise and flexibility. Furthermore, agencies may be more responsive to public desires, because they can often act more quickly than Congress can enact legislation, and they benefit from the President's accountability to a national electorate.[i]

In recent years, the nondelegation doctrine has also enjoyed an indirect revival at the Supreme Court level. Although "the Court has not

---

i. See also Adrian Vermeule, *Judging Under Uncertainty: An Institutional Theory of Legal Interpretation* (2006) (providing institutionalist defense of agency lawmaking and less aggressive judicial review); Elena Kagan, *Presidential Administration*, 114 Harv. L. Rev. 2245 (2001) (emphasizing delegations to the President); Edward L. Rubin, *Law and Legislation in the Administrative State*, 89 Colum. L. Rev. 369 (1989) (offering a pragmatic justification for broad delegations); David Spence & Frank Cross, *A Public Choice Case for the Administrative State*, 89 Geo. L.J. 97 (2000) (using public choice theory to defend broad delegations).

invalidated a statute on [nondelegation] grounds since the 1930s," the Court now "refers to the nondelegation idea as a canon of statutory interpretation rather than as an enforceable constitutional doctrine."[j] When agencies aggressively assert a broad jurisdiction not supported by a congressional authorization, clearly expressed in the statute, the Court will sometimes overrule the agency and insist on a more targeted statutory authorization. Examples include *Whitman*, which rejected a constitutional nondelegation challenge to the Clean Air Act but construed the Act narrowly in light of the apparent limiting principle, and in *MCI v. AT & T* (§ 3 of this chapter), which narrowly construed a telecommunications law on the ground that the broad revisionary authority claimed by the FCC had to be more clearly stated on the face of the statute for the Court to give it effect. See also *FDA v. Brown & Williamson Tobacco Co.* (Chapter 2, § 3B3). If a court is faced with an extremely broad delegation that might implicate constitutional concerns, it uses the canon to adopt a narrow interpretation that would restrain agency discretion. This approach is similar to the one used in *Yakus* or *Amalgamated Meat Cutters*, discussed above, where the courts poured meaning into general statutory language to find intelligible guidelines and procedural requirements to limit agency discretion.

SECTION 2. CONGRESSIONAL INFLUENCE OVER STATUTORY IMPLEMENTATION

As we have seen, Congress delegates a great deal of rulemaking and adjudicatory authority to administrative agencies, subject to the very lenient limits set by the nondelegation doctrine and other more specific limitations explored in this section. Why would Congress hand off so many policy decision to strangers (agencies)? Here is the logic. If legislators decide to enact very specific laws through normal congressional procedures, they face the following costs: information costs as they gather and analyze the data necessary to make wise policy in a detailed way; procedural costs as the laws meet constitutional requirements like bicameralism and presentment; and bargaining costs as they assemble majority support through logrolling. See David Epstein & Sharyn O'Halloran, *Delegating Powers: A Transaction–Cost Approach to Policymaking Under Separate Powers* (1999).

The foregoing logic does not obviate the main problem with delegation, however. If legislators choose to delegate broadly, they face monitoring costs because bureaucrats may have their own policy objectives that diverge from Congress's. Economists would call this an *agency problem* (an

---

j. William N. Eskridge Jr. & Philip P. Frickey, *Quasi–Constitutional Law: Clear Statement Rules as Constitutional Lawmaking*, 45 Vand. L. Rev. 593, 607 (1992). See also Lisa Schultz Bressman, Schechter Poultry *at the Millennium: A Delegation Doctrine for the Administrative State*, 109 Yale L.J. 1399 (2000) (making a similar argument that the doctrine survives in the judicial requirement that agencies adopt rules to limit its discretion). For support in the cases, see, e.g., *Mistretta*, 488 U.S. at 373 n.7; *Industrial Union Dep't, AFL–CIO v. American Petroleum Inst.*, 448 U.S. 607 (1980).

agent may shirk or cheat on duties delegated her by a principal); some political scientists call it *bureaucratic drift*. See Mathew D. McCubbins, Roger G. Noll, & Barry R. Weingast, *Structures and Process, Politics and Policy: Administrative Arrangements and the Political Control of Agencies*, 75 Va. L. Rev. 431, 439 (1989). The interactive structure of law implementation in our constitutional system entrenches the problem of bureaucratic drift.

Consider the creation and implementation of statutes as a political "game," a notion introduced in Chapter 1, § 2. See William N. Eskridge Jr. & John Ferejohn, *The Article I, Section 7 Game*, 80 Geo. L.J. 523 (1992). Each player in the game wants to impose its own policy preferences upon federal statutory policy, but no player will act in a way that subjects it to an immediate override; hence, the game is played backwards, each player anticipating the moves that would be made by the next (much as an attorney anticipates agency and judicial interpretations when she renders advice to a self-interested client). The following notations describe the important points in the game:

SQ	Existing policy (status quo)
H and S	Preferences of the median legislator in the two chambers of the legislature
P	Preferences of the President
h and s	Pivotal voter in veto override in the two chambers of the bicameral legislature
x	Statutory policy resulting from game

Under the circumstances of the Legislation Game, a statute will usually be enacted, for one example, when the status quo is objectionable from the perspectives of both Congress and the President, and their preferences for changing the status quo run in the same direction:

FIGURE 6–1
Legislative Compromise Involving Two Chambers and the President

		x		
P	**H**	**S**		**SQ**

The ultimate statutory policy will fall somewhere between the preferences of the two legislative chambers (H and S). Figure 6–1 describes the political alignments (left being more liberal) during the New Deal and the Great Society, when many modern regulatory statutes were enacted. Indeed, Figure 6–1 reflects the political landscape when Congress enacted the Civil Rights Act of 1964 (the Senate filibuster pushed "x" further to the right than we have it in Figure 6–1, however).

If Congress delegates authority to an executive agency, it is taking something of a political risk. As Figure 6–2 reveals, there is a chance that executive implementation of the statute (x*) will press it toward a much more leftward departure from the status quo than Congress wanted or expected.

FIGURE 6–2
Legislative Compromise, with Delegation to an Executive Agency

x*		x		
P	H	S		SQ
A				
h				

As you see, the agency can set policy virtually anywhere it wants, unless Congress would be stimulated to override the agency's choice. Thus, in Figure 6–2 situations the agency with policy preferences near those of the President can propose any policy, x*, at or to the right of the veto median of the more pro-presidential chamber (h), and Congress cannot successfully challenge this interpretation. Any attempt to do so would be successfully vetoed. Thus, instead of x—the policy that would have been adopted under Article I procedures—the administrative state (after a respectable delay) produces x*. (This is the argument Justice Rehnquist made in *Weber*, the affirmative action case in Chapter 1: the Civil Rights Act adopted a moderate race-blind policy, which the EEOC pressed leftward and the Court ultimately ratified.)

The game continues, of course, and changes policy yet again if a new President or agency is differently aligned from that of the original statute. This indeed happened after 1964. Since 1980, Presidents have been much more conservative than President Johnson, the leader who helped create the Civil Rights Act. Figure 6–3 maps the new preferences:

FIGURE 6–3
Legislative Compromise, with Agency Delegation and a New President

x*		x		x**	
P	H	S		P**	SQ
A				A**	

Thus, in addition to the problem of bureaucratic drift, Figure 6–3 reveals a further problem of a *bureaucratic yo-yo*, where statutory policy bounces around, depending on who is elected President. Thus, the Reagan Administration cut back on diversity and affirmative action policies in the 1980s, while the Clinton Administration sought to revive them in the 1990s. The yo-yo problem would trouble Congress because statutory policy would not only deviate from its aggregated preferences, but also because the stable rule of law itself would be threatened.

Neither the bureaucratic drift nor the yo-yo problem is, in practice, as dramatic as the three figures suggest. The reason is that Congress has responded with various mechanisms to protect against problems of drift and yo-yo'ing. As in the rest of politics and government, nothing works perfectly well (or perfectly badly), but everything has some effect, often unanticipated of course.

Some of the mechanisms—notably oversight (Part A of this section), budgetary pressures (Part B), and legislative vetoes (Part C)—are ways that later Congresses try to influence, control, or check agency implementation of earlier-adopted statutes. Over time, these mechanisms do little to protect the original deal, but they do help the agency update the deal to account for new political circumstances and they may help prevent the agency from straying too far from the statutory purposes. On the other hand, because congressional subgroups are disproportionately influential in these mechanisms, they offer opportunities for rent-seeking and partiality that might cut against the public interest as well as the original deal.

Other mechanisms—tenure protections (Part D), agency design (Part E), and judicial review (Part F)—offer potentially greater protection for the original legislative policy choices and, perhaps, the public interest as well. This chapter's case study of the Motor Vehicle Safety Act, however, counsels against undue optimism on this front as well. Tenure protections might keep incompetents in place, design features often work poorly and will have unintended consequences over time, and judicial review is not the cure-all that law professors have traditionally maintained.

A. Legislative Oversight and Investigation

A Congress that has delegated much of its lawmaking authority to agencies would rationally seek to monitor those agencies to assure their continued adherence to the original legislative delegation. Before 1933, there were few agencies to oversee, and Congress devoted little effort to monitoring. Agencies proliferated during the New Deal. Congress responded with the Legislative Reorganization Act of 1946, 60 Stat. 812, codified at 2 U.S.C. § 31 et al., which signaled a new commitment to oversight and started a process by which Congress and its committees added legislative staff to accomplish this goal. The goal of such legislation was to assure majoritarian (i.e., congressional) monitoring of agency implementation. See generally Frederick M. Kaiser, Report: Congressional Oversight (Cong., Res. Serv., updated Jan. 2006), available at http://www.fas.org/sgp/crs/misc/97-936.pdf (viewed Jan. 1, 2012).

Political scientists worry that structural problems impede effective legislative oversight.[a] Thus, legislative oversight committees may become captured by the same forces that capture agencies—interested persons and firms, who provide information, ideas, and encouragement. Also, motivations of legislators are more important in determining oversight activity than is the availability of resources. "Unless [oversight] reveals a scandalous situation with possibilities for favorable publicity for the legislators, the work is considered dull and potentially troublesome." Bernard Rosen,

---

a. E.g., Walter J. Oleszek, Congressional Procedure and the Policy Process 274–97 (2005); Morris Ogul, Congressional Oversight: Structures and Incentives, in Congress Reconsidered 317 (Lawrence Dodd & Bruce Oppenheimer eds., 2d ed. 1981).

Holding Government Bureaucracies Accountable 21 (1982). There are opportunity costs for oversight; time spent monitoring agencies is time away from fundraising, casework, and enacting new programs to benefit constituents. The latter are activities that often mean more to a legislator's reelection chances than tedious oversight. Finally, and most important, partisan politics can eviscerate oversight. In periods where Congress is controlled by the same political party as the President (1993–95, 2003–07, 2009–11), one would expect little critical oversight. On the other hand, when at least one branch of Congress and the President are controlled by different parties, as has been the norm (1981–93, 1995–2001, May 2001–03, 2007–09, 2011–13), one would expect to see more aggressive oversight.

Notwithstanding this analysis, between 1980 and 2010, committee hearings steadily declined in both the House and the Senate, with only half as many 2009–10 hearings in each body as there were in 1979–80.[b] This might suggest that oversight activity has fallen off greatly, but much of the oversight done by legislators is informal. Lawmakers jawbone agency officials as policy is formulated, or they intervene on behalf of constituents to present arguments and perspectives. Although rules prohibit some forms of *ex parte* communications, particularly during formal adjudication, there are numerous ways for members of Congress to communicate with bureaucrats as rules as being considered. Mark Moran and Barry Weingast, for example, argue that the FTC is strongly influenced by subtle messages sent outside the formal oversight process and that this influence is statistically significant for both enforcement and policymaking initiatives by the FTC.[c] See also Joel D. Auerbach, *Keeping A Watchful Eye: The Politics of Congressional Oversight* (1990), arguing that vigorous congressional oversight is responsive to public demands for greater government accountability.

Various mechanisms exist to provide members of Congress with information that alerts them to the need for aggressive oversight or that supports them as they engage in monitoring. Mathew D. McCubbins and Thomas Schwartz describe two kinds of monitoring strategies. See *Congressional Oversight Overlooked: Police Patrols Versus Fire Alarms*, 28 Am. J. Pol. Sci. 165 (1984). A *police patrol* strategy is time-consuming as legislators and their staffs regularly monitor to discover bureaucratic drift. In contrast, a *fire alarm* strategy saves congressional resources as members wait to hear the alarm raised by interest parties upset about agency policy. Once the alarm has been sounded, members can begin aggressive oversight, and they can ignore areas where no discontent is evident. In this way, lawmakers externalize some of the costs of oversight, perhaps

---

b. See Suzy Khimm, "The Decline of Congressional Oversight, in One Chart" (Nov. 29, 2011), available at http://www.washingtonpost.com/blogs/ezra-klein/post/the-decline-of-congressional-oversight-in-one-chart/2011/11/29/gIQAwq078N_blog.html (viewed Jan. 1, 2012).

c. Barry R. Weingast & Mark J. Moran, *Bureaucratic Discretion or Congressional Control? Regulatory Policymaking at the Federal Trade Commission*, 91 J. Pol. Econ. 765 (1983); Barry R. Weingast & Mark J. Moran, *The Myth of the Runaway Bureaucracy: The Case of the FTC*, Regulation, May/June 1982, at 33. See also John Ferejohn & Charles Shipan, *Congressional Influence on Bureaucracy*, 6 J.L. Econ. & Org. 1 (1990) (special issue).

engaging in police patrols only in arenas without much interest group activity and thus with less possibility of alarms.

Even when Congress engages in vigorous oversight activity, however, there are problems that concern thoughtful observers.

1. *The Problem of Regulatory Priorities and Efficacy.* Oversight hearings may push agencies away from their public-regarding agendas. With their scarce resources, committed agencies have their hands full devising workable strategies and fighting off industry attacks. If an oversight committee is controlled or influenced by the regulated industry, it can pressure the agency toward less intrusive (and often less efficacious) modes of regulation. Even well-intended oversight might undermine agency efficacy if it adds more to the agency's plate, as illustrated in the auto safety area.[d]

Recall that the NHTSA's biggest regulatory initiative was Standard 208, which required automakers to produce cars that would protect passengers against injury under specified performance criteria. Manufacturers could meet the standard with airbags, automatic seat belts, and other mechanisms. For various institutional reasons, after 1971, the only way to comply with the standard was an "ignition interlock" system, whereby the car would not start until all passengers engaged their seatbelts. The public was not pleased. Drivers disengaged their interlocks (which were mandatory for the 1974 auto market) and wrote their members of Congress against this intrusion into their "freedom to drive."

Responding to public outrage, Congress held several oversight hearings, and the result was a massive disruption in the agency's regulatory program. On the one hand, the auto industry and elected representatives alike had a field day deriding the interlock system. Senator Norris Cotton joked, to great laughter, that his car would not start when he placed groceries in the passenger's seat. Instead of placing them on the floor, the New Hampshire legislator seat-belted "a pound of cheese and a loaf of bread" to satisfy the system. Although the experts maintained that ignition interlocks saved lives, popular resentment about inconveniences and infringements on their freedom to drive overwhelmed the theoretical safety gains.

On the other hand, oversight focused on a minor problem: school bus design. Of the more than 54,000 annual deaths as a result of auto accidents, the agency found only a few dozen where an expensive school bus redesign might have saved the lives of schoolchildren. (As many as 80% of child deaths from school bus accidents occurred *outside* of the bus.) Even sympathetic members of Congress were appalled by agency's failure to focus on *children's deaths* because of school bus accidents. Representative Les Aspin, a liberal, berated the agency for "misusing the concept of cost-benefit analysis" (Mashaw, *Story of* State Farm, 363–65).

---

d. See Jerry L. Mashaw, *The Story of* State Farm, in *Administrative Law Stories* 334, 357–67 (Peter L. Strauss ed., 2006).

The upshot of all this oversight was the Motor Vehicle and Schoolbus Safety Amendments of 1974, described earlier. These amendments forbade imposition of the ignition interlock (which saved hundreds and probably thousands of lives each year) and required the agency to impose stringent new design requirements on schoolbuses (which might save a life or three each year, at much greater expense). As Professor Mashaw wearily concludes, "[i]f Congress had wanted to protect the lives of children, it would have done better to re-energize NHTSA's lagging standard-setting enterprise as it applied to the passenger car" (*id.* at 367).

2. *Congressional Oversight and Individual Rights.* When Congress or its committees exercise vigorous oversight power, there may be problems involving overreaching or violation of individual rights. In the 1950s, several congressional committees engaged in what many regard as a "witch hunt" for Communists and "homosexuals" in American government and society. The legislative investigations often seemed bent on ruining peoples' reputations rather than on serving valid legislative goals, and courts through the 1950s and 1960s sometimes overturned contempt citations against uncooperative witnesses.

The leading case was *Watkins v. United States*, 354 U.S. 178 (1957), in which the Supreme Court overturned a contempt conviction based upon its finding that the House Un–American Activities Committee had ventured far beyond its House-authorized arena of investigation. See also Judge Weinfeld's decision in *United States v. Lamont*, 18 F.R.D. 27 (S.D.N.Y. 1955), aff'd, 236 F.2d 312 (2d Cir. 1956), which made similar findings for the Senate's Permanent Subcommittee on Investigations (chaired by Joseph McCarthy). Chief Justice Warren's opinion in *Watkins* suggested, moreover, that legislative investigations are limited to building a factual record for proposed legislation and providing information for the exercise of legislative insight. "We have no doubt that there is no congressional power to expose for the sake of exposure," concluded Warren. 354 U.S. at 200.

Although *Watkins'* holding was based on lack of "pertinency" of the questions asked to the mission delegated to the committee by Congress, Chief Justice Warren's concerns included the process's threat to First Amendment freedoms (354 U.S. at 197):

> Abuses of the investigative process may imperceptibly lead to abridgment of protected freedoms. The mere summoning of a witness and compelling him to testify, against his will, about his beliefs, expressions or associations is a measure of governmental interference. And when those forced revelations concern matters that are unorthodox, unpopular, or even hateful to the general public, the reaction in the life of the witness may be disastrous. This effect is even more harsh when it is past beliefs, expressions or associations that are disclosed and judged by current standards rather than those contemporary with the matters exposed. * * *

3. *The Problem of Agency Defiance and Executive Privilege.* A final problem with legislative oversight is that even when it is vigorous and public-seeking—and respectful of individual rights—it may face frustrating obstacles to obtaining information from the agency, particularly one located in the executive branch. Some of the recent oversight hearings during the Clinton and Bush–Cheney Administrations demonstrate that difficulty, as well as the political aspects of oversight. Perhaps one of the best examples of an oversight proceeding stymied by the need to obtain data from the executive branch arose out of the 1982 skirmish between two House subcommittees and EPA Administrator Anne Burford Gorsuch over the EPA's allegedly lax enforcement of the Superfund Act's program for cleaning up existing hazardous waste-dumping sites.[e]

In the Gorsuch dispute, the EPA refused to turn over many documents which the subcommittees demanded. The General Counsel to the House Clerk opined that the subcommittees were entitled to those documents under their *Watkins* authority to investigate reported abuses in enforcement. In a memorandum analyzing the House position, the Office of Legal Counsel countered that the most relevant Supreme Court decision is *United States v. Nixon*, 418 U.S. 683 (1974), which found a constitutional basis for claims of executive privilege and held such claims superseded only in unusual circumstances, such as to provide evidence to be used in the criminal trials of former White House officials involved in the Watergate Scandal.

Ultimately, the Public Works Committee recommended that the House hold Gorsuch in contempt, which it did on December 16, 1982. See *United States v. House of Representatives of the United States*, 556 F.Supp. 150 (D.D.C. 1983) (dismissing Department of Justice lawsuit trying to head off contempt citation). In February and March 1983, the Administration reached compromises with the relevant subcommittees; in each case the Administration agreed to let the subcommittee examine enforcement documents, with protections to assure confidentiality. Gorsuch resigned as EPA Administrator on March 9, 1983.

B. Congress' Budgetary and Appropriations Power

Under Article I, Section 8, clauses 1 and 18 and Section 9, clause 7, Congress has virtually plenary power to determine how the United States' money will be spent. This power of the purse gives Congress an ongoing substantive power as well. For example, the power of the purse and oversight activities that we discussed previously are related. Much oversight occurs when programs are reauthorized or receive appropriations, not only in primary-purpose oversight hearings. Auerbach, *Keeping a Watchful Eye*, 130–33. The use of spending control to influence executive branch actions works in several different ways.

---

e. Our description is a synopsis of the detailed account in Harold H. Bruff & Peter M. Shane, *The Law of Presidential Powers: Cases and Materials* (1988); Peter M. Shane, *Legal Disagreement and Negotiation in a Government of Laws: The Case of Executive Privilege Claims Against Congress*, 71 Minn. L. Rev. 461 (1987).

The statute establishing a program or agency does not also appropriate money to fund its activities. With regard to discretionary spending programs, the authorization process is separate from the appropriations process. Thus, the level of funding for an agency will depend, in part, upon Congress' attitude toward the statutory scheme and the agency. An agency might have a strong incentive to move statutory policy close to the House or Senate position even though the agency's preferred policy would be protected by a presidential veto, if the agency fears that Congress will fail to fund it adequately in retaliation for the agency's policy position. This reveals a potential advantage the appropriations power gives Congress: Because the agency needs each Congress to act affirmatively to give it money, the agency has a strong and continuing incentive not to adopt policies that rile congressional, or even just committee, majorities.

It is hard to tell how important the appropriations power is, however. The main limitation involves a coordination problem: the oversight committee cannot routinely pressure the agency to adopt new substantive policies by threatening to cut off funds, because separate subcommittees of the chamber's appropriations committee control funding. Unless the two different congressional entities share the same political preferences *and* can coordinate their activities, the funding weapon will be hard to deploy. Moreover, the preferences of the two committees can be expected to diverge much of the time. Because of the requirements of the congressional budget process, the appropriations subcommittees are usually required to operate under a zero-sum mentality more often than the corresponding substantive committees: the primary goal of appropriations subcommittees is to meet certain budget needs, while the primary goal of substantive committees is to solve social or economic problems. The NHTSA was caught in this bind. It received ample funding in the 1960s but suffered budget cuts as a consequence of general tightening-the-belt during the Nixon Administration and beyond. Even though the substantive committees were still quite keen on auto safety, the President and the appropriations committees were much more concerned with other budgetary priorities. Moreover, when Congress did bestir itself to focus on auto safety concerns, as during the interlock controversy in 1973–74, it has been more likely to make the agency's job more difficult (with diminishing funds) by curtailing unpopular regulatory options and adding low priority issues (school bus safety) to the already crowded agency agenda.

Congress' spending power can be used as a mechanism of control in less direct ways than by underfunding a particular agency. For example, committee reports accompanying appropriations bills may include directives to agencies about how the money should be spent. Reports contain line items with specific instructions to fund particular projects, usually in the districts of key congressional players. Although language in committee reports is not legally binding, agencies usually follow the mandates in order to retain the goodwill of the appropriators whom they will face again next year.

Congress will sometimes include substantive restrictions in appropriations measures, which are legally binding because they meet the constitutional requirements for laws. This occurs even though congressional rules often forbid riders or other substantive legislation on an appropriations bill. The Congressional Research Service reports that Congress frequently—and successfully—deploys appropriations riders in order to influence agency enforcement priorities. See Curtis W. Copeland, Cong. Research Serv., *Congressional Influence on Rulemaking and Regulation Through Appropriations Restrictions* (2008).

The Supreme Court has conservatively applied substantive provisions in appropriations measures. For example, repeals by implication are especially disfavored in the appropriations context. E.g., *TVA v. Hill*, 437 U.S. 153, 190 (1978) (Chapter 2, § 3A), where the Court refused to credit continued congressional funding of the Tellico Dam as an amendment to the Endangered Species Act (ESA). On the other hand, Congress may amend substantive law in an appropriations statute, as long as it does so clearly. E.g., *Robertson v. Seattle Audubon Society*, 503 U.S. 429 (1992), where the Court applied an appropriations rider to allow timber-cutting that threatened the habitat of an endangered species (the spotted owl), which would otherwise have been a violation of the ESA. For a skeptical examination of the Court's approach, see Matthew D. McCubbins & Daniel B. Rodriguez, *Canonical Construction and Statutory Revisionism: The Strange Case of the Appropriations Canon*, 14 Law & Contemp. Probs. 669 (2005).

C. The Legislative Veto of Agency Rules

Another response to the tension between administrative lawmaking and majoritarian government has been the development of the *legislative veto*. The legislative veto is generally any statutory mechanism that renders the implementation or the continuing implementation of agency decisions or actions subject to some further form of legislative review or control, usually for a specified time period. The purpose of the legislative veto is to provide a quick mechanism to slow down or overturn administrative actions that are unresponsive to the legislature's aims in the original authorizing statute, without going through the obstacle course of the full legislative process. Hence, the power to nullify an administrative decision has been vested in joint action of both chambers of the legislature, action by only one house, or action by a legislative committee. (At the state level, there have been mechanisms for suspension, rather than veto, of agency decisions by joint legislative committees.) Any of these procedures is more streamlined than the normal legislative process; even a two-house legislative veto avoids the presentment clause. Getting around the President is important because he would presumably veto most legislative nullifications of regulations passed by agencies in his government, thereby requiring a supermajority in each house to implement congressional preferences.

The form of the veto can be either negative or positive. A *negative veto provision* (the typical one) stipulates that administrative decisions will be effective, unless the legislature or its designated subgroup actually disapproves the decisions. A *positive veto provision* requires legislative approval of the administrative decision before it becomes effective. A related concept is *laying over*: The executive or an agency is required to submit proposed decisions to the legislature or a designated subgroup, and the decisions do not go into effect for a specified period of time so that the full legislature can have an opportunity to study and take action on the proposed decisions. The Congressional Review Act of 1996, Pub. L. No. 104–121, establishes such a procedure. The law requires agencies promulgating rules to submit those rules to Congress, which has 60 days to disapprove or overturn it through enactment of a joint resolution signed by the President or passed over his veto.

The negative legislative veto was used sporadically in the early part of this century and was an important part of the Reorganization Act of 1932, 47 Stat. 382. Although President Hoover objected to the legislative veto in the 1932 Act as violating separation of powers, he accepted the provision in order to get the power to make changes in the executive branch. It was not until the 1970s that the negative legislative veto became a popular mechanism for greater legislative oversight of the administrative process. A Library of Congress study for the period 1932 to 1975 found 295 congressional review provisions in 196 federal statutes; for the year 1975 alone, there were 58 provisions in 21 statutes. Clark Norton, *Congressional Review, Deferral and Disapproval of Executive Actions: A Summary and Inventory of Statutory Authority* 8–12 (1976). When Congress revisited the Motor Vehicle Safety Act in 1974, it required that any future regulation of passive restraints be subject to a two-house legislative veto.

The concept of the legislative veto also drew criticisms from political scientists, who argued that they created as many problems for popular government as they solved, and from legal scholars, who argued that they were hard to reconcile with the concept of separation of powers. These constitutional concerns, and the political objections, generated a series of challenges to legislative vetoes at both the state and federal level.

Immigration & Naturalization Service v. Chadha, 462 U.S. 919 (1983). Section 244(c)(2) of the Immigration and Nationality Act (8 U.S.C. § 1254(c)(2)) authorized one chamber of Congress, by resolution, to invalidate a decision by the executive to allow a deportable alien to remain in the United States. Chadha was an East Indian born in Kenya and holding a British passport. Pursuant to the Act, Chadha was able to obtain a suspension of his deportation. He had been deportable because he remained in the United States after the expiration of his nonimmigrant student visa. At the behest of Representative Eilberg, Chair of the Judiciary Committee Subcommittee on Immigration, the House overrode the suspension of Chadha's deportation. After the House action, the immigration judge reopened Chadha's case and ordered him deported. Chadha appealed the order through the Department of Justice, and then to the federal courts. The Ninth Circuit declared § 244(c)(2) unconstitutional. The Supreme Court affirmed.

Chief Justice Burger's opinion for the Court relied on Article I, Section 7, the bicameralism and presentment requirements for congressional statutes and resolutions having the force of law. "These provisions of Art. I are integral parts of the constitutional design for the separation of powers." Thus, the presentment clauses of Article I, Section 7 were carefully debated at the Philadelphia Convention. "The decision to provide the President with a limited and qualified power to nullify proposed legislation by veto was based on the profound conviction of the Framers that the powers conferred on Congress were the powers to be most carefully circumscribed. It is beyond doubt that lawmaking was a power to be shared by both Houses and the President. In The Federalist No. 73 (H. Lodge ed., 1888), [Alexander] Hamilton focused on the President's role in making laws:

'If even no propensity had ever discovered itself in the legislative body to invade the rights of the Executive, the rules of just reasoning and theoretic propriety would of themselves teach us that the one ought not to be left to the mercy of the other, but ought to possess a constitutional and effectual power of self-defense.' *Id.*, at 457–458.

See also The Federalist No. 51 [(James Madison)]. In his Commentaries on the Constitution, Joseph Story makes the same point. 1 J. Story, Commentaries on the Constitution of the United States 614–615 (3d ed. 1858).

"The President's role in the lawmaking process also reflects the Framers' careful efforts to check whatever propensity a particular Congress might have to enact oppressive, improvident, or ill-considered measures. The President's veto role in the legislative process was described later during public debate on ratification:

'It establishes a salutary check upon the legislative body, calculated to guard the community against the effects of faction, precipitancy, or of any impulse unfriendly to the public good which may happen to influence a majority of that body * * *. The primary inducement to conferring the power in question upon the Executive is to enable him to defend himself; the secondary one is to increase the chances in favor of the community against the passing of bad laws through haste, inadvertence, or design.' The Federalist No. 73, *supra*, at 458 (A. Hamilton).

See also *The Pocket Veto Case*, 279 U.S. 655, 678 (1929); *Myers v. United States*, 272 U.S. 52, 123 (1926). The Court also has observed that the Presentment Clauses serve the important purpose of assuring that a 'national' perspective is grafted on the legislative process:

'The President is a representative of the people just as the members of the Senate and of the House are, and it may be, at some times, on some subjects, that the President elected by all the people is rather more representative of them all than are the members of either body of the Legislature whose constituencies are local and not country-wide. . . .' *Myers v. United States*, [272 U.S. 52, 123 (1926)].

"The bicameral requirement of Art. I, §§ 1, 7 was of scarcely less concern to the Framers than was the Presidential veto and indeed the two concepts are interdependent. By providing that no law could take effect without the concurrence of the prescribed majority of the Members of both Houses, the Framers reemphasized their belief, already remarked upon in connection with the Presentment Clauses, that legislation should not be enacted unless it has been carefully and fully considered by the Nation's elected officials. In the Constitutional Convention debates on the need for a bicameral legislature, James Wilson, later to become a Justice of this Court, commented:

> 'Despotism comes on mankind in different shapes. Sometimes in an Executive, sometimes in a military, one. Is there danger of a Legislative despotism? Theory & practice both proclaim it. If the Legislative authority be not restrained, there can be neither liberty nor stability; and it can only be restrained by dividing it within itself, into distinct and independent branches. In a single house there is no check, but the inadequate one, of the virtue & good sense of those who compose it.' 1 M. Farrand, *supra*, at 254. * * *

These observations are consistent with what many of the Framers expressed, none more cogently than Madison in pointing up the need to divide and disperse power in order to protect liberty:

> 'In republican government, the legislative authority necessarily predominates. The remedy for this inconveniency is to divide the legislature into different branches; and to render them, by different modes of election and different principles of action, as little connected with each other as the nature of their common functions and their common dependence on the society will admit.' The Federalist No. 51, *supra*, at 324.

See also The Federalist No. 62 [(James Madison)]."

For those reasons, Chief Justice Burger concluded that the Court must strictly enforce both the presentment and the bicameralism requirements whenever Congress was seeking to exercise its *legislative* power. "Not every action taken by either House is subject to the bicameralism and presentment requirements of Art. I. Whether actions taken by either House are, in law and fact, an exercise of legislative power depends not on their form but upon 'whether they contain matter which is properly to be regarded as legislative in its character and effect.' S.Rep. No. 1335, 54th Cong., 2d Sess., 8 (1897)."

The House resolution abrogating the suspension of Chadha's deportation was such an action, because it "had the purpose and effect of altering the legal rights, duties and relations of persons, including the Attorney General, Executive Branch officials and Chadha, all outside the legislative branch. Section 244(c)(2) purports to authorize one House of Congress to require the Attorney General to deport an individual alien whose deportation otherwise would be cancelled under § 244. The one-House veto operated in this case to overrule the Attorney General and mandate Chadha's deportation; absent the House action, Chadha would remain in the United States. Congress has *acted* and its action has altered Chadha's status."

"The veto authorized by § 244(c)(2) doubtless has been in many respects a convenient shortcut; the 'sharing' with the Executive by Congress of its authority over aliens in this manner is, on its face, an appealing compromise. In purely practical terms, it is obviously easier for action to be taken by one House without submission to the President; but it is crystal clear from the records of the Convention, contemporaneous writings and debates, that the Framers ranked other values higher than efficiency. The records of the Convention and debates in the states preceding ratification underscore the common desire to define and limit the exercise of the newly created federal powers affecting the states and the people. There is unmistakable expression of a determination that legislation by the national Congress be a step-by-step, deliberate and deliberative process."

Justice Powell concurred only in the Court's judgment. He was unwilling to strike down the hundreds of legislative veto provisions that Congress had included in laws since the New Deal. "One reasonably may disagree with Congress' assessment of the veto's utility, but the respect due its judgment as a coordinate branch of Government cautions that our holding should be no more extensive than necessary to decide those cases. In my view, the case may be decided on a narrower ground. When Congress finds that a particular person does not satisfy the statutory criteria for permanent residence in this country it has assumed a judicial function in violation of the principle of separation of powers."

The argument of Justice Powell's opinion proceeded in three steps: First, the policy underlying constitutional separation of powers is that "[t]he accumulation of all powers legislative, executive and judiciary in the same hands * * * may justly be pronounced the very definition of tyranny." The Federalist No. 47 (James Madison). Second, the greatest separation of powers concern at the time the Constitution was adopted was that the legislature would arrogate too much power in its own hands. Some of the state legislatures had offended justice by deciding essentially judicial controversies involving individual rather than group rights. See The Federalist No. 48 (James Madison). Third, this is exactly what happened in *Chadha*: By applying a general rule to the six specific immigration cases, part of the legislature was doing something that appeared, to Justice Powell, to be "clearly adjudicatory." This situation, therefore, "raises the very danger the Framers sought to avoid—the exercise of unchecked power." Justice Powell also warned that because Congress does not operate in a judicial tradition, with regularized due process and other procedural safeguards, its adventitious intervention is most likely to deprive persons of their rights arbitrarily.

Justice White was the only dissenter. He characterized the legislative veto as "an important if not indispensable political invention that allows the President and Congress to resolve major constitutional and policy differences, assures the accountability of independent regulatory agencies, and preserves Congress' control over lawmaking. Perhaps there are other means of accommodation and accountability, but the increasing reliance of Congress upon the legislative veto suggests that the alternatives to which Congress must now turn are not entirely satisfactory."

"The history of the legislative veto also makes clear that it has not been a sword with which Congress has struck out to aggrandize itself at the expense of the other branches—the concerns of Madison and Hamilton. Rather, the veto has been a means of defense, a reservation of ultimate authority necessary if Congress is to fulfill its designated role under Article I as the Nation's lawmaker. While the President has often objected to particular legislative vetoes, generally those left in the hands of congressional committees, the Executive has more often agreed to legislative review as the price for a broad delegation of authority. To be sure, the President may have preferred unrestricted power, but that could be precisely why Congress thought it essential to retain a check on the exercise of delegated authority."

Justice White expressed concern that the Court should leap to invalidate all legislative vetoes on constitutional grounds when (1) the Constitution seems to offer no specific objection to the legislative veto; (2) Congress in the last 50 years has enacted hundreds of legislative vetoes without apparent constitutional qualms; (3) commentators are, at best, divided over the usefulness or invalidity of the device. Given the deep ambiguity of the constitutional or policy issues, the Court is unwise to sweep so broadly with its reasoning.

"The Court's holding today that all legislative-type action must be enacted through the lawmaking process ignores that legislative authority is routinely delegated to the Executive Branch, to the independent regulatory agencies, and to private individuals and groups. * * * There is no question but that agency rulemaking is lawmaking in any functional or realistic sense of the term. The Administrative Procedure Act, 5 U.S.C. § 551(4) provides that a 'rule' is an agency statement 'designed to implement, interpret, or prescribe law or policy.' When agencies are authorized to prescribe law through substantive rulemaking, the administrator's regulation is not only due deference, but is accorded 'legislative effect.' See, *e.g., Schweiker v. Gray Panthers*, 453 U.S. 34, 43–44 (1981); *Batterton v. Francis*, 432 U.S. 416 (1977). These regulations bind courts and officers of the federal government, may pre-empt state law, see, *e.g., Fidelity Federal Savings & Loan Assoc. v. De la Cuesta*, 458 U.S. 141 (1982), and grant rights to and impose obligations on the public. In sum, they have the force of law.

"If Congress may delegate lawmaking power to independent and executive agencies, it is most difficult to understand Article I as prohibiting Congress from also reserving a check on legislative power for itself. Absent the veto, the agencies receiving delegations of legislative or quasi-legislative power may issue regulations having the force of law without bicameral approval and without the President's signature. It is thus not apparent why the reservation of a veto over the exercise of that legislative power must be subject to a more exacting test. In both cases, it is enough that the initial statutory authorizations comply with the Article I requirements."

NOTES ON THE LEGISLATIVE VETO AND STRUCTURAL SEPARATION OF POWERS

1. *Different Visions of the Structure of the Constitution.* The three *Chadha* opinions offer different visions of the structures of constitutional law. The opinions of Justices Powell and White (who would allow legislative vetoes in many instances) take a functional approach to the separation of powers concept. Their main concern is that Congress should not usurp duties given to the executive (Justice White) or judicial (Justice Powell) powers. See U.S. Const. arts. I–III.[f]

The Chief Justice's opinion seems to focus on a distinct but related issue of the circumstances under which Congress can legislate, pursuant to Article I, § 7. Because the Framers considered the lawmaking branch the most dangerous arm of government, they limited the instances in which Congress could act decisively by erecting anti-majoritarian barriers within the legislative process—bicameralism and presentment to the President. If Congress can make "law" without going through both Houses of Congress and the President, then there is a greater danger of abuse of legislative power, Chief Justice Burger contends. Is the Chief Justice right in focusing on this feature of the Constitution, and treating it so strictly? His approach has been termed a formalist one, in contrast to the more functional approach reflected in the other opinions. How do Justices Powell and White justify their different focus?

2. *Policy Arguments.* Underlying the different constitutional visions of the various opinions in *Chadha* are probably different attitudes about the necessity or usefulness of the legislative veto. See generally Jessica Korn, *The Power of Separation: American Constitutionalism and the Myth of the Legislative Veto* (1997), and the articles cited in note "f."

The chief argument for the legislative veto is that once the Court has allowed Congress to delegate enormous lawmaking power to agencies, with virtually no enforceable guidelines, Congress ought to be allowed to attach "strings" to that delegation, especially strings that allow the democratic

---

f. For a variety of well-informed, thoughtful perspectives on the separation of powers questions entailed in the legislative veto debate, see, Stanley Brubaker, *Slouching Toward Constitutional Duty: The Legislative Veto and the Delegation of Authority,* 1 Const. Comment. 81 (1984); E. Donald Elliott, INS v. Chadha: *The Administrative Constitution, the Constitution, and the Legislative Veto,* 1983 Sup. Ct. Rev. 125; Victoria F. Nourse, *The Vertical Separation of Powers,* 49 Duke L.J. 749 (1999), and Nourse, *Toward a New Anatomy of Constitutional Structure,* 56 Stan. L. Rev. 835 (2004).

process (Congress) to provide agencies with feedback having greater bite than oversight hearings. Moreover, the legislative veto provides flexibility in the conduct of public affairs in situations that could not have been foreseen by the Framers. Congress does not have the capacity to oversee the complicated regulatory state, and if it attempted to do so, the machinery of government would grind to a halt.

There are a number of policy arguments against the legislative veto. First, the legislative veto might distort the legislative process. Legislation that would otherwise fail will pass if key legislators know that later they will have the opportunity to block offending provisions through the use of the legislative veto. This allows Congress to appear to be addressing hard questions, when in fact the legislative veto will thwart any substantial action by an administrative agency to address those questions.

Second, the legislative veto makes agencies vitally concerned with the views of entities other than the enacting Congress, which may be problematic. For example, because interest in the legislation will be lower when, months or years after its passage, the agency proposes implementing regulations, the task of reviewing those regulations will fall upon the congressional committees and subcommittees. "Thus a likely and apparently common occurrence is a significant skewing of the original legislative intent towards the interest of the congressmen on the overseeing committee or subcommittee and the groups and people most responsible for their re-election." Brubaker, *Legislative Veto,* 92. If committees are comprised of members with preferences more extreme than that of the body, a one-committee legislative veto may produce regulations far away from the preferences of the median legislator. In addition, the legislative veto allows subsequent Congresses a great deal of influence over the implementation of statutes passed in the past. Although this may allow for useful updating of policy without going through the procedural hurdles to enact new legislation, it may also allow for substantial shifts from the original intent of the enactors. Consider how a committee in a conservative Republican Congress might influence policies enacted by more liberal Democratic Congresses with very different ideological commitments. Is that legitimate?[g]

Third, the legislative veto may have encouraged very broad delegations because Congress could exert continuing and effective control over the agencies as they exercised their delegated authority. In other words, the incentive to constrain agency discretion *ex ante* by enacting detailed and precise statutes is less compelling if Congress has *ex post* tools to constrain agencies. For those who object to broad delegations, perhaps on the ground that they reduce political accountability, this possibility is disturbing. An excellent empirical study of the legislative veto suggests that it had some effect on the breadth of congressional delegations. See Korn, *The Power of Separation.* For example, after *Chadha* invalidated the legislative veto, members of Congress rescinded broad authority given the Secretary of Education with respect to Pell Grants and enacted their policy preferences more precisely. But other

---

g. See Michael E. Herz, *The Legislative Veto in Times of Political Reversal:* Chadha *and the 104th Congress,* 14 Const. Comment. 319 (1997) (using game theory to demonstrate how legislative vetoes could radically shift regulatory outcomes when the partisan makeup of Congress changes). See also Eskridge & Ferejohn, *Article I, Section 7 Game.*

forces, practical and political, continue to discourage legislators from using specific and detailed statutory directive to reduce agency discretion, so the effect of *Chadha* in this area has not been substantial.

3. *Severability of Unconstitutional Legislative Veto Provisions.* In *Alaska Airlines v. Brock*, 480 U.S. 678 (1987), the Supreme Court held that a legislative veto provision contained in the Airlines Deregulation Act of 1978, 92 Stat. 1705, was severable from the remainder of the statute. The Court suggested the following approach (*id.* at 685):

> In considering this question [of severability] in the context of a legislative veto, it is necessary to recognize that the absence of the veto necessarily alters the balance of powers between the Legislative and Executive Branches of the Federal Government. Thus, it is not only appropriate to evaluate the importance of the veto in the original legislative bargain, but also to consider the nature of the delegated authority that Congress made subject to a veto. Some delegations of power to the Executive or to an independent agency may have been so controversial or so broad that Congress would have been unwilling to make the delegation without a strong oversight mechanism. The final test, for legislative vetoes as well as for other provisions, is the traditional one: the unconstitutional provisions must be severed unless the statute created in its absence is legislation that Congress would not have enacted.

Under this approach, the provision would seem nonseverable: The employee protections title was the only one in which Congress inserted a legislative veto, and that title was controversial. One concern about the title was that it would be administered by the Secretary of Labor, and therefore not under the normal oversight of the transportation committees. A House sponsor specifically spoke of the importance of the legislative veto to the employee protection title, and no one said anything to the contrary. Yet the Court found the legislative veto severable, mainly by starting with a presumption of severability. See *Heckler v. Mathews*, 465 U.S. 728, 738 & n.5 (1984). Is this defensible?

4. *The Impact of* Chadha. Congressional scholar Louis Fisher reports that many statutes enacted after *Chadha* continue to include legislative vetoes, and administrative agencies regularly attend to them as though they were the "law," seeking committee permission for certain decisions. See Louis Fisher, *The Legislative Veto: Invalidated, It Survives*, 56 Law & Contemp. Probs. 273 (1993).

On the other hand, Jessica Korn argues that other mechanisms, constitutional under *Chadha*, can and do work just as well as the legislative veto. She examines the subsequent history of the legislative veto in the Jackson–Vanik Amendment to the Trade Act of 1974, which terminated most-favored nation (MFN) trade status upon the vote of one house of Congress. Korn, *Power of Separation*, 91–115. By Korn's account, the main value of the veto was as a fast-track vehicle for Congress to express frustration with presidential trade actions and to put pressure on the President to press congressional human rights concerns in negotiations with specific countries. Because members wanted their views considered but did not want to be seen as upsetting foreign policy, Congress did not actually "veto" any MFN status until after *Chadha*. In any event, Korn argues, joint resolutions "conditioning" MFN status upon meeting human rights conditions have been a more effective vehicle for expression of Congress's concerns. Since such resolutions can be and usually are vetoed by the President, Congress can and does express concern without hurting foreign policy.

Korn's comprehensive study leads her to conclude that the practice was never a particularly important weapon in the arsenal of congressional oversight. "Members did not need the legislative shortcut to force executive branch officials to attend to congressional concerns, because the most useful sources of congressional oversight power—the power to make laws, and the power to require the executive branch and independent agency officials report [to committees] proposed actions before implementation—are well nestled in the authorities granted to members by Article I of the Constitution." Korn, *Power of Separation*, 116. Of fourteen potential oversight mechanisms, some of which we discuss in this section, the legislative veto ranked last in terms of frequency of use and ninth in terms of effectiveness, according to Joel D. Auerbach, *Keeping a Watchful Eye: The Politics of Congressional Oversight* 132 tbl. 6–1, 135 tbl. 6–2 (1990).

Does it make sense to think that *Chadha* has had *no* effect, as these scholars seem to maintain? Are they not making the same error the Supreme Court made in *Alaska Airlines*, that is, thinking that legislative vetoes were just symbolic "add-ons"? Doesn't the *threat* of a one-House veto change the bargaining game between Congress and the President or an agency?

5. *The Line Item Veto Case*. In 1995, Congress enacted the Line Item Veto Act, 110 Stat. 1200, which authorized the President to "cancel" statutory items relating to discretionary spending or tax benefits if the President determined that cancellation would help reduce the budgetary deficit, not impair essential government functions, and not harm the national interest. In *Clinton v. City of New York*, 524 U.S. 417 (1998), the Supreme Court invalidated the line item veto as inconsistent with Article I, Section 7, as interpreted in *Chadha*. Justice Stevens's opinion for the Court contrasted the President's constitutional role *before* statutory enactment (the President can "return" an unacceptable bill with his "veto") with this unconstitutional role of cancellation *after* statutory enactment. Does the reasoning of *Chadha* support this result? Is the line item veto as problematic as the legislative veto? You might recall the Eskridge and Ferejohn "Article I, Section 7 Game" as a way of thinking about this matter.

In dissent, Justice Breyer argued that the President was not creating a statute—he was simply exercising authority (routinely given him in prior statutes) not to spend all the money appropriated by Congress.[h] Justice Stevens's answer was that the Item Veto Act authorized the President to cancel statutory provisions and thereby prevent them from "having legal force or effect," 2 U.S.C. § 691e(4)(B)–(C), which is *legislative* in nature and not *implementational*. If the Act had not contained the "legal force or effect" language, the Court may have been more lenient. Justice Breyer responded, however, that Congress had previously given the Court and the President

---

h. Congress has allowed the President discretion in the spending arena, e.g., *Train v. City of New York*, 420 U.S. 35 (1975), but not in the tax arena. Thus, the cancellation power might be more constitutionally problematic as to tax benefits than for discretionary spending.

similar "force and effect" powers, e.g., 28 U.S.C. § 2072, without perceived constitutional difficulty.

Justice Breyer and Justice Scalia (in a separate dissenting opinion) believed that Congress's ability to give the President cancellation authority is limited by the nondelegation doctrine, but the statute easily revealed an "intelligible principle" to guide the President's exercise of discretion. Justice Breyer also asked: "Has the Congress given the President the 'wrong' kind of power, i.e., 'non-Executive' power?" To answer that question, he analyzed the item veto under the criteria in *Bowsher v. Synar*, excerpted in the next part of this section.

Query: If Congress really wants the President to have something like a line item veto authority, as a way of restraining Congress's tendency to undertax and over-spend, is there a way to do that after *Clinton*? See Elizabeth Garrett, *Accountability and Restraint: The Federal Budget Process and the Line Item Veto Act*, 36 Cardozo L.J. 871 (1999).

D. *Legislative Control Through Power Over Agency Officials*

As a matter of formal constitutional law, Congress can directly influence agency officials through the appointment and removal process. (1) It may legislate a means by which "inferior Officers" are appointed and removed from office. U.S. Const. art. II, § 2, cl. 2; see *Morrison v. Olson*, 487 U.S. 654 (1988) (Congress can vest appointment of Independent Counsel "in Courts of Law"). (2) Although the President must name "other Officers of the United States," the President can only do so "with the Advice and Consent of the Senate." *Id.*; cf. *id.* art. II, § 2, cl. 3 (President may make recess appointments without advice and consent). (3) The House may impeach and the Senate may remove any "civil Officer[] of the United States." *Id.* art. I, § 2, cl.5; art. I, § 3, cls. 6–7; art. II, § 4.

Jonathan R. Macey, *Organizational Design and Political Control of Administrative Agencies*, 8 J.L. Econ. & Org. 93, 100–08 (1992), argues that Congress has sometimes used this kind of formal authority in an innovative way, by insulating appointees from political pressure and removal. Thus, Congress's desire to establish a central banking authority that would keep inflation in check was a key reason why it ensured that the Federal Reserve Board would be an "independent" agency. Had the Board been part of the executive branch, debtor groups (who benefit from inflation) would have more influence with the agency, through pressure from the President and congressional committees. The Federal Reserve Bank Act of 1914 has been very successful in this regard, but one might wonder whether its insulation of the agency from *presidential* control (the President cannot remove Fed officials as he can those in the executive branch) is a violation of Article II. Federal Reserve Board members are not "inferior Officers" under the Appointments Clause, and Article II might be read to deny Congress the right to design agencies in ways that denigrate from the "executive" authority to direct statutory implementation.[i]

The New Deal created several "independent" agencies having this feature. In *Humphrey's Executor v. United States*, 295 U.S. 602 (1935), the Supreme Court upheld a statute preventing the President from removing an FTC Commissioner unless for cause. Characterizing the independent agency as performing both adjudicative and "quasi-legislative" duties, the Court reasoned that Congress could restrict presidential power over such officers in ways it could not do for officials in purely executive agencies, under *Myers v. United States*, 272 U.S. 52 (1926). *Humphrey's Executor* suggested that Congress might have some room within the constitutional scheme to exercise direct control over officials implementing "quasi-legislative" duties. This hypothesis was tested in the litigation arising out of the famous Gramm–Rudman–Hollings balanced budget law.

Bowsher v. Synar, 478 U.S. 714 (1986). The Gramm–Rudman–Hollings (GRH) Act was designed to eliminate the budget deficit through adherence to a set of deficit targets. If Congress failed to make spending and taxing changes in any year sufficient to meet the target, then a sequester would take place that would implement pro rata spending reductions in all eligible programs.

These automatic reductions were to be accomplished in three steps each year: (1) The executive Office of Management and Budget (OMB) and the legislative Congressional Budget Office (CBO) each estimated the federal deficit for the forthcoming fiscal year. If the projected deficit exceeded the targeted deficit, each calculated the program-by-program reductions needed to meet the target. The Directors of each independently reported all this information to the Comptroller General of the General Accounting Office (GAO), who is an agent of Congress (appointed by the President but removable by Congress). (2) The Comptroller General reviewed these reports and made his own report to the President. The Act required the President to issue a "sequestration order" to implement the spending reductions specified by the Comptroller General. (3) Congress had an opportunity to alter or implement the reductions by legislation. If nothing were done, the sequestration order automatically became effective.

The Supreme Court invalidated the enforcement provision of GRH. Having just read *Chadha*, you might think that GRH has the same structural problem as the legislative veto: It delegated important law-creating authority to an agent of the legislature, without requiring bicameral approval and presentment. **Justice Stevens** believed that the Act's enforcement provisions were invalid for this reason. He was convinced

---

i. The argument in text is especially compelling if it is true that Article II establishes a *unitary executive*, which must constitutionally be under the exclusive authority of the President. See Steven G. Calabresi & Christopher S. Yoo, *The Unitary Executive: Presidential Power from Washington to Bush* (2008); Steven G. Calabresi & Saikrishna Prakash, *The President's Power to Execute the Laws*, 104 Yale L.J. 541 (1994). But arguments against the constitutionality of independent agencies go beyond the unitary executive theory. E.g., Gary Lawson, *Delegation and Original Meaning*, 88 Va. L. Rev. 327 (2002).

that Congress cannot delegate to one of its subgroups *or* agents the power "to make policy determinations that bind the Nation." But Justice Stevens spoke only for himself and for Justice Marshall, in an opinion concurring with the result reached by a majority of the Court.

Chief Justice Burger's opinion for the Court majority accepted Congress's characterization of sequestration as executive in nature; in other words, the Comptroller General was merely implementing a congressional policy decision. Executive actions can be delegated to executive branch entities and independent agencies without raising constitutional concerns. Consistent with this conclusion, the sequestration provisions included a number of specific guidelines to constrain the discretion of the implementing institution. GRH specified which programs were eligible for cuts and which were exempt; it required uniformity; and it required pro rata cuts at the program, project and activity level.

Rather than applying his own opinion in *Chadha*, the Chief Justice picked up on the theme sounded by Justice Powell's *Chadha* concurring opinion: separation of powers concerns are greatest when the legislature (the most powerful branch) tries to usurp judicial (*Chadha*) or executive (*Bowsher*) power. Chief Justice Burger's opinion argued that GRH "usurped" executive power by giving an officer of Congress the authority to execute the laws. Such power can be constitutionally delegated to an executive branch entity; it cannot be retained by a direct agent of Congress. Burger's analysis is subject to several objections.

Justices White and **Blackmun** (dissenting) and Justices Marshall and Stevens (concurring in the judgment) found unrealistic the Court's suggestion that the Comptroller General would be "subservient" to Congress. The Comptroller General enjoys a 15–year term and may only be removed by Congress for (i) permanent disability; (ii) inefficiency; (iii) neglect of duty; (iv) malfeasance; or (iv) felony or conduct involving moral turpitude. 31 U.S.C. § 703(e)(1)(B). A Comptroller General has never been removed for policy reasons. Is there *any* reason to think that official might kowtow to Congress under the Gramm–Rudman Act? Aren't the Comptroller General's duties under the Act substantially limited by the OMB and CBO projections anyway?

Justices Marshall and Stevens argued that if the Court's opinion were taken literally—Congress may not "control" an official who performs "executive" rather than "legislative" powers—it would be an absurdity. The Capitol Police who arrest lawbreakers, the Sergeant-at-Arms who manages the congressional payroll, and the Capitol Architect who maintains the grounds are all agents of Congress who "execute" laws. Do those positions violate the Constitution?

NOTES ON THE GRAMM-RUDMAN CASE

1. *The Constitutionality of Independent Agencies?* Perhaps one reason *Bowsher* did not pursue the *Chadha* analysis is that the Court wanted to be

careful not to question the constitutionality of independent agencies. In footnote 4 of its opinion, the Court made quite a point of the ease by which independent agencies, whose members are removable only by the President (if at all), pass muster under a test focusing on whether an executive official is controlled by Congress. This returns us to *Chadha*: If you *really* believe the Court's analysis there, how can you accept all the lawmaking that goes on in independent agencies? This was a focus of Justice White's *Chadha* dissent. The *Chadha* Court never faced up to this dilemma, and the *Bowsher* Court sidestepped the problem.

2. *Does* Bowsher *Caution Against Congressional Micromanagement?* One might read *Bowsher* as suggesting a broad principle against *excessive* congressional control of statutory implementation. The vice in *Bowsher* was handing over statutory implementation to a congressional agent, but what if Congress hands over statutory implementation to an "independent" agency that Congress bullies into policy shifts because of *ex parte* pressure by Members of Congress, threats of funding cutoffs, or bad publicity and brutal accusations during oversight hearings? Surely, none of these mechanisms of congressional control is per se unconstitutional under *Bowsher*, but is there a *Bowsher* line that Congress would cross if it went "too far"? How might you define such a line?

This reading of *Bowsher* suggests that Congress could have avoided the constitutional problem rather easily, namely, by delegating the executive functions entailed in GRH to a true executive agency, such as the Office of Management and Budget (OMB) and then authorizing OMB to assign those functions to the Comptroller General. Indeed, Congress has done precisely that double delegation in the Legislative Branch Appropriations Act for Fiscal Year 1996, Pub. L. No. 104–53, § 211, and the General Accounting Office Act of 1996, Pub. L. No. 104–316.

3. *Implications of* Bowsher *and* Chadha *for Statutory Interpretation.* Recall the new textualist philosophy of statutory interpretation developed by Judge Easterbrook and Justice Scalia (Chapter 2, § 3A); one of the main themes of this philosophy is its disinclination to consider the legislative history of a statute to illuminate plain or clear statutory text (Chapter 4, § 2). Construct an argument from *Chadha* and *Bowsher*, to the effect that the new textualist position enjoys support of constitutional dimensions. Compare John F. Manning, *Textualism as a Nondelegation Doctrine*, 97 Colum. L. Rev. 673 (1997), with Jonathan R. Siegel, *The Use of Legislative History in a System of Shared Powers*, 53 Vand. L. Rev. 1457 (2000), with Victoria F. Nourse, *Misunderstanding Congress: Statutory Interpretation, the Supermajoritarian Difficulty, and the Separation of Powers*, 99 Geo. L.J. 1119 (2011).

NOTE ON WHITE HOUSE REVIEW OF AGENCY RULES

The President has many mechanisms available to control even the independent agencies: (1) The President appoints the agency heads. Although the appointment is subject to Senate rejection, the President, as the "first mover," has a lot of discretion to choose someone whose regulatory philosophy is compatible with his or her own. (2) The President's Office of Management and Budget (OMB) prepares the budget, which the President sends to Congress, which Congress of course changes, which the President can veto, and which the President then spends. Thus, the President has control at three points in the process. The President can use that power to punish agencies whose policies he disfavors and reward agencies the President favors. (3) The White House has assumed a power to override some agency rules. This important authority requires a bit of explanation.[j]

The process of White House regulatory review began immediately after the "new" public interest agencies (NHTSA, EPA) were created; the Nixon, Ford, and Carter OMBs asked some agencies for cost-benefit justifications for their legislative rules. President Ronald Reagan's Executive Order 12,291, 3 C.F.R. 127 (1982), required agencies to submit proposed rules and a cost-benefit analysis to the OMB's Office of Information and Regulatory Affairs (OIRA). OIRA not only reviewed the rules, but also delayed rules that did not meet its cost-benefit specifications. OSHA and EPA were the main victims of OIRA's cutting analyses. Presidents Clinton, Bush, and Obama have tweaked this Reagan-era policy in various ways but have also continued the practice of OMB/OIRA substantive review of proposed agency regulations. This exercise of presidential authority has been controversial. Critics argue that OMB/OIRA regulatory analysis has been highly partisan, substituting the President's ideological preferences for those embedded in policies more liberal Congresses have adopted.[k]

One line of defense posed by political theorists is that the President, and only the President, can impose rationality upon the nation's regulatory policy. See Terry Moe & Scott Wilson, *Presidents and the Politics of Structure*, 57 L. & Contemp. Probs. 1 (1994). The President may have several institutional advantages in this respect. The main one is that there is a single President, usually with a mandate from a national electorate. Another is the Constitution's failure to shackle the Presidency with the procedural limitations like those visited upon Congress. Compare U.S. Const. art. I, § 7 with *id.* art. II, § 2. The President therefore has both electoral (reelection) or personal (place in history) incentive and constitutional freedom to create institutions which tend toward policy coherence and rationality, rather than the cobbled together compromises and disorganization characteristic of congressional policymaking (at least according to critics of Congress). Taking a different point of view is Jide Nzelibe, *The Fable of the Nationalist President and the Parochial Congress*, 53 UCLA L. Rev. 1217 (2006), who argues that the majoritarian-mandate argument for presidential primacy has been overstated. On any given issue, the President is not as likely as Congress to reflect the preferences of the median voter. Moreover, the President is hardly immune from rent-seeking pressures and, on some issues, may be more corrupt than Congress in this regard.

Recall the history of the NHTSA's airbag rule. In 1971 NHTSA had proposed Standard 208, requiring that passive restraints be adopted in all

---

j. See Thomas McGarity, *Reinventing Rationality: The Role of Regulatory Analysis in the Federal Bureaucracy* (1991); Richard B. Stewart, *Administrative Law in the Twenty–First Century,* 78 NYU L. Rev. 437 (2003).

k. See, e.g., William F. West, *The Institutionalization of Regulatory Review: Organizational Stability and Responsive Competence at OIRA,* 35 Pres. Stud. Q. 76–93 (2005).

cars. The auto industry objected to the cost of airbags and other restraints, but they were willing to put "interlocks" on their cars. Interlocks would prevent the car from being started unless the passengers fastened their seatbelts; an interlock would only add $40 to the cost of a car. NHTSA was uninterested, however. According to Mashaw & Harfst, *Auto Safety,* 132–33, Henry Ford II and Lee Iacocca met with President Nixon on April 27, 1971, where they objected to the cost pinch that NHTSA was putting on the Big Three. Apparently, John Ehrlichman, the President's Domestic Advisor, directed the Department of Transportation to drop or delay airbags and adopt interlocks as the preferred technology. Transportation Secretary John Volpe objected but was overridden in October 1971. NHTSA announced that passive protections would not be required until August 15, 1975 and that until then compliance with Standard 208 could be accomplished through an interlock. When the courts enjoined most of the alternatives required by Standard 208, the interlock (which was fine under the court's decision) became the only way to comply with the standard. Its introduction into cars during 1974 triggered a public outcry that fueled the congressional revolt against the NHTSA-safety coalition later that year.

The next stage in the airbag story is more interesting still (see Mashaw & Harfst, *Auto Safety,* 205–10). President Carter's Secretary of Transportation, Brock Adams, revived passive restraints in a 1977 order. The stage seemed set for delivery on the decade-long process, but implementation of the order by the industry was not due until President Carter's second term—an event derailed by the voters in 1980. President Reagan had run on a platform of getting the government out of people's lives, and one of the most intrusive agencies was NHTSA. On February 12, 1981, the agency proposed a one-year delay in the imposition of passive restraint requirements. Automakers supported the proposed delay, on the grounds that it was unclear whether passive restraints would yield any increase in safety. The argument was that airbags are too expensive, so the industry would comply through passive seatbelts. But the public insisted that seatbelts be detachable. If, however, they were detachable, people would detach them, and they would have the same effect as manual belts, which cars already had. NHTSA accepted this argument, and on October 1981 the agency rescinded its passive restraints rule entirely. The Inside-the-Beltway belief is that the White House called the shot that killed Standard 208.

Assume that the Reagan White House killed Standard 208. In light of *Humphrey's Executor* and the separation of powers embedded in Articles I–III of the Constitution, is this exercise of presidential power constitutional? Cf. Neal Kumar Katyal, *Internal Separation of Powers: Checking Today's Most Dangerous Branch from Within,* 115 Yale L.J. 2314, 2324–27 (2006) (arguing that excessive presidential control of agencies can reduce the flow of valuable information from agencies to the President). Jot down your thoughts and then consider a more recent presidential initiative, for OMB review has been popular with Presidents of all ideologies.

In January 2011, President Barack H. Obama issued Executive Order 13,563, directing executive agencies to review existing regulations to assure that they remain cost-effective. The President's Council on Jobs and Competitiveness had urged action to reduce the number of agency regulations that imposed unnecessary costs on businesses. This was the same philosophy that motivated the Reagan White House to veto Standard 208. If you object to President Reagan's override of Standard 208, can you defend President Obama's executive order?

In Executive Order 13,579, *Regulation and Independent Regulatory Agencies* (July 11, 2011), available at http://www.whitehouse.gov/the-press-office/2011/07/11/executive-order-regulation-and-independent-regulatory-agencies (viewed Jan. 1, 2012), President Obama extended this cost-benefit reevaluation mandate to independent agencies, in the following language:

Sec. 2. Retrospective Analyses of Existing Rules. (a) To facilitate the periodic review of existing significant regulations, independent regulatory agencies should consider how best to promote retrospective analysis of rules that may be outmoded, ineffective, insufficient, or excessively burdensome, and to modify, streamline, expand, or repeal them in accordance with what has been learned. Such retrospective analyses, including supporting data and evaluations, should be released online whenever possible.

(b) Within 120 days of the date of this order, each independent regulatory agency should develop and release to the public a plan, consistent with law and reflecting its resources and regulatory priorities and processes, under which the agency will periodically review its existing significant regulations to determine whether any such regulations should be modified, streamlined, expanded, or repealed so as to make the agency's regulatory program more effective or less burdensome in achieving the regulatory objectives.

Does § 2 of the executive order raise constitutional concerns?

E. Congress' Policy Control Through Design of the Agency's Structure and Procedures

Oversight, *ex parte* contacts, the legislative veto, and appropriations pressure are all *ex post* methods for Congress to control the agencies to which it has delegated power. That is, these methods are after-the-fact: The agency does something Congress doesn't like, and Congress responds. Another way to control agency policy is *ex ante*: By careful design of the agency's procedure, jurisdiction, and composition, the enacting coalition can press agency policy in desired directions. McNollgast have called this "hardwiring" the agency.[1]

By the design of the agency's procedures and jurisdiction, the enacting Congress can create a powerful or a weak agency. When Congress created the Equal Employment Opportunity Commission (EEOC) in the Civil Rights Act of 1964, for example, it created procedural complexities and denied substantive rulemaking authority to the agency as part of the deal with conservative Senator Dirksen, who wanted to protect small

---

1. McNollgast (i.e., Mathew D. McCubbins, Roger G. Noll, and Barry R. Weingast), *Administrative Procedures as Instruments of Political Control*, 3 J.L. Econ. & Org. 243 (1987). See also Jonathan R. Macey, *Separated Powers and Positive Political Theory: The Tug of War Over Administrative Agencies*, 80 Geo. L.J. 671 (1992).

businesses against too much federal meddling in their affairs.[m] Although the EEOC has been a more successful policy entrepreneur than Dirksen probably would have wanted, his deal has ensured that the more conservative Supreme Court is a more constant check on EEOC interpretations than has been the case for other agencies (§ 3A of this chapter).

Relatedly, Congress made several judgments when it vested more interpretive authority in the Supreme Court than in the EEOC when it crafted Title VII. When an agency has primary lawmaking authority (as through explicit delegations), legislators can expect less consistency and greater political responsiveness over time; often the agency will also create a legal framework that is more internally coherent than the courts will accomplish. On the other hand, vesting the courts with primary lawmaking authority, legislators can expect greater consistency as to any given issue over time, but less flexibility. See Matthew C. Stephenson, *Legislative Allocation of Delegated Power: Uncertainty, Risk, and the Choice Between Agencies and Courts*, 119 Harv. L. Rev. 1036 (2006). Scott Shapiro makes the important point that these kinds of judgments involve matters of trust and comparative competence: If the enacting coalition believes that judges are more trustworthy and capable of carrying out legislative goals than the agency is, Congress is less likely to delegate lawmaking authority to the agency. See Shapiro, *Legality* chs. 11–13 (2010).

Another design questions are these: How many different interests is the agency going to represent? Will the agency have to fight for regulatory turf? For instance, the SEC is much more influenced by the New York Stock Exchange than the EEOC is influenced by employers, because the SEC works only with a handful of stock exchanges across the country and must compete with Commodities Future Trading Commission (CFTC) and the Comptroller of the Currency for regulatory "turf" in the financial world. The EEOC, in contrast, must deal with hundreds of different companies in a wide range of businesses. See also Edward Zelinsky, *James Madison and Public Choice at Gucci Gulch: A Procedural Defense of Tax Expenditures and Tax Institutions*, 102 Yale L.J. 1165 (1993) (making this point about the scope of interest group conflict in the tax arena).

Thus, if the enacting congressional coalition wants an agency's policy to be highly sensitive to the needs of the regulated industry, it will give the agency a small clientele and make it battle with other agencies for regulatory responsibilities. If the enacting coalition wants the agency to deal with industry in a more adversarial way, the enacting Congress will give the agency a wide-ranging clientele with competing interests and give the agency a monopoly on that type of regulation. Moreover, Congress might insulate the agency from political pressure, as it has done with the Federal Reserve Board, by ensuring long terms for agency heads, forbidding *ex parte* communications, and the like.

---

m. For an excellent exegesis of the complex "deal" with Dirksen, see Daniel B. Rodriguez & Barry R. Weingast, *The Positive Political Theory of Legislative History: New Perspectives on the 1964 Civil Rights Act and Its Interpretation*, 151 U. Pa. L. Rev. 1417 (2003).

Perhaps most important are the procedural rules established for the agency. The Supreme Court has discouraged the federal judiciary from adding procedural requirements to those in the APA and in the agency's particular enabling act. Hence, there is great room for congressional differentiation among agencies. By requiring more extensive notice and comment for rules than is required by the APA, Congress can hamper the agency's ability to move decisively. Responding to criticism that the FTC was promulgating too many "unfair competition" regulations (including those that affected doctors, lawyers, funeral home directors, auto manufacturers, used car dealers, advertisers, oil companies, and cereal producers), Congress imposed more burdensome procedures on FTC rulemaking. The agency had to hold actual hearings on proposed rules and allow cross-examination. The hybrid rulemaking procedure "made it impossible for the FTC to develop industry-wide rules away from public scrutiny." Korn, *Separation of Powers*, 55.

The enabling statute can require consultation with advisory groups, or with designated types of experts, and can insist that a diversity of perspectives be heard. The statute can provide counsel fees for certain groups appearing before an agency. These requirements serve two functions, according to McNollgast, *Structure and Process, Politics and Policy: Administrative Arrangements and the Political Control of Agencies*, 75 Va. L. Rev. 431, 472–73 (1989). First, they enfranchise particular groups of people who now have an enhanced right to have their views heard and considered. Second, the structure improves the fire alarm system of congressional monitoring because it more widely disseminates relevant information. Another increasingly popular method of control through institutional design is to require the agency to conduct extensive cost-benefit analysis before regulating. See Pablo Spiller & Emerson Tiller, *Decisions Costs and the Strategic Design of Administrative Process and Judicial Review*, 26 J. Legal Stud. 347 (1997). Not only may this analysis change the substance of the regulation by making costs and benefits more salient, but requiring agencies to expend limited resources on these studies also means they will have fewer funds for other activities. Spiller and Tiller conclude that Congress can control agencies by requiring certain allocations of decision costs and resources and that this is often accomplished through structure and institutional design.

McNollgast's hardwiring hypothesis remains to be tested, but we should caution that it is very hard to predict the long-term consequences of a certain institutional arrangement. The creators of the NHTSA sincerely wanted the agency to be a success, gave it great independence and full control over its regulatory turf, sought to assure broad participation in the agency's rulemaking proceedings, and insisted upon scientific and objective bases for the agency's standards. Yet, very early on the agency ran into more troubles than its creators expected: the retirement of President Johnson and election of Richard Nixon undermined the agency and drained its budget, the requirement that the first agency rules be tied to existing standards started the agency off on a conservative footing from which it never fully escaped, the notice and comment rulemaking procedures and accompanying judicial review became crippling once the Big Three automakers organized themselves and decided to take an aggressive stance in court challenges—challenges that were being initiated at exactly the time when the judicial and academic culture was becoming enamored of hard look judicial review.

Also, it is not always accurate to speak of an "enacting coalition" that "designs" the agency. Most agencies are designed over a period of years, reflecting the inputs of several "coalitions," sometimes even in the same year. For example, the NHTSA's design—which was none too coherent in 1966—was less coherent after 1974, when three different coalitions effected statutory changes: (1) The original safety-at-almost-any-cost coalition was able to add rulemaking authority and recall authority to buttress the agency. (2) A coalition reflecting the consumer revolt against "interlocks" inserted substantive and procedural restrictions into the statute at the same time. (3) Yet another coalition forced the NHTSA to regulate school buses, which the agency had decided were not cost-effective to regulate before 1974.

Connor A. Raso, *Procedural Constraints on Agency Rulemaking* (Ph. D. Diss., Stanford University, Political Science Dep't, 2010). Raso explores the many ways that Congress tries to build *ex ante* controls on the administrative process by imposing various requirements on agency rulemaking. Among the statutes following such a strategy are the following:

National Environmental Policy Act, 1969, 42 U.S.C. § 4321 et seq., which requires environmental impact statements before federal projects can proceed;

Administrative Procedure Act, 1946, 5 U.S.C. § 553, which requires public notice and comment before most agency rules can be adopted;

Consumer Products Safety Act Amendments, 1981, 15 U.S.C. § 2058, which imposes new requirements before the Consumer Product Safety Commission (CPSC) issues new regulations, including a major curtailment in the role of consumer groups and the accountability of the CPSC to such groups;

Regulatory Flexibility Act, 1980, 5 U.S.C. § 601 et seq., which requires a "regulatory flexibility" analysis from agency action imposing significant costs on small businesses;

Congressional Review Act, 1995, 5 U.S.C. § 801, which requires agencies to report new rules to Congress and prevents their taking effect for 60 days so that Congress can overturn them, through a resolution that must be adopted by both chambers and presented to the President but is not subject to the Senate filibuster;

Unfunded Mandates Reform Act, 1995, 2 U.S.C. § 658 et al., which requires agencies to disclose new costs its rules will impose on private parties or state/local governments and to consider alternatives to those "unfunded" costs.

Raso evaluates the efficacy of these structural restrictions, determining whether agencies actually follow the new rules and whether the restrictions have had the effect desired by their sponsors. The evidence is clear that the first three statutes have been reasonably effective, while the latter three have had no discernible effect on agency rulemaking.

As a general matter, Raso concludes that "constraints on the rulemaking process are more likely to be effective if they (1) do not include broad exemptions; (2) empower early interest group involvement; (3) enable judicial review; (4) charge an executive agency with enforcement responsibility; (5) create a dedicated monitoring process within the legislative branch. Satisfying each of these criteria increases the probability that a constraint will be effective." Id. at 36.

Thus, NEPA has been a model of effectiveness because (1) the statute sets forth a broad and easily understood directive, with few exemptions; (2) empowers environmental groups to participate early in the process of creating and responding to environmental impact statements; and assures compliance through (3) judicial review and (4) executive branch monitoring (NEPA created a Council on Environmental Quality within the White House). In contrast, the Regulatory Flexibility Act (RFA), even as strengthened in 1996, has been ineffective because (1) the statute contains big loopholes that can easily be exploited by agencies; (2) does not empower interested groups to have much influence early in the process; and (3–5) has no effective monitoring (the 1996 amendment added limited judicial review, but to little effect).

PROBLEM 6–3

Designing a Statutory Scheme to Influence Enforcement

You are a presidential adviser, and there is a window of opportunity to revisit the landmark auto safety law (discussed in § 1 of this chapter) and redesign the statutory scheme to protect more Americans from auto fatalities. Although such fatalities had dropped to 32,788 deaths in 2010, assume that they are rising again. Do some internet research on what causes these fatalities and what might be the most useful approach to reduce those fatalities—and then redesign the enforcement scheme in a way that will save lives at a reasonable cost. Use what you have learned to design a statutory scheme that will avoid both paralysis and capture by the auto industry.

F. JUDICIAL REVIEW OF AGENCY RULES AND ORDERS

Another way that Congress can regulate agencies is by assuring judicial review of agency action under the Administrative Procedure Act (APA), discussed in § 1. If the federal courts were able to enforce Congress' original directives upon the agency, then Congress could feel more comfortable about delegating lawmaking authority to those agencies. Consistent with this idea and with the further idea that judicial review can counteract "capture" of the agency by "special interests," administrative law in the 1960s and 1970s grew more aggressive, especially in the Court of Appeals for the District of Columbia Circuit. The main developments were (1) the establishment of a strong presumption in favor of judicial review of agency action or inaction, and the enlargement of the class of interests which can invoke judicial review; (2) more searching judicial review based upon a detailed agency justification for its decision, including an indication that reasonable alternatives were considered; and (3) judicial policing of informal lobbying of agency officials by special interests. See Richard B. Stewart, *The Reformation of American Administrative Law*, 88 Harv. L. Rev. 1669, 1716 (1975). As you examine these developments, consider the drawbacks of expanded judicial review.

1. *Expanding Judicial Review of Discretionary Administrative Action.* As noted above, the APA explicitly provides for judicial review of agency actions. Formal adjudication and rulemaking must be supported by "substantial evidence"; informal action, including notice and comment rulemaking, must not be "arbitrary and capricious." In *Citizens to Preserve Overton Park, Inc. v. Volpe*, 401 U.S. 402 (1971), the Supreme Court applied the arbitrary and capricious standard in the context of an informal adjudication, where there was a written record and only a few public hearings, none of which rose to the level of a judicial proceeding. The Department of Transportation Act of 1966, 80 Stat. 931, codified at 49 U.S.C. § 1653(f) (1964, Supp. V, 1969), and the Federal–Aid Highway Act of 1966, 80 Stat. 771, codified at 23 U.S.C. § 138 (1964, Supp. V, 1969), prohibited the Secretary of Transportation from authorizing the use of federal funds to finance construction of highways through public parks if a "feasible and prudent" alternative route existed. Proposed Interstate 40 would have cut across Overton Park, a 342–acre park in Memphis, Tennessee. Pursuant to the above statutes, the Secretary approved the highway project in 1968; concerned citizens and a national environmental group sued the Secretary, on the ground that it would be "feasible and prudent" to route I–40 around Overton Park.

The lower courts dismissed the lawsuit because of the Secretary's broad discretion to approve highway routes. The Supreme Court, in an opinion by Justice Marshall, reversed. The Court made short shrift of the Government's argument that informal, discretionary decisions are not reviewable. The Court saw nothing to meet the Court's standard of " 'clear and convincing evidence' of a * * * legislative intent" to restrict access to judicial review. *Abbott Laboratories v. Gardner*, 387 U.S. 136, 141 (1967). "Similarly, the Secretary's decision here does not fall within the exception for action 'committed to agency discretion.' This is a very narrow exception. * * * The legislative history of the Administrative Procedure Act indicates that it is applicable in those rare instances where 'statutes are drawn in such broad terms that in a given case there is no law to apply.' S. Rep. No. 752, 79th Cong., 1st Sess., 26 (1945)." Both relevant statutes provided that the Secretary "shall not approve any program or project" that requires the use of any public parkland "unless (1) there is no feasible and prudent alternative to the use of such land, and (2) such program includes all possible planning to minimize harm to such park * * *." Such language was sufficiently directive to foreclose a finding that these determinations were committed to agency discretion.

The Court determined that review should be limited, however, to whether the Secretary's action was "arbitrary or capricious" under APA § 706(2)(A). The reviewing court should conduct a review that is "thorough, probing, indepth" and "must consider whether the [agency] decision was based on a consideration of the relevant factors and whether there has been a clear error of judgment. * * * Although this inquiry into the facts is to be searching and careful, the ultimate standard of review is a narrow one. The court is not empowered to substitute its judgment for that of the agency." In *Overton Park*, the Court remanded the case to the district court to obtain from the Secretary a statement of reasons that might be reviewed. The Secretary on remand was ultimately unable to justify his decision and so declined to approve the parkland route. See *Citizens to Preserve Overton Park, Inc. v. Brinegar*, 494 F.2d 1212 (6th Cir. 1974), *cert. denied*, 421 U.S. 991 (1975). After more back-and-forth between local authorities and the Nixon, Ford, and Carter Administrations, the whole idea of an east-west expressway through Memphis was abandoned. Because most of I–40's east-west path had already been completed, the interstate now dead-ends when it reaches the park.

Peter Strauss has reassessed *Overton Park*.[n] Professor Strauss found the statutory directive much less clear than Justice Marshall did and credited legislative history which assumed that the Secretary would consider the importance of the parkland, along with cost, community disruption, and other factors. The Secretary did consider park values, and plans were changed several times in response to park concerns. By requiring that parklands be given paramount rather than ordinary consideration, the Court was imposing values by judicial dictate on the Secretary that were not clearly those Congress had put into the statute. Strauss maintains that the political balance between park values and efficient road-building values was disrupted by the Court's hurried decision.

The Supreme Court struck a different balance in *Heckler v. Chaney*, 470 U.S. 821 (1985), which upheld the refusal by the Food and Drug Administration (FDA) to investigate the applicability of the federal food and drug standards to the use of lethal injections in some states as their means of imposing the death penalty. Justice Rehnquist's opinion for the Court stated that an agency's decision not to prosecute or enforce, whether through civil or criminal process, is a decision generally committed to an agency's absolute discretion. "[A]n agency decision not to enforce often involves a complicated balancing of a number of factors

---

n. Peter L. Strauss, Citizens to Preserve Overton Park v. Volpe—*Of Politics and Law, Young Lawyers and the Highway Goliath*, in *Administrative Law Stories* 258–332 (Peter L. Strauss ed., 2006).

which are peculiarly within its expertise. Thus, the agency must not only assess whether a violation has occurred, but whether agency resources are best spent on this violation or another, whether the agency is likely to succeed if it acts, whether the particular enforcement action requested best fits the agency's overall policies, and indeed, whether the agency has enough resources to undertake the action at all." Additionally, when an agency refuses to prosecute, "it generally does not exercise its *coercive* power over an individual's liberty or property rights, and thus does not infringe upon areas that courts often are called upon to protect."

2. *How Scrutinizing Should Judicial Review Be? The "Hard Look Doctrine."* The *Overton Park* litigation was a signal not just that a presumption of reviewability under the APA was to be enthusiastically applied, but also that judicial scrutiny should have teeth. Such review has become known as the *hard look doctrine*, because courts scrutinize agency rationales and justifications so closely. See Harold Leventhal, *Environmental Decisionmaking and the Role of the Courts*, 122 U. Pa. L. Rev. 509 (1973); *Ethyl Corp. v. EPA*, 541 F.2d 1, 68–69 (D.C. Cir. 1976) (Leventhal, J., concurring). Hard look review requires that the agency examine all relevant evidence, to explain its decisions in detail, to justify departures from past practices, and to consider all reasonable alternatives before reaching a final policy decision. Hard look requires a well-reasoned explanation of agency policy; courts in most cases do not pass on the merits of the decision, merely the support the agency provides. Thus, in some cases, a rule that is remanded to the agency for further consideration is adopted again in similar form, but the agency provides a better explanation.

Critics of the hard look approach of aggressive review of agency policy (*Overton Park*) worry that it has led to agency *ossification* because second-guessing by nonexpert courts has undermined agencies' ability to act decisively on important national policies.° Mashaw and Harfst provide a specific example. NHTSA's Standard 208 proposed in 1969 that automakers be required by 1973 to adopt "passive" restraints (ones that consumers had no choice but to use, like airbags and automatic seat belts) that would meet the agency's performance criteria. The criteria were phrased in terms of the effects produced on an anthropomorphic "dummy" in frontal barrier crashes at 30 miles per hour. Standard 208, expected to save thousands of lives at relatively low cost, was delayed substantially by judicial hard looks. The Sixth Circuit enjoined implementation of Standard 208 in *Chrysler Corp. v. Department of Transportation*, 472 F.2d 659

---

o. See e.g., Shep Melnick, *Administrative Law and Bureaucratic Reality*, 44 Admin. L. Rev. 245, 246 (1992). But see William Jordan, *Ossification Revisited: Does Arbitrary and Capricious Review Significantly Interfere with Agency Ability to Achieve Regulatory Goals Through Informal Rulemaking?*, 94 Nw. U. L. Rev. 393 (2000) (arguing that review for arbitrary and capricious decisionmaking has not significantly impeded agencies in pursuit of policy goals). See also Mark Seidenfeld, *Demystifying Deossification: Rethinking Recent Proposals to Modify Judicial Review of Notice and Comment Rulemaking*, 75 Tex. L. Rev. 483 (1997) (surveying and analyzing arguments and reform proposals); Matthew C. Stephenson, *A Costly Signaling Theory of "Hard Look" Judicial Review*, 58 Ad. L. Rev. 753 (2006) (providing an alternative justification for hard look review, where a high-quality explanation by the government serves as a proxy for the confidence the government has in the utility of the rule).

(6th Cir. 1972), on the ground that the test dummy approach specified in the regulation did not provide a sufficiently "objective" standard in light of the Safety Act legislative history. But the history only suggested that standards be phrased in "objective terms," and the parties had all but ignored the issue until the judicial hard look made it central. Just as *Overton Park* threw road planning into turmoil for the rest of the 1970s, so *Chrysler* and other hard look decisions criticizing Standard 208 threw the NHTSA into turmoil for the remainder of the decade (Harfst & Mashaw, *Auto Safety*, ch. 5).

Kevin McDonald disputes the ossification theory in general and Mashaw and Harfst's view that judicial review undermined the NHTSA. McDonald, *Shifting Out of Park*, 96–97. From the industry's point of view, the NHTSA has had a winning record in court and has been able to impose most of the design changes it believes will improve highway safety. As McDonald sees it, the NHTSA's (and the nation's) big problem is that, since 1974, Congress has not shared the agency's priorities. (McDonald thinks that Congress has been misguided in focusing on minor defects that are the objects of recalls and in failing to focus on driver errors, which cause the overwhelming majority of accidents.)

In any event, judges have backed away from the hard-look doctrine. In *Syracuse Peace Council v. FCC*, 867 F.2d 654 (D.C. Cir. 1989), Judge Stephen Williams accepted the FCC's decision to reject the "fairness doctrine" that it had applied in the past to require broadcast media licensees to provide coverage of issues of public interest and to provide opportunities for the airing of contrasting viewpoints. The FCC claimed, *inter alia*, that the requirements of the fairness doctrine actually discouraged broadcasters from covering controversial issues. The study that "proved" a chilling effect on speech was based primarily on the representations of broadcasters in a survey. At its height, the hard look doctrine would have been applied to call into question this sort of evidence from arguably self-interested parties. Judge Williams' opinion seems more willing to give the benefit of the doubt to the expert regulatory commission, however. Furthermore, although Williams explicitly found that the FCC rule was based on a misunderstanding of the law, he did not remand it to the agency for a reconsideration. Rather, the correct understanding "appear[s] so obvious and compelling that a remand to extract the magic words from the Commission would be pure waste."

In a similar use of a soft glance rather than a hard look analysis, Judge Richard Posner upheld regulations adopted by OSHA regulating occupational exposure to blood-borne pathogens, a rule designed to protect health care workers from hepatitis and AIDS. *American Dental Ass'n v. Martin*, 984 F.2d 823 (7th Cir. 1993), *cert. denied*, 510 U.S. 859 (1993). The opinion has a much more deferential tone than *Overton Park* and its progeny. Much regulation occurs under conditions of uncertainty, Posner argues, and in such cases, the conclusions of experts on technical issues "are entitled to respect by the nonspecialist, biomedically unsophisticated Article III judiciary, at least in the absence of a more systematic showing of harms" by the challengers. Whether these cases represent a trend away from hard look review, at least in the context of notice-and-comment rulemaking and other informal decisions, remains to be seen.

3. *Procedural Requirements in Rulemaking Proceedings.* When an agency engages in informal rulemaking, it is acting like a legislature (APA § 553) and so does not have to follow the formal procedures of adjudication (APA § 554), where the agency is acting like a court. Under a benign view of agency decisionmaking, this makes perfect sense. But if one fears that the agency has been captured by special interests, one fears that the informal rulemaking process might easily be "corrupted." A few decades ago, the D.C. Circuit considered procedural ways to open up such rulemaking, a process ostensibly halted by the Supreme Court. See Gillian Metzger, *The Story of* Vermont Yankee*: A Cautionary Tale of Judicial Review and Nuclear Waste*, in *Administrative Law Stories* 124–67 (Peter L. Strauss ed., 2006) (excellent account, from which we liberally draw).

The D.C. Circuit in *Home Box Office, Inc. v. FCC*, 567 F.2d 9 (D.C. Cir. 1977), overturned rules easing limitations on cable and pay television programming in part because of evidence that the public docket for the proposed rules was "a sham" and the "real" deliberations had been conducted privately between the Commissioners and industry representatives. The Court read *Overton Park* to require that agency decisions be rendered upon a record that discloses all relevant evidence and argumentation that the agency considered. Hence, a decision in which there were undisclosed *ex parte* communications was invalid.

Home Box Office generated great criticism. The introduction of this feature into informal rulemaking threatened a valuable flow of information. Not only do members of the industry have detailed, first-hand information that is intrinsically useful, but it could be a check on the information developed by agency staffs. The dialogue between administrators and the private sector is a necessary part of regulation. Retreating from *Home Box Office*, the D.C. Circuit in *Sierra Club v. Costle*, 657 F.2d 298, 402–04 (D.C. Cir. 1981), only required the EPA to docket descriptions of oral communications which are of "central relevance" to the rulemaking proceedings. The Court in *Sierra Club* also faced objections that the EPA's rule was invalid because of undisclosed contacts between agency decisionmakers and the White House and one Member of Congress, Senator Byrd (D–W.V.). Judge Wald's opinion exempted most such contacts from the rule that *ex parte* communications be docketed, based upon principles of separation of powers.

Home Box Office was something of a judicial disaster, but its core idea—that agencies should observe judicial norms of openness when they affect private parties and the public interest—did not die. In the 1970s, the D.C. Circuit in some instances required some form of oral hearings, with cross-examination, in § 553 informal rulemaking. E.g., *Mobil Oil Corp. v. Federal Power Comm'n*, 483 F.2d 1238 (D.C. Cir. 1973); *International Harvester Co. v. Ruckelshaus*, 478 F.2d 615 (D.C. Cir. 1973) (Leventhal, J.). But see Stephen Williams, *"Hybrid Rulemaking" Under the Administrative Procedure Act: A Legal and Empirical Analysis*, 42 U. Chi. L. Rev. 401 (1975) (critical view of this form of review).

The Supreme Court, however, was hostile to "judicializing" rulemaking proceedings. E.g., *United States v. Florida East Coast Railway Co.*, 410 U.S. 224 (1973) (overriding lower court imposition of new requirements for agency rulemaking not required by the APA or the substantive statute). The Court's decision in *Vermont Yankee Nuclear Power Co. v. Natural Resources Defense Council, Inc.*, 435 U.S. 519 (1978), is a milestone for the administrative state because the Court passed on the legitimacy of judicially imposed hybrid procedures. See Metzger, *The Story of* Vermont Yankee, for a comprehensive analysis. In 1971, Vermont Yankee applied to the Atomic Energy Commission for a license to operate a nuclear plant in Vernon, Vermont. NRDC opposed the application, in part because of alleged environmental effects of operations to reprocess fuel or to dispose of wastes resulting from the reprocessing operations. The environmental issue was excluded from consideration by the Licensing Board which conducted the adjudicatory hearing, but in 1972 the Commission itself began rulemaking proceedings on the issue of what consideration should be given by the Licensing Board to the environmental effects of the uranium fuel cycle. The Commission's notice set forth two possible rules. In 1973, the Commission scheduled a hearing on the alternative rules and made available to the public an Environmental Survey prepared by its staff. Both written and oral comments were received, and the Commission in 1974 issued a rule requiring consideration of such environmental impact. Although that rule was inconsistent with the practice of the Licensing Board in the Vermont Yankee proceeding, the Commission affirmed the grant of an operating license to Vermont Yankee. On appeal, although the Commission had followed all the § 553 procedures for informal rulemaking, the D.C. Circuit found the procedures inadequate overall and remanded for the agency to follow procedures permitting greater public scrutiny of information upon which the Commission relied.

The Supreme Court pointedly criticized the D.C. Circuit's "Monday morning quarterbacking" of the agency's procedures. The Court cited *Florida East Coast Railway* for the proposition that § 553 of the APA "established the maximum procedural requirements which Congress was willing to have the courts impose upon agencies in conducting rulemaking procedures." While "[t]his is not to say necessarily that there are no circumstances which would ever justify a court in overturning agency action because of a failure to employ procedures beyond those required by statute * * * such circumstances, if they exist, are extremely rare." Moreover, apart from the APA, "this Court has for more than four decades emphasized that the formulation of procedures was basically to be left within the discretion of the agencies to which Congress had confided the responsibility for substantive judgments." The Court reversed the D.C. Circuit's invalidation of the procedures used in the agency's informal rulemaking and remanded to the D.C. Circuit to review the rule on the merits.

Does *Vermont Yankee* implicitly overrule *Home Box Office? Mobil Oil?* Is there any way to distinguish those cases? Notwithstanding *Vermont Yankee*, federal courts of appeals have continued to impose procedural requirements on "informal" rulemaking—but under cover of liberally "interpreting" the notice-and-comment requirements of § 553, rather than imposing them as a matter of administrative common law. See Gary Lawson, *Federal Administrative Law* 240–83 (4th ed. 2007) (disapproving); Metzger, *Story of Vermont Yankee* (acquiescent).

PROBLEM 6–4

Judicial Review of NHTSA Proposal

The NHTSA in 1970 proposed to amend Standard 108's provisions governing turn signals and warning flashers. Later, the agency indicated that it would abandon the "sampling" methodology it had allowed in the past (a random sample of flashers were tested) and would require testing of all automobiles. Since the agency did not propose to relax performance criteria, the proposal would upgrade the standard significantly. Wagner Electric Company objected that this sampling change was not indicated in the earlier notice of proposed rulemaking, and NHTSA issued a new notice which proposed to eliminate sampling.

Among the comments, Wagner and other companies urged relaxation of the performance criteria if sampling were adopted and urged, further, that yet another round of notice-and-comment should be commenced, so that the issues could be considered together. NHTSA's final rule, issued in 1971, eliminated sampling but also downgraded the performance criteria. Wagner sued to overturn the rule, on the ground that there was no single notice that the agency was considering both elimination of sampling and downgrading performance criteria. NHTSA responded that its sampling notice contained the usual reservation that its rule might encompass related matters and that several commenters had, like Wagner, fully commented on the matter.

Will the court overturn the rule? See *Wagner Electric Corp. v. Volpe*, 466 F.2d 1013 (3d Cir. 1972). Would a judicial invalidation be inconsistent with *Vermont Yankee*? Reconsider your answer after reading the next case.

MOTOR VEHICLE MANUFACTURERS ASS'N v. STATE FARM MUTUAL AUTOMOBILE INS. CO.

Supreme Court of the United States, 1983
463 U.S. 29, 103 S.Ct. 2856, 77 L.Ed.2d 443

JUSTICE WHITE delivered the opinion of the Court.

The development of the automobile gave Americans unprecedented freedom to travel, but exacted a high price for enhanced mobility. Since 1929, motor vehicles have been the leading cause of accidental deaths and injuries in the United States. * * * Congress responded by enacting the

National Traffic and Motor Vehicle Safety Act of 1966. The Act, created for the purpose of "reduc[ing] traffic accidents and deaths and injuries to persons resulting from traffic accidents," 15 U.S.C. § 1381, directs the Secretary of Transportation or his delegate to issue motor vehicle safety standards that "shall be practicable, shall meet the need for motor vehicle safety, and shall be stated in objective terms." 15 U.S.C. § 1392(a). In issuing these standards, the Secretary is directed to consider "relevant available motor vehicle safety data," whether the proposed standard "is reasonable, practicable and appropriate" for the particular type of motor vehicle, and the "extent to which such standards will contribute to carrying out the purposes" of the Act. 15 U.S.C. § 1392(f)(1), (3), (4).

The Act also authorizes judicial review under the provisions of the Administrative Procedure Act (APA), 5 U.S.C. § 706, of all "orders establishing, amending, or revoking a Federal motor vehicle safety standard," 15 U.S.C. § 1392(b). Under this authority, we review today whether NHTSA acted arbitrarily and capriciously in revoking the requirement in Motor Vehicle Safety Standard 208 that new motor vehicles produced after September 1982 be equipped with passive restraints to protect the safety of the occupants of the vehicle in the event of a collision. Briefly summarized, we hold that the agency failed to present an adequate basis and explanation for rescinding the passive restraint requirement and that the agency must either consider the matter further or adhere to or amend Standard 208 along lines which its analysis supports.

[I] As originally issued by the Department of Transportation in 1967, Standard 208 simply required the installation of seatbelts in all automobiles. 32 Fed.Reg. 2408, 2415 (Feb. 3, 1967). It soon became apparent that the level of seatbelt use was too low to reduce traffic injuries to an acceptable level. The Department therefore began consideration of "passive occupant restraint systems"—devices that do not depend for their effectiveness upon any action taken by the occupant except that necessary to operate the vehicle. Two types of automatic crash protection emerged: automatic seatbelts and airbags. The automatic seatbelt is a traditional safety belt, which when fastened to the interior of the door remains attached without impeding entry or exit from the vehicle, and deploys automatically without any action on the part of the passenger. The airbag is an inflatable device concealed in the dashboard and steering column. It automatically inflates when a sensor indicates that deceleration forces from an accident have exceeded a preset minimum, then rapidly deflates to dissipate those forces. The life-saving potential of these devices was immediately recognized, and in 1977, after substantial on-the-road experience with both devices, it was estimated by NHTSA that passive restraints could prevent approximately 12,000 deaths and over 100,000 serious injuries annually. 42 Fed.Reg. 34,298.

In 1969, the Department formally proposed a standard requiring the installation of passive restraints, 34 Fed.Reg. 11,148 (July 2, 1969), thereby commencing a lengthy series of proceedings. In 1970, the agency revised Standard 208 to include passive protection requirements, 35

Fed.Reg. 16,927 (Nov. 3, 1970), and in 1972, the agency amended the standard to require full passive protection for all front seat occupants of vehicles manufactured after August 15, 1975. 37 Fed.Reg. 3911 (Feb. 24, 1972). In the interim, vehicles built between August 1973 and August 1975 were to carry either passive restraints or lap and shoulder belts coupled with an "ignition interlock" that would prevent starting the vehicle if the belts were not connected. On review, the agency's decision to require passive restraints was found to be supported by "substantial evidence" and upheld. *Chrysler Corp. v. Dep't of Transportation*, 472 F.2d 659 (CA6 1972).

In preparing for the upcoming model year, most car makers chose the "ignition interlock" option, a decision which was highly unpopular, and led Congress to amend the Act to prohibit a motor vehicle safety standard from requiring or permitting compliance by means of an ignition interlock or a continuous buzzer designed to indicate that safety belts were not in use. Motor Vehicle and Schoolbus Safety Amendments of 1974, Pub.L. 93–492, § 109, 88 Stat. 1482, 15 U.S.C. § 1410b(b). The 1974 Amendments also provided that any safety standard that could be satisfied by a system other than seatbelts would have to be submitted to Congress where it could be vetoed by concurrent resolution of both houses. 15 U.S.C. § 1410b(b)(2).

The effective date for mandatory passive restraint systems was extended for a year until August 31, 1976. 40 Fed.Reg. 16,217 (April 10, 1975); *id.*, at 33,977 (Aug. 13, 1975). But in June 1976, Secretary of Transportation William T. Coleman, Jr., initiated a new rulemaking on the issue, 41 Fed.Reg. 24,070 (June 9, 1976). After hearing testimony and reviewing written comments, Coleman extended the optional alternatives indefinitely and suspended the passive restraint requirement. Although he found passive restraints technologically and economically feasible, the Secretary based his decision on the expectation that there would be widespread public resistance to the new systems. He instead proposed a demonstration project involving up to 500,000 cars installed with passive restraints, in order to smooth the way for public acceptance of mandatory passive restraints at a later date. Department of Transportation, The Secretary's Decision Concerning Motor Vehicle Occupant Crash Protection (December 6, 1976).

Coleman's successor as Secretary of Transportation disagreed. Within months of assuming office, Secretary Brock Adams decided that the demonstration project was unnecessary. He issued a new mandatory passive restraint regulation, known as Modified Standard 208. 42 Fed.Reg. 34,289 (July 5, 1977); 42 CFR § 571.208 (1978). The Modified Standard mandated the phasing in of passive restraints beginning with large cars in model year 1982 and extending to all cars by model year 1984. The two principal systems that would satisfy the Standard were airbags and passive belts; the choice of which system to install was left to the manufacturers. In *Pacific Legal Foundation v. Dep't of Transportation*, 593 F.2d 1338 (CADC), cert. denied, 444 U.S. 830 (1979), the Court of

Appeals upheld Modified Standard 208 as a rational, nonarbitrary regulation consistent with the agency's mandate under the Act. The standard also survived scrutiny by Congress, which did not exercise its authority under the legislative veto provision of the 1974 Amendments.

Over the next several years, the automobile industry geared up to comply with Modified Standard 208. As late as July, 1980, NHTSA reported:

> "On the road experience in thousands of vehicles equipped with airbags and automatic safety belts has confirmed agency estimates of the life-saving and injury-preventing benefits of such systems. When all cars are equipped with automatic crash protection systems, each year an estimated 9,000 more lives will be saved and tens of thousands of serious injuries will be prevented."

NHTSA, Automobile Occupant Crash Protection, Progress Report No. 3, p. 4. In February 1981, however, Secretary of Transportation Andrew Lewis reopened the rulemaking due to changed economic circumstances and, in particular, the difficulties of the automobile industry. 46 Fed.Reg. 12,033 (Feb. 12, 1981). Two months later, the agency ordered a one-year delay in the application of the standard to large cars, extending the deadline to September 1982, 46 Fed.Reg. 21,172 (April 9, 1981) and at the same time, proposed the possible rescission of the entire standard. 46 Fed.Reg. 21,205 (April 9, 1981). After receiving written comments and holding public hearings, NHTSA issued a final rule (Notice 25) that rescinded the passive restraint requirement contained in Modified Standard 208.

[II] In a statement explaining the rescission, NHTSA maintained that it was no longer able to find, as it had in 1977, that the automatic restraint requirement would produce significant safety benefits. Notice 25,46 Fed.Reg. 53,419 (Oct. 29, 1981). This judgment reflected not a change of opinion on the effectiveness of the technology, but a change in plans by the automobile industry. In 1977, the agency had assumed that airbags would be installed in 60% of all new cars and automatic seatbelts in 40%. By 1981 it became apparent that automobile manufacturers planned to install the automatic seatbelts in approximately 99% of the new cars. For this reason, the life-saving potential of airbags would not be realized. Moreover, it now appeared that the overwhelming majority of passive belts planned to be installed by manufacturers could be detached easily and left that way permanently. Passive belts, once detached, then required "the same type of affirmative action that is the stumbling block to obtaining high usage levels of manual belts." 46 Fed.Reg., at 53421. For this reason, the agency concluded that there was no longer a basis for reliably predicting that the standard would lead to any significant increased usage of restraints at all.

In view of the possibly minimal safety benefits, the automatic restraint requirement no longer was reasonable or practicable in the agency's view. The requirement would require approximately $1 billion to implement and the agency did not believe it would be reasonable to impose such substantial costs on manufacturers and consumers without more adequate assurance that sufficient safety benefits would accrue. In addition, NHTSA concluded that automatic restraints might have an adverse effect on the public's attitude toward safety. Given the high expense and limited benefits of detachable belts, NHTSA feared that many consumers would regard the standard as an instance of ineffective regulation, adversely affecting the public's view of safety regulation and, in particular, "poisoning ... popular sentiment toward efforts to improve occupant restraint systems in the future." 46 Fed.Reg., at 53424.

[The United States Court of Appeals for the District of Columbia Circuit invalidated the agency's rule rescinding the passive restraint requirement, on the ground that it was arbitrary and capricious and therefore in violation of the APA. 680 F.2d 206 (1982).]

[III. The Court held that the APA fully applied to NHTSA's rulemaking proceeding, and that a reviewing court has an obligation to set aside any rule found to be "arbitrary, capricious, an abuse of discretion, or otherwise not in accordance with law." 5 U.S.C. § 706(2)(A); see *Overton Park*. The Court rejected Motor Vehicle's argument that an agency's rescission of a rule should be governed by the same narrow standard as the agency's refusal to issue a rule in the first place.]

[Justice White explained the "arbitrary and capricious" standard of review.] [T]he agency must examine the relevant data and articulate a satisfactory explanation for its action including a "rational connection between the facts found and the choice made." *Burlington Truck Lines Inc. v. United States*, 371 U.S. 156, 168 (1962). In reviewing that explanation, we must "consider whether the decision was based on a consideration of the relevant factors and whether there has been a clear error of judgment." *Bowman Transp. Inc. v. Arkansas–Best Freight System*, [419 U.S. 281, 285 (1974)]. Normally, an agency rule would be arbitrary and capricious if the agency has relied on factors which Congress has not intended it to consider, entirely failed to consider an important aspect of the problem, offered an explanation for its decision that runs counter to the evidence before the agency, or is so implausible that it could not be ascribed to a difference in view or the product of agency expertise. The reviewing court should not attempt itself to make up for such deficiencies; we may not supply a reasoned basis for the agency's action that the agency itself has not given. * * * For purposes of these cases, it is also relevant that Congress required a record of the rulemaking proceedings to be compiled and submitted to a reviewing court, 15 U.S.C. § 1394, and intended that agency findings under the Motor Vehicle Safety Act would be supported by "substantial evidence on the record considered as a whole." S.Rep. No. 1301, 89th Cong., 2d Sess. 8 (1966); H.R.Rep. No. 1776, 89th Cong., 2d Sess. 21 (1966).

[In Part IV, Justice White rejected the lower court's requirement that NHTSA was obligated to provide "increasingly clear and convincing reasons" for its action. The Court of Appeals relied on post–1974 congressional signals (such as Congress's failure to override the Carter-era NHTSA initiatives) to infer a "congressional commitment to the concept of automatic crash protection devices for vehicle occupants." Justice White found the lower court's reading of the materials misguided. Also, "this Court has never suggested that the *standard* of review is enlarged or diminished by subsequent congressional action. While an agency's interpretation of a statute may be confirmed or ratified by subsequent congressional failure to change that interpretation, *Bob Jones University* [Chapter 8, § 2B6], in the cases before us, even an unequivocal ratification—short of statutory incorporation—of the passive restraint standard would not connote approval or disapproval of an agency's later decision to rescind the regulation. That decision remains subject to the arbitrary and capricious standard."]

[V] The ultimate question before us is whether NHTSA's rescission of the passive restraint requirement of Standard 208 was arbitrary and capricious. We conclude, as did the Court of Appeals, that it was. We also conclude, but for somewhat different reasons, that further consideration of the issue by the agency is therefore required. * * *

[A] The first and most obvious reason for finding the rescission arbitrary and capricious is that NHTSA apparently gave no consideration whatever to modifying the Standard to require that airbag technology be utilized. Standard 208 sought to achieve automatic crash protection by requiring automobile manufacturers to install either of two passive restraint devices: airbags or automatic seatbelts. There was no suggestion in the long rulemaking process that led to Standard 208 that if only one of these options were feasible, no passive restraint standard should be promulgated. Indeed, the agency's original proposed Standard contemplated the installation of inflatable restraints in all cars. Automatic belts were added as a means of complying with the standard because they were believed to be as effective as airbags in achieving the goal of occupant crash protection. 36 Fed.Reg. 12,858, 12,859 (July 8, 1971). At that time, the passive belt approved by the agency could not be detached. Only later, at a manufacturer's behest, did the agency approve of the detachability feature—and only after assurances that the feature would not compromise the safety benefits of the restraint. Although it was then foreseen that 60% of the new cars would contain airbags and 40% would have automatic seatbelts, the ratio between the two was not significant as long as the passive belt would also assure greater passenger safety.

The agency has now determined that the detachable automatic belts will not attain anticipated safety benefits because so many individuals will detach the mechanism. Even if this conclusion were acceptable in its entirety, standing alone it would not justify any more than an amendment of Standard 208 to disallow compliance by means of the one technology which will not provide effective passenger protection. It does not cast doubt on the need for a passive restraint standard or upon the efficacy of airbag technology. In its most recent rulemaking, the agency again acknowledged the lifesaving potential of the airbag:

> "The agency has no basis at this time for changing its earlier conclusions in 1976 and 1977 that basic airbag technology is sound and has been sufficiently demonstrated to be effective in those vehicles in current use. . . ."

NHTSA Final Regulatory Impact Analysis (RIA) at XI–4 (Oct. 1981). Given the effectiveness ascribed to airbag technology by the agency, the mandate of the Act to achieve traffic safety would suggest that the logical response to the faults of detachable seatbelts would be to require the installation of airbags. At the very least this alternative way of achieving the objectives of the Act should have been addressed and adequate reasons given for its abandonment. But the agency not only did not require compliance through airbags, it also did not even consider the possibility in its 1981 rulemaking. Not one sentence of its rulemaking statement discusses the airbags-only option. * * * [W]hat we said in *Burlington Truck Lines v. United States* is apropos here:

> "There are no findings and no analysis here to justify the choice made, no indication of the basis on which the [agency] exercised its expert discretion. We are not prepared to and the Administrative Procedure Act will not permit us to accept such ... practice.... Expert discretion is the lifeblood of the administrative process, but 'unless we make the requirements for administrative action strict and demanding, *expertise*, the strength of modern government, can become a monster which rules with no practical limits on its discretion.'"

We have frequently reiterated that an agency must cogently explain why it has exercised its discretion in a given manner, and we reaffirm this principle again today.

The automobile industry has opted for the passive belt over the airbag, but surely it is not enough that the regulated industry has eschewed a given safety device. For nearly a decade, the automobile industry waged the regulatory equivalent of war against the airbag and lost—the inflatable restraint was proved sufficiently effective. Now the automobile industry has decided to employ a seatbelt system which will not meet the safety objectives of Standard 208. This hardly constitutes cause to revoke the Standard itself. Indeed, the Motor Vehicle Safety Act was necessary because the industry was not sufficiently responsive to safety concerns. The Act intended that safety standards not depend on current technology and could be "technology-forcing" in the sense of inducing the development of superior safety design. If, under the statute, the agency should not defer to the industry's failure to develop safer cars, which it surely should not do, *a fortiori* it may not revoke a safety standard which can be satisfied by current technology simply because the industry has opted for an ineffective seatbelt design. * * *

[In Part VB, Justice White ruled that NHTSA was "too quick to dismiss the safety benefits of automatic seatbelts." Although an agency may decline to issue and may revoke a safety standard "on the basis of serious uncertainties about its efficacy, those uncertainties must be supported in the administrative record and reasonably explained. In this case, there was no direct evidence in the record supporting NHTSA's finding that detachable automatic belts cannot be predicted to yield a substantial increase in usage. Evidence in the record revealed more than a doubling of seat belt use under those circumstances. For one example, Volkswagen between 1975 and 1980 sold 350,000 Rabbits equipped with passive seatbelts guarded by an ignition interlock. NHTSA found that seatbelt use in Rabbits averaged 34% where the cars had regular manual belts, and 84% for the detachable passive belts. Although Justice White maintained that the agency had discretion to refuse to generalize from studies of Rabbit drivers to the general population of drivers, the agency was required to consider a fact that it neglected but that critically distinguishes detachable automatic belts and ordinary manual ones: A detachable passive belt requires an affirmative act to detach it, while a manual belt can be safely ignored. "Thus, inertia—a factor which the agency's own studies have found significant in explaining the current low usage rates for seatbelts—works in *favor* of, not *against*, use of the protective device." This would suggest that seatbelt use by occasional users would be substantially increased by detachable passive belts. "Whether this is in fact the case is a matter for the agency to decide, but it must bring its expertise to bear on the question."]

The agency is correct to look at the costs as well as the benefits of Standard 208. The agency's conclusion that the incremental costs of the requirements were no longer reasonable was predicated on its prediction that the safety benefits of the regulation might be minimal. Specifically, the agency's fears that the public may resent paying more for the automatic belt systems is expressly dependent on the assumption that detachable automatic belts will not produce more than "negligible safety benefits." 46 Fed.Reg., at 53,424. When the agency reexamines its findings as to the likely increase in seatbelt usage, it must also reconsider its judgment of the reasonableness of the monetary and other costs associated with the Standard. In reaching its judgment, NHTSA should bear in mind that Congress intended safety to be the preeminent factor under the Motor Vehicle Safety Act. [Quoting committee reports for the Safety Act.]
* * *

JUSTICE REHNQUIST, with whom THE CHIEF JUSTICE [BURGER], JUSTICE POWELL, and JUSTICE O'CONNOR join, concurring in part and dissenting in part.

I join Parts I, II, III, IV, and V–A of the Court's opinion. In particular, I agree that, since the airbag and continuous spool automatic seatbelt were explicitly approved in the standard the agency was rescinding, the agency should explain why it declined to leave those requirements intact. In this case, the agency gave no explanation at all. Of course, if the agency can provide a rational explanation, it may adhere to its decision to rescind the entire standard.

I do not believe, however, that NHTSA's view of detachable automatic seatbelts was arbitrary and capricious. The agency adequately explained its decision to rescind the standard insofar as it was satisfied by detachable belts.

The statute that requires the Secretary of Transportation to issue motor vehicle safety standards also requires that "[e]ach such … standard shall be practicable [and] shall meet the need for motor vehicle safety." 15 U.S.C. § 1392(a). The Court rejects the agency's explanation for its conclusion that there is substantial uncertainty whether requiring installation of detachable automatic belts would substantially increase seatbelt usage. The agency chose not to rely on a study showing a substantial increase in seatbelt usage in cars equipped with automatic seatbelts and an ignition interlock to prevent the car from being operated when the belts were not in place *and* which were voluntarily purchased with this equipment by consumers. It is reasonable for the agency to decide that this study does not support any conclusion concerning the effect of automatic seatbelts that are installed in all cars whether the consumer wants them or not and are not linked to an ignition interlock system.

The Court rejects this explanation because "there would seem to be grounds to believe that seatbelt use by occasional users will be substantially increased by the detachable passive belts," and the agency did not adequately explain its rejection of these grounds. It seems to me that the agency's explanation, while by no means a model, is adequate. The agency acknowledged that there would probably be some increase in belt usage, but concluded that the increase would be small and not worth the cost of mandatory detachable automatic belts. 46 F.R. 53421–54323 (1981). The agency's obligation is to articulate a " 'rational connection between the facts found and the choice made.' " I believe it has met this standard.
* * *

The agency's changed view of the standard seems to be related to the election of a new President of a different political party. It is readily apparent that the responsible members of one administration may consider public resistance and uncertainties to be more important than do their counterparts in a previous administration. A change in administration brought about by the people casting their votes is a perfectly reasonable basis for an executive agency's reappraisal of the costs and benefits of its programs and regulations. As long as the agency remains within the bounds established by Congress, it is entitled to assess administrative records and evaluate priorities in light of the philosophy of the administration.

NOTES ON STATE FARM

1. *Right or Wrong?* Did the Court do the right thing in this case—either from the Court's point of view, or the nation's? Write down your answer in the margin, and read on.

2. *The Proper Role of the Judiciary in the Implementation of Public Policy?* In light of your experience with the implementation of the Safety Act, what do you think the role of the Court should be: (1) Agent of Congress? If so, which Congress—the enacting one, the amending one, or the current one? (2) Independent principal, imposing the Court's own values, thwarting agencies implementing bad policies, and rewarding agencies that protect the Court's conception of the public interest? (3) Independent principal, imposing rule of law values? If so, what does the rule of law require in *State Farm?*

Chapter 11 of Mashaw and Harfst's book asks this question: Does the participation of the judiciary in the statutory implementation game advance the public interest? Their analysis suggests some doubt that the Court performs a useful role. The judiciary is the forum of choice whenever the government tries to upset traditional ways of doing things (ways easily translated into "rights"). Thus, the courts were a forum for the auto industry to harass the agency and delay implementation of its rules. The proceduralization of the rulemaking process rendered it less decisive and more vulnerable to shifts in public opinion and presidential leadership. Recall the wild shifts in Standard 208 from the Johnson Administration to the Nixon–Ford Administration to the Carter Administration to the Reagan Administration.

Adverse judicial decisions in the 1970s (the hard look decade) directly contributed to the interlock debacle and contributed less directly to an increasingly cautious attitude toward regulation. For example, *Chrysler* required "objective" testing standards that the agency's "dummy" regulations did not meet. This requirement discouraged the agency from imposing rules before it had "objective" scientific evidence well in hand, and thereby prevented the sort of experimentation and technology-forcing rules that the early experts thought were necessary to make genuine advances to reduce auto injuries and fatalities. More generally, the adverse judicial decisions discouraged NHTSA from proceeding by rulemaking, which had been the agency's original mandate and was probably its only hope for regulatory success. Favorable judicial decisions in response to NHTSA's recall campaigns, on the other hand, encouraged the agency to rely more and more heavily on that less effective regulatory mechanism. Like a Pavlovian dog, NHTSA was trained by the judiciary to quail at the thought of rules and salivate at the prospect of recalls.

Mashaw and Harfst are pessimistic about the role of the "legal culture" and of multiple principals in our administrative state of separated powers. "[T]he combination of congressional oversight and appropriations, Executive Office intervention and monitoring, and judicial review, has sharply limited the degree to which NHTSA could translate [its regulatory] aspirations into concrete technological requirements." (Mashaw & Harfst, *Auto Safety,* 228).

Do you find this level of pessimism persuasive? Jot down your initial thoughts in the margin, and then read the next note.

3. *The Aftermath of* State Farm. Transportation Secretary Elizabeth Dole initiated rulemaking to answer the Court's inquiries, and 7,800 comments were filed. On July 17, 1984, Dole issued the final rule, which (1) dropped mandatory airbags like a lead balloon and (2) required phasing in "automatic occupant restraints" (including airbags as a option for the manufacturer) between 1986 and 1989, unless (3) before April 1, 1989, two-thirds of the U.S. population are covered by state mandatory seat belt use laws meeting NHTSA's conditions. 49 Fed. Reg. 28,962–63 (1984).

By endorsing state mandatory seat belt laws as the preferred form of regulation, the agency seemed to revert to the old command-and-control regime that had been ineffective and to retreat from the proven-to-be-effective mandatory-redesign regime. State Farm challenged this rule, but the D.C. Circuit held the lawsuit premature. *State Farm Mutual Automobile Ins. Co. v. Dole*, 802 F.2d 474 (D.C. Cir. 1986).

With the support of the auto industry as well as new groups such as Mothers Against Drunk Driving (MADD), almost all the states adopted mandatory seat belt laws—but most were careful *not* to satisfy the requirements of the Dole rule. "As a consequence, the American public got both airbags and mandatory use laws." Mashaw, *Story of* State Farm, 385. Most surprisingly, *both* kinds of regulations captured the imagination of Americans. We the People started buckling up in record numbers *and* demanded more airbags from manufacturers than the law required. Although Professor Mashaw reports these results with no dimming of his customary pessimism about judicial review, do they suggest that the judiciary might play a productive role in the evolution of statutory policy?

Contrast McDonald's more recent account. Looking back on more than a generation of expensive federal regulation of auto safety, he argues that the NHTSA's focus on passive standards has reduced occupant fatality risk by only 15–20%, not an impressive amount given the tens of billions of dollars in cost and the much greater traffic safety achieved in Canada, Europe, and Australia, which focus on seat belts and driver error. McDonald, *Shifting Out of Park*, 18–19; Leonard Evans, *Traffic Safety* 117 (2004). Indeed, in the United States, reducing the speed limit has had greater safety effects than all the design changes posed by the NHTSA. McDonald, *Shifting Out of Park,* 42 n.65.

FCC v. Fox Television Stations, Inc., 556 U.S. 502 (2009). Federal law prohibits the broadcasting of "any ... indecent ... language," 18 U.S.C. § 1464, which includes expletives referring to sexual or excretory activity or organs, see *FCC v. Pacifica Foundation*, 438 U.S. 726 (1978). For many years, the FCC followed an announced regulatory approach that banned sexual or excretory "expletives" only if their use was "deliberate and repetitive"; mere "fleeting" expletives would generally be allowed. Even as the FCC expanded its indecency standard to encompass ever more words and phrases, it preserved this approach—until a 2006 FCC ruling against Fox. In that ruling, the FCC rejected its longstanding distinction between "expletive" and "literal" uses of terms like "fuck" as "artificial." Also, the FCC ended its tolerance for "fleeting" expletives, finding that they have the power to offend parents and children and that permitting "fleeting" expletives gives broadcasters too much freedom to be offensive.

Invoking the Supreme Court's decision in *State Farm*, the Second Circuit overturned the agency's order against Fox, on the ground that the FCC had not adequately explained why it was jettisoning its longstanding rule. The Supreme Court reversed, in an opinion by **Justice Scalia**. "We find no basis in the Administrative Procedure Act or in our opinions for a requirement that all agency [action that changes prior policy] be subjected to more searching review. The Act mentions no such heightened standard. And our opinion in *State Farm* neither held nor implied that every agency action representing a policy change must be justified by reasons more substantial than those required to adopt a policy in the first instance. That case, which involved the rescission of a prior regulation, said only that such action requires 'a reasoned analysis for the change beyond that which may be required when an agency *does not act* in the first instance.' ([E]mphasis added). Treating failures to act and rescissions of prior action differently for purposes of the standard of review makes good sense, and has basis in the text of the [APA], which likewise treats the two separately. It instructs a reviewing court to 'compel agency action unlawfully withheld or unreasonably delayed,' 5 U.S.C. § 706(1), and to 'hold unlawful and set aside agency action, findings, and conclusions found to be [among other things] . . . arbitrary [or] capricious,' § 706(2)(A). The statute makes no distinction, however, between initial agency action and subsequent agency action undoing or revising that action."

"To be sure, the requirement that an agency provide reasoned explanation for its action would ordinarily demand that it display awareness that it *is* changing position. An agency may not, for example, depart from a prior policy *sub silentio* or simply disregard rules that are still on the books. And of course the agency must show that there are good reasons for the new policy. But it need not demonstrate to a court's satisfaction that the reasons for the new policy are *better* than the reasons for the old one; it suffices that the new policy is permissible under the statute, that there are good reasons for it, and that the agency *believes* it to be better, which the conscious change of course adequately indicates. This means that the agency need not always provide a more detailed justification than what would suffice for a new policy created on a blank slate. Sometimes it must—when, for example, its new policy rests upon factual findings that contradict those which underlay its prior policy; or when its prior policy has engendered serious reliance interests that must be taken into account. It would be arbitrary or capricious to ignore such matters. In such cases it is not that further justification is demanded by the mere fact of policy change; but that a reasoned explanation is needed for disregarding facts and circumstances that underlay or were engendered by the prior policy."

Under this understanding of the law, Justice Scalia ruled that the FCC's order was not "arbitrary and capricious." The FCC had "forthrightly acknowledged" that it was creating new policy and repudiating inconsistent prior actions taken by the Commission and staff. Also, the FCC's reasons for its decision were "entirely rational." It was reasonable for the FCC to conclude that the literal-expletive distinction was nonsensical given that both kinds of uses could cause offense and subject children to a harmful "first blow" of indecency; given technological advances, it was reasonable for the FCC to expect broadcasters to "bleep out" even fleeting expletives.

Justice Kennedy joined Justice Scalia's opinion as to all of the foregoing matters but issued a concurring opinion which nonetheless took a somewhat different approach than Justice Scalia's opinion, which needed Kennedy's vote to represent a majority. "The question whether a change in policy requires an agency to provide a more-reasoned explanation than when the original policy was first announced is not susceptible, in my view, to an answer that applies in all cases."

"The question in each case is whether the agency's reasons for the change, when viewed in light of the data available to it, and when informed by the experience and expertise of the agency, suffice to demonstrate that the new policy rests upon principles that are rational, neutral, and in accord with the agency's proper understanding of its authority. * * *

"Where there is a policy change the record may be much more developed because the agency based its prior policy on factual findings. In that instance, an agency's decision to change course may be arbitrary and capricious if the agency ignores or countermands its earlier factual findings without reasoned explanation for doing so. An agency cannot simply disregard contrary or inconvenient factual determinations that it made in the past, any more than it can ignore inconvenient facts when it writes on a blank slate." This is the lesson Justice Kennedy drew from *State Farm*. "The present case does not raise the concerns addressed in *State Farm*," because the FCC had based its prior policy not on factual findings, but on its interpretation of the Court's *Pacifica* ruling, and had given appropriate reasons for changing its policy.

Justice Stevens dissented in an opinion emphasizing the FCC's status as an independent agency, which, he believed, should be relatively free from political influence. "The FCC, like all agencies, may revise its regulations from time to time, just as Congress amends its statutes as circumstances warrant. But the FCC is constrained by its congressional mandate. There should be a strong presumption that the FCC's initial views, reflecting the informed judgment of independent commissioners with expertise in the regulated area, also reflect the views of the Congress that delegated the Commission authority to flesh out details not fully defined in the enacting statute. The rules adopted after *Pacifica* have been in effect for decades and have not proved unworkable in the intervening years. * * * [B]roadcasters have a substantial interest in regulatory stability; the threat of crippling financial penalties looms large over these entities. The FCC's shifting and impermissibly vague indecency policy only imperils these broadcasters and muddles the regulatory landscape. It therefore makes eminent sense to require the Commission to justify why its prior policy is no longer sound before allowing it to change course. The FCC's congressional charter, the Administrative Procedure Act, § 706(2)(A) (instructing courts to 'hold unlawful and set aside ... arbitrary [or] capricious' agency action), and the rule of law all favor stability over administrative whim."

Justice Breyer (joined by Justices Stevens, Souter, and Ginsburg) dissented. He started with the premise that, as an independent agency, the

FCC was relatively insulated from political oversight. "That insulation helps to secure important governmental objectives, such as the constitutionally related objective of maintaining broadcast regulation that does not bend too readily before the political winds. But that agency's comparative freedom from ballot-box control makes it all the more important that courts review its decisionmaking to assure compliance with applicable provisions of the law— including law requiring that major policy decisions be based upon articulable reasons." Additionally, the agency must act consistently, and when it changes its own rules the agency must focus on the fact of change and explain the basis for that change.

"To explain a change requires more than setting forth reasons why the new policy is a good one. It also requires the agency to answer the question, 'Why did you change?' And a rational answer to this question typically requires a more complete explanation than would prove satisfactory were change itself not at issue." *State Farm* "requires the agency here to focus upon the reasons that led the agency to adopt the initial policy, and to explain why it now comes to a new judgment."

"I recognize that *sometimes* the ultimate explanation for a change may have to be, 'We now weigh the relevant considerations differently.' But at other times, an agency can and should say more. Where, for example, the agency rested its previous policy on particular factual findings; or where an agency rested its prior policy on its view of the governing law; or where an agency rested its previous policy on, say, a special need to coordinate with another agency, one would normally expect the agency to focus upon those earlier views of fact, of law, or of policy and explain why they are no longer controlling. Regardless, to say that the agency here must answer the question 'why change' is not to require the agency to provide a justification that is '*better* than the reasons for the old [policy].' It is only to recognize the obvious fact that *change* is sometimes (not always) a relevant background feature that sometimes (not always) requires focus (upon prior justifications) and explanation lest the adoption of the new policy (in that circumstance) be 'arbitrary, capricious, an abuse of discretion.' "

Like the Second Circuit, Justice Breyer concluded that the FCC's decision violated the *State Farm* requirement that an agency making a policy change "consider . . . important aspect[s] of the problem." In particular, he faulted the FCC for failing adequately to consider its new policy's First Amendment implications and potential impact on local broadcasters, many of whom might not be able to afford the technology necessary to "bleep out" fleeting expletives. Justice Breyer dismissed as inadequate the various reasons the FCC had adduced for its policy change—in particular, the claim that the literal-expletive distinction was nonsensical and the claim that the new policy better protects children against "the first blow" of broadcast indecency. Neither of these claims, Justice Breyer argued, could justify the FCC's policy *change* since both claims remained conclusory, failing to address the rationales underlying the prior policy.

NOTES ON WHEN AGENCY POLICY SHIFTS ARE "ARBITRARY":
STATE FARM VERSUS FOX TELEVISION

State Farm can be read as trying to strike a balance between two kinds of risks attending judicial review of agency policy changes. On the one hand, if courts are too deferential, there is the "yo-yo" risk that agency policies will fluctuate too frequently. On the other hand, if courts are too scrutinizing, there is the "ossification" risk that agencies will become too loath to change their policies. While the *State Farm* Court and the *Fox* dissenters seem to be more troubled by the yo-yo risk than the ossification risk, the *Fox* Court seems to have the opposite concern. Is *Fox* therefore inconsistent with *State Farm*? If so, can the inconsistency be justified?

1. *Independent versus Executive Agencies?* The agency in *State Farm* was an executive department directly accountable to the President, while the agency in *Fox* was an independent agency. The dissenters argue that, because of the relative insulation of independent agencies from political pressures, policy changes made by independent agencies should be subject to *more* stringent judicial scrutiny than those made by executive agencies and, consequently, that *State Farm* applies a fortiori to *Fox*. But might the opposite be true? Might the relative insulation of independent agencies from political pressures lead one to expect their decisions to be generally *more* reasoned than the decisions of executive agencies and thus to merit *more* deference from courts?

Writing for a plurality of Justices (Part III.E of his opinion, which Justice Kennedy did not join), Justice Scalia argues that independent agencies like the FCC are subject to significant political pressures exerted by Congress through its oversight authority. Thus, "independent" agencies are not necessarily free from politics; the political pressure just comes from different branches of government. (In fact, Justice Scalia argues that the FCC's new policy in *Fox Television* was a direct consequence of congressional complaints that families were being subjected to inappropriate language during prime-time television.) But once again, might the opposite be true? Might the political accountability of independent agencies lead one to expect their decisions to be *as poorly* reasoned as those of executive agencies and thus to merit *as much* scrutiny from courts?

Should APA judicial review distinguish between the kind of agency promulgating the evolving policy that is being reviewed?

2. *Facts versus Norms.* Rather than trying to distinguish *State Farm* and *Fox* based on the different kinds of *agencies* involved in each, one might try to distinguish them based on the different kinds of *policies* involved in each. Whereas the policy in *State Farm* seemed to be based on a relatively technical cost-benefit analysis, the policy in *Fox* seemed to be based more on a social or moral judgment.

This difference might help to explain Justice Scalia's observation about the difficulty of obtaining data about the harmfulness of fleeting expletives in broadcasts and the comparative ease of obtaining data about the benefits of passive restraints in automobiles. Perhaps the FCC's policy change rested on the judgment that, whatever the tangible harm caused by fleeting expletives, it was simply *wrong* or *immoral* to expose the public—and especially children—to such indecency. If this was in fact the nature of the FCC's judgment, should courts be more or less willing to defer to it than they would be to defer to a more technical cost-benefit analysis?

Note also that the moral judgment represented in *Fox* raises important First Amendment concerns not present in the cost-benefit judgment represented in *State Farm*: Isn't a "fleeting expletive" a classic example of free expression? Cf. *Cohen v. California*, 403 U.S. 15 (1971) (invalidating state censorship of a young man with "Fuck the Draft" on his jacket). As *Pacifica* held, Congress has greater leeway to regulate indecent speech on the radio and television than in newspapers and the print media—but the regulatory authority is not unlimited. Shouldn't there be more specific guidance from Congress as to such important matters—or is Justice Scalia probably right, that Congress was behind the FCC's tighter rule?

3. *The Difference Process Might Make?* Should process distinguish *State Farm* from *Fox Television*? The obvious process difference is that the former was a rulemaking proceeding, while the latter was an agency adjudication—but that difference might just as easily cut the other way. That is, a shift in agency policy might be more legitimate in the kind of rulemaking that *State Farm* overturned than in an adjudication that *Fox Television* sanctioned. In notice-and-comment rulemaking, for example, a greater variety of interests will submit formal analyses, and the agency must consider them—in contrast to adjudication, where the agency must only respond to the parties' presentations.

Another possible process distinction is that the DOT's auto safety policy had been a political football through several administrations, and the *State Farm* Court might have felt that the agency needed to buckle down and take its law work more seriously. In contrast, perhaps, the FCC's policy was more stable over several administrations. Although the FCC was moving policy toward greater regulation in *Fox Television*, it was making a small step (expanding the longstanding policy to include "fleeting" expletives), and a step that was arguably justified by proliferation of fleeting expletives during prime time (when more children are watching TV) and by technology allowing networks to bleep out fleeting expletives. Are any of these distinctions persuasive—or is *Fox Television* simply a precedent-narrowing reading of *State Farm*? Should *State Farm* be reframed, or even overruled?

SECTION 3. JUDICIAL DEFERENCE TO AGENCY INTERPRETATIONS

Earlier chapters have focused on statutory interpretation by courts. Jerry L. Mashaw, *Agency Statutory Interpretation*, Issues in Legal Scholarship, Issue 3: Dynamic Statutory Interpretation (2002): Article 9, *available at* www.bepress.com/ils/iss3/art9, argues that agencies and courts will and *ought to* follow different approaches to statutory interpretation, because of their different institutional competences and responsibilities. The table below is reproduced from his article and encapsulates his normative suggestions.

Mashaw Table of Canons for Agency and Court Statutory Interpretation

Canon for Statutory Interpretation	Appropriate for Agencies?	Appropriate for Courts?
1. *Follow presidential directives unless clearly outside your authority*	Yes	No
2. *Interpret to avoid raising constitutional questions*	No	Yes
3. *Use legislative history as a primary interpretive guide*	Yes	No
4. *Interpret to give energy and breadth to all legislative programs within your jurisdiction*	Yes	No
5. *Engage in activist lawmaking*	Yes	No
6. *Respect all judicial precedent*	No	Yes
7. *Interpret to lend coherence to the overall legal order*	No	Yes
8. *Pay particular attention to the strategic parameters of interpretive efficiency*	Yes	No
9. *Interpret to secure hierarchical control over subordinates*	Yes	No
10. *Pay constant attention to your contemporary political milieu*	Yes	No

* Source: Mashaw, *Agency Statutory Interpretation*

Many items in Mashaw's table might be questioned. For example, item 5 strikes us as meaningless without a careful definition of "activist" (which for most lawyers means any interpretation they strongly disagree with). And Trevor Morrison, *Constitutional Avoidance in the Executive Branch*, 106 Colum. L. Rev. 1189 (2006), vigorously argues, contra Mashaw, that agencies should consider the avoidance canon when they interpret statutes. Consider a dramatic example of statutory interpretation "outside the courts," in the following problem.

PROBLEM 6–5

Executive Department Interpretation of Wiretapping Authority

In the wake of the al Qaeda-organized attacks on the World Trade Center and the Pentagon on 9/11/01, President Bush authorized the National Security Agency (NSA) to intercept international communications into and out of the United States of persons linked to al Qaeda or related terrorist organizations. The President subsequently explained that his purpose was to "establish an early warning system to detect and prevent another catastrophic terrorist attack on the United States." Presidential Press Conference, December 19, 2005. "[A] two-minute phone conversation between somebody linked to al Qaeda here and an operative overseas could lead directly to the loss of thousands of lives." *Id.* (Since 9/11, al Qaeda leaders have repeatedly promised to deliver another attack on American soil. The group has done so successfully in Spain, Indonesia, and the United Kingdom since 9/11.)

Because terrorists pose such a huge threat and move quickly from place to place, the President maintains that protocols Congress set in place in 1978 for long-term electronic communications monitoring are no longer appropriate and must be supplemented with emergency shorter-term measures. NSA activities are "carefully reviewed every 45 days to ensure that [they are] being used properly." *Id.* The Attorney General monitors for legality, and NSA officials themselves monitor to assure protection of civil liberties.

Civil libertarians assailed the NSA wiretapping program, and Members of Congress expressed concern. You are the General Counsel to the Senate Judiciary Committee, chaired in 2006 by Senator Arlen Specter (R–Pa.). Senator Specter wonders whether the NSA program is legal. It might violate the Fourth Amendment, which the Supreme Court has construed to require warrants and probable cause for wiretaps, e.g., *Katz v. United States*, 389 U.S. 347 (1967), but the Court has never definitively ruled on the Fourth Amendment validity of surveillance to investigate foreign-sponsored terrorist activities. See *United States v. United States District Court*, 407 U.S. 297 (1972) (reserving this issue).

Set the Fourth Amendment questions aside. Instead, Senator Specter asks you to tell him whether the NSA program is a legitimate exercise of the President's authority, especially in light of prior legislation. The following materials will help you frame an answer to Senator Specter.[a]

January 9, 2006 Letter from Scholars and Former Government Officials [Curtis A. Bradley et al.] to Congressional Leadership in Response to Justice Department Letter of December 22, 2005.[b] In 1978, Congress enacted the Foreign Intelligence Surveillance Act (FISA). "With minor exceptions, FISA authorizes electronic surveillance only upon certain specified showings, and only if approved by a court. The statute specifically allows for warrantless *wartime* domestic electronic surveillance— but only for the first fifteen days of a war. 50 USC § 1811. It makes criminal any electronic surveillance not authorized by statute, *id.* § 1809; and it expressly establishes FISA and specified provisions of the federal criminal code (which govern wiretaps for criminal investigation) as the 'exclusive means by which electronic surveillance ... may be conducted.' 18 USC § 2511(2)(f) (emphasis added)."

The Department of Justice conceded that FISA did not authorize the NSA program, but argued that the AUMF [Authorization for the Use of Military Force] did. Signed on September 18, 2001, the AUMF empowers the President to use "all necessary and appropriate force against" al Qaeda. According to the DOJ, collecting "signals intelligence" on the enemy, including U.S. phone tapping, is a "fundamental incident of war" authorized by the AUMF.

The scholars advanced several reasons they thought the President was wrong about that: (1) The statute specifically addressing the matter of wiretaps (FISA) governs the more generally phrased law (AUMF), under accepted principles of statutory interpretation. Also, (2) repeals by implica-

---

a. These materials are taken from the appendices to David Cole & Martin Lederman, *The National Security Agency's Domestic Spying Program: Framing the Debate*, 81 Ind. L.J. 1363–1424 (2006).

b. This Letter, 81 Ind. L.J. at 1363–72, was a response to the December 22, 2005 Letter from Department of Justice to the Leadership of the Senate Select Committee on Intelligence and House Permanent Select Committee on Intelligence. *Id.* at 1359–62.

tion, the effect of the DOJ's broad AUMF interpretation, are disfavored in the law. Finally, (3) Members of Congress advised the Attorney General that legislation amending the FISA to allow this program would not be feasible. "It is one thing, however, to say that foreign battlefield capture of enemy combatants is an incident of waging war that Congress intended to authorize. It is another matter entirely to treat unchecked warrantless *domestic* spying as included in that authorization, especially where an existing statute specifies that other laws are the 'exclusive means' by which electronic surveillance may be conducted and provides that even a declaration of war authorizes such spying only for a fifteen-day emergency period."

" * * * [T]he [old] federal law involving wiretapping specifically provided that '[n]othing contained in this chapter or in section 605 of the Communications Act of 1934 shall limit the constitutional power of the President . . . to obtain foreign intelligence information deemed essential to the security of the United States.' 18 USC § 2511(3) (1976).

"But FISA specifically repealed that provision, FISA § 201(c), 92 Stat. 1797, and replaced it with language dictating that FISA and the criminal code are the 'exclusive means' of conducting electronic surveillance. In doing so, Congress did not deny that the President has constitutional power to conduct electronic surveillance for national security purposes; rather, Congress properly concluded that 'even if the President has the inherent authority in the absence of legislation to authorize warrantless electronic surveillance for foreign intelligence purposes, Congress has the power to regulate the conduct of such surveillance by legislating a reasonable procedure, which then becomes the exclusive means by which such surveillance can be conducted.' HR Rep. No. 95–1282 (1978). * * *

"Congress plainly has authority to regulate domestic wiretapping by federal agencies under its Article I powers, and the DOJ does not suggest otherwise. Indeed, when FISA was enacted, the Justice Department agreed that Congress had power to regulate such conduct, and could require judicial approval of foreign intelligence surveillance. [S. Rep. No. 95–604, pt. 1, at 16 (1977), et al.] * * * "

U.S. Department of Justice, "Legal Authorities Supporting the Activities of the National Security Agency Described by the President," January 19, 2006.[c] "As Congress expressly recognized in the AUMF, 'the President has authority under the Constitution to take action to deter and prevent acts of international terrorism against the United States,' AUMF pmbl., especially in the context of the current conflict. Article II of the Constitution vests in the President all executive powers of the United States, including the power to act as Commander in Chief of the Armed Forces, *see* U.S. Const. Art. II, § 2, and authority over the conduct of the Nation's foreign affairs. As the Supreme Court has explained, '[t]he President is the sole organ of the nation in its external relations, and its sole representative with foreign nations.' *United States v. Curtiss–Wright Export Corp.*, 299 U.S. 304 (1936). In this way, the Constitution gives the President inherent power to protect the Nation from foreign attack, *see, e.g., The Prize Cases*, 67 U.S. 635, 668

---

c. This Letter, 81 Ind. L.J. at 1373–1413, was a response to the Scholars' Letter of January 9 and a detailed elaboration of arguments suggested in the Department's Letter of December 22.

(1863), and to protect national security information, *see, e.g., Department of the Navy v. Egan*, 484 U.S. 518, 527 (1988).

"To carry out these responsibilities, the President must have authority to gather information necessary for the execution of his office. The Founders, after all, intended the federal Government to be clothed with all authority necessary to protect the Nation. *See, e.g., The Federalist* * * * No. 41 (James Madison) ('Security against foreign danger is one of the primitive objects of civil society.... The powers requisite for attaining it must be effectually confided to the federal councils.'). Because of the structural advantages of the Executive Branch, the Founders also intended that the President would have the primary responsibility and necessary authority as Commander in Chief and Chief Executive to protect the Nation and to conduct the Nation's foreign affairs. See, e.g., *The Federalist* No.70, at 471–72 (Hamilton); *see also Johnson v. Eisentrager*, 339 U.S. 763, 788 (1950) ('this [constitutional] grant of war power includes all that is necessary and proper for carrying these powers into execution'). Thus, it has long been recognized that the President has the authority to use secretive means to collect intelligence necessary for the conduct of foreign affairs and military campaigns. [*Curtiss–Wright* et al.]

"In reliance on these principles, a consistent understanding has developed that the President has inherent constitutional authority to conduct warrantless searches and surveillance within the United States for foreign intelligence purposes. Wiretaps for such purposes thus have been authorized by Presidents at least since the administration of Franklin Roosevelt in 1940. *See, e.g., United States v. United States District Court*, 444 F.2d 651, 669–71 (6th Cir. 1971) (reproducing as an appendix memoranda from Presidents Roosevelt, Truman, and Johnson). In a Memorandum to Attorney General Jackson, President Roosevelt wrote on May 21, 1940:

> You are, therefore, authorized and directed in such cases as you may approve, after investigation of the need in each case, to authorize the necessary investigation agents that they are at liberty to secure information by listening devices directed to the conversation or other communications of persons suspected of subversive activities against the Government of the United States, including suspected spies. You are requested furthermore to limit these investigations so conducted to a minimum and limit them insofar as possible to aliens. *Id.* at 670 (appendix A).

President Truman approved a memorandum drafted by Attorney General Tom Clark in which the Attorney General advised that 'it is as necessary as it was in 1940 to take the investigative measures' authorized by President Roosevelt to conduct electronic surveillance 'in cases vitally affecting the domestic security.' *Id.* Indeed, while the FISA was being debated during the Carter Administration, Attorney General Griffin Bell testified that 'the current bill recognizes no inherent power of the President to conduct electronic surveillance, and I want to interpolate here to say that *this does not take away the power [of] the President under the Constitution.*' Foreign Intelligence Electronic Surveillance Act of 1978: Hearings on H.R. 5764 [et al.] Before the Subcomm. on Legislation of the House Comm. on Intelligence, 95th Cong., 2d Sess. 15 (1978) (emphasis added) * * *.

"On September 14, 2001, in its first legislative response to the attacks of September 11th, Congress gave its express approval to the President's military campaign against al Qaeda and, in the process, confirmed the well-accepted understanding of the President's Article II powers. *See* AUMF § 2(a). In the preamble to the AUMF, Congress stated that 'the President has authority under the Constitution to take action to deter and prevent acts of international terrorism against the United States,' AUMF pmbl., and thereby acknowledged the President's inherent constitutional authority to defend the United States. This clause 'constitutes an extraordinarily sweeping recognition of independent presidential *constitutional* power to employ the war power to combat terrorism.' Michael Stokes Paulsen, Youngstown *Goes to War*, 19 Const. Comment. 215, 252 (2002). This striking recognition of presidential authority cannot be discounted as the product of excitement in the immediate aftermath of September 11th, for the same terms were repeated by Congress more than a year later in the Authorization for the Use of Military Force Against Iraq Resolution of 2002. Pub. L. No. 107–243, pmbl., 116 Stat. 1498, 1500 (Oct. 16, 2002) ('The President has authority under the Constitution to take action in order to deter and prevent acts of international terrorism against the United States. . . .'). In the context of the conflict with al Qaeda and related terrorist organizations, therefore, Congress has acknowledged a broad executive authority to 'deter and prevent' further attacks against the United States.

"The AUMF passed by Congress on September 14, 2001, does not lend itself to a narrow reading. Its expansive language authorizes the President 'to use all *necessary and appropriate force* against those nations, organizations, or persons *he determines* planned, authorized, committed, or aided the terrorist attacks that occurred on September 11, 2001.' AUMF § 2(a) (emphasis added). In the field of foreign affairs, and particularly that of war powers and national security, congressional enactments are to be broadly construed where they indicate support for authority long asserted and exercised by the Executive Branch. * * * This authorization transforms the struggle against al Qaeda and related terrorist organizations from what Justice Jackson called 'a zone of twilight,' in which the President and Congress may have concurrent powers whose 'distribution is uncertain,' *Youngstown* (Jackson, J., concurring), into a situation in which the President's authority it at its maximum because 'it includes all that he possesses in his own right plus all that Congress can delegate,' *id.* With regard to these fundamental tools of warfare—and, as demonstrated below, warrantless electronic surveillance against the declared enemy is one such tool—the AUMF places the President's authority at its zenith under *Youngstown*. * * *

"The Supreme Court's interpretation of the scope of the AUMF in *Hamdi v. Rumsfeld*, 542 U.S. 507 (2004), strongly supports this reading of the AUMF. In *Hamdi*, five members of the Court [the O'Connor plurality plus the Thomas dissent] found that the AUMF authorized the detention of an American within the United States, notwithstanding a statute that prevents the detention of U.S. citizens 'except pursuant to an Act of Congress.' 18 U.S.C. § 4001(a). Drawing on historical materials and 'longstanding law-of-war principles,' a plurality of the Court concluded that detention of combatants who fought against the United States as part of an organization 'known to have supported' al Qaeda 'is so fundamental and accepted an incident to war as to be an exercise of the "necessary and appropriate force" Congress has authorized the President to use.' *Id.* at 518; *see also id.* at 587 (Thomas, J., dissenting) (agreeing with the plurality that the joint resolution authorized the President to 'detain those arrayed against our troops'); *accord, Quirin,* 317 U.S. at 26–29, 38 (recognizing the President's authority to capture and try agents of the enemy in the United States even if they had never 'entered the theatre or zone of active military operations'). Thus, even though the AUMF does not say anything expressly about detention, the Court nevertheless found that it satisfied section 4001(a)'s requirement that detention be congressionally authorized. * * *

"The history of warfare—including the consistent practice of Presidents since the earliest days of the Republic—demonstrates that warrantless intelligence surveillance against the enemy is a fundamental incident of the use of military force, and this history confirms the statutory authority provided by the AUMF. Electronic surveillance is a fundamental tool of war that must be included in any natural reading of the AUMF's authorization to use 'all necessary and appropriate force.' "

The Department argued that, from General Washington onward, American leaders have "intercepted communications for wartime intelligence purposes and, if necessary, has done so within its own borders." This practice continued during World War II and, according to one historian, "helped shorten the war by perhaps two years."

" * * * [S]ection 109 of FISA prohibits any person from intentionally 'engag[ing] . . . in electronic surveillance under color of law *except as authorized by statute.*' 50 U.S.C. § 1809(a)(1) (emphasis added). * * *

"The AUMF qualifies as a 'statute' authorizing electronic surveillance within the meaning of section 109 of FISA. * * * As explained above, it is not necessary to demarcate the outer limits of the AUMF to conclude that it encompasses electronic surveillance targeted at the enemy. Just as a majority of the Court concluded in *Hamdi* that the AUMF authorizes detention of U.S. citizens who are enemy combatants without expressly mentioning the President's long-recognized power to detain, so too does it authorize the use of electronic surveillance without specifically mentioning the President's equally long-recognized power to engage in communications intelligence targeted at the enemy. And just as the AUMF satisfies the requirement in 18 U.S.C. § 4001(a) that no U.S. citizen be detained 'except pursuant to an Act of Congress,' so too does it satisfy section 109's requirement for statutory authorization of electronic surveillance. * * * "

Section 111 of FISA, 50 USC § 1811, which capped presidential surveillance even in time of war without court authorization at fifteen days, "cannot reasonably be read as Congress's final word on electronic surveillance during wartime. * * * Rather, section 111 represents Congress's recognition that it would likely have to return to the subject and provide additional authorization to conduct warrantless electronic surveillance outside FISA during time of war. * * *

"Nothing in the terms of section 111 disables Congress from authorizing such electronic surveillance as a traditional incident of war through a broad,

conflict-specific authorization for the use of military force, such as the AUMF.
* * *

" * * * Nevertheless, some might argue that sections 109 and 111 of the
FISA, along with section 2511(2)(f)'s 'exclusivity' provision and section
2511(2)(e)'s liability exception for officers engaged in FISA-authorized surveillance, are best read to suggest that FISA requires that subsequent authorizing legislation specifically amend FISA in order to free the Executive from
FISA's enumerated procedures. As detailed above, this is not the better
reading of FISA. But even if these provisions were ambiguous, any doubt as to
whether the AUMF and FISA should be understood to allow the President to
make tactical military decisions to authorize surveillance outside the parameters of FISA must be resolved to avoid the serious constitutional questions
that a contrary interpretation would raise.

"It is well established that the first task of any interpreter faced with a
statute that may present an unconstitutional infringement on the powers of
the President is to determine whether the statute may be construed to avoid
the constitutional difficulty. '[I]f an otherwise acceptable construction of a
statute would raise serious constitutional problems, and where an alternative
interpretation of the statute is "fairly possible," then we are obligated to
construe the statute to avoid such problems.' *INS v. St. Cyr*, 533 U.S. 289,
299–300 (2001); *Ashwander v. TVA*, 297 U.S. 288, 345–48 (1936) (Brandeis, J.,
concurring). Moreover, the canon of constitutional avoidance has particular
importance in the realm of national security, where the President's constitutional authority is at its highest. See *Department of the Navy v. Egan*, 484
U.S. 518, 530 (1988); William N. Eskridge, Jr., *Dynamic Statutory Interpretation* 325 (1994) (describing '[s]uper-strong rule against congressional interference with the President's authority over foreign affairs and national security')." The AUMF should be interpreted broadly, and FISA narrowly, to avoid
constructions where FISA would unconstitutionally obstruct the President's
commander-in-chief powers.

The concluding portion of the Letter argued that the NSA program did
not violate the Fourth Amendment.

**February 2, 2006 Letter from Scholars and Former Government
Officials to Congressional Leadership in Response to Justice Department White Paper of January 19, 2006.** The Scholars found no authorization for illegal wiretapping in the AUMF, especially in light of section 111.
"An amendment to FISA of the sort that would presumably be required to
authorize the NSA program here would be a momentous statutory development, undoubtedly subject to serious legislative debate. It is decidedly *not* the
sort of thing that Congress would enact *inadvertently*. As the Supreme Court
recently noted, ' "Congress does not alter the fundamental details of a
regulatory scheme in vague terms or ancillary provisions—it does not, one
might say, hide elephants in mouseholes." ' *Gonzales v. Oregon*, 126 S.Ct. 904,
921 (2006) (quoting *Whitman v. American Trucking Ass'ns*, 531 U.S. 457, 468
(2001))."

Section 111 also distinguishes this situation from that in *Hamdi*. The
detention statute in *Hamdi* did not mention detention of citizens in wartime.
"Had there been a statute on the books providing that when Congress

declares war, the President may detain Americans as 'enemy combatants' *only* for the first fifteen days of the conflict, the Court could not reasonably have read the AUMF to authorize silently what Congress had specifically sought to limit. Yet that is what the DOJ's argument would require here. [See also 18 U.S.C. § 2511(2)(f), which specifies that FISA and the criminal code are the 'exclusive means' by which electronic surveillance can be conducted. DOJ concedes that its interpretation requires an implicit repeal of § 2511, which is strongly disfavored in the law.]

"The argument that conduct undertaken by the Commander in Chief that has some relevance to 'engaging the enemy' is immune from congressional regulation finds no support in, and is directly contradicted by, both case law and historical precedent. *Every* time the Supreme Court has confronted a statute limiting the Commander-in-Chief's authority, it has upheld the statute. No precedent holds that the President, when acting as Commander in Chief, is free to disregard an Act of Congress, much less a *criminal statute* enacted by Congress, that was designed specifically to restrain the President as such. [See, e.g., *Little v. Barreme*, 6 U.S. 170 (1804), holding unlawful a presidential seizure of a ship coming *from* France during the Quasi–War with France, when Congress authorized seizure only of ships going *to* France.]

"In fact, as cases such as *Hamdi* and *Rasul* demonstrate, Congress has routinely enacted statutes regulating the Commander-in-Chief's 'means and methods of engaging the enemy.' It has subjected the Armed Forces to the Uniform Code of Military Justice, which expressly restricts the means they use in 'engaging the enemy.' It has enacted statutes setting forth the rules for governing occupied territory. And, most recently, it has enacted statutes prohibiting torture under all circumstances, 18 USC §§ 2340–2340A, and prohibiting the use of cruel, inhuman, and degrading treatment. Pub. L. No. 109–148, Div. A, tit X, § 1003, 119 Stat. 2739–40 (2005). These limitations make ample sense in light of the overall constitutional structure. Congress has the explicit power 'To make Rules for the Government and Regulation of the land and naval Forces.' US Const., art. I, § 8, cl. 14. The President has the explicit constitutional obligation to 'take Care that the Laws be faithfully executed,' U.S. Const., art. II, § 3—including FISA. And Congress has the explicit power to 'make all Laws which shall be necessary and proper for carrying into Execution . . . all . . . Powers vested by this Constitution in the Government of the United States, or in any Department or Officer thereof.' US Const., art. I, [§ 8, cl. 18].

"If the DOJ were correct that Congress cannot interfere with the Commander in Chief's discretion in 'engaging the enemy,' all of these statutes would be unconstitutional. Yet the President recently conceded that Congress may constitutionally bar him from engaging in torture. Torturing a suspect, no less than wiretapping an American, might provide information about the enemy that could conceivably help prevent a terrorist attack, yet the President has now conceded that Congress can prohibit that conduct. * * * "

The Letter also argued that FISA does not unduly interfere with the President's ability to gather intelligence. FISA only applies if the target is a U.S. person in the U.S., or where the surveillance "acquisition" occurs in the U.S. 50 U.S.C. § 1801(f)(1)–(2). FISA does not prohibit wiretapping; it only requires approval, including after-the-fact approval so long as the petition is filed within 72 hours. 50 U.S.C. § 1805(f). "As such, the statute cannot reasonably be said to intrude impermissibly upon the President's ability to 'engage the enemy,' and certainly does not come anywhere close to 'prohibit[ing] the President from undertaking actions necessary to fulfill his constitutional obligation to protect the Nation from foreign attack.' DOJ Memo."

Queries: This exchange illustrates most of Mashaw's *proposed* canons for agencies and the executive to interpret statutes. Is this a model that seems attractive to you? If not, can you come up with one that would work better? Relevant to the Mashaw–Morrison debate, do you think the executive branch handled the constitutional arguments productively?

Final question: Assume that one of the Americans subject to the President's wiretapping brought a justiciable claim in federal court, challenging the President's authority under FISA. How would the Supreme Court handle this case? More to the point: How much, if at all, would the Court "defer" to the executive interpretation of FISA and AUMF? How much deference *should* the Court give? What considerations should influence the deference equation?

A. THE BASIC FRAMEWORK: *SKIDMORE* AND *CHEVRON*

The New Deal approach to deference was founded on the comparative expertise of courts and agencies: the former should defer to the experts who worked with the statute day-in and day-out and developed wisdom about what worked and what did not. The leading case was *Skidmore v. Swift & Co.*, 323 U.S. 134 (1944). Employees sued their employer to recover overtime pay unlawfully withheld under the Fair Labor Standards Act. The employer argued that the "extra" time they alleged was inactive time and not "hours worked" for purposes of the Act.

The Administrator (the Department of Labor official charged with implementing the Act) filed an *amicus* brief with the Supreme Court which described the flexible approach he had taken to the "inactive duty" issue. In his view, the on-call duty time spent sleeping and eating should not be included in "hours worked," but the remainder of the on-call time should be.

Justice Jackson's opinion for the *Skidmore* Court observed that the Administrator's practices and his recommendation in this case did not constitute a "binding" interpretation of the statute, but they were entitled to "respect," because they "constituted a body of experience and informed judgment" regarding workplace practices. "The weight of such a judgment in a particular case will depend upon the thoroughness evident in its consideration, the validity of its reasoning, its consistency with earlier and later pronouncements, and all those factors which give it power to persuade, if lacking power to control." The Court followed the Administrator's judgment and reversed the court below upon this point of law.

Soon after the APA's adoption, in 1946, Louis Jaffe explained how the modern administrative state fit into the traditional statutory interpretation framework, while at the same time altering it subtly. Louis L. Jaffe, *Judicial Review: Question of Law*, 69 Harv. L. Rev. 239 (1955). Consistent with *Marbury* and APA § 706, the Supreme Court remained the expositor of what the law is, but when interpreting vague or ambiguous regulatory statutes the Court was and ought to be open to agency inputs. Sometimes the Court found that the statute was relatively clear, but other times statutory vagueness suggested a range of possible meanings and the Court was willing to accept the agency's interpretation if it were within that range, as in *Skidmore* and later decisions such as *Udall v. Tallman*, 380 U.S. 1, 16 (1965).

Professor Jaffe also believed that the New Deal had regularized a different kind of agency role. In many statutes, Congress had (consistent with the APA) delegated to agencies the authority to create binding "law," usually through formal adjudications and legislative rules. Under those circumstances, Jaffe suggested that the role of the Court was more like deferential judicial review that the New Deal Court applied to social and economic legislation. Likewise, when reviewing agency *lawmaking*, the Court should give the agency's rule the benefit of the doubt and overturn it only if it was *unreasonable*, in light of the statutory text and purposes. Jaffe, *Judicial Review*, 243–44. This idea was the germ for what would become the famous "*Chevron* Doctrine," introduced in this part.

General Electric Co. v. Gilbert, 429 U.S. 125 (1976). General Electric provided for all of its employees a disability plan which paid weekly nonoccupational sickness and accident benefits. Excluded from the plan's coverage were disabilities arising from pregnancy. Female employees challenged this plan as sex discrimination in violation of Title VII. The Supreme Court, in an opinion by **Justice Rehnquist,** held that the exclusion of pregnancy was not sex discrimination, relying on *Geduldig v. Aiello*, 417 U.S. 484 (1974), where the Court stated that state discrimination in employee plans on the basis of pregnancy did not violate the Fourteenth Amendment. The reasoning for both decisions was that failure to provide pregnancy benefits is not "discrimination based upon gender as such." Justice Rehnquist conceded that Title VII, as interpreted by the Court, prohibited discriminatory effects as well as intended discrimination. But he concluded that query with the assertion that there was insufficient evidence that the plan in question selected risks that had discriminatory effects. "As there is no proof that the package is in fact worth more to men than to women, it is impossible to find any gender-based discrimination in the scheme simply because women disabled as a result of pregnancy do not receive benefits * * *."

The employees relied on a 1972 regulation issued by the EEOC and urged the Court to defer to it. The Court ruled that the EEOC regulation was not entitled to deference. To begin with, Title VII did not confer upon the EEOC authority to promulgate substantive rules. The proper level of deference for such informal agency views was set forth in *Skidmore v. Swift & Co.*, 323 U.S. 134, 140 (1944). [The Court quoted the language from the beginning of this part.]

The 1972 guideline fared badly under this standard, first, because it was not a "contemporaneous interpretation of Title VII, since it was first promulgated eight years after the enactment of that Title. More important, the 1972 guideline flatly contradicted the position which the agency had enunciated at an earlier date, closer to the enactment of the governing statute," specifically, an opinion letter by the General Counsel of the EEOC, dated October 17, 1966, which opined that an employer policy excluding pregnancy from its disability policy did not violate Title VII. Most important, the EEOC interpretation was inconsistent with the interpretation of the Wage and Hour Administrator of § 6(d) of the Equal Pay Act to permit employers to offer different levels of disability benefits to male and female employees. Section 703(h) of Title VII explicitly permits practices allowed under § 6 of the Equal Pay Act.

Justice Brennan (joined by Justice Marshall) dissented, disputing the majority's concept of what is "sex discrimination" and urging deference to the EEOC, as the Court did in *Albemarle Paper Co. v. Moody*, 422 U.S. 405, 431 (1975); *Griggs v. Duke Power Co.*, 401 U.S. 424, 433–34 (1971). Justice Brennan argued that the EEOC moved slowly and deliberatively toward a policy on pregnancy and maternity, because the agency needed more information and study of this difficult issue:

> Therefore, while some eight years had elapsed prior to the issuance of the 1972 guideline, and earlier opinion letters had refused to impose liability on employers during this period of deliberation, no one can or does deny that the final EEOC determination followed thorough and well-informed consideration. Indeed, realistically viewed, this extended evaluation of an admittedly complex problem and an unwillingness to impose additional, potentially premature costs on employers during the decisionmaking stages ought to be perceived as a practice to be commended. It is bitter irony that the care that preceded promulgation of the 1972 guideline is today condemned by the Court as tardy indecisiveness, its unwillingness irresponsibly to challenge employers' practices during the formative period is labeled as evidence of inconsistency, and this indecisiveness and inconsistency are bootstrapped into reasons for denying the Commission's interpretation its due deference.

Justice Brennan maintained that the 1972 EEOC rule was consistent with congressional actions also occurring in the 1970s (a series of statutes extending various employment protections to pregnant women), and with studies showing that "pregnancy exclusions built into disability programs both financially burden women workers and act to break down the continuity of the employment relationship, thereby exacerbating women's comparatively transient role in the labor force. In dictating pregnancy coverage under Title VII, the EEOC's guideline merely settled upon a solution now accepted by every other Western industrial country."

Postscript: Congress responded to *Gilbert* with the Pregnancy Discrimination Act of 1978, Pub. L. No. 95–555, 92 Stat. 2076, codified at 42

U.S.C. § 2000e(k), which establishes that "discrimination on the basis of * * * sex" in Title VII includes denial of pregnancy benefits. The Supreme Court in *Newport News Shipbuilding & Dry Dock Co. v. EEOC*, 462 U.S. 669 (1983), held that the 1978 amendment not only overruled the *Gilbert* result, but also invalidated the *Gilbert* Court's narrow approach to discrimination.

CHEVRON, U.S.A., INC. v. NATURAL RESOURCES DEFENSE COUNCIL

Supreme Court of the United States, 1984
467 U.S. 837, 104 S.Ct. 2778, 81 L.Ed.2d 694

JUSTICE STEVENS delivered the opinion of the Court.

In the Clean Air Act Amendments of 1977, Pub. L. 95–95, 91 Stat. 685, Congress enacted certain requirements applicable to States that had not achieved the national air quality standards established by the Environmental Protection Agency (EPA) pursuant to earlier legislation. The amended Clean Air Act required these "nonattainment" States to establish a permit program regulating "new or modified major stationary sources" of air pollution. Generally, a permit may not be issued for a new or modified major stationary source unless several stringent conditions are met.[1] The EPA regulation promulgated to implement this permit requirement allows a State to adopt a plantwide definition of the term "stationary source."[2] Under this definition, an existing plant that contains several pollution-emitting devices may install or modify one piece of equipment without meeting the permit conditions if the alteration will not increase the total emissions from the plant. The question presented by these cases is whether EPA's decision to allow States to treat all of the pollution-emitting devices within the same industrial grouping as though they were encased within a single "bubble" is based on a reasonable construction of the statutory term "stationary source." * * *

[II] When a court reviews an agency's construction of the statute which it administers, it is confronted with two questions. First, always, is the question whether Congress has directly spoken to the precise question at issue. If the intent of Congress is clear, that is the end of the matter, for the court, as well as the agency, must give effect to the unambiguously expressed intent of Congress.[9] If, however, the court determines Congress

---

1. Section 172(b)(6), 42 U.S.C. § 7502(b)(6), provides:

"The plan provisions required by subsection (a) shall—* * *

"(6) require permits for the construction and operation of new or modified major stationary sources in accordance with section 173 (relating to permit requirements)." 91 Stat. 747.

2. "(i) 'Stationary source' means any building, structure, facility, or installation which emits or may emit any air pollutant subject to regulation under the Act.

"(ii) 'Building, structure, facility, or installation' means all of the pollutant-emitting activities which belong to the same industrial grouping, are located on one or more contiguous or adjacent properties, and are under the control of the same person (or persons under common control) except the activities of any vessel." 40 CFR §§ 51.18(j)(1)(i) and (ii) (1983).

9. The judiciary is the final authority on issues of statutory construction and must reject administrative constructions which are contrary to clear congressional intent. If a court, employ-

has not directly addressed the precise question at issue, the court does not simply impose its own construction on the statute, as would be necessary in the absence of an administrative interpretation. Rather, if the statute is silent or ambiguous with respect to the specific issue, the question for the court is whether the agency's answer is based on a permissible construction of the statute.[11]

"The power of an administrative agency to administer a congressionally created ... program necessarily requires the formulation of policy and the making of rules to fill any gap left, implicitly or explicitly, by Congress." If Congress has explicitly left a gap for the agency to fill, there is an express delegation of authority to the agency to elucidate a specific provision of the statute by regulation. Such legislative regulations are given controlling weight unless they are arbitrary, capricious, or manifestly contrary to the statute. Sometimes the legislative delegation to an agency on a particular question is implicit rather than explicit. In such a case, a court may not substitute its own construction of a statutory provision for a reasonable interpretation made by the administrator of an agency.

We have long recognized that considerable weight should be accorded to an executive department's construction of a statutory scheme it is entrusted to administer, and the principle of deference to administrative interpretations

> "has been consistently followed by this Court whenever decision as to the meaning or reach of a statute has involved reconciling conflicting policies, and a full understanding of the force of the statutory policy in the given situation has depended upon more than ordinary knowledge respecting the matters subjected to agency regulations.

> "... If this choice represents a reasonable accommodation of conflicting policies that were committed to the agency's care by the statute, we should not disturb it unless it appears from the statute or its legislative history that the accommodation is not one that Congress would have sanctioned." *United States v. Shimer*, 367 U.S. 374, 382, 383 (1961).

In light of these well-settled principles it is clear that the Court of Appeals misconceived the nature of its role in reviewing the regulations at issue. Once it determined, after its own examination of the legislation, that Congress did not actually have an intent regarding the applicability of the bubble concept to the permit program, the question before it was not whether in its view the concept is "inappropriate" in the general context of a program designed to improve air quality, but whether the Administrator's view that it is appropriate in the context of this particular program is

---

ing traditional tools of statutory construction, ascertains that Congress had an intention on the precise question at issue, that intention is the law and must be given effect.

    11. The court need not conclude that the agency construction was the only one it permissibly could have adopted to uphold the construction, or even the reading the court would have reached if the question initially had arisen in a judicial proceeding.

a reasonable one. Based on the examination of the legislation and its history which follows, we agree with the Court of Appeals that Congress did not have a specific intention on the applicability of the bubble concept in these cases, and conclude that the EPA's use of that concept here is a reasonable policy choice for the agency to make.

[The 1977 Amendments added a definition of "major stationary source," as "any stationary facility or source of air pollutants which directly emits, or has the potential to emit, one hundred tons per year or more of any air pollutant." Justice Stevens found this definition ambiguous. Examining the legislative history, he found only that Congress sought to accommodate both the "economic interest in permitting capital improvements to continue and the environmental interest in improving air quality." There was no clear evidence as to how Congress expected this balance to be carried out with regard to stationary sources.]

In these cases the Administrator's interpretation represents a reasonable accommodation of manifestly competing interests and is entitled to deference: the regulatory scheme is technical and complex, the agency considered the matter in a detailed and reasoned fashion, and the decision involves reconciling conflicting policies. Congress intended to accommodate both interests, but did not do so itself on the level of specificity presented by these cases. Perhaps that body consciously desired the Administrator to strike the balance at this level, thinking that those with great expertise and charged with responsibility for administering the provision would be in a better position to do so; perhaps it simply did not consider the question at this level; and perhaps Congress was unable to forge a coalition on either side of the question, and those on each side decided to take their chances with the scheme devised by the agency. For judicial purposes, it matters not which of these things occurred.

Judges are not experts in the field, and are not part of either political branch of the Government. Courts must, in some cases, reconcile competing political interests, but not on the basis of the judges' personal policy preferences. In contrast, an agency to which Congress has delegated policymaking responsibilities may, within the limits of that delegation, properly rely upon the incumbent administration's views of wise policy to inform its judgments. While agencies are not directly accountable to the people, the Chief Executive is, and it is entirely appropriate for this political branch of the Government to make such policy choices—resolving the competing interests which Congress itself either inadvertently did not resolve, or intentionally left to be resolved by the agency charged with the administration of the statute in light of everyday realities.

When a challenge to an agency construction of a statutory provision, fairly conceptualized, really centers on the wisdom of the agency's policy, rather than whether it is a reasonable choice within a gap left open by Congress, the challenge must fail. In such a case, federal judges—who have no constituency—have a duty to respect legitimate policy choices made by those who do. The responsibilities for assessing the wisdom of such policy choices and resolving the struggle between competing views of the public interest are not judicial ones: "Our Constitution vests such responsibilities in the political branches." *TVA v. Hill*, 437 U.S. 153, 195 (1978). * * *

The judgment of the Court of Appeals is reversed.

JUSTICE MARSHALL and JUSTICE REHNQUIST did not participate in the consideration or decision of these cases.

JUSTICE O'CONNOR did not participate in the decision of these cases.

NOTES ON *CHEVRON* AND *DEFERENCE TO ADMINISTRATIVE INTERPRETATIONS*

1. *Traditional Doctrine of Deference to Agency Interpretations. Gilbert* reflects the *Skidmore* approach to deference. The Court majority saw the EEOC as an agency that could not make up its mind as to exactly how the sex discrimination bar should apply to pregnancy-based employer exclusions. One might even find some suggestion in the opinion that the Court thought the EEOC was a captive of civil rights groups.

The Court's *Skidmore* jurisprudence had become quite complicated by the time *Gilbert* was decided. Colin S. Diver, *Statutory Interpretation in the Administrative State*, 133 U. Pa. L. Rev. 349, 562 n.95 (1985), set forth a "partial list"(!) of circumstances which the Court had considered in deciding whether to defer to administrative interpretations:

> A partial list of the factors cited by the Court would include: (1) whether the agency construction was rendered contemporaneously with the statute's passage, *see, e.g.*, Norwegian Nitrogen Prods. Co. v. United States, 288 U.S. 294, 315 (1933); (2) whether the agency's construction is of longstanding application, *see, e.g.*, NLRB v. Bell Aerospace Co., 416 U.S. 267, 275 (1974); (3) whether the agency has maintained its position consistently (even if infrequently), *see, e.g.*, Haig v. Agee, 453 U.S. 280, 293 (1981); (4) whether the public has relied on the agency's interpretation, *see, e.g.*, Udall v. Tallman, 380 U.S. 1, 18 (1965); (5) whether the interpretation involves a matter of "public controversy," *see, e.g.*, United States v. Rutherford, 442 U.S. 544, 545 (1979); (6) whether the interpretation is based on "expertise" or involves a "technical and complex" subject, *see, e.g.*, Aluminum Co. of Am. v. Central Lincoln People's Util. Dist., [467 U.S. 380 (1984)]; (7) whether the agency has rulemaking authority, *see, e.g.*, FCC v. National Citizens Comm. for Broadcasting, 436 U.S. 775, 793 (1978); (8) whether agency action is necessary to set the statute in motion, *see, e.g.*, Ford Motor Credit Co. v. Milhollin, 444 U.S. 555, 565–66 (1980); (9) whether Congress was aware of the agency interpretation and failed to repudiate it, *see, e.g.*, Zemel v. Rusk, 381 U.S. 1, 11 (1965); and (10) whether the agency has expressly addressed the application of the statute to its proposed action, *see, e.g.*, Investment Co. Inst. v. Camp, 401 U.S. 617, 627–28 (1971).

Does Diver's list support the Court's application *of Skidmore* in *Gilbert*? How would this list apply to the issue in *Chevron*?

2. *The Accidental Birth of a New Regime.* The "bubble concept" adopted by the EPA was twice rebuffed in the D.C. Circuit, but the Department of Justice pressed it before the Supreme Court in an effort to reduce judicial interference with its deregulatory agency initiatives. Representing the EPA, Deputy Solicitor General Paul Bator came up with a brilliant legal argument to counter the D.C. Circuit's conclusion that the bubble concept went beyond the statute. Bator argued that Congress's purpose was complex—to clean up the nation's air (the lower court's focus), but at a reasonable cost to industry (the EPA's focus). Because the statute was fairly open-ended, the EPA had considerable discretion in setting this policy balance, and federal judges should not upset that balance unless the EPA's view was clearly contrary to the statute.[d]

Penned by the first "political" deputy within the SG's Office, Bator's brief was a roadmap for relief from excessive regulatory burdens that was a hallmark of the Reagan Administration (1981–89). Liberal Justice William Brennan was suspicious of Bator's framework, but the Administration caught some lucky breaks as Justices dropped out of the case like flies in a hailstorm.[e] Their biggest break, though, was that the legality of the bubble concept was impossibly complicated for the Court. Apparently the shakiest voice in the original 4–3 conference vote to reverse the D.C. Circuit, Justice Stevens explained his tentative willingness to side with the EPA: "When I am so confused, I go with the agency." (Conference Notes by Justice Blackmun.) Encouraged by Justice White, the assigning Justice in the case, Justice Stevens not only accepted Bator's argument from complex statutory purpose, but went further to write an opinion that was analytically quite innovative.

3. *The Different Approach of* Chevron. *Chevron* reflects a different analytical approach to deference issues than *Gilbert* does. To begin with, the new approach is more formal and much simplified: Step One asks whether Congress specifically addressed the interpretive question. Justice Stevens' opinion, refreshingly, says this is an issue Congress fudged. In that event, the Court moved to Step Two, which asks whether the agency's interpretation is "reasonable." If so, the Court has an obligation to defer. "Where an agency acts pursuant to delegated legislative authority, the task of interpretation is merely to define the boundaries" of what Peter Strauss calls the "zone of indeterminacy" within which Congress has authorized the agency to act.[f]

---

d. On the Bator brief and its background, see Thomas W. Merrill, *The Story of* Chevron USA Inc. v. Natural Resources Defense Council, Inc.: *Sometimes Great Cases Are Made, Not Born*, in *Statutory Interpretation Stories* 164, 177–80 (Eskridge, Frickey & Garrett eds., 2011).

e. Although liberal Justice Brennan voted to affirm the D.C. Circuit, his liberal colleague Thurgood Marshall was absent due to illness. After voting with Brennan to affirm, Justice O'Connor also dropped out of the case because of a potential conflict of interest after her father died. See Memorandum from O'Connor to the Conference, June 14, 1984, in the Papers of Harry A. Blackmun, Library of Congress, Madison Building, Box 397, Folder 7. Also out of the case was Justice Rehnquist, who would probably have been a voice for deference. (As O'Connor mentioned during Conference, the bubble concept was helpful to smelters and other ailing industries in Arizona, her and Rehnquist's home state. See Blackmun's Conference Notes for *Chevron.*)

f. Peter L. Strauss, *One Hundred and Fifty Cases Per Year: Some Implications of the Supreme Court's Limited Resources for Judicial Review of Agency Action*, 87 Colum. L. Rev. 1093, 1124 (1987); accord. Michael E. Herz, *Deference Running Riot: Separating Interpretation and Lawmaking under* Chevron, 6 Admin. L.J. Am. U. 187, 199 (1992).

Chevron is also an important recognition of dynamic statutory interpretation in the modern administrative state, because it recognizes that first-order statutory interpretation will usually be accomplished by politically accountable—and therefore politically protean—agencies; because it further recognizes that under general statutory language that does not target the interpretive issue (Step One) there may be several "reasonable" agency interpretations, any of which must be upheld (Step Two); and because it recognizes that agency interpretations may themselves change over time. "An initial agency interpretation is not carved in stone. On the contrary, the agency, to engage in informal rulemaking, must consider varying interpretations and the wisdom of its policy on a continuing basis." *Chevron,* 467 U.S. at 863–64.

Finally, *Chevron* rests the idea of deference on the greater democratic legitimacy that agencies enjoy over courts in making policy choices that have been left open by Congress. This is both more and less formalist than the approach followed in *Gilbert.* It is less formalist, because deference ought not depend on whether Congress has officially delegated rulemaking responsibilities to the agency, or on whether the agency's opinion was contemporaneous with the enactment of the statute. It is more formalist, because *Chevron* seems to require deference even when the agency is responding to pressure from the President to move statutory policy in ways that Congress would not have adopted. This may have been the case with *Chevron* itself. The liberal Democratic House of Representatives would probably not have favored the bubble concept, but the Reagan Administration very much did.

4. *Hostile Critical Reception. Chevron* was controversial from the very beginning. Then–Judge Breyer objected that a broad reading of *Chevron* is inconsistent with the judicial role articulated in both *Marbury* and in the APA. Both require courts to exercise independent judgment to declare what the law of the land is. See Stephen G. Breyer, *Judicial Review of Questions of Law and Policy,* 38 Admin. L. Rev. 363, 370 (1986); see also Cynthia R. Farina, *Statutory Interpretation and the Balance of Power in the Administrative State,* 89 Colum. L. Rev. 452 (1989) (developing this objection in detail). "[T]he present law of judicial review of administrative decisionmaking, the heart of administrative law, contains an important anomaly," Breyer continued. "The law (1) requires courts to defer to agency judgments about *matters of law,* but (2) it also suggests that courts conduct independent, 'in-depth' reviews of agency judgments about *matters of policy.* [E.g., *State Farm,* in this chapter.] Is this not the exact opposite of a rational system? Would one not expect courts to conduct a stricter review of matters of law, where courts are more expert, but more lenient review of matters of policy, where agencies are more expert?" Breyer, *Judicial Review,* 397.

John F. Duffy, *Administrative Common Law in Judicial Review,* 77 Tex. L. Rev. 113, 199–302 (1998), maintained that the APA and *Chevron* can be reconciled only by understanding that regulatory statutes delegate to agencies the power to interpret ambiguous statutory commands, so long as the agencies' decisions do not conflict with other provisions of law. "Thus, *Chevron* is primarily a case about delegation, not deference." *Id.* at 202. Should Professor Duffy's argument, however, require the kind of statute-specific inquiry that (now) Justice Breyer suggests?

5. *Was There a* Chevron *Revolution? Preliminary Soundings.* The conventional wisdom in administrative law is, or at least until recently was, that *Chevron* was a revolutionary decision which ushered in a new period of greater deference to agency interpretations of statutes they are charged with enforcing. This might be questioned or qualified.

On the one hand, deference to agencies was a trend long preceding *Chevron*. Peter Schuck & E. Donald Elliott, *To the* Chevron *Station: An Empirical Study of Federal Administrative Law*, 1990 Duke L.J. 984, conclude from a lengthy historical study of federal appellate review of agency determinations that long before *Chevron* agency affirmance rates were on the rise in the federal courts—especially during the 1970s, even though that was the heyday of hard look review in the D.C. Circuit (which supposedly subjected administrative decisions to a greater degree of review).

On the other hand, it is not clear how much *Chevron* changed the prevailing Supreme Court practice. Since the New Deal, the Court had been deferential to agency decisions, sometimes with language presaging *Chevron*. In *Batterton v. Francis*, 432 U.S. 416 (1977), the Court held that when Congress delegates lawmaking authority to an agency, "Congress entrusts to the [agency], rather than to the courts, the primary responsibility for interpreting the statutory term." Once the agency has authoritatively construed the statute through legislative rules, the reviewing court "is not free to set aside the agency regulations simply because it would have interpreted the statute in a different manner."

Just as the Court was often highly deferential before *Chevron*, it was often pretty scrutinizing after *Chevron*. For example, in *INS v. Cardoza–Fonseca*, 480 U.S. 421 (1987), the Court not only rejected the INS's interpretation of its obligations not to deport noncitizens who have a "well-founded fear" of political persecution, 8 U.S.C. § 1158(a), but laid out a detailed legal regime for the INS to follow. Justice Stevens (the author of *Chevron*) wrote the majority opinion, which dissenting Justice Powell felt was not very deferential to the INS.

Moreover, the Supreme Court reaffirmed the approach it took in *Gilbert*. Not only has the Court reiterated that it will not defer to the EEOC (absent a special reason to do so), see *EEOC v. Aramco*, 499 U.S. 244 (1991), but the Court in *Christensen v. Harris County*, 529 U.S. 576, 586–88 (2000), *id.* at 596–97 (Breyer, J., dissenting on other grounds), reaffirmed the *Skidmore* standard for weighing the views of an agency when expressed through informal opinions and letters. In both cases, Justice Scalia objected that the *Chevron* theory for deference (the superior legitimacy agencies had in filling in genuine statutory gaps) should apply to the EEOC and to informal but public rulings by the agency, but agreed that the EEOC's interpretations should be set aside because they were inconsistent with the statute.

6. *Think Critically about What "Deference" Means.* In *Cardoza–Fonseca, Aramco,* and *Christensen,* Justice Scalia found plain meanings inconsistent with the agency views and so voted against the agencies even under the *Chevron* deference standard. Can a judge be "deferential" to agency constructions of ambiguous laws yet still overturn many agency constructions, on the ground that the laws are unambiguous? Should a "deferential" approach

extend to an agency's practical understanding of statutory language in cases such as *Aramco*?

For institutional, selection-of-case reasons, a highly deferential Supreme Court need not actually *agree* with agencies in most cases. If agencies are winning most of the cases at the lower court level, because those judges are *Chevron*-deferring, then the cases actually making it to the Supreme Court might reflect even more agency goose eggs (bad interpretations) than would otherwise be the case.[g] Consider the following case: agency goose egg? Or raw deal for an energetic agency trying to ease regulatory burdens?

MCI TELECOMMUNICATIONS CORP. v. AT & T
Supreme Court of the United States, 1994
512 U.S. 218, 114 S.Ct. 2223, 129 L.Ed.2d 182

JUSTICE SCALIA delivered the opinion for the Court.

Section 203(a) of Title 47 of the United States Code requires communications common carriers to file tariffs with the Federal Communications Commission, and § 203(b) authorizes the Commission to "modify" any requirement of § 203. These cases present the question whether the Commission's decision to make tariff filing optional for all nondominant long-distance carriers is a valid exercise of its modification authority.

[The Communications Act of 1934, 48 Stat. 1064, as amended, authorized the FCC to regulate the rates charged for communication services to ensure that they were reasonable and nondiscriminatory. The requirements of § 203 that common carriers file their rates with the Commission and charge only the filed rate were the centerpiece of the Act's regulatory scheme. For the next 40 years, AT & T had a virtual monopoly over the nation's telephone service, but in the 1970s new competitors emerged. During the 1980s, the Commission allowed, and briefly required, nondominant carriers an exemption from the tariff requirements. The Supreme Court accepted AT & T's challenge to the agency rule.]

The dispute between the parties turns on the meaning of the phrase "modify any requirement" in § 203(b)(2). Petitioners [MCI and the FCC] argue that it gives the Commission authority to make even basic and fundamental changes in the scheme created by that section. We disagree. The word "modify"—like a number of other English words employing the root "mod-" (deriving from the Latin word for "measure"), such as "moderate," "modulate," "modest," and "modicum"—has a connotation of increment or limitation. Virtually every dictionary we are aware of says that "to modify" means to change moderately or in minor fashion. See,

---

g. Schuck & Elliott, Chevron *Station*, found that the D.C. Circuit's agency agreement rates went up significantly in the years immediately after *Chevron*. Other scholars have found an ongoing *Chevron* effect at the lower court level, e.g., Thomas Miles & Cass R. Sunstein, *Do Judges Make Regulatory Policy? An Empirical Examination of* Chevron, 73 U. Chi. L. Rev. 823 (2006) (examining court of appeals decisions reviewing EPA and NLRB decisions). See also Kristin Hickman & Mathew Krueger, *In Search of the Modern* Skidmore *Standard*, 108 Colum. L. Rev. (2008), finding a statistically significant amount of *Skidmore* deference among the courts of appeals.

e.g., Random House Dictionary of the English Language 1236 (2d ed. 1987) ("to change somewhat the form or qualities of; alter partially; amend"); [similar references from Webster's Third New International Dictionary, Oxford English Dictionary, and Black's Law Dictionary].

In support of their position, petitioners cite dictionary definitions contained in, or derived from, a single source, Webster's Third New International Dictionary 1452 (1981) (Webster's Third), which includes among the meanings of "modify," "to make a basic or important change in." Petitioners contend that this establishes sufficient ambiguity to entitle the Commission to deference in its acceptance of the broader meaning, which in turn requires approval of its permissive detariffing policy. See *Chevron.* In short, they contend that the courts must defer to the agency's choice among available dictionary definitions. * * *

Most cases of verbal ambiguity in statutes involve * * * a selection between accepted alternative meanings shown as such by many dictionaries. One can envision (though a court case does not immediately come to mind) having to choose between accepted alternative meanings, one of which is so newly accepted that it has only been recorded by a single lexicographer. (Some dictionary must have been the very first to record the widespread use of "projection," for example, to mean "forecast.") But what petitioners demand that we accept as creating an ambiguity here is a rarity even rarer than that: a meaning set forth in a single dictionary (and, as we say, its progeny) which not only *supplements* the meaning contained in all other dictionaries, but *contradicts* one of the meanings contained in virtually all other dictionaries. Indeed, contradicts one of the alternative meanings contained in the out-of-step dictionary itself—for * * * Webster's Third itself defines "modify" to connote *both* (specifically) major change *and* (specifically) minor change. It is hard to see how that can be. When the word "modify" has come to mean *both* "to change in some respects" *and* "to change fundamentally" it will in fact mean *neither* of those things. It will simply mean "to change," and some adverb will have to be called into service to indicate the great or small degree of the change.

If that is what the peculiar Webster's Third definition means to suggest has happened—and what petitioners suggest by appealing to Webster's Third—we simply disagree. "Modify," in our view, connotes moderate change. It might be good English to say that the French Revolution "modified" the status of the French nobility—but only because there is a figure of speech called understatement and a literary device known as sarcasm. And it might be unsurprising to discover a 1972 White House press release saying that "the Administration is modifying its position with regard to prosecution of the war in Vietnam"—but only because press agents tend to impart what is nowadays called "spin." Such intentional distortions, or simply careless or ignorant misuse, must have formed the basis for the usage that Webster's Third, and Webster's Third alone, reported.[3] It is perhaps gilding the lily to add this: In 1934, when the Communications Act became law—the most relevant time for determining a statutory term's meaning, see *Perrin v. United States*, 444 U.S. 37, 42–45 (1979)—Webster's Third was not yet even contemplated. To our knowledge *all* English dictionaries provided the narrow definition of "modify," including those published by G. & C. Merriam Company. We have not the slightest doubt that is the meaning the statute intended. * * *

Since an agency's interpretation of a statute is not entitled to deference when it goes beyond the meaning that the statute can bear, *Chevron*, the Commission's permissive detariffing policy can be justified only if it makes a less than radical or fundamental change in the Act's tariff-filing requirement. The Commission's attempt to establish that no more than that is involved greatly understates the extent to which its policy deviates from the filing requirement, and greatly undervalues the importance of the filing requirement itself. [Tariff-filing is at the heart of the regulatory scheme, because it provides the data by which the FCC can police rate-discrimination and unreasonableness in charges.]

Bearing in mind, then, the enormous importance to the statutory scheme of the tariff-filing provision, we turn to whether what has occurred here can be considered a mere "modification." The Commission stresses that its detariffing policy applies only to nondominant carriers, so that the rates charged to over half of all consumers in the long-distance market are on file with the Commission. It is not clear to us that the proportion of customers affected, rather than the proportion of carriers affected, is the proper measure of the extent of the exemption (of course *all* carriers in the long-distance market are exempted, except AT & T). But even assuming it is, we think an elimination of the crucial provision of the statute for 40% of a major sector of the industry is much too extensive to be considered a "modification." What we have here, in reality, is a fundamental revision of the statute, changing it from a scheme of rate regulation in long-distance common-carrier communications to a scheme of rate regulation only where effective competition does not exist. That may be a good idea, but it was not the idea Congress enacted into law in 1934. * * *

[JUSTICE O'CONNOR took no part in the consideration or decision of these cases.]

JUSTICE STEVENS, with whom JUSTICE BLACKMUN and JUSTICE SOUTER join, dissenting. * * *

Although the majority observes that further relaxation of tariff-filing requirements might more effectively enhance competition, it does not take issue with the Commission's conclusions that mandatory filing of tariff

---

3. That is not an unlikely hypothesis. Upon its long-awaited appearance in 1961, Webster's Third was widely criticized for its portrayal of common error as proper usage. See, e.g., Follett, Sabotage in Springfield, 209 Atlantic 73 (Jan. 1962); Barzun, What is a Dictionary? 32 The American Scholar 176, 181 (spring 1963); Macdonald, The String Unwound, 38 The New Yorker 130, 156–157 (Mar. 1962). An example is its approval (without qualification) of the use of "infer" to mean "imply". * * *

schedules serves no useful purpose and is actually counterproductive in the case of carriers who lack market power. As the Commission had noted in its prior detariffing orders, if a nondominant carrier sought to charge inflated rates, "customers would simply move to other carriers." Moreover, an absence of market power will ordinarily preclude firms of any kind from engaging in price discrimination. The Commission plausibly concluded that any slight enforcement benefits a tariff-filing requirement might offer were outweighed by the burdens it would put on new entrants and consumers. Thus, the sole question for us is whether the FCC's policy, however sensible, is nonetheless inconsistent with the Act.

In my view, each of the Commission's detariffing orders was squarely within its power to "modify any requirement" of § 203. Section 203(b)(2) plainly confers at least some discretion to modify the general rule that carriers file tariffs, for it speaks of "*any* requirement." Section 203(c) of the Act, ignored by the Court, squarely supports the FCC's position; it prohibits carriers from providing service without a tariff "*unless otherwise provided by or under authority of this Act.*" Section 203(b)(2) is plainly one provision that "otherwise provides," and thereby authorizes, service without a filed schedule. The FCC's authority to modify § 203's requirements in "particular instances" or by "general order applicable to special circumstances or conditions" emphasizes the expansive character of the Commission's authority: modifications may be narrow or broad, depending upon the Commission's appraisal of current conditions. From the vantage of a Congress seeking to regulate an almost completely monopolized industry, the advent of competition is surely a "special circumstance or condition" that might legitimately call for different regulatory treatment.
* * *

According to the Court, the term "modify," as explicated in all but the most unreliable dictionaries, rules out the Commission's claimed authority to relieve nondominant carriers of the basic obligation to file tariffs. Dictionaries can be useful aids in statutory interpretation, but they are no substitute for close analysis of what words mean as used in a particular statutory context. Even if the sole possible meaning of "modify" were to make "minor" changes,[3] further elaboration is needed to show why the detariffing policy should fail. The Commission came to its present policy through a series of rulings that gradually relaxed the filing requirements for nondominant carriers. Whether the current policy should count as a cataclysmic or merely an incremental departure from the § 203(a) baseline depends on whether one focuses on particular carriers' obligations to file (in which case the Commission's policy arguably works a major shift) or on the statutory policies behind the tariff-filing requirement (which remain satisfied because market constraints on nondominant carriers obviate the need for rate filing). When § 203 is viewed as part of a

---

3. As petitioner MCI points out, the revolutionary consent decree providing for the breakup of the Bell System was, per AT & T's own proposal, entitled "Modification of Final Judgment." See *United States v. American Telephone & Telegraph Co.*, 552 F.Supp. 131 (D.C. 1982), aff'd, 460 U.S. 1001 (1983).

statute whose aim is to constrain monopoly power, the Commission's decision to exempt nondominant carriers is a rational and "measured" adjustment to novel circumstances—one that remains faithful to the core purpose of the tariff-filing section. See Black's Law Dictionary 1198 (3d ed. 1933) (defining "modification" as "A change; an alteration which introduces new elements into the details, or cancels some of them, but leaves *the general purpose and effect of the subject-matter* intact").

The Court seizes upon a particular sense of the word "modify" at the expense of another, long-established meaning that fully supports the Commission's position. That word is first defined in Webster's Collegiate Dictionary 628 (4th ed. 1934) as meaning "to limit or reduce in extent or degree." The Commission's permissive detariffing policy fits comfortably within this common understanding of the term. The FCC has in effect adopted a general rule stating that "if you are dominant you must file, but if you are nondominant you need not." The Commission's partial detariffing policy—which excuses nondominant carriers from filing *on condition that* they remain nondominant—is simply a relaxation of a costly regulatory requirement that recent developments had rendered pointless and counterproductive in a certain class of cases.

A modification pursuant to § 203(b)(1), like any other order issued under the Act, must of course be consistent with the purposes of the statute. On this point, the Court asserts that the Act's prohibition against unreasonable and discriminatory rates "would not be susceptible of effective enforcement if rates were not publicly filed." That determination, of course, is for the Commission to make in the first instance. But the Commission has repeatedly explained that (1) a carrier that lacks market power is entirely unlikely to charge unreasonable or discriminatory rates, (2) the statutory bans on unreasonable charges and price discrimination apply with full force regardless of whether carriers have to file tariffs, (3) any suspected violations by nondominant carriers can be addressed on the Commission's own motion or on a damages complaint filed pursuant to § 206, and (4) the FCC can reimpose a tariff requirement should violations occur. The Court does not adequately respond to the FCC's explanations, and gives no reason whatsoever to doubt the Commission's considered judgment that tariff filing is altogether unnecessary in the case of competitive carriers; the majority's ineffective enforcement argument lacks any evidentiary or historical support. * * *

The filed tariff provisions of the Communications Act are not ends in themselves, but are merely one of several procedural *means* for the Commission to ensure that carriers do not charge unreasonable or discriminatory rates. The Commission has reasonably concluded that this particular means of enforcing the statute's substantive mandates will prove counterproductive in the case of nondominant long-distance carriers. Even if the 1934 Congress did not define the scope of the Commission's modification authority with perfect scholarly precision, this is surely a paradigm case for judicial deference to the agency's interpretation, particularly in a statutory regime so obviously meant to maximize administrative flexibility. Whatever the best reading of § 203(b)(2), the Commission's reading cannot in my view be termed unreasonable. It is informed (as ours is not) by a practical understanding of the role (or lack thereof) that filed tariffs play in the modern regulatory climate and in the telecommunications industry. Since 1979, the FCC has sought to adapt measures originally designed to control monopoly power to new market conditions. It has carefully and consistently explained that mandatory tariff-filing rules frustrate the core statutory interest in rate reasonableness. The Commission's use of the "discretion" expressly conferred by § 203(b)(2) reflects "a reasonable accommodation of manifestly competing interests and is entitled to deference: the regulatory scheme is technical and complex, the agency considered the matter in a detailed and reasoned fashion, and the decision involves reconciling conflicting policies." *Chevron.* The FCC has permissibly interpreted its § 203(b)(2) authority in service of the goals Congress set forth in the Act. We should sustain its eminently sound, experience-tested, and uncommonly well-explained judgment.

NOTES ON *MCI,* THE NEW TEXTUALISM, AND "EXCESSIVE" LEGISLATIVE DELEGATIONS TO AGENCIES

1. *The New Textualism and* Chevron: *Should the Court Consider Legislative History?* In *INS v. Cardoza–Fonseca,* 480 U.S. 421 (1987) (discussed in the previous set of notes), Justice Scalia alone adhered to the view that *Chevron* permits overturning agency action only when the agency view clashes with a clear statutory text. All other Justices consulted the legislative history to determine the validity of the agency view under *Chevron.* Justice Scalia has continued to press his view that statutory text and structure are the only relevant inquiries in Step One of the *Chevron* analysis (has Congress specifically addressed the issue?). Justice Stevens's approach, that other traditional tools such as legislative history and purpose are also relevant in Step One, seemed to lose ground on the Court after *Cardoza–Fonseca.* E.g., *MCI v. AT & T*; *Sutton v. United Airlines. Inc.,* 527 U.S. 471, 482 (1999).

An interesting example is *City of Chicago v. Environmental Defense Fund,* 511 U.S. 328 (1994).[h] The issue in the case was whether waste combustion ash generated by a municipal resource recovery incinerator was exempt from hazardous waste regulation under Subtitle C of the Resource Conservation and Recovery Act (RCRA). Without explicit statutory support, the EPA had supported a RCRA exemption for municipal waste incineration in the early 1980s, and in 1984 Congress added § 3001(i) to provide that "[a] resource recovery facility recovering energy from the mass burning of municipal solid waste" would not be "deemed to be treating, storing, disposing of, or otherwise managing hazardous wastes for the purposes of [Subtitle C],"42 U.S.C. § 6921(i). Municipalities assumed that § 3001(i) also allowed them to dispose of the ash created in such process without the expensive protections required

---

h. Our discussion of *City of Chicago* draws from Richard Lazarus & Claudia Newman, City of Chicago v. Environmental Defense Fund: *Searching for Plain Meaning in Unambiguous Ambiguity,* 4 N.Y.U. Env. L.J. 1 (1995).

by Subtitle C. The EPA sent mixed signals on the ash issue, before siding with the municipalities in a 1992 memorandum developed in connection with the *City of Chicago* case. The EPA memorandum argued that the statutory balance of environmental protection and reasonable costs could best be achieved through a broad exemption, because cities faced enormous costs if they had to dispose of ash under Subtitle C. Moreover, the legislative history of § 3001(i) supported this balance. The Senate report accompanying § 3001(i) said that "[a]ll waste management activities of such a facility, including the *generation*, transportation, treatment, storage and disposal of waste shall be covered by the exclusion." All this background persuaded Justice Stevens, but he found himself in dissent. Justice Scalia's opinion for the Court ruled § 3001(i) unambiguous: the *facility* is exempt from Subtitle C, but there is no mention and therefore no exemption for the *ash* produced in the facility and subsequently disposed of by the city. Scalia not only refused to credit the Senate report with any value, but deployed it to prove his point: the report included *generation* of waste as one of the activities exempted by section 3001(i), a term notably absent from the statute itself.

On the other hand, there have also been many post-*MCI* decisions in which the Court considered legislative history and other nontextual arguments when doing a *Chevron* analysis. E.g., *FDA v. Brown & Williamson Tobacco Corp.* (Chapter 2, § 3B3); *Babbitt v. Sweet Home* (Chapter 3, § 1C). In *Wisconsin Public Intervenor v. Mortier*, 501 U.S. 597, 610 n.4 (1991), the Court *Chevron*-deferred to an agency interpretation that the federal pesticide law did not preempt state law. In determining whether Congress had directly addressed this question (*Chevron* Step One), the Court examined the legislative history as well as the statutory text. Justice White's opinion marshaling legislative history won over the votes of Chief Justice Rehnquist and Justice O'Connor, who had originally thought that the statutory scheme "occupied the field" and therefore preempted state law (according to Justice Blackmun's conference notes). In dissent, Justice Scalia mounted a full-scale assault on the Court's reliance on legislative history—an assault that drew no support from any other Justice. See also William N. Eskridge Jr. & Lauren E. Baer, *The Continuum of Deference: Supreme Court Treatment of Agency Statutory Interpretations from* Chevron *to* Hamdan, 96 Geo. L.J. 1083 (2008) (finding that the Court relies on legislative history *more* often in *Chevron* cases than in other statutory interpretation cases).

Consider a suggestion made by the Seventh Circuit in *Bankers Life & Cas. Co. v. United States*, 142 F.3d 973 (1998). "While this circuit has examined legislative history during the first step of *Chevron*, we now seem to lean toward reserving consideration of legislative history and other appropriate factors until the second *Chevron* step." This suggested approach would focus on statutory text and structure to determine whether the law is ambiguous (Step One) and, if so, would consider legislative history and the statutory purpose evaluating the reasonableness of the agency's construction (Step Two). One might evaluate *Sweet Home* (the spotted owl case) along these lines. The statutory text was ambiguous as to whether destruction of habitat constituted a taking of endangered animals, and so the Justices should have evaluated the agency's position under step two of *Chevron*. The various legislative discussions surrounding the 1973 statute (relied on by dissenting

Justice Scalia) and its 1982 amendment (relied on by Justice Stevens' opinion for the Court) would then have been relevant to the reasonableness of the agency's choice.

2. *The Implications of the New Textualism for Deference, More Generally.* If Justice Scalia's position on *Chevron* were adopted by the Court, agency rules might be *more* prone to reversal than under Justice Stevens' position. Justice Scalia explains why this might be so in *Judicial Deference to Administrative Interpretation of Law*, 1989 Duke L.J. 511, 521:

> * * * One who finds *more* often (as I do) that the meaning of a statute is apparent from its text and from its relationship with other laws, thereby finds *less* often that the triggering requirement for *Chevron* deference exists. It is thus relatively rare that *Chevron* will require me to accept an interpretation which, though reasonable, I would not personally adopt. Contrariwise, one who abhors a "plain meaning" rule, and is willing to permit the apparent meaning of a statute to be impeached by legislative history, will more frequently find agency-liberating ambiguity. * * *

That a textualist approach to *Chevron* might be less deferential to agency interpretations is supported by Professor Merrill's empirical study, which found that in 1988–90 (the period of new textualist ascendancy) *Chevron*'s framework was applied in more cases than it had been in 1985–86 (51% to 32%) but that the agency view had prevailed much less often overall (59% to 72%). Thomas W. Merrill, *Judicial Deference to Executive Precedent*, 101 Yale L.J. 969, 992 (1992) (Table 3). Merrill speculates that textualism may lead to a "permanent subordination of the *Chevron* doctrine."[i]

A milder conclusion suggested by Justice Scalia's law review article would be that the new textualism is more likely to resolve cases at Step One of *Chevron* (the agency is either right or wrong) and is less likely to get to Step Two, which is where deference really kicks in (the law is unclear, so the agency can make a choice the judges would not have otherwise made). Others are skeptical that methodology per se is decisive. See Eskridge & Baer, *Continuum of Deference* (reporting relatively low agency agreement rates for textualist Justices Scalia and Thomas, but even lower rates for Justice

---

i. Thomas W. Merrill, *Textualism and the* Chevron *Doctrine*, 72 Wash. U.L.Q. 351, 372 (1994):

This has to do with the style of judging associated with textualism. Intentionalism mandates an "archeological" excavation of the past, producing opinions written in the style of the dry archivist sifting through countless documents in search of the tell-tale smoking gun of congressional intent. Textualism, in contrast, seems to transform statutory interpretation into a kind of exercise in judicial ingenuity. The textualist judge treats questions of interpretation like a puzzle to which it is assumed there is one right answer. The task is to assemble the various pieces of linguistic data, dictionary definitions, and canons into the best (most coherent, most explanatory) account of the meaning of the statute. This exercise places a great premium on cleverness. In one case the outcome turns on the place of a comma, in another on the inconsistency between a comma and rules of grammar, in a third on the conflict between quotation marks and the language of the text. One day arguments must be advanced in support of broad dictionary definitions; the next day in support of narrow dictionary definitions. New canons of construction and clear statement rules must be invented and old ones reinterpreted.

This active, creative approach to interpretation is subtly incompatible with an attitude of deference toward other institutions—whether the other institution is Congress or an administrative agency. In effect, the textualist interpreter does not *find* the meaning of the statute so much as *construct* the meaning. Such a person will very likely experience some difficulty in deferring to the meanings that other institutions have developed.

Stevens, who relies on legislative history). Indeed, there are plenty of cases where Justice Scalia's textualism is more lenient toward agency interpretations than it was in *MCI* or *Sweet Home*. E.g., *Massachusetts v. EPA*, 549 U.S. 497 (2007) (Scalia, J., dissenting) (deferring to EPA interpretation narrowly construing its broad statutory authority over greenhouse gases allegedly contributing to global warming).

3. MCI, *Dictionaries, and Excessive Delegations. MCI* is a leading case for the Court's well-honed deployment of dictionaries. The Court faults *Webster's Third* for too readily incorporating ordinary usage—which would seem to be most desirable for discerning the meaning an ordinary reader would draw from the statute. One might argue, however, that legislative drafters use language more formally, and thus more consistently with the prescriptive approach of *Webster's Second*. *MCI* also involves a methodological debate over the extent to which policy context matters.

One reading of *MCI* is that it supports a rule or presumption against excessive delegations. Recall from § 1 of this chapter, the Supreme Court will not enforce the nondelegation doctrine anymore—it will not strike down, as a constitutional violation, even extremely broad legislative delegations of law-making authority to administrative agencies. The Court can still give this "underenforced constitutional norm" some teeth, however, by "canonizing" it. Thus, the Court will be reluctant to read statutory delegations broadly, for fear that this will encourage the legislature to make excessive delegations. Does this reading make *MCI* a more persuasive opinion? How can this be reconciled with *Chevron*?

This reading of *MCI* reappeared in *FDA v. Brown & Williamson* (Chapter 2, § 3B3), where the Court said:

Deference under *Chevron* to an agency's construction of a statute that it administers is premised on the theory that a statute's ambiguity constitutes an implicit delegation from Congress to the agency to fill in the statutory gaps. In extraordinary cases, however, there may be reason to hesitate before concluding that Congress has intended such an implicit delegation.

* * * Owing to its unique place in American history and society, tobacco has its own unique political history. Congress, for better or for worse, has created a distinct regulatory scheme for tobacco products, squarely rejected proposals to give the FDA jurisdiction over tobacco, and repeatedly acted to preclude any agency from exercising significant policymaking authority in the area. Given this history and the breadth of the authority that the FDA has asserted, we are obliged to defer not to the agency's expansive construction of the statute, but to Congress' consistent judgment to deny the FDA this power. [The Court then discussed *MCI*.]

As in *MCI*, we are confident that Congress could not have intended to delegate a decision of such economic and political significance to an agency in so cryptic a fashion.

Brown & Williamson, 529 U.S. at 159–60. Is this a persuasive deployment of *MCI*? Should this precept have counseled a different result in some of the other cases where the Court has deferred to agencies, such as *Sweet Home* (Chapter 3, § 1C)? *Bob Jones* (Chapter 4, § 2F)?

UNITED STATES v. MEAD CORP.

Supreme Court of the United States, 2001
533 U.S. 218, 121 S.Ct. 2164, 150 L.Ed.2d 292

JUSTICE SOUTER delivered the opinion of the Court.

The question is whether a tariff classification ruling by the United States Customs Service deserves judicial deference. The Federal Circuit rejected Customs's invocation of *Chevron* in support of such a ruling, to which it gave no deference. We agree that a tariff classification has no claim to judicial deference under *Chevron*; there being no indication that Congress intended such a ruling to carry the force of law, but we hold that under *Skidmore*, the ruling is eligible to claim respect according to its persuasiveness. * * *

[II.A] When Congress has "explicitly left a gap for an agency to fill, there is an express delegation of authority to the agency to elucidate a specific provision of the statute by regulation," *Chevron*, and any ensuing regulation is binding in the courts unless procedurally defective, arbitrary or capricious in substance, or manifestly contrary to the statute. See APA, 5 U.S.C. § 706(2)(A), (D). But whether or not they enjoy any express delegation of authority on a particular question, agencies charged with applying a statute necessarily make all sorts of interpretive choices, and while not all of those choices bind judges to follow them, they certainly may influence courts facing questions the agencies have already answered. "[T]he well-reasoned views of the agencies implementing a statute 'constitute a body of experience and informed judgment to which courts and litigants may properly resort for guidance,'" *Bragdon* v. *Abbott,* 524 U.S. 624, 642 (1998) (quoting *Skidmore*), and "[w]e have long recognized that considerable weight should be accorded to an executive department's construction of a statutory scheme it is entrusted to administer...." *Chevron* (footnote omitted).

The fair measure of deference to an agency administering its own statute has been understood to vary with circumstances, and courts have looked to the degree of the agency's care, its consistency, formality, and relative expertness, and to the persuasiveness of the agency's position, see *Skidmore.* * * * Justice Jackson summed things up in *Skidmore:*

"The weight [accorded to an administrative] judgment in a particular case will depend upon the thoroughness evident in its consideration, the validity of its reasoning, its consistency with earlier and later pronouncements, and all those factors which give it power to persuade, if lacking power to control."

Since 1984, we have identified a category of interpretive choices distinguished by an additional reason for judicial deference. This Court in *Chevron* recognized that Congress not only engages in express delegation of specific interpretive authority, but that "[s]ometimes the legislative delegation to an agency on a particular question is implicit." Congress, that is, may not have expressly delegated authority or responsibility to implement a particular provision or fill a particular gap. Yet it can still be apparent from the agency's generally conferred authority and other statutory circumstances that Congress would expect the agency to be able to speak with the force of law when it addresses ambiguity in the statute or fills a space in the enacted law, even one about which "Congress did not actually have an intent" as to a particular result. When circumstances implying such an expectation exist, a reviewing court has no business rejecting an agency's exercise of its generally conferred authority to resolve a particular statutory ambiguity simply because the agency's chosen resolution seems unwise, but is obliged to accept the agency's position if Congress has not previously spoken to the point at issue and the agency's interpretation is reasonable; *cf.* 5 U.S.C. §§ 706(2) (a reviewing court shall set aside agency action, findings, and conclusions found to be "arbitrary, capricious, an abuse of discretion, or otherwise not in accordance with law").

We have recognized a very good indicator of delegation meriting *Chevron* treatment in express congressional authorizations to engage in the process of rulemaking or adjudication that produces regulations or rulings for which deference is claimed. [Citing cases, including *Gilbert*, that apply only *Skidmore* deference to EEOC interpretations.] It is fair to assume generally that Congress contemplates administrative action with the effect of law when it provides for a relatively formal administrative procedure tending to foster the fairness and deliberation that should underlie a pronouncement of such force. Thus, the overwhelming number of our cases applying *Chevron* deference have reviewed the fruits of notice-and-comment rulemaking or formal adjudication. That said, and as significant as notice-and-comment is in pointing to *Chevron* authority, the want of that procedure here does not decide the case, for we have sometimes found reasons for *Chevron* deference even when no such administrative formality was required and none was afforded, see, *e.g., NationsBank of N. C., N. A.* v. *Variable Annuity Life Ins. Co.,* 513 U.S. 251, 256–257, 263 (1995). The fact that the tariff classification here was not a product of such formal process does not alone, therefore, bar the application of *Chevron.*

There are, nonetheless, ample reasons to deny *Chevron* deference here. The authorization for classification rulings, and Customs's practice in making them, present a case far removed not only from notice-and-comment process, but from any other circumstances reasonably suggesting that Congress ever thought of classification rulings as deserving the deference claimed for them here.

[II.B] No matter which angle we choose for viewing the Customs ruling letter in this case, it fails to qualify under *Chevron.* On the face of the statute, to begin with, the terms of the congressional delegation give no indication that Congress meant to delegate authority to Customs to issue classification rulings with the force of law. We are not, of course, here making any global statement about Customs's authority, for it is true that the general rulemaking power conferred on Customs authorizes some regulation with the force of law, or "legal norms" * * *. It is true as well that Congress had classification rulings in mind when it explicitly authorized, in a parenthetical, the issuance of "regulations establishing procedures for the issuance of binding rulings prior to the entry of the merchandise concerned," 19 U.S.C. § 1502(a). The reference to binding classifications does not, however, bespeak the legislative type of activity that would naturally bind more than the parties to the ruling, once the goods classified are admitted into this country. And though the statute's direction to disseminate "information" necessary to "secure" uniformity, *ibid.*, seems to assume that a ruling may be precedent in later transactions, precedential value alone does not add up to *Chevron* entitlement; interpretive rules may sometimes function as precedents, see Strauss, *The Rulemaking Continuum*, 41 Duke L.J. 1463, 1472–1473 (1992), and they enjoy no *Chevron* status as a class. In any event, any precedential claim of a classification ruling is counterbalanced by the provision for independent review of Customs classifications by the CIT [Court of International Trade]; the scheme for CIT review includes a provision that treats classification rulings on par with the Secretary's rulings on "valuation, rate of duty, marking, restricted merchandise, entry requirements, drawbacks, vessel repairs, or similar matters," § 1581(h). It is hard to imagine a congressional understanding more at odds with the *Chevron* regime.

It is difficult, in fact, to see in the agency practice itself any indication that Customs ever set out with a lawmaking pretense in mind when it undertook to make classifications like these. Customs does not generally engage in notice-and-comment practice when issuing them, and their treatment by the agency makes it clear that a letter's binding character as a ruling stops short of third parties; Customs has regarded a classification as conclusive only as between itself and the importer to whom it was issued, and even then only until Customs has given advance notice of intended change. Other importers are in fact warned against assuming any right of detrimental reliance.

Indeed, to claim that classifications have legal force is to ignore the reality that 46 different Customs offices issue 10,000 to 15,000 of them each year. Any suggestion that rulings intended to have the force of law are being churned out at a rate of 10,000 a year at an agency's 46 scattered offices is simply self-refuting. Although the circumstances are less startling here, with a Headquarters letter in issue, none of the relevant statutes recognizes this category of rulings as separate or different from others; there is thus no indication that a more potent delegation might have been understood as going to Headquarters even when Headquarters provides developed reasoning, as it did in this instance.

Nor do the amendments to the statute made effective after this case arose disturb our conclusion. The new law requires Customs to provide notice-and-comment procedures only when modifying or revoking a prior classification ruling or modifying the treatment accorded to substantially identical transactions; and under its regulations, Customs sees itself obliged to provide notice-and-comment procedures only when "changing a practice" so as to produce a tariff increase, or in the imposition of a restriction or prohibition, or when Customs Headquarters determines that "the matter is of sufficient importance to involve the interests of domestic industry." 19 C.F.R. §§ 177.10(c)(1), (2). The statutory changes reveal no new congressional objective of treating classification decisions generally as rulemaking with force of law, nor do they suggest any intent to create a *Chevron* patchwork of classification rulings, some with force of law, some without.

In sum, classification rulings are best treated like "interpretations contained in policy statements, agency manuals, and enforcement guidelines." *Christensen*. They are beyond the *Chevron* pale.

[II.C] To agree with the Court of Appeals that Customs ruling letters do not fall within *Chevron* is not, however, to place them outside the pale of any deference whatever. *Chevron* did nothing to eliminate *Skidmore*'s holding that an agency's interpretation may merit some deference whatever its form, given the "specialized experience and broader investigations and information" available to the agency, and given the value of uniformity in its administrative and judicial understandings of what a national law requires.

There is room at least to raise a *Skidmore* claim here, where the regulatory scheme is highly detailed, and Customs can bring the benefit of specialized experience to bear on the subtle questions in this case: whether the daily planner with room for brief daily entries falls under "diaries," when diaries are grouped with "notebooks and address books, bound; memorandum pads, letter pads and similar articles"; and whether a planner with a ring binding should qualify as "bound," when a binding may be typified by a book, but also may have "reinforcements or fittings of metal, plastics, etc." A classification ruling in this situation may therefore at least seek a respect proportional to its "power to persuade," *Skidmore*. Such a ruling may surely claim the merit of its writer's thoroughness, logic and expertness, its fit with prior interpretations, and any other sources of weight.

[II.D] Underlying the position we take here, like the position expressed by Justice Scalia in dissent, is a choice about the best way to deal with an inescapable feature of the body of congressional legislation authorizing administrative action. That feature is the great variety of ways in which the laws invest the Government's administrative arms with discretion, and with procedures for exercising it, in giving meaning to Acts of Congress. Implementation of a statute may occur in formal adjudication or the choice to defend against judicial challenge; it may occur in a central board or office or in dozens of enforcement agencies dotted across the country; its institutional lawmaking may be confined to the resolution of minute detail or extend to legislative rulemaking on matters intentionally left by Congress to be worked out at the agency level.

Although we all accept the position that the Judiciary should defer to at least some of this multifarious administrative action, we have to decide how to take account of the great range of its variety. If the primary objective is to simplify the judicial process of giving or withholding deference, then the diversity of statutes authorizing discretionary administrative action must be declared irrelevant or minimized. If, on the other hand, it is simply implausible that Congress intended such a broad range of statutory authority to produce only two varieties of administrative action, demanding either *Chevron* deference or none at all, then the breadth of the spectrum of possible agency action must be taken into account. Justice Scalia's first priority over the years has been to limit and simplify. The Court's choice has been to tailor deference to variety. This acceptance of the range of statutory variation has led the Court to recognize more than one variety of judicial deference, just as the Court has recognized a variety of indicators that Congress would expect *Chevron* deference.

Our respective choices are repeated today. Justice Scalia would pose the question of deference as an either-or choice. On his view that *Chevron* rendered *Skidmore* anachronistic, when courts owe any deference it is *Chevron* deference that they owe. Whether courts do owe deference in a given case turns, for him, on whether the agency action (if reasonable) is "authoritative." The character of the authoritative derives, in turn, not from breadth of delegation or the agency's procedure in implementing it, but is defined as the "official" position of an agency, and may ultimately be a function of administrative persistence alone.

The Court, on the other hand, said nothing in *Chevron* to eliminate *Skidmore*'s recognition of various justifications for deference depending on statutory circumstances and agency action; *Chevron* was simply a case recognizing that even without express authority to fill a specific statutory gap, circumstances pointing to implicit congressional delegation present a particularly insistent call for deference. Indeed, in holding here that *Chevron* left *Skidmore* intact and applicable where statutory circumstances indicate no intent to delegate general authority to make rules with force of law, or where such authority was not invoked, we hold nothing more than we said last Term in response to the particular statutory circumstances in *Christensen*, to which Justice Scalia then took exception, see 529 U.S., at 589, just as he does again today.

We think, in sum, that Justice Scalia's efforts to simplify ultimately run afoul of Congress's indications that different statutes present different reasons for considering respect for the exercise of administrative authority or deference to it. Without being at odds with congressional intent much of the time, we believe that judicial responses to administrative action must continue to differentiate between *Chevron* and *Skidmore*, and that continued recognition of *Skidmore* is necessary for just the reasons Justice Jackson gave when that case was decided.

Since the *Skidmore* assessment called for here ought to be made in the first instance by the Court of Appeals for the Federal Circuit or the CIT, we go no further than to vacate the judgment and remand the case for further proceedings consistent with this opinion.

JUSTICE SCALIA, dissenting.

Today's opinion makes an avulsive change in judicial review of federal administrative action. Whereas previously a reasonable agency application of an ambiguous statutory provision had to be sustained so long as it represented the agency's authoritative interpretation, henceforth such an application can be set aside unless "it appears that Congress delegated authority to the agency generally to make rules carrying the force of law," as by giving an agency "power to engage in adjudication or notice-and-comment rulemaking, or . . . some other [procedure] indicati[ng] comparable congressional intent," and "the agency interpretation claiming deference was promulgated in the exercise of that authority." What was previously a general presumption of authority in agencies to resolve ambiguity in the statutes they have been authorized to enforce has been changed to a presumption of no such authority, which must be overcome by affirmative legislative intent to the contrary. And whereas previously, when agency authority to resolve ambiguity did not exist the court was free to give the statute what it considered the best interpretation, henceforth the court must supposedly give the agency view some indeterminate amount of so-called *Skidmore* deference. We will be sorting out the consequences of the *Mead* doctrine, which has today replaced the *Chevron* doctrine, for years to come. I would adhere to our established jurisprudence, defer to the reasonable interpretation the Customs Service has given to the statute it is charged with enforcing, and reverse the judgment of the Court of Appeals.

[I.A] As to principle: The doctrine of *Chevron*—that all *authoritative* agency interpretations of statutes they are charged with administering deserve deference—was rooted in a legal presumption of congressional intent, important to the division of powers between the Second and Third Branches. When, *Chevron* said, Congress leaves an ambiguity in a statute that is to be administered by an executive agency, it is presumed that Congress meant to give the agency discretion, within the limits of reasonable interpretation, as to how the ambiguity is to be resolved. By committing enforcement of the statute to an agency rather than the courts, Congress committed its initial and primary interpretation to that branch as well.

There is some question whether *Chevron* was faithful to the text of the Administrative Procedure Act (APA), which it did not even bother to cite. But it was in accord with the origins of federal-court judicial review. Judicial control of federal executive officers was principally exercised through the prerogative writ of mandamus. That writ generally would not issue unless the executive officer was acting plainly beyond the scope of his authority.

> "The questions mooted before the Secretary and decided by him were whether the fund is a tribal fund, whether the tribe is still existing and whether the distribution of the annuities is to be confined to members of the tribe.... These are all questions of law the solution of which requires a construction of the act of 1889 and other related acts. A reading of these acts shows that they fall short of plainly requiring that any of the questions be answered in the negative and that in some aspects they give color to the affirmative answers of the Secretary. That the construction of the acts insofar as they have a bearing on the first and third questions is sufficiently uncertain to involve the exercise of judgment and discretion is rather plain....

> "From what has been said it follows that the case is not one in which mandamus will lie." *Wilbur v. United States ex rel. Kadrie*, 281 U.S. 206, 221–222 (1930).

Statutory ambiguities, in other words, were left to reasonable resolution by the Executive.

The basis in principle for today's new doctrine can be described as follows: The background rule is that ambiguity in legislative instructions to agencies is to be resolved not by the agencies but by the judges. Specific congressional intent to depart from this rule must be found—and while there is no single touchstone for such intent it can generally be found when Congress has authorized the agency to act through (what the Court says is) relatively formal procedures such as informal rulemaking and formal (and informal?) adjudication, and when the agency in fact employs such procedures. The Court's background rule is contradicted by the origins of judicial review of administrative action. But in addition, the Court's principal criterion of congressional intent to supplant its background rule seems to me quite implausible. There is no necessary connection between the formality of procedure and the power of the entity administering the procedure to resolve authoritatively questions of law. The most formal of the procedures the Court refers to—formal adjudication—is modeled after the process used in trial courts, which of course are not generally accorded deference on questions of law. The purpose of such a procedure is to produce a closed record for determination and review of the facts—which implies nothing about the power of the agency subjected to the procedure to resolve authoritatively questions of law.

As for informal rulemaking: While formal adjudication procedures are *prescribed* (either by statute or by the Constitution), informal rulemaking is more typically *authorized* but not required. Agencies with such authority are free to give guidance through rulemaking, but they may proceed to administer their statute case-by-case, "making law" as they implement their program (not necessarily through formal adjudication). Is it likely— or indeed even plausible—that Congress meant, when such an agency chooses rulemaking, to accord the administrators of that agency, *and their* *successors*, the flexibility of interpreting the ambiguous statute now one way, and later another; but, when such an agency chooses case-by-case administration, to eliminate all future agency discretion by having that same ambiguity resolved authoritatively (and forever) by the courts? Surely that makes no sense. It is also the case that certain significant categories of rules—those involving grant and benefit programs, for example, are exempt from the requirements of informal rulemaking. See 5 U.S.C. § 553(a)(2). Under the Court's novel theory, when an agency takes advantage of that exemption its rules will be deprived of *Chevron* deference, *i.e.*, authoritative effect. Was this either the plausible intent of the APA rulemaking exemption, or the plausible intent of the Congress that established the grant or benefit program? * * *

[In Part II.B, Justice Scalia lamented the terrible "practical effects" of the Court's new rule.] (1) The principal effect will be protracted confusion. As noted above, the one test for *Chevron* deference that the Court enunciates is wonderfully imprecise: whether "Congress delegated authority to the agency generally to make rules carrying the force of law, . . . as by . . . adjudication[,] notice-and-comment rulemaking, or . . . some other [procedure] indicati[ng] comparable congressional intent." But even this description does not do justice to the utter flabbiness of the Court's criterion, since, in order to maintain the fiction that the new test is really just the old one, applied consistently throughout our case law, the Court must make a virtually open-ended exception to its already imprecise guidance: In the present case, it tells us, the absence of notice-and-comment rulemaking (and "[who knows?] [of] some other [procedure] indicati[ng] comparable congressional intent") is not enough to decide the question of *Chevron* deference, "for we have sometimes found reasons for *Chevron* deference even when no such administrative formality was required and none was afforded." The opinion then goes on to consider a grab bag of other factors—including the factor that used to be the sole criterion for *Chevron* deference: whether the interpretation represented the *authoritative* position of the agency. It is hard to know what the lower courts are to make of today's guidance.

(2) Another practical effect of today's opinion will be an artificially induced increase in informal rulemaking. Buy stock in the GPO. Since informal rulemaking and formal adjudication are the only more-or-less safe harbors from the storm that the Court has unleashed; and since formal adjudication is not an option but must be mandated by statute or constitutional command; informal rulemaking—which the Court was once careful to make voluntary unless required by statute—will now become a virtual necessity. As I have described, the Court's safe harbor requires not merely that the agency have been given rulemaking authority, but also that the agency have *employed* rulemaking as the means of resolving the statutory ambiguity. (It is hard to understand why that should be so. Surely the mere *conferral* of rulemaking authority demonstrates—if one accepts the Court's logic—a congressional intent to allow the agency to resolve ambiguities. And given that intent, what difference does it make

that the agency chooses instead to use another perfectly permissible means for that purpose?) Moreover, the majority's approach will have a perverse effect on the rules that do emerge, given the principle (which the Court leaves untouched today) that judges must defer to reasonable agency interpretations of their own regulations. Agencies will now have high incentive to rush out barebones, ambiguous rules construing statutory ambiguities, which they can then in turn further clarify through informal rulings entitled to judicial respect.

(3) Worst of all, the majority's approach will lead to the ossification of large portions of our statutory law. Where *Chevron* applies, statutory ambiguities remain ambiguities subject to the agency's ongoing clarification. They create a space, so to speak, for the exercise of continuing agency discretion. As *Chevron* itself held, the Environmental Protection Agency can interpret "stationary source" to mean a single smokestack, can later replace that interpretation with the "bubble concept" embracing an entire plant, and if that proves undesirable can return again to the original interpretation. For the indeterminately large number of statutes taken out of *Chevron* by today's decision, however, ambiguity (and hence flexibility) will cease with the first judicial resolution. *Skidmore* deference gives the agency's current position some vague and uncertain amount of respect, but it does not, like *Chevron, leave* the matter within the control of the Executive Branch for the future. Once the court has spoken, it becomes *unlawful* for the agency to take a contradictory position; the statute now *says* what the court has prescribed. It will be bad enough when this ossification occurs as a result of judicial determination (under today's new principles) that there is no affirmative indication of congressional intent to "delegate"; but it will be positively bizarre when it occurs simply because of an agency's failure to act by rulemaking (rather than informal adjudication) before the issue is presented to the courts.

One might respond that such ossification would not result if the agency were simply to readopt its interpretation, after a court reviewing it under *Skidmore* had rejected it, by repromulgating it through one of the *Chevron*-eligible procedural formats approved by the Court today. Approving this procedure would be a landmark abdication of judicial power. It is worlds apart from *Chevron* proper, where the court does not *purport* to give the statute a judicial interpretation—except in identifying the scope of the statutory ambiguity, as to which the court's judgment is final and irreversible. (Under *Chevron* proper, when the agency's authoritative interpretation comes within the scope of that ambiguity—and the court therefore approves it—the agency will not be "overruling" the court's decision when it later decides that a different interpretation (still within the scope of the ambiguity) is preferable.) By contrast, under this view, the reviewing court will not be holding the agency's authoritative interpretation within the scope of the ambiguity; but will be holding that the agency has not used the "delegation-conferring" procedures, and that the court must therefore *interpret the statute on its own*-but subject to reversal if and when the agency uses the proper procedures.

* * * I know of no case, in the entire history of the federal courts, in which we have allowed a judicial interpretation of a statute to be set aside by an agency—or have allowed a lower court to render an interpretation of a statute subject to correction by an agency. As recently as 1996, we rejected an attempt to do *precisely* that. In *Chapman* v. *United States*, 500 U.S. 453 (1991) [affirming *Marshall* v. *United States*, excerpted and discussed in Chapter 7, § 3B], we had held that the weight of the blotter paper bearing the lysergic acid diethylamide (LSD) must be counted for purposes of determining whether the quantity crossed the 10–gram threshold of 21 U.S.C. § 841(b)(1)(A)(v) imposing a minimum sentence of 10 years. At that time the United States Sentencing Commission applied a similar approach under the Sentencing Guidelines, but had taken no position regarding the meaning of the statutory provision. The Commission later changed its Guidelines approach, and, according to the petitioner in *Neal* v. *United States*, 516 U.S. 284 (1996), made clear its view that the statute bore that meaning as well. The petitioner argued that we should defer to that new approach. We would have none of it.

> "Were we, for argument's sake, to adopt petitioner's view that the Commission intended the commentary as an interpretation of §§ 841(b)(1), and that the last sentence of the commentary states the Commission's view that the dose-based method is consistent with the term 'mixture or substance' in the statute, he still would not prevail. The Commission's dose-based method cannot be squared with *Chapman*.... In these circumstances, we need not decide what, if any, deference is owed the Commission in order to reject its alleged contrary interpretation. Once we have determined a statute's meaning, we adhere to our ruling under the doctrine of *stare decisis*, and we assess an agency's later interpretation of the statute against that settled law."

There is, in short, no way to avoid the ossification of federal law that today's opinion sets in motion. What a court says is the law after according *Skidmore* deference will be the law forever, beyond the power of the agency to change even through rulemaking.

(4) And finally, the majority's approach compounds the confusion it creates by breathing new life into the anachronism of *Skidmore*, which sets forth a sliding scale of deference owed an agency's interpretation of a statute that is dependent "upon the thoroughness evident in [the agency's] consideration, the validity of its reasoning, its consistency with earlier and later pronouncements, and all those factors which give it power to persuade, if lacking power to control"; in this way, the appropriate measure of deference will be accorded the "body of experience and informed judgment" that such interpretations often embody. Justice Jackson's eloquence notwithstanding, the rule of *Skidmore* deference is an empty truism and a trifling statement of the obvious: A judge should take into account the well-considered views of expert observers.

It was possible to live with the indeterminacy of *Skidmore* deference in earlier times. But in an era when federal statutory law administered by federal agencies is pervasive, and when the ambiguities (intended or unintended) that those statutes contain are innumerable, totality-of-the-circumstances *Skidmore* deference is a recipe for uncertainty, unpredictability, and endless litigation. To condemn a vast body of agency action to that regime (all except rulemaking, formal (and informal?) adjudication, and whatever else might now and then be included within today's intentionally vague formulation of affirmative congressional intent to "delegate") is irresponsible.

[In Part II of his dissenting opinion, Justice Scalia criticized the majority's approach as an important departure from the Court's post-*Chevron* precedents as well as *Chevron* itself. In Part III, Justice Scalia explained why *Chevron*, properly understood, required deference to the Customs Service. "*Chevron* sets forth an across-the-board presumption, which operates as a background rule of law against which Congress legislates: Ambiguity means Congress intended agency discretion. Any resolution of the ambiguity by the administering agency that is authoritative—that represents the official position of the agency—must be accepted by the courts if it is reasonable." Given that precept as his starting point, Justice found nothing in the customs statute to rebut the presumptive discretion Congress gave the Service to draw lines as to tariff categories. In Part IV, Justice Scalia maintained that deference was required by *Nations Bank of North Carolina, N. A.* v. *Variable Annuity Life Ins. Co.*, 513 U.S. 251 (1995), which the Court acknowledged as an instance in which *Chevron* deference is warranted notwithstanding the absence of formal adjudication, notice-and-comment rulemaking, or comparable administrative formality.]

[Justice Scalia ended his opinion with a flourish, first dissenting from the Court's holding, that the case be remanded for the lower court to apply *Skidmore* deference, instead of reversing and remanding for the lower court to affirm the agency's interpretation.] I dissent even more vigorously from the reasoning that produces the Court's judgment, and that makes today's decision one of the most significant opinions ever rendered by the Court dealing with the judicial review of administrative action. Its consequences will be enormous, and almost uniformly bad.

NOTES ON MEAD AND RECENT REPORTS ON THE "CHEVRON REVOLUTION"

1. *The Grounding of* Chevron *on the Notion of Delegated Authority to Issue Orders or Rules Having the Force of Law: The Court's Uneven Application.* The Court's decision in *Mead* makes clear that the normative basis for *Chevron*'s deference-plus regime is congressional intent to delegate *lawmaking* authority to agencies. See Thomas W. Merrill & Kristin E. Hickman, Chevron's *Domain*, 89 Geo. L.J. 833 (2001), as well as Thomas W. Merrill, *Rethinking Article I, Section 1: From Nondelegation to Exclusive Delegation*, 104 Colum. L. Rev. 2097 (2004). Again over the dissents of Justice Scalia, the

Court reaffirmed this understanding in *National Cable & Telecommunications Ass'n v. Brand X Internet Services*, 545 U.S. 967 (2005), and *Gonzales v. Oregon*, 546 U.S. 243 (2006) (excerpted below).

Although this is the Court's official test, it is one that the post-*Chevron* Court has applied unevenly, at best. On the one hand, the Court does not seem to have a clear idea of when Congress has vested agencies with authority to create rules or orders having the "force of law." Thus, the Court often treats NLRB orders as having the force of law, even though that is clearly incorrect as a technical or historical matter: the NLRA says that the agency's orders would *not* have legal effect unless the agency or a party went to court and obtained an order to that effect. See Thomas W. Merrill & Kathryn Tongue Watts, *Agency Rules with the Force of Law: The Original Convention*, 116 Harv. L. Rev. 467 (2002). Indeed, the EPA rule in *Chevron* was not, in 1984, a rule having the force of law. *Id.* at 587.

The Court's approach is further complicated in *Mead*, where the Court says that Congress might implicitly delegate lawmaking authority to an agency. See also *Barnhart v. Walton*, 535 U.S. 212 (2002) (providing an even more functional *Skidmore*-like approach to *Chevron* than *Mead*). It is far from clear what kinds of statutory schemes would amount to an "implicit" delegation, and the lower courts have shown evidence of increased confusion since *Mead*.[j]

On the other hand, the Court's deployment of *Chevron* has been underwhelming even in those cases where there has been an explicit grant of lawmaking authority, liberally defined to include statutes that grant formal adjudication authority (e.g., NLRA) or substantive rulemaking authority (e.g., Clean Air Act). The Eskridge and Baer study surveyed 1014 post-*Chevron* Supreme Court decisions between 1984 and 2006 where an agency statutory interpretation was presented to the Court. In 8.3% of those cases, the Court majority applied the *Chevron* framework, even though almost 27% of those cases involved agency decisions pursuant to explicit grants of formal adjudicatory or legislative (substantive) rulemaking authority. About 10% of the *Chevron* cases involved very informal agency action clearly not derived from lawmaking grants—agency letters, interpretive guidances, and even opinions voiced in *amicus* briefs. See William N. Eskridge Jr. & Lauren E. Baer, *The Continuum of Deference: Supreme Court Treatment of Agency Statutory Interpretations from* Chevron *to* Hamdan, 96 Geo. L.J. 1083 (2008).

The Eskridge and Baer study also found that, as of 2006, the Court followed pre-*Chevron* deference-plus (i.e., non-*Skidmore*) regimes in 4.8% of their 1014 case database. Most of these involved deference to NLRB, IRS, HHS, and FDA interpretations. The conceptual basis for these cases fell somewhere between *Chevron* and *Skidmore*: Congress has vested such-and-such agency with authority to carry out the statutory purpose; to carry out the congressional purpose, the agency needs interpretational breathing room; hence, courts ought to defer to reasonable agency readings of the statute. E.g.,

---

j. See Lisa Schultz Bressman, *Has* Mead *Muddled Judicial Review of Agency Action?*, 58 Vand. L. Rev. 1443 (2005) (yes, *Mead* has muddled judicial review of agency action); Adrian Vermeule, *Mead in the Trenches*, 71 Geo. Wash. L. Rev. 347 (2003) (*Mead* has created very muddled trenches).

Beth Israel Hospital v. NLRB, 437 U.S. 483 (1978), applied in *Auciello Iron Works v. NLRB*, 517 U.S. 781 (1996) (NLRB); *National Muffler Dealers v. United States*, 440 U.S. 472 (1979), recently overruled in *Mayo Foundation v. United States*, 131 S.Ct. 704 (2011) (requiring that *Chevron* replace *National Muffler* as the deference standard in tax cases where there has been a delegation of lawmaking authority to the IRS).

2. *The Survival—Indeed, Flourishing—of* Skidmore. *Mead* confirmed the survival of *Skidmore* as the default deference regime. The Eskridge and Baer study identified 6.7% of the cases in their database as ones where the Court explicitly applied *Skidmore* deference, almost as many cases where the Court applied *Chevron* during their time period (1984–2006). Moreover, in 17.8% of the cases Eskridge and Baer collected, the Court relied on or was clearly influenced by an agency rule or *amicus* brief (the format followed by the agency in *Skidmore*), but without citation of *Skidmore* or an announcement that the Court was "deferring." The authors call this last group of cases *Skidmore*-Lite. Not only has *Skidmore* not been overruled, but it has perhaps been the dominant deference regime within the Supreme Court.

The Eskridge and Baer study confirmed the importance of the *Skidmore* norm, based upon the agency's comparative competence, by analyzing agency win-rates by subject area. The chart below is a small but representative sampling of their findings:

Statutory Subject Matter	Primary Deference Regime/Secondary Regime	Agency Win Rate
Pensions	No deference/*Skidmore*-Lite	82.5%
Foreign Affairs etc.	No deference/*Skidmore*	78.5%
Tax	No deference/*Skidmore*	75.7%
Bankruptcy	No deference/*Skidmore*-Lite	75.0%
Entitlements	No deference/*Chevron*	71.9%
Environmental Law	No deference/*Chevron*	68.4%
Civil Rights	No deference/*Skidmore*	61.0%
Indian Law	No deference/*Skidmore*	51.6%

Source: Eskridge & Baer, *Continuum of Deference.*

Even this summary illustrates the authors' argument that the primary mechanism for agency success at the Supreme Court level is neither formal lawmaking delegation nor *Chevron* deference, but some combination of institutional acquiescence and statutory subject matter. For all statutes, the Solicitor General usually persuades the Court that the government's construction of the statute is correct, even in cases (like civil rights) where the Justices have strong opinions themselves. For statutes that are technical and instrumental to some routine economic or foreign affairs goal, the Justices have less strong opinions and are cognizant that they do not have full command of the technical considerations important to these cases; hence, the Justices are super-deferential in those cases.

A final way that *Skidmore* has persevered is that its contextual factors have proven to be influential even in cases where the agency decision was pursuant to a congressional delegation of lawmaking authority, precisely the cases where *Chevron* is supposed to be the governing approach. Yet in those cases, agency success rates were significantly higher when the agency interpretation had been consistent over time, did not raise thorny constitutional issues, and had generated discernible public or private reliance.

3. *Evidence of Ideological Voting by the Justices in Agency Deference Cases.* In the wake of *Mead*, a number of academic studies found evidence of ideological voting in agency deference cases. For example, consider the Eskridge and Baer study of 1014 cases in which agency interpretations were in play found the following pattern of voting:

Agreement with Agency Interpretations, by Justice (*Chevron* to *Hamdan*)

Supreme Court Justice (Tenure)	Agreement with Agency Overall	Agreement with Liberal Agency Interpretations	Agreement with Conservative Agency Interpretations
Warren Burger (1969–86)	82.3%	75.9%	87.0%
Byron White (1962–93)	74.0%	71.9%	76.3%
Lewis Powell (1971–87)	72.7%	73.9%	73.0%
Stephen Breyer (1994–)	72.0%	79.5%	64.9%
William Rehnquist (1971–2006)	70.6%	59.4%	79.1%
Ruth Bader Ginsburg (1993–)	69.5%	77.1%	61.9%
Anthony Kennedy (1986–)	69.3%	61.9%	74.0%
David Souter (1990–2009)	68.7%	75.6%	62.5%
Sandra Day O'Connor (1981–2007)	68.6%	61.5%	73.7%
Harry Blackmun (1970–1993)	65.1%	80.6%	55.3%
Antonin Scalia (1986–)	64.5%	53.8%	71.6%
Clarence Thomas (1991–)	63.1%	46.8%	75.8%
John Paul Stevens (1975–2010)	60.9%	79.2%	49.6%
Thurgood Marshall (1967–91)	55.6%	84.8%	38.8%
William Brennan (1956–90)	52.6%	81.6%	36.7%

Source: Eskridge & Baer, *Continuum of Deference.*

These data reveal a wide variance of judicial willingness to go along with agency interpretations: Warren Burger, Byron White, and Lewis Powell were quite deferential, while William Brennan and Thurgood Marshall went against agency views most of the time. Surprisingly, John Paul Stevens, the author of *Chevron*, is one of the least deferential. Exactly as he suggested in his law review article, Justice Scalia is not as deferential as other Justices.

Eskridge and Baer found pretty much the same pattern when they limited their analysis to the *Chevron* cases in their database or to the 267 cases involving agency interpretations pursuant to delegated lawmaking authority. (The Justices had slightly higher deference rates, but the ideological pattern remained the same.) Analyzing only cases citing and following *Chevron* for a shorter time period, Cass Sunstein and Thomas Miles found somewhat more pronounced ideological voting and report that Justice Scalia is far less deferential (59%) than Justices Breyer (89.5%), Ginsburg (86%), Souter (81%), and Stevens (73%). See Thomas J. Miles & Cass R. Sunstein, *Do Judges Make Regulatory Policy? An Empirical Investigation of* Chevron, 73 U. Chi. L. Rev. 823 (2006).

Eskridge and Baer caution that there may be a selection bias at work, especially during the Clinton Administration, which was the focus of the Miles and Sunstein study. Between 1993 and 2001, a Democratic Administration may have had more success getting its liberal positions before the Court than in persuading the Justices that its positions were correct. If the liberal agency decisions were relatively "weaker" on the merits, that would explain the lower deference rates for conservative Justices like Scalia.

B. IMPORTANT *CHEVRON* ISSUES

So long as the Supreme Court sticks with the *Mead* understanding of *Chevron*, the linchpin is whether the agency interpretation is pursuant to a congressional delegation of authority to issue orders or rules having the force of law. The implications of this conceptual basis for *Chevron* are spelled out in Thomas W. Merrill & Kristin E. Hickman, Chevron's *Domain*, 89 Geo. L.J. 833 (2001). Consider some of these issues as the Supreme Court has wrestled with them.

1. Is the Agency Acting Within Its Delegated Authority?

If the *Chevron* deference boost rests upon congressional delegation of lawmaking authority, then the Court should make sure that Congress has delegated such authority to the agency in general *and* as applied to the issue in suit. Merrill & Hickman, Chevron's *Domain*, call this Step Zero of *Chevron*. Although written as a Step One opinion, *MCI v. AT & T* may be read as an early example of Step Zero. Consider the following case, which is clearly Step Zero and illustrates the complexity that Step Zero inquiries might have.

GONZALES v. OREGON

Supreme Court of the United States, 2006
546 U.S. 243, 126 S.Ct. 904, 163 L.Ed.2d 748

JUSTICE KENNEDY delivered the opinion of the Court.

In 1994, Oregon became the first State to legalize assisted suicide when voters approved a ballot measure enacting the Oregon Death With Dignity Act (ODWDA). ODWDA, which survived a 1997 ballot measure seeking its repeal, exempts from civil or criminal liability state-licensed physicians who, in compliance with the specific safeguards in ODWDA, dispense or prescribe a lethal dose of drugs upon the request of a terminally ill patient.

The drugs Oregon physicians prescribe under ODWDA are regulated under a federal statute, the Controlled Substances Act (CSA or Act). 84 Stat. 1242, as amended, 21 U.S.C. § 801 et seq. The CSA allows these particular drugs to be available only by a written prescription from a registered physician. In the ordinary course the same drugs are prescribed in smaller doses for pain alleviation.

A November 9, 2001 Interpretive Rule issued by the Attorney General addresses the implementation and enforcement of the CSA with respect to ODWDA. It determines that using controlled substances to assist suicide is not a legitimate medical practice and that dispensing or prescribing them for this purpose is unlawful under the CSA. The Interpretive Rule's validity under the CSA is the issue before us.

[I] We turn first to the text and structure of the CSA. Enacted in 1970 with the main objectives of combating drug abuse and controlling the legitimate and illegitimate traffic in controlled substances, the CSA creates a comprehensive, closed regulatory regime criminalizing the unauthorized manufacture, distribution, dispensing, and possession of substances classified in any of the Act's five schedules. 21 U.S.C. § 841; 21 U.S.C. § 844. The Act places substances in one of five schedules based on their potential for abuse or dependence, their accepted medical use, and their accepted safety for use under medical supervision. Schedule I contains the most severe restrictions on access and use, and Schedule V the least. 21 U.S.C. § 812. Congress classified a host of substances when it enacted the CSA, but the statute permits the Attorney General to add, remove, or reschedule substances. He may do so, however, only after making particular findings, and on scientific and medical matters he is required to accept the findings of the Secretary of Health and Human Services (Secretary). These proceedings must be on the record after an opportunity for comment. See 21 U.S.C. § 811.

The present dispute involves controlled substances listed in Schedule II, substances generally available only pursuant to a written, nonrefillable prescription by a physician. 21 U.S.C. § 829(a). A 1971 regulation promulgated by the Attorney General requires that every prescription for a controlled substance "be issued for a legitimate medical purpose by an individual practitioner acting in the usual course of his professional practice." 21 CFR § 1306.04(a) (2005).

To prevent diversion of controlled substances with medical uses, the CSA regulates the activity of physicians. To issue lawful prescriptions of Schedule II drugs, physicians must "obtain from the Attorney General a registration issued in accordance with the rules and regulations promulgated by him." 21 U.S.C. § 822(a)(2). The Attorney General may deny, suspend, or revoke this registration if, as relevant here, the physician's registration would be "inconsistent with the public interest." § 824(a)(4); § 822(a)(2). When deciding whether a practitioner's registration is in the public interest, the Attorney General "shall" consider:

"(1) The recommendation of the appropriate State licensing board or professional disciplinary authority.

"(2) The applicant's experience in dispensing, or conducting research with respect to controlled substances.

"(3) The applicant's conviction record under Federal or State laws relating to the manufacture, distribution, or dispensing of controlled substances.

"(4) Compliance with applicable State, Federal, or local laws relating to controlled substances.

"(5) Such other conduct which may threaten the public health and safety." § 823(f).

The CSA explicitly contemplates a role for the States in regulating controlled substances, as evidenced by its pre-emption provision.

"No provision of this subchapter shall be construed as indicating an intent on the part of the Congress to occupy the field in which that provision operates ... to the exclusion of any State law on the same subject matter which would otherwise be within the authority of the State, unless there is a positive conflict between that provision ... and that State law so that the two cannot consistently stand together." § 903.

[After Oregon voters adopted that state's DWDCA in 1994 and reaffirmed it in a 1997 referendum, several senators, including John Ashcroft of Missouri, petitioned Attorney General Janet Reno to override the Oregon law through an interpretation of the CSA declaring that use of controlled substances for "assisted suicide" was a federal crime. Reno declined, but when Ashcroft himself became Attorney General, he issued the Directive. The Ninth Circuit rejected his interpretation, and Ashcroft appealed. He argued that his Interpretive Rule was entitled to *Chevron* deference. Because Congress had not directly addressed the issue of "assisted suicide," the Court should defer to his interpretation. (Ashcroft also argued that he was entitled to super-deference because he was interpreting the 1971 regulation.)]

[II After rejecting Ashcroft's argument for super-deference because he was construing a Department rule, the Court considered his *Chevron* deference argument and posed the *Mead* question: Has Congress delegated lawmaking authority to the Attorney General to preempt this kind of state law?] The Attorney General has rulemaking power to fulfill his duties under the CSA. The specific respects in which he is authorized to make rules, however, instruct us that he is not authorized to make a rule declaring illegitimate a medical standard for care and treatment of patients that is specifically authorized under state law. * * *

The CSA gives the Attorney General limited powers, to be exercised in specific ways. His rulemaking authority under the CSA is described in two provisions: (1) "The Attorney General is authorized to promulgate rules and regulations and to charge reasonable fees relating to the registration and control of the manufacture, distribution, and dispensing of controlled substances and to listed chemicals," 21 U.S.C. § 821; and (2) "The Attorney General may promulgate and enforce any rules, regulations, and procedures which he may deem necessary and appropriate for the efficient execution of his functions under this subchapter," 21 U.S.C. § 871(b). As is evident from these sections, Congress did not delegate to the Attorney General authority to carry out or effect all provisions of the CSA. Rather, he can promulgate rules relating only to "registration" and "control," and "for the efficient execution of his functions" under the statute.

Turning first to the Attorney General's authority to make regulations for the "control" of drugs, this delegation cannot sustain the Interpretive Rule's attempt to define standards of medical practice. Control is a term of art in the CSA. "As used in this subchapter," § 802—the subchapter that includes § 821—

> "The term 'control' means to add a drug or other substance, or immediate precursor, to a schedule under part B of this subchapter, whether by transfer from another schedule or otherwise." § 802(5).

To exercise his scheduling power, the Attorney General must follow a detailed set of procedures, including requesting a scientific and medical evaluation from the Secretary. See 21 U.S.C. §§ 811, 812. The statute is also specific as to the manner in which the Attorney General must exercise this authority: "Rules of the Attorney General under this subsection [regarding scheduling] shall be made on the record after opportunity for a hearing pursuant to the rulemaking procedures prescribed by [the Administrative Procedure Act, 5 U.S.C. § 553]." 21 U.S.C. § 811(a). The Interpretive Rule now under consideration does not concern the scheduling of substances and was not issued after the required procedures for rules regarding scheduling, so it cannot fall under the Attorney General's "control" authority. * * *

We turn, next, to the registration provisions of the CSA. Before 1984, the Attorney General was required to register any physician who was authorized by his State. The Attorney General could only deregister a physician who falsified his application, was convicted of a felony relating to controlled substances, or had his state license or registration revoked. The CSA was amended in 1984 to allow the Attorney General to deny registration to an applicant "if he determines that the issuance of such registration would be inconsistent with the public interest." 21 U.S.C. § 823(f). Registration may also be revoked or suspended by the Attorney General on the same grounds. § 824(a)(4). In determining consistency with the public interest, the Attorney General must * * * consider five factors, including: the State's recommendation; compliance with state, federal, and local laws regarding controlled substances; and public health and safety. § 823(f).

The Interpretive Rule cannot be justified under this part of the statute. It does not undertake the five-factor analysis and concerns much more than registration. Nor does the Interpretive Rule on its face purport to be an application of the registration provision in § 823(f). It is, instead, an interpretation of the substantive federal law requirements (under 21 CFR § 1306.04 (2005)) for a valid prescription. It begins by announcing that assisting suicide is not a "legitimate medical purpose" under

§ 1306.04, and that dispensing controlled substances to assist a suicide violates the CSA. 66 Fed. Reg. 56608 (2001). Violation is a criminal offense, and often a felony, under 21 U.S.C. § 841. The Interpretive Rule thus purports to declare that using controlled substances for physician-assisted suicide is a crime, an authority that goes well beyond the Attorney General's statutory power to register or deregister.

The Attorney General's deregistration power, of course, may carry implications for criminal enforcement because if a physician dispenses a controlled substance after he is deregistered, he violates § 841. The Interpretive Rule works in the opposite direction, however: it declares certain conduct criminal, placing in jeopardy the registration of any physician who engages in that conduct. To the extent the Interpretive Rule concerns registration, it simply states the obvious because one of the five factors the Attorney General must consider in deciding the "public interest" is "[c]ompliance with applicable State, Federal, or local laws relating to controlled substances." 21 U.S.C. § 823(f)(4). The problem with the design of the Interpretive Rule is that it cannot, and does not, explain why the Attorney General has the authority to decide what constitutes an underlying violation of the CSA in the first place. The explanation the Government seems to advance is that the Attorney General's authority to decide whether a physician's actions are inconsistent with the "public interest" provides the basis for the Interpretive Rule.

By this logic, however, the Attorney General claims extraordinary authority. If the Attorney General's argument were correct, his power to deregister necessarily would include the greater power to criminalize even the actions of registered physicians, whenever they engage in conduct he deems illegitimate. This power to criminalize—unlike his power over registration, which must be exercised only after considering five express statutory factors—would be unrestrained. It would be anomalous for Congress to have so painstakingly described the Attorney General's limited authority to deregister a single physician or schedule a single drug, but to have given him, just by implication, authority to declare an entire class of activity outside "the course of professional practice," and therefore a criminal violation of the CSA. * * * See also *Adams Fruit Co. v. Barrett,* 494 U.S. 638, 649–50 (1990) (holding that a delegation of authority to promulgate motor vehicle safety "*standards*" did not include the authority to decide the pre-emptive scope of the federal statute because "[n]o such delegation regarding [the statute's] enforcement provisions is evident in the statute").

The same principle controls here. It is not enough that the terms "public interest," "public health and safety," and "Federal law" are used in the part of the statute over which the Attorney General has authority. The statutory terms "public interest" and "public health" do not call on the Attorney General, or any other Executive official, to make an independent assessment of the meaning of federal law. The Attorney General did not base the Interpretive Rule on an application of the five-factor test generally, or the "public health and safety" factor specifically. Even if he had, it is doubtful the Attorney General could cite the "public interest" or "public health" to deregister a physician simply because he deemed a controversial practice permitted by state law to have an illegitimate medical purpose. * * *

The authority desired by the Government is inconsistent with the design of the statute in other fundamental respects. The Attorney General does not have the sole delegated authority under the CSA. He must instead share it with, and in some respects defer to, the Secretary [of the Department of Health and Human Services], whose functions are likewise delineated and confined by the statute. The CSA allocates decisionmaking powers among statutory actors so that medical judgments, if they are to be decided at the federal level and for the limited objects of the statute, are placed in the hands of the Secretary. In the scheduling context, for example, the Secretary's recommendations on scientific and medical matters bind the Attorney General. The Attorney General cannot control a substance if the Secretary disagrees. 21 U.S.C. § 811(b). See H.R. Rep. No. 91–1444, pt. 1, p. 33 (1970) (the section "is not intended to authorize the Attorney General to undertake or support medical and scientific research [for the purpose of scheduling], which is within the competence of the Department of Health, Education, and Welfare").

In a similar vein the 1970 Act's regulation of medical practice with respect to drug rehabilitation gives the Attorney General a limited role; for it is the Secretary who, after consultation with the Attorney General and national medical groups, "determine[s] the appropriate methods of professional practice in the medical treatment of ... narcotic addiction." 42 U.S.C. § 290bb–2a; see 21 U.S.C. § 823(g) (2000 ed. and Supp. II) (stating that the Attorney General shall register practitioners who dispense drugs for narcotics treatment when the Secretary has determined the applicant is qualified to treat addicts and the Attorney General has concluded the applicant will comply with record keeping and security regulations); H.R. Rep. No. 93–884, p 6 (1974) ("This section preserves the distinctions found in the [CSA] between the functions of the Attorney General and the Secretary.... All decisions of a medical nature are to be made by the Secretary.... Law enforcement decisions respecting the security of stocks of narcotics drugs and the maintenance of records on such drugs are to be made by the Attorney General").

Post enactment congressional commentary on the CSA's regulation of medical practice is also at odds with the Attorney General's claimed authority to determine appropriate medical standards. In 1978, in preparation for ratification of the Convention on Psychotropic Substances, Feb. 21, 1971, [1979–1980] 32 U. S. T. 543, T. I. A. S. No. 9725, Congress decided it would implement the United States' compliance through "the framework of the procedures and criteria for classification of substances provided in the" CSA. 21 U.S.C. § 801a (3). It did so to ensure that "nothing in the Convention will interfere with ethical medical practice in this country as determined by [the Secretary] on the basis of a consensus of the views of the American medical and scientific community." *Ibid.*

The structure of the CSA, then, conveys unwillingness to cede medical judgments to an Executive official who lacks medical expertise. In interpreting statutes that divide authority, the Court has recognized: "Because historical familiarity and policymaking expertise account in the first instance for the presumption that Congress delegates interpretive lawmaking power to the agency rather than to the reviewing court, we presume here that Congress intended to invest interpretive power in the administrative actor in the best position to develop these attributes." *Martin v. OSHRC*, 499 U.S. 144, 153 (1991). This presumption works against a conclusion that the Attorney General has authority to make quintessentially medical judgments. * * *

The idea that Congress gave the Attorney General such broad and unusual authority through an implicit delegation in the CSA's registration provision is not sustainable. "Congress, we have held, does not alter the fundamental details of a regulatory scheme in vague terms or ancillary provisions—it does not, one might say, hide elephants in mouseholes." *Whitman v. American Trucking Assns., Inc.*, 531 U.S. 457, 468 (2001); see *FDA v. Brown & Williamson* ("[W]e are confident that Congress could not have intended to delegate a decision of such economic and political significance to an agency in so cryptic a fashion").

The importance of the issue of physician-assisted suicide, which has been the subject of an "earnest and profound debate" across the country, [*Washington v. Glucksberg*, 521 U.S., 702, 735 (1997), which upheld a state prohibition on physician-assisted suicide, in part on the argument that the states should have discretion to decide such issues for themselves], makes the oblique form of the claimed delegation all the more suspect. Under the Government's theory, moreover, the medical judgments the Attorney General could make are not limited to physician-assisted suicide. Were this argument accepted, he could decide whether any particular drug may be used for any particular purpose, or indeed whether a physician who administers any controversial treatment could be deregistered. This would occur, under the Government's view, despite the statute's express limitation of the Attorney General's authority to registration and control, with attendant restrictions on each of those functions, and despite the statutory purposes to combat drug abuse and prevent illicit drug trafficking.

[III Finding no delegation, and therefore no *Chevron* deference, the Court considered the Attorney General's facts and arguments à la *Skidmore* as it interpreted the CSA to determine whether Congress meant to preempt laws like the ODWDA.] The statute and our case law amply support the conclusion that Congress regulates medical practice insofar as it bars doctors from using their prescription-writing powers as a means to engage in illicit drug dealing and trafficking as conventionally understood. Beyond this, however, the statute manifests no intent to regulate the practice of medicine generally. The silence is understandable given the structure and limitations of federalism, which allow the States " 'great latitude under their police powers to legislate as to the protection of the lives, limbs, health, comfort, and quiet of all persons.' " *Medtronic, Inc. v. Lohr*, 518 U.S. 470, 475 (1996).

* * * [W]e find only one area in which Congress set general, uniform standards of medical practice. Title I of the Comprehensive Drug Abuse Prevention and Control Act of 1970, of which the CSA was Title II, provides that

> "[The Secretary], after consultation with the Attorney General and with national organizations representative of persons with knowledge and experience in the treatment of narcotic addicts, shall determine the appropriate methods of professional practice in the medical treatment of the narcotic addiction of various classes of narcotic addicts, and shall report thereon from time to time to the Congress." § 4, 84 Stat. 1241, codified at 42 U.S.C. § 290bb–2a.

This provision strengthens the understanding of the CSA as a statute combating recreational drug abuse, and also indicates that when Congress wants to regulate medical practice in the given scheme, it does so by explicit language in the statute [and with consultation involving the medical experts in HHS]. * * *

JUSTICE SCALIA, joined by CHIEF JUSTICE ROBERTS and JUSTICE THOMAS, dissenting.

* * * Setting aside the implicit delegation inherent in Congress's use of the undefined term "prescription" in § 829, the Court's reading of "control" in § 821 is manifestly erroneous. The Court urges that "control" is a term defined in part A of the subchapter (entitled "Introductory Provisions") to mean "to add a drug or other substance ... to a schedule *under part B of this subchapter*," 21 U.S.C. § 802(5) (emphasis added). But § 821 is not included in "part B of this subchapter," which is entitled "Authority to Control; Standards and Schedules," and consists of the sections related to *scheduling*, 21 U.S.C.A. §§ 811–814 (main ed. and Supp. 2005), where the statutory definition is uniquely appropriate. Rather, § 821 is found in *part C* of the subchapter, §§ 821–830, entitled "Registration of Manufacturers, Distributors, and Dispensers of Controlled Substances," which includes all and only the provisions relating to the "manufacture, distribution, and dispensing of controlled substances," § 821. The artificial definition of "control" in § 802(5) has no conceivable application to the use of that word in § 821. Under that definition, "control" must take a *substance* as its direct object, see 21 U.S.C. § 802(5) ("to add a drug or other substance ... to a schedule")—and that is how "control" is consistently used throughout *part B*. See, *e.g.*, §§ 811(b) ("proceedings ... to *control* a drug or other substance"), 811(c) ("each drug or other substance proposed to be *controlled* or removed from the schedules"), 811(d)(1) ("If *control* is required ... the Attorney General shall issue an order *controlling* such drug ..."), 812(b) ("Except where

control is required ... a drug or other substance may not be placed in any schedule ...''). In § 821, by contrast, the term "control" has as its object, not "a drug or other substance," but rather the *processes* of "manufacture, distribution, and dispensing of controlled substances." It could not be clearer that the artificial definition of "control" in § 802(5) is inapplicable. It makes no sense to speak of "adding the manufacturing, distribution, and dispensing of substances to a schedule." We do not force term-of-art definitions into contexts where they plainly do not fit and produce nonsense. What is obviously intended in § 821 is the ordinary meaning of "control"—namely, "[t]o exercise restraining or directing influence over; to dominate; regulate; hence, to hold from action; to curb," Webster's Second 580. "Control" is regularly used in this ordinary sense elsewhere in *part C* of the subchapter.

When the word is given its ordinary meaning, the Attorney General's interpretation of the prescription requirement of § 829 plainly "relat[es] to the ... *control* of the ... dispensing of controlled substances," 21 U.S.C. § 821 (emphasis added), since a prescription is the chief requirement for "dispensing" such drugs, see § 829. The same meaning is compelled by the fact that § 821 is the first section not of part B of the subchapter, which deals entirely with "control" in the artificial sense, but of part C, every section of which relates to the "registration and control of the manufacture, distribution, and dispensing of controlled substances," § 821. It would be peculiar for the first section of this part to authorize rulemaking for matters covered by the *previous* part. The only sensible interpretation of § 821 is that it gives the Attorney General interpretive authority over the provisions of part C, all of which "relat[e] to the registration and control of the manufacture, distribution, and dispensing of controlled substances." These provisions include *both* the prescription requirement of § 829 and the criteria for registration and deregistration of §§ 823 and 824.

Even if the Directive were entitled to no deference whatever, the most reasonable interpretation of the Regulation and of the statute would produce the same result. Virtually every relevant source of authoritative meaning confirms that the phrase "legitimate medical purpose" does not include intentionally assisting suicide. "Medicine" refers to "[t]he science and art dealing with the prevention, cure, or alleviation of disease." Webster's Second 1527. The use of the word "legitimate" connotes an *objective* standard of "medicine," and our presumption that the CSA creates a uniform federal law regulating the dispensation of controlled substances means that this objective standard must be a federal one. As recounted in detail in the memorandum for the Attorney General that is attached as an appendix to the Directive (OLC Memo), virtually every medical authority from Hippocrates to the current American Medical Association (AMA) confirms that assisting suicide has seldom or never been viewed as a form of "prevention, cure, or alleviation of disease," and (even more so) that assisting suicide is not a "legitimate" branch of that "science and art." Indeed, the AMA has determined that " '[p]hysicianassisted suicide is fundamentally incompatible with the physician's role as a healer.'" *Glucksberg*. "[T]he overwhelming weight of authority in judicial decisions, the past and present policies of nearly all of the States and of the Federal Government, and the clear, firm and unequivocal views of the leading associations within the American medical and nursing professions, establish that assisting in suicide ... is not a legitimate medical purpose." OLC Memo. See also *Glucksberg* (prohibitions or condemnations of assisted suicide in 50 jurisdictions, including 47 States, the District of Columbia, and 2 Territories). * * *

Even if the Regulation did not exist and "prescription" in § 829 could not be interpreted to require a "legitimate medical purpose," the Directive's conclusion that "prescribing, dispensing, or administering federally controlled substances ... by a physician ... may 'render his registration ... inconsistent with the public interest' and therefore subject to possible suspension or revocation under 21 U.S.C. [§] 824(a)(4)," 66 Fed. Reg. 56608, would nevertheless be unassailable in this Court.

Sections 823(f) and 824(a) explicitly grant the Attorney General the authority to register and deregister physicians, and his discretion in exercising that authority is spelled out in very broad terms. He may refuse to register or deregister if he determines that registration is "inconsistent with the public interest," 21 U.S.C. § 823(f), after considering five factors, the fifth of which is "[s]uch other conduct which may threaten the public health and safety," § 823(f)(5). As the Court points out, these broad standards were enacted in the 1984 amendments for the specific purpose of *freeing* the Attorney General's discretion over registration from the decisions of state authorities.

The fact that assisted-suicide prescriptions are issued in violation of § 829 is of course sufficient to support the Directive's conclusion that issuing them may be cause for deregistration: such prescriptions would violate the fourth factor of § 823(f), namely "[c]ompliance with applicable ... Federal ... laws relating to controlled substances," 21 U.S.C. § 823(f)(4). But the Attorney General did not rely solely on subsection (f)(4) in reaching his conclusion that registration would be "inconsistent with the public interest"; nothing in the text of the Directive indicates that. Subsection (f)(5) ("[s]uch other conduct which may threaten the public health and safety") provides an independent, alternative basis for the Directive's conclusion regarding deregistration—provided that the Attorney General has authority to interpret "public interest" and "public health and safety" in § 823(f) to exclude assisted suicide.

Three considerations make it perfectly clear that the statute confers authority to interpret these phrases upon the Attorney General. First, the Attorney General is solely and explicitly charged with administering the registration and deregistration provisions. See §§ 823(f), 824(a). By making the criteria for such registration and deregistration such obviously ambiguous factors as "public interest" and "public health and safety," Congress implicitly (but clearly) gave the Attorney General authority to interpret those criteria—*whether or not* there is any explicit delegation provision in the statute. "Sometimes the legislative delegation to an agency on a particular question is implicit rather than explicit. In such a case, a court may not substitute its own construction of a statutory provision for a reasonable interpretation made by the administrator of an agency." *Chevron.* The Court's exclusive focus on the *explicit* delegation provisions is, at best, a fossil of our pre-*Chevron* era; at least since *Chevron*, we have not conditioned our deferral to agency interpretations upon the existence of explicit delegation provisions. *Mead* left this principle of implicit delegation intact.

Second, even if explicit delegation were required, Congress provided it in § 821, which authorizes the Attorney General to "promulgate rules and regulations . . . relating to the *registration and control* of the manufacture, distribution, and dispensing of controlled substances. . . ." (Emphasis added.) Because "dispensing" refers to the delivery of a controlled substance "pursuant to the lawful order of a practitioner," 21 U.S.C. § 802(10), the deregistration of such practitioners for writing impermissible orders "relat[es] to the registration . . . of the . . . dispensing" of controlled substances, 21 U.S.C.A. § 821 (Supp. 2005).

Third, § 821 also gives the Attorney General authority to promulgate rules and regulations "relating to the . . . control of the . . . dispensing of controlled substances." As discussed earlier, it is plain that the *ordinary* meaning of "control" must apply to § 821, so that the plain import of the provision is to grant the Attorney General rulemaking authority over all the provisions of part C of the CSA, 21 U.S.C. §§ 821–830. Registering and deregistering the practitioners who issue the prescriptions necessary for lawful dispensation of controlled substances plainly "relat[es] to the . . . control of the . . . dispensing of controlled substances." § 821.

The Attorney General is thus authorized to promulgate regulations interpreting §§ 823(f) and 824(a), both by implicit delegation in § 823(f) and by two grounds of explicit delegation in § 821. The Court nevertheless holds that this triply unambiguous delegation cannot be given full effect because "the design of the statute" evinces the intent to grant the Secretary of Health and Human Services exclusive authority over scientific and medical determinations. This proposition is not remotely plausible. The Court cites as authority for the Secretary's exclusive authority two specific areas in which his medical determinations are said to be binding on the Attorney General—with regard to the "scientific and medical evaluation" of a drug's effects that precedes its scheduling, § 811(b), and with regard to "the appropriate methods of professional practice in the medical treatment of the narcotic addiction of various classes of narcotic addicts," 42 U.S.C. § 290bb–2a. Far from establishing a general principle of Secretary supremacy with regard to all scientific and medical determinations, the fact that Congress granted the Secretary specifically defined authority in the areas of scheduling and addiction treatment, *without otherwise mentioning him* in the registration provisions, suggests, to the contrary, that Congress envisioned *no* role for the Secretary in that area—

where, as we have said, interpretive authority was both implicitly and explicitly conferred upon the Attorney General.

Even if we could rewrite statutes to accord with sensible "design," it is far from a certainty that the Secretary, rather than the Attorney General, ought to control the registration of physicians. Though registration decisions sometimes require judgments about the legitimacy of medical practices, the Department of Justice has seemingly had no difficulty making them. But unlike decisions about whether a substance should be scheduled or whether a narcotics addiction treatment is legitimate, registration decisions are not exclusively, or even primarily, concerned with "medical [and] scientific" factors. See 21 U.S.C. § 823(f). Rather, the decision to register, or to bring an action to deregister, an individual *physician* implicates all the policy goals and competing enforcement priorities that attend any exercise of prosecutorial discretion. It is entirely reasonable to think (as Congress evidently did) that it would be easier for the Attorney General occasionally to make judgments about the legitimacy of medical practices than it would be for the Secretary to get into the business of law enforcement. It is, in other words, perfectly consistent with an intelligent "design of the statute" to give the Nation's chief law enforcement official, not its chief health official, broad discretion over the substantive standards that govern registration and deregistration. That is *especially* true where the contested "scientific and medical" judgment at issue has to do with the legitimacy of physician-assisted suicide, which ultimately rests, not on "science" or "medicine," but on a naked value judgment. It no more depends upon a "quintessentially medical judgmen[t]" than does the legitimacy of polygamy or eugenic infanticide. And it requires no particular *medical* training to undertake the objective inquiry into how the continuing traditions of Western medicine have consistently treated this subject. The Secretary's supposedly superior "medical expertise" to make "medical judgments" is strikingly irrelevant to the case at hand.

The Court also reasons that, even if the CSA grants the Attorney General authority to interpret § 823(f), the Directive does not purport to exercise that authority, because it "does not undertake the five-factor analysis" of § 823(f) and does not "on its face purport to be an *application* of the registration provision in § 823(f)." This reasoning is sophistic. It would be improper—indeed, *impossible*—for the Attorney General to "undertake the five-factor analysis" of § 823(f) and to "appl[y] the registration provision" outside the context of an actual enforcement proceeding. But of course the Attorney General may issue regulations to clarify his interpretation of the five factors, and to signal how he will apply them in future enforcement proceedings. That is what the Directive plainly purports to do by citing § 824(a)(4), and that is why the Directive's conclusion on deregistration is couched in conditional terms: "Such conduct by a physician ... *may* 'render his registration ... inconsistent with the public interest' and therefore subject to *possible* suspension or revocation under 21 U.S.C. [§] 824(a)(4)." 66 Fed. Reg. 56608 (emphasis added).

It follows from what we have said that the Attorney General's authoritative interpretations of "public interest" and "public health and safety" in § 823(f) are subject to *Chevron* deference. As noted earlier, the Court does not contest that the absence of notice-and-comment procedures for the Directive renders *Chevron* inapplicable. And there is no serious argument that "Congress has directly spoken to the precise question at issue," or that the Directive's interpretations of "public health and safety" and "inconsistent with the public interest" are not "permissible." *Chevron*. On the latter point, in fact, the condemnation of assisted suicide by 50 American jurisdictions supports the Attorney General's view. The Attorney General may therefore weigh a physician's participation in assisted suicide as a factor counseling against his registration, or in favor of deregistration, under § 823(f).

In concluding to the contrary, the Court merely presents the conclusory assertion that "it is doubtful the Attorney General could cite the 'public interest' or 'public health' to deregister a physician simply because he deemed a controversial practice permitted by state law to have an illegitimate medical purpose." But why on earth not?—especially when he has interpreted the relevant statutory factors in advance to give fair warning that such a practice is "inconsistent with the public interest." The Attorney General's discretion to determine the public interest in this area is admittedly broad—but certainly no broader than other congressionally conferred Executive powers that we have upheld in the past.

NOTES ON THE *OREGON AID-IN-DYING* CASE AND DEFERENCE FOR ISSUES OF AGENCY AUTHORITY

1. *The Debate over Textual Authorization for the Attorney General.* The take-no-prisoners debate between Justices Kennedy and Scalia provides an occasion for the student to practice her or his skills with the statutory interpretation rules and practices covered in this casebook. Note especially the skillful combination of dictionary meanings, grammatical analyses, and structural points made in the dissent. Justice Scalia has excellent arguments for the proposition that the Ashcroft Directive is literally within at least one of the CSA delegations, maybe several of them. Such a reading may also fit with the CSA's purpose, which was to create a federal regulatory regime for the dispensation of drugs by doctors. Yet this deft wedding of Reagan Era textualism and New Deal purposivism is not persuasive to Justices Kennedy and O'Connor, Reagan conservatives who are probably not great friends to the death-with-dignity movement. Why are they not persuaded?

Here's one way of understanding why some pretty conservative jurists rejected Justice Scalia's legal arguments. Consider this: Parents A and B retain Babysitter C to look after their beloved child while they attend the opera. Their instructions to C: "You are in charge; we delegate you all decisions regarding his care while we are gone." In a tragic twist of fate, the baby has a terrible accident, and C rushes him to the hospital. The hospital asks C who has authority to make decisions about treatment options, risk assessment, and even possible termination of life support. Can C legitimately respond that she is "authorized" to make those decisions? A strict reading of the instructions might suggest "yes," but common sense makes us sure the answer is "no."

This is probably the point of the Court's invocation of the idea that Congress does not hide elephants in mouseholes. Assuming this point, however, why would Justices O'Connor and Kennedy consider the "assisted suicide" rule an "elephant" and not a "mouse"? If the CSA represented a federalization of drug regulation, why isn't the Ashcroft Directive simply the routine agency decision suggested by the dissenters? Does a negative answer to that question rest upon a reservation of a special judicial role for aid-in-dying issues?

2. *Deference to the Agency's View of Its Own Jurisdiction or Delegated Authority?* Justice Scalia has long argued that the Court should defer to agency interpretations of its own authority or jurisdiction. His reason is that there is "no discernible line between an agency's exceeding its own authority and an agency's exceeding authorized application of its authority." *Mississippi Power & Light v. Mississippi ex rel. Moore*, 487 U.S. 354, 381–82 (1988) (Scalia, J., concurring in the judgment). He does not press this point in *Oregon*, presumably because he believes his plain meaning arguments are unanswerable. Is there a cogent response to this concern?

Although the Supreme Court has not settled the broad question whether *Chevron* applies to expansive agency interpretations of its own authority, the logic of the Court's *Chevron*'s jurisprudence suggests the non-deferential approach taken by the *Oregon* majority. Because *Mead* held that *Chevron* rests upon Congress's delegation of lawmaking authority to the agency, courts ought to take care that there actually *has been such a delegation*.[k] Reflecting this logic, there are in fact a number of precedents where the Court has taken a non-deferential approach to agency interpretations of their own jurisdiction; the FDA Tobacco Case is one of them.

By the way, if *Chevron* deference does not apply to the agency's interpretation of its own delegated authority, should *Skidmore* deference apply to that issue? Would *Skidmore* have made a difference to the *Oregon* Court on the delegation issue? Assume that the Court applies *Skidmore* deference to the application of the CSA to the Oregon law, but *not* to the issue of delegation of lawmaking authority to the Attorney General.

3. *Deference When Congress Has Delegated Responsibilities to More than One Agency.* The Oregon Aid-in-Dying Case is an example of a growing range of controversies involving several possibly relevant agencies. Recall that one reason the *Gilbert* Court rejected the EEOC's understanding of pregnancy exclusions as being sex discrimination was that another body had reached a different interpretation. In addition to inter-agency *conflict* is the problem of *primacy* among agencies. As Justice Kennedy was in *Oregon*, the Court is

---

k. E.g., Ernest Gellhorn & Paul Verkuil, *Controlling Chevron–Based Delegations*, 20 Cardozo L. Rev. 989, 1006–17 (1999); Merrill & Hickman, Chevron's *Domain*, 89 Geo. L.J. 833; see also Bressman, *Has* Mead *Muddled*, 1469–74 (after *Mead*, lower courts have tended to avoid applying *Chevron* deference to issues of agency jurisdiction or authority); Eskridge & Baer, *Continuum of Deference* (finding relatively unimpressive agency win rates for issues where the agency was interpreting its own jurisdiction or authority). But see Kevin M. Stack, *The Statutory President*, 90 Iowa L. Rev. 539, 594–95 (2005) (agreeing with the Scalia position).

usually pretty particular about matching the most apparently authorized agency with an award of deference. E.g., *Martin v. OSHRC*, 499 U.S. 144 (1991), where the Court ruled that in OSHA cases deference was owed to the Department of Labor, which issues substantive rules, rather than the Commission which adjudicates controversies by applying rules to facts.

Sometimes, the Court has been very picky about this matching game. For example, in *Sutton v. United Air Lines, Inc.*, 527 U.S. 471 (1999), the Court interpreted the ADA's definition of "disability" to exclude conditions easily corrected for. (The plaintiffs lost their jobs as airline pilots because they had poor vision; the Court held that this was not a disability, because it could be corrected by eyeglasses. The employer's policy was that corrected vision was still disqualifying. Catch–22.) Although the EEOC had been given rulemaking authority for implementing the jobs title of the Act, which was the basis for Sutton's claims, the Court ruled that the EEOC was *not* delegated authority to determine the scope of the ADA's coverage of "disability," which was defined in a different title to the Act (as to which there was no agency with delegated lawmaking authority).

4. *Deference in Matters of Criminal Law.* The *Oregon* majority was troubled that Ashcroft was expansively interpreting a statute imposing serious criminal liability. Recall from Chapter 3, § 2A that the rule of lenity theoretically requires anti-deference—presumptive rejection of the agency's interpretation—when a criminal statute is ambiguous. Indeed, Justice Scalia is one of the few Justices who seems to apply the rule of lenity with rigor and even enthusiasm—but not in *Oregon*. Why not? Apparently, Justice Scalia views the notice and nondelegation policies underlying the rule of lenity to be satisfied by an open rule promulgated by the Attorney General pursuant to congressional authorization. Accord, Dan Kahan, *Is* Chevron *Relevant to Federal Criminal Law?*, 110 Harv. L. Rev. 469 (1996) (arguing that criminal law should move in precisely this direction).

Note that *Chevron* might apply in federal criminal sentencing law. Congress has vested the Sentencing Commission with substantive rulemaking authority as regards sentencing, and the Court sometimes gave *Chevron* deference to the Sentencing Guidelines before they were partially nullified. See *Stinson v. United States*, 508 U.S. 36 (1993). Should *Stinson* make us more willing to defer in cases like *Oregon*?

5. *Ideological Voting in* Chevron *Cases.* Recall that commentators are finding that ideology is a better predictor of the Justices' voting patterns in agency deference cases than doctrine. The Oregon Aid-in-Dying Case helps us see how this works. Notice the completely different linguistic as well as normative attitudes in the majority and chief dissenting opinions. Note the majority's repeated citations to *Glucksberg* (the constitutional "right to die" case) and its treatment of aid-in-dying as a matter for serious national debate. These and other bits of textual evidence suggest that the majority understands the matter as a possible privacy right of persons to choose "death with dignity." Is it for this *normative* reason that the majority thinks that aid-in-dying is an "elephant" that cannot hide in a normative "mousehole"? Consider, in addition, the federalism argument that Oregon ought to have authority to decide the question of aid in dying without federal intervention.

The dissenters, in contrast, rhetorically agree with Ashcroft that this is "assisted suicide," a half step away from murder. Because the matter has long been settled by religious doctrine, state law, and national policy, this is no "elephant," but is instead a mouse hiding in the mousehole. It is for this *normative* reason that the dissenters believe it outrageous for the majority to treat Oregon's law as a great matter for state experimentation and deviance from settled national policy.

The process by which the Justices are voting their norms more than their dictionaries is, by the way, probably unconscious. In our view, the process by which one's own normative horizon influences one's interpretation of canonical texts is not only unconscious, but inevitable. Social scientists would explain this phenomenon as an example of framing effects and cognitive dissonance: the way an interpreter frames the issue drives her thinking, and indeed she will filter evidence through the lens of this frame. Philosophers would cite this as an example of how interpretation is an activity by which we come to be who we are.

6. *Process Matters: Deliberative Agency Actions May Trigger More Deference.* Another way to read the Oregon Aid-in-Dying Case emphasizes the agency's public process and justifications. One of us argues that the Court was reluctant to defer in the case because the agency had tackled a big normative issue without the public process of information-gathering and deliberation that usually accompanies agency rulemaking. See William N. Eskridge Jr., *The Story of* Gonzales v. Oregon: *Death, Deference, Deliberation,* in *Statutory Interpretation Stories* 366–98 (Eskridge, Frickey & Garrett eds., 2011). Professor Eskridge endorses "deliberation-rewarding" canons of statutory interpretation, such as the Oregon Case, where the Court rewards public deliberation with greater deference. Is this a sensible canon? Does such a canon create too much complexity in an already complicated regime of rules and principles?

2. Does the Agency Have Broader Freedom to Interpret Its Own Rules?

Since the New Deal, the Supreme Court has sometimes given special super-deference to agency interpretations of their own regulations. Such interpretations are "controlling unless plainly erroneous or inconsistent with the regulation." *Bowles v. Seminole Rock & Sand Co.*, 325 U.S. 410, 414 (1945). The *Seminole Rock* rule apparently survives *Chevron*, as illustrated by *Auer v. Robbins*, 519 U.S. 452 (1997). This very issue was the first claim by the Attorney General in the Oregon Aid-in-Dying Case.

Gonzales v. Oregon, 546 U.S. 243 (2006). Under the Controlled Substances Act (CSA), Schedule II substances are generally available only pursuant to a written, nonrefillable prescription by a physician. 21 U.S.C. § 829(a). A 1971 regulation promulgated by the Department of Justice requires that every prescription for a controlled substance "be issued for a legitimate medical purpose by an individual practitioner acting in the usual course of his professional practice." 21 C.F.R. § 1306.04(a). Attorney General Ashcroft presented his Directive preempting the Oregon Death With Dignity Act, as an interpretation of the Department's 1971 regulation and therefore entitled to *Seminole Rock* super-deference.

Justice Kennedy's opinion for the Court rejected this assertion of deference. "*Auer* involved a disputed interpretation of the Fair Labor Standards Act of 1938 as applied to a class of law enforcement officers. Under regulations promulgated by the Secretary of Labor, an exemption from overtime pay depended, in part, on whether the employees met the 'salary basis' test. In this Court the Secretary of Labor filed an *amicus* brief explaining why, in his view, the regulations gave exempt status to the officers. We gave weight to that interpretation, holding that because the applicable test was 'a creature of the Secretary's own regulations, his interpretation of it is, under our jurisprudence, controlling unless plainly erroneous or inconsistent with the regulation.'

"In *Auer*, the underlying regulations gave specificity to a statutory scheme the Secretary was charged with enforcing and reflected the considerable experience and expertise the Department of Labor had acquired over time with respect to the complexities of the Fair Labor Standards Act. Here, on the other hand, the underlying regulation does little more than restate the terms of the statute itself. The language the Interpretive Rule addresses comes from Congress, not the Attorney General, and the near-equivalence of the statute and regulation belies the Government's argument for *Auer* deference. [21 U.S.C. §§ 812(b), 830(b)(3)(A)(ii).]

" * * * Simply put, the existence of a parroting regulation does not change the fact that the question here is not the meaning of the regulation but the meaning of the statute. An agency does not acquire special authority to interpret its own words when, instead of using its expertise and experience to formulate a regulation, it has elected merely to paraphrase the statutory language.

"Furthermore, * * * if there is statutory authority to issue the Interpretive Rule it comes from the 1984 amendments to the CSA that gave the Attorney General authority to register and deregister physicians based on the public interest. The regulation was enacted before those amendments, so the Interpretive Rule cannot be justified as indicative of some intent the Attorney General had in 1971. That the current interpretation runs counter to the 'intent at the time of the regulation's promulgation,' is an additional reason why *Auer* deference is unwarranted. *Thomas Jefferson Univ. v. Shalala*, 512 U.S. 504, 512 (1994)."

In dissent, **Justice Scalia** questioned whether there was any authority creating a "parroting" exception to *Auer*. "Even if there were an antiparroting canon, however, it would have no application here. The Court's description of 21 CFR § 1306.04 as a regulation that merely 'paraphrase[s] the statutory language' is demonstrably false. In relevant part, the Regulation interprets the word 'prescription' as it appears in 21 U.S.C. § 829, which governs the dispensation of controlled substances other than those on Schedule I (which may not be dispensed at all). Entitled '[p]rescriptions,' § 829 requires, with certain exceptions not relevant here, 'the written prescription of a practitioner' (usually a medical doctor) for the dispensation of Schedule II substances (§ 829(a)), 'a written or oral prescription' for substances on Schedules III and IV (§ 829(b)), and no prescription but merely a 'medical purpose' for the dispensation of Schedule V substances (§ 829(c)).

"As used in this section, 'prescription' is susceptible of at least three reasonable interpretations. First, it might mean any oral or written direction of a practitioner for the dispensation of drugs. Second, in light of the requirement of a 'medical purpose' for the dispensation of Schedule V substances, see § 829(c), it might mean a practitioner's oral or written direction for the dispensation of drugs that the practitioner believes to be for a legitimate medical purpose. See Webster's New International Dictionary 1954 (2d ed. 1950) (defining 'prescription' as '[a] written direction for the preparation and use of a *medicine*'); *id.*, at 1527 (defining 'medicine' as '[a]ny substance or preparation used in *treating disease*') (emphases added). Finally, 'prescription' might refer to a practitioner's direction for the dispensation of drugs that serves an *objectively* legitimate medical purpose, regardless of the practitioner's *subjective* judgment about the legitimacy of the anticipated use. See *ibid.*

"The Regulation at issue constricts or clarifies the statute by adopting the last and narrowest of these three possible interpretations of the undefined statutory term: 'A prescription for a controlled substance to be effective must be issued for a legitimate medical purpose. . . .' 21 CFR § 1306.04(a) (2005). * * *

"The Court points out that the Regulation adopts some of the phrasing employed in unrelated sections of the statute. This is irrelevant. A regulation that significantly clarifies the meaning of an otherwise ambiguous statutory provision is not a 'parroting' regulation, *regardless* of the sources that the agency draws upon for the clarification. Moreover, most of the statutory phrases that the Court cites as appearing in the Regulation, see *ibid.* (citing 21 U.S.C. §§ 812(b) ('currently accepted medical use'), 829(c) ('medical purpose'), 802(21) ('in the course of professional practice')), are inapposite because they do *not* 'parrot' the *only* phrase in the Regulation that the Directive purported to construe. None of them includes the key word 'legitimate,' which gives the most direct support to the Directive's theory that § 829(c) presupposes a uniform federal standard of medical practice.

"Since the Regulation does not run afowl (so to speak) of the Court's newly invented prohibition of 'parroting'; and since the Directive represents the agency's own interpretation of that concededly valid regulation; the only question remaining is whether that interpretation is 'plainly erroneous or inconsistent with the regulation'; otherwise, it is 'controlling.' *Auer.* This is not a difficult question. The Directive is assuredly valid insofar as it interprets 'prescription' to require a medical purpose that is 'legitimate' as a matter of *federal* law—since that is an interpretation of 'prescription' that we ourselves have adopted. *Webb v. United States*, 249 U.S. 96 (1919), was a prosecution under the Harrison Act of a doctor who wrote prescriptions of morphine 'for the purpose of providing the user with morphine sufficient to keep him comfortable by maintaining his customary use.' The dispositive issue in the case was whether such authorizations were 'prescriptions' within the meaning of § 2(b) of the Harrison Act, predecessor to the CSA. We held that 'to call such an order for the use of morphine a physician's prescription would be so plain a perversion of meaning that no discussion of the subject is required.' Like the Directive, this interprets 'prescription' to require medical purpose that is legitimate as a matter of federal law. And the Directive is also assuredly valid insofar as it interprets 'legitimate medical purpose' as a matter of federal law to exclude physician-assisted suicide, because that is not only a permissible but indeed the most natural interpretation of that phrase.' "

NOTE ON AGENCY INTERPRETATIONS OF ITS OWN REGULATIONS

Although he does not answer the Court's chronology point (the incongruity of the Department's using new 1984 rulemaking authority to "interpret" a 1971 administrative rule), Justice Scalia presents a typically powerful legal analysis in defense of the Attorney General's *Seminole–Auer* argument for deference. Technically speaking, the Attorney General's Directive does seem like an "interpretation" of the 1971 Rule. One might wonder why this legal point was not more persuasive to more Justices. Consider a few observations.

Agency interpretations of its own rules can come in a variety of formats—*amicus* briefs (as in *Auer*), directives or interpretive rules/guidances (as in *Oregon*), opinion letters (SEC and IRS especially), and so forth. Generally, agency interpretations in these formats are entitled to *Skidmore* deference, as in the Oregon Aid-in-Dying Case—but if the agency can relate them somehow to an existing *Chevron*-eligible rule, then it can not only jump *Skidmore*, but also jump *Chevron*, all the way to *Seminole–Auer*. This concern with "agency bootstrapping" is probably what worried Justice Kennedy, and it has certainly worried other Justices, e.g., *Thomas Jefferson Univ.*, 512 U.S. at 525 (Thomas, J., dissenting), and commentators, e.g., John F. Manning, *Constitutional Structure and Judicial Deference to Agency Interpretations of Agency Rules*, 96 Colum. L. Rev. 612 (1996).

The Eskridge and Baer survey of 1014 Supreme Court cases between *Chevron* and *Hamdan* identified 155 cases where an agency said it was interpreting its own prior rules—yet the Court applied *Seminole–Auer* superdeference in only 12 of those cases, a surprisingly low number unless the bootstrapping concern is at work. See Eskridge & Baer, *Continuum of Deference*. Perhaps *Seminole* is most relevant under the circumstances identified in *Auer*: the regulatory concept in play is one that the agency itself created (pursuant to a valid congressional delegation) and is now interpreting. Otherwise, the Justices are cautious. Contrast the following case with the Oregon Aid-in-Dying Case.

COEUR ALASKA, INC. v. SOUTHEAST ALASKA CONSERVATION COUNCIL

Supreme Court of the United States, 2009
557 U.S. 261, 129 S.Ct. 2458, 174 L.Ed.2d 193

JUSTICE KENNEDY delivered the opinion of the Court.

[Coeur Alaska proposed to reopen a defunct gold mine in Alaska. To extract the gold, it planned to use a technique known as "froth flotation" in which crushed rock from the mine would be churned in tanks of chemical-laden, frothing water. Gold-bearing minerals would float to the surface, where they would be skimmed off. Coeur Alaska sought permission to discharge the remaining mixture of crushed rock and water, known as slurry, into Lower Slate Lake, a navigable waterway of the United States subject to the Clear Water Act (CWA or Act). The discharge would eventually raise the lakebed to the current surface, significantly expanding the lake's area.

[Respondents, a coalition of three environmental groups known as SEACC, challenged the decision of the Army Corps of Engineers to grant Coeur Alaska a permit for the discharge on two grounds: (1) that only the EPA, not the Corps, had authority under the CWA to grant the permit and (2) that even if the Corps had permitting authority, it could not grant the permit without violating an EPA regulation, known as a "new source performance standard," promulgated under the CWA.]

[II.A] Section 402 gives the EPA authority to issue "permit[s] for the discharge of any pollutant," with one important exception: The EPA may not issue permits for fill material that fall under the Corps' § 404 permitting authority. Section 402(a) states:

"*Except as provided in . . . [CWA § 404, 33 U.S.C. § 1344]*, the Administrator may . . . issue a permit for the discharge of any pollutant, . . . notwithstanding [CWA § 301(a), 33 U.S.C. § 1311(a)], upon condition that such discharge will meet either (A) all applicable requirements under [CWA § 301, 33 U.S.C. § 1311(a), and other enumerated provisions], or (B) prior to the taking of necessary implementing actions relating to all such requirements, such conditions as the Administrator determines are necessary to carry out the provisions of this chapter." 33 U.S.C. § 1342(a)(1) (emphasis added). * * *

The Act is best understood to provide that if the Corps has authority to issue a permit for a discharge under § 404, then the EPA lacks authority to do so under § 402.

Even if there were ambiguity on this point, the EPA's own regulations would resolve it. Those regulations provide that "[d]ischarges of dredged or fill material into waters of the United States which are regulated under section 404 of CWA" "do not require [§ 402] permits" from the EPA. 40 CFR § 122.3. * * * Before us, the EPA confirms this reading of the regulation. Brief for Federal Respondents 27. The agency's interpretation is not "plainly erroneous or inconsistent with the regulation"; and so we accept it as correct. *Auer.*

The question whether the EPA is the proper agency to regulate the slurry discharge thus depends on whether the Corps of Engineers has authority to do so. If the Corps has authority to issue a permit, then the EPA may not do so. We turn to the Corps' authority under § 404.

[II.B] Section 404(a) gives the Corps power to "issue permits . . . for the discharge of dredged or fill material." 33 U.S.C. § 1344(a). As all parties concede, the slurry meets the definition of fill material agreed upon by the agencies in a joint regulation promulgated in 2002. That regulation defines "fill material" to mean any "material [that] has the effect of . . . [c]hanging the bottom elevation" of water—a definition that includes "slurry, or tailings or similar mining-related materials." 40 CFR § 232.2. * * *

Rather than challenge the agencies' decision to define the slurry as fill, SEACC instead contends that § 404 contains an implicit exception. According to SEACC, § 404 does not authorize the Corps to permit a discharge of fill material if that material is subject to an EPA new source performance standard.

But § 404's text does not limit its grant of power in this way. Instead, § 404 refers to all "fill material" without qualification. Nor do the EPA regulations support SEACC's reading of § 404. The EPA has enacted guidelines, pursuant to § 404(b), to guide the Corps permitting decision. 40 CFR pt. 230. Those guidelines do not strip the Corps of power to issue permits for fill in cases where the fill is also subject to an EPA new source performance standard. * * *

[III] A second question remains: In issuing the permit did the Corps act in violation of a statutory mandate so that the issuance was "not in accordance with law"? 5 U.S.C. § 706(2)(A). SEACC contends that the slurry discharge will violate the EPA's new source performance standard and that the Corps permit is made "unlawful" by CWA § 306(e). Petitioners and the agencies argue that the permit is lawful because the EPA performance standard, and § 306(e), do not apply to fill material regulated by the Corps. In order to determine whether the Corps permit is lawful we must answer the question: Do EPA performance standards, and § 306(e), apply to discharges of fill material? * * *

[III.A] As for the statutory argument, SEACC claims the CWA § 404 permit is unlawful because § 306(e) forbids the slurry discharge. Petitioners and the federal agencies, in contrast, contend that § 306(e) does not apply to the slurry discharge.

(1) To address SEACC's statutory argument, it is necessary to review the EPA's responsibilities under the CWA. As noted, § 306 empowers the EPA to regulate the froth-flotation gold mining industry. Pursuant to this authority, EPA promulgated the new source performance standard relied upon by SEACC. The standard is stringent. If it were to apply here, it

would allow "no discharge of process wastewater" from the mine. 40 CFR § 440.104(b)(1).

The term "process wastewater" includes solid waste. So the regulation forbids not only pollutants that dissolve in water but also solid pollutants suspended in water—what the agency terms "total suspended solids," or TSS. See § 440.104(a) (limiting the amount of TSS from other kinds of mines) * * *.

When the performance standard applies to a point source, § 306(e) makes it "unlawful" for that point source to violate it: "[I]t shall be unlawful for any owner or operator of any new source to operate such source in violation of any standard of performance applicable to such source." CWA § 306(e), 33 U.S.C. § 1316(e).

SEACC argues that this provision, § 306(e), forbids the mine from discharging slurry into Lower Slate Lake. SEACC contends the new source performance standard is, in the words of § 306(e), "applicable to" the mine. * * *

(2) For their part, the State of Alaska and the federal agencies claim that the Act is unambiguous in the opposite direction. They rely on § 404 of the Act. As explained above, that section authorizes the Corps of Engineers to determine whether to issue a permit allowing the discharge of the slurry. Petitioners and the agencies argue that § 404 grants the Corps authority to do so without regard to the EPA's new source performance standard or the § 306(e) prohibition discussed above.

Petitioners and the agencies make two statutory arguments based on § 404's silence in regard to § 306. First, they note that nothing in § 404 requires the Corps to consider the EPA's new source performance standard or the § 306(e) prohibition. That silence advances the argument that § 404's grant of authority to "issue permits" contradicts § 306(e)'s declaration that discharges in violation of new source performance standards are "unlawful."

Second, petitioners and the agencies point to § 404(p), which protects § 404 permitees from enforcement actions by the EPA or private citizens:

"Compliance with a permit issued pursuant to this section ... shall be deemed compliance, for purposes of sections 1319 [CWA § 309] and 1365 [CWA § 505] of this title, with sections 1311 [CWA § 301], 1317 [CWA § 307], and 1343 [CWA § 403] of this title." 33 U.S.C. § 1344(p).

Here again, their argument is that silence is significant. Section 404(p) protects the permitee from lawsuits alleging violations of CWA § 301 (which bars the discharge of "any pollutant" "except as in compliance" with the Act), § 307 (which bars the discharge of "toxic pollutants"); and § 403 (which bars discharges into the sea). But § 404(p) does not in express terms protect the permitee from a lawsuit alleging a violation of § 306(e) or of the EPA's new source performance standards. Section 404(p)'s silence regarding § 306 is made even more significant because a parallel provision in § 402 does protect a § 402 permitee from an enforcement action alleging a violation of § 306. CWA § 402(k), 33 U.S.C. § 1342(k).

In our view, Congress' omission of § 306 from § 404, and its inclusion of § 306 in § 402(k), is evidence that Congress did not intend § 306(e) to apply to Corps § 404 permits or to discharges of fill material. If § 306 did apply, then the Corps would be required to evaluate each permit application for compliance with § 306, and issue a permit only if it found the discharge would comply with § 306. But even if that finding were made, it is not clear that the § 404 permitee would be protected from a suit seeking a judicial determination that the discharge violates § 306.

(3) The CWA is ambiguous on the question whether § 306 applies to discharges of fill material regulated under § 404. On the one hand, § 306 provides that a discharge that violates an EPA new source performance standard is "unlawful—without any exception for fill material. On the other hand, § 404 grants the Corps blanket authority to permit the discharge of fill material—without any mention of § 306. This tension indicates that Congress has not "directly spoken" to the "precise question" of whether § 306 applies to discharges of fill material. *Chevron*.

[III.B] Before turning to how the agencies have resolved that question, we consider the formal regulations that bear on §§ 306 and 404. See *Mead*. The regulations, like the statutes, do not address the question whether § 306, and the EPA new source performance standards promulgated under it, apply to § 404 permits and the discharges they authorize. There is no regulation, for example, interpreting § 306(e)'s text—"standard of performance applicable to such source"—to mean that a performance standard ceases to be "applicable" the moment the discharge qualifies as fill material, which would resolve the cases in petitioners' favor. Nor is there a regulation providing that the Corps, in deciding whether to grant a permit under § 404, must deny that permit if the discharge would violate § 306(e), which would decide the cases for SEACC.

Rather than address the tension between §§ 306 and 404, the regulations instead implement the statutory framework without elaboration on this point. Each of the two principal regulations, which have been mentioned above, seems to stand on its own without reference to the other. The EPA's new source performance standard contains no exception for fill material; and it forbids any discharge of "process wastewater," a term that includes solid wastes. 40 CFR § 440.104(b)(1). The agencies' joint regulation defining fill material is also unqualified. It includes "slurry, or tailings or similar mining-related materials" in its definition of a "discharge of fill material," 40 CFR § 232.2; and it contains no exception for slurry that is regulated by an EPA performance standard. * * *

[III.C.] The regulations do not give a definitive answer to the question whether § 306 applies to discharges regulated by the Corps under § 404, but we do find that agency interpretation and agency application of the regulations are instructive and to the point. *Auer*. The question is addressed and resolved in a reasonable and coherent way by the practice and policy of the two agencies, all as recited in a memorandum written in May 2004 by Diane Regas, then the Director of the EPA's Office of Wetlands, Oceans and Watersheds, to Randy Smith, the Director of the EPA's regional Office of Water with responsibility over the mine. (Regas Memorandum). The Memorandum, though not subject to sufficiently formal procedures to merit *Chevron* deference, see *Mead*, is entitled to a measure of deference because it interprets the agencies' own regulatory scheme. See *Auer*.

The Regas Memorandum explains:

"As a result [of the fact that the discharge is regulated under § 404], the regulatory regime applicable to discharges under section 402, including effluent limitations guidelines and standards, such as those applicable to gold ore mining ... do not apply to the placement of tailings into the proposed impoundment [of Lower Slate Lake]. See 40 CFR § 122.3(b)."

The regulation that the Memorandum cites—40 CFR § 122.3—is one we considered above and found ambiguous. That regulation provides: "[d]ischarges of dredged or fill material into waters of the United States which are regulated under section 404 of CWA" "do not require [§ 402] permits." The Regas Memorandum takes an instructive interpretive step when it explains that because the discharge "do[es] not require" an EPA permit, the EPA's performance standard "do[es] not apply" to the discharge. The Memorandum presents a reasonable interpretation of the regulatory regime. We defer to the interpretation because it is not "plainly erroneous or inconsistent with the regulation[s]." *Auer*. Five factors inform that conclusion.

First, the Memorandum preserves a role for the EPA's performance standard. It confines the Memorandum's scope to closed bodies of water, like the lake here. When slurry is discharged into a closed body of water, the Memorandum explains, the EPA's performance standard retains an important role in regulating the discharge into surrounding waters. The Memorandum does not purport to invalidate the EPA's performance standard.

Second, the Memorandum acknowledges that this is not an instance in which the discharger attempts to evade the requirements of the EPA's performance standard. The Kensington Mine is not, for example, a project that smuggles a discharge of EPA-regulated pollutants into a separate discharge of Corps-regulated fill material. The instant cases do not present a process or plan designed to manipulate the outer boundaries of the definition of "fill material" by labeling minute quantities of EPA-regulated solids as fill. The Memorandum states that when a discharge has only an "incidental filling effect," the EPA's performance standard continues to govern that discharge.

Third, the Memorandum's interpretation preserves the Corps' authority to determine whether a discharge is in the public interest. See 33 CFR

§ 320.4(a)(1); 40 CFR § 230.10. The Corps has significant expertise in making this determination. Applying it, the Corps determined that placing slurry in the lake will improve that body of water by making it wider, shallower, and so more capable of sustaining aquatic life. The Corps determined, furthermore, that the alternative—a heap of tailings larger than the Pentagon placed upon wetlands—would cause more harm to the environment. Because the Memorandum preserves an important role for the Corps' expertise, its conclusion that the EPA's performance standard does not apply is a reasonable one.

Fourth, the Regas Memorandum's interpretation does not allow toxic pollutants (as distinguished from other, less dangerous pollutants, such as slurry) to enter the navigable waters. The EPA has regulated toxic pollutants under a separate provision, § 307 of the CWA, and the EPA's § 404(b) guidelines require the Corps to deny a § 404 permit for any discharge that would violate the EPA's § 307 toxic-effluent limitations. 40 CFR § 230.10(b)(2).

Fifth, as a final reason to defer to the Regas Memorandum, we find it a sensible and rational construction that reconciles §§ 306, 402, and 404, and the regulations implementing them, which the alternatives put forward by the parties do not. SEACC's argument, that § 402 applies to this discharge and not § 404, is not consistent with the statute and regulations, as already noted. See Part II, *supra.* * * *

[III.D Justice Kennedy then proceeded to reject SEACC's argument that three agency statements—a 1986 "memorandum of understanding" between the EPA and the Corps regarding the definition of fill material, the preamble to the agencies' fill regulation (i.e., 40 CFR § 122.3), and remarks made by the agencies in response to public comments on the proposed fill regulation—contradicted the Regas Memorandum's interpretation of the memorandum.]

JUSTICE BREYER, concurring.

As I understand the Court's opinion, it recognizes a legal zone within which the regulating agencies might reasonably classify material either as "dredged or fill material" subject to § 404 of the Clean Water Act, 33 U.S.C. § 1344(a), or as a "pollutant," subject to §§ 402 and 306, 33 U.S.C. §§ 1342(a), 1316(a). Within this zone, the law authorizes the environmental agencies to classify material as the one or the other, so long as they act within the bounds of relevant regulations, and provided that the classification, considered in terms of the purposes of the statutes and relevant regulations, is reasonable.

This approach reflects the difficulty of applying §§ 402 and 306 literally to *every* new-source-related discharge of a "pollutant." The Environmental Protection Agency (EPA) applies § 306 new source "performance standards" to a wide variety of discharges * * *. These "standards of performance" "reflect the greatest degree of effluent reduction which the Administrator determines to be achievable through application of the best available demonstrated control technology ... including, where practicable, a standard permitting no discharge of pollutants." 33 U.S.C. § 1316(a)(1). (1996).

To literally apply these performance standards so as to forbid the use of any of these substances as "fill," even when, say, they constitute no more than trace elements in dirt, crushed rock, or sand that is clearly being used as "fill" to build a levee or to replace dirt removed from a lake bottom may prove unnecessarily strict, cf. § 1362(6) (defining "pollutant" to include "rock"), to the point that such application would undermine the objective of § 404, which foresees the use of "dredged or fill material" in certain circumstances and with approval of the relevant agencies. § 1344. At minimum, the EPA might reasonably read the statute and the applicable regulations as allowing the use of such material, say crushed rock, as "fill" in some of these situations. Cf. *Chevron*; *Auer*.

At the same time, I recognize the danger that Justice Ginsburg warns against, namely, that "[w]hole categories of regulated industries" might "gain immunity from a variety of pollution-control standards," if, say, a § 404–permit applicant simply adds "sufficient solid matter" to a pollutant "to raise the bottom of a water body," thereby turning a "pollutant" governed by § 306 into "fill" governed by § 404.

Yet there are safeguards against that occurring. For one thing, as the Court recognizes, it is not the case that *any* material that has the " 'effect of . . . [c]hanging the bottom elevation' " of the body of water is automatically subject to § 404, not § 402. The EPA has never suggested that it would interpret the regulations so as to turn § 404 into a loophole, permitting evasion of a "performance standard" simply because a polluter discharges enough pollutant to raise the bottom elevation of the body of water. For another thing, even where a matter is determined reasonably to be "fill" and consequently falls within § 404, the EPA can retain an important role in the permitting process. That is because the EPA may veto any § 404 plan that it finds has an "unacceptable adverse effect on municipal water supplies, shellfish beds and fishery areas . . . , wildlife, or recreational areas." § 1344(c). Finally, EPA's decision not to apply § 306, but to allow permitting to proceed under § 404, must be a reasonable decision; and court review will help assure that is so. 5 U.S.C. § 706.

In these cases, it seems to me that the EPA's interpretation of the statute as permitting the EPA/Corps of Engineers "fill" definition to apply to the cases at hand is reasonable, hence lawful. * * *

I cannot say whether the EPA's compromise represents the best overall environmental result; but I do believe it amounts to the kind of detailed decision that the statutes delegate authority to the EPA, not the courts, to make (subject to the bounds of reasonableness). I believe the Court's views are consistent with those I here express. And with that understanding, I join its opinion.

JUSTICE SCALIA, concurring in part and concurring in the judgment.

I join the opinion of the Court, except for its protestation that it is not according *Chevron* deference to the reasonable interpretation set forth in the [Regas Memorandum]—an interpretation consistently followed by both EPA and the Corps of Engineers, and adopted by both agencies in the proceedings before this Court. See *Chevron*. The opinion purports to give this agency interpretation "a measure of deference" because it involves an interpretation of "the agencies' own regulatory scheme," and "'the regulatory regime,'" (citing *Auer*). *Auer*, however, stands only for the principle that we defer to an agency's interpretation *of its own ambiguous regulation*. But it becomes obvious from the ensuing discussion that the referenced "regulatory scheme," and "regulatory regime" for which the Court accepts the agency interpretation includes not just the agencies' own regulations but also (and indeed primarily) the conformity of those regulations with the ambiguous governing statute, which is the primary dispute here.

Surely the Court is not adding to our already inscrutable opinion in *Mead* the irrational fillip that an agency position which otherwise does not qualify for *Chevron* deference *does* receive *Chevron* deference if it clarifies not just an ambiguous statute but *also* an ambiguous regulation. One must conclude, then, that if today's opinion is *not* according the agencies' reasonable and authoritative interpretation of the Clean Water Act *Chevron* deference, it is according some *new* type of deference—perhaps to be called in the future *Coeur Alaska* deference—which is identical to *Chevron* deference except for the name.

The Court's deference to the EPA and the Corps of Engineers in today's cases is eminently reasonable. It is quite impossible to achieve predictable (and relatively litigation-free) administration of the vast body of complex laws committed to the charge of executive agencies without the assurance that reviewing courts will accept reasonable and authoritative agency interpretation of ambiguous provisions. If we must not call that practice *Chevron* deference, then we have to rechristen the rose. Of course the only reason a new name is required is our misguided opinion in *Mead*, whose incomprehensible criteria for *Chevron* deference have produced so much confusion in the lower courts that there has now appeared the phenomenon of *Chevron* avoidance—the practice of declining to opine whether *Chevron* applies or not.

I favor overruling *Mead*. Failing that, I am pleased to join an opinion that effectively ignores it.

JUSTICE GINSBURG, with whom JUSTICE STEVENS and JUSTICE SOUTER join, dissenting. * * *

The litigation before the Court * * * presents a single question: Is a pollutant discharge prohibited under § 306 of the Act eligible for a § 404 permit as a discharge of fill material? In agreement with the Court of Appeals, I would answer no. The statute's text, structure, and purpose all mandate adherence to EPA pollution-control requirements. A discharge covered by a performance standard must be authorized, if at all, by EPA.

[I.A] Congress enacted the Clean Water Act in 1972 "to restore and maintain the chemical, physical, and biological integrity" of the waters of the United States. 33 U.S.C. § 1251(a). "The use of any river, lake, stream or ocean as a waste treatment system," the Act's drafters stated, "is unacceptable." S.Rep. No. 92–414, p. 7 (1971). Congress announced in the Act itself an ambitious objective: to eliminate, by 1985, the discharge of all pollutants into the Nation's navigable waters. 33 U.S.C. § 1251(a). * * *

The Act instructs EPA to establish various technology-based, increasingly stringent effluent limitations for categories of point sources. *E.g.,* §§ 1311, 1314. * * *

Of key importance, new sources must meet stringent "standards of performance" adopted by EPA under § 306. That section makes it "unlawful for *any* . . . new source to operate . . . in violation of" an applicable performance standard. 33 U.S.C. § 1316(e) (emphasis added). * * *

In 1982, EPA promulgated new source performance standards for facilities engaged in mining, including those using a froth-flotation milling process. Existing mills, the Agency found, were already achieving zero discharge; it was therefore practicable, EPA concluded, for new mills to do as well. Accordingly, under 40 CFR § 440.104(b)(1), new mines using the froth-flotation method, as Coeur Alaska proposes to do, may not discharge wastewater directly into waters of the United States. * * *

[II] Is a pollutant discharge prohibited under § 306(e) eligible to receive a § 404 permit as a discharge of fill material? All agree on preliminary matters. Only one agency, the Corps or EPA, can issue a permit for the discharge. Only EPA, through the [§ 402 permitting scheme], issues permits that implement § 306. Further, § 306(e) and EPA's froth-flotation performance standard, unless inapplicable here, bar Coeur Alaska's proposed discharge. * * *

Section 404, stating that the Corps "may issue permits" for the discharge of "dredged or fill material," does not create an exception to § 306(e)'s plain command. 33 U.S.C. § 1344(a). Section 404 neither mentions § 306 nor states a contrary requirement. The Act can be home to both provisions, with no words added or omitted, so long as the category of "dredged or fill material" eligible for a § 404 permit is read in harmony with § 306. Doing so yields a simple rule: Discharges governed by EPA performance standards are subject to EPA's administration and receive permits under [§ 402], not § 404.

This reading accords with the Act's structure and objectives. It retains, through [§ 402], uniform application of the Act's core pollution-control requirements, and it respects Congress' special concern for new sources. Leaving pollution-related decisions to EPA, moreover, is consistent with Congress' delegation to that agency of primary responsibility to administer the Act. Most fundamental, adhering to § 306(e)'s instruction honors the overriding statutory goal of eliminating water pollution, and Congress' particular rejection of the use of navigable waters as waste disposal sites.

The Court's reading, in contrast, strains credulity. A discharge of a pollutant, otherwise prohibited by firm statutory command, becomes lawful if it contains sufficient solid matter to raise the bottom of a water body, transformed into a waste disposal facility. Whole categories of regulated industries can thereby gain immunity from a variety of pollution-control standards. * * *

Congress, we have recognized, does not "alter the fundamental details of a regulatory scheme in vague terms or ancillary provisions—it does not, one might say, hide elephants in mouseholes." *Whitman v. American Trucking Assns., Inc.,* 531 U.S. 457, 467–468 (2001). Yet an alteration of that kind is just what today's decision imagines. Congress, as the Court reads the Act, silently upended, in an ancillary permitting provision, its painstaking pollution-control scheme. Congress did so, the Court holds, notwithstanding the lawmakers' stated effort "to restore and maintain the chemical, physical, and biological integrity" of the waters of the United States, 33 U.S.C. § 1251(a); their assignment to EPA of the Herculean task of setting strict effluent limitations for many categories of industrial sources; and their insistence that new sources meet even more ambitious standards, not subject to exception or variance. Would a rational legislature order exacting pollution limits, yet call all bets off if the pollutant, discharged into a lake, will raise the water body's elevation? To say the least, I am persuaded, that is not how Congress intended the Clean Water Act to operate. * * *

NOTES ON *COEUR ALASKA* AND **DEFERENCE TO AGENCY INTERPRETATIONS OF ITS OWN RULES**

1. *The Bootstrapping Concern with* Auer *Deference.* Justice Kennedy depicts the Regas Memorandum as an interpretation of the "regulatory scheme" and the "regulatory regime." Was the memorandum interpreting only the ambiguous EPA regulation, or was it construing the relevant provisions of the CWA as well?

If Justice Kennedy is treating the memorandum as an interpretation not only of the regulation, but also, by extension, of the statute, then he seems to be countenancing the kind of "bootstrapping" that concerned him in *Gonzales v. Oregon.* Here, the EPA promulgated an ambiguous regulation to implement an ambiguous statute. It then interpreted the regulation in an internal memorandum. As an interpretation of the regulation, the memorandum should be assessed under *Auer* and should receive deference so long as that interpretation is not "plainly erroneous or inconsistent with the regulation." But insofar as the interpretation of the regulation also resolves an ambiguity in the statute, the memorandum should be assessed under *Chevron* or under *Skidmore* (if the memorandum does not meet *Chevron* Step Zero). To assess the agency's *statutory* interpretation under *Auer*, simply because it is embedded in an interpretation of a regulation, would be to permit the agency to bootstrap that interpretation from *Skidmore* or *Chevron* to the more deferential *Auer* regime.

Justice Kennedy fails—at least explicitly—to assess the memorandum under the *Skidmore* or *Chevron* standard. Instead, he concludes his analysis by asserting that the memorandum satisfies the *Auer* standard. Insofar as the memorandum also interprets the statute, Justice Kennedy should have taken the further step of asking whether, per *Chevron*, there had been a delegation of lawmaking authority and that the agency lawmaking was "reasonable." See *Mead*.

This amounts to both substantive and procedural bootstrapping. It is *substantive*, as it enables an agency to shift its statutory interpretation from one regime of judicial review (*Skidmore* or *Chevron*) to a more deferential one (*Auer*). It is *procedural*, as it enables the agency to reap the advantages of lawmaking without considering whether Congress has delegated that kind of authority (*Mead*). It does not appear that the Regas Memorandum was issued under a delegation of lawmaking authority, however. Thus, if the majority is tacitly treating the memorandum as a *statutory* interpretation, then it is allowing the agency to circumvent *Mead*. (Justice Kennedy elides this point, but Justice Scalia waves it like a bloody flag.)

Justice Ginsburg's dissenting opinion drives home the bootstrapping charge in another way: under cover of *Auer*, the agency has radically amended the statutory scheme, creating a huge loophole for "fill" material to elbow out the strict no-tolerance EPA policy toward mining slurry. Her elephants-not-in-mouseholes argument is very similar to the one that Justice Kennedy found cogent in *Oregon*. (What *does* distinguish *Oregon* from *Coeur Alaska* for Justice Kennedy?)

2. *The Difference Between* Chevron *and* Auer, *and the Closeted Role of* Skidmore. Justice Scalia suggests that the majority is actually applying *Chevron* deference to the Regas Memorandum, despite its claim to be applying *Auer* deference. Is there any practical difference between the two regimes? That is, will judges be any more deferential under a "clearly erroneous" (*Auer*) standard than under a "reasonableness" (*Chevron*) one? Or will they simply make an independent, policy-based judgment about the merits of deference in any given case, regardless of the particular deference regime they ultimately announce? This might be an implication of Justice Breyer's concurring opinion here, as well as his opinions in earlier cases. From Breyer's perspective, there is in reality just one deference regime: *Skidmore*, with its various factors for assessing whether deference is warranted.

Bring these two points together and relate them to the majority opinion. Justice Kennedy claims to be according the Regas Memorandum "a measure of deference"—a phrase that appears to equivocate between *Chevron* and *Auer* deference. Note also that the five factors he adduces for deferring to the memorandum (especially the third, agency expertise) seem to sit comfortably within the *Skidmore* framework.

3. *The Agency's Highly Dynamic Interpretation.* SEACC argued that the Regas interpretation was contradicted by three previous agency statements: a 1986 "memorandum of understanding" between the EPA and the Corps regarding the definition of fill material, which, though not subject to notice and comment procedures, was published in the Federal Register; the preamble of the current fill regulation; and remarks made by the agencies in response

to public comments on the proposed fill regulation, remarks that were incorporated by reference into the administrative record.

Justice Kennedy concluded that the previous statements did not in fact contradict the Regas Memorandum, but there was strong evidence going the other way. G. Tracy Mehan, III, the former EPA Assistant Administrator for Water (2001–03) who oversaw the promulgation of the fill rule, filed an *amicus* brief supporting SEACC. Mehan advocated an interpretation of the rule that contradicted the one advanced in the Regas Memorandum, citing some of the very same agency statements noted above. Does an agency enjoy *Auer* deference even after it has radically changed earlier constructions? Justice Kennedy did not answer that question, because he believed the EPA had been reasonably consistent in its approach to these issues.

The most dramatic agency about-face, however, was the Corps' reinterpretation of "fill material." Given the Corps' longstanding jurisdiction over river-based construction and fill projects, the agency had apparently not, before the second Bush Administration, understood fill material to include elements that were mainly "pollutants" regulated primarily by EPA. Indeed, § 404 may cement the traditional definition of "fill material" into the statute. To begin with, § 404's use of the term "fill material" presumptively entails the materials the Corps had traditionally regulated, which were construction-related matter where the primary concern was that they would elevate water levels. Moreover, § 404(f)(1) exempts from Corps regulation fill materials resulting from construction or navigation activities (like constructing "farm roads," "dams," and the like). Finally, this reading of "fill material" contrasts with "pollutant," the matter regulated by the EPA. As a structural matter, this helps us understand why Congress treated §§ 402 and 404 as different regulatory regimes that presumptively did not overlap. (An *amicus* brief from Members of Congress serving on committees regulating environmental matters made these points.)

Yet Justice Kennedy treated the Corps' definition of "fill material" (to include slurry) as settled between the parties and therefore not available for judicial second-guessing. Was this well founded? (*Amicus* briefs filed by both Tracy Mehan and the Members of Congress vigorously disputed this assertion and viewed it as central to the case.) Is the Bush–Cheney Administration's expansion of the definition of fill material a regulatory elephant sneaking in through the statutory mousehole? Is the majority doing a disservice to the rule of law by going along with an administrative revision of the CWA—a revision that the *amici* felt were a wholesale abandonment of the statute's purpose, to clean up the nation's waterways? See Brief for Tracy Mehan as Amicus Curiae in Support of Respondent, *Coeur Alaska*, 40–41 (Nos. 07–984, 07–990). How might Justice Breyer's concurring opinion help explain, or defend, the majority's approach?

3. Should Courts Defer When the Agency Interpretation Presents Serious Constitutional Difficulties?

Yet another way to read the Oregon Aid-in-Dying Case is through a constitutional lens. Five Justices (O'Connor, Stevens, Souter, Ginsburg, Breyer), all in the *Oregon* majority, had opined in *Washington v. Glucks-*

berg that they were open to recognizing a "constitutionally cognizable interest in controlling the circumstances of his or her imminent death," in at least some instances. Without any constitutional nuance or case-by-case reservation, the Ashcroft Directive made aid-in-dying a crime under any and all circumstances. Justice Kennedy's opinion mentioned the "earnest and profound debate" over the constitutionality of state efforts to ban all forms of euthanasia as one reason the Court was reluctant to find a congressional delegation to the Attorney General on this issue. Most and perhaps all of the majority Justices found the Ashcroft Directive constitutionally problematic in the breadth of its intrusion into private decision-making and state policymaking. It is likely that none of the dissenting Justices had these constitutional problems. See Eskridge, *Story of* Gonzales v. Oregon, 366–75, 384–94.

Does the existence of potential constitutional problems make a difference in the Court's overall willingness to defer? What would be the theoretical basis for that? One might presume that Congress does not normally delegate to agencies the authority to press constitutional limits, and so constitutional concerns would show up at Step Zero, as in the *Oregon* case. Or one might invoke the avoidance canon in Step One: when there are two possible meanings of statutory language, the Court should for institutional process reasons follow the one that does not raise constitutional problems. (In that event, the avoidance canon would trump *Chevron*. The Court has in fact gone that route in some *Chevron*-eligible cases. E.g., *Department of Commerce v. U.S. House of Representatives* (Chapter 3, § 3B).) One can even imagine the constitutional analysis coming in *Chevron* Step Two: an agency interpretation is not "reasonable" if it raises constitutional concerns when a more cautious interpretation would just as easily subserve congressional goals.

Do these arguments lose their cogency when fewer than five Justices flag constitutional problems? Perhaps surprisingly, the Eskridge and Baer study suggests not. They identified 75 cases where at least one Justice flagged a constitutional concern with the agency's interpretation: the agency view prevailed only 45.3 percent of the time, while the agency view won in 70.7 percent of the cases where no Justice raised constitutional concerns. Eskridge & Baer, *Continuum of Deference*. This is the most dramatic differential in their study and strongly suggests that agencies do *not* get nearly as much deference when there are constitutional concerns with their interpretations.

PROBLEM 6–6

Deference When There Are Constitutional Concerns

In 1970, Congress enacted Title X of the Public Health Service Act, 84 Stat. 1499, 1504, which provides federal funding for family-planning services. The purposes of the Act expressed in § 2 are:

> (1) to assist in making comprehensive voluntary family planning services readily available to all persons desiring such services; * * *

(5) to develop and make readily available information (including educational materials) on family planning and population growth to all persons desiring such information.

The Act authorizes the provision of federal funds to support the establishment and operation of voluntary family planning projects and empowers the Secretary of Health and Human Services to promulgate regulations imposing conditions on grant recipients to ensure that "grants will be effectively utilized for the purposes for which made."

Section 1 of the Act authorizes the Secretary to "make grants to and enter into contracts with public or nonprofit private entities to assist in the establishment and operation of voluntary family planning projects which shall offer a broad range of acceptable and effective family planning methods and services." Section 1008 provides: "None of the funds appropriated under this Act shall be used in programs where abortion is a method of family planning." According to the conference report for the Act, the § 1008 restriction was to ensure that Title X funds would "be used only to support preventive family planning services, population research, infertility services, and other related medical, informational, and educational opportunities."

The Secretary's 1971 regulations implementing the Act described the kind of services that grant recipients had to provide in order to be eligible for federal funding. Pursuant to section 1008, the regulations stipulated that "the project will not provide abortions as a method of family planning." The 1971 regulations, even as revised in 1986, did not regulate the form of counseling or the distribution of information at federally funded projects.

In 1988, the Secretary promulgated new regulations to clarify the "family planning" services that Title X funds may be used to assist. Section 59.2 of the new regulations limits Title X services to "preconceptual counseling, education, and general reproductive health care (including obstetric or prenatal care)." Section 59.8(a)(1) specifies that henceforth a "Title X project may not provide counseling concerning the use of abortion as a method of family planning or provide referral for abortion as a method of family planning." Section 59.8(a)(2)–(3) makes clear that Title X programs have to refer pregnant women to other services, but doctors in the program cannot "steer" expectant mothers to health care providers who perform abortions. Even if the client specifically requests referral to an abortion provider, the Title X program cannot do so, nor can doctors associated with the program. According to § 59.8(b)(5), the appropriate response is that "the project does not consider abortion an appropriate method of family planning and therefore does not counsel or refer for abortion."

Grantees and doctors immediately challenge the new regulations. What arguments can they invoke against the Secretary's interpretation of § 1008? What arguments should the Secretary make in response? How would the Supreme Court analyze and decide this issue? Compare *Rust v. Sullivan*, 500 U.S. 173 (1991).

PALM BEACH COUNTY CANVASSING BOARD v. HARRIS

Supreme Court of Florida, 2000
772 So.2d 1220 *vacated and remanded sub nom. Bush v.
Palm Beach Canvassing Bd.*, 531 U.S. 70 (2000).

[On November 8, 2000, the Florida Division of Elections reported that George W. Bush had received 2,909,135 votes for President in that state, narrowly winning Florida over Albert Gore, Jr., who received 2,907,351 votes. An automatic recount narrowed the gap between the candidates, with Bush still in the lead. On November 9, the Florida Democratic Party Executive Committee requested that manual recounts be conducted in Broward, Palm Beach, and Volusia Counties. The Florida Division of Elections determined, however, in Advisory Opinion DE 00–10, that absent unforeseen circumstances, returns from all counties must be received by 5:00 p.m., November 14, 2000, in order to comply with Fla. Stat. § 101.111(1). Based on this advisory opinion, the Florida Secretary of State announced that she would ignore returns submitted after that cut-off time.

[Volusia County, joined by Palm Beach County, went to court for an injunction barring the Secretary from ignoring returns after that time. The trial court ruled on November 14 that the deadline was mandatory but that the Secretary had discretion to accept amended returns filed after that date. The Secretary announced on November 15 that she would not exercise her discretion to accept amended returns from Volusia and Palm Beach Counties; Gore and the Democratic Party filed suit to compel the Secretary to accept the amended returns. The trial court denied relief, and the Florida Supreme Court accepted an expedited appeal to consider, first, the circumstances authorizing an elections board to require a county-wide manual recount under § 102.166(5) and, second, whether the Secretary could accept the recounts submitted after the passing of the § 101.111(1) deadline.]

[II] Twenty-five years ago, this Court commented that the will of the people, not a hyper-technical reliance upon statutory provisions, should be our guiding principle in election cases:

[T]he real parties in interest here, not in the legal sense but in realistic terms, are the voters. They are possessed of the ultimate interest and it is they whom we must give primary consideration. The contestants have direct interests certainly, but the office they seek is one of high public service and of utmost importance to the people, thus subordinating their interest to that of the people. Ours is a government of, by and for the people. Our federal and state constitutions guarantee the right of the people to take an active part in the process of that government, which for most of our citizens means participation via the election process. *The right to vote is the right to participate; it is also the right to speak, but more importantly the right to be heard.* We must tread carefully on that right or we risk the unnecessary and unjustified muting of the public voice. By refusing to recognize an otherwise valid exercise of the right of a citizen to vote for the sake of sacred, unyielding adherence to statutory scripture, we would in effect nullify that right.

Boardman v. Esteva, 323 So. 2d 259, 263 (Fla. 1975) (emphasis added). We consistently have adhered to the principle that the will of the people is the paramount consideration. Our goal today remains the same as it was a quarter of a century ago, i.e., to reach the result that reflects the will of the voters, whatever that might be. This fundamental principle, and our traditional rules of statutory construction, guide our decision today. * * *

[IV] The first issue this Court must resolve is whether a County Board may conduct a countywide manual recount where it determines there is an error in vote tabulation that could affect the outcome of the election. Here, the Division issued opinion DE 00–13, which construed the language "error in vote tabulation" to exclude the situation where a discrepancy between the original machine return and sample manual recount is due to the manner in which a ballot has been marked or punched.

Florida courts generally will defer to an agency's interpretation of statutes and rules the agency is charged with implementing and enforcing. Florida courts, however, will not defer to an agency's opinion that is contrary to law. We conclude that the Division's advisory opinion regarding vote tabulation is contrary to law because it contravenes the plain meaning of section 102.166(5).

Pursuant to section 102.166(4)(a), a candidate who appears on a ballot, a political committee that supports or opposes an issue that appears on a ballot, or a political party whose candidate's name appeared on the ballot may file a written request with the County Board for a manual recount. This request must be filed with the Board before the Board certifies the election results or within seventy-two hours after the election, whichever occurs later. Upon filing the written request for a manual recount, the canvassing board may authorize a manual recount. The decision whether to conduct a manual recount is vested in the sound discretion of the Board. If the canvassing board decides to authorize the manual recount, the recount must include at least three precincts and at least one percent of the total votes cast for each candidate or issue, with the person who requested the recount choosing the precincts to be recounted. If the manual recount indicates an "error in the vote tabulation which could affect the outcome of the election," the county canvassing board "shall":

(a) Correct the error and recount the remaining precincts with the vote tabulation system;

(b) Request the Department of State to verify the tabulation software; *or*

(c) Manually recount all ballots. § 102.166(5)(a)–(c), Fla. Stat. (2000) (emphasis added).

The issue in dispute here is the meaning of the phrase "error in the vote tabulation" found in section 102.166(5). The Division opines that an "error in the vote tabulation" only means a counting error resulting from incorrect election parameters or an error in the vote tabulating software. We disagree.

The plain language of section 102.166(5) refers to an error in the vote tabulation rather than [in] the vote tabulation system. On its face, the statute does not include any words of limitation; rather, it provides a remedy for any type of mistake made in tabulating ballots. The Legislature has utilized the phrase "vote tabulation system" and "automatic tabulating equipment" in section 102.166 when it intended to refer to the voting system rather than the vote count. Equating "vote tabulation" with "vote tabulation system" obliterates the distinction created in section 102.166 by the Legislature.

Sections 101.5614(5) and (6) also support the proposition that the "error in vote tabulation" encompasses more than a mere determination of whether the vote tabulation system is functioning. Section 101.5614(5) provides that "[n]o vote shall be declared invalid or void if there is a clear indication of the intent of the voter as determined by the canvassing board." Conversely, section 101.5614(6) provides that any vote in which the board cannot discern the intent of the voter must be discarded. Taken together, these sections suggest that "error in the vote tabulation" includes errors in the failure of the voting machinery to read a ballot and not simply errors resulting from the voting machinery.

Moreover, section 102.141(4), which outlines the board's responsibility in the event of a recount, states that the Board "shall examine the counters on the machines or the tabulation of the ballots cast in each precinct in which the office or issue appeared on the ballot and determine whether the returns correctly reflect the votes cast." § 102.141, Fla. Stat. (2000). Therefore, an "error in the vote tabulation" includes a discrepancy between the number of votes determined by a voter tabulation system and the number of voters determined by a manual count of a sampling of precincts pursuant to section 102.166(4).

Although error cannot be completely eliminated in any tabulation of the ballots, our society has not yet gone so far as to place blind faith in machines. In almost all endeavors, including elections, humans routinely correct the errors of machines. For this very reason, Florida law provides a human check on both the malfunction of tabulation equipment and error in failing to accurately count the ballots. Thus, we find that the Division's opinion DE 00–13 regarding the ability of county canvassing boards to authorize a manual recount is contrary to the plain language of the statute.

Having concluded that the county canvassing boards have the authority to order countywide manual recounts, we must now determine whether the Commission [i.e., the Secretary of State, the Director of the Division of Elections, and the Governor] must accept a return after the seven-day deadline set forth in sections 102.111 and 102.112 under the circumstances presented. * * *

[VI] The provisions of the Code are ambiguous in two significant areas. First, the time frame for conducting a manual recount under section 102.166(4) is in conflict with the time frame for submitting county returns under sections 102.111 and 102.112. Second, the mandatory language in section 102.111 conflicts with the permissive language in 102.112.

[A. *The Recount Conflict.*] Section 102.166(1) states that "[a]ny candidate for nomination or election, or any elector qualified to vote in the election related to such candidacy, shall have the right to protest the returns of the election as being erroneous by filing with the appropriate canvassing board a sworn written protest." The time period for filing a protest is "prior to the time the canvassing board certifies the results for the office being protested or within 5 days after midnight of the date the election is held, whichever occurs later."

Section 102.166(4)(a), the operative subsection in this case, further provides that, in addition to any protest, "any candidate whose name appeared on the ballot ... or any political party whose candidates' names appeared on the ballot may file a written request with the county canvassing board for a manual recount" accompanied by the "reason that the manual recount is being requested." Section 102.166(4)(b) further provides that the written request may be made prior to the time the Board certifies the returns or within seventy-two hours after the election, whichever occurs later:

> (4)(a) Any candidate whose name appeared on the ballot, any political committee that supports or opposes an issue which appeared on the ballot, or any political party whose candidates' names appeared on the ballot may file a written request with the county canvassing board for a manual recount. The written request shall contain a statement of the reason the manual recount is being requested.
>
> (b) *Such request must be filed with the canvassing board prior to the time the canvassing board certifies the results for the office being protested or within 72 hours after midnight of the date the election was held, whichever occurs later.* § 102.166, Fla. Stat. (2000) (emphasis added).

[The Board "may" then authorize a recount, including at least three precincts and 1% of the total votes for the protesting candidate. If the manual recount then indicates an error in the vote tabulation which could affect the election, the Board "shall" either "(a) [c]orrect the error and recount the remaining precincts * * *; (b) [r]equest the Secretary of State to verify the tabulation software; or (c) [m]anually recount all ballots." § 102.166(5).]

Under this scheme, a candidate can request a manual recount at any point prior to certification by the Board and such action can lead to a full recount of all the votes in the county. Although the Code sets no specific deadline by which a manual recount must be completed, logic dictates that the period of time required to complete a full manual recount may be substantial, particularly in a populous county, and may require several days. The protest provision thus conflicts with section 102.111 and 102.112, which state that the Boards "must" submit their returns to the Elections Canvassing Commission by 5:00 p.m. of the seventh day following the election or face penalties. For instance, if a party files a pre-certification protest on the sixth day following the election and requests a manual recount and the initial manual recount indicates that a full countywide recount is necessary, the recount procedure in most cases could not be completed by the deadline in sections 102.111 and 102.112, i.e., by 5:00 p.m. of the seventh day following the election.

[B. *The "Shall" and "May" Conflict.*] In addition to the conflict in the above statutes, sections 102.111 and 102.112 contain a dichotomy. Section 102.111, which sets forth general criteria governing the State Canvassing Commission, was enacted in 1951 as part of the Code and provides as follows:

(1) * * * The Elections Canvassing Commission shall, as soon as the official results are compiled from all counties, certify the returns of the election and determine and declare who has been elected for each office. * * * *If the county returns are not received by the Department of State by 5 p.m. of the seventh day following an election, all missing counties shall be ignored*, and the results shown by the returns on file shall be certified. § 102.111, Fla. Stat. (2000) (emphasis added).

The Legislature in 1989 revised chapter 102 to include section 102.112, which provides that returns not received after a certain date "may" be ignored and that members of the County Board "shall" be fined:

(1) The county canvassing board or a majority thereof shall file the county returns for the election of a federal or state officer with the Department of State immediately after the certification of the election returns. Returns must be filed by 5 p.m. on the 7th day following the first primary and general election and by 3 p.m. on the 3rd day following the second primary. *If the returns are not received by the department by the time specified, such returns may be ignored* and the results on file at that time may be certified by the department. * * *

[Subsection (2) sets forth fines against board members "for each day such returns are late," and (3) establishes a procedure for board members to appeal such fines.] § 102.112, Fla. Stat. (2000) (emphasis added).

The above statutes conflict. Whereas section 102.111 is mandatory, section 102.112 is permissive. While it is clear that the Boards must submit returns by 5 p.m. of the seventh day following the election or face penalties, the circumstances under which penalties may be assessed are unclear.

[VII] Legislative intent—as always—is the polestar that guides a court's inquiry into the provisions of the Florida Election Code. Where the language of the code is clear and amenable to a reasonable and logical interpretation, courts are without power to diverge from the intent of the Legislature as expressed in the plain language of the Code. As noted above, however, chapter 102 is unclear concerning both the time limits for submitting the results of a manual recount and the penalties that may be assessed by the Secretary. In light of this ambiguity, the Court must resort to traditional rules of statutory construction in an effort to determine legislative intent.

First, it is well-settled that where two statutory provisions are in conflict, the specific statute controls the general statute. In the present case, whereas section 102.111 in its title and text addresses the general makeup and duties of the Elections Canvassing Commission, the statute only tangentially addresses the penalty for returns filed after the statutory date, noting that such returns "shall" be ignored by the Department. Section 102.112, on the other hand, directly addresses in its title and text both the "deadline" for submitting returns and the "penalties" for submitting returns after a certain date; the statute expressly states that such returns "may" be ignored and that dilatory Board members "shall" be fined. Based on the precision of the title and text, section 102.112 constitutes a specific penalty statute that defines both the deadline for filing returns and the penalties for filing returns thereafter and section 102.111 constitutes a non-specific statute in this regard. The specific statute controls the non-specific statute.

Second, it also is well-settled that when two statutes are in conflict, the more recently enacted statute controls the older statute. In the present case, the provision in section 102.111 stating that the Department "shall" ignore returns was enacted in 1951 as part of the Code. On the other hand, the penalty provision in section 102.112 stating that the Department "may" ignore returns was enacted in 1989 as a revision to chapter 102. The more recently enacted provision may be viewed as the clearest and most recent expression of legislative intent.

Third, a statutory provision will not be construed in such a way that it renders meaningless or absurd any other statutory provision. In the present case, section 102.112 contains a detailed provision authorizing the assessment of fines against members of a dilatory County Canvassing Board. The fines are personal and substantial, i.e., $200 for each day the returns are not received. If, as the Secretary asserts, the Department were required to ignore all returns received after the statutory date, the fine provision would be meaningless. For example, if a Board simply completed its count late and if the returns were going to be ignored in any event, what would be the point in submitting the returns? The Board would simply file no returns and avoid the fines. But, on the other hand, if the returns submitted after the statutory date would not be ignored, the Board would have good reason to submit the returns and accept the fines. The fines thus serve as an alternative penalty and are applicable only if the Department may count the returns.

Fourth, related statutory provisions must be read as a cohesive whole. As stated in *Forsythe v. Longboat Key Beach Erosion Control Dist.*, 604 So. 2d 452, 455 (Fla. 1992), "all parts of a statute must be read together in order to achieve a consistent whole. Where possible, courts must give effect to all statutory provisions and construe related statutory provisions in harmony with another." In this regard we consider the provisions of section 102.166 and 102.168.

Section 102.166 states that a candidate, political committee, or political party may request a manual recount any time before the County Canvassing Board certifies the results to the Department and, if the initial manual recount indicates a significant error, the Board "shall" conduct a countywide manual recount in certain cases. Thus, if a protest is filed on the sixth day following an election and a full manual recount is required, the Board, through no fault of its own, will be unable to submit its returns to the Department by 5:00 p.m. on the seventh day following the election. In such a case, if the mandatory provision in section 102.111 were given effect, the votes of the county would be ignored for the simple reason that the Board was following the dictates of a different section of the Code. The Legislature could not have intended to penalize County Canvassing Boards for following the dictates of the Code.

And finally, when the Legislature enacted the Code in 1951, it envisioned that all votes cast during a particular election, including absentee ballots, would be submitted to the Department at one time and would be treated in a uniform fashion. Section 97.012(1) states that it is the Secretary's responsibility to "[o]btain and maintain uniformity in the application, operation, and interpretation of the election laws." Chapter 101 provides that all votes, including absentee ballots, must be received by the Supervisor no later than 7 p.m. on the day of the election. Section 101.68(2)(d) expressly states that "[t]he votes on absentee ballots shall be included in the total vote of the county." Chapter 102 requires that the Board submit the returns by 5 p.m. on the seventh day following the election.

The Legislature thus envisioned that when returns are submitted to the Department, the returns "shall" embrace all the votes in the county, including absentee ballots. This, of course, is not possible because our state statutory scheme has been superseded by federal law governing overseas voters; overseas ballots must be counted if received no later than ten days following the election (i.e., the ballots do *not* have to be received by 7 p.m. of the day of the election, as provided by state law). In light of the fact that overseas ballots cannot be counted after until the seven day deadline has expired, the mandatory language in section 102.111 has been supplanted by the permissive language of section 102.112.

Further, although county returns must be received by 5 p.m. on the seventh day following an election, the "official results" that are to be compiled in order to certify the returns and declare who has been elected must be construed in pari materia with section 101.5614(8), which specifies that "write-in, absentee *and manually counted results* shall constitute the official return of the election." (Emphasis added).

Under this statutory scheme, the County Canvassing Boards are required to submit their returns to the Department by 5 p.m. of the seventh day following the election. The statutes make no provision for exceptions following a manual recount. If a Board fails to meet the deadline, the Secretary is not required to ignore the county's returns but rather is permitted to ignore the returns within the parameters of this statutory scheme. To determine the circumstances under which the Secretary may lawfully ignore returns filed pursuant to the provisions of section 102.166 for a manual recount, it is necessary to examine the interplay between our statutory and constitutional law at both the state and federal levels.

[VIII] * * * To the extent that the Legislature may enact laws regulating the electoral process, those laws are valid only if they impose no "unreasonable or unnecessary" restraints on the right of suffrage:

The declaration of rights expressly states that "all political power is inherent in the people." Article I, Section 1, Florida Constitution. The right of the people to select their own officers is their sovereign right, and the rule is against imposing unnecessary and unreasonable [restraints on that right].... *Unreasonable or unnecessary* restraints on the elective process are prohibited.

Treiman v. Malmquist, 342 So. 2d 972, 975 (Fla. 1977) (emphasis added).

Because election laws are intended to facilitate the right of suffrage, such laws must be liberally construed in favor of the citizens' right to vote:

Generally, the courts, in construing statutes relating to elections, hold that the same should receive a liberal construction in favor of the citizen whose right to vote they tend to restrict and in so doing to prevent disfranchisement of legal voters and the intention of the voters should prevail when counting ballots.... It is the intention of the law to obtain an honest expression of the will or desire of the voter.

State ex rel. Carpenter v. Barber, 198 So. 49, 51 (Fla. 1940). Courts must not lose sight of the fundamental purpose of election laws: The laws are intended to facilitate and safeguard the right of each voter to express his or her will in the context of our representative democracy. Technical statutory requirements must not be exalted over the substance of this right.

Based on the foregoing, we conclude that the authority of the Florida Secretary of State to ignore amended returns submitted by a County

Canvassing Board may be lawfully exercised only under limited circumstances as we set forth in this opinion. The clear import of the penalty provision of section 102.112 is to deter Boards from engaging in dilatory conduct contrary to statutory authority that results in the late certification of a county's returns. This deterrent purpose is achieved by the fines in section 102.112, which are substantial and personal and are levied on each member of a Board. The alternative penalty, i.e., ignoring the county's returns, punishes not the Board members themselves but rather the county's electors, for it in effect disenfranchises them.

Ignoring the county's returns is a drastic measure and is appropriate only if the returns are submitted to the Department so late that their inclusion will compromise the integrity of the electoral process in either of two ways: (1) by precluding a candidate, elector, or taxpayer from contesting the certification of an election pursuant to section 102.168; or (2) by precluding Florida voters from participating fully in the federal electoral process. In either case, the Secretary must explain to the Board her reason for ignoring the returns and her action must be adequately supported by the law. To disenfranchise electors in an effort to deter Board members, as the Secretary in the present case proposes, is unreasonable, unnecessary, and violates longstanding law. [The Secretary made no such claim in this case.] * * *

Because of the unique circumstances and extraordinary importance of the present case, wherein the Florida Attorney General and the Florida Secretary of State have issued conflicting advisory opinions concerning the propriety of conducting manual recounts, and because of our reluctance to rewrite the Florida Election Code, we conclude that we must invoke the equitable powers of this Court to fashion a remedy that will allow a fair and expeditious resolution of the questions presented here.

Accordingly, in order to allow maximum time for contests pursuant to section 102.168, amended certifications must be filed with the Elections Canvassing Commission by 5 p.m. on Sunday, November 26, 2000 and the Secretary of State and the Elections Canvassing Commission shall accept any such amended certifications received by 5 p.m. on Sunday, November 26, 2000, provided that the office of the Secretary of State, Division of Elections is open in order to allow receipt thereof. If the office is not open for this special purpose on Sunday, November 26, 2000, then any amended certifications shall be accepted until 9 a.m. on Monday, November 27, 2000. The stay order entered on November 17, 2000, by this Court shall remain in effect until the expiration of the time for accepting amended certifications set forth in this opinion. The certificates made and signed by the Elections Canvassing Commission pursuant to section 102.121 shall include the amended returns accepted through the dates set forth in this opinion.

NOTES ON PALM BEACH CANVASSING BOARD AND THE ROLE OF CANONS IN JUDICIAL EVALUATION OF AGENCY INTERPRETATIONS

1. *The Subsequent History of* Palm Beach Canvassing Bd. v. Harris. The U.S. Supreme Court unanimously vacated the foregoing opinion, on the ground that the Florida court's interpretation of the statutes may have been influenced by their view of the state constitution. *Bush v. Palm Beach County Canvassing Bd.*, 531 U.S. 70 (2000) (per curiam). The Court's reasoning was as follows. In normal cases, the Supreme Court would not second-guess a state court in this way. Article II of the U.S. Constitution,[l] however, as well as a federal statute, 3 U.S.C. § 5,[m] vest the state "Legislature," alone, with the authority to determine the procedures by which the state chooses its electors for President. Thus, the Constitution has delegated an important federal role to the state legislature, not to the legislature-cum-court. The state court's only role is to determine what procedures the legislature has *actually* chosen, not what procedures the state constitution—superseded on this point by federal law—would require the legislature to choose in state elections. The Supreme Court remanded the case to the state courts. (On remand, the Florida Supreme Court reaffirmed its prior interpretation.) For a discussion of the Article II issue, see Samuel Issacharoff, Pamela Karlan & Richard Pildes, *When Elections Go Bad* (2001).

On November 26, the Florida Elections Canvassing Commission certified the Bush electors for that state. Vice President Gore immediately challenged the certification under the state contest law, Fla. Stat. § 102.168, which allows a contest if there is "[r]eceipt of a number of illegal votes or rejection of a number of legal votes sufficient to change or place in doubt the result of the election." Reversing the trial court in several respects, a divided Florida Supreme Court in *Gore v. Harris*, 772 So.2d 1243 (Dec. 8, 2000), ruled that Miami–Dade and other counties must conduct manual recounts of "under-votes," those ballots the machines did not count but where the intent of the voter might be discerned through examination of "chads" created by a partial punch-through in the ballot and even of "dimples," or indentations not amounting to punch-throughs. The court ruled that the "intent of the voter" was the standard each county must follow. The recounts were to be completed by December 12, the federal safe-harbor date under 3 U.S.C. § 5 (if a state has chosen electors by that date, they cannot be challenged). (A second date, December 18, was also important, because that's when the electors would cast their votes for President.) The recounts began but were stayed by the U.S.

---

l. "Each state shall appoint, in such Manner as the Legislature thereof may direct, a Number of Electors, equal to the whole Number of Senators and Representatives to which the State may be entitled in the Congress * * *." U.S. Const., art. I, § 1, cl. 2.

m. "If any State shall have provided, by laws enacted prior to the day fixed for the appointment of the electors, for its final determination of any controversy or contest concerning the appointment of all or any of the electors of such State, by judicial or other methods or procedures, and such determination shall have been made at least six days before the time fixed for the meeting of the electors, such determination made pursuant to such law so existing on said day, and made at least six days prior to said time of meeting of the electors, shall be conclusive, and shall govern in the counting of the electoral votes as provided in the Constitution, and as hereinafter regulated, so far as the ascertainment of the electors appointed by such State is concerned." 3 U.S.C. § 5.

Supreme Court on December 9. *Bush v. Gore*, 531 U.S. 1046 (2000). The Supreme Court reversed the second Florida Supreme Court decision on December 12, on the ground that the state recount procedures violated the Equal Protection Clause. *Bush v. Gore*, 531 U.S. 98 (2000) (per curiam). Florida certified its Bush electors, and the next day candidate Gore conceded the election to Governor Bush.

2. *Was the Florida Supreme Court's Statutory Interpretation Beyond the Pale? Should the Court Have Deferred?* A concurring opinion in *Bush v. Gore* maintained that the state court constructions of the state statutes violated Article II on the ground that they rewrote the Legislature's directives. 531 U.S. at 113 (Rehnquist, C.J., joined by Scalia and Thomas, JJ., concurring). The Chief Justice maintained that the state court's interpretation misread the legislature's election-contest law, in its view that a fraction of "undervote" ballots were "legal votes" that needed to be counted and in its remedy of new manual recounts, which threatened Florida's compliance with the safe-harbor December 12 deadline. These were criticisms of the Florida court's December 8 opinion, not its November 21 opinion, but other criticisms applied to the earlier opinion as well. The Chief Justice would have ruled that "[n]o reasonable person would call [an undervote, where the voter did not completely punch through] 'an error in the vote tabulation,' " within the meaning of § 102.166(5). (Hint: look up *tabulate* in the dictionary.) The Chief Justice also criticized the Florida court for failing to defer to the "reasonable interpretation" offered by the administrative official (Secretary of State Katharine Harris, the Bush campaign chief in the state) and insisting instead on its "peculiar one." *Id.* at 537.

The dissenting opinions essentially took the position that the Florida court made a reasonable interpretation of its own state law and, therefore, should receive the deference the Chief reserved for the administrators. *Id.* at 542 (Stevens, J., dissenting); *id.* at 544 (Souter, J., dissenting); *id.* at 546–52 (Ginsburg, J., dissenting). In short, while the Florida justices would have appreciated more deference to their efforts to make sense of the statutory scheme and construct a fair but expeditious recount procedure, the Florida election administrators would have appreciated more deference to their efforts to bring the contentious election to a close. Even under the Florida Supreme Court's opinion, the Secretary of State had discretion in receiving late vote tallies because of manual recounts. Why was it that the Secretary was found to have abused her discretion? Was there no room for deference—at least as to that?

The answer in *Palm Beach Canvassing Board* seems to have been, in part, that the Secretary was not giving proper weight to the state constitutional right to vote. The U.S. Supreme Court's first opinion rejected reliance on the state constitution—but the state court could then have relied on the federal constitutional right to vote. But under federal precedents, it appears doubtful that a decision by a state election board to call a halt to manual recounts in order to meet a statutory deadline would violate anyone's federal right to vote. (It's hard to imagine a different result under the Florida Constitution, but there are fewer precedents to guide prediction.) If that's right, then the interpretive principle seems to have no traction. This recalls the quandary we raised in connection with *Catholic Bishop* in Chapter 3,

§ 2B: Should a court go out of its way to avoid a constitutional difficulty if it's clear that both statutory approaches actually are constitutional? So should the state court have deferred to the Secretary in the exercise of her discretion? Is there good reason for a court not to defer in matters of voting law?

Another angle, unexamined in the various opinions, is that agency *litigating positions* are not entitled to *Chevron* deference under federal law. See *Bowen v. Georgetown Univ. Hosp.*, 488 U.S. 204 (1988); *United States v. Western Elec. Co.*, 900 F.2d 283, 297 (D.C. Cir. 1990). For example, in the rule of lenity cases, courts do not defer to Department of Justice guidelines for implementing criminal laws, in part because they are developed for purposes of litigation. To the extent that the administrative interpretations in *Palm Beach Canvassing Board* were "litigating positions," they are probably not entitled to deference. But were they litigating positions?

3. *Deference and Canons of Construction.* Deference to administrative interpretations is, among other things, one of the canons of statutory construction. But under the *Chevron* framework, that canon has no application if the statute is otherwise clear. One way to determine whether the statute is clear is to examine it through the lens of the various canons—precisely as the Florida Supreme Court did (and it found the statute clear, so deference was unwarranted). The debate rehearsed in our note about legislative history after *Chevron* can be understood in this light.

All judges agree that determination of statutory clarity under *Chevron* Step One requires consideration of the textual canons or the principles embedded in them. Thus, U.S. Supreme Court Justices have refused to defer to agency interpretations when their Step One inquiry has found a statutory plain meaning based on such canonical chestnuts as the rule against surplusage, e.g., *National Credit Union Admin. v. First Nat'l Bank & Trust Co.*, 522 U.S. 479, 500, 502 (1998); noscitur a sociis, e.g., *Sweet Home* (Chapter 3, § 1C) (Scalia, J., dissenting); inclusio unius, e.g., *City of Chicago, supra*; the dictionary rule, e.g., *MCI, supra*; and so forth.

The role of substantive canons in the *Chevron* analysis is even murkier. Like the Florida Supreme Court, the U.S. Supreme Court seems to consider such canons highly relevant in determining whether there is a statutory plain meaning that terminates the inquiry with step one. See Elizabeth Garrett, *Legal Scholarship in the Age of Legislation*, 34 Tulsa L.J. 679, 695–96 (1999) (discussing the relationship between substantive canons and textualism). Note the irony, therefore, in the U.S. Supreme Court's first and second decisions reviewing the Florida court. The kind of substantive canon the Florida court invoked in *Palm Beach Canvassing Board* is, according to the U.S. Supreme Court in other cases, a part of the plain meaning inquiry. The message of the earlier U.S. Supreme Court cases is that the interpretive process itself requires a court to consider substantive canons—a message in some tension with the first opinion in the Bush and Gore election mess. Moreover, the concurring Justices in the second Supreme Court opinion (Rehnquist, Scalia, Thomas) are aggressive users of constitutional clear statement rules—yet they faulted the Florida court for a milder invocation of the kinds of rules that they regularly deploy.

NOTE ON DEFERENCE TO AGENCIES IN THE STATE COURTS[n]

Chevron has received a mixed reception in the state courts. The dominant view is probably a posture of weak deference, in which courts give complete deference (akin to *Chevron* Step Two) to agency interpretations only in limited circumstances, such as where the interpretation is long-standing or the product of the agency's particular expertise. Otherwise, these courts cling to their traditional prerogative to review questions of law de novo, which allows them to substitute their judgment for that of the agency where they believe the agency has incorrectly construed the statute. See Eric Lane, *How to Read a Statute*, 28 Hofstra L. Rev. 85, 123–24 (1999). A smaller, but nonetheless significant, number of states have adopted full *Chevron* deference (or something akin to it), while another group goes to the opposite extreme, affording agencies little or no respect on question of statutory construction. See Michael Asimow et al., *State and Federal Administrative Law* § 9.2 (1998).

The majority position is well illustrated by *Connecticut State Medical Society v. Connecticut Board of Examiners in Podiatry*, 546 A.2d 830 (Conn. 1988). There, the state's podiatry board had interpreted the statutory term "foot" to include the ankle. The **Connecticut** Supreme Court overturned this construction, holding that the dictionary definition of the word, rather than the agency's understanding of the legislature's intent, provided the proper resolution of the interpretation question. The court's approach to the *Chevron* issue is interesting and instructive. First, the court describes statutory interpretation as "purely a question of law," which requires less deference to the agency than would normally be shown in judicial review of administrative action. The court then suggests that only when the statute has previously been subjected to judicial scrutiny or to "time-tested agency interpretations" should a court afford the agency's interpretation any "special deference." Here, the court held that because "neither the board nor the courts have previously ruled on the issue presented ... such deference is not due."

Also representative of this relaxed deference approach are **Michigan**, see *West Bloomfield Hospital. v. Certificate of Need Bd.*, 550 N.W.2d 223, 227 (Mich. 1996) ("The appellate courts, on judicial review, will give the agency's construction such weight as it concludes is appropriate on full consideration of the statutory criteria and the record of the case on review."); **New Jersey**, see *In re Petition For Authorization To Conduct A Referendum On Withdrawal Of North Haledon School Dist. From Passaic County Manchester Regional High School*, 854 A.2d 327 (N.J. 2004) (courts are "in no way bound by the agency's interpretation of a statute or its determination of a strictly legal issue. * * * The judiciary may intervene in those rare circumstances in which an agency action is clearly inconsistent with [the agency's] statutory mission or with other State policy"); *In re Distribution of Liquid Assets*, 168 N.J. 1, 773 A.2d 6 (2001) (citing *Chevron*, but nonetheless concluding that courts are "in no way bound" by agency interpretations and do not sit simply to "rubber stamp" agency determinations); *James v. Board of Trustees of Public Employ-*

---

 n. Brian Willen (Yale Law, Class of 2001) provided the research and first draft for this Note.

ees' Retirement System, 753 A.2d 1061, 1066 (N.J. 2000) (suggesting that where an administrative interpretation is not "longstanding and consistent," the courts are within their power to construe the statute on their own by trying to ascertain the intent of the legislature); **New York**, see *Lorillard Tobacco Co. v. Roth*, 786 N.E.2d 7, 10 (2003) ("[A]n agency's interpretation of the statutes it administers must be upheld absent demonstrated irrationality or unreasonableness," but where "the question is one of pure statutory reading and analysis, dependent only on accurate apprehension of legislative intent, there is little basis to rely on any special competence or expertise of the administrative agency"); *Seittelman v. Sabol*, 697 N.E.2d 154, 157 (N.Y. 1998) (holding that though deference is the norm, where "the question is one of pure statutory reading and analysis, dependent only on accurate apprehension of legislative intent," courts need not rely on the agency, and remain "free to ascertain the proper interpretation from the statutory language and legislative intent"); and **Ohio**, see *State ex rel. Celebrezze v. Natl. Lime & Stone Co.*, 627 N.E.2d 538 (Ohio 1994) (substituting a *Chevron*-style rule with a different interpretive canon, a substantive one holding that any uncertainty about the scope of an environmental law should be resolved "in favor of the person or entity (manufacturer or otherwise) affected by the law," regardless of how the agency has construed the statute).

States that have adopted a *Chevron*-like posture include **Colorado**, see *Coffman v. Colorado Common Cause*, 102 P.3d 999 (Colo. 2004) (noting that while agency review "is not binding on this court," agency decisions "will be sustained unless arbitrary or capricious"); *North Colorado Medical Center, Inc. v. Committee on Anticompetitive Conduct*, 914 P.2d 902, 907 (Colo. 1996) (citing *Chevron* for the proposition that the "interpretation of a statute by the agency charged with enforcement of that statute is generally entitled to deference"); *El Paso County Bd. of Equalization v. Craddock*, 850 P.2d 702, 704–05 (Colo. 1993) (observing that while agency constructions of statutes are not binding, courts nonetheless "afford deference to the interpretation given the statute by the officer or agency charged with its administration"); **Florida**, see *Donato v. AT & T*, 767 So.2d 1146, 1153 (Fla. 2000) (adopting a two-step, *Chevron-style* analysis in which courts show great deference to agency construction of statutes of "doubtful meaning," but are not bound by such interpretations where the text is not ambiguous); **Massachusetts**, see *Protective Life Ins. Co. v. Sullivan*, 682 N.E.2d 624, 627–28 (Mass. 1997) (granting "substantial deference" to agency interpretations, so long as not contrary to the "plain language of the statute and its underlying purpose"); and **Pennsylvania**, see *Tool Sales & Service Co. v. Commonwealth*, 637 A.2d 607, 613 (Pa. 1993) (holding that an agency's interpretation is to be afforded deference when it does not clearly contradict the statutory language and that the state courts are not to disregard administrative interpretations unless they are "clearly erroneous"). **West Virginia** has explicitly adopted *Chevron* itself for reviewing interpretations offered by the state's administrative agencies. See *Shroyer v. Harrison County Bd. of Educ.*, 564 S.E.2d 425 (W.Va. 2002) (citing *Chevron* for the proposition that "the court first must ask whether the Legislature has directly spoken to the precise question at issue. If the intention of the Legislature is clear, that is the end of the matter, and the agency's position only can be upheld if it conforms to the Legislature's intent.

No deference is due the agency's interpretation at this stage."); *Maikotter v. University of West Virginia Bd. of Trustees*, 527 S.E.2d 802 (W.Va. 1999).

Other states, such as **Washington**, have articulated a formal *Chevron* approach, but have, in practice, departed from a posture of deference. Compare *Waste Management of Seattle, Inc. v. Utilities and Transp. Comm'n*, 869 P.2d 1034, 1038 (Wash. 1994) ("Where an agency is charged with the administration and enforcement of a statute, the agency's interpretation of an ambiguous statute is accorded great weight in determining legislative intent.") with *Sebastian v. Department of Labor and Industries*, 12 P.3d 594 (Wash. 2000) (finding that the text of the statute at issue was ambiguous, but refusing to show deference to the relevant agency construction and instead applying, over a vigorous dissent, a different interpretive canon: the rule that coverage provisions of remedial statutes are to be construed broadly, and the limitations on coverage narrowly).

Such backsliding also characterizes the situation in **California**. The state supreme court's basic approach is to show substantial deference to administrative agencies. See *People ex rel. Lungren v. Superior Court*, 926 P.2d 1042, 1051 (Cal. 1996) ("Although not necessarily controlling, as where made without the authority of or repugnant to the provisions of a statute, the contemporaneous administrative construction of [an] enactment by those charged with its enforcement is entitled to great weight, and courts generally will not depart from such construction unless it is clearly erroneous or unauthorized."). However, in certain circumstances, the state courts have departed significantly from the *Chevron* principle. E.g., *Henning v. Industrial Welfare Comm'n*, 762 P.2d 442, 451 (Cal. 1988) (holding that while "in the abstract, a current administrative interpretation would ordinarily be entitled to great weight," a non-contemporaneous interpretation that "flatly contradicts the position which the agency had enunciated at an earlier date, closer to the enactment of the statute" cannot command significant deference). In *Henning*, Justice Broussard, concurring, went even further, arguing that because statutory interpretation is an act of judicial power, once the court has endorsed "a particular interpretation of a statute, an administrative agency lacks authority to interpret the statute differently." *Id.* at 455. In *City of Long Beach v. Department of Industrial Relations*, 102 P.3d 904, 910 (Cal. 2004), the California Supreme Court reaffirmed the court's role as the ultimate arbiter of statutory interpretation, despite the court's commitment in *Lungren* to agency deference: "[A]lthough we give the Department's interpretation great weight * * * this court bears the ultimate responsibility for construing the statute."

An example of a no-deference state is **Delaware**, which has explicitly declined to adopt *Chevron*. See *Public Water Supply Co. v. DiPasquale*, 735 A.2d 378, 382–83 (Del. 1999) ("A reviewing court may accord due weight, but not defer, to an agency interpretation of a statute administered by it. A reviewing court will not defer to such an interpretation as correct merely because it is rational or not clearly erroneous.")

4.   Does Agency Deference Apply to Issues of Preemption?

The Supremacy Clause of Article VI requires that federal statutes be the supreme law of the land and that state courts enforce them rather than state law when they are inconsistent, or "preempted." There are three different circumstances when state law, such as the Oregon Death With Dignity Act, is preempted by federal law. First, a valid federal statute can stipulate that it preempts state law, and the Court will follow that statutory directive (unless there is a constitutional problem). E.g., *Shaw v. Delta Airlines*, 463 U.S. 85 (1983). Of course, Congress can also write a "non-preemption," *saving clause* into legislation, which will direct courts not to find preemptive force to the legislation.

Second, a federal statute will preempt state law whose operation is inconsistent with that of the federal statutory scheme. This applies not only "where compliance with both federal and state regulations is a physical impossibility," *Florida Lime & Avocado Growers, Inc. v. Paul*, 373 U.S. 132, 142–43 (1963), but also where the state law "stands as an obstacle to the accomplishment and execution of the full purposes and objectives of Congress." *Hines v. Davidowitz*, 312 U.S. 52, 67 (1941).

Third is "field" preemption. "The scheme of federal regulations may be so pervasive as to make reasonable the inference that Congress left no room for the States to supplement it. Or the Act of Congress may touch a field in which the federal interest is so dominant that the federal system will be assumed to preclude enforcement of state laws of the same subject." *Rice v. Santa Fe Elevator Corp.*, 331 U.S. 218, 230 (1947). Areas such as immigration, naturalization, and regulation of noncitizens are examples of fields where federal legislation is likely to be preemptive. E.g., *Toll v. Moreno*, 458 U.S. 1 (1982).

Assume you have a federal statute, such as the Motor Vehicle Safety Act explored in this chapter, which delegates lawmaking and other authority to an agency such as the NHTSA. The agency might have important input in a court's determination of the scope of federal preemption. First, Congress might give the agency direct authority to preempt state law through notice-and-comment rulemaking. Such rules would be subject to *Chevron* deference. Second, Congress might delegate to the agency the authority to adopt substantive rules which could then be the basis for federal preemption the same as explicit statutory rules would. The validity of such rules would be evaluated under *Chevron*, but the agency's understanding of their preemptive force would probably entail only *Skidmore* deference. Third, the agency might, on its own, present its views, usually through interpretive guidances or in *amicus* briefs. What level of deference should that entail?

As you ponder that question, recall that the Supreme Court has recognized a substantive canon that is relevant: "The historic police powers of the States [are] not to be superseded by . . . Federal Act unless that [is] the clear and manifest purpose of Congress." *Cipollone v. Liggett Group, Inc.*, 505 U.S. 504, 516 (1992). How does this canon relate to the three different kinds of preemption *and* to the three kinds of agency inputs? Consider the following case.

GEIER v. HONDA MOTOR CO.

United States Supreme Court, 2000
529 U.S. 861, 120 S.Ct. 1913, 146 L.Ed.2d 914

JUSTICE BREYER delivered the opinion of the Court.

[In 1992, petitioner Alexis Geier, driving a 1987 Honda Accord, collided with a tree and was seriously injured. The car was equipped with manual shoulder and lap belts which Geier had buckled up at the time. The car was not equipped with airbags or other passive restraint devices. Geier and her parents, also petitioners, sued the car's manufacturer, American Honda under District of Columbia tort law. They claimed that American Honda had designed its car negligently and defectively because it lacked a driver's side airbag. The District Court dismissed the lawsuit on grounds of preemption: Because Geier's lawsuit sought to establish a stricter safety standard (an airbag requirement) than FMVSS 208 (which permits choice between airbags and passive restraints), the asserted tort claim was pre-empted by a provision of the Safety Act of 1966 which pre-empts "any safety standard" that is not identical to a federal safety standard applicable to the same aspect of performance, 15 U.S.C. § 1392(d). Disagreeing, the Supreme Court held that the pre-emption provision was inapplicable because of a saving provision, which says that "compliance with" a federal safety standard "does not exempt any person from any liability under common law." 15 U.S.C. § 1397(k). The saving clause assumes that there are some significant number of common-law liability cases to save.]

[III] We have just said that the saving clause *at least* removes tort actions from the scope of the express pre-emption clause. Does it do more? In particular, does it foreclose or limit the operation of ordinary pre-emption principles insofar as those principles instruct us to read statutes as pre-empting state laws (including common-law rules) that "actually conflict" with the statute or federal standards promulgated thereunder? Petitioners concede, as they must in light of *Freightliner Corp. v. Myrick*, 514 U.S. 280 (1995), that the pre-emption provision, by itself, does not foreclose (through negative implication) "any possibility of implied [conflict] pre-emption." But they argue that the saving clause has that very effect. * * *

Nothing in the language of the saving clause suggests an intent to save state-law tort actions that conflict with federal regulations. The words "compliance" and "does not exempt" sound as if they simply bar a special kind of defense, namely, a defense that compliance with a federal standard automatically exempts a defendant from state law, whether the Federal Government meant that standard to be an absolute requirement or only a minimum one. See Restatement (Third) of Torts: Products Liability § 4(b), Comment *e* (1997) (distinguishing between state-law compliance defense and a federal claim of pre-emption). It is difficult to understand why Congress would have insisted on a compliance-with-federal-regulation precondition to the provision's applicability had it wished the Act to "save" all state-law tort actions, regardless of their potential threat to the objectives of federal safety standards promulgated under that Act. Nor does our interpretation conflict with the purpose of the saving provision, say by rendering it ineffectual. As we have previously explained, the saving provision still makes clear that the express pre-emption provision does not of its own force pre-empt common-law tort actions. And it thereby preserves those actions that seek to establish greater safety than the minimum safety achieved by a federal regulation intended to provide a floor.

Moreover, this Court has repeatedly "declined to give broad effect to saving clauses where doing so would upset the careful regulatory scheme established by federal law." *United States v. Locke*, 529 U.S. 89 (2000). We find this concern applicable in the present case. And we conclude that the saving clause foresees—it does not foreclose—the possibility that a federal safety standard will pre-empt a state common-law tort action with which it conflicts. We do not understand the dissent to disagree, for it acknowledges that ordinary pre-emption principles apply, at least sometimes. * * *

Why, in any event, would Congress not have wanted ordinary pre-emption principles to apply where an actual conflict with a federal objective is at stake? Some such principle is needed. In its absence, state law could impose legal duties that would conflict directly with federal regulatory mandates, say, by premising liability upon the presence of the very windshield retention requirements that federal law requires. Insofar as petitioners' argument would permit common-law actions that "actually conflict" with federal regulations, it would take from those who would enforce a federal law the very ability to achieve the law's congressionally mandated objectives that the Constitution, through the operation of ordinary pre-emption principles, seeks to protect. To the extent that such an interpretation of the saving provision reads into a particular federal law toleration of a conflict that those principles would otherwise forbid, it permits that law to defeat its own objectives, or potentially, as the Court has put it before, to " 'destroy itself.' " We do not claim that Congress lacks the constitutional power to write a statute that mandates such a complex type of state/federal relationship. But there is no reason to believe Congress has done so here. * * *

[IV] The basic question, then, is whether a common-law "no airbag" action like the one before us actually conflicts with FMVSS 208. We hold that it does.

In petitioners' and the dissent's view, FMVSS 208 sets a minimum airbag standard. As far as FMVSS 208 is concerned, the more airbags, and the sooner, the better. But that was not the Secretary's view. DOT's comments, which accompanied the promulgation of FMVSS 208, make clear that the standard deliberately provided the manufacturer with a range of choices among different passive restraint devices. Those choices would bring about a mix of different devices introduced gradually over time; and FMVSS 208 would thereby lower costs, overcome technical safety problems, encourage technological development, and win widespread consumer acceptance—all of which would promote FMVSS 208's safety objectives. See generally 49 Fed. Reg. 28962 (1984).

[Justice Breyer surveyed the history of rule 208, already explicated in this chapter.] Read in light of this history, DOT's own contemporaneous explanation of FMVSS 208 makes clear that the 1984 version of FMVSS 208 reflected the following significant considerations. First, buckled up seatbelts are a vital ingredient of automobile safety. Second, despite the enormous and unnecessary risks that a passenger runs by not buckling up manual lap and shoulder belts, more than 80% of front seat passengers would leave their manual seatbelts unbuckled. Third, airbags could make up for the dangers caused by unbuckled manual belts, but they could not make up for them entirely.

Fourth, passive restraint systems had their own disadvantages, for example, the dangers associated with, intrusiveness of, and corresponding public dislike for, nondetachable automatic belts. Fifth, airbags brought with them their own special risks to safety, such as the risk of danger to out-of-position occupants (usually children) in small cars.

Sixth, airbags were expected to be significantly more expensive than other passive restraint devices, raising the average cost of a vehicle price $320 for full frontal airbags over the cost of a car with manual lap and shoulder seatbelts (and potentially much more if production volumes were low). And the agency worried that the high replacement cost—estimated to be $800—could lead car owners to refuse to replace them after deployment. Seventh, the public, for reasons of cost, fear, or physical intrusiveness, might resist installation or use of any of the then-available passive restraint devices—a particular concern with respect to airbags.

FMVSS 208 reflected these considerations in several ways. Most importantly, that standard deliberately sought variety—a mix of several different passive restraint systems. It did so by setting a performance requirement for passive restraint devices and allowing manufacturers to choose among different passive restraint mechanisms, such as airbags, automatic belts, or other passive restraint technologies to satisfy that requirement. And DOT explained why FMVSS 208 sought the mix of devices that it expected its performance standard to produce. DOT wrote that it had *rejected* a proposed FMVSS 208 "all airbag" standard because of safety concerns (perceived or real) associated with airbags, which concerns threatened a "backlash" more easily overcome "if airbags" were "not the only way of complying." It added that a mix of devices would help develop data on comparative effectiveness, would allow the industry time to overcome the safety problems and the high production costs associated with airbags, and would facilitate the development of alternative, cheaper, and safer passive restraint systems. And it would thereby build public confidence necessary to avoid another interlock-type fiasco.

The 1984 FMVSS 208 standard also deliberately sought a *gradual* phase-in of passive restraints. It required the manufacturers to equip only 10% of their car fleet manufactured after September 1, 1986, with passive restraints. It then increased the percentage in three annual stages, up to 100% of the new car fleet for cars manufactured after September 1, 1989. And it explained that the phased-in requirement would allow more time for manufacturers to develop airbags or other, better, safer passive restraint systems. It would help develop information about the comparative effectiveness of different systems, would lead to a mix in which airbags and other nonseatbelt passive restraint systems played a more prominent role than would otherwise result, and would promote public acceptance. * * *

In effect, petitioners' tort action depends upon its claim that manufacturers had a duty to install an airbag when they manufactured the 1987 Honda Accord. Such a state law—*i.e.*, a rule of state tort law imposing such a duty—by its terms would have required manufacturers of all similar cars to install airbags rather than other passive restraint systems, such as automatic belts or passive interiors. It thereby would have presented an obstacle to the variety and mix of devices that the federal regulation sought. It would have required all manufacturers to have installed airbags in respect to the entire District-of-Columbia-related portion of their 1987 new car fleet, even though FMVSS 208 at that time required only that 10% of a manufacturer's nationwide fleet be equipped with any passive restraint device at all. It thereby also would have stood as an obstacle to the gradual passive restraint phase-in that the federal regulation deliberately imposed. In addition, it could have made less likely the adoption of a state mandatory buckle-up law. Because the rule of law for which petitioners contend would have stood "as an obstacle to the accomplishment and execution of" the important means-related federal objectives that we have just discussed, it is pre-empted. * * *

One final point: We place some weight upon DOT's interpretation of FMVSS 208's objectives and its conclusion, as set forth in the Government's brief, that a tort suit such as this one would " 'stand as an obstacle to the accomplishment and execution' " of those objectives. Brief for United States as *Amicus Curiae* 25–26 (quoting *Hines v. Davidowitz*, 312 U.S. 52, 67 (1941)). Congress has delegated to DOT authority to implement the statute; the subject matter is technical; and the relevant history and background are complex and extensive. The agency is likely to have a thorough understanding of its own regulation and its objectives and is "uniquely qualified" to comprehend the likely impact of state requirements. And DOT has explained FMVSS 208's objectives, and the interference that "no airbag" suits pose thereto, consistently over time. In these circumstances, the agency's own views should make a difference. * * *

[We omit the dissenting opinion of JUSTICE STEVENS, joined by JUSTICES SOUTER, THOMAS, and GINSBURG. Most of the dissenters' arguments are mentioned in the notes following the decision.]

NOTES ON GEIER AND FEDERAL PREEMPTION OF STATE LAW

1. *The Debate Among the Justices.* Key to Justice Breyer's opinion is the Court's belief that allowing state courts to find that airbags are sometimes required to satisfy the manufacturer's duty of care would undermine the federal statute's compromise, whereby manufacturers would have choices. Justice Stevens's dissent objected that case-by-case adjudications would not establish a hard-and-fast rule that airbags were required; not only could different juries reach different results, but manufacturers could win all the cases if they showed airbags to be ineffective or other methods just as effective. See generally Peter L. Strauss, *The Story of* Geier v. American Honda Motor Co.: *Statutes, Regulation, and the Common Law*, in *Statutory Interpretation Stories* 294, 320–32 (Eskridge, Frickey & Garrett eds., 2011).

The dissenters also argued that the Court ignored the *Cipollone* presumption and was too willing to preempt the state tort suit. Was it clear that preemption was required by the "clear and manifest purpose of Congress"? Justice Stevens also insisted that the majority's holding was in tension with the saving clause: "The saving clause in the Safety Act unambiguously expresses a decision by Congress that compliance with a federal safety standard does not exempt a manufacturer from *any* common-law liability. In light of this reference to common-law liability in the saving clause, Congress surely would have included a similar reference in § 1392(d) if it had intended to pre-empt such liability. Cf. *Chicago v. Environmental Defense Fund,* 511 U.S. 328, 338 (1994) (noting presumption that Congress acts intentionally when it includes particular language in one section of a statute but omits it in another)." Should the Court be especially chary of preempting state common law under "inconsistent application" preemption when there is a saving clause?

Note, finally, that state law is essentially preempted by an agency rule and not by a statutory provision. Although the agency had authority to issue the rule, see *State Farm*, the Court ought to think twice before giving the rule preemptive authority to displace state law, especially in light of the federalism presumption of *Cipollone*. Should the Court allow agency opinions to venture too far into constitutionally murky territory or should the Justices essentially remand the issue for Congress, not just the agency, to make such constitutionally sensitive policy choices. Should this argument have had some weight in *Geier*?

2. *Titanic Concerns: Underenforcement versus Overenforcement of Safety Norms?* Addressing this issue, Ralph Nader and Joe Page had argued in *Automobile–Design Liability and Compliance with Federal Standards*, 64 Geo. Wash. L. Rev. 415, 419 (1996), that the statutory minimum should not preclude state regulation that raised the floor. Apart from the saving clause, which seemed to embody this philosophy, Nader and Page invoked the *Titanic* precedent. That famous vessel had fully "complied with British governmental regulations setting minimum requirements for lifeboats when it left port on its final, fateful voyage with boats capable of carrying only about [half] of the people on board," W. Wade, *The Titanic: End of a Dream* 68 (1986), yet one might reasonably conclude that the *Titanic* had not satisfied its duty of care

to the other half of the passengers who lost their lives when the ship sunk in ice-cold waters. Because people's lives are at stake just as much in auto safety regulation, Nader and Page maintained that states ought to be able to raise the floor. The dissenting Justices agreed and cited their article and its *Titanic* analogy. Their position was that the majority was standing in the way of permissible enforcement of the safety norm. The Court may have even been seen as pandering to the auto industry's determination to *underenforce* safety norms.

The majority did not respond but might have said that the regulatory scheme sought a balance of safety and cost. To be blunt, NHTSA was willing to trade off human lives (more people would die in accidents each year) for cost savings by manufacturers. This may seem terrible, but don't forget that the nation's decision to allow automobiles on the road and to travel 65 miles per hour has predictable costs in human lives each year—lives that could be saved if all of us suffered the inconvenience of not being able to drive (or drive so fast) on the open road. The majority's view was that Congress had authorized the agency to make these kinds of trade-offs (recall Justice White's opinion in *State Farm*, not to mention Justice Stevens's opinion in *Chevron*). Hence, the dissenters' position would have *overenforced* safety norms.

3. *Should the Court Defer to the Agency in Preemption Cases?* How should *Chevron/Skidmore* interact with *Cipollone* in these cases? Justice Thomas has reconciled the different authorities with the suggestion that the Court should be *less* deferential if the federal agency is pushing for preemption and *more* deferential when the agency is arguing against preemption, especially in conflict or field preemption cases. *Pharmaceutical Res. & Mfrs. v. Walsh*, 538 U.S. 644, 675–83 (2003) (Thomas, J., concurring in the judgment). This is consistent with his dissenting vote in *Geier*, but not his dissenting vote in the Oregon Aid-in-Dying Case. And, of course, the *Geier* majority gives significant credit to the Department's views.

Nina A. Mendelson, Chevron *and Preemption*, 102 Mich. L. Rev. 737 (2004), argues against *Chevron* deference for agency views regarding preemption. Although she demonstrates that agencies are more accountable to state interests than the Court or (surprisingly) Congress, she cautions against *Chevron* deference because courts continue to have some comparative advantages in evaluating preemption claims and because agencies will often tend to expand their own authority at the expense of the states. Mendelson believes that agencies often have useful contributions and so favors *Skidmore* deference as appropriate—the same accommodation reached by Justice Breyer in *Geier* and Justice Kennedy in *Oregon*.

Wyeth v. Levine, 555 U.S. 555 (2009). Directly injecting the drug Phenergan into a patient's vein creates a significant risk of catastrophic consequences. A Vermont jury found that Wyeth, the manufacturer of the drug, had failed to provide an adequate warning of that risk and awarded damages to Diana Levine to compensate her for the amputation of her arm. Because the warnings on Phenergan's label had been deemed sufficient by the federal Food and Drug Administration (FDA) when it approved Wyeth's new drug application in 1955 and when it later approved changes in the drug's labeling, Wyeth challenged the state tort verdict on the ground that it was preempted by the Food, Drug & Cosmetic Act of 1938 (FDCA), which bars unsafe drugs.

Justice Stevens's opinion for the Court (joined by Justices Kennedy, Souter, Ginsburg, and Breyer) ruled that the FDCA did not preempt these state tort claims. Justice Stevens started with this presumption: "[i]n all preemption cases, and particularly in those in which Congress has 'legislated . . . in a field which the States have traditionally occupied,' . . . we 'start with the assumption that the historic police powers of the States were not to be superseded by the Federal Act unless that was the clear and manifest purpose of Congress.'" (quoting *Medtronic, Inc. v. Lohr,* 518 U.S. 470, 485 (1996)).

Wyeth's main argument rested upon a 2007 amendment to the FDCA that required FDA approval of drug labels. Because the FDA had okayed the warning that was the basis for the state tort suit, Wyeth argued that state tort law was implicitly preempted because it would be impossible for Wyeth to comply with both its federal duty to use the approved label and its state duty to provide more detailed warnings (the doctrine of "impossibility preemption"). In an *amicus* brief, the FDA agreed and urged the Court to find preemption here. Justice Stevens rejected that argument, in part because federal law allowed Wyeth to amend its label without FDA approval based on safety concerns of the sort raised by the state tort suit. Thus, it was *not* impossible for Wyeth to comply with both federal law and state law. More generally, Justice Stevens ruled that the federal statute vests primary responsibility for labeling with drug companies, not the FDA, which is merely a monitor.

Wyeth and the FDA also argued that state tort liability undermined the purposes of federal law (the doctrine of "obstacle preemption"). In a preface to a 2006 rule, the FDA had opined that drug standards in the statute represented *both* a floor *and* a ceiling for manufacturers; hence, state tort liability was preempted when the manufacturer was following the label requirements of the federal law.

"In prior cases, we have given 'some weight' to an agency's views about the impact of tort law on federal objectives when 'the subject matter is technica[l] and the relevant history and background are complex and extensive.' *Geier.* Even in such cases, however, we have not deferred to an agency's *conclusion* that state law is pre-empted. Rather, we have attended to an agency's explanation of how state law affects the regulatory scheme. While agencies have no special authority to pronounce on pre-emption absent delegation by Congress, they do have a unique understanding of the statutes they administer and an attendant ability to make informed determinations about how state requirements may pose an 'obstacle to the accomplishment and execution of the full purposes and objectives of Congress.' [See *Geier.*] The weight we accord the agency's explanation of state law's impact on the federal scheme depends on its thoroughness, consistency, and persuasiveness. Cf. *Mead*; *Skidmore.*

"Under this standard, the FDA's 2006 preamble does not merit deference. When the FDA issued its notice of proposed rulemaking in December 2000, it explained that the rule would 'not contain policies that have federalism implications or that preempt State law.' In 2006, the agency finalized the rule and, without offering States or other interested parties notice or opportunity for comment, articulated a sweeping position on the FDCA's pre-emptive effect in the regulatory preamble. The agency's views on state law are inherently suspect in light of this procedural failure.

"Further, the preamble is at odds with what evidence we have of Congress' purposes, and it reverses the FDA's own longstanding position without providing a reasoned explanation, including any discussion of how state law has interfered with the FDA's regulation of drug labeling during decades of coexistence. The FDA's 2006 position plainly does not reflect the agency's own view at all times relevant to this litigation. Not once prior to Levine's injury did the FDA suggest that state tort law stood as an obstacle to its statutory mission. To the contrary, it cast federal labeling standards as a floor upon which States could build and repeatedly disclaimed any attempt to pre-empt failure-to-warn claims. For instance, in 1998, the FDA stated that it did 'not believe that the evolution of state tort law [would] cause the development of standards that would be at odds with the agency's regulations.' It further noted that, in establishing 'minimal standards' for drug labels, it did not intend 'to preclude the states from imposing additional labeling requirements.' "

Justice Breyer (the author of *Geier*) wrote a concurring opinion, reserving judgment on the possibility that the FDA could in the future adopt a rule having preemptive force (as in *Geier*) if the agency found a specific clash between federal policy and state tort lawsuits.

Justice Thomas concurred in the judgment. "I have become increasingly skeptical of this Court's 'purposes and objectives' pre-emption jurisprudence. Under this approach, the Court routinely invalidates state laws based on perceived conflicts with broad federal policy objectives, legislative history, or generalized notions of congressional purposes that are not embodied within the text of federal law." Drawing from the Tenth Amendment, the Constitution's federal structure, and Article I, Section 7, Justice Thomas argued that, as a matter of constitutional principle, state law remains the default law for citizens unless there is a *federal statutory text* that preempts it under Article VI (the Supremacy Clause). Hence, he was skeptical of obstacle preemption doctrine entirely and would apply impossibility preemption doctrine very cautiously—and was unwilling to apply either doctrine to the Levine case.

Justice Alito (joined by Chief Justice Roberts and Justice Scalia) dissented. Justice Alito relied on the notion that the FDA is responsible for determining drug safety and, hence, that its determinations are both a floor and a ceiling for a manufacturer's legal responsibility. Cf. *Riegel v. Medtronic, Inc.*, 552 U.S. 312, (2008) (ruling that federal regulation preempts state tort suits for warning defects for medical devices, also regulated by the FDA). Indeed, Justice Alito believed the case was controlled by *Geier*.

"Notwithstanding the statute's saving clause, and notwithstanding the fact that Congress gave the Secretary authority to set only "minimum" safety standards, we held Geier's state tort suit pre-empted. In reaching that result, we relied heavily on the view of the Secretary of Transportation—expressed in an *amicus* brief—that Standard 208 " 'embodies the Secretary's policy judgment that safety would best be promoted if manufacturers installed *alterna-*

tive protection systems in their fleets rather than one particular system in every car." ' Because the Secretary determined that a menu of alternative technologies was 'safe,' the doctrine of conflict pre-emption barred Geier's efforts to deem some of those federally approved alternatives 'unsafe' under state tort law.

"The same rationale applies here. Through Phenergan's label, the FDA offered medical professionals a menu of federally approved, 'safe' and 'effective' alternatives—including IV push—for administering the drug. Through a state tort suit, respondent attempted to deem IV push 'unsafe' and 'ineffective.' To be sure, federal law does not prohibit Wyeth from contraindicating IV push, just as federal law did not prohibit Honda from installing airbags in all its cars. But just as we held that States may not compel the latter, so, too, are States precluded from compelling the former. If anything, a finding of pre-emption is even more appropriate here because the FDCA—unlike the National Traffic and Motor Safety Vehicle Act—contains no evidence that Congress intended the FDA to set only 'minimum standards,' and the FDCA does not contain a saving clause."

NOTE ON *WYETH* AND AGENCY VIEWS IN PREEMPTION CASES

Recall that Professor Nina Mendelson argued in Chevron *and Preemption*, 102 Mich. L. Rev. 737 (2004), that *Chevron* deference should presumptively not be available for agency interpretations preempting state law. *Wyeth* seems consistent with her position and reasoning. Consider other patterns we have discerned in the Supreme Court preemption decisions between 1984 and 2006:

• The Court was more skeptical of agency interpretations that expanded national power than of those that respected the regulatory authority of the states. When an agency argued against preemption (39 cases, 1984–2006) the Court agreed with its assessment 84.6% of the time, an astounding rate of agreement. So *Wyeth* was squarely in the mainstream of Supreme Court practice in this regard.

• For technical areas of law, as in *Geier,* the Court was super-deferential: For the 31 cases involving transportation, energy, and communications, the Court agreed with agency recommendations (usually favoring preemption) a whopping 87.1% of the time. Health law cases, such as *Wyeth* and *Riegel*, had lower but still impressive agreement rates. Normative areas such as civil rights and criminal law saw much less impressive agency performances.

• There was no significant difference between agency win rates for express preemption cases (97 cases, with 72.2% agreement rate) and for conflict or obstacle preemption cases (29 cases, with 72.4% agreement rate), perhaps surprising in light of the Article I, § 7 and the federalism concerns raised by Justice Thomas against conflict or obstacle preemption in *Wyeth* and other cases.

See William N. Eskridge Jr., *Vetogates,* Chevron, *Preemption*, 83 Notre Dame L. Rev. 1441 (2008) (reporting and analyzing these data).

Note that federalism-loving Justice Scalia dissented in *Wyeth* and is probably unsympathetic to the Mendelson position. Why would a strong federalist favor an agency-driven preemption of traditional state law? Justice Thomas's position, also from a strong federalist orientation, is very different from Justice Scalia's. Accord, Bradford R. Clark, *Separation of Powers as a Safeguard of Federalism*, 79 Tex. L. Rev. 1321 (2001). Is there any principled reason a federalist should follow Justice Scalia over Justice Thomas as to this issue?

5. Deference and Stare Decisis

In *National Cable & Telecommunications Ass'n v. Brand X Internet Servs.*, 545 U.S. 967 (2005), the Supreme Court *Chevron*-deferred to FCC interpretations even though they went against lower court constructions of the statute. *Brand X* confirmed the longstanding view that agencies can refuse to acquiesce in lower court interpretations and can continue to litigate statutory issues. But what if the Supreme Court has construed the statute? Under what circumstances should the Court *Chevron*-defer in the face of contrary Supreme Court precedent?

Neal v. United States, 516 U.S. 284 (1996). In *Chapman v. United States*, 500 U.S. 493 (1991), the Court had interpreted 18 U.S.C. § 841(b)(1)(A)(v)'s mandatory minimum sentence for LSD to include blotter paper in determining weight of the substance possessed by the defendant. (*Chapman* affirmed the Seventh Circuit's judgment in *Marshall*, Chapter 2, § 2.) In 1991, the Sentencing Commission also considered the blotter paper in determining the base sentence for defendants convicted of LSD possession. The Commission reversed that position in 1993, retroactively amending its Guidelines to assign a smaller weight for each LSD dose.

Having been convicted for selling 11,456 doses of LSD on blotter paper, Meirl Neal moved to reduce his sentence, not only under the Guidelines, but also beneath the ten-year mandatory minimum of § 841. He argued that the Court should reconsider *Chapman* in light of the Commission's revision of the Guidelines. Writing for a unanimous Court, **Justice Kennedy** rejected Neal's argument.

To begin with, Justice Kennedy found that the Commission's Guideline was only intended to affect the base sentence level, and not the 1986 statute fixing mandatory minimum sentences for drug offenses. (Indeed, the Guidelines recognize the distinct regulatory goals, as well as the tensions, of the two sentencing regimes.) This was a tacit acknowledgment by the Commission that it has no authority to override the 1986 statute, as authoritatively construed by the Supreme Court.

"Once we have determined a statute's meaning, we adhere to our ruling under the doctrine of *stare decisis*, and we assess an agency's later interpretation of the statute against that settled law." The Court will overrule precedents when (1) there is "compelling evidence bearing on Congress's original intent"; (2) new legal developments have weakened the "conceptual underpinnings" of the prior decisions; or (3) the prior decisions are irreconcilable with "competing legal doctrines or policies."

E.g., *Patterson v. McLean Credit Union*, 491 U.S. 164, 173 (1989). But the new Guideline did not create such a compelling case, and the Court held firm to *stare decisis*. "Congress, not this Court, has the responsibility for revising its statutes. Were we to alter our statutory interpretations from case to case, Congress would have less reason to exercise its responsibility to correct statutes that are thought to be unwise or unfair."

Justice Kennedy concluded with a reservation. Hypothetical situations involving very heavy carriers and very little LSD (such as one dose in a glass of juice) could present due process problems that the routine case would not. In light of the earlier materials, how should the Court handle such cases? Should it strike down the statute as applied, or construe it narrowly?

NOTE ON *CHEVRON* AND STARE DECISIS: *THE CASE OF THE "OVER-REGULATED" WETLANDS*

An issue not settled in *Neal* is whether a Supreme Court decision, such as *Chevron* itself, deferring to an agency interpretation within the zone of reasonableness left by the statute, then bars the agency from changing its interpretation. The reasoning of *Chevron* suggests not: "An initial agency interpretation is not carved in stone. On the contrary, the agency, to engage in informal rulemaking, must consider varying interpretations and the wisdom of its policy on a continuing basis." 467 U.S. at 863–64.

Periodically, the Court or individual Justices will signal this flexibility to agencies. In *Rapanos v. United States*, 547 U.S. 715 (2006), the Court evaluated the broad understanding held by the Army Corps of Engineers of its jurisdiction protecting "waters of the United States," 33 U.S.C. § 1362(7). The Corps took the position that private backfilling of wetlands adjacent to a non-navigable tributary could not be pursued without a permit. A plurality of the Court rejected the Corps' broad assertion of jurisdiction, mainly because it went beyond the statute's plain meaning, *Rapanos* (Scalia, J., plurality opinion), but also because the Corps' sweeping definition would be an "unprecedented intrusion into traditional state authority" over wetlands, *id.* (citing *BFP*, Chapter 2, § 3), and "stretches the outer limits of Congress's commerce power and raises difficult questions about the ultimate scope of that power." *Id.* Concurring only in the judgment, Justice Kennedy read into the statute a requirement that the Corps' jurisdiction depends on a "significant nexus between the wetlands in question and the navigable waters in the traditional sense." *Rapanos* (concurring opinion).

All five majority Justices were bothered by the Corps' disinclination to admit any significant limiting principle to its jurisdiction over wet places in the United States. In a separate concurring opinion, Chief Justice Roberts urged the Corps or the EPA to clarify the reach of their jurisdiction through legislative notice-and-comment rulemaking, as they had started to do in 2003 (after an earlier Supreme Court defeat). "Given the broad, somewhat ambiguous, but nonetheless clearly limiting terms Congress employed in the Clean Water Act, the Corps and the EPA would have enjoyed plenty of room to operate in developing *some* notion of an outer bound to the reach of their authority." *Rapanos* (concurring opinion). Justice Kennedy agreed, and Justice Breyer (in dissent) urged the Corps to develop regulations addressing Justice Kennedy's nexus approach.

Although a particularly dramatic example, the Case of the Backfilled Wetlands illustrates the reach and limits of *stare decisis* in *Chevron* cases. (All nine Justices agreed that the Corps' interpretation was governed by *Chevron*.) On the one hand, the Corps is probably bound by the Kennedy "nexus" requirement, as it reflected the outer bound of jurisdiction adopted by a Court majority. On the other hand, the Corps has considerable discretion to develop particular rules and/or standards for different scenarios. Justice Kennedy's test is so general that the agency surely has a lot of room for discretionary but reasoned judgment. Note that the *Chevron* room for discretionary judgment depends in large part on how broadly (Kennedy) or narrowly (Scalia) the Court writes its opinion about what the statute *requires* of the agency.

For other cases where concurring Justices have made similar pitches, see *Norfolk Southern Ry. v. Shankin*, 529 U.S. 344 (2000) (Breyer, J., concurring); *Christensen v. Harris County*, 529 U.S. 576 (2000) (Souter, J., concurring).

6. Deference in National Security and Foreign Affairs

In *United States v. Curtiss–Wright Export Co.*, 299 U.S. 304 (1936), the Court opined that "congressional legislation ... within the international field must often accord to the President a degree of discretion and freedom from statutory restriction which would not be admissible were domestic affairs alone involved." The source of this discretion in statutory enforcement was grounded in Article II—in the inherent powers of the President to represent the nation in foreign matters and to protect America's security interests.

Curtiss–Wright deference is theoretically distinguishable from *Chevron* deference. Because it rests upon the President's Article II powers, rather than Congress's Article I authority, *Curtiss–Wright* deference does not necessarily depend upon a statutory delegation of lawmaking responsibilities, although the power of its presumption might be augmented by such delegation. Moreover, the *Curtiss–Wright* rule is a more deferential standard than *Chevron:* the executive department interpretation prevails not only in cases of statutory ambiguity, but also in cases where Congress has not clearly trumped the agency or presidential construction.

For example, the Court in *Department of the Navy v. Egan*, 484 U.S. 518 (1988), ruled against judicial review of presidential revocation of security clearances. Given the President's broad powers to protect national security and conduct foreign policy, the Court reasoned that, "unless Congress specifically has provided otherwise, courts traditionally [should be] ... reluctant to intrude upon the authority of the Executive in military and national security affairs." *Egan* is a strong post-*Chevron* statement of *Curtiss–Wright* deference, but is a rare instance where the Court invokes such deference. See Eskridge & Baer, *Deference Continuum* (reporting that the Court invoked *Curtiss–Wright* deference in fewer than

10% of its foreign affairs and national security docket). For a recent debate over this doctrine, consider the following case.

Hamdan v. Rumsfeld, 548 U.S. 557 (2006). The Supreme Court ruled that presidential military commissions dispensing summary justice could not legally try Salim Ahmed Hamdan, a Yemeni national apprehended by American allies in Afghanistan and turned over to American authorities; since 2002, he has been detained at our naval base in Guantanamo. The government claimed that Hamdan was the chauffeur of terrorist Osama bin Laden and had engaged in various activities supporting al Qaeda. In 2003, President Bush deemed Hamdan triable by a military commission as defined in the Military Order of November 13, 2001. In 2004, the United States charged him with "conspiracy to commit crimes triable by military commission" and ruled that the commissions would not follow the procedures provided for court martials in the Uniform Code of Military Justice (UCMJ) or for prisoners of war stipulated in the Geneva Conventions.

In a petition for habeas corpus, Hamdan challenged the legality of such a trial. Reversing the D.C. Circuit, the Supreme Court, in an opinion by **Justice Stevens**, agreed with Hamdan. **Justice Kennedy** concurred in most of the Stevens opinion and wrote a lengthy separate statement. Three Justices (Scalia, Thomas, Alito) dissented; Chief Justice Roberts did not participate (as he had joined the lower court opinion the Court was reviewing, and reversing).

Justice Stevens' opinion provided the following background which was not disputed among the Justices: "The common law governing military commissions may be gleaned from past practice and what sparse legal precedent exists. Commissions historically have been used in three situations. First, they have substituted for civilian courts at times and in places where martial law has been declared. Their use in these circumstances has raised constitutional questions, see *Duncan v. Kahanamoku*, 327 U.S. 304 (1946); [*Ex parte*] *Milligan*, 4 Wall. 2, 121–122 [1866], but is well recognized. Second, commissions have been established to try civilians 'as part of a temporary military government over occupied enemy territory or territory regained from an enemy where civilian government cannot and does not function.' *Duncan*, 327 U. S., at 314 see *Milligan*, 4 Wall., at 141–142 (Chase, C.J., concurring in judgment) (distinguishing '*martial law proper*' from '*military government*' in occupied territory). Illustrative of this second kind of commission is the one that was established, with jurisdiction to apply the German Criminal Code, in occupied Germany following the end of World War II. See *Madsen v. Kinsella*, 343 U.S. 341, 356 (1952).

"The third type of commission, convened as an 'incident to the conduct of war' when there is a need 'to seize and subject to disciplinary measures those enemies who in their attempt to thwart or impede our military effort have violated the law of war,' [*Ex parte*] *Quirin*, 317 U.S. [1], at 28–29 [1942], has been described as 'utterly different' from the other two. Not only is its jurisdiction limited to offenses cognizable during time of war, but its role is primarily a factfinding one—to determine, typically on the battlefield itself, whether the defendant has violated the law of war. The last time the U.S. Armed Forces used the law-of-war military commission was during World War II. In *Quirin*, this Court sanctioned President Roosevelt's use of such a tribunal to try Nazi saboteurs captured on American soil during the War. And in *Yamashita*, we held that a military commission had jurisdiction to try a Japanese commander for failing to prevent troops under his command from committing atrocities in the Philippines. 327 U.S. 1 [1946]."

The Administration's military commissions were of the third type. Most of the debate within the Court involved three fascinating matters of statutory interpretation and military law.

1. *Justiciability.* **Justice Stevens'** opinion for the Court ruled that neither the Detainee Treatment Act of 2005 (DTA) (which sharply curtailed judicial review in many respects) nor principles of abstention supported the United States' position that the Court should dismiss Hamdan's habeas petition on justiciability grounds. The Court worried that a broad interpretation of the DTA would "rais[e] grave questions about Congress' authority to impinge upon this Court's appellate jurisdiction, particularly in habeas cases." Speaking for the three dissenters, **Justice Scalia** argued that the case should have been dismissed on these grounds. Justice Scalia summarily dismissed Hamdan's argument that curtailment of judicial review raised constitutional concerns. The DTA provides a narrow mechanism for Hamdan to present his constitutional arguments, and the Exceptions Clause of Article III allows Congress wide latitude to regulate the Court's appellate jurisdiction.

2. *Authorization: The Framework.* The main issue was whether the President had the authority to deploy these military commissions to impose sanctions (including death) on suspected enemy combatants. **Justice Stevens** emphasized the primacy of Congress in setting rules for military engagement. "Exigency alone, of course, will not justify the establishment and use of penal tribunals not contemplated by Article I, § 8 and Article III, § 1 of the Constitution unless some other part of that document authorizes a response to the felt need. See *Ex parte Milligan* ('Certainly no part of the judicial power of the country was conferred on [military commissions]'). And that authority, if it exists, can derive only from the powers granted jointly to the President and Congress in time of war. *Yamashita*.

"The Constitution makes the President the 'Commander in Chief of the Armed Forces,' Art. II, § 2, cl. 1, but vests in Congress the powers to 'declare War . . . and make Rules concerning Captures on Land and Water,' Art. I, § 8, cl. 11, to 'raise and support Armies,' *id.*, cl. 12, to 'define and punish . . . Offences against the Law of Nations,' *id.*, cl. 10, and 'To make Rules for the Government and Regulation of the land and naval Forces,' *id.*, cl. 14.

"The interplay between these powers was described by Chief Justice Chase in the seminal case of *Ex parte Milligan*:

'The power to make the necessary laws is in Congress; the power to execute in the President. Both powers imply many subordinate and auxiliary powers. Each includes all authorities essential to its due exercise. But neither can the President, in war more than in peace, intrude upon the proper authority of Congress, nor Congress upon the proper authority of the President.... Congress cannot direct the conduct of campaigns, nor can the President, or any commander under him, without the sanction of Congress, institute tribunals for the trial and punishment of offences, either of soldiers or civilians, unless in cases of a controlling necessity, which justifies what it compels, or at least insures acts of indemnity from the justice of the legislature.' 4 Wall., at 139–140.

Whether Chief Justice Chase was correct in suggesting that the President may constitutionally convene military commissions 'without the sanction of Congress' in cases of 'controlling necessity' is a question this Court has not answered definitively, and need not answer today."

Writing for the three dissenters, **Justice Thomas** emphasized that "the structural advantages attendant to the Executive Branch—namely, the decisiveness, 'activity, secrecy, and dispatch' that flow from the Executive's 'unity' (quoting The Federalist No. 70, p. 472 (J. Cooke ed. 1961) (A. Hamilton))—led the Founders to conclude that the 'President ha[s] primary responsibility—along with the necessary power—to protect the national security and to conduct the Nation's foreign relations.' Consistent with this conclusion, the Constitution vests in the President '[t]he executive Power,' Art. II, § 1, provides that he 'shall be Commander in Chief' of the Armed Forces, § 2, and places in him the power to recognize foreign governments[.] This Court has observed that these provisions confer upon the President broad constitutional authority to protect the Nation's security in the manner he deems fit. See, e.g., *Prize Cases*, 67 U.S. 635, 2 Black 635, 668 (1863) ('If a war be made by invasion of a foreign nation, the President is not only authorized but bound to resist force by force ... without waiting for any special legislative authority'); *Fleming v. Page*, 9 How. 603, 615 (1850) (acknowledging that the President has the authority to 'employ [the Nation's Armed Forces] in the manner he may deem most effectual to harass and conquer and subdue the enemy').

"Congress, to be sure, has a substantial and essential role in both foreign affairs and national security. But 'Congress cannot anticipate and legislate with regard to every possible action the President may find it necessary to take or every possible situation in which he might act,' and '[s]uch failure of Congress ... does not, "especially ... in the areas of foreign policy and national security," imply "congressional disapproval" of action taken by the Executive.' *Dames & Moore v. Regan*, 453 U.S. 654, 678 (1981). Rather, in these domains, the fact that Congress has provided the President with broad authorities does not imply—and the Judicial Branch should not infer—that Congress intended to deprive him of particular powers not specifically enumerated. See *Dames & Moore.* ("[T]he enactment of legislation closely related to the question of the President's authority in a particular case which evinces legislative intent to accord the President broad discretion may be considered to invite measures on independent presidential responsibility.')." Following a *Curtiss–Wright* approach strongly deferential to presidential authority, Justice Thomas argued that application of that framework in military matters required *expansive* interpretation of congressional authorizations to meet the unpredictable demands of war.

3. *Authorization: Statutory Analysis.* The Court ruled that the Administration's deployment of a military commission in Hamdan's case was "incompatible with the expressed or implied will of Congress." The dissenters, in contrast, found the matter to fall within the President's "authority is at its maximum, for it includes all that he possesses in his own right plus all that Congress can delegate."

The Court ruled that UCMJ Article 21, adopted in 1950, did *not* authorize the Bush Administration military commissions. **Justice Stevens** offered three reasons: (1) Article 21 authorizes military commissions to try "offenders or offenses" that "by statute or by the law of war may be tried by" such commissions. The government could point to no statute, and conspiracy to commit war crimes is not a recognized violation of the law of war. In contrast, the sabotage in *Quirin* was an accepted violation of the law of war. This reason commanded only a plurality of the eight-Justice Court (Stevens, Souter, Ginsburg, Breyer), but the other two commanded a majority. (2) The military commissions did not comport with UCMJ Article 36(b), which requires uniformity in procedural rules under the UCMJ unless "impracticable." The Court ruled that Article 36(b) creates a baseline whereby the court-martial procedures presumptively apply to military commissions; the Bush Administration's commission's relaxed evidentiary rules and its failure to give the defendant access to all the evidence against him were important departures from the court-martial rules that the Administration could not justify. (3) Until Hamdan is judged to be an enemy combatant, the 1949 Geneva Conventions require that he be subject to punishment only by a "regularly constituted court affording all the judicial guarantees which are recognized as indispensable by civilized peoples."

Justice Kennedy's concurring opinion emphasized the following procedural differences between the Bush Administration military commissions and court-martials that were not justified: (a) quasi-independent military judges preside over court-martials, while any military lawyer can preside over a military commission; (b) the Appointing Authority controls the number of judges and various procedural appeals for military commissions, but not for court-martials; (c) military commissions follow relaxed evidentiary rules and consider evidence without the accused even being present.

Writing for the three dissenters, **Justice Thomas** sharply disagreed. He argued that (a) UCMJ Article 21 constituted an explicit congressional authorization for the military commission in Hamdan's case, and Article 36 constituted virtually a blank check for the President to devise special procedures for those tribunals; (b) the Iraq War Authorization for Military Force was a separate congressional authorization; and (c) the Geneva Conventions create no judicially enforceable rights for unlawful combatants in Hamdan's position. Also speaking for the three dissenters, **Justice Alito** argued that the military commissions satisfy the Geneva Conventions and the requirements of UCMJ Articles 21 and 36.

In his extensive analysis, Justice Thomas approached the same statutory materials that the Court analyzed, but did so with a more expansive eye. Specifically, he deferred to the President's judgment about what was needed to fight terrorism effectively and his interpretation of the relevant statutes and treaties, considered past practice relevant and read it expansively, and stressed the process that the President's Military Order and the DTA afforded accused terrorists like Hamdan.

As to the last point, consider the Government's Brief, page 4: "Petitioner is entitled to appointed military legal counsel, 32 C.F.R. 9.4(c)(2), and may retain a civilian attorney (which he has done), 32 C.F.R. 9.4(c)(2)(iii)(B). Petitioner is entitled to the presumption of innocence, 32 C.F.R. 9.5(b), proof beyond a reasonable doubt, 32 C.F.R. 9.5(c), and the right to remain silent, 32 C.F.R. 9.5(f). He may confront witnesses against him, 32 C.F.R. 9.5(i), and may subpoena his own witnesses, if reasonably available, 32 C.F.R. 9.5(h). Petitioner may personally be present at every stage of the trial unless he engages in disruptive conduct or the prosecution introduces classified or otherwise protected information for which no adequate substitute is available and whose admission will not deprive him of a full and fair trial, 32 C.F.R. 9.5(k); Military Commission Order No. 1 (Dep't of Defense Aug. 31, 2005) § 6(B)(3) and (D)(5)(b). If petitioner is found guilty, the judgment will be reviewed by a review panel, the Secretary of Defense, and the President, if he does not designate the Secretary as the final decisionmaker. 32 C.F.R. 9.6(h). The final judgment is subject to review in the Court of Appeals for the District of Columbia Circuit and ultimately in this Court. See DTA § 1005(e)(3), 119 Stat. 2743; 28 U. S. C. 1254(1)."

NOTE ON CURTISS-WRIGHT *DEFERENCE*

In considering the cogency of Justice Thomas's dissenting opinion, consider the President's "inherent powers" under Article II. (This was the conceptual basis for *Curtiss–Wright* itself.) If there were no statute, the President as Commander-in-Chief would have inherent authority to deal with prisoners of war and enemy combatants. This would include the authority to establish tribunals for the summary trial of enemy agents, prisoners, etc. The UCMJ (1950) channels and perhaps cabins that authority, but the issue in *Hamdan* was what limits the UCMJ actually placed on the President. Article II might require, as *Curtiss–Wright* suggests, that the UCMJ be read to displace the President's inherent authority only when it has clearly done so. See *Egan*. Is there any flaw in this argument?

The issues of military justice and the conduct of the war on terror would seem even more centrally implicated by *Curtiss–Wright* than those adjudicated in *Egan*, yet the *Hamdan* Court applied neither *Curtiss–Wright* nor *Chevron* deference. Is there a sufficient distinction between the two cases? Why were the majority Justices so undeferential in *Hamdan*?

C. QUO VADIS THE *"CHEVRON* REVOLUTION"?

Commentators and judges agree there has been a *"Chevron* Revolution" of some sort, but its contours remain unclear, especially after *Mead*. Schuck & Elliott, Chevron *Station*, demonstrates that *Chevron* had an immediate impact in the D.C. Circuit, at least for the short term. Subsequent scholars report that *Chevron* is now the most cited Supreme Court decision in our history, because lower courts are citing *Chevron* extensively. E.g., Orin S. Kerr, *Shedding Light on* Chevron: *An Empirical Study of the* Chevron *Doctrine in the U.S. Courts of Appeals*, 15 Yale J. on Reg. 1 (1998). Moreover, lower court judges have not only applied *Skidmore* deference in many non-*Chevron* cases, but have applied it with serious attention to agency inputs. See Kristin E. Hickman & Mathew D. Krueger, *In Search of the Modern* Skidmore *Standard*, 107 Colum. L. Rev. 1235 (2007).

There is also anecdotal evidence that agencies themselves have internalized the new *Chevron* regime as freeing them up to make more decisions on policy or political rather than legal lines. See E. Donald Elliot, Chevron *Matters: How the* Chevron *Doctrine Redefined the Roles of Congress, Courts, and Agencies in Environmental Law*, 16 Vill. Envtl. L.J. 1, 11–12 (2005). There is even more systematic evidence that the lower courts are not only applying *Skidmore,* but have agreed with agency interpretations in more than 60% of the *Skidmore* cases decided in the last five years. See Hickman & Krueger, *Modern* Skidmore *Standard*.

The evidence is most equivocal at the Supreme Court itself, however. The Court was highly deferential to agency rules and interpretations before *Chevron* and has continued to be deferential after *Chevron*. It remains unclear whether *Chevron* has had any influence at the Supreme Court level—beyond creating the increasingly complicated legisprudence that we have presented in this section. Consider matters concretely. Is there any reason to believe that the Court would have decided the leading cases in this chapter any differently in the pre-*Chevron* era? Except for Justice Breyer's opinion in *Geier*, the opinions for the Court were *reasoned* differently under the *Chevron* criteria, but the fundamental role of agency views, the key precepts, and the results in the cases are not affected at all in our view.

Also, the Supreme Court follows a more elaborate *deference continuum* than is captured by the simple *Chevron–Skidmore* dichotomy. The

Eskridge and Baer study gives us a complete lay of the land in cases between *Chevron* and *Hamdan* where there was an agency interpretation.

Supreme Court Deference Regimes, *Chevron* to *Hamdan*

Deference Regime (% Cases)	Deference Accorded	Basis for Deference	Subject Areas
Curtiss–Wright (0.9%)	Super-strong deference in national security cases	Article II + Congressional Delegation	Foreign Affairs; Immigration; National Security
Seminole Rock/Auer (1.1%)	Strong deference for agency interpretations of own regulations	Congressional Delegation + Agency Expertise	Entitlements; Tax; Telecommunications
Chevron (8.3%)	Defer to reasonable interpretations unless Congress has directly addressed the issue	Congressional Delegation	Energy; Envir'l; Entitlements; Immigration; Labor; Securities; Transportation
Diaz/Beth Israel (4.8%)	Defer to reasonable interpretations if consistent with statute	Congressional Purposes	Health; Immigration; Labor; Taxation
Skidmore (6.7%)	Consider agency views for persuasive value (e.g., policy goals and reliance interests)	Agency Expertise and Experience	Civil Rights; Education; Energy; Environmental; Transportation
Skidmore-Lite (17.8%)	Consider agency-generated factual materials + background rules	Agency Expertise and Experience	Antitrust; Bankruptcy; Civil Rights; Energy; Intellectual Property; Indian Law; Pensions
No Deference (53.6%)	Court follows ordinary, ad hoc judicial reasoning	No basis for deference	All areas of Supreme Court practice are dominated by this category
Anti-Deference (6.8%)	Presumption *against* agency interpretation	Constitutional Values	Criminal Law; Immigration

Source: William N. Eskridge Jr. & Lauren E. Baer, *The Continuum of Deference: Supreme Court Treatment of Agency Statutory Interpretations from* Chevron *to* Hamdan, 96 Geo. L.J. 1083 (2008).

Assume that this chart accurately reflects the Court's practice since *Chevron*. Eskridge and Baer also report that when the Court applies the *Chevron* framework the agency wins 76.2% of the time, a very high agreement rate. But the agency win rate is also very high when the Court invokes other deference regimes: 80.6% when the Court follows a *Skidmore*–Lite approach; 73.5% when the Court invokes *Skidmore*; 73.5% when it invokes *Beth Israel*; 90.9% when it invokes *Seminole Rock*; and 100.0% when it invokes *Curtiss–Wright* deference. All these figures are inflated by the fact that the Court probably cites these deference regimes primarily when it is inclined to decide in favor of the agency. Recall Eskridge and Baer's finding that the Court follows *Chevron* in only one-third of the cases where it is potentially applicable (and in some cases where it is not, under *Mead*). The same is even truer of the other regimes: they are rarely applied even when theoretically applicable.

What a mess.

Surely this elaborate continuum can be simplified, and if simplified maybe the Justices would follow it more faithfully. But how should the continuum be simplified? Different Justices and academic commentators have come up with a dizzying array of proposed simplifications—which cut in all sorts of different directions. In concluding this chapter, we offer you several clusters of theories, and you are responsible for developing the approach that makes the best legal sense. You might want to apply these theories to some of the harder cases presented in this and the previous chapters, namely, *Weber*, where the Court followed the EEOC; *Brown & Williamson*, where the Court rejected an FDA rule; *Sweet Home*, where the Court followed a Department of Interior rule; *Oregon*, where the Court rejected a Department of Justice Directive; and the FISA debate between President George W. Bush and Congress (the problem opening this section).

1. Sharpen *Chevron* and *Skidmore* Within the *Mead* Framework

The dominant impulse among judges and law professors has been to work within the assumptions of *Mead* and to formulate and consistently apply *Chevron* and *Skidmore* accordingly. Most of these commentators would be happy to absorb *Beth Israel* and *Seminole Rock* into *Chevron*, and to jettison or deemphasize *Curtiss–Wright* deference. See Kristin E. Hickman, *The Need for* Mead: *Rejecting Tax Exceptionalism in Deference Cases*, 90 Minn. L. Rev. 1537 (2006), proposing that the Supreme Court jettison the special *National Muffler* deference regime for tax cases and just apply *Chevron*, a proposal the Court unanimously followed in *Mayo Foundation v. United States*, 131 S.Ct. 704 (2011).

Many commentators would reject *Mead*'s notion that Congress can delegate lawmaking authority *implicitly*. This notion has created confusion among lower courts. E.g., Lisa Schultz Bressman, *How* Mead *Has Muddled Judicial Review of Agency Action*, 58 Vand. L. Rev. 1443 (2005).

Different authors, of course, have come up with somewhat different prescriptions. More important, different authors have emphasized different normative underpinnings of *Mead*.

(a) *Legislative supremacy.* Probably the most important normative assumption of *Mead* is legislative supremacy: both judges and administrators are faithful agents of congressional directives embodied in statutes. Congress's intent as to who decides is just as important as its intent as to what the decision ought to be. For an excellent constitutional analysis of Congress's power to delegate lawmaking authority to agencies, see Thomas W. Merrill, *Rethinking Article I, Section 1: From Nondelegation to Exclusive Delegation*, 104 Colum. L. Rev. 2097 (2004).

In Chevron's *Domain*, Professors Thomas Merrill and Kristen Hickman anticipated *Mead*'s holding that an agency interpretation is entitled to *Chevron* deference *only* when it is pursuant to congressional delegation of lawmaking authority to the agency. They lay out the doctrinal consequences for this foundation, including the notion that courts should *not* *Chevron*-defer to an agency's interpretation of its own jurisdiction or authority. Thus, for them, *Chevron* Step Zero is critical, and the Oregon Aid-in-Dying Case exemplifies the kind of inquiry the Court should be engaging.

Professors Thomas W. Merrill and Kathryn Tongue Watts complicate the implications of *Mead* in *Agency Rules with the Force of Law: The Original Convention*, 116 Harv. L. Rev. 467 (2002). They demonstrate that the longstanding legislative tradition for delegating "lawmaking" authority required an expression of direct sanctions for violation of an agency rule or order. Many of the cases where the Court has applied *Chevron* deference—including *Chevron* itself—did not meet this conventional test. Because they require a court order to be enforceable, NLRB orders are not properly considered "lawmaking" delegations for this reason. The authors discuss various ways their discoveries could push the *Chevron* line of cases but come to no firm conclusions.

(b) *Democratic legitimacy.* In our democracy, the legitimacy of legislation (the moral reason we accept and obey its commands) rests in part on popular participation or, at least, the accountability of elected representatives to We the People for the laws they adopt. In the modern administrative state, most of the actual rules are developed by unelected agencies, and so there is a potential democracy deficit.

Henry Richardson, *Democratic Autonomy: Public Reasoning About the Ends of Policy* (2003), argues that agencies can contribute to rather than derogate from democratic decisionmaking when they engage in notice-and-comment rulemaking which replicates the legislative process (proposal, popular feedback, deliberated decision, with opportunity for people to object). Professor Richardson's focus, therefore, would not be the fact of legislative *delegation,* but instead the manner in which delegated *lawmaking* is accomplished. Thus, the agency decisions in *Mead, Oregon,* and *Hamdan* (administrative or presidential fiat) do not deserve *Chevron* deference—while the decision in *Chevron* (notice-and-comment rulemaking) does.

Complementing Richardson's analysis, Lisa Schultz Bressman, *Beyond Accountability: Arbitrariness and Legitimacy in the Administrative State*, 78 N.Y.U. L. Rev. 461 (2003), argues that we ought to be even more concerned about administrative arbitrariness than political accountability. Professor Bressman's prescription is that notice-and-comment rulemaking is most likely to produce decisions that reflect reasoned judgment and not arbitrary fiat. Accord, Mark Seidenfeld, *A Syncopated* Chevron: *Emphasizing Reasoned Decisionmaking in Reviewing Agency Interpretations of Statutes*, 73 Tex. L. Rev. 83 (1994).

(c) *Institutional competence.* Few scholars have focused on *Skidmore,* which is not only the default regime under the *Chevron* jurisprudence, but is a default regime that both dominates *Chevron* and generates high agency win rates. In recent empirical articles, one focusing on the Supreme Court and the other on lower courts, scholars have sought to clarify *Skidmore* with a focus on *institutional competence.* Competence is the old

New Deal theme: agencies are better qualified than judges to make certain kinds of policies. In *Continuum of Deference,* Eskridge and Baer found that the Justices' inability to handle technical issues in the fields of intellectual property, telecommunications, taxation, pensions, and bankruptcy generated high levels of deference to agency interpretations, whatever the deference regime the Court invoked. In contrast, more normative arenas such as criminal, Indian affairs, civil rights, and labor law found the Justices agreeing less often, again regardless of the deference regime invoked or applicable. (An implication of their empirical study, which Eskridge and Baer endorse normatively, is that *Skidmore* factors like institutional competence show up in *Chevron* cases as well.)

Focusing on *Skidmore* as the critical regime even before *Mead,* Eskridge and Baer urge the Court to focus on three factors: (1) the rule of law, including agency consistency and public reliance on agency interpretations; (2) comparative institutional competence, with technical issues, matters of regulatory tradeoffs, and uncertainty better handled by agencies and bigger normative issues as those where courts should be more scrutinizing; and (3) legitimacy, with open processes and public participation being pluses for the agency. For a *Skidmore* sliding scale that emphasizes dangers of agency capture, see Hickman & Krueger, *supra.*

2. Reject *Mead* in Favor of Greater Deference to Agency Interpretations

A number of other commentators reject or would go beyond *Mead* and would read *Chevron* much more expansively than the Supreme Court has thus far been willing to do. These scholars are broadly critical of judicial "interference" in the ongoing administration of statutory schemes and urge that agency monitoring is better left to the political than the judicial process. Most of these scholars favor an expanded reading of *Chevron,* a vigorous revival of *Curtiss–Wright,* and a diminished role for *Skidmore* (which they tend to reject as exemplifying what is wrong with the Court's deference jurisprudence).

As before, there are many theoretical ways to reach this conclusion.

(a) *Agencies rather than courts as the preferred congressional agents.* A respected administrative law scholar before his appointment as a judge, Justice Scalia finds no inconsistency between congressional supremacy and a broad reading of *Chevron* that defers to any interpretation adopted by the head of an agency that is not a litigating position. His argument is that any ambiguity or gap that Congress leaves in a statute is an implicit delegation of lawmaking authority to the agency Congress has charged with enforcing the statute. *Mead,* 533 U.S. at 256–57 (dissenting opinion); Antonin Scalia, *Judicial Deference to Administrative Interpretations of Law,* 1989 Duke L.J. 511, 516.

Professor John F. Duffy, *Administrative Common Law in Judicial Review,* 77 Tex. L. Rev. 113, 193–99 (1998), responds that such a broad reading of *Chevron* is inconsistent with the text, structure, and original meaning of the Administrative Procedure Act (APA), especially 5 U.S.C. §§ 558(b) (limits on agency sanctions) and 706(2) (judicial review of agency action), which Duffy believes codify a *Marbury* model of judicial review for agency decisions (under which it is the responsibility of the judiciary to say what the law is). Justice Scalia does not read the APA so restrictively, and scholars are now thinking about deeper responses he might have to Professor Duffy's critique.

Jack Goldsmith and John F. Manning, *The President's Completion Power*, 115 Yale L.J. 2280 (2006), argue for a "completion power" in Article II, namely "the President's authority to prescribe incidental details needed to carry into execution a legislative scheme, even in the absence of any congressional authorization to complete that scheme." The authors rely on historical practice, where the President has exercised such a "completion power" with the acquiescence of both Congress and the Court. E.g., *Dames & Moore v. Regan*, 453 U.S. 654 (1981); Proposed Executive Order Entitled "Federal Regulation," 5 Op. O.L.C. 59 (1981) (defending presidential cost-benefit review of proposed agency rules).

Goldsmith and Manning justify a broad reading of *Chevron* in light of the completion power: "while Congress can legitimately give either courts or agencies ultimate authority to resolve statutory ambiguities or fill up statutory interstices, it is more consistent with the background premises of our constitutional democracy to embrace a default rule that Congress prefers to leave such completion power in the hands of the more accountable executive." 115 Yale L.J. at 2299. This constitutional default rule would inform one's reading of the APA as well as *Chevron* and would provide Justice Scalia with an argument for his notion that statutory ambiguities represent an implicit delegation of lawmaking authority to agencies, not courts. Interestingly, Professors Goldsmith and Manning do not maintain that *Mead* is wrongly decided, but do argue for a narrow reading of *Mead* that leaves plenty of room for a broad reading of *Chevron*.

(b) *Democratic legitimacy.* Recall that *Chevron* emphasized the relatively greater accountability of agencies (responsible to the nationally elected President) compared with federal courts (responsible to the unelected Supreme Court). Dean (now Justice) Elena Kagan, *Presidential Administration*, 114 Harv. L. Rev. 2245 (2001), takes this normative point one step further to support something like the Scalia position. When the President has taken a role in an agency interpretation *or* it has been adopted by the President's appointee (the agency head), see David Barron & Elena Kagan, Chevron's *Nondelegation Doctrine*, 2001 Sup. Ct. Rev. 201, 234–57 (amending the suggestions of her earlier article), then federal judges ought to *Chevron*-defer. According to then-Dean (now Justice) Kagan, the main advantage of this approach would be *national transparency*. The buck stops with the President, and any policy option he or she chooses will be subject to national examination and critique—much more legitimate checks than those offered by judicial review. 114 Harv. L. Rev. at 2332–33.

Professor Bressman, *Beyond Accountability*, 503–13, wonders how Dean Kagan's proposal would work as a practical matter. Pointing to numerous examples, Bressman questions whether presidential interventions are either transparent or public-regarding. A lot of presidential interventions are either behind-the-scenes or below the media radar, but can easily be trumpeted by the Solicitor General if needed to give an agency interpretation a boost. Moreover, many presidential interventions represent the worst sort of rent-seeking politics. It is not clear that the balance of rent-seeking and public-regarding presidential interventions weighs in favor of the latter. See also Jide Nzelibe, *The Fable of the Nationalist President and the Parochial Congress*, 53 UCLA L. Rev. 1217 (2006), arguing that the President does not necessarily represent a national majoritarian constituency any better than Congress does.

A more modest proposal is that made in Kevin Stack, *The Statutory President*, 90 Iowa L. Rev. 539 (2005). Professor Stack argues that *Chevron* deference ought to apply to congressionally authorized lawmaking by the President. Other scholars would go much further in situations where the President is acting to protect national security or engage in matters touching foreign affairs. For example, Curtis Bradley & Jack Goldsmith, *Congressional Authorization and the War on Terrorism*, 118 Harv. L. Rev. 2047, 2100–06 (2005), argue that congressional authorizations for the President's use of force against foreign enemies should be interpreted to include previous presidential practices *and* should be interpreted not to interfere with the President's inherent powers to respond to international emergencies and threats.

(c) *Institutional competence.* Professor Neil Komesar argues in *Imperfect Alternatives: Choosing Institutions in Law, Economics, and Public Policy* (1994), that lawmakers and commentators must consider the institutional costs as well as the benefits of having judges involved in public policy decisions. His book points out that the structural limitations of the judiciary create significant costs for statutory as well as constitutional judicial review. Although he does not address *Chevron,* Professor Komesar's analytical framework is playing an important role in the *Chevron* debate, with some of the most judge-critical voices explicitly invoking his framework. Professor Frank Cross, *Pragmatic Pathologies of Judicial Review of Administrative Rulemaking*, 78 N.C. L. Rev. 1013 (2000), for example, argues that judges should play little if any role in second-guessing agency rules, for they are ignorant and easy prey for rent-seeking special interests. See also David Spence & Frank Cross, *A Public Choice Case for the Administrative State*, 89 Geo. L.J. 97 (2000).

Also following Professor Komesar's framework, Professor Adrian Vermeule argues in *Judging Under Uncertainty* (2006) that judges should always defer to agencies (even their litigating positions) and indeed should defer to agency choices about what substantive canons of statutory interpretation should govern their own positions. Professor Vermeule would not only overturn *Mead*, but would go further than Justice Scalia. Under his approach, a federal judge could only overrule an agency interpretation if it were inconsistent with the plain text of the statute, without *any* reference to contextual considerations such as statutory structure, the whole act, other parts of the U.S. Code, or legislative history.

Less ambitious institutional criticisms have been made by other commentators. They maintain that judicial review of agency rulemaking has been counterproductive because judges are not sufficiently knowledgeable, because judicial interventions tend to be legalistic and thereby derogate from the agency's purposive activities, and because even well-considered judicial interventions may have counterproductive side effects. These problems are illustrated by Jerry Mashaw and Harfst's *The Struggle for Auto Safety* (1990), which we have summarized at various points in this chapter. Professor Mashaw, in particular, has urged courts to be more deferential in the sense that judges need to leave agencies alone so that they can do the jobs Congress has given them. For this reason, he supports a broad reading of *Chevron*. See Jerry L. Mashaw, *Prodelegation: Why Administrators Should Make Political Decisions*, 1 J.L. Econ. & Org. 81, 91–99 (1985). Professor Mashaw would probably be even more deferential in practice than Justice Scalia has been, because he would allow agencies a wide berth in construing statutory language that Justice Scalia would often consider clear and therefore confining.

3. Synthesize *Chevron* and *Skidmore*

Justice Breyer has long been a critic of *Chevron* deference as inconsistent with the judicial role. E.g., Stephen G. Breyer, *Judicial Review of Questions of Law and Policy*, 38 Admin. L. Rev. 363 (1986); accord. Cynthia R. Farina, *Statutory Interpretation and the Balance of Power in the Administrative State,* 89 Colum. L. Rev. 452 (1989). Yet he has not urged the overruling of *Chevron* or the abandonment of its two-step framework. Instead, Justice Breyer seems to apply *Chevron* as a special case of general *Skidmore* (Article III) deference, and the *Mead* notion of congressionally delegated lawmaking authority as a big "plus" in the *Skidmore* scale.

For example, in *Barnhart v. Walton*, 535 U.S. 212 (2002), decided soon after *Mead*, Justice Breyer wrote for the Court in affirming a recent rule adopted by the Social Security Administration. His opinion cheerfully announced that *Chevron* was applicable, because Congress had delegated lawmaking authority to the agency. But the opinion continued the threshold analysis with the further observations that *Chevron*'s applicability was confirmed by the agency's expertise and its longstanding adherence to that interpretation for years before the rule was adopted—classic *Skidmore* considerations. *Id.* at 219–22.

The upshot of Breyer's point of view would be that *Skidmore* is the rule, with pluses awarded for congressional delegation (as in *Chevron*), agency expertise (as in *Chevron* or perhaps *Egan*, the security clearance case) or foreign affairs subject matter (as in *Curtiss–Wright*), and minuses subtracted for agency wishi-washiness, secret processes, or lack of obvious expertise (all exemplified in *Gonzales v. Oregon*). Although this sounds kind of radical after almost a quarter century of *Chevron*, Justice Breyer's approach is not so dissimilar from what the Supreme Court has actually been doing. According to Eskridge & Baer, *Deference Continuum*, agency success rates have no correlation with announced deference regime and strong correlation with perceived agency expertise and consistency of the agency's position over time (the same *Skidmore* factors Justice Breyer emphasized in *Barnhart*).

Notice, finally, that Justice Breyer is the most deferential Justice on the current Court, according to the Eskridge and Baer study.

APPENDIX A

THE CONSTITUTION OF THE UNITED STATES

■ ■ ■

1787

Preamble

We the People of the United States, in Order to form a more perfect Union, establish Justice, insure domestic Tranquility, provide for the common defence, promote the general Welfare, and secure the Blessings of Liberty to ourselves and our Posterity, do ordain and establish this Constitution for the United States of America.

Article I

Section 1. All legislative Powers herein granted shall be vested in a Congress of the United States, which shall consist of a Senate and House of Representatives.

Section 2. [1] The House of Representatives shall be composed of Members chosen every second Year by the People of the several States, and the Electors in each State shall have the Qualifications requisite for Electors of the most numerous Branch of the State Legislature.

[2] No Person shall be a Representative who shall not have attained to the Age of twenty five Years, and been seven Years a Citizen of the United States, and who shall not, when elected, be an Inhabitant of that State in which he shall be chosen.

[3] [Representatives and direct Taxes shall be apportioned among the several States which may be included within this Union, according to their respective Numbers, which shall be determined by adding to the whole Number of free Persons, including those bound to Service for a Term of Years, and excluding Indians not taxed, three fifths of all other Persons.] The actual Enumeration shall be made within three Years after the first Meeting of the Congress of the United States, and within every subsequent Term of ten Years, in such Manner as they shall by Law direct. The Number of Representatives shall not exceed one for every thirty Thousand, but each State shall have at Least one Representative; and until such enumeration shall be made, the State of New Hampshire shall be entitled to chuse three, Massachusetts eight, Rhode Island and

Providence Plantations one, Connecticut five, New York six, New Jersey four, Pennsylvania eight, Delaware one, Maryland six, Virginia ten, North Carolina five, South Carolina five, and Georgia three.

[4] When vacancies happen in the Representation from any State, the Executive Authority thereof shall issue Writs of Election to fill such Vacancies.

[5] The House of Representatives shall chuse their Speaker and other Officers; and shall have the sole Power of Impeachment.

Section 3. [1] [The Senate of the United States shall be composed of two Senators from each State, chosen by the Legislature thereof, for six Years; and each Senator shall have one Vote.]

[2] Immediately after they shall be assembled in Consequence of the first Election, they shall be divided as equally as may be into three Classes. The Seats of the Senators of the first Class shall be vacated at the Expiration of the Second Year, of the second Class at the Expiration of the fourth Year, and of the third Class at the Expiration of the sixth Year, so that one third may be chosen every second Year; [and if Vacancies happen by Resignation, or otherwise, during the Recess of the Legislature of any State, the Executive thereof may make temporary Appointments until the next Meeting of the Legislature, which shall then fill such Vacancies.]

[3] No Person shall be a Senator who shall not have attained to the Age of thirty Years, and been nine Years a Citizen of the United States, and who shall not, when elected, be an Inhabitant of that State for which he shall be chosen.

[4] The Vice President of the United States shall be President of the Senate, but shall have no Vote, unless they be equally divided.

[5] The Senate shall chuse their other Officers, and also a President pro tempore, in the Absence of the Vice President, or when he shall exercise the Office of President of the United States.

[6] The Senate shall have the sole Power to try all Impeachments. When sitting for that Purpose, they shall be on Oath or Affirmation. When the President of the United States is tried, the Chief Justice shall preside: And no Person shall be convicted without the Concurrence of two thirds of the Members present.

[7] Judgment in Cases of Impeachment shall not extend further than to removal from Office, and disqualification to hold and enjoy any Office of honor, Trust, or Profit under the United States: but the Party convicted shall nevertheless be liable and subject to Indictment, Trial, Judgment, and Punishment, according to Law.

Section 4. [1] The Times, Places and Manner of holding Elections for Senators and Representatives, shall be prescribed in each State by the Legislature thereof; but the Congress may at any time by Law make or alter such Regulations, except as to the Places of chusing Senators.

[2]   The Congress shall assemble at least once in every Year, and such Meeting shall be on the first Monday in December, unless they shall by Law appoint a different Day.

Section 5. [1] Each House shall be the Judge of the Elections, Returns, and Qualifications of its own Members, and a Majority of each shall constitute a Quorum to do Business; but a smaller Number may adjourn from day to day, and may be authorized to compel the Attendance of absent Members, in such Manner, and under such Penalties as each House may provide.

[2]   Each House may determine the Rules of its Proceedings, punish its Members for disorderly Behaviour, and, with the Concurrence of two thirds, expel a Member.

[3]   Each House shall keep a Journal of its Proceedings, and from time to time publish the same, excepting such Parts as may in their Judgment require Secrecy; and the Yeas and Nays of the Members of either House on any question shall, at the Desire of one fifth of those Present, be entered on the Journal.

[4]   Neither House, during the Session of Congress, shall, without the Consent of the other, adjourn for more than three days, nor to any other Place than that in which the two Houses shall be sitting.

Section 6. [1] The Senators and Representatives shall receive a Compensation for their Services, to be ascertained by Law, and paid out of the Treasury of the United States. They shall in all Cases, except Treason, Felony and Breach of the Peace, be privileged from Arrest during their Attendance at the Session of their respective Houses, and in going to and returning from the same; and for any Speech or Debate in either House, they shall not be questioned in any other Place.

[2]   No Senator or Representative shall, during the Time for which he was elected, be appointed to any civil Office under the Authority of the United States, which shall have been created, or the Emoluments whereof shall have been increased during such time; and no Person holding any Office under the United States, shall be a Member of either House during his Continuance in Office.

Section 7. [1] All Bills for raising Revenue shall originate in the House of Representatives; but the Senate may propose or concur with Amendments as on other Bills.

[2]   Every Bill which shall have passed the House of Representatives and the Senate, shall, before it become a Law, be presented to the President of the United States; If he approve he shall sign it, but if not he shall return it, with his Objections to the House in which it shall have originated, who shall enter the Objections at large on their Journal, and proceed to reconsider it. If after such Reconsideration two thirds of that House shall agree to pass the Bill, it shall be sent together with the Objections, to the other House, by which it shall likewise be reconsidered, and if approved by two thirds of that House, it shall become a Law. But in

all such Cases the Votes of both Houses shall be determined by Yeas and Nays, and the Names of the Persons voting for and against the Bill shall be entered on the Journal of each House respectively. If any Bill shall not be returned by the President within ten Days (Sundays excepted) after it shall have been presented to him, the Same shall be a Law, in like Manner as if he had signed it, unless the Congress by their Adjournment prevent its Return in which Case it shall not be a Law.

[3] Every Order, Resolution, or Vote, to Which the Concurrence of the Senate and House of Representatives may be necessary (except on a question of Adjournment) shall be presented to the President of the United States; and before the Same shall take Effect, shall be approved by him, or being disapproved by him, shall be repassed by two thirds of the Senate and House of Representatives, according to the Rules and Limitations prescribed in the Case of a Bill.

Section 8. [1] The Congress shall have Power to lay and collect Taxes, Duties, Imposts and Excises, to pay the Debts and provide for the common Defence and general Welfare of the United States; but all Duties, Imposts and Excises shall be uniform throughout the United States;

[2] To borrow money on the credit of the United States;

[3] To regulate Commerce with foreign Nations, and among the several States, and with the Indian Tribes;

[4] To establish an uniform Rule of Naturalization, and uniform Laws on the subject of Bankruptcies throughout the United States;

[5] To coin Money, regulate the Value thereof, and of foreign Coin, and fix the Standard of Weights and Measures;

[6] To provide for the Punishment of counterfeiting the Securities and current Coin of the United States;

[7] To Establish Post Offices and Post Roads;

[8] To promote the Progress of Science and useful Arts, by securing for limited Times to Authors and Inventors the exclusive Right to their respective Writings and Discoveries;

[9] To constitute Tribunals inferior to the supreme Court;

[10] To define and punish Piracies and Felonies committed on the high Seas, and Offenses against the Law of Nations;

[11] To declare War, grant Letters of Marque and Reprisal, and make Rules concerning Captures on Land and Water;

[12] To raise and support Armies, but no Appropriation of Money to that Use shall be for a longer Term than two Years;

[13] To provide and maintain a Navy;

[14] To make Rules for the Government and Regulation of the land and naval Forces;

[15] To provide for calling forth the Militia to execute the Laws of the Union, suppress Insurrections and repel Invasions;

[16]   To provide for organizing, arming, and disciplining, the Militia, and for governing such Part of them as may be employed in the Service of the United States, reserving to the States respectively, the Appointment of the Officers, and the Authority of training the Militia according to the discipline prescribed by Congress;

[17]   To exercise exclusive Legislation in all Cases whatsoever, over such District (not exceeding ten Miles square) as may, by Cession of particular States and the Acceptance of Congress, become the Seat of the Government of the United States, and to exercise like Authority over all Places purchased by the Consent of the Legislature of the State in which the Same shall be, for the Erection of Forts, Magazines, Arsenals, dock-Yards, and other needful Buildings;—And

[18]   To make all Laws which shall be necessary and proper for carrying into Execution the foregoing Powers, and all other Powers vested by this Constitution in the Government of the United States, or in any Department or Officer thereof.

Section 9. [1] The Migration or Importation of Such Persons as any of the States now existing shall think proper to admit, shall not be prohibited by the Congress prior to the Year one thousand eight hundred and eight, but a Tax or duty may be imposed on such Importation, not exceeding ten dollars for each Person.

[2]   The privilege of the Writ of Habeas Corpus shall not be suspended, unless when in Cases of Rebellion or Invasion the public Safety may require it.

[3]   No Bill of Attainder or ex post facto Law shall be passed.

[4]   No Capitation, or other direct, Tax shall be laid, unless in Proportion to the Census or Enumeration herein before directed to be taken.

[5]   No Tax or Duty shall be laid on Articles exported from any State.

[6]   No Preference shall be given by any Regulation of Commerce or Revenue to the Ports of one State over those of another: nor shall Vessels bound to, or from, one State be obliged to enter, clear, or pay Duties in another.

[7]   No money shall be drawn from the Treasury, but in Consequence of Appropriations made by Law; and a regular Statement and Account of the Receipts and Expenditures of all public Money shall be published from time to time.

[8]   No Title of Nobility shall be granted by the United States: And no Person holding any Office of Profit or Trust under them, shall, without the Consent of the Congress, accept of any present, Emolument, Office, or Title, of any kind whatever, from any King, Prince, or foreign State.

Section 10. [1] No State shall enter into any Treaty, Alliance, or Confederation; grant Letters of Marque and Reprisal; coin Money; emit Bills of Credit; make any Thing but gold and silver Coin a Tender in

Payment of Debts; pass any Bill of Attainder, ex post facto Law, or Law impairing the Obligation of Contracts, or grant any Title of Nobility.

[2]   No State shall, without the Consent of the Congress, lay any Imposts or Duties on Imports or Exports, except what may be absolutely necessary for executing it's inspection Laws: and the net Produce of all Duties and Imposts, laid by any State on Imports or Exports, shall be for the Use of the Treasury of the United States; and all such Laws shall be subject to the Revision and Controul of the Congress.

[3]   No State shall, without the Consent of Congress, lay any Duty of Tonnage, keep Troops, or Ships of War in time of Peace, enter into any Agreement or Compact with another State, or with a foreign Power or engage in War, unless actually invaded, or in such imminent Danger as will not admit of delay.

Article II

Section 1. [1] The executive Power shall be vested in a President of the United States of America. He shall hold his Office during the Term of four Years, and, together with the Vice President, chosen for the same Term, be elected, as follows:

[2]   Each State shall appoint, in such Manner as the Legislature thereof may direct, a Number of Electors, equal to the whole Number of Senators and Representatives to which the State may be entitled in the Congress; but no Senator or Representative, or Person holding an Office of Trust or Profit under the United States, shall be appointed an Elector.

[3]   [The Electors shall meet in their respective States, and vote by Ballot for two Persons, of whom one at least shall not be an Inhabitant of the same State with themselves. And they shall make a List of all the Persons voted for, and of the Number of Votes for each; which List they shall sign and certify, and transmit sealed to the Seat of the Government of the United States, directed to the President of the Senate. The President of the Senate shall, in the Presence of the Senate and House of Representatives, open all the Certificates, and the Votes shall then be counted. The Person having the greatest Number of Votes shall be the President, if such Number be a Majority of the whole Number of Electors appointed; and if there be more than one who have such Majority, and have an equal Number of Votes, then the House of Representatives shall immediately chuse by Ballot one of them for President; and if no Person have a Majority, then from the five highest on the List the said House shall in like Manner chuse the President. But in chusing the President, the Votes shall be taken by States, the Representation from each State having one Vote; A quorum for this Purpose shall consist of a Member or Members from two thirds of the States, and a Majority of all the States shall be necessary to a Choice. In every Case, after the Choice of the President, the Person having the greater Number of Votes of the Electors shall be the Vice President. But if there should remain two or more who

have equal Votes, the Senate shall chuse from them by Ballot the Vice President.]

[4]   The Congress may determine the Time of chusing the Electors, and the Day on which they shall give their Votes; which Day shall be the same throughout the United States.

[5]   No person except a natural born Citizen, or a Citizen of the United States, at the time of the Adoption of this Constitution, shall be eligible to the Office of President; neither shall any Person be eligible to that Office who shall not have attained to the Age of thirty five Years, and been fourteen Years a Resident within the United States.

[6]   In case of the removal of the President from Office, or of his Death, Resignation or Inability to discharge the Powers and Duties of the said Office, the Same shall devolve on the Vice President and the Congress may by Law provide for the Case of Removal, Death, Resignation or Inability, both of the President and Vice President, declaring what Officer shall then act as President, and such Officer shall act accordingly, until the Disability be removed, or a President shall be elected.

[7]   The President shall, at stated Times, receive for his Services, a Compensation, which shall neither be increased nor diminished during the Period for which he shall have been elected, and he shall not receive within that Period any other Emolument from the United States, or any of them.

[8]   Before he enter on the Execution of his Office, he shall take the following Oath or Affirmation: "I do solemnly swear (or affirm) that I will faithfully execute the Office of President of the United States, and will to the best of my Ability, preserve, protect and defend the Constitution of the United States."

Section 2. [1] The President shall be Commander in Chief of the Army and Navy of the United States, and of the militia of the several States, when called into the actual Service of the United States; he may require the Opinion, in writing, of the principal Officer in each of the Executive Departments, upon any Subject relating to the Duties of their respective Offices and he shall have Power to grant Reprieves and Pardons for Offenses against the United States, except in Cases of Impeachment.

[2]   He shall have Power, by and with the Advice and Consent of the Senate, to make Treaties, provided two thirds of the Senators present concur; and he shall nominate, and by and with the Advice and Consent of the Senate, shall appoint Ambassadors, other public Ministers and Consuls, Judges of the supreme Court, and all other Officers of the United States, whose Appointments are not herein otherwise provided for, and which shall be established by Law; but the Congress may by Law vest the Appointment of such inferior Officers, as they think proper, in the President alone, in the Courts of Law, or in the Heads of Departments.

[3]   The President shall have Power to fill up all Vacancies that may happen during the Recess of the Senate, by granting Commissions which shall expire at the End of their next Session.

Section 3. He shall from time to time give to the Congress Information of the State of the Union, and recommend to their Consideration such Measures as he shall judge necessary and expedient; he may, on extraordinary Occasions, convene both Houses, or either of them, and in Case of Disagreement between them, with Respect to the Time of Adjournment, he may adjourn them to such Time as he shall think proper; he shall receive Ambassadors and other public Ministers; he shall take Care that the Laws be faithfully executed, and shall Commission all the Officers of the United States.

Section 4. The President, Vice President and all civil Officers of the United States, shall be removed from Office on Impeachment for, and Conviction of, Treason, Bribery, or other high Crimes and Misdemeanors.

Article III

Section 1. The judicial Power of the United States, shall be vested in one supreme Court, and in such inferior Courts as the Congress may from time to time ordain and establish. The Judges, both of the supreme and inferior Courts, shall hold their Offices during good Behaviour, and shall, at stated Times, receive for their Services a Compensation, which shall not be diminished during their Continuance in Office.

Section 2. [1] The judicial Power shall extend to all Cases, in Law and Equity, arising under this Constitution, the Laws of the United States, and Treaties made, or which shall be made, under their Authority;—to all Cases affecting Ambassadors, other public Ministers and Consuls;—to all Cases of admiralty and maritime Jurisdiction;—to Controversies to which the United States shall be a Party;—to Controversies between two or more States;—between a State and Citizens of another State;—between Citizens of different States;—between Citizens of the same State claiming Lands under the Grants of different States, and between a State, or the Citizens thereof, and foreign States, Citizens or Subjects.

[2]   In all Cases affecting Ambassadors, other public Ministers and Consuls, and those in which a State shall be a Party, the supreme Court shall have original Jurisdiction. In all the other Cases before mentioned, the supreme Court shall have appellate Jurisdiction, both as to Law and Fact, with such Exceptions, and under such Regulations as the Congress shall make.

[3]   The trial of all Crimes, except in Cases of Impeachment, shall be by Jury; and such Trial shall be held in the State where the said Crimes shall have been committed; but when not committed within any State, the Trial shall be at such Place or Places as the Congress may by Law have directed.

Section 3. [1] Treason against the United States, shall consist only in levying War against them, or, in adhering to their Enemies, giving them Aid and Comfort. No Person shall be convicted of Treason unless on the Testimony of two Witnesses to the same overt Act, or on Confession in open Court.

[2] The Congress shall have Power to declare the Punishment of Treason, but no Attainder of Treason shall work Corruption of Blood, or Forfeiture except during the Life of the Person attainted.

Article IV

Section 1. Full Faith and Credit shall be given in each State to the public Acts, Records, and judicial Proceedings of every other State. And the Congress may by general Laws prescribe the Manner in which such Acts, Records and Proceedings shall be proved, and the Effect thereof.

Section 2. [1] The Citizens of each State shall be entitled to all Privileges and Immunities of Citizens in the several States.

[2] A Person charged in any State with Treason, Felony, or other Crime, who shall flee from Justice, and be found in another State, shall on demand of the executive Authority of the State from which he fled, be delivered up, to be removed to the State having Jurisdiction of the Crime.

[3] No Person held to Service or Labour in one State, under the Laws thereof, escaping into another, shall, in Consequence of any Law or Regulation therein, be discharged from such Service or Labour, but shall be delivered up on Claim of the Party to whom such Service or Labour may be due.

Section 3. [1] New States may be admitted by the Congress into this Union; but no new State shall be formed or erected within the Jurisdiction of any other State; nor any State be formed by the Junction of two or more States, or Parts of States, without the Consent of the Legislatures of the States concerned as well as of the Congress.

[2] The Congress shall have Power to dispose of and make all needful Rules and Regulations respecting the Territory or other Property belonging to the United States; and nothing in this Constitution shall be so construed as to Prejudice any Claims of the United States, or of any particular State.

Section 4. The United States shall guarantee to every State in this Union a Republican Form of Government, and shall protect each of them against Invasion; and on Application of the Legislature, or of the Executive (when the Legislature cannot be convened) against domestic Violence.

Article V

The Congress, whenever two thirds of both Houses shall deem it necessary, shall propose Amendments to this Constitution, or, on the Application of the Legislatures of two thirds of the several States, shall call a Convention for proposing Amendments, which, in either Case, shall be valid to all Intents and Purposes, as part of this Constitution, when ratified by the Legislatures of three fourths of the several States, or by Conventions in three fourths thereof, as the one or the other Mode of Ratification may be proposed by the Congress; Provided that no Amendment which may be made prior to the Year One thousand eight hundred and eight shall in any Manner affect the first and fourth Clauses in the Ninth Section of the first Article; and that no State, without its Consent, shall be deprived of its equal Suffrage in the Senate.

Article VI

[1] All Debts contracted and Engagements entered into, before the Adoption of this Constitution, shall be as valid against the United States under this Constitution, as under the Confederation.

[2] This Constitution, and the Laws of the United States which shall be made in Pursuance thereof; and all Treaties made, or which shall be made, under the Authority of the United States, shall be the supreme Law of the Land; and the Judges in every State shall be bound thereby, any Thing in the Constitution or Laws of any State to the Contrary notwithstanding.

[3] The Senators and Representatives before mentioned, and the Members of the several State Legislatures, and all executive and judicial Officers, both of the United States and of the several States, shall be bound by Oath or Affirmation, to support this Constitution; but no religious Test shall ever be required as a Qualification to any Office or public Trust under the United States.

Article VII

The Ratification of the Conventions of nine States shall be sufficient for the Establishment of this Constitution between the States so ratifying the Same.

DONE in Convention by the Unanimous Consent of the States present the Seventeenth Day of September in the Year of Our Lord one thousand seven hundred and Eighty seven and of the Independence of the United States of America the Twelfth. IN WITNESS whereof We have hereunto subscribed our Names,

Go. WASHINGTON—
Presidt.
and deputy from Virginia

New Hampshire

JOHN LANGDON

NICHOLAS GILMAN

Massachusetts

NATHANIEL GORHAM

RUFUS KING

Connecticut

WM. SAML. JOHNSON

ROGER SHERMAN

New York

ALEXANDER HAMILTON

New Jersey

WIL: LIVINGSTON   WM. PATERSON
DAVID BREARLEY   JONA: DAYTON

Pennsylvania

B. FRANKLIN   THOS. FITZSIMONS
THOMAS MIFFLIN   JARED INGERSOLL
ROBT. MORRIS   JAMES WILSON
GEO. CLYMER   GOUV MORRIS

Delaware

GEO: READ   RICHARD BASSETT
GUNNING BEDFORD JUN   JACO: BROOM
JOHN DICKINSON

Maryland

JAMES MCHENRY   DANL. CARROLL
DAN OF ST THOS. JENIFER

Virginia

JOHN BLAIR   JAMES MADISON, JR.

North Carolina

WM. BLOUNT   HU WILLIAMSON
RICHD. DOBBS SPAIGHT

South Carolina

J. RUTLEDGE   CHARLES PINCKNEY
CHARLES COTESWORTH PINCKNEY   PIERCE BUTLER

Georgia

WILLIAM FEW   ABR BALDWIN
Attest   WILLIAM JACKSON
                                         Secretary

ARTICLES IN ADDITION TO, AND AMENDMENT OF, THE CONSTI-
TUTION OF THE UNITED STATES OF AMERICA, PROPOSED BY
CONGRESS, AND RATIFIED BY THE LEGISLATURES OF THE
SEVERAL STATES PURSUANT TO THE FIFTH ARTICLE OF
THE ORIGINAL CONSTITUTION.

Amendment [I] [1791]

Congress shall make no law respecting an establishment of religion,
or prohibiting the free exercise thereof; or abridging the freedom of
speech, or of the press; or the right of the people peaceably to assemble,
and to petition the Government for a redress of grievances.

Amendment [II] [1791]

A well regulated Militia, being necessary to the security of a free
State, the right of the people to keep and bear Arms, shall not be
infringed.

Amendment [III] [1791]

No Soldier shall, in time of peace be quartered in any house, without
the consent of the Owner, nor in time of war, but in a manner to be
prescribed by law.

Amendment [IV] [1791]

The right of the people to be secure in their persons, houses, papers, and effects, against unreasonable searches and seizures, shall not be violated, and no Warrants shall issue, but upon probable cause, supported by Oath or affirmation, and particularly describing the place to be searched, and the persons or things to be seized.

Amendment [V] [1791]

No person shall be held to answer for a capital, or otherwise infamous crime, unless on a presentment or indictment of a Grand Jury, except in cases arising in the land or naval forces, or in the Militia, when in actual service in time of War or public danger; nor shall any person be subject for the same offence to be twice put in jeopardy of life or limb; nor shall be compelled in any criminal case to be a witness against himself, nor be deprived of life, liberty, or property, without due process of law; nor shall private property be taken for public use, without just compensation.

Amendment [VI] [1791]

In all criminal prosecutions, the accused shall enjoy the right to a speedy and public trial, by an impartial jury of the State and district wherein the crime shall have been committed, which district shall have been previously ascertained by law, and to be informed of the nature and cause of the accusation; to be confronted with the witnesses against him; to have compulsory process for obtaining witnesses in his favor, and to have the Assistance of Counsel for his defence.

Amendment [VII] [1791]

In Suits at common law, where the value in controversy shall exceed twenty dollars, the right of trial by jury shall be preserved, and no fact tried by jury, shall be otherwise re-examined in any Court of the United States, than according to the rules of the common law.

Amendment [VIII] [1791]

Excessive bail shall not be required, nor excessive fines imposed, nor cruel and unusual punishments inflicted.

Amendment [IX] [1791]

The enumeration in the Constitution, of certain rights, shall not be construed to deny or disparage others retained by the people.

Amendment [X] [1791]

The powers not delegated to the United States by the Constitution, nor prohibited by it to the States, are reserved to the States respectively, or to the people.

Amendment [XI] [1798]

The Judicial power of the United States shall not be construed to extend to any suit in law or equity, commenced or prosecuted against one of the United States by Citizens of another State, or by Citizens or Subjects of any Foreign State.

Amendment [XII] [1804]

The Electors shall meet in their respective states and vote by ballot for President and Vice–President, one of whom, at least, shall not be an inhabitant of the same state with themselves; they shall name in their ballots the person voted for as President, and in distinct ballots the person voted for as Vice–President, and they shall make distinct lists of all persons voted for as President, and of all persons voted for as Vice–President, and of the number of votes for each, which lists they shall sign and certify, and transmit sealed to the seat of the government of the United States, directed to the President of the Senate;—The President of the Senate shall, in the presence of the Senate and House of Representatives, open all the certificates and the votes shall then be counted;—The person having the greatest number of votes for President, shall be the President, if such number be a majority of the whole number of Electors appointed; and if no person have such majority, then from the persons having the highest numbers not exceeding three on the list of those voted for as President, the House of Representatives shall choose immediately, by ballot, the President. But in choosing the President, the votes shall be taken by states, the representation from each state having one vote; a quorum for this purpose shall consist of a member or members from two-thirds of the states, and a majority of all the states shall be necessary to a choice. And if the House of Representatives shall not choose a President whenever the right of choice shall devolve upon them before the fourth day of March next following, then the Vice–President shall act as President, as in the case of the death or other constitutional disability of the President.—The person having the greatest number of votes as Vice–President, shall be the Vice–President, if such number be a majority of the whole number of Electors appointed, and if no person have a majority, then from the two highest numbers on the list, the Senate shall choose the Vice–President; a quorum for the purpose shall consist of two-thirds of the whole number of Senators, and a majority of the whole number shall be necessary to a choice. But no person constitutionally ineligible to the office of President shall be eligible to that of Vice–President of the United States.

Amendment XIII [1865]

Section 1. Neither slavery nor involuntary servitude, except as a punishment for crime whereof the party shall have been duly convicted, shall exist within the United States, or any place subject to their jurisdiction.

Section 2. Congress shall have power to enforce this article by appropriate legislation.

Amendment XIV [1868]

Section 1. All persons born or naturalized in the United States, and subject to the jurisdiction thereof, are citizens of the United States and of the State wherein they reside. No State shall make or enforce any law which shall abridge the privileges or immunities of citizens of the United States; nor shall any State deprive any person of life, liberty, or property, without due process of law; nor deny to any person within its jurisdiction the equal protection of the laws.

Section 2. Representatives shall be apportioned among the several States according to their respective numbers, counting the whole number of persons in each State, excluding Indians not taxed. But when the right to vote at any election for the choice of electors for President and Vice President of the United States, Representatives in Congress, the Executive and Judicial officers of a State, or the members of the Legislature thereof, is denied to any of the male inhabitants of such State, being twenty-one years of age, and citizens of the United States, or in any way abridged, except for participation in rebellion, or other crime, the basis of representation therein shall be reduced in the proportion which the number of such male citizens shall bear to the whole number of male citizens twenty-one years of age in such State.

Section 3. No person shall be a Senator or Representative in Congress, or elector of President and Vice President, or hold any office, civil or military, under the United States, or under any State, who having previously taken an oath, as a member of Congress, or as an officer of the United States, or as a member of any State legislature, or as an executive or judicial officer of any State, to support the Constitution of the United States, shall have engaged in insurrection or rebellion against the same, or given aid or comfort to the enemies thereof. But Congress may by a vote of two-thirds of each House, remove such disability.

Section 4. The validity of the public debt of the United States, authorized by law, including debts incurred for payment of pensions and bounties for services in suppressing insurrection or rebellion, shall not be questioned. But neither the United States nor any State shall assume or pay any debt or obligation incurred in aid of insurrection or rebellion against the United States, or any claim for the loss or emancipation of any slave; but all such debts, obligations and claims shall be held illegal and void.

Section 5. The Congress shall have power to enforce, by appropriate legislation, the provisions of this article.

Amendment XV [1870]

Section 1. The right of citizens of the United States to vote shall not be denied or abridged by the United States or by any State on account of race, color, or previous condition of servitude.

Section 2. The Congress shall have power to enforce this article by appropriate legislation.

Amendment XVI [1913]

The Congress shall have power to lay and collect taxes on incomes, from whatever source derived, without apportionment among the several States, and without regard to any census or enumeration.

Amendment [XVII] [1913]

[1]   The Senate of the United States shall be composed of two Senators from each State, elected by the people thereof, for six years; and each Senator shall have one vote. The electors in each State shall have the qualifications requisite for electors of the most numerous branch of the State legislatures.

[2]   When vacancies happen in the representation of any State in the Senate, the executive authority of such State shall issue writs of election to fill such vacancies: *Provided, that the legislature of any State may empower the executive thereof to make temporary appointments until the people fill the vacancies by election as the legislature may direct.*

[3]   This amendment shall not be so construed as to affect the election or term of any Senator chosen before it becomes valid as part of the Constitution.

Amendment [XVIII] [1919]

Section 1. After one year from the ratification of this article the manufacture, sale, or transportation of intoxicating liquors within, the importation thereof into, or the exportation thereof from the United States and all territory subject to the jurisdiction thereof for beverage purposes is hereby prohibited.

Section 2. The Congress and the several States shall have concurrent power to enforce this article by appropriate legislation.

Section 3. This article shall be inoperative unless it shall have been ratified as an amendment to the Constitution by the legislatures of the several States, as provided in the Constitution, within seven years from the date of the submission hereof to the States by the Congress.

Amendment [XIX] [1920]

[1]   The right of citizens of the United States to vote shall not be denied or abridged by the United States or by any State on account of sex.

[2]   Congress shall have power to enforce this article by appropriate legislation.

Amendment [XX] [1933]

Section 1. The terms of the President and Vice President shall end at noon on the 20th day of January, and the terms of Senators and

Representatives at noon on the 3d day of January, of the years in which such terms would have ended if this article had not been ratified; and the terms of their successors shall then begin.

Section 2. The Congress shall assemble at least once in every year, and such meeting shall begin at noon on the 3d day of January, unless they shall by law appoint a different day.

Section 3. If, at the time fixed for the beginning of the term of the President, the President elect shall have died, the Vice President elect shall become President. If the President shall not have been chosen before the time fixed for the beginning of his term, or if the President elect shall have failed to qualify, then the Vice President elect shall act as President until a President shall have qualified; and the Congress may by law provide for the case wherein neither a President elect nor a Vice President elect shall have qualified, declaring who shall then act as President, or the manner in which one who is to act shall be selected, and such person shall act accordingly until a President or Vice President shall have qualified.

Section 4. The Congress may by law provide for the case of the death of any of the persons from whom the House of Representatives may choose a President whenever the right of choice shall have devolved upon them, and for the case of the death of any of the persons from whom the Senate may choose a Vice President whenever the right of choice shall have devolved upon them.

Section 5. Sections 1 and 2 shall take effect on the 15th day of October following the ratification of this article.

Section 6. This article shall be inoperative unless it shall have been ratified as an amendment to the Constitution by the legislatures of three-fourths of the several States within seven years from the date of its submission.

Amendment [XXI] [1933]

Section 1. The eighteenth article of amendment to the Constitution of the United States is hereby repealed.

Section 2. The transportation or importation into any State, Territory, or possession of the United States for delivery or use therein of intoxicating liquors, in violation of the laws thereof, is hereby prohibited.

Section 3. This article shall be inoperative unless it shall have been ratified as an amendment to the Constitution by conventions in the several States, as provided in the Constitution, within seven years from the date of the submission hereof to the States by the Congress.

Amendment [XXII] [1951]

Section 1. No person shall be elected to the office of the President more than twice, and no person who has held the office of President, or acted as President, for more than two years of a term to which some other person was elected President shall be elected to the office of President more than once. But this Article shall not apply to any person holding the office of President when this Article was proposed by the Congress, and shall not prevent any person who may be holding the office of President, or acting as President, during the term within which this Article becomes operative from holding the office of President or acting as President during the remainder of such term.

Section 2. This article shall be inoperative unless it shall have been ratified as an amendment to the Constitution by the legislatures of three-fourths of the several States within seven years from the date of its submission to the States by the Congress.

Amendment [XXIII] [1961]

Section 1. The District constituting the seat of Government of the United States shall appoint in such manner as the Congress may direct:

A number of electors of President and Vice President equal to the whole number of Senators and Representatives in Congress to which the District would be entitled if it were a State, but in no event more than the least populous state; they shall be in addition to those appointed by the states, but they shall be considered, for the purposes of the election of President and Vice President, to be electors appointed by a state; and they shall meet in the District and perform such duties as provided by the twelfth article of amendment.

Section 2. The Congress shall have power to enforce this article by appropriate legislation.

Amendment [XXIV] [1964]

Section 1. The right of citizens of the United States to vote in any primary or other election for President or Vice President, for electors for President or Vice President, or for Senator or Representative in Congress, shall not be denied or abridged by the United States or any State by reason of failure to pay any poll tax or other tax.

Section 2. The Congress shall have power to enforce this article by appropriate legislation.

Amendment [XXV] [1967]

Section 1. In the case of the removal of the President from office or of his death or resignation, the Vice President shall become President.

Section 2. Whenever there is a vacancy in the office of the Vice President, the President shall nominate a Vice President who shall take office upon confirmation by a majority vote of both Houses of Congress.

Section 3. Whenever the President transmits to the President pro tempore of the Senate and the Speaker of the House of Representatives his written declaration that he is unable to discharge the powers and duties of his office, and until he transmits to them a written declaration to the contrary, such powers and duties shall be discharged by the Vice President as Acting President.

Section 4. Whenever the Vice President and a majority of either the principal officers of the executive departments or of such other body as Congress may by law provide, transmit to the President pro tempore of the Senate and the Speaker of the House of Representatives, their written declaration that the President is unable to discharge the powers and duties of his office, the Vice President shall immediately assume the powers and duties of the office as Acting President.

Thereafter, when the President transmits to the President pro tempore of the Senate and the Speaker of the House of Representatives his written declaration that no inability exists, he shall resume the powers and duties of his office unless the Vice President and a majority of either the principal officers of the executive department or of such other body as Congress may by law provide, transmit within four days to the President pro tempore of the Senate and the Speaker of the House of Representatives their written declaration that the President is unable to discharge the powers and duties of his office. Thereupon Congress shall decide the issue, assembling within forty-eight hours for that purpose if not in session. If the Congress, within twenty-one days after receipt of the latter written declaration, or, if Congress is not in session, within twenty-one days after Congress is required to assemble, determines by two-thirds vote of both Houses that the President is unable to discharge the powers and duties of his office, the Vice President shall continue to discharge the same as Acting President; otherwise, the President shall resume the powers and duties of his office.

Amendment [XXVI] [1971]

Section 1. The right of citizens of the United States, who are eighteen years of age or older, to vote shall not be denied or abridged by the United States or by any State on account of age.

Section 2. The Congress shall have power to enforce this article by appropriate legislation.

Amendment [XXVII] [1992]

No law, varying the compensation for the services of the Senators and Representatives, shall take effect, until an election of Representatives shall have intervened.

APPENDIX B

THE REHNQUIST-ROBERTS COURT'S CANONS OF STATUTORY INTERPRETATION

■ ■ ■

This is a collection of canons invoked by the Supreme Court from the 1986 through the 2006 Terms and divided into categories that parallel the typology provided in Chapter 3.*

TEXTUAL CANONS

- Plain meaning rule: follow the plain meaning of the statutory text,[1] except when textual plain meaning requires an absurd result[2] or suggests a scrivener's error.[3]

LINGUISTIC INFERENCES

- *Expressio* (or *inclusio*) *unius*: expression of one thing suggests the exclusion of others.[4] Inapplicable if context suggests listing is not comprehensive.[5]

---

* Diana Rusk, Yale Law School Class of 2009, provided invaluable assistance in the preparation of this appendix.

1. Massachusetts v. EPA, 549 U.S. 497 (2007); Arlington Cent. Sch. Dist. Bd. of Educ. v. Murphy, 548 U.S. 291 (2006); Barnhart v. Thomas, 540 U.S. 20, 26–29 (2003); West Virginia Univ. Hosps. v. Casey, 499 U.S. 83 (1991); United States v. Providence Journal Co., 485 U.S. 693, 700–01 (1988).

2. Zuni Pub. Sch. Dist. No. 89 v. Department of Educ., 550 U.S. 81 (2007) (majority and concurring opinion); United States v. Wilson, 503 U.S. 329, 334 (1992); Green v. Bock Laundry Mach. Co., 490 U.S. 504, 509–11 (1989). This exception is controversial within the Court, e.g., *Zuni*, 550 U.S. at 108–15 (Scalia, J., dissenting).

3. Lamie v. United States Trustee, 540 U.S. 526, 530–31 (2004); United States Nat'l Bank v. Independent Ins. Agents, 508 U.S. 439, 462 (1993).

4. Hinck v. United States, 550 U.S. 501 (2007); TRW, Inc. v. Andrews, 534 U.S. 19 (2001); City of Chicago v. Environmental Def. Fund, 511 U.S. 328 (1994); United States v. Smith, 499 U.S. 160 (1991); Mississippi Band of Choctaw Indians v. Holyfield, 490 U.S. 30, 46–47 & n.22 (1989); Chan v. Korean Air Lines, Ltd., 490 U.S. 122, 133–34 (1989).

5. Marrama v. Citizens Bank of Mass., 549 U.S. 365 (2007); Christensen v. Harris County, 529 U.S. 576, 583–84 (2000); Burns v. United States, 501 U.S. 129, 136 (1991); Sullivan v. Hudson, 490 U.S. 877, 891–92 (1989).

- *Noscitur a sociis*: interpret a general term to be similar to more specific terms in a series.[6] *Noscitur* is often not helpful when applied to a technical statute whose details were hammered out through a complex process.[7]

- *Ejusdem generis*: interpret a general term to reflect the class of objects reflected in more specific terms accompanying it.[8] *Ejusdem* might be trumped by other canons, such as the rule against redundancy.[9]

- Follow ordinary usage of terms, unless Congress gives them a specified or technical meaning.[10]

- Where Congress uses terms that have settled meaning, either by common usage or through the common law, interpreters should apply that settled meaning.[11]

- Defer to experts, including agencies, regarding the meaning of technical terminology.[12]

- Follow dictionary definitions of terms,[13] unless Congress has provided a specific definition.[14] Consider dictionaries of the era in which the statute was enacted.[15] For technical terms, consult specialized dictionaries.[16] Do not credit nonstandard, "idiosyncratic" dictionary definitions.[17]

- Rules of Construction Act, 1 U.S.C. § 1 et seq., contains default definitions that apply if Congress fails to define a particular term.[18]

- A statute has an ordinary meaning if you'd use its terminology at a cocktail party, and "no one would look at you funny."[19]

---

6. Gustafson v. Alloyd Co., 513 U.S. 561, 575 (1995); Beecham v. United States, 511 U.S. 368, 371 (1994); Dole v. United Steelworkers of Am., 494 U.S. 26, 36 (1990); Massachusetts v. Morash, 490 U.S. 107, 114–15 (1989).

7. S.D. Warren Co. v. Maine Bd. of Envtl. Prot., 547 U.S. 370 (2006).

8. James v. United States, 550 U.S. 192 (2007); Circuit City Stores, Inc. v. Adams, 532 U.S. 105 (2001); Hughey v. United States, 495 U.S. 411, 419 (1990); Norfolk & Western Ry. Co. v. American Train Dispatchers' Ass'n, 499 U.S. 117, 129 (1991).

9. Babbitt v. Sweet Home Chapter of Communities for a Great Oregon, 515 U.S. 687 (1995).

10. Lopez v. Gonzales, 549 U.S. 47 (2006); Pasquantino v. United States, 544 U.S. 349, 355 (2005); Will v. Michigan Dep't of State Police, 491 U.S. 58, 64 (1989).

11. Stewart v. Dutra Constr. Co., 543 U.S. 481, 487 (2005); Scheidler v. NOW, Inc., 537 U.S. 393, 402 (2003); United States v. Wells, 519 U.S. 482, 491 (1997); Community for Creative Non-Violence v. Reid, 490 U.S. 730, 739 (1989).

12. Zuni Pub. Sch. Dist. No. 89 v. Department of Educ., 550 U.S. 81 (2007).

13. Limtiaco v. Comacho, 549 U.S. 483 (2007) (Black's); Rapanos v. United States, 547 U.S. 715 (2006) (plurality opinion of Scalia, J.) (Webster's Second); Muscarello v. United States, 524 U.S. 125 (1998) (Oxford English); Pittston Coal Group v. Sebben, 488 U.S. 105, 113 (1988) (Webster's Third).

14. Babbitt v. Sweet Home Chapter of Communities for a Great Oregon, 515 U.S. 687 (1995).

15. Permanent Mission of India to the United Nations v. City of New York, 127 S.Ct. (2007); Cook County v. United States *ex rel.* Chandler, 538 U.S. 119, 125–27 (2003); St. Francis College v. Al-Khazraji, 481 U.S. 604 (1987).

16. Zuni Pub. Sch. Dist. No. 89 v. Department of Educ., 550 U.S. 81 (2007).

17. MCI v. AT & T, 512 U.S. 218 (1994) (disrespecting *Webster's Third* for including colloquial as well as standard definitions).

18. Stewart v. Dutra Constr. Co., 543 U.S. 481 (2005).

19. Johnson v. United States, 529 U.S. 694, 718 (2000) (Scalia, J., dissenting).

GRAMMAR AND SYNTAX

- · Punctuation rule: Congress is presumed to follow accepted punctuation standards, so that placements of commas and other punctuation are assumed to be meaningful.[20]

- Grammar rule: Congress is presumed to follow accepted standards of grammar.[21]

- Rule of the last antecedent: referential and qualifying words or phrases refer only to the last antecedent, unless contrary to the apparent legislative intent derived from the sense of the entire enactment.[22] Do not have to apply this rule if not practical.[23]

- "May" is usually precatory and connotes decisionmaking discretion,[24] while "shall" is usually mandatory and suggests less discretion.[25]

- "Or" means in the alternative.[26]

TEXTUAL INTEGRITY (WHOLE ACT RULE)

- Each statutory provision should be read by reference to the whole act.[27] Statutory interpretation is a "holistic" endeavor.[28]

- The statute's preamble may provide clues to statutory meaning,[29] as may the title.[30]

- Presumption against redundancy: avoid interpreting a provision in a way that would render other provisions of the statute superfluous or unnecessary.[31] This presumption must give way when offset by other evidence of statutory meaning, however.[32]

---

20. Jama v. Immigration & Customs Enforcement, 543 U.S. 335, 344 (2005) (significance of periods); United States v. Ron Pair Enters., 489 U.S. 235, 241–42 (1989) (comma placement); San Francisco Arts & Athletics, Inc. v. United States Olympic Comm'n, 483 U.S. 522, 528–29 (1987).

21. Limtiaco v. Camacho, 549 U.S. 483 (2007); Rapanos v. United States, 547 U.S. 715 (2006) (plurality opinion of Scalia, J.); Jama v. Immigration & Customs Enforcement, 543 U.S. 335 (2005).

22. Jama v. Immigration & Customs Enforcement, 543 U.S. 335 (2005); Barnhart v. Thomas, 540 U.S. 20, 26 (2003); Nobelman v. American Savs. Bank, 508 U.S. 324, 330 (1993).

23. Nobelman v. American Sav. Bank, 508 U.S. 324, 330–31 (1993).

24. Jama v. Immigration & Customs Enforcement, 543 U.S. 335 (2005); Lopez v. Davis, 531 U.S. 230 (2001) ("may" vests wide discretion in agency).

25. Mallard v. United States Dist. Ct., 490 U.S. 296, 302 (1989).

26. Hawaiian Airlines v. Norris, 512 U.S. 246, 253–54 (1994).

27. Ledbetter v. Goodyear Tire & Rubber Co., 550 U.S. 618 (2007); Gonzales v. Oregon, 546 U.S. 243, 273–74 (2006); Doe v. Chao, 540 U.S. 614 (2004) (considering uncodified parts of the "whole act"); Clark v. Martinez, 543 U.S. 371 (2005); Babbitt v. Sweet Home Chapter of Communities for a Great Oregon, 515 U.S. 687 (1995); Pavelic & Leflore v. Marvel Entm't Group, 493 U.S. 120, 123–24 (1989); Massachusetts v. Morash, 490 U.S. 107, 114–15 (1989).

28. United Sav. Ass'n v. Timbers of Inwood Forest Assocs., Ltd., 484 U.S. 365, 371 (1988).

29. Sutton v. United Airlines, Inc., 527 U.S. 471 (1999); id. (Ginsburg, J., concurring).

30. Porter v. Nussle, 534 U.S. 516, 524 (2002). This is an exceedingly weak canon and has not been a key reason in any Rehnquist–Roberts Court case.

31. Circuit City Stores, Inc. v. Adams, 532 U.S. 105 (2001); United States v. Alaska, 521 U.S. 1 (1997); Walters v. Metropolitan Educ. Enters., Inc., 519 U.S. 202 (1997); Rake v. Wade, 508 U.S. 464 (1993); Kungys v. United States, 485 U.S. 759, 778 (1988) (plurality opinion by Scalia, J.).

32. Gutierrez v. Ada, 528 U.S. 250 (2000); Landgraf v. USI Film Prods., 511 U.S. 240, 259–60 (1994).

- Presumption of statutory consistency: interpret the same or similar terms in a statute the same way.[33] Presumption rebutted when other evidence suggests Congress was using the same term in different ways.[34]

- Presumption of meaningful variation: different statutory wording suggests different statutory meaning,[35] especially when Congress considered and rejected the alternate wording.[36] Presumption inapplicable when there is a reasonable explanation for variation (e.g., different provisions are enacted at different times).[37]

- Avoid interpreting a provision in a way that is inconsistent with the overall structure of the statute[38] *or* with another provision[39] *or* with a subsequent amendment to the statute[40] *or* with another statute enacted by a Congress relying on a particular interpretation.[41]

- Presumption of purposive amendment: statutory amendments are meant to have real and substantial effect.[42]

- Avoid the implication of broad congressional delegation of agency authority when statute carefully limits agency authority in particular matters.[43]

- Avoid broad readings of statutory provisions if Congress has specifically provided for the broader policy in more specific language elsewhere.[44]

- Broad term is presumptively ambiguous if Congress has elsewhere used more targeted terminology.[45]

---

33. Powerex Corp. v. Reliant Energy Servs., Inc., 551 U.S. 224 (2007); IBP, Inc. v. Alvarez, 546 U.S. 21, 34 (2005); Commissioner v. Lundy, 516 U.S. 235, 249–50 (1996); Gustafson v. Alloyd Co., 513 U.S. 561, 570 (1995); Sullivan v. Stroop, 496 U.S. 478, 484 (1990); United Sav. Ass'n v. Timbers of Inwood Forest Assocs., Ltd., 484 U.S. 365, 371 (1988).

34. Environmental Defense v. Duke Energy Corp., 127 S.Ct. 1423, 1432 (2007); Robinson v. Shell Oil Co., 519 U.S. 337, 343–44 (1997); Dewsnup v. Timm, 502 U.S. 410, 417 & n.3 (1992)

35. Lawrence v. Florida, 127 S.Ct. 1079, 1083–84 (2007); Lopez v. Gonzales, 549 U.S. 47 (2006); Lindh v. Murphy, 521 U.S. 320 (1997); Keene Corp. v. United States, 508 U.S. 200, 208 (1993); Gozlon–Peretz v. United States, 498 U.S. 395, 404–05 (1991). The leading case is Russello v. United States, 464 U.S. 16, 23 (1983).

36. Hamdan v. Rumsfeld, 126 S.Ct. 2749, 2765–66 (2006).

37. Gutierrez v. Ada, 528 U.S. 250 (2000); Field v. Mans, 516 U.S. 59, 67–69 (1995).

38. Ledbetter v. Goodyear Tire & Rubber Co., 550 U.S. 618 (2007); Beck v. PACE Int'l Union, 127 S.Ct. 2310 (2007).

39. Babbitt v. Sweet Home Chapter of Communities for a Great Oregon, 515 U.S. 687 (1995); Gade v. National Solid Wastes Management Ass'n, 505 U.S. 88, 100–01 (1992); United Sav. Ass'n v. Timbers of Inwood Forest Assocs., Ltd., 484 U.S. 365, 371 (1988).

40. Gonzales v. Oregon, 546 U.S. 243, 257–58 (2006).

41. FDA v. Brown & Williamson Tobacco Corp., 529 U.S. 120, 144 (2000).

42. Rumsfeld v. Forum for Academic & Institutional Rights, Inc., 547 U.S. 47 (2006); Babbitt v. Sweet Home Chapter of Communities for a Great Oregon, 515 U.S. 687 (1995).

43. Gonzales v. Oregon, 547 U.S. 243, 262–63 (2006).

44. Arlington Cent. Sch. Dist. Bd. of Educ. v. Murphy, 548 U.S. 291 (2006); Jama v. Immigration & Customs Enforcement, 543 U.S. 335 (2005); Custis v. United States, 511 U.S. 485, 491 (1994); West Virginia Univ. Hosps. v. Casey, 499 U.S. 83, 99 (1991).

45. Zuni Pub. Sch. Dist. No. 89 v. Department of Educ., 127 S.Ct. 1534, 1545 (2007).

- Specific provisions targeting a particular issue apply instead of provisions more generally covering the issue.[46]

- Provisos and statutory exceptions should be read narrowly.[47]

- Do not create exceptions in addition to those specified by Congress.[48]

EXTRINSIC SOURCE CANONS

AGENCY INTERPRETATIONS

- *Skidmore* deference. Agency interpretations are entitled to respect to the extent that they have "power to persuade" based upon consistency, factual basis, and expertise.[49] Contrariwise, agency views that are shifting or insufficiently developed have little or no persuasive value.[50]

- Even informal and unsettled agency interpretations (such as those embodied in handbooks or litigation briefs) may be useful confirmations for the interpreter's interpretation of statutory language.[51]

- *Chevron* deference. "Reasonable" agency interpretations pursuant to congressional delegation of lawmaking authority are binding on courts unless Congress has directly addressed the issue.[52] *Chevron* might also apply to notice-and-comment rules filling statutory gaps that the agency reasonably treats as binding on itself and the public.[53] The agency's discretion is at its height when the agency decides not to enforce a statute.[54]

- For *Chevron* purposes, whether Congress has delegated the agency lawmaking authority is itself a matter of statutory interpretation.[55] Presumption against congressional delegation of authority for agency to make fundamental changes in the statute.[56] The Court demands a clear statement authorizing agency constructions that press the envelope of

---

46. Green v. Bock Laundry Mach. Co., 490 U.S. 504, 524–26 (1989); Crawford Fitting Co. v. J.T. Gibbons, Inc., 482 U.S. 437, 444–45 (1987).

47. Cherokee Nation of Oklahoma v. Leavitt, 543 U.S. 631 (2005); Commissioner v. Clark, 489 U.S. 726, 739 (1989).

48. United States v. Smith, 499 U.S. 160, 166–67 (1991).

49. Beck v. PACE Int'l Union, 127 S.Ct. 2310 (2007); Gonzales v. Oregon, 546 U.S. 243, 255–56 (2006); United States v. Mead Corp., 533 U.S. 218, 226–27 (2001); EEOC v. Arabian Am. Oil Co., 499 U.S. 244 (1991). The leading case is Skidmore v. Swift & Co., 323 U.S. 134, 140 (1944).

50. Burlington Northern & Santa Fe Ry. v. White, 126 S.Ct. 2405, 2413–14 (2006).

51. S.D. Warren Co. v. Maine Bd. of Envtl. Prot., 126 S.Ct. 1843, 1848–49 (2006).

52. Zuni Pub. Sch. Dist.No. 89 v. Department of Educ., 550 U.S. 291 (2007) (majority and concurring opinions); National Cable & Telecommunications Ass'n v. Brand X Internet Servs., 545 U.S. 967 (2005); ABF Freight Sys., Inc. v. NLRB, 510 U.S. 317, 324 (1994); Sullivan v. Everhart, 494 U.S. 83, 88–89 (1990); K Mart Corp. v. Cartier, Inc., 486 U.S. 281, 291–92 (1988) The leading case is Chevron U.S.A., Inc. v. Natural Resources Defense Council, 467 U.S. 837 (1984).

53. Long Island Care at Home, Ltd. v. Coke, 127 S.Ct. 2339 (2007).

54. Massachusetts v. EPA, 127 S.Ct. 1438, 1459 (2007).

55. Gonzales v. Oregon, 546 U.S. 243 (2006).

56. Gonzales v. Oregon, 546 U.S. 243 (2006); FDA v. Brown & Williamson Tobacco Corp., 529 U.S. 120 (2000); MCI v. AT & T, 512 U.S. 218 (1994).

constitutional validity.[57]

- *Seminole Rock* deference. Agency interpretation of its own regulations is controlling unless "plainly erroneous or inconsistent with the regulation."[58] Rule does not apply when agency rule merely "parrots" the statute,[59] or where agency interpretation has been unstable over time.[60]

- *Curtiss-Wright* deference. In matters of foreign affairs and national security, presidential or executive statutory interpretations enjoy a super-strong presumption of correctness.[61] (The executive is still bound by statutory and treaty directives.[62]) Similar deference for executive branch views of federal jurisdiction over foreign states.[63]

- Courts accord great weight to executive department interpretation of treaties.[64]

CONTINUITY IN LAW

- Super-strong presumption of correctness for statutory precedents,[65] sometimes including statutory precedents whose narrow holding has been overridden by Congress.[66] The super-strong rule against overruling statutory precedents is inapplicable to the Sherman Act, which is a common law statute.[67]

- Wrongly decided precedents that are also inconsistent with recent legal developments can be overruled.[68]

---

57. Rapanos v. United States, 126 S.Ct. 2208, 2224–25 (2006) (plurality opinion of Scalia, J.); Edward J. Debartolo Corp. v. Florida Gulf Coast Building & Constr. Trades Council, 485 U.S. 568, 575 (1988).

58. Auer v. Robbins, 519 U.S. 452, 461–63 (1997); Thomas Jefferson Univ. v. Shalala, 512 U.S. 504, 512 (1994); Mullins Coal Co. v. Director, Office of Workers' Compensation Programs, 484 U.S. 135, 159 (1987). The leading case is Bowles v. Seminole Rock & Sand Co., 325 U.S. 410, 414 (1945).

59. Gonzales v. Oregon, 546 U.S. 243, 257 (2006).

60. Commissioner v. Schleier, 515 U.S. 323 (1995); Bowen v. Georgetown Univ. Hosp., 488 U.S. 204 (1988).

61. Hamdi v. Rumsfeld, 542 U.S. 507, 518 (2004) (plurality opinion of O'Connor, J.); id. at 580–81 (Thomas, J., concurring in part, with a stronger statement); Cheney v. U.S. Dist. Court, 542 U.S. 367 (2004); Crosby v. National Foreign Trade Council, 530 U.S. 363 (2000); Department of Navy v. Egan, 484 U.S. 518 (1988). The leading case is United States v. Curtiss–Wright Export Corp., 299 U.S. 304 (1936).

62. Hamdan v. Rumsfeld, 126 S.Ct. 2749 (2006).

63. Republic of Austria v. Altmann, 541 U.S. 677, 689–90 (2004).

64. Sanchez-Llamas v. Oregon, 126 S.Ct. 2669 (2006); El Al Israel Airlines v. Tsui Yuan Tseng, 525 U.S. 155 (1999).

65. Rita v. United States, 168 L.Ed.2d 203, 220–24 (2007) (Stevens, J., concurring); id. at 224 (Scalia, J., concurring in the judgment); Hohn v. United States, 524 U.S. 236, 251 (1998); Neal v. United States, 516 U.S. 284 (1996); California v. FERC, 495 U.S. 490, 498–99 (1990); Patterson v. McLean Credit Union, 491 U.S. 164 (1989).

66. Ledbetter v. Goodyear Tire & Rubber Co., 127 S.Ct. 2162 (2007); Arlington Cent. Sch. Dist. Bd. of Educ. v. Murphy, 126 S.Ct. 2455 (2006). This canon is controversial within the Court. See *Ledbetter*, 127 S.Ct. at 2182–84 (Ginsburg, J., dissenting).

67. Leegin Creative Leather Prods. v. PSKS, Inc., 127 S.Ct. 2705 (2007); State Oil Co. v. Khan, 522 U.S. 3 (1997).

68. Leegin Creative Leather Prods. v. PSKS, Inc., 127 S.Ct. 2705 (2007); Bowles v. Russell, 127 S.Ct. 2360 (2007); Rodriguez de Quijas v. Shearson/American Express, Inc., 490 U.S. 477, 480–81 (1989).

- Where Supreme Court decision follows an agency interpretation filling a gap in the law left by Congress (*Chevron*), a revised agency interpretation through rulemaking is not barred by *stare decisis*.[69]

- Presumption of continuity: Congress does not create discontinuities in legal rights and obligations without some clear statement.[70]

- Presumption against repeals by implication.[71] But where there is a clear repugnancy between a more recent statutory scheme and an earlier one, partial repeal will be inferred.[72]

- Presumption against hiding elephants in mouseholes: Congress usually does not alter the fundamental details of a regulatory scheme in vague or ancillary provisions.[73]

- Presumption that Congress uses same term consistently in different statutes.[74]

- Presumption that statutes be interpreted consistent with international law and treaties.[75] But international agreements do not trump the plain meaning of federal statutes.[76]

- Borrowed statute rule: when Congress borrows a statute, it adopts by implication interpretations placed on that statute,[77] absent indication to the contrary.[78]

- In pari materia rule: when similar statutory provisions are found in comparable statutory schemes, interpreters should presumptively apply them the same way.[79]

---

69. Central Laborers' Pension Fund v. Heinz, 541 U.S. 739, 751 (2004) (Breyer, J., concurring); Norfolk Southern Ry. v. Shankin, 529 U.S. 344 (2000) (Breyer, J., concurring); Christensen v. Harris County, 529 U.S. 576, 589 (2000) (Souter, J., concurring); United States v. Watts, 519 U.S. 148 (1997) (Breyer, J., concurring).

70. Green v. Bock Laundry Mach. Co., 490 U.S. 504, 521–22 (1989); Finley v. United States, 490 U.S. 545, 554 (1989).

71. Hamdan v. Rumsfeld, 126 S.Ct. 2749, 2775 (2006); Granholm v. Heald, 544 U.S. 460 (2005); Branch v. Smith, 538 U.S. 254, 273 (2003); Pittsburgh & Lake Erie R.R. v. Railway Labor Executives' Ass'n, 491 U.S. 490, 509 (1989); Traynor v. Turnage, 485 U.S. 535, 547–48 (1988). The leading case is Morton v. Mancari, 417 U.S. 535 (1974).

72. Credit Suisse Securities (USA) LLC v. Billing, 127 S.Ct. 2383 (2007).

73. Gonzales v. Oregon, 546 U.S. 243, 267 (2006); Whitman v. American Trucking Ass'ns, Inc., 531 U.S. 457, 468 (2001); FDA v. Brown & Williamson Tobacco Corp., 529 U.S. 120, 160 (2000).

74. Hawaiian Airlines v. Norris, 512 U.S. 246, 254 (1994); Smith v. United States, 508 U.S. 223, 234–35 (1993); Pierce v. Underwood, 487 U.S. 552 (1988).

75. Spector v. Norwegian Cruise Line Ltd., 545 U.S. 119 (2005); id. at 142 (Ginsburg, J., concurring in part and in the judgment); Hamdi v. Rumsfeld, 542 U.S. 507 (2004) (plurality opinion of O'Connor, J.); INS v. Cardoza–Fonseca, 480 U.S. 421 (1987) (strong presumption when statute is implementing an international agreement).

76. Societe Nationale Industrielle Aerospatialle v. U.S. Dist. Ct., 482 U.S. 522, 538–39 (1987).

77. Molzof v. United States, 502 U.S. 301, 307 (1992); Metropolitan Life Ins. Co. v. Taylor, 481 U.S. 58, 65–66 (1987).

78. Shannon v. United States, 512 U.S. 573, 581 (1994).

79. Ledbetter v. Goodyear Tire & Rubber Co., 127 S.Ct. 2162, 2176–78 (2007) (finding NLRA but not EPA analogous to Title VII for limitations purposes).

- Re-enactment rule: when Congress re-enacts a statute, it incorporates settled interpretations of the re-enacted statute.[80] The rule is inapplicable when there is no settled standard Congress could have known.[81]

- Acquiescence rules: consistent agency or Supreme Court interpretation known to Congress is presumed correct.[82] Also, consider unbroken line of lower court decisions interpreting statute, but do not give them decisive weight.[83]

EXTRINSIC LEGISLATIVE SOURCES

- · Statutory history (the formal evolution of a statute, as Congress amends it over the years) is always potentially relevant.[84]

- Consider legislative history (the internal evolution of a statute before enactment) if the statute is ambiguous.[85] But legislative history of an obsolete provision is unlikely to be probative.[86]

- Committee reports (especially conference committee reports reflecting the understanding of both House and Senate) are the most authoritative legislative history,[87] but cannot trump a textual plain meaning,[88] and should not be relied on if they are themselves ambiguous or imprecise.[89]

- Committee report language that cannot be tied to a specific statutory provision cannot be credited.[90] House and Senate reports inconsistent

---

80. Davis v. United States, 495 U.S. 472, 482 (1990); Pierce v. Underwood, 487 U.S. 552 (1988).

81. Jama v. Immigration & Customs Enforcement, 543 U.S. 335 (2005).

82. Zuni Pub. Sch. Dist.No. 89 v. Department of Educ., 127 S.Ct. 1534, 1541 (2007) (agency interpretation); FDA v. Brown & Williamson Tobacco Corp., 529 U.S. 120 (2000) (agency).

83. Gonzalez v. Crosby, 545 U.S. 524 (2005); General Dynamics Land Sys., Inc. v. Cline, 540 U.S. 581 (2004); National Archives & Records Admin. v. Favish, 541 U.S. 157 (2004); Monessen Sw. Ry. Co. v. Morgan, 486 U.S. 330, 338–39 (1988).

84. Powerex Corp. v. Reliant Energy Servs., Inc., 127 S.Ct. 2411 (2007) (Scalia, J.); Ballard v. Commissioner, 544 U.S. 40 (2005). Unlike reference to internal legislative materials, this canon is *not* controversial within the Court.

85. Safeco Ins. Co. of Am. v. Burr, 127 S.Ct. 2201 (2007); Zuni Pub. Sch. Dist. No. 89 v. Department of Educ., 127 S.Ct. 1534 (2007); Gonzales v. Oregon, 546 U.S. 243, 257–58 (2006); Rumsfeld v. Forum for Academic & Institutional Rights, 547 u.S. 47 (2006); Koons Buick Pontiac GMC, Inc. v. Nigh, 543 U.S. 50, 62–64 (2004); id. at 65–66 (Stevens, J., concurring); FDA v. Brown & Williamson Tobacco Corp., 529 U.S. 120 (2000); Babbitt v. Sweet Home Chapter of Communities for a Great Oregon, 515 U.S. 687 (1995); Wisconsin Pub. Intervenor v. Mortier, 501 U.S. 597, 610 n.4 (1991). This canon is controversial within the Court. See id. at 616–17 (Scalia, J., concurring in the judgment).

86. James v. United States, 127 S.Ct. 1586, 1593 (2007).

87. Tellabs, Inc. v. Makor Issues & Rights, Ltd., 127 S.Ct.2499 (2007); Rumsfeld v. Forum for Academic & Institutional Rights, 547 U.S. 47 (2006); Cherokee Nation of Oklahoma v. Leavitt, 543 U.s. 631 (2005); Intel Corp. v. Advanced Micro Devices, Inc., 542 U.S. 241 (2004); Jones v. R.R. Donnelley & Sons Co., 541 U.S. 369 (2004); Boeing Co. v. United States, 537 U.S. 437 (2003); Johnson v. DeGrandy, 512 U.S. 997, 1010–11 & n.9 (1994).

88. Arlington Cent. Sch. Dist. Bd. of Educ. v. Murphy, 126 S.Ct. 2455, 2463 (2006); id. at 2464–65 (Ginsburg, J., concurring in part); City of Chicago v. Environmental Def. Fund, 511 U.S. 328, 337 (1994); American Hosp. Ass'n v. NLRB, 499 U.S. 606, 613 (1991). This canon is controversial within the Court. See *Murphy*, 126 S.Ct. at 2466–68 (Breyer, J., dissenting).

89. Marrama v. Citizens Bank of Mass., 127 S.Ct. 1105, 1110 (2007); Small v. United States, 544 U.S. 385 (2005).

90. Shannon v. United States, 512 U.S. 573, 583 (1994).

with one another should be discounted.[91]

- Caution against interpretation considered and rejected by floor vote of a chamber of Congress or committee.[92] Cautionary principle inapplicable when it is not clear why Congress rejected the proposal.[93]

- Floor statements, especially by statutory sponsors, can be used to confirm apparent meaning.[94]

- Public give-and-take between Members of Congress and executive department drafters or sponsors during committee hearings are relevant if they illuminate a shared meaning of statutory language by the participants closest to the process.[95]

- The "dog didn't bark" canon: presumption that prior legal rule should be retained if no one in legislative deliberations even mentioned the rule or discussed any changes in the rule.[96]

- Views of a subsequent Congress are a hazardous basis for inferring the intent of an earlier one,[97] but are sometimes relevant.[98] Subsequent legislation clearly incorporating these views is relevant and persuasive.[99]

SUBSTANTIVE POLICY CANONS

Constitution-Based Canons

- Avoidance canon: avoid interpretations that would render a statute unconstitutional *or* that would raise serious constitutional difficulties.[100]

---

91. Moreau v. Klevenhagen, 508 U.S. 22, 26 (1993).

92. Hamdan v. Rumsfeld, 126 S.Ct. 2749, 2765–66 (2006); Doe v. Chao, 540 U.S. 614 (2004); F. Hoffman–LaRoche, Ltd. v. Empangran S.A., 540 U.S. 1088 (2004); FDA v. Brown & Williamson Tobacco Corp., 529 U.S. 120, 144 (2000); Department of Revenue v. ACF Indus., 510 U.S. 332, 345–36 (1994).

93. Safeco Ins. Co. of Am. v. Burr, 127 S.Ct. 2201 (2007); Rapanos v. United States, 126 S.Ct. 2208 (2006) (plurality opinion of Scalia, J.); Solid Waste Agency v. Army Corps of Eng'rs, 531 U.S. 159, 169 (2001).

94. Hamdan v. Rumsfeld, 126 S.Ct. 2749, 2767 n.10, 2769 (2006); Department of Revenue v. ACF Indus., Inc., 510 U.S. 332, 345–46 (1994).

95. General Dynamics Land Sys., Inc. v. Cline, 540 U.S. 581 (2004); FDA v. Brown & Williamson Tobacco Corp., U.S. (2000); Hagen v. Utah, 510 U.S. 399, 418 (1994); Darby v.Cisneros, 509 U.s. 137, 147–51 (1993).

96. Zuni Pub. Sch. Dist. No. 89 v. Department of Educ., 127 S.Ct. 1534, 1541 (2007); Chisom v. Roemer, 501 U.S. 380, 396 & n.23 (1991).

97. Masschusetts v. EPA, 127 S.Ct. 1438, 1460 (2007); Doe v. Chao, 540 U.S. 614 (2004); Solid Waste Agency v. Army Corps of Eng'rs, 531 U.S. 159, 170 (2001); Sullivan v. Finkelstein, 496 U.S. 617, 628 n.8 (1990).

98. Musick, Peeler & Garrett v. Employers Ins. of Wassau, 508 U.S. 286, 293 (1993). This canon is controversial within the Court. Sullivan v. Finkelstein, 496 U.S. 617, 631–32 (1990) (Scalia, J., concurring in part).

99. FDA v. Brown & Williamson Tobacco Corp., 529 U.S. 120, 144 (2000); Babbitt v. Sweet Home Chapter of Communities for a Great Oregon, 515 U.S. 687 (1995); Franklin v. Gwinnett County Pub. Sch., 503 U.S. 60 (1990); id. at 77–78 (Scalia, J., concurring in the judgment); Bowen v. Yuckert, 482 U.S. 137, 149–51 (1987).

100. Rapanos v. United States, 126 S.Ct. 2208, 2224–25 (2006) (plurality opinion of Scalia, J.); Cherokee Nation of Oklahoma v. Leavitt, 543 U.S. 631 (2005); Zadvydas v. Davis, 533 U.S. 678, 696–99 (2001); Public Citizen v. United States Dep't of Justice, 491 U.S. 440, 465–66 (1989);

Inapplicable if statute would clearly survive constitutional attack, or if statutory text is clear.[101]

1. *Separation of Powers*

- Super-strong rule against congressional interference with President's inherent powers, his executive authority.[102] Avoid interpretations whereby judges would interfere with foreign affairs.[103]

- Rule against review of President's core executive actions for "abuse of discretion."[104]

- Where Congress appropriates money without specific textual restrictions, the executive has leeway as to its expenditure, unlimited by more informal signals.[105]

- Rule of special treatment of President and Vice–President as litigants, affording them special privileges so as not to interfere with their official duties.[106]

- Rule against congressional curtailment of the judiciary's "inherent powers" or its "equity" powers.[107]

- Rule against congressional expansion of Article III injury in fact to include intangible and procedural injuries.[108]

- Presumption that Congress does not delegate authority without sufficient guidelines.[109]

- Presumption against "implying" causes of action into federal statutes.[110]

- Presumption that U.S. law conforms to U.S. international obligations.[111] Presumption that Congress takes account of the legitimate sovereign interests of other nations when it writes American laws.[112]

Edward J. Debartolo Corp. v. Florida Gulf Coast Building & Constr. Trades Council, 485 U.S. 568, 575 (1988).

101. Peretz v. United States, 501 U.S. 923, 932 (1991); Rust v.Sullivan, 500 U.S. 173, 182 (1991).

102. Department of Navy v. Egan, 484 U.S. 518, 527 (1988); Morrison v. Olson, 487 U.S. 654, 682–83 (1988); Carlucci v. Doe, 488 U.S. 93, 99 (1988); United States v. Johnson, 481 U.S. 681, 690–91 (1987).

103. Sosa v. Alvarez–Machain, 542 U.S. 692 (2004).

104. Franklin v. Massachusetts, 505 U.S. 788, 800–01 (1991).

105. Cherokee Nation of Oklahoma v. Leavitt, 543 U.S. 631 (2005); Lincoln v. Vigil, 508 U.S. 182, 191 (1993).

106. Cheney v. U.S. Dist. Court, 542 U.S. 367 (2004).

107. Chambers v. Nasco, Inc., 501 U.S. 32, 43–44 (1991).

108. Lujan v. Defenders of Wildlife, 504 U.S. 555, 557–61 (1992); id. at 579–80 (Kennedy, J., concurring in part).

109. Mistretta v. United States, 488 U.S. 361, 373 n.7 (1989).

110. Virginia Bancshares, Inc. v. Sandberg, 501 U.S. 1083, 1102–05 (1991); Thompson v.Thompson, 484 U.S. 174, 179 (1988).

111. Hamdan v. Rumsfeld, 126 S.Ct. 2749, 2793–98 (2006); id. at 2802–04 (Kennedy, J., concurring in part and in the judgment); Sale v. Haitian Centers Council, 509 U.S. 155, 173–74 (1993).

112. Microsoft Corp. v. AT & T, 127 S.Ct. 1746, 1758 (2007); F. Hoffmann–LaRoche Ltd. v. Empagran S.A., 542 U.S. 155, 164 (2004).

- Rule against congressional abrogation of Indian treaty rights.[113]

- Presumption favoring severability of unconstitutional provisions.[114]

2. Federalism

- Super-strong rule against federal invasion of "core state functions."[115] Strong presumption against statutory interpretations that would alter the federal-state balance.[116]

- Super-strong rule against federal abrogation of states' Eleventh Amendment immunity from lawsuits in federal courts.[117] Eleventh Amendment rules does not apply to municipalities and counties.[118]

- Super-strong rule against inferring conditions on federal grants to the states under the Spending Clause; conditions must be expressed clearly and unambiguously.[119] Sometimes the Court will require less than targeted statutory language, so long as states are reasonably on notice of conditions, as through agency guidances to that effect.[120]

- Presumption against federal preemption of traditional state regulation.[121] Presumption trumped if clear statutory language or the statutory purpose requires preemption.[122]

- Presumption against federal regulation of intergovernmental taxation by the states.[123]

---

113. South Dakota v. Bourland, 508 U.S. 679, 687 (1993).

114. Alaska Airlines, Inc. v. Brock, 480 U.S. 678, 684 (1987).

115. Rapanos v. United States, 126 S.Ct. 2208, 2224–25 (2006) (plurality opinion of Scalia, J.); Nixon v. Missouri Municipal League, 541 U.S. 125 (2004); BFP v. Resolution Trust Corp., 511 U.S. 531, 544 (1994); Gregory v. Ashcroft, 501 U.S. 452, 461–64 (1991).

116. Gonzales v. Oregon, 546 U.s. 243 (2006); Owasso Indep. Sch. Dist. v. Falvo, 534 U.S. 426 (2002); Raygor v. Regents of the Univ. of Minn., 534 U.S. 533 (2002); BFP v. Resolution Trust Corp., 511 U.S. 531, 544 (1994); Gregory v. Ashcroft, 501 U.S. 452, 461–64 (1991); Will v. Michigan Dep't of State Police, 491 U.S. 58, 65 (1989).

117. Nevada Dep't of Human Resources v. Hibbs, 538 U.S. 721 (2003) (finding abrogation); Raygor v. Regents of the Univ. of Minn., 534 U.S. 533 (2001); Blatchford v. Native Village of Noatak, 501 U.S. 775, 779 (1991); Dellmuth v. Muth, 491 U.S. 223, 227–28 (1989); Pennsylvania v. Union Gas, 491 U.S. 1, 7 (1989) (finding abrogation). The leading case is Atascadero State Hosp. v. Scanlon, 473 U.S. 234, 241 (1985).

118. Jinks v. Richland County, 538 U.S. 456 (2003).

119. Arlington Cent. Sch. Dist. Bd. of Educ. v. Murphy, 126 S.Ct. 2455, 2458–59 (2006); Barnes v. Gorman, 536 U.S. 181 (2002); Gonzaga Univ. v. Doe, 536 U.S. 273 (2002); Blessing v. Freestone, 520 U.S. 329 (1997); Suter v. Artist M., 503 U.S. 347 (1991). The leading case is Pennhurst State Sch. & Hosp. v. Halderman, 451 U.S. 1 (1981).

120. Davis v. Monroe County Bd. of Educ., 526 U.S. 629 (1999); Franklin v. Gwinnett County Pub. Sch., 503 U.S. 60 (1992).

121. Bates v. Dow Agrosciences LLC, 544 U.S. 431 (2005); Rush Prudential HMO v. Moran, 536 U.S. 355 (2002); Medtronic, Inc. v. Lohr, 518 U.S. 470 (1996); Hawaiian Airlines v. Norris, 512 U.S. 246, 252 (1994); BFP v. Resolution Trust Corp., 511 U.S. 531, 544 (1994); Cipollone v. Liggett Group, Inc., 505 U.S. 504 (1992); California v. ARC Am. Corp., 490 U.S. 93, 100–01 (1989); Rose v. Rose, 481 U.S. 619, 635–36 (1987) (O'Connor, J., concurring in part).

122. Geier v. Honda Motor Co., 529 U.S. 861 (2000).

123. Davis v. Michigan Dep't of Treasury, 489 U.S. 803, 810 (1989).

- Presumption against application of federal statutes to state and local political processes,[124] except when statutory plain meaning or other factors counsel in favor of such application.[125]

- Presumption against congressional derogation from state's land claims based upon its entry into Union on an "equal footing" with all other states.[126] Presumption that upon statehood, the new state acquires title to the land under navigable rivers.[127]

- Rule against federal habeas review of state criminal convictions unless prisoner has properly exhausted state remedies.[128] Rule against against federal habeas review of state criminal convictions supported by independent state ground.[129]

- Presumption of finality of state convictions for purposes of habeas review.[130]

- Narrow construction of federal court jurisdictional grants that would siphon cases away from state courts.[131]

- Rule against reading an ambiguous federal statute to authorize states to engage in activities that would violate the dormant commerce clause.[132]

- Rule favoring concurrent state and federal court jurisdiction over federal claims.[133]

- Rule that Indian sovereignty is limited to Indian Tribe members and designated tribal territories.[134]

- Presumption that states can tax activities within their borders, including Indian tribal activities,[135] but also presumption that states cannot tax on Indian lands.[136]

- Principle that federal equitable remedies must consider interests of state and local authorities.[137]

---

124. City of Columbia v. Omni Outdoor Advertising, Inc., 499 U.S. 365, 373 (1991); McCormick v. United States, 500 U.S. 257, 269 n.6 (1988); McNally v. United States, 483 U.S. 350, 361 n.9 (1987).

125. Evans v. United States, 504 U.S. 255, 270–71 (1992).

126. Utah Div'n of State Lands v. United States, 482 U.S. 193, 196 (1987).

127. Idaho v. United States, 533 U.S. 262 (2001).

128. O'Sullivan v. Boerckel, 526 U.S. 838, 845 (1999).

129. Sanchez-Llamas v. Oregon, 126 S.Ct. 2669, 2682 (2006); Massaro v. United States, 538 U.S. 500, 504 (2003); Wright v. West, 505 U.S. 277, 289 (1992); Coleman v. Thompson, 501 U.S. 722, 729 (1991).

130. Brecht v. Abrahamson, 507 U.S. 619, 635–38 (1993).

131. Kokkonen v. Guardian Life Ins. Co. of Am., 511 U.S. 375, 377 (1994); Finely v. United States, 490 U.S. 545, 552–54 (1989).

132. Granholm v. Heald, 544 U.S. 460 (2005); Wyoming v. Oklahoma, 502 U.S. 437, 458 (1992).

133. Tafflin v. Levitt, 493 U.S. 455, 458 (1990); Yellow Freight Sys., Inc. v. Donnelly, 494 U.S. 820, 823 (1990).

134. Atkinson Trading Co. v. Shirley, 532 U.S. 645 (2001).

135. Cotton Petroleum Corp. v. New Mexico, 490 U.S. 163, 174 (1989).

136. Oklahoma Tax Comm'n v. Sac and Fox Nation, 508 U.S. 114 (1993); County of Yakima v. Confederates Tribes & Bands of the Yakima Indian Nation, 502 U.S. 251, 268 (1992).

137. Raygor v. Regents of the Univ. of Minn., 534 U.S. 533 (2002); Spallone v. United States, 493 U.S. 265, 276 (1990).

- Presumption that Congress borrows state statutes of limitations for federal statutory schemes.[138]

3. Due Process

- Rule of lenity: rule against applying punitive sanctions if there is ambiguity as to underlying criminal liability or criminal penalty.[139] Rule is trumped when Congress clearly intended to criminalize the conduct in question.[140]

- Rule of lenity may apply to civil sanction that is punitive or when underlying liability is criminal.[141]

- Rule against criminal penalties imposed without showing of specific intent.[142] But willfulness requirement in civil sanction cases typically includes to reckless conduct as well.[143]

- Super-strong rule against implied congressional abrogation or repeal of habeas corpus.[144]

- Rule against interpreting statutes to be retroactive,[145] even if statute is curative or restorative.[146]

- Rule against interpreting statutes to deny a right to jury trial.[147]

- Presumption in favor of judicial review,[148] especially for constitutional questions, but not for agency decisions not to prosecute.

- Presumption against pre-enforcement challenges to implementation.[149]

- Presumption against exhaustion of remedies requirement for lawsuit to enforce constitutional rights.[150]

---

138. Wallace v. Kato, 127 S.Ct. 1091 (2007); Lampf, Pleva, Lipkind, Prupis & Petigrow v. Gilbertson, 501 U.S. 350, 355–56 (1991).

139. Arthur Andersen LLP v. United States, 544 U.S. 696 (2005); Cleveland v. United States, 531 U.S. 12 (2000) (explaining both notice and nondelegation rationales); United States v. Aguilar, 515 U.S. 593 (1995); United States v. Granderson, 511 U.S. 39 (1994); United States v. Kozminski, 487 U.S. 931, 939 (1988).

140. Muscarello v. United States, 524 U.S. 125 (1998); Chapman v. United States, 500 U.S. 453, 463–64 (1991).

141. Crandon v. United States, 494 U.S. 152, 158 (1990). The Court applies this canon very unevenly. E.g., Babbitt v. Sweet Home Chapter of Communities for a Great Oregon, 515 U.S. 687 (1995).

142. Arthur Andersen LLP v. United States, 544 U.S. 696 (2005); Bryan v. United States, 524 U.S. 184, 191–92 (1998); Ratzlaf v. United States, 510 U.S. 135, 137 (1994); Cheek v. United States, 498 U.S. 192, 200–01 (1991).

143. Safeco Ins. Co. of Am. v. Burr, 127 S.Ct. 2201 (2007); McLaughlin v. Richland Shoe Co., 486 U.S. 128, 132–33 (1988).

144. Demore v. Kim, 538 U.S. 510 (2003); INS v. St. Cyr, 533 U.S. 289 (2001).

145. Fernandez-Vargas v. Gonzales, 126 S.Ct. 2422 (2006); Landgraf v. USI Film Prods., 511 U.S. 244 (1994).

146. Rivers v. Raodway Express, 511 U.S. 298 (1994).

147. Gomez v. United States, 490 U.S. 858, 863 (1989).

148. Demore v. Kim, 538 U.S. 510 (2003); Webster v. Doe, 486 U.S. 592 (1988).

149. Thunder Basin Coal Co. v. Reich, 510 U.S. 200, 208–10 (1994).

150. McCarthy v. Madigan, 503 U.S. 140, 146–49 (1992).

- Presumption that judgments will not be binding upon persons not party to adjudication.[151]

- Presumption against national service of process unless authorized by Congress.[152]

- Presumption against foreclosure of private enforcement of important federal rights.[153]

- Presumption that preponderance of the evidence standard applies in civil cases.[154]

COMMON LAW-BASED CANONS

- Presumption in favor of following common law usage and rules where Congress has employed words or concepts with well-settled common law traditions.[155] Presumption inapplicable when Congress has directly addressed the issue[156] or when common law usage is inconsistent with statutory purpose.[157]

- Rule against extraterritorial application of U.S. law.[158] Presumption that Congress legislates with domestic concerns in mind.[159]

- American laws apply to foreign-flag ships in U.S. territory and affecting Americans, but will not apply to the "internal affairs" of a foreign-flag ship unless there is a clear statutory statement to that effect.[160]

- Super-strong rule against waivers of United States sovereign immunity.[161] Once sovereign immunity has been waived, equitable doctrines might be applied.[162]

---

151. Martin v. Wilks, 490 U.S. 755, 761–62 (1989).

152. Omni Capital Int'l v. Rudolf Wolff & Co., 484 U.S. 97, 107–08 (1987).

153. Wilder v. Virginia Hosp. Ass'n, 496 U.S. 498, 520–21 (1990). This presumption is probably no longer viable. See Gonzaga Univ. v. Doe, 536 U.S. 273 (2002).

154. Grogan v. Garner, 498 U.S. 279, 286 (1991).

155. Permanent Mission of India to the United Nations v. City of New York, 127 S.Ct. 2352 (2007) (FSIA); Wallace v. Kato, 127 S.Ct. 1091, 1095 (2007) (§ 1983); Norfolk Southern Ry. v. Sorrell, 127 S.Ct. 799 (2007) (FELA); Hamdan v. Rumsfeld, 126 S.Ct. 2749, 2775–86 (2006) (UCMJ); Dixon v. United States, 126 S.Ct. 2437 (2006) (defense to federal crimes); Dura Pharmaceuticals, Inc. v. Broudo, 544 U.S. 336 (2005) (§ 10(b)); Stewart v. Dutra Constr. Co., 543 U.S. 481, 487 (2005) (LWHCA); United States v. Texas, 507 U.S. 529, 534 (1993) (Debt Collection Act); Nationwide Mut. Ins. Co. v. Darden, 503 U.S. 318 (1992) (ERISA); Kamen v. Kemper Fin. Servs., Inc., 500 U.S. 90, 98–99 (1991) (Investment Company Act); Community for Creative Nonviolence v. Reid, 490 U.S. 730, 739–40 (1989) (Copyright Act).

156. Pasquantino v. United States, 544 U.S. 349, 356 (2005).

157. Taylor v. United States, 495 U.S. 575, 593–95 (1990).

158. Microsoft Corp. v. AT & T, 127 S.Ct. 1746, 1758 (2007); F. Hoffman–LaRoche, Ltd. v. Empangran S.A., 540 U.S. 1088 (2004); Sale v. Haitian Centers Council, 509 U.S. 155 (1993); EEOC v. Arabian Am. Oil Co., 499 U.S. 244, 248 (1991); Argentine Republic v. Amerada Hess Shipping Corp., 488 U.S. 428, 440 (1989).

159. Small v. United States, 544 U.S. 385 (2005); Smith v. United States, 507 U.S. 197, 204 n.5 (1993).

160. Spector v. Norwegian Cruise Line Ltd., 545 U.S. 119 (2005).

161. United States v. White Mt. Apache Tribe, 537 U.S. 465, 472–73 (2003); United States v. Nordic Village, Inc., 503 U.S. 30 (1992); Ardestani v. INS, 502 U.S. 129 (1991); United States v. Dalm, 494 U.S. 596, 608 (1990).

162. Irwin v. Department of Veterans Affairs, 498 U.S. 89, 94–96 (1990).

- Super-strong rule against congressional abrogation of state immunity from suit.[163] Common law rule does not apply to counties and other subdivisions created by the states.[164]

- Rule that debts to the United States shall bear interest[165]

- Presumption against conveyance of U.S. public lands to private parties.[166]

- Rule presuming against attorney fee-shifting in federal courts and federal statutes,[167] and narrow construction of fee-shifting statutes to exclude costs that are not explicitly identified.[168]

- Presumption that jury finds facts, judge declares law.[169]

- Rule presuming that law takes effect on date of enactment.[170]

- Presumption that public (government) interest not be prejudiced by negligence of federal officials.[171]

- Presumption that federal agencies launched into commercial world with power to "sue and be sued" are not entitled to sovereign immunity.[172]

- Presumption favoring enforcement of forum selection clauses.[173]

- Presumption that federal judgment has preclusive effect in state administrative proceedings.[174]

- Presumption importing common law immunities into federal civil rights statutes.[175]

STATUTE-BASED CANONS

- Purposive construction: interpret ambiguous statutes so as best to carry out their statutory purposes.[176] Avoid "incongruous results."[177] Cau-

---

163. Alden v. Maine, 527 U.S. 706, 713 (1999) (announcing that state immunity from suit was based on common law, not just Eleventh Amendment). This canon is controversial within the Court. See id. at 760 (Souter, J., dissenting).

164. Northern Ins. Co. of N.Y. v. Chatham County, 126 S.Ct. 1689, 1693 (2006).

165. United States v. Texas, 507 U.S. 529 (1993).

166. Utah Div. of State Lands v. United States, 482 U.S. 193, 197–98 (1987).

167. Key Tronic Corp. v. United States, 511 U.S. 809 (1994). The leading case is Alyeska Pipeline Serv. Co. v. Wilderness Society, 421 U.S. 240 (1975).

168. Arlington Cent. Sch. Dist. Bd. of Educ. v. Murphy, 126 S.Ct. 2455, 2461–63 (2006); West Virginia Univ. Hosps., Inc. v. Casey, 499 U.S. 83 (1991).

169. Shannon v. United States, 512 U.S. 573 (1994).

170. Gozlon-Peretz v. United States, 498 U.S. 395 (1991).

171. United States v. Montalvo–Murillo, 495 U.S. 711, 717–18 (1990).

172. Loeffler v. Frank, 486 U.S. 549, 554–55 (1988).

173. Carnival Cruise Lines v. Shute, 499 U.S. 585, 589 (1991); Stewart Org. v. Ricoh Corp., 487 U.S. 22, 33 (1988) (Kennedy, J., concurring).

174. Astoria Fed. Sav. & Loan Ass'n v. Solimino, 501 U.S. 104, 108 (1991).

175. Burns v. Reed, 500 U.S. 478, 484–85 (1991); Forrester v. White, 484 U.S. 219, 225–26 (1988).

176. Zuni Pub. Sch. Dist. No. 89 v. Department of Educ., 127 S.Ct. 1534 (2007); Massachusetts v. EPA, 127 S.Ct. 1438, 1462–63 (2007); Burlington Northern & Santa Fe Ry. v. White, 126 S.Ct. 2405, 2412–14 (2006); Jones v. R.R. Donnelley & Sons Co., 541 U.S. 369 (2004); PGA Tour, Inc.v. Martin, 532 U.S. 661 (2001); Reves v. Ernst & Young, 494 U.S. 56, 60–61 (1990).

177. Winkelman v. Parma City Sch. Dist., 127 S.Ct. 1994, 2004–05 (2007); Nixon v. Missouri Municipal League, 541 U.S. 125 (2004).

tion: no law pursues its purpose at all costs, and text-based limits on a law's scope are part of its "purpose."[178]

1. General canons

- · Presumption against repeals by implication.[179] But where there is a clear repugnancy between a more recent statutory scheme and an earlier one, partial repeal will be inferred.[180]

- *In pari materia*: similar statutes should be interpreted similarly,[181] unless legislative history or purpose suggests material differences.[182]

- Presumption *against* private right of action unless statute expressly provides one,[183] but once recognized a private right of action carries with it all traditional remedies.[184] Regulations cannot create a private cause of action not authorized by the statute.[185]

- A precisely drawn, detailed statute preempts or governs a more general statute or remedies.[186]

- When Congress enacts a specific remedy when no remedy was clearly recognized previously, the new remedy is regarded as exclusive.[187]

- Presumption against creating exemptions in a statute that has none.[188] Narrow interpretation of explicit exemptions.[189]

- Allow *de minimis* exceptions to statutory rules, so long as they do not undermine statutory policy.[190]

2. Process canons

- Presumption that adjudicative bodies are vested with inherent authority to sanction abusive litigation practices.[191] Judges presumptively have discretion to raise procedural errors sua sponte.[192]

---

178. Rapanos v. United States, 126 S.Ct. 2208, 2232 (2006) (plurality opinion of Scalia, J.).

179. See sources in note 71 *supra.*

180. Credit Suisse Securities (USA) LLC v. Billing, 127 S.Ct. 2383 (2007).

181. Powerex Corp. v. Reliant Energy Servs., Inc., 127 S.Ct. 2411 (2007); Ledbetter v. Goodyear Tire & Rubber Co., 127 S.Ct. 2162 (2007); John Hancock Mut. Life Ins. Co. v. Harris Trust & Sav. Bank, 510 U.S. 86, 101–06 (1993); Morales v. TWA, Inc., 504 U.S. 374 (1992); Communciations Workers v. Beck, 487 U.S. 735, 750–52 (1988); Wimberly v. Labor & Indus. Relations Comm'n, 479 U.S. 511, 517 (1987).

182. Ledbetter v. Goodyear Tire & Rubber Co., 127 S.Ct. 2162 (2007); Fogerty v. Fantasy, Inc., 510 U.S. 517 (1994).

183. Gonzaga Univ. v. Doe, 536 U.S. 273 (2002); Blessing v. Freestone, 520 U.S. 329 (1997); Suter v. Artist M., 503 U.S. 347 (1992).

184. Franklin v. Gwinnett County Pub. Sch., 503 U.S. 60 (1992).

185. Alexander v. Sandoval, 532 U.S. 275 (2001).

186. Credit Suisse Securities (USA) LLC v. Billing, 127 S.Ct. 2383 (2007); EC Term of Years Trust v. United States, 127 S.Ct. 1763, 1767 (2007). The leading case is Brown v. General Serv. Admin., 425 U.S. 820, 834 (1976).

187. Hinck, v. United States, 127 S.Ct. 2011 (2007).

188. City of Chicago v. Environmental Def. Fund, 511 U.S. 328, 337 (1994).

189. John Hancock Mut. Life Ins. Co. v. Harris Trust & Sav. Bank, 510 U.S. 86, 96–97 (1994); United States Dep't of Justice v. Landano, 508 U.S. 165 (1993); Citicorp Indus. Credit, Inc. v. Brock, 483 U.S. 27, 33–35 (1987).

190. Wisconsin Dep't of Revenue v. William Wrigley, Jr., Co., 505 U.S. 214 (1992).

191. Marrama v. Citizens Bank of Mass., 127 S.Ct. 1105, 1112 (2007).

192. Day v. McDonough, 547 U.S. 198 (2006).

- Presumption that statutory exhaustion requirements entail implicit requirements that the petitioner follow the proper procedures; failing that, the petitioner has not met statutory exhaustion requirements.[193]

- Strict construction of statutes authorizing appeals.[194] Rule that Court of Claims is proper forum for Tucker Act claims against federal government.[195]

- Rule that "sue and be sued" clauses waive sovereign immunity and should be liberally construed.[196] Presumption that statute creating agency and authorizing it to "sue and be sued" also creates federal subject matter jurisdiction for lawsuits by and against the agency.[197]

- American rule: strong presumption that each side bears its own costs in adjudications.[198] Super-strong rule against finding statutory authorization of witness fees as costs unless the statute refers explicitly to witness fees.[199]

- Rule that the burden of proof is on the party requesting benefits or entitlements from the state.[200]

- Rule that nonjurisdictional process objections (e.g., exhaustion of remedies, venue) are waived if not timely raised.[201]

3. Specific statutory subject areas

- **Antitrust.** Sherman Act should be applied in light of its overall purpose of benefitting consumers.[202]

- Presumption against application of Sherman Act to activities authorized by states.[203]

---

193. Woodford v. Ngo, 126 S.Ct. 2378, 2384–86 (2006); see also O'Sullivan v. Boerckel, 526 U.S. 838, 845 (1999) (similar rule in habeas corpus law).

194. Bowles v. Russell, 127 S.Ct. 2360 (2007); Hohn v. United States, 524 U.S. 236, 247 (1998); California Coastal Comm'n v. Granite Rock Co., 480 U.S. 572, 579 (1987).

195. Preseault v. ICC, 494 U.S. 1, 11–12 (1990).

196. FDIC v. Meyer, 510 U.S. 471 (1994).

197. American Nat'l Red Cross v. S.G., 505 U.S. 247 (1992).

198. Buckhannon Bd. & Care Home, Inc. v. West Virginia Dep't Health & Human Resources, 532 U.S. 598 (2001). The leading case is Alyeska Pipeline Serv. Co. v. Wilderness Soc'y, 421 U.S. 240 (1975).

199. Arlington Cent. Sch. Dist. Bd. of Educ. v. Murphy, 126 S.Ct. 2455, 2462 (2006); Crawford Fitting Co. v. J.T. Gibbons, Inc., 482 U.S. 437, 445 (1987).

200. NLRB v. Kentucky River Community Care, Inc., 532 U.S. 706 (2001).

201. Kontrick v. Ryan, 540 U.S. 443 (2004).

202. Weyerhauser v. Ross–Simmons Hardwood Lumber, 127 S.Ct. 1069 (2007).

203. City of Columbia v. Omni Outdoor Advertising, Inc., 499 U.S. 365, 370 (1991).

- Exemption from antitrust liability should not be lightly inferred.[204] Principle that statutes should not be interpreted to create anti-competitive effects.[205]

- **Arbitration.** Federal court deference to arbitral awards, even where the Federal Arbitration Act is not by its terms applicable.[206]

- Strong presumption in favor of arbitration and of enforcing labor arbitration agreements.[207]

- Rule favoring arbitration of federal statutory claims.[208]

- **Banking.** National Bank Act policy shielding national banks from "burdensome" state regulation.[209] But national banks are subject to state laws not conflicting with the NBA's purposes.[210]

- **Bankruptcy.** Bankruptcy Act should be construed in light of its overall purpose, to give a fresh start to the class of "honest but unfortunate debtors."[211]

- Presumption that the Bankruptcy Act of 1978 preserved prior bankruptcy doctrines.[212]

- Where statute is ambiguous, courts should create gapfilling rules that are familiar, objective, and less expensive to administer.[213]

- **Civil Procedure & Jurisdiction.** Subject-matter jurisdictional rules will be strictly enforced and applied.[214] Court-created "exceptions" to statutory jurisdictional grounds are strongly disfavored[215] and, even if recognized, will be narrowly construed.[216]

- Federal Rules of Civil Procedure apply in habeas cases, except to the extent they are inconsistent with the Habeas Corpus Rules.[217]

---

204. Credit Suisse Securities (USA) LLC v. Billing, 127 S.Ct. 2383 (2007).

205. Two Pesos, Inc. v. Taco Cabana, Inc., 505 U.S. 763 (1992).

206. United Paperworkers Int'l Union v. Misco, Inc., 484 U.S. 29, 36–37 (1987).

207. Howsam v. Dean Witter Reynolds, Inc., 537 U.S. 79, 83 (2002); Groves v. Ring Screw Works, Ferndale Fastener Div'n, 498 U.S. 168, 173 (1990).

208. Circuit City Stores, Inc. v. Adams, 532 U.S. 105 (2001); Gilmer v. Interstate/Johnson Lane Corp., 500 U.S. 20, 26 (1991); Shearson/American Express, Inc. v. McMahon, 482 U.S. 220, 226–27 (1987).

209. Watters v. Wachovia Bank, 127 S.Ct. 1559, 1566–67 (2007); Beneficial Nat'l Bank v. Anderson, 539 U.S. 1, 10 (2003); Barnett Bank of Marion County, N.A. v. Nelson, 517 U.S. 25, 32–34 (1996).

210. Atherton v. FDIC, 519 U.S. 213, 221–22 (1997).

211. Marrama v. Citizens Bank of Mass., 127 S.Ct. 1105, 1111 (2007).

212. Dewsnup v. Timm, 502 U.S. 410 (1992).

213. Till v. CSC Credit Corp., 541 U.S. 465 (2004) (plurality opinion of Stevens, J.).

214. Bowles v. Russell, 127 S.Ct. 2360 (2007);

215. Bowles v. Russell, 127 S.Ct. 2360 (2007).

216. Marshall v. Marshall, 547 U.S. 293 (2006) (narrow interpretation of "probate exception"); Ankenbrandt v. Richards, 504 U.S. 689 (1992) (narrow interpretation of "domestic relations exception").

217. Woofard v. Garceau, 538 U.S. 202, 208 (2003).

- Presumption that time-limitation periods, venue, and other nonjurisdictional requirements are waivable.[218]

- **Civil Rights.** Aspects of section 1983 not governed by state law are governed by federal rules conforming to common law tort principles.[219]

- Title VII of the Civil Rights Act should be interpreted to effectuate its goal of a workplace where individuals are not discriminated against because of their racial, ethnic, religious, or gender-based status.[220] But Title VII does not set forth a general code of workplace civility.[221]

- Voting Rights Act should be interpreted in light of its core purpose of preventing race discrimination in voting and fostering a transformation of America into a society no longer fixated on race.[222]

- **Criminal Law and Sentencing.** Rule of lenity: ambiguities in criminal statutes shall be decided in favor of the accused.[223] Likewise, ambiguous sentencing provisions should be interpreted against the government.[224]

- Failure of U.S. Attorneys to initiate criminal prosecutions in the past is evidence that the Attorney General's current reading of the statute is too broad.[225]

- Even when courts are not bound by Sentencing Commission interpretations, such interpretations may be considered.[226]

- **Environmental Law.** Environmental laws should be applied in light of their overall purpose of cleaning up the environment at a reasonable cost.[227]

- NEPA contains an implicit "rule of reason," relieving agencies of filing environmental impact statements that would serve no statutory purpose.[228]

- **Immigration.** Construe ambiguities in deportation statutes in favor of aliens.[229]

---

218. Eberhart v. United States, 546 U.S. 12, 17–18 (2006) (per curiam).

219. Wallace v. Kato, 127 S.Ct. 1091, 1095 (2007).

220. Burlington Northern & Santa Fe Ry. v. White, 126 S.Ct. 2405, 2412 (2006).

221. Oncale v. Sundowner Offshore Servs., Inc., 523 U.S. 75, 80 (1998); Faragher v. Boca Raton, 524 U.S. 775, 788 (1998).

222. League of United Latin Am. Citizens v. Perry, 126 S.Ct. 2594, 2618 (2006); Georgia v. Ashcroft, 539 U.S. 461, 490 (2003).

223. See sources in note 138 *supra.*

224. United States v. R.L.C., 503 U.S. 291 (1992).

225. Lopez v. Gonzales, 127 S.Ct. 625, 632 (2006).

226. James v. United States, 127 S.Ct. 1586, 1595–96 (2007).

227. Massachusetts v. EPA, 127 S.Ct. 1438 (2007).

228. Department of Transportation v. Public Citizen, 541 U.S. 752 (2004); Marsh v. Oregon Natural Resources Council, 490 U.S. 360, 373–74 (1989).

229. INS v. St. Cyr, 533 U.S. 289, 320 (2001); INS v. Cardoza–Fonseca, 480 U.S. 421, 449 (1987). This canon is applied with an unusual level of unpredictability. Compare, e.g., INS v. Elias–Zacarias, 502 U.S. 478 (1992).

- **Indian Law.** Rule against state taxation of Indian tribes and reservation activities.[230]

- Presumption against national "diminishment" of Indian lands.[231]

- Longstanding assertion of state jurisdiction over Indian lands creates justifiable expectations of sovereign authority.[232]

- Presumption against criminal jurisdiction by an Indian tribe over a nonmember.[233]

- Presumption that party cannot invoke federal jurisdiction until she has exhausted her remedies in Indian tribal courts.[234]

- **Labor Law.** Rule against statutory interference in labor-management discipline disputes.[235]

- **Patent Law.** Practice and precedent of Patent Office are particularly persuasive evidence of statutory meaning in this area, given the much greater competence of that Office.[236]

- Especially strong presumption against extraterritorial application of federal patent law.[237]

- **Taxation.** Presumption that IRS tax assessments are correct.[238]

- Narrow interpretation of exemptions from federal taxation.[239] Presumption against taxpayer claiming income tax deduction.[240]

- Presumption that tax valuation statutes follow majority approach, and that departures from the majority approach would be signaled with clear statutory language.[241]

- **Veterans Benefits.** Principle that veterans' benefits statutes be construed liberally for their beneficiaries.[242]

---

230. California v. Cabazon Band of Mission Indians, 480 U.S. 202, 208 (1987). This canon seems to have had little bite in recent decades.

231. Hagen v. Utah, 510 U.S. 399 (1994).

232. City of Sherrill v. Oneida Indian Nation of N.Y., 544 U.S. 197 (2005); Hagen v. Utah, 510 U.S. 399, 421 (1994).

233. Duro v. Reina, 495 U.S. 676, 693–94 (1990).

234. Iowa Mut. Ins. Co. v. LaPlante, 480 U.S. 9, 15–17 (1987).

235. Eastern Associated Coal Corp. v. UMW Dist. 17, 531 U.S. 57 (2000).

236. Festo Corp. v. Shoketsu Kinzoku Kogyo Kabushiki Co., 535 U.S. 722 (2002).

237. Microsoft Corp. v. AT & T, 127 S.Ct. 1746, 1758–59 (2007).

238. United States v. Fior D'Italia, 536 U.S. 238, 242–43 (2002).

239. United States v. Burke, 504 U.S. 229 (1992) (Souter, J., concurring in the judgment); United States v. Wells Fargo bank, 485 U.S. 351, 357 (1988).

240. INDOPCO, Inc. v. Commissioner, 503 U.S. 79 (1992).

241. Limitiaco v. Camacho, 127 S.Ct. 1413, 1420 (2007).

242. King v. St. Vincent's Hosp., 502 U.S. 215 (1991).

INDEX

References are to Pages

†